Lecture Notes in Computer Science   13870

Founding Editors

Gerhard Goos
Juris Hartmanis

Editorial Board Members

The series Lecture Notes in Computer Science (LNCS), including its subseries Lecture Notes in Artificial Intelligence (LNAI) and Lecture Notes in Bioinformatics (LNBI), has established itself as a medium for the publication of new developments in computer science and information technology research, teaching, and education.

LNCS enjoys close cooperation with the computer science R & D community, the series counts many renowned academics among its volume editors and paper authors, and collaborates with prestigious societies. Its mission is to serve this international community by providing an invaluable service, mainly focused on the publication of conference and workshop proceedings and postproceedings. LNCS commenced publication in 1973.

Catia Pesquita · Ernesto Jimenez-Ruiz ·
Jamie McCusker · Daniel Faria · Mauro Dragoni ·
Anastasia Dimou · Raphael Troncy ·
Sven Hertling
Editors

The Semantic Web

20th International Conference, ESWC 2023
Hersonissos, Crete, Greece, May 28 – June 1, 2023
Proceedings

Springer

Editors
Catia Pesquita (iD)
Universidade de Lisboa
Lisbon, Portugal

Ernesto Jimenez-Ruiz (iD)
University of London
London, UK

Jamie McCusker (iD)
Rensselaer Polytechnic Institute
Troy, MI, USA

Daniel Faria (iD)
Universidade de Lisboa
Lisbon, Portugal

Mauro Dragoni (iD)
Fondazione Bruno Kessler
Povo, Trento, Italy

Anastasia Dimou (iD)
KU Leuven
Sint-Katelijne-Waver, Belgium

Raphael Troncy (iD)
EURECOM
Biot, France

Sven Hertling (iD)
University of Mannheim
Mannheim, Germany

ISSN 0302-9743 ISSN 1611-3349 (electronic)
Lecture Notes in Computer Science
ISBN 978-3-031-33454-2 ISBN 978-3-031-33455-9 (eBook)
https://doi.org/10.1007/978-3-031-33455-9

This Springer imprint is published by the registered company Springer Nature Switzerland AG
The registered company address is: Gewerbestrasse 11, 6330 Cham, Switzerland

Preface

This volume contains the main proceedings of the 20th edition of the Extended Semantic Web Conference (ESWC 2023). ESWC is a major venue for discussing the latest in scientific results and innovations related to the semantic web, knowledge graphs, and web data. This year, we celebrate our 20th anniversary with a packed program that focuses on reflecting how far we have come as a community, where we are now headed, and the many exciting developments we can expect in the next two decades.

ESWC 2023's Research track addressed the theoretical, analytical, and empirical aspects of the Semantic Web, semantic technologies, knowledge graphs, and semantics on the Web in general. The In-use track focused on contributions that reuse and apply state-of-the-art semantic technologies or resources to real-world settings, broadening the scope of the track from previous years. The Resource track welcomed resource contributions that are on the one hand innovative or novel and on the other hand sharable and reusable and provide the necessary scaffolding to support the scientific publications and advance the state of the art.

The main scientific program of ESWC 2023 contained 41 papers selected out of 167 submissions (98 research, 23 in-use, 46 resource): 19 papers in the research track, 9 in the in-use track, and 13 in the resource track. The overall acceptance rate was 24% (19% research, 39% in-use, 28% resource). In keeping with the ESWC tradition of experimenting with different formats and processes, this year we changed our review process to not include a final overall assessment before the rebuttal phase. This enabled reviewers to focus on posing specific questions whose answers would help them reach a recommendation decision. The program chairs are grateful to the 54 senior PC members and 372 PC members and 52 external reviewers for providing their feedback on the scientific program and to their other community members. Each paper received an average of 3.95 reviews, with both the Research and In-Use being double-blind and Resource being single-blind.

We welcomed invited keynotes from three world-renowned speakers, spanning industry and academia and in keeping with our theme of painting the future landscape of the Semantic Web: Marieke Van Erp (KNAW Humanities Cluster), Efthymia Tsamoura (Samsung AI, Cambridge) and Alexander Gray (IBM).

The 20th anniversary panel invited researchers who have been pivotal to the development of the Semantic Web to reflect on and discuss the community's achievements and how we can build on this success. John Domingue (Open University, UK) moderated a lively panel with Dieter Fensel (University of Innsbruck, Austria), Asunción Gómez Pérez (UPM, Spain), Stefan Decker (RTH AU, Fraunhofer FIT), and Ian Horrocks (University of Oxford, UK).

The Next 20 Years track welcomed bold and paradigm-shifting ideas that illustrate the future landscape of ESWC 2043 and culminated with an exciting discussion of where we will be in 20 year's time, moderated by the track chairs, Irene Celino and Heiko Paulheim.

The conference also offered other opportunities to discuss the latest research and innovation work, including a poster and demo session, workshops and tutorials, a PhD symposium, an EU project networking session, and an industry track. We thank Mehwish Alam and Cassia Trojahn for organising the Workshop and Tutorials track, which hosted twelve workshops and tutorials covering topics ranging from knowledge graph construction to deep learning with knowledge graphs. We are also thankful to Hala Skaf-Molli and Vasilis Efthymiou for successfully running the Posters and Demos track with a record number of submissions. We are grateful to Sabrina Kirrane and Axel Ngonga for coordinating the PhD Symposium, which welcomed 12 PhD students who had the opportunity to present their work and receive feedback in a constructive environment. Thanks go to Diego Collarana and Renato Cerqueira for their management of the Industry track, which welcomed submissions from several large industry players. We also thank Armando Stellato and Maria Poveda-Villalón for increasing the networking potential of ESWC by running the Project Networking Session. A special thanks to Eleni Ilkou and Romana Pernisch for their amazing job as Web and Publicity chairs, and to Sven Hertling for preparing this volume with Springer. We thank STI International for supporting the conference organization, and in particular Julia Weninger for her quick reactions. We thank our sponsors for supporting ESWC 2023 and also our sponsorship chairs Albert Meroño and Joe Raad for securing them. Finally, we are also grateful to John Domingue, Elena Simperl, Paul Groth, and the ESWC 2022 organising committee for their invaluable support and advice.

As we reflect on both the past and the future, and our role as researchers and technologists, our thoughts go out to all those impacted by war.

April 2023

Catia Pesquita
Ernesto Jimenez-Ruiz
Jamie McCusker
Daniel Faria
Mauro Dragoni
Anastasia Dimou
Raphael Troncy
Sven Hertling

Organization

General Chair

Catia Pesquita   LASIGE, FC, Universidade de Lisboa, Portugal

Research Track Program Chairs

Ernesto Jimenez-Ruiz   City, University of London, UK & SIRIUS,
                                        Norway
Jamie McCusker   Rensselaer Polytechnic Institute, USA

Resource Track Program Chairs

Anastasia Dimou   KU Leuven, Belgium
Raphael Troncy   EURECOM, France

In-Use Track Program Chairs

Daniel Faria   INESC-ID, IST, Universidade de Lisboa, Portugal
Mauro Dragoni   Fondazione Bruno Kessler, Italy

Workshops and Tutorials Chairs

Mehwish Alam   Télécom Paris, Institut Polytechnique de Paris,
                                        France
Cassia Trojahn   IRIT, France

Poster and Demo Chairs

Hala Skaf-Molli   University of Nantes, France
Vasilis Efthymiou   FORTH-ICS, Greece

Symposium Chairs

Sabrina Kirrane   Technische Universität Dresden, Germany
Axel Ngonga   Universität Paderborn, Germany

Industry Track Program Chairs

Diego Collarana   Fraunhofer IAIS, Germany
Renato Cerqueira   IBM Research - Brazil, Brazil

Sponsorship

Albert Meroño   Kings College London, UK
Joe Raad   University of Paris-Saclay, France

Project Networking

Armando Stellato   University of Rome Tor Vergata, Italy
María Poveda-Villalón   Universidad Politécnica de Madrid, Spain

Web and Publicity

Eleni Ilkou   L3S Research Center, Leibniz Universität
                                 Hannover, Germany
Romana Pernisch   Vrije Universiteit Amsterdam, The Netherlands

Proceedings

Sven Hertling   University of Mannheim, Germany

ESWC: The Next 20 Years

Heiko Paulheim   University of Mannheim, Germany
Irene Celino   Cefriel, Italy

ESWC: 20th Anniversary

John Domingue   Knowledge Media Institute, The Open University,
                                 UK

Program Committee

Ibrahim Abdelaziz   IBM Research, USA
Maribel Acosta   Ruhr University Bochum, Germany
Nitish Aggarwal   Roku Inc., USA
Shqiponja Ahmetaj   Vienna University of Technology, Austria
Mehwish Alam   Télécom Paris, Institute Polytechnique de Paris,
                                France
Céline Alec   Université de Caen-Normandie, France
Vladimir Alexiev   Ontotext Corp., Bulgaria
Panos Alexopoulos   Textkernel B.V., The Netherlands
Alsayed Algergawy   University of Jena, Germany
José Luis Ambite   University of Southern California, USA
Vito Walter Anelli   Politecnico di Bari, Italy
Grigoris Antoniou   University of Huddersfield, UK
Julián Arenas-Guerrero   Universidad Politécnica de Madrid, Spain
Natanael Arndt   eccenca GmbH, Germany
Luigi Asprino   University of Bologna, Italy
Ghislain Auguste   Atemez-Mondeca, France
Maurizio Atzori   University of Cagliari, Italy
Sören Auer   TIB Leibniz Information Centre for Science &
                                Technology and University of Hannover,
                                Germany
Nathalie Aussenac-Gilles   IRIT CNRS, France
Amr Azzam   Vienna University of Business and Economics,
                                Austria
Carlos Badenes-Olmedo   Universidad Politécnica de Madrid, Spain
Ratan Bahadur Thapa   University of Oslo, Norway
Booma Sowkarthiga   University of Illinois at Chicago, USA
   Balasubramani
Rafael Berlanga   Universitat Jaume I, Spain
Nikos Bikakis   Athena Research Center, Greece
Russa Biswas   FIZ Karlsruhe, Leibniz Institute for Information
                                Infrastructure & KIT Karlsruhe, Germany
Christian Bizer   University of Mannheim, Germany
Peter Bloem   Vrije Universiteit Amsterdam, The Netherlands
Eva Blomqvist   Linköping University, Sweden
Carlos Bobed   everis / NTT Data - University of Zaragoza, Spain

Fernando Bobillo	University of Zaragoza, Spain
Iovka Boneva	University of Lille, France
Georgeta Bordea	Bordeaux Population Health Research Center, Université de Bordeaux
Alex Borgida	Rutgers University, USA
Paolo Bouquet	University of Trento, Italy
Zied Bouraoui	CRIL - CNRS & Université d'Artois, France
Loris Bozzato	Fondazione Bruno Kessler, Italy
Janez Brank	Jožef Stefan Institute, Slovenia
Anna Breit	Semantic Web Compny, Austria
Carlos Buil Aranda	Universidad Técnica Federico Santa María, Chile
Davide Buscaldi	LIPN, Université Sorbonne Paris Nord, France
Jean-Paul Calbimonte	University of Applied Sciences and Arts Western Switzerland HES-SO, Switzerland
Pablo Calleja	Universidad Politécnica de Madrid, Spain
Antonella Carbonaro	University of Bologna, Italy
Leyla Jael Castro	ZB MED Information Centre for Life Sciences, Germany
Sylvie Cazalens	LIRIS - INSA de Lyon, France
Irene Celino	Cefriel, Italy
Renato Cerqueira	IBM Research - Brazil, Brazil
Yoan Chabot	Orange Labs, France
Pierre-Antoine Champin	LIRIS, Université Claude Bernard Lyon1, France
Vinay Chaudhri	none
David Chaves-Fraga	Universidad Politécnica de Madrid, Spain
Jiaoyan Chen	University of Oxford, UK
Gong Cheng	Nanjing University, China
Sijin Cheng	Linköping University, Sweden
Philipp Cimiano	Bielefeld University, Germany
Andrea Cimmino Arriaga	Universidad Politécnica de Madrid, Spain
Michael Cochez	Vrije Universiteit Amsterdam, The Netherlands
Diego Collarana Vargas	Fraunhofer IAIS, Germany
Pieter Colpaert	Ghent University, Belgium
Oscar Corcho	Universidad Politécnica de Madrid, Spain
Francesco Corcoglioniti	Free University of Bozen-Bolzano, Italy
Julien Corman	Free University of Bozen-Bolzano, Italy
Marco Cremaschi	Università di Milano-Bicocca, Italy
Vincenzo Cutrona	University of Applied Sciences and Arts of Southern Switzerland (SUPSI), Switzerland
Claudia d'Amato	University of Bari, Italy
Enrico Daga	The Open University, UK
Jérôme David	Inria, France

Victor de Boer	Vrije Universiteit Amsterdam, The Netherlands
Daniele Dell'Aglio	Aalborg University, Denmark
Elena Demidova	University of Bonn, Germany
Ronald Denaux	Amazon, Spain
Gayo Diallo	ISPED & LABRI, University of Bordeaux, France
Stefan Dietze	GESIS - Leibniz Institute for the Social Sciences, Germany
Anastasia Dimou	KU Leuven, Belgium
Milan Dojchinovski	Czech Technical University in Prague, Czech Republic
John Domingue	The Open University, UK
Elvira Domínguez	Universidad Politécnica de Madrid, Spain
Ivan Donadello	Free University of Bozen-Bolzano, Italy
Hang Dong	University of Liverpool, UK
Mauro Dragoni	Fondazione Bruno Kessler, Italy
Vasilis Efthymiou	FORTH-ICS, Greece
Shusaku Egami	National Institute of Advanced Industrial Science and Technology, Japan
Fajar J. Ekaputra	Vienna University of Economics and Business (WU), Austria
Vadim Ermolayev	Ukrainian Catholic University, Ukraine
Paola Espinoza Arias	Universidad Politécnica de Madrid, Spain
Lorena Etcheverry	Universidad de la República, Uruguay
Pavlos Fafalios	FORTH-ICS, Greece
Alessandro Faraotti	IBM, Italy
Daniel Faria	INESC-ID, IST, Universidade de Lisboa, Portugal
Catherine Faron	Université Côte d'Azur, France
Anna Fensel	Wageningen University and Research, The Netherlands
Alba Fernandez-Izquierdo	BASF Digital Solutions, Spain
Javier D. Fernández	F. Hoffmann-La Roche AG, Switzerland
Mariano Fernández López	Universidad San Pablo CEU, Spain
Jesualdo Tomás Fernández-Breis	Departamento de Informatica y Sistemas. Universidad de Murcia, Spain
Sebastián Ferrada	Linköping University, Sweden
Sebastien Ferre	Univ Rennes, CNRS, IRISA, France
Erwin Filtz	Siemens AG Österreich, Austria
Giorgos Flouris	FORTH-ICS, Greece
Flavius Frasincar	Erasmus University Rotterdam, The Netherlands
Naoki Fukuta	Shizuoka University, Japan
Adam Funk	University of Sheffield, UK
Michael Färber	Karlsruhe Institute of Technology, Germany

Daniel Hernandez	University of Stuttgart, Germany
Nathalie Hernandez	IRIT, France
Sven Hertling	University of Mannheim, Germany
Rinke Hoekstra	Elsevier, The Netherlands
Aidan Hogan	DCC, Universidad de Chile, Chile
Andreas Hotho	University of Würzburg, Germany
Wei Hu	Nanjing University, China
Eero Hyvönen	Aalto University and University of Helsinki, Finland
Ali Hürriyetoğlu	Koç University, Turkey
Luis Ibanez-Gonzalez	University of Southampton, UK
Ryutaro Ichise	Tokyo Institute of Technology, Japan
Ana Iglesias-Molina	Universidad Politécnica de Madrid, Spain
Eleni Ilkou	Leibniz Universität Hannover, Germany
Antoine Isaac	Europeana, France
Hajira Jabeen	GESIS, Germany
Prateek Jain	Nuance Communications Inc., USA
Krzysztof Janowicz	University of California, Santa Barbara, USA
Ernesto Jimenez-Ruiz	City, University of London, UK
Clement Jonquet	MISTEA (INRAE) and University of Montpellier, France
Jan-Christoph Kalo	KRR, VU Amsterdam, The Netherlands
Maulik R. Kamdar	Optum Health, USA
Naouel Karam	Frauenhofer, Germany
Tomi Kauppinen	Department of Computer Science, Aalto University, Finland
Mayank Kejriwal	University of Southern California, USA
Ilkcan Keles	TomTom, The Netherlands
Ali Khalili	Deloitte, The Netherlands
Ankesh Khandelwal	Amazon, USA
Sabrina Kirrane	Vienna University of Economics and Business, Austria
Kjetil Kjernsmo	Inrupt Inc., Norway
Tomas Kliegr	Prague University of Economics and Business, Czech Republic
Matthias Klusch	DFKI, Germany
Haridimos Kondylakis	Institute of Computer Science, FORTH, Greece
Stasinos Konstantopoulos	NCSR Demokritos, Greece
Roman Kontchakov	Birkbeck, University of London, UK
Dimitris Kotzinos	ETIS Lab/CY Cergy Paris University, France
Manolis Koubarakis	National and Kapodistrian University of Athens, Greece

Kouji Kozaki	Osaka Electro-Communication University, Japan
Ralf Krestel	ZBW - Leibniz Information Centre for Economics & Kiel University, Germany
Tobias Käfer	Karlsruhe Institute of Technology, Germany
Jose Emilio Labra Gayo	Universidad de Oviedo, Spain
Frederique Laforest	INSA Lyon, France
Sarasi Lalithsena	IBM Watson, USA
Patrick Lambrix	Linköping University, Sweden
Andre Lamurias	Aalborg University, Denmark
Danh Le Phuoc	TU Berlin, Germany
Maxime Lefrançois	MINES Saint-Etienne, France
Huanyu Li	Linköping University, Sweden
Sven Lieber	Royal Library of Belgium, Belgium
Pasquale Lisena	EURECOM, France
Wenqiang Liu	Xi'an Jiaotong University, China
Jun Ma	Amazon, USA
Maria Maleshkova	University of Siegen, Germany
Claudia Marinica	Polytech Nantes, France
Beatrice Markhoff	Université de Tours, France
Maria Vanina Martinez	IIIA-CSIC, Spain
Miguel A. Martinez-Prieto	University of Valladolid, Spain
Jose L. Martinez-Rodriguez	Autonomous University of Tamaulipas, Mexico
Jamie McCusker	Rensselaer Polytechnic Institute, USA
Lionel Medini	CNRS, France
Albert Meroño-Peñuela	King's College London, UK
Nandana Mihindukulasooriya	IBM Research AI, USA
Daniel Miranker	Department of Computer Sciences, Institute for Cell and Molecular Biology, The University of Texas at Austin, USA
Pascal Molli	University of Nantes - LS2N , France
Gabriela Montoya	Aalborg University, Denmark
Jose Mora	Universidad Politécnica de Madrid, Spain
Boris Motik	University of Oxford, UK
Enrico Motta	The Open University, UK
Diego Moussallem	Paderborn University, Germany
Summaya Mumtaz	University of Oslo, Norway
Raghava Mutharaju	IIIT-Delhi, India
Ralf Möller	University of Lübeck, Germany
Hubert Naacke	Sorbonne Université, France
Shinichi Nagano	Toshiba Corporation, Japan
Natthawut Kertkeidkachorn	Japan Advanced Institute of Science and Technology, Japan

María Navas-Loro	Universidad Politécnica de Madrid, Spain
Axel Ngonga	Universität Paterborn, Germany
Tuan-Phong Nguyen	Max Planck Institute for Informatics, Germany
Vinh Nguyen	National Library of Medicine, USA
Andriy Nikolov	AstraZeneca, UK
Andrea Giovanni Nuzzolese	University of Bologna, Italy
Cliff O'Reilly	City, London University, UK
Femke Ongenae	Ghent University, Belgium
Andreas L. Opdahl	University of Bergen, Norway
Fabrizio Orlandi	ADAPT, Trinity College Dublin, Ireland
Francesco Osborne	The Open University, UK
Ankur Padia	UMBC, USA
Matteo Palmonari	University of Milan-Bicocca, Italy
Jeff Z. Pan	University of Edinburgh, UK
George Papadakis	National Technical University of Athens, Greece
Pierre-Henri Paris	CNAM, France
Heiko Paulheim	University of Mannheim, Germany
Terry Payne	University of Liverpool, UK
Tassilo Pellegrini	University of Applied Sciences St. Pölten, Austria
Maria Angela Pellegrino	Università degli Studi di Salerno, Italy
Bernardo Pereira Nunes	Australian National University, Australia
Sujan Perera	IBM Watson, USA
Nathalie Pernelle	LIPN, Université Sorbonne Paris Nord, France
Romana Pernisch	Vrije Universiteit Amsterdam, The Netherlands
Catia Pesquita	LASIGE, FC, Universidade de Lisboa, Portugal
Alina Petrova	University of Oxford, UK
Rafael Peñaloza	University of Milan-Bicocca, Italy
Patrick Philipp	Continental Automotive, Germany
Guangyuan Piao	National University of Ireland, Ireland
Francesco Piccialli	University of Naples Federico II, Italy
Lydia Pintscher	Wikimedia Deutschland, Germany
Alessandro Piscopo	BBC, UK
Dimitris Plexousakis	Institute of Computer Science, FORTH, Greece
Axel Polleres	Vienna University of Economics and Business - WU, Austria
María Poveda-Villalón	Universidad Politécnica de Madrid, Spain
Nicoleta Preda	University of Versailles Saint-Quentin-en-Yvelines, France
Valentina Presutti	University of Bologna, Italy
Cédric Pruski	Luxembourg Institute of Science and Technology, Luxembourg
Guilin Qi	Southeast University, China

Joe Raad	Vrije Universiteit Amsterdam, The Netherlands
Alexandre Rademaker	IBM Research and EMAp/FGV, Brazil
David Ratcliffe	Microsoft, Australia
Simon Razniewski	Bosch Center for AI, Germany
Diego Reforgiato	Università degli studi di Cagliari, Italy
Achim Rettinger	Trier University, Germany
Juan L. Reutter	Pontificia Universidad Católica de Chile, Chile
Artem Revenko	Semantic Web Company GmbH, Austria
Mariano Rico	Universidad Politécnica de Madrid, Spain
Petar Ristoski	eBay Inc., USA
Giuseppe Rizzo	LINKS Foundation, Italy
Sergio José Rodríguez Méndez	School of Computing / College of Engineering & Computer Science. The Australian National University, Australia
Edelweis Rohrer	Facultad de Ingeniería - Universidad de la República, Uruguay
Julian Rojas	Ghent University, Belgium
Maria Del Mar Roldan-Garcia	Universidad de Málaga, Spain
Julien Romero	Samovar, Télécom SudParis, France
Oscar Romero	Universitat Politècnica de Catalunya, Spain
Miguel Romero Orth	Universidad Adolfo Ibáñez, Chile
Henry Rosales-Méndez	University of Chile, Chile
Catherine Roussey	INRAE, France
Jose Rozanec	Jozef Stefan Institute, Slovenia
Sebastian Rudolph	TU Dresden, Germany
Anisa Rula	University of Brescia, Italy
Marta Sabou	Vienna University of Economics and Business, Austria
Harald Sack	FIZ Karlsruhe, Leibniz Institute for Information Infrastructure & KIT Karlsruhe, Germany
Angelo Antonio Salatino	The Open University, UK
Muhammad Saleem	AKSW, University of Leipzig, Germany
Emanuel Sallinger	TU Wien, Austria
Uli Sattler	University of Manchester, UK
Fatiha Saïs	LRI (Paris Sud University &CNRS8623), Paris Saclay University, France
Ralf Schenkel	Trier University, Germany
Stefan Schlobach	Vrije Universiteit Amsterdam, The Netherlands
Jodi Schneider	University of Illinois Urbana-Champaign, USA
Daniel Schwabe	PUC-Rio, Brazil
Jetzabel Maritza Serna Olvera	Universitat Politècnica de Catalunya, Spain
Patricia Serrano-Alvarado	LS2N - University of Nantes, France

Baris Sertkaya   Frankfurt University of Applied Sciences,
                                Germany
Cogan Shimizu   Kansas State University, USA
Pavel Shvaiko   Informatica Trentina, Italy
Lucia Siciliani   Dipartimento di Informatica - University of Bari
                                Aldo Moro, Italy
Gerardo Simari   Universidad Nacional del Sur (UNS) and
                                CONICET, Argentina
Kuldeep Singh   Cerence GmbH and Zerotha Research, Germany
Sneha Singhania   Max Planck Institute for Informatics, Germany
Hala Skaf-Moli   University of Nantes, France
Xingyi Song   University of Sheffield, UK
Rita Sousa   LASIGE, FC, Universidade de Lisboa, Portugal
Blerina Spahiu   Università degli Studi di Milano-Bicocca, Italy
Marc Spaniol   Université de Caen Normandie, France
Kavitha Srinivas   IBM, USA
Steffen Staab   IPVS, Universität Stuttgart, Germany and WAIS,
                                University of Southampton, UK
Kostas Stefanidis   Tampere University, Finland
Nadine Steinmetz   TU Ilmenau, Germany
Armando Stellato   University of Rome, Tor Vergata, Italy
Lise Stork   Vrije Universiteit Amsterdam, The Netherlands
Umberto Straccia   ISTI-CNR, Italy
Zequn Sun   Nanjing University, China
Vojtěch Svátek   Prague University of Economics and Business,
                                Czech Republic
Danai Symeonidou   INRAE, France
Ruben Taelman   Ghent University, Belgium
Valentina Tamma   University of Liverpool, UK
David Tena Cucala   University of Oxford, UK
Andrea Tettamanzi   Univ. Nice Sophia Antipolis, France
Andreas Thalhammer   Roche Diagnostics, Switzerland
Krishnaprasad Thirunarayan   Wright State University, USA
Steffen Thoma   FZI Research Center for Information Technology,
                                Germany
Ilaria Tiddi   Vrije Universiteit Amsterdam, The Netherlands
Konstantin Todorov   LIRMM/University of Montpellier, France
Riccardo Tommasini   INSA Lyon, France
Sebastian Tramp   eccenca GmbH, Germany
Cassia Trojahn   IRIT, France
Raphael Troncy   EURECOM, France
Yannis Tzitzikas   University of Crete and FORTH-ICS, Greece

Additional Reviewers

Aghaei, Sare
Akaichi, Ines
Badenes-Olmedo, Carlos
Bento, Alexandre
Bernardy, Laura
Biancofiore, Giovanni Maria
Blin, Inès
Braun, Christoph
Chen, Jiaoyan
Chhetri, Tek Raj
Darnala, Baptiste
Domínguez, Elvira
Dsouza, Alishiba
Emamirad, Ehsan
Ilkou
Jain, Monika
Jradeh, Khadija
Khajeh Nassiri, Armita
Lamprecht, David
Liu, Xiangyu
Majumdar, Abhishek
Markwald, Marco
Marx, Edgard
Massimino, Giulia
Mehrotra, Shubham
Mohammadi, Hossein

Morales Tirado, Alba Catalina
Moro, Gianluca
Möller, Cedric
Nararatwong, Rungsiman
Nayyeri, Mojtaba
Noullet, Kristian
Porena, Margherita
Quercini, Gianluca
Reyero Lobo, Paula
Rovetto, Robert
Sain, Joy
Sanguinetti, Manuela
Shen, Zhejun
Simonne, Lucas
Singh, Gunjan
Tan, Yiming
Tauqeer, Amar
Tian, Xiaobin
Tounsi Dhouib, Molka
Troullinou, Georgia
Werner, Simon
Wu, Hong
Xiong, Bo
Yacoubi Ayadi, Nadia
Zeginis, Chrysostomos
Zhao, Tianzhe

Sponsors

Gold Sponsors

metaphacts is a German software company that empowers customers to drive knowledge democratization and decision intelligence using knowledge graphs. Built entirely on open standards and technologies, our product metaphactory delivers a low-code, FAIR Data platform that supports collaborative knowledge modeling and knowledge generation and enables on-demand citizen access to consumable, contextual and actionable knowledge. metaphacts serves customers in areas such as life sciences and pharma, engineering and manufacturing, finance and insurance, retail, cultural heritage, and more. For more information about metaphacts and its products and solutions please visit https:// www.metaphacts.com.

VideoLectures.NET is an award-winning free and open-access educational video lectures repository. The lectures are given by distinguished scholars and scientists at the most important and prominent events like conferences, summer schools, workshops and science promotional events from many fields of Science. The portal is aimed at promoting science, exchanging ideas and fostering knowledge sharing by providing high-quality didactic contents not only to the scientific community but also to the general public. All lectures, accompanying documents, information and links are systematically selected and classified through the editorial process taking into account also users' comments.

Silver Sponsors

Ontotext is a global leader in enterprise knowledge graph technology and semantic database engines. Ontotext employs big knowledge graphs to enable unified data access and cognitive analytics via text mining and integration of data across multiple sources. Ontotext GraphDB engine and Ontotext Platform power business critical systems in the biggest banks, media, market intelligence agencies, car and aerospace manufacturers. Ontotext technology and solutions are widespread across the value chain of the most knowledge intensive enterprises in financial services, publishing, healthcare, pharma, manufacturing and public sectors. Leveraging AI and cognitive technologies, Ontotext helps enterprises get competitive advantage, by connecting the dots of their proprietary knowledge and putting it in the context of global intelligence.

Semantic Technology Institute (STI) Innsbruck is a leading research group in semantic technology at the Department of Computer Science at the University of Innsbruck, Austria, engaged in research and development to bring information and communication technologies of the future into today's world.

Springer is part of Springer Nature, a leading global research, educational and professional publisher, home to an array of respected and trusted brands providing quality content through a range of innovative products and services. Springer Nature is the world's largest academic book publisher, publisher of the world's most influential journals and a pioneer in the field of open research. The company numbers almost 13,000 staff in over 50 countries and has a turnover of approximately 1.5 billion. Springer Nature was formed in 2015 through the merger of Nature Publishing Group, Palgrave Macmillan, Macmillan Education and Springer Science+Business Media.

Eccenca In parallel with the 20th anniversary of the ESWC this year, eccenca is proud to announce the launch of the Community Edition Sandbox. Through eccenca.my you can register and evaluate the creation of Knowledge Graphs made easy and intuitive. No code. No bugs. No time.

Eccenca Corporate Memory is cutting-edge Knowledge Graph technology. It digitally captures the expertise of knowledge workers so that it can be accessed and processed by machines. The fusion of human knowledge with large amounts of data, coupled with the computing power of machines, results in powerful artificial intelligence that enables companies to execute existing processes as well as innovation projects of all kinds at high speed and low cost. And it creates an impressive competitive advantage.

Join pioneers like BOSCH, SIEMENS, Astra Zeneca and many other global market leaders - our world-class team of Linked Data Experts is ready when you are.

Bronze Sponsors

IOS Press is an independent, international STM publishing house established in 1987 in Amsterdam. One of our guiding principles is to embrace the benefits a lean organization offers. While our goal is to keep things simple, we strive to meet the highest professional standards. Our business practices are straightforward, transparent and ethical. IOS Press serves the information needs of scientific and medical communities worldwide. IOS Press now publishes more than 100 international journals and approximately 75 book titles each year on subjects ranging from computer sciences and mathematics to medicine and the natural sciences. Please visit iospress.com to find out more.

Contents

In-Use

Research

Explainable Drug Repurposing in Context via Deep Reinforcement Learning

Lise Stork[1]([✉])(iD), Ilaria Tiddi[1](iD), René Spijker[2,3](iD), and Annette ten Teije[1](iD)

[1] Vrije Universiteit Amsterdam, Amsterdam, The Netherlands
l.stork@vu.nl
[2] Cochrane Netherlands, Julius Center for Health Sciences and Primary Care,
Utrecht, The Netherlands
[3] University Medical Center Utrecht, Utrecht University, Utrecht, The Netherlands

Abstract. Biomedical knowledge graphs encode domain knowledge as biomedical entities and relationships between them. Graph traversal algorithms can make use of these rich sources for the discovery of novel research hypotheses, e.g. the repurposing of a known drug. Traversed paths can serve to explain the underlying causal mechanisms. Most of these models, however, are trained to optimise for accuracy w.r.t. known gold standard drug-disease pairs, rather than for the explanatory mechanisms supporting such predictions. In this work, we aim to improve the retrieval of these explanatory mechanisms by improving path quality. We build on a reinforcement learning-based multi-hop reasoning approach for drug repurposing. First, we define a metric for path quality based on coherence with context entities. To calculate coherence, we learn a set of phenotype annotations with rule mining. Second, we use both the metric and the annotations to formulate a novel reward function. We assess the impact of contextual knowledge in a quantitative and qualitative evaluation, measuring: (i) the effect training with context has on the quality of reasoning paths, and (ii) the effect of using context for explainability purposes, measured in terms of plausibility, novelty, and relevancy. Results indicate that learning with contextual knowledge significantly increases path coherence, without affecting the interpretability for the domain experts.

Keywords: Explainable AI · Multi-hop Reasoning · Reinforcement Learning · Drug Repurposing

1 Introduction

Drug discovery is challenging and costly [8]: it can take very long, an average of ∼9 years for a drug to get approved by the relevant bodies [5]. Repurposing an already approved drug is a good alternative: it may reveal new interesting drug targets and pathways. However, considerable background knowledge about the biochemical properties of drugs and diseases, their relationships, and the causal mechanisms between them is required. By making knowledge about biomedical associations and processes machine-readable, automated methods can aid

© The Author(s), under exclusive license to Springer Nature Switzerland AG 2023
C. Pesquita et al. (Eds.): ESWC 2023, LNCS 13870, pp. 3–20, 2023.
https://doi.org/10.1007/978-3-031-33455-9_1

experts in coming up with interesting new purposes for known drugs, to be further tested in clinical trials.

Modern Semantic Web technologies have shown a huge effort being directed toward the generation of structured biomedical knowledge, with the use of shared ontologies such as SNOMED-CT[1], DrugBank[2], the Cochrane Linked Data Vocabulary[3] or UMLS[4]. Researchers have aimed at linking such independent knowledge bases into federated biomedical networks with a.o. genes, pathways, biological processes, compounds and diseases [1,16,17], in support of automated drug repurposing or, more broadly, the discovery of new knowledge. The problem of drug repurposing on structured data can be formulated as a link prediction task in which known drug-disease pairs are used as gold standard data to predict novel ones [3,9,22,32].

Reinforcement learning (RL)-based multi-hop reasoning for drug repurposing has the advantage that reasoning paths can serve as explanations for newly discovered links, but the key challenge is the discovery of meaningful paths. Liu et al. [22] use logical rules, specifically *metapaths* (node types + relations between them), mined using AnyBurl [24] to guide the RL agent in discovering paths between diseases and compounds. Such metapaths can then be ranked by domain experts in order to assess the interpretability of the paths following these rules [23,35]. In most biomedical knowledge graphs, however, metapaths have many distinct instantiations. An example being the metapath *Compound–binds–Gene–associates–Disease* in Hetionet[5], of which the *Gene-associates-Disease* relation alone has an average number of ∼94 gene associations per disease[6]. The gene-disease associations catalogued by Gwas (See Footnote 6) are statistical, meaning that variations in these genes *may* contribute to the development of diseases or traits. This demonstrates that, often, only a subset of instantiated paths describe valid causal mechanisms, and not only the metapath but also the instantiated path, i.e., its entities, dictates their relevance.

In this work, we propose to guide the reinforcement agent's path traversal using auxiliary contextual knowledge about the phenotype(s) of a disease, i.e., its known symptoms. We formulate the task of drug repurposing as a *contextual* link prediction problem, in which we guide multi-hop reasoning using knowledge about a set of context entities. In RL-based multi-hop reasoning for drug repurposing [6], an agent traverses a graph of entities from disease to drug, rewarded when a terminal entity is reached. In our work, additional knowledge about the clinical phenotype of a disease is used to guide the path traversal of such agent (for an example, see Fig. 4). To the best of our knowledge, no research so far has focused on RL-based multi-hop reasoning using context entities.

We apply our methodology to Hetionet (See Footnote 5), a single integrative KG connecting biological entities such as genes and pathways. We assess the

---

[1] https://www.snomed.org/.

[2] https://go.drugbank.com/.

[3] https://data.cochrane.org/concepts/.

[4] https://www.nlm.nih.gov/research/umls/index.html.

[5] https://het.io/.

[6] https://www.ebi.ac.uk/gwas/.

impact of contextual knowledge in a quantitative and qualitative evaluation and aim at measuring: (i) the effect training with context has on the reasoning paths, and (ii) the effect of using context in causal explanations about phenotype-drug tuples on the plausibility, novelty and relevancy of these explanations as assessed by domain experts. Lastly, we present a real-world dataset consisting of patient populations (one or more diseases and symptoms), extracted from systematic reviews, that can be used for phenotype or population-based drug repurposing. Our contribution is twofold:

1. a RL method for multi-hop reasoning based on context, named CoCo (Coherent with Context), for the discovery of interesting clinical hypotheses;
2. a real-world dataset of small graphs representing patient populations (diseases, conditions, symptoms and comorbidities) from clinical trials.

2   Related Work

First, we discuss automated scientific discovery in general. Then, we move to AI for medicine, and finally multi-hop reasoning for drug repurposing.

Machine-Supported Scientific Discovery. Automated hypothesis discovery has been subject of study for a long time, since seminal works such as [2,33]. These works aimed at supporting scientists formulating testable hypotheses, either through suggesting literature or by discovering co-occurrences and correlations in data, sometimes using structured knowledge such as Medical Subject Headings (MeSH)-terms. The Knowledge Integration Toolkit (KnIT) [26] used methods such as matrix factorisation and graph diffusion to generate testable hypotheses in the biomedical domain. Methods for generated data insights were also presented in other fields, such as astronomy, geoscience or neuroscience [12,27]. These models create variants of hypotheses, which scientists can then refine and assess empirically.

One way to formulate the task of hypothesis generation, is through link prediction over knowledge graphs [3,9,22,32], or the generation of a small graph representing complex hypotheses. Attempts in this direction are the work of [15], where social sciences hypotheses are generated using a specific set of ontological classes, or [7] using generative adversarial models (GANs) for the prediction of small molecular graphs. Predictions made by such models are, however, not easily explained, which hampers trust especially in sensitive domains such as clinical medicine [19].

AI for Medicine. Through rapid technological developments and data digitisation, AI has found many applications in the pharmaceutical domain, from drug design through protein structure prediction with AlphaFold [18], to drug screening through toxicity prediction, and drug repurposing [28]. A downside of using common machine learning techniques for applications in medicine is the black-box nature of most of the prediction systems, hampering trust in such systems in sensitive domains such as medicine. Explainable AI methods tackle this issue by providing transparent reasoning for the models in a variety of tasks, prediction included. These systems generally provide explanations either by eliciting the models' inner workings (e.g. visual cues or anchors [25]) or by using feature importance [20,30]. Supplying an AI model with structured, machine-readable background knowledge about known cause and effect relationships within the problem domain [4] can instead support both the generation of hypotheses as well as their explanation [3,9,10,22]. Rule mining [13,24] or path-search algorithms over large-scale knowledge graphs [6,34], which carry the potential to provide predictions with understandable explanations, have proven to be effective in more recent years. RL-based multi-hop reasoning for drug repurposing is an example task.

Table 1. Hetionet metaedges (predicates + types) and number of facts.

Metaedge	Count
participates(Gene, Biol.Proc.)	559504
expresses(Anatomy, Gene)	526407
regulates(Gene, Gene)	265672
includes(Gene, Gene)	147164
causes(Compound, Symptom)	138944
downregulates(Anatomy, Gene)	102240
upregulates(Anatomy, Gene)	97848
participates(Gene, Mol.Func.)	97222
participates(Gene, Pathway)	84372
participates(Gene, Cell.Comp.)	73566
covariates(Gene, Gene)	61690
downregulates(Compound, Gene)	21102
upregulates(Compound, Gene)	18756
associates(Disease, Gene)	12623
binds(Compound, Gene)	11571
upregulates(Disease, Gene)	7731
downregulates(Disease, Gene)	7623
resembles(Compound, Compound)	6486
localizes(Disease, Anatomy)	3592
presents(Disease, Symptom)	3357
includes(Pharma.Class, Compound)	1029
resembles(Disease, Disease)	543
treats(Compound, Disease)	483
palliates(Compound, Disease)	390

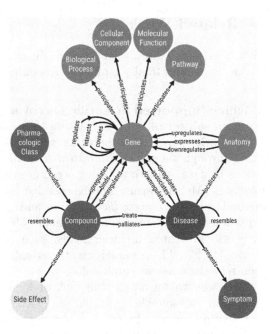

Fig. 1. Semantic schema of Hetionet.

Multi-hop Reasoning for Drug Repurposing. Link prediction has been proposed for the task of drug repurposing, in which a link between a disease and compound is predicted. Himmelstein et al. [16] for instance, obtained and integrated data from publicly available sources about biomedicine to create Hetionet (See Footnote 5) (see Fig. 1) and identified network patterns, call *meta-paths*, to distinguish treatments from non-treatments, e.g., *Compound-binds-Gene-associates-Disease*. Sosa et al. [32] used the Global Network of Biomedical

Relationships (GNBR) [29] to develop a knowledge graph embedding-based drug repurposing method to predict novel treatments for diseases. They assessed the validity of these hypotheses using a variety of sources, and, similarly to Himmelstein et al. [16], discovered meaningful metapaths explaining newly discovered links.

One of the challenges to RL-based multi-hop reasoning, is that RL agents learn without the help of gold standard reasoning paths. An agent can therefore learn from nonsensical or meaningless search trajectories that incidentally lead to a correct answer [21]. Finding meaningful higher-order neighbourhoods is challenging. The injection of additional knowledge in the path traversal can guide multi-hop reasoning to learn from a more meaningful subset of trajectories. For instance, [22] used metapaths from [16] to train a RL agent to walk a graph of biomedical knowledge, receiving a reward if the path found for the *Compound-treats-Disease*, or vice-versa, matched a metapath.

In our work, we hypothesise that not only metapaths dictate the meaningfulness of a path, but also its entities. Therefore, we train a RL agent by rewarding paths of which the entities are coherent with the phenotype of a disease.

3   Multi-hop Reasoning Coherent with Context (CoCo)

We present preliminaries (Sect. 3.1), after which we discuss our main approach (Sect. 3.2).

3.1   Preliminaries

Domain Knowledge. As auxiliary knowledge to drive the learning of multi-hop patterns between diseases and compounds, we use knowledge of symptoms (i.e. phenotypes). We base our choice on a few assumptions from biomedicine:

Assumption 1. *A detailed understanding of how a condition's symptoms relate to underlying molecular processes can help in elucidating the molecular mechanisms underlying these conditions, useful for identifying new drug targets [31, 37].*

Assumption 2. *Shared symptoms can indicate shared genes between diseases [31]. Symptoms can thus serve as additional knowledge for representation learning of diseases and their associations with genes and other genotypes.*

Biomedical Knowledge Graphs. A biomedical knowledge graph $\mathcal{G}$ is a collection of biomedical facts $\{(e_1, r, e_2)\} \subseteq \mathcal{E} \times \mathcal{R} \times \mathcal{E}$ where $\mathcal{E}$ and $\mathcal{R}$ are a set of entities (such as, genes or proteins, compounds, molecular functions, cellular components, biological processes, pathways, diseases) and relations (binds, associates, treats, downregulates, etc.), respectively. Inverse relations are indicated by an underscore: binds $\rightarrow$ _binds.

Logical Rules. Rule mining methods such as AnyBurl [24] or GPFL [13] mine logical rules from large knowledge graphs for the task of link prediction. Logical rules can be written in the form $head \leftarrow body$, in which the body can be seen as evidence for the head. We use lowercase letters to denote constants (ground entities e and relations $r \in \mathcal{G}$) and uppercase letters to denote variables. An example of a ground path rule of length n is shown below. Straight ground rules, rules without cycles in the body, can be divided into cyclic ($e_1 = e_{n+1}$), or acyclic rules ($e_1 \neq e_{n+1}$).

$$r_0(e_0, e_1) \leftarrow r_1(e_1, e_2), \ldots, r_n(e_n, e_{n+1}) \tag{1}$$

With rule mining, path rules are generalised into different rule types. Every method has a *language bias*, dictating what kind of rules can be learned. In this work, we focus on Both Anchored Rules (BAR) or instantiated rules, as they are capable of expressing relationships between pairs of entities. BAR rules are generalisations of acyclic straight rules in which an atom in the head e_i and the tail atom e_j are anchored by a constant, cfr. Eq. 2.

$$\textbf{BAR } :r_t(X, e_i) \leftarrow r_1(X, V1), r_2(V1, e_j) \tag{2}$$

We exemplify this with data from our use case, as shown in Eq. 3, which expresses that if a disease presents *Sensorineural Hearing Loss*, it was often associated with a gene that participates in the *positive regulation of Fc receptor mediated stimulatory signaling* pathway, with a confidence of α. For readability, we will call these associations *rule-based phenotype annotations*.

$$\alpha = 0.56 \quad presents(X, e_i) \leftarrow associates(X, V1), participates(V1, e_j)$$
$$e_i = \text{Sensorineural Hearing Loss} \tag{3}$$
$$e_j = \text{positive regulation of Fc receptor mediated stimulatory signaling}$$

The confidence score α refers to standard confidence [11], and is calculated by the number of correct predictions the rule suggests over the training set (support), divided by the number of possible groundings of the body atom of the rule.

Knowledge Graph Multi-hop Reasoning. Given a query $(e_{q1}, treats, ?)$ or $(?, treats, e_{q2})$, this approach aims to predict the missing element ?, through a k-hop reasoning path $e_1 \xrightarrow{r_1} e_2 \xrightarrow{r_2} \ldots \xrightarrow{r_k} e_{k+1}$. We extend the task to reasoning in context. Given a query $(e_{q1}, treats, ?, c_q)$, or $(?, treats, e_{q1}, c_q)$, in which c_q refers to additional knowledge about the query q, knowledge graph reasoning in context aims to predict the missing element ? through a k-hop reasoning path $p_q = e_1 \xrightarrow{r_1} e_2 \xrightarrow{r_2} \ldots e_{k+1}$, coherent with $c_q = \{e_1, \ldots, e_n\}$.

3.2 Proposed Approach

Link prediction through graph traversal as a Markov decision process has been proposed in the MINERVA algorithm [6]. Our methodology, which we call CoCo

(Coherent with Context), extends the MINERVA algorithm, with the novelty that we (i) formulate our queries as ternary relations $(e_{q1}, r_q, e_{q2}, c_q)$: a treats relation between a disease and drug, given a (set of) symptom(s), respectively, which we (ii) train and evaluate using a novel path coherence metric as reward. A schematisation of our method is presented in Fig. 2.

Path Coherence. We define Path Coherence (PC) as a score between a reasoning path p_q and context c_q for a given query q. Symptoms in the Hetionet graph do not contain any direct links to genes, pathways or other biomedical entities other than diseases. The human phenotype ontology[7], includes curated phenotype annotations, but the coverage is rather low. Therefore, we use GPFL [13] to mine these associations in the form of Both Anchored Rules (BAR), as exemplified in Eq. 4, with the added advantage of interpretability.

$$\alpha = 0.33 \quad presents(X, h_i) \leftarrow associates(X, t_j)$$
$$h_i = \text{Ataxia Telangiectasia} \tag{4}$$
$$t_j = \text{Gene ATP7B}$$

Path Coherence (Eq. 5) will be calculated based on these associations. In Eq. 5, $\mathbf{p}_q$ refers to the multi-hop reasoning path, $(t_j, \alpha_j) \in \mathbf{r}_{c_q}$ refers to the subset of rule-based phenotype annotations for which the head entity h_j is in the set of context entities c_q. t_j then refers to the tail entity of the rule, and α_j to the standard confidence. The metric sums up standard confidences for rule-based phenotype annotations that link a query's context entities to its path entities.

$$PC(\mathbf{p}_q, \mathbf{c}_q) = \sum_{e_i \in \mathbf{p}_q} \sum_{(t_j, \alpha_j) \in \mathbf{r}_{c_q}} \alpha_{j\{e_i = t_j\}} \tag{5}$$

States. The state of the RL agent is encoded by the current location of the agent e_t, the entity e at time t, as well as the query (e_{q1}, r, e_{q2}). More formally, $S_t \in S = \left(e_t, (e_{q1}, r, e_{q2}) \right)$.

Actions. The set of possible actions available to the agent at state S_t is encoded as $\mathcal{A}_{S_t}$, and denotes all outgoing edges from the current entity e_t, as well as their tail entities. $\mathcal{A}_t$ denotes an action taken at time t. As with the MINERVA algorithm, we include self loops, allowing an entity to stay at the current node in case the agent requires fewer steps to reach e_{q2}.

Environment. The environment evolves according to the transition function $\delta : S \times \mathcal{A} \leftarrow S$, the action chosen by the agent, by updating the current state S_t to the new state S_{t+1}.

---

[7] https://hpo.jax.org/app/data/annotations.

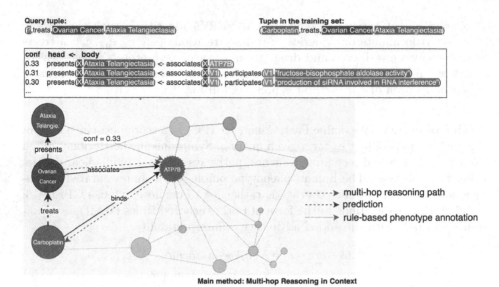

Fig. 2. A graphical representation of our methodology during training. First, the subset of rule-based phenotype annotations belonging to the query tuple's phenotype are retrieved. Second, A RL agent is trained to traverse the KG from disease to compound or vice versa. If the correct query entity is reached, a terminal reward of 1 is given. If the path is associated with the context via a rule-based annotation, an additional reward is given equal to the standard confidence of the rule (here PC = 0.33).

Policy Network. The history of our agent up to step t is denoted as $H_t = (H_{t-1}, A_{t-1})$. The policy network encodes the agent's transition history, and is parameterised by a long-term-short-term memory network (LSTM) [14], allowing for long-term dependencies between graph traversals.

$$\mathbf{h}_t = LSTM(\mathbf{h}_{t-1}, \mathbf{a}_{t-1}) \qquad (6)$$

In Eq. 6, $\mathbf{a}_{t-1}$ refers to the vector space embedding of the previous action, which consists of $[\mathbf{r}_{t-1}, \mathbf{e}_t]$: the embedding of the action relation and its tail entity. If there is no previous action, $\mathbf{a}_{t-1}$ refers to the zero vector. The history-dependent action space distribution is given by Eq. 7 below, where $\mathbf{W_1}$ and $\mathbf{W_2}$ in Eq. are weight matrices learned during training. By stacking the embeddings for all the outgoing actions we obtain $\mathbf{A}_t$. A next action A_t is sampled according to Eq. 8.

$$\mathbf{d}_t = softmax(\mathbf{A}_t(\mathbf{W_2}ReLU(\mathbf{W_1}[\mathbf{h}_t; \mathbf{a}_t; \mathbf{r}_q]))) \qquad (7)$$

$$A_t \sim Categorical(\mathbf{d}_t) \qquad (8)$$

For each step made by the agent, we repeat Eq. (7)–(9) until the maximum path length is reached. The parameters of the LSTM network together with $\mathbf{W_1}$ and $\mathbf{W_2}$ form the parameters θ of the policy network π_θ.

Rewards. Rewards are given according to Eq. 9 at the end of k transitions, where k refers to the length of the reasoning path.

$$R(S_{k+1}) = 1_{\{t(e_{k+1})=t(e_{q2})\}} + \tau_{\{e_{k+1}=e_{q2}\}} + \rho_{\{t(e_{k+1})=t(e_{q2})\}} \sum_{e_i \in \mathbf{p}_q} \sum_{(t_j, \alpha_j) \in \mathbf{r}_{c_q}} \alpha_j_{\{e_i=t_j\}}$$

(9)

The first part of the equation reflects a type reward: it is set to 1 if the correct type $t(e_{q2})$ is reached, and 0 otherwise. The second part of the function assigns a reward of τ when the target entity is reached, 0 otherwise. The last part of the equation adds a path coherence (PC) reward, multiplied by ρ, which is only given when at least the correct type is reached $\{t(e_{k+1}) = t(e_{q2})\}$, 0 otherwise. We experimented with a stricter rule reward, only given when the agent reached e_{q2}, but hyperparameter optimisation showed this impacted accuracy.

Optimisation. As MINERVA, we employ the REINFORCE [36] algorithm to optimise the expected rewards. The agent's optimisation problem is given by Eq. 10, where $\mathcal{D}$ refers to the true underlying distribution of the $(e_{q1}, treats, e_{q2})$ triples.

$$\arg \max \mathbb{E}_{(e_{q1},treats,e_{q2})\sim\mathcal{D}} \; \mathbb{E}_{A_1,A_2,...,A_L\sim\pi_\theta} \Big[R(S_{k+1})|e_{q1}, e_{q2} \Big] \qquad (10)$$

The second expectation is calculated over multiple rollouts (sampled trajectories) for each training example.

4 Experiments

Section 4.1 describes datasets used. Section 4.2 describes the rule-based phenotype annotations, and Sect. 4.3 describes the evaluation of our method.

4.1 Datasets

Hetionet Training, Validation and Test Set. Hetionet (See Footnote 5) consists of declarative knowledge within the biomedical domain, represented as binary relations between biomedical entities. Even though the graph contains binary relations between diseases and compounds, as well as between diseases and symptoms, it does not contain complex n-ary relations such as a relation between a disease, a set of symptoms, and a compound. Table 1 and 2 show statistics of the Hetionet graph. It's schema is shown in Fig. 1.

Table 2. Hetionet general dataset statistics.

Entities	Relations	Triples	Avg. node degree
47,031	24	2,250,197	95.8

For training and evaluation, we thus artificially construct such n-ary relations. First, we retrieve all *treats* triples as well as all *presents* triples from

Hetionet. From those triples, we construct tuples (all valid combinations) of the form *(Compound, Disease, Symptom)* and split them into training, validation and test set. As we are interested in discovering paths that give insight into the mechanics of drug treatments, we remove the edges *resembles* and *palliates*. Table 3 shows final train, test and validation-set statistics.

Real-World Dataset. Additionally, we extract a real-world dataset of populations from Cochrane's systematic reviews, which exemplifies how our approach can be used to predict drug targets or compounds based on complex phenotypes. The Cochrane Linked Data Project[8] has semantically annotated a collection of systematic reviews–a syntheses of clinical trials belonging to a specific research question–according to the PICO ontology[9], producing a small graph for each systematic review (a "PICO"). First, we extract unique patient populations and their diseases, conditions and symptoms from the PICO graphs[10]. In order to reason over the extracted subgraphs, we join them with the Hetionet graph in the following manner:

1. *Filtering PICO graph.* Using a SPARQL query, we extract populations and their disease or phenotype entities. In PICO graphs, these are all entities from the Cochrane Linked Data Vocabulary (CLDV)[11] of type `condition`. The query used to create these simplified graphs can be found online[12].
2. *Linking populations to Hetionet.* Both the CLVD and Hetionet use different codes to uniquely describe their biomedical entities. In order to join both graphs, we therefore replace all relevant nodes with UMLS identifiers using the steps enumerated below. The script used for this processing step can be found online (See Footnote 12).
   (a) `owl:sameAs` links are added between nodes in the CLDV and equivalent concepts from widely used vocabularies[13]. The CLDV maps disease and outcome entities to the following vocabulaires: MedDRA, MeSH, and SNOMED-CT.
   (b) vocabularies that are used to represent diseases and symptoms in Hetionet are DOID and UMLS, respectively. Both vocabularies, as well as those mentioned in (a), are downloaded from UMLS version 2021AA[14].
   (c) downloaded vocabularies are preprocessed by extracting all medical entities and linking them their respective UMLS identifiers using `owl:sameAs`.

---

[8] https://linkeddata.cochrane.org/.

[9] https://linkeddata.cochrane.org/pico--ontology.

[10] Initially, intervention nodes were extracted as well, but many of these proved too coarse grained—e.g. *viral agents*—to be useful for multi-hop reasoning.

[11] https://data.cochrane.org/concepts/.

[12] https://github.com/lisestork/coco.

[13] See the following concept for diabetes: https://data.cochrane.org/concepts/r4hp38bjj6qx, which they indicate is linked to unique codes from MedDRA: (10012594,10012601), MeSH: (D003920), and UMLS: (C0011849).

[14] https://download.nlm.nih.gov/umls/kss/2021AA/umls-2021AA-full.zip.

   (d) RDFpro[15] is used to smush all preprocessed vocabularies, meaning that
       all identifiers are replaced by their respective UMLS identifiers.
   (e) all `owl:sameAs` links are removed, such that all disease, drug and symp-
       toms are represented by codes from the UMLS vocabulary.
3. *Appending types.* As a last step, types are appended to the UMLS codes, e.g.
   `Disease::C0348393` to ensure the graph remains compliant with the Hetionet
   ontology after smushing, given that some UMLS codes are used to represent
   distinct types in the Hetionet ontology (e.g., to describe a side effect as well
   as a disease).

   After preprocessing, we end up with 357 population tuples. Statistics are
shown in Table 3. An example tuple: a patient population with Haematological
malignancy, as well as Cardiac death, Cytomegalovirus infection, and Herpes
simplex. The dataset can be found online (See Footnote 12). Further investigation is needed to evaluate these results, as it does not yet include gold standard
annotated drug targets (i.e., genes) or compounds.

Table 3. Hetionet training, validation and test set statistics: dataset split, total number
of triples n, total number of *(Drug, Disease, Symptom)* tuples n_+, number of diseases
n_d, number of compounds n_c and number of symptoms n_s.

dataset	n	n_+	n_d	n_c	n_s
Hetionet train	950	27,632	71	272	372
Hetionet validation	236	–	41	97	–
Hetionet test	300	9,200	56	119	363
Real-world dataset	357	–	60	–	276

4.2   Rule-Based Phenotype Annotations

To create a set of rule-based phenotype annotations, we applied GPFL [13] to
the full Hetionet graph to mine rules for the relation *Disease-presents-Symptom*,
as GPFL specialises in learning BAR rules (see Sect. 3.1). Recall that the set
of rule-based phenotype annotations **r** is needed in the reward function used to
train the policy network of the graph traversal algorithm (see Sect. 3.2), and is
used for evaluation. We preprocessed the rules before use, by taking only high
quality rules (which [13] defines as rules with a confidence score > 0.1, and a
head coverage of > 0.01), and only those for which the head constant was a
symptom (not a disease). Subsequently, we turned these rules into a rule set **r**
(cfr. Eq. 11).

$$\mathbf{r} = \{(h_0, t_0, \alpha_0), ...(h_n, t_n, \alpha_n)\} \tag{11}$$

The final ruleset consists of 4,981,259 rules with 1,746 unique head atoms and
33,449 unique tail atoms, and can be found online (See Footnote 12). On average,
each head atom has 2,853 rules (min: 1, max: 48,961).

---

[15] https://rdfpro.fbk.eu/.

4.3   Experimental Results

We evaluate our model on Hetionet in a quantitative and qualitative evaluation. We aim at measuring: (i) the effect training with contextual knowledge has on the quality of the reasoning paths, (ii) the effect training with contextual knowledge has on accuracy for the drug repurposing task, and (iii) the effect of using context in causal explanations on plausibility, novelty and relevancy as assessed by domain experts.

Quantitative Evaluation. We apply our method CoCo to Hetionet, as discussed in Sect. 3.2. After hyperparameter optimisation, we ran CoCo as well as MINERVA ten times using the following hyperparameters: learning rate: 0.004, $\rho = 2$, $\tau = 3$, 2 LSTM layers, and a hidden layer size of 128.

Results. To evaluate path quality, we calculate Path Accuracy (PA):

$$\text{PA} = \frac{n \text{ correct preds with } PC > 0}{n \text{ correct preds}} \tag{12}$$

We average PA over ten runs per model (CoCo and MINERVA), see Table 4. Moreover, to show that learning with context does not sacrifice hits@k scores, we compare CoCo to MINERVA on the basis of hits@1, hits@5 and Mean Reciprocal Rank (MRR), averaged over ten runs per model. Lastly, to demonstrate the difference in predictions and explanations between CoCo and MINERVA, we show statistics for the hits@1 predictions (Table 5): entities of correct predictions, as well as statistics of rewarded tail entities t_i. We trained both models for path length (PL) $\in \{2,4\}$, as training with a PL = 3 yielded significantly worse results. We hypothesise this is due to Hetionet's semantics: the number of path patterns between disease and compound are reduced to a less meaningful subset.

Table 4. APA(%), Hits@k(%) and MRR (%) scores ($\pm$ standard deviation) for CoCo and the model without context (MINERVA), averaged over 10 runs, for path length (PL) $\in \{2,4\}$.

Model	PL	APA	Hits@1	Hits@5	MRR
CoCo	2	**65.61** ($\pm$23.19)	**9.64** ($\pm$2.4)	14.11 ($\pm$2.25)	11.60 ($\pm$2.10)
MINERVA	2	**59.63** ($\pm$14.94)	**9.14** ($\pm$2.98)	14.64 ($\pm$3.74)	11.79 ($\pm$3.10)
CoCo	4	**57.45**($\pm$6.98)	**8.68** ($\pm$1.44)	**18.15** ($\pm$1.87)	**13.44** ($\pm$1.47)
MINERVA	4	45.87 ($\pm$4.25)	**8.58** ($\pm$2.15)	18.44 ($\pm$1.60)	13.37 ($\pm$1.72)

We observe from Table 4 and Table 5 that for CoCo, APA as well as the number of distinct rewarded tail entities t_i, has increased significantly for paths of length 4 (paired t-test, $p < 0.5$). This can indicate that patterns have been discovered between diseases and genes based on disease phenotypes. From Table 4, we additionally observe that hits@k results have not decreased nor increased significantly.

Figure 3 shows rewarded rule tail types $t(t_i)$ during training. We can see that rewarded entities are mostly of type *Gene* and *Anatomy*, and that these numbers are increasing during training, indicating that a relationship between disease-drug tuples and these entities is learned. Other entities are not rewarded often during training. By observing Fig. 1, we hypothesise that this is likely due to path length, as entities of type *Molecular Function, Biological Process, Cellular Component* and *Pathway* are more hops away from diseases and compounds.

Qualitative Evaluation. For our qualitative evaluation, we evaluate the multi-hop reasoning paths on the basis of plausibility, novelty and relevancy to the domain, through an online survey. For both models (CoCo and MINERVA), we extracted the path of the highest-ranked prediction for each example from the test set. From this subset, we randomly sampled paths from the five most used metapaths, making sure that half of those had a PC of > 0.

Table 5. Hits@1 statistics: path length (PL), number of rule hits n_r (number of unique rewarded rule tail atoms n_t), number of unique diseases n_d, number of unique compounds n_c, and number of unique drug-disease triples n_t.

Model	PL	n_r (n_t)	n_d	n_c	n_t
CoCo	2	143 (19)	26	46	49
MINERVA	2	109 (23)	27	61	63
CoCo	4	**191 (56)**	30	64	73
MINERVA	4	115 (41)	27	65	70

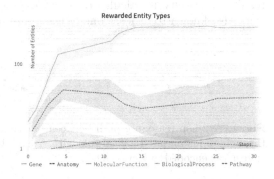

Fig. 3. Rewarded tail atom types $t(t_i)$ during training, averaged over ten runs. Note that the y-axis has a log scale.

Plausibility. For plausibility, we asked four annotators to rate each explanation with one of three categories: *implausible, partially plausible, plausible*. Amongst these annotators, the Krippendorff's inter annotator agreement was α_k 0.17, indicating a slight agreement ($0.01 < \alpha_k < 0.20$). The average plausibility score was 0.70, with a statistically insignificant difference between scores for paths generated by the model trained with and without context—0.73 and 0.66, respectively. Path length did influence interpretability scores significantly, with a score of 0.82 and 0.57 for path length 2 and 4 respectively, indicating that background knowledge about path semantics (for instance using metapaths in the reward function [22]) during training is needed to improve interpretability of longer paths.

Unexpectedly, using context in the explanation, as shown in Fig. 4, had a negative impact on the plausiblity score, 0.58 versus 0.86 for with and without context, respectively. We believe the result to be due to the associations (such as *Ovarian cancer → Ataxia Telangiectasia*) being unclear or difficult to interpret by the annotators due to the semantics of the *Disease-presents-Symptom* relation. Annotators indicated issues with semantics, i.e., *"Ataxia Telangiectasia is not a symptom of Ovarian cancer"*. Some annotators indicated a clearer description of the exact association would be more insightful *"association lacks further explanation of mechnism or relation"*. Framing such explanations differently, or in more detail, might therefore improve plausibility.

Novelty. To measure novelty, we asked annotators to indicate whether the fact was new to them or not, *True* or *False*. Amongst four annotators, the Krippendorff's α_k was −0.20, indicating a less than chance agreement ($\alpha_k < 0$). Given the varying expertise among the annotators (pharmacovigilance, geriatrics and multimorbidity, evidence synthesis, immunology, and molecular biology, drug therapies and safe use), we argue that the result is to be expected. No other result for novelty is calculated, as all explanations that were found plausible were also known to at least one of the annotators.

Fig. 4. A 2-hop reasoning path between Ovarian cancer and Carboplatin, associated through an instantiated logical rule with Ataxia Telangiectasia, a symptom of Ovarian cancer (as encoded in Hetionet).

Relevancy. For relevancy, we asked annotators to indicate, on a five point Likert Scale (*Strongly disagree-Strongly agree*), whether a fact was relevant to the domain of biomedicine. To three of the four annotators, the causal explanations were generally found relevant to the domain, given that in only 4 of the 24 cases one of the annotators chose *Neutral* or *Disagree/Strongly disagree*. The four cases that were rated as less relevant to the domain proved to be semantically incorrect. For one case, the symptom appeared to be the cause of the disease rather than a symptom, as noted by two annotators: *"fetal hypoxia is a cause of epilepsy, rather than a symptom"*. Moreover, in two cases, the metapath appeared not relevant, such as: *Disease-associates-Gene-associates-Disease-associates-Gene-_binds-Compound*, for which annotators indicated they did not understand the reasoning. One annotator was less optimistic about path relevancy, specifically for paths of length two. It was indicated that, even though these were plausible, they were deemed less relevant as they would be easier to devise by humans. Longer paths, on the other hand, are deemed less plausible, but potentially more relevant, as it is more challenging for humans to think up longer chains of reasoning.

Table 6. Predictions for Cochrane's populations for $PC = 0$ and $PC > 0$, with their systematic review codes.

Prediction	α	Review
Haematological malignancy & Herpes simplex → Raloxifene	0	CD012601
Haematological malignancy & Herpes simplex → Dactinomycin	0.11	CD012601
ADHD & Hyperkinesis → Haloperidol	0.15	CD005042
ADHD & Hyperkinesis → Thioridazine	0	CD005042
Hypertension & Hypervigilance → Ciclopirox	0.70	CD004351
Hypertension & Hypervigilance → L-Aspartic Acid	0	CD004351
Gestational diabetes & Hypertension → L-Glutamine	1	CD005542
Gestational diabetes & Hypertension→ Dinoprostone	1.15	CD005542

Lastly, we ran CoCo on our real-world dataset of populations from Cochrane systematic reviews. The full dataset including predictions, as exemplified in Table 6, can be found online (See Footnote 12). Examples from Table 6 show that predictions can be ranked based on path coherence (PC), where predictions with a $PC < 0$ do not take into account a disease's phenotype, and those with a $PC > 0$ are related to the disease's phenotype. Given that a detailed understanding of how a condition's symptoms relate to underlying molecular processes can help in elucidating the molecular mechanisms underlying these conditions, such predictions can be useful for identifying interesting drug targets. However, without gold standard annotations of these populations with drug targets and compounds, it is challenging to quantify the exact improvement.

5   Conclusion

Based on two assumptions (Assumption 1 and 2), we employed a novel approach for drug repurposing in context. We based our work on a RL-based multi-hop reasoning approach for drug repurposing. First, we defined a metric for path quality based on path coherence with a set of context entities (symptoms). Second, we annotated the context entities with biomedical entities using logical rule mining. Third, we used the measure for path coherence as a reward during training. We evaluated: (i) the effect of training with these logical rules on the reasoning paths, (ii) whether including these associations increased the interpretability of the paths when presented to domain experts. Moreover, we presented a real-world dataset of populations for multi-hop reasoning.

First, we discovered that after training with context, reasoning paths extracted for predictions on the test set changed significantly. They were found to be more coherent with their context without sacrificing prediction accuracy. Second, we found that an increased path length was found more interesting, given that longer reasoning chains would be more challenging to discover by humans.

However, longer reasoning paths were also found less plausible or semantically incorrect. The addition of metapaths (as done in [22]) to our methodology would resolve this issue.

A limitation of our method is that it only learns from the similarity of diseases based on their phenotype, whereas it does not take into account differences between phenotypes of related diseases nor restrictions for drug treatments due to co-occurring diseases. Moreover, even though we prove that paths discovered during testing appear more coherent with context, it is challenging to quantify the exact improvement without a larger gold standard dataset of drug-symptom-disease tuples. This will be looked at in future work.

Acknowledgements. The authors would like to thankfully acknowledge Lotty Hooft and Alexandre Renaux for their valuable opinions and discussions related to this work. This work is supported by the EU Horizon 2020 research programme MUHAI, grant no. 951846.

References

1. Agrawal, M., Zitnik, M., Leskovec, J.: Large-scale analysis of disease pathways in the human interactome. In: Pacific Symposium on Biocomputing, no. 212669, pp. 111–122 (2018). https://doi.org/10.1142/9789813235533_0011
2. Bahler, D., Stone, B., Wellington, C., Bristol, D.W.: Symbolic, neural, and Bayesian machine learning models for predicting carcinogenicity of chemical compounds. J. Chem. Inf. Comput. Sci. **40**(4), 906–914 (2000). https://doi.org/10.1021/ci990116i
3. Bakal, G., Talari, P., Kakani, E.V., Kavuluru, R.: Exploiting semantic patterns over biomedical knowledge graphs for predicting treatment and causative relations. J. Biomed. Inform. **82**(January), 189–199 (2018). https://doi.org/10.1016/j.jbi.2018.05.003
4. Blomqvist, E., Alirezaie, M., Santini, M.: Towards causal knowledge graphs-position paper. In: KDH@ ECAI (2020)
5. Brown, D.G., Wobst, H.J.: A decade of FDA-approved drugs (2010–2019): trends and future directions. J. Med. Chem. **64**(5), 2312–2338 (2021). https://doi.org/10.1021/acs.jmedchem.0c01516
6. Das, R., et al.: Go for a walk and arrive at the answer: reasoning over paths in knowledge bases using reinforcement learning. In: 6th International Conference on Learning Representations, ICLR 2018 - Conference Track Proceedings (2018)
7. De Cao, N., Kipf, T.: MolGAN: an implicit generative model for small molecular graphs. arXiv preprint arXiv:1805.11973 (2018)
8. DiMasi, J.A., Grabowski, H.G., Hansen, R.W.: Innovation in the pharmaceutical industry: new estimates of R&D costs. J. Health Econ. **47**, 20–33 (2016). https://doi.org/10.1016/j.jhealeco.2016.01.012
9. Drancé, M., Boudin, M., Mougin, F., Diallo, G.: Neuro-symbolic XAI for computational drug repurposing. In: KEOD, vol. 2, pp. 220–225 (2021)
10. Fu, G., Ding, Y., Seal, A., Chen, B., Sun, Y., Bolton, E.: Predicting drug target interactions using meta-path-based semantic network analysis. BMC Bioinform. **17**(1), 1–10 (2016)

11. Galárraga, L., Teflioudi, C., Hose, K., Suchanek, F.M.: Fast rule mining in onto-logical knowledge bases with AMIE+. VLDB J. **24**(6), 707–730 (2015). https://doi.org/10.1007/s00778-015-0394-1
12. Garijo, D., et al.: Towards automated hypothesis testing in neuroscience. In: Gadepally, V., et al. (eds.) DMAH/Poly -2019. LNCS, vol. 11721, pp. 249–257. Springer, Cham (2019). https://doi.org/10.1007/978-3-030-33752-0_18
13. Gu, Y., Guan, Y., Missier, P.: Towards learning instantiated logical rules from knowledge graphs. arXiv preprint arXiv:2003.06071 (2020)
14. Guo, L., Sun, Z., Hu, W.: Learning to exploit long-term relational dependencies in knowledge graphs. In: International Conference on Machine Learning, pp. 2505–2514. PMLR (2019)
15. de Haan, R., Tiddi, I., Beek, W.: Discovering research hypotheses in social science using knowledge graph embeddings. In: Verborgh, R., et al. (eds.) ESWC 2021. LNCS, vol. 12731, pp. 477–494. Springer, Cham (2021). https://doi.org/10.1007/978-3-030-77385-4_28
16. Himmelstein, D.S., et al.: Systematic integration of biomedical knowledge prioritizes drugs for repurposing. Elife **6**, e26726 (2017)
17. Jaundoo, R., Craddock, T.J.: DRUGPATH: the drug gene pathway meta-database. Int. J. Mol. Sci. **21**(9), 3171 (2020). https://doi.org/10.3390/ijms21093171
18. Jumper, J., et al.: Highly accurate protein structure prediction with AlphaFold. Nature **596**(7873), 583–589 (2021)
19. Kundu, S.: AI in medicine must be explainable. Nat. Med. **27**(8), 1328 (2021). https://doi.org/10.1038/s41591-021-01461-z
20. Lakkaraju, H., Kamar, E., Caruana, R., Leskovec, J.: Interpretable & explorable approximations of black box models. arXiv preprint arXiv:1707.01154 (2017)
21. Lin, X.V., Socher, R., Xiong, C.: Multi-hop knowledge graph reasoning with reward shaping. In: Proceedings of the 2018 Conference on Empirical Methods in Natural Language Processing (EMNLP 2018) (2018)
22. Liu, Y., Hildebrandt, M., Joblin, M., Ringsquandl, M., Raissouni, R., Tresp, V.: Neural multi-hop reasoning with logical rules on biomedical knowledge graphs. In: Verborgh, R., et al. (eds.) ESWC 2021. LNCS, vol. 12731, pp. 375–391. Springer, Cham (2021). https://doi.org/10.1007/978-3-030-77385-4_22
23. Lv, X., et al.: Is multi-hop reasoning really explainable? Towards benchmarking reasoning interpretability. arXiv preprint arXiv:2104.06751 (2021)
24. Meilicke, C., Chekol, M.W., Ruffinelli, D., Stuckenschmidt, H.: Anytime bottom-up rule learning for knowledge graph completion. In: Proceedings of the 28th International Joint Conference on Artificial Intelligence (IJCAI). IJCAI/AAAI Press (2019)
25. Montavon, G., Samek, W., Müller, K.R.: Methods for interpreting and understanding deep neural networks. Digit. Sig. Process. **73**, 1–15 (2018)
26. Nagarajan, M., et al.: Predicting future scientific discoveries based on a networked analysis of the past literature. In: Proceedings of the 21th ACM SIGKDD International Conference on Knowledge Discovery and Data Mining, pp. 2019–2028 (2015)
27. Pankratius, V., et al.: Computer-aided discovery: toward scientific insight generation with machine support why scientists need machine support for discovery search. IEEE Intell. Syst. **31**(4), 3–10 (2016). https://doi.org/10.1109/MIS.2016.60
28. Paul, D., Sanap, G., Shenoy, S., Kalyane, D., Kalia, K., Tekade, R.K.: Artificial intelligence in drug discovery and development. Drug Discov. Today **26**(1), 80 (2021)

29. Percha, B., Altman, R.B.: A global network of biomedical relationships derived from text. Bioinformatics **34**(15), 2614–2624 (2018)
30. Ribeiro, M.T., Singh, S., Guestrin, C.: "Why should i trust you?" Explaining the predictions of any classifier. In: Proceedings of the 22nd ACM SIGKDD International Conference on Knowledge Discovery and Data Mining, pp. 1135–1144 (2016)
31. Saik, O.V., et al.: Novel candidate genes important for asthma and hypertension comorbidity revealed from associative gene networks. BMC Med. Genomics **11**(1), 61–76 (2018)
32. Sosa, D.N., Derry, A., Guo, M., Wei, E., Brinton, C., Altman, R.B.: A literature-based knowledge graph embedding method for identifying drug repurposing opportunities in rare diseases. In: Pacific Symposium on Biocomputing 2020, pp. 463–474. World Scientific (2020)
33. Swanson, D.R., Smalheiser, N.R.: An interactive system for finding complementary literatures: a stimulus to scientific discovery. Artif. Intell. **91**(2), 183–203 (1997). https://doi.org/10.1016/S0004-3702(97)00008-8
34. Tiddi, I., D'Aquin, M., Motta, E.: Walking linked data: a graph traversal approach to explain clusters. In: CEUR Workshop Proceedings (2014)
35. Wilcke, W.X., de Boer, V., de Kleijn, M.T., van Harmelen, F.A., Scholten, H.J.: User-centric pattern mining on knowledge graphs: an archaeological case study. J. Web Semant. **59**, 100486 (2019). https://doi.org/10.1016/j.websem.2018.12.004
36. Williams, R.J.: Simple statistical gradient-following algorithms for connectionist reinforcement learning. Mach. Learn. **8**(3), 229–256 (1992)
37. Zhou, X., Menche, J., Barabási, A.L., Sharma, A.: Human symptoms-disease network. Nat. Commun. **5**(1), 1–10 (2014)

A Comparative Study of Stream Reasoning Engines

Nathan Gruber(✉)🆔 and Birte Glimm🆔

Ulm University, Helmholtzstraße 16, 89081 Ulm, Germany
nathan.gruber@tum.de, birte.glimm@uni-ulm.de

Abstract. The diverse research efforts in recent years in the area of stream reasoning (SR) led to a wide range of SR engines. However, the lack of standardization and the diverse choices in SR (e.g., tuple-driven vs. time-driven engines, streaming all results vs. newly derived ones, ...) mean that real comparability among the engines is hardly given. A first step towards achieving comparability and standardization is the RSP-QL model, implemented in the RSP4J framework, which allows for describing and formalizing the semantics of SR engines. To further advance the state of the art in comparative research of stream reasoning, we present the results of a survey to quantify the in-use importance of several key performance indicators (KPIs) and features and compare SR engines along these KPIs with the CityBench and the CSRBench oracle. Our analysis shows that the two RSP4J implementations C-SPARQL2.0 and YASPER outperform the well-known C-SPARQL implementation in terms of performance and configurability. Our comparison against a naive SR extension of the incremental reasoning engine RDFox shows that SR engines still have potential for improvement. To avoid a costly integration of engines into several different benchmarking environments, we finally present a unifying interface, already aligned with the City-Bench and CSRBench, for benchmarking SR engines.

Keywords: Stream Reasoning · RSP4J · RDFox · C-SPARQL · CityBench · CSRBech · Benchmarking Interface

1 Introduction

Research in the area of stream reasoning (SR) has gained popularity in recent years [10] because the fields of application are vast, reaching from smart cities [11] over industry 4.0 scenarios [12] to the internet of things [22]. Stream reasoning aims at making sense of dynamic data streams combined with static background knowledge in real-time. To meet the requirements necessary for reaching this vision, researchers theoretically investigated the area of stream reasoning, suggested approaches and models that tackle some requirements, and built stream reasoning engines, mainly as proof of concept implementations, to test their approaches and compare them in practice. Examples for such stream reasoning engines are C-SPARQL [4], SPARQL$_{STREAM}$ [6], and CQELS [16].

© The Author(s), under exclusive license to Springer Nature Switzerland AG 2023
C. Pesquita et al. (Eds.): ESWC 2023, LNCS 13870, pp. 21–37, 2023.
https://doi.org/10.1007/978-3-031-33455-9_2

Since these engines have been developed individually by different research groups, each having their own ideas and no binding standard being established, there are significant differences in the engines' behavior, performance, and functionality. Multiple query languages have been proposed as well, which fostered the breadth of research but hindered a fair comparison between stream reasoning engines. In order to identify and name differences in the operational semantics of existing engines, Botan et al. [5] came up with the descriptive SECRET model for stream reasoning engines that was then extended into a unifying standard model for the semantics of SR engines, the RSP-QL model [8]. The recently published RSP4J framework [23] implements this standard and proposes prototype engines. In this paper, we present the following contributions:

- While it is broadly recognized that benchmarking fosters research and applications by helping to identify superior techniques and best practices, it is less clear which measurable KPIs are the most relevant ones in practice. We empirically evaluate the in-use importance of several KPIs and features through a survey, which gives a clearer context for benchmark results.
- We analyze four stream reasoning engines theoretically and compare their performance regarding several KPIs using common SR benchmarks. The engines C-SPARQL2.0[1] and YASPER [24] are based on the newly introduced RSP4J framework, while another one is the commonly known baseline implementation C-SPARQL [4]. The last one is the high-performance incremental reasoning engine RDFox [17], which we extended for its use as SR engine.
- In order to avoid the time-consuming task of integrating one SR engine at a time into different benchmarking environments, we developed a flexible, unifying interface for benchmarking SR engines. Two popular benchmarks, namely CityBench and CSRBench, are already aligned with the interface and can, hence, directly be used with any SR engine adapting the interface.

The paper is structured as follows: Sect. 2 introduces the definitions that are necessary for understanding what follows. Section 3 gives an overview of related work and, in Sect. 4, we introduce the considered engines and provide a theoretical categorization. In Sect. 5, we showcase and discuss the results of our survey as well as of our benchmarking efforts before we present the unifying interface for SR benchmarks in Sect. 6. Section 7 sums up our findings and gives an outlook on open issues that should be addressed in future research.

2 Preliminaries

We assume interested readers to be familiar with the basics of the RDF data model [19] and the SPARQL query language [2]. In the following, we focus on RDF Stream Processing (RSP) aspects, i.e., on extensions of RDF and SPARQL for dealing with the continuous processing of (RDF) data streams.

Stream reasoning engines work on (static) RDF graphs in combination with dynamic RDF streams. Those streams are RDF triples combined with a monotonously increasing timestamp that indicates the arrival time of the triples:

---

[1] https://github.com/streamreasoning/csparql2.

Definition 1 (RDF Streams). *Let $t_0, \ldots, t_n$ be RDF triples and $\tau_0, \ldots, \tau_n$ timestamps such that, for each $0 \leq i < j \leq n$, $\tau_i < \tau_j$, then the sequence $(\langle t_0, \tau_0 \rangle, \ldots, \langle t_n, \tau_n \rangle)$ is an RDF stream.*

Note that we can see an RDF stream $(\langle t_0, \tau_0 \rangle, \ldots, \langle t_n, \tau_n \rangle)$ w.r.t. a current timestamp τ_c, $\tau_0 \leq \tau_c \leq \tau_n$, such that the sub-sequence $(\langle t_0, \tau_0 \rangle, \ldots, \langle t_i, \tau_i \rangle)$, $\tau_0 \leq \tau_i < \tau_c$, consists of past and the sub-sequence $(\langle t_j, \tau_j \rangle, \ldots, \langle t_n, \tau_n \rangle)$, $\tau_c < \tau_j \leq \tau_n$ consists of future (timestamped) triples.

Most SR engines work on snapshots of the data streams, so-called *windows*, which consist of a sub-sequence of the streamed data w.r.t. some point in time.

Definition 2 (Windows). *Given an RDF stream $(\langle t_0, \tau_0 \rangle, \ldots, \langle t_n, \tau_n \rangle)$ and a current timestamp τ_c, $\tau_0 \leq \tau_c \leq \tau_n$, a physical window of (window) size $w \in \mathbb{N}$ is the sub-sequence $(\langle t_i, \tau_i \rangle, \ldots, \langle t_c, \tau_c \rangle)$ of $(\langle t_0, \tau_0 \rangle, \ldots, \langle t_n, \tau_n \rangle)$ such that $\#\{\tau_i, \ldots, \tau_c\} = w$, i.e., the window consists of the last w triples.*

Given an RDF stream $(\langle t_0, \tau_0 \rangle, \ldots, \langle t_n, \tau_n \rangle)$, a starting time τ_0, a window size $w \in \mathbb{N}$, and a step size $s \in \mathbb{N}$ ($s \leq w$), the ith logical window W_i opens at $\tau_o = \tau_0 + i * s$, closes at $\tau_c = \tau_o + w$ and contains the (timestamped) triples $\{\langle t, \tau \rangle \mid \tau_o \leq \tau < \tau_c\}$. A logical window is called a tumbling window, if $s = w$, and it is called a sliding window if $s < w$.

Note that in practice, one might also consider initial physical windows that contain less than w triples, whereas the current definition considers the first window to be defined only when w triples are available at the current point in time. Note further that the contents of tumbling windows are always non-overlapping, whereas sliding windows have an overlap.

Since most SR engines perform reasoning and query answering on the (static) windows, we distinguish three types of necessary operators: *Stream-To-Relation (S2R)*, *Relation-to-Relation (R2R)*, and *Relation-to-Stream (R2S)*, where S2R operators typically perform some kind of windowing on data streams, R2R operators usually process SPARQL-like queries that produce static variable bindings (i.e., again relational data), and R2S operators transform these bindings back into data streams [3]. Regarding R2S operators, we distinguish RStreams, which emit the current solution mappings, IStreams, which emit the difference between the current and the previous solution mappings, and DStreams, which emit the difference between the previous and the current solution mappings.

Most SR query languages are extensions of SPARQL that additionally allow for setting the necessary information to execute SPARQL-like queries continuously over given data streams. An example is given in Listing 1.1, which registers a query as an RStream (Line 3) and specifies windows over which patterns are to be executed (Lines 5 and 7).

Window-based querying opens up several choices in terms of query execution semantics. The SECRET model [5] allows for characterizing these choices along four complementary dimensions: **S**cop**E**, **C**ontent, **RE**port, and **T**ick. Given a query's window parameters, *ScopE* defines the time interval for the active window. *Content* then specifies the elements of a stream that are in scope. *REport* states under what conditions those window contents become visible to the query

```
1   PREFIX ses: <http://www.insight-centre.org/dataset/SampleEventService#>
2   PREFIX ssn: <http://purl.oclc.org/NET/ssnx/ssn#>
3   REGISTER RSTREAM <q1> AS
4   SELECT ?obId1
5   FROM NAMED WINDOW <w1> ON ses:AarhusTrafficData182955 [RANGE PT3S STEP PT1S]
6   FROM <http://localhost/WebGlCity/RDF/SensorRepository.rdf>
7   WHERE { WINDOW <w1> { ?obId1 ssn:observedBy ses:AarhusTrafficData182955 . } }
```

Listing 1.1. An example (streaming) query

processor for evaluation and result reporting. Possible report strategies include the *window close* strategy, where results are reported, when a window closes, *periodic* (time-based) reporting, and reporting when the current window contains changed content (*content change*), or is non-empty (*non-empty content*). Finally, *Tick* (aka "window state change" or "window re-evaluation") models what drives an SR engine to take action on its input, which can, for example, be tuple-driven (when a triple arrives) or time-driven.

3   Related Work

To enable meaningful benchmarking in the area of stream reasoning, descriptive models are needed that can characterize the differences between existing engines and, thus, raise the comparability. On the other hand, benchmarks should push the systems to their limits in various respects and automatically measure the corresponding KPIs.

Correctness and Comparability. Only if the SECRET primitives of different engines are aligned and well understood, a fair comparison can be made. The SECRET framework is the basis for the RSP-QL model [8], which aims at unifying the semantics of SR engines. RSP-QL extends the SECRET model with data types like time-varying graphs, instantaneous graphs, and R2S operators and, thus, allows for a formal definition of correctness in SR systems. The correctness of SR engines can be checked automatically using the CSRBench [9], which comes with a configurable oracle that compares the answers of an SR engine with expected answers w.r.t. its SECRET primitives and for different start times. The RSP4J framework [23] is the first RSP-QL compliant Java API designed to facilitate the building of new SR engines and to foster the comparability among these systems.

Benchmarking. Scharrenbach et al. consider inference support over background knowledge or correct and efficient time modeling as essential properties of stream processing systems and, against this background, propose seven commandments for effective benchmarking of stream processing systems [21]. The benchmarks should challenge the systems in different dimensions including load balancing, various joins and aggregates, as well as the usage of various types of background knowledge. These proposals and the CityBench [1], which is based on real sensor data collected within the CityPulse project, combined with imaginary

Table 1. Properties of the considered SR engines

C-SPARQL	C-SPARQL2.0 & YASPER	RDFox
Scope		
physical & logical windows	logical windows	logical windows
start time cannot be set	start time can be set	start time cannot be set
Content / RSP-QL Dataset		
content merged into default graph	individually named windows	content merged into default graph
Report		
window close & non-empty content	configurable	periodic
Tick		
time-driven	configurable	time-driven (configurable interval)
R2S Operator		
RStream	configurable	RStream
empty relations are transmitted	empty relations are not transmitted	empty relations are not transmitted

movement data, are the basis of our work. The CityBench allows for various configurations, from the input stream rate to different sized background data files, over queries with variable numbers of input streams, to a configurable number of queries to be executed in parallel. Meanwhile, the CityBench measures the latency, memory consumption, and completeness of the considered engines.

Because it is time-consuming to integrate several SR engines into multiple benchmarks individually, Tommasini et al. proposed approaches to unify parts of the SR engines with Heaven [25] and RSPLab [26] and Kolchin et al. developed the YABench as an extensive benchmarking framework with multiple supported KPIs [14]. In addition, the results of some practical comparisons of the performances of existing engines have been published, e.g., comparing the performance of C-SPARQL and CQELS [7,20].

The HOBBIT platform[2] aims at providing a general, distributed, open-source, evaluation platform for semantic technologies. Due to its generality, the platform is more complex than a dedicated SR benchmark, while it is not targeting SR intricacies such as aligning the systems along the SECRET primitives.

4 Stream Reasoning Engines

In the following, we introduce the evaluated SR engines and compare them with regard to their SECRET and RSP-QL primitives (see Sect. 2 for the necessary definitions). Table 1 summarizes the categorization of the engines.

C-SPARQL. Continuous SPARQL (C-SPARQL) was introduced in 2010 by Barbieri et al. [4] as a query language extension for SPARQL. It came along with an open-source proof-of-concept Java implementation, the C-SPARQL engine,

---

[2] https://project-hobbit.eu/.

which is still a common baseline implementation. The C-SPARQL engine is provided as an open-source Java project on GitHub.[3]

C-SPARQL2.0 and YASPER. C-SPARQL2.0[4] and YASPER [24] are the first two prototype engines based on RSP4J, provided as Java open-source projects. While C-SPARQL2.0 uses Esper[5] for windowing and Jena[6] for querying, YASPER is a from-scratch implementation within RSP4J. C-SPARQL2.0 can be used to evaluate the performance of the RSP4J framework whereas YASPER, with its high degree of abstraction, is built for teaching. RSP4J-based engines allow for configuring their SECRET primitives and as they are RSP-QL compliant, using RSP-QL as a query language, they are more expressive than, for example, C-SPARQL due to the naming of the time-varying graphs.

RDFox. RDFox [17] is a highly-scalable, parallelized in-memory RDF store, which is currently commercially licensed and maintained by Oxford Semantic Technologies.[7] RDFox is not a stream reasoning engine per se, but it supports incremental (datalog) reasoning, has an extensive query support and shows an excellent performance. Hence, a comparison with RDFox gives an interesting perspective on the performance of dedicated SR engines.

For extending RDFox into an SR engine, we used similar SECRET primitives as those of C-SPARQL and implemented logical windowing. We parse queries in two parts: first, the information about the static/dynamic data and the windows is read, before the actual SPARQL query is parsed. We deliberately store the static and streamed data in the same data store (within the default graph) this allows for processing all data at the same time and perform reasoning on it. Since C-SPARQL follows a time-driven tick and a window-close report strategy, which is no different from a time-driven report strategy except for the first window, we implemented a time-driven tick and report strategy. We update the data store at the periodic step size interval of every stream (*report*) and evaluate the query every 15 milliseconds (*tick*).[8] Implemented optimizations include the adjustment of the tick interval and the adding of an offset to the data store updates depending on the number of concurrent queries, as well as the aggregation of the streamed data prior to the execution of data store updates. Since the internal dictionary for recording resources in RDFox grows with newly arriving triples, we regularly refreshed the data store (exported and reimported the triples) depending on the relative size of the dictionary. This prevents the RDFox server from growing linearly during the runtime and only has a negligible impact on the latency. We refer interested readers to GitHub[9] for the complete implementation details.

---

[3] https://github.com/streamreasoning/CSPARQL-engine.

[4] https://github.com/streamreasoning/csparql2.

[5] https://www.espertech.com/esper/.

[6] https://jena.apache.org/.

[7] https://www.oxfordsemantic.tech/.

[8] The tick interval of 15 milliseconds was chosen experimentally as it was a good trade-off between low latency and not putting too much load on the engine.

[9] https://github.com/SRrepo/CityBench-CSPARQL-RDFox/tree/master/src/org/java/aceis/utils/RDFox.

5 Evaluation

In this section, we present the results of our survey on the in-use importance of features and KPIs of SR engine as well as the benchmarking results.

5.1 Features and Key Performance Indicators

We start by introducing a list of features and KPIs which are the structured sum of previous publications and community discussions [1,9,20]. We further provide a short theoretical comparison of the considered SR engines regarding each feature (see Table 2) while the presented benchmarking results cover the remaining KPIs.

Latency. The latency of a stream reasoning engine refers to the average amount of time between the input arrival and the output generation for every triple. This performance indicator can be measured within the CityBench testbed. All considered engines internally use a periodic/time-driven tick strategy, which is essential for a fair comparison. A fair comparison with CQELS [16], for example, would not be possible because CQELS instantly reacts to the arrival of each triple and, therefore, offers a better latency.

Memory Consumption. The memory consumption of a stream reasoning engine refers to the average amount of memory used by the engine during its runtime. The CityBench testbed provides a possibility to measure this performance indicator. However, it also impurifies the results because it does not distinguish between the memory consumption of the engine and the memory consumption of the testing environment (which, for instance, stores the processed answers). To give a finer-grained picture, we analyzed the memory consumption during every execution in detail.

Completeness. The completeness of a stream reasoning engine refers to the percentage of correctly processed input triples. In our setup of the CityBench testbed, completeness is measured by setting the number of unique observations captured by the SR engine ($\#CO$) in relation to the number of unique observations produced by the test bed generator ($\#PO$), i.e., we compare $\#CO/\#PO$.

Maximum Throughput. An SR engine's maximum throughput characterizes the maximum amount of RDF triples that the engine can handle per time unit. This performance indicator cannot be measured automatically by any (existing) benchmarking environment because the maximum throughput depends, for example, on the complexity of the query, the size of the static background data, and the number of concurrent queries. The CityBench, however, allows for configuring the frequency and rate of input streams. In the following, we compare the latency, memory consumption, and completeness of the engines as a function of the input rate of the streams. Especially the dependencies between the input rate and the latency/completeness allow for making statements about the maximum throughput of the engines.

Correctness/Approximation Quality. We refer to correctness in the context of stream reasoning engines in terms of RSP-QL correctness [8]. To validate the functional correctness of the engines with respect to their execution semantics, we used the CSRBench oracle.

Table 2. Features of the considered SR engines

C-SPARQL	C-SPARQL2.0 & YASPER	RDFox
Support of Background Data		
supported	supported	supported
(RDFS-)Reasoning / Inference Support		
RDF entailment	OWL 2 entailment	OWL 2 entailment
Distributed Streams		
supported	supported	supported
Distribution Computation		
not supported	not supported	parallelization/distribution across physical cores
Guaranteed Performance Level		
not supported	not supported	not supported
Intern Mode of Operation		
	see Table 1	
Special Query Language Features / Expressiveness		
timestamp function	naming of streams	extensive datalog reasoning
Maintenance and Further Development		
research group maintained	research group maintained	commercial software
no active development	under active development	under active development

Support of Background Data. This feature refers to an SR engines' ability to process queries with respect to static background data and streamed data.

(RDFS-)Reasoning/Inference Support. Stream reasoning engines generally allow for reasoning under a specific entailment regime. This means, they can entail new facts from given data and knowledge [13].

Distribution. The distribution of an SR engine can either refer to its ability to process distributed data streams or its ability to work on multiple physical machines in parallel.

Guaranteed Performance Level. If an SR engine supports a guaranteed performance level, it allows for configuring a maximum time interval between the initiation and the answering of a query (e.g., 50 ms). The answers might be incomplete or approximated, but in time.

Intern Mode of Operation. For some applications, the intern mode of operation (e.g., the supported windowing technique, the tick strategy, or the supported R2S operators) of an SR engine might be relevant.

Special Query Language Features/Expressiveness. We consider features that are rarely supported by SR engines and suit a particular application use case, as special features. Expressiveness refers to the complexity of queries that are supported by the respective query language of an engine.

Maintenance and Further Development. The level of maintenance, support, and the regularity of updates for an engine can be important factors for users of SR engines.

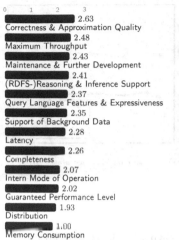

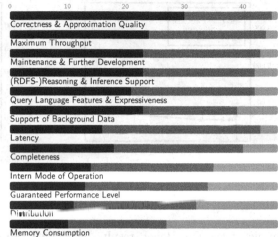

(a) Survey Results: On Feature Importance in Applications

(b) Survey Results: Detailed Assessments very important = black, important = dark gray and not so important = light gray

Fig. 1. Survey Results

5.2   Survey Results

Given the multitude of features and KPIs, the question arises as to which of them are particularly important for many real-world applications. To address this question, we conducted a survey with 46 developers, who worked on applications that internally use an SR engine. We asked them to assess the importance of each feature and performance indicator for their application on a scale of 1 (*not so important*), 2 (*important*), and 3 (*very important*). The results are presented in Fig. 1 with full details available on GitHub.[10]

The results indicate, that the correctness of a stream reasoning engine is essential to almost any application. It is, therefore, very important for an SR engine to pass the CSRBench (or YABench [14]). The survey results also suggest that many developers consider the maximum throughput of an SR engine to be more important for their application than the engines' latency. Furthermore, developers need SR engines to be reliable and maintained to benefit from their usage. The distribution (to multiple physical machines) and the memory consumption were rated as least important features/KPIs.

5.3   Benchmarking Setup

We performed all our experiments with the CityBench on a Lenovo ThinkPad T480 with 8 Intel(R) Core(TM) i5-8350U CPUs clocked at 1.70GHz and 8 GB RAM. Note that due to space limitations, we can only present a representative

---

[10] https://github.com/SRrepo/SurveyResults.

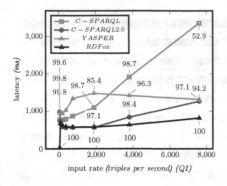 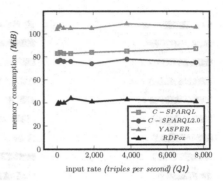

Fig. 2. Change of KPIs with a varying input rate

sample of the CityBench results below. All the setups (CityBench and CSR-Bench) and complete results are available in GitHub.[11] We used RDFox 5.4 and left the number of allowed threads to the default, which is the number of logical cores. For all other engines, we used their latest versions from GitHub.[12]

To improve the runtime efficiency, we performed two warm-up runs that lasted 130 s each before we started the experiments, which lasted 10 min or until all the available data was streamed.

5.4   CityBench Results

To examine the performance of the engines from different angles and to push the systems to their capacity limits in various ways, we used four scalability factors: the input rate, the number of concurrent queries (duplicity), the size of background data, and the number of parallel input streams. The following diagrams show the changes in latency, memory consumption, and completeness of the engines as a function of these scalability factors. The completeness is marked as a percentage next to the latency.

We used *Query 1* of the CityBench for the presented experiments with the input rate and duplicity and variants of *Query 1* which use larger background files for the experiments with varying background data. For the experiments with an increasing number of input streams, we used variants of *Query 10*. Note that the complexity of the chosen queries is rather low as they neither include calculations, filters, and aggregations nor UNION and OPTIONAL, which are computationally more complex operators [18].

Input Rate. The results in Fig. 2 show that the RDFox-based engine can handle large data streams without problems using its incremental maintenance

---

[11] https://github.com/SRrepo/.
[12] C-SPARQL2.0 commit number: f682cdc427d85594b39f9b4aa8d86e04833c8368,
YASPER commit number: aea74443955e1ab3b95de7b0ef65f7c1dbd51d08,
C-SPARQL commit number 4be27dd5ca23550da6bf7fb4e3420b0eb75132f0.

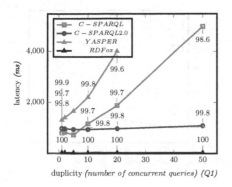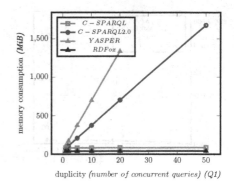

Fig. 3. Change of KPIs with a varying number of concurrent queries

algorithm. The implementation can be seen as a baseline in terms of completeness because it does not drop input triples when it faces an overload and is built in a way that no input is missed at the boundaries of a window. Meanwhile, the system's memory consumption is minimal. The RSP4J-based engines can also handle large amounts of input triples without losing much in terms of completeness. Their completeness decreases in dependence of how many input triples get lost at the boundaries of a window. C-SPARQL, on the other hand, successfully processes the query with an increased latency at a high completeness level up to around 5500 triples per second before its completeness suddenly collapses.

Duplicity. The results for concurrently executed queries are shown in Fig. 3. If the number of queries to be executed in parallel rises, the SR extension of RDFox increases its tick interval and adds an offset. Because the same query is executed multiple times and the results are evaluated centrally in the City-Bench testbed, no significant changes in performance can be detected. If different queries were executed, the latency would increase to a uniform but overall higher level, depending on the tick interval, while the completeness would remain the same. The memory consumption would rise because multiple data stores were needed. With the RSP4J-based engines, significant memory consumption can be observed because these engines cache the static data for each query individually. The latency of C-SPARQL2.0 remains almost constant, whereas YASPER was not able to execute 50 queries in parallel because the available system memory was exceeded. C-SPARQL shows an increasing latency, while its memory usage remains constant in the trade-off between memory consumption and latency.

Background Data. Figure 4 shows the results of our experiments with background data sets of different sizes. The RDFox extension once again exhibits a low latency because its periodic report is initiated exactly after the first receipt of input triples. Only the latency of C-SPARQL is affected negatively by an increased amount of background data. On the other hand, the results indicate that RDFox manages large amounts of data in a very memory-efficient way compared to the conventional SR engines.

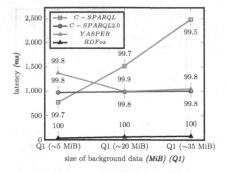
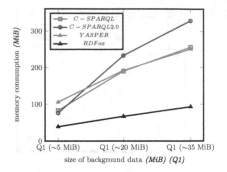

Fig. 4. Change of KPIs with a varying size of background data

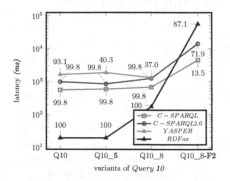
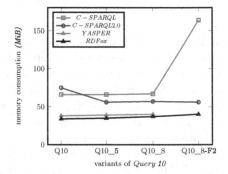

Fig. 5. Change of KPIs with a varying number of input streams

Number of Input Streams. Finally, our findings in combination with different numbers of input streams are depicted in Fig. 5. We used *Query 10*, *Query 10_5*, and *Query 10_8* of the CityBench and increased the frequency of *Query 10_8* to 2 (Q10_8-F2). These queries do not only test the engines' capabilities to process multiple input streams, but also their ability to handle a large number of answers because *Query 10_8* produces 3^8 (6^8) output bindings per second at a frequency level of 1 (2). The results show that RDFox and C-SPARQL2.0 are able to handle a large number of query answers per time unit while C-SPARQL and YASPER face an overload.

Discussion. Generally, our performance measurements for C-SPARQL are consistent with most previous work [1,15,20] though the presentation of our results differs from previous publications as we directly relate completeness to latency. Thus, it is noticeable when stable latency is measured for an engine simply because it no longer processes all results correctly. The presented results indicate that RDFox, which is (one of) the most efficient and highly optimized incremental reasoning engines, is also competitive when being used as SR engine. Furthermore, the empirical results illustrate the potential for improvement that

Table 3. RSP-QL correctness of SR engines using the CSRBench oracle

	C-SPARQL	C-SPARQL2.0	YASPER	RDFox
Query 1	✓	✓	✓	✓
Query 2	✓	✓	✓	✓
Query 3	✓	✓	✓	✓
Query 4	✓	✓	_a	✓
Query 5	×	×b	×b	✓
Query 6	✓	✓	✓	✓
Query 7	✓	✓	✓	✓

[a]YASPER does not yet support the AVG-function, which is necessary for *Query 4*.
[b]For a sliding window with a window size of 5 time units and a step size of 1 time unit and assuming an RStream, C-SPARQL2.0 and YASPER are expected to return every answer five times. While most answers are indeed returned five times, some are only returned four times. We conjecture that this is due to internal temporal imprecisions introduced by a processing overhead.

still exists in the prototypical and not fully optimized implementations of the RSP4J framework.

5.5 CSRBench Results

Since our survey underlines the importance of the correct functioning of SR engines, the results of the CSRBench take on special significance. Table 3 shows the results of our experiments with the CSRBench oracle. All queries but Query 5 of the CSRBench use tumbling windows, for which the periodic and the window-close report strategies are equivalent (see Sect. 2). While C-SPARQL's answers do not match the expected answers for Query 5 because it reports the first window before it closes [9], the answers of our RDFox extension were accepted, even though the engine uses a periodic report strategy which is not supported by the oracle. This is because RDFox does not return empty answers and the first open windows do not contain any data that produces answers.

6 A Unifying Interface for Stream Reasoning Benchmarks

As it is very time-consuming to integrate one SR engine at a time into multiple benchmarking environments, we suggest a unifying interface for SR benchmarks that should speed up future benchmarking. The proposed interface is divided into three consecutive phases: the *initialization* (see Fig. 6), the *processing* (see Fig. 7), and the *evaluation* phase (see Fig. 8). Some parameters such as the *engine name* and specific *benchmark parameters* are required. Optional parameters include the *RDF serialization format* in which the data is streamed, the *configuration URL*, the *answers URL*, the *query language* of the engine, and the *waiting time* after the streams end. Reasonable defaults for the parameters

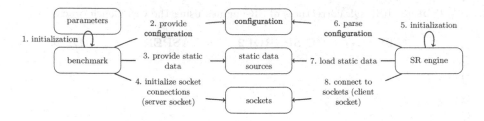

Fig. 6. Sequence and steps of the initialization phase

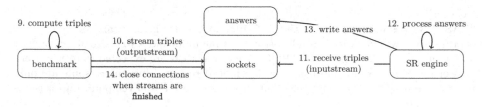

Fig. 7. Sequence and steps of the processing phase

are foreseen and can be found in GitHub.[13] The interface comes along with several advantages:

Alignment of CityBench and CSRBench. We already aligned the City-Bench[14] and the CSRBench[15] with the interface. Using these proof-of-concept implementations, we were able to reproduce the results presented in the last section with an aligned C-SPARQL[16], and central classes of these projects can easily be used for the alignment of further benchmarks.

Speed Up. The unifying interface speeds up benchmarking for developers of benchmarks as well as SR engines. For simplicity, let us assume that three SR

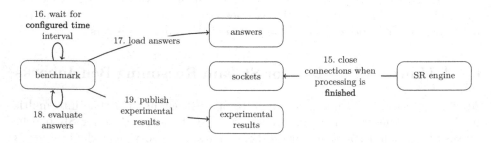

Fig. 8. Sequence and steps of the evaluation phase

[13] https://github.com/SRrepo/CSRBench-Aligned/blob/master/Parameters.md.
[14] https://github.com/SRrepo/CityBench-Aligned.
[15] https://github.com/SRrepo/CSRBench-Aligned.
[16] https://github.com/SRrepo/CSPARQL-Running-Example-For-Unifying-Interface.

engines and three benchmarks exist. Currently, if a new SR engine is developed and should be benchmarked, it has to be integrated into all three benchmarks individually. Since the developer first has to understand each benchmark's functionality, this process takes at least one week per benchmark, according to our experience. If all benchmarks were aligned with the interface, the developer would only have to write one single wrapper that implements the interface for the engine. Since dealing with the functionality of each individual benchmark is not needed any more and large parts of our C-SPARQL example can be adopted, this process probably takes less than one week. Analogously, the development time of a new benchmark can be significantly reduced by using the interface. In agreement with the developers of RSP4J, a standardized RSP4J runner component could even be used to automatically test every RSP4J-based engine with all aligned benchmarks, regardless of its implementation details.

Engine Independence. Another advantage of the interface is that the SR engine runs independently of the benchmark in a separate process. This allows for measuring, e.g., the memory consumption more cleanly and, by using sockets, standardized RDF formats, and JSON for the communication between benchmark and engine, we enable a smooth benchmarking of SR engines that are not written in Java or already compiled.

Expandability. As the engines store all data in a time-annotated fashion and the benchmark evaluates the performance retrospectively, future benchmarks can easily introduce new KPIs.

7   Conclusions

In this work, we empirically demonstrated RSP4J to be sound and performant. We also highlighted its advantages over C-SPARQL in the prototype implementations C-SPARQL2.0 and YASPER. Furthermore, this work reveals how a high-performant SR engine can be built on top of the incremental reasoning engine RDFox. The presented survey highlights the importance of functional correctness in SR engines for real-world applications and the unifying interface for SR benchmarks forms the basis for simplified future benchmarking.

Future research could, on the one hand, extend the RSP4J framework with a unified benchmark-runner and, on the other hand, further optimize RSP4J, e.g., by introducing algorithmic optimizations on its operators. In addition, it is worth supplementing this comparison with other engines, especially from the EP area, and building a standardized database for benchmarking results of SR engines. More generally, it is certainly useful to test other programming languages than Java in the context of SR engines. Last but not least, the incompleteness of SR engines endangers their use in real-world applications. There is an urgent need to explore theoretically and in practice how the completeness and reliability of SR engines can be raised. If an SR engine drops input to prevent an overload, for instance, it will be crucial to investigate how priorities can be assigned to certain inputs or how the dropping of input can be realized in a way that affects the query results as little as possible and, ideally, in a quantifiable manner.

References

1. Ali, M.I., Gao, F., Mileo, A.: CityBench: a configurable benchmark to evaluate RSP engines using smart city datasets. In: Arenas, M., et al. (eds.) ISWC 2015. LNCS, vol. 9367, pp. 374–389. Springer, Cham (2015). https://doi.org/10.1007/978-3-319-25010-6_25
2. Aranda, C.B., et al.: SPARQL 1.1 overview. W3C recommendation, W3C (2013). https://www.w3.org/TR/2013/REC-sparql11-overview-20130321/
3. Arasu, A., et al.: STREAM: the Stanford data stream management system. In: Data Stream Management. DSA, pp. 317–336. Springer, Heidelberg (2016). https://doi.org/10.1007/978-3-540-28608-0_16
4. Barbieri, D.F., Braga, D., Ceri, S., Valle, E.D., Grossniklaus, M.: C-SPARQL: a continuous query language for RDF data streams. Int. J. Semant. Comput. **4**(01), 3–25 (2010)
5. Botan, I., Derakhshan, R., Dindar, N., Haas, L., Miller, R.J., Tatbul, N.: Secret: a model for analysis of the execution semantics of stream processing systems. Proc. VLDB Endow. **3**(1–2), 232–243 (2010)
6. Calbimonte, J.-P., Corcho, O., Gray, A.J.G.: Enabling ontology-based access to streaming data sources. In: Patel-Schneider, P.F., et al. (eds.) ISWC 2010. LNCS, vol. 6496, pp. 96–111. Springer, Heidelberg (2010). https://doi.org/10.1007/978-3-642-17746-0_7
7. Dao-Tran, M., Beck, H., Eiter, T.: Contrasting RDF stream processing semantics. In: Qi, G., Kozaki, K., Pan, J.Z., Yu, S. (eds.) JIST 2015. LNCS, vol. 9544, pp. 289–298. Springer, Cham (2016). https://doi.org/10.1007/978-3-319-31676-5_21
8. Dell'Aglio, D., Della Valle, E., Calbimonte, J.P., Corcho, O.: RSP-QL semantics: a unifying query model to explain heterogeneity of RDF stream processing systems. Int. J. Semant. Web Inf. Syst. **10**, 17–44 (2014). https://doi.org/10.4018/ijswis.2014100102
9. Dell'Aglio, D., Calbimonte, J.P., Balduini, M., Corcho, O., Della Valle, E.: On correctness in RDF stream processor benchmarking. In: Alani, H., et al. (eds.) Semantic Web Conference, pp. 326–342. Springer, Heidelberg (2013). https://doi.org/10.1007/978-3-642-41338-4_21
10. Dell'Aglio, D., Della Valle, E., van Harmelen, F., Bernstein, A.: Stream reasoning: a survey and outlook. Data Sci. **1**(1–2), 59–83 (2017)
11. D'Aniello, G., Gaeta, M., Orciuoli, F.: An approach based on semantic stream reasoning to support decision processes in smart cities. Telemat. Inform. **35**(1), 68–81 (2018). https://doi.org/10.1016/j.tele.2017.09.019. https://www.sciencedirect.com/science/article/pii/S0736585317304768
12. Giustozzi, F., Saunier, J., Zanni-Merk, C.: Abnormal situations interpretation in industry 4.0 using stream reasoning. Procedia Comput. Sci. **159**, 620–629 (2019). https://doi.org/10.1016/j.procs.2019.09.217. https://www.sciencedirect.com/science/article/pii/S1877050919314012. Knowledge-Based and Intelligent Information & Engineering Systems: Proceedings of the 23rd International Conference KES2019
13. Glimm, B., Ogbuji, C.: SPARQL 1.1 entailment regimes. W3C recommendation, W3C (2013). https://www.w3.org/TR/2013/REC-sparql11-entailment-20130321/
14. Kolchin, M., Wetz, P., Kiesling, E., Tjoa, A.M.: YABench: a comprehensive framework for RDF stream processor correctness and performance assessment. In: Bozzon, A., Cudre-Maroux, P., Pautasso, C. (eds.) ICWE 2016. LNCS, vol. 9671, pp. 280–298. Springer, Cham (2016). https://doi.org/10.1007/978-3-319-38791-8_16

15. Lachhab, F., Bakhouya, M., Ouladsine, R., Essaaidi, M.: Performance evaluation of linked stream data processing engines for situational awareness applications. Concurr. Comput. Pract. Exp. **30**(12), e4380 (2018)
16. Le-Phuoc, D., Dao-Tran, M., Xavier Parreira, J., Hauswirth, M.: A native and adaptive approach for unified processing of linked streams and linked data. In: Aroyo, L., et al. (eds.) ISWC 2011. LNCS, vol. 7031, pp. 370–388. Springer, Heidelberg (2011). https://doi.org/10.1007/978-3-642-25073-6_24
17. Nenov, Y., Piro, R., Motik, B., Horrocks, I., Wu, Z., Banerjee, J.: RDFox: a highly-scalable RDF store. In: Arenas, M., et al. (eds.) ISWC 2015. LNCS, vol. 9367, pp. 3–20. Springer, Cham (2015). https://doi.org/10.1007/978-3-319-25010-6_1
18. Pérez, J., Arenas, M., Gutierrez, C.: Semantics and complexity of SPARQL. In: Cruz, I., et al. (eds.) ISWC 2006. LNCS, vol. 4273, pp. 30–43. Springer, Heidelberg (2000). https://doi.org/10.1007/11926078_3
19. Raimond, Y., Schreiber, G.: RDF 1.1 primer. W3C note, W3C (2014), https://www.w3.org/TR/2014/NOTE-rdf11-primer-20140624/
20. Ren, X., Khrouf, H., Kazi-Aoul, Z., Chabchoub, Y., Curé, O.: On measuring performances of C-SPARQL and CQELS. arXiv preprint arXiv:1611.08269 (2016)
21. Scharrenbach, T., Urbani, J., Margara, A., Della Valle, E., Bernstein, A.: Seven commandments for benchmarking semantic flow processing systems. In: Cimiano, P., Corcho, O., Presutti, V., Hollink, L., Rudolph, S. (eds.) ESWC 2013. LNCS, vol. 7882, pp. 305–319. Springer, Heidelberg (2013). https://doi.org/10.1007/978-3-642-38288-8_21
22. Su, X., Gilman, E., Wetz, P., Riekki, J., Zuo, Y., Leppänen, T.: Stream reasoning for the internet of things: challenges and gap analysis. In: Proceedings of the 6th International Conference on Web Intelligence, Mining and Semantics, WIMS 2016. Association for Computing Machinery, New York (2016). https://doi.org/10.1145/2912845.2912853
23. Tommasini, R., Bonte, P., Ongenae, F., Della Valle, E.: RSP4J: an API for RDF stream processing. In: Verborgh, R., et al. (eds.) ESWC 2021. LNCS, vol. 12731, pp. 565–581. Springer, Cham (2021). https://doi.org/10.1007/978-3-030-77385-4_34
24. Tommasini, R., Della Valle, E.: Yasper 1.0: towards an RSP-QL engine. In: International Semantic Web Conference (Posters, Demos & Industry Tracks) (2017)
25. Tommasini, R., Della Valle, E., Balduini, M., Dell'Aglio, D.: Heaven: a framework for systematic comparative research approach for RSP engines. In: Sack, H., Blomqvist, E., d'Aquin, M., Ghidini, C., Ponzetto, S.P., Lange, C. (eds.) ESWC 2016. LNCS, vol. 9678, pp. 250–265. Springer, Cham (2016). https://doi.org/10.1007/978-3-319-34129-3_16
26. Tommasini, R., Della Valle, E., Mauri, A., Brambilla, M.: RSPLab: RDF stream processing benchmarking made easy. In: d'Amato, C., et al. (eds.) ISWC 2017. LNCS, vol. 10588, pp. 202–209. Springer, Cham (2017). https://doi.org/10.1007/978-3-319-68204-4_21

Join Ordering of SPARQL Property Path Queries

Julien Aimonier-Davat[✉][iD], Hala Skaf-Molli[iD], Pascal Molli[iD],
Minh-Hoang Dang, and Brice Nédelec

LS2N, University of Nantes, 2 Rue de la Houssinière - BP 92208,
44322 Nantes Cedex 3, France
{julien.aimonier-davat,hala.skaf-molli,pascal.molli,
minh-hoang.dang,brice.nedelec}@univ-nantes.fr

Abstract. SPARQL property path queries provide a succinct way to
write complex navigational queries over RDF knowledge graphs. However, their evaluation remains difficult as they may involve the execution
of transitive closures. As a result, many property path queries just timeout when executed on public online RDF knowledge graphs. One solution to speed up their execution is to find optimal join orders. Although
the join ordering problem has been extensively studied for traditional
SPARQL queries, the presence of property path patterns biases existing approaches. In this paper we focus on $C2RPQ_{UF}$ queries (conjunctive SPARQL property path queries with UNION and FILTER), and we
present a query optimizer that is able to capture the cost of $C2RPQ_{UF}$
queries using an appropriate cost model and a sampling-based cardinality estimator. On the latest Wikidata Query Benchmark, we empirically
demonstrate that our approach finds significantly better join orders than
Virtuoso and BlazeGraph.

Keywords: Join Order · SPARQL Property Path · Random Walks ·
Sampling

1 Introduction

Context and Motivation: SPARQL 1.1 [30] introduced property paths to
add extensive navigational capabilities to the SPARQL query language. Property path queries (PPQs) are intensively used on Wikidata; they account for
38% of the entire query log [5]. Transitive closures are a crucial part of property
paths as they allow to match paths of arbitrary length. According to the log
of Wikidata, transitive closures are used by 66% of the property path queries.
However, transitive closures make the evaluation of property path queries challenging [33], and many of them cannot terminate in less than 60s. For example,
the query presented in Fig. 1a searches for road bicycle races in Central America
and time-out on Wikidata.

Related Works: Speeding up the processing of PPQs received much attention from the semantic web community [2]. One approach relies on a dedicated

```
SELECT ?x1 ?x3 WHERE {
    ?x3 wdt:P361 wd:Q27611 .    # tp1 (9)
    ?x1 wdt:P17 ?x3 .           # tp2 (13M)
    ?x1 wdt:P641* wd:Q3609 .    # tp3 (47K)
}
```

(a) $Q_1^{J_1}$: BlazeGraph's join order

```
SELECT ?x1 ?x3 WHERE {
    hint:Query hint:optimizer "None" .
    ?x1 wdt:P641* wd:Q3609 . # tp3
    hint:Prior hint:gearing "reverse" .
    ?x1 wdt:P17 ?x3 .           # tp2
    ?x3 wdt:P361 wd:Q27611 .    # tp1
}
```

(b) $Q_1^{J_2}$: Hand-crafted join order

Fig. 1. Query Q_1 comes from the Wikidata Query Benchmark [3] and returns road bicycle races located in Central America. $Q_1^{J_1}$ is the join order decided by BlazeGraph while $Q_1^{J_2}$ is a hand-crafted join order. The "hint:Query" triple pattern in $Q_1^{J_2}$ is used to force the join order in BlazeGraph. Commented numbers are triple patterns cardinality. On the Wikidata Query Service $Q_1^{J_1}$ time-out ($>$60s) while $Q_1^{J_2}$ terminates in less than 3 s.

index [28] that improves PPQs execution time, but requires the construction and maintenance of the index. Other works propose new dedicated operators to process transitive closures [1,4,27,32,33]. Such approaches are very effective but focus on evaluating property path patterns (PPPs) alone, while most of the time PPPs are just part of a PPQ. For instance, tp_3 is just a pattern among others in the query Q_1 in Fig. 1. In this paper, we propose to improve PPQs execution time by finding better join orders. Compared to previous works, finding better join orders allows us to improve PPQs execution time on existing engines, without new indexes and new operators. To illustrate the impact of finding good join orders, Q_1 has been executed on the Wikidata query service using two different join orders: (1) a join order $J_1 = ((tp1 \bowtie tp2) \bowtie tp3)$ that has been decided by BlazeGraph, the SPARQL engine behind Wikidata (2) a join order $J_2 = ((tp3 \bowtie tp2) \bowtie tp1)$ that has been hand-crafted. Following J_1 the query $Q_1^{J_1}$ time-out on Wikidata, i.e. $Q_1^{J_1}$ requires more than 60 s to complete, while $Q_1^{J_2}$ terminates in less than 3 s. Although the join ordering problem has been extensively studied in the context of conjunctive queries with filters [12,13,17], it has been poorly explored when considering property path queries [10,11]. It is currently unclear how current engines consider path patterns, i.e. how the cost of a join order that contains PPPs is computed, and why it should be computed like that.

Approach and Contributions: This paper focuses on the class of conjunctive two-way regular path queries with UNION and FILTER, denoted $C2RPQ_{UF}$ in [5]. For $C2RPQ_{UF}$ queries, we propose a query optimizer that can find efficient join orders without changing existing SPARQL engines. Finding such join orders is challenging; depending on the join order, a path pattern may behave as a transitive closure or a reachability pattern. The changing nature of path patterns is biasing traditional cost models that fail to find efficient join orders. The contributions of this paper are the following:

1. This paper proposes a cost model along with a dynamic programming (DP) algorithm able to capture the cost of evaluating PPQs using traditional PPP operators. Compared to state-of-the-art, the proposed DP algorithm can

rewrite PPPs such that their cost remain observable to existing cost functions as the one defined in [18].
2. Any cost model requires accurate cardinality estimates. However, there is currently no cardinality estimator able to handle property path patterns. Consequently, this paper proposes a cardinality estimator for PPQs based on random walks. Random walks can be computed for cheap thanks to B-Tree indexes, widely used to index RDF data. Compared to state-of-the-art, the proposed cardinality estimator extends the WanderJoin approach [18] to handle property path patterns.
3. The approach is evaluated on BlazeGraph and Virtuoso using the newly proposed Wikidata Query Benchmark [3]. Experimental results demonstrate that our approach significantly improves SPARQL property path queries performance in terms of execution time. Compared to BlazeGraph, the execution time is divided by at least 14.

The rest of the paper is organized as follows: Section 2 presents our approach, preliminaries, and the problem of ordering joins in the presence of property path patterns. Section 3 introduces a cost model for property path queries. Section 4 presents our cardinality estimator for property path queries. Section 5 details our experimental results. Finally, after discussing related works in Sect. 6, we present our conclusions and future work in Sect. 7.

2 Query Optimization of Property Path Queries

This paper follows the traditional query optimizer architecture of the system R [26]. The optimizer takes a property path query as input and returns a physical plan that minimizes a cost function. For each property path pattern, the optimizer also decides in which direction it should be evaluated, i.e. from subjects to objects (*forward navigation*) or from objects to subjects (*backward navigation*). The query optimizer enumerates valid join orders using a dynamic programming algorithm. Based on cardinality estimates, the cost model chooses the cheapest alternative among the valid join orders. The goal of this paper is to target mainstream SPARQL engines, consequently two hypotheses are assumed: (1) There are no indexes dedicated to transitive closures, such as the FERRARI index [28] (2) Property path patterns are evaluated using the traditional ALP procedure (a BFS-style algorithm) defined in the SPARQL specification [30] as it is done in JENA or BlazeGraph, or using transitive closure operators as in Virtuoso.

2.1 Preliminaries

SPARQL Query: This paper follows the notations from [24,25] and considers three disjoint sets I (IRIs), L (literals) and B (blank nodes). Let $T = I \cup L \cup B$ be the set of RDF terms, an RDF triple $(s, p, o) \in (I \cup B) \times I \times T$ connects a subject s through a predicate p to an object o. An RDF graph G is a finite set of RDF triples. Let V be an infinite set of variables, disjoint from the previous sets. A graph pattern P is defined recursively as follows:

1. A tuple from $(I \cup B \cup V) \times (I \cup V) \times (T \cup V)$ is a triple graph pattern.
2. If P_1 and P_2 are graph patterns, then $(P_1$ AND $P_2)$ and $(P_1$ UNION $P_2)$ are respectively a conjunctive graph pattern and an union graph pattern.
3. If P is a graph pattern and R is a SPARQL built-in condition, then $(P$ FILTER $R)$ is a filter graph pattern.

Given P a graph pattern, $var(P)$ is the set of variables found in P. The semantics of SPARQL queries is defined in terms of mappings. A mapping μ is a partial function $\mu : V \rightarrow T$. The domain of μ, denoted $dom(\mu)$, is the subset of V on which μ is defined. Given a triple pattern tp, $\mu(tp)$ is the image of tp under μ, i.e. the triple obtained by replacing the variables in tp according to μ. Letting $\mu(P)$ denote the image of P under μ, with respect to the latter definition, the evaluation of a graph pattern P over an RDF graph G is defined as $[\![P]\!]_G = \{ \mu \mid dom(\mu) = var(P) \wedge \mu(P) \subseteq G \}$. To simplify explanations around random walks, this paper assumes that the evaluation of a triple pattern tp over an RDF graph G returns a set of triples, i.e. $[\![tp]\!]_G = \{ \mu(tp) \mid dom(\mu) = var(tp) \wedge \mu(tp) \subseteq G \}$.

SPARQL Property Path Query (PPQ): A property path query is a SPARQL query with at least one property path pattern (PPP). A PPP is a tuple in $(I \cup B \cup V) \times E \times (T \cup V)$ where E is the set of property path expressions. Based on [16], property path expressions are defined by the grammar: $e := a \mid e^- \mid e_1 \cdot e_2 \mid e_1 + e_2 \mid e^+ \mid e^* \mid e? \mid !a_1, ..., a_k \mid !a_1^-, ..., a_k^-$ where $a, a_1, ..., a_k \in I$. This paper assumes non-transitive property path expressions to be evaluated using traditional SPARQL algebra operators [30]. Thus, the paper focuses only on the evaluation of transitive property path expressions, i.e. e^+ and e^*. Nested stars, e.g. $(a+)+$, are not considered and will be the subject of future work.

2.2 The Join Ordering Problem with Property Paths

$$C_{mm}(P,G) = \begin{cases} |[\![P]\!]_G| & \text{if } P = tp \vee P = \sigma(tp) \\ C_{mm}(P_1) + & \text{if } P = P_1 \overset{NLJ}{\bowtie} P_2, \\ |[\![P_1]\!]_G| \times max(\frac{|[\![P_1 \bowtie tp]\!]_G|}{|[\![P_1]\!]_G|}, 1) & (P_2 = tp \vee P_2 = \sigma(tp)) \end{cases}$$

Let us consider the C_{mm} cost function defined above, which is a simplified version of the one presented in [17]. For simplicity, only index-nested-loop joins and left-deep trees are considered, but our proposal holds in the general case. Most cost functions rely on cardinality estimates. For instance, the C_{mm} function defines the cost of evaluating a triple pattern as its cardinality [17]. Indeed, considering traditional indexes SPO, POS, OSP as available, any triple pattern tp can be evaluated over an RDF graph G in $\mathcal{O}(|[\![tp]\!]_G|log(|G|))$. Thus, for conjunctive queries with filters, minimizing a cardinality-based cost function such as the C_{mm} effectively leads to good join orders [7,17]. While the cost of evaluating a triple pattern is correlated with its cardinality, it is not always true for property

```
SELECT ?x1 ?x3 WHERE {                              SELECT ?x1 ?x3 WHERE {
  ?x3 wdt:P361 wd:Q27611 .        # tp1 (9)           ?x3 wdt:P361 wd:Q27611 .         # tp1 (9)
  ?x1 wdt:P17 ?x3 .               # tp2 (13M)          ?x1 wdt:P17 ?x3 .                # tp2 (13M)
  ?x1 wdt:P641* ?relax .                               ?relax wdt:P641* wd:Q3609 .      # tp3 (47K)
  FILTER (?relax = wd:Q3609) .    # tp3 (47K)          FILTER (?relax = ?x1) .
}                                                    }
```

(a) $Q_1^{J_1^F}$: Forward relaxation of J_1.   (b) $Q_1^{J_1^B}$: Backward relaxation of J_1.

Fig. 2. Forward and Backward relaxations of tp_3 in J_1 of query Q_1.

path patterns (PPPs). Assuming PPPs are evaluated using ALP, a BFS-style algorithm defined by the standard [30], two cases can be distinguished:

Case 1, Transitive-pattern Let $tp = (s, p, o)$ be a PPP such that at least the subject or the object is a variable, i.e. $s \in V \lor o \in V$. Let o be in V and N be the set of nodes reachable from s. Using the ALP algorithm, the evaluation of tp returns N that can be computed in $\mathcal{O}(|N| log(|G|))$ over an RDF graph G. As $|[\![tp]\!]_G| = |N|$, the cost of evaluating tp is correlated with its cardinality.

Case 2, Reachability-pattern Let $tp = (s, p, o)$ be a PPP such that both the subject and the object are bounded, i.e. $s, o \notin V$. According to [30], the cardinality of a fully bounded PPP is 1 if o can be reached from s, 0 otherwise. However, to check the reachability between s and o, the ALP algorithm first computes the set of nodes N reachable from s, then checks if $o \in N$. Consequently, the cost of evaluating a fully bounded PPP is not correlated with its cardinality.

To illustrate the problem on a concrete example, let us compute the cost of $Q_1^{J_1}$ and $Q_1^{J_2}$ depicted in Fig. 1. Using the true cardinalities[1], we calculate $C_{mm}(Q_1^{J_1}) \approx 91K$ and $C_{mm}(Q_1^{J_2}) \approx 168K$. Despite $Q_1^{J_1}$ being estimated less costly than $Q_1^{J_2}$, $Q_1^{J_1}$ time-out on Wikidata while $Q_1^{J_2}$ completes in less than 3 s. Focusing on property path patterns, tp_3 appears as a transitive-pattern in $Q_1^{J_2}$, while it appears as a reachability-pattern in $Q_1^{J_1}$. Because the cost of computing N is not captured by the cardinality of a reachability-pattern, the cost of $Q_1^{J_1}$ is largely underestimated. Thus, a cost function purely based on cardinalities, such as the C_{mm}, cannot correctly estimate the cost of a PPQ. *The scientific challenge is to define a cost model that, given any join order, can capture the cost of a PPP whether it appears as a transitive-pattern or a reachability-pattern.*

3   Cost-Model for Property Path Queries

Given a join order J, the key idea is to relax fully bounded property path patterns (PPPs) such that J no longer contains reachability-patterns. If all PPPs behave as transitive-patterns, then cardinality-based cost functions are able to correctly estimate the cost of J. Whether a PPP behaves as a transitive-pattern or a reachability-pattern depends on the join order. Therefore, the general approach

---

[1] True cardinalities were computed using SPARQL COUNT queries on the Wikidata SPARQL endpoint as of December 5, 2022.

is to detect reachability-patterns during enumeration of join orders, and relax them before ordering them.

Definition 1 (Reachability-pattern relaxation). *Let Q be a SPARQL property path query, J a join order, and $tp = (s, p, o) \notin J$ a fully bounded property path pattern with respect to J, i.e. $var(tp) \subseteq var(J)$. A forward relaxation of tp generates a filter graph pattern of the form $((s, p, v) \; FILTER \; (v = o))$ such that $v \notin var(Q)$. A backward relaxation of tp generates a filter graph pattern of the form $((v, p, o) \; FILTER \; (v = s))$ such that $v \notin var(Q)$.*

Using a BFS-style algorithm, a reachability-pattern can be evaluated following two strategies. One can decide to navigate from the subject to the object (forward strategy), another can decide to go from the object to the subject (backward strategy). In this context, the forward and backward relaxations allow to estimate which strategy is the cheapest one. According to [33], the cost of going forward or backward can be drastically different. Selecting the best strategy is therefore important to expect good performance. For instance, BlazeGraph evaluates tp_3 in $Q_1^{J_1}$ starting from the object. Using the forward and backward relaxations, we can rewrite $Q_1^{J_1}$ as $Q_1^{J_1^F}$ and $Q_1^{J_1^B}$ as depicted in Fig. 2. If we use the true cardinalities to compute the cost of both strategies, we get $C_{mm}(Q_1^{J_1^F}) = 95K$ and $C_{mm}(Q_1^{J_1^B}) = 2.6B$. Thus, $Q_1^{J_1}$ time-out on Wikidata because BlazeGraph chose the wrong strategy to evaluate tp_3.

Algorithm 1: Dynamic Programming with Relaxation

Require: Q: SPARQL Property Path Query, G: RDF Graph
Data: $dpTable$: keeps the best join order for a set S of triple/property path patterns

1   **for** $\forall tp \in Q$ **do** $dpTable[\{tp\}] = tp$
2   **for** $\forall n \in 1..|Q| - 1$ **do**
3   **for** $\forall S \in dpTable : |S| = n$ **do**
4   **for** $\forall tp \in Q : tp \notin S$ **do**
5   **if** $var(tp) \cap var(dpTable[S]) = \emptyset$ **then continue**
6         $S' = S \cup \{tp\}$; $C = \emptyset$
7   **if** tp is a $PPP \wedge var(tp) \subseteq var(dpTable[S])$ **then**
8           $C = C \cup \{dpTable[S] \bowtie ForwardRelaxation(Q, tp)\}$
9           $C = C \cup \{dpTable[S] \bowtie BackwardRelaxation(Q, tp)\}$
10   **else**
11          $C = C \cup \{dpTable[S] \bowtie tp\}$
12   **for** $\forall P \in C$ **do**
13   **if** $S' \notin dpTable \vee C_{mm}(P, G) < C_{mm}(dpTable[S'], G)$ **then**
14          $dpTable[S'] = P$

15 **return** $UndoRelaxation(dpTable[Q])$

Algorithm 1 is a custom dynamic programming algorithm that integrates relaxation. When the algorithm detects a reachability-pattern tp with respect to a join order $J = dpTable[S]$ (Line 7), it uses relaxation so that the cost function is able to correctly estimate the cost of tp in J. Moreover, to select the

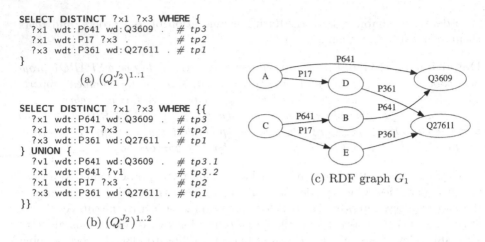

```
SELECT DISTINCT ?x1 ?x3 WHERE {
  ?x1 wdt:P641 wd:Q3609 .   # tp3
  ?x1 wdt:P17 ?x3 .          # tp2
  ?x3 wdt:P361 wd:Q27611 .  # tp1
}
```

(a) $(Q_1^{J_2})^{1..1}$

```
SELECT DISTINCT ?x1 ?x3 WHERE {{
  ?x1 wdt:P641 wd:Q3609 .   # tp3
  ?x1 wdt:P17 ?x3 .          # tp2
  ?x3 wdt:P361 wd:Q27611 .  # tp1
} UNION {
  ?v1 wdt:P641 wd:Q3609 .   # tp3.1
  ?x1 wdt:P641 ?v1           # tp3.2
  ?x1 wdt:P17 ?x3 .          # tp2
  ?x3 wdt:P361 wd:Q27611 .  # tp1
}}
```

(b) $(Q_1^{J_2})^{1..2}$

(c) RDF graph G_1

Fig. 3. RDF graph G_1 and rewrites of the query $Q_1^{J_2}$ used to estimate the cost of J_2 with random walks.

best strategy to evaluate tp both relaxations are used, generating two candidates that are stored in C (Line 8-9). One of them will evaluate tp using the forward strategy, while the other will use the backward strategy. Next, the cost function is used to keep the cheapest alternative (Line 12-14). At the end, the algorithm returns the cheapest join order, with relaxed property path patterns in their original form.

4 Cardinality Estimation of Property Path Queries

This section introduces a new cardinality estimator for property path queries based on random walks. Random walks [19] offer several advantages: (1) They proved to be the best approach for estimating the cardinality of conjunctive SPARQL queries [23] (2) They do not require maintaining statistics [10] (3) They can be efficiently implemented just by relying on traditional SPO, POS, and OSP indexes that are widely available on existing triple stores [18]. Before moving to the contribution, we first recall how to estimate the cardinality of conjunctive SPARQL queries using random walks. Next, we address the case of SPARQL property path queries. For the sake of simplicity, we assume that property path queries are conjunctive queries with a single property path pattern. However, the approach can be generalized to $C2RPQ_{UF}$ queries that contain multiple property path patterns.

4.1 Cardinality Estimates of Conjunctive Queries

Let Q be a conjunctive SPARQL query, and $J = \langle tp_1, ..., tp_n \rangle$ be the join order used to perform random walks. Based on [19] a random walk $\gamma = \langle t_1, ..., t_n \rangle$ is computed over an RDF graph G by randomly picking t_1 in $[\![tp_1]\!]_G$, and each subsequent t_i $(i > 1)$ in $[\![t_{i-1} \bowtie tp_i]\!]_G$. Thus, the probability of sampling γ is $P(\gamma) = |[\![tp_1]\!]_G|^{-1} \prod_{i=2}^{n} |[\![t_{i-1} \bowtie tp_i]\!]_G|^{-1}$. Let $\Gamma = \langle \gamma_1, ..., \gamma_k \rangle$ be a multiset of k random walks, the cardinality of Q is estimated as $card(\Gamma) = |\Gamma|^{-1} \sum_{i=1}^{|\Gamma|} P(\gamma_i)^{-1}$. For instance, let us estimate the cardinality of $(Q_2^{J_2})^{1..1}$ on the RDF graph G_1 with a budget of 2 random walks. Both $(Q_2^{J_2})^{1..1}$ and G_1 are depicted in Fig. 3. Let γ_1 and γ_2 be the two random walks we picked following J_2:

$$\gamma_1 \begin{vmatrix} tp_3 \\ tp_2 \\ tp_1 \end{vmatrix} \begin{array}{l} \text{picking } t_1 = (\mathbf{A}, P641, Q3609) \quad \text{in } [\![(?x1, P641, Q3609)]\!]_{G_1} \\ \text{picking } t_2 = (A, P17, \mathbf{D}) \qquad\quad \text{in } [\![(\mathbf{A}, P17, ?x3)]\!]_{G_1} \\ \text{picking } t_3 = (D, P361, Q27611) \;\; \text{in } [\![(\mathbf{D}, P361, Q27611)]\!]_{G_1} \end{array}$$

$$\gamma_2 \begin{vmatrix} tp_3 \end{vmatrix} \text{ picking } t_1 = (\mathbf{B}, P641, Q3609) \text{ in } [\![(?x1, P641, Q3609)]\!]_{G_1}$$

In this example, $P(\gamma_1) = \frac{1}{2} \times \frac{1}{1} \times \frac{1}{1} = \frac{1}{2}$, while $P(\gamma_2) = 0$. Indeed, when it becomes impossible for a random walk γ to sample t_i for some $i \leq n$, e.g. t_2 in γ_2 because $[\![(B, P17, ?x3)]\!]_{G_1} = \emptyset$, γ is classified as invalid, and its probability of being sampled is 0. Thus, the estimated cardinality of $(Q_2^{J_2})^{1..1}$ is $\frac{1}{2} \times (P(\gamma_1)^{-1} + P(\gamma_2)^{-1}) = \frac{2+0}{2} = 1$.

4.2 Cardinality Estimates of Property Path Queries

Definition 2. *Let Q be a conjunctive SPARQL property path query. Let $tp_i \in Q$ be a property path pattern. We denote Q^d the conjunctive SPARQL query obtained by rewriting tp_i into a chain $tp_i^1, ..., tp_i^d$ of triple patterns. If $J = \langle tp_1, ..., tp_i, ..., tp_{|Q|} \rangle$ is a join order associated to Q, we denote $J^d = \langle tp_1, ..., tp_i^1, ..., tp_i^d, ..., tp_{|Q|} \rangle$ the equivalent join order associated to Q^d.*

To estimate the cardinality of a SPARQL property path query Q, the key idea is to rewrite Q into an equivalent query Q' that does not contain property paths. For instance, let us consider the query $Q_1^{J_2}$ depicted in Fig. 1b. Assuming that the diameter d of the relation $P641$ is known, and let $d = 2$, $Q_1^{J_2}$ is equivalent to the query $(Q_1^{J_2})^{1..2}$ described in Fig. 3b, i.e. both return the same result. Knowing d, any PPP can be rewritten as an UNION graph pattern with d clauses, each clause matching paths of different lengths from 1 to d. Thus, assuming a budget of k random walks, the cardinality of Q' can be estimated by uniformly distributing random walks over the d clauses of the UNION, ending up with d multisets of random walks $\Gamma_1, ..., \Gamma_d$. The cardinality of Q' is then estimated as $\sum_{i=1}^{d} card(\Gamma_i)$. In other words, we consider clauses of the UNION as individual queries $Q^1, ..., Q^d$, for which we estimate the cardinality, and the cardinality of Q is the sum of the estimated cardinalities of $Q^1, ..., Q^d$.

According to the SPARQL semantics, PPPs are evaluated following a set-semantics [30]. For instance, no matter how many paths they are between wd:Q3609 and A, evaluating tp_3 over G_1 must return A only once. Thus, for the rewriting to be correct, a DISTINCT modifier must be introduced in the rewriting of Q into Q'. However, to the best of our knowledge, estimating the cardinality of DISTINCT queries using random walks has not been studied. To cope with this issue, the DISTINCT modifier is just ignored, aware that the estimator will overestimate cardinalities. On dense graphs, cardinalities can be significantly overestimated, preventing the optimizer from finding good join orders. Nevertheless, we assume that in practice, removing the DISTINCT modifier will not prevent the optimizer from finding good join orders.

Algorithm 2: Cardinality Estimation with Property Paths

Require: Q: SPARQL query where tp_i is a property path pattern, J: Join order, G: RDF
     graph, k: Number of random walks, $dMax$: Depth exploration limit
Data: d: Length of the longest path explored, Γ: Multisets of random walks

1 $d = 1$
2 **while** $\sum_j |\Gamma_j| < k$ **do**
3      $d' \sim \mathcal{U}\{1, d\}$; $\gamma = \langle t_1, ..., t_n \rangle = randomWalk(Q^{d'}, J^{d'}, G)$
4   **if** $P(\gamma) > 0 \wedge t_i^1, ..., t_i^{d'} \in \gamma$ *are pairwise distinct* **then**
5        $\mid$ $\Gamma_{d'} = \Gamma_{d'} \cup \{\gamma\}$
6   **else**
7        $\mid$ $\Gamma_{d'} = \Gamma_{d'} \cup \{\gamma'\}$ with $P(\gamma') = 0$
8   **end**
9   **if** $|\gamma| \geq i + d - 1 \wedge t_i^1, ..., t_i^d \in \gamma$ *are pairwise distinct* **then**
10       $\mid$ $d = min(d + 1, dMax)$
11   **end**
12 **end**
13 **return** $\sum_{j=1}^{d} card(\Gamma_j)$

Rewriting a property path pattern tp requires to know the diameter d of the subgraph recognized by tp. To avoid relying on statistics, Algorithm 2 computes d while performing random walks. Given a SPARQL property path query Q where tp_i is a PPP, and a budget k, Algorithm 2 starts with $d = 1$. At each iteration, the algorithm computes a random walk $\gamma = \langle t_1, ..., t_n \rangle$ from $Q^{d'}$, following the join order $J^{d'}$, where d' is drawn uniformly at random between 1 and d. Each time $d' = d$, the algorithm checks if γ has found a path of length d matching tp_i. Given $J^d = \langle tp_1, ..., tp_i^1, ..., tp_i^d, ..., tp_{|Q|} \rangle$, a path of length d has been found if γ matches at least $\langle tp_1, ..., tp_i^1, ..., tp_i^d \rangle$, i.e. if $|\gamma| \geq |\langle tp_1, ..., tp_i^1, ..., tp_i^d \rangle|$ or $|\gamma| \geq i + d - 1$. In this case, it may exist a path of length $d + 1$ matching tp_i, and d is increased by 1.

Algorithm 2 increases d each time a random walk finds a path of length d matching tp_i. However, in the presence of cycles, d may increase forever, significantly impacting the accuracy of estimates. To address this issue, Algorithm 2 enforces a simple path semantics. Under a simple path semantics [20], a random walk can go through a node only once when matching PPPs. In other words, let $\gamma = \langle t_1, ..., t_i^1, ..., t_i^{d'}, ..., t_{|Q|} \rangle$ be a random walk sampled from $Q^{d'}$, with $t_i^1, ..., t_i^{d'}$ matching $tp_i^{d'}$, γ is valid if and only if $t_i^1, ..., t_i^{d'}$ are pairwise distinct. Thus, considering an infinite number of random walks, Algorithm 2 ensures that d

Table 1. Characteristics of the workload used in the experiments

#queries	#joins	#triples	#path patterns	#constants	#join variables
213	1–8	2–9	1–2	1–5	1–6

converges to the size of the longest simple path in the subgraph recognized by tp_i, which is equal to or larger than the diameter of the subgraph.

Even without cycles, d can quickly reach large values. Because the budget k is distributed between queries $Q^1, ..., Q^d$ to sample paths of length 1 to d, with a small budget, the algorithm may end up with too few random walks in each multiset Γ_j to compute accurate estimates. To address this issue, d can be clipped to a maximum value $dMax$. As the computation time of a random walk is proportional to its size, clipping d can also improve optimization times.

5   Experimental Study

The goal of this experimental study is to empirically answer the following questions: (1) Does our approach improve total workload execution time compared to baselines? (2) What is the impact of our approach on each query? (3) How do the budget k and the depth exploration limit $dMax$ impact performance?

5.1   Experimental Setup

Datasets and Queries. Our experiments use the newly proposed Wikidata Graph Query Benchmark (WDBench) [3], which extracts real-world SPARQL queries from the public query logs of the Wikidata SPARQL endpoint. The WDBench provides a RDF dataset of 1,257,169,959 triples built from the dump of Wikidata. To create our workload, all non-property path queries have been filtered out, as well as queries with cross-products. The resulting workload contains 213 queries and is described in Table 1. To ensure that queries return the same result for all engines, we added the DISTINCT modifier to all queries.

Compared Approaches. To demonstrate that random walks have the potential to be used to improve the join order of SPARQL property path queries, we compare our approach with Virtuoso v.OS-7.2.7 [8] (one of the most deployed engine in practice [6], as well as the SPARQL endpoint behind DBpedia), and BlazeGraph v.2.1.4 [31] (used by the Wikidata Query Service [21]). BlazeGraph comes with two different optimizers; a first optimizer based on simple statistics such as the cardinality of triple patterns, and another one, named RTO, that relies on sampling to estimate the cost of join orders. Because RTO supports property paths and is adapted from ROX [15], which is related to our proposal, our approach is compared to both optimizers.

Implementation and Experimental Protocol. We implemented our query optimizer as a standalone Python 3.9 program. Random walks are performed

Table 2. TET=Total Execution Time, T=Timeouts, E=Errors.

Engine	Optimizer	TET [Seconds]	T	E
BlazeGraph	Default	20270	15	9
	RTO	35107	36	64
	Proposal (k=1000, d=5)	1429 ± 130	0	0
Virtuoso	Default	419	0	0
	Proposal (k=1000, d=5)	362 ± 11	0	0

over the WDBench dataset stored in HDT [9]. The generated plans of our query optimizer are translated into SPARQL queries using BlazeGraph and Virtuoso query hints. Query hints allow us to force the join order and the direction in which property path patterns are evaluated by the engine[2][3][4]. Virtuoso and BlazeGraph have been tuned for a system with 64GB, following engine recommendations. Code and configurations can be found online for reproducibility purposes[5] As random walks are not deterministic, the workload is optimized 5 times for each tested configuration, and each query is executed 3 times after a warmup execution. All queries are executed with a timeout of 900 s.

Evaluation Metrics. In our experiments, the following metrics are used: (1) The *Total Execution Time* is the time spent by Virtuoso or BlazeGraph executing a SPARQL query with the Optimization Time. (2) The *Execution Time* is the time spent by Virtuoso or BlazeGraph executing a SPARQL query without the Optimization Time. (3) The *Optimization Time* is the time spent by our query optimizer to optimize a SPARQL query. Each query is executed three times and the metrics are computed on the average of these 3 executions.

Hardware. All experiments ran on a single machine with Ubuntu 20.04.4 LTS, AMD EPYC 7513 32-Core Processor, 64GB of RAM, and a logical volume of 2TB on a remote SSD accessible through the LAN.

5.2   Experimental Results

Does Our Approach Improve Total Workload Execution Time Compared to Baselines? Table 2 presents the total execution time of the workload for all engines. Our proposal is configured with a budget of 1000 random walks (k=1000), and the depth limit for property paths is set to 5 (d=5). As our proposal relies on random walks, the workload has been optimized 5 times. Averages and standard deviations are reported in Table 2.

---

[2] https://docs.openlinksw.com/virtuoso/rdfsparqlimplementatiotrans.
[3] https://docs.openlinksw.com/virtuoso/rdfperfcost.
[4] https://github.com/blazegraph/database/wiki/QueryHints.
[5] https://github.com/JulienDavat/Join-Ordering-of-SPARQL-Property-Path-Queries.

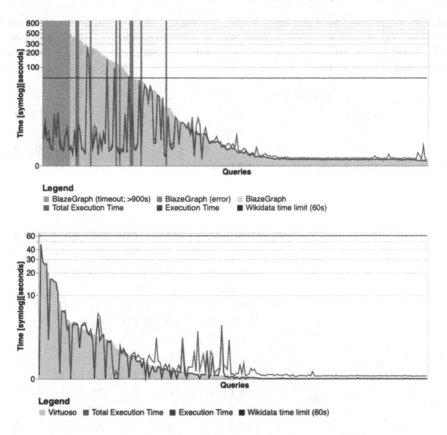

Fig. 4. Average execution time on BlazeGraph (top) and Virtuoso (bottom) with a budget of 1000 random walks and an exploration depth limited to 5.

First, Virtuoso is much faster than BlazeGraph on this workload. While BlazeGraph requires more than 20270 s, Virtuoso only needs 419 s. Moreover, BlazeGraph is not able to execute 24 queries. For the first 15 queries, Blaze-Graph reaches the time-out set to 900 s in our experiments. An Out-Of-Memory exception occurs for the nine remaining queries. Note that queries that time-out account for 900 s in the total execution time, while queries that result in an error account for 0. On its side, Virtuoso processes all 213 queries. Despite being recommended when there are join ordering issues, the RTO optimizer delivers the worst results. Given a SPARQL query Q, to estimate the cost of a join order J, RTO samples the first triple pattern in J and executes Q^J on this sample. Unfortunately, evaluating Q^J, even on a small sample, can take a very long time. As a result, many queries time-out or crash because of the optimization step. In the end, our proposal outperforms both BlazeGraph and Virtuoso. The workload total execution time is divided by at least 14 on BlazeGraph. It can be much more depending on the queries that time-out. Compared to Virtuoso, we observe a 14% improvement on the execution time.

Table 3. Global results of our experiments. For each configuration, queries have been optimized 5 times and executed 3 times after a warmup execution. DL=Depth Limit, TET=Total Execution Time (secs), ET=Execution Time (secs), OT=Optimization Time (secs), T=Timeouts, E=Errors.

		Walks	DL	TET	ET	OT	T	E
Blaze Graph	Default			20270			15	9
	RTO			35107			36	64
	Proposal	1000	10	1635 (± 195)	1577 (± 195)	58 (± 2)	0	0
			5	1429 (± 130)	1383 (± 128)	37 (± 14)	0	0
			3	1629 (± 207)	1583 (± 206)	46 (± 4)	0	0
			1	2046 (± 219)	2006 (± 222)	40 (± 13)	0	0
		10000	10	1890 (± 286)	1530 (± 288)	361 (± 4)	0	0
			5	1545 (± 134)	1226 (± 127)	319 (± 14)	0	0
			3	1583 (± 206)	1290 (± 206)	293 (± 8)	0	0
			1	2087 (± 15)	1847 (± 11)	241 (± 6)	0	0
Virtuoso	Default			419	415	4	0	0
	Proposal	1000	10	365 (± 18)	317 (± 18)	48 (± 0)	0	0
			5	362 (± 11)	319 (± 11)	43 (± 0)	0	0
			3	356 (± 29)	317 (± 29)	39 (± 0)	0	0
			1	346 (± 5)	315 (± 5)	31 (± 0)	0	0
		10000	10	613 (± 17)	300 (± 12)	314 (± 9)	0	0
			5	594 (± 15)	303 (± 15)	291 (± 1)	0	0
			3	570 (± 16)	301 (± 35)	269 (± 1)	0	0
			1	528 (± 3)	308 (± 3)	220 (± 0)	0	0

What is the Impact of Our Approach on Each Query? Figure 4 presents a per-query view of the results summarized in Table 2. Queries are ordered on the x-axis according to the total execution time of the baseline. Focusing first on BlazeGraph, the 15 queries that exceed the time limit are depicted in dark gray, while the nine queries that result in an error are in red. As depicted by the blue curve in Fig. 4, our optimizer makes the difference on the long-running queries by finding better join orders. When looking at the optimization time, i.e. the ratio between the blue and green curves, they are irregularities. It comes from the HDT storage that cannot draw a random triple in constant time using the POS index. We can draw the same conclusion on Virtuoso. For short-running queries, the generated join orders are close to Virtuoso. However, long-running queries can benefit from significant improvements. For instance, the longest query on Virtuoso takes 63 s to complete. Using our optimizer we are able to find a join order that reduces the execution time to 110 ms.

How do the Budget k and The Depth Exploration Limit $dMax$ Impact Performance? In our approach, two parameters impact performance; the budget k, i.e. the number of random walks used to estimate the cardinality of joins, and the limit $dMax$ on the exploration depth for property paths. To measure the impact of these two parameters, we tested different configurations that are summarized in Table 3.

First, let us focus on the execution time. As expected, given $dMax$, increasing k systematically leads to better performance. Moreover, increasing the budget tends to decrease the variance between measurements, i.e. estimates become more reliable. However, despite multiplying the number of random walks by ten, the gain in terms of execution time is not that large, especially on Virtuoso. When using a bottom-up approach (as a DP algorithm), the quality of join orders mainly depends on the quality of the first joins, as highlighted in [18]. Thus, accuracy on 1-way, 2-way, or 3-way joins is often enough to get good join orders and does not require a large budget.

If increasing the budget always leads to better performance, increasing $dMax$ may negatively impact the execution time. Random walks are uniformly distributed over the interval $1..dMax$. The larger the interval is, the fewer walks remain to estimate each part, i.e. the more inaccurate the estimator is. Consequently, with a small budget, it is better to reduce $dMax$ to have more accurate cardinalities. Even if property path patterns may be underestimated (because they are not fully explored), estimates will be more reliable. However, with a larger budget, it is worth looking for a larger $dMax$ to better capture the real cost of property path patterns. The budget k being the most impacting factor in optimization time, a good strategy to define k and $dMax$ is to define a budget first, and then select $dMax$ by testing different values until the quality of join orders deteriorates. For instance, with a budget of 1000 random walks on Blaze-Graph, setting $dMax = 5$ results in good performance, but increasing $dMax$ to 10 starts deteriorating the execution time.

6 Related Works

Different approaches have been proposed to speed up the evaluation of SPARQL property path queries [2]. Some approaches rely on indexes to improve the evaluation of property path patterns. For instance, [28] proposes an index named FERRARI that encodes transitive closures into a compact representation. This index is then used in RDF-3X [11] to evaluate property path queries efficiently. In [4], authors combine a novel index to represent sets of triples with a new algorithm based on the Glushkov automaton. Although using indexes can drastically improve property path patterns execution, maintaining them on large and dynamic knowledge graphs is costly [27]. This paper requires no additional indexes, only those currently used in SPARQL engines.

Other approaches rely on innovative property path pattern operators [1, 4, 27, 32, 33]. For instance, to find the best strategy to evaluate a property pattern, Waveguide [33] introduces a new operator that mixes idea from relational and graph databases. To improve the execution time of property path queries, [27] relies on an approximate operator to compute, with a fixed error rate, the reachability between two nodes. All these approaches are really exciting but focus only on evaluating property path patterns alone. This paper focuses on optimizing property path queries, where a property path pattern is just one part of a query. By choosing the proper join orders, queries execution time can be significantly improved without changing the underlying engines.

Closer to our approach, [14] focuses on the optimization of conjunctive regular path queries, i.e. not just property path patterns. In [14], the authors propose a new algebra, with a set of rewriting rules, allowing optimizers to explore query plans that could not be considered before. While their approach consists in enriching the search space of query plans, we propose a solution to accurately compare the different plans in order to choose the best one. Thus both approaches can be used together.

The importance of finding good join orders for property path queries has already been pointed out in RDF-3X [10,11]. However, to estimate the cardinality of property path patterns, the FERRARI index is used. Other approaches based on synopses or statistics can also be used to estimate cardinalities, such as characteristic sets [22] or SumRDF [29]. However, they suffer from the same problem as index-based approaches; synopses and statistics need to be maintained. A well-known alternative is sampling. Sampling allows gathering information when no indexes or statistics are available. For instance, the RTO engine of BlazeGraph relies on sampling, while Virtuoso commonly uses sampling to estimate the selectivity of filters. One drawback of using sampling to estimate cardinalities is its cost. However, [18] demonstrates that sampling can be both accurate and cheap when using traditional index structures such as existing B-Tree indexes. Following the same basic principles, WanderJoin [19] uses random walks to evaluate aggregate queries, and can be used as a cardinality estimator. As demonstrated in [23], WanderJoin outperforms other cardinality estimators. Compared to [18] and [19], our cardinality estimator handles property path queries.

7   Conclusions and Future Work

This paper introduces a new query optimizer that relies on the relaxation of reachability-patterns and a sampling-based cardinality estimator to find efficient join orders for $C2RPQ_{UF}$ queries. The experimental study demonstrates that our proposal outperforms existing engines. On the newly proposed Wikidata Query Benchmark, the workload execution time is divided by 14 compared to BlazeGraph. This work opens several perspectives. First, optimization times can be significantly improved using a better budget model such as the one defined in [18]. Moreover, computing the confidence interval of estimators [19] may allow us to adapt the budget to each join order, rather than systematically computing k random walks. Generalizing our approach to nested stars is also part of our research agenda. Finally, this paper relies on random walks to estimate the cardinality of $C2RPQ_{UF}$ queries. Another exciting line of research would be to study how random walks can be used to estimate the cardinality of SPARQL queries in the presence of the MINUS, OPTIONAL and FILTER NOT EXISTS operators.

Acknowledgments. This work is supported by the ANR project DeKaloG (Decentralized Knowledge Graphs), ANR-19-CE23-0014, CE23 - Intelligence artificielle, and the CominLabs project MikroLog (The Microdata Knowledge Graph).

References

1. Aimonier-Davat, J., Skaf-Molli, H., Molli, P.: Processing SPARQL property path queries online with web preemption. In: Verborgh, R., et al. (eds.) ESWC 2021. LNCS, vol. 12731, pp. 57–72. Springer, Cham (2021). https://doi.org/10.1007/978-3-030-77385-4_4
2. Ali, W., Saleem, M., Yao, B., Hogan, A., Ngomo, A.C.N.: A survey of RDF stores & SPARQL engines for querying knowledge graphs. VLDB J., 1–26 (2021)
3. Angles, R., Aranda, C.B., Hogan, A., Rojas, C., Vrgoč, D.: WDBench: a wikidata graph query benchmark. In: Angles, R., Aranda, C.B., Hogan, A., Rojas, C., Vrgoč, D., et al. (eds.) The Semantic Web—ISWC 2022. ISWC 2022. Lecture Notes in Computer Science, vol. 13489, pp. 714–731. Springer, Cham (2022). https://doi.org/10.1007/978-3-031-19433-7_41
4. Arroyuelo, D., Hogan, A., Navarro, G., Rojas-Ledesma, J.: Time-and space-efficient regular path queries. In: 38th International Conference on Data Engineering (ICDE), pp. 3091–3105. IEEE (2022)
5. Bonifati, A., Martens, W., Timm, T.: Navigating the maze of wikidata query logs. In: The World Wide Web Conference, pp. 127–138 (2019)
6. Buil-Aranda, C., Hogan, A., Umbrich, J., Vandenbussche, P.-Y.: SPARQL web-querying infrastructure: ready for action? In: Alani, H., et al. (eds.) ISWC 2013. LNCS, vol. 8219, pp. 277–293. Springer, Heidelberg (2013). https://doi.org/10.1007/978-3-642-41338-4_18
7. Cluet, S., Moerkotte, G.: On the complexity of generating optimal left-deep processing trees with cross products. In: Gottlob, G., Vardi, M.Y. (eds.) ICDT 1995. LNCS, vol. 893, pp. 54–67. Springer, Heidelberg (1995). https://doi.org/10.1007/3-540-58907-4_6
8. Erling, O., Mikhailov, I.: RDF support in the virtuoso DBMS. In: n: Pellegrini, T., Auer, S., Tochtermann, K., Schaffert, S. (eds.) Networked Knowledge - Networked Media. Studies in Computational Intelligence, vol. 221, pp. 7–24. Springer, Berlin, Heidelberg (2009). https://doi.org/10.1007/978-3-642-02184-8_2
9. Fernández, J.D., Martínez-Prieto, M.A., Gutiérrez, C., Polleres, A., Arias, M.: Binary RDF representation for publication and exchange (HDT). J. Web Seman. **19**, 22–41 (2013)
10. Gubichev, A.: Query processing and optimization in graph databases. Ph.D. thesis, Technische Universität München (2015)
11. Gubichev, A., Bedathur, S.J., Seufert, S.: Sparqling kleene: fast property paths in RDF-3x. In: First International Workshop on Graph Data Management Experiences and Systems, pp. 1–7 (2013)
12. Gubichev, A., Neumann, T.: Exploiting the query structure for efficient join ordering in SPARQL queries. In: 17th International Conference on Extending Database Technology, EDBT (2014)
13. Hertzschuch, A., Hartmann, C., Habich, D., Lehner, W.: Simplicity done right for join ordering. In: CIDR (2021)
14. Jachiet, L., Genevès, P., Gesbert, N., Layaïda, N.: On the optimization of recursive relational queries: application to graph queries. In: Proceedings of the 2020 ACM SIGMOD International Conference on Management of Data, pp. 681–697 (2020)

15. Kader, R.A., Boncz, P.A., Manegold, S., van Keulen, M.: ROX: run-time optimization of XQueries. In: Çetintemel, U., Zdonik, S.B., Kossmann, D., Tatbul, N. (eds.) International Conference on Management of Data, SIGMOD. ACM (2009)
16. Kostylev, E.V., Reutter, J.L., Romero, M., Vrgoč, D.: SPARQL with property paths. In: Arenas, M., et al. (eds.) ISWC 2015. LNCS, vol. 9366, pp. 3–18. Springer, Cham (2015). https://doi.org/10.1007/978-3-319-25007-6_1
17. Leis, V., Gubichev, A., Mirchev, A., Boncz, P.A., Kemper, A., Neumann, T.: How good are query optimizers, really? VLDB Endow. **9**(3), 204–215 (2015)
18. Leis, V., Radke, B., Gubichev, A., Kemper, A., Neumann, T.: Cardinality estimation done right: Index-based join sampling. In: CIDR (2017)
19. Li, F., Wu, B., Yi, K., Zhao, Z.: Wander join and XDB: online aggregation via random walks. ACM Trans. Database Syst. **44**(1), 1–41 (2019). https://doi.org/10.1145/3284551
20. Losemann, K., Martens, W.: The complexity of regular expressions and property paths in SPARQL. ACM Trans. Database Syst. (TODS) **38**(4), 1–39 (2013)
21. Malyshev, S., Krötzsch, M., González, L., Gonsior, J., Bielefeldt, A.: Getting the most out of Wikidata: semantic technology usage in Wikipedia's knowledge graph. In: Vrandečić, D., et al. (eds.) ISWC 2018. LNCS, vol. 11137, pp. 376–394. Springer, Cham (2018). https://doi.org/10.1007/978-3-030-00668-6_23
22. Neumann, T., Moerkotte, G.: Characteristic sets: accurate cardinality estimation for RDF queries with multiple joins. In: 27th International Conference on Data Engineering. IEEE (2011)
23. Park, Y., Ko, S., Bhowmick, S.S., Kim, K., Hong, K., Han, W.S.: G-care: a framework for performance benchmarking of cardinality estimation techniques for subgraph matching. In: International Conference on Management of Data (SIGMOD) (2020)
24. Pérez, J., Arenas, M., Gutiérrez, C.: Semantics and complexity of SPARQL. ACM Trans. Database Syst. **34**(3), 1–45 (2009)
25. Schmidt, M., Meier, M., Lausen, G.: Foundations of SPARQL query optimization. In: Database Theory - ICDT 2010, pp. 4–33 (2010)
26. Selingerl, P., Astrahan, M., Chamberlin, D., Lorie, R., Price, T.: Access path selection in a relational database management system. In: ACM SIGMOD (1979)
27. Sengupta, N., Bagchi, A., Ramanath, M., Bedathur, S.: Arrow: approximating reachability using random walks over web-scale graphs. In: International Conference on Data Engineering (ICDE), pp. 470–481. IEEE (2019)
28. Seufert, S., Anand, A., Bedathur, S., Weikum, G.: Ferrari: flexible and efficient reachability range assignment for graph indexing. In: 29th International Conference on Data Engineering (ICDE), pp. 1009–1020. IEEE (2013)
29. Stefanoni, G., Motik, B., Kostylev, E.V.: Estimating the cardinality of conjunctive queries over RDF data using graph summarisation. In: The World Wide Web Conference, pp. 1043–1052 (2018)
30. Steve, H., Andy, S.: SPARQL 1.1 query language. In: Recommendation W3C (2013)
31. Thompson, B., Personick, M., Cutcher, M.: The bigdata® RDF graph database. In: Linked Data Management, pp. 221–266. Chapman and Hall/CRC, Boca Raton (2016)
32. Wadhwa, S., Prasad, A., Ranu, S., Bagchi, A., Bedathur, S.: Efficiently answering regular simple path queries on large labeled networks. In: International Conference on Management of Data, pp. 1463–1480 (2019)
33. Yakovets, N., Godfrey, P., Gryz, J.: Query planning for evaluating SPARQL property paths. In: International Conference on Management of Data, pp. 1875–1889 (2016)

Refining Large Integrated Identity Graphs Using the Unique Name Assumption

Shuai Wang[1(✉)] , Joe Raad[2] , Peter Bloem[1] , and Frank van Harmelen[1]

[1] Department of Computer Science, Vrije Universiteit Amsterdam,
Amsterdam, The Netherlands
{shuai.wang,p.bloem,frank.van.harmelen}@vu.nl
[2] LISN, University of Paris-Saclay, Orsay, France
joe.raad@lisn.fr

Abstract. The Unique Name Assumption (UNA) supposes that two terms with distinct identifiers from the same knowledge base do not refer to the same real-world entity. The UNA can be used to detect errors in large integrated knowledge bases. For example, some identity link can be erroneous if they are in a path that connects two entities (that refer to different real-world objects) defined in the same knowledge base. For large knowledge bases, however, the UNA does not always hold due to redundant IRIs that capture various encodings, languages, namespaces, versions, letter cases, etc. The UNA can still be useful for identifying erroneous links provided good adaption to the exceptions. For this, we propose a concrete definition of the UNA with tolerance towards multiple exceptions, namely the internal UNA (iUNA). To compare the iUNA and other variants of the UNA, we propose a generic algorithm that can be used for refinement. The algorithm employs an SMT (Satisfiability Modulo Theory) solver and takes advantage of the latter's ability to efficiently reason over equality. For evaluation, we identify erroneous links in an identity graph of half a billion triples extracted from the LOD Cloud, and compare our approach against community detection methods (Louvain and Leiden) as well as other identity refinement approaches.

1 Introduction

The question *"What is an entity?"* and the related question *"When are two entities equal?"* are not only longstanding philosophical questions[1] but are also longstanding technical issues in information systems [7]. The Semantic Web, and in its wake, Linked Open Data, have operationalised the notion of an "entity" as an Internationalized Resource Identifier (IRI): each is represented as an IRI, and using the same IRI implies referring to the same entity. Entities are connected by the identity links (e.g. `owl:sameAs`) to form identity graphs. Many existing approaches for detecting errors in identity graphs require information such as

---

[1] https://plato.stanford.edu/entries/object/.

© The Author(s), under exclusive license to Springer Nature Switzerland AG 2023
C. Pesquita et al. (Eds.): ESWC 2023, LNCS 13870, pp. 55–71, 2023.
https://doi.org/10.1007/978-3-031-33455-9_4

vocabulary alignments, textual descriptions [8,17] or the presence of a large number of ontology axioms and alignment of the vocabularies [11,14]. However, such information is often restricted to certain languages or simply not always available [8,17], thus not appropriate for refinement tasks at web scale. Identity graphs on the web exhibit special properties which must be considered: they are integrated from multiple sources, sources can be multilingual, many suffer from a lack of maintenance and some have multiple encoding schemes.

Since `owl:sameAs` is a symmetric relation, we reduce the directed graph to a simple, undirected graph. In an undirected graph G, a *Connected Component* (CC) is a maximal subgraph with any two vertices connected by a path (Fig. 1a). A *gold standard* is the ground truth that maps each node (IRI) to the real-world entity, which can be used for evaluation (Fig. 1b). An *equivalence class* (EC) is a set of vertices corresponding to the same real-world entity (may or may not be connected by a path). In an identity graph, a CC is an EC if and only if all its nodes refer to the same real-world entity[2].

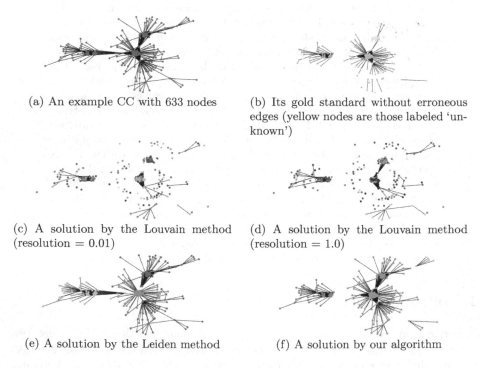

(a) An example CC with 633 nodes

(b) Its gold standard without erroneous edges (yellow nodes are those labeled 'unknown')

(c) A solution by the Louvain method (resolution = 0.01)

(d) A solution by the Louvain method (resolution = 1.0)

(e) A solution by the Leiden method

(f) A solution by our algorithm

Fig. 1. An example of a connected component (No. 4170), its gold standard, and solutions by the Louvain algorithm, the Leiden algorithm, and our algorithm.

---

[2] However, when constructing the gold standard by annotating IRIs extracted from the Web, some may be annotated 'unknown' if the subject cannot be established.

The Unique Name Assumption (UNA) supposes that two terms with distinct IRIs do not refer to the same real-world entity. Although the UNA does not always hold due to redundant IRIs that capture various encodings, languages, namespaces, versions, letter cases, the UNA can still be useful for identifying erroneous links. We design a refinement algorithm that removes a minimal number of edges with good precision (Fig. 1f). We compare the results against the Louvain algorithm (Fig. 1c and 1d) and the Leiden algorithm (Fig. 1e).

This paper focuses on four research questions:

RQ1 How can we define a UNA for large integrated knowledge graphs?
RQ2 How do we validate various definitions of the UNA?
RQ3 Can the UNA give a reliable indication of errors in practise?
RQ4 Can we develop an efficient UNA-based algorithm for refinement?

We present existing definitions of the UNA and related work in Sect. 2. In Sect. 3, we propose a new definition of the UNA and we test the different UNA definitions and examine their reliability for error detection in Sect. 4, by validating them over data of the LOD cloud. In Sect. 5, we present our refinement algorithm and we evaluate it in Sect. 6. Finally, discussion and future work are presented in Sect. 7. Our main contributions[3] are as follows:

1. We propose a new definition of the UNA, namely the iUNA and check it against a large integrated knowledge graph together with other definitions.
2. We design an inconsistency-based refinement algorithm that evaluates definitions of the UNA by employing an SMT solver.
3. We publish a gold standard of over 8K manually annotated entities (200K owl:sameAs links) together with some additional information such as redirection and equivalence under different encoding schemes.
4. We introduce new evaluation metrics and provide a benchmark using our gold standard and algorithm.

2   Related Work

Estimates of the proportion of erroneous identity links in the semantic web range from around 3% [11,15] to 20% [10]. Existing approaches for detecting errors in identity graphs fall into three categories [17]. *Content-based* approaches exploit the descriptions associated with each resource for evaluating the correctness of an identity link. They typically rely on additional information such as vocabulary alignments and textual descriptions for each entity. However, such information is not always available [8,17] on open Web datasets, and in practice, such algorithms often do not scale to the size of the LOD Cloud. The *network-based* approaches [9,16] take advantage of graph-theoretical algorithms for the detection of erroneous links. For instance, [16] rely on the Louvain community detection algorithm for assigning an error degree for each identity link. This error

---

[3] The data is published on Zenodo (https://zenodo.org/record/7765113) with DOI 10.5281/zenodo.7765113.

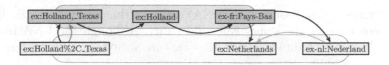

Fig. 2. An example CC with links expressing identity (black), redirection (red), and encoding equivalence (blue) (see also Sect. 3). (Color figure online)

degree is based on the density of the community in which an identity link occurs in, and the weight of the `owl:sameAs` (i.e. reciprocally asserted owl:sameAs have a lower error degree, hence a higher chance of correctness). These error degrees are published online as part of the MetaLink dataset [3]. However, the accuracy of these methods is limited due to a lack of understanding of the underlying semantics. Finally, the *inconsistency-based* approaches [11,14] hypothesise that `owl:sameAs` links that lead to logical inconsistencies have a higher chance of being incorrect. They typically require the presence of a large number of ontology axioms and alignment of the vocabularies.

The use of the UNA to detect errors in identity graphs is an inconsistency-based approach. This idea has been explored in [12,19]. Despite that UNA is a well-defined definition in relational database theory (a.k.a. Unique Name Axiom) [18], the lack of an agreed-upon definition of UNA in semantic web leads to different conclusions. The primitive adaption of UNA in semantic web postulates that any two ground terms with distinct names are non-identical [12]. In the scope of integrated knowledge graphs, Valdestilhas et al. [19] formalise this as any two URIs in the same knowledge base cannot refer to the same thing in the real world. We name this definition *naive UNA*, or *nUNA* for short. In practice, an integrated knowledge graph violates the nUNA if at least one of its connected components (from the identity graph) has two entities from the same source.

Figure 2 is a fictional example of six entities from two knowledge bases (corresponding to nodes in light grey and dark grey, respectively). The six entities connected by the black edges form a connected component. The two equivalence classes are about the Netherlands (the three nodes on the right), and a city in Texas named Holland (the two nodes on the left). The node `ex:Holland` can be confusing (could be annotated as "unknown"). The blue arrow is an example how encoding schemes can lead to redundancy. Due to transitivity, the mistake between `ex:Holland,_Texas`, `ex:Holland` and `ex-fr:Pays-Bas` was carried over to other entities such as `ex-nl:Nederland`. This example shows how entities in various languages can be confusing. This connected component violates the nUNA: for the knowledge base of light grey, there are three entities in the connected components. This helps the detection of spurious links. Note that removing the links between `ex:Holland,_Texas` and `ex:Holland` and `ex-fr:Pays-Bas` results in three connected components, which are correct but still violate the nUNA.

De Melo [12] points out that the Semantic Web is very different from traditional closed scenarios because multiple parties can publish data about the same entity using different identifiers. Thus, they propose to use a quasi-unique name constraint (*quasi UNA*, or *qUNA*) for entities: they use the namespace of an IRI as its source of provenance, with a focus on 6 major hubs including DBLP, DBpedia, FreeBase, GeoNames, MusicBrainz, and UniProt. This definition also takes into account some exceptions: two DBpedia entities from the same dataset/source do not violate the UNA if one redirects to the other, or either is a dead node (those that can no longer be resolved).

These definitions have several drawbacks in practice. First, both the nUNA and the qUNA lack a clear definition of *provenance*, i.e. the source of entities. The algorithm using the nUNA relies on LinkLion[4] for computing the provenance of entities [19]. That of the qUNA takes an entities' namespace as the source by default. As for DBpedia, the paper studied only the namespace http://dbpedia.org/resource/ for violation and redirection. The algorithm developed based on nUNA outputs only partitions of the identity graph rather than the edges to remove [19]. Despite that the paper proposed to handle cases of DBpedia with exception, qUNA is restricted to awareness of redirect within DBpedia [12]. In fact, recent work estimates that between 45% and 83% of redirection links can be taken as identity link[5] [13]. Furthermore, the work in [12] does not specify how redirection and dead nodes were obtained. In addition, we believe that there are other forms of exceptions that must be considered. For example, the IRIs `wikidata.dbpedia.org/resource/Q6453410`, `www.wikidata.org/entity/Q6453410` and `wikidata.org/entity/Q6453410` are about the same entity but in different versions of Wikidata. Despite issues with the definition, the refinement algorithm using these two UNA definitions takes violations as hard constraints: entities are considered different as long as the UNA is violated. Due to the lack of a gold standard, neither definition was validated on real-world data, or compared with other existing baselines. In this work, we propose a new definition of the UNA that is suited for large integrated graphs on the Web and compare it with the existing UNA variations previously proposed by [12,19].

3   The iUNA

When examining the data in the LOD Cloud, we note that identity links are often used to connect the same entity in different language, versions or encodings. Therefore, we propose our own definition of the UNA, which we call the internal UNA (iUNA), to take these differences into account. Our iUNA definition assumes that two different IRIs $e1$ and $e2$ within the same namespace should refer to distinct real-world entities only when: a) they are in the same knowledge base according to a certain provenance information, b) they don't satisfy any of the following exceptions:[6]

---

[4] LinkLion (https://www.linklion.org/) is no longer available.

[5] The uncertainty is due to the presence of a large number of 'unknown' entities.

[6] These exceptions are based on our manual examination of the entities in the linksets.

Table 1. Comparing the definition of the UNA

	nUNA	qUNA	iUNA
Definition	Two URIs in the same KB cannot refer to the same thing	Refinement of nUNA, considering exceptions of DBpedia	Refinement of nUNA by considering multiple exceptions and provenance estimations
Provenance	Rely on LinkLion	Namespace (in 6 major hubs)	Three means of provenance
Exceptions	None	Redir. between some DBpedia entities	Encoding variants, redirection, dead nodes
Algorithm (see sections below)	Violation as hard constraint; returns partitions that are contradiction free	Violation as hard constraint; remove links that violate qUNA	Violations as hard and soft constraints; remove fewer identity links
Limitations (see sections below)	No tolerance towards exceptions; relies on an external server for provenance	Not enough exceptions taken into consideration; restricted definition of provenance; violations taken as hard constraints	Not every exception is included or handled explicitly. Can be relaxed by taking violations as soft constraints

1. if $e1$ can be percent encoded/decoded into e_2 by one or more steps,[7]
2. if e_1 redirects to e_2 (or vice versa), or both redirect to the same location,
3. if at least one of e_1 and e_2 is a dead node, not found, unresolvable, redirects until reaching some error or has a timeout error while resolving.

To check whether two entities violate the iUNA, condition (a) requires us to check whether they are from the same knowledge base. This requires some form of provenance to determine where an entity is defined. The nUNA relies on the provenance information of LinkLion, which consists of multiple linksets. It is questionable if linksets can in fact be taken as the knowledge base where the entities are defined, not to mention that LinkLion is no longer available. As for the qUNA, it takes the namespace of an entity to define its knowledge base (regardless of the actual knowledge bases where the corresponding identity links are). This can be problematic for popular namespaces: an entity in DBpedia can be defined in one knowledge base but used in other knowledge bases. Authors can specify where an entity is defined using `rdfs:isDefinedBy`, but an ad-hoc examination shows that this information is rare. We therefore propose two additional means for the estimation of provenance of an entity e. Table 1 provides a comparison of the three UNA definitions.

Explicit sources: an explicit source of e is the object in any triple with subject e and predicate `rdfs:isDefinedBy` (or any equivalent or sub-properties).

Implicit label-like sources: an implicit label-like source of e is the RDF file containing triples where e is the subject and `rdfs:label` (or any of its equivalent or sub-properties) is the predicate.

Implicit comment-like sources: an implicit comment-like source of e is the RDF file containing triples where e is the subject and `rdfs:comment` (or any of its equivalent or sub-properties) is the predicate.

---

[7] For example, `ex:Bandon_(Oreg%C3%B3n)` and `ex:Bandon_(Oregón)` can be equivalent.

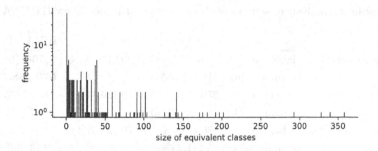

Fig. 3. Size distribution of the equivalence classes in the gold standard.

4   Testing the UNA

4.1   Dataset and Gold Standard

We use the http://sameas.cc dataset [4], which provides the transitive closure
of 558 million distinct `owl:sameAs` statements. These identity statements were
extracted from the 2015 LOD Laundromat crawl [2] that provides more than
38 billion triples from over 650K RDF files. The identity links are distributed
over 49 million connected components (CCs), with each CC being associated
with a unique ID. We manually annotated all IRIs from 28 CCs with fewer than
1K nodes each. Our gold standard consists of 8,394 manually annotated entities
covering a total of 232,311 `owl:sameAs` links. There are 987 entities (11.75%)
annotated as 'unknown'. A total of 209,160 edges (90.02%) are between nodes
with the same annotation while 3,678 edges (1.58%) link entities with different
manual annotations. The remaining edges involve at least one node annotated as
'unknown'. Based on this manual examination, we estimate the error rate to be
between 1.58% and 9.98%. We divide our gold standard randomly into two parts
of 14 files each for training and evaluation respectively. To better understand the
gold standard, we show their size ECs and their distribution in Fig. 3. The plot
shows that redundancy is common in the LOD cloud. The majority of ECs
contain fewer than 200 nodes, while there could be as many as 358 identifiers
referring to the same real-world entity at the right end of the spectrum. This
gives a reference for the setting of parameters in our algorithms in Sect. 5.

4.2   Validating the UNA

Using the gold standard, we validate our definitions (RQ2). For this, we use the
sources of entities in our gold standard retrieved also from LOD Laundromat.
Our examination shows that only 0.71% of the entities have an explicit source.
In contrast, 61.97% of the entities have at least one implicit label-like source and
40.71% have a comment-like source. This indicates that explicit sources are too
rare and thus we only use two variants of iUNA in this work: *iUNA-label* and
iUNA-comment corresponding to label-like sources and comment-like sources
respectively.

Table 2. Analysis of sources of the gold standard that follow the UNA

		nUNA	qUNA	iUNA
one unique entity	label-like	1,351 (77.78%)	204 (59.48%)	**1,566 (90.15%)**
	comment-like	519 (68.56%)		**670 (88.51%)**
up to two entities	label-like	250 (14.40%)	69 (20.11%)	119 (6.85%)
	comment-like	153 (20.21%)		57 (7.53%)
more than two entities	label-like	136 (7.82%)	70 (20.41%)	52 (2.99%)
	comment-like	85 (11.23%)		30 (3.96%)

For each source, we analyze the number of entities in each EC. Although the original work that examines qUNA was restricted to only 6 major hubs' namespace as provenance, it can be easily adapted to any namespace. Thus, we generalize its definition of provenance in the experiments below. Considering that the nUNA lacks a proper definition of provenance, we use the label-/comment-like source defined for iUNA for the sake of comparison. Table 2 provides the proportion of sources with the number of entities in each implicit label-/comment-like source in the equivalence classes. A source follows the UNA if there is only one unique entity in the EC. An estimate of 1,351 out of 1,737 label-like sources follows the nUNA. On the other hand, 14.40% of the sources violate the nUNA by having two entities in at least one equivalence class in the gold standard, and an additional 7.82% of the sources violate the nUNA by having more than two entities. Table 2 shows that the iUNA is better than the nUNA and the qUNA in terms of capturing how the community is implementing the UNA in their knowledge bases. This also shows that taking encoding equivalence and redirection can indeed align the UNA with its use in practice. Thus, the algorithm should not remove all edges that violate the UNA when refining the identity graphs.

4.3   Detecting Errors Using UNA

In this section, we focus on **RQ3:** can the UNA give a reliable indication of identity errors in practice? Our analysis shows that the errors can be classified as two types. The first type are erroneous edges between entities that refer to two real-world entities. The others are edges involving nodes annotated as 'unknown'. Thus, we provide upper and lower bound of error rate depending on how these edges are treated. First, we study how two random entities in a connected component are identical. For this, in each connected component G in the gold standard, we sample $|V|$ (i.e. the number of nodes) different pairs of entities at random. The estimated error (proportion of non-identical pairs) is between 47.0% and 68.1%, depending on the interpretation of the nodes labeled "unknown" in the gold standard. We use this as our baseline for the analysis below (see the first row of Table 3).

For these same sampled pairs, we test the error rate and the UNA violation percentage for the three UNA definitions. The second row in Table 3 shows that

Table 3. Percentage of pairs violating different definitions of the UNA with the lower/upper bound of their error rates using different sources

		Violation (%)	Lower bound (%)	Upper bound(%)
random		-	47.0	68.1
nUNA	label	61.9	33.4	49.8
	comment	42.5	32.6	46.2
iUNA	label	0.3	8.5	75.9
	comment	0.1	11.7	35.0
qUNA		1.4	16.1	61.3

when using label-like sources, 61.9% of the sampled pairs violate the nUNA, the estimated error is between 33.4% and 49.8%. In contrast, only 0.3% sampled pairs violates iUNA, with an error rate between 8.5% and 75.9%. Recall that 11.75% nodes were annotated "unknown". This analysis also indicates that such nodes are heavily involved in pairs violating the UNA. More pairs violate the UNA when using label-like sources than when using comment-like sources. In all cases, the lower bounds of error reduce when compared against that of randomly sampled pairs. Using iUNA with comment-like sources reaches the lowest error rate for the lower bound. These selected pairs are then used in the algorithm to identify erroneous edges in the paths that connect them.

Next, we study the impact of redirection. There are in total 13,922 nodes in the graphs that capture redirect relations[8]. We find that 3,072 out of 8,394 entities were redirected. Among them, 5,528 correspond to new IRIs that are in the extended graph but not in the original graphs. There are in total 6,991 edges in the redirect graphs. Among them, 546 are between entities in the original graph with 504 correct ones and 8 erroneous ones. That is, the error rate is between 1.47% and 7.69%. In addition, we have 12,531 pairs of entities that redirect to the same entity in the extended graph. The error rate is between 4.29% and 6.32%.

Next we study the equivalent entities suffering from different encodings (recall the example given in Fig. 2). We have 1,818 pairs of entities in the gold standard.[9] Among them, there are edges between 1,130 pairs in the original identity graphs with an error rate between 2.21% and 8.50%. We discovered 688 new pairs that differ only by encoding with an error rate between 1.16% and 14.83%. Finally, there is a pair of entities whose IRIs in alternative encoding are the same but they actually refer to different real-world entities. We conclude that though the exception do not always hold, they are often useful.

---

[8] Redirection was tested with the *requests* Python package using the *get* function with a max timeout of 5 s for connection and 25 s for reading.

[9] We used the *parse* function in the *rfc3987* and *urllib* Python library.

Algorithm 1: partition

---

1 **Input:** an identity graph G, a weighting scheme w, a graph of redirect G^R, a
  graph of equivalence under various encodings G^E
  Result: status s, a set of edges removed A, the graph of partitions G_P
2 initiate A as an empty set (to store removed edges);
3 initiate H_{ccs} as a set of the connected components of G;
4 **while** $|A|$ *is increasing (no new edge to remove) and H_{ccs} is not empty* **do**
5   **foreach** $H_{cc} \in H_{ccs}$ **do**
6   (optional: obtain the corresponding subgraphs H_{cc}^R, H_{cc}^E from G^R, G^E);
7          $(N_{ccs}, A') = $ partition_iter$(H_{cc}, w, H_{cc}^R, H_{cc}^E)$;
8          $A := A \cup A'$;
9   remove H_{cc} from H_{ccs};
10   add new graphs N_{ccs} that are not singleton to H_{ccs}.

11 remove A from G to get G_P;
12 return (A, G_P).

---

5 Algorithm Design

We limit the scope of refinement algorithms in this paper to removing erroneous
identity links and forego identifying erroneous entities or adjoining additional
links. The intuition is that for two inter-connected clusters, if there is more force
pushing them apart than holding them together, then some edge(s) should be
removed to split the clusters apart. The "force" that pushes the clusters apart are
between pairs of entities violating the UNA. These pairs might not be directly
connected, but they can be connected through multiple paths. The removed
edges as the output of the algorithm is a *cut* for the graph. Computing an
optimal cut whose removal makes the graph consistent within each CC is APX-
hard (i.e. where there are polynomial-time approximation algorithms) [12]. We
can encode this problem (as soft and hard clauses) to an optimization problem
and employing an SMT solver [5]. The goal is to maximise the sum of weights
over all soft clauses while satisfying all the hard clauses. We choose this approach
because it enables fast reasoning over weighted constraints of relations of equality
and inequality and it returns a sub-optimal answer in case of timeout.

5.1 Algorithm Using UNA

Since the iUNA/nUNA requires the same parameters, we present the algorithm
using the iUNA. That of qUNA can be derived simply by removing the parameters of redirect graphs and that of encoding equivalence. Algorithm 1 takes as
input a graph G, the corresponding redirect graph G^R, the graph of equivalence
under various encodings G^E, and a weighting scheme w. As a first step, we load
H_{css} with the connected components of G. We obtain the corresponding sub-
graphs H_{cc}^R, H_{cc}^E from G^R, G^E respectively. G_{ccs}, together with G_{cc}^R, G_{cc}^E and the

---

Algorithm 2: partition_iter

---

1 **Input:** a graph of connected component G_{cc}, a weighting scheme w, a graph of
   redirect G_{cc}^R, a graph of equivalence under various encodings G_{cc}^E
   Result: a set of graphs of connected components N_{ccs}, edges removed A_{cc}
2 obtain random pairs of nodes, select only those that violates the iUNA, as P;
3 **if** $|P| \leq 1$ **then**
4 $\quad$ return $(G_{cc}, \emptyset)$.

5 initiate an SMT solver o;
6 **foreach** *entity e in G_{cc}* **do**
7 $\quad$ introduce an integer variable I_e in the SMT solver;
8 $\quad$ assert **hard clauses** $(0 \leq I_e)$ and $(I_e \leq M)$ in o.

9 **foreach** *pair (s,t) in P* **do**
10 $\quad$ assert in o a **soft clause** NOT$(I_s == I_t)$ with weight according to w.

11 let F be the minimum spanning forest of G_{cc};
12 sample a small amount of additional edges from G_{cc} as B;
13 **foreach** *pair (s,t) in $F \cup B$* **do**
14 $\quad$ assert in o a **soft clause** $(I_s == I_t)$ with weight according to w.

15 obtain $G_{cc}'^R$ the undirected graph of the (directed) graph G_{cc}^R;
16 **foreach** *pair (s,t) in G_{cc}'* **do**
17 $\quad$ **if** *there is a path between s and t in $G_{cc}'^R$* **then**
18 $\quad\quad$ initiate/update the weight of a **soft clause** c_r in o according to w.

19 **foreach** *pair (s,t) in G_{cc}^E* **do**
20 $\quad$ initiate/update the weight of a **soft clause** $(I_s == I_t)$ in o according to w.

21 let m be the model of o after solving;
22 extract the removed edges A_{cc} from m;
23 remove A_{cc} from G_{cc};
24 compute N_{ccs} as the connected components without singletons;
25 **return** (N_{ccs}, A_{cc}).

---

weighting scheme is then taken as the input of Algorithm 2. The removed edges
are collected in A. The algorithm stops when no more edges can be removed.

In the while-loop of Algorithm 1, there is a repeated call to Algorithm 2 that
examines each graph of a connected component in H_{ccs} (line 7). Algorithm 2
takes advantage of an SMT solver's power of reasoning over weighted relations
of equality and returns a solution within a given time bound. We first randomly
sample some pairs of nodes. We keep those that violates the iUNA, denoted P
(line 2). If there is at most one pair in graph G_{cc} that violates the iUNA, we
keep the graph as it is (line 4). Otherwise, we initiate an SMT solver (line 5).
For each node, we introduce a integer variable. We encode two hard clauses to
ensure the values to be between 0 and M in the model m. These integer variables
will eventually be assigned an integer value in the model m after solving.

Next we explain how the soft clauses are generated. For each pair (s, t) in P,
we obtain a clause NOT$(I_s = I_t)$ and associate it with a weight according to the

weighting scheme w (line 10). Instead of taking all the edges of G_{cc}, we take the edges of its minimum spanning forest and a small sample of the edges to reduce the load on the SMT solver. In line 11, we obtain the minimum spanning forest F. For efficiency, we keep a set of edges in B (line 12) for the back propagation process of SMT's internal algorithm design. The edges of $F \cup B$ forms the set of edges in G_{cc} to examine this round (line 11–14). Recall that in Sect. 4.3, our analysis showed that it provides relatively reliable information when considering redirection and equivalence under different encoding. We therefore encode the edges of the redirection (line 15–18) as soft clauses. The undirected graph is used for the checking of convergence of redirection of two entities (line 15, 17).

While not every soft clause is true in the model, all the hard clauses must be satisfied. The goal is to maximise the sum of weights over all soft clauses while satisfying all the hard clauses. Note that if an SMT solver fails to get an optimal solution within the timeout, it will return the best sub-optimal solution (line 21). The edge (s, t) remains if and only if I_s equals I_t in the model m (line 22).

The weighting scheme w consists of a series of functions that map clauses to weights: $w = (f_G, f_R, f_E, f_P)$. We used the training dataset to fine-tune the weighting scheme. For a soft clause c_e corresponding to an edge e, the weight is $f_G(c_e) + f_R(c_e) + f_E(c_e) + f_P(c_e)$. The first weighting scheme w_1 consists of four functions: f_G assigns the clause of each edge in the $F \cup B$ a weight of 5, the rest 0; Similarly, f_P assignes the clauses corresponding to pairs in P a weight of 2. f_R and f_E both increase the weight by 1 for that of $G_{cc}'^R$ and $G_c^E c$ respectively. After some manual tuning, we provide an alternative weighting scheme w_2 with the corresponding values being 31, 16, 5, and 5, respectively. Other parameters and hyper parameters were set according to Sect. 4.1 and fine-tuned. The upper bound M was set to $2 + |G_{cc}|/50$. A random selection of 12% of the edges from the original graph were kept in B. Finally, based on our experience with Z3, the timeout bound for SMT solving was set to $(|G_{cc}|/100 + 0.5)$ second.

6   Evaluation

6.1   Implementation

We used the *networkx* Python package[10] for the computation of the connected components and the minimum spanning forests. For the manual annotation of the entities, we used ANNit[11]. We used the implementation of the Leiden algorithm and the Louvain algorithm in CDlib[12]. As for SMT solver, we employed Z3[13] and used its Python binding [5]. We published all the code as an open source

---

[10] https://networkx.github.io.

[11] ANNit is a user-friendly interface for fast annotation of entities and triples. See https://github.com/shuaiwangvu/ANNit for details.

[12] Community Discovery Library is a meta-library for community discovery in complex networks: https://pypi.org/project/cdlib/.

[13] https://github.com/Z3Prover/z3.

project[14]. All our experiments were conducted on the LOD Labs machine. It has 32 64-bit Intel Xeon CPUs (E5-2630 v3 @ 2.40GHz) with a RAM of 264GB.

6.2 Evaluation Metrics

While precision and recall are commonly used in evaluation metrics [17], the presence of 'unknown' annotations makes them less suitable for this task since no edge involving entity of 'unknown' counts toward precision or recall. Thus, precision and recall do not adequately capture the qualities. Moreover, we noticed that 11 graphs in our gold standard has no erroneous edges except those with nodes labelled "unknown". Therefore, we provide an additional metric. In its design, we focus on two properties that the equivalence classes should possess within the CCs resulting from refinement. (a) the equivalence class should not be separated over multiple CCs; (b) two equivalence classes should not share the same CC. This leads to the following metric for the graph G' that results from applying a refinement algorithm to G:

$$\Omega(G') = \sum_{C \in G'_{ccs}} \sum_{Q_e \in E(C)} \frac{|Q_e|}{|V|} \frac{|Q_e|}{|O_e|} \frac{|Q_e|}{|C|}.$$

Here, C iterates over all connected components in G', and $E(C)$ is a partitioning of the nodes in C by equivalence class, so that Q always represents the set of nodes within a given C that refers to the same real-world entity e. V represents the total number of vertices, and O_e is the set of all entities in G' referring to e.

Within the summation, there are three factors. The first, $|Q_e|/|V|$ is the proportion of the current set of vertices to the total. This turns $\Omega(G')$ into a weighted sum over all subsets $|Q|$, with the weights summing to the total proportion of nodes not annotated "unknown". The second, $|Q_e|/|O_e|$, is 1 if all references to e are in C, and lower if there are more references in other connected components. This penalizes deviating from (a). The third, $|Q_e|/|C|$, is 1 if all nodes in C refer to e and lower if the connected component is shared with nodes referring to other entities. This penalizes deviating from (b). Note that if the graph contains no "unknown" nodes, the max. of Ω is 1.

6.3 Evaluation Results

We compare our algorithm using two variants of sources (implicit label-like and comment-like sources) with two weighting schemes (w_1 and w_2, as defined in Sect. 5) against the Louvain algorithm [6], the Leiden algorithm [1], as well as the result of MetaLink with two threshold values [3,16]. Table 4 presents the results of the average of 5 runs for each method with best results highlighted. The Louvain algorithm removes the most amount of edges. It has the highest

---

[14] The code and implementation details are at https://github.com/shuaiwangvu/ sameAs-iUNA together with the results of several parametric settings.

recall but relatively low precision. Recall the example in Fig. 2, the results of Louvain can be smaller isolated components. This problem also exhibits in our evaluation, due to the significant amount of edges removed, its Ω values are low despite varying its resolution parameter from 0.01 to 1.0. Compared with Louvain, the result of the Leiden algorithm shows obvious improvements. There are fewer edges removed while the precision and Ω have improved for both the training set and the evaluation set. As for Metalink, we run the algorithm with two thresholds: 0.9 and 0.99 (only links with an error degree higher than the threshold are considered erroneous). There are fewer edges removed in both cases, with higher Ω values compared against that of Leiden and Louvain.

Table 4. Evaluation of the Louvain algorithm with two resolution values, the Leiden algorithm, MetaLink with two threshold values, and our algorithm using different UNA and settings.

		Training set				Evaluation set			
		precision	recall	Ω	$|A|$	precision	recall	Ω	$|A|$
Louvain	res=0.01	0.020	**0.803**	0.091	39,471.4	0.042	**0.727**	0.087	42,424.2
	res=1.0	0.020	0.778	0.087	39,226.2	0.042	0.660	0.084	43,610.0
Leiden		0.249	0.198	0.377	3,398.4	0.068	0.323	0.439	2,782.6
MetaLink	t=0.9	0.076	0.029	0.522	241	0.086	0.032	0.524	337
	t=0.99	0.036	0.004	0.591	58	0.013	0.001	0.635	99
nUNA	label, w1	0.126	0.150	0.590	406.2	0.042	0.063	0.597	684.6
	label, w2	0.153	0.181	0.591	529.0	0.061	0.075	0.580	697.4
	comment, w1	0.201	0.146	0.595	263.0	0.098	0.040	0.618	356.4
	comment, w2	0.209	0.178	0.597	360.2	0.063	0.036	0.606	431.2
qUNA	w1	0.258	0.152	**0.641**	492.0	0.058	0.036	0.662	706.4
	w2	0.227	0.174	0.640	566.6	0.101	0.054	**0.671**	634.2
iUNA	label, w1	**0.333**	0.127	0.606	78.0	0.122	0.013	0.652	236.8
	label, w2	0.204	0.118	0.616	125.8	**0.136**	0.028	0.647	235.0
	comment, w1	0.267	0.090	0.598	63.8	0.097	0.002	0.636	141.2
	comment, w2	0.258	0.117	0.607	133.2	0.117	0.003	0.638	173.8

In almost all cases, using comment-like sources results in better precision values while having fewer edges removed. The difference of Ω between using label-like sources and comment-like sources is minor. In general, fewer links were removed when using the UNA and Metalink for refinement. Comparing the nUNA with the iUNA, we can see that using the nUNA results in more edges removed with a lower precision. When comparing the qUNA with the iUNA, we find as well that the qUNA removes a larger amount of edges, which leads to a slightly higher recall. In almost all settings, using the iUNA results in higher precision, which could be the benefit of better modeling using exceptions. The best Ω values in both sets are obtained using the qUNA, while using the iUNA results in better precision with similar Ω values. Compared with Metalink, our algorithm shows higher precision and better Ω values. Overall, our evaluation indicates that different algorithms have different advantages, but using the UNA shows clear benefits.

As for time efficiency, the Louvain and Leiden algorithm completes processing both the training and evaluation sets within 40 s. For the algorithm using the UNA, it takes around 8 min to process the training set in contrast to up to 27 min for the evaluation set. In addition, we note that up to three graphs in the evaluation set can suffer from timeout using our algorithm[15]. When there is a timeout, the SMT solver returns a sub-optimal solution. Our manual examination shows that some "harder" and larger graphs were distributed to the evaluation set when constructing the two sets.

7   Discussion and Future Work

In this paper, we studied three definitions of UNA and proposed a UNA-based identity refinement approach. RQ1 was answered by defining the iUNA that considers certain exceptions that are common in large integrated graphs. For RQ2 and RQ3, we created a gold standard and compared the reliability of iUNA against the qUNA and the nUNA. For RQ4, we proposed an identity refinement algorithm and evaluated its performance on different definitions of UNA.

Strictly speaking, our gold standard is not large enough for an accurate estimate of the error rate of the entire identity graph. Using our sample, we found that among the 3,678 erroneous edges, only 5 entities have multiple label-like or comment-like sources. This indicates that the UNA can be used for refinement but redundancy is not the direct cause of error. This is contrary to the conclusion of [12] (see type 2 error: consistency and conciseness error).

The performance of our algorithm is sensitive to the parameters and hyperparameters. For example, the upper bound for each integer value M can significantly influence the results if too small. Future work includes studying how our algorithm scales with different time limits, automatic tuning of the parameters, and extending the gold standard. The results of some other parametric settings are included in the supplementary material in the repository.

The performance of MetaLink is comparable with the best outcome of our algorithms. However, our analysis shows that no more than 10% edges removed are shared between Metalink and our algorithms in various settings. It could be promising to explore a hybrid approach in future work. Since our evaluation confirms the superiority of the communities detected using the Leiden algorithm compared to Louvain, it is also reasonable to quest how far the results can be improved if MetaLink uses Leiden's outputs for calculating its error degree.

The identity graph we study contains a large number of connected components of size two, as well as two very large connected components. The biggest CC in this dataset has 177,794 entities and 2,849,426 edges (No. 4073). The second biggest has 21,191 entities and 101,269 edges (No. 142063). The rest are

---

[15] The connected components with the IDs 14872, 4635725, and 37544.

significantly smaller with no more than 5076 nodes. Some past attempts using SMT solvers have also discovered the bottleneck in scalability [20,21]. Our initial experiments show that removing the disambiguation entities has some potential to reduce the size of connected components. In future work, we plan to design scalable algorithms following a divide-and-conquer approach for the handling of large connected components using pairs of entities that violate the UNA as heuristics.

References

1. Traag, V.A., et al.: From Louvain to Leiden: guaranteeing well-connected communities. CoRR abs/1810.08473 (2018). arXiv: 1810.08473. http://arxiv.org/abs/1810.08473
2. Beek, W., Rietveld, L., Bazoobandi, H.R., Wielemaker, J., Schlobach, S.: LOD laundromat: a uniform way of publishing other people's dirty data. In: Mika, P., et al. (eds.) ISWC 2014. LNCS, vol. 8796, pp. 213–228. Springer, Cham (2014). https://doi.org/10.1007/978-3-319-11964-9_14
3. Beek, W., Raad, J., Acar, E., van Harmelen, F.: MetaLink: a travel guide to the LOD cloud. In: Harth, A., et al. (eds.) ESWC 2020. LNCS, vol. 12123, pp. 481–496. Springer, Cham (2020). https://doi.org/10.1007/978-3-030-49461-2_28
4. Beek, W., Raad, J., Wielemaker, J., van Harmelen, F.: sameAs.cc: the closure of 500M owl:sameAs statements. In: Gangemi, A., et al. (eds.) ESWC 2018. LNCS, vol. 10843, pp. 65–80. Springer, Cham (2018). https://doi.org/10.1007/978-3-319-93417-4_5
5. Bjørner, N.: Engineering theories with Z3. In: Yang, H. (ed.) APLAS 2011. LNCS, vol. 7078, pp. 4–16. Springer, Heidelberg (2011). https://doi.org/10.1007/978-3-642-25318-8_3
6. Blondel, V.D., et al.: Fast unfolding of communities in large networks. J. Stat. Mech. Theory Exp. **2008**(10), P10008 (2008)
7. Chen, P.P.-S.: The entity-relationship model–toward a unified view of data. ACM Trans. Database Syst. (TODS) **1**(1), 9–36 (1976)
8. Cuzzola, J., Bagheri, E., Jovanovic, J.: Filtering inaccurate entity co-references on the linked open data. In: Chen, Q., Hameurlain, A., Toumani, F., Wagner, R., Decker, H. (eds.) DEXA 2015. LNCS, vol. 9261, pp. 128–143. Springer, Cham (2015). https://doi.org/10.1007/978-3-319-22849-5_10
9. Guéret, C., Groth, P., Stadler, C., Lehmann, J.: Assessing linked data mappings using network measures. In: Simperl, E., Cimiano, P., Polleres, A., Corcho, O., Presutti, V. (eds.) ESWC 2012. LNCS, vol. 7295, pp. 87–102. Springer, Heidelberg (2012). https://doi.org/10.1007/978-3-642-30284-8_13
10. Halpin, H., Hayes, P.J., McCusker, J.P., McGuinness, D.L., Thompson, H.S.: When owl:sameAs isn't the same: an analysis of identity in linked data. In: Patel-Schneider, P.F., et al. (eds.) ISWC 2010. LNCS, vol. 6496, pp. 305–320. Springer, Heidelberg (2010). https://doi.org/10.1007/978-3-642-17746-0_20
11. Hogan, A., et al.: Scalable and distributed methods for entity matching, consolidation and disambiguation over linked data corpora. J. Web Semant. **10**, 76–110 (2012). ISSN 1570-8268. https://doi.org/10.1016/j.websem.2011.11.002. https://www.sciencedirect.com/science/article/pii/S1570826811000813
12. de Melo, G.: Not quite the same: identity constraints for the web of linked data. In: AAAI (2013)

13. Nasim, I., et al.: What does it mean when your URIs are redirected? Examining identity and redirection in the LOD cloud. In: Workshop on Managing the Evolution and Preservation of the Data Web (MEPDaW) (2022)
14. Papaleo, L., et al.: Logical detection of invalid sameas statements in RDF data. In: EKAW (2014)
15. Raad, J.: Identity management in knowledge graphs. Doctoral dissertation. PhD thesis, University of Paris-Saclay (2018)
16. Raad, J., Beek, W., van Harmelen, F., Pernelle, N., Saïs, F.: Detecting erroneous identity links on the web using network metrics. In: Vrandečić, D., et al. (eds.) ISWC 2018. LNCS, vol. 11136, pp. 391–407. Springer, Cham (2018). https://doi.org/10.1007/978-3-030-00671-6_23
17. Raad, J., et al.: The sameas problem: a survey on identity management in theweb of data. CoRR abs/1907.10528 (2019). arXiv: 1907.10528. http://arxiv.org/abs/1907.10528
18. Reiter, R.: Towards a logical reconstruction of relational database theory. In: Brodie, M.L., Mylopoulos, J., Schmidt, J.W. (eds.) On Conceptual Modelling: Perspectives from Artificial Intelligence, Databases, and Programming Languages, pp. 191–238. Springer, New York (1984). https://doi.org/10.1007/978-1-4612-5196-5_8
19. Valdestilhas, A., et al.: CEDAL: time-efficient detection of erroneous links in large-scale link repositories. In: Proceedings of the International Conference on Web Intelligence (2017). https://doi.org/10.1145/3106426.3106497
20. Wang, S., Raad, J., Bloem, P., van Harmelen, F.: Refining transitive and pseudo-transitive relations at web scale. In: Verborgh, R., et al. (eds.) ESWC 2021. LNCS, vol. 12731, pp. 249–264. Springer, Cham (2021). https://doi.org/10.1007/978-3-030-77385-4_15
21. Wang, S., et al.: SUBMASSIVE: resolving subclass cycles in very large knowledge graphs. In: Workshop on Large Scale RDF Analytics (2020)

Structural Bias in Knowledge Graphs for the Entity Alignment Task

Nikolaos Fanourakis[1]([✉]), Vasilis Efthymiou[1], Vassilis Christophides[2],
Dimitris Kotzinos[2], Evaggelia Pitoura[3], and Kostas Stefanidis[4]

[1] FORTH-ICS, Heraklion, Greece
{fanourakis,vefthym}@ics.forth.gr
[2] Lab. ETIS, CY Cergy Paris University, ENSEA, CNRS UMR 8051, Cergy, France
Vassilis.Christophides@ensea.fr, Dimitrios.Kotzinos@cyu.fr
[3] University of Ioannina, Ioannina, Greece
pitoura@uoi.gr
[4] Tampere University, Tampere, Finland
konstantinos.stefanidis@tuni.fi

Abstract. Knowledge Graphs (KGs) have recently gained attention for representing knowledge about a particular domain and play a central role in a multitude of AI tasks like recommendations and query answering. Recent works have revealed that KG embedding methods used to implement these tasks often exhibit direct forms of bias (e.g., related to gender, nationality, etc.) leading to discrimination. In this work, we are interested in the impact of indirect forms of bias related to the structural diversity of KGs in entity alignment (EA) tasks. In this respect, we propose an exploration-based sampling algorithm, SUSIE, that generates challenging benchmark data for EA methods, with respect to structural diversity. SUSIE requires setting the value of a single hyperparameter, which affects the connectivity of the generated KGs. The generated samples exhibit similar characteristics to some of the most challenging real-world KGs for EA tasks. Using our sampling, we demonstrate that state-of-the-art EA methods, like RREA, RDGCN, MultiKE and PARIS, exhibit different robustness to structurally diverse input KGs.

Keywords: Knowledge Graphs · Entity Alignment · Structural Bias

1 Introduction

Knowledge Graphs (KGs) provide interlinked descriptions of real-world entities (e.g., persons, places, etc.) that play a central role in a multitude of AI tasks like recommendations [25] and query answering [37]. Recently, graph representation learning techniques have been used to automate several KG construction tasks, such as link prediction [42,46], node classification [41,52], and entity alignment (EA) [22,51]. The key idea of these methods is to embed the nodes (entities) and the edges (relations or attributes) of a KG into a low-dimensional vector space in such a way that similar entities in the original KG are close to each other in the embedding space, while dissimilar entities lie far from each other [38,56,57].

C. Pesquita et al. (Eds.): ESWC 2023, LNCS 13870, pp. 72–90, 2023.
https://doi.org/10.1007/978-3-031-33455-9_5

However, recent studies have shown that KG embeddings may reflect or even amplify biases that exist in the original KGs, for example biases related to gender, nationality, or popularity [8,9,45]. In this paper, we focus on a different type of bias. Specifically, we focus on whether structural characteristics of the original KGs introduce biases in the KG entity alignment (EA) task used to find pairs of nodes in two input KGs that refer to the same real-world entity [16,51].

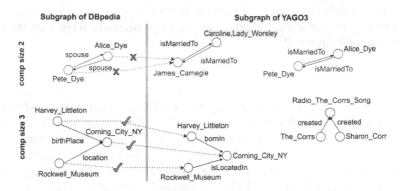

Fig. 1. Correct (check) and incorrect (X) matches suggested by RREA [38] for nodes belonging to connected components of different sizes on the D-Y dataset.

Several methods have been proposed for the EA task that rely on factual (attribute based) or structural (relation based) information of the entities in the KGs (e.g., [13,38,53]). Experimental studies have shown that their performance depends on the factual and structural heterogeneity of the input KGs [22,51]. Since most state-of-the-art EA methods exploit the structural characteristics of entities [22], we focus on structural diversity. Embedding-based EA methods seem to favor the alignment of entities from *rich structural neighborhoods in the two KGs* [22,51].

Example 1. Consider the two KGs (DBpedia and YAGO3) of Fig. 1, where it is seemingly trivial to align entities based on their labels (e.g., "Pete Dye" and "Alice Dye" in DBpedia should be aligned to "Pete Dye" and "Alice Dye", respectively, in YAGO). RREA [38], a state-of-the-art KG embedding-based EA method, fails to find some of these trivial matches and instead, maps Alice_Dye to James_Carnegie and also Pete_Dye to James_Carnegie, as shown by the dotted lines (RREA mappings), as these entities exhibit the same structural cues. In contrast, RREA, as a relation-based EA method that exploits the structural similarity of entities, matches correctly all the entities in a component of size three (Harvey Littleton, Rockwell Museum and Corning City NY), where the structural information is richer [52]. The point is that EA systems face difficulties to correctly match entities when they belong to small graph components, since there are many more entities that have similar structures, unless we consider additional similarity evidence sources than just the entity structure. Figure 1 illustrates this problem over entity subgraphs of two real KGs.

In many cases, structural bias in a KG can be seen as an instance of indirect bias against protected groups defined over sensitive attributes (e.g., gender, race), since structural bias often reflects sampling and representation bias [7], where members of protected groups are incompletely described. This is because missing relations and values in KGs are frequent manifestations of several latent causes: protected group members are more reluctant to provide information that could be used against them, sensitive information may be erased by human curators, or data acquisition may be less complete for protected groups [39].

Following previous work, we quantify structural diversity relying on the number and size of connected components and on node degrees [26,27,47,59]. To generate KGs with adjustable levels of structural diversity for the EA task, we propose an exploration-based sampling method (SUSIE). Our sampling method directly controls the number of connected components, while component sizes and node degrees are affected indirectly. Our evaluation shows that state-of-the-art KG embedding-based EA methods exhibit indirect bias, due to structural diversity, against smaller, less connected regions of the benchmark datasets.

Unlike existing benchmarking (e.g., [15,18,58]) and sampling methods (e.g., Fairwalk [45], IDS [51], div2vec [28]), our exploration-based sampling produces EA datasets (i.e., two KGs and their alignment) of varying structural diversity. As highlighted by previous empirical studies [14,55], and also confirmed experimentally in the current study, real-life KGs are characterized by power-law distributions with respect to the number of connected components and node degrees. Our KG sampling aims to assess to what extent EA methods leave the long tail of entities of KGs under-represented in the correct matches (true positives). In summary, the contributions of this work are the following:

- We introduce the problem of structural-based indirect bias in the EA task.
- We propose SUSIE, an exploration-based sampling method to generate benchmark datasets with varying structural diversity, resembling the characteristics of real-world KGs that are typically left out of EA evaluations. Our method can be used to evaluate the trade-off between the matching accuracy and fairness of existing EA methods, covering the lack of publicly available related benchmarks as pointed out by recent surveys [15,18].
- We show experimentally that state-of-the-art KG embedding-based EA methods exhibit structural bias against smaller, less connected regions of the KGs.

The source code used in this work is publicly accessible[1].

Outline. The rest of the paper is organized as follows. In Sect. 2, we introduce the basic notation used throughout the paper. In Sect. 3, we describe the sampling strategy followed to generate EA datasets of varying structural diversity. In Sect. 4, we report the experimental results that showcase the benefits of our sampling method. In Sect. 5, we position our study with respect to existing works, and we conclude the paper in Sect. 6.

---

[1] https://github.com/fanourakis/Sampling_for_Entity_Alignment.git.

2 Preliminaries

Let $KG = (E, R, T)$ be a knowledge graph, consisting of a set of entities E (i.e., nodes), a set of relation types R (i.e., edge labels), and a set of triples T (i.e., edges). The problem of entity alignment (EA) is defined as follows: Given two knowledge Graphs $KG_1 = (E_1, R_1, T_1)$ and $KG_2 = (E_2, R_2, T_2)$, identify the set of node pairs $M \subseteq E_1 \times E_2$ that refer to the same entity. The following assumptions are common in the EA literature:

- One-to-one assumption (bijection): every node $e \in E_1$ should be mapped to exactly one node $e' \in E_2$ and vice-versa.
- Seed alignment: for training purposes, a subset $S \subseteq M$ of truly matching pairs is known in advance, commonly called the *seed alignment*.

A key notion in our sampling strategy, as well as its evaluation, is that of *weakly connected components*. Given a knowledge graph KG, a weakly connected component is a subgraph of KG where all nodes are connected to each other by some path, ignoring the direction of edges[2]. From now on, we may simply refer to weakly connected components as *connected components*, or just *components*.

Then, we adapt the component-based definition of structural diversity from [26, 54], as follows:

Definition 1 (Structural diversity). *The structural diversity of a knowledge graph $KG = (E, R, T)$ is the number of connected components in KG whose size, measured by the number of vertices, is larger than or equal to an integer t, where $1 \leqslant t \leqslant |E|$.*

To measure structured diversity of KGs, we rely on the following graph-based metrics most of which (or unnormalized variations) have been previously investigated in [27, 59] for social networks analysis.

Ratio of Weakly Connected Components ($wccR$). The number of weakly connected components ($wcc(KG)$) indicates the connectivity of a KG. For a fixed number of nodes, the higher the number of weakly connected components, the less this graph is connected, i.e., there are many, small components in this graph. On the contrary, the fewer the connected components, in a graph of fixed size, the bigger those components are, i.e., bigger regions of the graph are connected. Intuitively, big components are easier to align than small ones, since the big components carry more relational information. To have a normalized score, we report here the ratio of the number of weakly connected components divided by the number of nodes in the knowledge graph (KG): $wccR(KG) = |wcc(KG)|/|E|$.

The number of weakly connected components has been previously used in [27, 59] for measuring the structural diversity. According to [27], large number of weakly connected components, corresponds to high structural diversity.

---

[2] As opposed to strongly connected components, where edge directions matter.

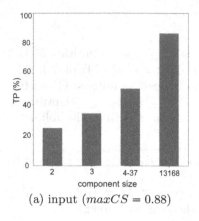
(a) input ($maxCS = 0.88$)

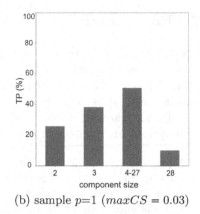
(b) sample $p=1$ ($maxCS = 0.03$)

Fig. 2. Percentage of true matching pairs (TP) found by RREA for different sizes of connected components on KG_1 of the D-Y dataset. D-Y (a) consists of 15k nodes; its sample (b) consists of 1k nodes.

Max Component Size ($maxCS$). This measure is inspired by our early findings (Fig. 2(a)), indicating that a large portion of the existing benchmark data belonged to a single connected component. Thus, the effectiveness of existing methods on the biggest connected component largely determines the effectiveness of the method for the entire dataset. The effectiveness of the same method for smaller connected components is typically lower. To normalize this measure, we divide the size of the largest connected component to the number of nodes in the KG: $maxCS(KG) = \left(\max_{CC \in wcc(KG)}(|CC|)\right)/|E|$. In Fig. 2(a) the largest component has 13,168 nodes and the entire dataset has 15k nodes ($maxCS = 0.88$), while in a sample of the same dataset with 1k nodes (Fig. 2(b)), the largest component has 28 nodes ($maxCS = 0.028$).

Average Node Degree ($\overline{deg}$). The average node degree of a KG is defined as the ratio of the total number of incoming and outgoing edges ($deg(e)$) of each node e, divided by the number of nodes: $\overline{deg}(KG) = \frac{1}{|E|} \sum_{e_i \in E} deg(e_i)$. A low average node degree corresponds to high structural diversity [27].

To measure the effectiveness of each EA method, we report the values of the following standard measures.

Hits@k (H@k) measures the proportion of correctly aligned entities ranked in the top k candidates r: $Hits@k = \frac{|\{r \in \mathcal{I} | r \leqslant k\}|}{|\mathcal{I}|}$, where $\mathcal{I}$ is an individual ranked list of candidates, generated for each entity of the test set. $H@k \in [0,1]$. This measure is easy to interpret, but it considers only top-k ranks.

Mean Reciprocal Rank (MRR) is the inverse of the harmonic mean rank: $MRR = \frac{1}{|\mathcal{I}|} \sum_{r \in \mathcal{I}} \frac{1}{r}$, where $MRR \in (0,1]$. This metric is affected more by the top-ranked values rather than the bottom ones. Thus, MRR is less sensitive to outliers, while it considers all ranks in $\mathcal{I}$.

3   Exploration-Based Sampling Algorithm

In this section, we introduce an exploration-based[3] sampling algorithm (SUSIE) for generating benchmark EA datasets out of two KGs given as input. SUSIE samples parts of both input graphs by performing small random walks on each graph, before jumping/switching to the other graph. This way, it allows exploring diverse areas of both knowledge graphs, with respect to the size of the connected components that it samples. In this respect, it requires to define a desired output sample size s, measured in number of nodes in each KG, the desired minimum component size t to consider, from Definition 1, as well as a hyper-parameter p, controlling the jump probability.

SUSIE is described in Algorithm 1. In summary, it first computes the weakly connected components (Lines 3–4) and groups the nodes by the size of the components they belong to (Lines 5–6). Then, starting from KG_1 (Line 7), it performs uniform sampling on the component sizes limited by t (Line 8) and another uniform sampling to select a random node belonging to a component of this size (Line 9). While the desired sample size s has not been reached (Line 10), the algorithm adds the currently selected node, as well as one of its in- or out-neighbors (Lines 11–12) randomly, and adds them to the sampled nodes (Line 13), while also adding their aligned nodes, as given by the ground truth M (Line 14), also updating the generated seed alignment (Lines 15–16). Based on the given jump probability p, the algorithm then proceeds with a jump (Lines 19–26), also switching KGs (Line 20), or continues a random walk on the current KG (Lines 27–28). In the case of a jump, the algorithm prefers to jump to one of the nodes that may have been left disconnected (i.e., without neighbors) so far (Lines 24–26). Finally, the algorithm copies all edges between the selected sampled nodes from the original KGs, while also checking for any newly added disconnected nodes (Lines 29–34).

Complexity. The time complexity of Algorithm 1 is $O\left(2\left|E\right|\left(\left|E\right|+\left|R\right|\right)\right)$, which is the time complexity of generating the weakly connected components.

4   Experiments

In this section, we present our results of using our sampling algorithm to evaluate indirect fairness of state-of-the-art EA methods. A key takeaway is that we can use our sampling algorithm to measure how much existing EA methods are robust to structural diversity of the input KGs.

Experimental Setup. In our experiments, we have set the sample size s to 1,000, and the minimum component size t to 1 (Definition 1), and tested values 0, 0.15, 0.5, 0.85, and 1 for the jump probability p, with 0 corresponding to no jumps. For the experiments of EA methods, we used the code provided by

---

[3] According to the sampling taxonomy proposed in [34].

Algorithm 1: SUSIE algorithm.

Input: $KG_1 = (E_1, R_1, T_1)$, $KG_2 = (E_2, R_2, T_2)$, ground truth M, jump probability p,
    sample size s, min component size t
Output: $KG'_1 = (E'_1, R'_1, T'_1)$, $KG'_2 = (E'_2, R'_2, T'_2)$, ground truth M'

1 $E'_1, E'_2, R'_1, R'_2, T'_1, T'_2, M' \leftarrow \varnothing$
2 $DE_1, DE_2 \leftarrow \varnothing$ `// disconnected nodes`
3 $wcc_1 \leftarrow KG_1.getWeaklyConnectedComponents()$
4 $wcc_2 \leftarrow KG_2.getWeaklyConnectedComponents()$
5 $cbs_1 \leftarrow groupByComponentSize(wcc_1)$
6 $cbs_2 \leftarrow groupByComponentSize(wcc_2)$
7 $i \leftarrow 1$ `// start from `KG_1
8 $compSize \leftarrow uniSampl(t, cbs_i.keys())$ `// `$t \leqslant$` random size `$\leqslant |cbs_i.keys|$
9 $e \leftarrow uniSampl(cbs_i.nodes(compSize))$ `// a random node`
10 **while** $(|M'| < s)$ **do**
11     $candNeighbs \leftarrow KG_i.get1HopInOutNeighbors(v)$
12     $neigh \leftarrow uniSampl(candNeighbs)$
13     $E'_i \leftarrow E'_i \cup e \cup neigh$
14     $E'_j \leftarrow E'_j \cup matchOf(e, M) \cup matchOf(neigh, M)$ `// `$j = (i\%2) + 1$
15     $M' \leftarrow M' \cup \{(e, matchOf(e, M))\}$ `// reversed, if `$i=2$
16     $M' \leftarrow M' \cup \{(neigh, matchOf(neigh, M))\}$
17     $wcc_i \leftarrow wcc_i \setminus (e \cup neigh)$
18     $jump \leftarrow Binomial(p, 1 - p)$ `// Prob(jump) is `p
19   **if** $jump$ **then** `// jump case`
20        $i \leftarrow (i\%2) + 1$ `// switch KG`
21   **if** $DE_i = \varnothing$ **then**
22           $compSize \leftarrow uniSampl(cbs_i.keys())$
23           $e \leftarrow uniSampl(cbs_i.nodes(compSize))$
24   **else**
25           $e \leftarrow uniSampl(DE_i)$
26           $DE_i \leftarrow DE_i \setminus e$
27   **else** `// random walk case`
28        $e \leftarrow neigh$
       `// get all edges between sampled nodes`
29   **for** $i \in \{1, 2\}$ **do**
30   **foreach** $(h, r, t) \in T_i$, *where* $h, t \in E'_i$ **do**
31           $T'_i \leftarrow T'_i \cup \{(h, r, t)\}$
32           $R'_i \leftarrow R'_i \cup \{r\}$
33        $update(DE_i)$ `// update the disconnected nodes`
34 **return** KG'_1, KG'_2, M'

RREA[4], OpenEA[5] and entity-matchers[6]. Particularly, there are two versions for MultiKE and PARIS; one that uses both relational and factual information (i.e., literal values) and another one that uses only relational information. In our work, we use the relation-based, since our sampling algorithm considers only relational information for structural diversity, while the structural diversity based on attribute information is left for future work.

Datasets. The benchmark datasets from the EA literature that we employ in our experiments, are summarized in Table 1 and briefly described next. **D-Y** [51] was constructed from DBpedia and YAGO3 KGs, describing actors, musicians, writers, films, songs, cities, football players and football teams. **D-W** [51] was constructed from DBpedia and Wikidata KGs, describing the same entity

---

4 https://github.com/MaoXinn/RREA.
5 https://github.com/nju-websoft/OpenEA.
6 https://github.com/epfl-dlab/entity-matchers.

Table 1. Datasets Characteristics.

	Entities ($|E_1|/|E_2|$)	Relations ($|R_1|/|R_2|$)	Triples ($|T_1|/|T_2|$)
D-Y	15,000/15,000	165/28	30,291/26,638
D-W	15,000/15,000	248/169	38,265/42,746
BBC-D	9,396/9,396	9/98	15,478/45,561
MEM-E	69,444/32,311	173/121	1,617,357/323,400

types as D-Y. **BBC-D** [20] was constructed from BBCmusic and DBpedia[7], describing various music-related entity types, such as bands, musicians, and their birth places. **MEM-E** [3] was constructed by Memory Alpha [4] and Star Trek Expanded Universe [6], describing TV series related to Star Trek.

Entity Alignment Methods. In our experiments, we employ the top-performing (according to recent experimental reviews [11,22,35,51]) embedding-based relational methods (i.e., using the structural information of KGs) for EA, namely RREA [38], RDGCN [56] and MultiKE [57].

RREA [38] integrates *Graph Convolutional Networks* (GCNs) and *Graph Attention Networks* (GATs) with a *relational reflection transformation* operation in order to obtain relation-specific embeddings for KG entities. More precisely, RREA stacks multiple layers and uses weight coefficients (similar to GATs), for capturing and aggregating useful multihop-neighborhood information for the entity embeddings. The final entity embeddings come from the concatenation of the embedding of each layer and then, they are refined by minimizing the aligned (from seed alignment) entities' distance in the embedding space. RREA is a semi-supervised method, since, in each iteration, it enriches the training data with entity pairs that are mutually nearest aligned.

RDGCN [56] also utilizes GCNs and GATs. Differently to RREA, RDGCN uses dual relation graphs (i.e., graphs whose vertices are the relations of the input, primal KGs) for incorporating relational information in the entity embeddings and a GAT to encourage the interactions between the dual and the primal KGs. The generated embeddings are fed to a GCN in order to collect relation-aware entity embeddings from the primal graph and then, they are refined by learning a matrix (which is used as a linear transformation from the entities of KG_1), aiming to minimize the distance of the linearly transformed entity and its aligned entity (from seed alignment) in the embedding space. Unlike RREA, RDGCN is a supervised method, and it uses the pre-trained word embeddings of the entity names for the initialization of entity embeddings, instead of the random initialization in RREA.

MultiKE [57] learns the entity embeddings by adopting a translation-based method, TransE [57]. Particularly, given a relation triple $<h, r, t>$ in a KG, where h is a head entity, t is a tail entity, and r is a relation between the entities, it interprets the relation as a translation vector from h to t, aiming to minimize the distance $\mathbf{h}+\mathbf{r}-\mathbf{t}$ of the entity embeddings $\mathbf{h}$ and $\mathbf{t}$, plus the relation embedding $\mathbf{r}$. MultiKE, unlike RREA and RDGCN, considers only the one-hop neighbors. In

---

[7] https://www.csd.uoc.gr/~vefthym/minoanER/datasets.html.

Table 2. The impact of jump probability (p) values on the sampled datasets, using graph connectivity measures.

p			input	0	0.15	0.5	0.85	1
D-Y	wccR	KG_1	0.03	0.01	0.15	0.24	0.28	0.28
		KG_2	0.04	0.05	0.18	0.24	0.28	0.29
	maxCS	KG_1	0.87	0.90	0.13	0.03	0.02	0.02
		KG_2	0.83	0.70	0.06	0.03	0.02	0.02
	$\overline{deg}$	KG_1	4.03	3.65	3.41	2.94	2.71	2.78
		KG_2	3.55	2.31	2.59	2.35	2.16	2.17
D-W	wccR	KG_1	0.01	0.01	0.14	0.24	0.28	0.29
		KG_2	0.02	0.03	0.11	0.20	0.24	0.24
	maxCS	KG_1	0.95	0.91	0.47	0.18	0.11	0.10
		KG_2	0.93	0.85	0.57	0.34	0.24	0.26
	$\overline{deg}$	KG_1	5.10	3.68	2.79	2.50	2.47	2.44
		KG_2	5.69	3.31	2.94	2.37	2.28	2.19
BBC-D	wccR	KG_1	0.18	0.16	0.23	0.29	0.34	0.36
		KG_2	0.07	0.01	0.16	0.24	0.28	0.31
	maxCS	KG_1	0.31	0.26	0.02	0.01	0.01	0.02
		KG_2	0.78	0.92	0.27	0.03	0.04	0.02
	$\overline{deg}$	KG_1	3.29	3.44	3.09	2.73	2.47	2.43
		KG_2	9.69	11.69	6.52	6.07	5.43	5.11
MEM-E	wccR	KG_1	0.00004	0.009	0.003	0.003	0.007	0.006
		KG_2	0.00009	0.001	0.003	0.005	0.011	0.008
	maxCS	KG_1	0.99	0.99	0.78	0.76	0.74	0.77
		KG_2	0.99	1	0.80	0.78	0.78	0.79
	$\overline{deg}$	KG_1	46.58	27.64	24.46	18.76	13.50	14.70
		KG_2	20.01	24.76	14.53	11.25	9.24	8.74

parallel with learning the entity embeddings, it also aligns the relations using the relation embeddings. As for the refinement of the generated entity embeddings, it follows a variation of the method that RREA uses, enriching the training data with new triples that come from the replacement of either h or t of existing triples with their aligned entities from the seed alignment.

PARIS [50] is a probabilistic, holistic approach, i.e., it aligns both instances (entities) and schema, by estimating probabilities of equivalence (for matching), without learning KG embeddings, as previous methods do. More precisely, the estimation of the probabilities, relies on quasi-functional relations, i.e., relations that for a given head entity, the expected number of tail entities is close to 1.

Finally, it is worth mentioning that the evaluation of EA methods commonly relies on the one-to-one assumption and a complete ground truth of matches, i.e., the size of seed alignment $|S|$ is the same as $|E_1|$ and $|E_2|$. Yet, recent efforts [58] have shown ways of dropping this assumption (e.g., by removing a percentage of entities from each KG). We have included a dataset (MEM-E) that does not conform to these assumptions. However, RDGCN and MultiKE could not by-pass this assumption and are thus, not evaluated on this dataset.

4.1   Experimental Results

In this section, we report our experimental findings, divided into three parts. First, we discuss how our sampling method affects the graph-related measures

Table 3. $wccR$ and $maxCS$ scores of some real-world KGs.

	LOCAH [2]	Restaurants [5]	Airlines [1]	IMDb [43]	TMDb [43]	TVDb [43]
$wccR$	0.34	0.33	0.14	0.06	0.06	0.02
$maxCS$	0.001	0.008	0.07	0.27	0.24	0.28

of the given datasets, for different values of the hyperparameter p. Then, we see how the choice of p also affects the effectiveness of the state-of-the-art evaluated EA methods. Finally, we check if there are statistically significant correlations between those graph measures and the methods' effectiveness, which in essence, reveals whether and how much an evaluated method is robust (no correlations) or not (correlations exist) to changes in the structural diversity of the input KGs.

Effects of Sampling on Dataset-Related Measures. We first report the structure-based results of the generated (sampled) datasets, when varying the hyperparameter value p (jump probability). Due to space limitations, we report in Table 2 only results for $t = 1$. Note that samples generated by SUSIE with $t = 5$ from D-Y for $p = 0.5$, yield, for KG_1 and KG_2, a $wccR$ of 0.17 and 0.18, $maxCS$ 0.03 and 0.03, and $\overline{deg}$ 3.27 and 2.62, respectively. As expected, larger t values make the samples easier for EA methods, since larger components are sampled something that justifies the default choice of $t = 1$ in our experiments.

Note that the denominator $|E|$ in all three graph-related measures ($wccR$, $maxCS$, $\overline{deg}$) is fixed in the generated samples, determined by the value of s. This means that, in this study, the scores of those measures are only determined by their nominators. Intuitively, we expect that more jumps (i.e., higher p) imply more connected components, of smaller size, and lower average node degree.

We first observe that in all cases, the connectivity of the input KGs to our sampling algorithm, is closer to the case of $p = 0$ (no jumps). As expected, while p is increasing, the number of weakly connected components (and $wccR$, since $|E|$ remains the same, as it is controlled by the parameter s) is also increasing, i.e., with more frequent jumps, we get more weakly connected components. We observe that $wccR$ scores are almost identical between the KGs in D-Y, D-W and MEM-E. Interestingly, this is not the case for small values of p in BBC-D, but the $wccR$ values of KG_1 and KG_2 start to converge to similar values as p increases, mostly affecting (increasing) the $wccR$ value of KG_2. Unlike other datasets, the $wccR$ of MEM-E it is much smaller, due to the limited number of weakly connected components, even in the KGs given as input to SUSIE.

Since the size of the KG remains the same, the more the weakly connected components the smaller they are. This is confirmed by the size of the largest connected component, which decreases as more jumps are performed. We further observe that the largest component sizes across the two KGs are very similar in D-Y and D-W ($maxCS$ >0.8 of the KG sizes in the input graphs and the sampled ones with $p = 0$), while the values of $maxCS$ for the two KGs of BBC-D are very different (even by an order of magnitude in the case of $p = 0.15$); another indicator about the heterogeneity of this dataset, explaining the lower effectiveness of EA methods. As for MEM-E, the largest component sizes across

Table 4. The impact of sampling on the effectiveness of RREA, as the jump probability p increases.

p		input	0	0.15	0.5	0.85	1
D-Y	H@1	.807	.804	.500	.454	.367	.384
	H@10	.928	.931	.792	.717	.652	.682
	MRR	.855	.844	.605	.541	.467	.486
D-W	H@1	.697	.730	.465	.372	.354	.421
	H@10	.898	.918	.725	.640	.604	.672
	MRR	.772	.802	.554	.454	.435	.499
BBC-D	H@1	.389	.466	.404	.347	.315	.271
	H@10	.611	.707	.570	.477	.401	.392
	MRR	.472	.556	.473	.399	.350	.317
MEM-E	H@1	.249	.154	.134	.079	.064	.131
	H@10	.616	.591	.463	.333	.320	.416
	MRR	.367	.277	.237	.175	.152	.223

Table 5. The impact of sampling on the effectiveness of RDGCN.

p		input	0	0.15	0.5	0.85	1
D-Y	H@1	.924	.928	.908	.847	.908	.865
	H@10	.967	.973	.974	.947	.967	.948
	MRR	.940	.946	.934	.887	.934	.900
D-W	H@1	.526	.631	.500	.450	.438	.437
	H@10	.730	.820	.727	.642	.638	.640
	MRR	.591	.699	.586	.527	.518	.514
BBC-D	H@1	.067	.071	.080	.084	.102	.102
	H@10	.114	.146	.138	.140	.164	.154
	MRR	.080	.101	.106	.108	.126	.127

Table 6. The impact of sampling on the effectiveness of MultiKE.

p		input	0	0.15	0.5	0.85	1
D-Y	H@1	.554	.431	.264	.261	.247	.218
	H@10	.802	.763	.602	.570	.510	.511
	MRR	.636	.544	.382	.370	.340	.316
D-W	H@1	.286	.367	.235	.200	.225	.214
	H@10	.579	.727	.548	.400	.428	.418
	MRR	.377	.484	.347	.274	.296	.286
BBC-D	H@1	.247	.292	.270	.252	.255	.208
	H@10	.531	.674	.540	.452	.408	.387
	MRR	.342	.426	.377	.332	.314	.280

the two KGs are very similar, while $maxCS$ is much larger (even in the highest values of p), indicating that this dataset contains huge components.

Finally, the average node degree decreases as p increases, which implies that, as expected, the generated knowledge graph samples become sparser as we perform more random jumps. Again the average node degrees in D-Y and D-W are very similar between KG_1 and KG_2, which is not the case for BBC-D and MEM-E. It worth mentioning that the KGs in MEM-E are much denser than the ones of the other datasets.

As Table 3 demonstrates, there are many real-world KGs that exhibit similar $maxCS$ and/or $wccR$ to our sampled KGs. For instance, LOCAH exhibits $wccR$ = 0.34 and $maxCS$ = 0.001, while the sample generated by SUSIE for D-Y and $p = 0.5$ exhibits very similar characteristics ($wccR$ = 0.24 and $maxCS$ = 0.03).

Effects of Sampling on the Effectiveness of EA Methods. Next, we report the effectiveness results of the employed EA methods on the generated (sampled) datasets, when varying the hyperparameter value p (jump probability). Those results are summarized in Tables 4 (for RREA), 5 (for RDGCN), 6 (for MultiKE) and 7 (for PARIS).

Table 7. The impact of sampling on the effectiveness (H@1) of PARIS.

p	input	0	0.15	0.5	0.85	1
D-Y	.979	.454	.267	.265	.271	.221
D-W	.841	.460	.242	.184	.213	.209
BBC-D	.387	.325	.302	.267	.288	.242
MEM-E	.082	.060	.047	.019	.011	.031

Again, we observe that in all cases, the behavior of the EA algorithms in the input KGs (i.e., before sampling) is closer to the case of $p = 0$ (no jumps). In Table 4, for all datasets, the effectiveness of RREA are dropping while p is incrementally increasing from 0 to 0.85. The biggest effect is when comparing the effectiveness on samples of $p = 0$ to those of $p = 0.15$. In both BBC-D and MEM-E, unlike D-Y and D-W, the impact of changing p from 0.15 to 0.5 is also large. In all cases, the impact of changing p from 0.5 to 0.85 is much smaller, while changing p from 0.85 to 1 seems to have a negligible effect on the effectiveness of RREA. Overall, the effects of increasing p on the effectiveness of RREA are larger (e.g., there is a 44% drop in H@1 for D-Y) for the datasets (D-Y and D-W) in which RREA was having good results on the original input graphs, and smaller ($\leqslant$18% and 22% for any measure) for BBC-D and MEM-E, in which RREA was struggling. As mentioned in Sect. 4.1, we further include some indicative experiments, setting $t = 5$ with the corresponding H@1, H@10 and MRR for $p = 0.5$ for RREA: 0.460, 0.808, 0.592, showcasing that higher values of t make the EA datasets less challenging (since small components are excluded).

In Table 5, we see that the effectiveness RDGCN is not affected so much by changing the jump probability values, compared to RREA. There is no change larger than 9.2% (H@10 in D-W) for any measure. This is probably due to the impact of initializing the embeddings with entity names in RDGCN, as opposed to random initialization in RREA. Having an additional source of alignment information helps RDGCN to get better results when the relational information become poorer (i.e., when p increases), as compared to RREA that relies entirely on relational information. RDGCN, was unable to run on MEM-E, due to one-to-one assumption, so we excluded this dataset from this experiment.

In Table 6, for all datasets, we see that the effectiveness of MultiKE, similarly to RREA, is dropping while p is incrementally increasing from 0 to 1. The largest impact in the effectiveness of the method due to our sampling algorithm, is observed when we increase p from 0 to 0.15 for D-Y and D-W. When changing p from 0.15 to 0.50, from 0.5 to 0.85 and from 0.85 to 1, the effect on the scores is much smaller compared to RREA and in some cases negligible (e.g., H@1 on D-Y when changing p from 0.15 to 0.5). This is probably due to the already bad results on the original input graphs, since unlike RREA and RDGCN, MultiKE considers only the one-hop neighbors and unlike RDGCN, it does not consider entity names as matching evidence. MultiKE could not run on MEM-E, either. Finally, we further extend our experiments by investigating the robustness of

Table 8. Spearman's correlations between the connectivity of sampled datasets and effectiveness results $Hits@k$ ($H@k$) and MRR. Dashed cells denote statistically not significant correlation, with p-values > 0.05.

		wccR		maxCS		$\overline{deg}$	
		KG_1	KG_2	KG_1	KG_2	KG_1	KG_2
RREA	H@1	−0.90	−0.81	0.81	0.71	0.86	-
	H@10	−0.85	−0.65	0.79	0.56	0.77	-
	MRR	−0.88	−0.75	0.79	0.65	0.84	-
RDGCN	H@1	-	-	-	-	-	−0.66
	H@10	-	-	-	-	-	−0.65
	MRR	-	-	-	-	-	−0.65
MultiKE	H@1	−0.70	−0.70	0.46	0.55	0.84	-
	H@10	−0.87	−0.77	0.68	0.61	0.93	-
	MRR	−0.80	−0.72	0.56	0.54	0.90	-
PARIS	H@1	−0.65	−0.68	0.49	0.60	0.81	0.51

EA systems, like the version of MultiKE that accounts also textual facts, to structural diversity. The results showcase that it remains unaffected (Hits@1 scores in D-Y dataset, which are 0.90, 0.85, 0.92, 0.92, for input, p = 0, 0.15, 1, respectively) to structural diversity.

In Table 7, we consider F1-score (that PARIS reports) equal to H@1, since in the test phase, each source entity gets a list of candidates [51]. We observe that the effectiveness of PARIS is dropping while p is increasing. The largest impact on the effectiveness of PARIS, due to our sampling algorithm, is observed when p goes from 0 to 0.15 for D-Y and D-W. When changing p from 0.15 to 0.50, from 0.50 to 0.85 and from 0.85 to 1, the effect on the effectiveness of PARIS is negligible. This happens because PARIS uses only the functional relations, in contrast to the other methods that use all the relations for the embeddings.

Correlations Between Graph Measures and EA Effectiveness. Table 8 reports the statistically significant Spearman's correlations between data measures ($wccR$, $maxCS$, $\overline{deg}$) and effectiveness measures (H@k, MRR), while cells with a dash ('-') are those without statistically significant correlations. In this correlation analysis, we used only D-Y, D-W and BBC-D, since RDGCN and MultiKE were unable to run with MEM-E.

This table shows that in RREA, MultiKE and PARIS, $wccR$ is negatively correlated with effectiveness (i.e., bigger $wccR$ comes with worse results) of the methods, while $maxCS$ and $\overline{deg}$ are positively correlated (i.e., higher average node degree and bigger size of the largest component, are both associated with better results). In RDGCN, $\overline{deg}$ in KG_2 is negatively correlated with the method effectiveness (i.e., smaller average node degree comes with better results).

Discussion. We observe that probabilistic, non-embedding-based methods like PARIS, assuming that the input graphs are isomorphic and few relations are more important than others (i.e., quasi-functional), outperform embedding-based methods, but they are not robust even to the slightest structural variations (i.e., even with small values of p).

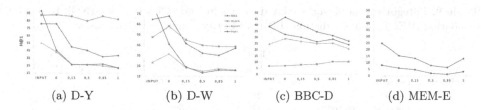

| (a) D-Y | (b) D-W | (c) BBC-D | (d) MEM-E |

Fig. 3. Robustness of EA methods' effectiveness (H@1) to structural diversity brought by SUSIE sampling.

On the other hand, the robustness of embedding-based methods against the structural diversity of input graphs depends on the factual information (e.g., attributes values, entity names) that they exploit to align entities. For example, RDGCN is the most robust method to structural diversity, RREA is the least robust, while MultiKE lies somewhere in the middle. Unlike RREA, which only relies on the relational structure, RDGCN heavily relies on the naming of entities, which is not affected by our sampling. The small difference on the impact of structural diversity between RREA and MultiKE is due to the fact that RREA considers multi-hop neighbors, while MultiKE stops at hop-1 neighbors.

Finally, we observe that our sampling significantly impacts the evaluation of EA methods, as it changes the entity ranking of the top-performing methods, even in the same input KGs. This behavior is illustrated in Fig. 3, where the performance of EA methods is measured using Hits@1 (similar observations hold for the other measures). For example, we observe that in D-Y, PARIS is the top-performing method for the input KGs, but it is the worst-performing method for our samples, for all values of p. Moreover, for D-W, PARIS has the same behavior as in D-Y, but also RREA and RDGCN outperform each other for different values of p; RDGCN starts outperforming RREA for $p \geq 0.15$. Overall, SUSIE reveals the performance differences of EA methods that enable to assess their robustness against increasing structural diversity of input graphs.

5 Related Work

In this section, we position our contributions w.r.t. previous works related to bias in KG-embedding-based prediction tasks (summarized in Table 9), as well as, to existing KG sampling algorithms.

Bias in KG Embeddings. The majority of works on KG embeddings focus on direct forms of bias[8] (group fairness). Among them, only few are related to EA tasks, aiming to mitigate bias by satisfying fairness constraints [21], or to identify name matching bias using string similarity measures [31]. Most of the bias related work focuses on link prediction [23,24,32,49], node classification [33] and recommendation [8,10,36,45] tasks.

---

[8] [18,44] investigate direct forms of bias on "flat", tabular data.

Table 9. Categorization of works related to bias in Node Classification (NC), Recommendation (REC), Link Prediction (LP) and Entity Alignment (EA) tasks.

		NC	REC	LP	EA
Direct	Group	[33]	[8,10,36,45]	[8,10,23,24,32,33,36,45,49]	[21,31]
Indirect	Individual	[17,19]	–	[17,29,40,48]	–
	Degree-related	[12,30,52]	[28]	[28,47]	[11]
	Connectivity-related	–	[27]	[27,59]	–

Fairwalk [45] is an embedding method based on modified random walks, that weights the edges between the node and their one-hop neighbors, in order the latter to be chosen equiprobably and independently to the sensitive group they belong to. Crosswalk [33] is also a random walk-based embedding method, but, unlike Fairwalk, extends the range of the weighting including multi-hop neighbors. Few works recently consider indirect forms of bias, such as graph modularity/homophily in node classification [19], link prediction [40] or complex networks [48]. We should also mention [17,29] that investigate individual fairness on GNNs from a ranking perspective. The main difference to these tasks is that EA involves two, instead of one, KGs.

To the best of our knowledge, no previous work addressed indirect forms of bias related to the structural diversity w.r.t. connected components of KGs in EA. Only the impact of node degree in the message passing protocol of GNNs has been investigated so far in node classification [12,30,52], link prediction or recommendation [28,47] tasks. Additionally, Div2vec [28] proposes a random walk-based method for generating diverse node embeddings, with the probability of a node to be selected being inversely proportional to its degree. Finally, some works investigate connectivity-related fairness in social networks [27,59]. Two of our evaluation measures ($wccR$ and $\overline{deg}$) are adaptations of the measures proposed in [27,59], while other measures like k-core and k-brace decomposition are not relevant to our sampling method that was not designed to affect them. Our work essentially covers the lack of publicly available benchmark data for assessing fairness of EA tasks, as pointed out by recent surveys [15,18].

Graph Sampling Algorithms. In order to reduce the size of the initial graphs while preserving their structural properties, different sampling methods have been proposed that fall under three categories [34]: random node, edge selection, and sampling by exploration.

Random Node selection by uniform sampling does not retain the power-law node degree distribution, while non-uniform sampling (Random PageRank and Random Degree Node), produces very dense KG samples, with too many high-degree nodes. Random Edge sampling aims to retain as much as possible the degree distribution, but by keeping only a subset of edges, we end up with sampled KGs with possibly different neighborhoods compared to the initial graphs (some edges in the input graphs may not exist in the sampled graphs).

On the other hand sampling by exploration, the category to which SUSIE belongs, selects a node uniformly at random and explores the nodes in its vicinity using random walks [34]. This allows us to control the probability with which the output sample will include entities of diverse connected component sizes. Motivated by the aforementioned works, Iterative Degree-based Sampling [51] preserves the degree distribution of the initial graphs, by removing nodes with probability proportional to the nodes PageRank scores. In addition, the sampling of [11] aims to reduce name bias of KGs while preserving the structural properties (e.g., degree distribution) of the input KGs. Unlike graph sampling methods used in embeddings (e.g., Fairwalk, Crosswalk, div2vec), or in node classification and link prediction tasks, our sampling method is the first exploration-based sampling that allows to control (directly) the number and (indirectly) the size of connected components of the two input KGs for the task of EA.

6 Conclusions

In this work, we have shown that the structural diversity of EA benchmark data, which has not been evaluated before, is a factor that affects the performance of state-of-the-art EA methods. To do that, we have introduced an exploration-based sampling algorithm (SUSIE) that detects challenging subgraphs of a given EA benchmark dataset, with respect to structural diversity. We have further shown that methods like RDGCN, that do not rely exclusively on relational data, but also consider other sources of alignment information (e.g., entity names) are more robust to such diversity, than other EA methods like RREA, relying exclusively on the graph structure of the input KGs.

Assessing diversity in EA is only the first step in our ongoing work for a method that exploits spectral GNNs for structural matching, as well as attributes and entity names. Thus, we plan to extend our sampling method to consider not only structural diversity, but also diversity in factual information (i.e., literal values), as well as to examine additional diversity measures and to determine the number and size distribution of the sampled connected components.

Acknowledgement. The work of N. Fanourakis and V. Efthymiou was funded from the Hellenic Foundation for Research and Innovation (HFRI) and the General Secretariat for Research and Technology (GSRT), under GA No 969.

References

1. Airlines dataset. https://archive.org/download/kasabi. Accessed 02 Mar 2023
2. Locah dataset. http://data.archiveshub.ac.uk/. Accessed 02 Mar 2023
3. Mem-e dataset from oaei 2022. http://oaei.ontologymatching.org/2022/knowledgegraph/index.html. Accessed 02 Mar 2023
4. Memory-alpha dataset. http://memory-alpha.wikia.com/. Accessed 02 Mar 2023
5. Restaurants dataset from oaei 2010. http://oaei.ontologymatching.org/2010/im/. Accessed 02 Mar 2023
6. Star trek expanded universe dataset. http://stexpanded.wikia.com/. Accessed 02 Mar 2023
7. Biemer, P.P., et al.: Total Survey Error in Practice. Wiley, Hoboken (2017)

8. Bose, A.J., Hamilton, W.L.: Compositional fairness constraints for graph embeddings. In: ICML, vol. 97, pp. 715–724 (2019)
9. Bourli, S., Pitoura, E.: Bias in knowledge graph embeddings. In: ASONAM, pp. 6–10 (2020)
10. Buyl, M., Bie, T.D.: DeBayes: a Bayesian method for debiasing network embeddings. CoRR abs/2002.11442 (2020)
11. Chaurasiya, D., et al.: Entity alignment for knowledge graphs: progress, challenges, and empirical studies. CoRR abs/2205.08777 (2022)
12. Chen, M., Wei, Z., Huang, Z., Ding, B., Li, Y.: Simple and deep graph convolutional networks. CoRR abs/2007.02133 (2020)
13. Chen, M., Tian, Y., Chang, K., Skiena, S., Zaniolo, C.: Co-training embeddings of knowledge graphs and entity descriptions for cross-lingual entity alignment. In: IJCAI, pp. 3998–4004 (2018)
14. Cheng, W., Wang, C., Xiao, B., Qian, W., Zhou, A.: On statistical characteristics of real-life knowledge graphs. In: Zhan, J., Han, R., Zicari, R.V. (eds.) BPOE 2015. LNCS, vol. 9495, pp. 37–49. Springer, Cham (2016). https://doi.org/10.1007/978-3-319-29006-5_4
15. Choudhary, M., Laclau, C., Largeron, C.: A survey on fairness for machine learning on graphs. CoRR abs/2205.05396 (2022)
16. Christophides, V., Efthymiou, V., Stefanidis, K.: Entity Resolution in the Web of Data. Morgan & Claypool Publishers (2015)
17. Dong, Y., Kang, J., Tong, H., Li, J.: Individual fairness for graph neural networks: a ranking based approach. In: KDD, pp. 300–310 (2021)
18. Dong, Y., Ma, J., Chen, C., Li, J.: Fairness in graph mining: a survey. CoRR abs/2204.09888 (2022)
19. Dwork, C., Hardt, M., Pitassi, T., Reingold, O., Zemel, R.S.: Fairness through awareness. In: Innovations in Theoretical Computer Science, pp. 214–226 (2012)
20. Efthymiou, V., Stefanidis, K., Christophides, V.: Big data entity resolution: from highly to somehow similar entity descriptions in the web. In: IEEE BigData, pp. 401–410 (2015)
21. Efthymiou, V., Stefanidis, K., Pitoura, E., Christophides, V.: FairER: entity resolution with fairness constraints. In: CIKM, pp. 3004–3008 (2021)
22. Fanourakis, N., Efthymiou, V., Kotzinos, D., Christophides, V.: Knowledge graph embedding methods for entity alignment: an experimental review. CoRR abs/2203.09280 (2022)
23. Fisher, J.: Measuring social bias in knowledge graph embeddings. CoRR abs/1912.02761 (2019)
24. Fisher, J., Mittal, A., Palfrey, D., Christodoulopoulos, C.: Debiasing knowledge graph embeddings. In: EMNLP, pp. 7332–7345 (2020)
25. Guo, Q., et al.: A survey on knowledge graph-based recommender systems. IEEE Trans. Knowl. Data Eng. **34**(8), 3549–3568 (2022)
26. Huang, X., Cheng, H., Li, R., Qin, L., Yu, J.X.: Top-K structural diversity search in large networks. VLDB J. **34**, 319–343 (2015). https://doi.org/10.1007/s00778-015-0379-0
27. Huang, X.L., Tiwari, M., Shah, S.: Structural diversity in social recommender systems. In: RecSys (2013)
28. Jeong, J., Yun, J., Keam, H., Park, Y., Park, Z., Cho, J.: div2vec: diversity-emphasized node embedding. In: RecSys (2020)
29. Kang, J., He, J., Maciejewski, R., Tong, H.: InFoRM: individual fairness on graph mining. In: KDD, pp. 379–389 (2020)

30. Kang, J., Zhu, Y., Xia, Y., Luo, J., Tong, H.: RawlsGCN: towards Rawlsian difference principle on graph convolutional network. CoRR abs/2202.13547 (2022)
31. Karakasidis, A., Pitoura, E.: Identifying bias in name matching tasks. In: EDBT, pp. 626–629 (2019)
32. Keidar, D., Zhong, M., Zhang, C., Shrestha, Y.R., Paudel, B.: Towards automatic bias detection in knowledge graphs. In: EMNLP, pp. 3804–3811 (2021)
33. Khajehnejad, A., Khajehnejad, M., Babaei, M., Gummadi, K.P., Weller, A., Mirzasoleiman, B.: CrossWalk: fairness-enhanced node representation learning. In: AAAI, pp. 11963–11970 (2022)
34. Leskovec, J., Faloutsos, C.: Sampling from large graphs. In: SIGKDD, pp. 631–636 (2006)
35. Li, J., Song, D.: Uncertainty-aware pseudo label refinery for entity alignment. In: WWW, pp. 820–837 (2022)
36. Li, P., Wang, Y., Zhao, H., Hong, P., Liu, H.: On dyadic fairness: exploring and mitigating bias in graph connections. In: ICLR (2021)
37. Luo, Y., Yang, B., Xu, D., Tian, L.: A survey: complex knowledge base question answering. In: ICICSE, pp. 46–52 (2022)
38. Mao, X., Wang, W., Xu, H., Wu, Y., Lan, M.: Relational reflection entity alignment. In: CIKM, pp. 1095–1104 (2020)
39. Martínez-Plumed, F., Ferri, C., Nieves, D., Hernández-Orallo, J.: Missing the missing values: the ugly duckling of fairness in machine learning. Int. J. Intell. Syst. 36(7), 3217–3258 (2021)
40. Masrour, F., Wilson, T., Yan, H., Tan, P., Esfahanian, A.: Bursting the filter bubble: fairness-aware network link prediction. In: AAAI, pp. 841–848 (2020)
41. Molokwu, B.C., Shuvo, S.B., Kar, N.C., Kobti, Z.: Node classification in complex social graphs via knowledge-graph embeddings and convolutional neural network. In: Krzhizhanovskaya, V.V., et al. (eds.) ICCS 2020. LNCS, vol. 12142, pp. 183–198. Springer, Cham (2020). https://doi.org/10.1007/978-3-030-50433-5_15
42. Nathani, D., Chauhan, J., Sharma, C., Kaul, M.: Learning attention-based embeddings for relation prediction in knowledge graphs. In: ACL, pp. 4710–4723 (2019)
43. Obraczka, D., Schuchart, J., Rahm, E.: EAGER: embedding-assisted entity resolution for knowledge graphs. CoRR abs/2101.06126 (2021)
44. Quy, T.L., Roy, A., Iosifidis, V., Zhang, W., Ntoutsi, E.: A survey on datasets for fairness-aware machine learning. WIREs Data Min. Knowl. Discov. 12(3), e1452 (2022)
45. Rahman, T.A., Surma, B., Backes, M., Zhang, Y.: Fairwalk: towards fair graph embedding. In: IJCAI, pp. 3289–3295 (2019)
46. Rossi, A., Barbosa, D., Firmani, D., Matinata, A., Merialdo, P.: Knowledge graph embedding for link prediction: a comparative analysis. ACM Trans. Knowl. Discov. Data 15(2), 14:1–14:49 (2021)
47. Sanz-Cruzado, J., Pepa, S.M., Castells, P.: Structural novelty and diversity in link prediction. In: WWW, pp. 1347–1351 (2018)
48. Saxena, A., Fletcher, G., Pechenizkiy, M.: HM-EIICT: fairness-aware link prediction in complex networks using community information. J. Comb. Optim. 44(4), 2853–2870 (2021)
49. Sinha, A., Cazabet, R., Vaudaine, R.: Systematic biases in link prediction: comparing heuristic and graph embedding based methods. In: Aiello, L.M., Cherifi, C., Cherifi, H., Lambiotte, R., Lió, P., Rocha, L.M. (eds.) COMPLEX NETWORKS 2018. SCI, vol. 812, pp. 81–93. Springer, Cham (2019). https://doi.org/10.1007/978-3-030-05411-3_7

50. Suchanek, F.M., Abiteboul, S., Senellart, P.: PARIS: probabilistic alignment of relations, instances, and schema. PVLDB **5**(3), 157–168 (2011)
51. Sun, Z., et al.: A benchmarking study of embedding-based entity alignment for knowledge graphs. Proc. VLDB Endow. **13**(11), 2326–2340 (2020)
52. Tang, X., et al.: Investigating and mitigating degree-related biases in graph convolutional networks. In: CIKM, pp. 1435–1444 (2020)
53. Trisedya, B.D., Qi, J., Zhang, R.: Entity alignment between knowledge graphs using attribute embeddings. In: AAAI, pp. 297–304 (2019)
54. Ugander, J., Backstrom, L., Marlow, C., Kleinberg, J.M.: Structural diversity in social contagion. Proc. Natl. Acad. Sci. U.S.A. **109**(16), 5962–5966 (2012)
55. Wang, S.: On the analysis of large integrated knowledge graphs for economics, banking and finance. In: EDBT/ICDT Workshops, vol. 3135 (2022)
56. Wu, Y., Liu, X., Feng, Y., Wang, Z., Yan, R., Zhao, D.: Relation-aware entity alignment for heterogeneous knowledge graphs. In: IJCAI, pp. 5278–5284 (2019)
57. Zhang, Q., Sun, Z., Hu, W., Chen, M., Guo, L., Qu, Y.: Multi-view knowledge graph embedding for entity alignment. In: IJCAI 2019 (2019)
58. Zhang, R., Trisedya, B.D., Li, M., Jiang, Y., Qi, J.: A benchmark and comprehensive survey on knowledge graph entity alignment via representation learning. VLDB J. **31**(5), 1143–1168 (2022). https://doi.org/10.1007/s00778-022-00747-z
59. Zhang, Y., Wang, L., Zhu, J.J.H., Wang, X., Pentland, A.S.: The strength of structural diversity in online social networks. CoRR abs/1906.00756 (2019)

A Framework to Include and Exploit Probabilistic Information in SHACL Validation Reports

Rémi Felin$^{(\boxtimes)}$ [ID], Catherine Faron [ID], and Andrea G. B. Tettamanzi [ID]

Université Côte d'Azur, Inria, I3S, Sophia-Antipolis, France
{remi.felin,catherine.faron}@inria.fr,
andrea.tettamanzi@univ-cotedazur.fr

Abstract. The Shapes Constraint Language (SHACL) is a W3C recommendation which allows to represent constraints in RDF– shape graphs –, and validate RDF data graphs against these constraints. A SHACL validator produces a validation report whose result is false for a shape graph as soon as there is at least one node in the RDF data graph that does not conform to the shape. This Boolean result of the validation of an RDF data graph against an RDF shape graph is not suitable for discovering new high-potential shapes from the RDF data. In this paper, we propose a probabilistic framework to accept shapes with a realistic proportion of nodes in an RDF data graph that does not conform to it. Based on this framework, we propose an extension of the SHACL validation report to express a set of metrics including the generality and likelihood of shapes and we define a method to test a shape as a hypothesis test. Finally, we present the results of experiments conducted to validate a test RDF data graph against a set of shapes.

Keywords: RDF · SHACL · Shape Testing · Data Validation · Probabilistic Assessment

1 Introduction

The notable growth of the semantic Web has led to the emergence of new research areas such as the quality of RDF data. SHACL is the language recommended by the W3C to express patterns that RDF data must respect in order to ensure the dataset consistency.

We observe that violations generated during a SHACL validation of a shape are a significant factor. As soon as we observe at least one violation the shape is inconsistent with the RDF data. Considering a large collaborative RDF dataset with a massive and constant increase of RDF triples (e.g., DBPedia), we assume that a large number of RDF data violations against a set of shapes seems inevitable due to incomplete and/or incorrect data. In practice, a more in-depth investigation of the data seems necessary. An expert could develop a strategy for updating the data or the shapes depending on the rate or the nature of the violations. This problem has a direct impact on SHACL shape mining and limits domain knowledge learning. We tackle the following research question:

C. Pesquita et al. (Eds.): ESWC 2023, LNCS 13870, pp. 91–104, 2023.
https://doi.org/10.1007/978-3-031-33455-9_6

How to design a validation process considering physiological errors in real-life data?

Our contribution addresses the problem by suggesting a framework based on a probabilistic model to consider a rate of violations p assumed to be contained in an RDF dataset. p represents the proportion of errors that RDF data contains. We define a *measure of likelihood* to observe a given number of violations. We assess a given RDF dataset against a set of shapes to verify the consistency of the dataset considering a theoretical error rate.

This paper is organized as follows: In Sect. 2, we summarise the related work and the positioning of our work. In Sect. 3 we present our probabilistic model (3.1), our extension of the SHACL validation report model (3.2), and our proposal of an extended shape validation process as a test of hypothesis (3.3). We present the results of our experiments in Sect. 4. We conclude and discuss further research in Sect. 5.

2   Related Work

Given that SHACL is a fairly new recommendation, dating from 2017 [13], its interactions with other standards are subject to ongoing research. In particular, we find work on the interactions with inference rules [20], with OWL [2], description logic reasoning [15] and Ontology Design Pattern [18]. Moreover, extensions regarding SHACL validation are emerging, e.g., a SHACL validation engine based on the study of the connectivity of a given RDF graph and the collection of data in this same graph [11]. The expressiveness and semantics of SHACL is a rich subject in the literature [1,15]: it highlights a semantics based on $\mathcal{SROIQ}$, one of the most expressive description logics.

The validation of RDF data with SHACL is a timely research question largely addressed in the literature [3,7,9,12,14,19]. All these works consider a standard use of SHACL: an RDF dataset is valid against a shape if it verifies the expressed constraints. Our approach extends the standardized SHACL validation process to overcome its binary character by considering a possible acceptable violation rate.

SHACL constraint generation [10,22,23] can be carried out in several ways, some using data-based and statistical approaches, others based on ontologies [5]. The different approaches lead to different ways of tackling the validation of these shapes: The statistical-based approach requires expert analysis to define the consistency of a shape, while the ontology-based approach relies on the described RDF Schema properties (`rdfs:range`; `rdfs:domain`; ...) to provide a set of shapes based on this ontology, which can be validated if the quality of the ontology is assured. Knowledge graph profiling [21] is an important issue in order to induce constraints from large KGs [17]. The work presented in this article is focused on RDF data validation against shapes and is in line with the logic of providing expertise on the consistency of RDF data by considering the inescapable errors that they may contain, against a set of shapes that may be generated automatically or provided by an expert.

3   A Probabilistic Framework for Shape Assessment

3.1   Probabilistic Model

In a real-life context, RDF datasets are imperfect, incomplete (in the sense that expected data is missing) and containing errors of various natures. The quality control of RDF data and efficient data integration guaranteeing RDF data consistency are use cases that can be tackled using SHACL. In another respect, SHACL shapes mining from RDF data is a promising approach to learn domain knowledge (domain constraints). Candidate SHACL shapes are those triggering a few violations in the data, but this is directly correlated with the quality (error rate, which, however, is unknown) of the RDF dataset considered.

We propose to extend the evaluation of RDF data against SHACL shapes by considering a physiological theoretical error proportion p in real-life RDF data. In this context, mathematical modeling of the SHACL evaluation process, combined with an error proportion p, is based on a probabilistic model.

Definition 1. *The cardinality (or support) of a shape s, v_s, is the set of RDF triples targeted by s and tested during the validation. We define its cardinality as the **reference cardinality**: $\|v_s\|$.*

The Confirmations and Violations of a shape s, respectively v_s^+ and v_s^-, $v_s^+ \cap v_s^- = \emptyset$, are the disjoint sets that correspond, respectively, to the triples that are consistent with s and those that violate s.

Remark 1. The sum of the number of confirmations and the number of violations of a shape s equals to the total number of triples targeted by s:

$$v_s = v_s^+ \cup v_s^- \tag{1}$$

The Modelling is based on the assessment process where we define a random variable X which conceptualises a set of observations from the validation of a shape s, i.e., a set of triples v_s; each triple $t \in v_s$ can be either a *confirmation*, $t \in v_s^+$, or a *violation*, $t \in v_s^-$.

Let us assume a single selection among v_s for which we have two possible values: **1** if $v_1 \in v_s^-$, **0** otherwise. We conclude that a binomial distribution models this probabilistic approach, with $X \sim B(n, p)$ where $n = \|v_s\|$ and p corresponds to the unavoidable theoretical error proportion, i.e. $X \sim B(\|v_S\|, p)$.

Definition 2. *Considering X as a random variable with the following binomial distribution $X \sim B(n, p)$ and $\Omega = \{0, 1, \ldots, n\}$, the probability to obtain exactly k success among n attempts is:*

$$\forall k \in \Omega, P(X = k) = \binom{n}{k} \cdot p^k \cdot (1 - p)^{n-k} \tag{2}$$

The **likelihood measure** L_k determines the plausibility of obtaining k violations, i.e. $k = ||v_S^-||$, under the hypothesis of following a binomial distribution. The calculation is based on Formula 2 (see Definition 3).

Definition 3. *The **likelihood** to observe a number of violations $||v_S^-||$ among the nodes concerned by a shape S, i.e. $||v_S||$, considering $X \sim B(||v_S||, p)$ is*

$$L_{||v_S^-||} = P(X = ||v_S^-||) = \binom{||v_S||}{||v_S^-||} \cdot p^{||v_S^-||} \cdot (1-p)^{||v_S^+||}. \tag{3}$$

3.2 Extension of the SHACL Validation Report Model

We propose an enriched model of the SHACL validation report to express additional information for each shape considered in the report. We defined an extension to the SHACL Validation Report Vocabulary denoted by prefix psh.[1] For each source shape considered in the validation of an RDF graph we generate additional triples: property psh:summary links the validation report to a blank node of type psh:ValidationSummary which is the subject of several properties whose values are the result of the computation of various metrics relative to the source shape.

The **focus shape** is the value of property psh:focusShape. It is the source shape of the validation result further described in the validation summary.

The **reference cardinality of a shape** s $||v_s||$ is the value of property psh:referenceCardinality (see Definition 1).

The **numbers of confirmations and violations** of a shape s, respectively $||v_s^+||$ and $||v_s^-||$, are the values of properties psh:numConfirmation and psh:numViolation.

The **generality** $G(s) \in [0, 1]$ of a shape s measures the *representativeness* of s considering the whole RDF graph v:

$$G(s) = \frac{||v_s||}{||v||}. \tag{4}$$

It is the value of property psh:generality.

The **likelihood** of a shape s in an RDF graph v as defined in Sect. 3.1 is the value of property psh:likelihood.

Figure 1 presents an excerpt of an example validation report where:

- the SHACL shape s_1 is described by URI :s1;
- the cardinality of the RDF graph being validated is $||v|| = 1000$;
- the parameter of the binomial distribution is $p = 0.1$.

---

[1] prefix psh: <http://ns.inria.fr/probabilistic-shacl/>.

```
[ a sh:ValidationReport ;
    sh:conforms boolean ;
    sh:result r ;
    # Probabilistic SHACL extension
    psh:summary [
        a psh:ValidationSummary ;
        psh:referenceCardinality ||v_S|| ;
        psh:numConfirmation ||v_S^+|| ;
        psh:numViolation ||v_S^-|| ;
        psh:generality G(S) ;
        psh:likelihood L_{||v_S^-||} ;
        psh:focusShape S
    ] ;
] .
```

Fig. 1. Structure of the extended SHACL validation report.

3.3   Data Graph Validation Against a Shape as a Hypothesis Test

The decision-making process for a given shape S is based on the probabilistic model proposed in Sect. 3.1, which is based on the hypothesis that a given observation follows a binomial distribution, such that $X \sim B(||v_S||, p)$. However, the question concerning the consistency of the model is relevant as it can lead to incorrect conclusions. We propose an approach based on hypothesis testing which highlights the consistency of our hypothesis and a methodology to validate our shapes.

The acceptance of a SHACL Shape s considers the proportion of violations for s, i.e. $\hat{p} = \frac{||v_s^-||}{||v_s||}$. We suggest accepting the shape s as consistent with the RDF data if the observed proportion is smaller than the theoretical violation proportion:

$$\hat{p} \leq p \implies KG \models s. \tag{5}$$

In the case where the observed proportion is greater than the theoretical proportion, we minimize the distance of this probability from the maximum values of the mass function of the binomial distribution $B(||v_s||, p)$ by using hypothesis testing. Figure 3 shows the proportion of the number of violations that we accept compared to the number that we reject with our method.

The Null and Alternate Hypothesis are (respectively) H_0: *data follow the given distribution*, i.e. the frequency of observed violations $\hat{p} = \frac{||v_S^-||}{||v_S||}$ is in line with the expected proportions of violations p and $X \sim B(||v_S||, p)$. Finally, H_1 indicates that *data do not follow the given distribution*.

```
@prefix sh: <http://www.w3.org/ns/shacl#> .
@prefix psh: <http://ns.inria.fr/probabilistic-shacl/> .
@prefix : <http://www.example.com/myDataGraph#> .


# SHACL Standard
:v1 a sh:ValidationResult ;
    sh:focusNode :n1 ;
    [...]
    sh:sourceShape :s1 .

:v2 a sh:ValidationResult ;
    sh:focusNode :n2 ;
    [...]
    sh:sourceShape :s1 .

[...]

[ a sh:ValidationReport ;
    sh:conforms false ;
    sh:result :v1 ;
    sh:result :v2 ;
    [...]
    # SHACL Extension
    # shape s1
    psh:summary [
        a psh:ValidationSummary ;
        psh:generality "0.2"^^xsd:decimal ;
        psh:numConfirmation 178 ;
        psh:numViolation 22 ;
        psh:likelihood "0.0806"^^xsd:decimal ;
        psh:referenceCardinality 200 ;
        psh:focusShape :s1
    ] ;
] .
```

Fig. 2. Example of an extended SHACL validation report for a shape :s1 with $||v|| = 1000$ and $p = 0.1$.

The testing for goodness of Fit verifies the alignment of our observations with a theoretical distribution: we define X_s^2 the **test statistic** for a shape s which follows $\chi_{k-1,\alpha}^2$ assuming H_0, i.e. $X_s^2 \sim \chi_{k-1,\alpha}^2$ (a chi-square distribution with $k-1$ degrees of freedom and a level of significance $1 - \alpha$) if X_s^2 verifies Definition 4. This test is performed at the α level defined at 5%. It considers k the total number of groups, i.e. $k = 2$, n_i the observed number of individuals and T_i the theoretical number of individuals. The test statistic X_s^2 is defined by

$$X_s^2 = \sum_{i=1}^{k} \frac{(n_i - T_i)^2}{T_i} \sim \chi_{k-1;\alpha}^2. \tag{6}$$

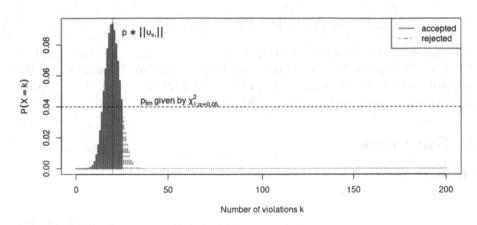

Fig. 3. Acceptance zone of shape s_1, considering $X \sim B(||v_{s_1}||, p)$ where $||v_{s_1}|| = 200$ and $p = 0.1$.

Remark 2. A shape s for which we observe very small support $||v_s||$ (let us say $||v_s|| = 5$) implies a proportion of violations and/or confirmations that are less than 5. Thus, the hypothesis test cannot be applied because the sample is not sufficiently representative of a Chi-square distribution (see Definition 4).

Definition 4. *The testing for goodness of fit is applicable (Formula 6) if* $\forall i \in [1, k], T_i \geq 5$.

The critical region i.e. the rejection region of H_0, is defined by the value $\chi^2_{k-1;\alpha}$. Considering $\alpha = 0.05$ and $k = 2$, we define the critical value: $\chi^2_{k-1;\alpha} = \chi^2_{1;\alpha=0.05} = 3.84$.

Remark 3. An alternative formula considers the acceptance interval I_a of a χ^2 distribution, i.e. $I_a = [0, \chi^2_{k-1;\alpha}]$ which accept H_0 if $X^2_s \in I_a$.

The acceptance of the null hypothesis, i.e., $X \sim B(||v_s||, p)$, implies that the value of our test statistic X^2_s is not included in the rejection zone of the $\chi^2_{k=1}$ distribution, such that

$$X^2_s \leq \chi^2_{k-1;\alpha}. \tag{7}$$

The acceptance of H_0 implies the acceptance of the considered shape s, i.e.,

$$X^2_s \leq \chi^2_{k-1;\alpha} \implies KG \models s. \tag{8}$$

Let us consider the case shown in Fig. 2 as an example of an application. We observe a proportion of violations that is slightly higher than expected, i.e., $\hat{p} = \frac{||v^-_{s_1}||}{||v_{s_1}||} = 0.11$ and $\hat{p} > p$: an analysis through the hypothesis test determines if this observation is inconsistent with the null hypothesis, and in which case we would reject H_0 and the shape :s1. We assume $\alpha = 5\%$ to assess $X^2_{s_1}$:

$$X_{s_1}^2 = \frac{(22-20)^2}{20} + \frac{(178-180)^2}{180} = \frac{4}{20} + \frac{4}{180} \approx 0.222.$$

The statistical test demonstrated that $X_{s_1}^2 \leq \chi_{1;\alpha=0.05}^2$ (i.e. 3.84) and so $X_{s_1}^2 \in I_\alpha$. We accept H_0 and validate the adequacy of this hypothesis, i.e. the assumption that our observations from the validation of :s1 follow a binomial distribution $X \sim B(200, 0.1)$, with a level of significance of $1 - \alpha$, i.e., 95%.

4   Experiments

These contributions lead to an extension of the validation report to cover the generation of a degree of probability expressed under the hypothesis that the samples follow a binomial distribution with a cardinality defined by the SHACL shapes (i.e. $||v_s||$) and a probability p defined *empirically* corresponding to the assumed proportion of violations that we accept from some RDF data. At the same time, we investigate whether such an approach can capture the knowledge domain in a larger way, i.e., a broader spectrum of accepted shapes for which they are considered consistent despite the observed violations. Considering a shape graph representative of an RDF dataset, the conclusion of an error rate p for which it is reasonable to consider the acceptance of shapes on a subset of the global dataset seems a relevant perspective for the evaluation of this work. This implies a detailed analysis of the characteristics of the considered subset, the proportions of accepted or rejected shapes and the impact of hypothesis testing on acceptance.

4.1   Experimental Setup

Our experiments use the *CovidOnTheWeb dataset*[2] [16] against **a set of 377 shapes** from a translation of the experimental results of Cadorel & al. [4] which are considered as **representative shapes** of the whole CovidOnTheWeb dataset. We run the probabilistic SHACL validation engine (see Sect. 3.2) implemented in the *Corese* semantic web factory. We will conduct an analysis of the theoretical error rate in order to find an optimal rate: we assume the values of p empirically such that $p \in \{0.05, 0.1, 0.15, \ldots, 0.95, 1\}$, which gives 20 values for p to be tested. The experiments were performed on a Dell Precision 3561 equipped with an Intel(R) 11th Gen Core i7-11850H processor, with 32 GB of RAM running under the Fedora Linux 35 operating system. The source code is available in a public repository.[3]

CovidOnTheWeb is an RDF knowledge graphs produced from *COVID-19 Open Research Dataset (CORD-19)*. It targets **articles**, described by URIs and **named entities** identified in these articles, disambiguated by *Entity-Fishing* and linked to *Wikidata* entities. Figure 4 shows an excerpt of RDF description

---

[2] https://github.com/Wimmics/CovidOnTheWeb.
[3] https://github.com/RemiFELIN/RDFMining/tree/eswc_2023.

in CovidOnTheWeb in *turtle* format and Table 1 shows the characteristics of the RDF dataset. We consider a subset containing approximately 18.79% of the articles and 0.01% of the named entities.

Table 1. Summary of the *CovidOnTheWeb* RDF subgraph considered for the experiment.

#RDF triples	226,647
#distinct articles	20,912
#distinct named entities	6,331
avg. #named entities per article	10.52

```
@prefix rdf:  <http://www.w3.org/1999/02/22-rdf-syntax-ns#>
        .
@prefix rdfs: <http://www.w3.org/2000/01/rdf-schema#> .
@prefix covid:    <http://ns.inria.fr/covid19/> .
@prefix entity:   <http://www.wikidata.org/entity/> .

covid:ec1[...]2c5   rdf:type    entity:Q4407  .
covid:fff[...]86d   rdf:type    entity:Q10876 .
[...]
entity:Q4407        rdfs:label  "methyl"@en .
entity:Q10876       rdfs:label  "bacteria"@en .
```

Fig. 4. Example of RDF data extracted from *CovidOnTheWeb*.

The candidate shapes describe association rules obtained by Cadorel & al. [4] from a subset of the *CovidOnTheWeb dataset*. These rules are not necessarily perfect, so we are interested in using them in our probabilistic approach. From the experimental results of Cadorel & al., we extracted the named entities corresponding to the antecedents and the consequents of these association rules. We have carried out a treatment allowing the conversion of these rules into SHACL shapes. We target articles belonging to a named entity, representing the *antecedent*, with the property `sh:targetClass`. Among the articles considered, we are interested in determining the affiliation to another named entity, representing the *consequent*: we use a constraint applied on the articles' type and target a named entity with the property `sh:hasValue`. In this context, a violation will invoke a violation of type `sh:HasValueConstraintComponent` for the current shape. An example of a shape formed after treatment is shown in Fig. 5.

```
@prefix : <http://www.example.com/myDataGraph#> .
@prefix sh: <http://www.w3.org/ns/shacl#> .
@prefix entity: <http://www.wikidata.org/entity/> .

:1 a sh:NodeShape ;
    sh:targetClass  entity:Q10295810 ;
    sh:property [
        sh:path rdf:type ;
        sh:hasValue entity:Q43656 ;
    ] .
```

Fig. 5. Example SHACL shape representing an association rule with `entity:Q10295810` (`"hypocholesterolemia"@en`) as an *antecedent* and `entity:Q43656` (`"cholesterol"@en`) as a *consequent*.

4.2 Results

Table 2 shows the first experimental results, notably the generality score which is relatively low, indicating a low average cardinality compared to the number of total triples in our dataset: approximately 106 RDF triples on average are targeted by our shapes (0.047% of the RDF triples). The rate of violations is relatively high but is nuanced by the rate of confirmations (33.19%). It highlights the interest in a probabilistic approach in order to check the consistency of our RDF dataset against the shape graph considering varying p error rates and understand how we can consider a reasonable error rate and a consistent number of valid shapes.

Table 2. Summary of the SHACL shape graph considered in the experiment.

#named entities represented	337 (*5.32%*)
avg. reference cardinality	106.69 (*0.0470%*)
avg. #confirmations	33.19 (*31.11%*)
avg. #violations	73.50 (*70.89%*)
avg. generality $G(S)$ (**Formula** 4)	0.0005%

Figure 6a shows an increasing evolution of the likelihood measure up to the value $p = 0.5$ and then a decrease. It appears that the most reasonable error rate is **50%**, as it maximises the mean likelihood value (0.0362%).

Figure 7 presents the set of decisions made on shapes (acceptance, rejection) as a function of the theoretical error proportion p and clearly shows the importance of hypothesis testing. The number of tests performed increases until $p = 0.3$ and then decreases. Similarly, hypothesis testing tends to reject shapes for "small" values of p and the trend reverses as p increases: the number of

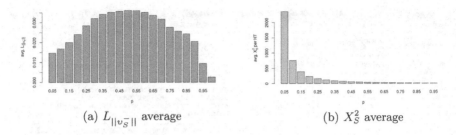

(a) $L_{\|v_S^-\|}$ average

(b) X_S^2 average

Fig. 6. Average value of (a) likelihood measures and (b) statistic test as functions of the theoretical error proportion p.

accepted shapes increases and the value of the test statistic decreases (see Fig. 6b). Further analysis of the results obtained with $p = 0.5$ shows that 63 shapes among the 187 accepted shapes are accepted after performing a hypothesis test, i.e. 33.7% of the accepted shapes. These same tests accepted 25.7% of the shapes that were tested, which shows its ability to efficiently filter with a risk of $\alpha = 0.05$ or 5% of being incorrect.

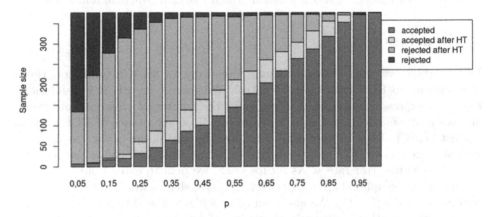

Fig. 7. Shapes acceptance as a function of the theoretical error proportion p (HT= Hypothesis Testing).

The production of the results in HTML format was performed with a STTL transformation [6]. STTL is an extension to the SPARQL query language to transform RDF in any template-specified text result format, which is populated with the results of a SPARQL query. In our case, we provided an HTML template including the desired values in its structure. An excerpt of 20 out of 377 results obtained for a theoretical error proportion of $p = 0.5$ is presented in Fig. 8.

We compared the computation time of our proposed probabilistic validation framework with that of standard validation. For our base of 377 shapes and our

antecedent	consequent	referenceCardinality	#violation	likelihood	generality	X²ₛ	Acceptance
two-hybrid screening	protein-protein interaction	48	19	0.041004809004459284	0.000211783081179910231		true
nidovirales	proteolysis	80	69	8.6669313322632E-12	0.00035297180196517053	42.05	false
intensive care medicine	acute respiratory distress syndrome	166	139	9.193409214822706E-20	0.0007324164890777288	75.56626506024097	false
astrocyte	central nervous system	70	34	0.09238587705330051	0.0003088503267195242		true
dopamine	serotonin	10	6	0.205078125	0.00004412147524564632	0.4	true
crystallography	crystal structure	20	7	0.0739288330078125	0.0000888242950491129263		true
human parainfluenza	adenoviridae	237	133	0.00800821375320367	0.0010456789633218177	3.548523206751055	true
carbohydrate	lectin	114	75	2.4200572197826046E-12	0.00050298481780 0368	11.368421052631579	false
mycoplasma bovis	bovine coronavirus	12	6	0.2255859375	0.0000529457029477558		true
crystallization	diffraction	31	21	0.020653086248785257	0.00013677657326150358	3.903225806451613	false
membrane raft	methyl	32	19	0.08087921887636185	0.0001411887207860682	1.125	true
ifitm1	ifitm3	27	9	0.0349195674061752	0.00011912798316324504		true
multiple sclerosis	myelin	139	97	1.0209205741082355E-6	0.0006132885059144837	21.762589928057555	false
wheeze	asthma	85	44	0.08188889187584301	0.00037503253958799367	0.10588235294117647	true
influenza a virus subtype h5n1	avian influenza	277	165	2.969648471686876E-4	0.001222216486430 4403	10.140794223826715	false
hepatocellular carcinoma	liver cirrhosis	72	46	0.005843155895129734	0.00031767462176865343	5.555555555555555	false
diffraction	x-ray crystallography	16	7	0.174560546875	0.0000705943603930341		true
feline infectious peritonitis	feline coronavirus	130	46	2.605193913325792E-4	0.000573579178193402		true
aedes aegypti	culicidae	21	4	0.002853870391845703	0.00000926550980158 5726		true
monomer	oligomer	83	70	5.4692741602999564E-11	0.0003662082445388644	39.144578313253014	false

Fig. 8. SHACL validation report in HTML format for $p = 0.5$.

extract of *CovidOnTheWeb* (226,647 triples), we observed an overall computation time of **1 min 35 s** for the probabilistic validation framework against **1 min 29 s** for standard validation: the probabilistic framework takes **6,31%** more time than standard validation and it is linear which makes it practical and scalable.

5 Conclusion

In this article, we propose a probabilistic framework for SHACL validation, thus contributing to RDF data quality control. We extend the SHACL validation report to express the likelihood measure for the number of violations observed and we propose a decision model for a probabilistic acceptance of RDF triples against SHACL shapes. Our experiments show the capabilities of our approach to validate a real-world RDF dataset against a set of SHACL shapes while accepting a reasonable error rate p. As future work, we plan to extend our proposed framework to complex shapes, especially recursive shapes which are the focus of ongoing research [3,8,19]. We also plan to investigate the automatic extraction or generation of SHACL shapes from reference RDF datasets, to capture domain knowledge as constraints.

Acknowledgements. This work has been partially founded by the 3IA Côte d'Azur "Investments in the Future" project managed by the National Research Agency (ANR) with the reference number ANR-19-P3IA-0002.

References

1. Bogaerts, B., Jakubowski, M., den Bussche, J.V.: Expressiveness of SHACL features. In: ICDT (2022)
2. Bogaerts, B., Jakubowski, M., Van den Bussche, J.: SHACL: a description logic in disguise (2021)

3. Boneva, I., Labra Gayo, J.E., Prud'hommeaux, E.G.: Semantics and validation of shapes schemas for RDF. In: d'Amato, C., Fernandez, M., Tamma, V., Lecue, F., Cudré-Mauroux, P., Sequeda, J., Lange, C., Heflin, J. (eds.) ISWC 2017. LNCS, vol. 10587, pp. 104–120. Springer, Cham (2017). https://doi.org/10.1007/978-3-319-68288-4_7

4. Cadorel, L., Tettamanzi, A.: Mining RDF data of COVID-19 scientific literature for interesting association rules. In: 2020 IEEE/WIC/ACM International Joint Conference on Web Intelligence and Intelligent Agent Technology (WI-IAT), pp. 145–152 (2020)

5. Cimmino, A., Fernández-Izquierdo, A., García-Castro, R.: Astrea: automatic generation of SHACL shapes from ontologies. In: Harth, A., et al. (eds.) ESWC 2020. LNCS, vol. 12123, pp. 497–513. Springer, Cham (2020). https://doi.org/10.1007/978-3-030-49461-2_29

6. Corby, O., Faron Zucker, C.: STTL: a SPARQL-based transformation Language for RDF. In: 11th International Conference on Web Information Systems and Technologies. Lisbon, Portugal (2015)

7. Corman, J., Florenzano, F., Reutter, J.L., Savković, O.: Validating SHACL constraints over a SPARQL endpoint. In: Ghidini, C., et al. (eds.) ISWC 2019. LNCS, vol. 11778, pp. 145–163. Springer, Cham (2019). https://doi.org/10.1007/978-3-030-30793-6_9

8. Corman, J., Reutter, J.L., Savković, O.: Semantics and validation of recursive SHACL. In: Vrandečić, D., et al. (eds.) ISWC 2018. LNCS, vol. 11136, pp. 318–336. Springer, Cham (2018). https://doi.org/10.1007/978-3-030-00671-6_19

9. Debruyne, C., McGlinn, K.: Reusable SHACL constraint components for validating geospatial linked data (short paper). In: GeoLD@ESWC (2021)

10. Fernandez-Álvarez, D., Labra-Gayo, J.E., Gayo-Avello, D.: Automatic extraction of shapes using sheXer. Knowl.-Based Syst. **238**, 107975 (2022). https://doi.org/10.1016/j.knosys.2021.107975, https://www.sciencedirect.com/science/article/pii/S0950705121010972

11. Figuera, M., Rohde, P.D., Vidal, M.E.: Trav-SHACL: efficiently validating networks of SHACL constraints. In: Proceedings of the Web Conference 2021, pp. 3337–3348. WWW 2021, Association for Computing Machinery, New York, NY, USA (2021). https://doi.org/10.1145/3442381.3449877

12. K Soman, R.: Modelling construction scheduling constraints using shapes constraint language (SHACL), pp. 351–358 (2019). https://doi.org/10.35490/EC3.2019.170

13. Kontokostas, D., Knublauch, H.: Shapes constraint language (SHACL). In: W3C Recommendation, W3C (2017). https://www.w3.org/TR/2017/REC-shacl-20170720/

14. Köcher, A., Vieira da Silva, L.M., Fay, A.: Constraint checking of skills using SHACL (2021)

15. Leinberger, M., Seifer, P., Rienstra, T., Lämmel, R., Staab, S.: Deciding SHACL shape containment through description logics reasoning. In: Pan, J.Z., et al. (eds.) ISWC 2020. LNCS, vol. 12506, pp. 366–383. Springer, Cham (2020). https://doi.org/10.1007/978-3-030-62419-4_21

16. Michel, F., et al.: Covid-on-the-web: knowledge graph and services to advance COVID-19 research. In: Pan, J.Z., et al. (eds.) ISWC 2020. LNCS, vol. 12507, pp. 294–310. Springer, Cham (2020). https://doi.org/10.1007/978-3-030-62466-8_19

17. Mihindukulasooriya, N., Rashid, M.R.A., Rizzo, G., García-Castro, R., Corcho, O., Torchiano, M.: RDF shape induction using knowledge base profiling, pp. 1952–

1959. SAC 2018, Association for Computing Machinery, New York, NY, USA (2018). https://doi.org/10.1145/3167132.3167341
18. Pandit, H., O'Sullivan, D., Lewis, D.: Using ontology design patterns to define SHACL shapes. In: WOP@ISWC, pp. 67–71. Monterey California, USA (2018)
19. Pareti, P., Konstantinidis, G.: A review of SHACL: from data validation to schema reasoning for RDF graphs. In: Šimkus, M., Varzinczak, I. (eds.) Reasoning Web. Declarative Artificial Intelligence. Reasoning Web 2021. Lecture Notes in Computer Science, vol. 13100, pp. 115–144. Springer, Cham (2021). https://doi.org/10.1007/978-3-030-95481-9_6
20. Pareti, P., Konstantinidis, G., Norman, T.J., Şensoy, M.: SHACL constraints with inference rules. In: Ghidini, C., et al. (eds.) ISWC 2019. LNCS, vol. 11778, pp. 539–557. Springer, Cham (2019). https://doi.org/10.1007/978-3-030-30793-6_31
21. Alva Principe, R.A., Maurino, A., Palmonari, M., Ciavotta, M., Spahiu, B.: ABSTAT-HD: a scalable tool for profiling very large knowledge graphs. VLDB J., 1–26 (2021). https://doi.org/10.1007/s00778-021-00704-2
22. Rabbani, K., Lissandrini, M., Hose, K.: SHACL and ShEx in the wild: a community survey on validating shapes generation and adoption. In: Companion Proceedings of the Web Conference 2022, pp. 260–263. WWW 2022, Association for Computing Machinery, New York, NY, USA (2022). https://doi.org/10.1145/3487553.3524253
23. Wright, J., Rodríguez Méndez, S.J., Haller, A., Taylor, K., Omran, P.G.: *Schímatos*: a SHACL-based web-form generator for knowledge graph editing. In: Pan, J.Z., et al. (eds.) ISWC 2020. LNCS, vol. 12507, pp. 65–80. Springer, Cham (2020). https://doi.org/10.1007/978-3-030-62466-8_5

Transformer Based Semantic Relation Typing for Knowledge Graph Integration

Sven Hertling$^{(\boxtimes)}$ [ID] and Heiko Paulheim [ID]

Data and Web Science Group, University of Mannheim, Mannheim, Germany
{sven,heiko}@informatik.uni-mannheim.de

Abstract. More and more knowledge graphs (KGs) are generated in various domains. Applications using more than one KG require an integrated view of those KGs, which, in the first place, requires a common schema or ontology. Merging schemas requires not only equivalence mappings between classes but also other semantic relations, like subclass, superclass, etc. In this paper, we introduce *TaSeR*, a **Ta**nsformer based model for **Se**mantic **R**elation Typing, which is able to decide which type of relation holds between two given classes. The approach can differentiate between equivalent class, sub-/superclass, part of/has part, cohyponym, and no relation at all. With the latter outcome, it is not only possible to refine given class alignments, but also filter incorrect correspondences. The models are trained based on examples from general knowledge graphs as well as fine-tuned on the test case at hand. The former models can be directly used to predict a relation without further training. We show that those models are able to outperform other approaches which solve a similar task. For the evaluation, a new measure is introduced which credits for proximal matches.

Keywords: Relation Typing · Ontology Matching · Knowledge Graph Integration · Transformers

1 Introduction

Data integration comprises different tasks, such as schema matching, entity matching, and data fusion. In most approaches, schema or ontology matching is carried out as a first step, trying to find correspondences between schema elements of different knowledge graphs (KGs).

Most existing ontology matching tools only identify equivalent classes in two schemas. This restriction, however, is very limiting when it comes to existing integration problems. For example, if one schema defines a class `Person` (without any subclasses), and another one defines a class `Artist` (without any superclasses), such tools can either not find any correspondence between the two classes, or erroneously identify them as equivalent.

Since both solutions – not finding a correspondence at all, or erroneously identifying equivalence – are suboptimal, we argue that schema matching tools should output a wider range of relations between classes in schemas.

C. Pesquita et al. (Eds.): ESWC 2023, LNCS 13870, pp. 105–121, 2023.
https://doi.org/10.1007/978-3-031-33455-9_7

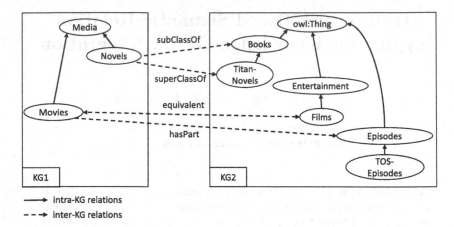

Fig. 1. Example of a matching task with semantic relations. All intra-KG relations represent rdfs:subClassOf.

In this work, we present *TaSeR*, a **T**ransformer based model for **Se**mantic **R**elation Typing. The input is a correspondence between two classes where the relation type is not yet determined. The task is to find out which type of relation actually holds between those inputs. We show that transformer based models can outperform state of the art approaches by fine-tuning them on general knowledge graphs such as DBpedia or Wikidata. The input KGs are further used to create a test case-specific model which often increases the performance.

Such models can be used to integrate ontologies of multiple KGs such as in the case of DBkWik [12]. Thousands of KGs are generated from Wikis by applying the DBpedia extraction framework. The result is a set of isolated KGs. When integrating their schemas, different relations can hold between their classes, not only equivalence.

Our contributions are: (1) a transformer based model for semantic relation prediction, (2) an existing dataset transformed to a new track at the OAEI, and (3) an improved evaluation measure for this task.

The paper is structured as follows: In the next section, we first define the task and present the relations our approach is able to predict. Afterwards related work is discussed. The following approach section is divided into training data generation, model tuning, and tuning on test cases. We evaluate the models on a gold standard in Sect. 5 and conclude with an outlook on future work.

2   Task Definition

Figure 1 shows an example of the task. Given two input KGs KG1 and KG2, the task is to find correspondences between them that are enriched with semantic relations. Thus only inter-KG relations are of interest in this work. Nevertheless, it is possible to use intra-KG relation as an additional training signal which is later discussed and evaluated.

Table 1. Mapping of linguistic relations to correspondence types.

Relation	DL	RDF representation	Correspondence	example
Synonym	$A \equiv B$	owl:equivalentClass	equivalence	home <-> domicile
Hyponym	$A \sqsubseteq B$	rdfs:subClassOf	subsumed	apple -> fruit
Hypernym	$A \sqsupseteq B$	rdfs:subClassOf^{-1}	subsume	fruit -> apple
Meronym	–	dcterms:isPartOf	part of	knee -> leg
Holonym	–	dcterms:hasPart	has a / has part	leg -> knee
Cohyponym	–	skos:related	cohyponym	dalmatian <-> poodle

The input is an alignment A consisting of correspondences defined as a 4-tuple $< x, y, r, c >$ where x and y are entities of KGs one and two, r represents the relation which holds between the entities (e.g., $=$ or $\sqsubseteq$), and finally a confidence value $c \in [0, 1]$. The output is an alignment A' with the same pairs (x, y), but potentially different relations and confidence scores.

In the example knowledge graph on the right, there is no equivalent class to novels. But many inter-KG correspondences can still be created e.g. novel is a subclass of book. Thus it is important to not only use equivalence relations between classes for integrating knowledge graphs.

The following semantic relations can be used between KGs: equivalence, sub-/super class of, part of/has part, cohyponym, and no relation at all (to filter correspondences). We now discuss how the relations should be used, their semantics, and how they relate to each other. Given the fact that class A is a subclass of class B means that all instances of A are also instances of class B (by RDFS semantics). Thus A is the more specific class whereas B is the more general class. The inverse relation is called superclass of. Whenever A is a subclass of B then B is always a superclass of A. The part of relation which represents a composition of concepts is often miss-used with the subclass relation[1]. As an example, a leg is a part of the body and not a subclass because each instance of a leg is not an instance of type body. The inverse relation is called has part or has a. Based on the definition of [1], the cohyponym relation consists of a pair of concepts that are both direct subclasses of a common superclass (e.g. A and C are related iff A is a subclass of B and C is a subclass of B).

3 Related Work

The first area of related work is *knowledge graph completion* [23]. The main task is to find links between entities that are true, but not explicitly stated in a KG. Technically, the systems are required to retrieve a ranked list of entities that are most likely for a given source entity and a relation - essentially object entity prediction. In a similar way, the subject entity should be predicted for a given target entity and relation. Some approaches also use the task of predicting

---

[1] https://www.w3.org/2001/sw/BestPractices/OEP/SimplePartWhole/.

the relation given both source and target entities as an additional training task. The approaches can be further divided into embedding-based approaches such as RESCAL [22], TransE [3], and ComplEx [29] as well as rule-based systems such as AnyBURL [18] and AMIE [7]. The main difference is that those approaches do only predict relations that are seen during training. This means that any relation which appears in the given KGs might be a candidate for the prediction. But in the presented use case the target relation is restricted to class relations.

The next field of related is the *natural language processing (NLP)* community. Given resources such as Wordnet [20] the relations between synsets can also be seen as semantic relations between classes in KGs. Table 1 shows the connection between linguistic relations used in Wordnet and relation types used in correspondences. [8] shows for example an approach to detect semantic relation between two given words/phrases using word embeddings [19]. The focus lies on the symmetric and asymmetric properties of the relations. Most of the datasets used in this work are derived from Wordnet.

[26] introduces a shared task about semantic relations. Based on this dataset, KEML, a meta learning framework for predicting lexical relations, is introduced [32].

Finally, the work in this paper falls into the area of *Knowledge Graph matching and fusion/integration* [13]. The closest related work is STROMA [1] which follows an enrichment strategy by refining given correspondences with a more meaningful relation than e.g. equivalence. The approach consists of five techniques consisting of linguistic approaches as well as the use of background knowledge (such as Wordnet).

The Tifi [5] approach combines multiple taxonomies together and uses lexical and graph features to determine if a given subsumption relation holds or not. The difference to our work is that the focus lies on the cleaning of those hierarchies and thus only intra-KG relations are analyzed. Furthermore, the prediction is binary and indicates only if two given concepts are subsumed. BERTSubs [4] focuses also on this relation. The idea is to embed concepts with BERT [6] by transforming classes and other OWL constructs such as restrictions into a textual representation. They evaluate their approach based on rankings. Given a concept A, they rank all other entities based on how likely it is that A is a subclass of this concept.

Except for STROMA [1], there is no system that can directly be applied to a given dataset to create correspondences between classes which includes semantic relations. Most of the approaches which use transformer based models, show specific techniques on how to train such models but do not create a usable model based on existing data. With TaSeR, we close this gap and present a model which is able to predict the relation type and can optionally be further fine-tuned on the test case at hand.

4   Approach

The overall approach is shown in Fig. 2. Given two knowledge graphs KG1 and KG2, the task is to find an alignment A consisting of correspondences with

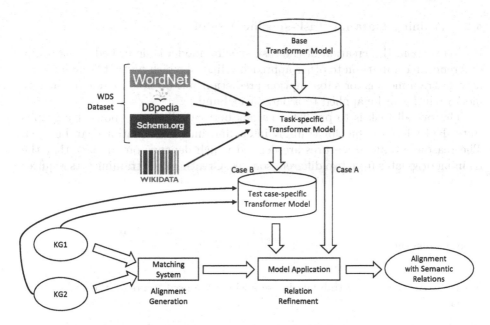

Fig. 2. Overall approach of TaSeR.

semantic relations (e.g. subsumption, equivalence, part of, etc.). TaSeR is a two-step approach. The first step is to generate candidate correspondences between classes where the relation is not yet specified (equivalence by default). This can be achieved by running various matching systems which are able to produce class correspondences. In a second step, the relation is further refined with the help of a transformer model. Two cases are analyzed: Case A) a task-specific model which is directly applied to the candidate set of correspondences. Such a model is trained on external datasets like DBpedia, Wordnet, and Schema.org. Case B) on top of the task-specific model, a further fine-tuned model is trained on test case data such as intra-KG subclass relations. In the further sections, each step is explained in more detail.

4.1 Creating Candidates/Blocking

Our approach TaSeR needs input class correspondences to further refine the relation. An advantage is that TaSeR is also able to filter correspondences in case they are not related at all. This allows using candidate generators that return many correspondences which may also contain incorrect correspondences (aligned classes that should not be connected at all, e.g. car and actor).

In general, any matching system or any combination of them can be used to generate candidates. A low threshold should be used to increase recall and allow the system to include also near matches. Due to the fact that this is not the focus of this work, LogMap [15] is chosen as it is a state of the art ontology matching system.

4.2 Training Data for Task-specific Model

In this section, the creation of the task-specific model is described. This is one difference in comparison to other approaches like [4] which present techniques on how to train models for subsumption prediction but do not provide a concrete model which can be applied to a dataset at hand.

The overall task is to predict relations between different knowledge graphs (inter-KG relations) but for training inter- and intra-KG relations can be used. The reason is that no features are derived which depends on the fact that the training originates from two different sources. Creating such training sets requires KGs which have a lot of relations useful for the models such as rdfs:subClassOf or skos:hasPart etc. In the following, we describe how each KG is used to create the training dataset. Wherever possible, for all kinds of relations examples are generated. Table 2 shows an analysis of all datasets and their counts for each type of relation.

Table 2. Analysis of the training datasets which are used to create the task-specific model.

dataset	equivalence	sub-/superclass of	part of/has part	cohyponym	negatives
Wordnet	215,672	84,501	9,092	44,329	410,960
DBpedia	58	246	0	198	0
Schema.org	0	1,421	0	826	0
Wikidata	927	127,659	230,897	0	0

Wordnet [20]: Other approaches like STROMA [1] use Wordnet as their main background knowledge because of the quality and coverage of concepts. Therefore in this work, Wordnet is also included.

Wordnet is structured by so-called synsets. They contain different lemmas which describe the same concept (synonyms). Each synset can have multiple relations to other synsets such as hypernym, hyponym, and holonym (see also Table 1). Generating examples for the equivalence relation is achieved by using all possible combinations between the words in a synset. This also includes the tuple where the word is equivalent to itself. In each synset the words "are ordered by estimated frequency of use"[2] e.g. "dog" is the most used word but "Canis familiaris" is also a synonym for it. The sub-/superclass examples are produced by following the hyponym/hypernym relations between the synsets. As a label, the first word is chosen as a representation of the synset. For the part of relations, the same approach is applied but following the meronym/holonym relations. The second last relation is called cohyponym. Examples are generated by listing all hypernyms of a given synset and creating combinations between them. Usually, there are many hypernyms of a given synset and thus only a maximum of five

---

[2] As stated in https://wordnet.princeton.edu/documentation/wn1wn.

examples are extracted per synset to not overemphasize this kind of relation. The last relation is an exception because its semantics is that no relation holds between the given concepts. The training data for this kind of negative example is generated by randomly sampling two synsets. It was ensured that no false negative is included by checking that the two synsets do not relate with either hyponym/hypernym and meronym/holonym relations.

DBpedia [2]: Beyond Wordnet, other KGs like DBpedia are used for training. The class hierarchy in DBpedia is manually created and curated in the mappings wiki[3]. The reason why such a mappings wiki exists is that the class information for each wiki page originates from the MediaWiki templates containing the text "infobox" which is usually rendered at the top right of the page to highlight some key facts of the concept. But many templates need to be mapped and processed to create a reasonable KG out of it e.g. the template infobox_aircraft_type[4] is mapped to the ontological class aircraft. Such a manual-created taxonomy is helpful in training subsumption relationships.

The training examples for equivalence relation from DBpedia are extracted by querying the official SPARQL endpoint[5] with the query in Listing 1.1 (the from statement was necessary to retrieve all results without duplicates). All English labels attached to the classes are queried in case they exist (optional statement). In cases where the label does not exist, the URI fragment[6] is used instead. In those fragments, no whitespaces are allowed and thus the text is split by camel case[7]. Hyphens and underscores are replaced by whitespace. Most of those equivalence mappings map two different datasets e.g. DBpedia to Schema.org and thus no label information is available for the external one. The YAGO mappings are skipped because the mapping only changes the URI but no label or textual representation. Still, in the resulting equivalence dataset of DBpedia, most examples map the exact same label to each other which is intentional. For sub-/superclass relationships, the same query as before is used but the property is replaced with `rdfs:subClassOf`. Due to the fact that there is no RDF property to express a superclass relation, the source and target entity of the subclass relation are switched. In the same way as for Wordnet, the examples with the cohyponym relation are created (at a maximum of five for each superclass). In the DBpedia ontology no further part of or has part relations are defined.

Schema.org [9]: Other public common knowledge graphs such as the first version of YAGO [28] also use Wordnet as their top-level ontology which is then used as a type system for all Wikipedia pages. Starting from YAGO 4 [24] they changed the top-level ontology to Schema.org. It is a taxonomy primarily used for encoding knowledge in websites with RDFa or Microdata. Consequently, this top-level ontology is also included as one source of training data.

---

[3] http://mappings.dbpedia.org.
[4] http://mappings.dbpedia.org/index.php/Mapping_en:Infobox_aircraft_type.
[5] https://dbpedia.org/sparql.
[6] The URI fragment is extracted by using the text after the last slash or hashtag.
[7] https://en.wikipedia.org/wiki/Camel_case.

Listing 1.1. DBpedia query to retrieve all equivalence relations.

```
PREFIX rdfs: <http://www.w3.org/2000/01/rdf-schema#>
PREFIX owl: <http://www.w3.org/2002/07/owl#>
SELECT *
FROM <http://dbpedia.org>
WHERE {
    ?left owl:equivalentClass ?right.
    OPTIONAL{
        ?left rdfs:label ?leftlabel.
        ?right rdfs:label ?rightlabel.
        FILTER (LANG(?leftlabel) = "en" &&
                LANG(?rightlabel) = "en" )
    }
}
```

For Schema.org the corresponding CSV (comma separated values) file[8] is downloaded and all subclass relations are extracted. Again, superclass and cohyponym examples are generated as in DBpedia. No part of or equivalence relations are available.

WDS Dataset: There are not many relations extracted from DBpedia and Schema.org. Thus a combination of Wordnet, DBpedia, and Schema.org is created. This WDS dataset will later be used to train the corresponding models with a rather limited set of data. In the next section, a larger dataset is presented which is extracted from Wikidata.

Wikidata [31]: Usually, more training data helps to improve the classification. Thus Wikidata is used as an additional dataset because it is one of the largest KGs available. Initially, the official endpoint[9] of Wikidata is used to retrieve all subclass and part of relations. Due to a large number of classes and relations, the endpoint runs into timeouts. Therefore the endpoint of Virtuoso[10] is used. The corresponding query is shown in Listing 1.2 which uses the P279 predicate to retrieve all subclass relations together with all labels. Due to the availability of labels and the size of Wikidata, the labels are marked as mandatory in the query. The high number of results forced us to execute all queries with limits and offsets to iterate over pages of results. In a similar way, the part of/has part relation examples are collected (by replacing the property with wdt:P361). For the equivalence relation wdt:P1709 is used (equivalent property to owl:equivalenceClass). Similarly to DBpedia, one concept (either source or target) does not have literals included in Wikidata. Thus the URI fragment is used again.

4.3   Training of Task-specific Model

Given the general training dataset constructed in the previous section, the question remains how a transformer based model is trained. Many of the pre-trained

---

[8] https://schema.org/version/latest/schemaorg-current-http-types.csv.

[9] https://query.wikidata.org.

[10] https://wikidata.demo.openlinksw.com/sparql.

Listing 1.2. Wikidata query to retrieve all subclass relations.

```
PREFIX rdfs: <http://www.w3.org/2000/01/rdf-schema#>
PREFIX wdt: <http://www.wikidata.org/prop/direct/>
PREFIX owl: <http://www.w3.org/2002/07/owl#>
SELECT *
FROM <http://dbpedia.org>
WHERE {
    ?left wdt:P279 ?right.
    ?left rdfs:label ?leftlabel.
    ?right rdfs:label ?rightlabel.
    FILTER (LANG(?leftlabel) = "en" &&
            LANG(?rightlabel) = "en" )
    LIMIT 10000
    OFFSET 0
}
```

transformer models such as BERT [6], RoBERTa [17], or Albert [16] are trained on large amounts of text. The training objective is called *masked language modeling* where the model should predict a masked token given that it can attend to the surrounding tokens bidirectionally. In this work, those models are used but with a different objective. The overall task is to classify a given example into one of seven classes (which represent the different relation types in Table 1 plus the negative class). Therefore each model gets an additional dropout and linear layer on top (this is also called the head of the model) which transforms the output of the model into seven neurons (each representing a relation type). For each example during training exactly one of them should result in the value of one and all others to zero. The binary cross entropy loss is used to reduce this error. Each model gets this classification head and is trained with the given examples. In addition, it is possible to only finetune the head and freeze all layers of the underlying model but in this work, we adjust all weights.

In the following, the input representation of the training concepts is described. For each class, a textual representation is generated. It is usually the `rdfs:label` of the class. In case there is more than one label, each label is transformed into a training example (cross-product in case both concepts have multiple labels). If no label is available, then the URI fragment is extracted and post-processed (camel case, hyphens, and underscores as in Sect. 4.2). The extraction of textual representations can be further customized.

To separate the textual representation of the source and target class, the pre-trained special token [SEP] is used as a separator. Thus a training example for the relation has part can look like "body[SEP]leg". This is similar to the BERTSubs [4] approach called isolated class (IC). They showed that adding path context (PC) or breadth-first context (BC) does not improve the result much (e.g. 0.002 for inter-ontology named subsumption prediction on the HeLiS-FoodOn test case for hits at one) or even make it worse (e.g. 0.016 less in hits at five for the same task).

In comparison to BERTSubs we do not only rely on BERT as one prominent representative of transformer based language models, but also use and evaluate more common models such as albert-base-v2, bert-base-uncased, distilbert-base-uncased, and roberta-base.

For the actual training, the transformers library of huggingface [33] is used. In more detail, the trainer class is executed with the default parameters except for the batch size to create a first model. The value for the batch size is increased as much as possible to A) decrease the training time and B) update the weights based on more examples with different target relations. Thus the weights are not changed drastically by a batch that e.g. contains only examples with the equivalence relation. Each model has different memory requirements and thus an approach is developed to automatically select the highest possible batch size given the dataset, model, and GPU. It works as follows: The data set is first sorted by the overall length of the two input texts such that the longest texts appear at the beginning. Afterwards different batch sizes b are tried out by starting with four and multiplying by two after each trial (iterating over the powers of two). The dataset is cut to the top b examples and only trained for one step in order to quickly test if the memory of the GPU is large enough to store everything. If the test works fine, the batch size is increased. If instead an out-of-memory error is detected, the batch size is divided by two to get the maximum working batch size. This approach allows for higher batches sizes than trying out the theoretical maximum which is a batch where each example exhausts the maximum number of tokens. In case the dataset consists only of rather short texts, this is an improvement because the batch size could be increased.

In addition to the default hyperparameter (HP) of the trainer, an HP tuning is executed. The training of transformer based models requires a lot of time and thus population based training [14] (PBT) is selected as the HP search algorithm. The underlying idea is based on evolutionary algorithms. In the beginning, there is a set of models with random HPs based on an initial distribution. After training and evaluating the models for some number of batches, the hyperparameters of good performing models are used as a replacement for models which perform worse. With such an approach the HP can change over time during training. Thus it is necessary to use the trained model directly because there is no fixed set of HP such that one can tune a new model based on it.[11]

4.4   Training of Test Case Specific Model

In the previous section, a task-specific model is created. It is trained on general knowledge graphs and can thus be used directly to predict a semantic relation for a given pair of classes. But given the input KGs there is more training data

---

[11] The number of trained models is fixed to ten and the following hyperparameters are tuned: learning rate (loguniform between 1e-6 and 1e-4), train epochs (between 1 to 10), seed (uniform distribution from 1 to 40), batch size (choice of 4, 8, 16, 32, 64, 128 until the maximum possible batch size). The mutations of HPs are defined by: weight decay (uniform between 0.0 and 0.3), learning rate (uniform between 1e-5 and 5e-5), batch size (choice of 4, 8, 16, 32, 64, 128 until the maximum possible batch size).

Table 3. Analysis of the evaluation datasets.

dataset	equivalence	subclass of	superclass of	part of	has part	cohyponym
g1-web	275	29	26	2	3	4
g2-diseases	316	27	11	0	1	0
g3-text	70	425	267	0	0	0
g4-furniture	13	107	4	0	11	1
g5-groceries	29	14	113	0	2	11
g6-clothing	10	0	124	0	8	0
g7-literature	12	18	52	1	0	0

available. The overall task is to predict inter-KG relationships between classes and thus intra-KG relations can be used to further fine-tune the model to a given test case (consisting of two KGs). This will incorporate some knowledge about the concepts which are later used in the prediction.

To select training examples for the subsumption, we use all triples in each of the input KG where rdfs:subClassOf is used as a relation. In addition, the source and target of this relation are switched to also generate examples for the inverse relation. Similarly, for the equivalence relation the owl:equivalentClass predicate is used. For all other relations, we use the vocabulary terms defined in Table 1.

In most of the input KGs, only a taxonomy is defined. This results in training examples consisting only of subsumption relations. Fine-tuning the task-specific model with such a training set causes the model to adapt to these relations. Thus another fine-tuning dataset is created. In addition to the examples extracted from the input KGs, the same number of equivalence examples are sampled from the corresponding task-specific training dataset. This fine-tuning approach is later called in the evaluation "test case +".

5   Evaluation

In this section, the approach TaSeR is evaluated. Due to the fact that it is a two-step approach, we first evaluate only the prediction of semantic relations and later define a new measure for evaluating the whole system. In the next section, the corresponding evaluation datasets are selected.

5.1   Datasets

Most of the existing datasets are not suitable to evaluate our approach because they do only evaluate equivalence relationships such as the Ontology Alignment Evaluation Initiative (OAEI) [25]. Only the complex track allows the matching system to create correspondence which are composed of multiple concepts. But this is not the same task as presented in this paper where the relation between two concepts should be evaluated. Thus the dataset of STROMA [1] is used for evaluation. It contains seven pairs of ontologies from different domains. Each dataset was in a different format such as tabular separated files and various OWL formats. Furthermore, the identifier for concepts is not defined by URIs but by the path of labels from the given concept to the top concept. Due to the possibility of multiple inheritance, this is not unique.

Therefore, all datasets are transformed into the OAEI standard format which consists of a source and target KG in RDF/XML. The reference alignment contains correspondences where each one consists of a source and target URI which needs to be present in the input KGs. This was explicitly checked and errors (in the KGs as well as in the reference alignment) were corrected.

All characteristics of the dataset are included in Table 3. It shows for each test case and semantic relation the number of correspondences included in the reference alignment. All correspondences are directed and thus the number of sub-/superclass and part of/has part are not symmetric.

5.2   Results

All trained models are evaluated on the before mentioned dataset. The experiments are executed on NVIDIA Tesla V100 graphic cards and Intel Xeon Gold 6230 processors (2.1GHz). Due to the fact that the models are either trained on external datasets or on the input KGs, no further train test split needs to be created. The provided gold standard is solely used for testing. In this section, we evaluate the predictions of semantic relations given the class correspondences. Thus not using any candidate generation step. In essence, this boils down to a multi-class classification task.

Table 5 shows the overall results for each trained model. The runtime of each model is always below one minute (exact runtimes are given in the supplementary material). We differentiate between the base model, the dataset, and the fine-tuning method. The WDS dataset consists of Wordnet, DBpedia, and Schema.org whereas WDS + Wikidata represents the same dataset but adds all training examples from Wikidata (this increases the number of examples drastically). To compare all models, the micro averaged F_1 is computed across all classes which in this case represents the kind of semantic relation. Micro averaged precision and recall are the same as F_1 because *all* false instances are counted. Thus the following equation holds true (c represents the classes): $\sum_c FP_c = \sum_c FN_c$.

For the test cases G1 and G2, the task-specific model outperforms the STROMA baseline by 0.038 and 0.053 F_1. This is achieved by directly applying the task-specific model to the dataset without any knowledge of the task. This shows the overall usability of such models. Starting from G3 one can see that the fine-tuning on the test cases is really helpful in deciding which relation holds true between the classes. Except for G6, it turns out that fine-tuning on the test case together with samples from the training dataset (the one where the corresponding task-specific model is trained on) is useful (higher F_1 for test case + than for test case). Only training on the subsumption relations of the input KGs usually gives too high weights to this relation such that the model

Table 4. Two aggregated confusion matrices for DistilBERT over all tasks.

		Prediction WDS						Prediction WDS+Wikidata					
		equivalence	subclass of	superclass of	part of	has part	cohyponym	equivalence	subclass of	superclass of	part of	has part	cohyponym
Actual	equivalence	654	24	15	8	15	9	298	93	55	118	156	5
	subclass of	173	428	9	0	0	10	23	475	15	93	8	6
	superclass of	202	20	358	0	2	15	27	24	386	30	120	10
	part of	3	0	0	0	0	0	0	0	3	0	0	0
	has part	20	2	0	0	0	3	1	7	0	3	13	1
	cohyponym	8	2	5	0	0	1	1	2	3	5	5	0

overly often predicts those relations. The F1 gains are significant (95% confidence interval) for test cases G2, G3, and G7.

We finally select the best model which works without test case fine-tuning such that the research community can directly apply the model without any changes. For the model selection, all F_1 scores are added and the model with the highest score is selected. It turns out, that more training data or hyperparameter optimization is not always helpful because DistilBERT trained on the WDS dataset is achieving the overall best performance (not regarding test case fine tuning). The training time of the task-specific models can take up to 48 h. The best model is shared on the huggingface model hub[12].

Table 4 shows two confusion matrices (values summed all over all tasks) of DistilBERT models. The left one is only trained on the WDS dataset (the chosen best model). Equivalence, subclass of, and superclass of can be detected quite well whereas part of and has part is not easy. The right confusion matrix is the result of the model trained on WDS and Wikidata (which contains more part of relations), therefore, the predictions for these types of relations are better.

5.3   Evaluation of the Complete System

To evaluate the complete system, the candidate generation step is added and all resulting relations of the correspondences are further refined with TaSeR. As already mentioned in [1], the system might find correspondences that are not in the reference alignment but still valid (especially for subclass relations) e.g. the system finds that movies are a subclass of entertainment (cf. Figure 1). Such statements would count as false positives which is incorrect.

Therefore we propose a new measure to circumvent this problem. The following closure approach is applied to each reference alignment as well as system alignment. If the alignment maps class A to class X with a subclass relation, then additionally all subclasses of A are also subclasses of X as well as all of

---

[12] https://huggingface.co/dwsunimannheim/TaSeR.

118   S. Hertling and H. Paulheim

Table 5. Micro averaged F_1 results of all trained models differentiated by base model, datasets used for training, and kind of fine-tuning. STROMA serves as a baseline that is optimized for this gold standard. The top three values are printed in bold.

Base model	Dataset	Fine-tuning	G1	G2	G3	G4	G5	G6	G7
Albert	WDS	Task	0.422	0.673	0.906	0.125	0.314	0.261	0.651
		Test case	0.127	0.096	0.886	0.728	0.621	0.824	0.771
		Test case +	0.434	0.746	0.912	0.721	0.663	0.761	**0.940**
	WDS +HP Tuning	Task	0.540	0.758	0.886	0.213	0.361	0.211	0.566
		Test case	0.091	0.096	0.895	0.757	0.645	0.810	0.807
		Test case +	0.575	0.797	0.878	**0.779**	0.710	0.817	0.687
	WDS +Wikidata	Task	0.121	0.273	0.941	0.375	0.485	0.451	0.627
		Test case	0.118	0.099	0.932	0.699	0.680	0.838	0.783
		Test case +	0.248	0.727	0.915	0.757	0.704	0.824	**0.880**
Bert	WDS	Task	0.534	0.752	0.919	0.228	0.385	0.261	0.639
		Test case	0.109	0.093	0.932	0.699	0.663	0.831	0.759
		Test case +	0.348	0.718	0.927	**0.779**	0.728	0.852	0.723
	WDS +HP Tuning	Task	0.560	0.741	0.896	0.250	0.385	0.268	0.651
		Test case	0.103	0.087	0.913	0.699	0.663	0.817	0.735
		Test case +	0.440	0.758	0.904	0.691	0.716	0.845	0.747
	WDS +Wikidata	Task	0.136	0.400	**0.944**	0.500	0.485	0.331	0.663
		Test case	0.124	0.115	**0.946**	0.772	0.680	0.852	0.783
		Test case +	0.428	0.775	**0.944**	0.691	0.710	0.845	**0.831**
DistilBERT	WDS	Task	**0.767**	**0.828**	0.929	0.154	0.420	0.268	0.590
		Test case	0.100	0.085	0.883	0.699	0.698	**0.852**	0.783
		Test case +	0.378	0.727	0.924	0.662	**0.746**	0.838	0.771
	WDS +HP Tuning	Task	0.720	0.786	0.925	0.191	0.373	0.197	0.566
		Test case	0.094	0.087	0.928	0.721	0.645	**0.852**	0.783
		Test case +	0.372	0.783	0.919	0.706	**0.769**	0.824	0.747
	WDS +Wikidata	Task	0.183	0.510	**0.946**	0.331	0.367	0.317	0.675
		Test case	0.115	0.144	0.942	0.728	0.704	**0.866**	0.771
		Test case +	0.419	0.735	0.934	0.743	0.734	0.838	0.771
Roberta	WDS	Task	**0.799**	**0.820**	0.916	0.272	0.373	0.204	0.554
		Test case	0.118	0.099	0.865	0.750	0.550	0.831	0.675
		Test case +	0.363	0.445	0.930	0.735	0.627	0.810	0.759
	WDS +HP Tuning	Task	**0.799**	**0.845**	0.841	0.250	0.296	0.155	0.494
		Test case	0.124	0.099	0.883	0.728	0.669	0.803	0.663
		Test case +	0.472	0.727	0.898	0.728	0.669	0.824	0.747
	WDS +Wikidata	Task	0.021	0.090	0.886	0.287	0.479	0.275	0.518
		Test case	0.115	0.101	0.883	0.728	0.680	0.838	0.771
		Test case +	0.268	0.811	0.882	0.743	**0.740**	0.831	0.771
STROMA	-	-	0.761	0.792	0.854	**0.765**	0.716	**0.866**	0.807

all superclasses of X. Thus many more (implicit) relations between concepts are added. The equivalence relation is handled as two subclass relations in both directions. After the reference and system alignment are processed, precision, recall, and f-measure are computed as usual. We call those measures $P_{closure}$,

Table 6. Evaluation of complete system (micro averaged).

Measure	G1	G2	G3	G4	G5	G6	G7
$P_{closure}$	0.701	0.401	0.422	0.688	0.946	0.715	0.825
$R_{closure}$	0.815	0.695	0.162	0.630	0.658	0.305	0.371
$F_{1-closure}$	0.754	0.508	0.234	0.658	0.776	0.428	0.512

$R_{closure}$, and $F_{1-closure}$. With such a definition, it is also possible to extend it to the case where the gold standard is not complete but partial.

We evaluate the complete system with this measure and show the results in Table 6. The recall can be increased by using candidate generation models which return more correspondences and are thus more recall-oriented (due to the fact that TaSeR is also able to filter correspondences that are not related at all).

6 Conclusion and Outlook

In this paper, we presented TaSeR, a transformer based model for semantic relation prediction. Most state of the art matching systems do only output equivalence relations for classes which is too imprecise to use it for KG integration. TaSeR is based on two steps: (1) Generate candidate correspondences with any matching system, and (2) predict the most appropriate relation between them.

In addition, we transformed a given gold standard into the OAEI format and plan to submit a new track in 2023. We show that transformer models trained on general knowledge graphs such as Wordnet, DBpedia, and Schema.org can outperform STROMA which is one strong system developed especially for the gold standard used here. It could be shown that fine-tuning on the test case (by using intra-KG relations) can further improve the prediction.

In the future, we plan to extend our model to also deal with multilingual input. This can be achieved by using multilingual transformer models such as bert-base-multilingual-uncased together with additional training data. Those can be created from datasets like EuroWordNet [30], Wiktionary [27], and Babel-Net [21]. Other datasets used in this approach like Wikidata also include labels for a concept in different languages which would also help. In such a case, one can also train the model to find semantic relations between classes of different languages e.g. car (English) is a subclass of vehículo (Spanish).

Another direction for future work is to increase the number of possible semantic relations. Probably the most interesting relation is the "is a" relation which is different from the subclass relationship because the former connects an instance to a class whereas the latter should only connect classes. In essence, this boils down to detecting if a concept is an instance or a class. Training data for this relation is not directly available in Wordnet, but in other knowledge graphs like DBpedia or Wikidata. It is still unclear how the training of such models should look like and how much data is actually necessary to achieve good results. Such a model could be used for WebIsALOD [11] to create a proper ontology.

In this work, we mainly used the dataset given by STROMA [1]. Other datasets do not contain many semantic relations but only one or two as in the case of BERTSubs [4]. Still, we would like to include more datasets in the future to get a higher variety of datasets even though some of them might only care about subsumption.

All supplementary materials can be found at figshare [10].

References

1. Arnold, P., Rahm, E.: Enriching ontology mappings with semantic relations. Data Knowl. Eng. **93**, 1–18 (2014). https://doi.org/10.1016/j.datak.2014.07.001
2. Auer, S., Bizer, C., Kobilarov, G., Lehmann, J., Cyganiak, R., Ives, Z.: DBpedia: A Nucleus for a Web of Open Data. In: Aberer, K., et al. (eds.) ASWC/ISWC - 2007. LNCS, vol. 4825, pp. 722–735. Springer, Heidelberg (2007). https://doi.org/10.1007/978-3-540-76298-0_52
3. Bordes, A., Usunier, N., Garcia-Duran, A., Weston, J., Yakhnenko, O.: Translating embeddings for modeling multi-relational data. Adv. Neural Inf. Process. Syst. **26**, 2787–2795 (2013)
4. Chen, J., He, Y., Geng, Y., Jimenez-Ruiz, E., Dong, H., Horrocks, I.: Contextual semantic embeddings for ontology subsumption prediction. arXiv preprint arXiv:2202.09791 (2022)
5. Chu, C.X., Razniewski, S., Weikum, G.: Tifi: taxonomy induction for fictional domains. In: The World Wide Web Conference (WWW), pp. 2673–2679 (2019). https://doi.org/10.1145/3308558.3313519
6. Devlin, J., Chang, M., Lee, K., Toutanova, K.: BERT: pre-training of deep bidirectional transformers for language understanding. In: Burstein, J., Doran, C., Solorio, T. (eds.) NAACL-HLT, pp. 4171–4186. Association for Computational Linguistics (2019). https://doi.org/10.18653/v1/n19-1423
7. Galárraga, L., Teflioudi, C., Hose, K., Suchanek, F.M.: Fast rule mining in ontological knowledge bases with AMIE+. VLDB J. **24**(6), 707–730 (2015)
8. Glavaš, G., Ponzetto, S.P.: Dual tensor model for detecting asymmetric lexico-semantic relations. In: Conference on Empirical Methods in Natural Language Processing, EMNLP. Association for Computational Linguistics (2017)
9. Guha, R.V., Brickley, D., Macbeth, S.: Schema. org: evolution of structured data on the web. Commun. ACM **59**(2), 44–51 (2016)
10. Hertling, S.: TaSeR, March 2023. https://doi.org/10.6084/m9.figshare.21750338.v1, https://figshare.com/articles/dataset/TaSeR/21750338
11. Hertling, S., Paulheim, H.: Webisalod: providing hypernymy relations extracted from the web as linked open data. In: ISWC, pp. 111–119 (2017)
12. Hertling, S., Paulheim, H.: Dbkwik: extracting and integrating knowledge from thousands of wikis. Knowl. Inf. Syst. **62**(6), 2169–2190 (2020)
13. Hertling, S., Paulheim, H.: The knowledge graph track at OAEI. In: Harth, A., et al. (eds.) ESWC 2020. LNCS, vol. 12123, pp. 343–359. Springer, Cham (2020). https://doi.org/10.1007/978-3-030-49461-2_20
14. Jaderberg, M., et al.: Population based training of neural networks. arXiv preprint arXiv:1711.09846 (2017)
15. Jiménez-Ruiz, E., Grau, B.C., Zhou, Y., Horrocks, I.: Large-scale interactive ontology matching: algorithms and implementation. In: ECAI, vol. 242, pp. 444–449 (2012)

16. Lan, Z., Chen, M., Goodman, S., Gimpel, K., Sharma, P., Soricut, R.: Albert: a lite bert for self-supervised learning of language representations. arXiv preprint arXiv:1909.11942 (2019)
17. Liu, Y., et al.: Roberta: a robustly optimized bert pretraining approach. arXiv preprint arXiv:1907.11692 (2019)
18. Meilicke, C., Chekol, M.W., Ruffinelli, D., Stuckenschmidt, H.: Anytime bottom-up rule learning for knowledge graph completion. In: International Joint Conference on Artificial Intelligence (IJCAI), pp. 3137–3143 (2019). https://doi.org/10.24963/ijcai.2019/435
19. Mikolov, T., Sutskever, I., Chen, K., Corrado, G.S., Dean, J.: Distributed representations of words and phrases and their compositionality. Adv. Neural Inf. Process. Syst. **26**, 3111–3119 (2013)
20. Miller, G.A.: Wordnet: a lexical database for English. Commun. ACM **38**(11), 39–41 (1995)
21. Navigli, R., Ponzetto, S.P.: Babelnet: the automatic construction, evaluation and application of a wide-coverage multilingual semantic network. Artif. Intell. **193**, 217–250 (2012)
22. Nickel, M., Tresp, V., Kriegel, H.P.: A three-way model for collective learning on multi-relational data. In: ICML (2011)
23. Paulheim, H.: Knowledge graph refinement: a survey of approaches and evaluation methods. Semant. Web **8**(3), 489–508 (2017)
24. Pellissier Tanon, T., Weikum, G., Suchanek, F.: YAGO 4: a reason-able knowledge base. In: Harth, A., et al. (eds.) ESWC 2020. LNCS, vol. 12123, pp. 583–596. Springer, Cham (2020). https://doi.org/10.1007/978-3-030-49461-2_34
25. Pour, M., et al.: Results of the ontology alignment evaluation initiative 2021. In: CEUR Workshop Proceedings 2021, vol. 3063, pp. 62–108. CEUR (2021)
26. Santus, E., Gladkova, A., Evert, S., Lenci, A.: The CogALex-V shared task on the corpus-based identification of semantic relations. In: Proceedings of the 5th Workshop on Cognitive Aspects of the Lexicon (CogALex-V), pp. 69–79 (2016)
27. Sérasset, G.: DBnary: wiktionary as a lemon-based multilingual lexical resource in RDF. Semant. Web **6**(4), 355–361 (2015)
28. Suchanek, F.M., Kasneci, G., Weikum, G.: Yago: a core of semantic knowledge. In: Proceedings of the 16th International Conference on World Wide Web, pp. 697–706 (2007)
29. Trouillon, T., Welbl, J., Riedel, S., Gaussier, É., Bouchard, G.: Complex embeddings for simple link prediction. In: International Conference on Machine Learning, pp. 2071–2080. PMLR (2016)
30. Vossen, P.: Eurowordnet: a multilingual database for information retrieval. In: Proceedings of the DELOS workshop on Cross-language Information Retrieval, 5–7 March 1997, Zurich. Vrije Universiteit (1997)
31. Vrandečić, D., Krötzsch, M.: Wikidata: a free collaborative knowledgebase. Commun. ACM **57**(10), 78–85 (2014)
32. Wang, C., Qiu, M., Huang, J., He, X.: KEML: a knowledge-enriched meta-learning framework for lexical relation classification. In: Proceedings of the AAAI Conference on Artificial Intelligence, vol. 35, pp. 13924–13932 (2021)
33. Wolf, T., et al.: Transformers: state-of-the-art natural language processing. In: Proceedings of the 2020 Conference on Empirical Methods in Natural Language Processing: System Demonstrations, pp. 38–45. Association for Computational Linguistics, Online, October 2020. https://www.aclweb.org/anthology/2020.emnlp-demos.6

Entity Linking for KGQA Using AMR Graphs

Nadine Steinmetz[1,2]([✉]) [ID]

[1] Technische Universität Ilmenau, Ilmenau, Germany
nadine.steinmetz@tu-ilmenau.de
[2] Bergische Universität Wuppertal, Wuppertal, Germany
steinmetz@uni-wuppertal.de

Abstract. Entity linking is an essential part of analytical systems for question answering on knowledge graphs (KGQA). The mentioned entity has to be spotted in the text and linked to the correct resource in the knowledge graph (KG). With this paper, we present our approach on entity linking using the abstract meaning representation (AMR) of the question to spot the surface forms of entities. We re-trained AMR models with automatically generated training data. Based on these models, we extract surface forms and map them to an entity dictionary of the desired KG. For the disambiguation process, we evaluated different options and configurations on QALD-9 and LC-QuaD 2.0. The results of the best performing configurations outperform existing entity linking approaches.

Keywords: Entity Linking · AMR · Data Augmentation

1 Introduction

The correct identification of named entities in a natural language (NL) question is a key challenge for question answering on knowledge graphs (KGQA) systems. In terms of analytical approaches, the challenge of entity linking includes two aspects: the correct recognition of the surface form of the named entity within the text, as well as the correct disambiguation of possibly ambiguous phrases.

With this paper, we present our approach on entity linking in the context of KGQA [17]. Our proposed approach on entity linking is bipartite: a trained approach for the identification of the surface form and an analytical approach for the disambiguation and linking process.

We utilize the abstract meaning representation (AMR) of the question to structure the input question in a graph and identify separate parts of the question. Several libraries provide pre-trained models for the transformation. These models are using language models for the analysis of the syntax of the question, and training data, e.g. by the Linguistic Data Consortium (LDC), to transform a NL sentence/question to an AMR graph. We identified several flaws of the pre-trained models. We therefore generated augmented training data and re-trained several AMR models to be evaluated. The models are available via Zenodo: https://zenodo.org/record/7442882.

N. Steinmetz—Work was done while at TU Ilmenau.

The second part of our approach is the actual entity linking process. We utilize dictionaries containing several context information for the named entities within the respective KG. We rank possible entity candidates and choose the candidate with the highest score as the most relevant for the input question and surface form.

For the evaluation of our approach, we generated test data from actual KGQA test datasets – QALD-9 [20] and LC-QuaD 2.0 [5]. We compared our approach to existing approaches and their results on those test datasets. The results show that our approach outperforms other competing approaches on both datasets.

We automatically generated training data to re-train our AMR model and eliminate the identified flaws of the existing model. Our evaluation results show that with this augmentation and re-training, our new model improves the entity linking by at least 5% in recall and precision. Overall, we processed 28 different configurations for each test dataset to identify the best performing configuration from three different categories: AMR model, context information, calculation of ranking score.

The remainder of the paper is structured as follows: Related work is described in Sect. 2. We introduce our data augmentation process and the parameters of the re-training of the AMR models in Sect. 4. The entity linking step including the description of the dictionary and the ranking process is depicted in Sect. 5. We evaluated our approach on two different data sets based on Wikidata and DBpedia. The results are shown and discussed in Sect. 6. We summarize our approach and discuss future work in Sect. 7.

2   Related Work

In 2008, Milne et al. presented their approach on *wikification* – linking mentions in text to Wikipedia pages [14]. Their approach is completely based on machine learning, trained on Wikipedia articles. Both steps, the identification of phrases within the text to be linked to Wikipedia pages as well as the disambiguation of ambiguous phrases are trained on their training dataset. The disambiguation process utilizes unambiguous phrases within the context of the ambiguous phrase to help find the correct meaning and Wikipedia page.

TagMe also links text to Wikipedia pages and has been published in 2010 by Ferragina et al. [6]. Their approach aims at very short texts – which corresponds to entity linking in the context of QA. Their approach also takes into account the context of the text and the authors claim to propose a method that computes ranking scores for all meanings (resp. candidates) very fast. The disambiguation includes the calculation of the *relatedness* of Wikipedia pages in the context.

One of the first approaches of entity linking on DBpedia was DBpedia Spotlight [13] in 2011. Mendes et al. presented an approach consisting of several sub steps: spotting, candidate mapping, disambiguation and linking. For the spotting, a string matching algorithm based on Aho-Corasick is used. Afterwards, candidates are selected using the DBpedia Lexicalization dataset[1]. This stage

---

[1] Unfortunately, the Lexicalization dataset is not available anymore.

of the process already pre-ranks the candidates. The subsequent disambiguation makes use of a vector space model where each candidate is a vector in the space. The disambiguation then uses context information of the input text/question to rank the candidates in the vector space.

Also in 2011, AIDA has been presented by Yosef et al. [21]. AIDA uses for the spotting of entities in a text the Stanford NER tagger[2]. The disambiguation process utilizes a graph-based approach. The nodes in the graph are mentions and entities. There are two types of edges: edges between entities and edges between a mention and an entity. For a text, such a graph is created using the mentions (surface forms) of the text and adding the respective entities as pre-defined. Then the entity-entity edges are added. The goal of their approach is to reduce the graph to a high density graph where each mention is linked to only one entity.

Falcon 2.0 originally has been introduced as entity and relation linking tool over Wikidata by Sakor et al. [16]. Meanwhile the authors provide an API and the annotation of text also includes links to DBpedia entities and relations. The spotting of the surface forms in a text utilizes tokenization and n-gram tiling to retrieve combined tokens as surface forms. To identify the correct candidates, the approach tries to find triples in the KG that involves pairs of relations and entities from the candidate lists. Each match within the KG increases the individual score of the entity and relation candidates.

As stated by Bender et al. [1], large language models (LLM), such as BERT [3], are claimed to understand the meaning of NL while they actually are trained to predict text based on linguistic form. These LLMs might not be able to understand NL, but they can help to analyze and transform NL to other formal languages. Therefore, those LLMs are also suitable for the task of entity linking.

BLINK is an entity linking tool that utilizes bi-encoder to spot entity mentions and a cross-encoder to disambiguate and link the mentions to Wikipedia pages. The authors utilized a fine-tuned BERT architecture for that purpose. Later, the BLINK architecture has been enhanced especially for entity linking on questions (ELQ) [12]. The major enhancement of the ELQ architecture is a performance boost by processing multiple entity mentions at once and the eliminated necessity of mention boundaries with the input. BLINK is integrated as built-in wikification service in several libraries for the generation of AMR graphs, such as amrlib.

The approach of OpenTapioca has been published in 2019 [2]. The author proposes a light weight model for the purpose of entity linking on Wikidata which can be used to be run or trained to keep a linking system up to date as the Wikidata KG changes. The approach takes into account the local compatibility of pairs of mentions and entities as well as semantic similarity of entities occurring as candidates in the same context of a text. These metrics are computed based on the actual KG and used for training the model.

In 2021, Jiang et al. presented their neuro-symbolic approach which includes interpretable rules and neural learning [8]. Amongst other, the authors evaluated

[2] http://nlp.stanford.edu/software/CRF-NER.shtml.

their approach on QALD-9, but their test dataset contains 174 target entities (compared to 125 in our test dataset). Probably, they test dataset includes also categories and subjects in addition to only named entities. Therefore, we did not include their results in our comparison of evaluation results.

In terms of data augmentation and improving AMR parsing, Lee et al. presented several experiments to improve AMR parsing on different data sets [10]. AMR graphs for the QALD-9 test and train datasets were created manually by three annotators over a year and they achieved a SMATCH score of 89.3. This score is only 1.6% higher than the score we achieved with our automatic data augmentation process (c.f. Sect. 4).

As discussed in Sect. 4.1, AMR are very suitable as intermediate representation for KGQA applications due to their graph nature. Besides our own approach [17], there are already other existing approaches on KGQA utilizing AMR in the transformation pipeline from NL to SPARQL, as e.g. [9,15]. Both latter approaches use BLINK for the entity linking process.

3 Approach Overview

Our presented approach consists of two main sub steps. The first step is independent from the desired KG and identifies the surface forms of potential named entities within the input question. In the second step, the surface form is mapped to the respective KG to identify and disambiguate the specific named entity.

The first step includes the generation of the AMR graph and the extraction of the relevant parts of the surface forms of the named entities. Named entities are referenced using a *name* node in the graph.

With this approach, we are able to outperform existing competing approaches for entity linking based on Wikidata and DBpedia. As shown in Sect. 6, our data augmentation is able to improve the AMR model. Based on the re-trained models, we apply the entity mapping and ranking. The results for the overall process are very promising compared to competing systems. Our approach is described more in detail in the next sections.

For the AMR generation, we evaluated several libraries and identified several problems with the pre-trained model. Therefore, we re-trained the model for the AMR generation. The motivation and data augmentation process are described in Sect. 4. The entity linking process after extracting the surface forms from the AMR graph is described in Sect. 5.

4 Data Augmentation and Training

There are already existing libraries and models for the generation of AMR graphs. The most prominent libraries are amrlib[3] and JAMR[4]. Both libraries provide pre-trained models. While JAMR is older in general, the pre-trained

---

[3] https://github.com/bjascob/amrlib.
[4] https://github.com/jflanigan/jamr.

model naturally has been trained on older training data provided by the Linguistic Data Consortium (LDC)[5]. In contrast, amrlib was updated last in June 2022[6]. The developer provides a pre-trained model based on BART Large [11] and utilizing AMR 3.0 training data by the LDC[7]. We utilize the amrlib library for our approach. Section 4.1 gives a short introduction on AMR graphs. Section 4.2 describes flaws of the pre-trained model and our motivation to re-train the model. Section 4.3 depicts the data augmentation process to generate more training data and eliminate the identified flaws of the pre-trained model.

4.1 Abstract Meaning Representation

AMR graphs are directed, labeled, acyclic graphs. Each graph corresponds to one sentence[8]. An important aspect of AMR graphs is the negligence of the specific syntax of natural language. Sentences with similar meaning are aimed to obtain the same AMR graph even if they are phrased differently. This characteristic is essential for KGQA as different natural language questions can lead to the same formal query.

The AMR specification[9] explains the roles (used as edge property) and node labels to describe NL in a graph. For QA, the `amr-unknown` node label is essential as it represents the unknown fact a question asks for. Consider the following AMR graph for the question *Who is the mayor of Berlin?*:

```
(z0 / mayor
    :domain (z1 / amr-unknown)
    :location (z2 / city
                  :name (z3 / name
                            :op1 "Berlin")))
```

The node `mayor` has two child nodes: the one for Berlin and the one for an unknown resource. This means, the query constructed to answer this question must find something which is connected to Berlin through a relationship called `mayor`. This syntax is very close to the way, how facts are represented in KGs. In this way, AMR graphs are eligible as intermediate representation between an NL question and the formal query[10].

Named entities are represented using a `name` node with a parent node that describes the name node in a categorical way (namely as `city` in our example). The child nodes of the `name` node contain the parts of the surface form. Thus, the identification of named entities is straightforward using AMRs: finding `name` nodes in the graph and collecting the labels of their child nodes.

However, the correctness of the graphs depends on the sample data utilized to train the model. For our purpose of entity linking, we identified some problems

---

[5] The newest model is trained on 2016 LDC training data.

[6] as of December 2022.

[7] https://catalog.ldc.upenn.edu/LDC2020T02.

[8] c.f. https://amr.isi.edu/index.html.

[9] http://www.isi.edu/~ulf/amr/help/amr-guidelines.pdf.

[10] as shown in [9,17].

with the existing models trained on the LDC AMR 3.0 dataset. The next section describes those issues in detail.

4.2 LDC Training Data and Its Flaws

Since 2013, the LDC released datasets containing sample AMR graphs. The latest dataset – AMR 3.0 – has been released in January 2020 containing 59,255 sample AMR graphs from 13 categories. The dataset contains manually generated AMR graphs for sentences "from broadcast conversations, newswire, weblogs, web discussion forums, fiction and web text"[11]. The main problem of this training data is the case sensitivity of all sentences. This means, the casing of the words and surface forms (for named entities) is always correct. But for user-generated content – especially in QA scenarios – correct casing cannot be expected and this is a critical issue for the generation of correct AMR graphs[12]. Consider the question *What type of film is on the nose?*. The question refers to the movie *On the Nose* released in 2001 starring Dan Aykroyd and Robbie Coltrane. Please observe the incorrect casing of the surface form of the movie. Unfortunately, the model trained on the LDC AMR 3.0 dataset produces the following AMR graph for the question with incorrect casing:

```
(o / on-the-nose
    :domain (f / film
            :mod (t / type
                    :mod (a / amr-unknown)))))
```

In addition, we identified another problem with the pre-trained model regarding the entity linking task. Surface forms of named entities containing single quotes are also problematic in some cases. For the question *What is the significance of artists of The Beatles' Story?* the pre-trained model only identifies *The Beatles* as a named entity of type *story*.

Therefore, we decided to re-train the model regarding these issues. The next section describes the process of generating the training data automatically.

4.3 Generation of Augmented Training Data

We utilized the train splits of the KGQA benchmark datasets LC-QuaD 2.0 (based on Wikidata) [5] and QALD-9 (based on DBpedia) [20] for our approach. Both datasets are QA datasets containing NL questions, the respective SPARQL queries, and the answers from the underlying KG.

For our purpose, we created entity linking datasets by extracting the named entities from the SPARQL queries. As we identified two different issues with the pre-trained model, we also followed different approaches to automatically generate training data. We describe the generation process briefly for both approaches in the following paragraphs.

---

[11] https://catalog.ldc.upenn.edu/LDC2020T02.

[12] cf. the training dataset of the SMART task challenge 2022: https://smart-task.github.io/2022/.

Casing Problem. For each question of the training dataset, we check if the main label(s) of the respective named entities are contained in the question in correct casing. If so, we utilize the pre-trained model to generate the AMR graph and check if all components of the main labels of the contained entities are correctly contained in the graph as child nodes of the `name` nodes. If so, the question and the phrases of the child nodes in the AMR graph are converted to lowercase again and the graph is added as training data. We generate more similar training records using named entities of the same type as the required named entity in the original question. For instance, *On the Nose* is of `rdf:type dbo:Film`. We retrieve more instances of type `Film` and repeat the data augmentation process with the main labels of those entities. In this way, we created over 100,000 additional training records regarding the casing issue.

Surface Forms with Single Quotes. Again, for each question of the training datasets, we retrieve the referenced named entities and their respective ontology types. If the entity is referenced in the question using the main label, we generate similar questions utilizing the main labels of named entities of the same type containing single quotes. We enclose the surface form of the referenced entity with double quotes and generate the AMR graph. In this way, we generate the question *Give me all actors starring in movies directed by and starring "Lil' JJ".* from the original of question of the QALD9 training dataset: *Give me all actors starring in movies directed by and starring William Shatner..* If all components of the surface form are contained as child nodes in the name node, we remove the double quotes in the question and add the graph to the training data. In this way, we generated another 2,500 training graphs.

Utilizing the generated training data, we re-trained three AMR models in addition to the already pre-trained model. In the remainder of the paper, the different models are referred to as following:

- LDC – model only trained on LDC AMR 3.0
- LDC+LC – model trained on LDC AMR 3.0 + augmented data for lower cased questions
- LDC+QU – model trained on LDC AMR 3.0 + augmented data with entities containing quotes in the label
- LDC+QU+LC – model trained on LDC AMR 3.0 + all augmented data

We utilized BART Large [11] as well as the PEGASUS language model[13] and evaluated different configurations on both options.

For the training process, the training data is split into train, dev and test splits (0.7 : 0.1 : 0.2) and the correctness of the predicted graphs are evaluated using a SMATCH score[14]. We achieved the best results utilizing BART Large with a batch size of 16 and 32 epochs for all models. The SMATCH scores for this configuration are 0.819 (LDC+QU) and 0.877 (LDC+LC and LDC+QU+LC) respectively. Hence, the best training process achieves a SMATCH score 4%

---

[13] https://huggingface.co/docs/transformers/model_doc/pegasus.
[14] https://amr.isi.edu/smatch-13.pdf.

higher than the score achieved only using AMR 3.0 as training data[15]. We evaluated all four models for our further entity linking process. The models are available as download[16] [17].

5 Entity Linking

The second part of our entity linking process is the actual mapping of extracted surface forms to the desired KG and choosing the most probable candidate in case of ambiguous phrases. Section 5.1 describes the extraction of the surface forms from the AMR graph in detail. Section 5.2 gives an insight into our mapping dictionary and the characteristics of the named entity candidates we take into account. The ranking process is described in Sect. 5.3.

5.1 Label Extraction from the AMR Graph

As already mentioned, named entities are referenced using a `name` node an associated child nodes in the AMR graph. For our sample question *what type of film is on the nose?* the child nodes are connected to the `name` node using the edge roles `:op1`, `:op2`, and `:op3`. We collect the node labels of the child nodes and order them according to their edge roles.

But, we noticed some remarkable results of the AMR generation. In some cases, the AMR graph contains phrases that are not contained in the input question. Consider the question *What file format is the environment of Grand Theft Auto III?*. Our re-trained model (and also the pre-trained model) generates an AMR graph that contains a name node for the phrase *Grand Watch Auto III*. Apparently, this results from the language model (in our case BART) which replaces the probable unknown node label with a known label.

Therefore, we generate all k-grams of the input question, where k is the number of token in the surface form extracted from the AMR graph. We calculate the similarity of all k-grams with the surface form using Levenshtein distance. The k-gram with the lowest distance – above the threshold of a minimum similarity of 70% – is chosen as the respective surface form.

5.2 Mapping to Underlying KB

For the dictionary of entities within the underlying KG, we utilize various information. The labels are collected from main labels and alternative labels. As we use RDF/OWL KGs – Wikidata and DBpedia, the main labels are collected using `rdfs:label` information. Alternative labels are collected differently, depending on the KG. For DBpedia, we use the main labels of redirects and disambiguation resources. Wikidata provides alternative labels using

---

[15] The SMATCH score for BART Large is stated as 0.837 trained on LDC AMR 3.0.
[16] https://doi.org/10.5281/zenodo.7442882.
[17] instructions on how to use the models with amrlib can be found here: https://github.com/bjascob/amrlib-models.

`skos:alternativeLabel` as property. With this collection, we receive a wide range of labels but also increase the ambiguity of many labels in our dictionary. Therefore, we added a score for each label that corresponds to the distance of the label to the main label of the entity. In general, we calculate the Levenshtein distance, but also take into account if the label is an abbreviation of the main label or a synonym or a commonly used substring, such as a family name of a person. The calculation of the score is described more in detail in [18].

In addition, we use the indegree of the entity when considered a node in the network of entities. For DBpedia, we utilize the incoming Wikipedia page links. Wikidata provides a property `sitelinks` which corresponds to the indegree of page links.

And lastly, we add some context information to the entities in the dictionary. For DBpedia, we collect all labels of classes the entity is an instance of (in terms of `rdf:type`). These classes include umbel, yago and DBpedia ontology classes. For Wikidata, we utilize the property `instance of` (P31) to collect descriptive information for the entities.

Overall, the dictionary for the lookup contains the following information:

- URI – identifier of the named entity
- lowercase – the lowercased label
- score – distance of the label to the main label of the entity
- lowercase_stemmed – the stemmed version of the lowercase label
- indegree – the page link indegree resp. sitelinks
- types – context information (`rdf:type` resp. `instance of`)

Our dictionary for DBpedia entities contains over 19 million entries and the dictionary for Wikidata contains over 96 million entries.

The mapping to the entity dictionary is processed in three levels where the respective next level is only accessed if the current level does not provide results:

1. unstemmed equal mapping on the lowercase column
2. stemmed equal mapping on the lowercase_stemmed column
3. fuzzy search on the lowercase column using similarity function

In general, we retrieve the top 10 results using the similarity score for the fuzzy search. But also the first two steps of equal mappings can result in more than one entity candidate. Therefore, a ranking of the results and subsequent choice of the most relevant candidate is necessary. The ranking process is described in the next section.

5.3 Ranking

The ranking process is necessary in case multiple entity candidates are retrieved during the mapping process. The entity candidates possess three different features: a score – either the distance to the main label or in case of fuzzy search the similarity to the surface form, between 0.0 and 1.0, indegree, and type information.

For the ranking, we take into account the label-based score (in the remainder of the paper referred to as label score s_l) and calculate two additional scores for each entity candidate:

- score for the indegree – referred to as indegree score s_i, and
- a context-based score based on the types of the candidate and the context information of the question, referred to as context score s_c.

All scores are normalized to a value between 0.0 and 1.0.

The context score s_c requires context information from the input question. In QA scenarios, this context information is often very little, but the AMR graph sometimes provides additional information not contained in the question. For instance, the parent node of the `name` node for "Berlin" – from the example above – has the node label `city`. This is information not contained in the question itself. Additional context information can be collected using the node labels of all nodes of the AMR graph except for operator nodes, such as `amr-unknown`. The context for ranking the entity candidates for *Berlin* would thereby constitute of *city*, and *mayor*[18].

We evaluated both options of context creation: only the label of the parent node or the labels of all nodes in the graph. We want to emphasize that we use the parent node (in terms of a categorical type of the named entity) as context information for the disambiguation process and do not restrict the entity candidates to this type when mapping to the KG. The KG might not contain that information or is erroneous. The context score is then calculated based on how much of the context information from the question is contained in the types of the entity candidates.

For the final ranking, we make use of these three scores s_i, s_l, and s_c, and calculate a ranking score s_r. For the evaluation, we tested various combinations of weights for the different scores. The results are shown in Table 2 and discussed in Sect. 6.

Finally, the entity candidate with the highest ranking score s_r is chosen.

6   Evaluation

We evaluated our approach on two datasets and against six other entity linking approaches. We want to emphasize the following aspects of our evaluation:

- influence of the data augmentation process on the model
- influence of different options of context information
- evaluation of different configurations regarding the different scores for label distance, indegree and context matching

We introduce the datasets in Sect. 6.1. The experiments and the results are described and discussed in Sect. 6.2.

---

[18] which would not be helpful for that disambiguation case.

6.1 Datasets

For the evaluation of our approach, we utilize two different datasets. We want to attach importance on datasets that are appropriate for the actual QA process. That means, the dataset should contain the SPARQL queries that are required to answer the questions based on the respective KG. Therefore, we decided to utilize QALD-9 [20] and LC-QuaD 2.0 [5]. A pure entity linking dataset, such as NILK[19], is therefore not under consideration for our evaluation. More insights regarding contained types etc. on QALD-9 and the previous version of LC-QuaD 2.0 can be found in [19].

6.2 Experiments

In a first step, we evaluated different configurations for our approach. There are three aspects of the configuration of our approach:

- choice of AMR model
- creation of context information – only the parent node of the **name** node or labels of all nodes in the graph
- calculation of the ranking score – consisting of the context score s_c, the label score s_l and the indegree score s_i

Taking into account the three different scores, we calculated seven different ranking scores s_r:

- all scores unweighted: $s_r = (s_i + s_l + s_c)/3$
- one score double weighted respectively (makes 3 additional configurations), e.g. $s_r = ((2 * s_i) + s_c + s_l)/4$
- combination of two scores double weighted (makes another 3 additional configurations), e.g. $s_r = ((2 * s_i) + (2 * s_c) + s_l)/5$

Overall, we generated 14 different configurations per dataset and model.

6.3 Results

In the following, we present and discuss the results for our specific focal points of the evaluation separately.

Choice of AMR Model. We generated the results for all 14 configurations for each model and dataset. Table 1 shows the best results respectively. For both datasets, we can observe that our data augmentation process was able to improve the results. All results on re-trained models using our augmented data are increased compared to the results on the basic AMR model. Remarkably, the overall best results are achieved using the LDC+LC model (as expected LDC+QU+LC would achieve best results). Apparently, the model creates less correct graphs when trained on LDC+QU+LC. The amount of augmented data might play a

---

[19] https://zenodo.org/record/6607514.

role here – over 100,000 graphs for LC versus 2,500 for QU. Also, the structure of the sentences repeat, as we utilized the same training dataset to generate the augmented data. Therefore, the same sentences with different entities appear multiple times in the training data. This might result in conflicting graphs and we will include this aspect in future work.

Table 1. Evaluation results for the respective best configuration utilizing the different AMR models and on both datasets.

| | AMR model | | | | | | | | | | | |
| | LDC | | | LDC+LC | | | LDC+QU | | | LDC+QU+LC | | |
Dataset	R	P	F1	R	P	F1	R	P	F1	R	P	F1
QALD-9	85.7	82.8	84.2	**89.1**	**85.7**	**87.4**	86.7	82.8	84.7	87.7	82.9	85.2
LC-QuaD 2.0	59.7	64.6	62.1	**65.3**	**70.3**	**67.7**	63.8	68.0	65.8	64.8	69.7	67.2

Table 2 shows the results for all configurations utilizing the best performing AMR model – LDC+LC – for each dataset. We will discuss our results regarding the aspects of context creation and ranking score in the next paragraphs.

Creation of Context Information. For the context aspect, the results are clear. For both datasets, recall and precision are higher when the context information only consists of the node label of the parent node of the **name** node. As the parent node is a descriptive node of the **name** node, this is the most specific information for the disambiguation of the **name** node. We assume, the rest of the AMR graph to be too distractive as it describes also other name nodes and of course the actual result of the question.

Ranking Score. The results for the calculation of the ranking score are not that clear at least for the different datasets. On QALD-9 the best results are achieved having all scores unweighted or doubled weight for indegree and context score – conf 1 and conf 7 respectively. Apparently, the weighting of the label score decreases the overall result. But, the differences of recall and precision are too marginal for a definite conclusion.

For LC-QuaD the differences between score calculations are again not too significant. And only one combination achieves the best results: a doubled weighting of the label score and the indegree score. For this dataset, the context information does not seem to be too relevant. A tentative conclusion could be the accentuation of the indegree score. As the questions in the dataset often provide only minimal context, the popularity of the mentioned named entities might be of importance. A high indegree score emphasizes the most popular of the entity candidates.

With the experiments as described above, we were able to identify the configurations that achieve the best results on the utilized datasets. We also compared our results – naturally for the best configuration – with competing approaches.

Table 2. Results of our approach for 14 different configurations on QALD-9 and LC-QuaD 2.0 using the AMR model trained on LDC 3.0 and AUG LC

training data	QALD-9						LC-QuaD 2.0					
context	parent			all nodes			parent			all nodes		
	R	P	F_1	R	P	F_1	R	P	F_1	R	P	F_1
conf 1: s_l, s_i, s_c	**89.1**	**85.8**	**87.4**	87.7	84.8	86.2	64.4	69.1	66.7	65.0	70.0	67.4
conf 2: s_l, s_i, $2s_c$	87.2	84.3	85.7	86.2	83.3	84.7	63.6	68.3	65.9	64.7	69.4	67.0
conf 3: $2s_l$, s_i, s_c	88.2	84.7	86,4	86.2	82.8	84.5	64.6	69.2	66.8	65.2	70.0	67.5
conf 4: s_l, $2s_i$, s_c	88.2	85.2	86.6	87.7	84.8	86.2	64.7	69.7	67.1	64.6	69.6	67.0
conf 5: $2s_l$, $2s_i$, s_c	88.2	85.2	86.6	87.7	84.8	86.2	**65.3**	**70.3**	**67.7**	65.1	70.1	67.5
conf 6: $2s_l$, s_i, $2s_c$	87.2	83.8	85.5	85.8	81.2	83.4	64.0	68.7	66.3	64.8	69.5	67.1
conf 7: s_l, $2s_i$, $2s_c$	**89.1**	**85.8**	**87.4**	87.7	84.8	86.2	64.0	68.7	66.3	64.5	69.5	66.9

Comparison with Competing Approaches. We compared the results of our approach to six competing systems: AIDA, DBpedia Spotlight, Falcon 2.0 API, OpenTapioca, TagMe, and BLINK. For the LC-QuaD 2.0 dataset, we used the results published by the developers ([16] for Falcon 2.0 API) and by Diomedi et al. for the results of AIDA, DBpedia Spotlight, OpenTapioca, and TagMe [4].

We also compared our results on QALD-9 to the results of DBpedia Spotlight, TagMe, and Falcon 2.0 API. We retrieved the results of them by using the provided APIs[20]. BLINK is available as built-in option in the amrlib for the AMR generation. Links to named entities referenced to the English Wikipedia respectively DBpedia within the AMR graph are referenced with a `:wiki` tag. BLINK is also available as standalone version without the use of AMR. We evaluated both options. OpenTapioca only provides results for Wikidata and AIDA does not provide an API feasible for evaluation tasks[21].

All results of the competing systems compared to our best results are shown in Table 3. The Falcon 2.0 API does not provide configuration parameters. For DBpedia Spotlight, we achieved the best results using a confidence score of 0.6. The response of the TagMe API contains a `rho` parameter which corresponds to a confidence score. Without threshold, the recall for TagMe is 73% and the precision as low as 30%. In [7] the authors used a threshold of 0.1 for the `rho` parameter (achieving recall= 73.1%, precision= 39.0, F_1-score= 50.9%), but we achieved the best result in terms of F_1-score using `rho`=0.2, c.f. Table 3.

Obviously, our approach outperforms the other approaches. For QALD-9, we achieve a more than 10% higher recall than Falcon 2.0 API and even over 17% higher precision. For LC-QuaD 2.0, the difference to the best competing system is as high as 6% in terms of recall compared to TagMe, but our precision is

---

[20] Falcon: https://labs.tib.eu/falcon/falcon2/api-use,
Spotlight: https://www.dbpedia-spotlight.org/api,
TagMe: https://sobigdata.d4science.org/web/tagme/tagme-help.
[21] The authors do not wish to use the JSON web service for evaluation comparison and it also responses with HTTP 404 as of December 10th 2022.

Table 3. Results of our approach compared to other approaches

	QALD-9			LC-QuaD 2.0		
	R	P	F_1	R	P	F_1
DBpedia Spotlight	73.1	70.1	71.6	52.5	23.3	30.8
TagMe	70.2	52.2	59.9	59.4	29.5	37.4
AIDA	n.a.	n.a.	n.a.	30.5	38.5	33.1
BLINK (amrlib built-in)	64.4	61.0	62.5	n.a.	n.a.	n.a.
BLINK (standalone)	79.0	74.6	76.7	n.a.	n.a.	n.a.
OpenTapioca	n.a.	n.a.	n.a.	42.0	29.0	35.0
Falcon 2.0 API	78.0	68.1	72.7	56.0	50.0	53.0
Our approach	**89.1**	**85.8**	**87.4**	**65.3**	**70.3**	**67.7**

20% higher than by Falcon 2.0 API. Overall, we could show that our approach is efficient and achieves very good results. We will discuss questions where our approach fails further in the next section.

6.4 Discussion

We identified several reasons for failures and wrong linking processes of our approach:

– wrong AMR generation,
– missing label for surface form in entity dictionary,
– disambiguation errors, and
– specific characteristics of the SPARQL query.

There are two different aspects of wrong AMR generation: wrong structure/identification of named entities, and the modification of question phrases in the AMR graph. In the first case, the AMR model is not able to identify the named entity in the question correctly and does not provide a **name** node or only parts of the actual surface form of the entity in the **name** node.

A second problem with the AMR generation is the modification of question parts within the AMR. As already described in Sect. 5.1, we compare the label constructed from the child nodes of the **name** nodes with n-grams of the question. Consider the question *When did Dracula's creator die?*. The AMR model modifies *Dracula* to *drago*. The levenshtein distance between *drago* and *Dracula* is 5 – when case sensitivity is considered – and too high for our pre-defined threshold.

The lexical gap is still a problem when it comes to QA scenarios as named entities can be referenced with multiple surface forms. For instance, the question *Which subsidiary of TUI Travel serves both Glasgow and Dublin?* asks for the airports of Dublin and Glasgow which both are represented by own named entities in the underlying KG. But, the airports are only referenced by mentioning the names of their location.

Disambiguation errors are also a major challenge especially when only little context is given. For instance, the QALD-9 dataset contains the question *What are the names of the Teenage Mutant Ninja Turtles?*. Our approach disambiguates the surface form *Teenage Mutant Ninja Turtles* to the entity of the movie dbr:Teenage_Mutant_Ninja_Turtles_(2014_film). But the query asks for the more general resource of the original series. We often see a similar behavior of our approach when the question asks for a movie or a movie character. Mostly, the most popular entity candidate (as per our best performing configuration) is chosen which is often not the entity for the original movie or character.

Lastly, another challenge is the comprehension of the underlying KG. In some cases the detected named entities are not relevant for the specific SPARQL query dependent on the KG. Or the SPARQL query requires more entities not even mentioned in the question to retrieve the answer for the question. Consider the task *Give me all taikonauts*. The required SPARQL query for that question based on DBpedia requires the ontology class dbo:Astronaut and references to the named entities of P.R. China. Our approach links *taikonauts* to dbr:Astronaut. Clearly, this challenge cannot be solved only using entity dictionaries.

7   Summary

We presented our two-fold approach that makes use of AMR graphs to analyze the syntax of a question. In the second step, we follow an analytical approach to avoid the out-of-vocabulary problem, but also to be able to apply our algorithm to any KG. With our data augmentation process, we were able to improve the AMR model by re-training it using automatically generated training data.

We provide an exhaustive evaluation taking into account context options and weights for the entity candidate ranking. Our results show that the categorical description of a name node should be preferred over using all information of the question as context for the disambiguation. Unfortunately, the evaluation of weights on the ranking scores does not show clear results to draw conclusions. The two datasets are using different KGs and therefore different characteristics of the KGs could be the cause. Future work would include evaluations on more datasets based on DBpedia and Wikidata.

We also discussed failures of our approach. Some of the issues might be eliminated by additional training data. For instance, the model could be trained to not split surface forms in case of consecutive words beginning with an upper case. Another problem is the modification of the phrases of the question in the AMR graph. We need to examine additional training and parsing parameters to prevent this modification.

Overall, our presented approach shows very promising results as it outperforms other existing entity linking systems. Our future work includes the further improvement of our approach as briefly discussed above.

Acknowledgement. The author wants to thank Khaoula Benmaarouf and Kanchan Shivashankar for their help in preparing some of the data utilized for this paper.

References

1. Bender, E.M., Koller, A.: Climbing towards NLU: on meaning, form, and understanding in the age of data. In: Proceedings of the 58th Annual Meeting of the Association for Computational Linguistics, pp. 5185–5198. Association for Computational Linguistics (2020). https://doi.org/10.18653/v1/2020.acl-main.463
2. Delpeuch, A.: OpenTapioca: Lightweight entity linking for Wikidata. CoRR abs/1904.09131 (2019). http://arxiv.org/abs/1904.09131
3. Devlin, J., Chang, M.W., Lee, K., Toutanova, K.: BERT: pre-training of deep bidirectional transformers for language understanding (2018). https://doi.org/10.48550/ARXIV.1810.04805
4. Diomedi, D., Hogan, A.: Entity linking and filling for question answering over knowledge graphs. In: Natural Language Interfaces for the Web of Data (NLIWOD) Workshop (2022)
5. Dubey, M., Banerjee, D., Abdelkawi, A., Lehmann, J.: LC-QuAD 2.0: a large dataset for complex question answering over Wikidata and DBpedia. In: Cruz, I., et al. (eds.) ISWC 2019. LNCS, vol. 11779, pp. 69–78. Springer, Cham (2019). https://doi.org/10.1007/978-3-030-30796-7_5
6. Ferragina, P., Scaiella, U.: Tagme: on-the-fly annotation of short text fragments (by Wikipedia entities). In: Proceedings of the 19th ACM International Conference on Information and Knowledge Management (CIKM 2010), pp. 1625–1628. Association for Computing Machinery, New York (2010). https://doi.org/10.1145/1871437.1871689
7. Ferragina, P., Scaiella, U.: Fast and accurate annotation of short texts with Wikipedia pages. IEEE Softw. **29**(1), 70–75 (2012). https://doi.org/10.1109/MS.2011.122
8. Jiang, H., et al.: LNN-EL: a neuro-symbolic approach to short-text entity linking. In: Proceedings of the 59th Annual Meeting of the Association for Computational Linguistics and the 11th International Joint Conference on Natural Language Processing, vol. 1, pp. 775–787. Association for Computational Linguistics (2021). https://doi.org/10.18653/v1/2021.acl-long.64
9. Kapanipathi, P., et al.: Leveraging abstract meaning representation for knowledge base question answering. In: Zong, C., Xia, F., Li, W., Navigli, R. (eds.) Findings of the Association for Computational Linguistics (ACL/IJCNLP 2021). Online Event, 1–6 August 2021. Findings of ACL, vol. ACL/IJCNLP 2021, pp. 3884–3894. Association for Computational Linguistics (2021). https://doi.org/10.18653/v1/2021.findings-acl.339
10. Lee, Y.S., Astudillo, R., Thanh Lam, H., Naseem, T., Florian, R., Roukos, S.: Maximum Bayes Smatch ensemble distillation for AMR parsing. In: Proceedings of the 2022 Conference of the North American Chapter of the Association for Computational Linguistics: Human Language Technologies, pp. 5379–5392. Association for Computational Linguistics, Seattle (2022). https://doi.org/10.18653/v1/2022.naacl-main.393
11. Lewis, M., et al.: BART: denoising sequence-to-sequence pre-training for natural language generation, translation, and comprehension (2019). https://doi.org/10.48550/ARXIV.1910.13461
12. Li, B.Z., Min, S., Iyer, S., Mehdad, Y., Yih, W.T.: Efficient one-pass end-to-end entity linking for questions. In: EMNLP (2020)

13. Mendes, P.N., Jakob, M., García-Silva, A., Bizer, C.: DBpedia spotlight: shedding light on the web of documents. In: Proceedings of the 7th International Conference on Semantic Systems (I-Semantics 2011), pp. 1–8. Association for Computing Machinery, New York (2011). https://doi.org/10.1145/2063518.2063519
14. Milne, D., Witten, I.H.: Learning to link with Wikipedia. In: Proceedings of the 17th ACM Conference on Information and Knowledge Management (CIKM 2008), pp. 509–518. Association for Computing Machinery, New York (2008). https://doi.org/10.1145/1458082.1458150
15. Neelam, S., et al.: SYGMA: system for generalizable modular question answering overknowledge bases. CoRR abs/2109.13430 (2021). https://arxiv.org/abs/2109.13430
16. Sakor, A., Singh, K., Patel, A., Vidal, M.E.: Falcon 2.0: an entity and relation linking tool over Wikidata. In: Proceedings of the 29th ACM International Conference on Information and Knowledge Management (CIKM 2020), pp. 3141–3148. Association for Computing Machinery, New York (2020). https://doi.org/10.1145/3340531.3412777
17. Shivashankar, K., Benmaarouf, K., Steinmetz, N.: From graph to graph: AMR to SPARQL. In: Proceedings of the 7th Natural Language Interfaces for the Web of Data (NLIWoD) co-located with the 19th European Semantic Web Conference (ESWC 2022), Hersonissos, Greece, 29th May 2022. CEUR Workshop Proceedings, vol. 3196 (2022). http://ceur-ws.org/Vol-3196
18. Steinmetz, N.: Context-aware semantic analysis of video metadata. Ph.D. thesis, University of Potsdam (2014). http://opus.kobv.de/ubp/volltexte/2014/7055/
19. Steinmetz, N., Sattler, K.U.: What is in the KGQA benchmark datasets? Survey on challenges in datasets for question answering on knowledge graphs. J. Data Semant. **10**(3–4), 241–265 (2021). https://doi.org/10.1007/s13740-021-00128-9
20. Usbeck, R., Gusmita, R.H., Ngomo, A.N., Saleem, M.: 9th challenge on question answering over linked data. In: Choi, K., et al. (eds.) Joint proceedings of the 4th Workshop on Semantic Deep Learning (SemDeep-4) and NLIWoD4: Natural Language Interfaces for the Web of Data and 9th Question Answering over Linked Data challenge (QALD-9) co-located with 17th International Semantic Web Conference (ISWC 2018), Monterey, California, United States of America, 8th–9th October 2018. CEUR Workshop Proceedings, vol. 2241, pp. 58–64 (2018). http://ceur-ws.org/Vol-2241/paper-06.pdf
21. Yosef, M.A., Hoffart, J., Bordino, I., Spaniol, M., Weikum, G.: AIDA: an online tool for accurate disambiguation of named entities in text and tables. Proc. VLDB Endow. **4**(12), 1450–1453 (2011). https://doi.org/10.14778/3402755.3402793

REGNUM: Generating Logical Rules with Numerical Predicates in Knowledge Graphs

Armita Khajeh Nassiri[1](✉)(iD), Nathalie Pernelle[1,2](✉)(iD), and Fatiha Saïs[1](✉)(iD)

[1] LISN, CNRS (UMR 9015), Paris Saclay University, 91405 Orsay, France
{armita.khajehnassiri,nathalie.pernelle,fatiha.sais}@lri.fr
[2] LIPN, CNRS (UMR 7030), University Sorbonne Paris Nord, Paris, France

Abstract. Mining logical rules from a knowledge graph (KG) can reveal useful patterns for predicting facts, curating the KG, and identifying trends. However, many rule mining systems face challenges when working with numerical data because numerical predicates can take a large number of values, leading to a huge search space. In this work, we present REGNUM, a system that addresses this issue by generating rules with numerical constraints. REGNUM extends the body of rules mined from a KG by using supervised discretization of numerical values with decision trees to increase the confidence of the rules without sacrificing significance. Our experimental results show that the numerical rules have a higher overall quality than the parent rules and are effective at making better predictions.

Keywords: Rule Mining · Numerical Predicates · KG Completion

1 Introduction

Knowledge graphs (KG) are large collections of facts about the world or a specific domain stored in a machine-readable format. There is no surprise that these large KGs incorporate different forms of knowledge within them. There has been a tremendous amount of work in the literature trying to capture and mine this knowledge. One such line of work is mining logical rules in KGs. These rules can serve to complete the KG, detect erroneous data, or uncover the knowledge that is not explicitly stated in the ontology. For instance, if we don't know one's place of residence, we could infer that they live in the same place as their spouse. In addition, rules can serve to debug the KG. If the spouse of someone lives in a different city, then this may indicate a problem. Finally, rules are useful in downstream applications such as fact-checking [1], ontology alignment [11,16], or predicting completeness [9]. Furthermore, such rules have the advantage of being explainable, interpretable, and transferable to unseen entities.

One challenge in finding logical rules in KGs lies in the exponential size of the search space, which varies depending on the considered language bias. To address this issue, several recent approaches have relied on sampling or approximate confidence calculations [10,30], and [23]. Another common technique [21,23,30], from standard

C. Pesquita et al. (Eds.): ESWC 2023, LNCS 13870, pp. 139–155, 2023.
https://doi.org/10.1007/978-3-031-33455-9_9

inductive logic programming (ILP), is to mine not all rules but only enough rules to cover the positive examples. Likewise, this speeds up the computation but may lose many interesting rules. While existing rule mining approaches are effective, they are unable to consider rules that involve constraints defined on numerical values. We believe that such constraints can be highly relevant in domains such as finance, public health, or life science as they can help uncover useful information, such as the increased like-lihood of a patient with heart disease having taken mood stabilizers for over five years. In this paper, we take a step forward toward incorporating numerical predicates into logical rules in a way that supports knowledge expansion. We focus on constraints that express the membership or non-membership to a value interval. One approach to imple-menting these constraints would be to discretize the values of the numerical predicates in a pre-processing step. However, this would not provide with relevant constraints for each rule and yield to loss of information. On the other hand, calculating constraints while the rule mining technique explores the search space (as it generalizes or refines the rule) results in having to re-calculate the interval at each step, making the approach time-consuming over large graphs. To this end, we propose a novel method that involves two steps: first, to obtain First-order logic (FOL) rules using existing efficient rule min-ing tools, and second, to enrich the rules with numerical predicates and constraints. For this second step, we consider the problem as a classification problem to obtain the inter-vals based on the correct and incorrect predictions of the rule, guided by the quality of the rules. The main contributions of our paper are:

- REGNUM is a novel approach that enhances the expressiveness of the rules gen-erated by a rule mining system by incorporating numerical constraints expressed through value intervals. To our knowledge, REGNUM is the first approach to utilize intervals in rules mined from large RDF graphs.
- REGNUM efficiently selects intervals that increase the rule's confidence using exist-ing supervised discretization techniques that best distinguish the correct and incor-rect predictions made by the rule.
- Since some value intervals can be too specific to lead to relevant rules, REGNUM considers both the membership and the non-membership of a value to an interval to offer more possibilities of generating a rule with high quality.
- The experimental evaluation shows that the numerical rules generated by REGNUM using the rules provided by two state-of-the-art rule mining systems, AMIE and AnyBURL, have a higher overall quality score and can potentially improve predic-tion results.

2   Related Work

Rule mining over a dataset has received a lot of attention from researchers, resulting in many published works on the subject.

Association Rule Mining. Association rule mining (ARM) is a widely used data min-ing technique that identifies frequent patterns among items and transactions based on a minimum number of observations. It typically generates if-then patterns, represented by association rules $X \rightarrow Y$, indicating that the presence of X suggests the pres-ence of Y in the same transaction. However, ARM faces challenges when dealing with numerical attributes since the values of these attributes rarely repeat themselves. To address this, a special type of association rule called quantitative association rules have been developed, which involves at least one numerical attribute in the rule, such as $(25 < age < 40) \wedge (3K < salary < 5K) \rightarrow (120K < loan < 200K)$. Quantitative association rule mining (QARM) can be achieved through different strategies, including discretization-based approaches such as pre-processing steps to partition numerical data [27] or statistical analysis of variables and distribution of the numerical variables [2], and optimization-based approaches where numeric attributes are optimized during the mining process, for instance with the use of genetic algorithms [15,20,26].

Nevertheless, these patterns or dependencies are restricted to single variables and are different from the logical rules relevant to complex relationships present in knowledge graphs.

Inductive Logic Programming (ILP). Inductive logic programming (ILP) systems can automatically find rules based on positive and negative examples. For example, WARMR [7] extends the Apriori algorithm to mine association rules in multiple relations. Other ILP-based approaches, such as DL-Learner [5], focus on learning expressive concept definitions, including numerical constraints. However, ILP is not suitable for the open world assumption (OWA) in large KGs, where counter-examples are not declared, and missing information cannot be treated as negative but rather unknown.

FOL Rule on Knowledge Graphs. Finding logical rules on large knowledge graphs (KGs) has been addressed in several works that use specific language biases, pruning criteria, and optimization strategies to scale the rule-mining process.

AMIE [17] is a state-of-the-art rule mining system for KGs. It is fast and exhaustive, i.e., it mines all connected and closed rules given thresholds defined on quality measures (e.g., confidence and head coverage) and a specified maximum number of atoms. AMIE can discover rules that involve constants (e.g., age(x,53)). However, these rules can be too specific and not interesting when it comes to these predicates. RuDiK [24] proposes a non-exhaustive approach to mine logical rules that are more expressive. RuDiK can predict the absence of a fact and allows us to perform comparisons beyond equality by using relationships from the set $rel \in \{<, \leq, \neq, \geq, >\}$. An example of such rules would be: $R_1 : p_1(x, v_0) \wedge p_2(y, v_1) \wedge v_0 > v_1 \Rightarrow p_3(x, y)$, where v_0 and v_1 are values from the KG itself, not thresholds.

Rule mining systems, such as AnyBURL [19], focus only on rules based on graph paths. AnyBURL is a bottom-up approach that starts with sampling specific paths and uses generalization techniques to expand it such that the obtained rule has a high confidence. An extension of AnyBURL [18] uses reinforcement learning to sample better paths from the start. The advantage of these systems is that they are any-time, meaning they can trade time for rule quality and quantity. However, like AMIE, AnyBURL is not able to find interesting rules with numerical predicates and can only consider them as constants.

Another family of rule mining systems is differentiable rule-based inference methods such as NeuralLP [29]. This body of work maps each entity to a vector and each relation to an adjacency matrix. DRUM [25] proposes changes to the NeuralLP to support variable-length rules. Another extension, NeuralLP-num [28], can learn rules involving numerical features. Like RuDiK, these rules can involve negative atoms or make pair-wise comparisons between numerical values of different atoms in the rules (e.g., R_1). Furthermore, the rules produced by NeuralLP-num can also include classification operators, which are sigmoid functions over numerical values of atoms with numerical predicates in the rule. For example, a rule with a classification operator could be of the form $f\{y_1, y_2 : p_1(X, y_1), p_2(X, y_2)\} > 0.5 \land p_3(X, Z) \Rightarrow p_4(X, Z)$ where f is the sigmoid function and p_1 and p_2 are numerical predicates.

To the best of our knowledge, RuDiK and NeuralLP-num are the only works in the literature that can mine interesting rules with numerical predicates on large KGs. However, both techniques are limited to using numerical values from the knowledge graph and applying functions or comparisons between them. They are unable to discover numerical intervals or thresholds as constraints to enhance the quality of the rules and derive additional knowledge. To fill this gap, REGNUM has been developed to incorporate such constraints into the rules.

3   Preliminaries

This section presents the definitions and notations used in the rest of the paper.

Definition 1. RDF Knowledge Graph. *In an RDF knowledge graph $\mathcal{G}$, a collection of facts is represented as triples of the form $\{(subject, predicate, object) \mid subject \in \mathcal{I}, predicate \in \mathcal{P}, object \in \mathcal{I} \cup \mathcal{L}\}$ where the set of entities is denoted as $\mathcal{I}$, the set of predicates is denoted as $\mathcal{P}$, and the set of literals (such as numbers and strings) is denoted as $\mathcal{L}$. Additionally, we define $\mathcal{P}_{num}$ as the subset of predicates whose range consists solely of numerical values.*

Definition 2. Atom. *An atom is a basic well-formed first-order logic formula of the form $p(X, Y)$, where p is a predicate[1] and X, Y are either constants or variables[2]. If an atom's arguments are constants, the atom is said to be "grounded" and can be treated as a fact.*

Definition 3. (Horn) Rule. *A rule $r : \mathcal{B} \Rightarrow H$ is a first-order logic formula where the body $\mathcal{B}$ is a conjunction of atoms $B_1, ..., B_n$ and the head H is a single atom. A rule is closed if every variable appears at least twice in the rule. Two atoms are connected if they share at least one variable. A rule is connected if all atoms in the rule are transitively connected.*

Definition 4. Prediction of a Rule. *Given a rule $r : \mathcal{B} \Rightarrow H$ and a substitution of the rule $\sigma(r)$, $\sigma(H)$ is a prediction for r if all the atoms of $\sigma(\mathcal{B})$ belong to the knowledge graph $\mathcal{G}$. A prediction is correct if $\sigma(H) \in \mathcal{G}$.*

For a rule $r : \mathcal{B} \Rightarrow H$, we have the following quality measures as defined in [17]. In the absence of identity links (i.e., *owl:sameAs*), we assume that the Unique Name Assumption (UNA) is fulfilled. If identity links exist, a pre-processing step is required to compute the quality measures and functionality score accurately.

Definition 5. Support. *The support $supp(r) := |\{(x, y) : \mathcal{B} \land H(x, y)\}|$ measures the number of correct predictions made by the rule.*

---

[1] Membership to a class, can also be represented with a binary predicate, i.e., type(X, Y).
[2] Variables are represented using lowercase letters whereas capitalized letters denote constants.

Definition 6. Head Coverage. *Head coverage represents the proportion of instantiations of the head atom that are correctly predicted by the rule.*

$$hc(r) = \frac{supp(r)}{|\{(x,y) : H(x,y) \in \mathcal{G}\}|}$$

In order to calculate the confidence of a rule, counter-examples are necessary. Knowledge graphs are based on the open world assumption (OWA), meaning they only contain positive examples, and missing facts are not necessarily false. We adhere to the Partial Completeness Assumption (PCA) to account for counter-examples.

Definition 7. Functionality Score. *The functionality score of a predicate is a value between 0 and 1 that measures the ratio of subjects that the property is related to in $\mathcal{G}$ to the total number of triples with that predicate. The inverse functionality score $ifun(p)$ is the functionality score for the inverse of the predicate p.*

$$fun(p) := \frac{|\{x : \exists y : p(x,y) \in \mathcal{G}\}|}{|\{(x,y) : p(x,y) \in \mathcal{G}\}|}$$

Under PCA, if a fact $p(x,y) \in \mathcal{G}$ and if $fun(p) > ifun(p)$, then no other fact for x holding with the predicate p is correct and can be considered as a counter-example (i.e., $p(x,y') \notin \mathcal{G}$). On the other hand, if $ifun(p) > fun(p)$, then all $p(x',y) \notin \mathcal{G}$.

Definition 8. PCA confidence. *The PCA confidence of the rule r measures the precision of the rule under the PCA, i.e., the ratio of correct predictions or support to the total number of predictions made by the rule. More precisely, if $fun(H) > ifun(H)$,*

$$pca\_conf(r) = \frac{supp(r)}{|\{(x,y) : \exists y' : \mathcal{B} \wedge H(x,y')\}|}$$

Based on definition of counter-examples under PCA, if $ifun(H) > fun(H)$, then the denominator, namely PCA body size, becomes $|\{(x,y) : \exists x' : \mathcal{B} \wedge H(x',y)\}|$ in the above equation.

4   REGNUM

In this section, we describe REGNUM, a system that automatically enriches the connected and closed rules mined on a given knowledge graph, regardless of the method used to mine them, with numerical predicates by constraining the introduced numerical values to specified intervals. REGNUM aims to enhance the PCA confidence in the considered rules while ensuring that the rules do not become overly specific.

4.1   Problem Statement

This approach aims to mine numerical rules that are defined as follows:

Definition 9. Numerical Rule. *A numerical rule is a first-order logic formula of the form:* $B \wedge C \Rightarrow H$, *where B is a conjunction of atoms of the KG and where the range values of the numerical atoms of B can be constrained using C, conjunction (resp. a disjunction) of atoms that express their membership (resp. their non-membership) to an interval* $[inf, sup]$.

Example 1. Here are two examples of numerical rules with constraints defined on numerical predicates:
r_1 : $\text{worksIn}(x,y) \wedge \text{hasPopulation}(y,w) \wedge w \in [1000, 5500] \wedge \text{hasHusband}(x,z) \Rightarrow \text{worksIn}(z,y)$
r_2 : $\text{worksIn}(x,y) \wedge \text{hasHusband}(x,z) \wedge \text{age}(z,a) \wedge \text{hasPopulation}(y,w) \wedge (w \notin [1000, 5500] \vee a \notin [50, \infty)) \Rightarrow \text{worksIn}(z,y)$

Generating the complete set of numerical rules that fulfill quality measure thresholds (e.g., $minHC$ and $minconf$ in [17]) can be very time-consuming. This is because the intervals used to constrain the range of numerical predicates must be recalculated each time a rule is generalized or refined as the search space is explored. This ensures that the constraints applied to the rule are appropriate for the updated rule.

To overcome this issue, we propose an approach that builds on the shoulders of the rules mined by an existing rule-mining technique (i.e., parent rules) and expands the body of these rules through an enrichment process to generate numerical rules. More precisely,

- A numerical rule is considered relevant if it improves the PCA confidence of its parent rule by at least a $marginC$ without its head coverage decreasing more than $marginHC$. This criterion guarantees that the rule has higher PCA confidence than its parent rule while preventing over-fitting the KG.
- The enrichment process of a parent rule is driven by considering diverse sets of numerical predicates. This means that once a numerical rule involving a particular numerical predicate p is relevant in a constraint that involves n numerical atoms, the approach will not consider larger sets of atoms that involve p.
- The search strategy to obtain constraints on the numerical predicates relies on tree-based algorithms.

4.2   Rule Enrichment with Numerical Predicates Algorithms

Given a knowledge graph $\mathcal{G}$, a set of closed rules $\mathcal{R}$ mined from $\mathcal{G}$, called *parent rules*, and thresholds $marginC$ and $marginHC$ as introduced in Sect. 4.1, our approach REGNUM is able to enrich the parent rules in $\mathcal{R}$ to obtain relevant and diverse numerical rules. The algorithm we describe in Algorithm 1 performs the following steps.

(1) Pre-processing Step [line 1 in Algorithm 1]. As a pre-processing step, we first identify the set of numerical predicates, denoted as $\mathcal{P}_{num}$ in $\mathcal{G}$. We use the domain and range definition axioms if they are available in the ontology, and if not, we discover them by considering the range of values they take. We also compute the functionality score, as defined in Definition 7, for all predicates in the head of the parent rules $\mathcal{R}$.

Algorithm 1: REGNUM

Input:
- $\mathcal{G}$: knowledge graph
- $\mathcal{R}$: set of parent rules mined on $\mathcal{G}$
- $marginHC, marginC$: margins on head coverage and PCA confidence

Output: $\mathcal{E}$: set of enriched rules

1   Identify P_{num} and compute functionality degree of predicates P
2   $\mathcal{E} = \emptyset$
3   **foreach** $r : \mathcal{B} \Rightarrow H$ *in* $\mathcal{R}$ **do**
4   compute quality measure $hc(r)$ and $pca\_conf(r)$; compute $minHC$ and $minC$; create an empty queue q_{atoms};
5   **for** $p_{num} \in P_{num}$ **do**
6   **if** $hc(p_{num}(x_i, x_{new}) \wedge \mathcal{B} \Rightarrow H) > minHC$ **then**
7   Enqueue $p_{num}(x_i, x_{new})$ in q_{atoms}
8
9   **end**
10      $ln = 1$ // number of numerical atoms
11   **while** $|q_{atoms}| > ln$ **do**
12   **for** $\mathcal{B}_{num}$ *created by combining* ln *atoms from* q_{atoms} **do**
13            $r_s : \mathcal{B}_{num} \wedge \mathcal{B} \Rightarrow H$
14   **if** $hc(r_s) > minHC$ **then**
15               $< X, Y > \leftarrow construct\_prediction\_classes(\mathcal{G}, r_s)$;
16               $r_{nodes} \leftarrow discretize(< X, Y >, minHC, minC)$;
17   **foreach** r_{node} *in* r_{nodes} **do**
18   **if** $hc(r_{node}) > minHC$ *and* $pca\_conf(r_{node}) > minC$ **then**
19   add $r_{node} \Rightarrow H$ to $\mathcal{E}$;
20
21   **end**
22
23   **end**
24   remove from q_{atoms} atoms that resulted in a numerical rule;
25         $ln\mathbin{+}= 1$
26   **end**
27   **end**
28   **return** $\mathcal{E}$;

Then, for each parent rule $r \in \mathcal{R}$, we proceed with the following steps.

(2) Computation of $minHC$ **and** $minC$ [line 4 in Algorithm 1]. A numerical rule obtained by enriching a parent rule r is considered relevant if its PCA confidence increases by at least $marginC$ and if its head coverage does not decrease by more than $marginHC$. We first query the KG to compute $pca\_conf(r)$ and $hc(r)$ if the rule mining system does not provide them, and we calculate the $minHC : (1 - marginHC) * hc(r)$ and $minC : (1 + marginC) * pca\_conf(r)$ that the enriched rule must satisfy in order to be considered relevant.

(3) Enqueue Numerical Atoms [lines 5–8 in Algorithm 1.] In this step, we find all possible numerical atoms that can enrich the parent rule and store them in q_{atoms}. We consider the set of all variables $vars = \{x_1, \ldots, x_n\}$ that appear in the rule r, and enqueue all the atoms $p_{num}(x_i, x_{new})$ with $x_i \in vars$, x_{new} is a new variable and such that the head coverage of $p_{num}(x_i, x_{new}) \wedge \mathcal{B} \Rightarrow H$ is greater than $minHC$. Otherwise, the atom is discarded since its conjunction with other atoms will only lead to lower head coverage due to monotonicity.

Example 2. Let $r_1 : \text{workPlace}(x_1, x_2) \Rightarrow \text{birthPlace}(x_1, x_2)$, be a parent rule. The atom involving the numerical predicate hasPopulation with variables x_1 will be pruned as the rule $\text{hasPopulation}(x_1, x_3) \wedge \text{workPlace}(x_1, x_2) \Rightarrow \text{birthPlace}(x_1, x_2)$ does not satisfy the $minHC$.

(4) Selection of Numerical Atoms and Generation of the Best Intervals [lines 11–20 in Algorithm 1]. Our objective is to identify relevant numerical rules that meet the quality measure requirements by utilizing the fewest numerical predicates. To construct these numerical rules, we iteratively search through the space of possible conjunctions of atoms in q_{atoms}. We begin with a single numerical atom ($ln = 1$) and continue until the queue q_{atoms} does not contain ln atoms or more. At iteration ln, we apply the following steps:

Enriching r with ln numerical atoms [lines 11–12 in Algorithm 1] We retrieve ln atoms from q_{atoms} and consider their conjunctions $\mathcal{B}_{num} : p_{num_1}(x_i, x_{n+1}) \wedge \cdots \wedge p_{num_l}(x_j, x_{n+l})$ to construct:

$$r_s : \mathcal{B}_{num} \wedge \mathcal{B} \Rightarrow H$$

We query the knowledge graph and proceed with the enrichment process only if r_s satisfies the $minHC$ as constraining the values of these numerical predicates will not satisfy $minHC$ either.

Example 3. At iteration 3, we can have $r_s : \text{worksIn}(x, y) \wedge \text{hasHusband}(x, z) \wedge \text{hasPopulation}(y, w) \wedge \text{age}(x, v) \wedge \text{hasRevenue}(x, u) \Rightarrow \text{worksIn}(z, y)$ involving three different numerical predicates hasPopulation, age and hasRevenue that satisfies the $minHC$.

Classification problem based on rule predictions [line 14 in Algorithm 1]. The rules r_s created in the previous step are used to classify the instantiations of $\mathcal{B}_{num} : p_{num_1}(x_i, x_{n+1}) \wedge \cdots \wedge p_{num_l}(x_j, x_{n+l})$ as correct or incorrect examples and define a binary classification problem.

In this classification step, we build a class A to represent the set of instantiations $(x_{n+1}, \ldots, x_{n+l})$ of the numerical values of $\mathcal{B}_{num}$ that lead to a correct prediction $H(x_a, x_b)$ for the rule r_s. The examples of A are defined as follows:

$$\{(x_{n+1}, \ldots, x_{n+l}) \mid \mathcal{B}(x_1, \ldots, x_n) \wedge \mathcal{B}_{num}(x_i, \ldots, x_j, x_{n+1}, \ldots, x_{n+l}) \wedge H(x_a, x_b)\}$$

Moreover, we build a class B to represent the set of instantiations $(x_{n+1}, \ldots, x_{n+l})$ of the numerical values of $\mathcal{B}_{num}$ that lead to an incorrect prediction for the rule r_s under

PCA if the $fun(H) > ifun(H)$, i.e., the predictions $H(x_a, x_b)$ such that $H(x_a, x_b) \notin \mathcal{G} \wedge \exists x_b' \, H(x_a, x_b') \in \mathcal{G}$.

$$\{(x_{n+1}, \ldots, x_{n+l}) \mid \mathcal{B}(x_1, \ldots, x_n) \wedge \mathcal{B}_{num}(x_i, \ldots, x_j, x_{n+1}, \ldots, x_{n+l}) \wedge \exists x_{b'} \, H(x_a, x_b')\}$$

If $ifun(H) > fun(H)$, we classify the instantiation as incorrect if a fact does not exist in the KG for the target object and if there exists at least one subject for this object.

We generate a data structure $< X, Y >$ that represents for each correct and incorrect prediction $H(x_a, x_b)$, the set of numerical values per numerical predicate of $\mathcal{B}_{num}$ (since the numerical predicates can be multi-valued), and the label Y. The correct and incorrect example values are retrieved from the KG through the queries defined for the label A and B.

Example 4. Let r_2 : worksIn$(x, y) \wedge$ hasHusband$(x, z) \Rightarrow$ worksIn(z, y) be the considered parent rule. One possible refinement r_s of this rule to consider in step 2 would be: hasPopulation$(y, w) \wedge$ worksIn$(x, y) \wedge$ hasHusband$(x, z) \wedge$ hasRevenue$(z, r) \Rightarrow$ worksIn(z, y) In this rule, the target variable is z since $ifun($worksIn$) < fun($worksIn$)$. Consider the following facts in $\mathcal{G}$: {worksIn$(Marie, Lyon)$, worksIn$(Marie, Gordes)$, worksIn$(Joe, Lyon)$, hasPopulation$(Lyon, 513\ 000)$, hasPopulation$(Gordes, 2\ 000)$, hasHusband$(Marie, Joe)$, hasRevenue$(Joe, 1500)$, hasRevenue$(Joe, 800)$}. The triple worksIn$(Joe, Lyon)$ is a correct prediction of r_s, and for the introduced numerical features $<$ hasPopulation$_y$, hasRevenue$_z >$ the two sets of numerical values $(513000, 800)$, and $(513000, 1500)$ are examples that belong to class A. worksIn$(Joe, Gordes)$ is an incorrect prediction. The numerical values $(2000, 800)$ and $(2000, 1500)$ are examples that belongs to class B. If we do not know where Joe works, the possible instantiations of the numerical values do not belong to any class.

Constraining the numerical rule to intervals [lines 16–19 in Algorithm 1]. To obtain a set of rules for classes A and B defined by a rule r_s, we can discretize the values of the numerical predicates. For this purpose, different methods can be considered, including decision-tree-based approaches, e.g., CART [4], sequential covering approaches, e.g., RIPPER [6], or FURIA [14], QARM techniques introduced in Sect. 2, or other discretization techniques.

We aim to find the purest intervals that can effectively differentiate between examples in class A and class B. However, if we limit ourselves to constraints that only express interval membership for correct groundings of class A, the resulting rule may have low head coverage if the interval is too specific. On the other hand, if we exclude intervals that lead to incorrect predictions, we may overlook rules with high confidence that can enhance the accuracy of predictions in KG completion tasks.

Therefore, we consider both candidate rules. For instance, it is common for people to work in the city where they were born if that city has between 50,000 and 500,000 inhabitants. However, we can also consider a rule that excludes megacities with over 1,000,000 inhabitants.

Hence, we decided to employ a supervised method to discretize the continuous values of numerical predicates in $\mathcal{B}_{num}$ and keep track of the number of correct and incorrect predictions falling in each interval to consider both membership and non-membership constraints. This method involves constructing a univariate CART Decision Tree (DT), where the numerical predicates serve as features. The DT is binary and built using impurity-based criteria, specifically entropy, as the splitting criteria.

The root of the tree corresponds to the numerical $r_s : \mathcal{B}_{num} \wedge C \wedge \mathcal{B} \Rightarrow H$ where C is initially empty. At each split, the instance space is divided into two subspaces by constraining the range values of one of the atoms in $\mathcal{B}_{num}$ to the split threshold and hence updating C. The rules at each child node r_{node} are created according to the rule of the parent node and the split made at that node.

More specifically, if a split is made using an atom $p(x,y)$ and a threshold α at node i, a membership constraint creates a rule for the left child by updating C with $\wedge y \in (-\infty, \alpha]$ and $\wedge y \in [\alpha, \infty)$ for the right child. A non-membership constraint, however, creates the rule for its left child by updating C with $\vee y \notin (-\infty, \alpha]$ for the left child and $\vee y \notin [\alpha, \infty)$ for the right child.

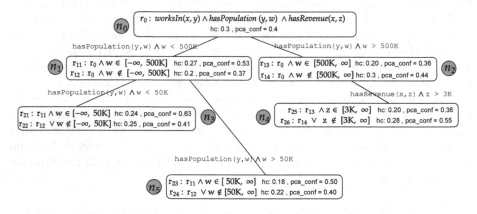

Fig. 1. Example of a part of the DT and the considered rules at each node

Example 5. Consider the parent rule $r :$ worksIn$(x,y) \Rightarrow$ livesIn(x,y) and enriching the body of r with two predicates $r_0 :$ worksIn$(x,y) \wedge$ hasPopulation$(y,w) \wedge$ hasRevenue(x,z). Figure 1 depicts the construction of the rules at each node for a part of the tree to constrain the values of w and z with membership or non-membership. The $minHC = 0.23$ and the $minC = 0.5$. Node n_1 shows the inclusion and exclusion rules as well as their respective head coverage and PCA confidence constructed using the constraint hasPopulation$(y,w) \wedge w < 500K$.

Furthermore, we ensure that each node only contains the most concise rule. This means that if an atom $p(x,y)$ has already been selected for a split in the path from the root to the child nodes, the constraint already exists in the body of the parent node. Therefore, instead of adding the constraint, we update the constraint on y (i.e., the range values of the atom $p(x,y)$).

Example 6. At node n_5, the rule r_{23} is expressed as worksIn(x, y) $\wedge$ hasPopulation(y, w) $\wedge$ $w \in [50K, 500K]$ $\wedge$ hasRevenue(x, z). At node r_{22}, the rule is worksIn(x, y) $\wedge$ hasPopulation(y, w) $\wedge$ $w \notin (-\infty, 50K]$ $\wedge$ hasRevenue(x, z). At node n_4, the rule r_{26} is expressed as worksIn(x, y) $\wedge$ hasPopulation(y, w) $\wedge$ hasRevenue(x, z) $\wedge$ $(w \notin [500K, \infty) \vee z \notin [3k, \infty))$.

We use the stopping criteria based on $minHC$ and $minC$ of each node's inclusion and exclusion rules to decide when to stop splitting further. To do this, we calculate the size of class A and B using $< X, Y >$ as defined in the previous step. We stop if the number of different instantiations for the head that belong to class A is less than $minHC * headsize(r)$, and if the number for class B is less than $pca\_bodysize(r_s) - \frac{supp(r_s)}{minC}$. In other words, if neither of the rules can satisfy the expected $marginC$ and $marginHC$, we stop splitting.

Example 7. In Fig. 1, rule r_{24} will not appear in node n_5 because generalizing r_{12} with the constraint of the split would not exclude enough incorrect predictions to satisfy the $minC$.

We could select all nodes that meet the requirements of $minHC$ and $minC$. However, to limit the number of generated numerical rules and avoid redundant rules covering the same instances, we have implemented a strategy that selects the most general rules along each path from the root to the leaves. Specifically, we choose the rules with the highest PCA body size.

Example 8. In Fig. 1, rules corresponding to nodes n_1, n_3, and n_4 in Fig. 1, namely r_{11}, r_{21}, and r_{25} respectively, meet the requirements of $minHC$ and $minC$. We include r_{11} and r_{25} in $\mathcal{E}$ because nodes r_{11} and r_{21} are along the same path from the root, and r_{11} is the more general rule.

Rule Diversity[line 21 in Algorithm 1]. In order to maintain diversity, after each iteration, we remove any atoms that have led to a numerical rule with parent rule r that meets the conditions of $minHC$ and $minC$ from q_{atoms}, as explained in Sect. 4.1.

5   Experimental Evaluation

We have conducted two groups of experiments. First, we evaluate the quality of the set of enriched rules vs. their parent rules. The parent rules have been obtained by running rule mining techniques of AMIE [17] and AnyBURL [18]. Secondly, we have evaluated the performance of KG completion task using these enriched rule sets.

Datasets. We consider three different benchmark datasets that involve numerical values. *FB15K-237-num* and *DB15K-num* are variants of Freebase and DBPedia knowledge graphs involving numerical predicates and values proposed in [12]. *LitWD19K* is one of the three datasets proposed in LiterallyWikidata [13], which is a recent dataset gathered from Wikidata and Wikipedia with a special focus on literals. Table 1 shows the statistics for these datasets.

Table 1. Statistics of the benchmark datasets.$|\mathcal{G}_t|$ denotes the size of test set.

Dataset	$|\mathcal{I}|$	$|\mathcal{P}|$	$|\mathcal{P}_{num}|$	$|\mathcal{G}|$	$|\mathcal{G}_t|$
DB15K-num	12,867	278	251	79,345	9,789
FB15K-237-Num	14,541	237	116	272,115	1,215
LitWD19K	18,986	182	151	260,039	14,447

Experimental Setup. All experiments are run on a single machine with a processor 2.7 GHz, 8 cores, and 16GB of RAM that runs Mac OS X 10.13. REGNUM is written in Python and we have used Stardog[3] RDF data management system. The source code and the datasets used in our experiments are publicly available[4]. The time taken for rule generation ranges from 20 minutes to 15 hours, depending on the number of parent rules, their quality, and the KG.

5.1 Rules Quality Assessment

In this first set of experiments, we compare the quality of the parent rules that could be enriched with the set of enriched rules. Specifically, we compare the percentage of gain in terms of PCA confidence and head coverage. To measure the overall quality of the rules, we rely on $F_r = 2 * \frac{pca\_conf(r)*hc(r)}{pca\_conf(r)+hc(r)}$, which is a harmonic mean between the pca_conf and hc. This is because just a high pca_conf or a high hc is not a good indicator of the overall quality of a rule (i.e., the rule can be too specific or not yield good predictions).

Setup. We have run AMIE with default values $minHC = 0.01$ and $min\_pca\_conf = 0.1$, and maximum rule length of 3, on the *LitWD19K* and *DBPedia15K* datasets. To limit the number of parent rules, we used an increased $minHC = 0.1$ when running AMIE on *FB15K-237-num*. As AMIE mines only closed rules, no post-processing of the rules obtained was needed. We have run AnyBURL with default parameters except for the maximum rule length being set to 3, and the rules are learned for 100s with the $min\_conf = 0.03$. We performed post-processing on the obtained rules to retain only closed rules. REGNUM enriches the parent rules with $marginC = 20\%$, $marginHC = 10\%$.

Table 2. Statistic of rules mined by AMIE, compared to numerical rules in terms of the quality measure.

Dataset	$|\mathcal{R}|$	$|\mathcal{R}_{enriched}|$	$|\mathcal{E}|$	level 1	level 2	level 3	g_{conf}	g_{hc}	g_F
DB15K-num	4,163	402	2,783	2,747	36	0	+38.3%	−1.2%	+9.9%
FB15K-237-num	9,591	1,187	5,434	4,640	789	5	+28.6%	−4.2%	+9.8%
LitWD19K	2,481	859	9,068	7,764	1,272	12	+31.2%	−2.5%	+3.5%

---

[3] https://www.stardog.com/.
[4] https://github.com/armitakhn/REGNUM.

Table 2 and Table 3 detail the number of parent rules mined $\mathcal{R}$ by AMIE and Any-BURL, respectively. The number of parent rules that could be enriched with numerical predicates $\mathcal{R}_{enriched}$ and the number of numerical rules obtained by REGNUM $\mathcal{E}$ are also presented. On the three datasets, we compute the average of the rules' pca_conf, hc, and F measure of $\mathcal{R}_{enriched}$ and on the numerical rules $\mathcal{E}$. In the Tables 2 and 3, we provide the percentage of improvement of PCA confidence, head coverage, and F measure of $\mathcal{E}$ over parent rules $\mathcal{R}_{enriched}$, denoted by g_{conf}, g_{hc}, and g_F, respectively. The results indicate that the pca_conf of the numerical rules increased significantly across all benchmark datasets, irrespective of the rule mining technique used for obtaining parent rules. This improvement has been achieved without sacrificing much head coverage, and the overall quality of the rules (F measure) increased.

When we set a more relaxed value for $marginHC$, we noticed a decrease in the overall quality of rules. However, we were able to obtain more numerical rules. For instance, setting $marginHC$ to 20% on FB15K-237-num in Table 2 reduces the g_F from 9.8% to 6.22%, but the number of enriched rules increases to 10,141 with 1,744 parent rules that could be enriched.

Table 3. Statistic of rules mined by AnyBURL, compared to numerical rules regarding the quality measure.

Dataset	$|\mathcal{R}|$	$|\mathcal{R}_{enriched}|$	$|\mathcal{E}|$	level 1	level 2	level 3	g_{conf}	g_{hc}	g_F
DB15K-num	1,539	515	2,184	2,052	132	0	+30.4%	−3.5%	+3.3%
FB15K-237-num	7,959	1,688	7,252	6,597	654	1	+29.1%	−3.5%	+8.1%
LitWD19K	1,758	787	7,721	6,407	1,266	48	+29.0%	−3.8%	+4.5%

Approximately 25% of the rules on across all datasets incorporate membership constraints that include intervals. For example, the LitWD19K dataset mines 2,585 rules with membership constraints and 6,483 rules with non-membership constraints using parent rules from AMIE. Similarly, the AnyBURL dataset comprises 2,157 numerical rules with membership and 5,564 numerical rules with non-membership. As elaborated in Sect. 4.2, we expect that membership rules will generally have lower head coverage and higher PCA confidence compared to non-membership rules, which exclude incorrect predictions. This is demonstrated to be true when we limit the rules to only inclusion or only exclusion rules. For instance, for the LitWD19K dataset, the membership rules obtained from AMIE parent rules show g_{conf} of 36.8%, and g_{hc} of −3.0%, whereas for non-membership rules g_{conf} is 30.1%, and g_{hc} is −2.2%. We observe the same trend in all datasets.

We have also explored the use of the Minimum description length principle (MDLP) [8], and Optimal Binning [22] as supervised discretization techniques. However, these methods can only discretize a single numerical predicate at a time and cannot handle combinations of numerical predicates. To ensure a fair comparison, we have limited the rules of REGNUM to level 1. We have found that DT can enrich more parent rules by providing more relevant intervals. For example, on the FB15K-237-num dataset in Table 2, using MDLP results in the enrichment of 940 parent rules ($|\mathcal{R}_{enriched}|$), leading to a total of 7,005 numerical rules ($|\mathcal{E}|$) with a g_F of 11.7%. On the same dataset, the results of Optimal Binning are $|\mathcal{R}_{enriched}| = 874$, $|\mathcal{E}| = 3{,}832$, and $g_F = 12.0\%$. Finally, using only REGNUM rules with one numerical predicate (level 1) enriches 1,042 parent rules, resulting in 4640 numerical rules and a g_F of 10.13%, which is higher than the other two methods.

5.2 KG Completion

In this second set of experiments, we focus on the task of knowledge graph completion, where we aim to evaluate the efficacy of integrating the numerical rules obtained via REGNUM with the parent rules for knowledge graph completion. KG completion aims to predict a missing object o in a fact $(s, p, o) \notin \mathcal{G}$. While most current research on KG completion employs sub-symbolic approaches that involve embedding the graph into a low-dimensional vector space, rule-based methods offer the advantage of interpretability and explainability.

For each test data (s, p, o), we examine all the rules mined with predicate p in the head of the rule, i.e., $p(x, y)$. For each such rule, we execute a SPARQL query by substituting x with the subject of the test data s and obtain a set of predictions generated by the rule. Each candidate c can be given by a set of rules $C = \{R_1, ..., R_n\}$. We use four different aggregation strategies to assign a score to each candidate based on the rules that predicted them. The aggregation methods we considered are:

1. The democracy aggregation where the score depends on the number of rules that fired a candidate $\mathcal{S}_c = |C|$.
2. The max-aggregation $\mathcal{S}_c = max\{pca\_conf(R_1), ..., pca\_conf(R_n)\}$ where the rule with the highest PCA confidence defines the score.
3. The noisy-or aggregation $\mathcal{S}_c = 1 - \prod_{i=1}^{n}(1 - pca\_conf(R_i))$.
4. The weighted-F aggregation $\mathcal{S}_c = \Sigma_{i=1}^{n} \frac{1}{\#Prediction(R_i)} * f(R_i)$ which penalizes the rules that result in many predictions (candidates).

The rules with statistics reported in Table 2 are used to find the candidates. To assess the performance of the rules, we report the Hits@10 result, which is the number of correct head terms predicted out of the top 10 predictions. Table 4 shows the results of KG completion on three datasets using the rules mined by AMIE vs. the numerical rules of REGNUM added to the set of rules of AMIE. The four different aggregations are used to score the candidates and report the hits@10 results in the filtered setting (i.e., a prediction that already exists in $\mathcal{G}$ or $\mathcal{G}_t$ will not be ranked).

On all three datasets, we found that adding the rules of REGNUM to the set of rules from AMIE improved the performance of knowledge graph completion when using the Max aggregation method. This suggests that numerical rules can improve predictions. With the Max aggregation method, we know that whenever a candidate is selected, it is because a numerical rule of REGNUM with higher confidence than its parent rule has been chosen. If no numerical rule exists, the parent rule will be chosen.

The marginal benefit of numerical rules on these benchmark datasets can be attributed to the small number of rules that could be enriched, as well as the generic nature of the datasets that do not heavily rely on numerical predicates for accurate predictions. Hence, to better understand the impact of the enriched rules, we focus only

Table 4. Hits@10 results of KG completion with rules of AMIE ($\mathcal{R}$) and numerical rules of REGNUM with the rules of AMIE ($\mathcal{R} \cup \mathcal{E}$)

	FB15K-237-num		DBPedia15K		LitWD19K	
	AMIE	AMIE+REGNUM	AMIE	AMIE+REGNUM	AMIE	AMIE+REGNUM
Democ	61.6	61.0	33.8	35.8	31.9	31.6
Max	70.5	71.7	34.5	36.9	32.4	32.6
Noisy-or	68.1	66.9	34.7	37.0	32.5	32.4
Weighted-F	69.1	68.3	34.7	37.0	32.9	32.8

on the rules that could be enriched, $\mathcal{R}_{enriched}$, and use them for knowledge graph completion. Table 5 shows the results using the Max aggregation method, indicating improvements in the accuracy of knowledge graph completion when enriched rules are combined with their respective parent rules.

Table 5. Hits@1 and Hits@10 results of KG completion with $\mathcal{R}_{enriched}$ and $\mathcal{R}_{enriched} \cup \mathcal{E}$

	AMIE		AMIE+REGNUM	
	Hits@1	Hits@10	Hits@1	Hits@10
DBPedia15K	4.6	7.7	6.4	10.2
FB15K-237-num	5.5	14.7	6.3	15.3
LitWD19K	12.6	22.5	13.9	23.6

6   Conclusion and Future Work

In this paper, we introduced REGNUM, a novel approach that builds numerical rules on the shoulders of the rules mined by a rule-mining system. The parent rules are enriched with numerical predicates, with their values being constraints to membership or non-membership to intervals obtained through supervised discretization. We showed that the enriched rules have a higher average quality and can assist in improving the accuracy of rule mining systems on the knowledge graph completion task.

Future work will explore alternative methods of obtaining constraints, such as using sequential covering approaches and applying numerical rules to other domains where numerical values are crucial for predictions. We also plan to investigate more complex aggregation techniques, such as latent-based Aggregation [3], and consider using an in-memory database to improve query run-time, as proposed in AMIE3 [17]. Ultimately, we intend to compare our results regarding both run-time and optimality with an approach that finds optimal intervals while mining the numerical rule. We expect our approach to be faster but less accurate.

Acknowledgements. This work has been supported by the project PSPC AIDA: 2019-PSPC-09 funded by BPI-France.

References

1. Ahmadi, N., Lee, J., Papotti, P., Saeed, M.: Explainable fact checking with probabilistic answer set programming. CoRR abs/1906.09198 (2019)
2. Aumann, Y., Lindell, Y.: A statistical theory for quantitative association rules. In: Proceedings of the Fifth ACM SIGKDD International Conference on Knowledge Discovery and Data Mining, KDD 1999, pp. 261–270. Association for Computing Machinery, New York (1999). https://doi.org/10.1145/312129.312243
3. Betz, P., Meilicke, C., Stuckenschmidt, H.: Supervised knowledge aggregation for knowledge graph completion. In: Groth, P., et al. (eds.) ESWC 2022. LNCS, vol. 13261, pp. 74–92. Springer, Cham (2022). https://doi.org/10.1007/978-3-031-06981-9_5
4. Breiman, L., Friedman, J., Stone, C.J., Olshen, R.A.: Classification and Regression Trees. Taylor & Francis, Milton Park (1984)
5. Bühmann, L., Lehmann, J., Westphal, P.: Dl-learner-a framework for inductive learning on the semantic web. J. Web Semant. **39**, 15–24 (2016)
6. Cohen, W.W.: Fast effective rule induction. In: Proceedings of the Twelfth International Conference on Machine Learning, pp. 115–123. Morgan Kaufmann (1995)
7. Dehaspe, L., Toironen, H.: Discovery of Relational Association Rules. In: Džeroski, S., Lavrač, N. (eds.) Relational Data Mining, pp. 189–208. Springer, Heidelberg (2001). https://doi.org/10.1007/978-3-662-04599-2_8
8. Fayyad, U.M., Irani, K.B.: Multi-interval discretization of continuous-valued attributes for classification learning. In: IJCAI (1993)
9. Galárraga, L., Razniewski, S., Amarilli, A., Suchanek, F.M.: Predicting completeness in knowledge bases. In: de Rijke, M., Shokouhi, M., Tomkins, A., Zhang, M. (eds.) Proceedings of the Tenth ACM International Conference on Web Search and Data Mining, WSDM 2017, Cambridge, United Kingdom, 6–10 February 2017, pp. 375–383. ACM (2017)
10. Galárraga, L., Teflioudi, C., Hose, K., Suchanek, F.M.: Fast rule mining in ontological knowledge bases with AMIE+. VLDB J. **24**(6), 707–730 (2015)
11. Galárraga, L.A., Preda, N., Suchanek, F.M.: Mining rules to align knowledge bases. In: Proceedings of the 2013 Workshop on Automated Knowledge Base Construction, AKBC@CIKM 2013, San Francisco, California, USA, 27–28 October 2013, pp. 43–48. ACM (2013)
12. García-Durán, A., Niepert, M.: KBLRN: end-to-end learning of knowledge base representations with latent, relational, and numerical features. In: Proceedings of the 34th Conference on Uncertainty in Artificial Intelligence (UAI) (2018)
13. Gesese, G.A., Alam, M., Sack, H.: LiterallyWikidata - a benchmark for knowledge graph completion using literals. In: Hotho, A., et al. (eds.) ISWC 2021. LNCS, vol. 12922, pp. 511–527. Springer, Cham (2021). https://doi.org/10.1007/978-3-030-88361-4_30
14. Hühn, J., Hüllermeier, E.: FURIA: an algorithm for unordered fuzzy rule induction. Data Mining Knowl. Discov. **19**(3), 293–319 (2009). https://doi.org/10.1007/s10618-009-0131-8
15. Jaramillo, I.F., Garzás, J., Redchuk, A.: Numerical association rule mining from a defined schema using the VMO algorithm. Appl. Sci. **11**(13), 6154 (2021). https://doi.org/10.3390/app11136154
16. Khajeh Nassiri, A., Pernelle, N., Saïs, F., Quercini, G.: Generating referring expressions from RDF knowledge graphs for data linking. In: The Semantic Web – ISWC 2020 (2020)
17. Lajus, J., Galárraga, L., Suchanek, F.: Fast and exact rule mining with AMIE 3. In: Harth, A., et al. (eds.) ESWC 2020. LNCS, vol. 12123, pp. 36–52. Springer, Cham (2020). https://doi.org/10.1007/978-3-030-49461-2_3
18. Meilicke, C., Chekol, M.W., Fink, M., Stuckenschmidt, H.: Reinforced anytime bottom up rule learning for knowledge graph completion. arXiv preprint arXiv:2004.04412 (2020)

19. Meilicke, C., Chekol, M.W., Ruffinelli, D., Stuckenschmidt, H.: Anytime bottom-up rule learning for knowledge graph completion. In: Proceedings of the Twenty-Eighth International Joint Conference on Artificial Intelligence, IJCAI 2019, pp. 3137–3143 (7 2019)

20. Minaei-Bidgoli, B., Barmaki, R., Nasiri, M.: Mining numerical association rules via multi-objective genetic algorithms. Inf. Sci. **233**, 15–24 (2013). https://doi.org/10.1016/j.ins.2013.01.028. https://www.sciencedirect.com/science/article/pii/S0020025513001072

21. Muggleton, S.: Learning from positive data. In: Muggleton, S. (ed.) ILP 1996. LNCS, vol. 1314, pp. 358–376. Springer, Heidelberg (1997). https://doi.org/10.1007/3-540-63494-0_65

22. Navas-Palencia, G.: Optimal binning: mathematical programming formulation abs/2001.08025 (2020). http://arxiv.org/abs/2001.08025

23. Ortona, S., Meduri, V.V., Papotti, P.: Robust discovery of positive and negative rules in knowledge bases. In: 2018 IEEE 34th International Conference on Data Engineering (ICDE), pp. 1168–1179 (2018)

24. Ortona, S., Meduri, V.V., Papotti, P.: Rudik: rule discovery in knowledge bases. Proc. VLDB Endow. **11**(12), 1946–1949 (2018)

25. Sadeghian, A., Armandpour, M., Ding, P., Wang, D.Z.: DRUM: End-to-End Differentiable Rule Mining on Knowledge Graphs. Curran Associates Inc., Red Hook (2019)

26. Salleb-Aouissi, A., Vrain, C., Nortet, C.: Quantminer: a genetic algorithm for mining quantitative association rules. In: IJCAI, pp. 1035–1040 (2007)

27. Srikant, R., Agrawal, R.: Mining quantitative association rules in large relational tables. In: ACM SIGMOD Conference (1996)

28. Wang, P.W., Stepanova, D., Domokos, C., Kolter, J.Z.: Differentiable learning of numerical rules in knowledge graphs. In: International Conference on Learning Representations (2020). https://openreview.net/forum?id=rJleKgrKwS

29. Yang, F., Yang, Z., Cohen, W.W.: Differentiable learning of logical rules for knowledge base reasoning. In: Guyon, I., et al. (eds.) Advances in Neural Information Processing Systems, vol. 30. Curran Associates, Inc. (2017)

30. Zeng, Q., Patel, J.M., Page, D.: Quickfoil: scalable inductive logic programming. Proc. VLDB Endow. **8**(3), 197–208 (2014)

Classifying Sequences by Combining Context-Free Grammars and OWL Ontologies

Nicolas Lazzari[1,3] , Andrea Poltronieri[2] , and Valentina Presutti[1(✉)]

[1] LILEC, University of Bologna, Bologna, Italy
{nicolas.lazzari3,valentina.presutti}@unibo.it
[2] Department of Computer Science and Engineering, University of Bologna, Bologna, Italy
andrea.poltronieri2@unibo.it
[3] Department of Computer Science, University of Pisa, Pisa, Italy

Abstract. This paper describes a pattern to formalise context-free grammars in OWL and its use for sequence classification. The proposed approach is compared to existing methods in terms of computational complexity as well as pragmatic applicability, with examples in the music domain.

Keywords: sequence classification · context-free grammar · ontologies · music

1 Introduction

The introduction of formal grammars by Chomsky in the 50 s [7], and in particular Context Free Grammars (CFG), led to prolific research in the area of Natural Language Processing. Methods based on statistical language modeling have mostly replaced formal grammars, nevertheless research in this area is still relevant as many domains and tasks benefit from their application. For example, an important application of formal grammars concerns high level programming languages. Through an efficient parsing process [1], machine-level instructions can be abstracted in human readable instructions. Theoretically, every problem that can be abstracted as a *sequence of symbols* can be modeled with formal grammars, which makes them a suitable tool for *sequence classification*, the task we focus on in this paper. In the biology field, the classification of RNA secondary structures has been performed using CFG [9,15,35]. Similarly, in the music field, CFG are used to classify different types of harmonic and melodic sequences [3,24,36,39,41,42].

Background. A *language* is a collection of sequences, each defined according to a finite set of symbols [8]. A *grammar* can be interpreted as a function of a language, having a set of symbols as its domain, and a set of sequences as its

---

Alphabetical order.

C. Pesquita et al. (Eds.): ESWC 2023, LNCS 13870, pp. 156–173, 2023.
https://doi.org/10.1007/978-3-031-33455-9_10

range. Defining a formal grammar is a complex task that requires deep knowledge of the application domain as well as good modeling skills, to obtain an efficiently parsable grammar. CFGs can be parsed in less than $O(n^3)$ [43], with n the length of the string. However when symbols have ambiguous semantics and require additional attributes to be disambiguated, parsing a sequence is NP-complete [14]. Ambiguous symbols are a common issue, for instance in the case of polysemous words in natural language or diminished chords in music. This problem can be mitigated through the use of complex notations, such as SMILES [44] to represent molecules in the biology field or Harte [18] to represent musical chords. Nevertheless, these notations are either hard to interpret, requiring additional tools to be converted back into a human understandable format, or they cause loss of information.

We address the problem of sequence classification by proposing a hybrid approach that combines the use of Context Free Grammar (CFG) parsers with OWL ontologies. We define a pattern to formalise CFG by providing a novel definition for CFG based on Description Logic. We define a set of algorithms to produce an OWL ontology based on this pattern that supports the alignment of symbols in a sequence to its classes. Our approach is based on the identification of sub-sequences according to the taxonomy defined in the ontology. We argue that our proposal has a relevant pragmatic potential as it enables sequence classification based on semantic web knowledge representation, therefore supporting the linking of Context Free Grammars to web ontologies and knowledge graphs.

The contribution of this research can be summarised as follows:

- defining a novel formalisation of Context Free Grammars based on Description Logic;
- providing an algorithm for the conversion of such formalisation in OWL;
- demonstrating the correctness, computational complexity and applicability of the proposed method in the music domain.

The paper is organized as follows: in Sect. 2, an overview of related works on sequence classification is presented. Section 3 provides relevant definitions for Context Free Grammars that are used later in Sect. 4, to describe the formalisation of CFGs in DL. Section 5 describes our approach to sequence classification. In Sect. 6 we evaluate our method on the task of sequence classification in the music domain. Finally, in Sect. 7, we summarize the contribution and discuss future development.

2   Related Work

Relevant work to this contribution include: techniques for sequence classification, sequence model with grammars, approaches to integrate CFG and semantic web technologies, and their application in the music domain (cf. Sect. 6).

Sequence Classification (SQ) is the task of predicting the class of an input, defined as a sequence over time or space, among a predefined set of classes [31]. SQ is relevant in several application fields, such as genomics research [26], health informatics, abnormality detection and information retrieval [47], Natural Language Processing (NLP) [6,28]. In [47] different methodologies for SQ are identified, such as feature-based classification, sequence distance-based classification and support vector machines (SVM). The most advanced approaches mainly rely on Deep Learning (DL) [5,30]. SQ is relevant in the music domain, as sequences are at its core, for instance melodic and harmonic sequences that span over a temporal dimension. An example of sequence classification applied to music is [31], which addresses the recognition of *raga* using recurrent neural networks (LSTM-RNN).

Sequence Model with Grammars. There is a close relationship between sequences and formal grammars. A classic related task (ranging from natural language processing [27] to bio-informatics [9]) is *grammar inference* [49]. Grammars are used for the classification of sequences of different types, mainly for analysing genetic sequences [15,35]. There are applications of grammars for music classification. The most renowned example is the generative theory of tonal music (GTTM) [29], analogous to Chomsky's transformational or generative grammar. [7]. Although GTTM does not explicitly provide generative grammar rules, this work has inspired the formalisation of a wide range of context-free rules, describing different music genres [24,39,41], melody [3] and harmony [36,42]. These works are relevant input to our work as they formalise aspects of certain types of sequences into rules.

Sequence Model with OWL. There are proposals to use OWL to classify sequences. However, one of the main challenges when dealing with sequences in OWL is to organise the elements being described in an ordered fashion, as proposed in [12]. For instance, OWL reasoning is employed for classifying genomic data [46]. A method for analysing jazz chord sequences is proposed in [33]. This system is based on an ontology which, through reasoning, produces a hierarchical jazz sequence analysis. Similarly, two OWL ontologies, $\mathcal{MEO}$ and $\mathcal{SEQ}$, are presented in [45] that combined with a CFG parser support sequence classification. Nevertheless, this method is only able to represent *safely-concatenable* CFG, while we overcome this limitation in our approach (cf. Sect. 5.3).

3 Preliminaries

This section introduces the notation and the definitions used in Sect. 4, based on [20] that the reader can consult for details.

Definition 1 (Context Free Grammar). *A Context Free Grammar (CFG)* $G = (V, \Sigma, R, S)$ *consists of a finite set of non-terminal V (variables), a set of terminals Σ such that $\Sigma \cap V = \emptyset$, a set of functions $R \subseteq V \times (V \times R)^*$ (production), and a starting symbol $S \in V$.*

Definition 2 (Language of a grammar). *The language of a grammar* $G(V, \Sigma, R, S)$ *is defined as $L(G) = \{w \in \Sigma^* : S \overset{*}{\Rightarrow} w\}$, where $S \overset{*}{\Rightarrow} w$ represents the consecutive application of production $f \in R$ starting from the initial symbol S, called derivation.*

Example 1 (Context Free Grammar). Let $G = (V, \Sigma, R, S)$ with

$$V = \{\text{Expression}, \text{Bit}\}$$
$$\Sigma = \{0, 1, +\}$$
$$R = \{\text{Expression} \rightarrow \text{Expression} + \text{Expression} \mid \text{Bit } 0 \mid \text{Bit } 1 \mid 0 \mid 1,$$
$$\text{Bit} \rightarrow \text{Bit } 0 \mid \text{Bit } 1 \mid 0 \mid 1 \}$$
$$S = \text{Expression}$$

where $X \rightarrow X_1 \mid \cdots \mid X_n$ is a shorthand for $\{X \rightarrow X_1, \cdots X \rightarrow X_n\}$

Example 1 shows a simple grammar used to parse the sum of two binary numbers. Its language L, as defined in Definition 2, is of the form $L = \{0+0, 0+1, 1+0, 10+0, \cdots, 11010+10, \cdots\}$.

In order to express a concise and effective conversion method and its corresponding proof we only consider grammars in Chomsky Normal Form, as defined in Definition 3. This results in homogeneous productions in the form

$$A \rightarrow BC \quad \text{or} \quad A \rightarrow t$$

where $A, B, C \in V$ and $t \in \Sigma$.

Definition 3 (Chomsky Normal Form). *A Context Free Grammar is in Chomsky Normal Form (CNF) if the set of functions $R \subseteq V \times (V \backslash \{S\} \times R)^2$*

Note that the imposed restriction does not imply any loss in expressiveness, since any context-free grammar can be converted in CNF [20]. For instance, Example 1, converted in CNF, results in the grammar in Example 2.

Example 2 (Example 1 in Chomsky Normal Form). Let $G = (V, \Sigma, R, S)$ with

$$V = \{\text{Expression}, \text{Expression}_0, \text{Bit}, \text{Zero}, \text{One}, \text{Plus}\}$$
$$\Sigma = \{0, 1, +\}$$
$$R = \{\text{Expression} \rightarrow \text{Expression}_0 \text{ Expression} \mid \text{Bit Zero} \mid \text{Bit One} \mid 0 \mid 1,$$
$$\text{Expression}_0 \rightarrow \text{Expression Plus},$$
$$\text{Bit} \rightarrow \text{Bit Zero} \mid \text{Bit One} \mid 0 \mid 1,$$
$$\text{Plus} \rightarrow +,$$
$$\text{Zero} \rightarrow 0,$$
$$\text{One} \rightarrow 1\}$$

When parsing a language based on a grammar, it is useful to visualise the derivation process as a parse tree.

Definition 4 (Parse tree of a CFG). *A parse tree T of $G = (V, \Sigma, R, S)$ is a tree in which each leaf $l \in (V \cup \Sigma)$ and each inner node $n_i \in V$. Given $c_1 \cdots c_n$ the children of an inner node n_i then $\exists f \in R$ s.t. $f : n_i \rightarrow c_1 \cdots c_n$. [20]*

Corollary 1. *Given T the parse tree of a CFG in CNF $\Rightarrow T$ is a binary tree.*

Corollary 1 follows from Definitions 3 and 4, since each production is either a unary or a binary function. Figure 1a shows the parse tree of the sequence *1+0* from the grammar defined by Example 1 and Fig. 1b shows the parse tree the grammar defined by Example 2.

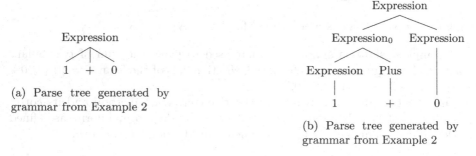

(a) Parse tree generated by grammar from Example 2

(b) Parse tree generated by grammar from Example 2

Fig. 1. Parse trees obtained from the sequence *1+0*

4   Formalising Context-Free Grammars Using Description Logic

As OWL is based on Description Logic (DL) theory, we define a DL-based formalisation of Context-Free Grammars (in Chomsky Normal Form), which we refer to as CFG-DL. CFG-DL is based on Definition 1, where variables and terminals are represented as concepts[1]. We demonstrate that any CFG can be converted in a CFG-DL (cf. Theorem 1) and that such conversion can be performed in $O(n)$ (cf. Theorem 2). Theorem 1 and its proof rely on the concept of *rolification*, which formalises axioms that act as rules in the form *if-then* [25]. For each concept C a corresponding axiom R_C is created and the restriction $C \equiv R_C.Self$ is imposed. By chaining together different axioms it is possible to define *if-then* rules. For a more in-depth explanation, please refer to Krisnadhi et al. [25].

Definition 5 (CFG-DL). *A CFG-DL $G_{DL} = (C_v, R, C_\Sigma, S)$ consists of a finite set of concepts C_v, a finite set of concepts C_Σ, a set of axioms R, and a starting concept $S \in C_v$.*

Theorem 1. *Every Context-Free Grammar G in Chomsky Normal Form can be converted in a CFG-DL G_{DL}.*

---

[1] DL concepts translate into OWL classes.

Proof. Given a Context-Free grammar $G = (V, \Sigma, R, S)$ in Chomsky Normal Form we can obtain the corresponding $G_{DL} = (C'_v, R', C'_\Sigma, S')$ as follows:

1. $\forall v \in V$ let C_v be a concept such that $C_v \sqsubseteq C'_v$
   $\implies \forall v \in V \exists C_v \sqsubseteq C'_v$, where C_v is the respective concept of the variable V.
2. $\forall t \in \Sigma$ let C_t be a concept such that $C_t \sqsubseteq C'_\Sigma$
   $\implies \forall t \in \Sigma \exists C_t \sqsubseteq C'_\Sigma$, where C_t is the respective concept of the terminal t.
3. Let $f \in R$. It follows from Definition 3 that f is of either type:
   (a) $R \to AB$ such that $R \in V$, $A, B \in V \cup \Sigma$.
   (b) $R \to t$ such that $R \in V$ and $t \in \Sigma$;
   Both cases can respectively be represented in DL as follows:
   (a) i. Let $C_R \sqsubseteq C'_v, C_A \sqsubseteq C'_v, C_B \sqsubseteq C'_v$ be the respective concepts of R, A, B definied in step 1
       ii. Let R_R, R_A, R_B be the rolification [25] of the concepts $\cup_R, \cup_A, \cup_B$ such that $C_R \equiv \exists R_R.Self$, $C_A \equiv \exists R_A.Self$, and $C_B \equiv \exists R_B.Self$.
       iii. Let R_{next} be the role such that $C_1 \circ R_{next} \circ C_2$ has semantic meaning C_1 *has as next element in the sequence* C_2, with $C_1 \sqsubseteq C'$ and $C_2 \sqsubseteq C'$
       iv. Let $V_1 \equiv \exists R_1.Self$ and $V_2 \equiv \exists R_2.Self$ be roles such that $R_A \circ R_{next} \circ R_B \sqsubseteq R_1$ and $R_B \circ R_{next}^{-1} \circ R_A \sqsubseteq R_2$.
   $$\xRightarrow{3(a)i,3(a)ii,3(a)iii,3(a)iv} R \to AB \iff (C_A \sqcap V_1) \sqcup (C_B \sqcap V_2) \sqsubseteq C_R.$$
   (b) Let $C_t \sqsubseteq C'_\Sigma$ be the concept of the terminal t defined in step 2 and $C_R \sqsubseteq C'_V$ be the concept of variable R defined in step 1
   $\Rightarrow R \to t \iff C_t \sqsubseteq C_r$
   $$\xRightarrow{3a,3b} f \in R', \forall f \in R .$$
4. $\xRightarrow{1} \exists C_s \sqsubseteq C'_V$ where C_s is the concept corresponding to S, as defined in step 1.

$$\xRightarrow{1,2,3,4} G_{DL} \equiv G. \qquad \blacksquare$$

Theorem 2. *The conversion between a CFG $G = (V, \Sigma, R, S)$ and a CFG-DL $G_{DL} = (C'_v, R', C'_\Sigma, S')$ can be performed in $O(n)$, in particular $O(|V| + |\Sigma| + |R|)$.*

Proof. It follows from the proof of Theorem 1 as we only need to loop through each element of V, Σ and R at most one time. $\qquad \blacksquare$

We remark that in Definition 5 terminals are modeled as concepts and stand at the same level of variables. At first, it might seem more intuitive to represent terminals as individuals. But this would radically change the semantic meaning of an element in a sequence. Take for example the sequence *10+11* from the language of grammar in Example 1. There are three occurrences of terminal *1*, but they are fundamentally different entities: the first occurrence of terminal *1* is characterized by its syntactic aspect as well as its position with respect to the whole sequence. If we represent each terminal as an individual then each occurrence of that terminal in a sequence would be represented by the very same individual. This would invalidate the semantics of the whole sequence and yield a wrong formalization. In order to address this issue, we need a proper definition of how to represent a sequence in description logic. We do that by adapting Definition 2 to CFG-DL.

Definition 6 (Language of a CFG-DL). *Let $G = (C_v, R, C_\Sigma, S)$ be a CFG-DL, we define as $L(G)$ the set of sequences $\overline{s}$ such that, given N the number of elements in the sequence $\overline{s}$, $\overline{s} \equiv (C_1 \sqcap \exists R_{next}.C_2) \sqcap \cdots \sqcap (C_{N-1} \sqcap \exists R_{next}.C_N)$, with R_{next} the role defined in step 3(a)iii of Theorem 1's proof and $C_t \sqsubseteq C_\Sigma, t \in [1, N]$.*

5   Sequence Classification Using CFG-DL

CFG-DL can be represented in OWL, as OWL2 direct semantics is based on Description Logic [22]. We devise an algorithm based on Definition 5 and on the respective constructive Proof 4 of Theorem 1. Algorithm 1 converts a CFG to OWL, without generating any intermediary CFG-DL. A similar algorithm can be defined to convert a CFG in CFG-DL, following the constructive Proof 4.

Triples are written in Manchester syntax [21]. We use the symbol ▶ to indicate the OWL triples that need to be created. We generally use $\overline{R}_{next}$ as the role R_{next} defined in step 3(a)iii of Thereom 1's proof. Any arbitrary OWL property can be used as $\overline{R}_{next}$ as long as it is a functional property, such as the *seq:directlyPrecedes* property from the *sequence* Ontology Design Pattern [19]. Algorithm 1 has also complexity $O(n)$: similarly to the considerations on Theorem 2, we only need to loop through each element of V, Σ and R at most one time.

The rolification of the classes $\overline{V}_1$ and $\overline{V}_2$ is performed by using the existential restriction on `owl:Thing`. This prevents the creation of non-simple properties due to the use of property chain later in the algorithm and allows the usage of reasoners such as Hermit [16] or Pellet [37].

Sequences must be converted to be used in the ontology obtained with Algorithm 1. Algorithm 2 presents an algorithm that performs such conversion in $O(n)$. It is based on Definition 6. Analogously to Algorithm 1, we express triples in Manchester syntax using the symbol ▶ and we use $\overline{R}_{next}$ as the role R_{next} defined in step 3(a)iii of Thereom 1's proof.

Figure 2, shows the grammar from Example 2, converted to a CFG-DL in OWL with Algorithm 1, used to parse the sequence *1 + 0*, converted using Algorithm 2. We can see how the whole sequence is correctly classified to be of class `Expression` and how `Expression_0` and `Expression` are classified as subclass of each other. Indeed, `Expression_0` and `Expression` are equivalent. This can be observed from the normalization process performed on Example 1 that resulted in Example 2: *Expression_0* variable is introduced to obtain a binary projection of *Expression → Expression + Expression*, as required by CNF. If we substitute every occurrence of *Expression_0* with its right hand side (*Expression + Expression*) an equivalent grammar, which is not in CNF, is obtained. The overall pattern in Fig. 3 can be generalized to every CFG converted in OWL.

Algorithm 1. CFG in OWL

Require: $G = (V, \Sigma, R, S)$

▶ ObjectProperty: $\overline{R}_1$

▶ ObjectProperty: $\overline{R}_2$

▶ Class: $\overline{V}_1$ EquivalentTo: $\overline{R}_1$ some

▶ Class: $\overline{V}_2$ EquivalentTo: $\overline{R}_2$ some

for $\overline{v} \in V$ **do**

    ▶ ObjectProperty: $R_{\overline{v}}$

    ▶ Class: $C_{\overline{v}}$ EquivalentTo: $R_{\overline{v}}$ some Self

end for

for $\overline{t} \in \Sigma$ **do**

    ▶ ObjectProperty: $R_{\overline{t}}$

    ▶ Class: $C_{\overline{t}}$ EquivalentTo: $R_{\overline{t}}$ some Self

end for

for $r \in R$ **do**

    if r is of type $R \rightarrow AB$ **then**

        with $\overline{C}_R, \overline{C}_A, \overline{C}_B$ being the respective concepts of R, A, B

        with $\overline{R}_A, \overline{R}_B$ being the respective rolification of A, B

        ▶ ObjectProperty: $\overline{R}_1$ SubPropertyChain: $\overline{R}_A$ o $\overline{R}_{next}$ o $\overline{R}_B$

        ▶ ObjectProperty: $\overline{R}_2$ SubPropertyChain: $\overline{R}_B$ o inverse($\overline{R}_{next}$) o $\overline{R}_A$

        ▶ $(\overline{C}_A$ and $\overline{V}_1)$ or $(\overline{C}_B$ and $\overline{V}_2)$ SubClassOf: $\overline{C}_R$

    else if r is of type $R \rightarrow t$ **then**

        with $\overline{C}_R, \overline{C}_t$ being the respective concepts of R, t

        ▶ Class: $\overline{C}_t$ SubClassOf: $\overline{C}_R$

    end if

end for

Algorithm 2. Sequence in OWL for CFG-DL

Require: $G = (V, \Sigma, R, S)$

Require: $s \subseteq \Sigma^*$ the sequence to represent

Require: N the length of the sequence s

for $i \in [1, N-1]$ **do**

    $s_i \leftarrow s[i]$

    $s_n \leftarrow s[i+1]$

    with $\overline{C}_i, \overline{C}_n$ being the respective concepts of the terminals s_i, s_n

    ▶ Individual: s_n Types: $\overline{C}_n$

    ▶ Individual: s_i Types: $\overline{C}_i$ Facts: $\overline{R}_{next}$ s_n

end for

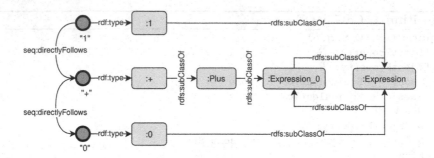

Fig. 2. Sequence *1+0* parsed by the grammar from Example 2 represented as CFG-DL in OWL

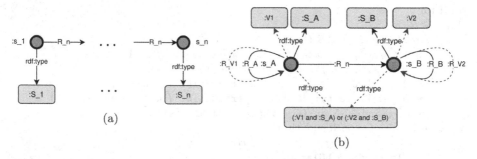

Fig. 3. General ontology patterns from Algorithms 1 (3a) and 2 (3b), for a rule of type $R \rightarrow A\ B$. The red arrows are created by the reasoner, due to the definition of the property chain and the general axiom. The pattern from a rule of type $R \rightarrow t$ is a simple subsumption relation.

5.1   Computational Complexity

An ontology produced by Algorithm 1 is in DL $\mathcal{SROIEL}$, which is contained in OWL 2 DL [25]. It has exponential complexity (NExpTime) for automated reasoning [23]. *Parsing* a sequence through a DL reasoner would be too complex compared to an external parser: parsing CFGs has complexity $O(n^3)$ [43] even in the case of ambiguous grammars [13]. Without the use of inverse properties the produced ontology is in DL $\mathcal{SROEL}$, which is within OWL-EL and solvable in polynomial time [23]. To mitigate the overall complexity we propose a hybrid approach combining CFG parsers and OWL reasoning, to perform sequence classification.

5.2 Combining CFG Parser with OWL-Based Reasoning

We claim that converting CFG in CFG-DL, besides being an interesting theoretical approach, constitutes a relevant pragmatic approach to perform automatic sequence classification that can benefit from an explicit knowledge representation, using OWL ontologies. In practice, given a CFG G, after recognising a sequence $s \in L(G)$ using a parser for G, the resulting parse tree can be converted, using Algorithm 3 to instantiate the OWL ontology O resulting from Algorithm 1, for G.

Algorithm 3. Parse tree in OWL

Require. $G = (V, \Sigma, R, S)$ in CNF
Require: $s \subseteq \Sigma^*$ with $s \in L(G)$
Require: T the parse tree obtained by parsing s with G
Ensure: T is a binary tree
  for all leaf l in R **do**
    with $\overline{C}_l$ being the concept of the terminal l
    for all ancestor a of l **do**
      with $\overline{C}_a$ being the concept of the variable a
      ▶ Class: C_l SubClassOf: $\overline{C}_a$
    end for
  end for

Algorithm 3 is based on Definitions 4 and 1.

The sequence s can be now classified by a DL reasoner according to the classes in O - or of any other ontology aligned to O. This process is demonstrated in Sect. 6 with a use case in the music domain.

The same approach can be used to convert the parse tree produced by algorithms such as Neural Network based Part of Speech tagging [2,4] or Constituency Parsing [32,40,48].

5.3 Comparison with $\mathcal{SEQ}$

The work presented in [45] introduces $\mathcal{SEQ}$, an ontology pattern used to model sequence of elements using Description Logic and OWL. The method performs sequence classification by identifying sub-sequences through a subsumption relation: the sequence that is being classified subsumes a set of patterns (subsequences). Those patterns classify the sequence. The author shows how this method is only able to represent *safely-concatenable* CFG. A CFG is *safely-concatenable* if its productions are in the form $R \to t_1 \cdots t_n X$, with $X, R \in V$ and $t_1 \cdots t_n \in \Sigma$ [45]. V and Σ are defined as in Definition 1. Such restrictions prevent the representation of *self-embedding* grammars [45], which are grammars that contain productions of the type $R \to \alpha R \beta$, with $R \in V$ and $\alpha, \beta \in (V \cup \Sigma)$ [8]. Our proposal overcomes this limitation by directly reflecting the semantics of a production, as shown in Proof 4 of Theorem 1.

6   Experiments

In this section we apply our approach to the music domain[2] to perform the automatic analysis of harmonic progressions. Harmonic progressions are defined as sequences of chords, their analysis consists in assessing the underlying function of each chord [33]. Traditionally, it is performed by trained musicians since a deep knowledge and understanding of the music domain is required. The correctness depends on the taxonomy used and on the context in which the sequence is analysed (e.g. the genre).

In music theory, harmony is a well-researched area, and several taxonomies have been proposed to perform this task [36]. Most approaches classify each chord based on its tonal function, according to western musical theory, using CFG [11,36] or Probabilistic CFG [17]. The implementation of these grammars can be problematic and relies on different techniques, such as Haskell datatypes in [11] or extensions to the definition of CFG in [17]. In [24] a CFG is used to detect sub-sequences, called *bricks*. *Bricks* are classes of chords sequences. Their combination defines new *bricks*. A similar approach is explored in [33], where the definition of *bricks* (called *idioms*) is performed through the use of a tree-like hierarchical ontology implemented using Object Oriented programming.

Our experiments are based on a subset of the rules implemented by [24], which we convert into an OWL ontology using Algorithm 1.

6.1   Grammar Subset

The CFG defined in [24] can be formalized as $G_k = (V, \Sigma, R, S)$ where the set of variables V is the set of sub-sequences that will be extracted from a harmonic progression, Σ is the set of chords, R is the set of productions that maps each sequence to the corresponding set of chords. The starting S can be assigned to a special variable $V_s \in V$ such that $\forall\ t \in \Sigma\ \exists f \in R\ :\ s.t.\ f(V_s) = t$. To obtain a more tractable example, we extract a subset of the whole grammar G_k: we will only use the variables, terminals, and productions that are sufficient to analyze the tune *Blue Bossa* by *Dorham Kenny*. We then expand the grammar to include a few other productions that should not appear in the final analysis, to investigate how accurately the ontology reflects a grammar-based approach. A correspondence between the analysis of [24] and our results provides empirical evidences of the method correctness.

Figure 4 shows the formalization of the rules strictly needed to classify *Blue Bossa* as performed in [24]. Using Algorithm 1 we convert the grammar in Fig. 4 into OWL. The resulting ontology contains 130 axioms. Using Algorithm 2 we convert the chord annotations of *Blue Bossa*, taken from [24] into OWL. The resulting ontology contains a total of 29 axioms. By joining the two ontologies, we obtain a final ontology with a total of 159 axioms. The ontology correctly parses the sequence, as can be seen from Table 1.

---

[2] The code of the experiments is available at https://github.com/n28div/CFGOwl under CC-BY License.

OnOffMinorIV_Cm → MinorOn_Cm Off_F

MinorOn_Cm → C:min | C:minmaj7 | C:min6 | C:min7

Off_F → F:7 | F | F:maj | F:min | F:min7 | F:minmaj7 | F:dim7

SadCadence_Cm → SadApproach_Cm MinorOn_Cm

| SadApproach_Cm MinorOn_Cm

| F:7(#11) MinorPerfectCadence_Cm

SadApproach_Cm → D:hdim7 G:7

MinorPerfectCadence_Cm → G:7 C:min7

StraightCadence_Db → StraightApproach_Db Db

| StraightApproach_Db Db:maj7

StraightApproach_Db → Eb:min7 StraightApproach_C_0

| Eb:min7 Ab:7

StraightApproach_C_0 → Ab:7 C:7/Bb

Fig. 4. Productions of grammar $G_{k_1} \subseteq G_k$. Only productions are listed. The set of terminals and variables is the one used in the productions.

Table 1. Parsing results for the harmonic progression of *Blue Bossa* using the grammar of Fig. 4. The class identified by [24] is represented in bold text

Chord	Inferred classes
C:min7	**OnOffMinorIV_Cm** VariableOne C:min7 MinorOn_Cm
F:min7	**OnOffMinorIV_Cm** VariableTwo F:min7 Off_F
D:hdim7	VariableOne SadApproach_Cm **SadCadence_Cm** D:hdim7
G:7	MinorPerfectCadence_Cm VariableTwo VariableOne G:7 SadApproach_Cm **SadCadence_Cm**
C:minmaj7	C:minmaj7 VariableTwo MinorOn_Cm **SadCadence_Cm**
Eb:min7	VariableOne StraightApproach_Db **StraightCadence_Db** Eb:min7
Ab:7	VariableTwo VariableOne StraightApproach_Db Ab:7 **StraightCadence_Db** StraightApproach_C_0
Db:maj7	VariableTwo Db:maj7 **StraightCadence_Db**
D:hdim7	VariableOne SadApproach_Cm **SadCadence_Cm** D:hdim7
G:7	MinorPerfectCadence_Cm VariableTwo VariableOne G:7 SadApproach_Cm **SadCadence_Cm**
C:minmaj7	C:minmaj7 VariableTwo MinorOn_Cm **SadCadence_Cm**

6.2   Reasoning Complexity

As discussed in Sect. 5.1, the computational complexity of parsing a sequence using a CFG-DL is exponential. On Fig. 5a we parse the song *Blue Bossa* using the grammar defined in Sect. 6.1. We then progressively add random productions to the grammar that do not affect the classification. At each iteration we add 5 new productions, which have a random number of right-hand sides sampled in the range $[1, 10]$. Each production is of type $R \to AB$ 80% of the time and $R \to t$ 20% of the time, to reflect the higher frequency of $R \to AB$ productions, especially when a CFG is expressed in CNF.

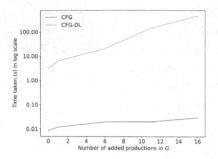

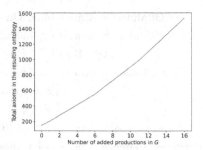

(a) Time taken (y axis, logarithmic) as random productions are added to the grammar (x axis). Parsing using DL is compared to the use of Earley parser on the corresponding CFG. The time taken by using the hybrid approach is 200% (3 orders of magnitude) than using DL parsing.

(b) Number of total axioms in the ontology (y axis) as random productions are added to the grammar (x axis). As more productions are added to the grammar, say N, roughly $10N$ axioms are inserted in the ontology. Since the computational complexity directly depends on the number of axioms in the ontology, the resulting CFG-DL is inefficient in real-world settings.

Fig. 5. Empirical results of the computational complexity when using a CFG-DL to parse the song *Blue Bossa*. (Color figure online)

In Fig. 5 empirical results from the described experiments are shown. Figure 5a shows how as productions are added to the grammar, the time complexity of CFG-DL increases exponentially. This is a consequence of the proportional increase of axioms as new productions are added (Fig. 5b). When using the hybrid approach of Sect. 5.2 the computational complexity is much lower. In Fig. 5a the time required to classify a sequence is significantly lower. All the experiments are executed using the Pellet reasoner [37] on a 2.4GHz Intel i5-6300U CPU and 8GB of RAM under regular computational load.

Even though the results of the two methods are indistinguishable, it is important to note that if the sequence is modified, Algorithm 3 need to be executed again, while a CFG-DL produced with Algorithm 1 would be able to classify the new element without any additional effort. We plan to address this aspect in future works, for instance by combining Algorithm 1 and Algorithm 3.

6.3   Subsequence Classification

A complete understanding of the CFG is required to interpret Fig. 4 and the results in Table 1. To obtain an higher interpretability, it is sufficient to expand the ontology produced by Algorithm 1 and increase the level of abstraction or by aligning other relevant ontologies. In the example of Fig. 6, we can align the results with a domain-specific ontology, such as the Music Theory Ontology [34]. Differently from [33], the grammar and ontology definitions are decoupled in our approach.

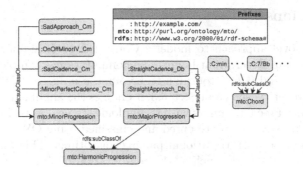

Fig. 6. Ontology imported by the ontology generated by Algorithm 1.

The classification in Table 2 is obtained using the ontology of Fig. 6. The results are arguably easier to interpret when compared to Table 1, without any update on the original CFG. By converting relevant grammars using Algorithm 1, a Knowledge Graph can be populated using the results of the parsing procedure. Additional classification can then be performed by aligning additional ontologies. For instance, to classify modal passages from a major to a minor progression (i.e. chord progression that transition from a major progression to a minor progression) as X it would be sufficient to define an axiom such as

▶((mto:MajorProgression and $\overline{V}_1$) or (mto:MinorProgression and $\overline{V}_2$)) SubClassOf: X

Table 2. Parsing results for the harmonic progression of *Blue Bossa* using the grammar of Fig. 4 and importing Music Theory Ontology as shown in Fig. 6.

Chord	Progression type
C:min7	Minor
F:min7	Minor
D:hdim7	Minor
G:7	Minor
C:minmaj7	Minor
Eb:min7	Major
Ab:7	Major
Db:maj	Major
D:hdim7	Minor
G:7	Minor
C:minmaj7	Minor

7   Conclusions

We present a novel approach to model a Context Free Grammar in Chomsky Normal Form using Description Logic. The computational complexity, as analysed in Sects. 5.1 and 6.2, is too high to favour the usage of OWL for parsing sequences. However, as shown in Sect. 6.3, it enables the alignment of approaches based on Context Free Grammars with technologies typically used in the Semantic Web. Sequences can be represented and classified using OWL in an effective way by combining it with traditional parsing algorithms. This form of classification can be used for tasks such as the computation of similarity between two sequences. The inference of these similarities is of great use in the Music Information Retrieval field, where it is hard to define a similarity metric between two harmonic progression. The same approach, however, can be applied to other fields where sequences have been modeled using formal grammar, such as natural language processing [27], bio-informatics [9] and programming languages [10]. The hybrid approach using CFG and OWL ontologies allows a shift in the grammar modeling process: existing extensions, such as Combinatory Categorical Grammars (CCG) [38], have been proposed to transparently take into account the semantics of a sequence, along-side the syntactical aspects. It is possible to formalize a CCG in terms of DL, with a similar approach as the one presented in Sect. 4, and develop grammars whose semantic information is fueled by an expressive ontology.

Acknowledgements. This project has received funding from the European Union's Horizon 2020 research and innovation programme under grant agreement No 101004746.

References

1. Aho, A.V., Johnson, S.C.: LR parsing. ACM Comput. Surv. (CSUR) **6**(2), 99–124 (1974)
2. Akbik, A., Blythe, D., Vollgraf, R.: Contextual string embeddings for sequence labeling. In: Proceedings of the 27th International Conference on Computational Linguistics, pp. 1638–1649 (2018)
3. Baroni, M., Jacoboni, C.: Proposal for a grammar of melody : the Bach chorales. Presses de l'Universite de Montreal Montreal (1978)
4. Bohnet, B., McDonald, R., Simoes, G., Andor, D., Pitler, E., Maynez, J.: Morphosyntactic tagging with a Meta-BiLSTM model over context sensitive token encodings. In: Gurevych, I., Miyao, Y., (eds.) Proceedings of the 56th Annual Meeting of the Association for Computational Linguistics, ACL 2018, Melbourne, Australia, 15–20 July 2018, Volume 1: Long Papers, pp. 2642–2652. Association for Computational Linguistics (2018)
5. Carrasco-Davis, R., et al.: Deep learning for image sequence classification of astronomical events. Publ. Astron. Soc. Pac. **131**(1004), 108006 (2019)
6. Chen, T., Xu, R., He, Y., Xia, Y., Wang, X.: Learning user and product distributed representations using a sequence model for sentiment analysis. IEEE Comput. Intell. Mag. **11**(3), 34–44 (2016)

7. Chomsky, N.: Three models for the description of language. IRE Trans. Inf. Theory **2**(3), 113–124 (1956)
8. Chomsky, N.: On certain formal properties of grammars. Inf. Control **2**(2), 137–167 (1959)
9. Damasevicius, R.: Structural analysis of regulatory DNA sequences using grammar inference and support vector machine. Neurocomputing **73**(4–6), 633–638 (2010)
10. de Aguiar, C.Z., de Almeida Falbo, R., Souza, V.E.S.: OOC-O: a reference ontology on object-oriented code. In: Laender, A.H.F., Pernici, B., Lim, E.-P., de Oliveira, J.P.M. (eds.) ER 2019. LNCS, vol. 11788, pp. 13–27. Springer, Cham (2019). https://doi.org/10.1007/978-3-030-33223-5_3
11. De Haas, W.B., Magalhães, J.P., Wiering, F., Veltkamp, R.C.: Automatic functional harmonic analysis. Comput. Music. J. **37**(4), 37–53 (2013)
12. Drummond, N., et al.: Putting OWL in order: patterns for sequences in OWL. In: Grau, B.C., Hitzler, P., Shankey, C., Wallace, E., (eds.) Proceedings of the OWLED*06 Workshop on OWL: Experiences and Directions, Athens, Georgia, USA, 10–11 November 2006, volume 216 of CEUR Workshop Proceedings. CEUR-WS.org. (2006)
13. Earley, J.: An efficient context-free parsing algorithm. Commun. ACM **13**(2), 94–102 (1970)
14. Barton, G.E., Berrywick, R.C., Ristad, E.S.: Computational complexity and natural language. J. Linguist. **24**(2), 573–575 (1987)
15. Giegerich, R.: Introduction to stochastic context free grammars. In: Gorodkin, J., Ruzzo, W.L. (eds.) RNA Sequence, Structure, and Function: Computational and Bioinformatic Methods. MMB, vol. 1097, pp. 85–106. Humana Press, Totowa, NJ (2014). https://doi.org/10.1007/978-1-62703-709-9_5
16. Glimm, B., Horrocks, I., Motik, B., Stoilos, G., Wang, Z.: HermiT: an OWL 2 reasoner. J. Autom. Reason. **53**(3), 245–269 (2014)
17. Harasim, D., Rohrmeier, M., O'Donnell, T.J.: A generalized parsing framework for generative models of harmonic syntax. In: ISMIR, pp. 152–159 (2018)
18. Harte, C., Sandler, M.B., Abdallah, S.A., Gómez, E.: symbolic representation of musical chords: a proposed syntax for text annotations. In: ISMIR, vol. 5, pp. 66–71 (2005)
19. Hitzler, P., Gangemi, A., Janowicz, K. (eds.).: Ontology Engineering with Ontology Design Patterns - Foundations and Applications, volume 25 of Studies on the Semantic Web. IOS Press, Amsterdam (2016)
20. Hopcroft, J.E., Motwani, R., Ullman, J.D.: Introduction to automata theory, languages, and computation. ACM SIGACT News **32**(1), 60–65 (2001)
21. Horridge, M., Drummond, N., Goodwin, J., Rector, A.L., Stevens, R., Wang, H.: The Manchester OWL syntax. In: OWLed, vol. 216 (2006)
22. Horrocks, I., Parsia, B., Sattler, U.: OWL 2 web ontology language direct semantics. World Wide Web Consort. 42–65 (2012)
23. Horrocks, I., Patel-Schneider, P.F.: Reducing OWL entailment to description logic satisfiability. In: Fensel, D., Sycara, K., Mylopoulos, J. (eds.) ISWC 2003. LNCS, vol. 2870, pp. 17–29. Springer, Heidelberg (2003). https://doi.org/10.1007/978-3-540-39718-2_2
24. Keller, R., Schofield, A., Toman-Yih, A., Merritt, Z., Elliott, J.: Automating the explanation of jazz chord progressions using idiomatic analysis. Comput. Music. J. **37**(4), 54–69 (2013)
25. Krisnadhi, A., Maier, F., Hitzler, P.: OWL and rules. In: Polleres, A., et al. (eds.) Reasoning Web 2011. LNCS, vol. 6848, pp. 382–415. Springer, Heidelberg (2011). https://doi.org/10.1007/978-3-642-23032-5_7

26. Kumar, S.: Gene sequence classification using K-mer decomposition and soft-computing-based approach. In: Sharma, T.K., Ahn, C.W., Verma, O.P., Panigrahi, B.K. (eds.) Soft Computing: Theories and Applications. AISC, vol. 1381, pp. 181–186. Springer, Singapore (2021). https://doi.org/10.1007/978-981-16-1696-9_17
27. Lawrence, S., Giles, C., Fong, S.: Natural language grammatical inference with recurrent neural networks. IEEE Trans. Knowl. Data Eng. **12**(1), 126–140 (2000)
28. Lei, J., Zhang, Q., Wang, J., Luo, H.: BERT based hierarchical sequence classification for context-aware microblog sentiment analysis. In: Gedeon, T., Wong, K.W., Lee, M. (eds.) ICONIP 2019. LNCS, vol. 11955, pp. 376–386. Springer, Cham (2019). https://doi.org/10.1007/978-3-030-36718-3_32
29. Lerdahl, F., Jackendoff, R.: A Generative Theory of Tonal Music. The MIT Press, Cambridge. MA (1983)
30. Lo Bosco, G., Di Gangi, M.A.: Deep learning architectures for DNA sequence classification. In: Petrosino, A., Loia, V., Pedrycz, W. (eds.) WILF 2016. LNCS (LNAI), vol. 10147, pp. 162–171. Springer, Cham (2017). https://doi.org/10.1007/978-3-319-52962-2_14
31. Madhusudhan, S.T., Chowdhary, G.: Deepsrgm - sequence classification and ranking in Indian classical music with deep learning. In: Flexer, A., Peeters, G., Urbano, J., Volk, A., (eds.) Proceedings of the 20th International Society for Music Information Retrieval Conference, ISMIR 2019, Proceedings of the 20th International Society for Music Information Retrieval Conference, ISMIR 2019, pp. 533–540. International Society for Music Information Retrieval (2019)
32. Mrini, K., Dernoncourt, F., Tran, Q., Bui, T., Chang, W., Nakashole, N.: Rethinking self-attention: towards interpretability in neural parsing. In: Cohn, T., He, Y., Liu, Y., (eds.) Findings of the Association for Computational Linguistics: EMNLP 2020, Online Event, 16–20 November 2020, volume EMNLP 2020 of Findings of ACL, pp. 731–742. Association for Computational Linguistics (2020)
33. Pachet, F.: Computer analysis of jazz chord sequence: is solar a blues? (2000)
34. Rashid, S.M., De Roure, D., McGuinness, D.L.: A music theory ontology. In: Proceedings of the 1st International Workshop on Semantic Applications for Audio and Music, pp. 6–14 (2018)
35. Rivas, E., Eddy, S.R.: The language of RNA: a formal grammar that includes pseudoknots. Bioinformatics **16**(4), 334–340 (2000)
36. Rohrmeier, M.: Towards a generative syntax of tonal harmony. J. Math. Music **5**(1), 35–53 (2011)
37. Sirin, E., Parsia, B., Grau, B.C., Kalyanpur, A., Katz, Y.: Pellet: a practical OWL-DL reasoner. J. Web Seman. **5**(2), 51–53 (2007)
38. Steedman, M., Baldridge, J.: Combinatory categorial grammar. non-transformational syntax: formal and explicit models of grammar. Wiley-Blackwell, pp. 181–224 (2011)
39. Steedman, M.J.: A generative grammar for jazz chord sequences. Music Percept.: Interdisc. J. **2**(1), 52–77 (1984)
40. Tian, Y., Song, Y., Xia, F., Zhang, T.: Improving constituency parsing with span attention. In: Cohn, T., He, Y., Liu, Y., (eds) Findings of the Association for Computational Linguistics: EMNLP 2020, Online Event, 16–20 November 2020, volume EMNLP 2020 of Findings of ACL, pp. 1691–1703. Association for Computational Linguistics (2020)
41. Tidhar, D.: A hierarchical and deterministic approach to music grammars and its application to unmeasured preludes. PhD thesis, Berlin Institute of Technology (2005)

42. Tojo, S., Oka, Y., Nishida, M.: Analysis of chord progression by HPSG. In: Proceedings of the 24th IASTED International Conference on Artificial Intelligence and Applications, AIA2006, USA, pp. 305–310. ACTA Press (2006)

43. Valiant, L.G.: General context-free recognition in less than cubic time. J. Comput. Syst. Sci. **10**(2), 308–315 (1975)

44. Weininger, D.: SMILES, a chemical language and information system. 1. introduction to methodology and encoding rules. J. Chem. Inf. Comput. Sci. **28**(1), 31–36 (1988)

45. Wissmann, J.: Chord sequence patterns in OWL. PhD thesis, City University London (2012)

46. Wolstencroft, K., Stevens, R., Haarslev, V.: Applying OWL reasoning to genomic data. In: Baker, C.J.O., Cheung, KH. (eds.) Semantic Web, pp. 225–248. Springer, Boston, MA (2007). https://doi.org/10.1007/978-0-387-48438-9_12

47. Xing, Z., Pei, J., Keogh, E.: A brief survey on sequence classification. SIGKDD Explor. Newsl. **12**(1), 40–48 (2010)

48. Yang, K., Deng, J.: Strongly incremental constituency parsing with graph neural networks. Advances in Neural Information Processing Systems, vol. 33, pp. 21687–21698 (2020)

49. Young-Lai, M.: Grammar inference. In: Liu, L., ÖZSU, M.T., (eds.) Encyclopedia of Database Systems, pp. 1256–1260, Springer, Boston, MA, US (2009)

NASTyLinker: NIL-Aware Scalable Transformer-Based Entity Linker

Nicolas Heist[(✉)][ID] and Heiko Paulheim[ID]

Data and Web Science Group, University of Mannheim, Mannheim, Germany
{nico,heiko}@informatik.uni-mannheim.de

Abstract. Entity Linking (EL) is the task of detecting mentions of entities in text and disambiguating them to a reference knowledge base. Most prevalent EL approaches assume that the reference knowledge base is complete. In practice, however, it is necessary to deal with the case of linking to an entity that is not contained in the knowledge base (NIL entity). Recent works have shown that, instead of focusing only on affinities between mentions and entities, considering inter-mention affinities can be used to represent NIL entities by producing clusters of mentions. At the same time, inter-mention affinities can help to substantially improve linking performance for known entities. With NASTyLinker, we introduce an EL approach that is aware of NIL entities and produces corresponding mention clusters while maintaining high linking performance for known entities. The approach clusters mentions and entities based on dense representations from Transformers and resolves conflicts (if more than one entity is assigned to a cluster) by computing transitive mention-entity affinities. We show the effectiveness and scalability of NASTyLinker on NILK, a dataset that is explicitly constructed to evaluate EL with respect to NIL entities. Further, we apply the presented approach to an actual EL task, namely to knowledge graph population by linking entities in Wikipedia listings, and provide an analysis of the outcome.

Keywords: NIL-Aware Entity Linking · Entity Discovery · Knowledge Graph Population · NILK · Wikipedia Listings · CaLiGraph

1 Introduction

1.1 Motivation and Problem

Entity Linking (EL), i.e., the task of detecting mentions of entities in text and disambiguating them to a reference knowledge base (KB), is crucial for many downstream tasks like question answering [9,40], or KB population and completion [16,19,31]. One main challenge of EL is the inherent ambiguity of mentioned entities in the text. Figure 1 shows four homonymous mentions of distinct entities with the name *James Lake* (a lake in Canada, a lake in the US, a musician, and a fictional character). Correctly linking the mentions in Fig. 1a and 1b is especially challenging as both point to lakes that are geographically close.

C. Pesquita et al. (Eds.): ESWC 2023, LNCS 13870, pp. 174–191, 2023.
https://doi.org/10.1007/978-3-031-33455-9_11

In a typical EL setting, we assume that the training data contains mentions of all entities to be linked against. This assumption is dropped in Zero-Shot EL [26], where a linking decision is made on the basis of entity information in the reference KB (e.g. textual descriptions, types, relations). In this setting, a seminal approach has been introduced with BLINK [41]. Its core idea is to create dense representations of mentions and entities with a Transformer model [10] in a bi-encoder setting, retrieve mention-entity candidates through Nearest Neighbor Search, and rerank candidates with a cross-encoder.

In a practical setting, we additionally encounter the problem of mentions without a corresponding entity in the reference KB (which we refer to as NIL mentions and NIL entities, respectively). In fact, the mention in Fig. 1a is the only one with a counterpart in the reference KB (i.e., Wikipedia). For the other mentions, a correct prediction based on Wikipedia entities is impossible. Instead, NIL-aware approaches could either (1) create an (intermediate) entity representation for the NIL entity to link, or (2) produce clusters of NIL mentions with all mentions in a cluster referring to the same entity.

While this problem has been largely ignored by EL approaches for quite some time, recent works demonstrate that reasonable predictions for NIL mentions can be made by clustering mentions on the basis of inter-mention affinities [1,24]. Both compute inter-mention and mention-entity affinities using a bi-encoder architecture on the basis of BLINK [41]. EDIN [24] is an approach of category (1) that uses a dedicated adaptation dataset to create representations for NIL entities in an unsupervised fashion. Hence, the approach can only link to a NIL entity if there is at least one mention of it in the adaptation dataset. For some EL tasks, especially as a prerequisite for KB population, creating an adaptation dataset with good coverage is not trivial because an optimal adaptation dataset has to contain mentions of all NIL entities. Agarwal et al. [1] present an approach of category (2) that creates clusters of mentions and entities in a bottom-up fashion by iteratively merging the two most similar clusters, always under the constraint that a cluster must contain at most one entity.

1.2   Approach and Contributions

With NASTyLinker, we present an EL approach that is NIL-aware in the sense of category (2) and hence avoiding the need for an adaptation dataset. Similar to Agarwal et al. [1], it produces clusters of mentions and entities on the basis of inter-mention and mention-entity affinities from a bi-encoder. NASTyLinker relies on a top-down clustering approach that – in case of a conflict – assigns mentions to the entity with the highest transitive affinity. Contrary to Agarwal et al., who discard cross-encoders completely due to the quadratic growth in complexity when evaluating inter-mention affinities, our experiments show that applying a cross-encoder only for the refinement of mention-entity affinities can result in a considerable increase of linking performance at a reasonable computational cost. Our evaluation on the NILK dataset [21], a dataset especially suited for the evaluation of NIL-aware approaches, shows that NASTyLinker manages to make competitive predictions for NIL entities while even slightly improving

Name	Township(s)	Coordinates	NTS map	Status	CGNDB id
Jackpine Lake	Banting, Chambers	47°8'44"N 79°56'3"W	031M/04	Official	FBRBM
James Lake	Best	47°10'41"N 79°44'26"W	031M/04	Official	FBRHD
Jamieson Lake	Banting	47°9'22"N 79°59'37"W	031M/04	Official	FBRHY
Jessie Lake	Strathcona	47°2'28"N 79°48'14"W	031M/04	Official	FBRSJ
Jumping Caribou Lake	Law, Olive	46°52'57"N 79°48'32"W	031L/13	Official	FBSOZ
Jumpingcat Lake	Belfast, Joan	47°1'46"N 80°9'59"W	041P/01	Official	FBSPA

(a) A lake in Ontario, CA.
Lakes of Temagami

- Elbow Lake, 46°21'53"N 113°01'31"W, el. 7,746 feet (2,361 m)[14]
- Evans Lake, 47°00'15"N 113°04'19"W, el. 4,193 feet (1,278 m)[15]
- Hagan Pond, 46°28'46"N 112°52'55"W, el. 5,000 feet (1,500 m)[16]
- James Lake, 47°04'32"N 113°12'43"W, el. 4,137 feet (1,261 m)[17]
- Jones Lake, 47°02'35"N 113°08'35"W, el. 4,088 feet (1,246 m)[18]
- Kleinschmidt Lake, 46°58'33"N 113°02'35"W, el. 4,186 feet (1,276 m)[19]

(b) A lake in Montana, US.
List of lakes of Powell County, Montana

Members [edit]

- Lionel Williams – vocals, various instruments (2007–present)

Associated musicians [edit]

- Bryan Lee – drums (2007–2010)
- Calin Stephensen – bass (2007–2008)
- James Lake – drums/synth (2011–2017)
- Ian Gibbs – various instruments (2011–2018)

(c) A musician in the band Vinyl Williams.
Vinyl Williams

Character	Actor/Actress	Duration
Joe Lacerra	Stephen Liska	1998–2005
Cindy Lake	DeAnna Robbins	1982–83
James Lake	Glenn Corbett	1983
Mary Margaret Lake	Fawne Harriman	1983
Sammy Lake	Danny McCoy Jr.	1978
Hilary Lancaster	Kelly Garrison	1991–93
Dr. Joshua Landers	Heath Kizzier	1996–98

(d) A character in a soap opera.
List of The Young and Restless characters

Fig. 1. Listings in Wikipedia containing the mention *James Lake*. All of the mentions refer to distinct entities. A dedicated Wikipedia page exists only for the entity of the mention in (a).

prediction performance for known entities. The approach is designed in a modular way to make existing EL models NIL-aware by post-processing the computed inter-mention and mention-entity affinities. By applying NASTyLinker to a knowledge graph population task, we demonstrate its ability to reliably link to known entities (up to 87% accuracy) and identify NIL entities (up to 90% accuracy).

To summarize, the contributions of this paper are as follows:

- We introduce the NASTyLinker approach, serving as an extension to existing EL approaches by using a top-down clustering mechanism to consistently link mentions to known entities and produce clusters for NIL mentions (Sect. 4).
- In our experiments, we demonstrate the competitive linking performance and scalability of the presented approach through an evaluation on the NILK dataset (Sect. 5.4).
- We use NASTyLinker for KB population by linking entities in Wikipedia listings. We report on the linking statistics and provide a qualitative analysis of the results (Sect. 5.5).

The produced code is part of the CaLiGraph extraction framework and publicly available on GitHub.[1]

2   Related Work

Entity Linking. Entity Linking has been studied extensively in the last two decades [33,37]. Initially, approaches relied on word and entity frequencies, alias

---

[1] https://github.com/nheist/CaLiGraph.

tables, or neural networks for their linking decisions [7,13,28]. The introduction of pre-trained transformer models [10] made it possible to create representations of mentions and entities from text without relying on other intermediate representations. Gillick et al. [14] show how to learn dense representations for mentions and entities, Logeswaran et al. [26] extend this by introducing the zero-shot EL task and demonstrating that reasonable entity embeddings can be derived solely from entity descriptions. Wu et al. [41] introduce BLINK, the prevalent bi-encoder and cross-encoder paradigm for zero-shot EL. Various improvements for zero-shot EL have been proposed based on this paradigm. KG-ZESHEL [35] adds auxiliary entity information from knowledge graph embeddings into the linking process; Partalidou et al. [30] propose alternative pooling functions for the bi-encoder to increase the accuracy of the candidate generation step.

Cross-Document Coreference Resolution. NIL-Aware EL is closely related to Cross-Document Coreference Resolution (CDC), the task of identifying coreferent entity mentions in documents without explicitly linking them to entities in a KB [5]. Dutta and Weikum [11] explicitly tackle CDC in combination with EL by applying clustering to bag-of-words representations of entity mentions. More recently, Logan IV et al. [25] evaluate greedy nearest-neighbour and hierarchical clustering strategies for CDC, however, without explicitly evaluating them with respect to EL.

Entity Discovery and NIL-Aware EL. The majority of EL approaches may identify NIL mentions (for instance, through a binary classifier or a ranking that explicitly includes *NIL*), but does not process them in any way [37,38]. In 2011, the TAC-KBP challenge [22] introduced a task that includes NIL clustering; in the NEEL challenge [36] that is based on microposts, NIL clustering was part of the task as well. Approaches that tackled these tasks typically applied clustering based on similarity measures over the entity mentions in the text [6,12,15,29,32]. More recently, Angell et al. [3] train two separate bi-encoders and cross-encoders to compute inter-mention and mention-entity affinities. Subsequently, they apply a bottom-up clustering for refined linking predictions within single biomedical documents. Agarwal et al. [1] extend the approach to cross-document linking through a clustering based on minimum spanning trees over all mentions in the corpus. Clusters are formed by successively adding edges to a graph as long as the constraint that a cluster can contain at most one entity is not violated. They omit the cross-encoder and employ a custom training procedure for the bi-encoder instead. They explicitly evaluate their approach w.r.t. NIL entity discovery by removing a part of the entities in the training set from zero-shot EL benchmark datasets. In our approach, we employ a similar method for computing affinities but employ a top-down clustering approach that aims to better identify clusters of NIL mentions. The EDIN pipeline [24] also applies clustering w.r.t. inter-mention and mention-entity affinities, but only to identify NIL mention clusters on a dedicated adaptation dataset. Subsequently, the entity index is enhanced with pooled representations of these clusters to make a prediction of NIL entities possible. In their clustering phase, they first produce groups of mentions and then identify NIL mention clusters by checking whether less than

70% of the mentions are referring to the same entity. As we aim to apply NIL-aware EL for KB population, relying on an adaptation dataset is not possible. Still, we include the clustering method of the EDIN pipeline in our experiments to compare how well the approaches detect NIL mention clusters.

3   Task Formulation

A document corpus $\mathcal{D}$ contains a set of textual entity mentions $\mathcal{M}$. Each of the mentions $m \in \mathcal{M}$ refers to an entity e in the set of all entities $\mathcal{E}$. Given a knowledge base K with known entities $\mathcal{E}^k$, the task in standard EL is to assign an entity $\hat{e} \in \mathcal{E}^k$ to every mention in $\mathcal{M}$. In this setting, we assume that $\mathcal{E} = \mathcal{E}^k$, i.e., all entities are contained in K.

In NIL-aware EL, we drop the assumption that every mention links to an entity contained in K. Instead there is a set of NIL entities $\mathcal{E}^n$ with $\mathcal{E}^k \cup \mathcal{E}^n = \mathcal{E}$ and $\mathcal{E}^k \cap \mathcal{E}^n = \emptyset$. For mentions $\mathcal{M}^k$ that refer to entities in K, the task is still to predict an entity $\hat{e} \in \mathcal{E}^k$. For mentions $\mathcal{M}^n$ that refer to entities not contained in K, the task is to predict a cluster identifier $c \in \mathcal{C}$ so that the clustering $\mathcal{C}$ resembles the distribution of mentions in $\mathcal{M}^n$ to entities in $\mathcal{E}^n$ as closely as possible. We assume that we are additionally operating in a zero-shot setting, i.e., the training portion $\mathcal{D}_{train}$ of the document corpus may not contain mentions for all entities in $\mathcal{E}$.

Note that, similar to related works [1,26], we assume that the textual entity mentions are already given. Further, we only investigate the relevant steps for KB population, i.e., detection and disambiguation of NIL entities. While we discard the indexing aspect, an EL model which includes the entities in $\mathcal{E}^n$ can still be created in a subsequent step by training a new model on the enhanced KB.

4   NASTyLinker: An Approach for NIL-Aware and Scalable Entity Linking

In this section, we describe our proposed approach for making NIL-aware EL predictions. Figure 2 depicts the three main phases of the NASTyLinker approach. In the *Linking Phase*, we first retrieve inter-mention and mention-entity affinities from an underlying EL model for the subsequent clustering. We define constraints for such a model and describe the one used in our experiments in Sect. 4.1. During the *Clustering Phase*, clusters of mentions and entity candidates are created using greedy nearest-neighbour clustering (Sect. 4.2). Finally, we retrieve entity candidates for every cluster. In the *Conflict Resolution Phase*, clusters are split based on transitive mention-entity affinities to ensure that a cluster contains at most one known entity (Sect. 4.3).

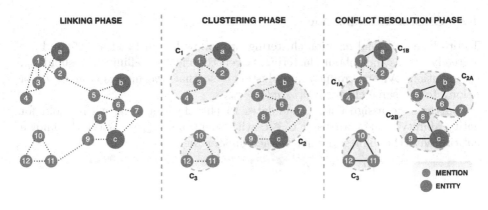

Fig. 2. Main phases of the NASTyLinker approach. Dotted lines show top-k affinity scores, solid lines indicate the highest transitive affinity scores.

4.1   Entity Linking Model

In the *Linking Phase* we compute the k most similar mentions and entities for every mention in $\mathcal{M}$ (dotted lines in Fig. 2). The underlying EL model has to provide a function ϕ with $\phi(m,e) \in [0;1]$ for the similarity between mention m and entity e as well as $\phi(m,m') \in [0;1]$ for the similarity between mentions m and m'. In addition to that, it must be possible to retrieve the top k mention and entity candidates for a given mention in an efficient manner.

For our experiments with NASTyLinker, we choose the BLINK architecture [41] as the underlying EL model as it provides the foundation for many state-of-the-art EL models. Furthermore, as the bi-encoder creates embeddings for mentions and entities alike, methods for an approximate nearest neighbour search like FAISS [23] can be used to retrieve linking candidates efficiently. As the application of the cross-encoder is the most time-consuming part of this model, we explore in our experiments the trade-off between linking performance and runtime when reranking only inter-mention affinities, only mention-entity affinities, or both.

Partalidou et al. [30] propose several layouts for structuring the input sequence of mentions and entities for the Transformer model. We achieved the best results with the mention layout

```
[CLS] [<type>] <mention label> [CTX] <mention context> [SEP]
```

and the entity layout

```
[CLS] [<type>] <entity title> [CTX] <entity description> [SEP]
```

where [CTX] is a special delimiter token and [<type>] is a placeholder for a special token of the mention type (POS-tag) or entity type (top-level type in the KB). For optimization, we stick to Wu et al. [41] and use in-batch (hard) negatives for the bi-encoder, and bi-encoder-generated negatives for the cross-encoder.

4.2　Cluster Initialization

To produce an initial mention clustering, we follow Logan IV et al. [25] and use a greedy nearest-neighbour clustering. Given the mention affinity threshold τ_m, the mentions $\mathcal{M}$ are grouped into clusters $\mathcal{C}$ so that two mentions $m, m' \in \mathcal{M}$ belong to the same cluster if $\phi(m, m') > \tau_m$.

Further, we assign entity candidates to the clusters using a threshold for entity affinity τ_e. For a cluster $C \in \mathcal{C}$ with mentions M_c, we select the known entities with the highest affinity to each cluster mention:

$$E_c^k = \bigcup_{m \in M_c} \{\underset{e \in \mathcal{E}^k}{argmax}\, \phi(m, e) : \phi(m, e) > \tau_e\}. \tag{1}$$

In Fig. 2, the dotted lines represent affinities greater than the thresholds τ_m and τ_e, respectively. Cluster C_1 contains four loosely connected mentions with m_1 and m_2 directly connected to the entity candidate e_a. Either all four mentions refer to e_a as they are transitively connected, or some mentions refer to an entity in $\mathcal{E}^n$ (e.g., a situation like in Fig. 1a and 1b). Cluster C_2 contains several mentions with two known entity candidates e_b and e_c, making a trivial assignment of mentions to entities impossible. Finally, cluster C_3 contains three connected mentions without any assigned entity candidates, most likely representing a NIL entity. Conflicts like the ones occurring in the former two clusters are resolved in the subsequent resolution phase.

4.3　Cluster Conflict Resolution

The objectives of the *Conflict Resolution Phase* are twofold: For every cluster $C \in \mathcal{C}$ we (1) find sub-clusters with $|E_c^k| = 1$ (c.f. C_{1B}, C_{2A}, and C_{2B} in Fig. 2), and (2) identify mentions in M_c that do not refer to any entity in E_c^k. For these, we create one or more sub-clusters representing the NIL entities E_c^n of C (c.f. C_{1A} and C_3 in Fig. 2).

For conflict resolution, we view a cluster $C \in \mathcal{C}$ as a graph G_c with $M_c \cup E_c^k$ as nodes, and affinities above threshold as edges. To ensure objective (1), we assign every mention in a cluster to the candidate entity with the highest transitive, defined as follows:

$$\phi^*(m, e) = \underset{m \sim e \in G_c}{max} \prod_{u,v}^{m \sim e} \phi(u, v) \tag{2}$$

with $m \sim e$ denoting a path from a mention m to an entity e in G_c and (u, v) a single edge. The rationale for this metric is to favour strong contextual similarity between mentions over the mediocre similarity between a mention and an entity. As the entity context is coming from a different data corpus (i.e., information from a KB) than the mention context, it is more likely to happen that the contexts for a mention and its linked entity are dissimilar than the contexts of two mentions linking to the same entity.

Example 1. With affinities $\phi(m_6, e_b) = 0.9$, $\phi(m_6, m_7) = 0.9$, $\phi(m_7, e_c) = 0.8$, and paths m_7–m_6–e_b, m_7–e_c from Fig. 2, we find that $\phi^*(m_7, e_b) = 0.81 >$

$\phi^*(m_7, e_c) = 0.8$, resulting in the assignment of m_7 to the cluster of e_b in spite of e_c being the most likely entity for m_7 w.r.t. ϕ.

To ensure objective (2), we introduce a threshold τ_a as a lower limit for the transitive affinity between a mention and an entity. We label mentions as NIL mentions if they do not have a transitive affinity higher than the threshold to any entity in E_c^k:

$$M_c^n = \{m \in M_c | \nexists e \in E_c^k : \phi^*(m, e) > \tau_a\} \tag{3}$$

From M_c^n we produce one or more mention clusters similar to the initialization step in Sect. 4.2.

Example 2. With $\tau_a = 0.75$, affinities $\phi(m_1, e_a) = 0.9$, $\phi(m_1, m_3) = 0.8$, $\phi(m_3, m_4) = 0.9$, and path m_4–m_3–m_1–e_a from Fig. 2, we find that $\phi^*(m_3, e_a) = 0.72 < \tau_a$ and $\phi^*(m_4, e_a) = 0.648 < \tau_a$. m_3 and m_4 are labelled as NIL mentions and form - due to their direct connection - the single cluster C_{1B}.

The function ϕ^* can be computed efficiently on a graph using Dijkstra's algorithm with $-log\phi$ as a function for edge weights. Edges are only inserted in the graph for $\phi > \tau_a$, avoiding undefined edge weights in the case of $\phi = 0$.

5   Experiments

We first describe the datasets and experimental setup used for the evaluation of NASTyLinker. Then, we compare the performance of our approach with related NIL-aware clustering approaches on the NILK dataset [21] and analyze its potential to scale. Finally, we report on the application of NASTyLinker for KB population by linking entities in Wikipedia listings.

5.1   Datasets

NILK. NILK is a dataset that is explicitly created to evaluate EL both for known and NIL entities. It uses Wikipedia as a text corpus and Wikidata [39] as reference KB. All entities contained in Wikidata up to 2017 are labelled as known entities and entities added to Wikidata between 2017 and 2021 are labelled as NIL entities. Mention and entity counts of NILK are displayed in Table 1. About 1% of mentions in NILK are NIL mentions, and about 6% of entities are NIL entities. NIL entities are probably slightly biased towards more popular entities, as the fact that they are present in Wikidata hints at a certain popularity, which may be higher than the popularity of an average NIL entity. Hence, the average number of mentions per NIL entity is quite high in this dataset: half of the entities are mentioned more than once, and more than 15% are even mentioned more than 5 times. Mention boundaries are already given and the authors define partitions for training, validation, and test, which are split in a zero-shot manner w.r.t. NIL entities. As mention context, the authors provide 500 characters before and after the actual mention occurrence in a Wikipedia page. As entity descriptions, we use Wikipedia abstracts.[2]

---

[2] While there are entities in Wikidata which do not have a Wikipedia page, this case does not occur in NILK by construction.

Table 1. Mention and entity occurrences in the partitions of the datasets. NIL mention counts for $\mathcal{D}^L$ are estimated w.r.t. partial completeness assumption. Furthermore, the number of NIL entities $\mathcal{E}^n$ in the listings dataset is not known. For $\mathcal{D}^L_{pred}$ a single mention count is displayed as we cannot know whether a mention in $\mathcal{M}$ links to an entity in $\mathcal{E}^k$ or $\mathcal{E}^n$.

Dataset		$|\mathcal{M}^k|$	$|\mathcal{M}^n|$	$|\mathcal{E}^k|$	$|\mathcal{E}^n|$
NILK	Training ($\mathcal{D}^N_{train}$)	85,052,764	1,327,039	3,382,497	282,210
	Validation ($\mathcal{D}^N_{val}$)	10,525,107	162,948	422,812	35,276
	Test ($\mathcal{D}^N_{test}$)	10,451,126	162,497	422,815	35,279
LISTING	Training ($\mathcal{D}^L_{train}$)	11,690,019	6,760,273	3,073,238	?
	Validation ($\mathcal{D}^L_{val}$)	3,882,641	2,272,941	1,695,156	?
	Test ($\mathcal{D}^L_{test}$)	3,884,066	2,259,072	1,701,015	?
	Prediction ($\mathcal{D}^L_{pred}$)	18,658,271		?	?

Wikipedia Listings. The LISTING dataset was extracted in prior work [20] and consists of entity mentions in enumerations and tables of Wikipedia. Instead of all possible mentions, the focus is only on *subject entities*, which we define as *all entities in a listing appearing as instances to a common concept* [19]. So every item in a listing is assumed to have one main entity the item is about. For example, in Fig. 1d, the soap opera characters are considered entity mentions, while the actors are not.

As reference KB we use CaLiGraph [17,18]. Mention and entity statistics are given in Table 1. We partition the data into train, validation, and test while making sure that listings on a page are all in the same split. Contrary to NILK, the LISTING dataset does not contain explicit labels for NIL entities. Instead, we define NIL entities using the partial completeness assumption (PCA). Given a listing with multiple mentions, we only incorporate them into training or test data if at least one mention is linked to a known entity. Then, by PCA, we assume that all mentions that can be linked are actually linked. All other mentions are assigned a new unique entity identifier. The prediction partition $\mathcal{D}^L_{pred}$, however, contains all mentions without a linked entity (i.e., they may link to a known or to a NIL entity). We use the text of the listing item as mention context for the dataset, and we use Wikipedia abstracts as entity descriptions.

We have considered further datasets that were used for evaluation of NIL-aware approaches for evaluation (e.g. from challenges like TAC-KBP or Microposts [8]), but discarded them due to their small size or not being free to use.

5.2 Metrics

Classification Metrics. We compute precision, recall, and F1-score as well as aggregations of the metrics on the instance level (micro average). As the evaluated approaches are not aware of the true NIL entities, they assign cluster identifiers to (what they assume to be) NIL mentions. To compute the classification metrics, it is necessary to map the cluster identifiers to actual NIL entities. Kassner et al. [24] allow the assignment of multiple cluster identifiers to the same NIL entity. This assumption would yield overly optimistic results. Instead, we only allow one-to-one mappings between cluster identifiers and NIL entities. Finding an optimal assignment for this scenario is equivalent to solving the linear sum assignment problem [2], for which efficient algorithms exist.

Clustering Metrics. Following related approaches [1,24], we additionally provide normalized mutual information (NMI) and adjusted rand index (ARI) as clustering metrics for the comparison of the approaches to settings where no gold labels of NIL entities may be available.[3] For known entities, however, the classification metrics will most likely be more expressive than the clustering metrics as the latter treat multiple clusters with the same known entity as their label still as separate clusters.

5.3 Evaluated Approaches

EL Model. We compute inter-mention and mention-entity affinities with a bi-encoder similar to BLINK [41]. As the reranking of bi-encoder results with a cross-encoder is costly, we evaluate different scenarios where the cross-encoder is omitted (*No Reranking*), applied to inter-mention affinities only (*Mention Reranking*), applied to mention-entity affinities only (*Entity Reranking*), or applied to both (*Full Reranking*). We use the Sentence-BERT implementation of the bi-encoder and cross-encoder [34] with *all-MiniLM-L12-v2* and *distilbert-base-cased* as respective base models. The base models are fine-tuned for at most one million steps on the training partitions of the datasets. Longer fine-tuning did not yield substantial improvements. We use a batch size of 256 for the bi-encoder and 128 for the cross-encoder. For efficient retrieval of candidates from the bi-encoder, we apply approximate nearest neighbour search with hnswlib [27].

We use the plain bi-encoder and cross-encoder predictions of the EL model as baselines. Additionally, we evaluate a trivial *Exact Match* approach, where we link a mention to an entity if their textual representations match exactly.[4] In case of multiple matches, the more popular entity (w.r.t. ingoing and outgoing links in the KB) is selected. Naturally, this approach cannot handle NIL entities.

Clustering Approaches. Apart from the NASTyLinker clustering as described in Sect. 4, we apply the clustering approaches of Kassner et al. [24] and Agarwal et al. [1] for comparison.[5] The clustering approach of Kassner et al., which we

---

[3] We implement further clustering metrics (B-Cubed+, CEAF, MUC) but do not list them as they are similar to or adaptations of the classification metrics.

[4] We apply simple preprocessing like lower-casing and removal of special characters.

[5] We tried to compare with the full approach of Agarwal et al. but they do not provide any code and our efforts to re-implement it did not yield improved results.

call *Majority Clustering*, applies a greedy clustering and assigns a known entity e to a cluster if at least 70% of mentions in the cluster have the highest affinity to e. Similarly to NASTyLinker, they use hyperparameters as thresholds for minimum inter-mention and mention-entity affinities.

The clustering approach of Agarwal et al., which we call *Bottom-Up Clustering*, starts with an empty graph and iteratively adds the edge with the highest affinity, as long as it does not violate the constraint of a cluster having at most one entity. They use a single hyperparameter as a threshold for the minimum affinity of an edge, be it inter-mention or mention-entity.

Hyperparameter Tuning. We select the hyperparameters of the EL model $(k, learning\_rate, warmup\_steps)$ and the thresholds of all three clustering approaches w.r.t. micro F1-score on the validation partition of the datasets. For a fair comparison, we also test multiple values for the threshold for entity assignment of Majority Clustering, which in the original paper was fixed at 0.7.

Our experiments are run on a single machine having 96 CPUs, 1 TB of RAM, and an NVIDIA RTX A6000 GPU with 48 GB of RAM.

5.4   Entity Linking Performance

We tune hyperparameters by evaluating on $\mathcal{D}_{val}^N$. For the EL model, we use a k of 4, a learning rate of 2e−5, and no warmup steps. For τ_m, a value between 0.8 and 0.9 works best for all approaches. For τ_e, the best values revolve around 0.9 for NASTyLinker and Bottom-Up Clustering, and around 0.8 for Majority Clustering. We use an affinity threshold τ_a of 0.75 for NASTyLinker and find that the 0.7 threshold of Majority Clustering produces the best results.

NILK Results. As shown in Table 2, we evaluate all clustering approaches on $\mathcal{D}_{test}^N$ in different reranking scenarios. We find Exact Match already to be a strong baseline for known entities with an F1 of 79.5%, which the Cross-Encoder outperforms by approximately 10%. Even without reranking, the three clustering approaches are able to achieve an F1-score between 40% and 50% for NIL entities. Overall, Majority Clustering is best suited to identify NIL entities. It is the only one to substantially benefit from reranking, increasing the F1-score by 10% when applying entity reranking. Especially for linking known entities, applying only entity reranking is the most favourable scenario, leading even to slight improvements over the baseline approaches that focus only on known entities.

As the reranking of mentions tends to lead to a decrease in results while considerably increasing runtime, we omit mention reranking (and hence, full reranking) in experiments with Wikipedia listings. In the remaining scenarios, NASTyLinker finds the best balance between the linking of known entities and the identification of NIL entities w.r.t. F1-score and NMI.

Table 2. Results for the test partition $\mathcal{D}_{test}^N$ of the NILK dataset.

Approach		Known			NIL			Micro		
		F1	NMI	ARI	F1	NMI	ARI	F1	NMI	ARI
No Clustering	Exact Match	79.5	—	—	0.0	—	—	78.1	—	—
	Bi-Encoder	80.8	—	—	0.0	—	—	79.1	—	—
	Cross-Encoder	89.0	—	—	0.0	—	—	87.1	—	—
Clustering & No Reranking	Bottom-Up	64.6	99.0	97.5	41.6	94.8	81.8	64.1	96.8	93.5
	Majority	59.4	99.3	98.0	49.8	92.7	82.7	59.2	96.6	**94.6**
	NASTyLinker	76.8	98.6	95.3	40.8	**95.2**	76.8	76.0	97.3	90.3
Clustering & Mention Reranking	Bottom-Up	65.7	97.1	98.9	41.5	94.6	10.0	65.1	96.0	66.0
	Majority	66.6	92.4	74.8	44.0	94.4	73.2	66.1	92.4	70.4
	NASTyLinker	74.2	99.0	96.6	39.2	85.6	16.5	73.5	95.5	81.6
Clustering & Entity Reranking	Bottom-Up	89.0	99.3	96.2	41.6	94.1	58.0	87.9	98.2	92.6
	Majority	74.2	99.1	**99.3**	**54.1**	89.3	**92.5**	73.7	96.6	**94.6**
	NASTyLinker	**90.4**	99.3	95.5	43.7	94.6	85.3	**89.4**	**98.5**	84.1
Clustering & Full Reranking	Bottom-Up	84.2	**99.6**	98.9	41.8	84.6	3.2	83.3	96.2	65.5
	Majority	80.3	95.1	95.9	51.7	90.0	39.2	79.6	93.9	70.4
	NASTyLinker	87.9	99.5	99.2	42.5	87.6	33.6	86.9	97.4	71.7

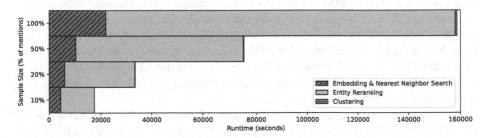

Fig. 3. Runtime of NASTyLinker components for predictions on samples of $\mathcal{D}_{test}^N$.

Runtime and Scalability. The fine-tuning of the bi-encoder and cross-encoder models took 2 h and 12 h, respectively. For prediction with a k of 4 on $\mathcal{D}_{test}^N$, the bi-encoder needed 6 h. Reranking entity affinities with the cross-encoder took 38 h. Clustering the results with any of the three approaches took an additional 8 to 12 min.

In Fig. 3 we give an overview of the runtime of NASTyLinker components, compared over various sample sizes of $\mathcal{D}_{test}^N$. Overall, we can see that the total runtime scales linearly. With a smaller sample size, the computation of embeddings and nearest neighbour search with the bi-encoder is responsible for a larger fraction of the total runtime. We find that this is due to the relatively large overhead of creating the index for the approximate nearest neighbour search. With increasing sample size, this factor is less important for the overall runtime. In general, entity reranking is responsible for most of the total runtime.

The runtime of the clustering itself is responsible for approximately 1% of total runtime and we do not expect it to increase substantially, as Dijkstra's algorithm has log-linear complexity and the size of mention clusters can be controlled by the threshold τ_m. Hence, the runtime of NASTyLinker is expected to grow proportionally to the runtime of BLINK [41] for increasing sizes of datasets. If runtime is an important factor, one might consider skipping entity reranking as NASTyLinker still produces reasonable results when relying on bi-encoder affinities only.

5.5   Linking Entities in Wikipedia Listings

As the average mention context length in the LISTING dataset is lower than the one in NILK, fine-tuning the EL models took only a total of 8 h. We find that most of the hyperparameters chosen for NILK are a reasonable choice for this dataset as well. For entity reranking, however, the approaches produce better results when the thresholds τ_m and τ_a are slightly increased to 0.9 and 0.85.

Results on Test Partition. Linking results for $\mathcal{D}_{test}^L$ are provided in Table 3. As we rely on PCA for the labelling of NIL mentions, we only know whether a mention is a NIL mention without knowing which NIL mentions refer to the same entity. Hence, we can only compute results for known entities and for overall predictions. For the latter, we simply assume that any prediction made for a NIL mention is incorrect. With this assumption, we are obviously not able to produce realistic performance estimates, but we are able to see the impact of being NIL-aware (and hence, make no prediction for NIL mentions) on the overall linking performance.

Due to their majority mechanism, Majority Clustering identifies known entities with very high precision, but at the cost of a reduced recall. The scores of Bottom-Up Clustering and NASTyLinker are comparable when considering known entities, but diverge w.r.t. the micro average. In the entity reranking scenario, NASTyLinker achieves the overall best micro F1-score with 86.7%. This, however, has to be taken with a grain of salt as we do not know how many of the heuristically labelled NIL mentions are actually referring to NIL entities and how many refer to known entities.

Knowledge Graph Population Statistics. The partition $\mathcal{D}_{pred}^L$ of the LISTING dataset contains only mentions for which we don't know whether they link to a known or to a NIL entity. To make predictions for these mentions, we run the NASTyLinker approach on the whole LISTING corpus, i.e. on a total of 38 million mentions, as we need representations of all known entities for the clustering step. These mentions were extracted from 2.9 million listings on 1.4 million Wikipedia pages. As reference KB, we use the knowledge graph CaLi-Graph which is based on Wikipedia and hence contains entities for all 5.8 million Wikipedia articles.

Table 3. Results for the test partition $\mathcal{D}_{test}^{L}$ of the LISTING dataset. No results for NIL are given because the real NIL entities $\mathcal{E}^n$ are not available for this dataset. For the micro average, we label every prediction made for a mention linked to an entity in $\mathcal{E}^n$ as incorrect.

Approach		Known			Micro		
		P	R	F1	P	R	F1
No Clustering	Exact Match	91.4	73.5	81.5	81.1	73.5	77.1
	Bi-Encoder	88.6	88.6	88.6	62.6	88.6	73.4
	Cross-Encoder	93.7	**93.8**	**93.8**	66.2	**93.8**	77.6
Clustering & No Reranking	Bottom-Up	89.7	84.9	87.2	63.9	84.9	72.9
	Majority	95.2	67.9	79.2	78.1	67.9	72.6
	NASTyLinker	90.6	78.5	84.1	70.7	78.5	74.4
Clustering & Entity Reranking	Bottom-Up	94.2	90.8	92.5	75.3	90.8	82.3
	Majority	**98.8**	76.2	86.0	**93.4**	76.2	83.9
	NASTyLinker	97.0	87.0	91.8	88.5	87.0	**87.7**

The total runtime was 62 h, with 14 h for the bi-encoder, 47 h for the cross-encoder, and 45 min for the clustering. We find 13.4 million mentions (i.e., 70%) to be NIL mentions which refer to 7.6 million NIL entities. The remaining 5.2 million mentions refer to 1.4 million entities that exist in CaLiGraph already. By integrating the discovered NIL entities into CaLiGraph, we would increase its entity count by 130%. Further, the discovered mentions for known entities can be used to enrich the representations of the entities in the knowledge graph through various knowledge graph completion methods [19].

Qualitative Analysis. To evaluate the actual linking performance on the set of unlabeled mentions $\mathcal{D}_{pred}^{L}$, we conducted a manual inspection of the results. We randomly picked 100 mentions and 100 clusters[6] and identified, if incorrect, the type of error.[7] The results of this evaluation are given in Table 4. Overall, we find the outcome to agree with the results of NASTyLinker on $\mathcal{D}_{test}^{L}$. Hence, the approach produces highly accurate results, which we observed even for difficult cases. For example, the approach correctly created NIL entity clusters for the mention *North Course* referring to a racing horse (in pages *Appleton Stakes* and *Oceanport Stakes*), a golf course in Ontario, CA (in page *Tournament Players Club*), and a golf course in Florida, US (in page *Pete Dye*).

While the linking performance is quite consistent for mentions, the correctness of clusters for known entities is significantly lower than for NIL entities.[8]

---

[6] The sampling of clusters was stratified w.r.t. cluster size.

[7] We evaluated the linking and clustering decision w.r.t. the top-4 mention and entity candidates produced by the bi-encoder. Although recall@4 for the bi-encoder is 97%, some relevant candidates might have been missed.

[8] For the evaluation to be significant, we treat all clusters referring to the same known entity as a single cluster.

Table 4. Results of the manual evaluation of 100 clusters and 100 mentions. Columns group the results by actual entity type (known, NIL, overall), rows group by prediction outcome. Accuracy values may deviate by ±9.6% for mentions and by ±7.0% for clusters (95% confidence).

Prediction	Mentions			Clusters		
	$\mathcal{E}^k$	$\mathcal{E}^n$	$\mathcal{E}$	$\mathcal{E}^k$	$\mathcal{E}^n$	$\mathcal{E}$
Correct	20	64	84	8	71	79
Incorrectly linked to NIL entity	3	—	3	1	—	1
Incorrectly linked to known entity	—	7	7	—	3	3
Not all mentions of entity in cluster	—	—	—	8	0	8
Mentions from multiple entities in cluster	—	—	—	1	4	5
Ignored (mention extracted incorrectly)	—	—	6	—	—	4
Total Count	23	71	94	18	78	96
Accuracy (%)	87.0	90.1	89.4	44.4	91.0	82.3

This drop in performance is not due to NASTyLinker being incapable of linking to known entities correctly (as the accuracy of 87% on mention-level shows). Instead, it can rather be attributed to the fact that clusters of known entities contain 3.8 mentions on average, while clusters of NIL entities contain 1.7 mentions on average. Hence, the likelihood of missing at least one mention is a lot higher, which is also the main error for known clusters.

Compared to the results on NILK, the linking accuracy for NIL mentions is much higher. We explain this with the different kinds of NIL entities contained in the two datasets. While an average NIL entity is mentioned 4.6 times in NILK, our results indicate that this number is approximately 1.7 for the LISTING dataset. The latter dataset may hence contain a lot of easy-to-link mentions by assigning them their own cluster.

6   Conclusion and Outlook

With NASTyLinker, we introduce a NIL-aware EL approach that is capable of making high-quality predictions for known and for NIL entities. In the practical setting of EL in Wikipedia listings, we show that our approach can be used to populate a knowledge graph with a large number of additional entities as well as to enrich representations of existing entities.

Although the results look promising at a first glance, there is still a lot to improve as even small errors can multiply in downstream applications. For future work, we plan to concentrate on establishing a full end-to-end pipeline that includes the detection of mention, as recent works demonstrate how this can substantially reduce runtime without a decrease in performance [4, 24]. This will also open the path to a training procedure that considers NIL entities already during the creation of embeddings. Additionally, we will explore how the dependencies between items in listings can be exploited to further improve predictions.

References

1. Agarwal, D., Angell, R., Monath, N., McCallum, A.: Entity linking and discovery via arborescence-based supervised clustering. arXiv preprint arXiv:2109.01242 (2021)
2. Alfaro, C.A., Perez, S.L., Valencia, C.E., Vargas, M.C.: The assignment problem revisited. Optim. Lett. **16**(5), 1531–1548 (2022). https://doi.org/10.1007/s11590-021-01791-4
3. Angell, R., Monath, N., Mohan, S., Yadav, N., McCallum, A.: Clustering-based inference for biomedical entity linking. In: Proceedings of the 2021 Conference of the North American Chapter of the Association for Computational Linguistics: Human Language Technologies, pp. 2598–2608 (2021)
4. Ayoola, T., Tyagi, S., Fisher, J., Christodoulopoulos, C., Pierleoni, A.: ReFinED: an efficient zero-shot-capable approach to end-to-end entity linking. arXiv preprint arXiv:2207.04108 (2022)
5. Bagga, A., Baldwin, B.: Entity-based cross-document coreferencing using the vector space model. In: COLING 1998 Volume 1: The 17th International Conference on Computational Linguistics (1998)
6. Blissett, K., Ji, H.: Cross-lingual NIL entity clustering for low-resource languages. In: Proceedings of the Second Workshop on Computational Models of Reference, Anaphora and Coreference, pp. 20–25 (2019)
7. Cucerzan, S.: Large-scale named entity disambiguation based on Wikipedia data. In: Proceedings of the 2007 Joint Conference on Empirical Methods in Natural Language Processing and Computational Natural Language Learning (EMNLP-CoNLL), pp. 708–716 (2007)
8. Dadzie, A., Preotiuc-Pietro, D., Radovanovic, D., Basave, A.E.C., Weller, K. (eds.): Proceedings of the 6th Workshop on 'Making Sense of Microposts' Co-Located with the 25th International World Wide Web Conference (WWW 2016), Montréal, Canada, 11 April 2016, CEUR Workshop Proceedings, vol. 1691. CEUR-WS.org (2016). http://ceur-ws.org/Vol-1691
9. Das, R., et al.: Multi-step entity-centric information retrieval for multi-hop question answering. In: Proceedings of the 2nd Workshop on Machine Reading for Question Answering, pp. 113–118 (2019)
10. Devlin, J., Chang, M.W., Lee, K., Toutanova, K.: BERT: pre-training of deep bidirectional transformers for language understanding. arXiv preprint arXiv:1810.04805 (2018)
11. Dutta, S., Weikum, G.: C3EL: a joint model for cross-document co-reference resolution and entity linking. In: Proceedings of the 2015 Conference on Empirical Methods in Natural Language Processing, pp. 846–856 (2015)
12. Fahrni, A., Heinzerling, B., Göckel, T., Strube, M.: HITS'Monolingual and cross-lingual entity linking system at TAC 2013. In: TAC. Citeseer (2013)
13. Ganea, O.E., Hofmann, T.: Deep joint entity disambiguation with local neural attention. In: Proceedings of the 2017 Conference on Empirical Methods in Natural Language Processing, pp. 2619–2629 (2017)
14. Gillick, D., et al.: Learning dense representations for entity retrieval. In: Proceedings of the 23rd Conference on Computational Natural Language Learning (CoNLL), pp. 528–537 (2019)
15. Greenfield, K., et al.: A reverse approach to named entity extraction and linking in microposts. In: # Microposts, pp. 67–69 (2016)

16. Heist, N., Hertling, S., Ringler, D., Paulheim, H.: Knowledge graphs on the web-an overview. In: Knowledge Graphs for eXplainable Artificial Intelligence, pp. 3–22 (2020)
17. Heist, N., Paulheim, H.: Uncovering the semantics of Wikipedia categories. In: Ghidini, C., et al. (eds.) ISWC 2019. LNCS, vol. 11778, pp. 219–236. Springer, Cham (2019). https://doi.org/10.1007/978-3-030-30793-6_13
18. Heist, N., Paulheim, H.: Entity extraction from Wikipedia list pages. In: Harth, A., et al. (eds.) ESWC 2020. LNCS, vol. 12123, pp. 327–342. Springer, Cham (2020). https://doi.org/10.1007/978-3-030-49461-2_19
19. Heist, N., Paulheim, H.: Information extraction from co-occurring similar entities. In: Proceedings of the Web Conference 2021, pp. 3999–4009 (2021)
20. Heist, N., Paulheim, H.: Transformer-based subject entity detection in Wikipedia listings. arXiv preprint arXiv:2210.01482 (2022)
21. Iurshina, A., Pan, J., Boutalbi, R., Staab, S.: NILK: entity linking dataset targeting NIL-linking cases. In: Proceedings of the 31st ACM International Conference on Information & Knowledge Management, pp. 4069–4073 (2022)
22. Ji, H., Grishman, R., Dang, H.T., Griffitt, K., Ellis, J.: Overview of the TAC 2010 knowledge base population track. In: Third Text Analysis Conference (TAC 2010), vol. 3, p. 3 (2010)
23. Johnson, J., Douze, M., Jégou, H.: Billion-scale similarity search with GPUs. IEEE Trans. Big Data 7(3), 535–547 (2019)
24. Kassner, N., Petroni, F., Plekhanov, M., Riedel, S., Cancedda, N.: EDIN: an end-to-end benchmark and pipeline for unknown entity discovery and indexing. arXiv preprint arXiv:2205.12570 (2022)
25. Logan IV, R.L., McCallum, A., Singh, S., Bikel, D.: Benchmarking scalable methods for streaming cross document entity coreference. In: Proceedings of the 59th Annual Meeting of the Association for Computational Linguistics and the 11th International Joint Conference on Natural Language Processing (Volume 1: Long Papers), pp. 4717–4731 (2021)
26. Logeswaran, L., Chang, M.W., Lee, K., Toutanova, K., Devlin, J., Lee, H.: Zero-shot entity linking by reading entity descriptions. In: Proceedings of the 57th Annual Meeting of the Association for Computational Linguistics, pp. 3449–3460 (2019)
27. Malkov, Y.A., Yashunin, D.A.: Efficient and robust approximate nearest neighbor search using hierarchical navigable small world graphs. IEEE Trans. Pattern Anal. Mach. Intell. 42(4), 824–836 (2018)
28. Milne, D., Witten, I.H.: Learning to link with Wikipedia. In: Proceedings of the 17th ACM Conference on Information and Knowledge Management, pp. 509–518 (2008)
29. Monahan, S., Lehmann, J., Nyberg, T., Plymale, J., Jung, A.: Cross-lingual cross-document coreference with entity linking. In: TAC (2011)
30. Partalidou, E., Christou, D., Tsoumakas, G.: Improving zero-shot entity retrieval through effective dense representations. In: Proceedings of the 12th Hellenic Conference on Artificial Intelligence, pp. 1–5 (2022)
31. Paulheim, H.: Knowledge graph refinement: a survey of approaches and evaluation methods. Semant. Web 8(3), 489–508 (2017)
32. Radford, W., Hachey, B., Honnibal, M., Nothman, J., Curran, J.R.: Naïve but effective NIL clustering baselines-CMCRC at TAC 2011. In: Proceedings of Text Analysis Conference (TAC 2011). Citeseer (2011)

33. Rao, D., McNamee, P., Dredze, M.: Entity linking: finding extracted entities in a knowledge base. In: Poibeau, T., Saggion, H., Piskorski, J., Yangarber, R. (eds.) Multi-Source, Multilingual Information Extraction and Summarization. NLP, pp. 93–115. Springer, Heidelberg (2013). https://doi.org/10.1007/978-3-642-28569-1_5
34. Reimers, N., Gurevych, I.: Sentence-BERT: sentence embeddings using siamese BERT-networks. In: Proceedings of the 2019 Conference on Empirical Methods in Natural Language Processing and the 9th International Joint Conference on Natural Language Processing (EMNLP-IJCNLP), pp. 3982–3992 (2019)
35. Ristoski, P., Lin, Z., Zhou, Q.: KG-ZESHEL: knowledge graph-enhanced zero-shot entity linking. In: Proceedings of the 11th on Knowledge Capture Conference, pp. 49–56 (2021)
36. Rizzo, G., Pereira, B., Varga, A., Van Erp, M., Cano Basave, A.E.: Lessons learnt from the Named Entity rEcognition and linking (NEEL) challenge series. Semant. Web 8(5), 667–700 (2017)
37. Sevgili, Ö., Shelmanov, A., Arkhipov, M., Panchenko, A., Biemann, C.: Neural entity linking: a survey of models based on deep learning. Semant. Web 13(3), 527–570 (2022)
38. Shen, W., Wang, J., Han, J.: Entity linking with a knowledge base: issues, techniques, and solutions. IEEE Trans. Knowl. Data Eng. 27(2), 443–460 (2014)
39. Vrandečić, D., Krötzsch, M.: Wikidata: a free collaborative knowledgebase. Commun. ACM 57(10), 78–85 (2014)
40. Wang, Z., Ng, P., Nallapati, R., Xiang, B.: Retrieval, re-ranking and multi-task learning for knowledge-base question answering. In: Proceedings of the 16th Conference of the European Chapter of the Association for Computational Linguistics: Main Volume, pp. 347–357 (2021)
41. Wu, L., Petroni, F., Josifoski, M., Riedel, S., Zettlemoyer, L.: Scalable zero-shot entity linking with dense entity retrieval. In: Proceedings of the 2020 Conference on Empirical Methods in Natural Language Processing (EMNLP), pp. 6397–6407 (2020)

iSummary: Workload-Based, Personalized Summaries for Knowledge Graphs

Giannis Vassiliou[1], Fanouris Alevizakis[2,3], Nikolaos Papadakis[1], and Haridimos Kondylakis[3(✉)]

[1] Department of Electrical and Computer Engineering, HMU, Heraklion, Greece
[2] Computer Science Department, UOC, Heraklion, Greece
[3] Institute of Computer Science, FORTH, Heraklion, Greece
kondylak@ics.forth.gr

Abstract. The explosion in the size and the complexity of the available Knowledge Graphs on the web has led to the need for efficient and effective methods for their understanding and exploration. Semantic summaries have recently emerged as methods to quickly explore and understand the contents of various sources. However, in most cases, they are static, not incorporating user needs and preferences, and cannot scale. In this paper, we present iSummary, a novel, scalable approach for constructing personalized summaries. As the size and the complexity of the Knowledge Graphs for constructing personalized summaries prohibit efficient summary construction, in our approach we exploit query logs. The main idea behind our approach is to exploit knowledge captured in existing user queries for identifying the most interesting resources and linking them, constructing as such high-quality, personalized summaries. We present an algorithm with theoretical guarantees on the summary's quality, linear in the number of queries available in the query log. We evaluate our approach using three real-world datasets and several baselines, showing that our approach dominates other methods in terms of both quality and efficiency.

Keywords: Semantic Summaries · RDF/S · Workload-based

1 Introduction

Daily, a tremendous amount of new information becomes available online. RDF Knowledge graphs (KGs) rapidly grow to include millions or even billions of triples that are offered through the web. For example, the Linked Open Data Cloud, currently includes more than 62 billion triples, organized in large and complex RDF data graphs [1].

The complexity and the size of those data sources limit their exploitation potential and necessitate effective and efficient ways to explore and understand their content [17]. In this direction, semantic summarization has been proposed as a way to extract useful, minimized information out of large semantic graphs that many applications can exploit instead of the original data graphs for performing certain tasks more efficiently such as visualization [13], exploration

C. Pesquita et al. (Eds.): ESWC 2023, LNCS 13870, pp. 192–208, 2023.
https://doi.org/10.1007/978-3-031-33455-9_12

[18,19], query answering, etc. [5]. Structural semantic summaries focus mostly on the structure of the graph for extracting the required information, whereas non-quotient structural semantic summaries try to select the most important parts of the graph for generating the result summaries.

The Problem. Most of the existing works in the area of structural, non-quotient semantic summarization, produce generic static summaries [5] that cannot be applied to big KGs. Further, as different persons have different data exploration needs the generated summaries should be tailored specifically to the individual's interests. Although this has already been recognized by the research community, the approaches offering personalized summaries so far, rely on node weights selected by the users, then followed by algorithms making various vague assumptions about the relevant subsets out of the semantic graph that should complement the initial user choice [3,24]. More recent approaches like [14] exploit the individual user queries for mining user preferences but still rely on the KG to compute the summary which makes it computationally hard. Further, capturing a complete individual user query set is usually not feasible.

The Solution. Instead of relying on node weights or on individual provided set of user queries, we exploit generic logs already available through the SPARQL endpoints of the various KGs available online. Then in order to generate a personalized summary we only require one or a few nodes the user is most interested in. As previous users have already identified through their queries, the most common connections to the specific user-selected nodes, we exploit this information in order to formulate the generated summaries. More specifically:

- We introduce, motivate and formulate the problem of λ/κ-Personalized Summary and we show that although a solution to the problem is rather useful, resolving the problem is both impractical (requires multiple weights assignments) and computationally expensive (NP-complete).
- We analytically show how we can resolve the problem relying on existing query logs and we provide a solution to both the multiple weight assignment required and also to the computational problem.
- We present an algorithm that provides theoretical guarantees on the summary's quality which is linear in the number of queries available in the query log.
- We experimentally evaluate our approach using three real-world datasets and the corresponding workloads, i.e. Wikidata, Bio2RDF, and DBPedia, showing the benefits of our approach maximizing coverage for user queries, dominating all baselines and competitors on both quality and efficiency.

To the best of our knowledge, this is the first approach to constructing personalized, structural, non-quotient semantic summaries exploiting generic query workloads. The rest of this paper is organized as follows: Sect. 2 provides preliminaries and problem definition. Then Sect. 3 presents our solution, iSummary, detailing the various steps for generating a personalized summary. Section 4 presents the experimental evaluation of our work, whereas Sect. 4 presents related work. Finally, Sect. 5 concludes this paper and presents directions for future work.

2   Preliminaries and Problem Definition

Preliminaries. In this paper, we focus on RDF Knowledge Graphs, as RDF is among the most widely-used standards for publishing and representing data on the Web, promoted by the W3C for semantic web applications. An *RDF KG* $\mathcal{G}$ is a set of *triples* of the form (s, p, o). A triple states that a *subject* s has the *property* p, and the value of that property is the *object* o. We consider only well-formed triples, according to the RDF specification [23]. These belong to $(\mathcal{U} \cup \mathcal{B}) \times \mathcal{U} \times (\mathcal{U} \cup \mathcal{B} \cup \mathcal{L})$, where $\mathcal{U}$ is a set of Uniform Resource Identifiers (URIs), $\mathcal{L}$ a set of typed or untyped literals (constants), and $\mathcal{B}$ a set of blank nodes (unknown URIs or literals); $\mathcal{U}, \mathcal{B}, \mathcal{L}$ are pairwise disjoint. Additionally, we assume an infinite set $\mathcal{X}$ of variables that is disjoint from the previous sets. Blank nodes are essential features of RDF allowing to support *unknown URI/literal tokens*. The RDF standard includes the `rdf:type` property, which allows specifying the type(s) of a resource. Each resource can have zero, one or several types. For querying, we use SPARQL [2], the W3C standard for querying RDF datasets. The basic building units of the SPARQL queries are triple pattern and Basic Graph Pattern (BGP). A triple pattern is a triple from $(\mathcal{U} \cup \mathcal{B} \cup \mathcal{X}) \times (\mathcal{U} \cup \mathcal{X})) \times (\mathcal{U} \cup \mathcal{B} \cup \mathcal{L} \cup \mathcal{X})$. A set of triple patterns constitutes a basic graph pattern (BGP).

Informal Problem Statement. Informally the problem we address may be described as follows: Given a knowledge graph G, a limited set of λ resources that the user wants his/her summary to be focused on, and a number κ denoting the size of the summary (in terms of nodes to be included), efficiently construct a personal summary $G\prime \in G$ that best captures the user's preferred information in G.

Resolving this problem is really important, as usually users visit a KG with a specific information request in mind, and are used in providing a starting point to begin the KG exploration that will lead to the information they are looking for. Usually, they are not interested in generic summaries of the overall graph, but they would like to identify information pertinent to a specific part of the graph [20].

Example 1. Consider as an example, the KG shown in Fig. 1, which includes information on the university domain. The figure visualizes persons and organizations and also presents some indicative instances. Note that prefixes are omitted from the figure for sake of clarity. Now assume that the user selects two nodes ($\lambda = 2$), i.e. *Plexousakis* and *Fanis* (the blue ones), and would like to get a personalized summary of size five ($\kappa = 5$). As such, three more nodes should be selected from the graph and linked with the two nodes provided by the user.

A way to select the three additional nodes and the edges for the result summary, used by previous approaches (e.g., [25]) is to have weights available on all (or some of) the nodes, and select the nodes maximizing the weight of the selected sub-graph. However, those weights should be specific to user requests. For example, *Publication* might not be of interest when requesting a summary for *Plexousakis* and *Fanis* whereas it might be of interest when requesting a summary for *Research*.

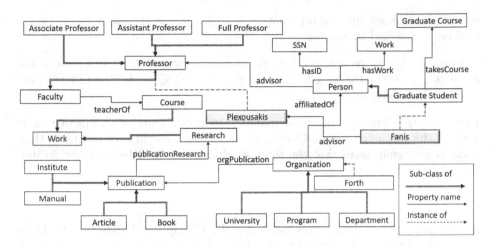

Fig. 1. Example RDF KG.

Formal Problem Statement. The previous example makes it obvious that requesting the user to provide weights each time for all (or a least some) of the nodes is impractical. Next, we formally present the problem of λ/κ-Personalized Summary and we show that, although useful, besides impractical it is also computationally expensive.

Definition 1 (λ/κ-Personalized Summary). *Given (1) a knowledge graph $G = (V, E)$, (2) a non-negative weight assignment to all nodes, capturing user preferences in G, (3) λ seed nodes, (4) and a number κ ($\lambda \leq \kappa$), find the smallest maximum-weight tree $G\prime = (V\prime, E\prime) \in G$ including the κ most preferred nodes.*

Not that we don't actually require a weight to be assigned to all nodes, as the weight of all nodes can be by default zero, and the user only adds weights to a subset of them. A solution to the λ/κ-Personalized Summary problem is not unique, as there might be many maximum-weight trees with the smallest size that are equally useful for the user. Next, we prove that the aforementioned problem is NP-complete.

Theorem 1. *The λ/κ-Personalized Summary problem is NP-complete.*

Proof. The Steiner tree problem [9], focuses on connecting selected nodes of a weighted graph at minimum cost. In our case, we normalize weight assignments from 0 to 1 and subtract them from 1. Further, we set the weight of the λ seed nodes to be equal to zero. Now instead of finding a maximum-weight tree, we search for a minimum-weight tree, connecting the seed nodes with the $\kappa - \lambda$ minimum weight nodes. As such our problem is equivalent to the Steiner tree problem which has been shown to be NP-complete.

A nice property of the λ/κ-Personalized Summaries is that their quality is *monotonically increasing* as the κ increases. This means that as the summary size increases more relevant information is added to the summary for the same seed nodes selected by the user.

Lemma 1. *Let S_κ be a λ/κ-Personalized Summary and $S_{\kappa+1}$ be a $\lambda/(\kappa + 1)$-Personalized Summary for G. Then $W(S_{\kappa+1}) \geq W(S_\kappa)$, where $W(S)$ the sum of all node weights in S.*

Proof. As S_k is a maximum-weight tree for λ including κ nodes, adding one more node in the summary and looking for the maximum-weight tree including that node as well guarantees that the total weight of S_{k+1} will be equal or greater than the total weight of S_k.

Over the years many approximations have been proposed for resolving the Steiner Tree problem [10,22] that could be exploited for resolving the λ/κ-Personalized Summary problem as well. CHeapeast INSertion (CHINS) one of the fastest approximation algorithms has a worst time complexity of $O(\kappa \times 2|V| \times log|V|)$. CHINS starts with a partial solution consisting of a single selected node and it incrementally adds the nearest one of the selected not yet in the solution. However, still, computing a Steiner Tree approximate solution over commodity hardware for a large KG such as WikiData is not feasible. For example, assuming $1\mu s$ for each operation, running CHINS for WikiData that includes 1.4 billion statements would require more than a year to calculate a 5/10-Personalized Summary.

For the rest of the paper, without loss of generality, we will focus on $1/\kappa$-Personalized Summaries (in short κ-Personalized Summaries), where the user provides only a single seed node as input, for not perplexing definitions and algorithms and due to space limitations. Extending the presented solution and algorithms for multiple seed nodes is straightforward.

3   iSummary

As we have shown in the previous section, computing the κ-Personalized Summary is both *impractical*, as different weights should be assigned to the graph nodes for each distinct user query, and computationally *expensive*, as it requires computing a Steiner Tree solution. In this section, we are going to provide an elegant approximate solution based on query workloads.

Resolving the Problem of Multiple Weight Assignments. Assume now that for the KG G we have available a query log $Q = \{q_1, \cdots, q_n\}$ available. This assumption is reasonable, as all big KGs offer a SPARQL endpoint that logs user queries for various purposes. Multiple studies already confirm this (e.g., [4]), and we were also able to easily get access to such logs for DBpedia, WikiData, and Bio2RDF (more about this in Sect. 4).

Having such a query log available, our first idea is that we can *use it to mine user preferences* for the specific seed node that the user is interested in. The idea here is that if a user is interested in a κ-Personalized Summary for s then we can use Q to identify *relevant queries* to s, i.e., queries that include s. In those queries, other nodes relevant to the user input will be available. In fact, as those queries have been issued by thousands of users, we assume that *the most useful related nodes will be the ones that appear more frequently* there.

Example 2. Assume that for our example KG, shown in Fig. 1, we have available a query log consisting of the following SPARQL queries:

```
Q1. SELECT ?x ?y WHERE
    {x? a Person. y? a Professor. ?x advisor ?y.}
Q2. SELECT ?x ?y WHERE
    {x? a Person. y? a Organization. ?y affiliatedOf ?x.}
Q3. SELECT ?x ?y WHERE
    {x? a Person. y? a Organization. ?y affilatedOf ?x.
    ?y orgName "FORTH".}
Q4. SELECT ?y WHERE
    {y? a Organization.}
Q5. SELECT ?y WHERE
    {y? a Publication. ?x authored ?y. ?x a Institute.}
```

Now assume that a user is interested in a 2-Personalized Summary for the node *Person*. Based on the query log we can identify that relevant queries to user input are $Q1$, $Q2$, and $Q3$. Examining those queries we can identify that the useful nodes are the *Professor* and *Organization*. In fact, as *Organization* is used in two queries it should be most useful according to the available query log. As we are looking for a 2-Personalized Summary it will be included in the result. On the other hand, if the user is interested in a 2-Personalized Summary for the node *Publication* the relevant query is $Q5$ which suggests that the *Institute* node should be included in the result.

Based on this assumption we can have multiple weight assignments, one per user input, as they occur from thousands of user queries that involve the provided user input and that are based on past users' preferences, as expressed in their queries. Note here that we don't need weights for the whole graph, as by default we can set the weight of the nodes that do not appear in the filtered user queries to zero.

Resolving the Computational Problem. Now that we have a way to assign personalized weights to the nodes, we will provide a computationally efficient procedure in order to link the selected nodes over a big graph. We will stick to the ideas proposed by the CHINS approximation algorithm. We will start with a solution including a single node, the s selected by the user, adding one node each time of the ones with the maximum weight till all remaining $k - 1$ nodes are included in the summary. However, for doing so we will not use the original data graph but again *relevant user queries*. The main idea here is the following: link s with the $k - 1$ maximum weight nodes using *the most frequent shortest paths* from the user queries.

Example 3. We now continue our example for constructing a 2-Personalized Summary for the node *Person*. As we have already explained the node

Organization has the higher frequency in queries involving *Person* and as such it will be selected to be included in the summary. Now instead of searching the graph shown in Fig. 1 for linking *Person* with *Organization* we will additionally filter queries including *Person* keeping only the ones including *Organization* as well. Those are Q2 and Q3. For each one of those queries, we calculate the shortest path for linking *Person* and *Organization* and we eventually select the most frequent shortest path to include in the summary. As such the 2-Personalized Summary for the node *Person* includes a single triple $t_1 : (Organization, addiliatedOf, Person)$.

In the case we are interested in a 3-Personalized Summary for the node *Person*, the summary would have to include the *Professor* node as well. To link *Person* with *Professor* we would filter the queries to keep only those where both *Professor* and *Person* appear, e.g. Q1. Then for linking those nodes we would keep the most frequent shortest path, i.e., $t_2 : (Person, advisor, Professor)$. Now the 3-Personalized Summary for *Person* would include both t_1 and t_2.

3.1   The Algorithm

Now we are ready to present the corresponding algorithm for constructing a κ-Personalized Summary for an input node s. The algorithm is presented in Algorithm 1 and receives as input κ, s and a query log Q. It starts by including the first node in the summary (line 2), the one selected by the user. Then it filters the queries to keep only Q_s, i.e., the ones including s (line 3). Next, it calculates the frequency of all nodes in Q_s and selects the $k - 1$ ones with the higher frequency to be included in the result summary (line 4), i.e., the top_{k-1} ones.

The next step is to visit one by one these nodes each time identifying an optimal way to link each one of those nodes not in the summary with the ones already added (lines 5–13). More specifically for each node in top_{k-1} not already in the summary we explore all nodes in the summary by filtering again the queries in Q_S retrieving Q_{sxy} that contains x and y (line 8). Then for each query in Q_{sxy}, we find the shortest path linking x with y (line 10) and we keep the most frequent one (line 11) to formulate the result summary. Eventually, we select to link the next node in the top_{k-1} with the most frequent shortest path linking that node with all nodes currently in the summary. However, as we identify paths in the queries, those might include variables that we should replace with actual resources. This is accomplished by replacing them with resources mined from other queries which might have both the specific resource and its neighbors instantiated (line 13). Finally, we return to the user the constructed set of triples S as a summary (line 14).

The result produced by the aforementioned algorithm is deterministic based on its implementation, as in the case of ties, these are broken by keeping the first choice. However as already explained a personalized workload-based summary might not be unique as many nodes can have the same frequency in the available queries, or there might be available many different shortest paths to connect

---

Algorithm 1. iSummary

Input: An user-selected node s, a query workload Q, the number of the most useful nodes to be included in the summary κ.
Output: S a κ-Personalized summary for s

1: $S \leftarrow \emptyset$
2: $visited \leftarrow \{s\}$
3: $Q_s \leftarrow filter(Q, \{s\})$
4: $top_{k-1} \leftarrow selectTopNodes(Q_s, k-1)$
5: **for all** $x \in top_{k-1}, x \notin visited$ **do**
6:    $selectedPath \leftarrow \emptyset$
7:    **for all** $pairs(x,y), y \in visited$ **do**
8:       $Q_{sxy} \leftarrow filter(Q_s, \{x,y\})$
9:       **for all** $q \in Q_{sxy}$ **do**
10:          $shortestPaths[q] \leftarrow getShortestPathFromQuery(q, \{x,y\})$
11:          $selectedPath \leftarrow findMostFrequent(shortestPaths, selectedPath)$
12:    $visited \leftarrow visited \cup \{x\}$
13:    $S \leftarrow S \cup resolveVariables(selectedPath, Q)$
14: **return** S

---

them. Next, we prove that iSummary is able to find an approximate solution with specific guarantees:

Theorem 2. *The iSummary algorithm finds an approximate solution to the κ-Personalized Summary problem with a worst-case bound of 2, i.e., $W/W_{opt} \leq 2 \times (1 - l/k)$, where W and W_{opt} denote the total weight of a feasible solution and an optimal solution respectively, and l a constant.*

Proof. (sketch) In essence, iSummary replicates the CHINS approximation algorithm which has been proved to have the aforementioned worst-case bound [7] using the queries in order to reconstruct the part of the interest of the original graph. For the remaining nodes that do not appear in the filtered queries, we set their weight to zero. The proof follows.

To identify the complexity of the algorithm we should first identify the complexity of its components. Assuming $|Q|$ the number of queries in the available workload we first need to scan them once for filtering and retrieving the top_{k-1} nodes, i.e. $O(|Q|)$. Then for each node in the top_{k-1} we need to gradually include them in the visited set by checking their connection to all existing nodes in the summary. This will result in k^2 iterations in each of which the Q_s queries should be filtered, i.e. $O(k^2 \times |Q_s|)$. Then for each query appearing in the filtering results we should run once the Dijkstra algorithm for getting the shortest path. At the worst case for each node we need to calculate the shortest paths for all queries, i.e. $O(k^2 \times |Q_s| \times |V_{Q_s}^2|)$, where $V_{Q_s}^2$ the maximum number of nodes that appear in the queries in the workload. Overall the complexity of the algorithm is

$$O(|Q|) + O(k^2 \times |Q_s| \times |V_{Q_s}^2|) \leq O(k^2 \times |Q| \times |V_Q^2|)$$

However, usually, the number of nodes requested by the user to be included in the summary is small. Also, the number of nodes in the queries is limited (usually ≤ 10), and as such we can safely replace V_Q^2 with a constant, eventually showing that the algorithm scales linearly to the number of queries in the workload.

Limitations. The aforementioned algorithm provides an elegant solution to the κ-Personalized Summary problem and can be trivially extended for the λ/κ-Personalized Summary problem as well, just by searching for queries including the λ nodes and then exploiting those queries to link them in the summary. However, it assumes that *adequate* queries are available in the query log. In other words, it assumes that a) there are queries available including user input, and b) that there are at least κ other nodes available in those queries. These assumptions hold for popular online KGs which can easily log user queries but might not hold for other less popular KGs. As such our approach should be considered complementary to approaches working directly on the graphs of the KGs. However, as we showed the problem is NP-complete, and neither existing approximate solutions nor competitors (as we will show) will terminate within a reasonable time.

4   Experimental Evaluation

In this chapter, we present the experiments performed for evaluating our approach using three real world datasets along with the corresponding query workloads. The source code and guidelines on how to download the datasets and the workloads are available online[1].

4.1   Setup

Implementation. The iSummary was developed using Java. In addition, the evaluation was performed using windows 10 with an Intel® Core™ i3 10100 CPU @ 3.60 GHz (4 cores) and 16 GB RAM.

Datasets. The first dataset we use is DBpedia v3.8 along with the corresponding query workload. DBpedia v3.8 consists of 422 classes, 1323 properties, and more than 2.3M instances. The available query workload is 16.3 MB including 58,610 queries.

WikiData is a free and open knowledge base that can be read and edited by both humans and machines. Wikidata contains 100 million items, and 1.4 billion statements and covers many general topics for knowledge exploration and data science applications. The query workload for WikiData was retrieved from [12] and includes 192,325 queries

Bio2RDF is a biological database that uses semantic web technologies to provide interlinked life science data and includes more than 11 billion triples [8]. The query workload for Bio2RDF was retrieved from the corresponding SPARQL endpoint and includes 3,616,330 queries.

---

[1] https://anonymous.4open.science/r/iSummary-47F2/.

4.2   Metrics

We already have proven the theoretical bound of our algorithm in terms of quality when compared to an optimal solution. In addition, as it is not feasible to compute the optimal solution for our big graphs for evaluating the quality of the generated algorithms we use **coverage**. Coverage has been proved rather useful in evaluating structural, non-quotient semantic summaries in the past [15,16,18,20,21]. The idea behind coverage is that, ideally, we would like to maximize the fragments of the queries that are answered by the summary. More specifically, a summary that is able to provide answers to bigger and more query fragments from the query workload is preferable. However, as we are generating personalized summaries, we would like the generated summaries to maximize the number and fragments that include the input provided by the user. As such, we define coverage as follows:

Definition 2 (Coverage). *Assuming a κ-Personalized summary S for s, a query workload Q, and two weights for nodes and edges, i.e. w_n and w_p, we define coverage as follows:*

$$Coverage(Q, S, s) = \frac{1}{n} \sum_{s \in q_i} (w_n \frac{snodes(S, q_i)}{nodes(q_i)} + w_p \frac{sedges(S, q_i)}{edges(q_i)}) \qquad (1)$$

where $nodes(q_i)$ and $edges(q_i)$ denote the number of nodes and edges respectively in q_i, and $snodes(S, q_i)$ and $sedges(S, q_i)$ denote the number of nodes and edges respectively that appear in S.

In our experiments, we set $w_n = 0.5$ and $w_p = 0.5$ as we perceive both nodes and edges as equally important in a summary.

4.3   Baselines and Competitors

To evaluate our system, we use for each query workload a percentage of the queries for constructing the personalized summary (train queries) and the remaining queries for evaluating node selection and coverage of the constructed summary (test queries).

We compare our approach with a *random* baseline, where we randomly select nodes and edges from the train queries that involve user selection to be included in the summary and then evaluate node selection and coverage over the test queries.

In addition, we compare our approach with another summarization method for personalized summaries *GLIMPSE* [14] which tries to maximize a user's inferred "utility" over a given KG, subject to a user- and device-specific constraint on the summary's size.

Finally, we explore an approximate version of the *personalized PageRank*[2] which works directly on the KG trying to identify the most important nodes and paths given a start node through random walks.

---

[2] https://github.com/asajadi/fast-pagerank

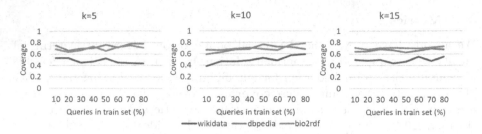

Fig. 2. Coverage as the number of queries increases.

4.4 Coverage for Various Query Log Sizes

In the first experiment, we try to understand what is the size of the query log required for getting high-quality results in terms of coverage for iSummary. As such, we keep a random 20% of the queries for testing and we use the remaining for the training. We gradually increase the percentage of queries considered and report the average coverage each time. We randomly pick a node to be used as a seed node for construction summaries for k = 5, 10, and 15. We repeat the experiment 10 times (10 fold-cross validation). The results are shown in Fig. 2.

As shown, query coverage even with 10% of the queries (i.e., 6000 queries for DBpedia) is more than 0.4. Further it is not significantly increased as more queries are considered for constructing the summary. This shows that our method is able to generate high coverage summaries even with relatively small size of queries.

In addition, we can see that the worst coverage is for wikidata. Trying to identify the reason for this we identified that in Wikipedia on average the queries include 3.9 triple patterns, in Bio2RDF 1.5 triple patterns, and in DBpedia 1 triple pattern. Based on this we can conclude that larger queries introduce more nodes on average for coverage evaluation (in the denominator of Eq. (1)), and as such the coverage drops.

4.5 Comparing Coverage

Next, we compare iSummary with baselines and competitors. For iSummary and Random we randomly select 80% of the queries for training and 20% for testing. For the same test queries each time we evaluate also coverage for PPR and GLIMPSE. We randomly select 10 seed nodes for generating a personalized summary for k = 5, 10, 15. We repeat 10 times the aforementioned procedure (10 fold cross-validation).

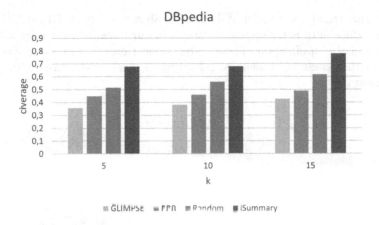

Fig. 3. DBpedia coverage for various k and baselines.

The results for DBpedia are shown in Fig. 3. As shown approaches that work on the data graph have worst coverage than the ones working directly on the queries. GLIMPSE performs worst for all cases, as providing just a node as an input is not enough for GLIMPSE to provide a high-quality summary in terms of coverage. PPR has better results than GLIMPSE, but still, it is outperformed by both Random and iSummary. Note that Random is not purely random as it randomly selects nodes and edges to construct a summary from the queries involving the input node. As shown iSummary outperforms all baselines almost two times when compared with GLIMPSE, random by 17–24% and PPR by 32–37%.

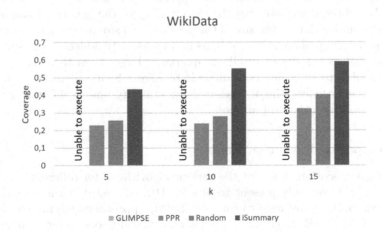

Fig. 4. Wikidata coverage for various k and baselines.

The same trend appears for WikiData as shown in Fig. 4. GLIMPSE is not able to produce output for such a big graph in our machine as it fully loads the memory and the application crashes after some time. In this case, iSummary dominates the remaining baselines, achieving in most of the cases a two times higher coverage.

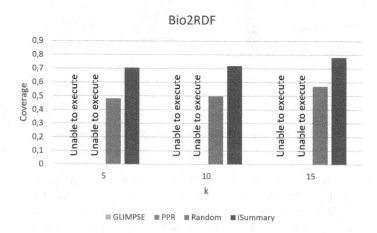

Fig. 5. Bio2RDF coverage for various k and baselines.

Finally, results for Bio2RDF are shown in Fig. 5. Now even PPR cannot process such a big graph and after 24 h and we stopped its execution. Again iSummary is better than Random by 25–30%.

Overall, as we can see in all cases our approach has consistently better results than all baselines, demonstrating the high quality of the generated summaries. We can also notice that as the size of the personalized summary increases ($\kappa = 5$, 10, 15) the coverage increases as well, as more nodes are added to the summary. Note also that as the size of WikiData queries is larger than the other datasets it is reasonable to be a bit more difficult to cover them and as such coverage is smaller. Nevertheless, the algorithm shows stability among different datasets always dominating other approaches.

4.6   Comparing Execution Time

The average execution times for the various algorithms, for different κ are presented in Fig. 6. We only present results for DBpedia as it is the only dataset that all competitors are able to run. As shown, approaches relying on the KG (PPR and GLIMPSE) to calculate the summary require one order of magnitude more execution time than the ones relying on query logs. iSummary is just a bit slower than Random showing that linking the k nodes using queries has a minimal impact on query execution, but highly improves summaries' quality. Further, we can observe that as the k grows, all algorithms require more time

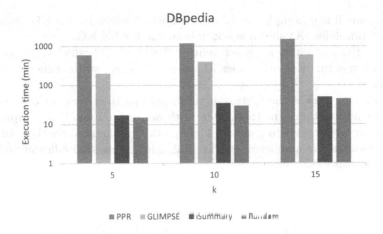

Fig. 6. Execution time for the various k and algorithms

to identify and link more nodes. Overall, however, iSummary is only 0.13 times slower than Random, 14 times faster than GLIMPSE, and 40 times faster than PPR, however dominating all baselines in terms of coverage.

5 Related Work

In this Section, we focus on personalized, structural, and non-quotient summaries and we present related works. For a complete overview of the works in the area, the interested reader is forwarded to relevant surveys available in the domain [6,11].

Among the first works that focused on generating personalized non-quotients is [25], that returns a summary of an RDF Sentence Graph. An RDF Sentence Graph is a weighted, directed graph where each vertex represents an RDF sentence. A link between two sentences exists if an object of one sentence belongs to another sentence as well. The creation of a sentence graph is customized by domain experts, who provide as input the desired summary size, and their navigation preferences, i.e. weights in the links they are most interested in. In Queiroz-Sousaet al. [3], on the other hand, the authors try to combine user preferences with the degree of centrality and the closeness to calculate the importance of a node, and then they use an algorithm to find paths that include the most important nodes in the final graph. However, in both these approaches, incorporating user preferences is neither explored in detail nor evaluated.

GLIMPSE [14] is the most relevant work to our approach and focuses on constructing personalized summaries of KG containing only the facts most relevant to individuals' interests. However, they require from the user to provide a set of relevant queries that would like relevant information to be included in the summary, whereas their algorithms are directly executed on the KG. However, it is difficult for a user to provide these queries and although the corresponding algorithm has linear complexity in the number of edges in the KG, still faces scalability problems. As shown is not able to run for big KGs.

Finally, there is latest approach named WBSUM [20] which exploits query logs for constructing KG summaries. However, those are static, generic, and not personalized.

Overall, our work is the first, structural, non-quotient, workload-based personalized summarization method. Our work accepts minimal user input, and exploits query workloads to generate high-quality summaries. Further our algorithm is linear in the number of queries available and as such efficient and scalable.

6   Conclusions

In this paper, we present a summarization method able to construct personalized, workload-based, semantic summaries with high quality. We formulate the problem of λ/κ-Personalized summaries and provide an elegant algorithm for resolving it, linear in the number of queries available in the query logs with theoretical guarantees. Our algorithm effectively identifies different weight assignments for different inputs and is able to efficiently and effectively identify how to link the selected nodes based on the available queries.

We experimentally show that even 5k queries are enough for generating high-quality summaries (10% of the query log in DBpedia) and we compare our approach with several baselines. We demonstrate that our approach strictly dominates all baselines in terms of query coverage (20–50% better coverage than Random and 33–56% better coverage than PPR and 40% better coverage than GLIMPSE) and it is highly efficient being orders of magnitude faster than relevant approaches working directly on the KG.

Future Work. As future work, we intend to explore alternative methods for linking the κ nodes to be used in the summary by exploiting the original data graph. The graph could be queried just once at the end for replacing the variables with the actual resources from the KG. This would introduce minimal overhead for querying the original graph and it would be quicker and possibly more effective than searching again all queries for filling the missing variables.

Another really interesting direction is to study how personalized summaries change over time for specific user input. As users' interests drift in time and we only require 4k–10k queries for generating high-quality summaries, it would be interesting to identify how the personalized summaries also change, considering that queries focus changes through time due to specific events, disasters, seasonality, or occasions.

Finally, as λ/κ-Personalized summaries are not unique, introducing the element of diversity would be interesting so that the users are not always presented with the same personalized summary.

References

1. The linked open data cloud. https://lod-cloud.net/. Accessed 22 Sep 2022
2. W3C Recommendation, SPARQL query language for RDF. https://www.w3.org/TR/rdf-sparql-query/. Accessed 09 Oct 2019
3. Alzogbi, A., Lausen, G.: Similar structures inside RDF-graphs. In: LDOW (2013)
4. Bonifati, A., Martens, W., Timm, T.: An analytical study of large SPARQL query logs. VLDB J. **29**(2-3), 655–679 (2020). https://doi.org/10.1007/s00778-019-00558-9
5. Čebirić, Š, Goasdoué, F., Kondylakis, H., Kotzinos, D., Manolescu, I., Troullinou, G., Zneika, M.: Summarizing semantic graphs: a survey. VLDB J. **28**(3), 295–327 (2018). https://doi.org/10.1007/s00778-018-0528-3
6. Čebirić, Š., et al.: Summarizing semantic graphs: a survey. VLDB J. **28**(3), 295–327 (2019)
7. Du, D.Z., Smith, J.M., Rubinstein, J.H. (eds.): Advances in Steiner Trees. Springer, New York (2000). https://doi.org/10.1007/978-1-4757-3171-2
8. Dumontier, M., et al.: Bio2rdf release 3: a larger, more connected network of linked data for the life sciences. In: Horridge, M., Rospocher, M., van Ossenbruggen, J. (eds.) Proceedings of the ISWC 2014 Posters & Demonstrations Track a track within the 13th International Semantic Web Conference, ISWC 2014, Riva del Garda, Italy, 21 October 2014. CEUR Workshop Proceedings, vol. 1272, pp. 401–404. CEUR-WS.org (2014)
9. Hakimi, S.L.: Steiner's problem in graphs and its implications. Networks **1**(2), 113–133 (1971). https://doi.org/10.1002/net.3230010203
10. Hwang, F.K., Richards, D.S.: Steiner tree problems. Networks **22**(1), 55–89 (1992). https://doi.org/10.1002/net.3230220105
11. Kellou-Menouer, K., Kardoulakis, N., Troullinou, G., Kedad, Z., Plexousakis, D., Kondylakis, H.: A survey on semantic schema discovery. VLDB J. **31**(4), 675–710 (2022). https://doi.org/10.1007/s00778-021-00717-x
12. Malyshev, S., Krötzsch, M., González, L., Gonsior, J., Bielefeldt, A.: Getting the most out of Wikidata: semantic technology usage in Wikipedia's knowledge graph. In: Vrandečić, D., et al. (eds.) ISWC 2018. LNCS, vol. 11137, pp. 376–394. Springer, Cham (2018). https://doi.org/10.1007/978-3-030-00668-6_23
13. Pappas, A., Troullinou, G., Roussakis, G., Kondylakis, H., Plexousakis, D.: Exploring importance measures for summarizing RDF/S KBs. In: Blomqvist, E., Maynard, D., Gangemi, A., Hoekstra, R., Hitzler, P., Hartig, O. (eds.) ESWC 2017. LNCS, vol. 10249, pp. 387–403. Springer, Cham (2017). https://doi.org/10.1007/978-3-319-58068-5_24
14. Safavi, T., Belth, C., Faber, L., Mottin, D., Müller, E., Koutra, D.: Personalized knowledge graph summarization: from the cloud to your pocket. In: Wang, J., Shim, K., Wu, X. (eds.) 2019 IEEE International Conference on Data Mining, ICDM 2019, Beijing, China, 8–11 November 2019, pp. 528–537. IEEE (2019). https://doi.org/10.1109/ICDM.2019.00063
15. Trouli, G.E., Pappas, A., Troullinou, G., Koumakis, L., Papadakis, N., Kondylakis, H.: Summer: structural summarization for RDF/S KGs. Algorithms **16**(1), 18 (2023). https://doi.org/10.3390/a16010018

16. Trouli, G.E., Troullinou, G., Koumakis, L., Papadakis, N., Kondylakis, H.: Summer: summarizing RDF/S KBs using machine learning. In: Seneviratne, O., Pesquita, C., Sequeda, J., Etcheverry, L. (eds.) Proceedings of the ISWC 2021 Posters, Demos and Industry Tracks: From Novel Ideas to Industrial Practice colocated with 20th International Semantic Web Conference (ISWC 2021), Virtual Conference, 24–28 October 2021. CEUR Workshop Proceedings, vol. 2980. CEUR-WS.org (2021)

17. Troullinou, G., Kondylakis, H., Lissandrini, M., Mottin, D.: SOFOS: demonstrating the challenges of materialized view selection on knowledge graphs. In: Li, G., Li, Z., Idreos, S., Srivastava, D. (eds.) SIGMOD 2021: International Conference on Management of Data, Virtual Event, China, 20–25 June 2021, pp. 2789–2793. ACM (2021). https://doi.org/10.1145/3448016.3452765

18. Troullinou, G., Kondylakis, H., Stefanidis, K., Plexousakis, D.: Exploring RDFS KBs using summaries. In: Vrandečić, D., et al. (eds.) ISWC 2018. LNCS, vol. 11136, pp. 268–284. Springer, Cham (2018). https://doi.org/10.1007/978-3-030-00671-6_16

19. Troullinou, G., Kondylakis, H., Stefanidis, K., Plexousakis, D.: RDFDigest+: a summary-driven system for KBs exploration. In: van Erp, M., Atre, M., López, V., Srinivas, K., Fortuna, C. (eds.) Proceedings of the ISWC 2018 Posters & Demonstrations, Industry and Blue Sky Ideas Tracks co-located with 17th International Semantic Web Conference (ISWC 2018), Monterey, USA, 8th - to - 12th October 2018. CEUR Workshop Proceedings, vol. 2180. CEUR-WS.org (2018)

20. Vassiliou, G., Troullinou, G., Papadakis, N., Kondylakis, H.: Wbsum: workload-based summaries for RDF/S KBs. In: Zhu, Q., Zhu, X., Tu, Y., Xu, Z., Kumar, A. (eds.) SSDBM 2021: 33rd International Conference on Scientific and Statistical Database Management, Tampa, FL, USA, 6–7 July 2021, pp. 248–252. ACM (2021). https://doi.org/10.1145/3468791.3468815

21. Vassiliou, G., Troullinou, G., Papadakis, N., Stefanidis, K., Pitoura, E., Kondylakis, H.: Coverage-based summaries for RDF KBs. In: Verborgh, R., et al. (eds.) ESWC 2021. LNCS, vol. 12739, pp. 98–102. Springer, Cham (2021). https://doi.org/10.1007/978-3-030-80418-3_18

22. Voß, S.: Steiner's problem in graphs: heuristic methods. Discret. Appl. Math. 40(1), 45–72 (1992). https://doi.org/10.1016/0166-218X(92)90021-2

23. W3C: Resource description framework. http://www.w3.org/RDF/

24. Wu, G., Li, J., Feng, L., Wang, K.: Identifying potentially important concepts and relations in an ontology. In: Sheth, A., et al. (eds.) ISWC 2008. LNCS, vol. 5318, pp. 33–49. Springer, Heidelberg (2008). https://doi.org/10.1007/978-3-540-88564-1_3

25. Zhang, X., Cheng, G., Qu, Y.: Ontology summarization based on RDF sentence graph. In: Proceedings of the 16th International Conference on World Wide Web, pp. 707–716 (2007)

Neural Class Expression Synthesis

N'Dah Jean Kouagou(✉) ⓘ, Stefan Heindorf ⓘ, Caglar Demir ⓘ,
and Axel-Cyrille Ngonga Ngomo ⓘ

Paderborn University, Paderborn, Germany
{ndah.jean.kouagou,heindorf,caglar.demir,axel.ngonga}@upb.de

Abstract. Many applications require explainable node classification in knowledge graphs. Towards this end, a popular "white-box" approach is class expression learning: Given sets of positive and negative nodes, class expressions in description logics are learned that separate positive from negative nodes. Most existing approaches are search-based approaches generating many candidate class expressions and selecting the best one. However, they often take a long time to find suitable class expressions. In this paper, we cast class expression learning as a translation problem and propose a new family of class expression learning approaches which we dub neural class expression synthesizers. Training examples are "translated" into class expressions in a fashion akin to machine translation. Consequently, our synthesizers are not subject to the runtime limitations of search-based approaches. We study three instances of this novel family of approaches based on LSTMs, GRUs, and set transformers, respectively. An evaluation of our approach on four benchmark datasets suggests that it can effectively synthesize high-quality class expressions with respect to the input examples in approximately one second on average. Moreover, a comparison to state-of-the-art approaches suggests that we achieve better F-measures on large datasets. For reproducibility purposes, we provide our implementation as well as pretrained models in our public GitHub repository at https://github.com/dice-group/NeuralClassExpressionSynthesis

Keywords: Neural network · Concept learning · Class expression learning · Learning from examples

1 Introduction

One of the most popular families of web-scale knowledge bases [16] is that of RDF knowledge bases equipped with an ontology in W3C's web ontology

This work is part of a project that has received funding from the European Union's Horizon 2020 research and innovation programme under the Marie Skłodowska-Curie grant No 860801 and the European Union's Horizon Europe research and innovation programme under the grant No 101070305. This work has also been supported by the Ministry of Culture and Science of North Rhine-Westphalia (MKW NRW) within the project SAIL under the grant No NW21-059D and by the Deutsche Forschungsgemeinschaft (DFG, German Research Foundation): TRR 318/1 2021 - 438445824.

C. Pesquita et al. (Eds.): ESWC 2023, LNCS 13870, pp. 209–226, 2023.
https://doi.org/10.1007/978-3-031-33455-9_13

language OWL [28]. Examples include DBpedia [3], Wikidata [40], and Cali-Graph [17]. One means to implement ante-hoc explainable machine learning on these knowledge bases is class expression learning (also called concept learning) [13,15,24,26,34,39]. Informally, class expression learning approaches learn a class expression that describes individuals provided as positive examples. Class expression learning has applications in several domains, including ontology engineering [25], bio-medicine [27] and Industry 4.0 [2]. There exist three main learning settings in class expression learning: (1) positive and negative learning, (2) positive-only learning, and (3) class-inclusion learning [23]. This paper tackles setting (1).

Several methods have been proposed to solve class expression learning problems; the best are based on refinement operators [13,20,23,24,26,34] and evolutionary algorithms [15]. A common drawback of these approaches is their lack of scalability. While the reasoning complexity of all learning approaches grows with the expressivity of the underlying description logic (DL) [19,32], those based on refinement operators and evolutionary algorithms further suffer from the exploration of an infinite conceptual space for each learning problem [34]. Another inherent limitation of existing methods for class expression learning from examples is their inability to leverage previously solved problems—their algorithm always starts from scratch for each new learning problem.

In view of the large sizes of modern knowledge bases, e.g., DBpedia [3] and Wikidata [40], we propose a new family of approaches, dubbed **neural class expression synthesizers** (NCES), for web-scale applications of class expression learning. The fundamental hypothesis behind this family of algorithms is that one should be able to capture enough semantics from latent representations (e.g., embeddings) of examples to directly synthesize class expressions in a fashion akin to machine translation, i.e., without the need for costly exploration. This hypothesis is supported by the significant improvement in the performance of machine translation approaches brought about by neural machine translation (NMT) [7,44]. NMT approaches translate from a source language to a target language by exploiting an intermediary representation of a text's semantics. NCES behave similarly but translate from the "language" of sets of positive/negative examples to the "language" of class expressions. We instantiate this new paradigm by implementing three NCES instances that target the description logic $\mathcal{ALC}$. We show that our NCES instances generate high-quality class expressions with respect to the given sets of examples while remaining scalable. In fact, NCES instances synthesize solutions for multiple learning problems at the same time as they accept batches of inputs. This makes NCES particularly fit for deployment in large-scale applications of class expression learning, e.g., on the web.

The rest of the paper is organized as follows: First, we present existing approaches for class expression learning and introduce the notations and prerequisites needed throughout the paper. Next, we describe the intuition behind NCES in detail and introduce three instantiations of this new family of algorithms. We then compare these instantiations with state-of-the-art approaches on four benchmark datasets. Finally, we discuss our results and draw conclusions from our experiments.

2 Related Work

Class expression learning has been of interest to many researchers in recent years. Of the proposed approaches, the most prominent include those based on evolutionary algorithms [15] and refinement operators [6,13,20,24,25,36]. The state-of-the-art EvoLearner [15] initializes its population by random walks on the knowledge graph which are subsequently converted to description logic concepts, represented as abstract syntax trees. These concepts are further refined by means of mutation and crossover operations. EvoLearner outperformed approaches based on refinement operators such as CELOE and OCEL from the DL-Learner framework [15]. Previously, Lehmann and Hitzler [26] studied different properties that a refinement operator can have, then designed a refinement operator to learn class expressions in description logics. Their learning algorithm, CELOE [25], is implemented in DL-Learner [23] alongside OCEL and ELTL [6]. CELOE extends upon OCEL by using a different heuristic function and is currently regarded as the best class expression learning algorithm in DL-Learner. Although ELTL was designed for the lightweight description logic $\mathcal{EL}$, we include it in this study to check whether our generated learning problems can be solved in a simpler description logic. ECII [36] is a recent approach for class expression learning that does not use a refinement operator and only invokes a reasoner once for each run. This approach was designed to overcome the runtime limitations of refinement operator-based approaches. Other attempts to prune the search space of refinement operator-based approaches include DL-Focl [34]. It is a modified version of DL-Foil [13] that is quintessentially based on omission rates. DL-Focl uses techniques such as lookahead strategy and local memory to avoid reconsidering sub-optimal choices.

Even though existing approaches for class expression learning have shown promising results, most of them are search-based. As a result, these approaches often use entailment checks—which are hard to compute, see Ozaki [32]—or compute classification accuracies at each step of the search process. In contrast, NCES only require a refinement operator for generating training data but not at prediction time. Hence, NCES are particularly suitable for solving many different learning problems consisting of positive and negative examples on the same dataset. As the training process of our synthesizers only involves instance data embeddings and a vocabulary of atoms, they can be extended to more expressive description logics such as $\mathcal{ALCHIQ(D)}$.

3 Background

3.1 Notation

DL is short for description logic, and DNN stands for deep neural network. Unless otherwise specified, $\mathcal{K} = (\mathit{TBox}, \mathit{ABox})$ is a knowledge base in $\mathcal{ALC}$, and $\mathcal{N}_I$ is the set of all individuals in $\mathcal{K}$. The *ABox* consists of statements of the form $C(a)$ and $R(a,b)$, whereas the *TBox* contains statements of the form $C \sqsubseteq D$, where C, D are concepts, R is a role, and a, b are individuals in $\mathcal{K}$. We use the representation of OWL knowledge bases as sets of triples to compute embeddings of individuals, classes and roles. The conversion into triples is carried out using standard libraries such as RDFLib [21]. We then use the knowledge graph representation of the knowledge bases to compute embeddings, which are essential to our proposed approach (see Fig. 1). The function $|.|$ returns the cardinality of a set. $\mathbb{1}$ denotes the indicator function, i.e., a function that takes two inputs and returns 1 if they are equal, and 0 otherwise. Let a matrix M and integers i, j be given. $M_{:,j}$, $M_{i,:}$, and M_{ij} represent the j-th column, the i-th row, and the entry at the i-th row and j-th column, respectively. Similar notations are used for higher-dimensional tensors.

We define the vocabulary *Vocab* of a given knowledge base $\mathcal{K}$ to be the list of all atomic concepts and roles in $\mathcal{K}$, together with the following constructs in any fixed ordering: " " (white space), "." (dot), "$\sqcup$", "$\sqcap$", "$\exists$", "$\forall$", "$\neg$", "(", and ")", which are all referred to as atoms. *Vocab*[i] is the atom at position i in *Vocab*. These constructs are used by NCES to synthesize class expressions in $\mathcal{ALC}$ (see Sect. 4 for details). Let C be a class expression, then $\bar{C}$ and $\hat{C}$ are the list (in the order they appear in C) and set of atoms in C, respectively.

3.2 Description Logics

Description logics [30] are a family of knowledge representation paradigms based on first-order logics. They have applications in several domains, including artificial intelligence, the semantic web, and biomedical informatics. In fact, the web ontology language, OWL, uses description logics to represent the terminological box of RDF ontologies. In this work, we focus on the description logic $\mathcal{ALC}$ (*A*ttributive *L*anguage with *C*omplement) [37] because of its simplicity and expressiveness. The syntax and semantics of $\mathcal{ALC}$ are presented in Table 1.

Table 1. $\mathcal{ALC}$ syntax and semantics. $\mathcal{I}$ is an interpretation and $\Delta^{\mathcal{I}}$ its domain.

Construct	Syntax	Semantics
Atomic concept	A	$A^{\mathcal{I}} \subseteq \Delta^{\mathcal{I}}$
Atomic role	R	$R^{\mathcal{I}} \subseteq \Delta^{\mathcal{I}} \times \Delta^{\mathcal{I}}$
Top concept	$\top$	$\Delta^{\mathcal{I}}$
Bottom concept	$\bot$	$\emptyset$
Conjunction	$C \sqcap D$	$C^{\mathcal{I}} \cap D^{\mathcal{I}}$
Disjunction	$C \sqcup D$	$C^{\mathcal{I}} \cup D^{\mathcal{I}}$
Negation	$\neg C$	$\Delta^{\mathcal{I}} \backslash C^{\mathcal{I}}$
Existential role restriction	$\exists\, R.C$	$\{a^{\mathcal{I}} \in \Delta^{\mathcal{I}} / \exists\, b^{\mathcal{I}} \in C^{\mathcal{I}}, (a^{\mathcal{I}}, b^{\mathcal{I}}) \in R^{\mathcal{I}}\}$
Universal role restriction	$\forall\, R.C$	$\{a^{\mathcal{I}} \in \Delta^{\mathcal{I}} / \forall\, b^{\mathcal{I}}, (a^{\mathcal{I}}, b^{\mathcal{I}}) \in R^{\mathcal{I}} \Rightarrow b^{\mathcal{I}} \in C^{\mathcal{I}}\}$

3.3   Refinement Operators

Definition 1 ([26]). *Given a quasi-ordered space* $(\mathcal{S}, \preceq)$, *a downward (respectively upward) refinement operator on* $\mathcal{S}$ *is a mapping* $\rho : \mathcal{S} \to 2^{\mathcal{S}}$ *such that for all* $C \in \mathcal{S}$, $C' \in \rho(C)$ *implies* $C' \preceq C$ *(respectively* $C \preceq C'$*)*.

A refinement operator can be finite, proper, redundant, minimal, complete, weakly complete or ideal. Note that some of these properties can be combined whilst others cannot [26]. For class expression learning in description logics, weakly complete, finite, and proper refinement operators are the most used.

3.4   Class Expression Learning

Definition 2. *Given a knowledge base* $\mathcal{K}$, *a target concept* $\mathcal{1}$, *a set of positive examples* $E^+ = \{e_1^+, e_2^+, \ldots, e_{n_1}^+\}$, *and a set of negative examples* $E^- = \{e_1^-, e_2^-, \ldots, e_{n_2}^-\}$, *the learning problem is to find a class expression* C *such that for* $\mathcal{K}' = \mathcal{K} \cup \{T \equiv C\}$, *we have* $\forall\ e^+ \in E^+\ \forall e^- \in E^-$, $\mathcal{K}' \models C(e^+)$ *and* $\mathcal{K}' \not\models C(e^-)$.

Most existing approaches use hard-coded heuristics or refinement operators to search for the solution C. When an exact solution does not exist, an approximate solution in terms of accuracy or F-measure is to be returned by the approaches. In this work, we exploit the semantics embedded in latent representations of individuals (instance data) to directly synthesize C.

3.5   Knowledge Graph Embedding

A knowledge graph can be regarded as a collection of assertions in the form of subject-predicate-object triples (s, p, o). Embedding functions project knowledge graphs onto continuous vector spaces to facilitate downstream tasks such as link prediction [5], recommender systems [47], and structured machine learning [20]. Many embedding approaches for knowledge graphs exist [9,41]. Some of them use only facts observed in the knowledge graph [4,31]. Others leverage additional available information about entities and relations, such as textual descriptions [42,45]. Most embedding approaches initialize each entity and relation with a random vector, matrix or tensor and learn the embeddings as an optimization problem. For example, TransE [5] represents entities and relations as vectors in the same space and aims to minimize the Euclidean distance between $s + p$ and o for each triple (s, p, o). In this work, we use ConEx [10] and TransE to evaluate NCES.

3.6   Permutation-Invariant Network Architectures for Set Inputs

We deal with set-structured input data as in 3D shape recognition [33], multiple instance learning [11], and few-shot learning [14,38]. These tasks benefit from machine learning models that produce the same results for any arbitrary reordering of the elements in the input set. Another desirable property of these models is the ability to handle sets of arbitrary size.

In recent years, several approaches have been developed to meet the aforementioned requirements. The most prominent of these approaches include Deep Set [46] and Set Transformer [22]. The Deep Set architecture encodes each element in the input set independently and uses a pooling layer, e.g., averaging, to produce the final representation of the set. In contrast, the Set Transformer architecture uses a self-attention mechanism to represent the set, which allows pair-wise and even higher-order interactions between the elements of the input set. As a result, the Set Transformer architecture shows superior performance on most tasks compared to Deep Set with a comparable model size [22]. In this work, we hence use the Set Transformer architecture (more details in Sect. 4) and refer to [22] for a description of its building blocks: Multi-head Attention Block (MAB), Set Attention Block (SAB), Induced Set Attention Block (ISAB), and Pooling by Multi-head Attention (PMA).

4 Neural Class Expression Synthesis

In this section, we present our proposed family of approaches for class expression learning from examples. We start with a formal definition of the learning problem that we aim to solve, then present our proposed approach in detail.

4.1 Learning Problem

We adapt the classical definition of a learning problem (see Definition 2) to our setting of class expression synthesis (Definition 3).

Definition 3. *Given a knowledge base $\mathcal{K}$, a set of positive examples $E^+ = \{e_1^+, e_2^+, \ldots, e_{n_1}^+\}$, and a set of negative examples $E^- = \{e_1^-, e_2^-, \ldots, e_{n_2}^-\}$, the learning problem is to synthesize a class expression C in $\mathcal{ALC}$ using atoms (classes and roles) in $\mathcal{K}$ that (ideally) accurately classifies the provided examples.*

In theory, there can be multiple solutions to a learning problem under both Definition 2 and Definition 3; our NCES generate only one. Moreover, the solution computed by a concept learner might be an approximation, e.g., there might be some false positives and false negatives. NCES aim to obtain high values for accuracy and F-measure.

4.2 Learning Approach (NCES)

We propose the following recipe to implement the idea behind NCES. First, given a knowledge base over $\mathcal{ALC}$, convert it into a knowledge graph (see Subsect. 3.1). Then, embed said knowledge graph into a continuous vector space using any state-of-the-art embedding model in the literature. In our experiments, we used two embedding models with different expressive power: ConEx which applies convolutions on complex-valued vectors, and TransE which projects entities and relations onto a Euclidean space and uses the Euclidean distance to model interactions. The computed embeddings are then used as features for a model able to take a set of embeddings as input and encode a sequence of atoms as output (see Fig. 1).

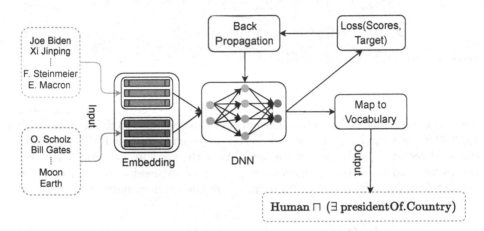

Fig. 1. NCES architecture. DNN stands for deep neural network that produces a sequence of tokens in the vocabulary (e.g., a sequence-to-sequence or a set-to-sequence model). The input consists of positive examples (upper left, dotted green box) and negative examples (bottom left, dotted red box). (Color figure online)

Neural Network Architectures. We conduct our experiments using the following network architectures: the Long Short-Term Memory (LSTM) [18], the Gated Recurrent Unit (GRU) [8], and the Set Transformer [22]. The latter is known to be permutation equivariant while the two others are not. Nonetheless, LSTM and GRU can handle set inputs as long as an ordering is defined since they deal well with sequential data [49,50]. In this work, we use the default ordering (the order in which we received the data) of the elements in each set during the data generation process (see Sect. 5.1).

Recurrent Networks (LSTM and GRU). We use two recurrent layers followed by three linear layers with the `relu` activation function and a batch normalization layer. A recurrent neural network produces a sequence of n hidden states h_i $(i = 1, \ldots, n)$ for each input sequence of length n. In this work, we are concerned with a sequence of n_1 positive examples and a sequence of n_2 negative examples which are processed separately with the same network:

$$h_1^{pos}, \ldots, h_{n_1}^{pos} = RNN(x_{pos}); \quad h_1^{neg}, \ldots, h_{n_2}^{neg} = RNN(x_{neg}); \qquad (1)$$

where x_{pos} and x_{neg} are the sequences of embeddings of positive and negative examples, respectively. *RNN* is a two-layer LSTM or GRU network. The hidden state vectors of the two sets of examples are summed separately, then concatenated and fed to a sequence of 3 linear layers:

$$h_{pos} := \sum_{t=1}^{T_1} h_t^{pos}; \quad h_{neg} := \sum_{t=1}^{T_2} h_t^{neg}; \quad h := \text{Concat}(h_{pos}, h_{neg}); \tag{2}$$

$$O = W_3(\text{bn}(W_2 f(W_1 h + b_1) + b_2)) + b_3. \tag{3}$$

Here, f is the `relu` activation function, bn is a batch normalization layer, and $W_1, b_1, W_2, b_2, W_3, b_3$ are trainable weights.

Set Transformer. This architecture comprises an encoder *Enc* and a decoder *Dec*, each with 4 attention heads. The encoder is a stack of two ISAB layers with $m = 32$ inducing points, and the decoder is composed of a single PMA layer with one seed vector ($k = 1$), and a linear layer. As in the previous paragraph, the sets of positive and negative examples for a given class expression are first encoded separately using the encoder. The outputs are then concatenated row-wise and fed to the decoder:

$$O_{pos} = Enc(x_{pos}); \quad O_{neg} = Enc(x_{neg}); \tag{4}$$

$$O = Dec(\text{Concat}(O_{pos}, O_{neg})). \tag{5}$$

Although the encoder captures interactions intra-positive and intra-negative examples separately, the decoder further captures interactions across the two sets of examples from the concatenated features through self-attention. This demonstrates the representational power of the Set Transformer model for our set-structured inputs for class expression synthesis.

The output O from Eq. 3 and Eq. 5 is reshaped into a $(1+|Vocab|) \times L$ matrix, where L is the length of the longest class expression that NCES instances can generate. These scores allow us to compute the loss (see Eq. 6) and update model weights through gradient descent during training.

Loss. We train our NCES instances using the loss function $\mathcal{L}$ defined by:

$$\mathcal{L}(x, y) = -\frac{1}{NL} \sum_{i=1}^{N} \sum_{j=1}^{L} \log \left(\frac{\exp(x_{i,y_{ij},j})}{\sum_{c=1}^{C} \exp(x_{i,c,j})} \right), \tag{6}$$

where N is the size of the minibatch, C is the number of classes, $x \in \mathbb{R}^{N \times C \times L}$ is the minibatch of predicted class scores for each position in the target sequence of atoms, and $y \in \mathbb{N}^{N \times L}$ is the minibatch of actual class indices. Minimizing $\mathcal{L}$ constrains the model to assign a high score to the entry corresponding to the correct token ($\exp(x_{i,y_{ij},j}) \approx 1$) while keeping the remaining scores relatively low ($\sum_{c=1, c \neq y_{ij}}^{C} \exp(x_{i,c,j}) \approx 0$). In this work, $C = 1 + |Vocab|$, where the additional $+1$ accounts for the special token "PAD" that we used to pad all class expressions to the same length. Contrarily to some works that omit this special token when computing the loss, we use it as an ordinary token during training. This way, we can generate class expressions more efficiently at test time with a single forward pass in the model, then strip off the generated tokens after the special token. To avoid exploding gradients and accelerate convergence during training, we adopt the gradient clipping technique [48].

Learning Metrics. Apart from the loss function, we introduce two accuracy measures to quantify how well neural networks learn during training: soft accuracy and hard accuracy. The former only accounts for the correct selection of the atoms in the target expression, while the latter additionally measures the correct ordering of the selected atoms. Formally, let T and P be the target and predicted class expressions, respectively. Recall the notation $\bar{C}$ and $\hat{C}$ introduced in Sect. 3.1 for any class expression C. The soft (Acc_s) accuracy and hard accuracy (Acc_h) are defined as follows:

$$Acc_s(T,P) = \frac{|\hat{T} \cap \hat{P}|}{|\hat{T} \cup \hat{P}|}; \quad Acc_h(T,P) = \frac{\sum_{i=1}^{\min(l_1,l_2)} \mathbb{1}(\bar{T}[i], \bar{P}[i])}{\max(l_1,l_2)}. \tag{7}$$

where l_1 and l_2 are the lengths of $\bar{T}$ and $\bar{P}$, respectively.

Class Expression Synthesis. We synthesize class expressions by mapping the output scores O (see Eqs. 3 and 5) to the vocabulary. More specifically, we select the highest-scoring atoms in the vocabulary for each position along the sequence dimension:

$$id_j = \underset{c \in \{1,...,C\}}{\arg\max}\ O_{c,j} \text{ for } j = 1, \ldots, L, \tag{8}$$

$$synthesized\_atom_j = Vocab[id_j]. \tag{9}$$

Model Ensembling. Ensemble learning has proven to be one of the most robust approaches for tasks involving complex noisy data [12,35]. In this work, we combine class expression synthesizers' predictions post training by averaging the predicted scores. Specifically, given the output scores $O_i \in \mathbb{R}^{C \times L}$ ($i = 1,2,3$) as defined in Eq. 3 and Eq. 5 for the three models LSTM, GRU, and Set Transformer, we consider four different ensemble models: three pairwise ensemble models, and one global ensemble model (LSTM, GRU, and Set Transformer are combined). Formally, the ensemble scores are computed as:

$$O = \frac{\sum_{i \in \mathcal{I}} O_i}{|\mathcal{I}|} \text{ with } \mathcal{I} \subseteq \{1,2,3\} \text{ and } |\mathcal{I}| \geq 2. \tag{10}$$

Then, the synthesized expression is constructed following Eqs. 8 and 9 using the average scores O.

Table 2. Detailed information about the datasets used for evaluation. |LPs| is the number of learning problems in the test set.

Dataset	|Ind.|	|Classes|	|Prop.|	|TBox|	|ABox|	|Train|	|LPs|	|Vocab|
Carcinogenesis	22,372	142	4	144	74,223	10,982	111	157
Mutagenesis	14,145	86	5	82	47,722	5,333	54	102
Semantic Bible	724	48	29	56	3,106	3,896	40	88
Vicodi	33,238	194	10	204	116,181	18,243	175	215

5 Evaluation

5.1 Experimental Setup

Datasets. We evaluated our proposed approach on the Carcinogenesis [43], Mutagenesis [43], Semantic Bible[1], and the Vicodi [29] knowledge bases. Carcinogenesis and Mutagenesis are knowledge bases about chemical compounds and how they relate to each other. The Semantic Bible knowledge base describes each named object or thing in the New Testament, categorized according to its class, including God, groups of people, and locations. The Vicodi knowledge base was developed as part of a funded project and describes European history. The statistics of each of the knowledge bases are given in Table 2.

Training and Test Data Construction. We generated class expressions of different forms from the input knowledge base using the recent refinement operator by Kouagou et al. [20] that was developed to efficiently generate numerous class expressions to serve as training data for concept length prediction in $\mathcal{ALC}$. The data that we generate is passed to the filtering process, which discards any class expression C such that an equivalent but shorter class expression D was not discarded. Note that each class expression comes with its set of instances, which are computed using the fast closed-world reasoner based on set operations described in [15]. These instances are considered positive examples for the corresponding class expression; negative examples are the rest of the individuals in the knowledge base. Next, the resulting data is randomly split into training and test sets; we used the discrete uniform distribution for this purpose. To ensure that our approach is scalable to large knowledge bases, we introduce a hyper-parameter $n = n_1 + n_2$ that represents the total number of positive and negative examples we sample for each class expression to be learned by NCES. Note that n is fixed for each knowledge base, and it depends on the total number of individuals.

Evaluation Metrics. We measure the quality of a predicted class expression in terms of accuracy and F-measure with respect to the positive/negative examples. Note that we cannot expect to exactly predict the target class expression in the test data since there can be multiple equivalent class expressions.

---

[1] https://www.semanticbible.com/ntn/ntn-overview.html.

Table 3. Hyper-parameter settings per dataset. Recall that m is the number of inducing points in the Set Transformer model, and n is the number of examples.

Dataset	epochs	opt.	lr	d	N	L	n	m	gc
Carcinogenesis	300	Adam	0.001	40	256	48	1,000	32	5
Mutagenesis	300	Adam	0.001	40	256	48	1,000	32	5
Semantic Bible	300	Adam	0.001	40	256	48	362	32	5
Vicodi	300	Adam	0.001	40	256	48	1,000	32	5

Table 4. Model size and training time. The training time is in minutes.

	Carcinogenesis		Mutagenesis		Semantic Bible		Vicodi	
	|Params.|	Time	|Params.|	Time	|Params.|	Time	|Params.|	Time
NCES$_{LSTM}$	1,247,136	31.50	906,576	16.94	819,888	6.65	1,606,272	50.82
NCES$_{GRU}$	1,192,352	21.61	851,792	12.28	765,104	5.39	1,551,488	34.15
NCES$_{ST}$	1,283,104	40.82	942,544	21.36	855,856	7.98	1,642,240	66.19

Hyper-parameter Optimization for NCES. We employed random search on the hyper-parameter space since it often yields good results while being computationally more efficient than grid search [1]; the selected values—those with the best results—are reported in Table 3. In the table, it can be seen that most knowledge bases share the same optimal values of hyper-parameters: the minibatch size N, the number of training epochs $epochs$, the optimizer $opt.$, the learning rate lr, the maximum output sequence length L, the number of embedding dimensions d, the number of inducing points m, and the gradient clipping value gc. Although we may increase n for very large knowledge bases, $n = \min(\frac{|N_I|}{2}, 1000)$ appears to work well with our evaluation datasets. This suggests that one can effortlessly find fitting hyper-parameters for new datasets.

Hardware and Training Time. We trained our chosen NCES instances on a server with 1 TB of RAM and an NVIDIA RTX A5000 GPU with 24 GB of RAM. Note that during training, approximately 8 GB of the 1 TB RAM is currently used by NCES. As search-based approaches do not require a GPU for class expression learning, we used a 16-core Intel Xeon E5-2695 with 2.30 GHz and 16 GB RAM to run all approaches (including NCES post training) for class expression learning on the test set. The number of parameters and training time of each NCES instance are reported in Table 4. From the table, we can observe that NCES instances are lightweight and can be trained within a few hours on medium-size knowledge bases. Note that training is only required once per knowledge base.

5.2   Results

Syntactic Accuracy. Our neural class expression synthesizers were trained for 300 epochs on each knowledge base. In Fig. 2, we only show the hard accuracy curves during training due to space constraints. The rest of the training curves can be found on our GitHub repository. The curves in Fig. 2 suggest that NCES instances train fast with an exponential growth in accuracy within the first 10 epochs. All models achieve over 95% syntactic accuracy on large knowledge bases (Carcinogenesis, Mutagenesis, and Vicodi). On the smallest knowledge base, Semantic Bible, we observe that $NCES_{ST}$ drops in performance as it only achieves 88% accuracy during training. On the other side, $NCES_{GRU}$ and $NCES_{LSTM}$ tend to overfit the training data. This suggests that NCES instances are well suited for large datasets. We validate this hypothesis through the quality of the synthesized solutions on the test set (see Table 5).

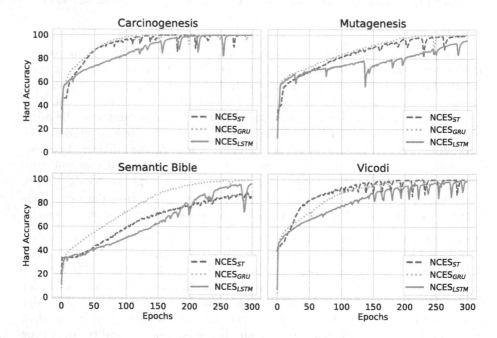

Fig. 2. Training accuracy curves.

Comparison to State-of-the-Art Approaches. We compare our approach against EvoLearner, CELOE, ECII, ELTL. The maximum execution time for CELOE and EvoLearner was set to 300 s per learning problem while ECII and ELTL were executed with their default settings, as they do not have the maximum execution time parameter in their original implementation. From Table 5, we can observe that our approach (with ensemble prediction) significantly outperforms all other approaches in runtime on all datasets, and in F-measure on Carcinogenesis and Vicodi. Table 6 shows that NCES performs slightly better

Table 5. Evaluation results per approach and dataset. NCES uses ConEx embeddings. The star (*) indicates statistically significant differences between the best search-based and the best synthesis-based approaches. ↑ indicates that the higher is better, and ↓ indicates that the lower is better. Underlined values are the second best.

| | F_1 (%) ↑ | | | |
	Carcinogenesis	Mutagenesis	Semantic Bible	Vicodi
CELOE	37.92 ± 44.25	82.95 ± 33.48	**93.18 ± 17.52***	35.66 ± 42.06
ELTL	13.35 ± 25.84	28.81 ± 34.44	42.77 ± 38.46	16.70 ± 33.31
ECII	15.74 ± 27.82	27.14 ± 31.64	33.97 ± 37.71	43.66 ± 36.13
EvoLearner	91.48 ± 14.30	**93.27 ± 12.95**	91.88 ± 10.14	92.74 ± 10.28
$NCES_{LSTM}$	82.21 ± 29.29	81.47 ± 27.77	72.32 ± 34.37	72.35 ± 35.34
$NCES_{GRU}$	89.51 ± 25.24	78.24 ± 30.99	52.37 ± 39.86	86.60 ± 26.84
$NCES_{ST}$	90.32 ± 25.12	80.55 ± 34.33	72.95 ± 38.68	77.75 ± 37.16
$NCES_{ST+GRU}$	96.77 ± 12.72	89.50 ± 26.09	84.32 ± 26.82	92.91 ± 20.14
$NCES_{ST+LSTM}$	96.72 ± 12.96	89.19 ± 26.16	80.78 ± 28.30	90.91 ± 21.57
$NCES_{GRU+LSTM}$	94.51 ± 15.39	81.49 ± 30.71	75.91 ± 32.48	88.28 ± 24.17
$NCES_{ST+GRU+LSTM}$	**97.06 ± 13.06***	91.39 ± 22.91	87.11 ± 24.05	**95.51 ± 12.14***

| | Accuracy (%) ↑ | | | |
	Carcinogenesis	Mutagenesis	Semantic Bible	Vicodi
CELOE	66.88 ± 24.87	94.39 ± 11.68	98.17 ± 4.95	85.38 ± 17.71
ELTL	24.96 ± 32.86	38.01 ± 39.26	47.31 ± 38.22	33.35 ± 41.88
ECII	25.95 ± 35.98	31.99 ± 38.36	30.35 ± 37.91	76.73 ± 35.22
EvoLearner	99.72 ± 1.44	**99.35 ± 2.03**	98.89 ± 3.45*	**99.27 ± 5.13**
$NCES_{LSTM}$	97.92 ± 11.19	98.04 ± 6.81	89.83 ± 23.59	94.03 ± 20.77
$NCES_{GRU}$	99.32 ± 4.16	98.02 ± 4.03	80.67 ± 30.80	98.10 ± 11.43
$NCES_{ST}$	97.16 ± 14.33	90.71 ± 25.49	84.19 ± 32.72	89.90 ± 27.89
$NCES_{ST+GRU}$	99.03 ± 9.28	97.27 ± 11.75	92.38 ± 21.39	97.11 ± 12.57
$NCES_{ST+LSTM}$	99.26 ± 5.69	96.93 ± 12.17	90.27 ± 21.60	95.78 ± 16.46
$NCES_{GRU+LSTM}$	**99.90 ± 0.31**	98.49 ± 5.35	87.16 ± 27.44	96.86 ± 14.99
$NCES_{ST+GRU+LSTM}$	99.04 ± 9.28	98.39 ± 6.45	94.70 ± 17.83	97.48 ± 11.71

| | Runtime (sec.) ↓ | | | |
	Carcinogenesis	Mutagenesis	Semantic Bible	Vicodi
CELOE	239.58 ± 132.59	92.46 ± 125.69	135.30 ± 139.95	289.95 ± 103.63
ELTL	23.81 ± 1.47	15.19 ± 12.50	4.12 ± 0.11	299.14 ± 202.21
ECII	22.93 ± 2.63	18.11 ± 4.93	6.45 ± 1.42	37.94 ± 28.25
EvoLearner	54.73 ± 25.86	48.00 ± 31.38	17.16 ± 9.20	213.78 ± 81.03
$NCES_{LSTM}$	0.16 ± 0.00	0.19 ± 0.00	0.08 ± 0.00	0.13 ± 0.00
$NCES_{GRU}$	0.15 ± 0.00	0.18 ± 0.00	0.08 ± 0.00	0.06 ± 0.00
$NCES_{ST}$	**0.08 ± 0.00***	**0.11 ± 0.00***	**0.07 ± 0.00***	**0.04 ± 0.00***
$NCES_{ST+GRU}$	0.16 ± 0.00	0.25 ± 0.00	0.11 ± 0.00	0.09 ± 0.00
$NCES_{ST+LSTM}$	0.23 ± 0.00	0.23 ± 0.00	0.11 ± 0.00	0.11 ± 0.00
$NCES_{GRU+LSTM}$	0.24 ± 0.00	0.32 ± 0.00	0.13 ± 0.00	0.17 ± 0.00
$NCES_{ST+GRU+LSTM}$	0.27 ± 0.00	0.31 ± 0.00	0.15 ± 0.00	0.15 ± 0.00

with ConEx embeddings than TransE embeddings except on the Carcinogenesis dataset. The standard deviation of NCES's prediction time is 0 because it performs batch predictions, i.e., it predicts solutions for all learning problems

Table 6. Evaluation results using TransE embeddings.

	F_1 (%) ↑			
	Carcinogenesis	Mutagenesis	Semantic Bible	Vicodi
$NCES_{LSTM}$	84.52 ± 27.01	76.45 ± 34.22	59.63 ± 34.98	79.06 ± 30.07
$NCES_{GRU}$	87.00 ± 27.43	77.77 ± 36.36	65.71 ± 33.51	79.81 ± 33.31
$NCES_{ST}$	86.66 ± 30.13	79.12 ± 34.23	68.14 ± 37.17	78.33 ± 36.35
$NCES_{ST+GRU}$	97.47 ± 9.63	91.05 ± 21.11	75.36 ± 32.88	89.27 ± 25.09
$NCES_{ST+LSTM}$	92.85 ± 21.88	90.01 ± 19.50	76.26 ± 34.07	89.37 ± 24.46
$NCES_{GRU+LSTM}$	91.83 ± 21.03	81.22 ± 33.05	76.17 ± 31.53	87.68 ± 24.54
$NCES_{ST+GRU+LSTM}$	97.56 ± 11.55	91.24 ± 21.27	85.82 ± 24.85	90.05 ± 23.67
	Accuracy (%) ↑			
	Carcinogenesis	Mutagenesis	Semantic Bible	Vicodi
$NCES_{LSTM}$	97.40 ± 14.19	96.59 ± 11.27	84.10 ± 24.91	97.17 ± 11.98
$NCES_{GRU}$	97.68 ± 12.82	95.20 ± 15.08	82.85 ± 29.44	95.86 ± 16.27
$NCES_{ST}$	93.59 ± 23.06	93.11 ± 21.15	82.47 ± 33.34	91.70 ± 25.01
$NCES_{ST+GRU}$	99.35 ± 5.52	99.07 ± 2.61	85.62 ± 27.76	96.45 ± 15.17
$NCES_{ST+LSTM}$	98.11 ± 11.18	99.00 ± 2.69	88.95 ± 23.69	95.05 ± 18.01
$NCES_{GRU+LSTM}$	98.91 ± 9.46	96.08 ± 13.64	89.25 ± 24.54	97.37 ± 12.60
$NCES_{ST+GRU+LSTM}$	98.99 ± 9.45	98.90 ± 4.70	93.53 ± 18.24	95.01 ± 18.53
	Runtime (sec.) ↓			
	Carcinogenesis	Mutagenesis	Semantic Bible	Vicodi
$NCES_{LSTM}$	0.09 ± 0.00	0.14 ± 0.00	0.06 ± 0.00	0.12 ± 0.00
$NCES_{GRU}$	0.05 ± 0.00	0.15 ± 0.00	0.06 ± 0.00	0.13 ± 0.00
$NCES_{ST}$	0.04 ± 0.00	0.09 ± 0.00	0.05 ± 0.00	0.05 ± 0.00
$NCES_{ST+GRU}$	0.08 ± 0.00	0.18 ± 0.00	0.08 ± 0.00	0.11 ± 0.00
$NCES_{ST+LSTM}$	0.09 ± 0.00	0.16 ± 0.00	0.08 ± 0.00	0.11 ± 0.00
$NCES_{GRU+LSTM}$	0.15 ± 0.00	0.22 ± 0.00	0.10 ± 0.00	0.15 ± 0.00
$NCES_{ST+GRU+LSTM}$	0.14 ± 0.00	0.22 ± 0.00	0.11 ± 0.00	0.14 ± 0.00

at the same time. The prediction time is averaged across learning problems and is therefore the same for each learning problem. We used the Wilcoxon Rank Sum test with a significance level of 5% and the null hypothesis that the compared quantities per dataset are from the same distribution. The best search-based approaches (CELOE and EvoLearner) only outperform NCES instances (including ensemble models) on the smallest datasets (Semantic Bible and Mutagenesis). The reason for this is that deep learning models are data-hungry and often fail to generalize well on small datasets. Our approach is hence well suited for large knowledge bases where search-based approaches are prohibitively slow.

5.3   Discussion

The hypothesis behind this work was that high-quality class expressions can be synthesized directly out of training data, i.e., without the need for an extensive search. Our results clearly undergird our hypothesis. While NCES is outperformed by CELOE and EvoLearner on small datasets, it achieves the best performance on Carcinogenesis with over 5% absolute improvement in F-measure. This large difference is due to the fact that most search-based approaches fail to find any suitable solution for some learning problems. For example, the first learning problem on the Vicodi knowledge base is (`Disaster` ⊔ `Military-Organisation`) ⊓ (¬`Engineer`). The solutions computed by each of the approaches are as follows: CELOE: `Flavour` ⊓ (¬`Battle`) ⊓ (¬`Person`) [F_1: 1.95%], ELTL: `Flavour` ⊓ (∃ `related`.(∃ `related`.`Role`)) [F_1: 0%], ECII: `Organisation` ⊔ ¬`VicodiOI` [F_1: 13.16%], EvoLearner: `Military-Organisation` ⊓ `Military-Organisation` [F_1: 73.17%], and NCES$_{ST+GRU}$[2]: (`Disaster` ⊔ `Military-Organisation`) ⊓ (¬`Engineer`) [F_1: 100%]. Here, our ensemble model NCES$_{ST+GRU}$ synthesized the exact solution, which does not appear in the training data of NCES, while the best search-based approach, EvoLearner, could only compute an approximate solution with an F-measure of 73.17%. On the other hand, CELOE, ECII, and ELTL failed to find any suitable solutions within the set timeout.

The scalability of the synthesis step of our approaches makes them particularly suitable for situations where many class expressions are to be computed for the same knowledge base. For example, taking into account the average training and inference time of the Set Transformer architecture, one can conjecture that the minimum number of learning problems from which the cost of deep learning becomes worthwhile is: 11 for NCES vs. CELOE, 25 for NCES vs. EvoLearner, 24 for NCES vs. ELTL, and 96 for NCES vs. ECII. These values are calculated by solving for n in $n \times T_{\text{algo\_learn}} > T_{\text{train}} + T_{\text{inference}}$, where $T_{\text{algo\_learn}}$, T_{train}, and $T_{\text{inference}}$ are the average learning time of a search-based approach, the training time, and the inference time of NCES, respectively.

6   Conclusion and Future Work

We propose a novel family of approaches for class expression learning, which we dub neural class expression synthesizers (NCES). NCES use neural networks to directly synthesize class expressions from input examples without requiring an expensive search over all possible class expressions. Given a set timeout per prediction, we showed that our approach outperforms all state-of-the-art search-based approaches on large knowledge bases. Taking training time into account, our approach is suitable for application scenarios where many concepts are to be learned for the same knowledge base. In future work, we will investigate means to transfer the knowledge acquired on one knowledge base to other knowledge bases. Furthermore, we plan to extend our approach to more expressive description logics such as $\mathcal{ALCHIQ(D)}$.

---

[2] Here, NCES uses ConEx embeddings.

References

1. Bergstra, J., Bengio, Y.: Random search for hyper-parameter optimization. J. Mach. Learn. Res. **13**, 281–305 (2012)
2. Bin, S., Westphal, P., Lehmann, J., Ngonga, A.: Implementing scalable structured machine learning for big data in the SAKE project. In: IEEE BigData, pp. 1400–1407. IEEE Computer Society (2017)
3. Bizer, C., et al.: DBpedia - a crystallization point for the web of data. J. Web Semant. **7**(3), 154–165 (2009)
4. Bordes, A., Glorot, X., Weston, J., Bengio, Y.: A semantic matching energy function for learning with multi-relational data - application to word-sense disambiguation. Mach. Learn. **94**(2), 233–259 (2014). https://doi.org/10.1007/s10994-013-5363-6
5. Bordes, A., Usunier, N., García-Durán, A., Weston, J., Yakhnenko, O.: Translating embeddings for modeling multi-relational data. In: NIPS, pp. 2787–2795 (2013)
6. Bühmann, L., Lehmann, J., Westphal, P.: DL-Learner - a framework for inductive learning on the semantic web. J. Web Semant. **39**, 15–24 (2016)
7. Cho, K., van Merrienboer, B., Bahdanau, D., Bengio, Y.: On the properties of neural machine translation: encoder-decoder approaches. In: SSST@EMNLP, pp. 103–111. ACL (2014)
8. Cho, K., et al.: Learning phrase representations using RNN encoder-decoder for statistical machine translation. In: EMNLP, pp. 1724–1734. ACL (2014)
9. Dai, Y., Wang, S., Xiong, N.N., Guo, W.: A survey on knowledge graph embedding: approaches, applications and benchmarks. Electronics **9**(5), 750 (2020)
10. Demir, C., Ngomo, A.-C.N.: Convolutional complex knowledge graph embeddings. In: Verborgh, R., et al. (eds.) ESWC 2021. LNCS, vol. 12731, pp. 409–424. Springer, Cham (2021). https://doi.org/10.1007/978-3-030-77385-4_24
11. Dietterich, T.G., Lathrop, R.H., Lozano-Pérez, T.: Solving the multiple instance problem with axis-parallel rectangles. Artif. Intell. **89**(1–2), 31–71 (1997)
12. Dong, X., Yu, Z., Cao, W., Shi, Y., Ma, Q.: A survey on ensemble learning. Front. Comput. Sci. **14**(2), 241–258 (2020). https://doi.org/10.1007/s11704-019-8208-z
13. Fanizzi, N., d'Amato, C., Esposito, F.: DL-FOIL concept learning in description logics. In: Železný, F., Lavrač, N. (eds.) ILP 2008. LNCS (LNAI), vol. 5194, pp. 107–121. Springer, Heidelberg (2008). https://doi.org/10.1007/978-3-540-85928-4_12
14. Finn, C., Abbeel, P., Levine, S.: Model-agnostic meta-learning for fast adaptation of deep networks. In: ICML, Proceedings of Machine Learning Research, vol. 70, pp. 1126–1135. PMLR (2017)
15. Heindorf, S., et al.: EvoLearner: learning description logics with evolutionary algorithms. In: WWW, pp. 818–828. ACM (2022)
16. Heist, N., Hertling, S., Ringler, D., Paulheim, H.: Knowledge graphs on the web - an overview. In: Knowledge Graphs for eXplainable Artificial Intelligence, Studies on the Semantic Web, vol. 47, pp. 3–22. IOS Press (2020)
17. Heist, N., Paulheim, H.: Uncovering the semantics of Wikipedia categories. In: Ghidini, C., et al. (eds.) ISWC 2019. LNCS, vol. 11778, pp. 219–236. Springer, Cham (2019). https://doi.org/10.1007/978-3-030-30793-6_13
18. Hochreiter, S., Schmidhuber, J.: Long short-term memory. Neural Comput. **9**(8), 1735–1780 (1997)
19. Konev, B., Ozaki, A., Wolter, F.: A model for learning description logic ontologies based on exact learning. In: AAAI, pp. 1008–1015. AAAI Press (2016)

20. Kouagou, N.J., Heindorf, S., Demir, C., Ngomo, A.N.: Learning concept lengths accelerates concept learning in ALC. In: Groth, P., et al. (eds.) ESWC. LNCS, vol. 13261, pp. 236–252. Springer, Cham (2022). https://doi.org/10.1007/978-3-031-06981-9_14

21. Krech, D.: RDFLib: a Python library for working with RDF (2006). https://github.com/RDFLib/rdflib

22. Lee, J., Lee, Y., Kim, J., Kosiorek, A.R., Choi, S., Teh, Y.W.: Set transformer: a framework for attention-based permutation-invariant neural networks. In: ICML, Proceedings of Machine Learning Research, vol. 97, pp. 3744–3753. PMLR (2019)

23. Lehmann, J.: DL-Learner: learning concepts in description logics. J. Mach. Learn. Res. **10**, 2639–2642 (2009)

24. Lehmann, J.: Learning OWL Class Expressions. Studies on the Semantic Web, vol. 6. IOS Press (2010)

25. Lehmann, J., Auer, S., Bühmann, L., Tramp, S.: Class expression learning for ontology engineering. J. Web Semant. **9**(1), 71–81 (2011)

26. Lehmann, J., Hitzler, P.: Concept learning in description logics using refinement operators. Mach. Learn. **78**(1–2), 203–250 (2010). https://doi.org/10.1007/s10994-009-5146-2

27. Lehmann, J., Völker, J.: Perspectives on Ontology Learning. Studies on the Semantic Web, vol. 18. IOS Press (2014)

28. McGuinness, D.L., Van Harmelen, F., et al.: OWL web ontology language overview. W3C Recommendation **10**(10), 2004 (2004)

29. Nagypál, G.: History ontology building: the technical view. In: Humanities, Computers and Cultural Heritage, p. 207 (2005)

30. Nardi, D., Brachman, R.J.: An introduction to description logics. In: Description Logic Handbook, pp. 1–40. Cambridge University Press (2003)

31. Nickel, M., Tresp, V., Kriegel, H.: Factorizing YAGO: scalable machine learning for linked data. In: WWW, pp. 271–280. ACM (2012)

32. Ozaki, A.: Learning description logic ontologies: five approaches. Where do they stand? Künstl. Intell. **34**(3), 317–327 (2020). https://doi.org/10.1007/s13218-020-00656-9

33. Qi, C.R., Su, H., Mo, K., Guibas, L.J.: PointNet: deep learning on point sets for 3D classification and segmentation. In: CVPR, pp. 652–660 (2017)

34. Rizzo, G., Fanizzi, N., d'Amato, C.: Class expression induction as concept space exploration: from DL-Foil to DL-Focl. Future Gener. Comput. Syst. **108**, 256–272 (2020)

35. Sagi, O., Rokach, L.: Ensemble learning: a survey. WIREs Data Min. Knowl. Discov. **8**(4), e1249 (2018)

36. Sarker, M.K., Hitzler, P.: Efficient concept induction for description logics. In: AAAI, pp. 3036–3043. AAAI Press (2019)

37. Schmidt-Schauß, M., Smolka, G.: Attributive concept descriptions with complements. Artif. Intell. **48**(1), 1–26 (1991)

38. Snell, J., Swersky, K., Zemel, R.S.: Prototypical networks for few-shot learning. In: NIPS, pp. 4077–4087 (2017)

39. Tran, T., Ha, Q., Hoang, T., Nguyen, L.A., Nguyen, H.S.: Bisimulation-based concept learning in description logics. Fundam. Informaticae **133**(2–3), 287–303 (2014)

40. Vrandecic, D., Krötzsch, M.: Wikidata: a free collaborative knowledgebase. Commun. ACM **57**(10), 78–85 (2014)

41. Wang, Q., Mao, Z., Wang, B., Guo, L.: Knowledge graph embedding: a survey of approaches and applications. IEEE Trans. Knowl. Data Eng. **29**(12), 2724–2743 (2017)

42. Wang, Z., Li, J.: Text-enhanced representation learning for knowledge graph. In: IJCAI, pp. 1293–1299. IJCAI/AAAI Press (2016)
43. Westphal, P., Bühmann, L., Bin, S., Jabeen, H., Lehmann, J.: SML-Bench - a benchmarking framework for structured machine learning. Semant. Web **10**(2), 231–245 (2019)
44. Wu, Y., et al.: Google's neural machine translation system: bridging the gap between human and machine translation. CoRR abs/1609.08144 (2016)
45. Xie, R., Liu, Z., Jia, J., Luan, H., Sun, M.: Representation learning of knowledge graphs with entity descriptions. In: AAAI, pp. 2659–2665. AAAI Press (2016)
46. Zaheer, M., Kottur, S., Ravanbakhsh, S., Póczos, B., Salakhutdinov, R., Smola, A.J.: Deep sets. In: NIPS, pp. 3391–3401 (2017)
47. Zhang, F., Yuan, N.J., Lian, D., Xie, X., Ma, W.: Collaborative knowledge base embedding for recommender systems. In: KDD, pp. 353–362. ACM (2016)
48. Zhang, J., He, T., Sra, S., Jadbabaie, A.: Why gradient clipping accelerates training: a theoretical justification for adaptivity. arXiv preprint arXiv:1905.11881 (2019)
49. Zhao, H., Sun, S., Jin, B.: Sequential fault diagnosis based on LSTM neural network. IEEE Access **6**, 12929–12939 (2018)
50. Zulqarnain, M., Ghazali, R., Ghouse, M.G., et al.: Efficient processing of GRU based on word embedding for text classification. JOIV **3**(4), 377–383 (2019)

Evaluating Language Models for Knowledge Base Completion

Blerta Veseli[1(✉)], Sneha Singhania[1], Simon Razniewski[2(✉)],
and Gerhard Weikum[1]

[1] Max Planck Institute for Informatics, Saarbrücken, Germany
bveseli@mpi-inf.mpg.de
[2] Bosch Center for AI, Renningen, Germany
srazniew@mpi-inf.mpg.de

Abstract. Structured knowledge bases (KBs) are a foundation of many intelligent applications, yet are notoriously incomplete. Language models (LMs) have recently been proposed for unsupervised knowledge base completion (KBC), yet, despite encouraging initial results, questions regarding their suitability remain open. Existing evaluations often fall short because they only evaluate on popular subjects, or sample already existing facts from KBs. In this work, we introduce a novel, more challenging benchmark dataset, and a methodology tailored for a realistic assessment of the KBC potential of LMs. For automated assessment, we curate a dataset called WD-KNOWN, which provides an unbiased random sample of Wikidata, containing over 3.9 million facts. In a second step, we perform a human evaluation on predictions that are not yet in the KB, as only this provides real insights into the added value over existing KBs. Our key finding is that biases in dataset conception of previous benchmarks lead to a systematic overestimate of LM performance for KBC. However, our results also reveal strong areas of LMs. We could, for example, perform a significant completion of Wikidata on the relations `nativeLanguage`, by a factor of ∼21 (from 260k to 5.8M) at 82% precision, and `citizenOf` by a factor of ∼0.3 (from 4.2M to 5.3M) at 90% precision. Moreover, we find that LMs possess surprisingly strong generalization capabilities: even on relations where most facts were not directly observed in LM training, prediction quality can be high. We open-source the benchmark dataset and code. (https://github.com/bveseli/LMsForKBC).

1 Introduction

Structured knowledge bases (KBs) like Wikidata [26], DBpedia [1], and Yago [25] are backbones of the semantic web and are employed in many knowledge-centric applications like search, question answering and dialogue. Constructing these KBs at high quality and scale is a long-standing research challenge and multiple knowledge base construction benchmarks exist, e.g., FB15k [2], CoDEx [21], and LM-KBC22 [24]. Text-extraction, knowledge graph embeddings, and LM-based knowledge extraction have continuously moved scores upwards on these tasks, and leaderboard portals like Paperswithcode[1] provide evidence to that.

Recently, pre-trained language models have been purported as a promising source for structured knowledge. Starting from the seminal LAMA paper [17], a throve of works have explored how to better probe, train, or fine-tune these LMs [12]. Nonetheless, we observe a certain divide between these late-breaking investigations, and practical knowledge base completion (KBC). While the recent LM-based approaches often focus on attractive and clean methodologies that produce fast results, practical KBC is a highly precision-oriented, extremely laborious process, involving a very high degree of manual labor, either for manually creating statements [26], or for building comprehensive scraping, cleaning, validation, and normalization pipelines [1,25]. We believe previous works fall short in three aspects:

1. *Focus on high precision:* On the KB side, part of Yago's success stems from its validated >95% accuracy, and the Google Knowledge Vault was not deployed into production, partly because it did not achieve 99% accuracy [27]. Yet, previous LM analyses balance precision and recall or report precision/hits@k values, implicitly tuning systems towards balanced recall scores resulting in impractical precision.
2. *Evaluation of completion potential:* Existing benchmarks often sample from popular subjects. This is useful for system comparison, but not for KBC. E.g., predicting capitals of countries with 99% accuracy does not imply practical value: they are already captured in established KBs like Wikidata.
3. *Prediction of missing facts:* Existing works test LMs on facts already stored in KBs, which does not provide us with a realistic assessment for completion. For KBC we need to predict objects for subject-relation pairs, previously not known to the KB.

It is also important to keep in mind the scale of KBs: Wikidata, for instance, currently contains around 100 Million entities, and 1.2B statements. The cost of producing such KBs is massive, one estimate from 2018 sets the cost per triple at 2 USD for manually curated triples [15], and 1 ct for automatically extracted ones.[2] Thus, even small additions in relative terms, might correspond to massive gains in absolute numbers. For example, even by the lower estimate of 1 ct/triple, adding one triple to just 1% of Wikidata humans, would come at a cost of 100k USD.

In this paper, *we conduct a systematic analysis of LMs for KBC*, where we focus on *high precision ranges* (90%). We evaluate by first using a new benchmark dataset WD-KNOWN, where we randomly sample facts from Wikidata (including many without any structured information, Wikipedia information, or English labels) and second by a manual evaluation on subject-relation pairs without object values, yet.

---

[1] https://paperswithcode.com/task/knowledge-graph-completion.
[2] Wikidata might broadly fall in between, as its aim is human-curated quality, but major portions are imported semi-automatically from other sources.

Technically, we focus on the BERT language model [7], and the Wikidata knowledge base. Although BERT has been superseded by newer LMs, its popularity is still matched only by the closed source GPT-3 and chatGPT models. Wikidata is by far the most prominent and comprehensive public KB, so evaluations against it provide the strongest yardstick.

Our main results are as follows:

1. In actual KBC, LMs perform considerably worse than benchmarks like LAMA indicated, but still achieve strong results for language-related, socio-demographic relations (e.g., *nativeLanguage*).
2. Simple changes on out-of-the-box LMs, in particular, vocabulary expansion and prompt formulation, can significantly improve their ability to output high-precision knowledge.
3. Using LMs, Wikidata could be significantly expanded for three relations, `nativeLanguage` by a factor of ~21 (from 260k to 5.8M) at precision 82%, `citizenOf` by a factor of ~0.3 (from 4.2M to 5.3M) at 90% precision and `usedLanguage` by a factor of ~2.08 (from 2.1M to 6.6M) at 82% precision.

2 Background and Related Work

KB Construction and Completion. Knowledge base construction is a field with considerable history. One prominent approach is by human curation, as done e.g., in the seminal CYC project [11], and this is also the backbone of today's most prominent public KB, Wikidata [26]. Another popular paradigm is the extraction from semi-structured resources, as pursued in Yago and DBpedia [1,25]. Extraction from free text has also been explored (e.g., NELL [4]). A popular paradigm has been embedding-based link prediction, e.g., via tensor factorization like Rescal [14], and KG embeddings like TransE [2].

An inherent design decision in KBC is the P/R trade-off – academic projects are often open to trade these freely (e.g., via F-1 scores), while production environments are often very critically concerned with precision, e.g., Wikidata generally discouraging statistical inferences[3], and industrial players likely using to a considerable degree human editing and verification [27]. Although the P/R trade-off is in principle tunable via thresholds, the high-precision range is hardly investigated. For example in all of Rescal, TransE, and LAMA, the main results focus on metrics like hits@k, MRR, or AUC, which provide no bounds on precision.

LMs for KB Construction. Knowledge extraction from language models provides fresh hope for the synergy of automated approaches and high-precision curated KBs. Knowledge-extraction from LMs provides remarkably straightforward access to very large text corpora: The basic idea by [17] is to just define one template per relation, then query the LM with subject-instantiated versions, and

---

[3] There is often a terminological confusion here: Automated editing is omnipresent on Wikidata, but the bots performing them typically execute meticulously pre-defined edit and insertion tasks (e.g., based on other structured sources), not based on statistical inference.

retain its top prediction(s). A range of follow-up works appeared, focusing, e.g., on investigating entities, improving updates, exploring storage limits, incorporating unique entity identifiers, and others [3,5,8,10,16,18–20,23]. Nonetheless, we observe the same gaps as above: The high-precision area, and real KBC, are underexplored.

Benchmarking KB Completion. KB completion (sometimes also referred to as link prediction) has a set of quasi-standard benchmarks. Here we review the important ones and outline why they do not help for the focus of our investigation.

Two of the most popular benchmarks, both introduced in [2], are **FB15k** and **WN18**. The former contains statements for 15k extremely popular entities from Freebase, entities that already in 2013, when KBs were small, had at least 100 statements. The latter contains 41k entities from WordNet, yet these are linguistic concepts where WordNet is already the authoritative reference, and the potential for completion is small. **DBP-5L** is a popular multilingual dataset of 14k entities, yet it is collected by iterative graph neighbourhood expansion, so by design is biased towards popular (well-connected) entities. **YAGO3-10** is another benchmark, that contains YAGO3 entities with at least 10 statements [6]. The recent **CoDEx** benchmark provides a much larger subset of Wikidata triples but again focuses on the more popular subjects, as even its hardest variant considers only entities with at least 5 statements [21]. The **LAMA** benchmark [16] is based on the T-REx dataset, which in turn restricts the scope of subjects to those having a Wikipedia page. **LAMA-UHN** [18] removes some surface correlations but does not remove the restriction to Wikipedia-known subjects. **LM-KBC22** [24] provides a curated mix of popular and long-tail subjects, but not a random sample, and only a small set of 12 relations. In summary, all these benchmarks provide non-random subject sets, and by taking ground truth from existing KBs, necessarily can not evaluate a method's real KB completion potential. The **PKGC** work [13] uses human evaluation to account for KB incompleteness, but also uses subjects from previous benchmarks focused on popular entities.

3   Method

3.1   Knowledge Base Completion Tasks

Established KBs like Wikidata store a large number of facts of the form *(subject, relation, object)*. However, such KBs still suffer from incompleteness, which limits their applicability. KBC tries to counteract this incompleteness and describes the task of predicting missing facts for a KB. KBC is often split into subtasks, such as predicting the relation, subject, or object slots in triples. In the following, we focus on the most prominent object slot filling task, i.e. predicting an object for a subject-relation pair without an object so far. Identifying plausible subject-relation pairs is another important task, as not every combination qualifies, e.g., (Albert Einstein, hasCapital,·) has no object.

We will refer to facts that are present in a KB as *existing facts* and *existing-fact prediction* describes predicting the object for a subject-relation pair for which the object value already exists in the KB. Similarly, we refer to facts that are missing in a KB as *missing facts* and *missing-fact prediction* describes predicting the object for a subject-relation pair with no object value yet.

3.2 Fact Prediction Using Pre-trained Language Models

The slot filling ability of an LM, i.e. predicting "Paris" for a pair (France, has-Capital), is essential for KBC. This is done by querying an LM using cloze-style statements, a.k.a. prompts, like "The capital of France is [MASK]." [17]. The LM's goal is to predict the token at the masked position, i.e. the object (Fig. 1).

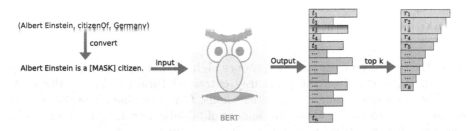

Fig. 1. To query the LM for an object slot, we convert triples into relation-specific prompts by masking the object, following [17]. The output is a probability vector over the model's vocabulary. We retain the top $k = 10$ predictions.

We probe the masked language model BERT [7] and query for facts of different relations by using relation-specific predefined prompts. The prompts contain placeholders for subject and object, so that the input for the LM can be automatically created by replacing the subject placeholder with the actual subject and the object placeholder with [MASK]. For each cloze-style query like "The capital of France is [MASK].", BERT returns a probability vector over its vocabulary $[t_1, .., t_n]$ (~29K tokens). From this vector, we select *top k* predictions $[r_1, .., r_k]$ with the highest probability as predictions for the object. We set $k = 10$.

3.3 Systematic Analysis Procedure

The goal of our analysis is to realistically assess the abilities of an LM for KBC. Therefore we perform a two-fold analysis by investigating 1) the existing-fact prediction ability of BERT in an automated evaluation and 2) the potential for KBC using LMs by predicting missing facts and evaluating the LM's predictions using human annotations.

The first analysis part includes the automated evaluation of existing facts in WD-KNOWN compared to the LAMA-T-REx benchmark in order to get a realistic estimate of an LM's prediction ability. Based on this evaluation we will extract relation-specific prediction thresholds considering precision and recall trade-offs to enable KBC on high precision and reasonable recall.

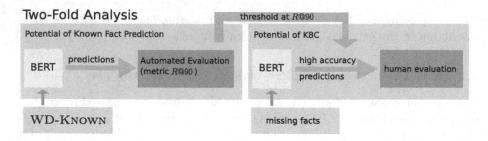

Fig. 2. Our systematic analysis is divided into two parts. First, we analyse existing-fact prediction by an automated evaluation computing the recall achieved at 90% precision ($R@P90$). The prediction at $R@P90$ is used as a threshold in the second part of the analysis. We analyse the potential of KBC for missing facts via a manual evaluation.

In the second analysis part, we produce high accuracy predictions for missing facts in Wikidata given the previously extracted threshold and evaluate the model's predictions using human annotations. Given the human evaluation, we will provide estimations about the amount of addable new facts to Wikidata. In Fig. 2 we show an overview of our systematic analysis.

4   Datasets

4.1   LAMA-T-REx

The LAMA-T-REx dataset [17] is derived from T-REx dataset [9], which is a subset of Wikidata and provides alignment between Wikidata (WD) triples and Wikipedia texts. LAMA-T-REx consists of 41 relations with ~1000 facts per relation sampled from T-REx. Included with the dataset are relation-specific, manually defined prompts, which [17] also refers to as templates. We use these 41 relations and their corresponding templates throughout our work. The scope of subjects in LAMA-T-REx is restricted to having a Wikipedia page and contains little data as shown in Table 1. This makes it difficult to realistically assess LMs for KBs.

4.2   WD-KNOWN

To realistically assess the usability of LMs for KBC, we created a large-scale dataset with random facts from Wikidata, without subject restrictions to pages such as Wikipedia. One must observe that, while WD-KNOWN is an unbiased sample from Wikidata's subject set per class, it is still biased towards reality, like Wikidata itself [22].

Creation. We extract facts from Wikidata for the same 41 relations as in LAMA-T-REx. We extract subject-relations pairs per relation and because these pairs may have multiple valid objects, e.g. N:M relations, we extract all associated valid objects along with the pairs. Otherwise, we would risk incomplete ground truth data. This would falsify our evaluation as an LM's prediction can not be recognized as correct when predicting another valid object than the extracted one. We sampled a maximum of 100,000 subject-relation pairs per relation along with all valid objects. If a relation contains fewer than 100,000 pairs, we extract all of them. The extracted facts consist of Wikidata-specific entity IDs, which we converted into natural language labels to allow probing an LM for facts. In contrast to [17], we do not remove multi-token objects like "Ball Aerospace & Technologies" because the inability to predict such objects is part of (some) LM's limitations and at the time KBC is performed it is unknown which objects are multi-token objects and which are not as KBC includes predicting missing facts, i.e. facts without ground truth object yet. This dataset feature enables the testing of LMs with multi-token prediction capability in comparison to uni-token predictions for KBC. Additionally, a large dataset like WD-KNOWN enables fine-tuning for fact prediction. In Table 1 we report some dataset statistics in comparison to LAMA-T-REx showing the larger size of WD-KNOWN. The dataset is available at https://github.com/bveseli/LMsForKBC.

Table 1. Our WD-KNOWN dataset in comparison to LAMA-T-REx. We report the total number of distinct objects (#unique objects), distinct subjects (#unique subjects), and the number of triples (#triples) as well as the total number of objects consisting of more than one token (#multi-token objects), and the average object entropy.

Dataset		#unique subjects	#unique objects	#triple	#multi-token objects	object dist. entropy
LAMA-T-REx	total	31,479	61,85	34,039	0	–
	average	767	150	830	0	0.76
WD-KNOWN	total	2,956,666	709,327	3,992,386	1,892,495	–
	average	72,113	17,300	97,375	46,158	0.67

5 Potential for Existing-Fact Prediction

Existing-fact prediction describes the prediction of an object for a subject-relation pair for which the ground truth object already exists in a KB. We will analyse the prediction ability of BERT given existing facts from Wikidata in an automated evaluation, focusing on the recall achieved at 90% precision ($R@P90$).

5.1 Metric

We use a rank-based metric and calculate the recall that our method achieves at 90% precision ($R@P90$). To compute $R@P90$, we sort the predictions in descending order of their prediction probability, and threshold predictions when average precision drops below 90%. When determining which prediction is true or false, we have to consider that a subject-relation pair can be associated with multiple valid objects. Therefore, a prediction is true, when it is among the valid objects and false otherwise.

5.2 Baselines

We want to check if BERT's fact prediction ability goes at least beyond just predicting statistically common objects, e.g. English for spokenLanguage. Therefore, we try two distribution-based baselines: random and majority vote. We compute relation-specific object distributions based on a relations ground truth data. In the case of a majority vote, we assign the most probable object to each fact and in the case of random, we assign a random object from the distribution. Additionally, we compare BERT to a relation extraction (RE) baseline and use the *Rosette Text Analytics*[4] relation extractor. Given a text snippet, the relation extractor can extract up to 17 relations. For the intersection of these 17 and our 41 relations, we subsampled relation-wise 200 facts from WD-KNOWN and align each fact with text. For text alignments, we consider two different source types: web texts and Wikipedia pages to cover facts with Wikipedia-unknown and Wikipedia-known subjects. Per relation, we align 100 facts with web texts, i.e. top 10 Google search results after googling the subject of a fact and 100 facts with wikipages, i.e. the summary of a subject's Wikipedia page. We get 200 facts with text alignments per relation headquarteredIn and citizenOf, 400 in total.

5.3 Evaluation and Results

Quantitative Analysis. In Table 2 we report $R@P90$ values achieved by BERT's predictions on our dataset WD-KNOWN in comparison to *LAMA-T-REx*. On WD-KNOWN the LM achieves significantly lower values (marked in bold) suggesting a more realistic assessment of BERT's fact prediction ability by WD-KNOWN. Only the relations nativeLanguage, spokenLanguage, officialLanguage show a smaller decrease and therefore stable results.

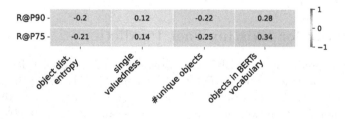

Fig. 3. Pearson Correlation Analysis

To investigate why BERT achieves low results, we perform a correlation analysis computing the Pearson correlation coefficient over $R@P90$ in Fig. 3. We notice a negative correlation between $R@P90$ and the object distribution entropy, meaning that a more uniform distribution makes the predictions harder. Furthermore, the number of unique objects is also negatively correlated with

---

[4] https://www.rosette.com/capability/relationship-extractor/#tech-specs.

Table 2. BERT's performance on data sets WD-KNOWN a LAMA-T-REx for the same 41 relations. Boldface marks significantly lower values, indicating an overestimation of BERT's fact predicting ability on LAMA.

Relation	WD-KNOWN	LAMA-T-REx	Relation	WD-KNOWN	LAMA-T-REx
	R@P90	R@P90		R@P90	R@P90
nativeLanguage	**0.61**	0.68	foundedIn	0.00009	0.001
spokenLanguage	**0.26**	0.33	deathPlace	0.00009	0
officialLanguage	**0.25**	0.37	namedAfter	0.00008	0
headquarteredIn	0.04	0.52	partOf	0.00006	0
developedBy	0.04	0.64	twinTown	0.00003	0.001
producedBy	0.03	0.86	sharesBorders	0.00001	0.001
countryOfJurisdiction	0.02	0.66	fieldOfWork	0	0
hasCapital	0.01	0.60	employedBy	0	0.002
locatedIn	0.008	0.20	hasReligion	0	0
bornIn	0.006	0.009	playerPosition	0	0
isCapital	0.006	0.81	subclassOf	0	0.01
CountryOfOrigin	0.005	0.08	holdsPosition	0	0
isA	0.004	0.06	diplomaticRelation	0	0
LanguageOfFilm	0.003	0	citizenOf	0	0
ownedBy	**0.0008**	0.16	consistsOf	0	0
hostCountry	0.0006	0.002	musicGenre	0	0
originalBroadcaster	0.0004	0.02	musicLabel	0	0.02
inTerritoryOf	0.0002	0.01	playsInstrument	0	0.003
writtenIn	**0.0001**	0.15	hasProfession	0	0
locationOfWork	0.0001	0	inContinent	0	0.004
memberOf	**0.0001**	0.52			

BERT's performance, i.e. fewer possible objects benefit the performance. The single valuedness, i.e. the relation-wise proportion of subject-relation pairs with only one object, shows a low but positive correlation. This indicates the performance is better on N:1 or 1:1 relations confirming the observation in [17]. The performance is also positively correlated with the number of objects in BERT's vocabulary, i.e. the more objects of a relation are covered by the LM's vocabulary, the better the performance. The vocabulary acts as a bottleneck, preventing the model from predicting facts.

Looking at the baselines in Table 3, we see that the majority baseline is quite solid with an average precision of 0.18. Access to the underlying distribution of relation-specific ground truth data has a noticeable impact on assigning objects to a subject-relation pair. Still, BERT achieving an average precision in a higher range (>75%) shows that the prediction ability is based on more than predicting statistically common objects. The RE baseline is outperformed by BERT for two tested relations, while BERT and RE show lower results on facts aligned with webtexts than on facts aligned with Wikipedia pages.

Qualitative Analysis. Since we are interested in high precision for KB completion and quantitative analysis showed low R@P90 values for most of the relations, we need to increase BERT's performance. We first perform a qualitative analysis of issues. Since analysing all 41 relations qualitatively is not feasible, we select a representative subset of relations. The subset is diverse regarding, e.g. semantics (e.g. language, demographic, goods), entity type (human, com-

Table 3. Random and Majority Baselines (left) and Relation Extraction (RE) Baseline for `citizenOf` and `headquarteredIn` (right). The RE Baseline is done on two datasets: 1) a (Wikipedia) dataset, where the triples are aligned with the Wikipedia summaries extracted from the subject's Wikipedia pages, and 2) a (Google search) dataset, where the triples are aligned with texts from the top 10 Google search results after searching for the subject of the respective triple. Scores were computed on a subset of WD-KNOWN with text alignments as described in Sect. 5.2.

Distribution vs. BERT	$\overline{P}$	$\overline{R}$	$F1$	RE vs. BERT	Wikipedia			Google search		
					$\overline{P}$	$\overline{R}$	$F1$	$\overline{P}$	$\overline{R}$	$F1$
Random	0.09	0.05	0.06	Rosette	0.32	0.05	0.08	0.21	0.01	0.02
Majority	0.18	0.09	0.03	BERT @P75	0.87	0.31	0.45	0.37	0.28	0.31
BERT @P75	0.75	0.43	0.54	BERT @P90	0.95	0.22	0.17	0.45	0.23	0.30
BERT @P90	0.90	0.35	0.48							

pany, places), performance (lower vs. higher scores), and possible objects (all languages vs. cities worldwide). The chosen relations are shown in Table 4. We aim to identify and eliminate or at least reduce systematic prediction errors for those relations. Common error categories are: 1) predicting the wrong hierarchy, i.e. country instead of a city; 2) predicting the wrong category, i.e. country instead of nationality and 3) ambiguous prompts, i.e. predicting "local" for "Albert Einstein is a [MASK] citizen". Such cases falsify the evaluation, since a distinction between actually true predictions ("German" or "Germany") and actually false predictions ("local" or "German") is not made. These errors are rooted in the conceptual discrepancy between LMs and KBs. While querying a KB is clearly defined and leads to unambiguous answers, an LM is queried by natural language prompts, which are as ambiguous as natural language itself. To use LMs for KBs we need to translate between them. Therefore we focus on three main model parts: input, model, and output: 1) input optimization by adjusting prompts; 2) model optimization by fine-tuning, and 3) output adjustment by converting ground truth and prediction into the same category. Input and model optimizations are done on relation-wise data splits for training and test $(80 - 20)$, where we split based on subject-relation pairs avoiding having the same subject in training and test.

Input Optimization. AutoPrompt [23] introduced an automatic way of prompt generation given a specific task, such as fact retrieval. We generate our prompts as suggested by [23] on relation-specific training splits of WD-KNOWN. In Table 4 the input optimization with AutoPrompts achieves notable improvements for $R@P90$, e.g. `hasReligion` increased from 0 to 0.21, `citizenOf` from 0 to 0.15. There is no deterioration in any of the relations.

Model Optimization. Fine-tuning not only allows us to optimize an LM on the searched output but also enables adding new words to the model's vocabulary as this has been shown to be a bottleneck for fact prediction. We fine-tune relation-specific LMs and for vocabulary extension, we add a *max.* of 2000 objects per relation. For fine-tuning the masked language model objective [7] is used as well as our training splits. We show results on two setups: 1) fine-tuning $BERT_{large}$, denoted FT, and 2) fine-tuning $BERT_{large}$ and with extended vocabulary, denoted FT_{vocab}. In Table 4 the model optimization shows the biggest improvements. Only developedBy, producedBy, headquarteredIn deteriorate at first in the FT setup, but producedBy and developedBy improve significantly in the FT_{vocab} setup. We found that after fine-tuning the model predicts substrings that match the ground truth object, e.g. in relation producedBy "Len" is predicted if the ground truth object is "Lenovo" or "Xiao" for "Xiaomi". The same happens in relation developedBy, e.g. "Core" for "Corel", and in relation headquarteredIn e.g. "Wind" for the city "Windhoek". After vocabulary expansion previously missing tokens like "Xiaomi" can now be fully predicted, so that $R@P90$ can increase in the FT_{vocab} setup. It is worth noting that producedBy and developedBy could only be improved significantly by expanding the vocabulary during fine-tuning. Only for headquarteredIn the precision does not improve. While headquarteredIn does degrade in precision, fine-tuning with an extended vocabulary increases the overall quality significantly (see Table 4, AVG $R@P90$).

Output Adjustment. To map prediction and ground truth, so a prediction "French" is correctly recognized for object "France", we use manually crafted dictionaries. Methods like string matching can always lead to incorrect mappings and sometimes even do not work for examples like the one shown. Therefore, we used two dictionaries mapping nationalities and countries on the one hand and religions and religious affiliations on the other hand. A prediction will be true if it belongs to the same entry in a relation-specific dictionary as the ground truth object and false otherwise. The creation of such mapping dictionaries involves tremendous manual labor, contradicting our search for automated KBC. Therefore, we evaluate on only two hasReligion and citizenOf as these relations were also most affected by the second error category mentioned above so that the output adjustment here might have the greatest effect. We find, that automated fine-tuning significantly outperforms this approach.

Table 4. Table shows $R@P90$ values. Improvement approaches to maximize BERT's performance on specific relations in comparison to pre-trained BERT-large (case-sensitive). Improvements were tested at three key points in the LM: *input, model, output.* Scores were computed on the test split of WD-KNOWN.

Relation	Base	Input Opt.	Model Opt.		Output Adjustment
	Pre-Trained	AutoPrompt	FT	FT_{vocab}	Manual Mapping
nativeLanguage	0.62	0.66	0.79	**0.79**	–
hasReligion	0	0.21	0.13	**0.27**	0.02
citizenOf	0	0.15	0.23	**0.23**	0.01
producedBy	0.03	0.03	0	**0.15**	–
developedBy	0.04	0.04	0.0004	**0.11**	–
headquarteredIn	**0.04**	0.04	0	0	–
spokenLanguage	0.26	0.42	**0.51**	0.5	–
LanguageOfFilm	0.003	0.04	**0.29**	0.27	–
AVG $R@P90$	0.12	0.20	0.24	**0.29**	0.015

Summary. We found that using biased datasets lead to an overestimation of an LM's performance for fact prediction. To neither over- nor underestimate BERT's performance, we tested it on the large dataset WD-KNOWN and implemented improvements to increase BERT's performance and perform KBC with high precision later on. We have seen the model's vocabulary to be a bottleneck for its performance. When fine-tuning with vocabulary extension, the model's performance can be significantly improved for fact prediction.

6 Potential for Knowledge Base Completion

In the following, we will obtain plausible missing facts from Wikidata, produce high accuracy predictions respective to $R@P90$, and let annotators from Amazon Mechanical Turk (mturk) manually evaluate the predictions given a five-value scale *true, plausible, unknown, implausible, false*. The relations in focus are the same as in Table 4, except for `hasReligion`, which appeared with too sparse information on the web.

6.1 Human Evaluation

Obtaining Missing Facts. The key to KBC with LMs is the ability to predict *missing facts*. Directly extracting empty subject-relation pairs from Wikidata is not possible, since Wikidata consists of existing facts (s, r, o). Also, randomly sampling an arbitrary subject to combine it with any relation would run the risk of violating our condition of plausible missing facts, where an object for a subject-relation pair exists (e.g. an implausible pair like (Albert Einstein, hasCapital,·) has no object). Therefore, we will only sample subject-relation pairs, where the subject has a relation-compatible entity type. Thus, we compute relation-wise the most frequent subject entity type within a relation. When sampling subject-relation pairs with missing objects, the subject is conditioned on having the most frequent entity type. This ensures extracting plausible missing facts. We randomly sample $10,000$ missing facts per relation, $70,000$ missing facts in total.

High Accuracy Predictions. To provide human annotators with reasonable predictions, we set a relation-specific prediction threshold to ensure the prediction quality and use the best possible model for predictions based on results in Table 4. Given these best models, the threshold is the prediction probability at $R@P90$ of each relation to respect the relation-specific precision and recall trade-offs. We keep only those missing facts, i.e. subject-relation pairs, whose predictions have a probability over the threshold. These are our *high accuracy predictions*.

Annotations. We filter the $70,000$ missing facts relation-wise by keeping only the facts with high accuracy predictions and then sample 50 missing facts with high accuracy predictions. This results in one prediction per subject-relation pair, i.e. 350 predicted missing facts in total. For these 350 missing facts, we use Amazon Mechanical Turk (mturk) for human annotations. An annotator is asked to evaluate a predicted missing fact. For readability reasons, each fact is formulated into relation-specific statements such as "The native language of Marcus Adams is English", where "English" is the prediction and nativeLanguage the relation. The annotators are given a five-value scale: true, plausible, unknown, implausible, and false. Before voting, we ask them to look up the fact on the web. They are required to give an evidence link and copy a text snippet supporting their voting. In case they vote unknown, they have to explain their voting. This way we ensure that annotators leave reasonable votes. We can say that all annotators left understandable insights regarding their voting.

We also self-annotated the 350 missing facts with ground truth and evidence links. Along with ground truth annotations, we annotated if the subject was known to English (en) Wikipedia; if the ground truth consists of more than one word; if the ground truth is in BERT's vocabulary, the position of the found evidence in Google search results and the search link used to find the ground truth. Furthermore, we rated each prediction using the same five-value scale as mturk annotators. We and mturk annotators reach an agreement of 69% given the five-value scale and an agreement of 94% given the upper categories true (true, plausible) and false (unknown, implausible, false).

Table 5. Overview of the results from the human evaluation. "True" denotes the summed up human ratings for "true with evidence" and "plausible" per relation. Similarly, "false" denotes the combined human ratings for "unknown", "implausible", and "false with evidence" per relation. The column "in Wikipedia (en)" describes the ratio of subjects with English Wikipedia articles to subjects without English Wikipedia articles per relation.

Relation	true	false	true with evidence	plausible	unknown	implausible	false with evidence	in Wikipedia (en)
nativeLanguage	82%	18%	48%	34%	6%	8%	4%	16%
spokenLanguage	82%	18%	46%	36%	6%	6%	6%	28%
headquarteredIn	82%	18%	34%	48%	6%	8%	4%	26%
developedBy	62%	38%	50%	12%	0%	0%	38%	74%
producedBy	22%	78%	20%	2%	6%	0%	72%	10%
LanguageOfFilm	76%	24%	56%	20%	0%	2%	22%	32%
citizenOf	90%	10%	52%	38%	4%	0%	6%	8%

6.2   Results

Quantitative Results. In Table 5, we see that the human annotators rate the model's predictions as highly correct. Based on these values we have determined the potential for KBC in Table 6. Given the number of missing facts and the proportion of high accuracy predictions, we can estimate the amount of addable facts at a relations-specific accuracy. This accuracy was achieved through human evaluation as shown in Table 5. Given the relation nativeLanguage we could

240   B. Veseli et al.

add $5,550,689$ new facts in a human-in-a-loop procedure or $7,871,085 \cdot 0.86 = 6,769,133$ with an accuracy of 82% automatically. In a human-in-a-loop procedure, the estimated costs of 2 USD (Sect. 1) for manually curated facts could drop to 40 Cents with approximately 2 min per annotation as we experienced with our mturk evaluation. Given our results in Table 6 we can perform significant KBC for relations `nativeLanguage` and `spokenLanguage` at precision 82% and `citizenOf` at precision 90%.

Qualitative Results. Looking into the annotations and predictions, we see that statements such as "Final Fantasy VII is developed by Square" are almost literally included in corresponding evidence links such as Wikipedia pages[5]. In contrast, relations like `nativeLanguage` include statements only implicitly, e.g. the native language of "Marcus Adams" is never mentioned explicitly in the corresponding Wikipedia page[6]. Yet, the LM achieves comparable results on most relations despite their more implicit or explicit factual basis.

Generalization or Retrieval? To investigate this further, we computed the proportion of subjects with English Wikipedia articles per relation. This enables us to estimate whether facts were mentioned in corresponding Wikipedia articles and thus, were present in BERT's training set. It can be shown that the language-related and socio-demographic relations achieve high results despite their lower occurrence in Wikipedia. This means that BERT predicts never seen facts with a high accuracy for these relations, showing a high generalization capability. When given facts such as the headquarters of "Universal de Televisión Peru", the model correctly predicts "Lima". Or given a fact such as the original language of the movie "Il mio paese", the model predicts "Italian" correctly. Socio-demographic relations such as `citizenOf`, `headquarteredIn` or language-related relations like `nativeLanguage`, `LanguageOfFilm` exhibit stronger correlations (e.g. person name and spoken language/origin country) than other relations (e.g. video game and developer, goods/products and manufacturer). These correlations are learned by the LM from the vast amounts of training data and used for the prediction. We recognize here that such learned correlations can be quite useful for fact prediction. Regarding the non-language or non-socio-demographic relations, we see that `producedBy` has the least Wikipedia-known subjects of 10% and shows also the lowest accuracy of 22%. In contrast, `developedBy` has the most Wikipedia-known subjects and still a high accuracy of 62% despite being a non-language or non-socio-demographic relation. In these relations, the model shows less generalization capability and is more in need of actual retrieval. As an example: the developer of "Pro Cycling Manager 2015" must be explicitly mentioned during training to know it, yet the model correctly predicts "Cyanide".

Conclusion. Given these qualitative examples and quantified numbers the model is capable of generalization as well as retrieval. But it is still unclear in what mixture and to what extent for example fact retrieval is possible. Regarding

---

[5] https://en.Wikipedia.org/wiki/Final_Fantasy_VII.
[6] https://en.Wikipedia.org/wiki/Marcus_Adams_(Canadian_football).

KBC both are beneficial. In case of precise retrieval, facts are addable automatically to an existing KB. In the case of generalization, which still achieves a high accuracy, human-in-a-loop procedures allow adding manually curated facts in a faster and cheaper way.

Table 6. The amount of missing facts and the percentage of high accuracy predictions denotes the number of new facts we could add at a relation-specific precision. The amount of addable facts indicates the number of potential new facts that could be added without error, e.g. in a human-in-a-loop procedure. The growth factor describes the potential growth of Wikidata given the current $cardinality^{WD}$ in Wikidata and the amount of addable facts.

Relation	$cardinality^{WD}$	#missing facts	high accuracy predictions(%)	accuracy	#addable facts	growth factor
nativeLanguage	264,778	7,871,085	86%	82%	5,550,689	20.96
spokenLanguage	2,148,775	7,090,119	77%	82%	4,476,701	2.08
headquarteredIn	409,309	55,186	8%	82%	3,443	0.008
developedBy	42,379	29,349	2%	62%	363	0.01
producedBy	123,036	31,239	0.8%	22%	55	0.0004
LanguageOfFilm	337,682	70,669	37%	76%	19,872	0.06
citizenOf	4,206,684	4,616,601	28%	90%	1,163,383	0.27

7   Discussion and Conclusion

In this paper, we investigated the potential of automated KB completion using LMs. We introduced a challenging benchmark dataset, WD-KNOWN, an unbiased random sample of Wikidata containing 3.9M existing facts. Using this dataset enabled a more realistic assessment of KB completion using LMs. This revealed that previous benchmarks lead to an overestimate of LM-based KB completion performance.

Our analysis showed that LMs are not able to obtain results at a high precision ($\sim$90%) for all relations equally, but LM-based knowledge covers language-related and socio-demographic relations particularly well. Furthermore, we discovered that an LM's vocabulary can limit the capability of fact prediction and we achieved significant improvements with fine-tuning and vocabulary expansion.

Since the prediction of facts non-existent to the KB is crucial for KB completion, we extracted plausible subject-relation pairs with non-existent objects in the KB. By probing the LM for these facts, we received actual novel facts previously unknown to the KB. Since the ground truth for these facts is missing, we performed a human evaluation. Annotators rated the LM's suggestions as highly correct. That showed a high potential for KB completion, either completely automated at a precision of up to 90% or as a strong recommender system for human-in-a-loop procedures. We demonstrated that in a human-in-a-loop procedure, LMs might reduce the costs for manually curated facts significantly, from approximately $2 to $0.4 per fact.

Moreover, we showed that LMs build surprisingly strong generalization capabilities for specific socio-demographic relations.

A promising direction for future work could be the construction of LMs specifically for KBs, which goes beyond fine-tuning. This could include defining specific vocabularies that are optimized for fact prediction.

References

1. Auer, S., Bizer, C., Kobilarov, G., Lehmann, J., Cyganiak, R., Ives, Z.: DBpedia: a nucleus for a web of open data. In: Aberer, K., et al. (eds.) ASWC/ISWC -2007. LNCS, vol. 4825, pp. 722–735. Springer, Heidelberg (2007). https://doi.org/10.1007/978-3-540-76298-0_52
2. Bordes, A., Usunier, N., Garcia-Duran, A., Weston, J., Yakhnenko, O.: Translating embeddings for modeling multi-relational data. In: NeurIPS (2013)
3. Cao, N.D., Aziz, W., Titov, I.: Editing factual knowledge in language models. In: EMNLP (2021)
4. Carlson, A., Betteridge, J., Kisiel, B., Settles, B., Hruschka, E.R., Mitchell, T.M.: Toward an architecture for never-ending language learning. In: AAAI (2010)
5. Cohen, R., Geva, M., Berant, J., Globerson, A.: Crawling the internal knowledge-base of language models. In: Findings of EACL (2023)
6. Dettmers, T., Minervini, P., Stenetorp, P., Riedel, S.: Convolutional 2D knowledge graph embeddings. In: AAAI (2018)
7. Devlin, J., Chang, M.W., Lee, K., Toutanova, K.: BERT: pre-training of deep bidirectional transformers for language understanding. In: NAACL (2019)
8. Elazar, Y., et al.: Measuring and improving consistency in pretrained language models. TACL **9**, 1012–1031 (2021)
9. Elsahar, H., Vougiouklis, P., Remaci, A., Gravier, C., Hare, J., Laforest, F., Simperl, E.: T-REx: a large scale alignment of natural language with knowledge base triples. In: LREC (2018)
10. Heinzerling, B., Inui, K.: Language models as knowledge bases: on entity representations, storage capacity, and paraphrased queries. In: EACL (2021)
11. Lenat, D.B.: CYC: a large-scale investment in knowledge infrastructure. CACM **38**, 33–38 (1995)
12. Liu, P., Yuan, W., Fu, J., Jiang, Z., Hayashi, H., Neubig, G.: Pre-train, prompt, and predict: a systematic survey of prompting methods in natural language processing. ACM CSUR **55**, 1–35 (2022)
13. Lv, X., et al.: Do pre-trained models benefit knowledge graph completion? A reliable evaluation and a reasonable approach. In: Findings of ACL (2022)
14. Nickel, M., Tresp, V., Kriegel, H.P.: A three-way model for collective learning on multi-relational data. In: ICML (2011)
15. Paulheim, H.: How much is a triple? Estimating the cost of knowledge graph creation. In: ISWC (2018)
16. Petroni, F., et al.: How context affects language models' factual predictions. In: AKBC (2020)
17. Petroni, F., et al.: Language models as knowledge bases? In: EMNLP (2019)
18. Poerner, N., Waltinger, U., Schütze, H.: E-BERT: efficient-yet-effective entity embeddings for BERT. In: Findings of EMNLP (2020)
19. Razniewski, S., Yates, A., Kassner, N., Weikum, G.: Language models as or for knowledge bases. In: DL4KG (2021)

20. Roberts, A., Raffel, C., Shazeer, N.: How much knowledge can you pack into the parameters of a language model? In: EMNLP (2020)
21. Safavi, T., Koutra, D.: CoDEx: a comprehensive knowledge graph completion benchmark. In: EMNLP (2020)
22. Shaik, Z., Ilievski, F., Morstatter, F.: Analyzing race and country of citizenship bias in wikidata (2021)
23. Shin, T., Razeghi, Y., Logan IV, R.L., Wallace, E., Singh, S.: AutoPrompt: eliciting knowledge from language models with automatically generated prompts. In: EMNLP (2020)
24. Singhania, S., Nguyen, T.P., Razniewski, S.: LM-KBC: Knowledge base construction from pre-trained language models. CEUR (2022)
25. Suchanek, F.M., Kasneci, G., Weikum, G.: YAGO: a core of semantic knowledge. In: WWW (2007)
26. Vrandečić, D., Krötzsch, M.: Wikidata: a free collaborative knowledge base. CACM **57**, 78–85 (2014)
27. Weikum, G., Dong, L., Razniewski, S., Suchanek, F.M.: Machine knowledge: creation and curation of comprehensive knowledge bases. In: FnT (2021)

Subsumption Prediction for E-Commerce Taxonomies

Jingchuan Shi[1]($\boxtimes$), Jiaoyan Chen[1], Hang Dong[1], Ishita Khan[2], Lizzie Liang[2], Qunzhi Zhou[2], Zhe Wu[2], and Ian Horrocks[1]

[1] Department of Computer Science, University of Oxford, Oxford, UK
{jingchuan.shi,jiaoyan.chen,hang.dong,ian.horrocks}@cs.ox.ac.uk
[2] eBay Inc., San Jose, USA
{ishikhan,lizliang,qunzhou,zwu1}@ebay.com

Abstract. Taxonomy plays a key role in e-commerce, categorising items and facilitating both search and inventory management. Concept subsumption prediction is critical for taxonomy curation, and has been the subject of several studies, but they do not fully utilise the categorical information available in e-commerce settings. In this paper, we study the characteristics of e-commerce taxonomies, and propose a new subsumption prediction method based on the pre-trained language model BERT that is well adapted to the e-commerce setting. The proposed model utilises textual and structural semantics in a taxonomy, as well as the rich and noisy instance (item) information. We show through extensive evaluation on two large-scale e-commerce taxonomies from eBay and AliOpenKG, that our method offers substantial improvement over strong baselines.

Keywords: Subsumption Prediction · E-Commerce Taxonomy · Pre-trained Language Model · BERT

1 Introduction

Taxonomies capture the *is-a* relationships between concepts, facilitating their storage, classification and organisation [4]. In e-commerce, taxonomy provides the basis for item categorisation, and is vital for search, inventory management and recommendation. Most e-commerce sites support two methods for users to locate a product: category browsing and keyword search. For the former, the taxonomy itself is presented to the user to navigate; for the latter, the taxonomy also provides important information to the search engine, which usually attempts to narrow the range of search results down to one or a few categories before retrieving and ranking items. For item recommendation, placement in the taxonomy is one of the most important heuristics in relevance scoring [31]. As such, the completeness and accuracy of the taxonomy has a major impact on sales and user experience.

Taxonomy-related research mainly includes taxonomy construction, curation and applications. These tasks have a close bond with natural language processing (NLP) and ontology engineering [13], the latter of which studies similar

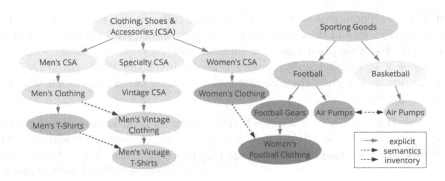

Fig. 1. Example of missing subsumptions in the e-commerce taxonomy

abstractions but typically involves more complex representations and utilises logical reasoning. Many taxonomies start as lightweight catalogues that can simply be curated by hand. However, as numerous taxonomies are constantly being created and existing ones constantly expanded, these tasks often become very labour intensive, and therefore their automation has become an important research topic. Among these tasks, subsumption prediction concerns adding new *is-a* relations between concepts, and is a major component of taxonomy curation.

The task of subsumption prediction is challenging. When taxa have complex, multifaceted semantics (e.g., e-commerce categories), the taxonomies are usually constructed in a way that each level specifies one or several facets (e.g., brand, material, function, etc.) on top of the parent category [18]. Theoretically, the order at which some facets are specified can be interchangeable, with no influence on the class's overall semantics. This leads to one kind of missing subsumption. For instance in Fig. 1, the categories *Men's Vintage Clothing* and *Men's Vintage T-Shirts*[1] should be considered subcategories of, respectively, *Men's Clothing* and *Men's T-Shirts*,[2] because all vintage clothing is clothing and all vintage t-shirts are t-shirts. Similarly, *Women's Football Clothing* is in reality a subcategory of *Women's Clothing*. However, these subsumptions may not be recognised because the categories belong to different branches in the hierarchy, although the two branches actually converge to a significant extent. A corollary of this observation is that while many taxonomies are organised into trees, the branches of these trees are not necessarily mutually exclusive; in our example there is some overlap between "Specialty CSA" and "Men's CSA".

While many missing subsumptions can be found by analysing the semantics of class labels, the underlying item level information could also be helpful. Each category in an e-commerce taxonomy is not only an abstract taxon, but also a label for a collection of inventory items. In Fig. 1, it is easy to judge from the class labels that *Football Air Pumps* and *Basketball Air Pumps*[3] are similar categories,

---

[1] Browse this category and the taxonomy around it at https://www.ebay.com/b/ 175781.

[2] https://www.ebay.com/b/15687.

[3] https://www.ebay.com/b/261761 and https://www.ebay.com/b/261791.

but it is not obvious that such pumps are compatible with each other and that the two categories should thus be mutually subsuming (i.e., equivalent). Discovering this kind of subsumption might be possible using a statistical approach based on the very large (and noisy) sets of relevant inventory items. However, it is unclear how to integrate the semantic understanding of category labels with the information from items.

Related Works. There is a large body of work on related areas, most prominently knowledge graph (KG) link prediction and taxonomy enrichment. KG link prediction is concerned with predicting relational facts (e.g., (*France, hasCapital, Paris*)) [29,30], often utilising different kinds of KG embedding models such as TransE [3], DistMult [38], and HolE [26]. However, these methods aim at relational facts, which can be understood as a multi-relation graph. They are not directly applicable in our e-commerce taxonomy curation given the taxonomy's noisy, multi-faceted, and hierarchical nature. Taxonomy enrichment [15] mines new concepts from a corpus and adds them to a taxonomy. Some enrichment methods can perform subsumption prediction for e-commerce taxonomies. Octet [24] is a two-stage pipeline that tackles edge prediction by applying a feed forward NN over features obtained from graph embeddings, word embeddings, and lexical metrics such as edit distance. While the model has achieved major improvements over non e-commerce specialised baselines, it uses non-contextual word embeddings, which leaves much room for improvement. AliCoCo [23] builds a massive, multi-layered KG of e-commerce concepts and links the concepts with items.

Another closely related field is ontology curation using deep learning. While numerous ontology embeddings such as OPA2Vec [34] and OWL2Vec* [6] can be applied to predict subsumptions, the amount of work focusing on optimising subsumption prediction is limited. BERTSubs [5] utilises BERT [9], a pre-trained language model (PLM) that has been shown to produce high quality contextual embeddings, and applies templates to convert candidate subsumptions into sentences for classification with BERT. The BERT is then attached to a classifier layer, and jointly fine-tuned using existing subsumptions. Evaluation on ontologies shows that BERTSubs can dramatically outperform early KG link prediction methods such as TransE and DistMult. However, BERTSubs ignores the aforementioned characteristics of e-commerce taxonomies, especially the existence of items.

In this work, we propose a new subsumption prediction approach that enhances previous work, taking into consideration the noisiness and richness of e-commerce taxonomies. Our approach features 1) BERT-based contextual embeddings with carefully designed templates; 2) a pipeline based on existing NLP tools to leverage lexical semantics in class labels; and 3) utilisation of instance data (i.e., product items). The practically optimal usage of BERT has been a long standing problem for researchers [22]. Our solution to this problem with templates and preprocessing proves to work well for subsumption prediction, and can generalise to other tasks of a similar nature. We propose two ways to combine instances with class label semantics, i.e., attention-based and template-based. Most BERT-based classification models use a feed forward neural network classifier that applies to a fixed amount of embedding vectors to make one prediction. In our instance-aware model, every prediction has to be based on a variably-sized set of embedding vectors, with one vector corresponding to one instance. Therefore, we also study two alternative classifiers besides feed forward layer: box embedding and extensional inference via k-nearest neighbours.

We evaluate our method on two large scale e-commerce taxonomies from eBay and AliOpenKG[4]. Both taxonomies are equipped with millions of items. Experiments have verified the effectiveness of the sentence processing pipeline and the consideration of items (instances), and clearly demonstrate that our solutions on path text preprocessing, templates and fine-tuning can help realise the full potential of BERT. We summarise our main contributions as follows:

1. Propose a taxonomy subsumption prediction framework based on contextual representations and also able to exploit instance data.
2. Extensively evaluate our framework and associated techniques on two e-commerce taxonomies.

2   Preliminaries

2.1   Pre-trained Language Model BERT

BERT, which stands for Bidirectional Encoder Representations from Transformers [9], is a transformer-based pre-trained language model (PLM) for contextual representations. It consists of a stack of encoder units (12 units in the original release `bert-base`) and self-attention heads. It is usually pre-trained with large, general-purpose corpora to learn sufficient understanding of the language itself. BERT is used in conjunction with a tokeniser based on WordPiece [32], where a single word may be split into multiple sub-word tokens, e.g. *stainless* into "`stain`" and "`##less`". The original BERT model is pre-trained on two tasks: masked language modelling (MLM) and next sentence prediction (NSP) [9]. MLM aims to predict some randomly masked tokens in the sentences, while NSP is to predict the following sentence of a given sentence. For a given sentence, standalone BERT can produce the contextual embedding of each individual token, as well as the embedding of the entire sentence, which is the embedding of a special token [CLS] added in front of the sentence.

An effective and popular way of applying BERT for downstream tasks is attaching an additional neural layer, and fine-tuning both BERT and the additional layer w.r.t. a task-specific loss and given samples. For classification, the textual input is either " [CLS] Sentence" for tasks on a single sentence, or " [CLS] Sentence A [SEP] Sentence B" for tasks on sentence pairs ([SEP] is a special token for separating two sentences). In our work, we adopt this fine-tuning paradigm as it allows BERT to adapt to the task's peculiarities, i.e. uncommon input and/or specialised classification objective.

---

[4] Code and data available at https://github.com/jingcshi/bert_subsumption.

2.2 Box Embeddings

The transitive, asymmetric nature of subsumption prohibits usage of symmetric similarity measures, e.g. Cosine similarity and Euclidean distance, when making predictions based on embeddings such as those produced by BERT. On the other hand, some geometric embeddings [10,27,28,36] have a natural ability to express subsumption and are thus suitable for embedding taxonomies. Box embeddings [37] have recently received attention as an effective taxonomic embedding method, where classes are mapped to high dimensional boxes and subsumption naturally translates to box containment. Informally, one may think of box embeddings as high dimensional Venn diagrams.

The original box embedding is a lattice structure in $\mathbb{R}^d$. A box is defined as $x = (x^m, x^M)$ where $x^m, x^M \in \mathbb{R}^d$ are the lower bound and upper bound coordinates, respectively. For two boxes x and y, the intersection $x \wedge y$ is naturally defined as their geometric intersection. The volume of a box x is $|x| = \prod_i (x_i^M - x_i^m)$. In order to learn embedding parameters from known subsumptions, a naïve loss function is to maximise proportional overlap:

$$\mathcal{L}(x, y) = \log |x \wedge y| - \log |x| \tag{1}$$

In other words, the ideal box embedding should have all child boxes completely submerged in parent boxes. Unfortunately, this loss function leads to poor performing models due to unbounded gradient and unfavorable local minima that hinder optimisation [8,19]. Therefore, numerous approaches have been investigated to soften the box boundaries [20] by redefining the box as a probabilistic distribution along each dimension. In this paper, we adopt the state-of-the-art soft box embedding to our knowledge, dubbed GumbelBox [8], that defines boxes as multi-dimensional Gumbel variables [12]. Key merits of Gumbel distribution are that 1) the max of two Gumbel variables with the same scale parameter β is another Gumbel variable, therefore with careful definition one can assure that the intersection of two Gumbel boxes is another Gumbel box; 2) it is smooth and mildly skewed, resulting in easier gradient descent.

3 Problem Statement

We define a *taxonomy* to be a set $T = (\mathcal{C}, \mathcal{R})$, where $\mathcal{C}$ is a set of classes and $\mathcal{R} \subseteq \mathcal{C} \times \mathcal{C}$ is a set of *is-a* relations. By definition, $\mathcal{R}$ is a partial ordering over $\mathcal{C}$, thus is transitive. We say C subsumes D if $(D, C) \in \mathcal{R}$ or (D, C) can be entailed from $\mathcal{R}$ via transitivity, and $C \equiv D$ if C subsumes D and D subsumes C. Note that many class hierarchies defined in OWL ontologies [2] can be regarded as a kind of taxonomy. The subsumption (is-a) relation between two OWL classes is defined by a built-in property *rdfs:subClassOf*.

We assume every class in the taxonomy has a text label and a set of instances which can be empty: $C = (l, P)$. In the e-commerce taxonomy we investigate, instances are items which are represented by a variety of modalities: text label, image, property-value pairs, etc. For the time being, we only consider the text

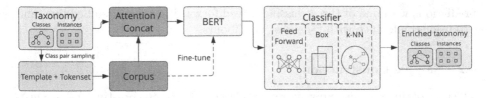

Fig. 2. Framework overview: (i) corpus construction, (ii) finc-tuning, (iii) joint embedding of label paths and instances, (iv) subsumption prediction using feed forward layer/box embedding/extensional inference with k-NN

modality and thus every $p_i \in P$ as well as every l_i are strings. We define the *label path* of a class to be the sequence of labels for all its ancestor classes and itself: If $C_0 \supseteq C_1 \supseteq \ldots \supseteq C_i$ is the longest possible subsumption chain for C_i, then the label path ("path" for simplicity) $\overline{l_i} = (l_0, l_1, \ldots, l_i)$. While the individual label for a class often misses important information, the path provides a more complete yet redundant textual description. The label for *Men's Vintage T-Shirts* is in fact just "T-Shirts" which is indistinguishable from many other classes, while the full path "Clothing, Shoes & Accessories $\to$ Specialty $\to$ Vintage $\to$ Men's Vintage Clothing $\to$ T-Shirts" has duplicate occurrences of "Clothing" and "Vintage", and one may consider the co-occurrence of "Clothing" and "T-Shirts" to be another type of redundancy since the former is a hypernym of the latter.

We model taxonomy subsumption prediction as a binary classification problem: given two classes $C_1 = (l_1, P_1)$ and $C_2 = (l_2, P_2)$ in a taxonomy $(\mathcal{C}, \mathcal{R})$, a score $s \in [0,1]$ indicating the likelihood of $C_1 \sqsubseteq C_2$ is expected. Subsumption can be interpreted in two ways, either intensionally or extensionally [7,35]: (i) intentionally, the abstract class defined by the semantics of $\overline{l_2}$ encompasses that of $\overline{l_1}$; (ii) extensionally, P_2 encompasses P_1 in the sense that any instance of P_1 either appears directly in P_2, or has a sufficiently close neighbour in P_2.

4 Methodology

4.1 Framework Overview

Our framework, as shown in Fig. 2, operates within the standard paradigm of BERT fine-tuning for classification. Given a taxonomy, we start by constructing the training corpus, consisting of instances and preprocessed label paths. A fast and simple label preprocessing technique (the process Tokenset) is used both as guidance for negative sampling and as a step in preparing the corpus. Next, we fine-tune the BERT model using existing positive subsumptions and negative subsumptions extracted from the previous step. We then use the trained BERT to obtain either instance embeddings when instances are present, or path embeddings, when instances are not present or not to be used. We ensure that instance embeddings contain class label semantics via either an attention mechanism or a concatenation template. Lastly, we convert the embeddings to subsumption predictions with one of three classifiers: feed forward layer, box embedding, and extensional inference with k-nearest neighbours.

4.2   Sample Construction

The goal of this stage is to obtain two sets of class pairs, one positive and one negative. The model first stores all the known subsumptions in a sparse matrix, and constructs the label path for each class. Since any two classes could potentially be a missing subsumption, it is difficult to safely sample negative pairs without hitting false negatives. To circumvent this problem, we designed Tokenset, a process that flattens out labels or paths into a list of keywords, allowing us to apply a filtering heuristic. Tokenset uses WordNet [25] to tokenise sentences, give part-of-speech tags to tokens and lemmatise them, as well as to identify and delete the hypernym in any hypernym-hyponym pair present in the list, thus removing the main source of noise in paths. An example of tokenset construction is the *Men's T-Shirt* class, whose label path is "Clothing, Shoes & Accessories → Men → Men's Clothing → Shirts → T-Shirts". Tokenset first produces the set {clothing, shoe, accessory, men, shirt, t-shirt}, then removes clothing and shirt in the hypernym reduction phase since both terms are hypernyms of t-shirt. The final representation {men, accessory, t-shirt, shoe} contains all the relevant information, i.e., men and t-shirt, and is much more concise. *Accessory* and *shoe* were not removed by this process because they are the irrelevant terms in a three way disjunction ("Clothing, Shoes & Accessories" really means "clothing" ∨ "shoes" ∨ "accessories"), and deletion of such terms would require construction of logical expressions from natural language, which adds further complexities; we leave this for future study.[5]

Once we obtain the abridged tokensets for two classes, we count the number of unique tokens that appear in one set but not the other. Such tokens usually represent semantic constraints that are unique to one of the classes. Taking into account the case where a tokenset may contain a hyponym of the other set's token, we apply the following criterion for negative sampling:

$$|\mathsf{Tokenset}(\overline{l_1} \cup \overline{l_2})| - \max\left(|\mathsf{Tokenset}(\overline{l_1})|, |\mathsf{Tokenset}(\overline{l_2})|\right) > 2 \qquad (2)$$

The equation demands that both tokensets contain at least three elements that are unique to themselves. It is very unlikely that classes satisfying this condition have a subsumption relationship.

We use all direct positive subsumptions as the positive set. For every positive pair (C_1, C_2), we replace C_2 with a random class and add the resulting pair to the negative set if the above negative sampling criterion is satisfied.

---

[5] The difficulty of such task is illustrated by labels featuring a mixture of conjunction and disjunction, e.g., *Suit Jackets & Blazers*, which means "Suit Jackets" ∨ "Blazers", and *North & Central America*, which means "North America" ∨ "Central America".

4.3 Corpus and Fine-tuning

The tokenset representation obtained above is close to the actual training corpus. In order to facilitate BERT's understanding of this unusual type of input, we place a fixed template "**A category of products defined by:**"[6] before the tokenset. The final input for *Men's T-Shirts* is therefore "**A category of products defined by: t-shirt, men, accessory, shoe**". The phrasing of this template is empirical, but the idea is to formulate the keyword-like taxonomic path as natural language. Evaluation results in the next section make it clear that such templates improve performance dramatically. A speculative explanation is that these templates establish the context for BERT so that it reads the following tokenset as related to categorisation, rather than as a random collection of words. A recent prompt learning study [17] reveals a similar phenomenon on GPT-3, another large PLM. It may be possible to improve the proposed templates by fine-tuning the embedding of the template tokens, similarly to learning a soft prompt [21]; we leave this for future study.

We denote the templated tokenset for a class C_i as $\overline{l_i}^*$. The actual fine-tuning task adds a feed forward layer on top of BERT as a classifier head for binary classification. For a pair (C_1, C_2), we feed the standard classification template [CLS] $\overline{l_1}^*$ [SEP] $\overline{l_2}^*$ into the model. In fine-tuning, we shuffle the order of tokens within each tokenset to prevent the model from simply learning to match exact sequences. The classifier uses the output of [CLS] token, a 768-dimensional vector as input, and returns a score $s \in [0,1]$ indicating the predicted subsumption likelihood. We use cross entropy loss over the corpus as the training objective, and fine-tune the BERT and the classifier jointly using an Adam optimiser [16]. We do not use instance data for fine-tuning because most instance data are noisy and have poorer quality compared to the human curated class labels.

4.4 Prediction

Prediction Without Instances. When instances are not present or are disabled, the model makes predictions with the feed forward NN classifier fine-tuned in Sect. 4.3. A broad list of candidate class pairs is either externally provided or manually generated. There is no single best method of generating candidate pairs, and we generate by ranking nearest neighbours w.r.t. Euclidean distances between the classes' embeddings. Note that the class embedding is the [CLS] token output of the fine-tuned BERT given the class's preprocessed tokensets. For each candidate, we take the output of the classifier directly as prediction.

Prediction with Instances. The prediction process is very different when instances are involved. First, the model input is no longer templated tokensets but instance labels. The model yields an embedding for each instance, where we

---

[6] For the Chinese AliOpenKG dataset (see Sect. 5.1), the template is " 产品类目： ".

apply either of the following two techniques to ensure the presence of class label information in item embeddings:

- **Attention.** For an instance $p = t_1 t_2 \ldots t_k$ in a class with path $\bar{l}$, we first separately compute the sentence embedding of $\bar{l}^*$, denoted e_l, and the contextual individual token embeddings of $t_1, t_2, \ldots, t_k$, denoted $E = [e_1, e_2, \ldots, e_k]^T$. The final instance embedding is a weighted sum of individual embeddings, where the weights are given by a softmax over the dot products between e_i and e_l:

$$e = \text{softmax}(\frac{e_l E^T}{\sqrt{d}}) E \tag{3}$$

where $d = 768$ is the embedding dimension. As an example, Fig. 3 shows the learned attention weights for the item titled "Original Kawasaki T-Shirt Iron-On Vintage 70s UNUSED Transfer" w.r.t. the category *Men's Vintage T-Shirts*. Attention places a higher weight on tokens closer to the label-based embedding, and consequently the instance embeddings gravitate towards it.
- **Concatenation.** Another approach is to concatenate the instance and label using the template "[CLS] Item: p in the category defined by: $\bar{l}^*$", which may vary for different taxonomies. For instance, we use "[CLS]产品名: p, 类目: $\bar{l}^*$" for the AliOpenKG dataset.

Token	Original	Kawasaki	T	-	Shirt	Iron
Weight	.0975	.0766	.0733	.0684	.0983	.0781
Token	-	On	Vintage	70s	UNUSED	Transfer
Weight	.0704	.0836	.1060	.0830	.0843	.0805

Fig. 3. Attention weights of tokens in an item title given the preprocessed label path "*vintage, accessory, t-shirt, men, specialty, shoe*".

After we embed each instance for both classes, we effectively have two vector clusters and the goal is to decide if one cluster encompasses the other. One of the following three classifier heads is used to obtain a prediction:

- **Feed forward.** As in the case without instances, we use the BERT with feed forward classifier. However, since the object is no longer a single sentence, we perform a simple but widely used ensemble technique, i.e., for each instance in the subclass, we pair it with a random instance in the superclass, predict each pair and report the average score.
- **Box embedding.** The motivation for using box embedding is to "draw a box around the cluster" and leverage the geometric properties of boxes. However, the 768 dimensional space where BERT outputs reside is not suitable for box embeddings, as volume and intersection become extremely unstable at such a

high dimension. Moreover, the vector clusters are often anisotropic and have irregular shapes. As such, we train a multilayer perceptron (MLP) that uses the means and standard deviations of a cluster along each dimension as input features, and projects this 1,536 dimensional feature to a low dimensional GumbelBox embedding [8]. The training data for this MLP is based on the same corpus for fine-tuning, with the label paths replaced by pre-computed features for each class. We employ the KL-divergence loss and use an Adam optimiser. The proportional box overlap $\frac{|c_1 \wedge c_2|}{|c_1|}$ is reported as the final score of the subsumption (C_1, C_2), where $|\cdot|$ measure the volumn of a box, c_1 and c_2 denote the boxes of C_1 and C_2, respectively.

- **Extensional inference with k-NN.** In the problem statement, we interpreted a possibility for subsumption as the instances of the parent encompassing those of the child. We call this approach extensional inference as the idea can trace its roots to the logical definition of hyponymy, where a hypernym tends to have wider extension (or more objects) than its hyponym [7,11,35]. We can thus find a concrete formulation of such idea in the context of two vector clusters of C_1 and C_2, given as:

$$C_1 \subseteq C_2 \leftrightarrow \forall x \in V(C_1).\exists\, y \in V(C_2).\,(\|x - y\| \leq d_0) \qquad (4)$$

where $V(\cdot)$ denotes the vectors of a class. In other words, all instances in the subclass's cluster are within distance d_0 from some instance in the superclass's cluster in embedding space, for some constant d_0 to be determined empirically. When the sizes of clusters are not formidably large, it is possible to chase this definition directly, and the resulting algorithm is a k-nearest neighbours (k-NN) with $k = 1$. Perfect containment is rarely feasible in reality, so we change the universal quantifier in the definition above to measuring the percentage of subclass instances that have sufficiently close neighbours in the superclass, reporting this percentage as the prediction score. Existing similarity searching libraries like Faiss [14] can speed up k-NN computation.

This bruteforce approach can be seen as an upper bound for any prediction method based on vector clusters. While it is slow and consumes massive memory storing all the vectors, it utilises full, uncompromised information from the instances, whereas box embedding loses significant information when downsampling the $n \times 768$ vector cluster to a 2×768 feature. Our expectation in evaluation is therefore not for the box embedding approach to beat k-NN, but to approximate k-NN to a sufficient degree.

5 Evaluation

5.1 Datasets and Setup

We conduct experiments on two taxonomies, the eBay taxonomy and the taxonomy extracted from the AliOpenKG ontology[7]. Since AliOpenKG stores the

---

[7] https://ali.openkg.org/.

classes and instances separately as TBox and ABox, we take the subset of TBox formed by product categories under *rdfs:subClassOf*, and link it with the subset of ABox formed by the label and category membership for each item. We publish this extracted dataset for benchmarking in other e-commerce curation tasks. Table 1 lists basic statistics for the two datasets. Note that both taxonomies in their original form are trees, therefore the number of direct subsumptions is one less than the number of classes.

Table 1. Metadata of the taxonomies used in evaluation

Taxonomy	#Classes	Max depth	Avg. depth	#Instances	Language
eBay	16,888	6	4.223	6.4M	English
Alibaba	7,100	4	3.896	3.1M	Chinese

Task. Manual labelling of subsumptions is difficult and expensive. Therefore, we evaluate by predicting masked subsumptions in the taxonomy. We hold out 10% of the direct subsumptions for testing, 10% for validation and use the remaining 80% for training. Note that membership of instances is inherited along the hierarchy, meaning that the non-leaf classes will automatically include instances from all their descendants, obtained by transitive closure of the direct subsumptions. We sample instance memberships prior to masking. To reflect masking and avoid data leakage, we remove some memberships and truncate some paths accordingly.

Metrics. We report results for mean reciprocal rank (MRR), hits@5 (H@5), precision (P) and recall (R). For each testing or validating subsumption (C_1, C_2), we create a set of negative subsumptions by replacing C_2 with false subsumers. False subsumers come from two sources:

1. Random classes that pass the Tokenset negativity test, which serve as the easy negatives.
2. Taxonomic neighbours. We consider the taxonomy as a graph and enumerate C_2's distance-1 and distance-2 neighbours. These classes will be the grandparents, parents, siblings, children and grandchildren of C_2. We select random classes from this pool and add them to the negative set if the selected class does not subsume C_1 in the original taxonomy. This process is repeated until either n negatives are found or the pool is exhausted, in which case we consider the distance-3 neighbors, then distance-4 neighbours, etc. We set $n = 20$ for both datasets. These classes serve as the hard negatives.

We maintain a 1:1 ratio of easy and hard negatives. The ranking set for each subsumption is therefore $\{C_2, C_{\text{neg1}}, \ldots, C_{\text{neg2}n}\}$ with a size of 41. To calculate P and R, we set a prediction threshold for each model by optimising F1 on the validation set, and apply the threshold to prediction scores on ranking sets.

Model. The eBay dataset is processed with `bert-base-cased`, while the Alibaba dataset is processed with `bert-base-chinese`. Both models can be found at

HuggingFace Transformers[8], and both are proven to have strong understanding of generic day-to-day language.

Baselines. Our set of baselines include three well established ontology embeddings, Onto2Vec [33], OPA2Vec [34], and OWL2Vec* [6], along with BERTSubs, a recent strong-performing subsumption prediction framework based on BERT fine-tuning [5]. Note that disabling instance data, path template and tokenset preprocessing from our method makes it effectively equivalent to the Path Context (PC) variant of BERTSubs for intra-ontology named subsumption prediction; further disabling paths, i.e., working with single class labels, is equivalent to the Isolated Class (IC) variant. Both methods use the output of the [CLS] token to represent a sequence and feed it to a classifier. Template formulations are identical in the case of IC, and differ minimally in the case of PC. We also take well-established ontology embeddings, including Onto2vec, OPA2Vec, and OWL2Vec*, which are all based on ontology tailored non-contextual word embeddings, as baselines.

Implementation. We ran all the experiments on a 6-core Intel Core i9 computer with 1x Tesla V100 GPU. We ran 5 epochs for fine-tuning with a learning rate of 5×10^{-5}, and 30 epochs for box embedding training with a learning rate of 2×10^{-5}. The MLP in box embedding has 4 hidden layers with a total of 1.9×10^{5} trainable parameters, producing 24 dimensional box embeddings.

5.2   Evaluation Results

Table 2 presents the results of our models and the baselines on predicting masked subsumptions in the eBay taxonomy. A common characteristic of all rows is that recall is significantly higher than precision, which is a consequence of the overwhelmingly negative ranking set. To optimise F1, the prediction thresholds are often set quite low. Consistent with [5], BERTSubs has a significant edge over ontological embedding baselines, showing the superiority of contextual word embedding by BERT. Unsurprisingly, the path-only variant outperforms BERTSubs-IC and BERTSubs-PC, thanks to the template introduced in Sect. 4.3 and the Tokenset pipeline.

Adding instances results in little if any improvement when the feed forward ensemble is used as the classifier. However, the benefit of instances gets pronounced when the classifier is designed for vector clusters. Both box embedding and k-NN show promising results, and box embedding is able to close the gap with the bruteforce approach to 2%, while running much more quickly and being more generalisable (more detailed account on inference speed in Sect. 5.3). Both box embedding and k-NN substantially outperform the feed forward classifier for two reasons. First, while BERT has been pre-trained and can handle item titles, the feed forward layer has not been trained with titles and should not be expected to perform well on them. Second, the ensemble mechanism does not

---

[8] https://huggingface.co/bert-base-cased   and   https://huggingface.co/bert-base-chinese.

Table 2. Results of predicting masked subsumptions of the eBay taxonomy

Method	Feed forward					Box embedding					k-NN				
	P	R	F1	MRR	H@5	P	R	F1	MRR	H@5	P	R	F1	MRR	H@5
Onto2Vec	.135	.709	.227	.265	.357	.166	.748	.272	.321	.414	.176	.754	.285	.335	.457
OPA2Vec	.160	.732	.263	.308	.401	.182	.781	.295	.347	.437	.189	.776	.304	.359	.462
OWL2Vec*	.174	.733	.281	.326	.436	.200	.772	.318	.369	.483	.207	.785	.328	.381	.495
BERTSubs-IC	.382	.869	.531	.557	.714	N/A					N/A				
BERTSubs-PC	.197	.840	.319	.493	.625	N/A					N/A				
Ours: P	.544	**.872**	.670	.601	.768	N/A					N/A				
Ours: P+I (att)	.463	.835	.596	.552	.729	.502	.854	.632	.611	.765	.585	.791	.673	**.633**	.783
Ours: P+I (con)	.456	.862	.596	.555	.736	.493	.840	.621	.618	.758	**.588**	.810	**.681**	.629	**.786**
Legend	P: path, I: instances, att: attention, con: concatenation														

Table 3. Results of predicting masked subsumptions of the Alibaba taxonomy

Method	Feed forward					Box embedding					k-NN				
	P	R	F1	MRR	H@5	P	R	F1	MRR	H@5	P	R	F1	MRR	H@5
Onto2Vec	.140	.658	.231	.223	.296	.137	.664	.227	.228	.296	.142	.696	.236	.228	.312
OPA2Vec	.151	.698	.248	.246	.327	.153	.689	.250	.245	.311	.155	.715	.254	.249	.333
OWL2Vec*	.189	.742	.301	.284	.380	.194	.736	.307	.290	.393	.199	.721	.311	.300	.408
BERTSubs-IC	.397	.796	.529	.468	.540	N/A					N/A				
BERTSubs-PC	.359	.783	.492	.432	.519	N/A					N/A				
Ours: P	.454	.806	.580	.503	.636	N/A					N/A				
Ours: P+I (att)	.485	.834	.613	.540	.667	.518	.828	.637	.562	.693	.532	.830	.648	**.583**	**.715**
Ours: P+I (con)	.480	**.838**	.610	.532	.656	.520	.831	.640	.569	.704	**.534**	.829	**.650**	.580	.713
Legend	P: path, I: instances, att: attention, con: concatenation														

fully capture the essence of subsumption in the vector cluster context, as defined by Eq. (4). The best results are achieved with k-NN on the attention variant, but otherwise attention and concatenation remain close in efficacy.

Results on the Alibaba taxonomy, shown in Table 3, displays a similar advantage for our method. In particular, the addition of instance data now gives an improvement even with the feed forward ensemble classifier. The baselines Onto2Vec, OPA2Vec and OWL2Vec* struggle more on this dataset since pretrained word embeddings are not available in Chinese. Combined with Table 2, the results on the two datasets compared against four baselines strongly confirm the effectiveness of our model.

Ablation Studies. We now investigate the individual effects of the template and Tokenset. Table 4 presents the results on the eBay masked taxonomy recovery task, using the setting of Path+Instance with attention. A significant loss in all metrics when the template is removed indicates that setting an appropriate semantic context is very useful when representing oddly shaped textual data with BERT and that a suitable template is one way to achieve this. Tokenset can give an additional boost to performance when the template is present, but it barely improves efficacy without the template. This suggests that removing duplicate information from the input may help BERT identify and concentrate

Table 4. Results of different preprocessing settings on predicting masked subsumptions of the eBay taxonomy

Template	Tokenset	Feed forward				
		P	R	F1	MRR	H@5
no	no	.215	.786	.338	.422	.578
no	yes	.228	.760	.351	.419	.557
yes	no	.441	.817	.573	.529	.671
yes	yes	**.463**	**.835**	**.596**	**.552**	**.729**

on key segments related to the problem, but only when the appropriate context has already been established.

5.3 Observations

Complexities. Due to the downsampling and approximative nature of box embedding based prediction, it is able to save much time and space compared to k-NN prediction. For a task with m child instances and n parent instances, k-NN consumes $O(m \log n)$ time and $O(m + n)$ space, while box embedding consumes $O(m + n)$ time and $O(1)$ space. In reality, a single k-NN inference with $m = n = 1000$ takes around 0.1s on the hardware in Sect. 5.1, while box embedding takes a few milliseconds.

Dependency on Labels. The Tokenset process makes an important contribution to our model's competitive performance, but it also makes a hidden assumption on class labels. By converting the path to a flat keyword list, Tokenset essentially treats each label as a conjunction of constraints. This treatment is inappropriate when the label contains disjunctive parts, as exemplified in Sect. 4.2. While disjunction handling could be solved by a more sophisticated approach, there are taxonomies/ontologies where the labels are convoluted, technical phrases that any bag-of-words style treatment cannot tackle accurately, e.g., medical terminology ontologies. Therefore, our approach works well when class labels are relatively short and concise. Another reason to prefer short labels is that paths are more valuable in this case. Tokenset is effective in combining information from multiple labels, since its motivation is to address the scenario where the class's own label does not provide a full description, but its path does. This is the case in most e-commerce taxonomies. One can also apply Tokenset to label sequences other than paths, e.g., the breadth-first context corpus constructed in BERTSubs [5]. Overall, the Tokenset preprocessing helps clean noisy labels, resulting in a more compact contextual representation of the class.

Dependency on Instances. For instances to contribute to subsumption prediction, they must either have good quality, or have abundant quantity that compensates for the quality. This condition is naturally met in our case of e-commerce taxonomy with the large pool of items. However, the language models used in our experiments are not pre-trained with e-commerce specific corpus, such as queries and item titles. It is a reasonable assumption that such pre-training can enhance the model's understanding of instance data and therefore overall performance. We will further investigate the role of instances and the impact of their quality in taxonomy curation in our future work.

6   Discussions and Conclusion

In this paper, we propose a new subsumption prediction model for taxonomies using PLMs such as BERT, with logical geometric embeddings and inferences. Inspired by the e-commerce setting, we design our model to utilise both class-level and instance-level information. At the class level, the model learns meaningful representations by using a template and preprocessing with lexical semantics to convert class labels into a concise list of tokens. At the instance level, we enrich the representations of class labels with instance data, and experiment with three classifier heads: feed forward, box embedding and extensional inference. Our evaluation on the eBay taxonomy in English and the Alibaba taxonomy in Chinese confirms our model's effectiveness. Furthermore, the experiments demonstrate the importance of templates and preprocessing, the advantage of instance-aware models with domain-specific PLM pretraining, and shows that box embedding is a promising alternative to the computationally expensive bruteforce method with either the feed forward classifier or direct extensional inference.

While this paper focuses on intra-taxonomy subsumption prediction, the techniques we describe could be applied to inter-taxonomy/ontology subsumption prediction. As shown in BERTSubs [5], inter-taxonomy subsumptions and indirect subsumptions inferred from existential restrictions can be expressed in templates and captured by PLMs. Furthermore, Tokenset and the modelling of ABox data can be directly generalised to the cases of inter-taxonomy and ontology.

Finally, we identify a few directions for future work: *Multi-modality* has drawn wide attention in recent machine learning and KG research [1,39]. E-commerce offers an ideal setting for investigating multi-modal KGs and multi-modal learning. Images, different kinds of properties and property values could be highly valuable complements to item titles for many taxonomy curation tasks, because most item titles are phrased to catch the eye and do not prioritise accurate and complete description of the item. Another interesting extension of this work would be taxonomy *enrichment* by inferring new classes from existing classes. In Fig. 1, we notice that applying facet constraints in different orders can lead to valid classes that are missing in the current taxonomy, e.g., *Vintage Clothing*, a concept that is currently split into *Men's Vintage Clothing* and *Women's Vintage Clothing* but does not exist on its own. The identification of these missing classes requires no external information, and in a sense fills the semantic "holes" of the taxonomy.

Acknowledgment. We would like to thank Mingjian Lu and Canran Xu for their work and constructive ideas. This work was supported by eBay and the EPSRC projects OASIS (EP/S032347/1), UK FIRES (EP/S019111/1) and ConCur (EP/V050869/1).

References

1. Baltrušaitis, T., Ahuja, C., Morency, L.P.: Multimodal machine learning: a survey and taxonomy. IEEE Trans. Pattern Anal. Mach. Intell. **41**(2), 423–443 (2018)
2. Bechhofer, S.: OWL web ontology language reference, W3C recommendation (2004). http://www.w3.org/TR/owl-ref/
3. Bordes, A., Usunier, N., Garcia-Duran, A., Weston, J., Yakhnenko, O.: Translating embeddings for modeling multi-relational data. In: Advances in Neural Information Processing Systems, vol. 26 (2013)
4. Centelles, M.: Taxonomies for categorization and organization in web sites. Hipertext.net (3) (2005). https://www.upf.edu/hipertextnet/en/numero-3/taxonomias.html
5. Chen, J., He, Y., Jimenez-Ruiz, E., Dong, H., Horrocks, I.: Contextual semantic embeddings for ontology subsumption prediction. arXiv preprint arXiv:2202.09791 (2022)
6. Chen, J., Hu, P., Jimenez-Ruiz, E., Holter, O.M., Antonyrajah, D., Horrocks, I.: OWL2Vec*: embedding of owl ontologies. Mach. Learn. **110**(7), 1813–1845 (2021)
7. Cruse, D.A.: Hyponymy and Its Varieties. In: Green, R., Bean, C.A., Myaeng, S.H. (eds.) The Semantics of Relationships, pp. 3–21. Springer, Dordrecht (2002). https://doi.org/10.1007/978-94-017-0073-3_1
8. Dasgupta, S., Boratko, M., Zhang, D., Vilnis, L., Li, X., McCallum, A.: Improving local identifiability in probabilistic box embeddings. Adv. Neural. Inf. Process. Syst. **33**, 182–192 (2020)
9. Devlin, J., Chang, M.W., Lee, K., Toutanova, K.: Bert: pre-training of deep bidirectional transformers for language understanding. arXiv preprint arXiv:1810.04805 (2018)
10. Dhingra, B., Shallue, C.J., Norouzi, M., Dai, A.M., Dahl, G.E.: Embedding text in hyperbolic spaces. arXiv preprint arXiv:1806.04313 (2018)
11. Dong, H., Wang, W., Coenen, F.: Rules for inducing hierarchies from social tagging data. In: Chowdhury, G., McLeod, J., Gillet, V., Willett, P. (eds.) iConference 2018. LNCS, vol. 10766, pp. 345–355. Springer, Cham (2018). https://doi.org/10.1007/978-3-319-78105-1_38
12. Gumbel, E.J.: Les valeurs extrêmes des distributions statistiques. In: Annales de l'institut Henri Poincaré, vol. 5, pp. 115–158 (1935)
13. Iqbal, R., Murad, M.A.A., Mustapha, A., Sharef, N.M., et al.: An analysis of ontology engineering methodologies: a literature review. Res. J. Appl. Sci. Eng. Technol. **6**(16), 2993–3000 (2013)
14. Johnson, J., Douze, M., Jégou, H.: Billion-scale similarity search with GPUs. IEEE Trans. Big Data **7**(3), 535–547 (2019)
15. Jurgens, D., Pilehvar, M.T.: Semeval-2016 task 14: semantic taxonomy enrichment. In: Proceedings of the 10th International Workshop on Semantic Evaluation (SemEval-2016), pp. 1092–1102 (2016)
16. Kingma, D.P., Ba, J.: Adam: a method for stochastic optimization. arXiv preprint arXiv:1412.6980 (2014)
17. Kojima, T., Gu, S.S., Reid, M., Matsuo, Y., Iwasawa, Y.: Large language models are zero-shot reasoners. arXiv preprint arXiv:2205.11916 (2022)

18. Lee, S., Park, Y.: The classification and strategic management of services in e-commerce: development of service taxonomy based on customer perception. Expert Syst. Appl. **36**(6), 9618–9624 (2009)
19. Lees, A., Welty, C., Zhao, S., Korycki, J., Mc Carthy, S.: Embedding semantic taxonomies. In: Proceedings of the 28th International Conference on Computational Linguistics, pp. 1279–1291 (2020)
20. Li, X., Vilnis, L., Zhang, D., Boratko, M., McCallum, A.: Smoothing the geometry of probabilistic box embeddings. In: International Conference on Learning Representations (2018)
21. Li, X.L., Liang, P.: Prefix-tuning: optimizing continuous prompts for generation. arXiv preprint arXiv:2101.00190 (2021)
22. Lu, Y., Bartolo, M., Moore, A., Riedel, S., Stenetorp, P.: Fantastically ordered prompts and where to find them: overcoming few-shot prompt order sensitivity. arXiv preprint arXiv:2104.08786 (2021)
23. Luo, X., et al.: Alicoco: alibaba e-commerce cognitive concept net. In: Proceedings of the 2020 ACM SIGMOD International Conference on Management of Data, pp. 313–327 (2020)
24. Mao, Y., et al.: Octet: online catalog taxonomy enrichment with self-supervision. In: Proceedings of the 26th ACM SIGKDD International Conference on Knowledge Discovery & Data Mining, pp. 2247–2257 (2020)
25. Miller, G.A.: Wordnet: a lexical database for english. Commun. ACM **38**(11), 39–41 (1995)
26. Nickel, M., Rosasco, L., Poggio, T.: Holographic embeddings of knowledge graphs. In: Proceedings of the AAAI Conference on Artificial Intelligence, vol. 30 (2016)
27. Nickel, M., Kiela, D.: Poincaré embeddings for learning hierarchical representations. In: Advances in Neural Information Processing Systems, vol. 30 (2017)
28. Nickel, M., Kiela, D.: Learning continuous hierarchies in the lorentz model of hyperbolic geometry. In: International Conference on Machine Learning, pp. 3779–3788. PMLR (2018)
29. Paulheim, H.: Knowledge graph refinement: a survey of approaches and evaluation methods. Semant. Web **8**(3), 489–508 (2017)
30. Rossi, A., Barbosa, D., Firmani, D., Matinata, A., Merialdo, P.: Knowledge graph embedding for link prediction: a comparative analysis. ACM Trans. Knowl. Discov. Data (TKDD) **15**(2), 1–49 (2021)
31. Schafer, J.B., Konstan, J.A., Riedl, J.: E-commerce recommendation applications. Data Min. Knowl. Disc. **5**(1), 115–153 (2001)
32. Schuster, M., Nakajima, K.: Japanese and Korean voice search. In: 2012 IEEE International Conference on Acoustics, Speech and Signal Processing (ICASSP), pp. 5149–5152. IEEE (2012)
33. Smaili, F.Z., Gao, X., Hoehndorf, R.: Onto2vec: joint vector-based representation of biological entities and their ontology-based annotations. Bioinformatics **34**(13), i52–i60 (2018)
34. Smaili, F.Z., Gao, X., Hoehndorf, R.: OPA2vec: combining formal and informal content of biomedical ontologies to improve similarity-based prediction. Bioinformatics **35**(12), 2133–2140 (2019)
35. Stock, W.G.: Concepts and semantic relations in information science. J. Am. Soc. Inform. Sci. Technol. **61**(10), 1951–1969 (2010)
36. Vendrov, I., Kiros, R., Fidler, S., Urtasun, R.: Order-embeddings of images and language. arXiv preprint arXiv:1511.06361 (2015)
37. Vilnis, L., Li, X., Murty, S., McCallum, A.: Probabilistic embedding of knowledge graphs with box lattice measures. arXiv preprint arXiv:1805.06627 (2018)

38. Yang, B., Yih, W.t., He, X., Gao, J., Deng, L.: Embedding entities and relations for learning and inference in knowledge bases. arXiv preprint arXiv:1412.6575 (2014)
39. Zhu, X., et al.: Multi-modal knowledge graph construction and application: a survey. arXiv preprint arXiv:2202.05786 (2022)

Two-View Graph Neural Networks
for Knowledge Graph Completion

Vinh Tong[1], Dai Quoc Nguyen[2], Dinh Phung[3], and Dat Quoc Nguyen[4(✉)]

[1] University of Stuttgart, Stuttgart, Germany
vinh.tong@ipvs.uni-stuttgart.de
[2] Oracle Labs, Brisbane, Australia
dai.nguyen@oracle.com
[3] Monash University, Melbourne, Australia
dinh.phung@monash.edu
[4] VinAI Research, Hanoi, Vietnam
v.datnq9@vinai.io

Abstract. We present an effective graph neural network (GNN)-based knowledge graph embedding model, which we name WGE, to capture entity- and relation-focused graph structures. Given a knowledge graph, WGE builds a single undirected entity-focused graph that views entities as nodes. WGE also constructs another single undirected graph from relation-focused constraints, which views entities and relations as nodes. WGE then proposes a GNN-based architecture to better learn vector representations of entities and relations from these two single entity- and relation-focused graphs. WGE feeds the learned entity and relation representations into a weighted score function to return the triple scores for knowledge graph completion. Experimental results show that WGE outperforms strong baselines on seven benchmark datasets for knowledge graph completion.

Keywords: Two-View · Graph Neural Networks · Knowledge Graph Completion · Link Prediction · WGE

1 Introduction

A knowledge graph (KG) is a network of entity nodes and relationship edges, which can be represented as a collection of triples in the form of *(h, r, t)*, wherein each triple *(h, r, t)* represents a relation r between a head entity h and a tail entity t. Here, entities are real-world things or objects such as music tracks, movies persons, organizations, places and the like, while each relation type determines a certain relationship between entities. KGs are used in many commercial applications, e.g. in such search engines as Google, Microsoft's Bing and Facebook's Graph search. They also are useful resources for many natural language processing tasks such as co-reference resolution [8,27], semantic parsing [2,18] and question answering [9,10]. However, an issue is that KGs are often incomplete, i.e., missing a lot of valid triples [4,23]. For an example of a specific

C. Pesquita et al. (Eds.): ESWC 2023, LNCS 13870, pp. 262–278, 2023.
https://doi.org/10.1007/978-3-031-33455-9_16

application, question answering systems based on incomplete KGs would not provide correct answers given correctly interpreted input queries. Thus, much work has been devoted towards KG completion to perform link prediction in KGs. In particular, many KG embedding models have been proposed to predict whether a triple not in KGs is likely to be valid or not, e.g., TransE [3], DistMult [37], ComplEx [33] and QuatE [39]. These KG embedding models aim to learn vector representations for entities and relations and define a score function such that *valid triples have higher scores than invalid ones* [23,40], e.g., the score of the valid triple (Sydney, city_in, Australia) is higher than the score of the invalid one (Sydney, city_in, Vietnam).

Recently, several KG completion works have adapted graph neural networks (GNNs) using an encoder-decoder architecture, e.g., R-GCN [30] and CompGCN [34]. In general, the encoder module customizes GNNs to update vector representations of entities and relations. Then, the decoder module employs an existing score function to return the triple score [3,5–7,20,33,37]. For example, R-GCN adapts Graph Convolutional Networks (GCNs) [17] to construct a specific encoder to update only entity embeddings. CompGCN modifies GCNs to use composition operations between entities and relations in the encoder module. Note that these existing GNN-based KG embedding models mainly consider capturing the graph structure surrounding entities as relation representations are used to update the entity embeddings only (as shown in Eqs. 3, 5 and 6; and see the last paragraph of Sect. 2 for a detailed discussion). Therefore, they might miss covering potentially useful information on relation structure.

To this end, we propose a new KG embedding model—named WGE that is equivalent to VVGE to abbreviate Two-View Graph Embedding—to leverage GNNs to capture both entity-focused graph structure and relation-focused graph structure for KG completion. In particular, WGE transforms a given KG into two views. The first view—a single undirected entity-focused graph—only includes entities as nodes to provide the entity neighborhood information. The second view—a single undirected relation-focused graph—considers both entities and relations as nodes, constructed from constraints (*subjective relation, predicate entity, objective relation*) e.g. (born_in, Sydney, city_in), to attain the potential dependence between two neighborhood relations. For instance, the knowledge about a potential dependence between "born_in" and "city_in" could be relevant for predicting some other relationship, e.g. "nationality" or "country of citizenship". Then WGE introduces a new GNN-based encoder module that directly takes these two graph views as input to better update entity and relation embeddings. WGE feeds the entity and relation embeddings into its decoder module that uses a weighted score function to return the triple scores for KG completion. In summary, our contributions are as follows:

– We present WGE for KG completion, that first proposes to transform a given KG into entity- and relation-focused graph structures and then introduces a new encoder architecture to learn entity and relation embeddings from these two graph structures.
– To verify model effectiveness, we conduct extensive experiments to compare our WGE with other strong GNN-based baselines on seven bench-

mark datasets, including FB15K-237 [32] and six new and difficult datasets of CoDEx-S, CoDEx-M, CoDEx-L, LitWD1K, LitWD19K and LitWD48K [11,28]. The experiments show that WGE outperforms the GNN-based baselines and other competitive KG embedding models on these seven datasets.

2   Related Work

Recently, GNNs become a central strand to learn low-dimensional continuous embeddings for nodes and graphs [14,29]. GNNs provide faster and more practical training and state-of-the-art results on benchmark datasets for downstream tasks [36,38]. In general, GNNs update the vector representation of each node by transforming and aggregating the vector representations of its neighbors [13,17,21,22,35].

We represent each graph $\mathcal{G} = (\mathcal{V}, \mathcal{E})$, where $\mathcal{V}$ is a set of nodes; and $\mathcal{E}$ is a set of edges. Given a graph $\mathcal{G}$, we formulate GNNs as follows:

$$\mathbf{h}_v^{(k+1)} = \text{AGGREGATION} \left(\left\{ \mathbf{h}_u^{(k)} \right\}_{u \in \mathcal{N}_v \cup \{v\}} \right) \tag{1}$$

where $\mathbf{h}_v^{(k)}$ is the vector representation of node v at the k-th layer; and $\mathcal{N}_v$ is the set of neighbours of node v.

There have been many designs for the AGGREGATION functions. The widely-used one is introduced in Graph Convolutional Networks (GCNs) [17] as:

$$\mathbf{h}_v^{(k+1)} = \mathbf{g} \left(\sum_{u \in \mathcal{N}_v \cup \{v\}} a_{v,u} \mathbf{W}^{(k)} \mathbf{h}_u^{(k)} \right), \forall v \in \mathcal{V} \tag{2}$$

where $\mathbf{g}$ is a nonlinear activation function such as ReLU; $\mathbf{W}^{(k)}$ is a weight matrix at the k-th layer; and $a_{v,u}$ is an edge constant between nodes v and u in the re-normalized adjacency matrix $\tilde{\mathbf{D}}^{-\frac{1}{2}} \tilde{\mathbf{A}} \tilde{\mathbf{D}}^{-\frac{1}{2}}$, wherein $\tilde{\mathbf{A}} = \mathbf{A} + \mathbf{I}$ where $\mathbf{A}$ is the adjacency matrix, $\mathbf{I}$ is the identity matrix, and $\tilde{\mathbf{D}}$ is the diagonal node degree matrix of $\tilde{\mathbf{A}}$.

It is worth mentioning that several KG embedding approaches have been proposed to adapt GNNs for knowledge graph link prediction [30,31,34]. For example, R-GCN [30] modifies the basic form of GCNs to introduce a specific encoder to update entity embeddings:

$$\mathbf{h}_e^{(k+1)} = \mathbf{g} \left(\sum_{r \in \mathcal{R}} \sum_{e' \in \mathcal{N}_e^r} \frac{1}{|\mathcal{N}_e^r|} \mathbf{W}_r^{(k)} \mathbf{h}_{e'}^{(k)} + \mathbf{W}^{(k)} \mathbf{h}_e^{(k)} \right) \tag{3}$$

where $\mathcal{R}$ is a set of relations in the KG; $\mathcal{N}_e^r = \{e' | (e, r, e') \in \mathcal{T} \cup (e', r, e) \in \mathcal{T}\}$ denotes the set of entity neighbors of entity e via relation edge r, wherein $\mathcal{T}$ denotes the set of knowledge graph triples; and $\mathbf{W}_r^{(k)}$ is a weight transformation matrix associated with r at the k-th layer. Then R-GCN uses DistMult [37] as its decoder module to compute the score of (h, r, t) as:

$$f(h, r, t) = \left\langle \mathbf{h}_h^{(K)}, \boldsymbol{v}_r, \mathbf{h}_t^{(K)} \right\rangle \tag{4}$$

where $\mathbf{h}_h^{(K)}$ and $\mathbf{h}_t^{(K)}$ are output vectors taken from the last layer of the encoder module; $\boldsymbol{v}_r$ denotes the embedding of relation r; and $\langle \rangle$ denotes a multiple-linear dot product $\langle \mathbf{a}, \mathbf{b}, \mathbf{c} \rangle = \sum_i^n \mathbf{a}_i \times \mathbf{b}_i \times \mathbf{c}_i$.

CompGCN [34] also customizes GCNs to consider composition operations between entities and relations in the encoder module as follows:

$$\mathbf{h}_e^{(k+1)} = g \left(\sum_{(e', r) \in \mathcal{N}_e} \boldsymbol{W}_{\text{type}(r)}^{(k)} \phi \left(\mathbf{h}_{e'}^{(k)}, \mathbf{h}_r^{(k)} \right) \right) \tag{5}$$

$$\mathbf{h}_r^{(k+1)} = \boldsymbol{W}^{(k)} \mathbf{h}_r^{(k)} \tag{6}$$

where $\mathcal{N}_e = \{(e', r) | (e, r, e') \in \mathcal{T} \cup (e', r, e) \in \mathcal{T}\}$ is the neighboring entity-relation pair set of entity e; and $\boldsymbol{W}_{\text{type}(r)}^{(k)}$ denotes relation-type specific weight matrix. CompGCN explores the composition functions (ϕ) inspired from TransE [3], DistMult, and HolE [24]. Then CompGCN uses ConvE [7] as the decoder module.

The existing GNN-based KG embedding models, e.g. R-GCN and CompGCN, mainly capture the graph structure surrounding entities. That is, as shown in Eqs. 3, 5 and 6, a relation's representation is *not* directly used to update another relation's representation and is only used to update entity embeddings, while entity embeddings are *not* used to update relation representations. Thus, these models might miss covering potentially useful relation structure information that is illustrated by the example (born_in, Sydney, city_in) in Sect. 1.

3   Our Model WGE

A knowledge graph $G = \{\mathcal{V}, \mathcal{R}, \mathcal{T}\}$ can be represented as a collection of factual valid triples *(head entity, relation, tail entity)* denoted as $(h, r, t) \in \mathcal{T}$ with $h, t \in \mathcal{V}$ and $r \in \mathcal{R}$, wherein $\mathcal{V}$, $\mathcal{R}$ and $\mathcal{T}$ denote the sets of entities, relations and triples, respectively.

To better capture the graph structure, as illustrated in Fig. 1, we introduce WGE as follows: (i) WGE transforms a given KG into two views: a single undirected entity-focused graph and a single undirected relation-focused graph. (ii) WGE introduces a new encoder architecture to update vector representations of entities and relations based on these two single graphs. (iii) WGE utilizes a weighted score function as the decoder module to compute the triple scores.

3.1   Two-View Construction

Entity-Focused View. WGE aims to obtain the entity neighborhood information. Thus, given a KG G, WGE constructs a single undirected graph $\mathcal{G}_{ef}$ viewing

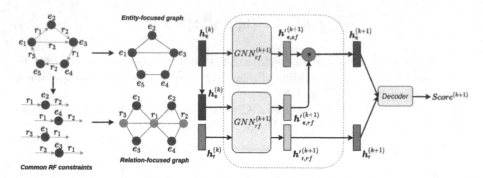

Fig. 1. An illustration of our proposed WGE. Here, $h_e^{(k)}$ and $h_r^{(k)}$ the vector representations of the entity e and the relation r at k-th layer of the encoder module, are computed following Eq. 13.

entities as individual nodes. Here, $\mathcal{G}_{ef} = \{\mathcal{V}_{ef}, \mathcal{E}_{ef}\}$, wherein $\mathcal{V}_{ef}$ is the set of nodes and $\mathcal{E}_{ef}$ is the set of edges. The number of nodes in $\mathcal{G}_{ef}$ is equal to the number of entities in G, i.e., $|\mathcal{V}_{ef}| = |\mathcal{V}|$. In particular, for each triple (h, r, t) in G, entities h and t become individual nodes in $\mathcal{G}_{ef}$ with an edge between them, as illustrated in Fig. 1. Here, $\mathcal{G}_{ef}$ is associated with an adjacency matrix A_{ef}:

$$A_{ef}(\mathsf{v}, \mathsf{u}) = \begin{cases} 1 & \text{if there is an edge between entity nodes } \mathsf{v} \text{ and } \mathsf{u} \\ 0 & \text{otherwise} \end{cases} \tag{7}$$

Relation-Focused View. WGE also aims to attain the potential dependence between two neighborhood relations (e.g. "child_of" and "spouse") to enhance learning representations. To do that, from G, our WGE extracts relation-focused (RF) constraints in the form of (*subjective relation, predicate entity, objective relation*), denoted as (r_s, e_p, r_o), wherein e_p is the tail entity for the relation r_s and also the head entity for the relation r_o, e.g. (born_in, Sydney, city_in). Here, WGE keeps a certain fraction β of common RF constraints based on ranking how often two relations r_s and r_o co-appear in all extracted RF ones. Then, WGE transforms those common obtained RF constraints into a single undirected relation-focused graph $\mathcal{G}_{rf} = \{\mathcal{V}_{rf}, \mathcal{E}_{rf}\}$ that views both entities and relations as individual nodes, wherein $\mathcal{V}_{rf}$ is the set of entity and relation nodes, $\mathcal{E}_{rf}$ is the set of edges. For example, as shown in Fig. 1, given an RF constraint (r_1, e_2, r_2), WGE considers r_1, e_2, and r_2 as individual nodes in $\mathcal{G}_{rf}$ with edges among them. $\mathcal{G}_{rf}$ is associated with an adjacency matrix A_{rf}:

$$A_{rf}(\mathsf{v}, \mathsf{u}) = \begin{cases} 1 & \text{if there is an edge between nodes } \mathsf{v} \text{ and } \mathsf{u} \\ 0 & \text{otherwise} \end{cases} \tag{8}$$

3.2   Encoder Module

Given a single graph $\mathcal{G} = (\mathcal{V}, \mathcal{E})$, we might adopt vanilla GNNs or GCNs directly on $\mathcal{G}$ and its adjacency matrix A to learn node embeddings. Recently,

QGNN—Quaternion Graph Neural Network [21]—has been proposed to learn node embeddings in the quaternion space as follows:

$$h_v^{(k+1),Q} = g \left(\sum_{u \in \mathcal{N}_v \cup \{v\}} a_{v,u} W^{(k),Q} \otimes h_u^{(k),Q} \right) \tag{9}$$

where the superscript Q denotes the quaternion space; k is the layer index; $\mathcal{N}_v$ is the set of neighbors of node v; $W^{(k),Q}$ is a quaternion weight matrix; $\otimes$ denotes the Hamilton product; and g is a nonlinear activation function such as tanh; $h_u^{(0),Q} \in \mathbb{H}^n$ is an input embedding vector for node u, which is randomly initialized and updated during training; and $a_{v,u}$ is an edge constant between nodes v and u in the Laplacian re-normalized adjacency matrix $\tilde{D}^{-\frac{1}{2}} \tilde{A} \tilde{D}^{-\frac{1}{2}}$ with $A = A + I$, where A is the adjacency matrix, I is the identity matrix, and $\tilde{D}$ is the diagonal node degree matrix of $\tilde{A}$. See quaternion algebra background in the Appendix. QGNN has demonstrated its superior performances for downstream tasks such as graph classification and node classification.

Our WGE thus proposes a new encoder architecture to learn entity and relation vector representations based on two different QGNNs, as illustrated in Fig. 1. This new encoder aims to capture both entity- and relation-focused graph structures to better update vector representations for entities and relations as follows:

$$h'^{(k+1),Q}_{v,ef} = g \left(\sum_{u \in \mathcal{N}_v \cup \{v\}} a_{v,u,ef} W^{(k),Q}_{ef} \otimes h^{(k),Q}_{u,ef} \right) \tag{10}$$

where the subscript ef denotes for QGNN on the entity-focused graph $\mathcal{G}_{ef}$, and we define $h^{(k),Q}_{u,ef}$ as:

$$h^{(k),Q}_{u,ef} = h'^{(k),Q}_{u,ef} * h'^{(k),Q}_{u,rf} \tag{11}$$

where $*$ denotes a quaternion element-wise product, and $h'^{(k),Q}_{u,rf}$ is computed following the Eq. 12:

$$h'^{(k+1),Q}_{v,rf} = g \left(\sum_{u \in \mathcal{N}_v \cup \{v\}} a_{v,u,rf} W^{(k),Q}_{rf} \otimes h^{(k),Q}_u \right) \tag{12}$$

where the subscript rf denotes for QGNN on the relation-focused graph $\mathcal{G}_{rf}$. We define $h^{(k),Q}_u$ as:

$$h^{(k),Q}_u = \begin{cases} h^{(k),Q}_{u,ef} & \text{if u is an entity node, as in Equation 11} \\ h'^{(k),Q}_{u,rf} & \text{if u is a relation node, following Equation 12} \end{cases} \tag{13}$$

WGE uses $h^{(k),Q}_e$ and $h^{(k),Q}_r$ as computed following Eq. 13 as the vector representations for entity e and relation r at the k-th layer of our encoder module, respectively. These vectors will be used as input for the decoder module.

Note that our encoder module is not merely using such a GNN but proposes a new manner where the two GNNs interact with each other to jointly learn entity and relation representations from two graphs. This interaction is crucial and novel and is directly responsible for the good performance of our model, showing that two-view modeling helps produce better scores than single-view modeling (See our ablation study in Sect. 4.3).

3.3   Decoder Module

As the encoder module learns quaternion entity and relation embeddings, WGE employs the quaternion KG embedding model QuatE [39] across all hidden layers of the encoder module to return a final score $f(h, r, t)$ for each triple (h, r, t) as:

$$f_k(h, r, t) = \left(\boldsymbol{h}_h^{(k),Q} \otimes \boldsymbol{h}_r^{\triangleleft,(k),Q} \right) \bullet \boldsymbol{h}_t^{(k),Q} \tag{14}$$

$$f(h, r, t) = \sum_k \alpha_k f_k(h, r, t) \tag{15}$$

where $\alpha_k \in [0, 1]$ is a fixed important weight of the k-th layer with $\sum_k \alpha_k = 1$; $\boldsymbol{h}_h^{(k),Q}$, $\boldsymbol{h}_r^{(k),Q}$, and $\boldsymbol{h}_t^{(k),Q}$ are quaternion vectors taken from the k-th layer of the encoder; $\otimes$, $\triangleleft$ and $\bullet$ denote the Hamilton product, the normalized quaternion and the quaternion-inner product, respectively.

3.4   Objective Function

We train WGE by using Adam [16] to optimize a weighted loss function as:

$$\mathcal{L} = - \sum_{(h,r,t) \in \{\mathcal{T} \cup \mathcal{T}'\}} \sum_k \alpha_k \Big(l_{(h,r,t)} \log \left(p_k(h, r, t) \right)$$

$$+ \left(1 - l_{(h,r,t)} \right) \log \left(1 - p_k(h, r, t) \right) \Big) \tag{16}$$

$$\text{in which, } l_{(h,r,t)} = \begin{cases} 1 & \text{for } (h, r, t) \in \mathcal{T} \\ 0 & \text{for } (h, r, t) \in \mathcal{T}' \end{cases}$$

$$\text{and } p_k(h, r, t) = \mathsf{sigmoid}\big(f_k(h, r, t) \big)$$

here, $\mathcal{T}$ and $\mathcal{T}'$ are collections of valid and invalid triples, respectively. $\mathcal{T}'$ is collected by corrupting valid triples in $\mathcal{T}$.

4   Experiments

We evaluate our proposed WGE for the KG completion task, i.e., link prediction [3], which aims to predict a missing entity given a relation with another entity, e.g., predicting a head entity h given $(?, r, t)$ or predicting a tail entity t given $(h, r, ?)$. The results are calculated by ranking the scores produced by the score function f on triples in the test set.

Table 1. Statistics of the experimental datasets.

Dataset	$|\mathcal{E}|$	$|\mathcal{R}|$	#Triples		
			Train	Valid	Test
CoDEx-S	2,034	42	32,888	1827	1828
CoDEx-M	17,050	51	185,584	10,310	10,311
CoDEx-L	77,951	69	551,193	30,622	30,622
LitWD1K	1,533	47	26,115	1,451	1,451
LitWD19K	18,986	182	260,039	14,447	14,447
LitWD48K	47,998	257	303,117	16,838	16,838
FB15K-237	14,541	237	272,115	17,535	20,466

4.1 Setup

Datasets. Recent works [11,28] show that there are some quality issues with previous existing KG completion datasets. For example, a large percentage of relations in FB15K-237 [32] could be covered by a trivial frequency rule [28]. Hence, they introduce six new KG completion benchmarks, consisting of CoDEx-S, CoDEx-M, CoDEx-L,[1] LitWD1K, LitWD19K and LitWD48K.[2] These datasets are more difficult and cover more diverse and interpretable content than the previous ones. We use the six new challenging datasets as well as the FB15K-237 dataset to compare different models. The statistics of these datasets are presented in Table 1.

Evaluation Protocol. Following the standard protocol [3], to generate corrupted triples for each test triple (h, r, t), we replace either h or t by each of all other entities in turn. We also apply the "Filtered" setting protocol [3] to filter out before ranking any corrupted triples that appear in the KG. We then rank the valid test triple as well as the corrupted triples in descending order of their triple scores. We report standard evaluation metrics: mean reciprocal rank (MRR) and Hits@10 (i.e. the proportion of test triples for which the target entity is ranked in the top 10 predictions). Here, a higher MRR/Hits@10 score reflects a better prediction result.

Our Model's Training Protocol. We implement our model using Pytorch [26]. We apply the standard Glorot initialization [12] for parameter initialization. We employ tanh for the nonlinear activation function g. We use the Adam optimizer [16] to train our WGE model up to 3000 epochs on all datasets. We use a grid search to choose the number K of hidden layers $\in \{1, 2, 3\}$, the Adam initial learning rate $\in \{1e^{-4}, 5e^{-4}, 1e^{-3}, 5e^{-3}\}$, the batch size $\in$

---

[1] https://github.com/tsafavi/codex [28].
[2] https://github.com/GenetAsefa/LiterallyWikidata [11].

Table 2. Experimental results on seven *test* sets. Hits@10 (H@10) is reported in %. The best scores are in bold, while the second best scores are in underline. The results of TransE [3], ComplEx [33], ConvE [7] and TuckER [1] on three CoDEx test sets are taken from [28]. The results of R-GCN [30] and CompGCN [34] and SimQGNN [21] on three CoDEx test sets are taken from [21]. The ComplEx results on three LitWD test sets are taken from [11]. The results of TransE, ComplEx, ConvE, R-GCN and CompGCN on the FB15K-237 test set are taken from [34]. The results of TuckER on FB15K-237 are taken from [1]. All results are reported using the same setup.

Method	CoDEx-S		CoDEx-M		CoDEx-L		LitWD1K		LitWD19K		LitWD48K		FB15K-237	
	MRR	H@10	MRR	H@10	MRR	H@10	MRR	H@10	MRR	H@10	MRR	H@10	MRR	H@10
TransE	0.354	63.4	0.303	45.4	0.187	31.7	0.313	51.3	0.172	26.4	0.269	41.3	0.294	46.5
ComplEx	**0.465**	64.6	0.337	47.6	0.294	40.0	0.413	67.3	0.181	29.6	0.277	42.8	0.247	33.9
ConvE	0.444	63.5	0.318	46.4	0.303	42.0	0.477	71.4	0.310	45.1	0.372	54.0	0.325	50.1
TuckER	0.444	63.8	0.328	45.8	0.309	43.0	0.498	74.4	0.311	46.3	0.391	58.7	**0.358**	54.4
R-GCN	0.275	53.3	0.124	24.1	0.073	14.2	0.244	46.2	0.211	34.1	0.238	44.2	0.248	41.7
CompGCN	0.395	62.1	0.312	45.7	0.304	42.8	0.323	52.8	0.319	47.4	0.379	58.4	0.355	53.5
SimQGNN	0.435	65.2	0.323	47.7	0.310	43.7	0.518	75.1	0.308	46.9	0.350	57.6	0.339	51.8
QuatE	0.449	64.4	0.323	48.0	0.312	44.3	0.514	73.1	0.341	49.3	0.392	58.6	0.342	52.9
WGE	0.452	66.4	**0.338**	48.5	**0.320**	44.5	**0.527**	76.2	**0.345**	49.9	**0.401**	59.5	0.348	53.6

$\{1024, 2048, 4096\}$, and the input dimension and hidden sizes of the QGNN hidden layers $\in \{32, 64, 128, 256, 512, 1024\}$. For the decoder module, we perform a grid search to select its mixture weight value $\alpha_0 \in \{0.3, 0.6, 0.9\}$, and fix the mixture weight values for the K layers at $\alpha_k = \dfrac{1 - \alpha_0}{K}$. For the percentage β of kept RF constraints, we grid-search $\beta \in \{0.1, 0.2, ..., 0.9\}$ for the CoDEx-S dataset, and the best value is 0.2; then we use $\beta = 0.2$ for all remaining datasets. We evaluate the MRR after every 10 training epochs on the validation set to select the best model checkpoint, and then apply the selected one to the test set.

Baselines' Training Protocol. For strong baseline models, we apply the same evaluation protocol. The training protocol is the same w.r.t. parameter initialization, the optimizer, the hidden layers, the initial learning rate values, the batch sizes and the number of training epochs as well as the best model checkpoint selection. We also use a model-specific configuration for each baseline. In particular, for TransE [3], ConvE [7], TuckER [1] and QuatE, we use grid search to choose the embedding dimension in $\{64, 128, 256, 512\}$. For the QGNN-based KG embedding model SimQGNN [21] that obtains state-of-the-art results on the CoDEx datasets, we successfully reproduce this model's reported results using its optimal hyper-parameters. For R-GCN and CompGCN, we use 2 GCN layers and vary the embedding size of the GCN layer from $\{64, 128, 256, 512\}$. For WGE variants in the Ablation study, we also set the same dimension value for both the embedding size and the hidden size, wherein we vary the dimension value in $\{64, 128, 256, 512\}$.

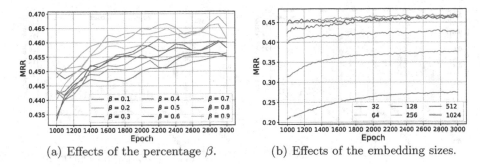

(a) Effects of the percentage β.   (b) Effects of the embedding sizes.

Fig. 2. Effects of hyper-parameters on the CoDEx-S validation set.

4.2   Main Results

Table 2 shows our results obtained for WGE and other strong baselines on seven experimental datasets. In general, our WGE obtains the highest MRR and Hits@10 scores on all three CoDEx and three LitDW challenge datasets (except the second highest MRR on CoDEx-S); and on FB15K-237, WGE obtains the third highest MRR and the second highest Hits@10. In particular, WGE gains substantial improvements compared to both R-GCN and CompGCN on all three CoDEx and three LitDW challenge datasets. Compared to the QGNN-based model SimQGNN, our WGE obtains 1.5% and 0.02 absolute higher Hits@10 and MRR scores averaged over all seven datasets than SimQGNN, respectively. We also find that QuatE obtains competitive performance scores when carefully tuning its hyper-parameters (e.g. generally outperforming SimQGNN),[3] however, it is still surpassed by WGE by about 1.1+% and 0.01 on averaged Hits@10 and MRR, respectively.

Hyper-parameter Sensitivity. We present in Figs. 2(a) and 2(b) the effects of essential hyper-parameters including the percentage β of kept RF constraints and the embedding sizes on the CoDEx-S validation set.

– **Percentage β of kept RF constraints**: As defined in Sect. 3.1, the hyper-parameter β aims to determine the number of common RF constraints to be kept in the relation-focused graph. We visualize the MRR scores according to the value of β in $\{0.1, 0.2, ..., 0.9\}$ in Fig. 2(a).[4] We find that WGE performs best with $\beta = 0.2$. Recall that the hyper-parameter $\beta = 0.2$ is tuned on the CoDEx-S validation set only, and then used for all remaining datasets.

---

[3] Note that the experimental setup is the same for both QuatE and WGE for a fair comparison as WGE uses QuatE for decoding. Zhang et al. [39] reported MRR at 0.348 and Hits@10 at 55.0% on FB15K-237 for QuatE. However, we could not reproduce those scores.

[4] Our training protocol monitors the MRR score on the validation set to select the best model checkpoint.

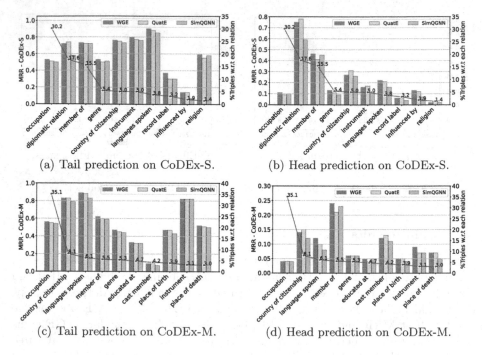

(a) Tail prediction on CoDEx-S.   (b) Head prediction on CoDEx-S.

(c) Tail prediction on CoDEx-M.   (d) Head prediction on CoDEx-M.

Fig. 3. MRR on the CoDEx-S and CoDEx-M validation sets w.r.t each relation. The right y-axis is the percentage of triples corresponding to each relation.

Here, the hyper-parameter $\beta = 0.2$ already helps our WGE to outperform strong baselines, as shown in Table 2. Our scores obtained on the remaining datasets are likely better if β is also tuned on those datasets. A limitation of our approach is that the mechanism of selecting kept RF constraints in the Relation-focused view is based on the observed co-occurrence frequency between entities and relations. This might not be optimal as some entity-relation pairs can have important interactions regardless of their small number of co-occurrences as the observed KG is incomplete (the actual number of co-occurrences could be larger). In future work, we would design a soft scoring mechanism that gives a score for each entity-relation pair and be able to adaptively prune the graph during training.

- **Embedding sizes:** Figure 2(b) illustrates the performance differences of WGE when varying the embedding size in $\{32, 64, 128, 256, 512, 1024\}$. Our WGE achieves the highest MRR when the embedding size is 256. We find that there are no substantial MRR gains when the size is larger than 256. We also observe similar findings for the remaining datasets.

Qualitative Study. We report the performances of WGE, QuatE and SimQGNN over different relation types on the CoDEx validation sets in Fig. 3 and 4. For each dataset, we select the top 10 frequent relations and compare

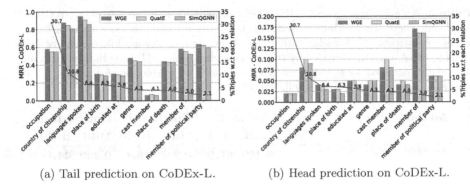

(a) Tail prediction on CoDEx-L.   (b) Head prediction on CoDEx-L.

Fig. 4. MRR on the CoDEx-L validation set w.r.t each relation. The right y-axis is the percentage of triples corresponding to each relation.

model performances over these 10 relations. We also separate the result into tail prediction (i.e., predicting the tail entity given $(h, r, ?)$) and head prediction (i.e., predicting the head entity given $(?, r, t)$). WGE generally works better than both QuatE and SimQGNN except for some special relation cases. For example, QuatE achieves higher head prediction scores for the relation "*country of citizenship*" than WGE as shown in Figs. 3(b), 3(d) and 4(b). A possible reason is that some useful RF constraints related to the relation "*country of citizenship*" have been omitted from the relation-focused graph construction. Note that there is a substantial performance gap between the head prediction and the tail prediction, wherein predicting the tail entities is easier than predicting the head entities. The reason might come from the fact that in the CoDEx datasets, each relation is associated with a small number of tail entities but with a large number of head entities. For example, head entity candidates for "*occupation*" relations can be any person nodes, while candidates for tail entities are limited by the number of job entities.

4.3 Ablation Analysis

Tables 3 and 4 present our ablation results on the validation sets for five variants of our proposed WGE, including:

- (1) **A variant without predicate entities:** This is a variant that only keeps relation nodes in the relation-focused view, i.e., *without using the predicate entities* as nodes from the extracted RF constraints.
- (2) **A variant with GCN:** This is a variant that uses GCN in the encoder module instead of using QGNN.
- (3) **A variant with only entity-focused view:** This is a variant that uses only the entity-focused view.
- (4) **A variant with only relation-focused view:** This is a variant that uses only the relation-focused view.

Table 3. Ablation results on CoDEx validation sets for five variants of our WGE. (1) A variant where the relation-focused view uses only relation nodes, without using the predicate entities. (2) A variant utilizes GCN in the encoder module instead of using QGNN. (3) A variant utilizes only the entity-focused view. (4) A variant utilizes only the relation-focused view. (5) A variant uses the Levi graph transformation, i.e. the entity-focused graph view with addition relation nodes.

Method	CoDEx-S		CoDEx-M		CoDEx-L	
	MRR	H@10	MRR	H@10	MRR	H@10
WGE	**0.469**	**67.9**	**0.339**	**48.4**	**0.320**	**44.1**
(1) w/o predicate entities	0.448	<u>67.1</u>	0.328	<u>47.1</u>	0.312	<u>43.1</u>
(2) w/ GCN	0.441	66.5	0.322	47.0	0.306	43.0
(3) w/ only entity-focused	0.452	66.9	<u>0.329</u>	46.5	<u>0.314</u>	43.0
(4) w/ only relation-focused	<u>0.455</u>	66.9	0.323	46.7	0.305	42.9
(5) w/ only Levi graph	0.447	63.5	0.320	45.7	0.288	41.1

Table 4. Ablation results on LitWD and FB15K-237 validation sets for five variants of our WGE.

Method	LitWD1K		LitWD19K		LitWD48K		FB15K-237	
	MRR	H@10	MRR	H@10	MRR	H@10	MRR	H@10
WGE	**0.518**	**75.5**	**0.343**	**49.5**	**0.402**	**59.3**	**0.351**	**53.6**
(1) w/o predicate entities	0.483	72.6	0.326	47.9	0.389	57.2	0.339	52.4
(2) w/ GCN	0.470	71.3	0.325	47.2	0.382	56.6	0.327	50.2
(3) w/ only entity-focused	0.497	73.3	0.336	48.1	<u>0.397</u>	<u>58.4</u>	<u>0.341</u>	<u>52.5</u>
(4) w/ only relation-focused	<u>0.498</u>	<u>73.7</u>	<u>0.338</u>	<u>48.4</u>	0.395	<u>58.4</u>	0.340	52.3
(5) w/ only Levi graph	0.484	72.8	0.331	48.2	0.387	56.9	0.336	50.8

– (5) **A variant with the Levi graph transformation:** This is a variant where a single Levi graph is used as the input of the encoder module. From the given KG, we investigate another strategy of constructing a single undirected graph, which can be considered as a direct extension of our entity-focused graph view with additional relation nodes, following the Levi graph transformation [19].

We find that WGE outperforms all of its variants, thus showing that: from (1), the predicate entities can help to better infer the potential dependence between two neighborhood relations; from (2), GCNs are not as effective as QGNNs; and from (3), (4) and (5), the modeling of two-view graphs of KGs helps produce better scores than single-view modeling of KGs, confirming the effectiveness of our two-view WGE approach. In addition, variant (5) obtains lower scores than variant (3), also showing that the Levi graph transformation is not as effective as the entity-focused graph transformation.

5   Conclusion

In this paper, we have introduced WGE—an effective GNN-based KG embedding model—to enhance the entity neighborhood information with the potential dependence between two neighborhood relations. In particular, WGE constructs two views from the given KG, including a single undirected entity-focused graph and a single undirected relation-focused graph. Then WGE proposes a new encoder architecture to update entity and relation vector representations from these two graph views. After that, WGE employs a weighted score function to compute the triple scores for KG completion. Extensive experiments show that WGE outperforms other strong GNN-based baselines and KG embedding models on seven KG completion benchmark datasets. Our WGE implementation is publicly available at: https://github.com/vinhsuhi/WGE.

Acknowledgment. Most of this work was done while Vinh Tong was a research resident at VinAI Research, Vietnam.

Appendix

The hyper-complex vector space has recently been considered on the Quaternion space [15] consisting of one real and three separate imaginary axes. It provides highly expressive computations through the Hamilton product compared to the Euclidean and complex vector spaces. We provide key notations and operations related to the Quaternion space required for our later development. Additional details can further be found in [25].

A quaternion $q \in \mathbb{H}$ is a hyper-complex number consisting of one real and three separate imaginary components [15] defined as:

$$q = q_r + q_i \mathbf{i} + q_j \mathbf{j} + q_k \mathbf{k} \tag{17}$$

where $q_r, q_i, q_j, q_k \in \mathbb{R}$, and $\mathbf{i}, \mathbf{j}, \mathbf{k}$ are imaginary units that $\mathbf{i}^2 = \mathbf{j}^2 = \mathbf{k}^2 = \mathbf{ijk} = -1$. The operations for the Quaternion algebra are defined as follows:

Addition. The addition of two quaternions q and p is defined as:

$$q + p = (q_r + p_r) + (q_i + p_i)\mathbf{i} + (q_j + p_j)\mathbf{j} + (q_k + p_k)\mathbf{k} \tag{18}$$

Norm. The norm $\|q\|$ of a quaternion q is computed as:

$$\|q\| = \sqrt{q_r^2 + q_i^2 + q_j^2 + q_k^2} \tag{19}$$

And the normalized or unit quaternion $q^\lhd$ is defined as: $q^\lhd = \frac{q}{\|q\|}$

Scalar Multiplication. The multiplication of a scalar λ and q is computed as follows:

$$\lambda q = \lambda q_r + \lambda q_i \mathbf{i} + \lambda q_j \mathbf{j} + \lambda q_k \mathbf{k} \tag{20}$$

Conjugate. The conjugate q^* of a quaternion q is defined as:

$$q^* = q_r - q_i\mathbf{i} - q_j\mathbf{j} - q_k\mathbf{k} \tag{21}$$

Hamilton Product. The Hamilton product $\otimes$ (i.e., the quaternion multiplication) of two quaternions q and p is defined as:

$$
\begin{aligned}
q \otimes p = \qquad & (q_r p_r - q_i p_i - q_j p_j - q_k p_k) \\
+ \qquad & (q_i p_r + q_r p_i - q_k p_j + q_j p_k)\mathbf{i} \\
+ \qquad & (q_j p_r + q_k p_i + q_r p_j - q_i p_k)\mathbf{j} \\
+ \qquad & (q_k p_r - q_j p_i + q_i p_j + q_r p_k)\mathbf{k}
\end{aligned} \tag{22}
$$

We can express the Hamilton product of q and p in the following form:

$$
q \otimes p =
\begin{bmatrix} 1 \\ \mathbf{i} \\ \mathbf{j} \\ \mathbf{k} \end{bmatrix}^\top
\begin{bmatrix}
q_r & -q_i & -q_j & -q_k \\
q_i & q_r & -q_k & q_j \\
q_j & q_k & q_r & -q_i \\
q_k & -q_j & q_i & q_r
\end{bmatrix}
\begin{bmatrix} p_r \\ p_i \\ p_j \\ p_k \end{bmatrix} \tag{23}
$$

The Hamilton product of two quaternion vectors $\boldsymbol{q}$ and $\boldsymbol{p} \in \mathbb{H}^n$ is computed as:

$$
\begin{aligned}
\boldsymbol{q} \otimes \boldsymbol{p} = \qquad & (\boldsymbol{q}_r \circ \boldsymbol{p}_r - \boldsymbol{q}_i \circ \boldsymbol{p}_i - \boldsymbol{q}_j \circ \boldsymbol{p}_j - \boldsymbol{q}_k \circ \boldsymbol{p}_k) \\
+ \qquad & (\boldsymbol{q}_i \circ \boldsymbol{p}_r + \boldsymbol{q}_r \circ \boldsymbol{p}_i - \boldsymbol{q}_k \circ \boldsymbol{p}_j + \boldsymbol{q}_j \circ \boldsymbol{p}_k)\mathbf{i} \\
+ \qquad & (\boldsymbol{q}_j \circ \boldsymbol{p}_r + \boldsymbol{q}_k \circ \boldsymbol{p}_i + \boldsymbol{q}_r \circ \boldsymbol{p}_j - \boldsymbol{q}_i \circ \boldsymbol{p}_k)\mathbf{j} \\
+ \qquad & (\boldsymbol{q}_k \circ \boldsymbol{p}_r - \boldsymbol{q}_j \circ \boldsymbol{p}_i + \boldsymbol{q}_i \circ \boldsymbol{p}_j + \boldsymbol{q}_r \circ \boldsymbol{p}_k)\mathbf{k}
\end{aligned} \tag{24}
$$

where $\circ$ denotes the element-wise product. We note that the Hamilton product is not commutative, i.e., $q \otimes p \neq p \otimes q$.

We can derived a product of a quaternion matrix $\boldsymbol{W} \in \mathbb{H}^{m \times n}$ and a quaternion vector $\boldsymbol{p} \in \mathbb{H}^n$ from Eq. 23 as follow:

$$
\boldsymbol{W} \otimes \boldsymbol{p} =
\begin{bmatrix} 1 \\ \mathbf{i} \\ \mathbf{j} \\ \mathbf{k} \end{bmatrix}^\top
\begin{bmatrix}
\boldsymbol{W}_r & -\boldsymbol{W}_i & -\boldsymbol{W}_j & -\boldsymbol{W}_k \\
\boldsymbol{W}_i & \boldsymbol{W}_r & -\boldsymbol{W}_k & \boldsymbol{W}_j \\
\boldsymbol{W}_j & \boldsymbol{W}_k & \boldsymbol{W}_r & -\boldsymbol{W}_i \\
\boldsymbol{W}_k & -\boldsymbol{W}_j & \boldsymbol{W}_i & \boldsymbol{W}_r
\end{bmatrix}
\begin{bmatrix} \boldsymbol{p}_r \\ \boldsymbol{p}_i \\ \boldsymbol{p}_j \\ \boldsymbol{p}_k \end{bmatrix} \tag{25}
$$

where $\boldsymbol{p}_r, \boldsymbol{p}_i, \boldsymbol{p}_j$, and $\boldsymbol{p}_k \in \mathbb{R}^n$ are real vectors; and $\boldsymbol{W}_r, \boldsymbol{W}_i, \boldsymbol{W}_j$, and $\boldsymbol{W}_k \in \mathbb{R}^{m \times n}$ are real matrices.

Quaternion-Inner Product. The quaternion-inner product $\bullet$ of two quaternion vectors $\boldsymbol{q}$ and $\boldsymbol{p} \in \mathbb{H}^n$ returns a scalar as:

$$\boldsymbol{q} \bullet \boldsymbol{p} = \boldsymbol{q}_r^\top \boldsymbol{p}_r + \boldsymbol{q}_i^\top \boldsymbol{p}_i + \boldsymbol{q}_j^\top \boldsymbol{p}_j + \boldsymbol{q}_k^\top \boldsymbol{p}_k \tag{26}$$

Quaternion Element-Wise Product. We further define the element-wise product of two quaternions vector $\boldsymbol{q}$ and $\boldsymbol{p} \in \mathbb{H}^n$ as follow:

$$\boldsymbol{p} * \boldsymbol{q} = (\boldsymbol{q}_r \circ \boldsymbol{p}_r) + (\boldsymbol{q}_i \circ \boldsymbol{p}_i)\mathbf{i} + (\boldsymbol{q}_j \circ \boldsymbol{p}_j)\mathbf{j} + (\boldsymbol{q}_k \circ \boldsymbol{p}_k)\mathbf{k} \tag{27}$$

References

1. Balažević, I., Allen, C., Hospedales, T.M.: TuckER: tensor factorization for knowledge graph completion. In: EMNLP, pp. 5185–5194 (2019)
2. Berant, J., Chou, A., Frostig, R., Liang, P.: Semantic parsing on freebase from question-answer pairs. In: EMNLP, pp. 1533–1544 (2013)
3. Bordes, A., Usunier, N., García-Durán, A., Weston, J., Yakhnenko, O.: Translating embeddings for modeling multi-relational data. In: NIPS, pp. 2787–2795 (2013)
4. Bordes, A., Weston, J., Collobert, R., Bengio, Y.: Learning structured embeddings of knowledge bases. In: AAAI, pp. 301–306 (2011)
5. Chen, X., Zhou, Z., Gao, M., Shi, D., Husen, M.N.: Knowledge representation combining quaternion path integration and depth-wise atrous circular convolution. In: UAI, pp. 336–345 (2022)
6. Demir, C., Ngomo, A. C.N.: Convolutional complex knowledge graph embeddings. In: Verborgh, R., et al. (eds.) ESWC 2021. LNCS, vol. 12731, pp. 409–424. Springer, Cham (2021). https://doi.org/10.1007/978-3-030-77385-4_24
7. Dettmers, T., Minervini, P., Stenetorp, P., Riedel, S.: Convolutional 2D knowledge graph embeddings. In: AAAI, pp. 1811–1818 (2018)
8. Dutta, S., Weikum, G.: Cross-document co-reference resolution using sample-based clustering with knowledge enrichment. Trans. ACL **3**, 15–28 (2015)
9. Fader, A., Zettlemoyer, L., Etzioni, O.: Open question answering over curated and extracted knowledge bases. In: KDD, pp. 1156–1165 (2014)
10. Ferrucci, D.A.: Introduction to "this is Watson". IBM J. Res. Dev. **56**(3), 235–249 (2012)
11. Gesese, G.A., Alam, M., Sack, H.: LiterallyWikidata - a benchmark for knowledge graph completion using literals. In: Hotho, A., et al. (eds.) ISWC 2021. LNCS, vol. 12922, pp. 511–527. Springer, Cham (2021). https://doi.org/10.1007/978-3-030-88361-4_30
12. Glorot, X., Bengio, Y.: Understanding the difficulty of training deep feedforward neural networks. In: AISTATS, pp. 249–256 (2010)
13. Hamilton, W.L., Ying, R., Leskovec, J.: Inductive representation learning on large graphs. In: NeurIPS (2017)
14. Hamilton, W.L., Ying, R., Leskovec, J.: Representation learning on graphs: methods and applications. IEEE Data Eng. Bull. **40**(3), 52–74 (2018)
15. Hamilton, W.R.: On quaternions; or on a new system of imaginaries in algebra. London Edinb. Dublin Philos. Mag. J. Sci. **25**(163), 10–13 (1844)
16. Kingma, D., Ba, J.: Adam: a method for stochastic optimization. In: ICLR (2015)
17. Kipf, T.N., Welling, M.: Semi-supervised classification with graph convolutional networks. In: ICLR (2017)
18. Krishnamurthy, J., Mitchell, T.: Weakly supervised training of semantic parsers. In: EMNLP-CoNLL, pp. 754–765 (2012)
19. Levi, F.W.: Finite Geometrical Systems: Six Public Lectues Delivered in February, 1940, at the University of Calcutta. University of Calcutta (1942)
20. Nguyen, D.Q., Nguyen, D.Q., Nguyen, T.D., Phung, D.: Convolutional neural network-based model for knowledge base completion and its application to search personalization. Semant. Web **10**(5), 947–960 (2019)
21. Nguyen, D.Q., Nguyen, T.D., Phung, D.: Quaternion graph neural networks. In: ACML (2021)
22. Nguyen, D.Q., Tong, V., Phung, D., Nguyen, D.Q.: Node co-occurrence based graph neural networks for knowledge graph link prediction. In: WSDM, pp. 1589–1592 (2022)

23. Nguyen, D.Q.: A survey of embedding models of entities and relationships for knowledge graph completion. In: TextGraphs, pp. 1–14 (2020)
24. Nickel, M., Rosasco, L., Poggio, T.: Holographic embeddings of knowledge graphs. In: AAAI, pp. 1955–1961 (2016)
25. Parcollet, T., Morchid, M., Linarès, G.: A survey of quaternion neural networks. Artif. Intell. Rev. **53**, 2957–2982 (2020)
26. Paszke, A., Gross, S., Massa, F., et al.: Pytorch: an imperative style, high-performance deep learning library. In: NeurIPS, pp. 8024–8035 (2019)
27. Ponzetto, S.P., Strube, M.: Exploiting semantic role labeling, wordnet and Wikipedia for coreference resolution. In: NAACL, pp. 192–199 (2006)
28. Safavi, T., Koutra, D.: CoDEx: a comprehensive knowledge graph completion benchmark. In: EMNLP, pp. 8328–8350 (2020)
29. Scarselli, F., Gori, M., Tsoi, A.C., Hagenbuchner, M., Monfardini, G.: The graph neural network model. IEEE Trans. Neural Netw. **20**(1), 61–80 (2009)
30. Schlichtkrull, M., Kipf, T.N., Bloem, P., van den Berg, R., Titov, I., Welling, M.: Modeling relational data with graph convolutional networks. In: Gangemi, A., et al. (eds.) ESWC 2018. LNCS, vol. 10843, pp. 593–607. Springer, Cham (2018). https://doi.org/10.1007/978-3-319-93417-4_38
31. Shang, C., Tang, Y., Huang, J., Bi, J., He, X., Zhou, B.: End-to-end structure-aware convolutional networks for knowledge base completion. In: AAAI, pp. 3060–3067 (2019)
32. Toutanova, K., Chen, D.: Observed versus latent features for knowledge base and text inference. In: CVSC, pp. 57–66 (2015)
33. Trouillon, T., Welbl, J., Riedel, S., Gaussier, É., Bouchard, G.: Complex embeddings for simple link prediction. In: ICML, pp. 2071–2080 (2016)
34. Vashishth, S., Sanyal, S., Nitin, V., Talukdar, P.: Composition-based multi-relational graph convolutional networks. In: ICLR (2020)
35. Veličković, P., Cucurull, G., Casanova, A., Romero, A., Liò, P., Bengio, Y.: Graph attention networks. In: ICLR (2018)
36. Wu, Z., Pan, S., Chen, F., Long, G., Zhang, C., Yu, P.S.: A comprehensive survey on graph neural networks. IEEE Trans. Neural Netw. Learn. Syst. **32**(1), 4–24 (2021)
37. Yang, B., Yih, W.T., He, X., Gao, J., Deng, L.: Embedding entities and relations for learning and inference in knowledge bases. In: ICLR (2015)
38. Zhang, D., Yin, J., Zhu, X., Zhang, C.: Network representation learning: a survey. IEEE Trans. Big Data **6**, 3–28 (2020)
39. Zhang, S., Tay, Y., Yao, L., Liu, Q.: Quaternion knowledge graph embeddings. In: NeurIPS, pp. 2731–2741 (2019)
40. Zhang, Y., Yao, Q., Dai, W., Chen, L.: AutoSF: searching scoring functions for knowledge graph embedding. In: ICDE, pp. 433–444 (2020)

GETT-QA: Graph Embedding Based T2T Transformer for Knowledge Graph Question Answering

Debayan Banerjee[1]([⊠]), Pranav Ajit Nair[2], Ricardo Usbeck[1],
and Chris Biemann[1]

[1] Universität Hamburg, Hamburg, Germany
{debayan.banerjee,ricardo.usbeck,chris.biemann}@uni-hamburg.de
[2] Indian Institute of Technology (BHU), Varanasi, Varanasi, India
pranavajitnair.cse18@itbhu.ac.in

Abstract. In this work, we present an end-to-end Knowledge Graph Question Answering (KGQA) system named GETT-QA. GETT-QA uses T5, a popular text-to-text pre-trained language model. The model takes a question in natural language as input and produces a simpler form of the intended SPARQL query. In the simpler form, the model does not directly produce entity and relation IDs. Instead, it produces corresponding entity and relation labels. The labels are grounded to KG entity and relation IDs in a subsequent step. To further improve the results, we instruct the model to produce a truncated version of the KG embedding for each entity. The truncated KG embedding enables a finer search for disambiguation purposes. We find that T5 is able to learn the truncated KG embeddings without any change of loss function, improving KGQA performance. As a result, we report strong results for LC-QuAD 2.0 and SimpleQuestions-Wikidata datasets on end-to-end KGQA over Wikidata.

1 Introduction

A Knowledge Graph (KG) is an information store where data is stored in the form of node-edge-node triples. Nodes represent entities and edges represent relationships between these entities. The aim of KGQA [21] is to produce answers from this KG given an input question in natural language, e.g., `Who is the father of Barack Obama ?`. Usually, the first step in KGQA is to perform Entity Linking (EL) where mention spans, e.g., `Barack Obama` representing the name of a person, place, etc., are linked to a KG node. The subsequent step is Relation Linking (RL), where the relationship of the entity to the potential answer in the KG is extracted, e.g., `father of`. Some KGQA systems attempt to fetch the answer based on the results of just the two steps above, which typically ends up being another entity (node) in the graph. However, for more complex questions, such as count queries or min/max aggregate queries (e.g.: `How many rivers are there in India?`) the answer does not lie in a node or edge in the graph, but instead, a formal query must be generated as a final step. To this end, semantic parsing is relevant to the problem of KGQA. Thus, our focus in this work is to generate a final SPARQL query that can be executed on the KG.

SPARQL is a popular graph query language for querying KGs. A sample SPARQL query for the running example over the Wikidata KG looks like the following:

```
SELECT ?o WHERE { wd:Q76 wdt:P22 ?o }
```

In the query above, `wd:Q76` stands for Barack Obama, while `wdt:P22` stands for the relation `father`. The `?o` variable represents the answer from the KG.

Recent works employ text-to-text (T2T) pre-trained language models (PLMs) for generating logical queries, e.g. SPARQL, from natural language questions. If the correct entity and relation IDs are already specified in the input, the accuracy of T2T models is high [2]. However, the absence of linked entity and relation IDs in the input presents a significant challenge to such models. PLMs are adept at generating linguistic tokens from within their weights. Yet, it is an entirely different proposition to query the KG and ground the entity and relations to specific IDs, as the variability of language creates impressive richness at generation while at the same time hampers the alignment to pre-defined KG items.

In this work, we demonstrate a novel method by which a T2T PLM, namely T5 [28], not only generates SPARQL queries, but also generates truncated KG embeddings, which aid in the subsequent process of grounding entities to the correct node in the KG. Our method produces strong results for end-to-end Question Answering on the LC-QuAD 2.0 and SimpleQuestions-Wikidata datasets over Wikidata KG. All code and data will be made available[1].

2   Related Work

Early KGQA systems could be divided on the basis of whether they can handle simple [44] or complex questions [21]. In a simple question, a node-edge-node triple is a sole basis on which a question is formed, whereas in a complex question there may be more than one such triple involved. Moreover, certain KGQA systems are built specifically to handle a certain class of questions better, e.g. temporal questions [18].

Another way of categorising KGQA systems is whether they form a formal query [1,3,8,35,39] versus whether they use graph search based methods without producing an explicit query [7,16,24,29,33,36,37,40].

Some KGQA systems work in a hybrid mode and can query from both KG and text-based sources. PullNet [36] and Graftnet [37] both use Relational-Graph Convolution Networks [34] to handle complex questions. UNIK-QA [25] verbalises all structured input from KG, tables and lists into sentences and adds them to a text corpora and proceeds to perform QA over this augmented text

---

[1] https://github.com/debayan/gett-qa.

corpora using deep passage retrieval techniques. UNIQORN [27] builds a context graph on-the-fly and retrieves question relevant pieces of evidence from KG and text corpora, using fine-tuned BERT models. They use group Steiner trees to identify the best answer in the context graph. We use the results of the KG components of these hybrid systems in our evaluation in Table 3, as reported by UNIQORN.

Platypus [39] and QAnswer [8] are two recent KGQA systems that work on Wikidata. Both of them use templates and ranking mechanisms to find the best query. We make no use of templates in our method since this inherently limits the flexibility of a system on unseen templates.

ElneuQA-ConvS2S [10] operates in a similar fashion to us, where they use a Neural Machine Translation (NMT) model to generate SPARQL queries with empty placeholders, while an entity linking and sequence labeling model fills the slots. In our case we also make use of NMT capabilities of T5 to generate a skeleton SPARQL query, however, we do not generate empty slots, and instead, generate entity and relation labels to be grounded later.

For simple questions, KEQA [17] targets at jointly recovering the question's head entity, predicate, and tail entity representations in the KG embedding spaces and then forming a query to retrieve the answer from a KG. Text2Graph [6] uses KEQA as a base, and improves on the embedding learning model by utilising CP tensor decomposition [15]. We include both these systems in our evaluation Table 4.

SGPT [31] and STAG [29] both use generative methods for forming the query using pre-trained language models, which is similar to what we do, however, neither of them generate the entity or relation label, or the embeddings. Instead STAG uses an external entity linking step, while SGPT attempts to generate entity and relation IDs directly. However such a method does not work well because for a KG like Wikidata, the IDs do not follow a hierarchical pattern, and hence the model is not able to predict an ID that it has not seen in training earlier.

One of our key ideas is to enable a PLM to learn KG Embeddings. There have been some recent efforts in the same direction such as KEPLER [43], K-BERT [23], KI-BERT [12], CoLAKE [38], BERT-MK [14] and JAKET [45]. These systems either try to inject KG embeddings into the input or intermediate layers of the model, or they try to augment the text corpora by including verbalised forms of the triple structural information. On the other hand, we ask the model to print the embeddings as output. This is a fundamentally different approach from what has been tried so far.

A related, yet different class of systems is that of conversational QA.

LASAGNE [19] and CARTON [26] are two notable systems in this category. They evaluate on the CSQA dataset [32], which is a conversational dataset answerable over a KG. In our case, we address only single sentence-long questions. The conversations in CSQA are arranged in sequence of turns of questions and answers. For the semantic parsing of logical forms, both LASAGNE and CARTON use a pre-defined grammar, while our approach is free of templated grammar rules. Both LASAGNE and CARTON use a Transformer architecture to generate base logical forms, however, LASAGNE uses, a Graph Attention Network [42] to resolve entities and relations while CARTON uses stacked pointer networks.

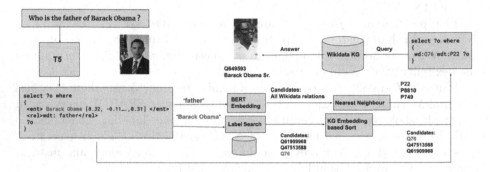

Fig. 1. Architecture of GETT-QA: T5 generates a skeleton SPARQL query with entity and relation labels and a truncated KG embedding string. The entity labels are grounded using label based search and embedding based sorting, while the relations are grounded using BERT embedding based sorting. The final query is executed against a KG to fetch the answer.

3   Method

As shown in Fig. 1, our system consists of five major steps:

- T5 generates a skeleton SPARQL query from input natural language question.
- The entity labels and truncated KG embeddings are extracted. A label search is performed to fetch entity candidates.
- The entity candidates are re-ranked using an embedding similarity metric.
- In parallel, the relation label is extracted and matched against Wikidata relations based on BERT embeddings.
- The final query is grounded to KG nodes and executed to receive the answer.

3.1   Truncated KG Embeddings

We teach T5 to generate truncated vector strings of KG embeddings. We use TransE [5] embeddings for Wikidata entities that were provided by Pytorch-BigGraph[2] [22]. These are 200-dimensional vectors of floats. The truncated KG embeddings we use are a shorter version of the same embeddings. For most of our experiments, we use the first 10 dimensions of these embeddings, and further reduce the precision of the floats to 3 digits after the decimal. We do so since T5

---

[2] https://github.com/facebookresearch/PyTorch-BigGraph.

is expected to produce these truncated KG embeddings while still in the text-to-text mode. In other words, T5 produces these vectors of floats considering them as a string. We use truncated KG embeddings instead of original embeddings to reduce the decoding load of T5. Our aim is not to learn the entire embedding space. Instead, we want to learn identifiers that can aid the entity disambiguation phase. We produce these truncated KG embeddings only for entities, not for relations.

3.2 Intuition

The initial idea behind our approach is to allow T5 to use its significant linguistic capability derived from pre-training over a large corpus for the task of semantic parsing. As a result, we use T5 to produce SPARQL tokens and entity and relation labels.

At first glance, it may appear that the production of entity labels is sufficient for grounding to KG entity nodes. However, in most KGs, several entities share the same labels. For example in Wikidata KG, the entity IDs Q76 and Q47513588 both share the label Barack Obama. In reality, Q76 represents the President while Q47513588 is the entity ID for a painting of the President. As a result of such collision of labels, a further step called *disambiguation* is required.

The next idea is to not just rely on T5's linguistic abilities but also to try and teach the model how to generate identifiers for the entities, which can aid the grounding and disambiguation process in a subsequent step. One way could be to generate the Wikidata IDs directly. However, the IDs do not correspond in any hierarchical way to the underlying entities. For example, while Q76 is Barack Obama, Q77 is Uruguay. Although the IDs are close to each other, the categories are completely different. Models cannot be expected to produce accurate IDs of this nature, especially on unseen input questions. As a result, we consider other schemes of entity identifiers that exhibit some hierarchical properties.

It turns out KG embeddings fulfill these requirements handsomely, and hence we decide to use truncated KG embeddings as the "soft" identifier of our choice. Another possibility would be to generate entity descriptions instead of truncated KG embeddings, however, roughly 50% of entities in Wikidata do not have corresponding descriptions (e.g.: Q67395985[3]), hence we focus on generating truncated KG embeddings instead.

While the production of such truncated embeddings may also aid the grounding of relations, we do not attempt this, since Wikidata only contains a few thousand relations, while the number of entities run into several millions. For the grounding of relations we use simpler text embedding based methods, as described later in Sect. 3.7.

3.3 Models

T5 [28], or text-to-text transfer transformer, is a transformer [41] based encoder-decoder architecture that uses a text-to-text approach. Every task, including

---

[3] https://www.wikidata.org/wiki/Q67395985.

translation, question answering, and classification, is cast as feeding the model text as input and training it to generate some target text. This allows using the same model, loss function, hyper-parameters, etc., across a diverse set of tasks. We experiment with fine-tuning two variants of the T5 model: T5-Small with 60 million parameters and T5-Base with 220 million parameters. For the GETT-QA system results reported in Tables 3 and 4 we use the T5-Base based model, whereas in the analysis Sect. 7.2 we present a comparative study against T5-Small.

3.4 Skeleton SPARQL

As shown in Fig. 1, the first step of our KGQA system is to generate a skeleton SPARQL query from the given natural language question. The skeleton query consists of SPARQL tokens such as SELECT, WHERE, {}, entity and relation labels, and truncated KG embeddings, which are an array of floats. Some additional tokens are used to surround the entity and relation labels, such as <ent>, </ent>,<rel>,</rel> so that in a later step their extraction can be performed using regular-expression operations. The extraction of the labels and the truncated KG embedding are essential for the subsequent grounding step. Notably, entity and relation IDs are not a part of a skeleton SPARQL query.

During training via fine-tuning, pairs of questions and skeleton SPARQL queries are presented to T5. For this purpose, we pre-process the original dataset, which contains gold SPARQL queries for each question. The SPARQL query is converted to a skeleton SPARQL query by replacing the entity and relation IDs with their gold labels while appending the entity labels with a truncated KG embedding. Hence, the following gold SPARQL query:

```
select ?o where {  wd:Q76 wdt:P22 ?o }
```

is converted to:

```
select ?o where
{
 <ent>Barack Obama [...] </ent>
 <rel>father</rel>
 ?o
}
```

for the purposes of training T5, where the truncated KG embedding is represented by [...].

3.5 Entity Candidates

During inference, when T5 generates a skeleton query, all entity and relation labels, as well as truncated KG embeddings, are extracted using regular expressions. For the entity labels, a BM-25-based [30] label search is performed on a database of all Wikidata entity labels, out of which top-k candidates are retrieved per entity label. For this text search we use the Elasticsearch database[4]. For our experiments, we fix k at 100.

3.6 Entity Candidates Re-ranking and Ordering

The top-3 entity candidates based on label matching are retained. For the next 3 candidates, we resort to truncated KG embedding-based sorting. For each item in the list of 100 entity candidates fetched, we also fetch their gold KG embeddings, and convert them to truncated KG embeddings. For the truncated KG embedding generated by T5, we compute its dot product against the gold truncated KG embeddings fetched and re-rank them in descending order. The dot product is used as a comparator because this was the same function that was used during the production of the TransE embeddings. From this re-ranked list based on truncated KG embedding similarity, top-3 candidates are retained.

We append these `top-3` truncated KG embedding-sorted candidates to the `top-3` label-sorted candidates, and proceed to the subsequent steps with a list of 6 candidate entities for each entity label.

3.7 Relation Candidates

We generate no truncated KG embeddings for relation IDs, as their numbers are orders of magnitudes smaller when compared to entities in Wikidata. From the relation labels generated by T5, we compute their BERT embeddings and compute the cosine similarity against the BERT embeddings of all Wikidata properties. The list of properties is sorted based on this similarity score, and the top-3 matches are considered for the subsequent steps.

3.8 Candidate Combinations

For a generated query, each entity label and each relation label has 6 and 3 candidates each, respectively. We preserve the serial order of the entities and relations as produced in the query, and generate all possible combinations of the entities and relations, which generates several queries of the same structure but different entity and relation IDs. For example, if the query contains just one entity and one relation, the number of possible SPARQL queries generated would be $6 \times 3 = 18$. We execute each query on the KG in sorted order of entity and relation IDs received in previous steps. We stop when the KG returns a non-empty response. This response is considered the output of our KGQA system. We consider the top 3 beams produced by T5 decoder as probable queries. The first beam producing a valid response from the KG is considered the output of our KGQA system.

---

[4] https://www.elastic.co/.

4   Dataset

We evaluate our approach on the LC-QuAD 2.0 [11] dataset, which consists of approximately 30,000 questions based on the Wikidata KG. Each question contains the corresponding SPARQL query as gold annotation. The dataset consists of a wide variety of questions, such as simple, complex, multi-hop, count, min/max, dual and boolean types. This dataset also uses the recently introduced hyper-relational [13] structure of the Wikidata KG.

Additionally, we evaluate our approach on the SimpleQuestions-Wikidata [9][5] dataset, which consists of 34,374 train questions and 9,961 test questions. This dataset is derived from the original SimpleQuestions dataset [4], which was later aligned with the Wikidata KG. A sample question from each dataset can be seen in Tables 1 and 2.

Table 1. Sample question from LC-QuAD 2.0

Question	SPARQL

Tell me the female beauty pageant that operates in all countries and contains the word model in it's name?	`SELECT DISTINCT ?sbj ?sbj_label`
	`  WHERE {`
	`?sbj wdt:P31 wd:Q58863414 .`
	`?sbj wdt:P2541 wd:Q62900839 .`
	`?sbj rdfs:label ?sbj_label .`
	`FILTER(CONTAINS(lcase(?sbj_label), "model")) .`
	`FILTER (lang(?sbj_label) = "en")`
	`}`
	`LIMIT 25`

Table 2. Sample question from SimpleQuestions-Wikidata

Question	SPARQL
What type of music does David Ruffin play?	`SELECT ?x WHERE { wd:Q1176417 wdt:P136 ?x }`

5   Evaluation

In Table 3, the results for UNIQORN, QAnswer, UNIK-QA, Pullnet, and Platypus are taken from UNIQORN [27]. UNIQORN uses a test split of 4,921 questions from the original LC-QuAD 2.0 test set of 6,046 questions for all the systems. We evaluate our approach on the same split as UNIQORN. Despite our best efforts we were unable to acquire the precise KG snapshot that UNIQORN used for evaluation. UNIQORN used a Wikidata dump dated 20 April 2021, which is no longer available either in the official Wikidata repository[6], or with the authors

---

[5] https://github.com/askplatypus/wikidata-simplequestions.
[6] https://dumps.wikimedia.org/wikidatawiki/entities/.

of UNIQORN. As a result, we ran the 4,921 questions against the NLIWOD[7] Wikidata dump[8,9], which is hosted on the docker hub for easy deployment, and also hosted as an API by the Universität Hamburg's SEMS group.

In Table 4 for SimpleQuestions-Wikidata, results for KEQA and Text2Graph are taken from MEKER [6]. They evaluate both systems on a smaller split of the SimpleQuestions-Wikidata test set. This subset contains those questions which are valid on a custom Wikidata version they call Wiki4M. We were provided the KG by the authors of MEKER and we evaluated our system on the same.

In Table 3, we report macro Precision@1 based on UNIQORN's reporting preference. In Table 4 we report macro F1 in line with MEKER. To compute metrics, we take the gold SPARQL and predicted SPARQL query and query the KG with both. We compare the results from the KG to compute true positives, false positives, and false negatives (TP, FP, FN).

Table 3. Results on LC-QuAD 2.0

	P@1
UNIK-QA	0.005
Pullnet	0.011
Platypus	0.036
QAnswer	0.308
UNIQORN	0.331
GETT-QA without truncated embeddings	0.327 ± 0.002
GETT-QA (with truncated embeddings)	$\mathbf{0.403} \pm 0.0$

Table 4. Results on SimpleQuestions-Wikidata

	F1
KEQA	0.405
Text2Graph	0.618
GETT-QA without truncated embeddings	0.752 ± 0.004
GETT-QA (with truncated embeddings)	$\mathbf{0.761} \pm 0.002$

6   Results

In Table 3, the bottom two rows contain the results of our system in two different settings for LC-QuAD 2.0. In the first case, our KGQA system uses the top-6 entity candidates based on label match, without the use of truncated KG

---

[7] https://www.nliwod.org/challenge.
[8] https://hub.docker.com/r/debayanin/hdt-query-service.
[9] https://skynet.coypu.org/#/dataset/wikidata/query.

embeddings for re-ranking. In the second case, we keep the top-3 entity candidates based on label match and append to it the top-3 candidates based on truncated KG embedding match. This is the same setting as described in Subsect. 3.6. The relation candidates in both cases remain top-3 as described in Subsect. 3.7.

The key finding in Table 3 is that when we compare the last two rows, our system performs better with an absolute gain of approximately 8% when truncated KG embeddings are used.

In Table 4, for SimpleQuestions-Wikidata our method without truncated KG embeddings already outperforms the nearest competitor by an absolute margin of 13%. This demonstrates the natural ability of T5 to predict the correct entity and relation labels given a question. Since the query structure of all the questions in this dataset is the same, no challenge is posed to T5 in trying to learn the query itself. It is noteworthy however, that after the inclusion of truncated KG embedding re-ranking, the performance remains similar. An insignificant margin of absolute improvement of 0.9% is seen. To investigate this gap when compared to the 8% improvement of LC-QuAD 2.0, we delve further into the nature of the two datasets and run some analysis. We find that in the case of LC-QuAD 2.0, the correct entity is found in the top-1 position of the candidate list based on text match 60% of the time, whereas in the case of SimpleQuestions-Wikidata, this number is significantly higher at 82%. This is so because the questions in SimpleQuestions-Wikidata contain the entity names in almost the exact form as their gold entity annotations, whereas in LC-QuAD 2.0, several entity labels are modified, misspelled or shortened by the human annotators. Hence, in the case of SimpleQuestions-Wikidata, label-only matching is in most cases sufficient, whereas in LC-QuAD 2.0, truncated KG embedding-based disambiguation holds greater importance.

Additionally, as mentioned in Sect. 2, STAG [29] and ElNeuQA-ConvS2S [10] are comparable generative KGQA systems. For STAG, no code, data or KG versions have been made public, while for ElNeuKGQA we were unable to run their code[10] as no instructions on how to run the code exists. For STAG on SimpleQuestions [4], on a test split of 2280 questions they report F1 61.0 while we report F1 78.1 on a larger test split of 9961 questions. Lastly, ElNeuQA-ConvS2S reports an F1 of 12.9 on WikidataQA while we report 17.8. WikidataQA is a 100 question test-subset created by the authors of ElNeuQA-ConvS2S. On LC-QuAD 2.0, they report F1 of 26.9 while we report 40.3.

6.1   Limitations

Although GETT-QA performs the best in Tables 3 and 4, we do not claim state-of-the-art results on the respective datasets. This is due to a variety of reasons: as mentioned in Subsect. 5, we could not procure the precise Wikidata KG version as the competing systems for LC-QuAD 2.0. In the case of LC-QuAD 2.0 and SimpleQuestions-Wikidata, evaluation was performed on a truncated subset of

---

[10] https://github.com/thesemanticwebhero/ElNeuKGQA.

the original test split of this dataset. As a result we can not claim that we have the best results on the entire dataset. Additionally, we could not find the code for, or run majority of systems we evaluated against, and hence resorted to using the results as reported by them.

7 Analysis

7.1 Error Analysis

In an attempt to find the common source of errors in LC-QuAD 2.0 we find that by far the largest cause of incorrect answers is the improper grounding of entities and relations to nodes in the KG. More than 95% of questions where the correct entities and relations were in the top-6 and top-3 candidates respectively, the right answer was eventually produced by the KG. Unfortunately, only in 41% of the questions, the correct entities and relations were found within the top-k candidates. This suggests that greater focus in the area of entity and relation linking will produce better results. One may also increase the size of k, at the cost of increased run time.

Less than 1% of the queries generated had incorrect truncated KG embedding length (e.g.: 11 instead of 10) however these were handled in code appropriately. Less than 1% of queries generated were improper SPARQL, where a critical keyword was missing rendering the query syntactically incorrect. This suggests that T5 learns how to generate valid SPARQL queries to a large extent. This is consistent with the findings of [2] where T5 crosses 90% accuracy when provided with grounded entity and relation IDs with their labels.

To explore the issue of lack of correct entities and relations in candidate lists, we observe that while 60% of questions contain the correct entity ID in the top-100 label-based search candidates, by the time we reduce this list to top-6, only 49% questions remain with the correct entity ID in the candidates list. On the other hand, for relation candidates, 45% of questions contain the correct relation IDs in the top-3 relation candidates.

When looking at the category of questions that return incorrect KG responses, irrespective of entity and relation grounding, we find that COUNT queries are the most common. This happens due to a quirk in SPARQL format. If a COUNT query is built around a family of triples that do not exist in the KG, the KG responds with count = 0, instead of producing a NULL value or an ERROR. This means that the very first query to be executed on the KG with the correct COUNT SPARQL syntax will return a valid response, even if it is count = 0 and we no longer explore subsequently ranked queries.

In the case of SimpleQuestions-Wikidata, all errors are either due to incorrect entity or relation linking. The model produced an accuracy of 70% for entity linking and 94% for relation linking.

7.2 Truncated KG Embedding Learning

We discover that T5 is able to produce a vector of floats while still in the text-to-text mode of decoding. For this functionality, no change of loss function or

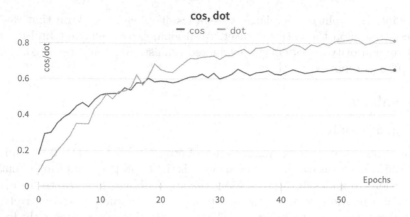

Fig. 2. Cosine and Dot Product based similarities of truncated KG embeddings

decoding scheme is made in our experiments. It effectively learns a simplified embedding space, but with certain limitations. To further explore this ability of T5, we performed some additional experiments on the 200 questions dev set of LC-QuAD 2.0 with T5-Small.

In Fig. 2, we compare how the model learns the embedding space with each epoch of training. The TransE embeddings have an angular component and a magnitude component. Since the dot operation was used to train the original embeddings, the magnitude of each embedding may be greater than 1. It appears in Fig. 2 that around step 20 the angular component of the embeddings has been learned by T5 to the best of its abilities, and it proceeds to learn the magnitude component (denoted by the orange line) further.

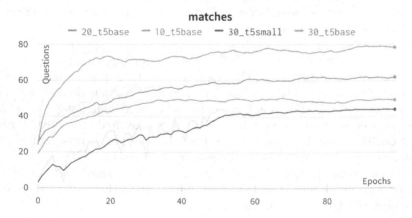

Fig. 3. Dev Set matches for varying truncated KG embedding lengths (Color figure online)

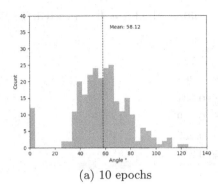
(a) 10 epochs

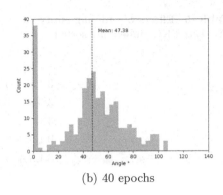
(b) 40 epochs

Fig. 4. Distribution of angular difference between gold and predicted truncated KG embeddings on LC-QuAD 2.0 dev set. The mean angular difference can be seen reducing as the epochs progress, suggesting that the model is learning the embedding space.

In Fig. 3 we chart the LC-QuAD 2.0 dev set performance of T5-Small and T5-Base in varying truncated KG embedding lengths. For T5-Small (pink line) we set the truncated KG embedding length at 30, so this should only directly be compared against T5-Base with truncated KG embedding length 30 (green line). In the matches metric, which only looks at the keywords and labels produced in the skeleton SPARQL query (truncated KG embeddings have been removed from the generated query), the two reach similar performance. This suggests that a larger number of parameters helps learn the embedding space better, but for the textual component the extra number of parameters of T5-Base remain unused.

With a truncated KG embedding length of 10 (yellow line), we see the best label match accuracy and hence we persist with this family of models for reporting results in Table 3.

In Fig. 4, we plot the distribution of the angular difference between the gold and predicted truncated embeddings on the LC-QuAD 2.0 dev set. The model seems to learn the embedding space in two distinctly different manners: firstly, for several entities it is able to print the exact embedding, with an angular difference of 0°. Secondly, for the entities which it is unable to learn the embedding of exactly, it produces a more familiar distribution, where the mean shifts every few epochs, reducing the angular difference. This suggests that the model is learning the embedding space effectively.

Table 5. Effects of ordering entity candidates differently. LS = Label sorted, TS = Truncated KG embedding sorted

	F1
3 LS + 3 TS	0.365
3 TS + 3 LS	0.331
3 LS + 0 TS	0.289
0 LS + 3 TS	0.236
6 LS + 0 TS	0.319
0 LS + 6 TS	0.256

7.3   Candidate Ordering

As mentioned in Subsect. 3.6, our results reported in Table 3 come from a configuration of our system where the entity candidates are layered in two parts: the first three candidates are sorted based on label match, while the bottom three candidates are sorted based on the truncated KG embedding dot product similarity. It is observed in Table 5 that the ordering of these two categories affects the eventual accuracy strongly. We take 200 questions at random from the LC-QuAD 2.0 test set and perform experiments to ascertain how the ordering of candidates affects accuracy. In the first row of the table, three entity candidates based on label sorting are followed by three candidates of truncated KG embedding sorting, while the next row of the table shows the result when we keep truncated KG embedding-sorted candidates above label-sorted candidates. The results show that keeping truncated KG embedding-sorted candidates at the top reduces accuracy, and hence, label-based matching for entities remains a stronger mode of fetching correct candidates. This is no surprise, since not all labels have multiple entity candidates requiring disambiguation. Kindly note that the accuracy drops because an earlier query formed due to candidate combinations (as explained in Subsect. 3.8) returns a non-empty result from the KG and this response turns out to be incorrect.

In the next two rows, we see how excluding either label-sorted candidates, or truncated KG embedding-sorted candidates entirely affects accuracy. Once more we see that label-sorted candidates still perform better when used in isolation. However, the crux of the table is the first row, i.e., when both the categories are appropriately sequenced and used in tandem, the accuracy is best.

In the bottom two rows, we see the effect of changing the number of candidates. It is no surprise that increasing k from 3 to 6 increases accuracy since more correct entities are included in the list. However, some systems also perform worse in such settings as the noise may increase adding to the disambiguation load. In our system, this does not seem to be the case.

Increasing the value of k further imposes a large cost on the run time of the system affecting the user experience adversely. Since the candidate combination step has exponential complexity, which depends on the number of entities and relations in a query, we need to keep the number of candidates in check. Too many candidates will produce too many SPARQL queries and the user must wait for all of them to be executed on the KG till one of them responds validly.

In our choice of setting k=6 for entities and k=3 for relations, we observe that on the test set of LC-QuAD 2.0, our system has an average response time of 1.2 s per question, which from a user experience perspective seems like an acceptable response time.

8 Hyperparameters and Hardware

For the evaluation of LC-QuAD 2.0 in Table 3, we fine-tune our models for 50 epochs with a learning rate of 1e-04 with the Adam optimizer [20]. For SimpleQuestions in Table 4 we fine-tune for 25 epochs, roughly half of LC-QuAD 2.0, since the train set is roughly twice as large as LC-QuAD 2.0. We use a batch size of 8. During this phase we had access to NVIDIA GeForce RTX 2080 Ti/1080 Ti graphics cards with approximately 11 GB of video memory. We do not fix a seed during training, and train and infer three times. We report mean and standard deviation for the three runs in the respective tables.

For the analysis in Sect. 7, we fine-tune our models for 100 epochs with a learning rate of 1e-05 with the Adam Optimizer [20] and we use a batch size of 20. During this phase we had access to larger GPUs, namely NVIDIA RTX A6000 with 48 GB of memory and RTX A5000 with 24 GB memory.

9 Conclusion and Future Work

In this work, we presented a novel KGQA pipeline called GETT-QA. We use no external entity or relation linking tool, and still achieve strong results on LC-QuAD 2.0 and SimpleQuestions-Wikidata datasets. Additionally, we discover the ability of T5 to learn KG embeddings. We demonstrate that in certain situations this ability helps in better question answering performance.

In future work, we will explore the ability of T5 in generating similar truncated KG embedding based queries with modified loss functions and a customised architecture towards the penultimate layers of the models, so that embeddings can be generated with more standard loss functions meant specifically for learning embeddings. Additionally, suitable identifiers other than embeddings can also be explored, for example, text description based identifiers.

Acknowledgement. This research was supported by grants from NVIDIA and utilized NVIDIA 2 x RTX A5000 24 GB. Furthermore, we acknowledge the financial support from the Federal Ministry for Economic Affairs and Energy of Germany in the project CoyPu (project number 01MK21007[G]) and the German Research Foundation in the project NFDI4DS (project number 460234259). This research is additionally funded by the "Idea and Venture Fund" research grant by Universität Hamburg, which is part of the Excellence Strategy of the Federal and State Governments.

References

1. Abujabal, A., Roy, R.S., Yahya, M., Weikum, G.: Never-ending learning for open-domain question answering over knowledge bases. In: Proceedings of the 2018 World Wide Web Conference on World Wide Web, WWW 2018, Lyon, France, pp. 1053–1062. ACM (2018). https://doi.org/10.1145/3178876.3186004
2. Banerjee, D., Nair, P., Kaur, J.N., Usbeck, R., Biemann, C.: Modern baselines for SPARQL semantic parsing. In: SIGIR 2022: The 45th International ACM SIGIR Conference on Research and Development in Information Retrieval, Madrid. ACM (2022). https://arxiv.org/abs/2204.12793
3. Bhutani, N., Zheng, X., Jagadish, H.V.: Learning to answer complex questions over knowledge bases with query composition. In: Proceedings of the 28th ACM International Conference on Information and Knowledge Management, CIKM 2019, Beijing, China, pp. 739–748. ACM (2019). https://doi.org/10.1145/3357384.3358033
4. Bordes, A., Usunier, N., Chopra, S., Weston, J.: Large-scale simple question answering with memory networks. CoRR abs/1506.02075 (2015). https://dblp.uni-trier.de/db/journals/corr/corr1506.html#BordesUCW15
5. Bordes, A., Usunier, N., García-Durán, A., Weston, J., Yakhnenko, O.: Translating embeddings for modeling multi-relational data. In: Advances in Neural Information Processing Systems 26: 27th Annual Conference on Neural Information Processing Systems 2013, Lake Tahoe, Nevada, United States, pp. 2787–2795 (2013). https://proceedings.neurips.cc/paper/2013/hash/1cecc7a77928ca8133fa24680a88d2f9-Abstract.html
6. Chekalina, V., Razzhigaev, A., Sayapin, A., Frolov, E., Panchenko, A.: MEKER: memory efficient knowledge embedding representation for link prediction and question answering. In: Proceedings of the 60th Annual Meeting of the Association for Computational Linguistics: Student Research Workshop, Dublin, Ireland, pp. 355–365. Association for Computational Linguistics (2022). https://aclanthology.org/2022.acl-srw.27
7. Christmann, P., Roy, R.S., Abujabal, A., Singh, J., Weikum, G.: Look before you hop: conversational question answering over knowledge graphs using judicious context expansion. In: Proceedings of the 28th ACM International Conference on Information and Knowledge Management, CIKM 2019, Beijing, China, pp. 729–738. ACM (2019). https://doi.org/10.1145/3357384.3358016
8. Diefenbach, D., Both, A., Singh, K.D., Maret, P.: Towards a question answering system over the semantic web. Semant. Web Interoperability Usability Applicability 11(3), 421–439 (2020). https://hal.archives-ouvertes.fr/hal-02013956
9. Diefenbach, D., Tanon, T.P., Singh, K.D., Maret, P.: Question answering benchmarks for Wikidata. In: Proceedings of the ISWC 2017 Posters & Demonstrations and Industry Tracks Co-Located with 16th International Semantic Web Conference (ISWC 2017), Vienna, Austria (2017). https://ceur-ws.org/Vol-1963/paper555.pdf
10. Diomedi, D., Hogan, A.: Question answering over knowledge graphs with neural machine translation and entity linking. arXiv preprint abs/2107.02865 (2021). https://arxiv.org/abs/2107.02865
11. Dubey, M., Banerjee, D., Abdelkawi, A., Lehmann, J.: LC-QuAD 2.0: a large dataset for complex question answering over Wikidata and DBpedia. In: Ghidini, C., et al. (eds.) ISWC 2019. LNCS, vol. 11779, pp. 69–78. Springer, Cham (2019). https://doi.org/10.1007/978-3-030-30796-7_5
12. Faldu, K., Sheth, A.P., Kikani, P., Akabari, H.: KI-BERT: infusing knowledge context for better language and domain understanding. arXiv preprint abs/2104.08145 (2021). https://arxiv.org/abs/2104.08145

13. Galkin, M., Trivedi, P., Maheshwari, G., Usbeck, R., Lehmann, J.: Message passing for hyper-relational knowledge graphs. In: Proceedings of the 2020 Conference on Empirical Methods in Natural Language Processing (EMNLP), pp. 7346–7359. Association for Computational Linguistics (2020). https://aclanthology.org/2020.emnlp-main.596

14. He, B., et al.: BERT-MK: integrating graph contextualized knowledge into pre-trained language models. In: Findings of the Association for Computational Linguistics: EMNLP 2020, pp. 2281–2290. Association for Computational Linguistics (2020). https://aclanthology.org/2020.findings-emnlp.207

15. Hitchcock, F.L.: The expression of a tensor or a polyadic as a sum of products. J. Math. Phys. **6**(1–4), 164–189 (1927). https://onlinelibrary.wiley.com/doi/abs/10.1002/sapm192761164

16. Huang, X., Zhang, J., Li, D., Li, P.: Knowledge graph embedding based question answering. In: Proceedings of the Twelfth ACM International Conference on Web Search and Data Mining, WSDM 2019, Melbourne, VIC, Australia, pp. 105–113. ACM (2019). https://doi.org/10.1145/3289600.3290956

17. Huang, X., Zhang, J., Li, D., Li, P.: Knowledge graph embedding based question answering. In: Proceedings of the Twelfth ACM International Conference on Web Search and Data Mining, WSDM 2019, pp. 105–113. Association for Computing Machinery, New York (2019). https://doi.org/10.1145/3289600.3290956

18. Jia, Z., Pramanik, S., Saha Roy, R., Weikum, G.: Complex temporal question answering on knowledge graphs. In: Proceedings of the 30th ACM International Conference on Information and Knowledge Management, CIKM 2021, pp. 792–802. Association for Computing Machinery, New York (2021). https://doi.org/10.1145/3459637.3482416

19. Kacupaj, E., Plepi, J., Singh, K., Thakkar, H., Lehmann, J., Maleshkova, M.: Conversational question answering over knowledge graphs with transformer and graph attention networks. In: Proceedings of the 16th Conference of the European Chapter of the Association for Computational Linguistics: Main Volume, pp. 850–862. Association for Computational Linguistics (2021). https://www.aclweb.org/anthology/2021.eacl-main.72

20. Kingma, D.P., Ba, J.: Adam: a method for stochastic optimization. In: 3rd International Conference on Learning Representations, ICLR 2015, San Diego, CA, USA, Conference Track Proceedings (2015). https://arxiv.org/abs/1412.6980

21. Lan, Y., He, G., Jiang, J., Jiang, J., Zhao, W.X., Wen, J.R.: A survey on complex knowledge base question answering: methods, challenges and solutions. In: Proceedings of the Thirtieth International Joint Conference on Artificial Intelligence, IJCAI-2021, pp. 4483–4491. International Joint Conferences on Artificial Intelligence Organization (2021). https://doi.org/10.24963/ijcai.2021/611. Survey track

22. Lerer, A., et al.: PyTorch-BigGraph: a large scale graph embedding system. In: Proceedings of Machine Learning and Systems 2019, MLSys 2019, Stanford, CA, USA. mlsys.org (2019). https://proceedings.mlsys.org/book/282.pdf

23. Liu, W., et al.: K-BERT: enabling language representation with knowledge graph. In: Proceedings of the AAAI Conference on Artificial Intelligence, vol. 34, no. 03, pp. 2901–2908 (2020)

24. Neelam, S., et al.: SYGMA: a system for generalizable and modular question answering over knowledge bases. In: Findings of the Association for Computational Linguistics: EMNLP 2022, Abu Dhabi, United Arab Emirates, pp. 3866–3879. Association for Computational Linguistics, December 2022. https://aclanthology.org/2022.findings-emnlp.284

25. Oguz, B., et al.: UniK-QA: unified representations of structured and unstructured knowledge for open-domain question answering (2020). https://arxiv.org/abs/2012.14610

26. Plepi, J., Kacupaj, E., Singh, K., Thakkar, H., Lehmann, J.: Context transformer with stacked pointer networks for conversational question answering over knowledge graphs. In: Verborgh, R., et al. (eds.) ESWC 2021. LNCS, vol. 12731, pp. 356–371. Springer, Cham (2021). https://doi.org/10.1007/978-3-030-77385-4_21

27. Pramanik, S., Alabi, J., Roy, R.S., Weikum, G.: UNIQORN: unified question answering over RDF knowledge graphs and natural language text. arXiv preprint abs/2108.08614 (2021). https://arxiv.org/abs/2108.08614

28. Raffel, C., et al.: Exploring the limits of transfer learning with a unified text-to-text transformer. J. Mach. Learn. Res. 21(1), 5485–5551 (2020)

29. Ravishankar, S., et al.: A two-stage approach towards generalization in knowledge base question answering. CoRR abs/2111.05825 (2021). https://arxiv.org/abs/2111.05825

30. Robertson, S.E., Walker, S.: Some simple effective approximations to the 2-Poisson model for probabilistic weighted retrieval. In: Annual International ACM SIGIR Conference on Research and Development in Information Retrieval (1994)

31. Rony, M.R.A.H., Kumar, U., Teucher, R., Kovriguina, L., Lehmann, J.: SGPT: a generative approach for SPARQL query generation from natural language questions. IEEE Access 10, 70712–70723 (2022). https://doi.org/10.1109/ACCESS.2022.3188714

32. Saha, A., Pahuja, V., Khapra, M.M., Sankaranarayanan, K., Chandar, S.: Complex sequential question answering: towards learning to converse over linked question answer pairs with a knowledge graph. In: AAAI 2018/IAAI 2018/EAAI 2018. AAAI Press (2018)

33. Saxena, A., Tripathi, A., Talukdar, P.: Improving multi-hop question answering over knowledge graphs using knowledge base embeddings. In: Proceedings of the 58th Annual Meeting of the Association for Computational Linguistics, pp. 4498–4507. Association for Computational Linguistics (2020). https://aclanthology.org/2020.acl-main.412

34. Schlichtkrull, M., Kipf, T.N., Bloem, P., van den Berg, R., Titov, I., Welling, M.: Modeling relational data with graph convolutional networks. In: Gangemi, A., et al. (eds.) ESWC 2018. LNCS, vol. 10843, pp. 593–607. Springer, Cham (2018). https://doi.org/10.1007/978-3-319-93417-4_38

35. Shen, T., et al.: Multi-task learning for conversational question answering over a large-scale knowledge base. In: Proceedings of the 2019 Conference on Empirical Methods in Natural Language Processing and the 9th International Joint Conference on Natural Language Processing (EMNLP-IJCNLP), Hong Kong, China, pp. 2442–2451. Association for Computational Linguistics (2019). https://aclanthology.org/D19-1248

36. Sun, H., Bedrax-Weiss, T., Cohen, W.: PullNet: open domain question answering with iterative retrieval on knowledge bases and text. In: Proceedings of the 2019 Conference on Empirical Methods in Natural Language Processing and the 9th International Joint Conference on Natural Language Processing (EMNLP-IJCNLP), Hong Kong, China, pp. 2380–2390. Association for Computational Linguistics (2019). https://aclanthology.org/D19-1242

37. Sun, H., Dhingra, B., Zaheer, M., Mazaitis, K., Salakhutdinov, R., Cohen, W.: Open domain question answering using early fusion of knowledge bases and text. In: Proceedings of the 2018 Conference on Empirical Methods in Natural Language

Processing, Brussels, Belgium, pp. 4231–4242. Association for Computational Linguistics (2018). https://aclanthology.org/D18-1455

38. Sun, T., et al.: CoLAKE: contextualized language and knowledge embedding. In: Proceedings of the 28th International Conference on Computational Linguistics, Barcelona, Spain, pp. 3660–3670. International Committee on Computational Linguistics (2020). https://aclanthology.org/2020.coling-main.327

39. Pellissier Tanon, T., de Assunção, M.D., Caron, E., Suchanek, F.M.: Demoing platypus – a multilingual question answering platform for Wikidata. In: Gangemi, A., et al. (eds.) ESWC 2018. LNCS, vol. 11155, pp. 111–116. Springer, Cham (2018). https://doi.org/10.1007/978-3-319-98192-5_21

40. Vakulenko, S., Garcia, J.D.F., Polleres, A., de Rijke, M., Cochez, M.: Message passing for complex question answering over knowledge graphs. In: Proceedings of the 28th ACM International Conference on Information and Knowledge Management, CIKM 2019, Beijing, China, pp. 1431–1440. ACM (2019). https://doi.org/10.1145/3357384.3358026

41. Vaswani, A., et al.: Attention is all you need. In: Advances in Neural Information Processing Systems 30: Annual Conference on Neural Information Processing Systems 2017, Long Beach, CA, USA, pp. 5998–6008 (2017). https://proceedings.neurips.cc/paper/2017/hash/3f5ee243547dee91fbd053c1c4a845aa-Abstract.html

42. Veličković, P., Cucurull, G., Casanova, A., Romero, A., Lió, P., Bengio, Y.: Graph attention networks. In: 6th International Conference on Learning Representations (2017)

43. Wang, X., et al.: KEPLER: a unified model for knowledge embedding and pre-trained language representation. Trans. Assoc. Comput. Linguist. 9, 176–194 (2021). https://aclanthology.org/2021.tacl-1.11

44. Yani, M., Krisnadhi, A.A.: Challenges, techniques, and trends of simple knowledge graph question answering: a survey. Information 12(7) (2021). https://www.mdpi.com/2078-2489/12/7/271

45. Yu, D., Zhu, C., Yang, Y., Zeng, M.: JAKET: joint pre-training of knowledge graph and language understanding. In: AAAI 2022 (2022). https://www.microsoft.com/en-us/research/publication/jaket-joint-pre-training-of-knowledge-graph-and-language-understanding/

Repairing $\mathcal{EL}$ Ontologies Using Weakening and Completing

Ying Li[1,2] and Patrick Lambrix[1,2,3(✉)]

[1] Linköping University, Linköping, Sweden
patrick.lambrix@liu.se
[2] The Swedish e-Science Research Centre, Linköping, Sweden
[3] University of Gävle, Gävle, Sweden

Abstract. The quality of ontologies in terms of their correctness and completeness is crucial for developing high-quality ontology-based applications. Traditional debugging techniques repair ontologies by removing unwanted axioms, but may thereby remove consequences that are correct in the domain of the ontology. In this paper we propose an interactive approach to mitigate this for $\mathcal{EL}$ ontologies by axiom weakening and completing. We present the first approach for repairing that takes into account removing, weakening and completing. We show different combination strategies, discuss the influence on the final ontologies and show experimental results. We show that previous work has only considered special cases and that there is a trade-off, and how to deal with it, involving the amount of validation work for a domain expert and the quality of the ontology in terms of correctness and completeness. We also present new algorithms for weakening and completing.

1 Introduction

Debugging ontologies aims to remove unwanted knowledge in the ontology. This can be knowledge that leads to logical problems such as inconsistency or incoherence (semantic defects) or statements that are not correct in the domain of the ontology (modeling defects) (e.g., [16]). The workflow consists of several steps including the detection and localization of the defects and the repairing. In this paper we assume we have detected and localized the defects, e.g., using traditional debugging techniques as in, e.g., [1,12–16,20,22,23,26–30,32], and we now need to repair the ontology. In the classical approaches for debugging the end result is a set of axioms to remove from the ontology that is obtained after detection and localization, and the repairing consists solely of removing the suggested axioms. However, first, these approaches are usually purely logic-based and therefore may remove correct axioms (e.g., [25]). Therefore, it is argued that a domain expert should validate the results of such systems. Furthermore, removing an axiom may remove more knowledge than necessary. Correct knowledge that is derivable with the help of the wrong axioms may not be derivable

---

Supplementary Information The online version contains supplementary material available at https://doi.org/10.1007/978-3-031-33455-9_18.

in the new ontology. In this paper we mitigate these effects of removing wrong axioms by, in addition to removing those axioms, also adding correct knowledge. Two approaches could be used. A first approach is to replace a wrong axiom with a weakened version of the axiom (e.g., [5,9,17,33]). Another approach is to complete[1] an ontology (e.g., [35]) which adds previously unknown correct axioms that allow to derive existing axioms, and that could be used on the results of weakening. These approaches have, however, not been studied together.

In this paper we focus on $\mathcal{EL}$ ontologies. $\mathcal{EL}$ is a description logic for which subsumption checking remains tractable and that is used (as is or with small extensions) by well-known ontologies such as SNOMED or Gene Ontology [2]. Further, we assume that we are given a set of wrong axioms W that we want to remove from the ontology and that when removing these axioms, they cannot be derived from the ontology anymore.

Our main contribution (i) (Sect. 5) is a framework for weakening and completing ontologies. It is the first work that combines removing with weakening and completing. For this framework we give a formal definition of the repairing problem, and introduce different operations for combining removing, weakening and completing approaches, and their relationships. Using the relationships between these operations, we show that different solutions to the repairing problem exist even using the same basic weakening and completing algorithms (an insight that no other work has discussed), that there is a trade-off involving completeness and correctness of the resulting ontologies with more validation effort for more complete ontologies (another insight that no other work has discussed), and we show how basic algorithms can be combined according to a preference for the level of completeness. Earlier work on weakening and earlier work on completing can be represented using our operators and their particular weakening and completing algorithms. Using the framework we can show that earlier work on weakening used one particular combination strategy (although with different weakening algorithms by different authors). Similarly, work on completing used one particular combination strategy. Our work shows thus that there are different variants of the earlier work by combining their basic algorithms in different ways, with trade-offs involving completeness, correctness and validation work.

In addition to the formal framework there are also other contributions. (ii) We show the trade-offs for 13 different combination strategies for 6 ontologies in experiments (Sect. 6). Further, in Sect. 4 (iii) we develop a new algorithm for weakening and a new algorithm for completing. For efficiency reasons, weakening algorithms restrict the search space, and we propose a new heuristic for this restriction. Our algorithm for completing is an extension of the approach in [35]. Finally, (iv) we provide two implemented systems, a Protégé plugin and a stand-alone system (Sect. 8).

---

[1] This term has been used with different meanings. In this paper we refer to completing as the dual task of weakening. The term has been used with other meanings in, e.g., [4,31]. Related terms are, e.g., ontology extension [21], ontology learning [6], ontology enrichment [11], and ontology revision [24].

2 Preliminaries

In this paper we assume that ontologies are represented using a description logic TBox. Description logics [3] are knowledge representation languages where concept descriptions are constructed inductively from a set N_C of atomic concepts and a set N_R of atomic roles and (possibly) a set N_I of individual names. Different description logics allow for different constructors for defining complex concepts and roles. An interpretation $\mathcal{I}$ consists of a non-empty set $\Delta^{\mathcal{I}}$ and an interpretation function $\cdot^{\mathcal{I}}$ which assigns to each atomic concept $P \in N_C$ a subset $P^{\mathcal{I}} \subseteq \Delta^{\mathcal{I}}$, to each atomic role $r \in N_R$ a relation $r^{\mathcal{I}} \subseteq \Delta^{\mathcal{I}} \times \Delta^{\mathcal{I}}$, and to each individual name[2] $i \in N_I$ an element $i^{\mathcal{I}} \in \Delta^{\mathcal{I}}$. The interpretation function is straightforwardly extended to complex concepts. A TBox is a finite set of axioms which in $\mathcal{EL}$ are *general concept inclusions* (GCIs). The syntax and semantics for $\mathcal{EL}$ are shown in Table 1.

Table 1. $\mathcal{EL}$ syntax and semantics. (Note that P and Q are arbitrary concepts. In the remainder we often use P and Q for atomic concepts.)

Name	Syntax	Semantics
top	$\top$	$\Delta^{\mathcal{I}}$
conjunction	$P \sqcap Q$	$P^{\mathcal{I}} \cap Q^{\mathcal{I}}$
existential restriction	$\exists r.P$	$\{x \in \Delta^{\mathcal{I}} \mid \exists y \in \Delta^{\mathcal{I}} : (x,y) \in r^{\mathcal{I}} \wedge y \in P^{\mathcal{I}}\}$
GCI	$P \sqsubseteq Q$	$P^{\mathcal{I}} \subseteq Q^{\mathcal{I}}$

An interpretation $\mathcal{I}$ is a *model* of a TBox $\mathcal{T}$ if for each GCI in $\mathcal{T}$, the semantic conditions are satisfied.[3] One of the main reasoning tasks for description logics is subsumption checking in which the problem is to decide for a TBox $\mathcal{T}$ and concepts P and Q whether $\mathcal{T} \models P \sqsubseteq Q$, i.e., whether $P^{\mathcal{I}} \subseteq Q^{\mathcal{I}}$ for every model of TBox $\mathcal{T}$. In this paper we update the TBox during the repairing and we always use subsumption with respect to the current TBox.

3 Problem Formulation

We can now formally define the repairing problem that we want to solve (Definition 1). We are given a set of wrong axioms W that we want to remove[4] from the ontology and that when they are removed, they cannot be derived from the

---

[2] As we do not deal with individuals in this paper, we do not use individuals in the later sections.

[3] We do not take up consistency of TBoxes, i.e., whether a model exists or not, in this paper as every $\mathcal{EL}$ TBox is consistent.

[4] We note that in this paper we deal with removing and not the full debugging problem, i.e., we assume that the axioms to be removed are already found. Removing can be seen as a simple kind of debugging, or as the second step of the debugging process.

TBox representing the ontology anymore. Further, to guarantee a high level of quality of the ontology (i.e., so that no correct information is removed or no incorrect information is added), domain expert validation is a necessity (e.g., [25]). Therefore, we assume an oracle (representing a domain expert) that, when given an axiom, can answer whether this axiom is correct or wrong in the domain of interest of the ontology. We have not required specific properties regarding the performance of the oracle. For instance, we did not require that an oracle always answers correctly or that the oracle gives consistent answers. As a first step we have chosen this way as it reflects reality. According to our long experience working with domain experts in ontology engineering, domain experts make mistakes. However, this does not necessarily mean that domain expert validation is not useful. In experiments in ontology alignment, it was shown that oracles making up to 30% mistakes were still beneficial (e.g., [8]). Further, requiring consistent answers seems to be a tough requirement for domain experts. This would require the ability to reason with long proof chains, while humans usually do well for chains of limited length. It is also not clear how to check that a particular domain expert would fulfil the required properties. Therefore, in this work we do not require such properties, but provide user support in our systems by providing warnings when incompatible validations are made and then allow the domain expert to revise the validations. We do acknowledge, however, that requiring such properties and thereby classifying types of domain experts, may allow us to guarantee certain properties regarding correctness and completeness and allow us to reduce the search space of possible repairs.

A repair for the ontology given the TBox $\mathcal{T}$, oracle Or, and a set of wrong axioms W, is a set of correct axioms that when added to the TBox where the axioms in W are removed will not allow deriving the axioms in W.

Definition 1. (Repair) Let $\mathcal{T}$ be a TBox. Let Or be an oracle that given a TBox axiom returns true or false. Let W be a finite set of TBox axioms in $\mathcal{T}$ such that $\forall \psi \in W$: $Or(\psi) = $ false. Then, a repair for Debug-Problem $\mathrm{DP}(\mathcal{T}, Or, W)$ is a finite set of TBox axioms A such that
(i) $\forall \psi \in A$: $Or(\psi) = $ true;
(ii) $\forall \psi \in W$: $(\mathcal{T} \cup A) \setminus W \not\models \psi$.

Our aim is to find repairs that remove as much wrong knowledge and add as much correct knowledge to our ontology as possible. Therefore, we introduce the preference relations *less incorrect* and *more complete* between ontologies (Definition 2) that formalize these intuitions, respectively.

Definition 2. (less incorrect/more complete - ontologies) Let $\mathcal{O}_1$ and $\mathcal{O}_2$ be two ontologies represented by TBoxes $\mathcal{T}_1$ and $\mathcal{T}_2$ respectively.
Then, $\mathcal{O}_1$ is *less incorrect* than $\mathcal{O}_2$ ($\mathcal{O}_2$ is *more incorrect* than $\mathcal{O}_1$) iff $(\forall \psi : (\mathcal{T}_1 \models \psi \wedge Or(\psi) = false) \rightarrow \mathcal{T}_2 \models \psi) \wedge (\exists \psi : Or(\psi) = false \wedge \mathcal{T}_1 \not\models \psi \wedge \mathcal{T}_2 \models \psi)$.
$\mathcal{O}_1$ and $\mathcal{O}_2$ are *equally incorrect* iff $\forall \psi : Or(\psi) = false \rightarrow (\mathcal{T}_1 \models \psi \leftrightarrow \mathcal{T}_2 \models \psi)$
Further, $\mathcal{O}_1$ is *more complete* than $\mathcal{O}_2$ (or $\mathcal{O}_2$ is *less complete* than $\mathcal{O}_1$) iff $(\forall \psi : (\mathcal{T}_2 \models \psi \wedge Or(\psi) = true) \rightarrow \mathcal{T}_1 \models \psi)) \wedge (\exists \psi : Or(\psi) = true \wedge \mathcal{T}_1 \models \psi \wedge \mathcal{T}_2 \not\models \psi)$.
$\mathcal{O}_1$ and $\mathcal{O}_2$ are *equally complete* iff $\forall \psi : Or(\psi) = true \rightarrow (\mathcal{T}_1 \models \psi \leftrightarrow \mathcal{T}_2 \models \psi)$

4 Weakening and Completing Algorithms

We now define algorithms for weakening and completing that we use in our experiments in Sect. 6. Completing is used on the results of weakening.

Basics. We assume that ontologies are represented by *normalized* $\mathcal{EL}$ TBoxes. A normalized $\mathcal{EL}$ TBox $\mathcal{T}$ contains only axioms of the forms $P \sqsubseteq Q$, $P \sqcap Q \sqsubseteq R$, $\exists r.P \sqsubseteq Q$ and $P \sqsubseteq \exists r.Q$ where P, Q, $R \in N_C$ and $r \in N_R$. Every $\mathcal{EL}$ TBox can in linear time be transformed into a normalized TBox that is a conservative extension, i.e., every model of the normalized TBox is also a model of the original TBox and every model of the original TBox can be extended to a model of the normalized TBox [2]. Further, we define the *simple complex concept set for a TBox* $\mathcal{T}$, which contains all atomic concepts in the ontology as well as the concepts that can be constructed by using one constructor ($\sqcap$ or $\exists$) and only atomic concepts and roles in the ontology (Definition 3). Note that $\top$ is not in SCC($\mathcal{T}$). Further, if the number of concepts in $N_C^{\mathcal{T}}$ is n and the number of roles in $N_R^{\mathcal{T}}$ is t, then the number of concepts in SCC($\mathcal{T}$) is $(n^2 + n)/2 + tn$.

Definition 3. For a normalized $\mathcal{EL}$ TBox $\mathcal{T}$ with $N_C^{\mathcal{T}}$ the set of atomic concepts occurring in $\mathcal{T}$ and $N_R^{\mathcal{T}}$ the set of atomic roles occurring in $\mathcal{T}$, we define the *simple complex concept set for* $\mathcal{T}$, denoted by SCC($\mathcal{T}$), as the set containing all the concepts of the forms P, $P \sqcap Q$, and $\exists r.P$ where $P, Q \in N_C^{\mathcal{T}}$ and $r \in N_R^{\mathcal{T}}$.

In our algorithms we use two basic operations which remove and add axioms to a TBox. The result of *Remove-axioms*($\mathcal{T}, D$) for a TBox $\mathcal{T}$ and a set of axioms D is the TBox $\mathcal{T} \setminus D$. If D contains only wrong axioms (such as W), then the ontology represented by Remove-axioms($\mathcal{T}, D$) is less (if at least one of the removed axioms cannot be derived anymore) or equally incorrect (if all removed axioms can still be derived), as well as less (if some correct axioms cannot be derived anymore by removing the wrong ones) or equally complete (if all correct axioms can still be derived), than the ontology represented by $\mathcal{T}$. The result of *Add-axioms*($\mathcal{T}, A$) for a TBox $\mathcal{T}$ and a set of axioms A is the TBox $\mathcal{T} \cup A$. If A contains only correct axioms then the ontology represented by Add-axioms($\mathcal{T}$, A) is more (if some added axiom was not derivable from the ontology) or equally complete (if all added axioms were derivable from the ontology), as well as more (if some wrong axioms can now be derived by adding the new ones) or equally incorrect (if no new wrong axioms can now be derived by adding the new ones), than the ontology represented by $\mathcal{T}$.

We also need to compute sub-concepts and super-concepts of concepts. However, to reduce the infinite search space of possible axioms to add during weakening and completing, we limit the use of nesting operators while computing sub- and super-concepts.[5] This we do by only considering sub- and super-concepts in the SCC of a TBox (Definition 4). As subsumption checking in $\mathcal{EL}$ is tractable, finding these sub- and super-concepts is tractable.

---

[5] Weaker limitations are possible, but the weaker the restriction, the larger the solution search space and the higher the probability of a less usable practical system.

Definition 4. (super- and sub-concepts in SCC)

$sup(P,\mathcal{T}) \leftarrow \{ sp \mid \mathcal{T} \models P \sqsubseteq sp \wedge sp \in \mathrm{SCC}(\mathcal{T})\}$

$sub(P,\mathcal{T}) \leftarrow \{ sb \mid \mathcal{T} \models sb \sqsubseteq P \wedge sb \in \mathrm{SCC}(\mathcal{T})\}$

Finally, as we work on normalized $\mathcal{EL}$ TBoxes, we need to make sure that when adding axioms, these are of one of the forms $P \sqsubseteq Q$, $P \sqcap Q \sqsubseteq R$, $\exists r.P \sqsubseteq Q$ and $P \sqsubseteq \exists r.Q$ where P, Q, $R \in N_C^{\mathcal{T}}$ and $r \in N_R^{\mathcal{T}}$. We note that new atomic concepts, not originally in the ontology, may be introduced.

Algorithm 1. Weakened axiom set

Input: TBox $\mathcal{T}$, Oracle Or, unwanted axiom $\alpha \sqsubseteq \beta$

Output: Weakened axiom set of $\alpha \sqsubseteq \beta$

1: $wt_{\alpha \sqsubseteq \beta} \leftarrow \{sb \sqsubseteq sp \mid sb \in sub(\alpha,\mathcal{T}) \wedge sp \in sup(\beta,\mathcal{T}) \wedge \mathrm{Or}(sb \sqsubseteq sp) = \mathrm{True} \wedge \neg \exists$
    $sb' \in sub(\alpha,\mathcal{T}), sp' \in sup(\beta,\mathcal{T})\colon (\mathrm{Or}(sb' \sqsubseteq sp') = \mathrm{True} \wedge ((sb \sqsubseteq sb' \wedge sp' \sqsubset sp) \vee$
    $(sb \sqsubset sb' \wedge sp' \sqsubseteq sp)))\}$

2: $w_{\alpha \sqsubseteq \beta} \leftarrow \emptyset$

3: **for each** $sb \sqsubseteq sp \in wt_{\alpha \sqsubseteq \beta}$ **do**

4: $\quad w_{\alpha \sqsubseteq \beta} \leftarrow w_{\alpha \sqsubseteq \beta} \cup \mathrm{Normalize}(sb \sqsubseteq sp)$

5: **end for**

6: **return** $w_{\alpha \sqsubseteq \beta}$

Algorithm 2. Completed axiom set

Input: TBox $\mathcal{T}$, Oracle Or, a wanted axiom $\alpha \sqsubseteq \beta$

Output: Completed axiom set of $\alpha \sqsubseteq \beta$

1: $ct_{\alpha \sqsubseteq \beta} \leftarrow \{sp \sqsubseteq sb \mid sp \in sup(\alpha,\mathcal{T}) \wedge sb \in sub(\beta,\mathcal{T}) \wedge \mathrm{Or}(sp \sqsubseteq sb) = \mathrm{True} \wedge \neg \exists$
    $sp' \in sup(\alpha), sb' \in sub(\beta)\colon (\mathrm{Or}(sp' \sqsubseteq sb') = \mathrm{True} \wedge (sp \sqsubseteq sp' \wedge sb' \sqsubset sb) \vee (sp \sqsubset$
    $sp' \wedge sb' \sqsubseteq sb)\}$

2: $c_{\alpha \sqsubseteq \beta} \leftarrow \emptyset$

3: **for each** $sb \sqsubseteq sp \in ct_{\alpha \sqsubseteq \beta}$ **do**

4: $\quad c_{\alpha \sqsubseteq \beta} \leftarrow c_{\alpha \sqsubseteq \beta} \cup \mathrm{Normalize}(sb \sqsubseteq sp)$

5: **end for**

6: **return** $c_{\alpha \sqsubseteq \beta}$

Weakening and Completing. Given an axiom, *weakening* aims to find other axioms that are weaker than the given axiom, i.e., the given axiom logically implies the other axioms. For an axiom $\alpha \sqsubseteq \beta$, this is often done by replacing α by a more specific concept or replacing β by a more general concept. For the repairing this means that a wrong axiom $\alpha \sqsubseteq \beta$ can be replaced by a correct weaker axiom, thereby mitigating the effect of removing the wrong axiom (Fig. 1). Algorithm 1 presents a tractable weakening algorithm for normalized $\mathcal{EL}$ TBoxes. For a given axiom $\alpha \sqsubseteq \beta$, it finds correct axioms $sb \sqsubseteq sp$ such that sb is a sub-concept in $\mathrm{SCC}(\mathcal{T})$ of α and sp is a super-concept in $\mathrm{SCC}(\mathcal{T})$ of β. Further, there should not be another correct axiom under these conditions that would add more correct knowledge to the ontology than $sb \sqsubseteq sp$. As we work

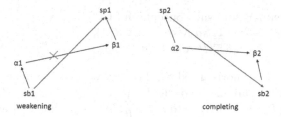

Fig. 1. Examples. Weakening: unwanted axiom $\alpha1 \sqsubseteq \beta1$ is replaced by correct axiom $sb1 \sqsubseteq sp1$; assumed that $\alpha1 \sqsubseteq sp1$ is not correct; formerly derivable correct axiom $sb1 \sqsubseteq sp1$ still entailed by repaired ontology. Completion: wanted axiom $\alpha2 \sqsubseteq \beta2$ is replaced by correct axiom $sp2 \sqsubseteq sb2$; $\alpha2 \sqsubseteq \beta2$ is still derivable and additional correct axiom $sp2 \sqsubseteq sb2$ in the repaired ontology.

with normalized $\mathcal{EL}$ TBoxes, the new axioms are normalized. The existence of such weaker axioms is not guaranteed.

Completing aims to find correct axioms that are not derivable from the ontology yet and that would make a given axiom derivable. It was introduced to aid domain experts when adding axioms to the ontology to find additional knowledge to add. While weakening is usually performed on unwanted axioms, completing is usually performed on wanted axioms. Algorithm 2 presents a tractable completion algorithm for normalized $\mathcal{EL}$ TBoxes. For a given axiom $\alpha \sqsubseteq \beta$, it finds correct axioms $sp \sqsubseteq sb$ such that sp is a super-concept in SCC($\mathcal{T}$) of α and sb is a sub-concept in SCC($\mathcal{T}$) of β (Fig. 1). This means that if $sp \sqsubseteq sb$ is added to $\mathcal{T}$, then $\alpha \sqsubseteq \beta$ would be derivable. Further, there should not be another correct axiom under these conditions that would add more correct knowledge to the ontology than $sp \sqsubseteq sb$. Similarly as for weakening, the new axioms are normalized. The completed axiom set is guaranteed to be not empty for a correct axiom $\alpha \sqsubseteq \beta$. It contains $\alpha \sqsubseteq \beta$ or other axioms that lead to the derivation of $\alpha \sqsubseteq \beta$.

Note that weakening and completing are dual operations where the former finds weaker axioms and the latter stronger axioms. This is reflected in the mirroring of the sub- and super-concepts of α and β in Algorithms 1 and 2.

5   Combination Strategies

Given a set of wrong axioms, there are different ways to repair the ontology using the removing, weakening and completing operations. There are choices to be made regarding the use of wrong axioms in the weakening and completing steps, regarding removing, weakening and completing all axioms at once or one at a time and in the latter case regarding the order the axioms are processed, as well as regarding when to update the ontology. Each of these choices may have an influence on the completeness and correctness of the repaired ontology. In general, using as much (possibly wrong) information as possible may lead to more complete ontologies, but also requires a larger validation effort. We have experimented with 13 different kinds of combinations. In this paper we show 4 representative algorithms that we use in the discussion as examples for general statements. We note that all proposed algorithms are tractable and find repairs as defined in Definition 1.

To show the trade-off between the choices regarding completeness and validation effort between the different algorithms, we define operators in Table 2 that can be used as building blocks in the design of algorithms. The operations represent choices regarding the use of wrong axioms by removing them (R) and adding them back (AB), regarding weakening (W) and completing (C) one at a time or all at once. Furthermore, update (U) is always used in combination with weakening or completing, and relates to when changes to the ontology are performed. For instance, when weakening an axiom, the weakened axioms could be added immediately to the ontology (and thus influence the ontology before weakening other axioms) or can be added after having weakened all axioms (and thus weakening one axiom does not influence weakening the next axiom). In the algorithms this is represented by the use of $\mathcal{T}$ or $\mathcal{T}_r$ as TBox. The operations have different effects on the completeness of the final ontology and validation effort. This is represented in the Hasse diagrams in Fig. 3 where the partial order represents more or equally complete final ontologies. For instance, Fig. 3b shows that weakening one axiom at a time and immediately updating the TBox (W-one,U-now) leads to a more complete ontology (and more validation effort) than the other choices. Figure 3c, shows that ontologies repaired by algorithms using one axiom at a time completing and immediate updates (C-one,U-now) are more complete than ontologies repaired using one axiom at a time completing and updating the ontology after each weakened axiom set for a wrong axiom (C-one,U-end_one). These ontologies are in turn more complete than for the other choices. Similar observations regarding removing are in Fig. 3a.

The combination algorithms can be defined by which of these building blocks are used and in which order. For instance, Algorithm C9 uses weaken one at a time, remove all wrong, complete one at a time, then add completed axiom sets at the end, while Algorithm C10 uses weaken one at a time, remove all wrong, add completed axiom sets one at a time. We can then compare algorithms using the Hasse diagrams. If the sequence of operators for one algorithm can be transformed to the sequence of operators of a second algorithm, by replacing some operators of the first algorithm using operators higher up in the lattices in Fig. 3, then the ontologies repaired using the second algorithm are more (or equally) complete than the ontologies repaired using the first algorithm. For instance, the sequence of Algorithm C9 can be rewritten into the sequence of Algorithm C10 by replacing the completion operator to a higher-level completion operator. Thus, repairing an ontology using Algorithm C10 leads to a more (or equally) complete ontology than repairing using Algorithm C9.

6 Experiments

In order to compare the use of the different combinations of strategies, we run experiments on several ontologies: Mini-GALEN (used as our running example),

Algorithm C2. Remove/weaken/add weakened axiom sets one at a time

Input: TBox $\mathcal{T}$, Oracle Or, set of unwanted axioms W
Output: A repaired TBox

1: $\mathcal{T}_r \leftarrow \mathcal{T}$
2: **for each** $\alpha \sqsubseteq \beta \in W$ **do**
3:     $\mathcal{T}_r \leftarrow$ Remove-axioms($\mathcal{T}_r$, $\{\alpha \sqsubseteq \beta\}$)
4:     $w_{\alpha \sqsubseteq \beta} \leftarrow$ weakened-axiom-set($\alpha \sqsubseteq \beta$, $\mathcal{T}_r$, Or)
5:     $\mathcal{T}_r \leftarrow$ Add-axioms($\mathcal{T}_r$,$w_{\alpha \sqsubseteq \beta}$)
6: **end for**
7: **return** $\mathcal{T}_r$

Algorithm C4. Remove all wrong, weaken/add weakened axiom sets one at a time

Input: TBox $\mathcal{T}$, Oracle Or, set of unwanted axioms W
Output: A repaired TBox

1: $\mathcal{T}_r \leftarrow$ Remove-axioms($\mathcal{T}$, W)
2: **for each** $\alpha \sqsubseteq \beta \in W$ **do**
3:     $w_{\alpha \sqsubseteq \beta} \leftarrow$ weakened-axiom-set($\alpha \sqsubseteq \beta$, $\mathcal{T}_r$, Or)
4:     $\mathcal{T}_r \leftarrow$ Add-axioms($\mathcal{T}_r$,$w_{\alpha \sqsubseteq \beta}$)
5: **end for**
6: **return** $\mathcal{T}_r$

PACO, NCI, OFSMR, EKAW and Pizza ontology (Table 3). We have used the parts of these ontologies that are expressible in $\mathcal{EL}$ in the sense that we removed the parts of axioms that used constructors not in $\mathcal{EL}$. We introduced new axioms in the ontologies by replacing existing axioms with axioms where the left-hand or right-hand side concepts of the existing axioms were changed. Further, we also flagged axioms as wrong in our full experiment set (e.g., in PACO). All axioms were validated manually.

For subsumption checking in the algorithms we used HermiT (http://www.hermit-reasoner.com/). We give results for Mini-GALEN (Fig. 2) which are representative for all experiments. Table 4 shows results for Algorithm C2 vs C4 regarding the number of sub-concepts of α and super-concepts of β for each wrong axiom $\alpha \sqsubseteq \beta$ when choosing to remove one wrong axiom at a time or all at once (while both update using the weakening result at once). In the table for each algorithm there is one sub and one sup set for each of the wrong axioms (e.g., for C2 for the first wrong axiom there are 3 concepts in the sup set and 2 in the sub set, resulting in 6 candidate weakened axioms). Further, the weakened axioms are shown. Table 5 shows the sizes of the sub and sup sets of the axioms (PPr$\sqsubseteq$IPr, IPr$\sqsubseteq$GPr, $\sqsubseteq$PPr), and the axioms to add using different orders of computing weakened axioms sets and adding them as soon as they are found for Algorithm C4. In Table 6 we show the sizes of the sub and sup sets for the completing step as well as the completed axioms for Algorithms C9 and C10.

Algorithm C9. Weaken one at a time, remove all wrong, complete one at a time, add completed axiom sets at end

Input: TBox $\mathcal{T}$, Oracle Or, set of unwanted axioms W
Output: A repaired TBox

1: **for each** $\alpha \sqsubseteq \beta \in W$ **do**
2:     $\mathcal{T}_r \leftarrow$ Remove-axioms($\mathcal{T}, \{\alpha \sqsubseteq \beta\}$)
3:     $w_{\alpha \sqsubseteq \beta} \leftarrow$ weakened-axiom-set($\alpha \sqsubseteq \beta, \mathcal{T}_r, Or$)
4: **end for**
5: $\mathcal{T}_r \leftarrow$ Remove-axioms($\mathcal{T}_r, W$)
6: **for each** $\alpha \sqsubseteq \beta \in W$ **do**
7:     $c_{\alpha \sqsubseteq \beta} \leftarrow \emptyset$
8:     **for each** $sb \sqsubseteq sp \in w_{\alpha \sqsubseteq \beta}$ **do**
9:         $c_{sb \sqsubseteq sp} \leftarrow$ completed-axiom-set($sb \sqsubseteq sp, \mathcal{T}_r, Or$)
10:         $c_{\alpha \sqsubseteq \beta} \leftarrow c_{\alpha \sqsubseteq \beta} \cup c_{sb \sqsubseteq sp}$
11.   end for
12: **end for**
13: $\mathcal{T}_r \leftarrow$ Add-axioms($\mathcal{T}_r, \bigcup_{\alpha \sqsubseteq \beta} c_{\alpha \sqsubseteq \beta}$)
14: **return** $\mathcal{T}_r$

7 Discussion

Choosing an Algorithm. The most preferred repair for an ontology with wrong axioms would lead to a more complete and less incorrect ontology than the original ontology. In general, however, this cannot be guaranteed unless we use a brute-force method that checks all axioms in an ontology. Although some optimizations are possible, this is in general not feasible. On the positive side, removing axioms does not introduce more incorrect knowledge and adding axioms does not remove correct knowledge. Unfortunately, removing wrong axioms may make the ontology less complete. For instance, when removing W from Mini-GALEN, the correct axiom PPr $\sqsubseteq$ NPr cannot be derived anymore. The weakening and completing alleviate this problem, but do not solve it completely. Adding correct axioms may make the ontology more incorrect in the case where some defects in the ontology were not yet detected or repaired and these lead to the derivation of new defects.

There is also a trade-off between using as much, but possibly wrong, knowledge as possible in the ontology and removing as much wrong knowledge as possible, when computing weakened and completed axiom sets (Fig. 3a). In the former case, more axioms (including more wrong axioms) are generated and need to be validated than in the latter case, but the final ontology in the former case may be more complete than in the latter case. For instance, Table 4 shows that sizes of the sup and sub sets for removing one axiom at a time are larger than or equal to the sizes of the sets for removing all at once (Algorithms C2 vs C4). When removing one at a time, the other wrong axioms can lead to more sub- and super-concepts and thus larger weakened axiom sets. This entails a higher validation effort by the domain expert, but it also leads to a more complete ontology as the axiom $PPr \sqsubseteq NPr$ is not always found by the approaches that remove all at once. Another choice is to add new correct axioms as soon as they

Algorithm C10. Weaken one at a time, remove all wrong, complete/add completed axiom sets one at a time

---

Input: TBox $\mathcal{T}$, Oracle Or, set of unwanted axioms W
Output: A repaired TBox

1: **for each** $\alpha \sqsubseteq \beta \in W$ **do**
2:     $\mathcal{T}_r \leftarrow$ Remove-axioms($\mathcal{T}$, $\{\alpha \sqsubseteq \beta\}$)
3:     $w_{\alpha \sqsubseteq \beta} \leftarrow$ weakened-axiom-set($\alpha \sqsubseteq \beta$, $\mathcal{T}_r$, Or)
4: **end for**
5: $\mathcal{T}_r \leftarrow$ Remove-axioms($\mathcal{T}$, W)
6: **for each** $\alpha \sqsubseteq \beta \in W$ **do**
7:     **for each** $sb \sqsubseteq sp \in w_{\alpha \sqsubseteq \beta}$ **do**
8:         $c_{sb \sqsubseteq sp} \leftarrow$ completed-axiom-set($sb \sqsubseteq sp$, $\mathcal{T}_r$, Or)
9:         $\mathcal{T}_r \leftarrow$ Add-axioms($\mathcal{T}_r$, $c_{sb \sqsubseteq sp}$)
10:     **end for**
11: **end for**
12: **return** $\mathcal{T}_r$

---

are found or wait until the end (Fig. 3b). In the former case they may be used to find additional information, but the end result may depend on the order that the axioms are handled. Also the order in which the axioms are processed, has an influence on the result as seen from Table 5 for Algorithm C4.

Similar observations can be made when completing is added to the removing and weakening (Fig. 3c). When the completed axioms are added one at a time during each iteration, the sizes of the sub and sup sets for each weakened axiom are larger than or equal to the sizes of the sets generated when adding them all at the end. In Table 6 we show this for Algorithms C9 and C10 that differ from each other in this aspect. Also here it entails a higher validation effort when adding one at a time, but it also leads to a more complete ontology.

In general, there is a trade-off between validation effort and the level of completeness and thus the choice of algorithm depends on the user's priority between these. For instance, earlier work on weakening discussed one combination strategy ((R-one, AB-none) with (W-one, U-now)) and did not show there were different options. In this work we show this trade-off. Further, by providing the Hasse diagrams we help deciding which features to use. Using features higher up in the diagrams means more validation work and more complete ontologies.

Domain Expert Validation in Practice. Introducing new concepts may make it hard for a domain expert to validate the axioms [5]. In our implemented systems we alleviate this problem by using a naming convention that reflects the logical description of the new concepts as they would be in a non-normalized TBox. For instance, we use names such as 'S-SOME-Q' and 'Q-AND-R'. This convention also allows the nesting of operators. In future work we will investigate the technique of 'forgetting' (e.g., [34]) to further alleviate this problem.

In [5] an ontology consists of a static part considered to be correct and a refutable part. If we would follow this approach, then in our setting wrong axioms in W can only be from the refutable part. Axioms from the static part

Table 2. Removing, weakening and completing - operations.

Operations	Description
R-all	Remove all the wrong axioms at once
R-one	Remove the wrong axioms one at a time
R-none	Remove nothing
W-all	Weaken all wrong axioms at once
W-one	Weaken the wrong axioms one at a time
C-all	Complete all weakened axioms at once
C-one	Complete the weakened axioms one at a time
AB-one	Add one wrong axiom back
AB-all	Add all wrong axioms back
AB-none	Add nothing back
U-now	Update the changes immediately
U-end_one	Update the changes after the iteration of each wrong axiom
U-end_all	Update the changes after iterations of all wrong axioms

Table 3. Ontologies

	Mini-GALEN	Pizza	EKAW	OFSMR	PACO	NCI
Concepts	9	74	100	159	224	3304
Roles	1	33	8	2	23	1
Axioms	20	341	801	1517	1153	30364

Table 4. Weakening for Mini-GALEN using C2 and C4. Three wrong axioms give 3 sup/sub-sets per algorithm.

	C2	C4
$\text{Sup}(\beta, \mathcal{T})$	3 2 2	1 2 1
$\text{Sub}(\alpha, \mathcal{T})$	2 1 1	1 1 1
Weakened	PPr $\sqsubseteq$ NPr IPr $\sqsubseteq$ NPr	IPr $\sqsubseteq$ NPr

do not need to be validated and should never be removed. Adding correct axioms should then grow the static part. We note that, in practise, it is not so clear how to divide an ontology in a static and a refutable part as, as mentioned before, according to our experience in assisting the development of ontologies in different domains, domain experts make mistakes even in the parts they think are correct.

8   Implemented Systems

We implemented two systems (see supplemental material). As Protégé is a well-known ontology development tool, we implemented a plugin for repairing based

N_C = {GPr (GranulomaProcess), NPr (NonNormalProcess),
PPh (PathologicalPhenomenon), F(Fracture), E (Endocarditis),
IPr (**InflammationProcess**), PPr (**PathologicalProcess**),
C (Carditis), CVD (CardioVascularDisease)};
N_R = { hAPr (hasAssociatedProcess) }
$\mathcal{T}$ = { CVD $\sqsubseteq$ PPh, F $\sqsubseteq$ PPh, $\exists$hAPr.PPr $\sqsubseteq$ PPh, E $\sqsubseteq$ C,
E $\sqsubseteq$ $\exists$hAPr.IPr, GPr $\sqsubseteq$ NPr, PPr $\sqsubseteq$ IPr, IPr $\sqsubseteq$ GPr, E $\sqsubseteq$ PPr };
W = { E $\sqsubseteq$ PPr, PPr $\sqsubseteq$ IPr, IPr $\sqsubseteq$ GPr }
Or returns $true$ for:
GPr $\sqsubseteq$ IPr, GPr $\sqsubseteq$ PPr, GPr $\sqsubseteq$ NPr, IPr $\sqsubseteq$ PPr, IPr $\sqsubseteq$ NPr,
PPr $\sqsubseteq$ NPr, CVD $\sqsubseteq$ PPh, F $\sqsubseteq$ PPh, E $\sqsubseteq$ PPh, E $\sqsubseteq$ C,
E $\sqsubseteq$ CVD, C $\sqsubseteq$ PPh, C $\sqsubseteq$ CVD, $\exists$hAPr.PPr $\sqsubseteq$ PPh,
$\exists$hAPr.IPr $\sqsubseteq$ PPh, E $\sqsubseteq$ $\exists$hAPr.IPr, E $\sqsubseteq$ $\exists$hAPr.PPh.
Note that for an oracle that does not make mistakes,
if Or(P $\sqsubseteq$ Q) = true, then also Or($\exists$r.P $\sqsubseteq$ $\exists$r.Q)=true and
Or(P $\sqcap$ O $\sqsubseteq$ Q)=true.
For other axioms P $\sqsubseteq$ Q with P, Q $\in$ N_C, Or(P $\sqsubseteq$ Q) = false.

Fig. 2. Mini-GALEN. (Visualized in supplemental material.)

Table 5. Adding weakened axioms in different order for Mini-GALEN by C4.Wrong axioms: ①PPr⊑IPr, ②IPr⊑GPr, ③E⊑PPr.

Wrong	①→②→③	①→③→②	②→①→③	②→③→①	③→①→②	③→②→①
$Sup(\beta, \mathcal{T})$	1 2 1	1 2 1	2 2 2	2 2 1	1 2 1	3 2 1
$Sub(\alpha, \mathcal{T})$	1 1 1	1 1 1	1 1 1	1 1 1	1 1 1	1 1 1
Weakened	IPr $\sqsubseteq$ NPr	IPr $\sqsubseteq$ NPr	IPr $\sqsubseteq$ NPr PPr $\sqsubseteq$ NPr	IPr $\sqsubseteq$ NPr PPr $\sqsubseteq$ NPr	IPr $\sqsubseteq$ NPr	IPr $\sqsubseteq$ NPr PPr $\sqsubseteq$ NPr

Table 6. Completing Mini-GALEN using C9 and C10.

	C9	C10
$Sup(\alpha, \mathcal{T})$	1 1	1 1
$Sub(\beta, \mathcal{T})$	2 2	2 3
Completed	PPr⊑NPr, IPr⊑NPr	PPr⊑NPr, IPr⊑PPr

on Algorithm C9. Using this algorithm the user can repair all wrong axioms at once. However, by iteratively invoking this plugin the user can also repair the wrong axioms one at a time. Further, we extended the $\mathcal{EL}$ version of the RepOSE system [19,35]. We allow the user to choose different combinations, thereby giving a choice in the trade-off between validation work and completeness. In the system, candidate weakened and completing axioms are shown in lists and also visualized using two sets of concepts. The axioms $\alpha \sqsubseteq \beta$ to be validated are the ones that can be constructed by choosing α from the first set and β from the second set. By showing them together, context of the solutions in the form of sub- and super-concepts is available. The domain expert can choose to validate such axioms by clicking in the different panes representing the sets of concepts.

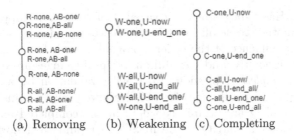

(a) Removing   (b) Weakening   (c) Completing

Fig. 3. Hasse diagrams. (a) remove and add back wrong axioms; (b) weakening and update; (c) completing and update. Combinations of operations higher up in the lattices lead to more validation work and more complete ontologies.

9 Related Work

We briefly discuss previous work on weakening and on completing. We are not aware of work that combines these.

Regarding *weakening*, previous work looks at the combination of debugging and weakening. Justifications for wrong axioms and a hitting set are computed. Then, instead of removing, weakened axioms are computed. In our approach we assume that the axioms to remove are given (e.g., by having computed a hitting set) and that when removing them they cannot be derived anymore. When this assumption is not made then, as pointed out in [5] (and ignored by older approaches) the weakening needs to be iterated to obtain a repair. We also note that none of the approaches explicitly state the use of a domain expert/oracle and they are purely logic-based. In practice, however, a domain expert/oracle is needed as otherwise axioms that are wrong in the domain of the ontology could be added. Regarding the *weakening algorithm*, in contrast to our approach, the other approaches work on non-normalized TBoxes. This means that they may find better solutions for the weakening, but the search space for solutions also becomes infinite. In [33] algorithms for weakening for $\mathcal{EL}$ and $\mathcal{ALC}$ are given with tractable and exponential complexity, respectively. They are based on refinement operators that are applied on the concepts of GCIs. The approach is extended in [7] for $\mathcal{SROIQ}$ TBoxes with an algorithm with almost-sure termination. Also in [9] an approach based on refinement operators is presented for $\mathcal{ALC}$. The nesting of operators is restricted based on the size of a concept. In [5] the right-hand side of axioms is generalized, but the left-hand side is not specialized to obtain a well-founded weakening relation (i.e., there is no infinite chain of weakenings). Essentially, our use of $sup(P, \mathcal{T})$ and $sub(P, \mathcal{T})$ in the weakening is a similar approach. As we have restricted the $sup(P, \mathcal{T})$ and $sub(P, \mathcal{T})$ to contain only concepts in SCC($\mathcal{T}$), we only have a finite number of possible axioms. Regarding the *strategy to combine removing with weakening*, in all these other approaches usually one-at-a-time removing (R-one, AB-none) and weakening (W-one, U-now) is used. From our Hasse diagrams we can see that this means the most complete ontologies and most validation work for weakening, but neither the most nor the least complete ontologies for removing. We note that using our Hasse diagrams, new variants of these other approaches can be created with another trade-off involving correctness and completeness. Further, the issue of the influence of the order is not addressed. In [17] parts of axioms to remove are pinpointed and harmful and helpful changes are defined.

Regarding *completing*, previous work with validation by a domain expert (e.g., [35] for the $\mathcal{EL}$ family, [18] for $\mathcal{ALC}$) allowed only axioms of the form $P \sqsubseteq Q$ where P and Q are atomic concepts in the completed axioms set while Algorithm 2 allows P and Q to be in SCC($\mathcal{T}$) (and then normalizes). That work used one particular combination strategy, i.e., (C-one, U-end-all). A non-interactive solution that is independent of the constructors of the description logic is proposed in [10]. This approach introduces justification patterns that can be instantiated with existing concepts or new concepts.

10   Conclusion

In this paper we proposed an interactive approach using weakening and completing to mitigate the negative effects of removing wrong axioms in $\mathcal{EL}$ ontologies. We presented a framework (and the first approach) for combining removing with weakening and completing. We showed that there are different combination strategies and that there is a trade-off involving correctness and completeness. We also introduced a way to compare combination strategies and showed that earlier work covered one type of combination strategy. Further, we presented new algorithms for weakening and completion and using these, showed the influence of 13 combination strategies on the completeness for 6 ontologies in experiments.

For future work we will investigate integrating the full debugging with weakening and completing. It is clear that, when for debugging we also add the step of finding which axioms to remove, that also this new step can be combined with removing, weakening and completing and thus leads to new combination strategies with different trade-offs. Further, for completing, we will look into other strategies for reducing the search space while still maintaining a practically feasible validation work for the domain expert. It is also interesting to investigate the problem for more expressive description logics.

Supplemental Material Statement. More details regarding the other algorithms, the full results of the experiments, diagram derivation and a short discussion on the difference of the combination strategies can be found in the supplemental material, which is available at https://www.ida.liu.se/~patla00/publications/ESWC2023/.

Acknowledgement. We thank Olaf Hartig for discussions leading to the Hasse diagrams. This work is financially supported by the Swedish e-Science Research Centre (SeRC) and the Swedish Research Council (Vetenskapsrådet, dnr 2018-04147).

References

1. Arif, M.F., Mencía, C., Ignatiev, A., Manthey, N., Peñaloza, R., Marques-Silva, J.: BEACON: an efficient SAT-based tool for debugging $\mathcal{EL}^+$ ontologies. In: Creignou,

N., Le Berre, D. (eds.) SAT 2016. LNCS, vol. 9710, pp. 521–530. Springer, Cham (2016). https://doi.org/10.1007/978-3-319-40970-2_32
2. Baader, F., Brandt, S., Lutz, C.: Pushing the $\mathcal{EL}$ envelope. In: IJCAI 2005: Proceedings of the 19th International Joint Conference on Artificial Intelligence, pp. 364–369 (2005)
3. Baader, F., Calvanese, D., McGuinness, D.L., Nardi, D., Patel-Schneider, P.F. (eds.): The Description Logic Handbook: Theory, Implementation, and Applications. Cambridge University Press, Cambridge (2003)
4. Baader, F., Ganter, B., Sertkaya, B., Sattler, U.: Completing description logic knowledge bases using formal concept analysis. In: IJCAI 2007: Proceedings of the 20th International Joint Conference on Artificial Intelligence, pp. 230–235 (2007)
5. Baader, F., Kriegel, F., Nuradiansyah, A., Peñaloza, R.: Making repairs in description logics more gentle. In: KR 2018: 16th International Conference on Principles of Knowledge Representation and Reasoning, pp. 319–328 (2018)
6. Buitelaar, P., Cimiano, P., Magnini, B.: Ontology Learning from Text: Methods, Evaluation and Applications. IOS Press (2005)
7. Confalonieri, R., Galliani, P., Kutz, O., Porello, D., Righetti, G., Troquard, N.: Towards even more irresistible axiom weakening. In: Proceedings of the 33rd International Workshop on Description Logics. CEUR, vol. 2663 (2020)
8. Dragisic, Z., Ivanova, V., Li, H., Lambrix, P.: Experiences from the anatomy track in the ontology alignment evaluation initiative. J. Biomed. Semant. 8(1), 56:1–56:28 (2017). https://doi.org/10.1186/s13326-017-0166-5
9. Du, J., Qi, G., Fu, X.: A practical fine-grained approach to resolving incoherent OWL 2 DL terminologies. In: CIKM 2014: Proceedings of the 23rd ACM International Conference on Conference on Information and Knowledge Management, pp. 919–928 (2014). https://doi.org/10.1145/2661829.2662046
10. Du, J., Wan, H., Ma, H.: Practical TBox abduction based on justification patterns. In: Proceedings of the Thirty-First AAAI Conference on Artificial Intelligence (AAAI 2017), pp. 1100–1106 (2017)
11. Ferré, S., Rudolph, S.: Advocatus Diaboli – exploratory enrichment of ontologies with negative constraints. In: ten Teije, A., et al. (eds.) EKAW 2012. LNCS (LNAI), vol. 7603, pp. 42–56. Springer, Heidelberg (2012). https://doi.org/10.1007/978-3-642-33876-2_7
12. Fleischhacker, D., Meilicke, C., Völker, J., Niepert, M.: Computing incoherence explanations for learned ontologies. In: Faber, W., Lembo, D. (eds.) RR 2013. LNCS, vol. 7994, pp. 80–94. Springer, Heidelberg (2013). https://doi.org/10.1007/978-3-642-39666-3_7
13. Ji, Q., Gao, Z., Huang, Z., Zhu, M.: An efficient approach to debugging ontologies based on patterns. In: Pan, J.Z., et al. (eds.) JIST 2011. LNCS, vol. 7185, pp. 425–433. Springer, Heidelberg (2012). https://doi.org/10.1007/978-3-642-29923-0_33
14. Kalyanpur, A., Parsia, B., Horridge, M., Sirin, E.: Finding all justifications of OWL DL entailments. In: Aberer, K., et al. (eds.) ASWC/ISWC -2007. LNCS, vol. 4825, pp. 267–280. Springer, Heidelberg (2007). https://doi.org/10.1007/978-3-540-76298-0_20
15. Kalyanpur, A., Parsia, B., Sirin, E., Cuenca-Grau, B.: Repairing unsatisfiable concepts in OWL ontologies. In: Sure, Y., Domingue, J. (eds.) ESWC 2006. LNCS, vol. 4011, pp. 170–184. Springer, Heidelberg (2006). https://doi.org/10.1007/11762256_15

16. Kalyanpur, A., Parsia, B., Sirin, E., Hendler, J.: Debugging unsatisfiable classes in OWL ontologies. J. Web Semant. **3**(4), 268–293 (2005). https://doi.org/10.1016/j.websem.2005.09.005
17. Lam, J.S.C., Sleeman, D.H., Pan, J.Z., Vasconcelos, W.W.: A fine-grained approach to resolving unsatisfiable ontologies. J. Data Semant. **10**, 62–95 (2008). https://doi.org/10.1007/978-3-540-77688-8_3
18. Lambrix, P., Dragisic, Z., Ivanova, V.: Get my pizza right: repairing missing is-a relations in ALC ontologies. In: Takeda, H., Qu, Y., Mizoguchi, R., Kitamura, Y. (eds.) JIST 2012. LNCS, vol. 7774, pp. 17–32. Springer, Heidelberg (2013). https://doi.org/10.1007/978-3-642-37996-3_2
19. Lambrix, P., Wei-Kleiner, F., Dragisic, Z.: Completing the is-a structure in light-weight ontologies. J. Biomed. Semant. **6** (2015). https://doi.org/10.1186/s13326-015-0002-8
20. Lehmann, J., Bühmann, L.: ORE - a tool for repairing and enriching knowledge bases. In: Patel-Schneider, P.F., et al. (eds.) ISWC 2010. LNCS, vol. 6497, pp. 177–193. Springer, Heidelberg (2010). https://doi.org/10.1007/978-3-642-17749-1_12
21. Li, H., Armiento, R., Lambrix, P.: A method for extending ontologies with application to the materials science domain. Data Sci. J. **18**(1) (2019). https://doi.org/10.5334/dsj-2019-050
22. Meyer, T., Lee, K., Booth, R., Pan, J.: Finding maximally satisfiable terminologies for the description logic ALC. In: Proceedings, The Twenty-First National Conference on Artificial Intelligence and the Eighteenth Innovative Applications of Artificial Intelligence Conference (AAAI 2006), pp. 269–274 (2006)
23. Moodley, K., Meyer, T., Varzinczak, I.J.: Root justifications for ontology repair. In: Rudolph, S., Gutierrez, C. (eds.) RR 2011. LNCS, vol. 6902, pp. 275–280. Springer, Heidelberg (2011). https://doi.org/10.1007/978-3-642-23580-1_24
24. Nikitina, N., Rudolph, S., Glimm, B.: Interactive ontology revision. J. Web Semant. **12–13**, 118–130 (2012). https://doi.org/10.1016/j.websem.2011.12.002
25. Pesquita, C., Faria, D., Santos, E., Couto, F.M.: To repair or not to repair: reconciling correctness and coherence in ontology reference alignments. In: Proceedings of the 8th International Workshop on Ontology Matching. CEUR, vol. 1111, pp. 13–24 (2013)
26. Rodler, P., Schmid, W.: On the impact and proper use of heuristics in test-driven ontology debugging. In: Benzmüller, C., Ricca, F., Parent, X., Roman, D. (eds.) RuleML+RR 2018. LNCS, vol. 11092, pp. 164–184. Springer, Cham (2018). https://doi.org/10.1007/978-3-319-99906-7_11
27. Schekotihin, K., Rodler, P., Schmid, W.: OntoDebug: interactive ontology debugging plug-in for Protégé. In: Ferrarotti, F., Woltran, S. (eds.) FoIKS 2018. LNCS, vol. 10833, pp. 340–359. Springer, Cham (2018). https://doi.org/10.1007/978-3-319-90050-6_19
28. Schlobach, S.: Debugging and semantic clarification by pinpointing. In: Gómez-Pérez, A., Euzenat, J. (eds.) ESWC 2005. LNCS, vol. 3532, pp. 226–240. Springer, Heidelberg (2005). https://doi.org/10.1007/11431053_16
29. Schlobach, S., Cornet, R.: Non-standard reasoning services for the debugging of description logic terminologies. In: IJCAI, pp. 355–360 (2003)
30. Schlobach, S., Huang, Z., Cornet, R., van Harmelen, F.: Debugging incoherent terminologies. J. Autom. Reason. **39**(3), 317–349 (2007). https://doi.org/10.1007/s10817-007-9076-z

31. Sertkaya, B.: ONTOCOMP: a PROTÉGÉ plugin for completing OWL ontologies. In: Aroyo, L., et al. (eds.) ESWC 2009. LNCS, vol. 5554, pp. 898–902. Springer, Heidelberg (2009). https://doi.org/10.1007/978-3-642-02121-3_78
32. Shchekotykhin, K.M., Friedrich, G., Fleiss, P., Rodler, P.: Interactive ontology debugging: two query strategies for efficient fault localization. J. Web Semant. **12**, 88–103 (2012). https://doi.org/10.1016/j.websem.2011.12.006
33. Troquard, N., Confalonieri, R., Galliani, P., Peñaloza, R., Porello, D., Kutz, O.: Repairing ontologies via axiom weakening. In: Proceedings of the Thirty-Second AAAI Conference on Artificial Intelligence (AAAI 2018), pp. 1981–1988 (2018). https://doi.org/10.1609/aaai.v32i1.11567
34. Wang, K., Wang, Z., Topor, R., Pan, J.Z., Antoniou, G.: Concept and role forgetting in $\mathcal{ALC}$ ontologies. In: Bernstein, A., et al. (eds.) ISWC 2009. LNCS, vol. 5823, pp. 666–681. Springer, Heidelberg (2009). https://doi.org/10.1007/978-3-642-04930-9_42
35. Wei-Kleiner, F., Dragisic, Z., Lambrix, P.: Abduction framework for repairing incomplete $\mathcal{EL}$ ontologies: complexity results and algorithms. In: Proceedings of the Twenty-Eighth AAAI Conference on Artificial Intelligence (AAAI 2014), pp. 1120–1127 (2014). https://doi.org/10.1609/aaai.v28i1.8858

Activity Recommendation for Business Process Modeling with Pre-trained Language Models

Diana Sola[1,2(✉)], Han van der Aa[2], Christian Meilicke[2],
and Heiner Stuckenschmidt[2]

[1] SAP Signavio, Walldorf, Germany
[2] Data and Web Science Group, University of Mannheim, Mannheim, Germany
{diana,han,christian,heiner}@informatik.uni-mannheim.de

Abstract. Activity recommendation in business process modeling is concerned with suggesting suitable labels for a new activity inserted by a modeler in a process model under development. Recently, it has been proposed to represent process model repositories as knowledge graphs, which makes it possible to address the activity-recommendation problem as a knowledge graph completion task. However, existing recommendation approaches are entirely dependent on the knowledge contained in the model repository used for training. This makes them rigid in general and even inapplicable in situations where a process model consists of unseen activities, which were not part of the repository used for training. In this paper, we avoid these issues by recognizing that the semantics contained in process models can be used to instead pose the activity-recommendation problem as a set of textual sequence-to-sequence tasks. This enables the application of transfer-learning techniques from natural language processing, which allows for recommendations that go beyond the activities contained in an available repository. We operationalize this with an activity-recommendation approach that employs a pre-trained language model at its core, and uses the representations of process knowledge as structured graphs combined with the natural-language-based semantics of process models. In an experimental evaluation, we show that our approach considerably outperforms the state of the art in terms of semantic accuracy of the recommendations and that it is able to recommend and handle activity labels that go beyond the vocabulary of the model repository used during training.

Keywords: activity recommendation · process models · semantic process analysis · language models · sequence-to-sequence models

1 Introduction

All organizations, from enterprises to governmental institutions, to healthcare providers, perform processes to deliver services or products to their internal and external customers [10]. Each of these processes consists of a number of

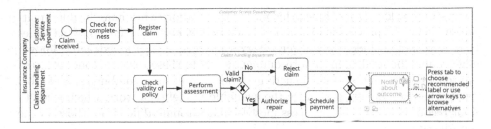

Fig. 1. A business process model under development

activities, which jointly turn an initial trigger into a desired outcome, such as *order-to-cash, purchase-to-pay*, or *ticket-to-resolution*. Process models are widely used artifacts to capture information on such processes, since they represent the semantics of a process in a structured manner, typically in the form of BPMN (Business Process Model and Notation) models or Petri nets. As graph-based process representations, they are a suitable basis for a variety of purposes, including process execution support, analysis, and improvement [8].

However, establishing process models is known to be a time-consuming and error-prone task [16,17], in part due to its dependence on knowledge from domain experts, who are typically not familiar with process modeling itself [10,44]. Furthermore, in cross-departmental settings, ensuring clarity and consistency in established process models is even harder [42], yet also crucial to avoid that process execution and analysis are conducted based on incorrect, incomplete, or inconsistent models [1,5]. Recognizing these issues, various methods have been proposed to support process modelers, which include methods that identify syntactic issues [12,29] or provide modeling recommendations [15] in the form of suggestions on how to expand a process model under development.

Activity recommendation represents the most common instantiation of such recommendation support [9,47,52], which aims to suggest suitable labels for new activities placed by modelers. Figure 1 shows an instance of this. The BPMN model in the figure depicts a process that starts when a claim has been received, after which various activities are performed to handle the claim. This involves a decision point, indicated by an *XOR-split gateway* (diamond shape with an *X*), where a claim is either rejected, or its payment is authorized and scheduled. Following this decision, the model synchronizes the two branches using an *XOR-join gateway*. After this gateway, a new activity has been inserted, for which the activity-recommendation task is to suggest one or more suitable labels. As shown, a recommended label is *"Notify about outcome"*. This label is fitting, because the preceding nodes indicate that the outcome of a claim has been determined, after which it is natural to inform the claimant.

To provide such recommendations, approaches typically extract knowledge from a repository of existing process models. This allows them to mine relations between activities in the available models and use the learned patterns to provide recommendations in the form of labels contained in the repository at hand [9,18,46,52]. However, such approaches are restricted to the knowledge contained in the model repository available for training, which is a strong limitation and results in two key issues. First, this makes these approaches inapplicable in situations where a process model under development entirely consists of activities that were not included in the repository's models, since the extracted knowledge cannot be used to make a recommendation in these cases. Second, existing approaches can only recommend activity labels (or, at best, combinations of label parts) that are already present in the available model repository, which leads to poor recommendations for process models that strongly differ from those in the repository.

To overcome these issues, an activity-recommendation approach should extend its recommendation capabilities to models and activities beyond those contained in the available training data. To achieve this, we propose to capture an instance of the activity-recommendation problem as a set of textual sequence-to-sequence tasks, which enables the application of transfer-learning techniques from natural language processing (NLP). Transfer learning, where a model is first pre-trained on a data-rich task to develop general-purpose abilities and then fine-tuned on a downstream task, has emerged as a powerful technique in NLP [43]. By applying such techniques to the activity-recommendation problem, we can use the general-purpose knowledge of pre-trained language models as an additional source to the problem-specific knowledge contained in a process model repository, thus enabling us to provide relevant recommendations in more settings.

We operationalize this by introducing BPART5 – a **B**usiness **P**rocess **A**ctivity **R**ecommendation approach using the pre-trained language model **T5** [43]. Using the—to this date—largest publicly available collection of process models, we evaluate the performance of BPART5 and compare it to a state-of-the-art rule-based approach for activity recommendation. The results reveal that BPART5 outperforms the rule-based approach in generating relevant recommendations in terms of semantic accuracy. Furthermore, we show that it is able to leverage the knowledge contained in the pre-trained language model to generate recommendations that go beyond the vocabulary of the model repository used for training. Specifically, BPART5 recommended numerous activities that were not present in the training data and was also able to provide better recommendations for process models consisting of unseen activities.

2   Background and Related Work

The semantics of a process model follow from the combination of two aspects [50]: the *formal semantics* of a modeling notation, which dictate how a modeled process should be executed (e.g., capturing the execution flow, including choices and concurrency), and the *label semantics* of individual model elements, which capture the meaning of the individual parts of a process model through natural language text. This dual nature opens up various opportunities for the integration of semantic technologies in process modeling and analysis, as, e.g., outlined in the overviews by Fellmann et al. [13,14]. Research directions in this context range from the development of an ontology for business process representation [2], the automated construction of process knowledge graphs [3], and general-purpose business process representation learning [41], to problem-specific applications of semantic technologies, such as for process model matching [30], process model similarity [11], and the focal point of our work: activity recommendation.

In the following, we consider how both aspects of process model semantics are considered by existing activity-recommendation approaches, focusing on methods exploiting formal model semantics in Sect. 2.1 and those that additionally incorporate label semantics in Sect. 2.2.

2.1 Activity Recommendation Based on Formal Semantics

Several activity-recommendation approaches use the formal semantics of process models to abstract them to directed graphs, followed by the application of graph-mining techniques to extract structural patterns from process models. Such approaches use, for example, common subgraph distance [6] or edit distance [6,9,32] to determine the similarity of extracted patterns from a given model repository and a process model under development. However, activity-recommendation approaches using graph-mining techniques reach their limits when applied to large repositories consisting of thousands of process models [52].

Another way of handling the formal semantics of a process models is the use of embeddings or rules. Wang et al. developed a representation-learning-based recommendation approach named RLRecommender [52], which embeds activities and relations between them. While their approach bases the recommendations of activities on one previous activity in the process model under development only, the rule-based approach from our earlier work [46] considers the entire process model under development when generating activity recommendations, which leads to better recommendations results. Based on problem-specific rule templates, our rule-based approach learns logical rules that capture activity inter-relations from the process models in a repository and applies the learned patterns to the model under development to generate activity recommendations.

Moreover, we show in an experimental study [45] that standard rule- and embedding-based knowledge graph completion methods can be applied to the activity-recommendation problem out of the box, but are not flexible enough to completely adapt to it. Compared to RLRecommender [52] and our rule-based approach [46], both specifically designed for activity recommendation, the knowledge graph completion methods performed comparably poor.

2.2 Activity Recommendation Based on Label Semantics

Several works go beyond the consideration of formal semantics, by also taking label semantics for activity recommendation into account.

In an extension of our rule-based approach [47], we generalize the information contained within activities of a repository. Through an additional analysis of the natural-language-based semantics of activities, actions and business-object patterns in the use of activity labels are leveraged to recommend also combinations of actions and business objects used in the repository.

Goldstein et al. [18] developed an approach that leverages semantic similarity of sequences in process models using the pre-trained language model Universal Sentence Encoder (USE) [7] and evaluated it both in experiments and in a user study [19]. Their approach compares an input sequence to the sequences in the training repository, recommending the label that followed the most similar training sequence. While their approach represents a first step towards the use of transfer-learning techniques from NLP for activity recommendation, it is limited to the use of a pre-trained language model without fine-tuning and recommendations of activities that exist in the given model repository for training.

3   Problem Statement

Our work is independent of a specific process modeling notation, which we achieve by representing process models as directed attributed graphs:

Definition 1 (Process model). *Let $\mathcal{L}$ be the universe of node labels and $\mathcal{T}$ be a set of node types. A process model is a tuple $M = (N, A, E, \tau, \lambda)$, where*

- *N is a set of nodes,*
- *$A \subseteq N$ is a set of activity nodes,*
- *$E \subseteq N \times N$ is a set of directed edges, such that all nodes of N are connected,*
- *$\tau : N \to \mathcal{T}$ is a function that maps a node to a type, and*
- *$\lambda : N \to \mathcal{L}$ is a function that maps a node to a label.*

This definition explicitly captures the set of activity nodes A, since these nodes are core to activity recommendation. Depending on the modeling notation, this set may contain nodes of multiple types, i.e., there exists a subset of activity types, $\mathcal{T}_A \subseteq \mathcal{T}$, such that $A = \{n \in N \mid \tau(n) \in \mathcal{T}_A\}$. For example, for BPMN, set A includes, among others, *tasks* (e.g., *reject claim*) and *events* (e.g., *claim received*), whereas *gateways* (e.g., *XOR splits*) are not included in A. Note that the edges in E can capture a partial order between nodes in N, to allow for concurrency and alternative executions paths in a process, such as the two choices following the XOR split in Fig. 1. We use $\bullet n = \{m \in N \mid (m, n) \in E\}$ to denote the *pre-set* of a node $n \in N$, i.e., the set of all nodes preceding n in the model.

Activity recommendation targets a situation in which a process model under development contains exactly one activity node that has not yet received a label[1], such as seen in Fig. 1. We refer to such a model as an *incomplete process model*:

Definition 2 (Incomplete process model). *An incomplete process model $M_I = (N, A, E, \tau, \lambda, \hat{n})$ is a process model (N, A, E, τ, λ) that has exactly one unlabeled activity node $\hat{n} \in A$ with a non-empty preset, i.e., $\lambda(n) \in \mathcal{L}$ is given for all $n \in N \setminus \{\hat{n}\}$, $\lambda(\hat{n}) = \bot$ and $\bullet \hat{n} \neq \emptyset$.*

Given an incomplete process model M_I, the *activity-recommendation problem* is to suggest one or more suitable labels for the unlabeled activity node $\hat{n}$.

---

[1] Note that process model nodes may have empty labels ($\lambda(n) = \epsilon$), such as the XOR-join in Fig. 1, which is different from a node being unlabeled ($\lambda(n) = \bot$).

4 The BPART5 Approach

This section presents our proposed BPART5 approach for activity recommendation, which uses the pre-trained sequence-to-sequence language model T5 at its core. Since T5 requires totally ordered, textual sequences as input, whereas process model nodes can be partially ordered, Sect. 4.1 describes how we lift activity recommendation to the format of sequence-to-sequence tasks. In Sect. 4.2, we describe how we use this procedure to fine-tune T5 for activity recommendation based on process knowledge encoded in a process model repository. Finally, Sect. 4.3 describes how we use our fine-tuned T5 model to solve instances of the activity-recommendation problem, for which we first solve multiple sequence-to-sequence tasks, whose results we then aggregate in order to return one or more label recommendations.

4.1 Sequence-to-Sequence Tasks for Activity Recommendation

Sequence-to-sequence tasks are concerned with finding a model that maps a sequence of inputs $(x_1, ..., x_T)$ to a sequence of outputs $(y_1, ..., y_{T'})$, where the output length T' is unknown a priori and may differ from the input length T [49]. A classic example of a sequence-to-sequence problem from the NLP field is machine translation, where the *input sequence* is given by text in a source language and the *output sequence* is the translated text in a target language.

In the context of activity recommendation, the *output sequence* corresponds to the activity label $\lambda(\hat{n})$ to be recommended for node $\hat{n}$, which consists of one or more words, e.g., *"notify about outcome"*. Defining the *input sequence* is more complex, though, since the input to an activity-recommendation task consists of an incomplete process model M_I, whose nodes may be partially ordered, rather than form a single sequence.

To overcome this, we turn a single activity-recommendation task into one or more sequence-to-sequence tasks. For this, we first extract multiple node sequences from M_I that each end in $\hat{n}$. Formally, we write that $S_l^{\hat{n}} = (n_1, ..., n_l)$ is a node sequence of length l, ending in node $\hat{n}$ ($n_l = \hat{n}$), for which it must hold that $n_i \in \bullet n_{i+1}$ for all $i = 1, ..., l - 1$. Finally, since an input sequence should consist of text, rather than of model nodes, we then apply *verbalization* to the node sequence, which strings together the types and (cleaned) labels of the nodes in $S_l^{\hat{n}}$, i.e., $\tau(n_1) \lambda(n_1) ... \tau(n_{l-1}) \lambda(n_{l-1}) \tau(\hat{n})$. For example, using sequences of length four, we obtain two verbalized input sequences for the recommendation problem in Fig. 1:

- *"task* authorize repair *task* schedule payment *xor task"*
- *"xor* valid claim *task* reject claim *xor task"*

We use this notion of sequence extraction and verbalization to fine-tune T5 for activity recommendation, as described next.

4.2 Fine-Tuning T5 for Activity Recommendation

For our approach, we use the sequence-to-sequence language model T5, which is based on the transformer architecture introduced by Vaswani et al. [51]. T5 is pre-trained on a set of unsupervised and supervised tasks, where each task is converted into a text-to-text format. We fine-tune T5 for activity recommendation by extracting a large number of sequence-to-sequence tasks from the models in an available process model repository $\mathcal{M}$. Specifically, for each model $M \in \mathcal{M}$, we extract all possible sequences of a certain length l that end in an activity node, i.e., $(n_1, ..., n_l)$ with $n_l \in A$. Afterwards, we apply verbalization on this node sequence to get the textual input sequence, as described in Sect. 4.1, whereas the output sequence corresponds to the label of n_l.

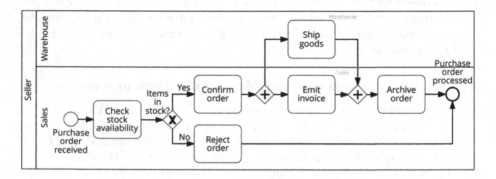

Fig. 2. An order-to-cash process model

As an example, consider the exemplary training process model depicted in Fig. 2. Setting $l = 4$, the model contains nine sequences of length four that end in an activity node. After verbalization, these result in the following textual *(input, output)* sequences we can use to fine-tune T5:

- (*start* purchase order received *task* check stock availability *xor* items in stock *task*, confirm order)
- (*start* purchase order received *task* check stock availability *xor* items in stock *task*, reject order)
- (*task* check stock availability *xor* items in stock *task* reject order *end*, purchase order processed)
- (*xor* items in stock *task* confirm order *and task*, ship goods)
- (*xor* items in stock *task* confirm order *and task*, emit invoice)
- (*and task* ship goods *and task*, archive order)
- (*and task* emit invoice *and task*, archive order)
- (*task* ship goods *and task* archive order *end*, purchase order processed)
- (*task* emit invoice *and task* archive order *end*, purchase order processed)

4.3   Generating Label Recommendations

Given an incomplete process model M_I with an unlabeled activity node $\hat{n}$, for which we want to provide label recommendations, we first extract all sequences of length l that end in $\hat{n}$. We then verbalize all these sequences and feed the resulting input sequences as sequence-to-sequence tasks into our fine-tuned T5 model. For instance, for the example of Fig. 1, this results in the two input sequences described earlier when using $l = 4$, which are:

- I_1: *task* authorize repair *task* schedule payment *xor task*
- I_2: *xor* valid claim *task* reject claim *xor task*

Output Sequence Generation. We solve the individual sequence-to-sequence tasks by feeding each input sequence into our fine-tuned T5 model, generating 10 alternative output sequences, i.e., 10 possible labels, per input. To do this, we use *beam search* [20] as a decoding method, with beam width $w = 10$. The beam search algorithm uses conditional probabilities to track the w most likely output sequences at each generation step.

A downside of the beam search algorithm is that it can lead to output sequences that repeat words or even short sequences, i.e., *n-grams*. Following activity labeling convention [36,37,42], we favor the suggestion of short labels that do not contain any recurring terms. For example, rather than suggesting labels such as *"check passport and check visa"*, our approach would suggest the non-repetitive alternative: *"check passport and visa"*. To achieve this, we apply n-gram penalties [26,40] during beam search. Specifically, we penalize the repetition of n-grams of any size (including single words) by setting the probability of next words that are already included in the output sequence to zero.

Tables 1a and 1b show the alternative output sequences (and probabilities) that the fine-tuned T5 model generates for input sequences I_1 and I_2.

Table 1. From two lists of T5-generated output sequences to one list of label recommendations using maximum strategy

Output sequences for I_1	Score	Output sequences for I_2	Score	Label recommendations	Score
notify about outcome	0.64	send email to customer	0.46	notify about outcome	0.64 (0.42)
send notification	0.48	email notification	0.46	send notification	0.48
inform about outcome	0.47	notify about outcome	0.42	inform about outcome	0.47
send claim rejection	0.38	send email to client	0.40	send email to customer	0.46
submit claim to system	0.37	customer notified	0.36	email notification	0.46
notify claim rejection	0.37	email	0.34	send email to client	0.40
notify customer	0.36	notification sent to customer	0.31	send claim rejection	0.38
send email notification	0.36	process end	0.29	submit claim to system	0.37
submit claim to management	0.34	send email notification	0.28	notify claim rejection	0.37
notify claimant	0.33	process claim	0.26	send email notification	0.36 (0.28)

(a) Output sequences and probabilities based on I_1	(b) Output sequences and probabilities based on I_2	(c) Final list of label recommendations

Result Aggregation. Finally, we aggregate the different lists of output sequences, obtained by using beam search to solve individual sequence-to-sequence tasks, in order to end up with a single list of recommended activity labels. To do this, we aggregate the contents of the lists using a *maximum strategy*, which is commonly used by rule-based methods to rank proposed entities according to the different confidence values of the rules that suggested them [35,38,46].

To apply the maximum strategy, we establish an aggregated recommendation list, sorted according to the maximal probability score that a recommended label received. For instance, the *notify about outcome* label receives a score of 0.64, from the output sequences generated for I_1, although the label also appears in I_2's list, yet with a score of 0.42. If two recommendations have the same maximum probability, we sort them based on their second-highest probability, if available. Analogously, if two recommendations share maximum and second-highest probability, we continue until we find a probability that makes a difference. In the end, BPART5 thus provides a list of ten label recommendations for the unlabeled node $\hat{n}$ that are the most probable candidates, according to the sequences contained in the model under development, the fine-tuned T5 model, and the maximum aggregation strategy.

The final list obtained for the running example is shown in Table 1c. Notably, the top five recommendations represent alternative manners to inform an applicant, e.g., in the form of *notify about outcome, send notification,* or *send email to customer*, which indeed appears to be the appropriate process step given the current state of the process model under development.

5   Experimental Study

In our experimental study[2], we evaluate the performance of BPART5 and compare it to the state-of-the-art approach from our earlier work [47]. We first describe the used dataset (Sect. 5.1), the experimental setup (Sect. 5.2) and the employed metrics (Sect. 5.3). Finally, we present the results of our experiments in Sect. 5.4.

5.1   Dataset

For our experimental evaluation, we employ the SAP Signavio Academic Models (SAP-SAM) [24] dataset. SAP-SAM is the—to this date—largest publicly available collection of business process models, which consists of over one million process models in different modeling notations and languages.

SAP-SAM contains models of varying complexity and quality. For our experiments, we aim to use a subset of the dataset where certain process modeling standards, as proposed in established work [36], are met. Following the recommendations for usage of the dataset provided by its publishers [48], we thus filter the dataset as follows. We select all BPMN 2.0 models in English with three to 30 nodes (including gateways), where each activity label is composed of at least three non-empty characters. In addition, we exclude default vendor-provided example models included in SAP-SAM[3]. Note that for filtering and

---

[2] We provide the source code of the employed implementation under this link: https://github.com/disola/bpart5.

[3] SAP-SAM contains a high number of vendor-provided example models. The publishers of the dataset recommend sorting them out as they negatively affect the diversity of the dataset.

pre-processing the models of SAP-SAM we apply label cleaning, in which we turn non-alphanumeric characters into whitespace, handle special cases as line breaks, change all letters into lowercase and delete unnecessary whitespace. This results in a filtered dataset, which consists of 77,239 process models containing an average of 14.7 nodes (median: 13) and a total of 241,283 unique node labels with an average length of 26.5 characters (median: 24).

5.2 Experimental Setup

Evaluated Approaches. In our experiments, we choose a sequence length $l = 4$ for our BPART5 approach, i.e., we extract sequences of length four that end in node $\hat{n}$. This choice follows findings from prior research [18], which showed that considering three previous nodes for activity recommondation works well across different datasets

We compare BPART5 to the rule-based approach from our earlier work [47], which has been shown to outperform several other recommendation approaches [22,23,45,46,52]. We also wanted to include the approach from Goldstein et al. [18], which is based on semantic similarity and the universal sentence encoder, but the source code of their approach is not available online, and also the authors did not provide us their source code after requesting it.

Implementation. Our implementation of BPART5 and the metrics uses the Huggingface library [53]. For tokenizing sequences, we used the *fast* T5 tokenizer backed by HuggingFace's tokenizer library, which is based on Unigram [27] in conjunction with SentencePiece [28]. We fine-tuned T5-Small[4] employing the Adam algorithm [25] with weight decay fix as introduced in [33] and constant learning rate 0.0003. Moreover, we set the batch size to 128 and trained the model until the validation loss did not improve for 20,000 steps. The experiments were carried out using two Nvidia RTX A6000 GPUs.

Data Split. We randomly divided the models in the filtered dataset into training, validation, and testing splits. More precisely, we train each approach on 85% of the process models while we use 7.5% of the models for validation and evaluation, respectively. From the training split, we extracted a total of 688.584 sequences, which we verbalized and used to fine-tune T5 for BPART5.

Evaluation Procedure. The testing split consists of process models, which the modelers have considered finished. However, we want to evaluate the ability of approaches to generate activity recommendations for process models under development, i.e., for incomplete process models. Given a finished process model, we thus simulate different stages of the model construction, which is a common practice for the evaluation of activity-recommendation approaches [18,47]. We use a breadth-first search inspired simulation technique, where we first select an activity node $\hat{n}$ from a finished process model as the one for which we want to recommend labels, and hide the label of $\hat{n}$. Then, we determine the shortest

---

[4] Compared to T5-Base with its 220 million parameters, T5-Small is a model checkpoint that has only 60 million parameters.

sequence from a source node (a node without preset) to $\hat{n}$ and denote the length of this sequence by s. Subsequently, we remove all nodes that are not contained in a sequence of length s starting from a source node and retain all other nodes and edges between them. The remaining process model is treated as the intermediate result of a model construction, and the task to recommend labels for the selected node $\hat{n}$ based on the remaining process model represents one evaluation case. For each process model in the testing split, we generate several such evaluation cases by carrying out this procedure for each activity node, where the shortest sequence to a source node has the minimum length three. This leads to a total of 36.143 evaluation cases, i.e., activity-recommendation tasks.

5.3 Metrics

We assess the performance of the activity-recommendation approaches using four different metrics, namely Hits@k, BLEU@k, METEOR@k and Cos@k:

Hits@k. First, we report on the standard *hit rate* Hits@k [21], which is frequently used in the context of activity recommendation [47,52] as well as for other recommendation applications, where it is sufficient that the recommendation list contains one item that the user selects [21]. Hits@k captures the proportion of hits in the top-k recommendations. In other words, it is the proportion of evaluation cases, where the ground truth, i.e., the actually used activity in a process model, is one of the k recommendations.

BLEU@k. The BLEU [39] metric is typically used in machine translation, where a candidate translation is compared to one or more reference translations. In the context of activity recommendation, BLEU basically compares n-grams of the recommended activity with n-grams of the ground-truth activity and calculates a modified precision based on n-gram matches. Similarly to the standard hit rate Hits@k, we can define the BLEU@k hit rate as the maximum BLEU score of the top-k recommendations. This results in a single score for a recommendation list of length k instead of the k BLEU scores of each recommendation in the list.

METEOR@k. Just as BLEU, the METEOR [4] metric is also typically used to assess the quality of machine translations[5]. In our context, METEOR evaluates the quality of an activity recommendation based on unigram matches with the ground-truth activity. In addition to exact matches, it also considers semantic similarity in the form of stemmed matches and wordnet-based synonym matches. Analogously to BLEU@k, the meteor hit rate METEOR@k is given by the maximum METEOR score of the first k recommendations.

---

[5] Note that BLEU and METEOR are designed for the comparison of (long) sentences or text corpora. Penalties in the definitions of the metrics can thus cause the metrics to be (close to) zero for short activity recommendations, even if ground truth and recommendation match. Therefore, we manually set the BLEU and METEOR scores to 1 if a recommended activity and the ground-truth activity are an exact match.

Table 2. Values of BLEU, METEOR and cosine similarity for different recommendations given the actual used activity *Notify about outcome*

Recommended activity label	BLEU	METEOR	Cosine Similarity
Notify about outcome	1.0	1.0	1.0
Send notification	0.0	0.0	0.46
Inform about outcome	0.58	0.63	0.80
Send email to customer	0.0	0.0	0.27

Cos@k. The cosine similarity [31] requires representations of the activity recommendation and the ground-truth activity as embeddings, enabling the calculation of the similarity of the two activities in the form of the cosine similarity of their embeddings. Cos@k is the maximum cosine similarity score of the top-k recommendations. In our evaluation, we use the universal sentence encoder [7] to generate the embeddings of activities, which allows Cos@k to consider the semantic similarity of the recommendations and the actual used activity.

Metric Relevance. In a recent user study, Goldstein et al. [19] showed that the employed metrics strongly correlate with experts' ratings of activity recommendations. Thus, they can be confidently used to measure the quality of activity recommendations.

Employing four metrics allows us to gain different kinds of insights. The standard hit rate, Hits@k, is a strict metric in the sense that a hit is realized only if a recommendation and the ground truth are an exact match. If, for example, a recommendation is given by *Notify about outcome* while *Inform about outcome* is used in the test process model, then the recommendation would not count as a hit and the recommendation approach would be considered unsuccessful in this case. However, given its similarity and the fact that there are several possible manners of describing an activity with a label, the recommendation would still be highly useful for the modeler. In this sense, the semantic hit rates BLEU@k, METEOR@k and Cos@k are more practice-oriented. By taking the similarity of recommendations to the ground truth into account, they measure the semantic accuracy of the recommendations. The values of the semantic hit rates are always bigger or equal to the Hits@k values. To illustrate the different levels of similarity that are measured by the three semantic hit rates, Table 2 shows the values of BLEU, METEOR and cosine similarity for four exemplary recommendations from the list in Table 1c, given that the actual used activity label is *Notify about outcome*.

5.4 Evaluation Results

In this section, we first consider the overall results, after which we assess how well BPART5 deals with the key limitations it aims to address: the ability to generate and handle activity labels not contained in the training data.

Table 3. Results of the evaluated approaches

List size	Approach	Hits@k	BLEU@k	METEOR@k	cos@k
$k = 10$	Sola et al. [47]	**0.3102**	0.3358	0.4149	0.5925
	BPART5	0.2800	**0.3876**	**0.5154**	**0.6679**
$k = 1$	Sola et al. [47]	**0.0625**	0.0714	0.1049	0.2539
	BPART5	0.0322	**0.1179**	**0.2269**	**0.4112**

Overall Results. The overall results of our experiments, in which we compare BPART5 to the rule-based recommendation approach from our earlier work [47], are shown in Table 3.[6] Considering a recommendation list of length $k = 10$, the rule-based approach outperforms BPART5 by 11% in terms of the rigid hit rate Hits@10. However, when considering the semantic hit rates, which recognize that activity recommendations that are semantically similar to the ground-truth activity are also useful for modelers, then BPART5 turns out to be superior. It outperforms the rule-based approach by 15%, 24%, and 12% in BLEU@10, METEOR@10, and Cos@10, respectively. Turning to the hit rates for $k = 1$, i.e., the hit rates of the top recommendation of each list, it is equally apparent that the rule-based approach performs better in terms of the standard hit rate, whereas BPART5 achieves better results in terms of the semantic hit rates. Thus, the results indicate that the rule-based approach is more accurate in giving recommendations that correspond exactly to the ground truth. BPART5 is better in generating recommendations that are not an exact match but have a high semantic similarity to the ground truth, though, which means that BPART5 provides in general more relevant recommendations.

Regarding the ranking of suitable activities within a recommendation list, Fig. 3 shows the courses of the standard hit rate Hits@k and the cosine hit rate Cos@k for recommendation lists of lengths $k = 1$ to $k = 10$ as examples. The curves of BLEU@k and METEOR@k, which are not depicted here, are comparable to the curves of Hits@k and Cos@k, respectively. Figure 3a shows that the lines from the Hits@1 to the Hits@10 values are rather straight. The likelihood of finding a—in terms of this metric—suitable recommendation thus increases linearly with each additional activity in the recommendation list. In the case of Cos@k (Fig. 3b), the curves rise more steeply for smaller lengths of the recommendation list, which indicates that both approaches are able to rank recommendations that are semantically similar to the ground truth on the first positions of the recommendation list.

Ability to Generate New Activity Labels. To investigate the ability of the approaches to generate new activity labels, i.e., labels that have not been used in the process models used for training, we performed an in-depth analysis of the labels recommended by both approaches. Overall, the approaches made a total of

---

[6] We performed t-tests for all reported differences between the evaluated approaches, which showed that the differences are statistically significant ($p < 0.001$).

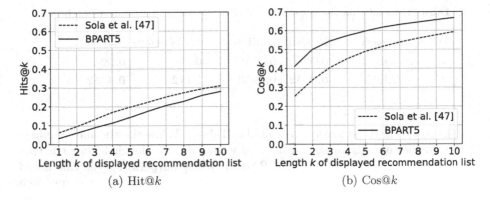

(a) Hit@k (b) Cos@k

Fig. 3. Results for different lengths of the displayed recommendation list

361.430 label recommendations, which corresponds to the number of evaluation cases (36.143) multiplied by the length of the generated recommendation list per evaluation case (ten). The proportion of recommended labels that are newly generated, i.e., do not exist in the process models in the training dataset, is 0% for the rule-based approach and 36.2% for BPART5. In the case of the rule-based approach, 16.551 of the recommended labels are unique, while BPART5 generated 98.857 unique label recommendations, of which 75.6% do not exist in the training dataset.

The difference in the unique numbers of generated label recommendations indicates that BPART5 achieves a higher diversity of recommended labels, while the rule-based approach is dependent on the knowledge in the process models used for training and thus more limited in its recommendations. From the percentages of newly generated labels, we can conclude that BPART5 is able to leverage the knowledge contained in the pre-trained language model and recommend activity labels that go beyond the vocabulary of the process models in the training set. On the one hand, BPART5 performs worse in terms of hit rate for this reason, on the other hand, this leads to less dependency on the given process models used for training and therefore a higher semantic accuracy of BPART5.

Handling Models with only Unseen Labels. Finally, we assess how well BPART5 is able to recommend activity labels for process models that are vastly different from those included in the training set, i.e., that only consist of unseen node labels. In general, such cases represent a considerable challenge for activity-recommendation approaches, as they face a recommendation task that is completely unfamiliar to them.

Out of the total of 36.143 evaluation cases, we found 1.726 evaluation cases from 589 process models that meet this criterion, i.e., where none of the node labels in the process model under development were contained in the training data. We evaluated the approaches on this subset in the same manner as in the evaluation on the whole set of evaluation cases.

Table 4. Results on the subset of evaluation cases with only unseen labels

Approach	Hits@10	BLEU@10	METEOR@10	cos@10
Sola et al. [47]	0.0070	0.0079	0.0628	0.2892
BPART5	**0.0232**	**0.0963**	**0.2112**	**0.4452**

The results of the study are presented in Table 4. While the absolute numbers of the metrics on this subset are naturally low, due to the challenging nature of the cases, the results show that BPART5 clearly outperforms the rule-based approach on the subset in terms of all metrics. Although the rule-based approach is restricted to the knowledge in the process model repository, it is able to generate a few useful recommendations in the form of default label recommendations. Specifically, it recommends the ten most often used activities of the repository whenever none of the rules it learned matches the process model under development, as is applicable to the cases at hand. Nevertheless, the difference between the results of both approaches is much larger than on the complete set of evaluation cases. This demonstrates that BPART5 is not only the better approach in terms of semantic accuracy in general, but also the approach of choice when it comes to recommendations for situations that differ considerably from the available training data.

6 Conclusion and Future Work

In this paper, we presented the BPART5 approach for activity-recommendation, which uses the formal and natural language semantics contained in process models to enable the application of pre-trained sequence-to-sequence language models. Our experiments showed that BPART5 outperforms a state-of-the-art rule-based approach in terms of semantic accuracy, which means that it provides in general more relevant recommendations. We also demonstrated that BPART5 is able to deal with input that differs considerably from what it has seen before, and can even generate label recommendations that go beyond the vocabulary of the model repository used for training. In this sense, it is the first activity-recommendation approach that fully leverages pre-trained models from the NLP domain.

In future work, we would like to address the three main limitations of our work. First, BPART5 requires node sequences of length l-1 (3 in our experiments) for providing recommendations. In future work, we want to investigate possible ways to use not only sequences of a particular length but arbitrary sequences of the process model under development to generate activity recommendations. Second, BPART5 does not yet incorporate information on task types or the organizational perspective, which we aim to include by extending BPART's verbalization procedure. For example, we could consider information about the organization, which owns the process model (pool label), or about the roles, systems or organization's departments that execute the process (lane labels). Additionally, we could also differentiate between gateway splits and gateway joins, or take edge labels into account. Third, our evaluation used artificial recommendation scenarios, whereas in the future we will study the perceived usefulness of our recommendations. In addition, similarly to the work by Meilicke et al. [34], who constructed a method to combine the outcomes of rule-based and latent approaches for knowledge base completion in a post-processing step, we also aim to develop an ensemble method that combines our rule-based approach [47] and BPART5 to generate better activity recommendations.

References

1. Abran, A., Moore, J.W., Bourque, P., Dupuis, R., Tripp, L.: Software Engineering Body of Knowledge. IEEE Computer Society, Angela Burgess (2004)
2. Annane, A., Aussenac-Gilles, N., Kamel, M.: BBO: BPMN 2.0 based ontology for business process representation. In: 20th European Conference on Knowledge Management (ECKM 2019), vol. 1, pp. 49–59 (2019)
3. Bachhofner, S., Kiesling, E., Revoredo, K., Waibel, P., Polleres, A.: Automated process knowledge graph construction from BPMN models. In: Strauss, C., Cuzzocrea, A., Kotsis, G., Tjoa, A.M., Khalil, I. (eds.) Database and Expert Systems Applications. DEXA 2022. LNCS, vol. 13426, pp. 32–47. Springer, Cham (2022). https://doi.org/10.1007/978-3-031-12423-5_3
4. Banerjee, S., Lavie, A.: Meteor: an automatic metric for mt evaluation with improved correlation with human judgments. In: Proceedings of the ACL Workshop on Intrinsic and Extrinsic Evaluation Measures for Machine Translation and/or Summarization, pp. 65–72 (2005)
5. Boehm, B.W., Papaccio, P.N.: Understanding and controlling software costs. IEEE Trans. Softw. Eng. **14**(10), 1462–1477 (1988)
6. Cao, B., Yin, J., Deng, S., Wang, D., Wu, Z.: Graph-based workflow recommendation: on improving business process modeling. In: CIKM, pp. 1527–1531. ACM (2012)
7. Cer, D., et al.: Universal sentence encoder (2018)
8. Davies, I., Green, P., Rosemann, M., Indulska, M., Gallo, S.: How do practitioners use conceptual modeling in practice? Data Knowl. Eng. **58**(3), 358–380 (2006)
9. Deng, S., et al.: A recommendation system to facilitate business process modeling. IEEE Trans. Cybern. **47**(6), 1380–1394 (2017)
10. Fundamentals of Business Process Management. Springer, Heidelberg (2018). https://doi.org/10.1007/978-3-662-56509-4_9
11. Ehrig, M., Koschmider, A., Oberweis, A.: Measuring similarity between semantic business process models. In: APCCM, vol. 7, pp. 71–80 (2007)
12. Fahland, D., Favre, C., Koehler, J., Lohmann, N., Völzer, H., Wolf, K.: Analysis on demand: instantaneous soundness checking of industrial business process models. Data Knowl. Eng. **70**(5), 448–466 (2011)
13. Fellmann, M., Delfmann, P., Koschmider, A., Laue, R., Leopold, H., Schoknecht, A.: Semantic technology in business process modeling and analysis. part 1: matching, modeling support, correctness and compliance. EMISA Forum **35**, 15–31 (2015)

14. Fellmann, M., Delfmann, P., Koschmider, A., Laue, R., Leopold, H., Schoknecht, A.: Semantic technology in business process modeling and analysis. part 2: Domain patterns and (semantic) process model elicitation. EMISA Forum **35**(2), 12–23 (2015)
15. Fellmann, M., Zarvic, N., Metzger, D., Koschmider, A.: Requirements catalog for business process modeling recommender systems. In: WI, pp. 393–407 (2015)
16. Frederiks, P.J., Van der Weide, T.P.: Information modeling: the process and the required competencies of its participants. DKE **58**(1), 4–20 (2006)
17. Friedrich, F., Mendling, J., Puhlmann, F.: Process model generation from natural language text. In: Mouratidis, H., Rolland, C. (eds.) CAiSE 2011. LNCS, vol. 6741, pp. 482–496. Springer, Heidelberg (2011). https://doi.org/10.1007/978-3-642-21640-4_36
18. Goldstein, M., González-Álvarez, C.: Augmenting modelers with semantic auto-completion of processes. In: Polyvyanyy, A., Wynn, M.T., Van Looy, A., Reichert, M. (eds.) BPM 2021. LNBIP, vol. 427, pp. 20–36. Springer, Cham (2021). https://doi.org/10.1007/978-3-030-85440-9_2
19. Goldstein, M., González-Álvarez, C.: Evaluating semantic autocompletion of business processes with domain experts. In: ASE, pp. 1116–1120 (2021)
20. Graves, A.: Sequence transduction with recurrent neural networks. arXiv preprint arXiv:1211.3711 (2012)
21. Gunawardana, A., Shani, G., Yogev, S.: Evaluating Recommender Systems. In: Ricci, F., Rokach, L., Shapira, B. (eds.) Recommender Systems Handbook, pp. 547–601. Springer, New York, NY (2022). https://doi.org/10.1007/978-1-0716-2197-4_15
22. Jannach, D., Fischer, S.: Recommendation-based modeling support for data mining processes. In: RecSys, pp. 337–340 (2014)
23. Jannach, D., Jugovac, M., Lerche, L.: Supporting the design of machine learning workflows with a recommendation system. ACM TiiS **6**(1), 1–35 (2016)
24. Kampik, T., et al.: Sap signavio academic models (2022). https://doi.org/10.5281/zenodo.7012043
25. Kingma, D.P., Ba, J.: Adam: a method for stochastic optimization. In: ICLR (2015)
26. Klein, G., Kim, Y., Deng, Y., Senellart, J., Rush, A.M.: Opennmt: open-source toolkit for neural machine translation. In: Proceedings of ACL 2017, System Demonstrations, pp. 67–72 (2017)
27. Kudo, T.: Subword regularization: improving neural network translation models with multiple subword candidates. In: Gurevych, I., Miyao, Y. (eds.) ACL, no. 1, pp. 66–75. Association for Computational Linguistics (2018)
28. Kudo, T., Richardson, J.: Sentencepiece: a simple and language independent sub-word tokenizer and detokenizer for neural text processing. CoRR abs/1808.06226 (2018)
29. de Leoni, M., Felli, P., Montali, M.: A holistic approach for soundness verification of decision-aware process models. In: Trujillo, J.C., et al. (eds.) ER 2018. LNCS, vol. 11157, pp. 219–235. Springer, Cham (2018). https://doi.org/10.1007/978-3-030-00847-5_17
30. Leopold, H., Niepert, M., Weidlich, M., Mendling, J., Dijkman, R., Stuckenschmidt, H.: Probabilistic optimization of semantic process model matching. In: Barros, A., Gal, A., Kindler, E. (eds.) BPM 2012. LNCS, vol. 7481, pp. 319–334. Springer, Heidelberg (2012). https://doi.org/10.1007/978-3-642-32885-5_25
31. Li, B., Han, L.: Distance weighted cosine similarity measure for text classification. In: Yin, H., et al. (eds.) IDEAL 2013. LNCS, vol. 8206, pp. 611–618. Springer, Heidelberg (2013). https://doi.org/10.1007/978-3-642-41278-3_74

32. Li, Y., et al.: An efficient recommendation method for improving business process modeling. IEEE Trans. Ind. Inf. **10**(1), 502–513 (2014)
33. Loshchilov, I., Hutter, F.: Decoupled weight decay regularization. In: International Conference on Learning Representations (2018)
34. Meilicke, C., Betz, P., Stuckenschmidt, H.: Why a naive way to combine symbolic and latent knowledge base completion works surprisingly well. In: 3rd Conference on Automated Knowledge Base Construction (2021)
35. Meilicke, C., Chekol, M.W., Ruffinelli, D., Stuckenschmidt, H.: Anytime bottom-up rule learning for knowledge graph completion. In: IJCAI, pp. 3137–3143. AAAI Press (2019)
36. Mendling, J., Reijers, H.A., van der Aalst, W.M.: Seven process modeling guidelines (7pmg). Inf. Softw. Technol. **52**(2), 127–136 (2010)
37. Mendling, J., Reijers, H.A., Recker, J.: Activity labeling in process modeling: empirical insights and recommendations. Inf. Syst. **35**(4), 467–482 (2010)
38. Ott, S., Meilicke, C., Samwald, M.: SAFRAN: an interpretable, rule-based link prediction method outperforming embedding models. In: 3rd Conference on Automated Knowledge Base Construction (2021)
39. Papineni, K., Roukos, S., Ward, T., Zhu, W.J.: Bleu: a method for automatic evaluation of machine translation. In: Proceedings of the 40th Annual Meeting of the Association for Computational Linguistics, pp. 311–318 (2002)
40. Paulus, R., Xiong, C., Socher, R.: A deep reinforced model for abstractive summarization. In: International Conference on Learning Representations (2018)
41. Pfeiffer, P., Lahann, J., Fettke, P.: Multivariate business process representation learning utilizing Gramian angular fields and convolutional neural networks. In: Polyvyanyy, A., Wynn, M.T., Van Looy, A., Reichert, M. (eds.) BPM 2021. LNCS, vol. 12875, pp. 327–344. Springer, Cham (2021). https://doi.org/10.1007/978-3-030-85469-0_21
42. Pittke, F., Leopold, H., Mendling, J.: Automatic detection and resolution of lexical ambiguity in process models. IEEE Trans. Softw. Eng. **41**(6), 526–544 (2015)
43. Raffel, C., et al.: Exploring the limits of transfer learning with a unified text-to-text transformer. J. Mach. Learn. Res. **21**(140), 1–67 (2020)
44. Rosemann, M.: Potential pitfalls of process modeling: part a. Bus. Process. Manag. J. **12**(2), 249–254 (2006)
45. Sola, D., Meilicke, C., van der Aa, H., Stuckenschmidt, H.: On the use of knowledge graph completion methods for activity recommendation in business process modeling. In: Marrella, A., Weber, B. (eds.) BPM 2021. LNBIP, vol. 436, pp. 5–17. Springer, Cham (2022). https://doi.org/10.1007/978-3-030-94343-1_1
46. Sola, D., Meilicke, C., van der Aa, H., Stuckenschmidt, H.: A rule-based recommendation approach for business process modeling. In: La Rosa, M., Sadiq, S., Teniente, E. (eds.) CAiSE 2021. LNCS, vol. 12751, pp. 328–343. Springer, Cham (2021). https://doi.org/10.1007/978-3-030-79382-1_20
47. Sola, D., Van der Aa, H., Meilicke, C., Stuckenschmidt, H.: Exploiting label semantics for rule-based activity recommendation in business process modeling. Inf. Syst. **108**, 102049 (2022)
48. Sola, D., Warmuth, C., Schäfer, B., Badakhshan, P., Rehse, J.R., Kampik, T.: Sap signavio academic models: a large process model dataset. arXiv e-prints pp. arXiv-2208 (2022)
49. Sutskever, I., Vinyals, O., Le, Q.V.: Sequence to sequence learning with neural networks. In: NIPS (2014)

50. Thomas, O., Fellmann, M.: Semantic process modeling - design and implementation of an ontology-based representation of business processes. Bus. Inf. Syst. Eng. 1(6), 438–451 (2009)
51. Vaswani, A., et al.: Attention is all you need. Adv. Neural Inf. Process. Syst. 30 (2017)
52. Wang, H., Wen, L., Lin, L., Wang, J.: RLRecommender: a representation-learning-based recommendation method for business process modeling. In: Pahl, C., Vukovic, M., Yin, J., Yu, Q. (eds.) ICSOC 2018. LNCS, vol. 11236, pp. 478–486. Springer, Cham (2018). https://doi.org/10.1007/978-3-030-03596-9_34
53. Wolf, T., et al.: Huggingface's transformers: state-of-the-art natural language processing. CoRR abs/1910.03771 (2019)

Resource

RELD: A Knowledge Graph of Relation Extraction Datasets

Manzoor Ali[✉][iD], Muhammad Saleem[iD], Diego Moussallem[iD],
Mohamed Ahmed Sherif[iD], and Axel-Cyrille Ngonga Ngomo[iD]

DICE Group, Department of Computer Science,
Paderborn University, Paderborn, Germany
manzoor@campus.uni-paderborn.de, saleem@informatik.uni-leipzig.de,
diego.moussallem@uni-paderborn.de, {mohamed.sherif,axel.ngonga}@upb.de
https://www.dice-research.org/

Abstract. Relation extraction plays an important role in natural language processing. There is a wide range of available datasets that benchmark existing relation extraction approaches. However, most benchmarking datasets are provided in different formats containing specific annotation rules, thus making it difficult to conduct experiments on different types of relation extraction approaches. We present RELD, an RDF knowledge graph of eight open-licensed and publicly available relation extraction datasets. We modeled the benchmarking datasets into a single ontology that provides a unified format for data access, along with annotations required for training different types of relation extraction systems. Moreover, RELD abides by the Linked Data principles. To the best of our knowledge, RELD is the largest RDF knowledge graph of entities and relations from text, containing ∼1230 million triples describing 1034 relations, 2 million sentences, 3 million abstracts and 4013 documents. RELD contributes to a variety of uses in the natural language processing community, and distinctly provides unified and easy modeling of data for benchmarking relation extraction and named entity recognition models.

Keywords: Knowledge graph · Relation extraction · benchmarks · Natural language processing. · ontology · RDF

Resource Type: Datasets
Repository: https://github.com/dice-group/RELD
Homepage: https://manzoorali29.github.io/index.html
License: GNU General Public License v3.0
Endpoint: http://reld.cs.upb.de:8890/sparql
Dumps/Local endpoint: https://hobbitdata.informatik.uni-leipzig.de/RELD/
DOI: 10.5281/zenodo.7429677

1 Introduction

Relation extraction (RE) aims to predict a relation between named entities in a natural language text. For example, the sentence *"YouTube is an online video sharing and social media platform owned by Google."* suggests that the relation owned_by holds between the two named entities with labels YouTube and Google, respectively. RE plays an important role in many natural language processing (NLP) applications, including question answering [30], knowledge base creation and completion [24], information extraction, and event identification [15]. Owing to the importance of RE, various machine learning and rule-based approaches have been proposed to extract relations from natural language text [10,17]. Consequently, different RE datasets [5,7,21,22] are also available to benchmark existing RE approaches.

However, benchmarking RE systems with existing RE datasets leads to several challenges. First, the datasets are in *different formats*. For example, NYT-FB [21], and Wikipedia-Wikidata [22] are in JSON, WEBNLG [5] is in XML, and SemEval 2010 Task 8 [7] is in text form. Second, datasets contain different styles of annotations. For example, the relation birthplace has the representation /people/person/place_of_birth in the NYT-FB dataset, while in the WEBNLG dataset, the same birthplace relation is labeled with birthPlace. The different formats and representation require extra work to benchmark the RE systems across different datasets. Third, these datasets are primarily from a single source, which in turn might bias the results achieved by RE systems. For example, the NYT-FB dataset is extracted from New York Times articles, while Wikipedia is the source of FewRel and Wikipedia-Wikidata datasets. Fourth, some datasets have poor or missing annotations (relations, sentences, named entities). For example, NYT-FB has only 2.1 % of the training sentences annotated with corresponding Freebase triplets [25]. Fifth, some of these datasets do not provide a natural language representation of relations. For example, the birthplace relation only has the label P19 in Wikipedia-Wikidata and FewRel [6] datasets. Sixth, some of these datasets focus on a limited number of relations and can hence only be used to benchmark very specific types of RE systems. For example, Google-RE has only four relations and targets binary relation extraction approaches. SemEval targets relation classification, and FewRel is for Few-shots [20] relation classification. To the best of our knowledge, no dataset is specialized for more than one type (binary, ternary, Few-shot, joint entity, relation extraction) of relation extraction. Finally, many of these datasets are imbalanced [23] and contain incorrect annotations [26]. All these shortcomings make it difficult to conduct a comprehensive evaluation of RE tools.

Keeping in view the aforementioned challenges, we present RELD, a single unified RDF representation of eight relation extraction and classification datasets. These datasets include well-known public and freely accessible[1] relation extraction datasets NYT-FB [21], Wikipedia-Wikidata [22], WEBNLG [5],

---

[1] We excluded datasets (e.g., TACRED) that are not freely available in this current version of the RELD. However, they can easily be included in the future.

SemEval 2010 Task 8 [7], Google-RE [16], FewRel [6], T-REx [4] and DocRed [29]. In RELD, each relation and corresponding sentence/document is modeled as a unique RDF resource, to which various statistics/annotations (for example, appearing entities, position of entities in a sentence) are attached in the form of properties. We used various NLP tools to attach the missing annotations. The resulting RELD RDF knowledge graph consists of 1,230 million triples, 1,034 unique relations, 2 million sentences, 3 million abstracts, and 4 thousand documents from different domains. To the best of our knowledge, RELD is the largest RDF dataset for relation extraction. We hope that the diversity of the relations, the unified model underlying the dataset and the improved relation annotations will contribute to easier and more comprehensive evaluations of RE systems.

The rest of this paper is structured as follows: Sect. 2 discusses the RELD data model. In Sect. 3, we outline a selection of use cases that illustrate the potential impact of our dataset and derive some requirements. Section 4 introduces the eight publicly available relation extraction datasets which are converted to RDF. We present details of the resulting RELD dataset and some statistics in Sect. 5. In Sect. 6, we describe the availability and reusability of RELD. Section 7 provides some concrete examples of SPARQL queries over the RELD dataset based on the motivating use cases from Sect. 3, and Sect. 8 concludes.

2   RDF Data Model

Our goal is to create an RDF knowledge graph of existing relation extraction labeled datasets available in different formats. This section describes the RDF data model we utilize to capture the features (see Sect. 3) for underlying NLP tasks (relation extraction, named entity recognition, entity linking, etc.). The design of this data model was based on the following premises:

i. **Generality:** The data model must provide means to represent features of sentences, relations, and entities. The resulting dataset should allow use cases to be implemented based on the meta-data alone without needing to parse sentence text.

ii. **Conciseness:** Since datasets contain millions of sentences and entities, the data model should be concise to keep the overall dataset size manageable.

iii. **Usability:** SPARQL queries over the dataset should execute efficiently without requiring numerous joins or complex filters.

iv. **Compatibility:** IRIs should be made dereferenceable per Linked Data Principles. Furthermore, well-known vocabularies and ontologies should be reused where appropriate.

From these high-level requirements, we can derive a list of more concrete features that should be captured by the RELD data model:

Relation representation: Relations should be modelled in a uniform style that contains corresponding sentences along with their types. Furthermore, equivalent relationships from different source datasets should be identified and interlinked.

Sentence features: The dataset should describe the features used in an individual sentence (e.g., entities position, entities direction) in such a manner that a sentence can be filtered according to the features they use/omit. Similarly, the number of sentences using a single characteristic can be determined.

Sentence statistics: The sentence metadata should likewise capture high-level information about the size and "complexity" of the sentences in terms of number of tokens, entity position, and number of entities tokens variables within a single sentence etc.

Named entities feature: The available named entities in a sentence should be identified along with additional statistics (e.g., types, labels). The correctness of the identified named entities is also key.

In Fig. 1, we provide an overview of the core of the schema for the RELD knowledge graph data model[2]. Listing 1.1 shows all the vocabularies used in RELD while listing 1.2 provides an example[3] output of the RELD knowledge graph.

Listing 1.1. List of all used vocabularies in RELD

```
@prefix reld: <http://reld.dice-research.org/schema/> .
@prefix reldr: <http://reld.dice-research.org/resource/> .
@prefix reldp: <http://reld.dice-research.org/property/> .
@prefix dbo: <http://dbpedia.org/ontology/> .
@prefix dc: <http://purl.org/dc/elements/1.1/> .
@prefix freebase: <http://rdf.freebase.com/ns> .
@prefix owl: <http://www.w3.org/2002/07/owl#> .
@prefix ps: <http://www.wikidata.org/prop/statement/> .
@prefix rdf: <http://www.w3.org/1999/02/22-rdf-syntax-ns#> .
@prefix rdfs: <http://www.w3.org/2000/01/rdf-schema#> .
@prefix xml: <http://www.w3.org/XML/1998/namespace> .
@prefix xsd: <http://www.w3.org/2001/XMLSchema#> .
@prefix prov: <http://www.w3.org/ns/prov#> .
@prefix schema: <http://schema.org/> .
@prefix dicom: <http://purl.org/healthcarevocab/v1> .
@prefix dcterms: <http://purl.org/dc/terms/> .
@prefix nif: <http://persistence.uni-leipzig.org/nlp2rdf/ontologies/nif-core#> .
@prefix foaf: <http://xmlns.com/foaf/0.1/> .
@prefix void: <http://rdfs.org/ns/void#> .
@prefix bibtex: <http://purl.org/net/nknouf/ns/bibtex#> .
@prefix dcat: <http://www.w3.org/ns/dcat> .
@prefix prof: <http://www.w3.org/ns/dx/prof/hasToken> .
```

Dataset: As a practical design decision, we create dataset instances for each dataset, whereby a dataset instance represents a single dataset that we consider for conversion to RDF for RELD. The `reld:Dataset` class contains the basic information about the datasets such as the homepage URL, the task for which the dataset is known, the type of the dataset such as document type or sentence type, title, and language of the dataset[4]. Every instance of `nif:String` (discussed next) linked with the dataset as a `prov:hadPrimarySource`.

---

[2] The detail information of schema, i.e., object properties, data properties, classes are available on RELD homepage.

[3] Due to page size limitation, some details and extra instances are truncated from Listing 1.2.

[4] We use VoID vocabulary to describe different metadata of the dataset.

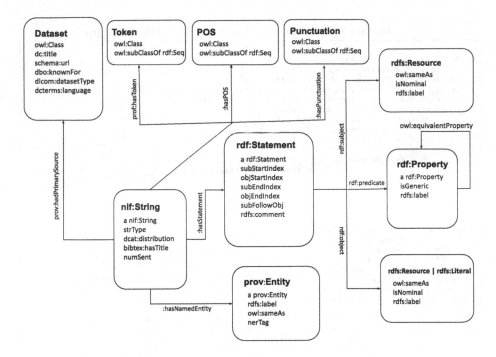

Fig. 1. RELD Data Model

String: For reusability, we use `nif:String` to model each sentence/document of the source dataset. The `nif:String` class avoids the ambiguity between sentences and documents. String class has a property `:strType` that differentiates a string as a sentence or document. Every instance of `nif:String` has an IRI <http://reld.dice-research.org/resource/S-147375> that contains a unique ID. Some datasets, e.g., DocRed contain titles for paragraphs or documents that we map in the RELD model using `bibtex:hasTitle`. RELD uses `dcat:distribution` to know the original distribution (train, test, validation) of a string in the parent datasets. Additionally, the `:numSent` property shows the number of sentences in a paragraph or document if mentioned in the source dataset.

Token, POS and Punctuation: An instance of a string connects to a `:Token` and `:POS` classes using the `prof:hasToken` and `:hasPOS` properties, respectively. `Token` and `POS` are the subclasses of `rdf:Seq`. An instance of a `Token` contains the words of a sentence or document in a sequence, where every token represents a word or punctuation mark in the same order as it appears in the original text.

Listing 1.2. An example listing of RELD knwoledge graph

```
# String Instance
reldr:S-147375 a nif:String ;
    reldr:hasPOS reldr:posSeq147375 ;
    reldr:hasPunctuation reldr:puncSeq147375 ;
    reld:hasNamedEntity reldr:1, reldr:2014, reldr:50000, reldr:koln ;
    reld:hasStatement reldr:Stmt1473750, reldr:Stmt1473751 ;
    reld:strType "sentence"^^xsd:string ;
    dcat:distribution "train"^^xsd:string ;
    prof:hasToken reldr:token_147375 ;
    prov:hadPrimarySource reldr:ds_05 .
# Dataset Instance
reldr:ds_05 a reld:Dataset ;
    dbo:knownFor "natural_language_generation"^^xsd:string ;
    dc:title "WebNLG"^^xsd:string ;
    dcterms:language "en"^^xsd:string ;
    dicom:datasetType "sentence"^^xsd:string ;
    schema:url <https://webnlg-challenge.loria.fr/> .
# Statement Instance
reldr:Stmt1473751 a rdf:Statement ;
    reld:objEndIndex 11 ;
    reld:objStartIndex 11 ;
    reld:subEndIndex 2 ;
    reld:subFollowObj false ;
    reld:subStartIndex 2 ;
    rdf:object reldr:50000 ;
    rdf:predicate reldr:numberOfMembers ;
    rdf:subject reldr:1_fc_k_ln .
# Token Instance
reldr:token_147375 a reld:Token ;
    rdf:_0 "2014"^^xsd:token ;
    rdf:_1 "saw"^^xsd:token ;
    rdf:_10 "have"^^xsd:token ;
    rdf:_11 "50000"^^xsd:token ;
    rdf:_12 "members"^^xsd:token ;
    rdf:_13 "."^^xsd:token ;
    rdf:_2 "1"^^xsd:token ;
    rdf:_3 "."^^xsd:token ;
    rdf:_4 "FC"^^xsd:token ;
    rdf:_5 "Koln"^^xsd:token ;
    rdf:_6 "participating"^^xsd:token ;
    rdf:_7 ","^^xsd:token ;
    rdf:_8 "and"^^xsd:token ;
    rdf:_9 "they"^^xsd:token .
# POS Instance
reldr:posSeq147375 a reld:POS ;
    rdf:_0 "CD"^^xsd:string ;
    rdf:_1 "VBD"^^xsd:string ;
    ...
    rdf:_12 "NNS"^^xsd:string ;
    rdf:_13 "."^^xsd:string ;
# Punctuation Instance
reldr:puncSeq147375 a reld:Punctuation ;
    rdf:_0 "."^^xsd:string ;
    rdf:_1 ","^^xsd:string ;
    rdf:_2 "."^^xsd:string .
# Object Instance
reldr:50000 a rdfs:Literal, prov:Entity ;
    rdfs:label "50000"^^xsd:string ;
    reld:nerTag "CARDINAL"^^xsd:string .
# Entity Instance
reldr:FC_koln a prov:Entity ;
    rdfs:label "koln"^^xsd:string ;
    reld:nerTag "ORG"^^xsd:string ;
    owl:sameAs dbr:FC_koln .
# Property Instance
reldr:numberOfMembers a rdf:Property ;
    rdfs:label "numberOfMembers"^^xsd:string .
# Subject Instance
reldr:1_fc_k_ln a rdfs:Resource ;
    rdfs:label "1_FC_K_ln"^^xsd:string .
```

Similarly, a POS instance represents a part of the speech tag for each corresponding token in the sentence/document. Listing 1.2 shows an example of a :Token and :POS. Likewise, in :Token and :POS classes, the :Punctuation class maps all the punctuation[5] of the original text. It is also the subclass of the rdf:Seq class. :hasPunctuation property links a nif:String to :Punctuation.

Statement: An instance of a nif:String may contain one or more annotated statements linked with them by a property :hasStatement. A Statement consists of a subject of type rdfs:Resource, an object of type rdfs:Resource or rdfs:Literal, and a predicate as rdf:Property. Properties like :subStartIndex, :subEndIndex, :objStartIndex, and :objEndIndex show the position of subject and object entities (also called head entity and tail entity) in a sentence or document. We annotate a statement with :subFollowObj boolean property as True if an object entity appears before a subject entity in the text, False otherwise. Remaining properties shown in the model diagram map further metadata related to each statement in the source dataset.

A subject and object both have a property :isNominal which indicates the sort of entity involved in a relation. For example, the sentence *"The suspect dumped the dead < /e2 >body< /e2 > into a local </e2>reservoir </e2>."* and the relation *"Entity-Destination(e1, e2)"* in SemEval2010 dataset has nominal entities. We take an open-world assumption and keep it True if we know that an entity is nominal.

To consolidate the subject and the object, we did not use any ID for them that enables multiple sentences pointing to a single subject or an object. In addition, the subject entity can appear as an object entity in another text and vice versa if both have type rdfs:Resource. To deal with the lexical variability (same entity but different representations), RELD keeps all of them separately but uses the owl:sameAs property to link the same entity to similar entities in other knowledge bases. For example, *Obama* and *Barack Obama*, we keep them separately, but both entities have owl:sameAs property linking to dbr:Barack_Obama.

rdf:Property: of a statement maintains the annotation of the relation in the source dataset. We disambiguate relations within each dataset, and if two relations represent the same relation, we link them using the owl:equivalentProperty. For example, the WEBNLG dataset has two different annotations for affiliation property *affiliation* and *affiliations*. To preserve the original annotation, RELD keeps both representations and links them using the owl:equivalentProperty. We have manually aligned similar properties based on the similarity information from the literature [13,28]. In the next version, we plan to use LIMES [14] and MAG [12] to score the similarity among properties and improve the linking. For relations like "Entity-Destination(e1,e2)" discussed earlier, RELD introduces the :isGeneric property. In the case of :isGeneric property, we also take an open-world assumption.

Entity: The number of entities plays an essential role in the relation prediction in a natural language text, whether it is not directly involved in the actual

---

[5] We use NLTK [9] for tokenization, parts of speech tagging, and punctuation.

relation [26]. Relation extraction datasets do not provide this information. To overcome this issue and increase the use cases of RELD, we annotate the text for named entities using Spacy [8]. A `String` instance can have zero or more named entities that may or may not be involved directly in a relation. RELD maps this information using the `prov:Entity` class. Using this information, the user can generate a custom benchmark that includes the required numbers of named entities [2]. Furthermore, the `owl:sameAs` property links the entity with other linked datasets[6].

To stick with conciseness, we avoid annotating features that affect the overall score of a relation extraction approach, but a SPARQL query can derive it from other basic annotations. For example, using the properties like `:subStartIndex`, `:subEndIndex`, `:objStartIndex`, and `:objEndIndex` in SPARQL user can retrieve the features such as the number of tokens before the subject entity, after the object entity, or between the two entities [1,3].

3   Impact

In this section, we cover several use cases for RELD to explain the potential impact and usage of the knowledge graph. These are the use cases we foresee going forward:

UC1 Custom Benchmarks The RELD dataset can be used to generate customized, use-case-specific benchmarks (called micro-benchmarks) by selecting the desired number of relations, length, and size of sentences with the desired number of mentioned entities within a sentence. Recently, the RELD dataset has already been used to generate micro-benchmarks according to the user-specified criteria [2]. We provided a sample query in Sect. 7 that shows the use-case-specific benchmarking of the RELD dataset.

UC2 Balanced Dataset Selection For better performance of a model, it requires a balanced dataset to train, where each relation has a similar number of sentences [23]. Using RELD, a balanced sub-dataset generation requires the execution of a single SPARQL query with desired filters. The sub-dataset can train a machine-learning algorithm on a large scale. Section 7 has a sample query that generates a balanced sub-dataset. In addition, the RELD dataset can be used for few-shot relation extraction [19], where a given relation is only found in a few sentences.

UC3 Generic model RELD contains relations and sentences of various types from diverse domains; hence, on top of RELD, we can train and test generic RE models.

UC4 Other NLP tasks In addition, the schema and data of RELD enable it for other underlying natural language processing tasks, such as:
  – **Causal relation classification:** Properties, i.e. `:isGeneric`, `:isNominal` enable RELD to be used for classifying casual relations. RELD contains

---

[6] The complete details of the mapping process and the tools used are available in the tutorial https://reld-tutorial.readthedocs.io/en/latest/tutorial.html.

the SemEval2010 Task 8, a causal relation classification dataset as named graph. Furthermore, the RELD schema can easily incorporate other such datasets.

- **Natural language generation:** The representation of entities and relations in statements makes the RELD schema compatible with the natural language generation datasets. Also, it contains the WebNLG dataset to fulfill this task.
- **Named entity recognition/disambiguation:** Entities annotation and linking with other knowledge bases add NER and NED use-cases to the RELD domain. Also, researchers can exploit RELD knowledge graphs for joint entity and relation extraction models.
- **Document-based Relation extraction:** Apart from sentence-based RE, RELD concisely includes document-based RE datasets, which can train an RE model on documents instead of sentences.

These are only a few use cases, and we can firmly imagine others.

4   Current Used Datasets

In this section, we briefly discuss the datasets that we used for building the RELD knowledge graph. In the current version, we only included those datasets that are publicly available, free of charge, and their license permits us to reuse the data in a different representation. To this end, we excluded datasets that are not free of charge. However, we are planning to include paid datasets (e.g., TACRED [31], ACE2005 [27]) in the future if their license permits. Currently, we also ignore datasets that target specific-purpose relation extraction, such as ChemProt [18], which is for biomedical relation extraction.

We wrote scripts to extract and normalize data from each dataset and map to the target schema explained in Sect. 2. In the current state, RELD consists of eight state-of-the-art open-sourced relation extraction datasets:

Wikipedia-Wikidata (WW) [22] WW dataset is extracted from Wikipedia text and aligned with the Wikidata relations. It is the second-largest dataset in RELD and consists of train, test, and validation sets in JSON format. The primary task of this dataset is the multi-relation (a single sentence can contain multiple relationships) extraction. In RELD, we keep the original annotation of the WW that are Wikidata identifiers. We also exploit Wikidata for the natural language representation of each relation and map it to the `rdfs:label` property.

FewRel [6] Like WW, FewRel's primary source is also Wikipedia for text and Wikidata for annotation. The primary task of this dataset is a few-shot relation classification. It is the only dataset in RELD that contains a balanced number of sentences (i.e., 700) for each relation. Due to the same sources, the basic structure of this dataset is also similar to WW.

NYT-FB [21] A dataset primarily created for distant supervision-based relation extraction is one of the most commonly used datasets in the relation extraction community. The dataset is extracted from New York Times articles and aligned with the freebase dataset. This dataset contains 24 relations, of which 50% are also available in other datasets, while the remaining 50% are unique.

WEBNLG [5] The primary purpose of this dataset is natural language generation. The dataset contains 354 relations that include 'Other' (a sentence may have a relationship, but that is not part of the defined set) relation. This dataset comprises the automatically generated sentences from DBpedia triples, where a sentence contains a range of 1 to 7 triples. This multi-triple nature of sentences in the WEBNLG dataset makes it perfect for the multi-relation extraction task.

Google-RE [16] Google relation extraction dataset consists of four relations represented in JSON format. The primary task of this dataset is binary relation extraction from sentences. Similar to the NYT-FB dataset, this dataset is also aligned with freebase. This dataset does not explicitly specify the train, test, and validation sets. Instead of only sentences, this dataset contains paragraphs for a single relation, so a relationship may appear between two entities that are not necessarily in a single sentence. The average length of the number of tokens is relatively higher than other datasets, which makes Google-RE a challenging dataset.

SemEval 2010 Task 8 [7] Instead of relation extraction, relation classification is the primary task of the SemEval2010 Task 8 dataset. It differs from the other relation extraction datasets as it does not contain a relation between two named entities. But it consists of sentences that have a generic relationship between two nominals. The sentence structure decides the subject and object entities, and the relationship depends on the direction of the two entities. We put :subFollowsObj in the RELD model to identify the order of entities in a sentence and identify the subject and object entities' position in the sentence. Furthermore, RELD handles generic relations using the :isGenric property and nominal entities using the :isNominal property.

DocRed [29] Unlike other datasets, DocRed is used for relation extraction from documents instead of sentences. This dataset is also different from the other relation extraction datasets because it consists of paragraphs (called documents) instead of sentences. It may have one or more relations between two named entities and also has a title. RELD has a property :title to identify the same document of various sentences and has a property :numSent which shows the number of sentences in a document.

T-REx [4] T-REx is the largest dataset mapped to RELD so far. It consists of more than six million sentences and 685 relations. Like FewRel and WW, its primary source is Wikipedia abstracts and Wikidata entities. We represent T-REx as a document-based dataset because of its similarity with the DocRed dataset.

5   RELD Dataset Statistics

Table 1 shows the relation extraction type, origin, number of relationships, and the total number of sentences/docs/abstracts in each selected dataset. It is worth noting that each dataset targets a particular kind of relation extraction that limits the use of a single dataset only for a single type of relation extraction. The RELD dataset contains a good variety in terms of the number of sentences corresponding to different relations. On average, WW provides the highest (5030 sentences) number of sentences per relation, followed by NYT-FB (4638), Google (4237), SemEval (1071), FewRel (700), WEBNLG (218), respectively. Table 2 shows the distribution of the relations and the corresponding sentences according to the train, test, and validation sets.

Table 1. Basic information of all the datasets used in RELD.

Datasets	RE Type	Source	# relation	# Sentences
WEBNLG	NL generation	DBpedia	354	53,786
NYT-FB	Sentence	Web-Freebase	24	111,327
FewRel	Few-shots	Wikipedia-Wikidata	80	56,000
SemEval	Classification	Crowd sourced	10	10,717
Google	Sentence	Web	4	16,948
WW	Sentence	Wikipedia-Wikidata	352	1,770,721
DocRed	Document	Wikipedia-Wikidata	96	4013 docs
T-REx	Sentence/Document	Wikipedia-Wikidata	685	3M abstracts

Table 2. Distribution of relations and sentences/documents in train, test and validation in different dataset. D represents documents, while M for a million

Dataset	Train		Validation		Test	
	relations	sent/docs	relations	sent/docs	relations	sent/docs
WEBNLG	246	74,779	186	72,719	246	80,710
NYT-FB	24	111,327	22	111,324	22	111,324
FewRel	64	44,800	16	11,200	0	0
SemEval	10	8,000	0	0	10	2,717
Google	4	16,948	0	0	0	0
WW	352	1,770,721	352	1,770,721	352	1,770,721
DocRed	96	3,053D	96	1000D	96	1000D
T-REx	685	6.02M/3M	0	0	0	0
Overall	**1,481**	**8.04M/3M~**	**672**	**0.36M/1K**	**726**	**1.96M/1K**

Table 3. Basic RDF statistics of the RELD datasets. SUB & OBJ represents subject and objects respectively, while R for resource and L for literal

Dataset	Triples	Resources	Named Entities	sameAs	Statements
SemEval	0.68M	7,592	8,941	907	10,717
NYT-FB	7.85M	14,663	365,373	17,179	111,327
FewRel	4.75M	71,940	231,122	23,969	56,000
WebNLG	1.02M	2,555	42,473	827	30,849
Google-RE	3.13M	20,028	169,319	14,169	14,458
WW	78.16M	515,422	3,701,186	512,010	1,770,721
DocRed	2.55M	25,675	84,066	9,408	50,503
T-REx	1132.08M	-	43,897,838	4,416,214	20,834,823

Table 3 shows various RDF-related features for each source dataset. In total, we have 1230 million triples, 48.5 million named entities, 5 million `owl:sameAs` links, and 23 million statements included in the final RELD dataset. Finally, Table 4 shows information about the structure and complexity of the sentences of the selected datasets, where average Before refers to the average number of tokens in the sentence before the subject entity of a relation. Similarly, AVG Between refers to the number of tokens between the subject and object entity, and AVG after refers to the number of tokens after the object entity. Clearly, the Google-RE dataset is more complex in terms of the number of tokens per sentence. Despite complex sentence structures, RE systems perform better (in terms of F scores) on Google-RE dataset [11]. This indicates that evaluation based on a single dataset with a small number of relations (4 in google dataset) might not sufficiently stress the RE systems. In total, there are 125 overlapping relations in the selected datasets. Overlapping relations have different representations in each dataset. For example, The Wikipedia-Wikidata dataset has a relation P19 that represents the place of birth; the same relationship is presented as /people/person/place_of_birth in NYT-FB and Google-RE, and is called birthPlace in the WEBNLG dataset. We use the `:equivalentProperty` to highlight the same relations from different datasets. Table 5 shows the top five relationships which appear in more than one dataset. Figure 2 shows the number of overlapping relationships among the three sentence-based datasets.

The `:equivalentProperty` increases the number of sentences for a given relation because it makes RELD capable of discovering all sentences that contain the given relationship in a different form. Figure 3 shows the range of sentences for a different number of relations that are available in more than one dataset. For example, Fig. 3a shows that 385 relationships have less than 100 sentences. However, in Fig. 3b this number reduces to 167 relationships by using `:equivalentProperty` information, which also increases the number of sentences for those relations. Furthermore, some datasets contain similar relations with different names, like *affiliation* vs. *affiliations* or *Leader* vs. *Leader-Name* in the WEBNLG dataset. We identify 22 such relations manually and use `:equivalentProperty` to relate all those relations.

Table 4. Tokens-related information from all the sentence based datasets.

Datasets	Avg Tokens	Tokens > 30	Avg Before	Avg Between	Avg After
WEBNLG	27	37%	2.6	7	14
NYT-FB	39	70%	12.6	9	14
FewRel	24	23%	6.5	6	7
SemEval	19	10%	5.1	4	7
Google	74	79%	0.07	4	68
WW	24	16%	7.3	6	7

Table 5. Top 5 relations that occurred in more than one dataset in RELD

Relation	WEBNLG	NYT-FB	FewRel	SemEval	Google	WW	DocRed	T-REx
birthDate	✓	✗	✗	✗	✓	✓	✓	✓
birthPlace	✓	✓	✗	✗	✓	✓	✓	✓
deathPlace	✓	✓	✗	✗	✓	✓	✓	✓
nationality	✓	✓	✓	✗	✗	✓	✓	✓
country	✓	✓	✓	✗	✗	✓	✓	✓
location	✓	✓	✓	✗	✗	✓	✓	✓

6   Resource Availability, Reusability, Sustainability

The resource is publicly available from the homepage, which contains the complete source code, data, and documentation. The homepage also links to the corresponding RELD ontology. The same home page will be used for sustainability and adding future datasets into the RELD. Paderborn Center for Parallel Computing PC2 will sustain the RELD resources. PC2 provides computing resources and consultation regarding their usage; to research projects at Paderborn University and external research groups. The Information and Media Technologies Center (IMT) at Paderborn University also provides a permanent IT infrastructure to host the RELD project. The open-source code available on GitHub is easily extendable to convert other datasets in the future. The RELD dataset is publicly available from the SPARQL endpoint, where the user can execute a SPARQL query for desired output.

7   RELD in Practice

We have made the RELD dataset available through three media: (i) dereferenceable Linked Data, (ii) flat dumps, and (iii) a SPARQL endpoint. In this section, we provide a few concrete queries that can be issued against the RELD SPARQL endpoint to derive insights relevant to some use cases discussed in Sect. 3.

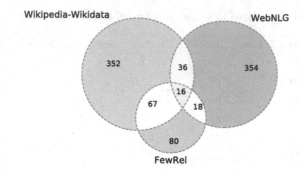

Fig. 2. Venn diagram for the number of overlapping relations in the three sentence-based datasets

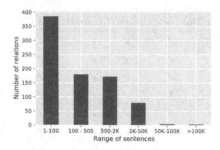

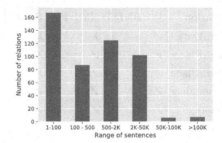

(a) Without `owl:equivalentProperty`   (b) With `owl:equivalentProperty`

Fig. 3. Number of relations in range of sentences in RELD

UC1 Facilitating Custom Benchmark Generation: RELD can help users to generate custom benchmark meeting defined criteria for a given use case.

Listing 1.3. UC1: Generate benchmark of having sentences length less than 50, and other required features

```
PREFIX reld: <http://reld.dice-research.org/schema/>
PREFIX nif: <http://persistence.uni-leipzig.org/nlp2rdf/ontologies/nif-core#>
PREFIX prof: <http://www.w3.org/ns/dx/prof/>

SELECT DISTINCT
?sent (count(?t) as Tokens) (count(?e) as ?Entities) (count(?stmt) as ?
    Statment)
WHERE
        {?sent a nif:String;
               reld:hasStatement ?stmt;
               reld:hasNamedEntity ?e;
               prof:hasToken ?token.
          ?token ?p ?t.
}
GROUP BY ?sent
HAVING(COUNT(?stmt) > 4 && COUNT(?e) > 10 && COUNT(?t) < 50)
```

Listing 1.3 is an example SPARQL query over RELD that selects a benchmark, each containing less than 50 tokens and more than 10 entities and more than four relations. RELD-based microbenchmarking framework for RE systems is presented in [2], where users can generate customized and more representative benchmarks by using different clustering techniques.

UC2 Balanced Dataset. To generate a balanced dataset, where all the selected relations should have the same number of relevant sentences. Listing 1.4 selects a benchmark of relations where each relationship has exactly 700 annotated sentences that contain this relation.

Listing 1.4. UC2: A balance dataset of relations each having 700 sentneces that contain the given relation.

```
PREFIX reld: <http://reld.dice-research.org/schema/>
PREFIX nif: <http://persistence.uni-leipzig.org/nlp2rdf/ontologies/nif-core#>
PREFIX prof: <http://www.w3.org/ns/dx/prof/>

SELECT DISTINCT ?properties  COUNT(?sent)
  WHERE {
          ?sent a nif:String;
          reld:hasStatement ?stmt.
          ?stmt rdf:predicate ?properties.
          }
GROUP BY ?properties
HAVING( COUNT(?sent) = 700)
```

8 Conclusion and Future Work

We presented RELD, to the best of our knowledge, the first publicly available knowledge graph for relation extraction that describes sentences with their annotation and labeled relations. We discussed various use cases for RELD with a detailed description of the model and basic statistics about the used datasets. Furthermore, we hope RELD can facilitate the benchmarking of the relation extraction tools. We are targeting to incorporate multilingual datasets to increase their use cases. The initial processing of multilingual datasets has already been in the final stages, and we will announce the integration to RELD on the project homepage. In addition, paid datasets such as TACRED [31] are also under consideration in the future. Finally, we plan to train a generic relation extraction model which extends the scope in terms of number relations and variability.

Acknowledgment. This work has been supported by the BMBF-funded EuroStars project PORQUE (01QE2056C), the European Union's Horizon Europe research and innovation programme ENEXA (101070305), the Ministry of Culture and Science of North Rhine-Westphalia (MKW NRW) within the project SAIL (NW21-059D) and the University of Malakand Pakistan.

References

1. Agichtein, E., Gravano, L.: Snowball: extracting relations from large plain-text collections. In: Proceedings of the Fifth ACM Conference on Digital Libraries, pp. 85–94 (2000)

2. Ali, M., Saleem, M., Ngomo, A.C.N.: Rebench: microbenchmarking framework for relation extraction systems. In: Sattler, U., et al. (eds.) ISWC 2022. LNCS, vol. 13489, pp. 643–659. Springer, Heidelberg (2022). https://doi.org/10.1007/978-3-031-19433-7_37

3. Batista, D.S., Martins, B., Silva, M.J.: Semi-supervised bootstrapping of relationship extractors with distributional semantics. In: Empirical Methods in Natural Language Processing. ACL (2015)

4. Elsahar, H., et al.: T-rex: a large scale alignment of natural language with knowledge base triples. In: Proceedings of the Eleventh International Conference on Language Resources and Evaluation (LREC 2018) (2018)

5. Gardent, C., Shimorina, A., Narayan, S., Perez-Beltrachini, L.: Creating training corpora for NLG micro-planners. In: Proceedings of the 55th Annual Meeting of the Association for Computational Linguistics (Volume 1: Long Papers), Vancouver, Canada, pp. 179–188. Association for Computational Linguistics (2017). https://doi.org/10.18653/v1/P17-1017. https://aclanthology.org/P17-1017

6. Han, X., et al.: Fewrel: a large-scale supervised few-shot relation classification dataset with state-of-the-art evaluation. In: EMNLP (2018)

7. Hendrickx, I., et al.: SemEval-2010 task 8: multi-way classification of semantic relations between pairs of nominals. In: Proceedings of the 5th International Workshop on Semantic Evaluation, Uppsala, Sweden, pp. 33–38. Association for Computational Linguistics (2010). https://aclanthology.org/S10-1006

8. Honnibal, M., Montani, I.: spacy 2: natural language understanding with bloom embeddings, convolutional neural networks and incremental parsing. $7(1)$, 411–420 (2017, to appear)

9. Loper, E., Bird, S.: Nltk: the natural language toolkit. arXiv preprint cs/0205028 (2002)

10. Martinez-Rodriguez, J.L., Hogan, A., Lopez-Arevalo, I.: Information extraction meets the semantic web: a survey. Semant. Web $11(2)$, 255–335 (2020)

11. Moreira, J., Oliveira, C., Macêdo, D., Zanchettin, C., Barbosa, L.: Distantly-supervised neural relation extraction with side information using BERT. In: 2020 International Joint Conference on Neural Networks (IJCNN), pp. 1–7 (2020). https://doi.org/10.1109/IJCNN48605.2020.9206648

12. Moussallem, D., Usbeck, R., Röeder, M., Ngomo, A.C.N.: Mag: a multilingual, knowledge-base agnostic and deterministic entity linking approach. In: Proceedings of the Knowledge Capture Conference, pp. 1–8 (2017)

13. Nadgeri, A., et al.: KGPool: dynamic knowledge graph context selection for relation extraction. In: Findings of the Association for Computational Linguistics: ACL-IJCNLP 2021, pp. 535–548. Association for Computational Linguistics (2021). https://doi.org/10.18653/v1/2021.findings-acl.48. https://aclanthology.org/2021.findings-acl.48

14. Ngonga Ngomo, A.C., et al.: LIMES - a framework for link discovery on the semantic web. KI-Künstliche Intelligenz, German Journal of Artificial Intelligence - Organ des Fachbereichs "Künstliche Intelligenz" der Gesellschaft für Informatik e.V. (2021). https://papers.dice-research.org/2021/KI_LIMES/public.pdf

15. Ning, Q., Feng, Z., Roth, D.: A structured learning approach to temporal relation extraction. arXiv preprint arXiv:1906.04943 (2019)

16. Orr, D.: 50,000 lessons on how to read: a relation extraction corpus. Online: Google Research Blog, vol. 11 (2013)

17. Pawar, S., Palshikar, G.K., Bhattacharyya, P.: Relation extraction: a survey. arXiv preprint arXiv:1712.05191 (2017)

18. Peng, Y., Yan, S., Lu, Z.: Transfer learning in biomedical natural language processing: an evaluation of BERT and ELMo on ten benchmarking datasets. arXiv preprint arXiv:1906.05474 (2019)
19. Qu, M., Gao, T., Xhonneux, L.P., Tang, J.: Few-shot relation extraction via Bayesian meta-learning on relation graphs. In: Daume III, H., Singh, A. (eds.) Proceedings of the 37th International Conference on Machine Learning. Proceedings of Machine Learning Research, vol. 119, pp. 7867–7876. PMLR (2020). https://proceedings.mlr.press/v119/qu20a.html
20. Ravi, S., Larochelle, H.: Optimization as a model for few-shot learning (2016)
21. Riedel, S., Yao, L., McCallum, A., Marlin, B.M.: Relation extraction with matrix factorization and universal schemas. In: Proceedings of the 2013 Conference of the North American Chapter of the Association for Computational Linguistics: Human Language Technologies, pp. 74–84 (2013)
22. Sorokin, D., Gurevych, I.: Context-aware representations for knowledge base relation extraction. In: Proceedings of the 2017 Conference on Empirical Methods in Natural Language Processing, Copenhagen, Denmark, pp. 1784–1789. Association for Computational Linguistics (2017). https://doi.org/10.18653/v1/D17-1188. https://aclanthology.org/D17-1188
23. Sui, D., Chen, Y., Liu, K., Zhao, J., Zeng, X., Liu, S.: Joint entity and relation extraction with set prediction networks. arXiv preprint arXiv:2011.01675 (2020)
24. Surdeanu, M., Tibshirani, J., Nallapati, R., Manning, C.D.: Multi-instance multi-label learning for relation extraction. In: Proceedings of the 2012 Joint Conference on Empirical Methods in Natural Language Processing and Computational Natural Language Learning, pp. 455–465 (2012)
25. Tran, T.T., Le, P., Ananiadou, S.: Revisiting unsupervised relation extraction. In: Proceedings of the 58th Annual Meeting of the Association for Computational Linguistics, pp. 7498–7505. Association for Computational Linguistics (2020). https://www.aclweb.org/anthology/2020.acl-main.669
26. Tran, T.T., Le, P., Ananiadou, S.: Revisiting unsupervised relation extraction (2020). https://doi.org/10.48550/ARXIV.2005.00087. https://arxiv.org/abs/2005.00087
27. Walker, C., Strassel, S., Medero, J., Maeda, K.: ACE 2005 multilingual training corpus. Linguistic Data Consortium, Philadelphia, vol. 57, p. 45 (2006)
28. Wang, Y., Yu, B., Zhang, Y., Liu, T., Zhu, H., Sun, L.: TPLinker: single-stage joint extraction of entities and relations through token pair linking. In: Proceedings of the 28th International Conference on Computational Linguistics, Barcelona, Spain, pp. 1572–1582. International Committee on Computational Linguistics (2020). https://doi.org/10.18653/v1/2020.coling-main.138. https://aclanthology.org/2020.coling-main.138
29. Yao, Y., et al.: Docred: a large-scale document-level relation extraction dataset. arXiv preprint arXiv:1906.06127 (2019)
30. Yu, M., Yin, W., Hasan, K.S., Santos, C.d., Xiang, B., Zhou, B.: Improved neural relation detection for knowledge base question answering. arXiv preprint arXiv:1704.06194 (2017)
31. Zhang, Y., Zhong, V., Chen, D., Angeli, G., Manning, C.D.: Position-aware attention and supervised data improve slot filling. In: Proceedings of the 2017 Conference on Empirical Methods in Natural Language Processing, pp. 35–45 (2017)

IMKG: The Internet Meme Knowledge Graph

Riccardo Tommasini[1]([✉]), Filip Ilievski[2], and Thilini Wijesiriwardene[3]

[1] LIRIS Lab (CNRS), INSA Lyon, Villeurbanne, France
riccardo.tommasini@insa-lyon.fr
[2] Information Sciences Institute, University of South California,
Los Angeles, CA, USA
ilievski@isi.edu
[3] Artificial Intelligence Institute of University of South Carolina (AIISC),
Columbia, SC, USA
thilini@sc.edu

Abstract. Internet Memes (IMs) are creative media that combine text and vision modalities that people use to describe their situation by reusing an existing, familiar situation. Prior work on IMs has focused on analyzing their spread over time or high-level classification tasks like hate speech detection, while a principled analysis of their stratified semantics is missing. Hypothesizing that Semantic Web technologies are appropriate to help us bridge this gap, we build the first *Internet Meme Knowledge Graph (IMKG)*: an explicit representation with 2 million edges that capture the semantics encoded in the text, vision, and metadata of thousands of media frames and their adaptations as memes. IMKG is designed to fulfil seven requirements derived from the inherent characteristics of IMs. IMKG is based on a comprehensive semantic model, it is populated with data from representative IM sources, and enriched with entities extracted from text and vision connected through background knowledge from Wikidata. IMKG integrates its knowledge both in RDF and as a labelled property graph. We provide insights into the structure of IMKG, analyze its central concepts, and measure the effect of knowledge enrichment from different information modalities. We demonstrate its ability to support novel use cases, like querying for IMs that are based on films, and we provide insights into the signal captured by the structure and the content of its nodes. As a novel publicly available resource, IMKG opens the possibility for further work to study the semantics of IMs, develop novel reasoning tasks, and improve its quality.

Keywords: internet memes · knowledge graphs · content enrichment

Resource type: Knowledge Graph
License: MIT
PURL: https://w3id.org/imkg
GitHub: https://github.com/riccardotommasini/imkg
DOI: https://doi.org/10.5281/zenodo.7457166.
The original version of this chapter was revised: the family name of the second author was corrected. The correction to this chapter can be found at https://doi.org/10.1007/978-3-031-33455-9_42

C. Pesquita et al. (Eds.): ESWC 2023, LNCS 13870, pp. 354–371, 2023.
https://doi.org/10.1007/978-3-031-33455-9_21

Fig. 1. Dissection of an Internet Meme.

1   Introduction

Internet Memes (IMs) can be defined as "a piece of culture, typically a joke, which gains influence through online transmission" [6]. An IM is based on a medium, typically an image representing a well-understood reference to a proto-typical situation within a certain community [32]. IMs have become very popular in today's Internet era where the real and the virtual are getting closer and closer, and almost any person, event, and idea have a Web counterpart. According to a recent survey by Facebook, 75% of people between 13 and 36 share Internet Memes (IMs), and 30% do it daily.[1] Thus, IMs easily traverse the Web, originating from niche platforms with low-moderation strategies and then migrating to mainstream social media [32]. During their migration, IMs change to gain the peculiar cultural fingerprint of each community until they become less relevant.

As potential vectors for misinformation [21] and political propaganda [25], but also as a novel digital medium for expressing complex and relatable ideas [5], IMs have been of interest to cognitive linguistics [5], psychology [13], and neuroscience [23]. Recent computer science research on IMs focuses on analyzing their spread (i.e., "virality") [18,22,31] or their relation to hate speech in fringe communities [10,14,15]. However, to our knowledge, no prior work has attempted to dissect the IM semantics at scale.

This paper is built on the premise that Knowledge Graphs (KGs) and their interlinking within the Semantic Web can adequately capture the semantics of IMs. We design and construct the first Internet Meme Knowledge Graph (IMKG), which explicitly represents the semantics encoded in the text, vision, and metadata of IMs. Based on the well-motivated characteristics of IMs from the literature, we derive a set of seven requirements that an IMKG should fulfil. We design a data model that aligns the notions of a media frame (i.e., the original scene that inspires the meme), the meme itself, and the underlying template that can be used to generate additional memes. We populate our KG with IM information scraped from a variety of popular IM sources: a meme encyclopedia, an IM generation website, and an open KG. We enrich the data by object detection from the meme image, entity extraction from the meme caption and

---

[1] https://www.facebook.com/notes/10158928003998415, accessed 17/12/2022.

background description, and Wikidata knowledge for adding background knowledge about the extracted entities and existing memes. We complete the IMKG construction by integrating the sources into a cohesive graph that is publicly available as RDF and a labelled property graph (LPG). Our analytics of IMKG shows that its data is centred around popular memes and slang terms, that the different modalities provide complementary information, and that it can support novel use cases like obtaining IMs that are based on films or meme matching by similarity. In summary, the paper makes the following contributions, described in detail in the indicated sections:

1. We study and motivate the need to study Internet Memes, pointing to their unique properties of multimodality, succinctness, relatability, and fluidity (Sect. 2). We formalize these properties into seven requirements for a comprehensive KG of IMs (Sect. 3).
2. We construct IMKG: the first Internet Meme Knowledge Graph that satisfies these requirements. The creation of IMKG consists of four main steps: KG modelling, data collection, knowledge enrichment, and knowledge integration (Sect. 4).
3. We provide insights into the structure of IMKG, analyze its central concepts, and measure the effect of knowledge enrichment from different information modalities. We demonstrate its ability to support novel use cases, like querying for IMs that are based on films, and we provide insights into the signal captured by the structure and the content of its nodes (Sect. 5).

2   Background

Origin of Internet Memes. The idea of IMs stems from Richard Dawkins' notion of biological memes, coined as a *"unit of cultural transmission, or a unit of imitation"* [7]. Dawkins draws an analogy between memes and genes, describing both as self-replicating entities: like genes, memes are transmitted between individuals, yet through imitation rather than duplication. Thus, memes propagate themselves through people and, then, through time. As a recent actualization of the meme phenomenon, IMs are concepts, customs, and habits, i.e., the building blocks of culture and society. According to Davison [6], a key defining aspect of IMs is *online transmission*, which requires IMs to be encoded into an internet-viable medium (visual, sound, text, or multimodal), and shared online. In the rest of the paper, we use "meme" and "Internet Meme" as synonyms.

Sources of IMs. On the Web, millions of minds work in tune to create, manipulate, adapt, and share IMs. The spread is extremely fast due to the hyperconnected nature of Web communities. Therefore, large **social media platforms**, such as Reddit, 4chan, and Twitter, are the natural habitat for IMs. An essential aspect of IMs' virality is their accessibility to the general public: anybody is a content creator on the Web. Meme **generators**, e.g., ImgFlip, are essential as they provide blank IMs templates for users to caption without

Table 1. Summary of Internet Meme Sources.

	Example	Open	Data Quality	Virality	Lore	Usage
Generators	ImgFlip	partially	medium	partially	no	yes
Encyclopedias	KYM	yes	high	yes	yes	partially
Large KGs	Wikidata	yes	high	no	partially	no
Social Media	reddit,twitter	partially	low	yes	no	yes

requiring editing skills. Central resources for IM knowledge are IM **encyclopedias:** non-academic efforts that collect and catalog IMs. A popular example is KnowYourMeme[2], which serves as a reference source for memes, analogous to how Wikipedia is the reference source for general world knowledge. Encyclopedias like KnowYourMeme provide essential background information about memes. They strive to explain their underlying lore and identify the IM origins, variations, usage, and, sometimes even interpretations of their meaning. Like Wikipedia, IM encyclopedias are collaborative, i.e., volunteers provide the information as unstructured and semi-structured text.

The popularity of IMs has reached a level that knowledge graphs like Wikidata [34], DBpedia [2], and Freebase [3] provide a wealth of background knowledge about IMs and their described concepts. As such, these sources promise to provide implicit knowledge not provided in IMs or their metadata. Among the listed sources, Wikidata has been found to have the highest quality [9], owing to its crowd-sourcing approach, semantic validation mechanisms, and active contributor pool. Wikidata has nearly 1.5 billion statements about nearly 100 million entities, including reliable links to thousands of other sources, including KnowYourMeme.

Table 1 summarises the characteristics of different IM sources. As apparent in this table, open and high-quality information about IMs is available in IM encyclopedias and large KGs, while the information type varies across sources. For instance, Lore is described in encyclopedias, and usage information is found in generators in social media. In this work, we focus on aggregating knowledge from generators, encyclopedias, and large KGs. We leave social media sources for future work, as these platforms are often restricted in their access and provide limited hints to IM interpretation.

Prior Work on IMs. IMs have been a prerogative subject of cognitive linguistics studies [5], although their relevance is noticeable also in psychology [13], neuroscience [23], and online communication studies [25]. Most prior works on IMs in AI have focused on understanding their virality and spread on social media over time [18,22,31]. Another popular direction has been detecting forms of hate speech in memes. The Hateful Memes Challenge and Dataset [14] is a competition and open-source dataset with over 10 thousand examples. The goal is to leverage vision and language understanding to identify memes that employ hate

---

[2] https://knowyourmeme.com/.

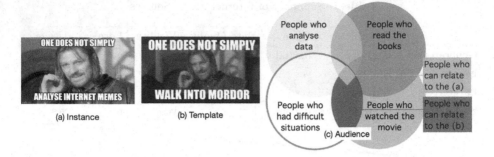

Fig. 2. Examples of multimodality and relatability explained.

speech. Kirk et al. [15] compare memes in this challenge to memes in the 'wild', observing that extracting captions is an open challenge and that open-world memes are more diverse than traditional memes. The Multimedia Automatic Misogyny Identification (MAMI) [10] challenge asks systems to identify misogynous IMs based on text and images in the input memes. MAMI has two subtasks: binary categorization of memes as misogynous or not misogynous, and finer categorization of types of misogyny as a stereotype, shaming, objectification, or violence. Methods for these challenges typically employ Transformer-based models that incorporate vision and language, like ViLBERT [20], UNITER [4], and CLIP [26]. Case-based reasoning methods that reason over instances or IM prototypes have been developed, providing explanations and visualizing them in a user-friendly interface [32]. Most similar to ours is the work by Sheratt [30] on organizing memes into genealogy with the goal to build a comprehensive knowledge base in the future. To our knowledge, no prior work has produced a KG to capture the stratified semantics of IMs provided explicitly in text or vision or implicitly through references to assumed background knowledge.

3 Problem Statement

Challenges. Prior works on memes are limited for two main reasons: 1) the multifaceted nature of IMs unveils a number of hard challenges for AI that make the automated analysis of IMs an open problem; 2) they limit their data work to few, exclusive yet limited datasets, a common pitfall for AI work [29]. A highly-curated and evolving Knowledge Graph of Internet Memes can address both issues. We identify four key challenges that concern the construction of a comprehensive KG about Internet Memes:

C1: IMs are **multimodal**, they come in different formats, generally visuals and text, but also gifs and sounds. At present, the integration of text and vision is a challenging problem for AI, relating to challenges of representation, information fusion, and reasoning [17]. IMs are constructed by overlaying a natural language

(i)   (ii)   (iii)   (iv)

Fig. 3. Examples of Variations.

caption over a visual medium, e.g., an image [5,36]. A meme overlays information over a visual medium, i.e., an image or video, with a natural language caption. Figure 2 a) and b) clarify the multimodality showing the template and an example of the IM "One does not simply walk into Mordor", which consists of a frame from Peter Jackson's 2002 movie adaptation depicting Sean Bean. The interplay between the visual and the textual information enables for a creative expression of ideas, be it humour or political commentary, and relies heavily on background knowledge [32].

C2: IMs are **succinct**, i.e., they convey complex messages with simple language. The IM succinctness owes to the stratified semantics that includes the original media frame, the template, a meme adaptation, and the background knowledge that constitutes the IMs' lore. Figure 1 shows such a stratification for the running example, illustrated with a reference frame *Difficulty in Action*. Namely, one can reuse the Lord of the Rings frame that symbolizes a futile undertaking [5] to express their perspective that analyzing memes is more difficult than expected. According to [19], memes should be considered as examples of multimodal similes, not multimodal metaphors, since the source and the target domain are not blended, but continue to be available as dissimilar, yet corresponding, domains.

C3: IMs are **relatable**, i.e., they are recognizable by the members of a certain community. Figure 2 c) exemplifies the community associated to the IM "One does not simply walk into Mordor" as we used in our example "One does not simply analyse internet memes". The target audience of our IM is clearly who normally analyse data, which are used to difficult tasks. Nonetheless, the IM results are clearer to those that have read the book and/or watched the movie. The IM relatability seems to alternate the sentiment of the referred situation, i.e., they trigger a sense of sympathy in the viewer, especially those who understand the lore. Thus, IMs can be powerful tools for social good, such as traumatic confessions and coping mechanisms [1], but also vehicles for political propaganda [25] and hate speech [14]. Relatability is often supported by a humorous and lightweight tone, however, IMs are not intrinsically funny. Indeed, Fig. 2 does not pass a positive message, yet the expected reaction from a target viewer is positive similar to "misery loves company".

C4: IMs are **fluid**, i.e., they are subject to variations and alterations. In one study by Meta, 121,605 different variants of one particular meme were posted across 1.14 million status updates. Figure 3 shows a few variations of the IM

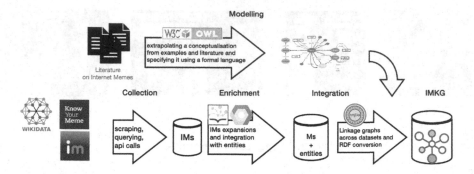

Fig. 4. IMKG Construction Pipeline

"One does not simply walk into Mordor". Such variations include, but are not limited to, (i) image and text to include community-specific slang; (ii) visual changes that further contextualise the caption; (iii) image redoing that extends the lore (e.g., setting from Dr Who), and (iv) image revision that crossover with extra source (e.g., Disney's logo).

It is important to distinguish, at the modelling level, between variations that are within the utilisation pattern of the IMs (e.g., captioning) and those that imply a change in the semantics, e.g., an extension of the meme lore or a change of sentiment. A deep understanding of the IM dynamics over time and across platforms is essential to grasping their semantics.

Notably, these four IM characteristics are tightly connected. Fluidity combines with relatability making IMs attractive for spreading across online communities. Relatability can impact multimodality because some communities are more present on social media networks with more video content than images.

Requirements. We transform these challenges into requirements for the construction and maintenance of an IMKG. Addressing *multimodality* requires constructing a KG that reliably captures both textual and visual information during its data collection and content provision. In other words, IMKG must collect information about *multiple modalities* (R1), and make that information *available* as appropriate (R2). To address the aspect of *succinctness*, IMKG must design a process that clearly dissects the IM stratification (R3). It also must provide the means for *exploring and interpreting* the various semantic layers (R4). To support *relatability*, the IMKG representation must represent links between communities that generate IMs (R5). To facilitate *fluidity*, it must record links to and between the original IM sources (R6). Moreover, fluidity requires that the IMKG incorporates *variations* of a given meme by recording the original media frame, its adaptations, and the common template (R7).

4   Construction of the Internet Meme Knowledge Graph

The construction of IMKG consists of four steps, as shown in Fig. 4. Namely, we start by designing a KG model that can capture the semantics of Internet

Memes, reflecting their multimodality, intended succinctness, relatability, and fluidity. We collect data from representative sources of internet memes, combining encyclopedias, meme generation sites, and open large KGs. We enrich the collected information based on textual processing, visual processing, and background knowledge. Finally, we integrate the extracted information following the developed model by using a schema mapping language and publish IMKG in RDF and LPG format.

Step 1: Data Modelling. We design an integrated conceptual model that can express key properties of IMs following data integration principles [16]. We scope the coverage of our IMKG to **Image macros**, common and representative subgenre of Internet Memes consisting of: (i) A background image that is chosen such that it is immediately recognizable by the intended audience and provides them context (ii) Superimposed text as a caption, whose position is fixed, and that contains the IMs message. The caption in an Image macro may take the form of a catchphrase or a snowclone (i.e., a phrasal template that can be recognized in multiple variants) and contain additional contextual information.

Figure 5 shows the conceptual model of IMKG. At the heart of IMKG's model lies the class `Media Frame`, which is defined as follows.

Definition 1. *A Media Frame is a multimedia object used to represent a "memeable" situation, i.e., one that is familiar to the creator and a broader community.*

For instance, the quote "One does not simply walk into Mordor" is a Media Frame that comes directly from the movie Lord of the Rings. Media Frames are instances of specific subclasses of Image macro, such as `kym:Catchphrase`, thus allowing the organization of IMs into a hierarchy. Media Frames are described in terms of their origin, spread, about, label, and year, and have connections to other media frames that are similar (`rdf:seeAlso`) or broader (`skos:broader`). Media Frames may refer to entities in their tags, about sections, or images.

Media frames can be adapted numerous times by a `Meme`. A Meme is, therefore, a notable example and an instance of a Media Frame. A Meme inherits the about section, tags, and image, but it builds on top of them by adding a new

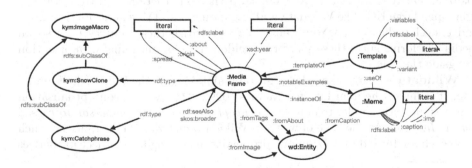

Fig. 5. Data Model of IMKG.

Fig. 6. Snippet of information on KYM (red box) and ImgFlip (green box). (Color figure online)

caption. The entities associated with a Meme are those present in the caption. For a Meme, we also store its textual label, caption, and image URI as strings.

To complete our model, we introduce the notion of `Template`, defined as:

Definition 2. *Templates are multimedia structures for a given Media Frame, typically consisting of an image and a placeholder for caption text.*

For a Media Frame to be used, IM generators publish a captionable blank image to generate a Meme. In ImgFlip, the template base structure is set but modifiable, e.g., the On Does Not Simply[3] template starts with two text boxes. In IMKG, we associate a template with two literals: its label and the default number of captions (variable). While a given Meme is generated by exactly one Template, multiple Templates can be associated with a given Media Frame. Indeed, Templates are user-proposed and can be duplicated or adapted over time, i.e., a Template can be a variant of another Template, e.g., One Does Not Simply Spiderman.[4]

Step 2: Data Collection. We bootstrap the construction of IMKG starting from open large KGs like Wikidata and expanding onto IM generators (ImgFlip) and encyclopedias (KnowYourMeme). We prioritize these sources over social media platforms since these platforms seldom provide meaningful information alongside the IMs.

Wikidata is an open knowledge graph maintained by the Wikimedia foundation. It includes the item Internet Memes (Q2927074), with a conceptualisation that is sufficiently similar to ours, i.e., *concept that spreads from person to person via the Internet.* At the time of writing, Wikidata includes 556 instances of such classes, characterised by *977* unique properties, including both object properties

---

[3] https://imgflip.com/meme/One-Does-Not-Simply.
[4] https://imgflip.com/memetemplate/20502958/one-does-not-simply-Spider-Man.

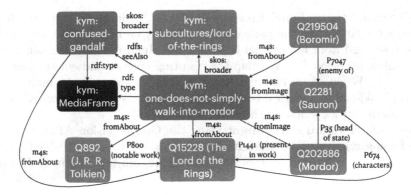

Fig. 7. Enrichment example for *kym:one-does-not-simply-walk-into-mordor*.

(that connect a given IM to other entities) and datatype properties. We denote the initial Wikidata IMs as *seeds* in the IMKG.

KnowYourMeme (KYM) is a well-known collaborative encyclopedia with information about IMs and people and events relevant to IM understanding. KYM provides the largest and most structured catalogue of internet memes and their lore, origin, and meaning. As KYM lacks an API or a similar method for programmatically querying this data, we crawl the entire KYM website, starting from a particular IM page and following the links to other pages describing related memes. The scraping focuses on collecting the following information: media frame (note 0 in Fig. 6), meme label (1), links to broader ("Part of a series on" section) and related ("View Related Entries") memes (2), popularity statistics (3), an infobox containing information about status, type, year, and origin of the meme (4), and the set of tags (5). Not shown in this figure, we also obtain the paragraphs describing a meme's about, origin, and spread. We scrape KYM by using Selenium, which takes two days.

ImgFlip is one of the most popular sites for meme generation, allowing users to quickly personalize one of the available meme templates using a custom caption. Moreover, registered users can vote and comment on the quality of the instantiated memes. ImgFlip organizes memes around templates, a blank version of the IM to be captioned. Users can also propose templates that others can adopt. Multiple Templates may be derived from any original Template, and many Memes may be created based on each of those Templates. For each Meme from ImgFlip, we recorded the media (6), title, author, views, and comment counts (7), the captioning text (8), upvotes (9), and the Template ID (10), which can be used to reconstruct the template URI.

Step 3: Data Enrichment. We perform three different types of enrichment: 1) textual, by extracting and linking entities from media frame descriptions and meme captions; 2) visual, by extracting entities from IM images by object detection; and 3) knowledge-based, by iteratively enriching information about memes and their entities with existing KGs.

We perform **textual enrichment** using DBpedia Spotlight [24]. Specifically, we extract entities from the paragraphs scraped from KYM, i.e., about, origin, and spread, and from the textual captions from ImgFlip. We filter out entities with confidence below 0.5. We map the resulting entities and entity types from DBpedia to Wikidata entities via the site links mapping file to maintain the usage of Wikidata as a central background resource. We also convert KYM tags to Wikidata entities following the same method.

We perform **visual enrichment** using the Google Vision API.[5] Given the cost of the service, we limit the extraction of objects to only the Media Frame image. The vision extraction tool detects objects and links them to Freebase. We map these entities to Wikidata by using the identifier property *P646*.

We perform two forms of **knowledge enrichment** using Wikidata. First, we obtain all information directly associated with the seed memes in Wikidata, i.e., we collect statements whose subject is one of the 556 seed memes. Second, we extract all Wikidata statements connecting two nodes (entities or memes) from the former enrichment steps. We use the Knowledge Graph Toolkit [12] to extract background knowledge about the meme seeds and entities from Wikidata.

An example snippet of an enriched graph for the media frame *kym:one-does-not-simply-walk-into-mordor* is shown in Fig. 7. The figure shows that this enrichment includes key entities such as Lord of the Rings, J.R.R. Tolkien, Mordor, Sauron, and Boromir, extracted from images or the about section in KnowYourMeme. The entities are tightly connected based on numerous Wikidata links, indicating for instance that Mordor is present in the work Lord of the Rings, created by Tolkien, that Boromir is the enemy of Sauron, and that Sauron is a character in Lord of the Rings. The figure also shows the effect of the data modelling, which allows us to connect similar media frames based on their broader subculture or explicit "rdfs:seeAlso" links in KnowYourMeme.

Step 4: Data Integration. We glue together the various datasets by deriving links across their entities. We obtain links between 276 memes in Wikidata and KYM via the property *P6760*. On the other hand, the KYM/ImgFlip linkage requires multiple steps. We first extract all direct ImgFlip links mentioned within our KYM crawled data and manually select the most reliable connections. Next, we perform a string match between memes titles in both datasets. We discovered about 60 matches above a safety threshold of 85% similarity. Finally, for the 276 seeds IMs identified above, we manually map the Templates (from ImgFlip) with the corresponding Media Frame (from KYM). Notably, given the user-based nature of ImgFlip templates, such a relationship is one-to-many, i.e., a given Media Frame has many templates, while a template is assigned to one and only one Media Frame, e.g., *One does not simply Spiderman.*[4]

Since the data comes in different formats (e.g., crawled data is in JSON, Wikidata in the KGTK TSV format [12]), we include a **data conversion** step with RML [8], a mapping language for KG construction. To sustain FAIR data management [35], we choose RDF as the data model of choice and N-Triples as the data format. We implement a parallel conversion pipeline from various

---

[5] https://cloud.google.com/vision.

Table 2. Overall statistics of IMKG and its constituent sources. I2K stands for the collection of links between ImgFlip templates and KYM memes.

source	#nodes	#edges	#rels	degree	#frames	#memes	#templates
KYM	167,662	914,941	18	10.91	12,585	12,585	0
ImgFlip	4,698,912	15,129,606	10	6.44	0	1,326,032	1,765
I2K	343	244	1	1.42	96	0	241
WD subset	85,917	504,781	805	11.75	242	242	0
IMKG	**4,850,636**	**16,549,810**	**836**	**6.82**	**12,585**	**1,338,617**	**2,006**

sources for scalability. For maintainability, we made an extensive effort to ensure the definition of identifiers: whenever possible, we reuse those from Wikidata, ImgFlip, and KYM. Notably, we avoid the use of blank nodes. Besides RDF, we also provide a property graph version of IMKG for scalable analytics.

5   Analysis

This section provides insights into the extent of knowledge covered in IMKG. We start by describing general graph statistics and indicators of centrality. We next explain how IMKG can support novel use cases. We then show how IMKG can facilitate hybrid applications based on both structural and content similarity.

Overall Statistics. Table 2 shows IMKG's general statistics. IMKG has 4.8M nodes described with 16.5M edges. Over a quarter of its nodes are memes, most of which come from ImgFlip. IMKG also has around two thousand templates, i.e., it has on average 2593 IMs per unique template and over twelve thousand frames that are linked to its memes. Most of the edges in IMKG, as can be expected, come from ImgFlip, whereas KnowYourMeme and Wikidata both contribute with hundreds of thousands of edges. The frames in IMKG come from KYM, the memes from practically all sources, and the templates primarily from ImgFlip. As such, IMKG is more than a sum of its parts, as it integrates knowledge in a compatible form.

The three most common relations in IMKG are `fromCaption`, `template`, and `image_url`. In total, IMKG has over 800 relations, most of which come from the enrichment with Wikidata. In terms of centrality, the Wikidata node for IM (*Q2927074*) has the largest PageRank values, followed by the Wikidata nodes Q978 (meme), Q336 (science), Q30 (United States), and Q11862829 (academic discipline). These statistics show that the Wikidata information that enriches the graph plays a key role in connecting the memes via background links.

Effect of Enrichment. In total, over 20% of IMKG consists of edges that connect memes to entities extracted from images or text, and over 3% (505k) of IMKG's edges come from the enrichment with background knowledge from Wikidata. Most of our entities come from captions (3,344,941), followed by 388,579 entities extracted from images, and 47,455 from the textual description. Table 3

Table 3. Most common entities extracted from each enrichment source: captions, images, and text description. "Org." stands for "Organization".

m4s:fromCaption	m4s:fromImage	m4s:fromAbout
Internet meme	font	image macro
meme	image	4chan
information technology	Internet meme	Internet meme
bling-bling	Know Your Meme	catchphrase
Batman	meme	YouTube
CAN bus	art	parody
human brain	happiness	Japanese
Hotline Bling	gesture	Tumblr
Kermit the Frog	illustration	meme
National Org. for Women	fictional character	United States of America

Table 4. Use-cases enabled by IMKG: for each, we show the KGTK query's match clause, the three matches of the results and the number of results in brackets.

Use case	Match query	Results
IMs that depict Sponge Bob	(h)-[:'m4s:fromImage']→(:Q83279), (h)-[:'rdf:type']→(:'kym:Meme')	kym:are-you-feeling-it-now-mr-krabs, kym:big-meaty-claws, kym:bold-and-brash,... (130)
Most meme-able person	(h)-[]→(person), (h)-[:'rdf:type']→(:'kym:Meme'), (person)-[:P31]→(:Q5)	Q22686 (Donald Trump), Q18738659 (Kyle Craven), Q15935 (Kanye West)
IMs based on films	(h)-[:'m4s:fromAbout']→(t), (t)-[:P31]→(:Q11424)	kym:hitlers-downfall-parodies→Q152857 (Downfall), kym:cat-transcendence → Q1534001 (The Prophecy),... (51)
Sex or gender distribution	()-[]→(person), (person)-[:P21]→(gender)	male: 10,333, female: 2,865, transgender female: 20,...

provides the top 10 most common entities extracted from each source. We observe that some more general entities are found in practically every modality (Internet meme, meme). Meanwhile, others are idiosyncratic to certain sources: for instance, bling-bling (Q44359) and Kermit the Frog (Q1107971) are dominantly extracted from meme captions, happiness (Q8) and art (Q735) from images, and Japanese language (Q5287) and USA (Q30) from textual descriptions. Notably, the most common Wikidata relations are P31 (instance-of) with 59K occurrences, P136 (genre) with 34K occurrences, and P106 (occupation) with 28K occurrences.

Illustrative Use Cases. We describe four novel use cases that are handled with simple queries over IMKG. These four use cases ask for IMs that depict Sponge Bob, for the most meme-able persons in IMKG, for Media Frames based on film scenes, and for sex or gender distribution of the people in IMKG (Table 4). We

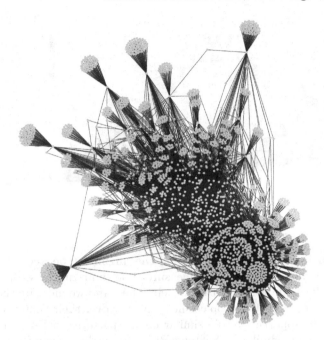

Fig. 8. Connections for media frames with the entity Sponge Bob Square Pants.

observe that there are 130 media frames that depict Sponge Bob in their image. We show a graph of these media frames with their one-hop information in Fig. 8. Curiously, the most meme-able people are a controversial modern-day politician (Donald Trump), a viral fictional character (Kyle Craven), and a controversial celebrity figure (Kanye West). While these entities are intuitively popular in memes, IMKG enables us to single them out statistically for the first time. Further, we learn that 413 of our media frames are based on films - for instance, the frame *kym:hitlers-downfall-parodies* is based on the 2004 film Downfall, while the frame *kym:cat-transcendence* on the 1995 film called The Prophecy. We find that over three-quarters of the people in IMKG are male, three times fewer are female, and dozens of people are trans women, intersex, or non-binary. While these use cases demonstrate a wide range of queries that can be asked about Internet memes for the first time, all of them are facilitated by the property of IMKG to harmonize data across sources (generators, encyclopedia, large open KGs), and to extract and enrich this data with entities and their relations from Wikidata.

Alignment Between Content and Structure. Our IMKG combines information encoded in its structure with information stored in its literals. As shown in Fig. 5, IMKG includes a number of literal properties, some of which are typically filled with long paragraphs of text. While we extract entities from these paragraphs, there is more information embedded in the text that can be naturally encoded with language models. We showcase the benefit of the hybrid informa-

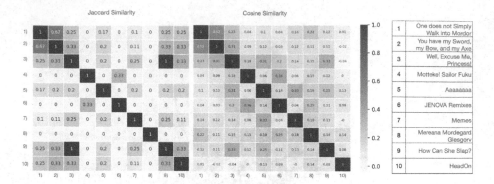

Fig. 9. Similarity heatmap of IM types vs Jaccard (left)/Cosine (right) of 'about'.

tion stored in IMKG here, by measuring the alignment between the IM types and the meme 'about' sections. We measure type similarity between two memes based on the Jaccard overlap between their types, and we measure the similarity of their 'about' sections based on cosine similarity over their SentenceBERT [27] embeddings. As apparent by the similar colour patterns in Fig. 9, memes that are considered more similar by SentenceBERT typically belong to similar types. Such an example is the meme 'One Does Not Simply Walk Into Mordor', of the types kym:snowclone, kym:catchphrase, and kym:pop-culture-reference, which is judged to be similar to the meme 'You Have My Sword, and My Bow, and My Axe', belonging to the types kym:snowclone and kym:catchphrase.

6 Conclusion and Outlook

This paper described the creation of the first Internet Meme Knowledge Graph. Starting from the meme characteristics of multimodality, reliability, succinctness, and fluidity, we defined seven requirements for a comprehensive IMKG. We created IMKG in four steps: data modelling, data collection, enrichment, and integration. The resulting IMKG consisted of over 2 million edges describing over 600K nodes collected from a popular meme encyclopedia (KnowYourMeme), a generation website (ImgFlip), and an open KG (Wikidata). Our analysis showed the importance of the extracted entities from images, captions, and text descriptions, and demonstrated how these entities can facilitate novel use cases such as obtaining all IMs based on films. To make IMKG knowledge was shown to be possible by a combination of IMKG with language model embeddings.

The current IMKG demonstrated the potential of our approach and the significance of aggregating the meme semantics following Semantic Web principles. We see two main directions for future work on IMKG. First, we propose to improve the coverage of IMKG as follows: (i) multimodality by studying videos in addition to images (ii) relatability by connecting user profiles to their meme comprehension based on crowdsourcing (iii) succinctness by incorporating frames from FrameNet [11] (iv) fluidity by further studying the similarity of the memes to other memes and to the original media frame.

Second, we propose that IMKG should be incorporated into methods for downstream reasoning tasks. IMKG may improve the accuracy and explainability of neuro-symbolic methods for IM, like hate speech detection and classification [14,32]. IMKG can facilitate the creation of novel reasoning tasks, such as Internet Meme QA. Third, we plan recurrent releases of the KGs, following emerging principles from the graph data management community to handle scalability in terms of volume [28] and velocity [33].

References

1. Akram, U., Irvine, K., Allen, S.F., Stevenson, J.C., Ellis, J.G., Drabble, J.: Internet memes related to the COVID-19 pandemic as a potential coping mechanism for anxiety. Sci. Rep. **11**(1), 22305 (2021)
2. Auer, S., Bizer, C., Kobilarov, G., Lehmann, J., Cyganiak, R., Ives, Z.: DBpedia: a nucleus for a web of open data. In: Aberer, K., et al. (eds.) ASWC/ISWC -2007. LNCS, vol. 4825, pp. 722–735. Springer, Heidelberg (2007). https://doi.org/10.1007/978-3-540-76298-0_52
3. Bollacker, K., Evans, C., Paritosh, P., Sturge, T., Taylor, J.: Freebase: a collaboratively created graph database for structuring human knowledge. In: ACM SIGMOD International Conference on Management of Data (2008)
4. Chen, Y.-C., et al.: UNITER: UNiversal image-TExt representation learning. In: Vedaldi, A., Bischof, H., Brox, T., Frahm, J.-M. (eds.) ECCV 2020. LNCS, vol. 12375, pp. 104–120. Springer, Cham (2020). https://doi.org/10.1007/978-3-030-58577-8_7
5. Dancygier, B., Vandelanotte, L.: Internet memes as multimodal constructions. Cogn. Linguist. **28**(3), 565–598 (2017)
6. Davison, P.: The Language of Internet Memes, pp. 120–134. New York University Press (2012)
7. Dawkins, R.: The Selfish Gene. Oxford University Press, Oxford (1976)
8. Dimou, A., Sande, M.V., Colpaert, P., Verborgh, R., Mannens, E., de Walle, R.V.: RML: a generic language for integrated RDF mappings of heterogeneous data. In: Bizer, C., Heath, T., Auer, S., Berners-Lee, T. (eds.) Proceedings of the Workshop on Linked Data on the Web co-located with the 23rd International World Wide Web Conference (WWW 2014), Seoul, Korea, 8 April 2014 (2014)
9. Färber, M., Bartscherer, F., Menne, C., Rettinger, A.: Linked data quality of dbpedia, freebase, opencyc, wikidata, and yago. Semant. Web **9**(1), 77–129 (2018)
10. Fersini, E., et al.: Semeval-2022 task 5: multimedia automatic misogyny identification. In: Proceedings of the 16th International Workshop on Semantic Evaluation (SemEval-2022), pp. 533–549 (2022)
11. Fillmore, C.J., Baker, C.F.: A frames approach to semantic analysis. In: The Oxford Handbook of Linguistic Analysis, pp. 313–339. Oxford University Press (2012)
12. Ilievski, F., et al.: KGTK: a toolkit for large knowledge graph manipulation and analysis. In: Pan, J.Z., et al. (eds.) ISWC 2020. LNCS, vol. 12507, pp. 278–293. Springer, Cham (2020). https://doi.org/10.1007/978-3-030-62466-8_18
13. Johann, M., Bülow, L.: One does not simply create a meme: conditions for the diffusion of internet memes. Int. J. Commun. **13**, 23 (2019)

14. Kiela, D., et al.: The hateful memes challenge: detecting hate speech in multimodal memes (2021)
15. Kirk, H.R., et al.: Memes in the wild: assessing the generalizability of the hateful memes challenge dataset. arXiv preprint arXiv:2107.04313 (2021)
16. Lenzerini, M.: data integration: a theoretical perspective. In: Popa, L., Abiteboul, S., Kolaitis, P.G. (eds.) Proceedings of the Twenty-first ACM SIGACT-SIGMOD-SIGART Symposium on Principles of Database Systems, 3–5 June, Madison, Wisconsin, USA, pp. 233–246. ACM (2002).https://doi.org/10.1145/543613.543644
17. Liang, P.P., Zadeh, A., Morency, L.: Foundations and recent trends in multimodal machine learning: Principles, challenges, and open questions. CoRR abs/2209.03430 (2022). https://doi.org/10.48550/arXiv.2209.03430
18. Ling, C., AbuHilal, I., Blackburn, J., De Cristofaro, E., Zannettou, S., Stringhini, G.: Dissecting the meme magic: Understanding indicators of virality in image memes. Proc. ACM Hum.-Comput. Interact. (CSCW) (2021)
19. Lou, A.: Multimodal simile: the "when" meme in social media discourse. Engl. Text Constr. 10(1), 106–131 (2017)
20. Lu, J., Batra, D., Parikh, D., Lee, S.: Vilbert: pretraining task-agnostic visiolinguistic representations for vision-and-language tasks. In: Advances in Neural Information Processing Systems, vol. 32 (2019)
21. Lynch, M.P.: Memes, misinformation, and political meaning. South. J. Philos. 60(1), 38–56 (2022)
22. Marino, G.: Semiotics of spreadability: a systematic approach to internet memes and virality (2015)
23. McNamara, A.: Can we measure memes? Front. Evol. Neurosci. (2011)
24. Mendes, P.N., Jakob, M., García-Silva, A., Bizer, C.: Dbpedia spotlight: shedding light on the web of documents. In: Proceedings of the 7th International Conference on Semantic Systems, pp. 1–8 (2011)
25. Nieubuurt, J.T.: Internet memes: leaflet propaganda of the digital age. Front. Commun. 5, 547065 (2021)
26. Radford, A., et al.: Learning transferable visual models from natural language supervision. In: International Conference on Machine Learning, pp. 8748–8763. PMLR (2021)
27. Reimers, N., Gurevych, I.: Sentence-bert: Sentence embeddings using Siamese Bert-networks. arXiv preprint arXiv:1908.10084 (2019)
28. Sakr, S., et al.: The future is big graphs: a community view on graph processing systems. Commun. ACM 64(9), 62–71 (2021). https://doi.org/10.1145/3434642
29. Sambasivan, N., Kapania, S., Highfill, H., Akrong, D., Paritosh, P.K., Aroyo, L.: "Everyone wants to do the model work, not the data work": data cascades in high-stakes AI. In: Kitamura, Y., Quigley, A., Isbister, K., Igarashi, T., Bjørn, P., Drucker, S.M. (eds.) CHI 2021: CHI Conference on Human Factors in Computing Systems, Virtual Event / Yokohama, Japan, pp. 39:1–39:15. ACM (2021)
30. Sherratt, V.: Towards contextually sensitive analysis of memes: Meme genealogy and knowledge base (2022)
31. Taecharungroj, V., Nueangjamnong, P.: The effect of humour on virality: The study of internet memes on social media. In: 7th International Forum on Public Relations and Advertising Media Impacts on Culture and Social Communication. Bangkok, August (2014)
32. Thakur, A.K., Ilievski, F., Sandlin, H.Â., Mermoud, A., Sourati, Z., Luceri, L., Tommasini, R.: Multimodal and explainable internet meme classification. arXiv preprint arXiv:2212.05612 (2022)

33. Tommasini, R., Bonte, P., Spiga, F., Della Valle, E.: Streaming Linked Data. Springer, Cham (2023)
34. Vrandečić, D., Krötzsch, M.: Wikidata: a free collaborative knowledgebase. Commun. ACM **57**(10), 78–85 (2014)
35. Wilkinson, M.D., et al.: The fair guiding principles for scientific data management and stewardship. Sci. Data **3**(1), 1–9 (2016)
36. Zenner, E., Geeraerts, D.: One does not simply process memes: Image macros as multimodal constructions, pp. 167–194. De Gruyter, Berlin (2018)

Describing and Organizing Semantic Web and Machine Learning Systems in the SWeMLS-KG

Fajar J. Ekaputra[1,2]($\boxtimes$), Majlinda Llugiqi[1], Marta Sabou[1],
Andreas Ekelhart[3,4], Heiko Paulheim[5], Anna Breit[6], Artem Revenko[6],
Laura Waltersdorfer[2], Kheir Eddine Farfar[7], and Sören Auer[7,8]

[1] WU (Vienna University of Economics and Business), Vienna, Austria
{fajar.ekaputra,majlinda.llugiqi,marta.sabou}@wu.ac.at
[2] TU Wien, Vienna, Austria
{fajar.ekaputra,laura.waltersdorfer}@tuwien.ac.at
[3] University of Vienna, Vienna, Austria
andreas.ekelhart@univie.ac.at
[4] SBA Research, Vienna, Austria
andreas.ekelhart@sba-research.org
[5] University of Mannheim, Mannheim, Germany
heiko.paulheim@uni-mannheim.de
[6] Semantic Web Company, Vienna, Austria
{anna.breit,artem.revenko}@semantic-web.com
[7] TIB Leibniz Information Centre for Science and Society, Hanover, Germany
{kheir.farfar,soren.auer}@tib.eu
[8] L3S Research Center, Leibniz University of Hannover, Hanover, Germany
auer@l3s.de

Abstract. The overall AI trend of creating neuro-symbolic systems is reflected in the Semantic Web community with an increased interest in the development of systems that rely on both *Semantic Web resources* and *Machine Learning components* (SWeMLS, for short). However, understanding trends and best practices in this rapidly growing field is hampered by a lack of standardized descriptions of these systems and an annotated corpus of such systems. To address these gaps, we leverage the results of a large-scale systematic mapping study collecting information about 470 SWeMLS papers and formalize these into one resource containing: (i) the *SWeMLS ontology*, (ii) the *SWeMLS pattern library* containing machine-actionable descriptions of 45 frequently occurring SWeMLS workflows, and (iii) *SWEMLS-KG*, a knowledge graph including machine-actionable metadata of the papers in terms of the SWeMLS ontology. This resource provides the first framework for semantically describing and organizing SWeMLS thus making a key impact in (1) understanding the status quo of the field based on the published paper corpus and (2) enticing the uptake of machine-processable system documentation in the SWeMLS area.

Keywords: Neuro-symbolic System · Semantic Web · Machine Learning · Knowledge Graphs

© The Author(s), under exclusive license to Springer Nature Switzerland AG 2023
C. Pesquita et al. (Eds.): ESWC 2023, LNCS 13870, pp. 372–389, 2023.
https://doi.org/10.1007/978-3-031-33455-9_22

Resource type: Knowledge Graph
License: https://creativecommons.org/licenses/by/4.0/
DOI: https://doi.org/10.5281/zenodo.7445917
URL: https://w3id.org/semsys/sites/swemls-kg/

1 Introduction

The field of Artificial Intelligence (AI) is currently witnessing a great interest in (more closely) integrating and bridging between symbolic and sub-symbolic (AI) [7] techniques. This substantial trend led to the establishment of the new sub-research field of *neuro-symbolic systems*[1] [6,12], which focuses on the the-oretical and practical aspects of creating such complex systems. Against this backdrop, it is not surprising that this AI trend is also reflected in the Seman-tic Web (SW) research community which has popularized AI-based knowledge representation techniques and resources in the last two decades [17]. There is increased interest in neuro-symbolic integration in the context of the Semantic Web [18], such as the development of systems that rely on both Semantic Web resources and Machine Learning components. We coined the term *Semantic Web and Machine Learning System* (SWeMLS) to refer to such systems [8].

For example, in [13] authors propose a system for automatic art analysis that can be classified as an SWeMLS. To that end, they augment a deep learning based system that classifies artistic images purely based on visual features with contex-tual art information in a form of a knowledge graph about painters, paintings, artistic schools, etc. Schematically, the system's workflow is depicted in Fig. 1 with the boxology notation introduced by [29]: starting with the sym1 knowledge graph, graph embeddings are created through ML1 which is a CNN deep learning model (sym1-ML1-data); subsequently, these embeddings together with visual data (i.e., images) are input to a CNN model (ML2) to create image classifications (sym2). Authors experimentally show that the inclusion of the SW component leads to performance increases by 7.3% in art classification and 37.24% in image retrieval tasks, thus demonstrating the potential of such systems.

Given the potential of SWeMLS and the increased interest in this field, the key *motivation* for our work was to gain a systematic understanding of the SWeMLS area by identifying trends among such systems and clustering them to better characterize the landscape of published systems. The main *challenges* in achieving a large-scale, data-driven, representative and systematic analysis of the SWeMLS field were:

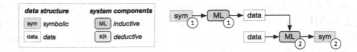

Fig. 1. Schematic representation of a SWeMLS workflow for art classification [13].

---

[1] The Neurosymbolic Artificial Intelligence journal will be launched in 2023: https://www.iospress.com/catalog/journals/neurosymbolic-artificial-intelligence.

- (i) a lack of understanding of important *system characteristics* that should be considered when analyzing SWeMLS. Approaches to characterise neuro-symbolic systems either focus on broader families of systems than SWeMLS [4, 21], or on a specific aspect of the systems (e.g., their internal processing flow [5,29]). Additionally, none are formalized for the purpose of using them as a basis for machine-actionable descriptions of the systems.
- (ii) the lack of a corpus of systematically collected (and therefore representative) papers annotated in terms of such characteristics, to allow for a data-driven research trend analysis. While a number of papers about systems that learn and reason were collected as a basis for the analysis described in [29], these were not offered as a corpus of annotated papers to the community.

We addressed both challenges by conducting a large-scale Systematic Mapping Study (SMS [23]) on SWeMLS [8], through which we (i) proposed a set of characteristics for describing SWeMLS and (ii) systematically collected, selected and extracted data from nearly 500 papers describing such systems. This led to the following artifacts which together are offered as one *resource*:

- *the SWeMLS ontology* that describes the main aspects of SWeMLS including their internal workflow in terms of boxology patterns as shown in Fig. 1. The ontology schema (i.e., capturing important SWeMLS characteristics, e.g., *StatisticalModel*) and relevant instances (e.g., *DeepLearningModel*) were derived systematically during the scoping and analysis phases of the SMS,
- *the SWeMLS-KG*: a knowledge graph containing the machine-actionable description of almost 500 systems in terms of the SWeMLS ontology, and
- *the SWeMLS Pattern Library* containing the machine-actionable description of 45 SWeMLS patterns and their associated SHACL-based validation constraints. This pattern library extends the initial pattern catalog of 10–15 patterns originally identified by [29] both *quantitatively* with additional patterns observed during the SMS and *qualitatively*, by offering the patterns in a machine-actionable rather than graphical representation.

This resource is *timely* considering the recent trend in the SW community (and beyond) to create systems that leverage both SW and ML components. To the best of our knowledge, it is also *novel* by (i) providing the first ontology (and associated pattern library) for describing SWeMLS in a machine-actionable way and (ii) a methodologically collected corpus of SWeMLS and their semantic description. The resource is of immediate benefit for (SW) researchers that aim to explore trends in the SWeMLS field by analysing the data in the SWeMLS-KG and as such promises to have an impact on the understanding of the status-quo in this emerging field. Furthermore, the resource provides a semantic framework for describing SWeMLS and their internal details, thus potentially strongly influencing this field in terms of being well-documented, data-driven, and transparent.

We continue by discussing the impact of this resource (Sect. 2) and then detail its main components and the methodology used to produce them (Sect. 3), availability (Sect. 4) and usage in two use cases (Sect. 5). We summarize related work in Sect. 6 and conclude with an outlook on future work in Sect. 7.

2   Impact of the Resource

This resource is interesting to the Semantic Web community both in terms of its immediate and potential future impact on the field. An *immediate impact* is *enabling the understanding of general trends in the emerging area of SWeMLS*. The SWeMLS-KG allows for the first time to perform data-driven analysis in order to better understand this family of systems. This can be achieved as part of two scenarios as described next and in more detail in Sects. 5.1 and 5.2.

- *Asking concrete research questions*, e.g., *What kind of processing patterns are the most frequent? Which ML methods are used most often in combination with which SW resources?* Such targeted analysis was performed as part of the SMS [8] from which the SWeMLS ontology and KG were derived. While we investigated a limited number of questions that were feasible within the scope of the SMS, by making this resource available openly we enable the research community at large to perform additional analysis.
- *Identifying new insights* (e.g., through graph embedding) allows uncovering a new understanding of the field by exploring latent semantics encoded in the data.

Furthermore, the presented resources could have an important future impact by enabling the following use cases:

- *Search for SWeMLS-related work.* Researchers that create a SWeMLS could more easily find related systems, as part of related work search, during the design, evaluation, and publishing of their own systems. The current resource supports answering questions such as: *Which system patterns/pattern types are most frequent for graph completion tasks in the medical domain?*
- *Machine readable documentation and validation of SWeMLS.* Researchers that want to document a SWeMLS, can now (1) describe the system in a machine-processable way in terms of the SWeMLS ontology and (2) verify the correctness of their description through the SHACL validation. While the core technical artifacts are in place to enable other researchers to document their systems, future work will focus on more user-friendly annotation tools to entice large-scale adoption of research documentation for SWeMLS.
- *Improved scientific reviewing and publication processes.* AI-related conferences are struggling with high numbers of submissions which leads to challenges (i) for conference organisers to meaningfully assign papers to reviewers; as well as (ii) for reviewers who are overloaded with receiving very diverse papers and challenged to compare new systems to related work. We envision that SWeMLS-related events could use the SWeMLS ontology as a basis for annotating the submitted system papers. Such in-depth annotation of the systems could support (i) assigning relevant/similar papers to reviewers by clustering papers in terms of (the intersection of) several dimensions (task solved, domain addressed, system pattern used); (ii) allow reviewers to more easily comprehend the design of the system by referring to a structured or even visual notation of the system besides its textual description in the paper. Naturally, reviewers could leverage other collections of annotated systems (e.g., the SWeMLS KG), to identify papers similar to the one reviewed to make an informed assessment of novelty.

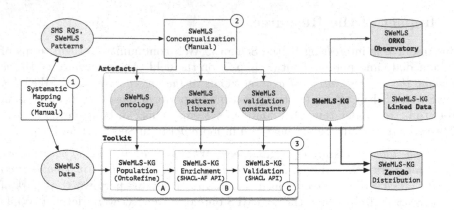

Fig. 2. Overview of the SWeMLS-KG construction process

To conclude, the proposed resource could have a major impact on the way the research-documentation-publication cycles of SWeMLS happen, leading to a data-driven field and supporting faster growth and shorter innovation cycles.

3   Knowledge Graph Construction

We hereby describe the overall methodology for the construction of SWeMLS-KG (Sect. 3.1) and focus on key elements in this process such as the SWeMLS ontology (Sect. 3.2), the SWeMLS pattern library (Sect. 3.3) and the SWeMLS-KG and its population process (Sect. 3.4).

3.1   SWeMLS-KG Construction Process and Methodology

Figure 2 depicts the process and methodology followed to construct the SWeMLS-KG. The starting point for the process was our prior large-scale SMS on the topic of SWeMLS [8] (cf. **Step 1** in Fig. 2) during which we collected information from 476 papers on SWeMLS in spreadsheet format. Starting from this SMS, we converted its results into a machine-processable format, through the next steps.

In **Step 2** we *conceptualised the SWeMLS related information* from two inputs provided in the SMS results: (i) the SMS research questions were a basis for the competency questions of the SWeMLS ontology, and (ii) the 45 SWeMLS patterns identified from the papers, which have been described and depicted as drawings but were not yet formalized in a machine-processable manner. From this step, we produce three types of outputs: (a) the SWeMLS ontology (Sect. 3.2), (b) the SWeMLS pattern library, which consists of pattern templates represented as RDF instances and SHACL-Advanced Features (SHACL-AF) rules, and (c) SWeMLS constraint definitions, which provide users with a mean to validate SWeMLS instances based on the existing patterns.

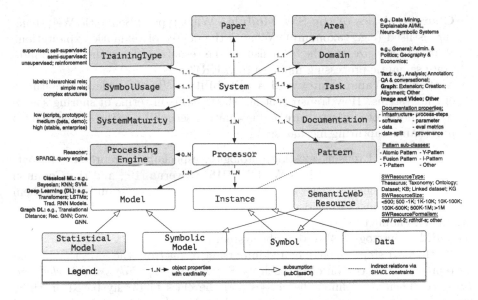

Fig. 3. SWeMLS Ontology Overview (adapted from [8])

In **Step 3** we perform the *population of SWeMLS-KG* using the SWeMLS data and the artifacts produced in Step 2. This step (detailed in Sect. 3.4) consists of three sub-steps: (3A) populating the KG with spreadsheet data extracted from the SMS, (3B) constructing workflows between components and variables linked to each SWeMLS, and (3C) validating the KG using pattern-specific validations. The integrated and validated SWeMLS-KG is published through three distribution channels: (i) Linked Data interface, (ii) ORKG observatory, and (iii) a Zenodo repository as further explained in Sect. 4.

3.2 The SWeMLS Ontology

Ontology Creation. To create the ontology, we followed the Ontology Development 101 guideline [25]. We started by determining the domain and the scope of the ontology, using SMS research questions as competency questions:

- **Bibliographic characteristics** - How are the publications temporally and geographically distributed? How are the systems positioned, and which keywords are used to describe them?
- **System Architecture** - What processing patterns are used in terms of inputs/outputs and what is the order of processing units?
- **Application Areas** - What kind of tasks are solved (e.g., text analysis)? In which domains are SWeMLS applied (e.g., life sciences)?
- **Characteristics of the ML Module** - What ML models are incorporated (e.g., SVM)? Which ML components can be identified (e.g., attention)? What training type(s) is used during the system training phase?

- **Characteristics of the SW Module** - What type of Semantic Web structure is used (e.g., taxonomy)? What is the degree of semantic exploitation? What are the size and the formalism of the resources? Does the system integrate semantic processing modules (i.e., KR)?
- **Maturity, Transparency and Auditability** - What is the level of maturity of the systems? How transparent are the systems in terms of sharing source code, details of infrastructure and evaluation setup? Does the system have a provenance-capturing mechanism?

We considered reusing existing ontologies, especially to represent the patterns' workflows such as Wings Workflow [15], Taverna [19], and the Common Workflow Language [1]. However, our patterns are very specific and none of them could be used. Thus, we decided to develop our own SWeMLS ontology by adapting and extending the P-PLAN ontology [14] to describe SWeMLS workflows and the OPMW ontology [24] to describe system patterns.

As the next step, we enumerated important terms from the SMS that should be represented in the ontology such as *System, Paper, Processor, Model*, and *Instance*. Then we defined the classes and the class hierarchy based on these terms, using a top-down approach, e.g., class *Model* has *Semantic Model* and *Statistical Model* as sub-classes. After establishing the classes and their hierarchy, we defined the class properties based on the data gathered from the SMS, e.g., system application area, task, and system maturity. Finally, we created individuals from the SMS data, i.e., *Data Mining* is an instance of *Area*.

Ontology Description. The resulting SWeMLS ontology is intended to represent the systems described in the publications reported in [8]. A high-level overview of its main classes, properties, and an excerpt of named individuals is shown in Fig. 3. Overall, the SWeMLS ontology includes: (i) paper details, (ii) system properties reported in such papers, and (iii) workflow-style representations of patterns:

- **Paper** details such as title, year of *publication, publication type, venue, authors' countries, keywords*, a short *summary*, and the *link* to the paper.
- **SWeMLS** properties such as the *targeted tasks, level of maturity, application domain, semantic web resources* being used, *machine learning model*, type of *semantic processor, the pattern* being used, as well as *documentation* properties which include: e.g., *infrastructure, provenance*, and *evaluation*.
- **SWeMLS patterns** representing the structure of each system workflow pattern with each pattern's component including their inputs/outputs. We detail the representation of the SWeMLS patterns in Sect. 3.3.

An example of how the terms defined by the ontology are used to describe a paper reporting a SWeMLS is presented in Sect. 3.1.

3.3   SWeMLS Pattern Library

Pattern Representation. We use the P-PLAN [14] and OPMW [24] as the basis for SWeMLS pattern representation. More specifically, we follow the separation of three major types of workflow structures outlined by Garijo et al. [14]:

- (i) Workflow Template (`opmw:WorkflowTemplate`), a generic pattern that indicates the type of steps in the workflow and their dataflow dependencies,
- (ii) Workflow Instance (`swemls:System` as a sub-class of `p-plan:Plan`), a workflow that specifies the application algorithms to be executed and data to be used, and
- (iii) Workflow Execution (`p-plan:Bundle`), a workflow execution trace containing details of what happened during an execution.

We focus on the first two types (i.e., Workflow Template and Instance) and plan for Workflow Execution as part of our future work.

The SWeMLS Pattern Library consists of the representation of 45 system processing patterns identified during the SMS (each pattern is captured in a .ttl file in the zenodo distribution of the resource). An example representation of the Workflow Template for pattern T-3 is shown in Listing 3.1. The template contains the definition of the patterns (e.g., `res:Pattern.T3`), its components/steps (i.e., `res:Pattern.T3.ML1` and `res:Pattern.T3.ML2`) and how they use or generate variables (e.g., `res:Pattern.T3.ML1` use `res:Pattern.T3.SW1` and generate `res:Pattern.T3.Data2`).

```
@prefix swemls: <https://w3id.org/semsys/ns/swemls#> .
@prefix res: <http://semantic-systems.net/swemls/> .
@prefix p-plan: <http://purl.org/net/p-plan#> .
@prefix opmw: <http://www.opmw.org/ontology/> .
/* ... rdf, rdfs are ommitted */

/* Pattern T3 as an instance of opmw:WorkflowTemplate */
res:Pattern.T3 a opmw:WorkflowTemplate ; rdfs:label "T3";
  rdfs:comment "[{sym -> ML -> data / data} -> ML -> sym]" .

/* Component T3.ML1 with T3.SW1 (SW resource) as input */
res:Pattern.T3.ML1 a swemls:WorkflowTemplateProcessML ;
  opmw:isStepOfTemplate res:Pattern.T3 ; opmw:uses res:Pattern.T3.SW1 .
/* Component T3.ML2 with T3.Data1 and T3.Data2 (data) as inputs */
res:Pattern.T3.ML2 a swemls:WorkflowTemplateProcessML ;
  p-plan:isPreceededBy res:Pattern.T3.ML1 ;
  opmw:isStepOfTemplate res:Pattern.T3; opmw:uses res:Pattern.T3.Data1 ,
      res:Pattern.T3.Data2 .

/* Variable T3.SW1 */
res:Pattern.T3.SW1 a swemls:TemplateArtifactSW ; opmw:isVariableOfTemplate
      res:Pattern.T3 .
/* Variable T3.Data1; used as input for component T3.ML2 */
res:Pattern.T3.Data1 a swemls:TemplateArtifactData;
  opmw:isVariableOfTemplate res:Pattern.T3 .
/* Variable T3.Data2; generated by T3.ML1; input for T3.ML2 */
res:Pattern.T3.Data2 a swemls:TemplateArtifactData ;
  opmw:isVariableOfTemplate res:Pattern.T3 ; opmw:isGeneratedBy
      res:Pattern.T3.ML1 .

/* Variable T3.SW2; generated by T3.ML2 as the final result of the System */
res:Pattern.T3.SW2 a swemls:TemplateArtifactSW ;
  opmw:isVariableOfTemplate res:Pattern.T3 ; opmw:isGeneratedBy
      res:Pattern.T3.ML2 .
```

Listing 3.1. T-3 pattern in turtle format

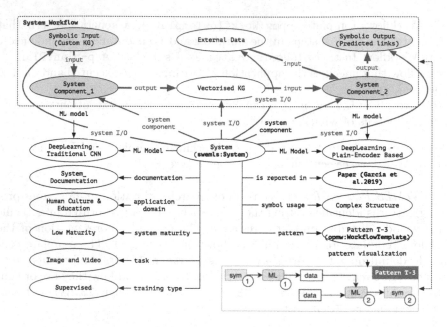

Fig. 4. Example of the semantic representation of paper [13] and the art classification SWeMLS described by it (adapted from [8]). *Green arrows* represent relations between a system and its components and variables, *Red arrows* represent workflow information generated with SHACL-AF rules. (Color figure online)

3.4   SWeML-KG Population and Update Mechanisms

After defining the underlying ontology, we populated the SWeMLS KG with the details of SWeMLS collected in the course of the SMS.

An example SWeMLS semantic description is depicted in Fig. 4 which shows the SWeMLS-KG instance of the SWeMLS discussed in Sect. 1 [13]. For this system, we display the paper in which it is reported, together with other paper details, such as title, keywords, and year of publication. In addition, the target task to be solved falls into the category of '*Image and Video*', the system maturity is reported as '*Low*', the application domain is listed as '*Human Culture and Education*', the training type as '*Supervised*' and the symbol usage as '*Complex Structure*'. The depicted system also contains documentation information, including transparency and auditability components of the system.

The chosen system instantiates pattern "T-3" (depicted visually in the bottom right of Fig. 4) which involves two symbolic data components, two machine learning components, and two data components in its workflow. The upper part of Fig. 4 shows the semantic representation of the system workflow: starting from custom KG as symbolic input to a traditional CNN machine-learning component, the model produces a vectorized KG, which, along with some external data, serves as input for a deep learning plain encoder-based model. Finally, the system produces predicted links as symbolic output.

The SWeMLS population process consisted of the following steps. We created a mapping to the SWeMLS Ontology[2] and transformed the SMS data into RDF format (**Step 3A** of Fig. 2). The generated RDF graphs from Step 3A already connect each system with its respective system components and I/O variables (cf. green arrows on Fig. 4). However, the connection between I/O variables and components is not yet available (cf. red arrows on Fig. 4). To build these connections, we ran an enrichment process (**Step 3B**) using SHACL-AF rules[3].

Lastly, we validated the resulting data against SHACL constraints (**Step 3C**). We defined a set of constraints for general SWeMLS as well as instances of specific SWEMLS patterns to ensure completeness, validity and conformance of the KG to the pattern definitions.

SWeML-KG Update Mechanisms. To promote community-based contributions, we published all the source code necessary for the KG creation (i.e., Ontotext refine projects and mapping files, SHACL-AF rules, and SHACL constraints). Furthermore, we plan to make updating the SWeMLS-KG with new system descriptions easier, for example, by relying on features provided by the Open Research Knowledge Graph to enable community-wide contributions.

4   Availability of the SWeMLS-KG

The SWeMLS-KG landing page[4] provides pointers to the various resources covered in this paper, i.e., the Linked Data resources[5], the SPARQL query interface[6], a Zenodo link for the complete RDF snapshots[7], the source code for SWeMLS toolkit[8]. This allows users to choose the most appropriate resources and access mechanisms most suitable for their context.

Publication as ORKG Observatory. SWeMLS-KG was also made available as part of the Open Research Knowledge Graph [3,20][9]. ORKG is a scholarly knowledge organization facility, where contributions conveyed in scientific articles are represented semantically in machine- and human-readable ways. The FAIR semantic description of research contributions facilitates a number of applications, such as overviews of the state-of-the-art for certain research questions (comparisons), visualizations, or leaderboards. The ORKG organizes the semantic contribution descriptions along research fields but also in thematic *observatories*, where a team of curators from one or several organizations curates the contributions related to a specific topic.

---

[2] We use Ontotext Refine https://www.ontotext.com/products/ontotext-refine/.
[3] Example SHACL-AF rules and SHACL validation constraints can be accessed in our GitHub repo, e.g., https://bit.ly/sweml-t3-pattern for pattern T-3.
[4] https://w3id.org/semsys/sites/swemls-kg/.
[5] e.g., Garcia et al. [13] https://semantic-systems.net/swemls/System_4QP5XAGX.
[6] https://semantic-systems.net/sparql/.
[7] https://doi.org/10.5281/zenodo.7445917.
[8] https://github.com/semanticsystems/swemls-toolkit.
[9] https://orkg.org.

Together with the ORKG development team, we imported the SWeMLS-KG, so that its data is browsable, accessible, citable and reusable. The ORKG observatory for SWeMLS-KG allows browsing patterns, instantiations of the patterns as well as searching and filtering contributions from articles by certain characteristics. An initial version of the SWeMLS-specific ORKG observatory is available online on the ORKG server[10], providing an overview of the collected papers as well as detailed metadata for each paper[11].

5 Use Cases

We hereby report on use cases that explore SWeMLS-KG via (i) SPARQL queries (Sect. 5.1, and (ii) Knowledge Graph Embedding methods (Sect. 5.2).

5.1 Use Case 1: Understanding SWeMLS Trends Through Querying the SWeMLS-KG

The SWeMLS-KG can support researchers and reviewers in exploring and understanding trends in the SWeMLS field through queries executed on the SPARQL enpoint of the KG. We first motivate exemplary knowledge questions in natural language, show their SPARQL representations, and discuss their results.

```
PREFIX swemls: <https://w3id.org/semsys/ns/swemls#>
PREFIX res: <http://semantic-systems.net/swemls/>
/* ... rdf, rdfs, and dc-terms are ommitted*/
select ?swModel ?statisticalModel ?trainingType ?title ?year
where {
  ?system a swemls:System ;
    swemls:hasApplicationDomain res:Domain.Medicine_Health ;
    swemls:hasTask res:Task.Patient_Diagnosis_Prediction ;
    swemls:hasTrainingType / rdfs:label ?trainingType .
  ?system swemls:hasSymbolIO / rdfs:label ?swModel .
  {
    select ?system (group_concat(?statisticalModelName;separator=",") as
        ?statisticalModel)
    where { ?system swemls:hasStatisticalModel / rdfs:label
        ?statisticalModelName}
    group by ?system
  }
  ?paper swemls:reports ?system ; terms:title ?title ; swemls:year ?year .
}
```

Listing 5.1. Query for components in the medical domain for diagnosis prediction

Task/domain Driven Queries for Components of SWeMLS. We want to support researchers and reviewers in identifying and exploring existing SWeMLS and their components: *What SWeMLS components (SW resources and ML models) have been used to solve a specific task x in the domain y?* A researcher might ask this question e.g., in the course of designing a new system as part of state-of-the-art research or when looking for additional datasets that have been used in a target domain. A reviewer on the other hand, could quickly

---

[10] https://orkg.org/observatory/Neurosymbolic_artificial_intelligence.
[11] e.g., Garcia et al. [13] in ORKG: https://orkg.org/paper/R574440.

Table 1. Query results for components in the medical domain for diagnosis prediction (excerpt)

swModel	statisticalModel	trainingType	title	year
CCS	Attention, GloVe, MLP, RNN	Self-supervised	GRAM: Graph-Based Attention Model for Healthcare Representation Learning	2017
UMLS	ARM	Self-supervised	Guiding supervised learning by bio-ontologies in medical data analysis	2018
ICD	Graph-based Attention Model, Knowledge Attention, Gated Recurrent Unit (GRU)	Supervised	KAME: Knowledge-based attention model for diagnosis prediction in healthcare	2018
DBpedia	SVM	Supervised	Improving rare disease classification using imperfect knowledge graph	2019

identify publications with similar components and use these to highlight the innovation and advantages of the submission under review. A SPARQL representation of this question in the domain **Medicine_Health** and for the task **Patient_Diagnosis_Prediction** is given in Listing 5.1. Table 1 shows an excerpt of the query results, which could be further explored.

Pattern-driven queries for SWeMLS are queries that explore the system workflow patterns' structure and its components. This allows researchers and reviewers to identify *structurally* identical or similar SWeMLS and their relevant aspects, i.e., the integration of ML models and SW resources: *What SWeMLS exist that use a specific SW resource x as input for a ML Model y that produces symbolic output?*

```
PREFIX swemls: <https://w3id.org/semsys/ns/swemls#>
PREFIX res: <http://semantic-systems.net/swemls/>
/* ... rdf, rdfs, skos, and dc-terms are ommitted */
select ?domain ?task ?pattern ?sw ?groupSw ?title ?year
where {
    ?system a swemls:System ; swemls:hasApplicationDomain ?domain ;
       swemls:hasTask ?task ; swemls:hasCorrespondingPattern ?pattern ;
          swemls:hasStepML ?ml .
    ?paper swemls:reports ?system ; terms:title ?title ; swemls:year ?year .
    ?sw a swemls:SemanticWebResource .
    { ?sw skos:broader res:Resource.Facebook }
    UNION {
       select ?sw (group_concat(?compoundSwInput;separator=",") as ?groupSw)
       where {
          ?sw swemls:hasCompoundElement ?compoundSwInput .
          ?compoundSwInput skos:broader res:Resource.Facebook
       } group by ?sw
    }
    ?ml swemls:componentInput ?sw .
    ?ml swemls:componentOutput/rdf:type swemls:SemanticWebResource .
    { ?ml swemls:componentModel res:StatisticalModel.TransX }
    UNION {
       ?ml swemls:componentModel ?compoundML .
       ?compoundML swemls:hasCompoundElement res:StatisticalModel.TransX
    }
}
```

Listing 5.2. SPARQL query for systems using a translation model on Facebook benchmark data, producing symbolic output as part of their architecture

Table 2. Query results for systems processing Facebook resources with a translation model, producing symbolic output (excerpt)

domain	task	pattern	sw	groupSw	title	year
General	KG_Completion	F4	...SW_cc6bef6e	FB122	Jointly embedding knowledge graphs ...	2016
General	KG_Completion	F2	...SW_d5ee1a61	FB_500K	Probabilistic Belief Embedding ...	2016
General	KG_Completion	A1	...SW_f27afb1c	FB13, FB15k	Learning Knowledge Embeddings by ...	2017
General	KG_Completion	A1	FB15k		Knowledge Graph Embedding via ...	2018
General	Question_Answering	F3	...SW_1fb71cdc	FB15k	Representation Learning of ...	2019

A SPARQL representation for this question is given in Listing 5.2. We search for systems that use a translation model (TransX) as ML module which operates on Facebook benchmark semantic web resources (e.g., FB15k, FB13, FB500k). Furthermore, the module has to generate symbolic output. The ML module can be placed anywhere in the system architecture, hence, we do not look for specific patterns or architectures.

Table 2 shows an excerpt of the found systems, including different patterns and specific SW resources. As an example, the system presented in the paper "Learning Knowledge Embeddings by Combining Limit-Based Scoring Loss", uses pattern A1 and two Facebook benchmark datasets, namely FB13 and FB15k, for KG completion.

5.2 Use Case 2: Embedding-Based Exploration of the SWeMLS KG

In order to allow further exploration of the SWeMLS-KG, we have computed RDF2vec embeddings [27] on the graph. With the help of those embeddings, visualizations can be generated, and additional queries, based on entity similarity in the embedding space, can be performed. Unlike the previous use case where the exploration of the data is guided by explicitly stated information needs, this use case explores the latent semantics encoded in the SWeMLS-KG.

Figure 5 shows scatter plots of embeddings for the statistical modeling methods and semantic web resources in the knowledge graph. Especially for the resources, one can observe that the grouping is actually sensible, forming, e.g., a cluster of DBpedia and YAGO-related resources in the top area.

Typical scenarios for searching in the embedding space would be triggered using one entity and then searching for further entities in the neighborhood. One typical example use case would be searching for alternative resources and methods. For example, a neighborhood query for the FB15k link prediction benchmark provides a list of other link prediction benchmark datasets, whereas a neighborhood query for DBpedia provides a list of other general-purpose knowledge graphs, such as YAGO or Wikidata. Likewise, neighborhood queries for

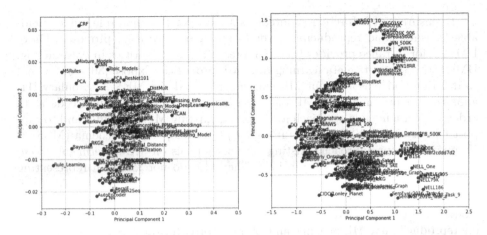

Fig. 5. Scatterplots of statistical model methods (left) and resources (right). For the plots, the embedding spaces have been reduced to 2D using principal component analysis.

methods can be conducted. For example, a neighborhood search for graph neural networks gives rule learning and On2vec as nearest neighbors[12].

Neighborhood queries can also be useful for finding related papers. We probed the embedding space with a randomly selected paper, describing a knowledge-graph-based recommender system using embeddings, attention networks, and freebase as a resource. The neighborhood contains mostly other papers describing knowledge-based recommenders and papers using the same pattern and/or resources for other purposes, such as question answering.

6 Related Work

Ontologies for describing neuro-symbolic/ML systems. For the proposed SWeMLS ontology, related work is represented by earlier efforts to characterize neuro-symbolic systems. For example, Bader and Hitzler [4] made an early attempt at such characterization and proposed eight dimensions for classification purposes. More recently, Van Harmelen and ten Teije [29] introduced a set of 13 design patterns, similar to design patterns in software engineering. This taxonomy has been extended with processes and models in [5]. Another taxonomy comprising six different types of systems but without focus on the internal architectures of the investigated systems has been presented by Kautz [21]. While all these efforts focus on the broader family of neuro-symbolic systems, in our recent work [8] we proposed a classification system tailored for SWeMLS. With the ontology presented here we provide the first machine-actionable (i.e., formally represented) system classification.

---

[12] Source code: https://w3id.org/semsys/sites/swemls-kg/rdf2vec.

To ensure that ML research outcomes are properly comparable, understandable, reusable, and reproducible several ontologies have been proposed. Onto-DM [26] for instance provides generic representations of entities in data mining, DMOP [22] supports meta-learning from ML processes, Exposé [30] can be used to describe and reason about ML experiments, and the MEX Vocabulary [11] aims to support managing ML outcomes and sharing of provenance data. In order to offer a flexible approach for mapping existing ML ontologies and to support extensions, a W3C Community Group[13] developed ML-Schema (MLS)[14]. Compared to our approach, existing ontologies focus on ML experiment *executions* and not on system descriptions. They also do not focus on representing SW elements of the systems. However, main ML concepts in our ontology can be mapped to ML-Schema, such as `mls:Experiment`, which is comparable to `swemls:System`, and `mls:Data` is similar to `swemls:Instance`. With a focus on reproducibility, ML-Schema and other approaches also cover detailed ML settings, such as hyperparameters and evaluation results. While this is not in the focus of our current work, we plan to extend our knowledge graph in this direction.

Machine-processable publication of domain-specific scientific knowledge is reported in several disciplines. For example, in social sciences, in the domain of human cooperation, experts annotated nearly 3,000 studies in terms of 60 features as part of the COoperation DAtabank initiative[15]. This systematically collected scientific knowledge has been published using semantic technologies as a knowledge graph [28] and as nanopublications [2] in order to support the automation of scientific tasks such as (comparative) meta-analysis and the detection of contradictory claims respectively.

Going beyond domain-specific efforts for publishing scientific knowledge, the Open Research Knowledge Graph (ORKG) aims to provide a platform for the publication of open research knowledge. ORKG describes scientific articles semantically in a machine- and human-readable way. It offers concepts and properties to classify articles, and extract various metadata such as authors and publication date, but also to describe research contributions and results. To contribute to this initiative, we mapped our ontology to the ORKG schema and published our SWeMLS results within the ORKG (see Sect. 4), thus being one of the first communities to leverage the capabilities of this system and to benefit by the sustainability of the data publication on a long term.

7   Conclusion and Future Work

In this work, we used a semantic technology approach to provide a machine-processable way to represent a large number of SWeMLS reported in scientific publications. We introduced the SWeMLS ontology and SWeMLS knowledge

---

[13] https://www.w3.org/community/ml-schema/.
[14] http://ml-schema.github.io/documentation/MLSchema.html.
[15] COoperation DAtabank: https://amsterdamcooperationlab.com/databank/.

graph to support researchers and reviewers using a more automated approach to search, conduct analysis and test existing SWeMLS. The SWeMLS-KG was also imported into ORKG, making the data browseable, accessible, citable, and reusable. The use cases we discussed have shown that the SWeMLS-KG is useful for researchers and reviewers on a variety of levels, including identifying and analyzing existing SWeMLS, drawing conclusions about the components being used, or identifying similar components using SPARQL queries and embedding-based exploration of the SWeMLS-KG.

Regarding future work, we plan to include audit support for SWeMLS by capturing Workflow Execution traces to complement the workflow templates (i.e., SWeMLS patterns) and workflow instances (i.e., SWeMLS instance), building on our prior work on auditability [10]. Furthermore, we strive to enable semi-automatized description extraction from SWeMLS papers and generation of SWeMLS pipeline code from patterns by building on existing works [9,16]. Finally, we want to support a two-way transformation of data from the SWeMLS-KG and the ORKG-observatory. Beyond the scope of our research, we hope to inspire broader research communities to provide their research results in a structured representation, which in turn will allow others to build their research *by standing on the shoulder of giants*.

Acknowledgments. This work has been supported by the Austrian Science Fund (FWF) under grant V0745 (HOnEst) and FFG Project OBARIS (Grant Agreement No 877389). SBA Research (SBA-K1) is a COMET Center within the COMET - Competence Centers for Excellent Technologies Programme and funded by BMK, BMAW, and the federal state of Vienna. The COMET Programme is managed by FFG. Moreover, financial support by the Christian Doppler Research Association, the Austrian Federal Ministry for Digital and Economic Affairs, the National Foundation for Research, Technology and Development, DFG NFDI4DataScience (No. 460234259) and ERC ScienceGRAPH (GA ID: 819536) is gratefully acknowledged.

References

1. Amstutz, P., et al.: Common workflow language, v1. 0 (2016). https://doi.org/10.6084/m9.figshare.3115156
2. Asif, I., Tiddi, I., Gray, A.J.G.: Using nanopublications to detect and explain contradictory research claims. In: 2021 IEEE 17th International Conference on eScience (eScience), pp. 1–10 (2021). https://doi.org/10.1109/eScience51609.2021.00010
3. Auer, S., et al.: Improving access to scientific literature with knowledge graphs. Bibliothek Forschung Praxis **44**(3), 516–529 (2020). https://doi.org/10.1515/bfp-2020-2042
4. Bader, S., Hitzler, P.: Dimensions of neural-symbolic integration - a structured survey. CoRR abs/cs/0511042 (2005). https://doi.org/10.48550/arXiv.cs/0511042
5. van Bekkum, M., de Boer, M., van Harmelen, F., Meyer-Vitali, A., Teije, A.: Modular design patterns for hybrid learning and reasoning systems. Appl. Intell. **51**(9), 6528–6546 (2021). https://doi.org/10.1007/s10489-021-02394-3

6. Besold, T.R., et al.: Neural-symbolic learning and reasoning: a survey and interpretation. In: Neuro-Symbolic Artificial Intelligence: The State of the Art, pp. 1–51. IOS Press (2021). https://doi.org/10.48550/arXiv.1711.03902
7. Booch, G., et al.: Thinking fast and slow in AI. In: AAAI. AAAI Press (2021). https://doi.org/10.48550/arXiv.2010.06002
8. Breit, A., et al.: Combining machine learning and semantic web: a systematic mapping study. ACM Comput. Surv. (2023). https://doi.org/10.1145/3586163. Just Accepted
9. Daga, E., Groth, P.: Data journeys: explaining AI workflows through abstraction. Semantic Web, pp. Early-Access (2023). http://oro.open.ac.uk/88012/
10. Ekaputra, F.J., et al.: Semantic-enabled architecture for auditable privacy-preserving data analysis. Semant. Web pre-press(Preprint), 1–34 (2021). https://doi.org/10.3233/SW-212883
11. Esteves, D., et al.: Mex vocabulary: a lightweight interchange format for machine learning experiments. In: Proceedings of the 11th International Conference on Semantic Systems, pp. 169–176 (2015). https://doi.org/10.1145/2814864.2814883
12. Garcez, A., Broda, K., Gabbay, D., et al.: Neural-Symbolic Learning Systems: Foundations and Applications. Springer, Heidelberg (2002). https://doi.org/10.1007/978-1-4471-0211-3
13. Garcia, N., Renoust, B., Nakashima, Y.: Context-aware embeddings for automatic art analysis. In: Proceedings of the 2019 on International Conference on Multimedia Retrieval, pp. 25–33 (2019). https://doi.org/10.1145/3323873.3325028
14. Garijo, D., Gil, Y., Corcho, Ó.: Towards workflow ecosystems through semantic and standard representations. In: Montagnat, J., Taylor, I.J. (eds.) Proceedings of the 9th Workshop on Workflows in Support of Large-Scale Science, WORKS 2014, New Orleans, Louisiana, USA, 16–21 November 2014, pp. 94–104. IEEE (2014). https://doi.org/10.1109/WORKS.2014.13
15. Gil, Y., et al.: Wings: intelligent workflow-based design of computational experiments. IEEE Intell. Syst. **26**(1), 62–72 (2011). https://doi.org/10.1109/MIS.2010.9
16. Grafberger, S., Groth, P., Stoyanovich, J., Schelter, S.: Data distribution debugging in machine learning pipelines. VLDB J. **31**(5), 1103–1126 (2022). https://doi.org/10.1007/s00778-021-00726-w
17. Hitzler, P.: A review of the semantic web field. Commun. ACM **64**(2) (2021). https://doi.org/10.1145/3397512
18. Hitzler, P., Bianchi, F., Ebrahimi, M., Sarker, M.K.: Neural-symbolic integration and the semantic web. Semant. Web **11**(1), 3–11 (2020). https://doi.org/10.3233/SW-190368
19. Hull, D., et al.: Taverna: a tool for building and running workflows of services. Nucleic Acids Res. **34**(Web-Server-Issue), 729–732 (2006). https://doi.org/10.1093/nar/gkl320
20. Jaradeh, M.Y., et al.: Open research knowledge graph: next generation infrastructure for semantic scholarly knowledge. In: Proceedings of the 10th International Conference on Knowledge Capture, K-CAP 2019, pp. 243–246. Association for Computing Machinery, New York (2019). https://doi.org/10.1145/3360901.3364435
21. Kautz, H.: The Third AI Summer, AAAI Robert S. Engelmore Memorial Lecture, 34th AAAI (2020). https://doi.org/10.1002/aaai.12036
22. Keet, C.M., et al.: The data mining optimization ontology. J. Web Semant. **32**, 43-53 (2015). https://doi.org/10.1016/j.websem.2015.01.001, https://www.sciencedirect.com/science/article/pii/S1570826815000025

23. Kitchenham, B., Charters, S., et al.: Guidelines for performing systematic literature reviews in software engineering. Technical report, Keele University and Durham University Joint Report (2007). https://www.researchgate.net/publication/302924724

24. Moreau, L., et al.: The open provenance model core specification (v1.1). Future Gener. Comput. Syst. **27**(6), 743–756 (2011). https://doi.org/10.1016/j.future.2010.07.005

25. Noy, N.F., McGuinness, D.L., et al.: Ontology development 101: a guide to creating your first ontology (2001). https://www.researchgate.net/publication/243772462

26. Panov, P., Džeroski, S., Soldatova, L.: OntoDM: an ontology of data mining. In: 2008 IEEE International Conference on Data Mining Workshops, pp. 752–760 (2008). https://doi.org/10.1109/ICDMW.2008.62

27. Ristoski, P., Paulheim, H.: RDF2Vec: RDF graph embeddings for data mining. In: Groth, P., Simperl, E., Gray, A., Saḅon, M., Krötzsch, M., Lecue, F., Flöck, F., Gil, Y. (eds.) ISWC 2016. LNCS, vol. 9981, pp. 498–514. Springer, Cham (2016). https://doi.org/10.1007/978-3-319-46523-4_30

28. Tiddi, I., Balliet, D., ten Teije, A.: Fostering scientific meta-analyses with knowledge graphs: a case-study. In: Harth, A., et al. (eds.) ESWC 2020. LNCS, vol. 12123, pp. 287–303. Springer, Cham (2020). https://doi.org/10.1007/978-3-030-49461-2_17

29. van Harmelen, F., ten Teije, A.: A boxology of design patterns for hybrid learning and reasoning systems. J. Web Eng. **18**(1–3), 97–124 (2019). https://doi.org/10.13052/jwe1540-9589.18133

30. Vanschoren, J., Soldatova, L.: Exposé: an ontology for data mining experiments. In: International Workshop on third Generation Data Mining: Towards Service-Oriented Knowledge Discovery (SoKD-2010), pp. 31–46 (2010). https://www.researchgate.net/publication/228525536

A Concise Ontology to Support Research on Complex, Multimodal Clinical Reasoning

Sabbir M. Rashid(✉)⊙, Jamie McCusker⊙, Daniel Gruen⊙,
Oshani Seneviratne⊙, and Deborah L. McGuinness⊙

Rensselaer Polytechnic Institute, Troy, NY, USA
{rashis2,mccusj2,gruend2,senevo}@rpi.edu, dlm@cs.rpi.edu

Abstract. When clinicians perform tasks involving clinical reasoning, such as the diagnosis or treatment of diabetes, multiple forms of reasoning, including deduction and abduction, are often employed. Ontologies designed to provide a foundation for clinical decision support systems have been encoded based on Clinical Practice Guidelines. Nevertheless, existing approaches solely allow deductive rules for clinical reasoning, with ontologies too large or complex to support tractable abductive reasoning. We follow existing guidelines and standards to design the Diabetes Pharmacology Ontology, a concise ontology – an ontology engineered by adhering to the Minimum Information to Reference an External Ontology Term principle and following an agile design approach. We claim that use cases that incorporate multiple forms of reasoning, such as those aimed at supporting both deduction and abduction, are better supported by concise, rather than complete and comprehensive, ontologies. We demonstrate how Personal Health Knowledge Graphs have been implemented using our ontology and evaluate the abductive capability of modules included with our ontology. We openly publish the resources that have resulted from this work, as listed below. This work demonstrates how multimodal semantic reasoning – deduction and abduction – can be used to emulate tasks involving clinical reasoning and thus has the potential to support practitioners with clinical decision-making.

- **Ontology:** https://purl.org/twc/dpo/ont/diabetes_pharmacology_ontology.ttl
- **Bioportal:** https://bioportal.bioontology.org/ontologies/DPCO
- **URL:** https://tetherless-world.github.io/diabetes-pharmacology-ontology
- **Documentation:** https://bit.ly/dpo_documentation
- **GitHub:** https://github.com/tetherless-world/diabetes-pharmacology-ontology
- **License:** https://www.apache.org/licenses/LICENSE-2.0
- **DOI:** https://doi.org/10.5281/zenodo.7454721

Keywords: Clinical Practice Guidelines · Standards · Case Studies · Diabetes · Ontology · Pharmacotherapy · Personal Health Knowledge Graph · Reasoning · Deductive Reasoning · Abductive Reasoning

Supported by Rensselaer Polytechnic Institute.

C. Pesquita et al. (Eds.): ESWC 2023, LNCS 13870, pp. 390–407, 2023.
https://doi.org/10.1007/978-3-031-33455-9_23

1 Introduction

The use of clinical reasoning, a complex process involving cognition, meta-cognition, and discipline-specific knowledge [25], is required for clinicians to complete complex medical tasks involving information comprehension and decision-making. Although the intricacies of how humans perform clinical reasoning is an ongoing topic encompassing much debate [30], it is clear that multiple distinct types of inference are used [2]. While the dialectics of logical philosophy is beyond the scope of this article, we find that the Select and Test Model (ST-Model), in which an expert chooses a plausible hypothesis that is subsequently confirmed or falsified through testing, is a practical epistemological framework for our research on medical reasoning [39, 44].

Since the ST-Model presents the cyclic and back and-forth nature of medical problem solving tasks in a manner resembling hierarchical decomposition, a divide-and-conquer approach employed by humans for solving large problems [27], we believe that for the purpose of our research, the ST-Model is representative enough of the type of reasoning a clinician may employ. To create a clinical decision support system capable of employing ST-Model-like reasoning, we initially focus on the facilitation of deduction and abduction.

We commence this research by incorporating domain-specific and semantic standards to design a knowledge representation that supports both types of reasoning. We present a guideline and standards-driven approach for crafting a clinical ontology. Given a specific use case for the diagnosis and treatment of type 2 diabetes mellitus, we design the Diabetes Pharmacology Ontology (DPO).

1.1 Motivation

While there are multiple factors that come into play when attempting to predict reasoning performance, empirically it has been shown that reasoning over large and complex ontologies can be very time-consuming [26]. Despite such concerns, existing diabetes ontologies focus on completeness and encoding as much knowledge as possible [15, 16]. These ontologies solely support deduction to accomplish clinical reasoning tasks such as differential diagnosis or therapy planning.

When a clinician reasons over patient information to perform clinical decision-making, multiple forms of reasoning are used, including abstraction, deduction, abduction, and induction [2]. Non-monotonic reasoning problems involving abduction are notoriously more challenging to solve than their monotonic counterparts [23] and have greater considerations in terms of tractability [12, 13, 40]. Therefore, this work is motivated by the need of supporting multiple forms of reasoning to better emulate how clinicians perform clinical reasoning tasks.

1.2 Contribution and Claims

The main contribution of this article is that we develop an approach for semantic knowledge representation that supports multimodal reasoning and demonstrate how the approach can be used for clinical decision-making by publishing a concise, FAIR-compliant ontology, the Diabetes Pharmacology Ontology (DPO), which is used in our approaches for differential diagnosis and therapy planning.

Due to performance and tractability concerns, it becomes important to consider the size and complexity of an ontology that will be used in any setting, which is often more important to consider when it is to be used for multimodal reasoning. We are able to support our use case involving clinical reasoning that incorporates multiple forms of reasoning by creating a concise, rather than complete and comprehensive, ontology. This is achieved by following the Minimum Information to Reference an External Ontology Term (MIREOT) [8] principle when linking to external vocabularies and using an agile [24] design strategy to create both an ontology and a Personal Health Knowledge Graph (PHKG) [20]. An agile approach allows us to meet the needs of our use case while limiting the number of concepts included, thus limiting the size of our ontology. Therefore, we define a concise ontology as one that adheres to both the MIREOT principle as well as an agile design methodology, where the minimum required amount of information for external classes is included and concepts in the ontology are limited to those required by a given use case.

One way we keep our ontology concise is by only including the pharmacotherapy factors and antihyperglycemic treatments found in Table 9.2[1] of Chap. 9 [7] of the ADA Guidelines, omitting other therapies from our ontology. In Sect. 8, we discuss the importance of conciseness as determined from the evaluation of abductive capability presented in Sect. 7 by answering a set of competency questions using the AAA Abox abduction solver [38]. Our ontology and PHKG support both deductive and abductive reasoning and can demonstrate how semantic reasoning can be used to emulate clinical decision-making tasks, including differential diagnosis and therapy planning.

Our ontology is based on existing standards and best practices. We leverage content from the American Diabetes Association (ADA) Clinical Practice Guidelines [3] to inform specific branches of the ontology. Additionally, we consider Ontology Design Patterns (ODPs) [18], the HCLS dataset specification [19], and the Data on the Web Best Practices [29] when designing, scoping, and annotating our ontology. The Fast Healthcare Interoperability Resources (FHIR) [4] specification is a standard for representing clinical information that employs a composition and constraint-based modeling approach. In Sect. 5, we demonstrate how a PHKG is created using either FHIR or an upper ontology.

The resources resulting from this research are FAIR [45], based on guiding principles for the discovery, use, and reuse of data, which we demonstrate by evaluating our ontology on principles for developing computational biomedical knowledge (CBK) infrastructure [32]. The ontology and PHKGs are published and readily available, use standard vocabulary, and are adequately documented.

---

[1] For easy reference, we include this table as supplementary material: tetherless-world.github.io/diabetes-pharmacology-ontology/#supplementary-material.

2   Related Work

2.1   Existing Diabetes Ontologies

To support Clinical Decision Support Systems (CDSS) with the diagnosis and treatment of diabetes, an ontological approach for incorporating recommendations from computerized Clinical Practice Guidelines is proposed [1]. While a relatively simple flat ontology (as opposed to hierarchical) is created including classes for diagnoses, lab tests, patient information, risk factors, and symptoms, diagnostic and therapy planning rules are written in SWRL [22], allowing for the categorization of patients in terms of both type 1 and type 2 prediabetes and diabetes. The concepts included in this ontology are similar to the top-level classes that we include in our ontology, but we expand upon each concept hierarchically, resulting in a richer representation.

Another ontology including SWRL rules for diabetes diagnosis is the Diabetes Diagnosis Ontology (DDO). This ontology was designed with the goal of systematically developing complete ontologies for the diagnosis of diabetes mellitus [15], resulting in the creation of comprehensive OWL2 diabetes knowledge representation interoperable with OBO Foundry [43] ontologies. A major limitation of DDO is the absence of support for therapy planning, addressed by the Diabetes Mellitus Treatment Ontology (DMTO) [16], an extension of DDO.

DMTO is an OWL 2 ontology based on the SHOIQ(D) description logic in which type 2 diabetes treatment plans are modeled based on CPGs which includes SWRL rules for diagnosis and treatment [16]. Unfortunately, when trying to run the rules ourselves, we ran into several errors. Furthermore, while DMTO is indeed a comprehensive ontology, resulting in great domain coverage, an ontology of this size is not compatible with timely abductive reasoning. Despite the inclusiveness of DMTO, it does not meet all the requisites to abductively plan treatments for patients, such as direct links from treatments to associated pharmacotherapy factors and appropriately represented concept restrictions to trigger the abductive reasoner used in our approach.

2.2   Clinical Practice Guidelines

Clinical Practice Guidelines (CPGs) are collections of statements intended to optimize patient care by assisting the understanding of factors involved in complex medical decision-making, including potential benefits, harms, or alternatives of a specific medical decision, as well as demographic and socioeconomic considerations [11]. For a set of guidelines to be trustworthy, they should be developed by experts from various associated disciplines through a systematic review of existing literature, should provide evidence, clear explanations, and quality ratings for recommendations, and should be revised appropriately in light of new findings. For this work, we leverage an existing CPG, the Standards of Medical Care in Diabetes [3] by the American Diabetes Association (ADA).

3 Ontology Design Approach

We now describe our design methodology for creating DPO, design-related scoping requirements, and our approach to linking external vocabularies.

3.1 Use Case

DPO arose from the need for a structured vocabulary to aid in clinical decision-making. We consider a use case with the goal of supporting clinicians with clinical reasoning tasks, such as differential diagnosis, therapy planning, or plan critiquing. We ground this in the setting where patients have elevated blood glucose levels.

A primary requirement of this use case is that the support provided should emulate the type of rationality a clinician is likely to apply. In particular, a proof of concept is required, where it must be demonstrated that the approach can support multimodal reasoning. We find that by adhering to the ST-Model, we can approximate human clinical decision-making involving multiple forms of reasoning. Inversely, the proof of concept requirement nullifies the requirement that complete coverage is realized. It is not necessary to demonstrate that any scenario in a given domain is addressable, but rather support for such content is possible with the proper extensions.

While complete domain coverage is not necessary, the use case does require that provided recommendations for the portion covered should align with domain-specific standards. As an elevated blood glucose level is an indicator of prediabetes or diabetes, a scoping requirement is that the technology created should center on these medical conditions. In particular, we focus on type 2 diabetes mellitus and leverage the well-used ADA Standards of Care Diabetes CPG. Since clinical decision-making employs multiple forms of reasoning and earlier work has been conducted involving the encoding of CPGs in ontologies, we found that the use of Semantic Web technologies was a natural choice for meeting these initial requirements.

Due to privacy considerations and to avoid HIPAA violations [42], the use of actual patient data is not a requirement for this use case. Nevertheless, it is required that the data used should resemble actual patient data. We find that a NetCE course [34] includes relevant case studies on diabetes and is a good reference point for constructing hypothetical patients.

3.2 Design Methodology

While an initial use case may be in mind when designing an ontology, it is arguably impossible to know all the future uses the ontology will have. We provide an initial set of concepts in our extensible ontology while remaining open to including additional concepts that may be needed as a consequence of growing use and reuse. Two ontology design approaches that allow for modular updates include the Agile [24] & eXtreme [5,35] Design (XD) methodologies. Approaches involving modular updates are often referred to as modular ontology design [21].

When using an agile design approach, simplicity is encouraged, especially when representing rudimentary ideas. Essential features should be implemented foremost, while additional features can be included in the future. Inspired by Agile, the XD methodology asserts that ontologies should only contain concepts and properties that are essential for the particular task for which the ontology is being designed. Extensions of an XD ontology typically transpire iteratively, where further improvements are incorporated by considering the needs of the end-user and involving the customer in the design process.

3.3   Design Requirement-Related Scoping

A design requirement is that our ontology must leverage a CPG so that intelligent systems that use the ontology can follow guideline recommendations. We scope our study to clinical cases relevant to type 2 diabetes mellitus. Therefore, the Standards of Medical Care in Diabetes by the American Diabetes Association (ADA) became an apparent choice of a CPG to use. Chapter 9 of the ADA guidelines [7], titled Pharmacologic Approaches to Glycemic Treatment, contains treatment information and factors that can be leveraged for diabetes therapy planning. Therefore, to create a concise rather than complete ontology, we scope the therapies and pharmacotherapy factors included in our ontology to those mentioned in this article, omitting additional diabetes-associated factors and therapies mentioned in the literature. For example, Licogliflozin and Sotagliflozin are SGLT2 inhibitors that we do not include in our ontology. Diagnostic factors and clinical measurements included in the ontology are scoped based on the diabetes-related NetCE case studies. To test the representation capability of the ontology, three of these case studies (patients K, H, and B in [34]) are used to create example patients.

3.4   Linking External Vocabularies

To make an ontology interoperable with other ontologies, it is necessary to link to external vocabularies. Unfortunately, importing entire ontologies using *owl:import* statements often results in unnecessarily large overhead, especially when the ontologies being imported have a substantial number of concepts, often including many concepts that are not directly applicable. It is not uncommon for an ontology to import other ontologies which are not even used.

The inclusion of *owl:import* statements introduces the risk of vastly increasing the size of an ontology, saturating it with unnecessary information, especially when multiple high-level ontologies are imported or an ontology is imported for the use of a single class or property. Too many classes can have a negative impact on reasoning complexity and computation time, especially with non-monotonic forms of reasoning, such as abduction.

Therefore, for our use case involving multimodal reasoning, it is necessary to minimize the number of external concepts included. The MIREOT guidelines provide specifications for the minimum amount of information required when including concepts from external ontologies. Rather than importing entire ontologies, only necessary concepts should be included. The MIREOT guidelines state that, for an external concept to be consistently referenced, the only required information includes the ontology namespace, the URI for the specific term being imported, and the URI for the superclass of the term being imported [8].

We adopt this approach in terms of directly including external concepts in our ontology as well as the minimal set of information required for reference. When including a superclass of a linked concept, in the cases that (i) the superclass is not directly linked to a term in the ontology, (ii) is not a subclass of another linked concept, or (iii) is a top-level class, we assign the superclass to be a subclass of the concept dpo:ExternalClass. By doing so, we reduce the hierarchical clutter by putting all external classes under a single branch.

In addition to the minimal set, we also include the labels of external concepts as also recommended in the MIREOT guidelines, simply to aid in readability. The external concepts are directly linked to internal concepts using *owl:equivalentClass*. For an external concept that includes a definition, we assign the definition to the linked internal concept. For all definitions acquired from external resources, we append a definition source attribution to the end of the definition string that references the external resource, concept, or URL that the definition is adopted from.

4 Diabetes Pharmacology Ontology

To address the needs of our use case, it is necessary to include in our ontology diagnostic factors, such as patient characteristics and test findings, therapies, and pharmacotherapy factors. Shown in Fig. 1 is a simplified representation of DPO, depicting key concepts that extend from the root concept, dpo:TherapyPlanningComponent, and some of their subclasses.

While additional classes extend from some of the concepts shown, due to space considerations we omit several branches of the ontology and limit this diagram to extend up to three concepts from the root. The three top-level branches are dpo:PharmacotherapyFactor, dpo:DiagnosticFactor, and dpo:Therapy. All other branches of the ontology extend from these top-level concepts. In addition to the existing concepts included in our ontology, DPO is extensible by allowing the incorporation of new classes as a subclass of an existing concept.

4.1 Pharmacotherapy Factor

Organized in the ADA CPG Table 9.2 are type 2 diabetes treatments based on drug-specific factors. Such factors, including efficacy, weight change association, cost, and risk correlations for several medical conditions or diseases, correspond to the columns of Table 9.2. The dpo:PharmacotherapyFactor branch is based off of this table, where the above-mentioned columns are used to form the immediate subclasses of dpo:PharmacotherapyFactor. In turn, potential values for each entry of a column informed the terms included under each of these concepts.

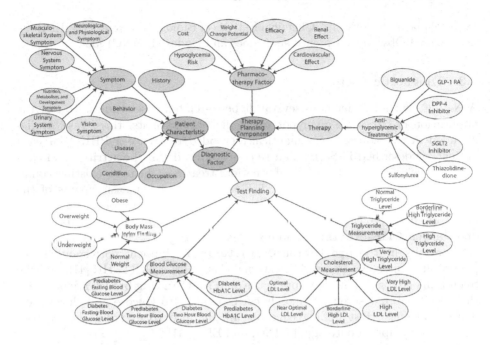

Fig. 1. DPO is rooted at `dpo:TherapyPlanningComponent`, which has three main branches. These top-level concepts include `dpo:PharmacotherapyFactor`, `dpo:DiagnosticFactor`, and `dpo:Therapy`. Diagnostic factors are split into `dpo:PatientCharacteristic`, shown in light red, and `dpo:Measurement`, shown in light orange. Pharmacotherapy factors are shown in light blue and therapies in light green. (Color figure online)

In addition to the factors mentioned above, Table 9.2 also incorporates a column titled "Additional Considerations". This column covers additional therapy considerations, such as FDA Black Box warnings [10] as well as additional known risks and reactions. To constrain the scope of the initial implementation of DPO, we have not yet included in our ontology the considerations from this column. This extension may be considered as part of future work. Pharmacotherapy factors are mapped to external classes from National Cancer Institute Thesaurus (NCIT) [28]. In particular, NCIT is used due to its broad coverage and since most of the concepts included in `dpo:PharmacotherapyFactor` is not included in the other external vocabularies we are linking.

4.2 Therapy

The rows of the ADA CPG Table 9.2 comprise of categorizations of therapies commonly used to treat type 2 diabetes. These categorizations are leveraged to inform the top-level therapies we included in our ontology. While there are many drugs associated with these therapy categorizations, it is not our intention to encode an exhaustive list of therapies. Instead, we limit our scope of therapies to include only those mentioned in Table 9.2. Therapy concepts are mapped to external classes from NCIT, Chemical Entities of Biological Interest (ChEBI) [9], and Logical Observation Identifiers Names and Codes (LOINC) [33].

4.3 Diagnostic Factor

A NetCE course [34] includes several diabetes-related case studies. To test the application of our work on hypothetical diabetes patients, three case studies included in this course are semantically encoded to create a PHKG for each patient, as described in Sect. 5. These case studies detail the attributes of each patient, including demographic information, treatment history, existing conditions, and symptoms. The case studies also include lab measurements of the patients taken at specific visits. The dpo:DiagnosticFactor branch is created based on the NetCE case studies, and is separated into two main branches, dpo:PatientCharacteristic and dpo:TestFinding.

Concepts in the dpo:PatientCharacteristic branch, corresponding to patient attributes, are mapped to external classes from NCIT, HP [41], and the Symptom ontology[2]. The concepts in the dpo:TestFinding branch are based on the NetCE lab measurement, mostly corresponding to glucose and cholesterol-related readings. Test finding concepts are mapped to external classes from NCIT, the Symptom ontology, LOINC, and EFO [31].

5 Personal Health Knowledge Graph

A Personal Health Knowledge Graph (PHKG) is a knowledge resource linking a patient's relevant medical information and personal data, typically for use in personalized health applications [20]. To test the applicability of our ontology, we have created PHKGs for several hypothetical patients based on diabetes-related NetCE case studies. A portion of one such PHKG is depicted in Fig. 2.

In addition to the use of concepts from DPO, our PHKGs leverage an upper ontology, such as the Semanticscience Integrated Ontology (SIO) [14]. We have also created a PHKG based on FHIR [4] rather than SIO for demonstration purposes and to provide support for a healthcare-related standard specification. Nevertheless, we find that the use of SIO results in a much more straightforward and concise representation. Both representation formats are included in our GitHub repository[3]. The file titled maria.ttl is the FHIR representation while the other files leverage SIO.

When using SIO, the patient is encoded as an instance of sio:Patient that has instances of attributes linked using *sio:hasAttribute*. Each attribute exists at an instance of a timepoint, linked using *sio:existsAt*, corresponding to the visit at which an attribute was recorded. Patient attributes include symptoms, conditions, demographic information, and measurement values. Deductive rules in the ontology can be used to make inferences regarding the recorded attributes.

---

[2] https://bioportal.bioontology.org/ontologies/SYMP/.

[3] https://github.com/tetherless-world/diabetes-pharmacology-ontology/tree/main/kb.

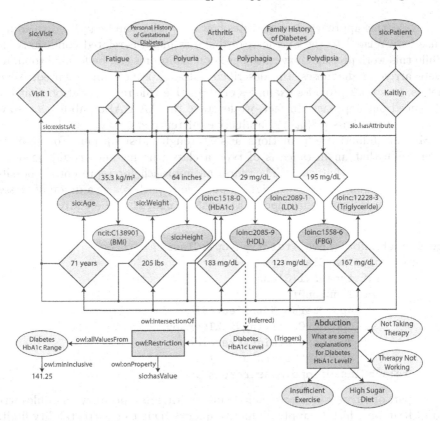

Fig. 2. A Personal Health Knowledge Graph includes instances of patients. A top-level ontology like SIO along with concepts in DPO is used for representing patient attributes. Deductive rules from the ontology are used to infer attribute categorizations. Ontology classes are shown as ellipses. External classes are pink while internal classes are color-coded as described in Fig. 1. Instances are shown as yellow diamonds. (Color figure online)

One such rule is depicted towards the bottom of Fig. 2, where a hemoglobin A1C (HbA1c) measurement is categorized to be in the diabetes range. Such categorizations can be used to trigger abductive hypotheses. One may ask the question, "What are some explanations for why the patient's HbA1c is in the diabetic range?" The encoding of this rule is discussed in the following section.

6 Application: Supporting Abductive Reasoning

The abductive reasoning problem arises when a knowledge base $\mathcal{K}$ does not entail an observation $\mathcal{O}$, that is $\mathcal{K} \not\models \mathcal{O}$, resulting in the search for an explanation $\mathcal{E}$ that when included with $\mathcal{K}$ would result in the entailment of the observation, $\mathcal{K} \cup \mathcal{E} \models \mathcal{O}$ [37]. For a sufficient solution, several constraints need to be considered, including consistency ($\mathcal{K} \cup \mathcal{E} \not\models \perp$), minimality ($\mathcal{E}$ is a '*minimal explanation*' for $\mathcal{O}$), relevance ($\mathcal{E} \not\models \mathcal{O}$), and explanatoriness ($\mathcal{K} \not\models \mathcal{O}, \mathcal{E} \not\models \mathcal{O}$) [17].

An existing approach demonstrates how abduction can be utilized to address a use case related to the diagnosis of diabetes mellitus-related conditions [36]. While this work presents how rules based on symptoms can be formed to abductively arrive at diagnoses, the described ontology is not implemented. Nevertheless, this work provides examples of abductive rule representation that have influenced our approach. In fact, we leverage the AAA ABox abduction solver by the same authors [38] as the abductive inference engine we employ.

Simple abductive explanations arise through subsumption. To entail the observation that an instance is of type a class, the instance could be one of the subclasses of that class. Therefore, an approach for representing possible abductive explanations is by assigning possible hypotheses as a union of classes. For example, we can define dpo:DiabetesHbA1cLevel to be equivalent to the union of classes that serve as potential explanations, as listed below.

```
dpo:DiabetesHbA1cLevel rdf:type owl:Class ;
    owl:equivalentClass
        [ rdf:type owl:Class ;
            owl:unionOf (
                dpo:TherapyNotEffective
                dpo:NotComplyingWithTherapy
                dpo:InsufficientExercise
                dpo:HighSugarDiet ) ] ;
    rdfs:subClassOf dpo:Measurement .
```

As part of our resources, we include in our GitHub repository[4] modules written in RDF on which to apply abductive queries. Due to the tractability limitations associated with abductive reasoning [40], we recommend the use of specific modules for targeted abductive queries rather than running the reasoner over the entire ontology. Nevertheless, if time and computational capability are not a deterrent, the modules can be combined with the ontology and/or additional knowledge to result in a more comprehensive set of explanations.

Included is a module for an example scenario involving unexpected weight gain, as well as modules related to the use case discussed in this article, such as a diagnostic module, HbA1c module, and therapy module. The therapy module represents specific antihyperglycemic medications prescribed based on pharmacotherapy factor considerations. We further include abductive queries for these modules in the form of commands[5] that can be sent to the abduction solver.

7 Evaluation

A recent article [32] promotes three guiding principles for developing computational biomedical knowledge (CBK) and its associated infrastructure; CBK

---

[4] https://github.com/tetherless-world/diabetes-pharmacology-ontology/tree/main/ont/modules.

[5] https://github.com/tetherless-world/diabetes-pharmacology-ontology/blob/main/abduction_commands.

should be FAIR, trustworthy, and open. We use these principles to evaluate the DPO, which we include in the Supplementary Materials section of our website.[6]

In addition to evaluating how our ontology met the principles for developing CBK, we evaluate the abductive reasoning support of our approach. To do so, we compile a set of competency questions that we test whether we can answer using abduction. These competency questions are listed as follows.

C_1 What are some causes for an HbA1c level in the diabetes range?
C_2 How can we explain the patient having insufficient exercise?
C_3 Why might the patient not be talking a medication?
C_4 What therapies have high efficacy?
C_5 What therapies have potential for weight loss?
C_6 What therapies have potential atherosclerotic cardiovascular disease benefit?

The first 3 questions are used to test diagnostic capability while the latter 3 relate to therapy planning. To test these competency questions, a Dell laptop with a Ubuntu 20.04.5 LTS operating system is used. The computer has an Intel Core i7-8550U CPU running at 1.8 GHz with 4 cores and 8 threads. The laptop contains 16 GB of RAM. Version 0.11 of the AAA Abox abduction solver[7] is used, with the negations and avoid loops parameters set to true, the abduction approach set to reduction, and the timeout set to 120 s.

Table 1. Modules used to evaluate competency questions. The columns correspond to ontology details returned by the AAA solver. "Concepts" refers to the number of classes in the module. "Roles" refers to the number of properties. "Individuals" refers to the number of instances. "Tbox" refers to the number of terminological axioms. "Abox" refers to the number of individual-associated assertions.

Module	Concepts	Roles	Individuals	TBox	ABox
hba1c	13	1	7	18	7
exercise	12	1	2	21	2
compliance	18	1	2	28	2
therapy	117	1	81	230	115

We use 4 modules with a varying number of concepts and individuals, as shown in Table 1. A unique module is used for each diagnostic question, while a single therapy module is used for the therapy-related questions. Abducibles are particular concepts, roles, or individuals that are provided to the reasoner to limit the reasoning space. Given the complete set of relevant abducibles, an abductive query can be run without providing any abducibles, by providing all of the relevant abducibles, or by segmenting the abducibles and running multiple

---

[6] https://tetherless-world.github.io/diabetes-pharmacology-ontology/#supplementary-material.

[7] Available here: https://dai.fmph.uniba.sk/~pukancova/aaa/.

queries using each of the segments. When creating segments, we keep necessary abducibles in all of the segments, such as those appearing in the observation, and split the rest. For this evaluation, we create at most 3 segments per query.

The depth of an explanation corresponds to the number of assertions that can appear in an explanation. We test each query with depths of 1, 2, and 3. For a depth n, we record the time t_n in seconds that it takes to find the set of explanations at that depth. If the set is not found within the time limit, which we have set to 2 min, the query times out, denoted using T/O. We also record the number of explanations found. The results of this evaluation are shown in Table 2. The full set of evaluation output logs are available on our GitHub.[8]

8 Discussion

We briefly discuss the results of the evaluation, the impact of this work, some limitations, and future research directions.

8.1 Results

We have evaluated the capability of competency questions to be answered abductively using modules included with our ontology. While the therapy-related queries did time out when specifying a depth of 3, upon examining the explanations provided, we found that for all of the modules, the set of expected explanations could be obtained using a depth of 2. Depending on the representation of the module, the expected explanations could even be reached using a depth of 1. Therefore, we have demonstrated that our approach allows us to abductively answer competency questions related to diagnosis and therapy planning.

These results demonstrate the importance of conciseness when performing abductive reasoning. Modules with fewer concepts allowed for abductive answers to be obtained faster and to a greater depth. We also found that greater depth calculations could be obtained by dividing the set of abducibles into segments. However, this requires knowledge of the set of relevant abducibles. Nevertheless, for simpler modules, such as the diagnostic modules, we can obtain the expected results without specifying abducibles, again showing the value of conciseness.

8.2 Scientific Impact

We have published an original ontology as well as PHKGs that exemplify how the ontology can be used with an upper ontology or as a FHIR adherent representation. We have introduced our resources in this article and have included further descriptions on a dedicated website. While other diabetes ontologies based on CPGs do exist, our work is innovative and advances the state-of-the-art in that we consider both deductive and abductive capabilities in its design. Unlike other

---

[8] https://github.com/tetherless-world/diabetes-pharmacology-ontology/tree/main/ evaluation_results.

Table 2. Abductive competency query results. For multiple segments, the number of abducibles per segment is shown as an average, and the computation times and number of unique explanations are shown as sums. *The second segment with 1 less abducible actually did finish computing after 109.48 s, but the first segment timed out.

CQ	#Segments	#Abducibles/Segment	Depth	t_1(s)	t_2(s)	t_3(s)	#Exp.	Module
C_1	0	∞	1	1.01	N/A	N/A	4	hba1c
			2	1.01	14.2	N/A	9	
			3	1.14	14.65	T/O	9	
	1	18	1	**0.91**	N/A	N/A	4	
			2	1.04	11.52	N/A	9	
			3	0.92	11.67	T/O	9	
	2	12	3	1.44	**6.04**	**49.04**	9	
C_2	0	∞	1	0.39	N/A	N/A	3	exercise
			2	0.38	0.66	N/A	3	
			3	0.39	0.66	1.33	3	
	1	9	1	0.38	N/A	N/A	3	
			2	**0.36**	**0.45**	N/A	3	
			3	0.39	0.49	**0.49**	3	
C_3	0	∞	1	0.49	N/A	N/A	6	compliance
			2	0.46	0.93	N/A	6	
			3	0.58	0.94	2.23	6	
	1	11	1	0.48	N/A	N/A	6	
			2	**0.38**	**0.48**	N/A	6	
			3	0.57	0.57	**0.57**	6	
C_4	0	∞	1	T/O	N/A	N/A	0	therapy
	1	26	1	8.26	N/A	N/A	14	
			2	8.47	T/O	N/A	14	
	2	13.5	2	7.64	T/O*	N/A	14	
	3	9.33	2	7.95	49.52	N/A	14	
			3	**7.4**	**48.75**	T/O	14	
C_5	0	∞	1	T/O	N/A	N/A	1	therapy
	1	26	1	7.76	N/A	N/A	11	
			2	7.25	T/O	N/A	12	
	2	13.5	2	6.86	T/O	N/A	12	
	3	9.33	2	**6.59**	**48.42**	N/A	11	
			3	7.07	48.95	T/O	12	
C_6	0	∞	1	T/O	N/A	N/A	0	therapy
	1	26	1	6.96	N/A	N/A	7	
			2	6.75	T/O	N/A	8	
	2	13.5	2	**5.68**	T/O	N/A	9	
	3	9.33	2	6.1	51.53	N/A	7	
			3	6.07	**50.51**	T/O	12	

diabetes ontologies, we focus on the creation of a concise rather than comprehensive ontology to better support tractable abductive reasoning. Our contributions include not just the shared resources, but also the approach that may be leveraged in other work. While we have not yet validated our technique using actual patient data, we do apply our approach to hypothetical diabetes case studies.

We apply our approach to the diagnosis and treatment of diabetes, a prevalent health problem affecting 37.3 million people in the United States (11.3% of the U.S. population), with an additional 96 million people aged 18 years or older (38.0% of the adult U.S. population) affected with prediabetes [6]. Our approach to designing the ontology and representing rules that can trigger abductive queries can also be generalized to other medical conditions. Therefore, this work and the resulting resources can potentially aid clinicians with a wide range of clinical decision-making tasks. Our resources and approach are of interest to the Semantic Web community since they illustrate how multimodal reasoning can be implemented for a practical application.

8.3   Limitations and Future Directions

Due to scoping considerations, only a subset of diabetes information is encoded in our ontology. This limitation is justified by the need for our approach to allow for abductive reasoning and the requirement of our use case for only a proof of concept rather than complete coverage. Nevertheless, a future extension of this work includes incorporating more knowledge. Another limitation is that for many queries to run quickly, such as those related to therapy planning, abducibles need to be explicitly specified to constrain the Abox abduction solver to only return explanations involving the expected concepts. This constraint reduces computation time but requires preexisting knowledge of the expected results.

We plan to encode additional components from the ADA guidelines. Moreover, we wish to review relevant literature to find further pharmacotherapy factor associations and allow support for more antiglycemic therapies. Since we test our approach using data based on diabetes-related case studies, one limitation of our PHKGs is that they are based on hypothetical rather than real patient data. Therefore, potential future research involves the validation of our approach using actual patient data.

9   Conclusion

We have introduced DPO, which we have used as the vocabulary and knowledge representation resource for our approach to supporting multimodal clinical reasoning for the diagnosis and treatment of diabetes. Unlike earlier ontologies that focus on comprehensiveness, we instead design a concise ontology able to support multimodal reasoning. We have presented and evaluated our approach, and have discussed the impact of this research, its limitations, and future work.

Acknowledgements. This work is supported by IBM Research AI through the AI Horizons Network. We would like to acknowledge Amar K. Das for his guidance. We also thank the members of the Tetherless World Constellation, especially Sola Shirai, Shruthi Chari, and Danielle Villa for their feedback.

References

1. Alharbi, R.F., Berri, J., El-Masri, S.: Ontology based clinical decision support system for diabetes diagnostic. In: 2015 Science and Information Conference (SAI), pp. 597–602. IEEE (2015)
2. Arocha, J.F., Wang, D., Patel, V.L.: Identifying reasoning strategies in medical decision making: a methodological guide. J. Biomed. Inform. **38**(2), 154–171 (2005)
3. Association, A.D.: Introduction: standards of medical care in diabetes-2022 (2022)
4. Bender, D., Sartipi, K.: HL7 FHIR: an agile and restful approach to healthcare information exchange. In: Proceedings of the 26th IEEE International Symposium on Computer-Based Medical Systems, pp. 326–331. IEEE (2013)
5. Blomqvist, E., Hammar, K., Presutti, V.: Engineering ontologies with patterns-the extreme design methodology (2016)
6. Centers for Disease Control and Prevention: National diabetes statistics report (2022). https://www.cdc.gov/diabetes/data/statistics-report/index.html
7. Committee, A.D.A.P.P., Committee: A.D.A.P.P.: 9. Pharmacologic approaches to glycemic treatment: Standards of medical care in diabetes-2022. Diab. Care **45**(Supplement_1), S125–S143 (2022)
8. Courtot, M., et al.: MIREOT: the minimum information to reference an external ontology term. Aug-2009 (2009)
9. Degtyarenko, K., et al.: ChEBI: a database and ontology for chemical entities of biological interest. Nucleic Acids Res. **36**(suppl_1), D344–D350 (2007)
10. Delong, C., Preuss, C.V.: Black box warning (2022)
11. of Medicine (US). Committee on Standards for Developing Trustworthy Clinical Practice Guidelines, I., Graham, R., Mancher, M., Miller Wolman, D.: Clinical practice guidelines we can trust. National Academies Press Washington, DC (2011)
12. Du, J., Qi, G., Shen, Y.D., Pan, J.Z.: Towards practical ABox abduction in large OWL DL ontologies. In: Twenty-Fifth AAAI Conference on Artificial Intelligence (2011)
13. Du, J., Wang, K., Shen, Y.D.: A tractable approach to ABox abduction over description logic ontologies. In: Twenty-Eighth AAAI Conference on Artificial Intelligence (2014)
14. Dumontier, M., et al.: The semanticscience integrated ontology (SIO) for biomedical research and knowledge discovery. J. Biomed. Semant. **5**(1), 1–11 (2014)
15. El-Sappagh, S., Ali, F.: DDO: a diabetes mellitus diagnosis ontology. Appl. Inform. **3**, 1–28 (2016)
16. El-Sappagh, S., Kwak, D., Ali, F., Kwak, K.S.: DMTO: a realistic ontology for standard diabetes mellitus treatment. J. Biomed. Semant. **9**(1), 1–30 (2018)
17. Elsenbroich, C., Kutz, O., Sattler, U.: A case for abductive reasoning over ontologies. In: OWLED, vol. 216 (2006)
18. Gangemi, A.: Ontology design patterns for semantic web content. In: Gil, Y., Motta, E., Benjamins, V.R., Musen, M.A. (eds.) ISWC 2005. LNCS, vol. 3729, pp. 262–276. Springer, Heidelberg (2005). https://doi.org/10.1007/11574620_21

19. Gray, A.J., Baran, J., Marshall, M.S., Dumontier, M.: Dataset descriptions: HCLS community profile. Interest group note, W3C (2015). http://www.w3.org/TR/hcls-dataset

20. Gyrard, A., Gaur, M., Shekarpour, S., Thirunarayan, K., Sheth, A.: Personalized health knowledge graph. In: CEUR Workshop Proceedings, vol. 2317. NIH Public Access (2018)

21. Hammar, K., Hitzler, P., Krisnadhi, A.: Advances in Ontology Design and Patterns, vol. 32. IOS Press (2017)

22. Horrocks, I., et al.: SWRL: a semantic web rule language combining OWL and RuleML. W3C Member Submission **21**(79), 1–31 (2004)

23. Hubauer, T., Lamparter, S., Pirker, M.: Automata-based abduction for tractable diagnosis. In: International Workshop on Description Logics, pp. 360–371 (2010)

24. Hunt, A., Thomas, D.: The trip-packing dilemma [agile software development]. IEEE Softw. **20**(3), 106–107 (2003)

25. Islam, R., Weir, C.R., Jones, M., Del Fiol, G., Samore, M.H.: Understanding complex clinical reasoning in infectious diseases for improving clinical decision support design. BMC Med. Inform. Decis. Mak. **15**(1), 1–12 (2015)

26. Kang, Y.B., Pan, J.Z., Krishnaswamy, S., Sawangphol, W., Li, Y.F.: How long will it take? Accurate prediction of ontology reasoning performance. In: Proceedings of the AAAI Conference on Artificial Intelligence, vol. 28 (2014)

27. Kindler, H., Fischer, B., Densow, D., Fliedner, T.M.: An architecture for medical knowledge-based assistance systems. In: Proceedings IEEE Symposium and Workshop on Engineering of Computer-Based Systems, pp. 442–449. IEEE (1996)

28. Kumar, A., Smith, B.: Oncology ontology in the NCI thesaurus. In: Miksch, S., Hunter, J., Keravnou, E.T. (eds.) AIME 2005. LNCS (LNAI), vol. 3581, pp. 213–220. Springer, Heidelberg (2005). https://doi.org/10.1007/11527770_30

29. Lóscio, B.F., Burle, C., Calegaro, N.: Data on the web best practices. W3C recommendation (2017). https://www.w3.org/TR/dwbp/

30. Loughlin, M., Copeland, S.M.: Humans, machines and decisions: clinical reasoning in the age of artificial intelligence, evidence-based medicine and COVID-19. J. Eval. Clin. Pract. **27**(3), 475 (2021)

31. Malone, J., et al.: Modeling sample variables with an experimental factor ontology. Bioinformatics **26**(8), 1112–1118 (2010)

32. McCusker, J., et al.: Guiding principles for technical infrastructure to support computable biomedical knowledge. Learn. Health Syst. **n/a**(n/a), e10352 (2022). https://doi.org/10.1002/lrh2.10352, https://onlinelibrary.wiley.com/doi/abs/10.1002/lrh2.10352

33. McDonald, C.J., et al.: LOINC, a universal standard for identifying laboratory observations: a 5-year update. Clin. Chem. **49**(4), 624–633 (2003)

34. NetCE: Diabetes pharmacology (2022). https://www.netce.com/coursecontent.php?courseid=2488

35. Presutti, V., Daga, E., Gangemi, A., Blomqvist, E.: eXtreme design with content ontology design patterns. In: Proceedings of Workshop on Ontology Patterns (2009)

36. Pukancová, J., Homola, M.: Abductive reasoning with description logics: Use case in medical diagnosis. In: Description Logics (2015)

37. Pukancová, J., Homola, M.: Tableau-based ABox abduction for the ALCHO description logic. In: Description Logics (2017)

38. Pukancová, J., Homola, M.: The AAA ABox abduction solver. KI-Künstliche Intell. **34**(4), 517–522 (2020)

39. Ramoni, M., Stefanelli, M., Magnani, L., Barosi, G.: An epistemological framework for medical knowledge-based systems. IEEE Trans. Syst. Man Cybern. **22**(6), 1361–1375 (1992)
40. Reyes-Cabello, A.L., Aliseda-Llera, A., Nepomuceno-Fernández, Á.: Towards abductive reasoning in first-order logic. Log. J. IGPL **14**(2), 287–304 (2006)
41. Robinson, P.N., Mundlos, S.: The human phenotype ontology. Clin. Genet. **77**(6), 525–534 (2010)
42. Schumaker, E.: What is a HIPAA violation? ABC News (2021)
43. Smith, B., et al.: The obo foundry: coordinated evolution of ontologies to support biomedical data integration. Nat. Biotechnol. **25**(11), 1251–1255 (2007)
44. Stefanelli, M., Ramoni, M.: Epistemological constraints on medical knowledge-based systems. In: Evans, D.A., Patel, V.L. (eds.) Advanced Models of Cognition for Medical Training and Practice. NATO ASI Series, vol. 97, pp. 3–20, Springer, Heidelberg (1992). https://doi.org/10.1007/070-3-662-02833-9_1
45. Wilkinson, M.D., et al.: The fair guiding principles for scientific data management and stewardship. Sci. Data **3**, 1–9 (2016)

LauNuts: A Knowledge Graph to Identify and Compare Geographic Regions in the European Union

Adrian Wilke[✉] and Axel-Cyrille Ngonga Ngomo

DICE Group, Department of Computer Science, Paderborn University,
Paderborn, Germany
adrian.wilke@uni-paderborn.de, axel.ngonga@upb.de
https://dice-research.org/

Abstract. The *Nomenclature of Territorial Units for Statistics* (NUTS) is a classification that represents countries in the European Union (EU). It is published at intervals of several years and organized in a hierarchical system where geographical areas are subdivided according to their population sizes. In addition to NUTS, there is a further subdivided hierarchy level, named *Local Administrative Units* (LAU), whose data are updated annually by EU member states. While both datasets are published by Eurostat as Excel files, an additional RDF dataset is available for NUTS up to the 2016 scheme. With this work, we provide the Linked Data community with an up-to-date Knowledge Graph in which NUTS and LAU data are linked and which contains population numbers as well as area sizes. We also publish an Open Source generator software for future released versions that will naturally arise due to changes in population numbers. These contributions can be used to enrich other datasets and allow comparisons among regions in the European Union. All resources are available at https://w3id.org/launuts.

Keywords: EU · European Union · Eurostat · Knowledge Graph · LAU · LauNuts · Linked Data · NUTS

1 Introduction: Extension Possibilities and Contributions

The *Nomenclature of Territorial Units for Statistics* (NUTS) is a hierarchical system in which regions of the European Union (EU) and related states are subdivided. There is an official Resource Description Framework (RDF) dataset

This work has been supported by the German Federal Ministry of Education and Research (BMBF) within the project EML4U under the grant no. 01IS19080B and by the German Federal Ministry of Transport and Digital Infrastructure (BMVI) within the project OPAL under the grant no. 19F2028A.
Resource type: Knowledge Graph
License: CC BY 4.0 International
DOIs: 10.5281/zenodo.7760179, 10.6084/m9.figshare.22272067.v2
Website: https://w3id.org/launuts

provided by Eurostat, which contains major NUTS concepts. Since some data is not included in the RDF dataset, the following possibilities for extension arise:

E.1 Extension by the finest geographical level, named *Local Administrative Units* (LAU). This level contains data of districts and municipalities and allows a more precise identification of regions.

E.2 Extension by the currently valid version (*NUTS 2021*). The published Eurostat RDF dataset is limited to data up to the *NUTS 2016* version.

E.3 Extension by URIs for different versions. The Eurostat RDF dataset focuses on the respective latest NUTS version. There are no unique URIs for obsolete versions, which would be helpful for, e.g., updating other datasets to revised NUTS versions, which are issued at intervals of three years.

With this work, we present the three following contributions to the Linked Data community:

C.1 A proposal to extend the existing Linked Data scheme by the additional LAU level as well as unique identifiers for published NUTS and LAU versions.

C.2 A Knowledge Graph (KG) generator, which can be used to build and update the KG to NUTS versions released in the future. The generator is implemented to automatically parse the file format used by Eurostat to publish new NUTS and LAU data, which are contained in Excel files.

C.3 A KG built upon the existing concepts as well as a scheme extension along with data officially published by Eurostat and links to additional entities.

The contributions can be used to enhance other KGs and scientific works which include relations to EU regions and their population. Also, tasks like Named Entity Recognition (NER) of geographical entities can be improved by including the hierarchical structure of named regions.

The remainder of this article is structured as follows: Sect. 2 introduces NUTS and LAU concepts and gives insights into related works. In Sect. 3, an extension of the existing *Eurostat: NUTS - Linked Open Data* dataset concepts is presented. This includes a description of the given scheme (Sect. 3.1), the added concepts of the extension (Sect. 3.2) and the data processing pipeline (Sect. 3.3). Sect. 4 lists statistics of the resulting KG. Finally, Sect. 5 provides a conclusion and an outlook towards future works.

2 Related Work: Existing Concepts and Their Usage

Related works comprise the data and schemes published by Eurostat (Sect. 2.1) and scientific works related to NUTS and LAU (Sect. 2.2).

2.1 NUTS and LAU: Hierarchial Geographical Regions

The *Nomenclature of Territorial Units for Statistics* (NUTS)[1] is a geographical hierarchy of regions. For every member state of the EU and for additional

---

[1] https://ec.europa.eu/eurostat/web/nuts/background.

Level	Minimum	Maximum	Example	Code 2021	Population
NUTS 0	Country level		France	FR	67.9 M
NUTS 1	3,000,000	7,000,000	Grand Est	FRF	5.5 M
NUTS 2	800,000	3,000,000	Alsace	FRF1	1.9 M
NUTS 3	150,000	800,000	Bas-Rhin	FRF11	1.1 M
LAU	-		Strasbourg	67482	0.3 M

Fig. 1. NUTS classification criteria based on population thresholds

states like the United Kingdom, respective geographical regions are sub-divided into three levels of detail. The subdivision into levels is based on thresholds of population sizes. The average population size of regions has to range between a minimum and a maximum. Figure 1 shows the specified thresholds as well as examples of NUTS levels and regions related to Strasbourg.

With exceptions, the current NUTS scheme version is updated every 3 years. The last three versions are 2021, 2016 and 2013. With regard to the version numbers, it has to be noted that there was no large delay in releasing the versions. The naming of the scheme was changed: Up to 2016, schemes were named after the technical date of adoptions, and from 2021, it is when data becomes available. *NUTS 2016* became valid in 2018 and *NUTS 2021* has been valid since 2021. The official description of the current NUTS version was published by Eurostat [4].

The current version *NUTS 2021* comprises sub-divided regions of the 27 EU states Austria (AT), Belgium (BE), Bulgaria (BG), Croatia (HR), Cyprus (CY), Czechia (CZ), Denmark (DK), Estonia (EE), Finland (FI), France (FR), Germany (DE), Greece (GR), Hungary (HU), Ireland (IE), Italy (IT), Latvia (LV), Lithuania (LT), Luxembourg (LU), Spain (ES), Malta (MT), Netherlands (NL), Poland (PL), Portugal (PT), Romania (RO), Slovakia (SK), Slovenia (SI) and Sweden (SE), as well as the United Kingdom (UK). These country regions are sub-divided into 104 regions at the *NUTS 1* level, 283 regions at *NUTS 2* level and 1,345 regions at *NUTS 3* level.

In addition to NUTS, there is one additional sub-divided level named *Local Administrative Units* (LAU). It consists of municipalities or equivalent units. Up to 2016, this level was sub-divided into two LAU levels. Additionally, it was named *NUTS 4* or rather *NUTS 5* up to 2003.

LAU is updated annually and in the current version (2021), it comprises the states of *NUTS 2021* (listed above) as well as additional data for Albania (AL), Iceland (IS), Liechtenstein (LI), Norway (NO), Switzerland (CH) and Turkey (TR). Related to the state of 2022-06-14, data for the following countries will also be added: Bosnia and Herzegovina (BA), Kosovo (XK), Montenegro (ME), Republic of North Macedonia (MK) and Serbia (RS). Along with the related NUTS regions, the respective area sizes and populations are published. This data has been used in statistical and scientific works.

2.2 Usage of NUTS and LAU in Statistical and Scientific Works

Statistical evaluations based on NUTS and LAU data were carried out in several domains. In the recent work *Coronis* [8], multiple public COVID-19 sources were combined with NUTS regions to compare rates of infection. The work is based on GeoVocab, which contains spatial data and was updated in 2011. In the economic domain, rental listings of Greece have been sub-divided into NUTS regions and visualized afterwards [1]. This approach could be applied to other countries and compared afterwards. Farm topology and spatial land in the German state of North Rhine-Westphalia have been combined with LAU level data [7]. It is an example of the usage of extended fine-granulated spatial data where "official statistics provide frequency tables [...] at NUTS 3 and higher level, only". Early works that focused on the UK used NUTS and the related harmonized statistics at the national level [2,3]. However, the URIs are not available anymore. In order to remain sustainably retrievable, our approach is based on a combination of open licensing of code and data, permanent identifiers via w3id.org and generator software that can parse official Eurostat data from the last 10 years and with which future releases can probably also be integrated effortlessly.

NUTS data has been combined with other data sources like postal codes, GeoNames[2] and OpenStreetMap[3] to enable users to search and retrieve information about geo entities [5]. Entities from OpenStreetMap itself have been transformed into RDF data [10].

There are also various visualizations of several domains, mainly published by Eurostat itself: Regions in Europe - 2022 interactive edition[4], Statistical Atlas[5], Statistics Illustrated[6], eurostat-map.js[7], NutsDorlingCartogramn[8], and Regions and Cities Illustrated[9]. To enable other EU projects to build equal works based on RDF, this work extends the existing NUTS Knowledge Graph by LAU data.

3 Extending the Existing NUTS Knowledge Graph

In order to extend the existing NUTS KG, we first analyze the officially published RDF data (Sect. 3.1). Based on the scheme characteristics, we propose an extension (Sect. 3.2). In addition, we describe the single steps of the generator software (Sect. 3.3).

---

[2] https://www.geonames.org/.
[3] https://www.openstreetmap.org/.
[4] https://ec.europa.eu/eurostat/cache/digpub/regions/.
[5] https://ec.europa.eu/statistical-atlas/viewer/.
[6] https://ec.europa.eu/eurostat/web/nuts/statistics-illustrated.
[7] https://github.com/eurostat/eurostat-map.js.
[8] https://github.com/eurostat/NutsDorlingCartogram.
[9] https://ec.europa.eu/eurostat/cache/RCI/.

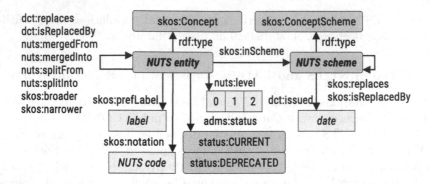

Fig. 2. Scheme of *Eurostat: NUTS - Linked Open Data*

3.1   The Eurostat Linked Open Data Scheme

The Eurostat LOD scheme comprises NUTS data from country level (NUTS 0) down to NUTS 3 data. For all levels, the NUTS schemes 2016, 2013 and 2010 are included. The dataset is focused on the newest included version; changes to prior versions are described, e.g. if a region was split. Single NUTS URIs (named *NUTS entities* afterwards) are provided with the related NUTS code, NUTS scheme, label and level. Figure 2 gives an overview and Table 1 lists the namespaces used in this paper.

The RDF dataset is well suited to describe the current NUTS state. However, the following disadvantages result: (a) The currently valid NUTS 2021 scheme is not included. (b) LAU-level data is not included. (c) There is no specific identifier for NUTS entities combined with related NUTS schemes. If additional data is added for a NUTS entity, e.g. population of a region, the related NUTS scheme cannot directly be addressed. (d) The NUTS level 3 is not included as literal; the data is limited to the literals 0, 1 and 2. (d) The properties *replaces* and *isReplacedBy* are part of the Dublin Core vocabulary, the RDF file erroneously uses SKOS. With regard to adding further details for regions, an extension of the scheme is necessary.

Table 1. Used prefixes, namespaces and related vocabularies

Prefix	URI
dct	http://purl.org/dc/terms/
dbo	https://dbpedia.org/ontology/
nuts	http://data.europa.eu/nuts/
owl	http://www.w3.org/2002/07/owl#
skos	http://www.w3.org/2004/02/skos/core#
status	http://publications.europa.eu/resource/authority/concept-status/

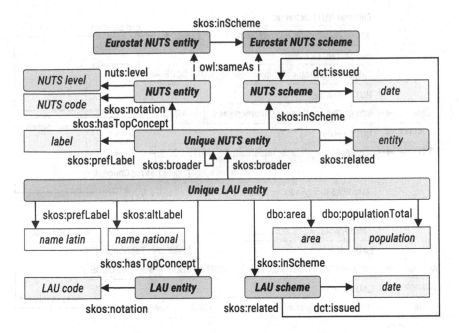

Fig. 3. Extension of Eurostat scheme with LAU data

3.2   Extension of the Eurostat Scheme

In order to uniquely address a NUTS entity, we introduce a combination of a *NUTS entity* and a related *NUTS scheme*. This combination is named *Unique NUTS entity* and is shown in Fig. 3. The figure also shows existing Eurostat concepts in blue, while all data generated in our approach is colored yellow and green. Additional concepts from Fig. 2 (e.g. the NUTS label) remain valid but are not additionally visualized. A *Unique NUTS entity* has a label (the name of the respective region in English) and can be related to other entities, e.g. the region URI in Wikipedia, Wikidata or DBpedia. The NUTS hierarchy is represented by *skos:broader* properties between pairs of *Unique NUTS entities*. The inverse narrower direction can easily be inferred and is not explicitly modelled to keep the amount of data to generate low.

In addition, we introduce the same NUTS concepts for LAU-level data. A *Unique LAU entity* is related to both a *LAU entity* with a code and a *LAU scheme* representing the issued year. In addition, we add the respective area and population sizes and use *skos:prefLabel* for Latin names and *skos:altLabel* for names using non-Latin characters. Figure 4 shows the symmetric design of the scheme and the single parts of URIs, which allow directly addressing NUTS and LAU codes of individual years. LAU entities can be listed by traversing scheme paths (e.g. using SPARQL) and be directly addressed by URIs. In addition to this scheme extension, we processed published data and built a KG.

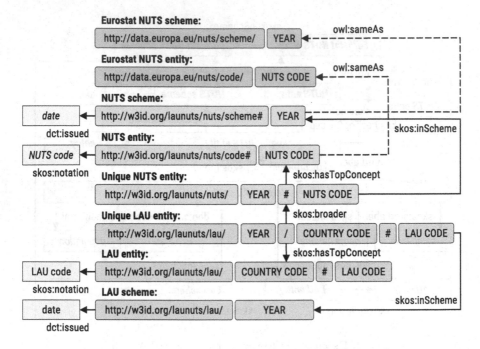

Fig. 4. Extension of Eurostat NUTS URIs with LAU and unique identifiers

3.3 Data Analysis and Processing

The LauNuts approach was developed in several iterations following the Linked Data life cycle [6] (Fig. 5). Actions such as *manual revision* and *quality analysis* towards the final KG generation are included implicitly in every stage of the workflow.

We first *explored* data sources and discovered, inter alia, the officially published sources for NUTS[10], LAU[11] and Linked Open Data[12]. The majority of the data is provided as Excel files. NUTS data is currently available as 7 Excel files for the schemes of the years 2021, 2016, 2013, 2010, 2006, 2003, 1999 and 1995 with 31 sheets in total; for LAU, there are 14 Excel files with 495 sheets for the years from 2010 to 2021. The RDF file related to Linked Open Data contains 20,001 triples.

The *extraction* started with sighting the data. Simply opening some of the Excel files was not possible for the following reasons: Google Sheets ("file is too large to preview"), LibreOffice Calc ("the maximum number of columns per sheet was exceeded") and Apache POI ("OutOfMemoryError: Java heap space"). We finally installed the following extraction queue, explicitly stated here as it could be interesting for other developers working on the topic: (1)

---

[10] https://ec.europa.eu/eurostat/web/nuts/history.

[11] https://ec.europa.eu/eurostat/web/nuts/local-administrative-units.

[12] https://ec.europa.eu/eurostat/web/nuts/linked-open-data.

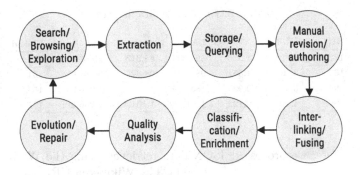

Fig. 5. The Linked Data life cycle

Converting XLS files to XLSX using LibreOffice (7.3.7.2). (2) Converting XLSX files to CSV using ssconvert/Gnumeric (1.12.51). (3) Extracting single sheet names using in2csv/csvkit (1.0.7). (4) Renaming CSV files. The additionally provided Eurostat RDF file could be read using Apache Jena (4.6.1) without any problems.

For further *querying*, the stored CSV and RDF data were used as a cache. To ensure reproducibility, even if the Excel source files are updated in the future, the pre-processed data are published on an FTP server[13].

The *manual revision* of the data started with data analysis of the RDF source. In order to reuse existing Semantic Web concepts, we created a scheme from the available RDF data (see Fig. 2). The scheme is extensible, and details of the most important nuts are provided. However, the predicates used in the RDF file *replaces* and *isReplacedBy* are not part of the used vocabulary SKOS, but DCT (see Table 1). Regarding the predicate *nuts:level* and related literals, the NUTS levels 0, 1 and 2 are included, and level 3 is not included. Additionally, the RDF data is limited to the NUTS schemes 2016, 2013, and 2010. The provided Excel files contain values that must be handled individually and partially cleaned. The LAU Excel files provide LAU codes, related NUTS codes, names in Latin characters, names in national (non-Latin) characters, and area and population data. The values of Latin names are sometimes duplicates of non-Latin names. In other cases, there are no Latin names given. Furthermore, some row headings describing the same concepts are named differently in single files. An example of required cleaning is the code FR7, which occurs twice in NUTS 2013. In addition, the LAU 2021 file contains a sheet with 1 million rows, where each contains a cell with a value 0. Overall, the data was evaluated to be usable with additional cleaning.

We *interlinked* the generated data with two data sources. First, the official Eurostat NUTS URIs have been reused. Second, as a proof of concept, we also created links to Wikipedia URIs[14] representing regions at NUTS levels 0

---

[13] https://hobbitdata.informatik.uni-leipzig.de/LauNuts/sources/.

[14] https://en.wikipedia.org/w/index.php?title=First-level_NUTS_of_the_European_Union&oldid=1126125069.

Table 2. Knowledge Graph sizes

	0	NUTS-1	NUTS-2	NUTS-3	LAU	Area	Population	Linked	Triples
2016	28	132	309	1,376	89,284	54,313	45,570	0	568,396
2021	37	162	371	1,551	98,891	98,825	90,074	151	707,816
2021b	65	294	680	2,927	188,175	153,138	135,644	151	1,181,549
All	177	829	1,992	9,122	1,591,703	1,151,106	1,266,290	151	8,039,437

and 1. Therefore, we processed JSON data retrieved using the Wikipedia API and parsed the embedded Markdown code. The Wikipedia URIs can be used to create additional *skos:relatedTo* links to Wikidata and DBpedia as these KGs are also linked to existing Wikipedia URIs.

Additional steps of the Linked Data life cycle are integrated into the used workflow. The *classification* of entities is built in as the overall data integration is based on the used RDF schemes. The *quality analysis* and *evolution* were conducted by several iterations during development and comparing official numbers about the data and concrete values with actually created entities in the KG. The development started in 2019 as part of the OPAL research project and has been used to access geo labels for Question Answering (QA) [9].

4   Results: Open Software and Knowledge Graph

This work provides three main contributions as listed in Sect. 1. The first contribution (C.1) is the scheme extension described in Sect. 3.2, which allows the integration of LAU data versions, which are updated annually. The scheme makes extensive use of common RDF vocabularies. Additionally, created URIs use permanent identifiers of w3id.org to be available in the future.

The generator software (C.2) is published as Open Source (*GNU AGPLv3* license) on GitHub[15]. This enables extensions or reuse of the code in other projects. It is designed to extract NUTS and LAU data in the format of published Eurostat data of the last 10 years; therefore, it is probably possible to effortlessly process data published in the future. The software is parameterized to process only single steps (e.g. data extraction or KG building) and subsets of available data (e.g. only specified NUTS or LAU versions or single country data).

Generated Knowledge Graphs (C.3) contain up to 7 NUTS versions (from 1999 to 2021) and 12 LAU versions (from 2010 to 2021) with labels, area, and population sizes. The current version is named *LauNuts2021b* to be referenced unambiguously and comprises the NUTS schemes 2021 and 2016 as well as LAU data from 2021 and 2020. In addition, entities of the NUTS levels 0 and 1 and the *NUTS 2021* scheme are linked to Wikipedia URIs. As new LAU versions are published annually, new KG versions are expected to be generated in the future. The KG is published under the *CC BY 4.0 International* license on FTP[16],

---

[15] https://github.com/dice-group/launuts.
[16] https://hobbitdata.informatik.uni-leipzig.de/LauNuts/.

Zenodo and Figshare and therefore is accessible by respective Document Object Identifiers (DOI). Table 2 shows an overview of contained entities and literals in the KG and sub-graphs for 2021 and 2016. The KG in version *LauNuts2021b* contains 1,181,549 triples.

5   Outlook and Conclusion

5.1   Possibilities for Future Work

Extending the KG with postal codes could enable a more precise linking to other KGs. Postal codes[17] are available for the NUTS schemes 2021, 2016, 2013, and 2010. For example, for NUTS 2021, there are lists for 35 countries. Mappings between geodata[18] and NUTS as well as LAU codes are available in different file formats and scales. An extension with geodata would enable the identification of geographic regions for given points of interest.

NUTS and LAU codes could complete mappings in well-known Knowledge Graphs independently from the LauNuts KG. In Wikidata, there is the property P605[19] which represents NUTS links. It is already used for entities, e.g. for Alsace[20]. In DBpedia, there is the property nutsCode[21]. It is used, e.g., for Cornwall[22]. The property is listed as an equivalent property to the Wikidata property P605[23].

The generated entities could be completely linked to Wikipedia URLs. For *NUTS 2021*, the levels 0 and 1 have already linked in this work as a proof of concept. Pages in the Wikipedia category *Nomenclature of Territorial Units for Statistics*[24] contain tables with NUTS codes and linked Wikipedia pages. These mappings could then be utilized for KG linking, as Wikipedia pages are also linked from Wikidata and DBpedia.

5.2   Conclusion

With this work, we extended the existing Eurostat KG with the suggestions listed in Sect. 1: We added (E.1) LAU data, (E.2) the current *NUTS 2021* version, and (E.3) URIs for different NUTS and LAU versions.

The KG can be utilized for tasks such as Named Entity Recognition or entity disambiguation by using the provided literals and geographical hierarchy. Other

---

[17] https://ec.europa.eu/eurostat/web/nuts/correspondence-tables/postcodes-and-nuts.

[18] https://ec.europa.eu/eurostat/web/gisco/geodata/reference-data/administrative-units-statistical-units.

[19] https://www.wikidata.org/wiki/Property:P605.

[20] https://www.wikidata.org/wiki/Q1142.

[21] https://dbpedia.org/property/nutsCode.

[22] http://dbpedia.org/resource/Cornwall.

[23] http://mappings.dbpedia.org/index.php/OntologyProperty:NutsCode.

[24] https://en.wikipedia.org/wiki/Category:Nomenclature_of_Territorial_Units_for_Statistics.

use cases are updates of outdated data to the newest NUTS and LAU versions or comparisons of EU regions based on population numbers.

The provided LauNuts KG and the generator software are available with open licensing and are ready to use for upcoming research projects related to EU regions and on the national level.

References

1. Boutsioukis, G., Fasianos, A., Petrohilos-Andrianos, Y.: The spatial distribution of short-term rental listings in Greece: a regional graphic. Reg. Stud. Reg. Sci. **6**(1), 455–459 (2019). https://doi.org/10.1080/21681376.2019.1660210
2. Correndo, G., Granzotto, A., Salvadores, M., Hall, W., Shadbolt, N.: A linked data representation of the nomenclature of territorial units for statistics. In: Auer, S. et al. (ed.) Proceedings of the Workshop on Linked Data in the Future Internet, vol. 700 (2010). http://ceur-ws.org/Vol-700/Paper1.pdf
3. Correndo, G., Shadbolt, N.: Linked nomenclature of territorial units for statistics. Semant. Web **4**(3), 251–256 (2013). https://doi.org/10.3233/SW-2012-0079
4. European Commission, Eurostat: Statistical regions in the European Union and partner countries : NUTS and statistical regions 2021 : 2022 edition. Publications Office of the European Union (2022). https://doi.org/10.2785/321792
5. Neumaier, S., Savenkov, V., Polleres, A.: Geo-semantic labelling of open data. In: Fensel, A. et al. (ed.) SEMANTiCS 2018. Procedia Computer Science, vol. 137, pp. 9–20. Elsevier (2018). https://doi.org/10.1016/j.procs.2018.09.002
6. Ngomo, A.-C.N., Auer, S., Lehmann, J., Zaveri, A.: Introduction to linked data and its lifecycle on the web. In: Koubarakis, M., et al. (eds.) Reasoning Web 2014. LNCS, vol. 8714, pp. 1–99. Springer, Cham (2014). https://doi.org/10.1007/978-3-319-10587-1_1
7. Pahmeyer, C., Schäfer, D., Kuhn, T., Britz, W.: Data on a synthetic farm population of the German federal state of North Rhine-Westphalia. Data Brief **36**, 107007 (2021). https://doi.org/10.1016/j.dib.2021.107007
8. Santipantakis, G.M., Vouros, G.A., Doulkeridis, C.: Coronis: Towards integrated and open COVID-19 data. In: Velegrakis, Y. et al. (ed.) EDBT 2021, pp. 686–689. OpenProceedings.org (2021). https://doi.org/10.5441/002/edbt.2021.84
9. Schmidt, M.: A Question Answering (QA) System for the Data Catalog Vocabulary (DCAT). Bachelor's thesis, Paderborn University (2020). https://github.com/projekt-opal/dcat-qa/blob/thesis/thesis.pdf
10. Stadler, C., Lehmann, J., Höffner, K., Auer, S.: LinkedGeoData: a core for a web of spatial open data. Semant. Web **3**(4), 333–354 (2012). https://doi.org/10.3233/SW-2011-0052

HHT: An Approach for Representing Temporally-Evolving Historical Territories

William Charles(✉), Nathalie Aussenac-Gilles, and Nathalie Hernandez

IRIT - Université de Toulouse, Toulouse, France
{william.charles,nathalie.aussenac-gilles,nathalie.hernandez}@irit.fr

Abstract. The notion of territory plays a major role in human and social sciences. Representation of this spatio-temporal object and computation of the changes occurring have been tackled in various ways. However, in an historical context, most approaches are irrelevant as they rely on geometric data, which is not available. In order to represent historical territories, we conceived the HHT ontology (Hierarchical Historical Territory) to represent hierarchical historical territorial divisions, without having to know their geometry. This approach relies on a notion of building blocks to replace polygonal geometry. This representation is further used to provide an algorithm to detect and characterize territorial changes in a knowledge graph. Said algorithm creates a knowledge graph of changes at multiple levels encompassing basic changes occurring in a single territory, and composite changes, which are the abstraction of several smaller changes into a large change. The approach was followed to produce 3 knowledge graphs available online. Each of these graphs allowed to set up an analysis of the evolution of the territories during the historical period they cover.

Keywords: Territory Ontology · Evolution Representation · Change Detection Algorithm · Digital Humanities

Resource Type: Ontology
License: Creative Common 4.0
DOI: https://doi.org/10.5281/zenodo.7451702
URL: https://w3id.org/HHT

Resource Type: Software and datasets
License: Creative Common 4.0
DOI: https://doi.org/10.5281/zenodo.7451408
URL: https://github.com/Brainchain09/HHT-SHACL

1 Introduction

In the context of digital humanities, representing territories as they once were is a keen issue. Among many issues arising when attempting to represent historical territories is their geometrical representation [13]. While it is common to use a vector geometry representation when tackling space-spanning entities, the available historical data generally has no geometric representation, which makes such approaches difficult to implement, whether it be for representation or reasoning about changes. In addition, in an historical approach, it is to be noted that representing the geometry of territories could be considered as a representation bias. It is known for example that, back in the 18th century, the typical representation of a territory was a list of places [6]. Another dimension of historical territories is their layered structure within multiple hierarchies. While current territorial hierarchies rely on a single territorial division, labeled as a nomenclature (example: INSEE in France), contexts such as the modern period in France call for several hierarchy layers depending on the power dimension considered (religious, administrative, etc.). As of now, to the best of our knowledge, no ontology nor change detection algorithm takes these two features into account. Thus, this paper proposes an algorithm to detect territorial changes relying on a data representation using an ontology we created, HHT (Historical Hierarchical Territories). Section 2 tackles the state of the art regarding historical territory representation. Section 3 addresses HHT, the ontology we propose for this purpose. Section 4 describes the algorithm used to detect and qualify changes in a knowledge graph relying on HHT. Finally, Sect. 5 presents the evaluation of said algorithm for multiple datasets displaying various particularities.

2 Representing Historical Territories and Changes

2.1 Inherent Difficulties in Representing Historical Territories

Representing historical territories is complex due to various factors. First, it is necessary to represent the hierarchical relations between the various territories. Several approaches exist to represent multi-level territorial divisions, whether they be context specific approaches (RAMON[1] for NUTS) or generic approaches (TSN [3]), they all describe hierarchies covering a whole territory according to a single nomenclature. It is, for example, impossible to simultaneously represent both an administrative territorial division and a religious one in TSN. Representing the geometry is also an issue for historical territories, as it is often found to be either missing or imprecise [13]. However, most approaches [3,15] rely on full geometry description, such as TSN which uses a GeoSPARQL representation.

2.2 Territories as Temporal Entities

When representing historical territories, temporal evolution is to be taken into account, thus inducing these territories to be considered as perdurant entities [3] as defined in the DOLCE ontology [8]. This ontology introduces the notions of perdurants, which are objects whose temporal properties evolve, as opposed to endurants which retain the same properties through their whole existence. Several approaches have been developed over the years to represent such entities. In [10], a general conceptual framework is proposed for temporal entities that distinguishes between SNAP (endurants) and SPAN (perdurants) ontologies. The 4D-Fluents approach [17] is also a common solution when representing perdurants [2]. It relies on representing perdurants as a series of time slices. More

---

[1] http://ec.europa.eu/eurostat/ramon/ontologies/geographic.rdf.

precisely, while an instance p represents the entity itself, it is attached to several time slices which represents its state at various points in time. Some recent work go further by generalizing this approach to describe any kind of statement context [9]. However, as pointed out in [1], the main drawback is the proliferation of entities represented due to the multiple time-slices, which both increases the size of the dataset and makes reasoning more complex. In TSN, as in other approaches [12], time-slicing is handled by creating a new version of the whole hierarchy for every change, regardless of whether every territory actually evolves or not. Regarding TSN, this approach is legitimate as they represent territory nomenclatures defined by a central organism which seldom issues a new version. In an historical context, however, territories and their hierarchies tend to evolve without a centralized management. The aforementioned approach would result in an overfragmentation of the time-slices in most cases. Other approaches, such as Temporal RDF [11] rely on time stamping properties. This can be achieved using several techniques, such as reification, named graphs, n-ary relations or RDF* [14]. However, representing and reasoning on temporally variable properties is still a challenge, as representing several temporal aspects of a single identity implies both a more complex representation and reasoning. In our approach we adapt the structure of TSN to an historical context by locating the versioning at the territory scale instead of the whole hierarchy.

2.3 Review of Change Representation and Reasoning

Change Ontological Representation. In approaches such as *fluents* [17], change representation is implicit. However approaches exist which rely on explicitly representing changes. The notion of Change Bridge is proposed in [13] to link two territory time slices (*input* and *output*) thus representing an evolution from one time slice to the other. A lightweight spatiotemporal vocabulary is defined, which describes changes in five classes (*Changepartof, Establishment, Merge, Namechange, Split*). Change representation can be furthered by defining changes on various scales. [7] introduces three levels of change representation: changes involving only one entity (such as an expansion), functional relations between two units (such as replacements), and composite changes (such as split or merge). TSN-Change [4] proposes a similar change representation. However, it only retains the single-entity and change categories, the last category being implicitly represented due to their hybrid approach relying on both *fluents* and change bridges. This ontology adds more categories in regard of identity, with the distinction between *Continuation* (identities are not impacted) and *Derivation* (identities are impacted) changes [16]. This ontology also provides a vocabulary to describe the relations between changes, and build a change graph. It notably defines a notion of *lowerChange* and *upperChange* which allows to define multiple levels of change. While the taxonomy of the latter is wide-ranged, the semantics of the relations between changes are not precise enough (for example, *lowerChange* is both used to link changes between various territories and between a territory and a nomenclature), and will be replaced with mereology relations in our approach.

Change Detection Algorithms. TSN provides an algorithm to automatically represent changes [4]. This algorithm is used to match entities in two consecutive versions of a nomenclature. It includes both a statistical identity preservation matching of entities, and an explicit qualification of changes. However, this algorithm is not intended to reason on an existing knowledge graph but rather to create a complete knowledge graph from raw data. Furthermore, part of the analysis carried out when computing the differences between two versions is a geometric comparison relying on geospatial vector files. This issue is partly tackled in the original change bridge approach [13]. This approach comes with an algorithm which relies on explicitly representing local changes (i.e. changes at the city scale, for example) in order to infer greater scale changes. However, this approach relies on knowing the extent of the surface of local entities ($50\,km^2$ for example), which is still not always available in an historical context.

3   The HHT Ontology for Historical Territories

3.1   Territory Representation and Link with TSN

To sum up, historical territories require an ontology that would allow representation of multiple overlaying hierarchies and their evolution, without knowledge of the territories' geometry. In order to take into account all these particularities of historical territory representation, the HHT ontology was proposed, basing on the TSN ontology [3], while focusing on units instead of nomenclatures. Figure 1a presents the main concepts and main properties of the territory representation proposed by HHT. All figures are available in the ontology documentation. It mostly revolves around the classes `hht:Unit` which represents a territorial unit, its subtype `hht:HistoricalTerritory` which adds the notion of control by an actor (not discussed in this paper), `hht:Level` which categorizes a hierarchical level, and `hht:HierarchicalCriterion` which corresponds to the criterion related to a level (example: Religious). This class is one of the main differences with TSN and enables the coexistence of multiple hierarchy layers on a single geographic space. However, we retain the level and unit versioning architecture. Instances of `hht:Unit` and `hht:Level` are bearers of the identity of the real world entities they represent. In order to represent their successive states, they are provided respectively with `hht:UnitVersion` and `hht:LevelVersion` through the adequate `hht:hasVersion` subproperty. Each unit version is a member of a level version which materializes its level in the hierarchy. Unit versions on a given level can be linked to Sub/Upper units that are members of the Sub/Upper level. Each of these `hht:Version` has property `hht:validityPeriod` providing the time stamp of the described state relying on *OWL-Time*'s interval concept. Considering that UnitVersions have their own validity period is one other main difference with TSN. In order to further reduce the fragmentation into slices, the impact of lower/upper territories on a `hht:UnitVersion` was tackled. It was first decided to redefine the time slices of a `hht:Unit` whenever one of its hierarchically linked territories was modified [5]. However, this naive approach was found to induce an over-fragmentation of the time slices. It was thus decided that

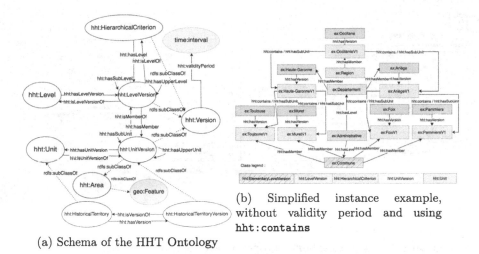

(a) Schema of the HHT Ontology

(b) Simplified instance example, without validity period and using hht:contains

Fig. 1. HHT Ontology: classes and instanciation

the timeline of a hht:Unit would only be fragmented (by increasing the number of its versions) whenever a change in lower territories induces a change of the territory's geometry (see Sect. 3.2). Hierarchical relations (hht:hasSubUnit and hht:hasUpperUnit) are thus valid only during the intersection of the validity intervals of the hht:UnitVersion it links. Note the existence of a super property for hht:hasSubUnit, hht:contains which describes geometry inclusion and is transitive. This property is notably used to access the building blocks of a version, as described in Sect. 3.2. Figure 1b presents a multi-level description of territories using HHT. It omits validity periods, which are considered to be the same for all versions. Figure 2 presents an example of representation using HHT, both with the current and the previous time fragmenting. In the current approach (left part of the figure), the renaming of ex:La-Chapelle-Blanche leads to this entity having two versions. However, as renaming does not affect the geometry of ex:Ploëmel, this hht:Unit retains only one hht:UnitVersion to which both versions of the lower territory are related through the hht:hasUpperUnit property (the validity of said property is implicitly the intersection of the validity intervals of both versions). In the former approach (right part of the figure), however, ex:Ploëmel gets two versions, resulting in a heavier knowledge graph (that would get heavier as we get higher in the hierarchy).

3.2   Discrete Geometry and Building Blocks

As mentioned in Sect. 2.1, geometry is an issue when representing historical territories. In order to address this, geometry representation is achieved by using a notion of *building block*, which are assumed to exist across the whole study period. A subclass of hht:LevelVersion, hht:ElementaryLevelVersion qualifies a hierarchical level version whose members (instances related to the level

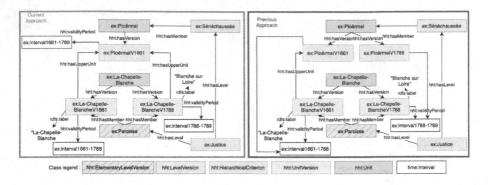

Fig. 2. Examples of current and previous version fragmentation

version with the `hht:isMemberOf` property) are territory versions that are building blocks of the geometry. In this approach, a territory geometry is discrete,
and is can be defined for every `hht:UnitVersion`. Considering such an entity v,
we define geometry as the set of `hht:Unit` that have a version contained by v
that is identified as a member of a `hht:ElementaryLevelVersion`. These units
are (by definition of the elementary level) hierarchically inferior to said territory. To guarantee a time-consistent geometry, we consider a set of `hht:Unit`,
and not of `hht:UnitVersion`. Building blocks can go through non-geometrical
evolutions (such as name changes), and thus have multiple versions even though
their geometry is considered as fixed. Formally, given u a `hht:UnitVersion`, we
can define its geometry as the set of versions of the lowest (elementary) level
territorial units that compose it:

$$geometry(u) = \{b | \exists bLevel, bVersion, hht : contains(u, bVersion) \wedge$$
$$hht : isMemberOf(bVersion, bLevel) \wedge hht : elementaryLevelVersion(bLevel) \wedge$$
$$hht : hasUnitVersion(b, bVersion)\} \quad (1)$$

In Fig. 1b, we have $geometry(ex : OccitanieV1) = \{ex : Muret, ex :$
$Toulouse, ex : Foix, ex : Pamiers\}$. This definition uses `hht:contains`, which
is transitive. However it does not imply that the geometry of a unit is the sum of
that of its direct sub units. This apparent flaw is legitimated in an historical context due to impreciseness in historical sources (an elementary level unit stated
to be inside a higher level unit without describing the intermediate hierarchy).
Note that despite describing the geometry of evolving territories, this definition
is devoid of any temporal component as it is defined for `hht:UnitVersion`, which
are already temporally stamped.

3.3   HHT-Change: Representing and Qualifying Change

So far, we presented how HHT allows to represent hierarchical territories through
time. The HHT ontology also allows to explicitly represent changes that occur
between versions, and to describe their nature. Change representation in HHT is

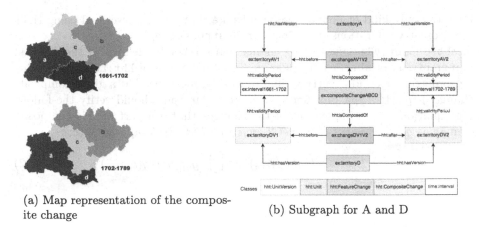

(a) Map representation of the composite change

(b) Subgraph for A and D

Fig. 3. An arbitrary composite change

strongly based on the TSN ontology in regard of change taxonomy [3]. However, the change description structure is quite different. While TSN-Change relies on a multi-level change genealogy, we distinguish between feature changes, which describe a change regarding a single change, and composite changes which are linked together using a mereology approach.

In this article, we focus on hht:FeatureChange and hht:CompositeChange, which are the two relevant classes when dealing with temporal evolution. Figure 3 displays an arbitrary composite change, and Fig. 3b presents a simplified subgraph for territories A and D which will be used to illustrate those examples.

hht:FeatureChange represents a change involving two hht:UnitVersion of the same hht:Unit. The nature of the change can be further qualified using subclasses. These classes include attribute changes (hht:NameChange), geometry changes (hht:GeometryChange), which can further be qualified with subclasses, and life cycle related changes (hht:Appearance, hht:Disappearance). Note that a feature change should be qualified using several subclasses whenever several properties are affected by it (hht:GeometryChange and hht:NameChange). A hht:FeatureChange is linked to the two versions of the hht:Unit it involves through the relations hht:before and hht:after, as seen in Fig. 3b. While hht:Appearance (respectively hht:Disappearance) instances will only have a hht:after (respectively hht:before) property, all other hht:FeatureChange should have exactly one value for each property, as it is intended to link two consecutive versions of the same hht:Unit.

Further in this article, given a feature change c, we refer to the hht:UnitVersion instance b verifying $hht : before(c, b)$ as c_{before} and, similarly, to the hht:UnitVersion instance a verifying $hht : after(c, a)$ as c_{after}.

As opposed to a hht:FeatureChange, a hht:CompositeChange is meant to represent a change that involves unit versions related to several hht:Unit. More accurately, the goal of the hht:CompositeChange class is to assemble several feature changes in order to make sense of those changes on a broader level. As of

now, the only kind of hht:CompositeChange that can be described using HHT
are geometry alterations (hht:GeometryRestructuring).

A hht:GeometryRestructuring change can further be defined as the smallest
non-empty set of hht:FeatureChange describing a unit of hht:Level l covering
a geometric area and occurring simultaneously, meaning that a given composite
change g (g rdf:type hht:GeometryRestructuring) should verify the following equations, denoting the set of the changes that are part of this composite
change as $g_{set} = \{c|htt : FeatureChange(c) \wedge hht : isComposedOf(c, g)\}$:

$$\bigcup_{c \in g_{set}} geometry(c_{before}) = \bigcup_{c \in g_{set}} geometry(c_{after}) \tag{2}$$

$$\forall c_s \subset g_{set} \bigcup_{c \in g_{set} \setminus c_s} geometry(c_{before}) \neq \bigcup_{c \in g_{set} \setminus c_s} geometry(c_{after}) \tag{3}$$

$$\forall c \in g_{set} \exists lversion, level|$$
$$(hht : isMemberOf(c_{before}, lversion) \wedge hht : hasLevelVersion(lversion, level))$$
$$\vee (hht : isMemberOf(c_{after}, lversion) \wedge hht : hasLevelVersion(lversion, level)) \tag{4}$$

$$\exists date|\forall c \in g_{set}$$
$$(\exists interval|hht : validityPeriod(c_{before}, interval) \wedge time : hasEnd(interval, date)) \vee$$
$$(\exists interval|hht : validityPeriod(c_{after}, interval) \wedge time : hasBeginning(interval, date))$$
$$\tag{5}$$

(2) guarantees that the geometry covered by the before and after territories
is equal, while (3) guarantees that the composite change found is not the fusion
of several composite changes. (4) guarantees that all changes that are part of g
affect territories at the same level. Finally (5) specifies that all feature changes
composing g should occur at the same date. Note that this last constraint prevents two changes linking versions of the same hht:Unit to be part of the same
hht:GeometryRestructuring, as there should not be two simultaneous feature
changes on a single territory.

HHT further defines subclasses to qualify the type of hht:GeometryRestruc-
turation an area undergoes. They are separated into three categories depending
on the type of geometry alteration (split, merge, redistribution) and further separated depending on their preserving the territories identity (continuation change)
or not (derivation change). Figure 4 presents examples of these categories.

4   Change Detection Algorithm

Building on HHT-Change, we now aim to automatically detect and qualify the
changes occurring between the various time slices described in a knowledge graph
using HHT to describe territories. A rule based algorithm was implemented in
order to achieve this goal. It is important to take into account some particularities
of the knowledge graphs on which said algorithm should be applied:

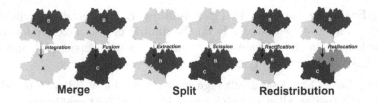

Fig. 4. The various types of `hht:GeometryRestructuring`

- Said knowledge graph should describe the territorial hierarchy only for a specified time period. The Third French Republic dataset used for evaluation in Sect. 5.1, for example, describes the French administrative hierarchy from 1870 to 1940. Such time boundaries are essential to properly detect appearances and disappearances. The instances of `hht:UnitVersion` described in the knowledge graph will have their validity interval truncated to fit in the focus of the knowledge graph, and no knowledge will be represented regarding the status of any territory before and after said time focus. Thus, the algorithm would be erroneous if it detected an appearance for each `hht:UnitVersion` being valid starting from 1870 and having no previous version in the knowledge graph, as this would be due to the graph focus.
- Instances of `hht:Unit` which are member of an elementary level should exist in the knowledge graph across its whole time focus.

The algorithm was designed to be implemented using SHACLRules which rely on SHACL and SPARQL to allow the user to write rules. Resulting implementation is available in the provided GitHub resource.

4.1 Algorithm Description

Algorithm 1. Change detection and qualification algorithmic steps
---
Add the "next version" property linking each version to its chronological successor
Add the feature changes
Qualify feature changes
Create composite changes depending on the feature changes
Qualify composite changes

Algorithm 1 presents the global steps involved in fully creating and qualifying the changes. This section will further detail how each step is achieved.

Finding the Next Version. The use of SHACLRules allows to carry out SPARQL queries to create new triples in a specified order. Thus, each of the steps of Algorithm 1 will be implemented using one or several SPARQL queries included in SHACL Shapes specifying to which graph nodes these queries should be applied.

Adding Feature Changes. This step from Algorithm 1 is actually divided into four steps. The first two steps rely on the finding of the next version that has been carried out in the previous step. Considering two versions $v1$ and $v2$ such as $hht : hasNextVersion(v1, v2)$, the steps proceed as follows:

- Adding basic hht:FeatureChange: wherever the validity interval of $v1$ meets $v2$'s (using Allen's algebra) we add a hht:FeatureChange c verifying $before(c, v1)$ and $after(c, v2)$. This case describes changes on two consecutive versions.
- Adding hht:Reappearance: wherever the validity interval of $v1$ does not meet $v2$'s, we add a hht:Disappearance d verifying $before(c, v1)$ and a hht:Reappearance verifying $after(c, v2)$. This case describes the disappearance of a hht:Unit followed by its reappearance.

The next two steps will allow the algorithm to add appearances and remaining disappearances. Considering a version $v1$ such as there is no $v2$ where $hht : hasNextVersion(v1, v2)$, the following steps consequently are:

- Adding hht:Disappearance: if $v1$'s end of validity interval is not the upper bound of the time focus of the knowledge graph, we add a hht:Disappearance d verifying $before(c, v1)$.
- Adding hht:Appearance: if $v1$'s start of validity interval is not the lower bound of the time focus of the knowledge graph, we add a hht:Appearance d verifying $before(c, v1)$.

It is to be noted that the time focus of the knowledge graph is as of now to be specified inside SHACLRules specification. Further work should include using graph annotation mechanisms to enable a more generic use of our algorithm.

Qualifying Feature Changes. The previous step created a set of hht:FeatureChange that we want to further qualify. Provided a c change, the algorithm will run several comparisons between c_{before} and c_{after}. For simple attributes such as name, the difference is quite easy to compute. Geometry comparisons however, considering our definition, require more fine grained analysis. Intuitively, a geometry change means that $geometry(c_{before}) \neq geometry(c_{after})$. Furthermore, HHT-Change goes further by defining subclasses to hht:geometryChange, which form a partition of the possible cases:

- A hht:Contraction describes the case where:

$$geometry(c_{before}) \not\subseteq geometry(c_{after}) \wedge geometry(c_{after}) \subseteq geometry(c_{before}) \tag{6}$$

In more common terms, a contraction describes the case of a loss of a geometry portion. As SPARQL is not designed to carry out set comparisons, it is calculated using cardinality comparisons regarding $card(geometry(c_{before}))$, $card(geometry(c_{after}))$ and $card(geometry(c_{before}) \cap geometry(c_{after}))$. Equation (6) is rephrased as:

$$card(geometry(c_{before})) > card(geometry(c_{after})) \wedge card(geometry(c_{after}))$$
$$= card(geometry(c_{before}) \cap geometry(c_{after})). \tag{7}$$

This condition can be implemented in SPARQL using several SPARQL COUNT inside the query.

- A hht:Expansion describes the case where:

$$geometry(c_{before}) \subseteq geometry(c_{after}) \land geometry(c_{after}) \not\subseteq geometry(c_{before}). \quad (8)$$

In more common terms, an expansion describes the case of a gain of a geometry portion. SPARQL however, is not designed to carry out set comparisons. In a similar fashion, (8) is rephrased as:

$$card(geometry(c_{before})) < card(geometry(c_{after})) \land card(geometry(c_{before}))$$
$$= card(geometry(c_{before}) \cap geometry(c_{after})). \quad (9)$$

- A hht:Deformation describes the case where:

$$geometry(c_{before}) \not\subseteq geometry(c_{after}) \land geometry(c_{after}) \not\subseteq geometry(c_{before}). \quad (10)$$

This case typically describes the simultaneous loss of some geometry portions and gain of others. Similarly, (10) is rephrased as follows:

$$card(geometry(c_{before})) > card(geometry(c_{before}) \cap geometry(c_{after}))$$
$$\land \, card(geometry(c_{after}))$$
$$> card(geometry(c_{before}) \cap geometry(c_{after})). \quad (11)$$

Adding Meaningful Geometry Restructurings from Feature Changes.
We now aim to add composite changes that will collect several related hht:FeatureChange. As mentioned in Sect. 3.3, as of now, composite changes are only geometry related. This section will tackle how we manage to create hht:CompositeChange which, provided the initial knowledge graph describes all building blocks across the whole graph's time focus, will respect Eqs. (2), (3), (4) and (5). First of all, it is mandatory to identify which hht:FeatureChange subclasses can be involved in a hht:GeometryRestructuring. In addition to hht:GeometryChange, all hht:Appearance, hht:Disppearance and hht:Reappearance induce a remapping of an area, and should thus be aggregated in order to form a coherent hht:GeometryRestructuring. More importantly, if all the hht:UnitVersion are described properly in regard of the building blocks they contain, any single instance of those subtypes of change should be involved in a hht:GeometryRestructuring. Assuming the knowledge graph description of building blocks is time-exhaustive, any building block b disappearing from the geometry of a territory $t1$ should appear in another territory $t2$. Thus, in order to aggregate hht:FeatureChange, the algorithm relies on finding other changes happening at the same time and featuring the adding/removing of the building blocks that are removed/added during a given hht:FeatureChange. In the example in Fig. 3, d loses part of its geometry to a and c. Starting from the hht:FeatureChange d goes through, we will thus find the changes involving a and c. Same goes for the gains. In order to properly aggregate changes, and

---

Algorithm 2. Create a composite change

Create a composite change for all geometry altering change which are not attached
to one already
Carry out the same operation for those who are attached
For all `hht:FeatureChange` involved in `hht:CompositeChange`, declare those to be
the same entity

---

considering the possibilities of SHACLRules, we propose Algorithm 2 to achieve
those steps.

To understand the need for those steps, consider a, b, c and d, as presented in
Fig. 3. Consider now an execution of the rule-based algorithm. During the first
step, the algorithm will create a new `hht:CompositeChange` ch_a attached to the
changes of d and a, as a absorbs part of d. Then comes b. A new composite
change ch_b is created, which is attached to the changes of c and b. c and d are
skipped during this step, as they have already been attached to a composite
change. In a second step, then, we aggregate the change of c to ch_a and d to ch_b,
due to the change of c. We now have reached a situation where we describe ch_a
et ch_b, which both represent parts of the same `hht:GeometryRestructuring`
(note that as of now, (1) is not verified by none of those changes). The third
step is thus there to unify those partial composite changes by linking them with
`owl:sameAs` properties.

Qualifying Composite Changes. With the composite changes being created,
the next step consists in qualifying them according to the categories displayed
in Fig. 4. This is achieved in two steps:

- Geometric nature of the composite change (Split, Merge, Redistribution):
  Similarly to what was done for feature changes, qualification boils down to
  cardinality considerations. However, the involved cardinalities are not those
  of geometries, but of territories before and after the change. Consider a
  `hht:GeometricRestructuring` g.
  We define $g_b = \{t|\exists c, tv|hht : isComposedOf(c, g) \land hht : before(c, tv) \land hht : hasUnitVersion(t, tv)\}$ and $g_a = \{t|\exists c, tv|hht : isComposedOf(c, g) \land hht : after(c, tv) \land hht : hasUnitVersion(t, tv)\}$. We then give those formal defi-
  nitions for Merge (12), Split (13), and Redistribution (14):

$$card(g_b) > 1 \land card(g_a) = 1 \tag{12}$$

$$card(g_b) = 1 \land card(g_a) > 1 \tag{13}$$

$$card(g_b) > 1 \land card(g_a) > 1 \tag{14}$$

- Identity Preservation: A `hht:DerivationChange` (15) is a change which preserves no identity. A `hht:ContinuationChange` (16) is a change that preserves the most identities considering the change type. Similarly, we provide

formal definitions that can be easily translated to SHACLRules. Note that these equations induce that derivation and continuation change are disjoint but not complementary. Redistribution can typically induce ambiguous cases where the identity of one territory is impacted while the others are not.

$$card(g_b \cap g_a) = 0 \qquad (15)$$

$$(card(g_a) > card(g_b) \wedge card(g_b \cap g_a) = card(g_b))$$
$$\vee \, card(g_b) > card(g_a) \wedge card(g_b \cap g_a) = card(g_a)) \qquad (16)$$

Those two steps being achieved, OWL inference will manage the qualification in the six final categories.

4.2   Extension for Flawed Data Detection

As mentioned, the algorithm properly qualifying changes rely on a time-exhaustive description of the geometric building blocks. Thus an extension was implemented to compensate for this. This extension, named HHT-SHACL FDD (for flawed data detection), adds a step after the detection of geometric changes during which geometric changes are scrutinized to determine whether the geometric change is due to an actual building block relocation (in which place said block can be traced to another territory) or to a building block unexpected appearance/disappearance. This extension can be used to avoid erroneous change qualification, and to detect lacking territory knowledge in the graph. Typically, some of the building blocks are bound to evolve across the time focus of the knowledge graph. Sometimes, however this evolution means that they appear/disappear at some time, mainly because they merge/split with another building block. These disappearances/appearances can also be due to data that exists but is missing from the knowledge graph. This will cause invalid detection of geometry changes. The algorithm will report such changes as Incomplete.

5   Evaluation

Our algorithm was evaluated on several datasets which all had particularities. Tests were carried out using the TopBraid API, which allows to evaluate SHACLRules. This section will tackle these evaluations, and their results. All datasets complemented with data description as well as the algorithm results are available online in the git resource. A script is also provided to convert CSV tables to HHT knowledge graphs. Finally, the git resource provides several SPARQL queries, and a query comparison with TSN.

5.1   French Third Republic

This dataset is the simplest the algorithm was tested on. It focuses on the French territory from 1870 to 1939. Only one hierarchy is represented, which has three levels (Commune, Arrondissement and Département). Data was represented using HHT, after being converted from CSV tables. Finally, all the building blocks (Communes, here) are described across the whole timespan of the knowledge graph, making this dataset fully-compliant with our approach. It is interesting to note that out of 211 `hht:CompositeChange`, only 181 are geometrically qualified. This difference is due to cases where a territory disappears to be replaced by another one occupying the exact same geometry, which were not considered in our approach. Such cases occur in this particular dataset mostly due to the reintegration of some part of the French territory following the first World War. The analysed changes were compared with results from an economists' study regarding territory evolution on this same period. The feature changes detected matched those found manually. Interestingly enough, it was shown that, by listing changes by year, it was possible to identify easily identify periods of great changes. In this dataset, for example, 241 feature changes occur in 1926, which coincides with the greatest territorial reform of the Third Republic. Humanities researches are also provided with a deeper analysis due to the aggregation of feature changes in composite changes. This dataset was also used to evaluate HHT-SHACL FDD. In order to have accurate results, it was mandatory to check that original data had been properly converted. The HHT-SHACL FDD approach was instrumental in that regard. Typically, the initial conversion script did not consider the possibility of some units disappearing to reappear afterwards. Those inconsistencies were pointed out by HHT-SHACL FDD, which allowed to reach a fully consistent knowledge graph.

5.2   NUTS

To evaluate our algorithm on a larger knowledge graph, it was used to detect changes in the NUTS (Nomenclature of territorial units for statistics)[2] nomenclature from 2010 to 2016. More precisely, this dataset describes the NUTS and LAU (Local Administrative Units)[3] nomenclatures for 14 of the 28 countries of the European Union, and was generated from an existing RDF dataset describing the NUTS hierarchy, and tables published on Eurostat describing the LAU levels. Some countries were removed due typically to arbitrary and non documented changes in territory IDs in the found data. The countries still described vary from the original dataset due to the removal of some LAU2 units which did not respect the hypothesis of description across the whole timespan. A high amount of name changes are found, mostly due to spelling variants. In addition, this particular dataset highlighted the high computing time involved whenever a territory with a large geometry (i.e. with a large number of building blocks) takes part in a geometry change (due to the computing of geometry intersection).

---

[2] https://ec.europa.eu/eurostat/web/nuts/background.
[3] https://ec.europa.eu/eurostat/web/nuts/local-administrative-units.

5.3   France: Region Reform

The goal of this evaluation was to test the behaviour of the algorithm when confronted to unproperly formalized data. This dataset was created by combining datasets provided by INSEE. Timeslicing was handled by creating one timeslice for each territory described in the original datasets, meaning that most territories are described as having two versions regardless of any difference between those two versions. As a consequence, in this dataset, Fragmentation is carried out poorly, with some hht:Unit having two temporally-consecutive hht:UnitVersion which describe the same properties. In addition, some building blocks aren't described across the whole timespan. Those inconsistencies with the algorithm's hypothesis lead to flaws in the results. Changes are detected between two versions that are describing the exact same properties, as they should be described as the same version. Geometry changes are detected where they should not, due to building block disappearances. 82 geometry changes are detected, but HHT-SHACL FDD denotes those 82 changes as Incomplete. Despite those erroneous change detections, it is to be noted that the composite changes are still properly aggregated. All the regions's fusions are detected, and qualified as merges.

6   Conclusion

Currently, the HHT approach allows to represent historical territories, by taking into account multiple overlaying hierarchies, providing a geometry definition that does not rely on knowledge of any vector geometry or surface figure. The evolution of territories can also be represented using an approach based on *fluents* [17]. This representation was chosen due to its being easily grasped by historians. However, it is important to highlight the high amount of time slices it induces, and the endeavor it requires in order to minimize overslicing. Further work will address the possible use of approaches relying on time stamping properties instead of creating new objects, notably in regard of a possible weight reduction of the final knowledge graph. Another representation dimension that is to be addressed by further work will be the linking of knowledge to the sources it has been extracted from inside the graph. The HHT approach also comes with an algorithm allowing to detect changes occurring for any territory, and aggregating those to reveal composite changes describing a global geometry remapping. Said algorithm is currently limited by the need to describe all the building blocks across the whole time focus of the graph. Though the FDD approach points out inconsistencies in the detected changes, this issue is to be further tackled. Various solutions are currently considered. The first would consist in a naive approach where disappearing/appearing building blocks would simply be ignored. A second possible approach would rely on applying part of the change bridge [13] algorithm by explicitly representing changes occurring at a local level. Finally, a third approach would consist in considering hybrid geometries, with some territories having a defined vector geometry.

434   W. Charles et al.

References

1. Batsakis, S., Petrakis, E.G.M.: SOWL: a framework for handling spatio-temporal information in OWL 2.0. In: Bassiliades, N., Governatori, G., Paschke, A. (eds.) RuleML 2011. LNCS, vol. 6826, pp. 242–249. Springer, Heidelberg (2011). https://doi.org/10.1007/978-3-642-22546-8_19
2. Batsakis, S., Petrakis, E.G., Tachmazidis, I., Antoniou, G.: Temporal representation and reasoning in OWL 2. Semant. Web **8**(6), 981–1000 (2017)
3. Bernard, C.: Immersing evolving geographic divisions in the semantic Web. Ph.D. thesis, Université Grenoble Alpes (2019)
4. Bernard, C., Villanova-Oliver, M., Gensel, J., Dao, H.: Modeling changes in territorial partitions over time: ontologies TSN and TSN-change. In: Proceedings of the 33rd Annual ACM Symposium on Applied Computing Pages (SAC 2018), pp. 866–875 (2018). https://doi.org/10.1145/3167132.3167227
5. Bourel, L., Hernandez, N.J., Aussenac-Gilles, N., Charles, W.: HHT: une ontologie modulaire pour représenter l'évolution des territoires en Histoire. In: Saïs, F. (ed.) 33ème Journées Francophones d'Ingénierie des Connaissances (IC 2022), pp. 131–136. IC 2022: Journées Francophones D'Ingénierie des Connaissances, Collège SIC (Science de l'Ingénierie des Connaissances) de l'AFIA, AFIA, Saint-Etienne, France (2022). https://hal.archives-ouvertes.fr/hal-03760559
6. Carbonnet, A.: Léonard dauphant, géographies. ce qu'ils savaient de la France (1100–1600). ceyzérieu, champ vallon, 2018, 318 p. Médiévales. Langues, Textes, Histoire **75**(75), 261–263 (2018)
7. Claramunt, C., Thériault, M.: Managing time in GIS an event-oriented approach. In: Clifford, J., Tuzhilin, A. (eds.) Recent Advances in Temporal Databases. Workshops in Computing, pp. 23–42. Springer, London (1995). https://doi.org/10.1007/978-1-4471-3033-8_2
8. Gangemi, A., Guarino, N., Masolo, C., Oltramari, A., Schneider, L.: Sweetening ontologies with DOLCE. In: Gómez-Pérez, A., Benjamins, V.R. (eds.) EKAW 2002. LNCS (LNAI), vol. 2473, pp. 166–181. Springer, Heidelberg (2002). https://doi.org/10.1007/3-540-45810-7_18
9. Giménez-García, J.M.: Formalizing, capturing, and managing the context of statements in the semantic web. Ph.D. thesis, Université Lyon (2022)
10. Grenon, P., Smith, B.: Snap and span: towards dynamic spatial ontology. Spatial Cogn. Comput. **4**, 104–69 (2004)
11. Gutierrez, C., Hurtado, C., Vaisman, A.: Temporal RDF. In: Gómez-Pérez, A., Euzenat, J. (eds.) ESWC 2005. LNCS, vol. 3532, pp. 93–107. Springer, Heidelberg (2005). https://doi.org/10.1007/11431053_7
12. Hyvönen, E., Tuominen, J., Kauppinen, T., Väätäinen, J.: Representing and utilizing changing historical places as an ontology time series. In: Ashish, N., Sheth, A.P. (eds.) Geospatial Semantics and the Semantic Web: Foundations, Algorithms, and Applications. ADSW, pp. 1–25. Springer, Boston (2011). https://doi.org/10.1007/978-1-4419-9446-2_1
13. Kauppinen, T., Hyvönen, E.: Modeling and reasoning about changes in ontology time series. In: Sharman, R., Kishore, R., Ramesh, R. (eds.) Ontologies, pp. 319–338. Springer, Cham (2007). https://doi.org/10.1007/978-0-387-37022-4_11
14. Lasolle, N.: Temporalité et représentation des connaissances pour un corpus en histoire : application à la correspondance d'Henri Poincaré (2022). https://hal.univ-lorraine.fr/hal-03681513, working paper or preprint

15. Lin, C., et al.: Building linked data from historical maps. In: SemSci@ ISWC, pp. 59–67 (2018)
16. Plumejeaud, C., Mathian, H., Gensel, J., Grasland, C.: Spatio-temporal analysis of territorial changes from a multi-scale perspective. Int. J. Geogr. Inf. Sci. **25**(10), 1597–1612 (2011)
17. Welty, C., Fikes, R., Makarios, S.: A reusable ontology for fluents in OWL. In: FOIS, vol. 150, pp. 226–236 (2006)

An Upper Ontology for Modern Science Branches and Related Entities

Said Fathalla[1,2(✉)], Christoph Lange[3], and Sören Auer[4]

[1] Institute of Computer Science, University of Bonn & Institute of Advanced Simulation - Materials Data Science and Informatics (IAS-9), Forschungszentrum Jülich, Jülich, Germany
[2] Faculty of Science, University of Alexandria, Alexandria, Egypt
sm_fathalla@alexu.edu.eg
[3] RWTH Aachen University, Germany & Fraunhofer FIT, Aachen, Germany
christoph.lange-bever@fit.fraunhofer.de
[4] TIB Leibniz Information Centre for Science and Technology & L3S Research Center, University of Hannover, Hannover, Germany
soeren.auer@tib.eu

Abstract. Recent developments in the context of semantic technologies have given rise to ontologies for modelling scientific information in various fields of science. Over the past years, we have been engaged in the development of the Science Knowledge Graph Ontologies (SKGO), a set of ontologies for modelling research findings in various fields of science. This paper introduces the Modern Science Ontology (ModSci), an upper ontology for modelling relationships between modern science branches and related entities, including scientific discoveries, phenomena, prominent scientists, instruments, etc. ModSci provides a unifying framework for the various domain ontologies that make up the Science Knowledge Graph Ontology suite. Well-known ontology development guidelines and principles have been followed in the development and publication of the resource. We present several use cases and motivational scenarios to express the motivation behind developing the ontology and, therefore, its potential uses. We deem that within the next few years, a science knowledge graph is likely to become a crucial component for organizing and exploring scientific work.

Keywords: Ontology Engineering · Knowledge Representation · Taxonomy · Modern Science · Hierarchical Classification

Resource type: Ontology
License: CC BY 4.0 International
PID: https://w3id.org/skgo/modsci

S. Fathalla—The majority of the research presented in this work was carried out at the University of Bonn.

C. Pesquita et al. (Eds.): ESWC 2023, LNCS 13870, pp. 436–453, 2023.
https://doi.org/10.1007/978-3-031-33455-9_26

1   Introduction

Ontologies have become widely used due to their ability to define relationships between different types of data, thus, improving data exploration strategies and enabling efficient data management and analysis. Ontologies provide an essential foundation for making data FAIR [32], primarily Interoperable and Reusable. For instance, the representation of scientific events metadata, including historical data about the publications, and submissions, in RDF format in EVENTS [8] and EVENTSKG datasets [9]. Knowledge-based representations of scientific data, which motivates the development of data models, ontologies, and knowledge graphs, will support a richer representation of this data, which makes it easier to query and process [2]. This greatly supports the analysis and exploration of scientific data, for example in digital libraries [8].

In this work, we present the Modern Science Ontology (ModSci), an upper ontology for providing a taxonomy of research fields, or fields of science. ModSci is a poly-hierarchical ontology that provides a hierarchical classification of various entities such as publications, events and scientists' research fields. Besides, classification allows research and experimental development activities to be categorized by field of study. Furthermore, it models the relationships between modern science branches and related entities, such as scientific discoveries, phenomena, prominent scientists, instruments, and common interlinking relationships. ModSci is a part of the Science Knowledge Graph Ontology Suite (SKGO) [7], which comprises ontologies describing scientific data in Physics [25], pharmaceutical science [26] and computer science [10]. Thus, the project is embedded within a wider setting of knowledge representation efforts covering diverse scientific disciplines aimed at making scientific knowledge FAIR. Indeed, ModSci provides a unifying framework for the various domain ontologies that make up the SKGO suite.

Motivation. The ModSci ontology is motivated by real-life requirements that we encounter during day-to-day research and supervision work: 1) finding fields of science that best match the interests of researchers in the early stages and what the applications of this field are, 2) gaining an insight into the instruments used in, and applications of, a particular field of science, 3) deriving a comprehensive overview of other fields of science that study a given phenomenon, and 4) indeed, the classification of research topics supports a diversity of research areas, such as information exploration (e.g., in digital libraries), scholarly data analytics and integration, and modelling research dynamics [19]. Therefore, this resource can be used in practice, for example, it helps editorial teams of multidisciplinary journals in positioning submissions according to the taxonomy of research topics, thus avoiding direct out-of-scope rejections. To the best of our knowledge, there is yet no semantic model that organizes major fields and related sub-fields of science and emerging areas of study. More details and four motivating scenarios are presented in Subsect. 3.1.

Potential Impact. The potential impacts of this work include but are not limited to the following: 1) ModSci can be used for internal classification by scholarly publishers, e.g., Springer Nature, for suggesting books, journals, and conference proceedings to readers, i.e., researchers interested in scholarly articles in a specific domain, 2) Cross-disciplinary indexing, and 3) ontology-based recommendation system for scholarly events as well as research papers, and classification of authors and organizations in digital libraries according to their research topics. ModSci is designed to afford high modelling capability and elasticity to deal with a wide variety of modern science branches and associated entities, which makes it applicable also to other areas besides research where the classification of science is an important aspect. ModSci powers two projects for semantically representing scholarly information: the Open Research Knowledge Graph [15] and the OpenResearch.org collaboration platform [28] (more details in Sect. 3).

2   Related Data Models

In the following, we present research efforts on developing ontologies for modelling research findings in different fields of science. Conversely, research efforts to develop taxonomies for modelling Computer Science subfields/subtopics are limited.

In computer science, one of the earliest efforts, dating back to 1998, is the traditional version of the ACM Computing Classification System (CCS) of the Association for Computing Machinery and its latest version in 2012, which is based on SKOS. The ACM context ontology [21] has been developed by ACM to provide a cognitive map of the computing space from the most common computer science fields, such as Applied Computing, to the most specific ones, such as Electronic commerce. In 2019, the large-scale Computer Science Ontology (CSO) [24] had been developed in order to represent scientific publications, mainly in Computer Science. In CSO, the `skos:broaderGeneric` property is used to express that a topic is a super-area of another one (e.g., the Information systems area is a super-area of Data management systems).

In the field of *Environmental Science*, the Semantic Web for Earth and Environmental Terminology (SWEET) ontology [22] models knowledge about Earth system science and related concepts, such as "Phenomena" and "Radiational-Cooling". In *Mathematics*, the Mathematics Subject Classification (MSC) is an alphanumerical classification scheme consisting of 63 macro-areas in mathematics, which is used by many mathematics journals for classifying articles; in an earlier work, we have proposed an implementation in SKOS. The latest version has been released in 2010; a revision is in progress[1].

In *Economics*, the Journal of Economic Literature (JEL)[2] classification system is a standard. JEL is available as a classification tree in a custom XML format (i.e., not implemented as an ontology); the latest update at the time of writing was performed at the end of 2018. Fields of Research (FoR) classification [23], last updated 2008, is one of the three classifications in the Australian

---

[1] https://msc2020.org/.
[2] https://www.aeaweb.org/econlit/jelCodes.php.

and New Zealand Standard Research Classification (ANZSRC) for classifying major sub-fields of research. The main disadvantage is that FoR is not available in a machine-readable format. The Dewey Decimal Classification (DDC) system is a general knowledge hierarchy in various disciplines, involving Computer science, Philosophy, and Social sciences [17]. Arabic numerals are used to represent each class in the DDC, e.g., 300 represents the Social Sciences class, and 320 represents the Political science subclass. The Library of Congress Classification (LCC), a classification system which organizes the book collections of the Library [16], is available in various machine-oriented formats including SKOS and the related MADS representation.

Despite these continuous efforts, none of the existing data models provides a complete view of the taxonomy of the various fields of science and their subfields, but rather focuses on the classification, in plain taxonomies, i.e., models with weak semantics, of knowledge belonging to a particular research area regardless of the overlap between them. What additionally distinguishes our work from the related work mentioned above is 1) the inclusion of related entities, 2) the representation of relationships between fields of science, and 3) the publication of the ontology considering FAIR principles and W3C standards and best practices.

3   Motivation and Usage Scenarios

Each of the modern science branches comprises various specialized yet overlapping scientific disciplines that often possess their own nomenclature and expertise [5]. For example, astrometrical studies use statistical methods to compute data estimates and error ranges; hence, an overlap between astrometry and statistics occurs here. In addition, there are collaborations between scientists from different fields of science. For example, biologists require mathematics to process, analyze and report experimental research data and to represent relationships between some biological phenomena. Statistics are also used in economics in the measurement of correlation, analyzing demand and supply, and forecasting through regression, interpolation, and time series analysis.

3.1   Motivating Scenarios

The objective of presenting the following scenarios is to express the motivation behind developing the ModSci ontology and, therefore, its potential uses.

Cross-Disciplinary Indexing: Cross-disciplinary research refers to research that embraces efforts conducted by researchers from two or more academic disciplines. Publications from this kind of research place obstacles to cross-disciplinary indexing and searching in digital libraries. Therefore, the classification of scholarly articles based on a rigid classification scheme is crucial.

Scholarly Information Classification: Classification of information is an important issue in wiki-based content management systems, such as Catawiki[3], Wik-

---
[3] https://www.catawiki.com/.

ispecies[4], and WikiAnswers[5]. In particular, developing a universal classification scheme of the various fields of science will greatly support information management in wikis devoted to research fields, such as nLab[6], Gene Wiki[7] and SNPedia[8]. The aforementioned motivation scenarios showed that such a classification makes a difference.

3.2   Real-World and Potential Use Cases

Several concrete real-world uses are presented to illustrate the added value of ModSci in various application areas, including interdisciplinary indexing, enriched bibliographic data, and network analysis within interdisciplinary scientific fields.

Open Research Knowledge Graph[9]: ModSci is being integrated into the Open Research Knowledge Graph (ORKG) [15] to support the classification of research papers. ORKG is a step towards the next generation of digital libraries for semantic scientific knowledge communicated in scholarly literature [15]. ModSci is being integrated into the step of selecting the research field of the research papers added to the knowledge graph, which provides more than 200 research fields in various fields of modern science. Besides, it can be used in browsing the research papers by fields through the "Browse by research field" feature.

Publication Classification: OpenResearch.org contains scholarly information in several fields of science, i.e., not restricted to particular fields. This semantic wiki aims at making scholarly information more accessible and shareable. ModSci is used to categorize information about scientific events, research projects, scientific papers, publishers, and journals.

Support Domain Ontologies Development: To name just a few, several classes and properties are in use by several emerging ontologies developed for consortia of the German National Research Data Infrastructure NFDI, including NFDI4Culture[10] and NFDI-MatWerk[11].

Publications and Scholarly Events Classification: ModSci can be used to classify research projects, research results, papers submitted to multidisciplinary journals and course contents. Poly-hierarchical ontologies can be used in digital libraries for categorizing published research articles as well as scholarly events. Furthermore, it supports exploring new features and unknown relationships between articles belonging to different fields of science to provide recommendations to end users [9].

---

[4] https://species.wikimedia.org/.
[5] https://www.answers.com/.
[6] https://ncatlab.org/.
[7] https://en.wikipedia.org/wiki/Gene_Wiki.
[8] https://www.snpedia.com/.
[9] https://projects.tib.eu/orkg/.
[10] https://nfdi4culture.de.
[11] https://nfdi-matwerk.de/.

4   Ontology Development

In the following, we present the decisions made during the development of the ontology.

- The Systematic Approach for Building Ontologies (SABiO) [1] has been followed in the development process of ModSci. It comprises five phases *ontology requirements elicitation, ontology capture and formalization, ontology design, ontology implementation,* and finally *ontology evaluation.*
- We have chosen a top-down approach because it makes more sense to start with the main branches of modern science and then classify them into specific hierarchies.
- The ontology is being developed in an iterative process which involves cross-disciplinary interaction between ontology engineers and researchers belonging to the respective fields of science. This process was continuing through the entire lifecycle of the ontology
- In the very beginning, we decided to define an initial version of the ontology and then to assess what we have at hand by discussing raised issues with the scientists involved, and finally performing changes accordingly. The assessment was done by drafting a set of competency questions that a knowledge base based on the ontology should answer to determine the usefulness of the ontology (i.e., whether it satisfies functional requirements). This helps the ontology engineer to identify relevant concepts and their properties, as well as constraints.
- The creation of classes' definitions and their properties are closely interlaced to better ingest the new class to the ontology. In addition, it also helps to define the scope of knowledge that the ontology encapsulates effectively.
- To make ModSci compatible with well-known classifications, we decided to reuse them.

4.1   Reusing External Vocabularies

Building the ontology hierarchy has been bootstrapped from the following resources: 1) reusing terms from existing models developed for describing the scientific work in various fields of science, such as BioAssay Ontology (BAO) [29], and the SWEET ontologies [22], FOAF, hence achieving FAIR's Interoperability (I2 and I3), 2) several taxonomies of research fields, such as the Field of Research (FoR) by ANZSRC [23], Dewey Decimal [17], DFG[12] structure of research areas, and Library of Congress Classification [16] have been integrated with ModSci for expanding various science branches, including mathematical, physical, and chemical sciences, 3) interviews with domain experts have been conducted in order to validate, remove or update identified concepts as well as add missing ones, and 4) research area classifications by universities (i.e. divisions of their research disciplines) have been considered.

---

[12] https://www.dfg.de/en/dfg_profile/statutory_bodies/review_boards/subject_areas/.

4.2   Core Concepts

The pivotal concepts of ModSci are the branches of modern science and its sub-branches. Several concepts (we follow the definitions found in [31]) related to such concepts, including scientific discovery, phenomenon, scientists, and scientific instruments, have been defined. Where possible, these concepts are mapped to well-known ontologies such as SWEET, SKOS and FOAF, and Role from Basic Formal Ontology (BFO) as well. Concretely, these entities are represented in ModSci as `owl:Class` as shown in Fig. 1.

We observed a great extent of collaboration between various fields of science, which in turn gave rise to new fields of science. For example, ecology, a branch of science that studies the distribution and interactions between living things and the physical environment, is a new field of science that combines methods and techniques from both biology and earth sciences. Thus, the `Ecology` class is defined as a subclass of both the `Biology` and the `EarthSciences` classes. Another example is `Biochemistry`, a subclass of both `Biology` and `Chemistry`. *Class specialization*: one example is the creation of `Ethology`, `Psychology`, `SocialPsychology`, and `Sociobiology` as sub-classes of `BehavioralSciences`. *Class Disjointness*: adding disjointness axioms to ontologies enables a wide range of noteworthy applications [30]. We explicitly asserted the pairwise disjointness of various classes in ModSci, for instance, the `AstronomicalPhenomena` class is disjoint with `BiologicalPhenomena`. *Class equivalence*: an example is the `LaboratoryInstrument` class which is equivalent to `ScientificInstrument`.

4.3   Semantic Relations

A full view of the properties defined in ModSci, including their domains and ranges, is shown in Fig. 1. Some properties have complex ranges and domains (i.e. *logical disjunction*), e.g., the domain of `discoveredByScience` is (Phenomenon ⊔ ScientificDiscovery), which means that a Phenomenon or a Scientific Discovery can be discovered by a particular Science.

Property Restrictions. A property restriction provides a type of logic-based constructor for complex classes by defining a particular type of class description, which is a class of all individuals that satisfy the restriction. OWL defines two kinds of property restrictions: value constraints (restricting the range of the property) and cardinality constraints (restricting the number of values a property can take). One example of a property restriction in ModSci is the use of `owl:minCardinality` for restricting `discoveredByScientist` to assure that a phenomenon is discovered by at least one scientist (`owl:someValuesFrom`). Another kind of property restriction is the *owl:allValuesFrom* constraint, which restricts the individuals used as objects with a given property to be either a member of a certain class or data values within a specified set of values. For instance, the property `discoveredByScientist` has been restricted by *owl:allValuesFrom* to the class `Scientist`.

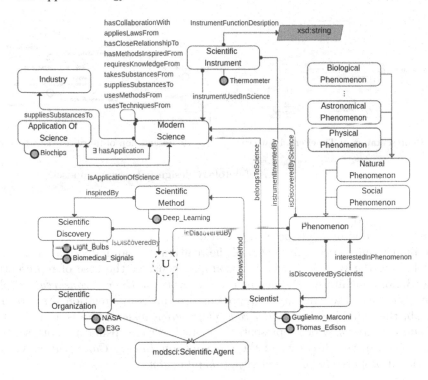

Fig. 1. The core concepts of ModSci and their interlinking relationships. Open arrowheads denote `subClassOf` properties between the classes. Several reflexive properties are represented as loops for better readability. The "U" symbol represents the `owl:unionOf`.

4.4 Design Patterns

Patterns provide a well-proven solution to a specific engineering problem, so they are recurrent solutions to design problems that can be reused when developing ontologies [4]. Several ontology design patterns (ODPs) [11], involving content, alignment and logical ODPs, have been applied to represent, for example, such as inverse relations and composition of relations. A full list of the ODPs can be found in the official catalogue[13] of ontology design patterns. Here, we list some examples of the used patterns. The *TimePeriod* content ontology design pattern (CP) [20] is used to represent the time periods in which the renowned scientists lived, as illustrated in Fig. 2a. An example of the Alignment ODPs is the *Class Union* pattern, which is used to define a class in one ontology as the union of two or more classes in another one(s). For instance, the `ScientificOrganization` class is defined as the union of both `ScientificAgent` and `foaf:Organization`. One common problem in ontology engineering is representing the N-ary relations ($N \geq 3$). An ordinary solution is to use the *N-ary relation pattern* [13]. In this pattern, the N-ary relation is reified by creating a class rather than a property

---

[13] http://ontologydesignpatterns.org/wiki/Community:ListPatterns.

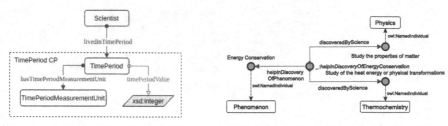

(a) Representation of TimePeriod pattern.   (b) Representation of n-ary relations pattern.

Fig. 2. Representations of ontology design patterns in modsci.

and uses N properties to point to the related entities [18]. Individuals of such classes are individuals of the N-ary relation and additional properties can provide binary links to each argument of the relation, i.e., an individual of the relation linking the N individuals. For example, consider the case of representing that Biology facilitated Physics in the discovery of *Energy conservation* phenomenon. This case can only be represented as an N-ary relation. As shown in Fig. 2b, the individual _:*helpInDiscoveryOfEnergyConservation* is an individual of *helpInDiscovery*, which represents a single object encapsulating both sciences that helped in the discovery of the phenomenon *Energy Conservation* via the functional property *helpInDiscoveryOfPhenomenon*.

4.5 Reasoning

To maximize ModSci's inference capability, several property characteristics, including reflexivity, symmetry, inverse, and transitivity, have been asserted [14]. To support the inference process, several symmetric relations have been defined. For instance, `hasCloseRelationshipTo` is a symmetric relation where Statistics is connected to Mathematics via this property, meaning the opposite also holds. Moreover, all corresponding inverse properties are created, where here possible to support bidirectional traversal between two concepts in the ontology network. For instance, `isApplicationOfScience` property being an inverse of `hasApplication` is an example of an inverse relation. Thus, if an application of science A, e.g., a Biochip, `isApplicationOfScience` S, then it can be inferred that S `hasApplication` A. Furthermore, some properties have the same domain and range, e.g., `hasCollaborationWith` has `ModernScience` as its domain and range, thus providing the information that there exist collaborations between two modern sciences. This property is additionally defined as a reflexive relation, i.e., scientists in a particular field of science have collaborations with themselves. An example of functional properties is the `inspiredBy` property, whereas a particular scientific method is inspired by either a phenomenon or a scientific discovery. For instance, *Deep Learning* is inspired by *Biomedical Signals*, the observations of the physiological activities of organisms. Finally, a set of SWRL rules have been defined for discovering new relationships and inferring new knowledge that is not explicitly given in the ontology. These rules have been semantically validated using the HermiT reasoner.

$$discoveredByScientist\,(x, y) \wedge \ discoveredByScience\,(x, z) \rightarrow undertakesResearch\,(y, z) \quad (1)$$

$$Scientist\,(x) \ \wedge \ isDiscoveredBy\,(a, x) \rightarrow isDiscoveredByScientist\,(a, x) \quad (2)$$

$$Scientist\,(x) \wedge undertakesResearch\,(x, s) \rightarrow scientistBelongsTo\,(x, s) \quad (3)$$

$$ScientificOrganization\,(x) \wedge isDiscoveredBy\,(a, x) \rightarrow isDiscoveredByOrganization\,(a, x) \quad (4)$$

5   Technical Specifications

Ontology Publishing: ModSci is published (following ontology publication best practices [3]) via a persistent identifier and dereferenced in HTML and OWL (both in RDF/XML and Turtle serialisations), hence achieving the FAIR's Findability (F1 and F4). Content negotiation is enabled via its PID in a way that requests from browsers get the HTML while others from semantic web applications or ontology editors (e.g. Protegé) get the requested representation (i.e. RDF serialization) of the ontology.

Interoperability: we implemented our ontology using OWL, hence achieving FAIR's Interoperability (I1).

Indexing and Availability: The ontology is licensed under the open CC-BY 4.0 license and its source is available from a *GitHub* repository[14], hence achieving FAIR's Reusability (R1). It can be browsed through a web-based repository front-end for browsing and visualizing published ontologies, such as BioPortal[15], and Linked Open Vocabularies[16]. Furthermore, these services also store the metadata of the ontology, hence achieving FAIR's Accessibility (A2).

Announcement: several mailing lists, such as the W3C LOD list (public-lod@w3.org), the discussion list of the open science community (open-science@lists.okfn.org), and discussion forums, such as those of the Open Knowledge Foundation (OKFN)[17] have been used for announcing the latest release of the ontology. We received valuable feedback, involving suggesting existing ontologies for reuse, presenting the ontology by explaining different parts of it and the composing concepts and improving the documentation from several parties (e.g., researchers in our community).

Logical Correctness: We validated the ontologies against inconsistencies using the HermiT reasoner, and OOPS! Ontology Pitfall Scanner[18].

---

[14] https://github.com/saidfathalla/Science-knowledge-graph-ontologies.
[15] http://bioportal.bioontology.org/ontologies/MODSCI.
[16] https://lov.linkeddata.es/dataset/lov/vocabs/modsci.
[17] https://discuss.okfn.org/.
[18] http://oops.linkeddata.es/.

Documentation: Widoco wizard for documenting ontologies [12] is used to create HTML documentation, thus enabling human understanding of the ontology and increasing its reusability. The documentation is available online through the persistent identifier of the ontology. The `rdfs:comment` property is used to provide a human-readable description of each resource.

Metadata Completion: A checklist[19] for completing the vocabulary metadata proposed has been used to complete the ontology's metadata (FAIR's Findability (F2 and F3)), e.g., authorship information in terms of Dublin Core and license. This makes it easier for academia and industry to identify and reuse the ontology effectively and efficiently.

Ontology Maintenance: Ontology maintenance includes fixing bugs (i.e. inconsistencies and inefficient implementation) and enhancing (i.e. improving coverage and integration with other models). The maintenance process is performed through the GitHub issue tracker with the possibility of submitting issues for either suggesting improvements, e.g., reusing related ontologies that may appear in the future, or reports of problems via *Improvement request* and *Problem report* issue templates (see Community collaboration part in the documentation page. Thus, enabling external collaboration in the development of the ontology to maintain its future sustainability.

6   Data-Driven Evaluation

The evaluation of the ontology has been carried out in two directions, 1) evaluating the success of the ontology in modelling a real-world domain (Formative evaluation) in which we use the verification and validation approach and 2) evaluating the quality of the ontology (Summative evaluation) in which we used a metric-based ontology quality analysis approach.

6.1   Test Data

To aid the development and testing of ModSci, we have created +150 individuals (including, `ScientificInstrumentManufacturer` (17), `ScientificInstrument` (35), `AtmosphericPhenomena` (5), `Scientist` (10), and `ScientificOrganization` (8)). These individuals have been created into a separate file to make it more modular. Figure 3 depicts the relationship between a sample of individuals in ModSci. These individuals help to assist in characterizing core concepts within the ontology and to provide links (where available) between ModSci and the reused ontologies. Even though some of these individuals are not required for evaluating the ontology, they are essential for understanding the domain; hence they help in the development process. Individuals are defined with individual axioms, also called "facts"; green circles in Fig. 1 and Fig. 3 present some of these individuals. Two types of facts have been created:

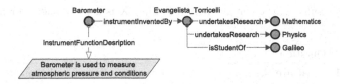

Fig. 3. Relationships between a sample of individuals (green circles) in ModSci. (Color figure online)

1) facts about class membership and property values of individuals: for example, deep learning algorithms (an individual of `algorithms`), or Non-Negative Matrix Factorization (NMF), are based on biological data called "biomedical signals" (also called *Biosignals*), and 2) facts about identical individuals. The OWL `owl:sameAs` construct is used to establish the identity of individuals, i.e., states that two URIs refer to the same individual.

6.2   Formative Evaluation

We performed ontology verification and validation (V&V) following the guidelines proposed in [1]. *Ontology verification* aims at ensuring that the ontology is being built correctly, while *ontology validation* (using test cases) aims at ensuring that the correct ontology is being built, i.e. it fulfills its intended purpose. After identifying motivational scenarios in a use-case fashion, the next step is to derive a set of competency questions (CQs)[20] from these scenarios. Competency questions can serve as a kind of functional requirement specification for an ontology. Therefore, a set of functional requirements have been identified from the CQs identified by domain experts and from the data sources (cf. subsection 4.1).

The verification is performed mainly to justify that the ontology being developed has adhered to these requirements, i.e it should be able to answer all CQs correctly. Some of these questions are defined at a high level of abstraction to help determine the scope of the ontology and its potential uses and others are more specific to cover potential use cases.

This evaluation has been conducted by means of expert judgment (ontology engineering experts), in which the concepts, relations and axioms defined in the ontology have been checked regarding whether they are able to answer the defined CQs [6] (cf. Table 1). Ontology engineers and scientists from different research fields, including Dentistry, Engineering and chemistry, have been recruited while developing both the ontology and CQs to validate, remove, add missing ones or update identified concepts. This approach enabled us not only to check whether the ontology is built correctly but also efficiently. For this reason, we performed this evaluation in parallel with the ontology development in an iterative manner, which significantly helped in improving the ontology. In

---

[20] The final set of competency questions is available at the GitHub repository.

Table 1. A sample of the competency questions. X is a placeholder for any suitable value.

Id	Question text
CQ1	What are the main branches of modern science and their sub-branches?
CQ2	Are there any collaborations of scientists from various fields of science to produce a product X? (*derived from F1*)
CQ3	What are the instruments used in a particular study X belonging to the scientific field Y?
CQ4	What are the phenomena discovered in science X?
CQ5	Which fields of science belong to two branches of science?

Table 2. A part of the verification process of ModSci.

CQ	Matched entities
CQ1	(AppliedScience, subClassOf, ModernScience) (HealthSciences, subClassOf, ModernScience) (ComputerScience, subClassOf, AppliedScience)
CQ3	(Thermometer, instrumentUsedInScience, Studying_biochemical_reactions) (Telescope, instrumentUsedInScience, Light_magnification)
CQ5	(BioChemistry, subClassOf, Biology and Chemistry) (Semiotics, subClassOf, SocialScience and InterdisciplinaryScience)

addition, it saves a lot of time by detecting defects at an early stage of the development process. After each iteration, a set of SPARQL queries have been run against the ontology to ensure that it meets the functional requirements. After five complete iterations (i.e. development-to-evaluation and vice versa), the final version of ModSci is obtained.

In Table 1, we present a sample of the CQs. These CQs have been derived from a set of facts either collected from interviewing researchers from various fields of science, including chemistry, biology and pharmaceutical science or have been collected from scientific articles. Some of these facts are *(F1) The production of psychiatric drugs is a result of studying the relationship between chemistry and psychology, (F2) Organic chemistry has a close relationship to biology since it supplies its substances* and *(F5) Biology applies natural physical laws since all living matter is composed of atoms.* Then, the CQs are translated into SPARQL queries, considering producing results which should be somehow informative for both non-experts and expert participants.

Overall, 25 queries were run against the ontology. The results have got 100% accuracy which means that ModSci fulfils all the specified functional requirements. This verified that ModSci is able to answer *all* competency questions

Table 3. Sample test cases.

Id	CQ	Input(s)	Expected Result(s)
T01	CQ01.01	Social Sciences	Linguistics, Natural Language Processing Anthropology, (no sub-classes)
T02	CQ01.02	Astronomy	Astrometry, Cosmology
T03	CQ02.01	Light magnification, Astronomy	Telescope
T04	CQ04.01	Physics	Conservation_of_energy

defined. Table 2 illustrates a part of the verification process of ModSci, showing matched entities corresponding to the CQs.

Ontology Validation. Generally, validation is a one-time process that starts after verification is completed to make sure that the ontology is suitable for its intended uses (i.e. the correctness). In this phase, the participation of domain experts and ontology engineers is essential. The validation is accomplished by preparing several test cases (derived from the predefined competency questions) in a competency question-driven approach for ontology testing. In order to design test cases, we derived more specific questions from the predefined CQs. For example, we have rewritten CQ01 more specifically as: *"CQ01.01: What are the main branches of Social Sciences and their sub-branches?"* and *"CQ01.02: What are the sub-fields of Astronomy?"*. In addition, we have rewritten CQ5 more specifically as: *"CQ05.01: List all phenomena discovered by Physics along with the scientists who discovered them?"*. Inspired by the white box testing method in software testing, we have prepared test cases so that each test case comprises three variables (i.e. input, actual output, and expected results). The objective is used to verify if the actual output of the CQs meets the anticipated output. Because of the space limit, we present sample test cases shown in Table 3 and we omitted the output column because it is identical to the expected results. The listing below shows the SPARQL query corresponding to CQ04.01, which is used in T04.

```
PREFIX mod: <https://w3id.org/skgo/modsci#>
SELECT DISTINCT ?phenom  ?scientist
WHERE {
  ?phenom          mod:isDiscoveredByScientist    ?scientist.
  ?scientist       mod:undertakesResearch         ?researchWork.
  ?researchWork    rdf:type                       ?science.
  FILTER (?science = mod:Physics)
}
```

After executing each test case, the returned results have been compared with the expected results, and the recall is computed. If the recall was less than 1.0, which means that not all required results (identified by experts) were returned, we analyzed the reason, iteratively adapted the ontology and re-executed the test case until all expected results were returned, i.e., we obtained a recall of

1.0. In this case, we marked the test case as *passed*. Algorithm 1 summarises the whole procedure. In the end, all the test cases are executed and results are reported.

6.3   Summative Evaluation

In this evaluation, we assess the richness/quality of the ontology by using OntoQA [27] evaluation model, a metric-based ontology quality analysis model. OntoQA evaluates the ontology using schema metrics and population/instance metrics. In this model, various metrics are calculated to asses different richness within the ontology. For ModSci, we found the most interesting metric is the *Inheritance Richness (IR)* describes the distribution of information across different levels of the ontology inheritance tree. IR indicates how knowledge is grouped into different classes and sub-classes in the ontology. Formally, IR is defined by

$$IR = \frac{\sum_{C_i \in C} |H^C(C_1, C_i)|}{|C|} \tag{5}$$

where H is the number of inheritance relationships and C is the number of classes. Strikingly, ModSci got a relatively high inheritance richness of 0.99, which indicates that knowledge/data can be well classified into different categories and subcategories in the ontology. In addition, it indicates that the ontology represents a wide range of general knowledge with a low level of detail.

Algorithm 1 White Box evaluation of ModSci

Require: $O \leftarrow$ initial version of the ontology
$\quad\quad\quad\quad FR \leftarrow$ set of functional requirements
Ensure: O is syntactically valid
 1: create sample individuals
 2: $CQ \leftarrow$ set of competency questions derived from FR
 3: $TC \leftarrow$ set of test cases derived from CQ
 4: $R \leftarrow 0$
 5: **while** $\exists T_i.passed == false$ **do**
 6:    **for all** $T_i \in TC$ **do**
 7:       run T_i
 8:       $R \leftarrow$ compute the recall of the results of T_i
 9:       **if** $R¡1.0$ **then**
10:          break
11:       **else**
12:          $T_i.passed = true$
13:       **end if**
14:    **end for**
15:    modify O accordingly
16: **end while**

---

7   Conclusions and Future Work

This paper presents the Modern Science Ontology, which models relationships between modern science branches and related entities, such as scientific discoveries, prominent scientists, instruments, phenomena, etc. Several design principles have been taken into consideration in the development of ModSci, such as configuration to support semantic web applications, registration in online services for ontology visualization and exploration, syntactic and semantic validation, human-readable documentation, and sustainability. The SABiO methodology has been followed when developing the ontologies, as well as FAIR principles for data publication. To maximize reasoning capability, 1) several property characteristics, such as reflexivity, symmetry, and transitivity, have been asserted, 2) disjointness of rules, and 3) several logic rules have been added to the ontologies. Motivating examples affirmed the usefulness and potential uses of ModSci ontologies. Two evaluation strategies have been carried out to assure the success of the ontology in modelling a real-world domain (Formative evaluation) and the quality of the ontology (Summative evaluation).

Our future work has three main directions: refining the formal representation of science in the ModSci ontology itself, covering further fields of science by dedicated ontologies, and realizing services on top of these ontologies. Regarding the formal representation of the scientific process and its entities, we aim at aligning ModSci's own model with existing formal models of science whose processes and structures have already been investigated in depth, i.e., Mathematics. Furthermore, we are studying the applicability of ModSci in cross-disciplinary indexing, enriched bibliographic data, and network analysis within cross-disciplinary scientific communities, among others. Finally, we intend to release a new version of ModSci that supports multilingualism and we plan to incorporate all the relevant catalogue information for more instruments, applications and scientific discoveries.

References

1. de Almeida Falbo, R.: SABiO: systematic approach for building ontologies. In: 1st Joint Workshop Onto. Com/ODISE on Ontologies in Conceptual Modeling and Information Systems Engineering (2014)
2. Auer, S., Kovtun, V., Prinz, M., Kasprzik, A., Stocker, M., Vidal, M.E.: Towards a knowledge graph for science. In: Proceedings of the 8th International Conference on Web Intelligence, Mining and Semantics. ACM, p. 1 (2018)
3. Berrueta, D., Phipps, J., Miles, A., Baker, T., Swick, R.: Best practice recipes for publishing RDF vocabularies. In: Working Draft, W3C (2008). http://www.w3.org/TR/swbp-vocab-pub/
4. Blomqvist, E.: Ontology patterns: typology and experiences from design pattern development. In: The Swedish AI Society Workshop 20–21 May 2010. Uppsala University. 048, pp. 55–64. Linköping University Electronic Press (2010)
5. Boyack, K., Klavans, D., Paley, W., Börner, K.: Scientific method: relationships among scientific paradigms. Seed Mag. **9**, 36–37 (2007)

6. Brank, J., Grobelnik, M., Mladenic, D.: A survey of ontology evaluation techniques. In: Proceedings of the Conference on Data Mining and Data Warehouses, pp. 166–170. Citeseer Ljubljana, Slovenia (2005)
7. Fathalla, S., Auer, S., Lange, C.: Towards the semantic formalization of science. In: Proceedings of the 35th Annual ACM Symposium on Applied Computing, pp. 2057–2059 (2020)
8. Fathalla, S., Lange, C.: EVENTS: a dataset on the history of top-prestigious events in five computer science communities. In: González-Beltrán, A., Osborne, F., Peroni, S., Vahdati, S. (eds.) SAVE-SD 2017-2018. LNCS, vol. 10959, pp. 110–120. Springer, Cham (2018). https://doi.org/10.1007/978-3-030-01379-0_8
9. Fathalla, S., Lange, C., Auer, S.: EVENTSKG: a 5-star dataset of top-ranked events in eight computer science communities. In: Hitzler, P., et al. (eds.) ESWC 2019. LNCS, vol. 11503, pp. 427–442. Springer, Cham (2019). https://doi.org/10.1007/978-3-030-21348-0_28
10. Fathalla, S., Vahdati, S., Auer, S., Lange, C.: SemSur: a core ontology for the semantic representation of research findings. Procedia Comput. Sci. **137**, 151–162 (2018)
11. Gangemi, A., Presutti, V.: Ontology design patterns. In: Staab, S., Studer, R. (eds.) Handbook on Ontologies. IHIS, pp. 221–243. Springer, Heidelberg (2009). https://doi.org/10.1007/978-3-540-92673-3_10
12. Garijo, D.: WIDOCO: a wizard for documenting ontologies. In: d'Amato, C., et al. (eds.) ISWC 2017. LNCS, vol. 10588, pp. 94–102. Springer, Cham (2017). https://doi.org/10.1007/978-3-319-68204-4_9
13. Giunti, M., Sergioli, G., Vivanet, G., Pinna, S.: Representing n-ary relations in the semantic web. Logic J. IGPL **29**(4), 697–717 (2021)
14. Grau, B.C., Horrocks, I., Motik, B., Parsia, B., Patel-Schneider, P., Sattler, U.: OWL 2: the next step for OWL. Web Seman. **6**(4), 309–322 (2008)
15. Jaradeh, M.Y., et al.:Open research knowledge graph: next generation infrastructure for semantic scholarly knowledge. In: Proceedings of the 10th International Conference on Knowledge Capture, pp. 243–246. ACM (2019)
16. Library of Congress contributors. Library of Congress Classification (2014). https://www.loc.gov/catdir/cpso/lcc.html. Accessed December 2022
17. Mitchell, J.S.: Relationships in the dewey decimal classification system. In: Bean, C.A., Green, R. (eds.) Relationships in the Organization of Knowledge. Information Science and Knowledge Management, vol 2, pp. 211–226. Springer, Dordrecht (2001). https://doi.org/10.1007/978-94-015-9696-1_14
18. Noy, N., Rector, A., Hayes, P., Welty, C.: Defining n-ary relations on the semantic web. In: W3C Working Group Note, vol. 12, no. 4 (2006)
19. Osborne, F., Salatino, A., Birukou, A., Motta, E.: Automatic classification of springer nature proceedings with smart topic miner. In: Groth, P., et al. (eds.) ISWC 2016. LNCS, vol. 9982, pp. 383–399. Springer, Cham (2016). https://doi.org/10.1007/978-3-319-46547-0_33
20. Presutti, V., Gangemi, A.: Content ontology design patterns as practical building blocks for web ontologies. In: Li, Q., Spaccapietra, S., Yu, E., Olivé, A. (eds.) ER 2008. LNCS, vol. 5231, pp. 128–141. Springer, Heidelberg (2008). https://doi.org/10.1007/978-3-540-87877-3_11
21. Priya, M., Aswani Kumar, C.: Construction and merging of ACM and sciencedirect ontologies. In: Abraham, A., Cherukuri, A.K., Melin, P., Gandhi, N. (eds.) ISDA 2018 2018. AISC, vol. 941, pp. 238–252. Springer, Cham (2020). https://doi.org/10.1007/978-3-030-16660-1_24

22. Raskin, R.G., Pan, M.J.: Knowledge representation in the semantic web for earth and environmental terminology (SWEET). Comput. Geosci. **31**(9), 1119–1125 (2005)
23. Rousseau, R., Ecoom, F.O.: The Australian and New Zealands fields of research (FoR) codes. ISSI Newslet. **14**(3), 59–61 (2018)
24. Salatino, A.A., Thanapalasingam, T., Mannocci, A., Osborne, F., Motta, E.: The computer science ontology: a large-scale taxonomy of research areas. In: Vrandečić, D., et al. (eds.) ISWC 2018. LNCS, vol. 11137, pp. 187–205. Springer, Cham (2018). https://doi.org/10.1007/978-3-030-00668-6_12
25. Say, A., Fathalla, S., Vahdati, S., Lehmann, J., Auer, S.: Semantic representation of physics research data. In: 12th International Conference on Knowledge Engineering and Ontology Development (KEOD 2020), pp. 64–75. Science and Technology Publications. LDA Setúbal, Portugal (2020)
26. Say, Z., Fathalla, S., Vahdati, S., Lehmann, J., Auer, S.: Ontology design for pharmaceutical research outcomes. In: Hall, M., Merčun, T., Risse, T., Duchateau, F. (eds.) TPDL 2020. LNCS, vol. 12246, pp. 119–132. Springer, Cham (2020). https://doi.org/10.1007/978-3-030-54956-5_9
27. Tartir, S., Arpinar, I.B., Moore, M., Sheth, A.P., Aleman-Meza, B.: OntoQA: metric- based ontology quality analysis. In: IEEE ICDM Workshop on Knowledge Acquisition from Distributed, Autonomous, Semantically Heterogeneous Data and Knowledge Sources (2005)
28. Vahdati, S., Arndt, N., Auer, S., Lange, C.: OpenResearch: collaborative management of scholarly communication metadata. In: EKAW (2016)
29. Visser, U., Abeyruwan, S., Vempati, U., Smith, R.P., Lemmon, V., Schürer, S.C.: BioAssay Ontology (BAO): a semantic description of bioassays and high-throughput screening results. BMC Bioinf. **12**(1), 257 (2011)
30. Völker, J., Fleischhacker, D., Stuckenschmidt, H.: Automatic acquisition of class disjointness. Web Seman. Sci. Serv. Agents World Wide Web **35**, 124–139 (2015)
31. Wikipedia contributors. Science - Wikipedia, The Free Encyclopedia (2019). http://en.wikipedia.org/w/index.php?title=Science&oldid=918085492. Accessed December 2022
32. Wilkinson, M.D., et al.: The FAIR Guiding Principles for scientific data management and stewardship. Sci. Data **3**, 1–9 (2016)

K-Hub: A Modular Ontology to Support Document Retrieval and Knowledge Extraction in Industry 5.0

Anisa Rula[1]([✉])[iD], Gloria Re Calegari[2][iD], Antonia Azzini[2][iD], Davide Bucci[2][iD], Alessio Carenini[2][iD], Ilaria Baroni[2][iD], and Irene Celino[2][iD]

[1] University of Brescia, Brescia, Italy
`anisa.rula@unibs.it`
[2] Cefriel – Politecnico di Milano, Milan, Italy
{`gloria.calegari,antonia.azzini,davide.bucci,alessio.carenini,`
`ilaria.baroni,irene.celino`}`@cefriel.com`

Abstract. Digitalization is entering the industrial sector and different needs are emerging to support shop floor operators; in particular, they need to retrieve information to support their operations (e.g., during maintenance activities), from structured and unstructured sources, as well as from other people's experience. Sharing knowledge and making it accessible to industrial workers is therefore a key challenge that Semantic Web technologies are able to address and solve. In this paper, we present a modular ontology that we engineered in order to support the collection, extraction and structuring of relevant information for industrial operators in a "knowledge hub" (K-Hub). In particular, our K-Hub ontology covers several aspects, from document annotation/retrieval to procedure support, from manufacturing domain concepts to company-specific information. We discuss its engineering process, extensibility and availability, as well as its current and future application scenarios to support industrial workers.

Keywords: Industry 5.0 · document retrieval · knowledge extraction

Resource type Ontology
Licencse CC BY 4.0 International
DOI https://doi.org/10.5281/zenodo.7443000
URL https://knowledge.c-innovationhub.com/k-hub/

1 Introduction

The manufacturing industry is advanced by a technological revolution, often referred to as Industry 4.0 [13], where the future trend lies in the convergence of several technologies including artificial intelligence, smart manufacturing, Internet of Things and web-based knowledge management. Moreover, the advent of the so-called Industry 5.0[1] is shedding light not only on the adoption of digital technologies, but also on their actual uptake by industry workers, thus making industry sustainable, human-centric and resilient. With specific reference to knowledge management, manufacturing companies face the challenge of managing, maintaining and transferring different kinds of knowledge between people and across company functions such as product design, process definition, production lines, system maintenance and customer service. This knowledge can be present in documents like user manuals, troubleshooting instructions, guidelines, internal processes and so on. Those documents should ensure optimal comprehensibility by the operator to safely and effectively install, operate, maintain and service the industrial systems. Given the high number and diversity of such documents, the operators often have to go through a laborious and time-consuming process of searching them and trying to filter their content to find the relevant information to answer their questions.

In this scenario, enterprises call for tools and methods for extracting knowledge from unstructured information encoded in documents (e.g., PDF or text files), using diverse state-of-the-art Natural Language Processing (NLP) [12] techniques that involve three main tasks: Named-Entity-Recognition (NER) [19], Entity-Linking (EL) [24] and Relation Extraction [1]. Methods to automatically extract or enrich the structure of documents have been a core topic in the context of the Semantic Web [17]; however, those automated methods may not solve the knowledge extraction process entirely. Indeed, extracting complex knowledge from unstructured sources is a challenge [21]: in the industrial domain, for example, troubleshooting documents may contain the description of long and articulated procedures (i.e., sequences of steps to be performed in a precise order and under specific conditions) and those natural language instructions may be represented in very different textual forms, thus making it hard for a knowledge extraction algorithm to correctly identify and structure the relevant information. Oftentimes, automatic extraction is followed by manual revision of domain experts. In any case, all machine-learning based methods require training data which is often not readily available, therefore novel approaches are emerging to exploit interactive dialogues and language models [2].

Even when the extraction is supported by suitable approaches, knowledge still requires to be represented in the structured form of a knowledge graph by means of ontologies. In the case of knowledge extraction from industrial documents, different aspects co-exist: domain concepts and company-specific terms are mixed with procedure/process information. The manufacturing domain is definitely multi-faceted and even recent surveys of the existing semantic vocabularies and ontologies identified a high number of efforts [6]. Therefore, to build knowledge graphs out of industrial documents, multiple ontologies are needed to cover all the relevant elements. In particular, our idea is to propose a set of vocabularies that improve the coverage of document annotations and knowledge extraction thereof, by means of ontology modularization [15], an interesting strategy to

---

[1] Cf. https://research-and-innovation.ec.europa.eu/research-area/industry/industry-50_en.

facilitate ontology reuse, since it allows for different ontology modules to cover specific subdomains.

In this paper, we present the K-Hub ontology, a modular conceptual model able to capture the different aspects of manufacturing knowledge management and to support the building of a "knowledge hub" that helps industrial operators like shop floor workers in their daily operations. The K-Hub ontology is made of a set of modules that identify and capture entities and relationships that are relevant for document retrieval and knowledge extraction: an annotation module, that covers the aspects of document analysis and knowledge extraction; a manufacturing module, which contains the most common domain topics that can be found in industrial documents; a procedure module, which addresses the challenges of representing complex process information; and company-specific modules that are necessary every time an enterprise uses dedicated names, terms and acronyms (often even characterized by privacy or confidentiality constraints).

The remainder of this paper is structured as follows: Sect. 2 illustrates our reference motivational scenario, based on the actual knowledge management needs of two different manufacturing companies; Sect. 4 describes the methodological approach and its application to the engineering of the K-Hub modular ontology; the details of the K-Hub ontology modules are explained in Sect. 5; Sect. 6 demonstrate the use of the K-Hub ontology, both in a document retrieval scenario implemented and tested by shop floor operators via a voice assistant, and in a scenario to support procedure execution; relevant work from state of the art is included in Sect. 3; finally, we offer our conclusions and delineate future lines of work in Sect. 7.

2   Motivational Scenario

The need for the K-Hub ontology emerged in a cooperative research and innovation project named "Manufacturing Knowledge Hub", with the final purpose to develop a voice assistant solution dedicated to supporting shop floor workers during maintenance processes. In this context, a huge number of documents must be managed and retrieved, in various digital formats: textual documents, pictures, spreadsheets, technical drawings, movies, presentations, etc. In the project, two different manufacturing companies provided their scenarios and specific needs and evaluated the project results.

The first one is Whirlpool, the multi-national home appliances manufacturer; in their maintenance procedures on the production lines, the real challenge is to find the relevant information within this universe of heterogeneous data (sometimes also including documents in paper format or in a scanned digital form), which can create an obstacle for an effective knowledge sharing, but which can represent a key element to take advantage of in the digitalization process. In Whirlpool, different plants, or even different production lines within the same plant, currently, adopt various practices to organize and search for information in the wealth of available documents.

The second involved company is Marposs, a large enterprise specialized in designing and manufacturing products and solutions for measurement, inspection and testing, widely used in very different sectors (e.g., automotive, aerospace, biomedical, energy, consumer electronics); in relation to Marposs' standard products, they already have well-structured documents, but also very long ones, with a lot of information; in this case, during maintenance activities, which employees often perform at the customer plants, the challenge is not only to find the right document but also to identify the relevant information within it, for example, to understand what maintenance or troubleshooting procedure to follow, especially in the case of novice operators.

Within the project, a voice assistant solution was designed and developed to simplify the access to the knowledge for the shop floor operators of both Whirlpool and Marposs. The K-Hub ontology described in this paper is a core part of this solution, with the purpose to facilitate document retrieval and knowledge extraction; as explained in the following, we engineered the K-Hub ontologies with the support of the domain experts from Whirlpool and Marposs, but we generalized their requirements so that our model can be reused in similar scenarios also beyond the two involved companies.

3   Related Work

This work involves ontology engineering through the modularization of different related conceptualizations, to combine in a "knowledge hub" relevant concepts and relations. As far as we were able to determine after the initial literature search at the beginning of this ontology development process, as well as during the identification of ontological resources to be reused, this is the first comprehensive and fully documented effort for the generation of a modular ontology "hub" in this area, which is born with the objective of serving further standardisation and community-driven initiatives around this domain [6].

We can mention some previous approaches reported in the literature, where vocabularies of workflows represent scientific experiments [4,7,10]. A popular vocabulary for describing activities is provided by PROV-O which relates activities to a plan but it does not allow for plans to be described. Therefore, P-Plan[2] [9] is proposed as an extension of `prov:Plan`. Other vocabularies such as ProvONE or its extension, ProvONE+[3] are general-purpose specification models for the control-flows in scientific workflows [4]. However, the only vocabulary describing closely the structure of procedures in our scenario is P-Plan. The Web Annotation Data Model[4] provides an extensible, interoperable framework for expressing annotations specifically for Web pages. It is possible to define our TopicAnnotation as a specialization of oa:Annotation for a higher level of expressivity.

In the domain of industrial and manufacturing, there are already a number of available vocabularies, but the critical aspect of this domain is that those belong to different areas such as product, systems and supply chain. Therefore,

---

[2] http://purl.org/net/p-plan.
[3] http://purl.org/provone.
[4] https://www.w3.org/TR/annotation-model/.

the definitions of the terms are very heterogeneous, as stakeholders view the manufacturing elements differently [6]. However, our extensible design of the K-Hub ontology allows for plugging-in other ontologies as additional modules, like for example SAREF4INMA [23], to cover other elements specific to the industry and manufacturing domain. We plan to register our vocabulary as part of the Industry Ontology Foundry (IOF) Initiative [14] which provides a repository for open reference ontologies to support the manufacturing and engineering industry needs and advance data interoperability.

Other works that aim at creating a modular ontology for the semantic annotation belonging to other domains are reported. The authors in [5] propose a network of ontologies for ICT infrastructures. They solved the problem of interoperability by homogeneously describing the core concepts and properties that are common across configuration and IT Service management databases. Similarly to our approach, the ontology network can be easily extended when new types of items appear. The authors in [22] construct a structure named emerging ontologies, which involves elements of more than one ontology. The idea is to provide a global view of several ontologies in one single structure which is useful for semantic annotation with concepts that come from more than one ontology.

4   Requirements and Methodology

We developed the K-Hub Ontology relying on the Linked Open Terms (LOT) Methodology [20], an industrial method for developing ontologies and vocabularies. The LOT methodology enriches the main workflow with Semantic Web-oriented best practices such as the reuse of terms (ontology classes, properties, and attributes) existing in already published vocabularies or ontologies and the publication of the built ontology according to Linked Data principles. The LOT methodology defines iterations over a basic workflow composed of the following activities: (i) ontological requirements specification, (ii) ontology implementation, (iii) ontology publication and (iv) ontology maintenance.

In this section, we focus on the process that we followed for all the steps of the LOT methodology, which are explained in detail in the following while Sect. 5 describes the contents of the final published ontology.

4.1   Ontology Requirements Specification

The ontology requirements specification activity was driven by the interviews conducted with domain experts and visits to the operating sites of the two companies. The interviews performed during the visits involved different stakeholders at different levels (management, technical support, end users). We collected information about their processes, their needs and pain points, to identify the main knowledge aspects they manage. This activity can be divided into the following sub-steps:

Use Case Specification: this activity has the goal to provide a list of use cases. We investigated specific use cases for each case study, with the respective goals to be achieved by the ontology data modeling. In the end, the two companies had similar needs that are captured by the following use cases.

UC1: The user (shop floor worker) wants to retrieve a document for supporting him/her during the maintenance process.

Description: this use case refers to a maintenance situation, focused on retrieving technical documents during specific maintenance activities. The maintenance activities may be based on the management of maintenance data on the shop floor, during daily activities performed by maintenance employees.

Actors: different types of actors are involved in maintenance operations: engineers, expert technicians, maintenance workers or new employees who need access to a specific document.

Flow: In the maintenance scenario, the documents relevant to the project are redacted by documentation workers and maintained within the company (in legacy systems and intranet networks). Engineers and technicians, both experts and novices, access those documents during maintenance activities or interventions related to problems or troubleshooting, for example, to find the most recent version of a document pertaining to a specific topic.

UC2: The user (shop floor worker) wants to be guided step-by-step in the correct execution of a company procedure during the maintenance process, especially if they are not an experienced employee.

Description: this use case refers to a maintenance situation, focused on guiding a shop floor worker in the execution of a specific maintenance process. Such a maintenance process is carried out by the execution of one or more procedures performed step by step, by the maintenance employee.

Actors: different kinds of actors may be involved in maintenance-specific procedures: technicians, maintenance workers and not-experienced employees who need to be guided step by step in the procedure execution.

Flow: in the maintenance scenario, shop floor engineers and technicians, both experts and novices, need to find the operational procedure to be applied to solve the problem at hand; they search for the most suitable procedure; they identify the relevant contextual information (e.g. tools to be used to execute the procedure, spare parts to have at disposal); they follow the procedure, possibly being guided in each step, getting information on what actions to perform in which order and, at the conclusion of each step, what is the next step to be followed. They can find all the relevant information within documents (similarly to UC1) or they can be supported by a digital tool that provides them interactive guidance within the procedure (e.g. an intelligent assistant).

The User Story generated by the identified use case *UC1* is **US1**.

US1: The user wants to retrieve a document and to open it at the most relevant page by specifying one or more topics/characteristics; some examples are: the type of document (e.g. installation manual), the machine/workstation/component on which the maintenance action will be performed, the action to be executed (e.g. replacement of a component, configuration, repair, etc.), the error to be solved in a troubleshooting.

The User Stories generated by the use case *UC2* are **US2**, **US3** and **US4**.

US2: The user wants to find a company procedure to be followed, that best suits the specific maintenance activity at hand by specifying one or more topics/characteristics; some examples are: the machine/workstation/component on which the maintenance activity will be performed, the procedure to be executed, the error to be solved.

US3: The user wants to know what the next step is to be executed in the current procedure by specifying the last executed step.

US4: The user wants to know what tools are needed to perform a specific procedure.

Data Exchange Identification. This activity aims to gather domain documents and resources. In particular, during the interviews conducted with the domain experts from the two companies, we obtained all the relevant information about the domain to be modeled. In particular, we gathered details on the documents a user wanted to retrieve including general aspects of the documents, access constraints, documents' topical content and the main search strategies that people use. During this collection activity, the company stakeholders also provided a list of sample documents (product and service manuals, schematic representations of electrical/mechanical/hydraulic/... components). The analysis of the collected information allowed us to provide a clear definition of the application domain and the appropriate terminology.

Functional Ontological Requirements. Competency Questions (CQs) are a well-known technique to define ontology functional requirements and in the form of a set of queries that the ontology should answer. On the other hand, preliminary definitions (or facts) are assertions that provide a description of the requirements associated with the considered domain terminology. We cooperated with the domain experts in the definition of both CQs and facts, thanks also to the selection of relevant documents described before. At the end of this stage, we provided the full list of competency questions and facts to the domain experts and user representatives, who performed their validation in terms of accuracy and completeness with respect to the identified use cases and user stories[5]. Some examples of CQs and facts are given, respectively, in Table 1 and Table 2, with their relation to use cases and user stories.

4.2 Ontology Implementation

The ontology implementation followed the LOT methodology. Our team of ontology engineers analysed the requirements and divided them into modules, since each module contains a subset of concepts and relations identifying an area

---

[5] The full list of CQs and facts is available at https://github.com/cefriel/k-hub-ontology/blob/main/PaperCompetencyQuestions_Facts.xlsx.

Table 1. Examples of competency questions.

UC	US	Identifier	Competency Question
UC1	US1	Cq-1	Which is the document about topic Z?
UC2	US2	Cq-2	Which is the procedure to do the action X on the component Y?
UC2	US3	Cq-3	Which is the next step to be executed?
UC2	US4	Cq-4	Which are the tools required for the procedure X?

Table 2. Examples of preliminary definitions.

UC	Identifier	Preliminary Definition (Fact)
UC1	Req-1	A document is associated to one or more topic annotation
UC1	Req-2	A topic can be one of: action, component, product, machine, workstation, document type, supplier, trouble, tool, spare part, error, configuration
UC2	Req-3	A step is associated to the next one
UC2	Req-4	A procedure requires one or more tools

of specialisation. The creation of modules is useful for facilitating the update and evolution of ontology in the future. After the ontological requirements were identified in the requirements specification process, we created the conceptual models using the Chowlk tool[6], which is a UML-based notation and provides a set of recommendations for ontology diagrams representation. We discussed the conceptual models with the domain experts on the basis of their graphical representation (as it is easier to understand for people with limited or no background on ontologies), then we proceeded to generate the formal representation in the OWL language, again using the capabilities of Chowlk. We carried out the ontology implementation phase iteratively, validating and refining it with some of the same domain experts that were involved in the requirements specification process. The OWL representations of the ontology modules are maintained in the GitHub repository.

We evaluated the ontology throughout the standard LOT process by asking for feedback to stakeholders: two persons from each company (among those interviewed at the beginning) were repeatedly involved to validate use cases, user stories, competency questions and facts. Moreover, when we adopted the ontology in the document retrieval system described in Sect. 6.1, the users indirectly evaluated the ontology by assessing the search results and comparing them to their expectations. In addition, regarding this methodology, we also used the OOPS tool to evaluate our ontology in terms of common pitfalls.

In the end, we performed a final assessment to verify that the ontology fulfills all the requirements, by checking the compliance between the ontology imple-

---

[6] Cf. https://chowlk.linkeddata.es/chowlk_spec.

mentation and the full list of competency questions and facts, and we also verified the absence of syntactic, modeling, or semantic errors.

4.3 Ontology Publication

The aim of the ontology publication activity is to provide an online ontology accessible both as a human-readable documentation and a machine-readable file from its URI, according to the FAIR principles. More specifically, we published the K-Hub Ontology online (cf. Sect. 5) following the best practice recipes for publishing vocabularies with content negotiation [3]. We documented the ontologies using WIDOCO[7] [8], a wizard that takes as input an ontology to generate a set of linked HTML (draft) pages containing a human-readable description of the ontology from the ontology content. It guides users through the steps to be followed when documenting an ontology, indicating missing metadata that should be included. As recommended by the LOT methodology, we created an extensible and modular ontology with the goal of making it available to support industrial workers covering several aspects; accordingly, we published and documented each of the modules of our ontology. We extended the automatically-generated HTML pages, by adding diagrams and other explanatory information.

As will be explained in more detail in the next section, our modular ontology contains both the knowledge of general use/availability and the specific knowledge of the two companies involved in this ontology engineering effort. With respect to the latter kind of knowledge, it is important to note that a critical requirement is to preserve the privacy of the information represented in the ontology [11]: for example, product names or supplier information may be covered by confidentiality constraints. Therefore, publishing their related details openly on the Web may be impossible, instead, a restricted access will be required. In order to cope with this situation, we managed the open/public and the private modules in partially different ways. For both cases, we adopted a GitHub repository and the content negotiation-based vocabulary publication best practices. While the public modules are maintained in a public GitHub repository with the machine-readable and human-readable representations openly reachable from the respective namespaces, the private modules are maintained in private GitHub repositories and their representations are password-protected and accessible only to those with the proper credentials. This double publication ensures the proper modularization and extensibility of the ontology, while at the same time preserving the business constraints of the two companies. We believe that this (simple) approach can be adopted in many other similar situations, in which privacy or confidentiality is a key requirement.

To complete the ontology publication, we also archived the public modules of the ontology in Zenodo[8], following the usual practices of Open Science.

---

[7] https://github.com/dgarijo/Widoco/.
[8] https://www.doi.org/10.5281/zenodo.7443000.

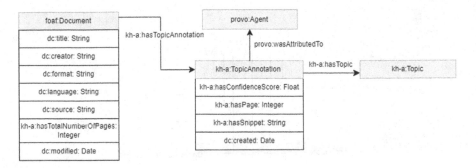

Fig. 1. Graphic representation of the Annotation Module

4.4   Ontology Maintenance

Our setup is now prepared for the ontology maintenance phase for the ontology, with the possibility of submitting issues through the GitHub repository (bugs, requests for additions, etc.) for each of the modules in the ontology, so as to facilitate discussions that may arise during future standardisation processes or ontology usage by other organizations that could extend and reuse its modules.

5   The K-Hub Ontology Modules

In this section, we describe the current version of the implementation of the Knowledge Hub Ontology and its modules, and the main decisions taken during their development.

Annotation Module

https://knowledge.c-innovationhub.com/k-hub/annotation

The annotation module of the Knowledge Hub Ontology represents the core of the ontology with concepts and properties used for describing the annotation of documents. This module is composed of 3 main concepts: `Document`, `Topic` and `TopicAnnotation`. The `Document` concept describes the document's information through general data properties such as the author, the edit date, the format, the language, and the url. The `TopicAnnotation` concept describes the semantic annotation of the snippet extracted from the document. The datatype properties describing the annotation include the page number of the document containing the annotation, the snippet containing the information to be annotated, the creator of the annotation, the creation date, and, if present, the annotation's confidence score. The `TopicAnnotation` also connects the document with its content information, expressed with a list of "topics". The `Topic` concept, therefore, refers to any subject, theme, entity or object contained in the document and which the final user may be interested to search. The `Topic` concept is further specialized in the others modules of the ontology and constitutes the main extension point of the ontology. During the analysis of existing vocabularies, we identify and reuse existing concepts and properties in the conceptual

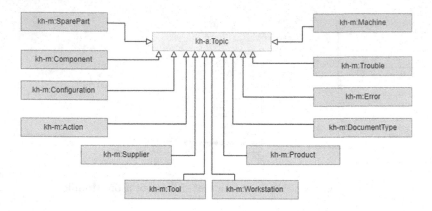

Fig. 2. Graphic representation of the Manufacturing Module

model: *FOAF* ontology for the definition of document concept, the *Dublin Core* ontology for describing the document's properties and the *PROV-O* ontology for modeling the provenance information about the annotations. Figure 1 displays the final version of this module.

Manufacturing Module
https://knowledge.c-innovationhub.com/k-hub/manufacturing
The manufacturing module of the K-Hub Ontology defines the specific topics for the domain of interest of the document. During the requirement collection phase, it was possible to define the list of concepts used for the maintenance process in the manufacturing domain. The identified concepts are represented as subclasses of the most general concept `Topic` defined in the Annotation Module, as displayed in Fig. 2. These subclasses describe general maintenance elements such as: `Component`, `Configuration`, `Supplier`, `DocumentType`, `Trouble`, `Action`, `Product`, `Machine`, `Workstation`, `SparePart`, `Error` and `Tool`. The implementation of this module was further enriched with a terminology of instances of the aforementioned concepts. This terminology represents a list of entities to be searched in the annotation of documents. The instances defined in this module are specific to the domain of interests given by a single company. The terminology was created thanks to the collaboration of the ontology developer team and the involved industrial partners and it contains a list of terms translated into English and Italian and a list of possible synonyms. The terminology was modeled using the *SKOS* vocabulary [18]. We defined Topic as skos:Concept and the hierarchy of topics as subClassOf Topic. We refer to "topics" as classes with instances and the annotations are expected to refer to those instances (e.g. `annotation1,hasTopic,productX`). The instances provide the indexer with a complete list of terms to be searched in the document for the annotation process.

Procedure Module
https://knowledge.c-innovationhub.com/k-hub/procedure

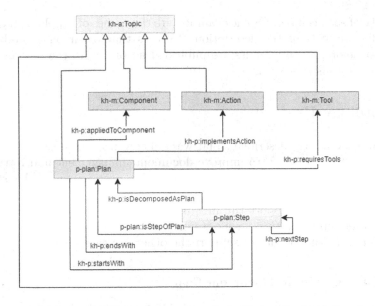

Fig. 3. Graphic representation of the Procedure Module

The procedure module of the K-Hub Ontology defines the concepts and properties for modeling the procedures described in the service manuals, usually composed of multiple atomic steps, for instance, guidelines for maintenance activities. As Fig. 3 shows, the ontology consists of 2 main concepts: Plan and Step, which are also defined as subclasses of Topic (from the annotation module). A procedure is an instance of the Plan concept and it can be considered as a pattern like "A *Procedure* to do an *Action* on a *Component* with a *Tool*". The object properties implementsAction, appliedToComponent and requiresTools implement these associations between the Plan concept and the Action, the Component and the Tool concepts respectively, as defined in the Manufacturing Module. Each atomic activity is an instance of the Step concept. A Plan is composed of one or multiple Steps, which must be executed in a given order. The object property nextStep defines the execution order of the steps, whereas the startsWith and endsWith properties indicate the first and last steps of a Plan. A Plan may be included as a Step of another plan and this association is expressed by the object property isDecomposedAsPlan. During the analysis of the existing vocabularies, we identified the P-Plan ontology [9] as a very interesting source for our modeling; therefore the Plan and Step concepts, as well as some of the properties of this module, reuse the respective P-Plan definitions.

Company Specific Modules
This part of the K-Hub Ontology is intended to model the private concepts and terms of industrial companies that may have privacy/confidentiality issues. For each company, we created a private module that contains context-specific instances related to the company's business. The included terms refer to the

specificity of each company. Some examples are the names of suppliers, the names of specific products or the description of errors that occur on a product. As explained before, those modules are published according to the best practices, but their access is protected.

6   Ontology Use

The modular ontology described so far was conceived in the context of the scenario illustrated in Sect. 2, to improve document management and retrieval in industrial maintenance for the Whirlpool and Marposs companies; this scenario was further detailed in the Use Cases described in Sect. 4. We fully implemented the entire tooling to support the first use case, which was also evaluated by industry user representatives, while we only started to lay the foundations for the tools and methodologies to support the other use cases.

6.1   Ontology Use in Document Search

The first use corresponds to the use case UC1, in which shop floor operators involved in a maintenance activity want to retrieve the right document for the case at hand. We employed the ontology to build a system that effectively supports this use case (cf. Fig. 4).

The ontology was used in the first step of document annotation: the relevant materials provided by the industrial partners were processed by a system that, for each document page, analyse its textual content in order to identify the most relevant Topics (operating, as such, an *entity linking* process): for example, the annotation can discover that a specific document contains information about a certain Product, mentions its Components or its SpareParts.

In case the automatic document annotation process does not perform correctly or this information is hard to identify automatically or the system (which is usually based on machine learning algorithms) requires a proper training set, the annotation step can also be performed manually by a domain expert[9].

The output of this phase – whether automatic or manual – is a set of TopicAnnotations which indicate, for each document, which topics were identified in which page(s); those annotations are stored and indexed in order to be ready for retrieval. We used a combination of a triple store and a full-text index to manage the annotation storage and provide a web API-based access layer to search applications.

Then, we set up a digital tool to support document retrieval for the shop floor operator: a voice assistant helps the user in finding the right document. This tool exploits the ontology in two ways: first, it elaborates the user requests/utterances in order to understand what is the main retrieval interest (e.g. if the person asks "how can I replace the battery of product X?", the system shall identify the

---

[9] We are currently working on an ontology-extension of the PAWLS tool for the manual annotation of PDF documents, cf. https://github.com/cefriel/onto-pawls.

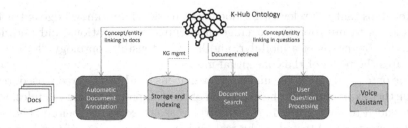

Fig. 4. Use of the K-Hub ontology in the document search scenario

"replace" Action, the "battery" Component and the "X" Product); then, it uses the identified Topics to match the most relevant TopicAnnotations and, consequently, to propose the user with a specific Document and to help them opening it and navigating to the right page, to find the answer to the original request.

6.2 Ontology Use to Support Procedure Execution

The second usage scenario corresponds to the use cases UC2 and UC3, in which a shop floor operator wants to be guided in the correct execution of a procedure. This scenario could be addressed like the previous one, in case the user is simply given back a relevant document that contains the explanation of a procedure. However, the vision here is to support the operator by giving them *instructions* rather than *documents*. In this sense, the first step of knowledge extraction is key, because the goal is not only to generate TopicAnnotations, but also to reconstruct the specific procedural knowledge (i.e. Plan and its Steps) and formalise it as structured knowledge, so to reuse it directly in user-supporting applications. As procedural knowledge is hard to formalise in a standard way [16], the knowledge extraction step would probably benefit from the manual annotation approach mentioned before.

The voice assistant application, implemented for the document retrieval scenario, could be exploited instead to provide the user with the exact instructions that they need. Thus, the user can first ask for the right procedure to follow, and then interactively ask the assistant to be supplied with the information required to perform the following step, with commands like "Give me the next step" which navigate the procedural knowledge graph by leveraging the nextStep property between Steps.

7   Conclusions and Future Work

In this paper, we presented the K-Hub ontology, a modular conceptual model able to capture the different aspects of manufacturing knowledge management and support industrial operators in their daily activities. In particular, the K-Hub ontology comprises a set of modules that identify and capture entities and relationships that are relevant for document retrieval and knowledge extraction. Our idea is to improve the coverage of document annotations and knowledge extraction by means of a modular, and hence extensible, ontology "hub" which facilitates the reuse of the conceptual model.

The ontology is available under an open license and can be freely used, reused and further extended with the exception of the company-specific modules, which are intended to have limited access for the reasons explained before. The ontology was created and tested in the real business environments of two large manufacturing companies, Whirlpool and Marposs. A permanent URI and all the resources are completely available online and in GitHub and archived in Zenodo (with a corresponding DOI).

Ontology requirements were collected from the interviews conducted with domain experts and visits to the operating sites of the two companies. The development followed state-of-the-art practices in ontology development – the LOT methodology as well as the best practices to publish vocabularies on the Web – that we are applying in all our ontology development projects.

In terms of impact, therefore, we consider that this work and its results can fill an important gap that has not been addressed sufficiently in the state of the art. This would be as well a resource of interest for the Semantic Web community, in general, demonstrating how ontologies and semantic technologies can be used in an area where knowledge is contained in documents and extracting and representing it by combining different aspects could hence benefit from this type of approach.

We have not demonstrated yet any further reuse of our K-Hub ontology outside our own efforts, given that it has been only created recently. We expect, though, that there may be an interest in the broader context of digitalization in the manufacturing sector, as well as in other sectors with similar requirements. Besides, the way in which the ontology has been structured, together with the rich set of documentation provided for it, should facilitate such reuse and extensibility in the future, even for situations that have not been originally foreseen. For example, the manufacturing related ontologies surveyed in [6] could be reused to provide additional lists of relevant domain concepts to be considered as subclasses of `Topic`, to annotate industry documents; the same approach could be used outside the manufacturing context, by reusing only the annotation module and plugging-in other domain ontologies (biomedical, tourism, commerce, etc.).

Our future work consists of the further maintenance, extension and application of the K-Hub ontology and its employment in document annotation scenarios. In particular, we are interested in exploring its use in further automatic knowledge extraction efforts with machine/deep learning techniques, as well as in manual annotation experiments involving domain experts.

Acknowledgments. This work was partially supported by the K-HUB "Manufacturing Knowledge Hub" project, co-funded by EIT Manufacturing (project id 22330). The authors would like to specifically thank the industrial partners of the project for their invaluable support in both the requirement elicitation and the ontology validation activities.

References

1. Bach, N., Badaskar, S.: A survey on relation extraction. Lang. Technol. Inst. Carnegie Mellon University **178**, 15 (2007)
2. Bellan, P., Dragoni, M., Ghidini, C.: Process extraction from text: state of the art and challenges for the future. CoRR abs/2110.03754 (2021)
3. Berrueta, D., Phipps, J.: Best Practice Recipes for Publishing RDF Vocabularies (2008). https://www.w3.org/TR/swbp-vocab-pub/
4. Butt, A.S., Fitch, P.: ProvONE+: a provenance model for scientific workflows. In: Huang, Z., Beek, W., Wang, H., Zhou, R., Zhang, Y. (eds.) WISE 2020. LNCS, vol. 12343, pp. 431–444. Springer, Cham (2020). https://doi.org/10.1007/978-3-030-62008-0_30
5. Corcho, O., et al.: A high-level ontology network for ICT infrastructures. In: Hotho, A., et al. (eds.) ISWC 2021. LNCS, vol. 12922, pp. 446–462. Springer, Cham (2021). https://doi.org/10.1007/978-3-030-88361-4_26
6. Franc, Y.L.: OntoCommons D3.2 - Report on existing domain ontologies in identified domains (2022). https://doi.org/10.5281/zenodo.6504553
7. Gangemi, A., Peroni, S., Shotton, D.M., Vitali, F.: The publishing workflow ontology (PWO). Semant. Web **8**(5), 703–718 (2017)
8. Garijo, D.: WIDOCO: a wizard for documenting ontologies. In: d'Amato, C., et al. (eds.) ISWC 2017. LNCS, vol. 10588, pp. 94–102. Springer, Cham (2017). https://doi.org/10.1007/978-3-319-68204-4_9. http://dgarijo.com/papers/widoco-iswc2017.pdf
9. Garijo, D., Gil, Y.: Augmenting prov with plans in p-plan: scientific processes as linked data. In: CEUR Workshop Proceedings (2012)
10. Garijo, D., Gil, Y., Corcho, Ó.: Abstract, link, publish, exploit: an end to end framework for workflow sharing. Future Gener. Comput. Syst. **75**, 271–283 (2017)
11. Grau, B.C.: Privacy in ontology-based information systems: a pending matter. Semant. Web **1**(1–2), 137–141 (2010)
12. Jurafsky, D., Martin, J.H.: Speech and Language Processing: An Introduction to Natural Language Processing, Computational Linguistics, and Speech Recognition, 2nd edn. Prentice Hall, Pearson Education International (2009)
13. Kamble, S.S., Gunasekaran, A., Gawankar, S.A.: Sustainable industry 4.0 framework: a systematic literature review identifying the current trends and future perspectives. Process Saf. Environ. Prot. **117**, 408–425 (2018)
14. Kulvatunyou, B.S., Wallace, E., Kiritsis, D., Smith, B., Will, C.: The industrial ontologies foundry proof-of-concept project. In: Moon, I., Lee, G.M., Park, J., Kiritsis, D., von Cieminski, G. (eds.) APMS 2018. IAICT, vol. 536, pp. 402–409. Springer, Cham (2018). https://doi.org/10.1007/978-3-319-99707-0_50
15. Le Clair, A., Marinache, A., El Ghalayini, H., Maccaull, W., Khedri, R.: A review on ontology modularization techniques - a multi-dimensional perspective. IEEE Trans. Knowl. Data Eng. **35**, 4376–4394 (2022)
16. Li, D., Landström, A., Fast-Berglund, Å., Almström, P.: Human-centred dissemination of data, information and knowledge in industry 4.0. Procedia CIRP **84**, 380–386 (2019)
17. Martínez-Rodríguez, J., Hogan, A., López-Arévalo, I.: Information extraction meets the semantic web: a survey. Semant. Web **11**(2), 255–335 (2020)
18. Miles, A., Bechhofer, S.: SKOS simple knowledge organization system reference (2009)

19. Nakashole, N., Tylenda, T., Weikum, G.: Fine-grained semantic typing of emerging entities. In: Proceedings of the 51st Annual Meeting of the Association for Computational Linguistics (Volume 1: Long Papers), pp. 1488–1497 (2013)
20. Poveda-Villalón, M., Fernández-Izquierdo, A., Fernández-López, M., García-Castro, R.: LOT: an industrial oriented ontology engineering framework. Eng. Appl. Artif. Intell. 111, 104755 (2022)
21. Rula, A., Re Calegari, G., Azzini, A., Bucci, D., Baroni, I., Celino, I.: Eliciting and curating procedural knowledge in industry: challenges and opportunities. In: Proceedings of the Third Conference on Digital Curation Technologies (Qurator 2022), Berlin, Germany, 19th–23rd September 2022. CEUR Workshop Proceedings, vol. 3234. CEUR-WS.org (2022). https://ceur-ws.org/Vol-3234/paper4.pdf
22. de Souza, H.C., Moura, A.M.D.C., Cavalcanti, M.C.: Integrating ontologies based on P2P mappings. IEEE Trans. Syst. Man Cybern. - Part A Syst. Hum. 40(5), 1071–1082 (2010). https://doi.org/10.1109/TSMCA.2010.2044880
23. Thakker, D., et al.: SAREF4INMA: a SAREF extension for the industry and manufacturing domain. Semant. Web 11(6), 911–926 (2020)
24. Wu, Z., Pan, S., Chen, F., Long, G., Zhang, C., Yu, P.S.: A comprehensive survey on graph neural networks. IEEE Trans. Neural Netw. Learn. Syst. 32(1), 4–24 (2021)

pyRDF2Vec: A Python Implementation and Extension of RDF2Vec

Bram Steenwinckel$^{(\boxtimes)}$, Gilles Vandewiele, Terencio Agozzino,
and Femke Ongenae

IDLab, Ghent University – imec, 9000 Gent, Belgium
bram.steenwinckel@ugent.be

Abstract. This paper introduces pyRDF2Vec, a Python software package that reimplements the well-known RDF2Vec algorithm along with several of its extensions. By making the algorithm available in the most popular data science language, and by bundling all extensions into a single place, the use of RDF2Vec is simplified for data scientists. The package is released under an MIT license and structured in such a way to foster further research into sampling, walking, and embedding strategies, which are vital components of the RDF2Vec algorithm. Several optimisations have been implemented in pyRDF2Vec that allow for more efficient walk extraction than the original algorithm. Furthermore, best practices in terms of code styling, testing, and documentation were applied such that the package is future-proof as well as to facilitate external contributions.

Keywords: RDF2Vec · walk-based embeddings · open source

1 Introduction

Knowledge Graphs (KGs) are an ideal candidate to perform hybrid Machine Learning (ML) where both background and observational knowledge are taken into account to construct predictive models. However, since KGs are symbolic data structures, they cannot be fed to ML algorithms directly and first require a non-trivial transformation step in which symbolic substructures of the graph are converted into numerical representations. These transformation techniques can typically be classified as being *feature*-based or *embedding*-based [26]. Feature-based approaches are often interpretable, but require domain knowledge about the task at hand and are effort-intensive. Embedding-based approaches, on the other hand, are typically agnostic to the task and are usually able to outperform their feature-based counterparts. Resource Description Framework To Vector (RDF2Vec) [18] is an unsupervised, task-agnostic, and embedding-based approach that has gained significant popularity over the past few years. RDF2Vec

---

Resource type: Software
License: MIT license
URL: https://github.com/IBCNServices/pyRDF2Vec.

builds on the popular Natural Language Processing (NLP) technique Word2Vec. The latter generates embeddings for different tokens present in a corpus, by training a neural network in an unsupervised way that must predict either a token based on its context (Continuous Bag of Words) or the context based on a token (Skip-Gram). The corpus, fed to Word2Vec, is constructed by extracting a large number of walks from the KG. A walk is a sequence of entities obtained from the KG by starting at a certain entity and traversing the directed edges.

Since its initial publication, in 2017, many extensions to the algorithm have been proposed. However, each of these extensions are individual implementations, which complicates combining several of them. Moreover, the original code for RDF2Vec was written in Java, which is significantly less popular than Python for data science, according to the Kaggle Survey 2022[1]. In Fig. 1, the answers to the question "What programming languages do you use on a regular basis?", where multiple answers were possible, are depicted. It should be noted that among the 3862 of the people who selected Java as being used regularly, only 461 did not pick Python. This makes it difficult to integrate the original RDF2Vec implementation into a data science pipeline, which is typically written in Python.

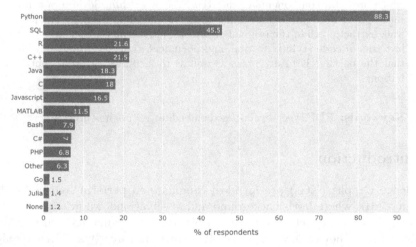

Fig. 1. Programming languages used by data scientists according to the Kaggle Survey 2021.

In this paper, we present `pyRDF2Vec`, a Python implementation of the original algorithm and many of its extensions. Moreover, various mechanisms are built, allowing to better handle large KGs. The code is released under an open-source license and is written in a way to facilitate further research into the different components of the RDF2Vec algorithm. The remainder of this paper is structured as follows. In Sect. 2, we provide background on representation learning

---

[1] https://www.kaggle.com/c/kaggle-survey-2022.

for KGs, followed by an in-depth discussion of RDF2Vec and its extensions. Then, in Sect. 3, we present the architecture of our pyRDF2Vec package and the mechanisms set in-place to easily allow for contributions by others. In Sect. 4, we discuss some studies and other software packages that have already made use of pyRDF2Vec. Finally, we conclude our paper in Sect. 6. In Appendix A, we provide a code snippet that shows how pyRDF2Vec can be used.

2   Background

In this section, we describe the necessary background to elaborate upon pyRDF2Vec. First, we will discuss related work regarding the transformation of a KG into numerical representations. Afterwards, we outline an in-depth overview of how RDF2Vec works and its extensions released over the past few years.

2.1   Representation Learning

As mentioned in the introduction, a *feature*-based or *embedding*-based transformation step is required that converts the symbolic KGs into numerical vectors before they can be used in ML models. Especially embedding-based approaches, which make use of Deep Learning techniques, have gained increasing popularity over the past few years as these can be applied out-of-the-box and can run efficiently on Graphical Processing Units (GPUs), which are quite commonly available today. Moreover, the largest advantage of embedding-based techniques is that they are typically task-agnostic and as such do not require extensive domain knowledge and/or significant effort, as opposed to feature-based approaches. A further distinction can be made between embedding-based techniques. The first category consists of techniques that learn embeddings either through tensor factorisation or through negative sampling [3,15,26], e.g. TransE [1]. A second category consists of Deep Learning architectures that make use of parameterised transformations, based on information from the neighbourhood of a node that is collected through message passing [19], e.g. Relational Graph Convolutional Networks (R-GCN). The parameters of this transformation are learned through back-propagation in a supervised fashion. A third, and final, category adapts existing NLP techniques, such as Word2Vec [13], to work on graph structures. RDF2Vec belongs to this final category [18].

2.2   RDF2Vec

RDF2Vec is an unsupervised, task-agnostic algorithm that achieves state-of-the-art performances on many benchmark datasets [18]. It extends Word2Vec to work on graph structures by first extracting walks that serve as a corpus. Each walk can be seen as a sentence of a corpus and each hop within such walks corresponds to a token. Word2Vec will then learn embeddings for each of these tokens in an unsupervised matter by learning to predict either a token based on its context

(Continuous Bag of Words), or the context based on a token (Skip-Gram). Over the past few years, several extensions to RDF2Vec have been suggested, which we will discuss subsequently. A good up-to-date overview of how RDF2Vec works, which extensions have been proposed over the last few years, and of applications that make use of RDF2Vec can be found on a website hosted by the original authors[2].

The number of walks that can be extracted quickly grows, depending on the depth of those walks and the size of the KG. As such, exhaustively extracting every possible walk becomes infeasible rather quickly. As a solution, Cochez et al. [4] proposed several sampling, or biased walking, techniques which enable only extracting a subset of walks that still capture most of the information. Recently, more sampling strategies have been proposed: (i) utilising page transition probabilities [25], (ii) using Metropolis-Hastings sampling [27], or (iii) other forms of prior knowledge [14].

Originally, the RDF2Vec algorithm used random walking and the Weisfeiler-Lehman paradigm to extract the corpus of walks for Word2Vec. However, within the domain of graph-based ML, walking techniques that are more advanced than random sampling have been suggested over the past few years. In addition, it has been shown that the Weisfeiler-Lehman paradigm introduces little to no extra information in the extracted walks. As such, Vandewiele et al. evaluated different walking strategies on several benchmark datasets to show that there is no one-size-fits-all strategy, and that tuning the strategy for the task at hand can result in increased performances [23].

Finally, Portisch et al. [17] applied an order-aware variant of Word2Vec to the corpus extracted by the walking and sampling strategies, which resulted in significantly increased predictive performances on multiple benchmark datasets.

3   pyRDF2Vec

In this section, we elaborate upon our pyRDF2Vec package. We first present its architecture, then give an overview of all the extensions available today and finally discuss the different mechanisms implemented to facilitate external contributions.

3.1   Architecture

In Fig. 2, an overview of the pyRDF2Vec workflow is provided. Seven main modules are used, which we now discuss subsequently.

1. **Connector**: coordinates the interaction with a local or remote graph. For KGs located on hard disk, pyRDF2Vec uses rdflib to load the graph into memory. If required, walk extraction from remote graphs is also possible

---

[2] www.rdf2vec.org.

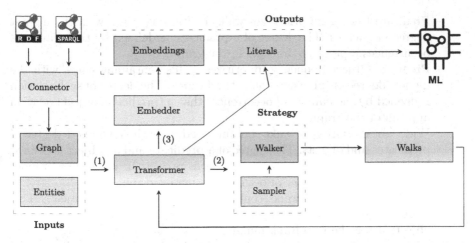

Fig. 2. Workflow of pyRDF2Vec. A Graph and collection of Entities are provided by the user to the Transformer (1), which is instantiated with a list of different strategies consisting of a Walker and Sampler (2). The latter are responsible for extracting walks from the Graph which are, in turn, fed to the embedder to calculate Embeddings (3). In addition, the Transformer also extracts Literals by following paths specified by the user.

through a SPARQL endpoint. Additional connectors can be implemented based on the provided Connector base class.

2. **Graph**: is the internal representation of the KG based on the representation of De Vries et al. [5]. It is used to efficiently traverse the graph and to store additional information regarding nodes and edges without being dependant upon other Python packages. As this representation removes the multi-relational aspect of the KG by transforming the edges to intermediate nodes, it enables pyRDF2Vec to create embeddings for predicates.

3. **Entities**: is the set of nodes within the graph for which we want to generate embeddings. These entities will serve as the starting points for the walk extraction and need to be provided by the user. It should however be noted that in fact all of the entities that appear in these extracted walks will have an associated embedding.

4. **Transformer**: the main interface for users that combines all other components.

5. **Sampler**: prioritises the use of some edges in the graph over others using a weight allocation strategy. The current pyRDF2Vec version implemented each of the sampling techniques described by Cochez et al. [4]. The currently supported sampling strategies are:
    - Uniform sampling: assigns a uniform weight to each edge.
    - Object frequency: prioritizes walks containing edges with the highest degree objects. The degree of an object is defined by the number of predicates present in its neighbourhood.

- Predicate frequency: prioritizes walks containing edges with the highest degree predicates. The degree of a predicate is defined by the number of occurrences a predicate appears in the graph.
- Predicate-Object frequency: prioritizes walks containing edges with the highest degree of (predicate, object) relations. The degree of such relation is defined by the number of occurrences that a (predicate, object) relation appears in the graph.
- Wide: gives priority to walks containing edges with the highest degree of predicates and objects. The degree of a predicate and an object is defined by the number of predicates and objects present in its neighbourhood, but also by their number of occurrences in the graph.
- PageRank: prioritizes walks containing the most frequent objects. This frequency is defined by assigning a higher weight to the most frequent objects using the PageRank ranking.

Additional sampling techniques can easily be implemented, according to the provided `Sampler` base class.

6. **Walker**: responsible for extracting walks from the KG. Different walking strategies, proposed by Vandewiele et al. [23] are incorporated in the current `pyRDF2Vec` version. The currently supported walking strategies are:
   - Random: equal probability to select a hop within our walk
   - Weisfeiler-Lehman: selecting hops based on the Weisfeiler-Lehman kernel.
   - Walklets: walks of length two containing the root node and one of the hops.
   - Anonymous: random walks but neglecting the label information
   - HALK: hierarchical random walks, removing rare hops
   - N-Gram: one-to-many mapping within walks by introducing wild cards
   - Community: provide a probability to hop to important (community) nodes within the graph.

   New walking strategies can be implemented using the `Walker` base class.

7. **Embedder**: is in charge of transforming the extracted walks into embeddings, based on a trained model. By default, Word2Vec is used within this embedder code to generate these embeddings. A fastText [9] embedder is also made available in the current `pyRDF2Vec` version and additional embedding techniques can be added by using the `Embedder` base class.

It is important to `Connector`, `Sampler`, `Walker`, and `Embedder` expose interfaces that can be implemented by users. That way, we hope to both facilitate and stimulate further research into these components of the RDF2Vec algorithm.

3.2 Optimizations and Extensions

The `pyRDF2Vec` implementation has several extensions, that speed up walk extraction and provide information in addition to the embeddings based on walks.

First, the `Transformer` takes a list of `Walker` strategies, with optionally associated `Sampler` strategies, which enables the combination of several strategies. This allows for further research into techniques similar to ensembling, where the information obtained from several strategies is combined. This combination can be done either (i) on corpus-level, by concatenating the walks extracted by the different strategies together before feeding them to the `Embedder`, (ii) on the embedding level, where embeddings are learned on the corpora of each strategy individually and then aggregated, or (iii) on prediction level, where the embeddings learned on each corpus are fed to a classifier to make predictions for the downstream task and then aggregated. The combination of different strategies is illustrated in the example code provided in Appendix A.

A second extension in the `pyRDF2Vec` allows the extraction of literal information in addition to the embeddings learned, based on the graph structure surrounding entities of interest. To achieve this, the user can specify a set of paths, starting from the nodes provided in `Entities`, for which literal information can be found. `pyRDF2Vec` will then traverse these paths and return (i) `NaN` if the literal cannot be found, (ii) a scalar in case exactly one literal can be found, and (iii) a list of literals in case the path to a literal can be found multiple times. From then on, the user can process this information and concatenate this to the provided embeddings. The usage of literal information is illustrated in the example code provided in Appendix A.

`pyRDF2Vec` enables reverse walking by traversing across incoming edges as opposed to outgoing edges. This is due to the fact that the direction of certain predicates is chosen rather arbitrarily [e.g., (`Brussels`, `isCapitalOf`, `Belgium`) vs. (`Belgium`, `hasCapital`, `Brussels`)]. This also allows for nodes from `Entities` to be in positions different from the starting position within walks.

Several mechanisms are implemented to speed up the extraction: (i) SPARQL requests to find the next hop in walks can be bundled together to reduce overhead introduced by HTTP when a remote KG is used, (ii) multi-threading is enabled to parallelize the extraction of walks, and (iii) caching is implemented to avoid redundant requests. To show the effect of these mechanisms, a benchmark evaluation on three well-known datasets from the original RDF2Vec paper was performed. In this benchmarking approach, a comparison was made between the fully optimized `pyRDF2Vec` library and a version resembling the original RDF2Vec approach. The results, for a varying amount of entities for which embeddings were created, are provided in Table 1. For large datasets, the reduction in time is more than 50%. For smaller datasets such as the MUTAG datasets, the optimized `pyRDF2Vec` package can be up to 10 times faster.

3.3 CI/CT/CD and Documentation

To facilitate contributions by the open-source community to our code repository, multiple mechanisms have been set up. First, Continuous Integration (CI), through the use of GitHub Actions[3], is implemented which makes sure that the

---

[3] https://github.com/features/actions.

Table 1. Evaluation of the SPARQL bundling, multi-threading and cache optimisations for different datasets in function of the number of entities. The time measurements are averages and their standard deviations over 10 different runs. The last column shows the relative speedup of `pyRDF2Vec` compared to the original, non-optimized, RDF2Vec implementation in Python.

Dataset	Entities	Depth	#Walks	Time (s)		Speedup
				(py)RDF2Vec	pyRDF2Vec	
MUTAG	25	4	500	74.85 ± 13.88	7.30 ± 0.34	10.25
	50			132.99 ± 24.02	14.75 ± 0.75	9.02
	100			255.83 ± 35.86	28.20 ± 1.06	9.07
AM	25	4	500	87.92 ± 17.87	9.83 ± 0.51	8.94
	50			207.97 ± 30.11	82.84 ± 4.61	2.51
	100			339.50 ± 39.52	87.68 ± 3.70	3.87
DBP:Cities	25	4	500	541.89 ± 29.63	218.43 ± 16.41	2.48
	50			1037.23 ± 84.15	401.44 ± 48.54	2.58
	100			1950.79 ± 132.02	764.23 ± 115.90	2.55

merge of the work of several developers does not impact the release of a project. With each push to one of the branches, several checks are performed, such as checking whether any styling guidelines have been violated. Second, Continuous Delivery (CD) is guaranteed as the `main` is always supposed to be the stable branch for which the checks performed by the CI pass. Added to that, the use of `poetry`[4] as dependency manager helps to facilitate future releases of `pyRDF2Vec` to the PyPI platform. Finally, a Continuous Testing (CT) mechanism executes a battery of unit tests, using `pytest`[5], for every push to the code repository. Afterwards, a coverage report is generated. With the help of these continuous methods, `pyRDF2Vec` has been able to release several new features and fix bugs to increase its stability, popularity, and notoriety.

Having an up-to-date and clear documentation is essential for the proper use of a library and its evolution. Good documentation will make it easier to use and contribute to a library. To improve the clarity of the documentation in Python, `mypy`[6], an optional static type checker, can also be used in addition to PyDoc. While Python is natively a dynamically typed language, the use of such a static type checker requires that consistent types are filled in, which improved documentation. Finally, this documentation generation is done with Sphinx[7] and is automatically updated on the online website hosted by Read the Docs, at each commit on the `main` branch.

---

[4] https://python-poetry.org/.
[5] www.pytest.org.
[6] http://mypy-lang.org/.
[7] https://www.sphinx-doc.org/.

4   Package Usage

At the time of writing, pyRDF2Vec has amassed 180 stars on Github and 24700 downloads according to PePy[8]. An overview of the number of downloads for the latest six months can be found in Fig. 3.

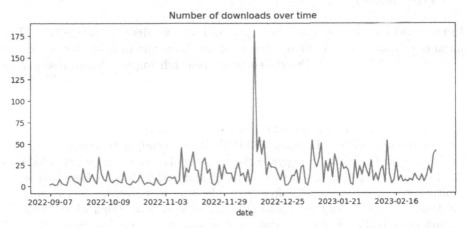

Fig. 3. The number of downloads of the last 180 days of our pyRDF2Vec package.

pyRDF2Vec has been used in several research projects and practical use cases. As of today, pyRDF2Vec appears in 40 studies published on Google Scholar[9]. We now give a brief overview of these studies. Ontowalk2vec [8] and Owl2Vec* [2] extend pyRDF2Vec to embed concepts by extracting walks from ontology information. Iana et al. [11] showed that applying reasoning to infer extra information in the KG before extracting walks results in little to no increased predictive performance. Portisch et al. [16] compared embedding techniques suited for link prediction and suited for data mining on both link prediction and data mining tasks. pyRDF2Vec was used as one of the data mining techniques during evaluation. In [12], pyRDF2Vec among many other embedding techniques, has been compared to non-embedding methods to better understand their semantic capabilities. In Sousa et al. [22] pyRDF2Vec is used to tailor aspect-oriented semantic similarity measures to fit a particular view on biological similarity or relatedness in protein-protein, protein function similarity, protein sequence similarity and phenotype-based gene similarity tasks. Engleitner et al. [7] compare pyRDF2Vec with other embedding techniques for news article tag recommendation. Shi et al. [20,21] use pyRDF2Vec to calculate semantic similarity between concepts in several datasets. Gurbuz et al. [10] evaluate many different techniques, including pyRDF2Vec, for explainable target-disease link prediction. Steenwinckel et al. [24] compare their newly proposed technique, INK, to state-of-the-art

---

[8] https://pepy.tech/project/pyRDF2Vec.
[9] https://scholar.google.com/scholar?q="pyRDF2Vec".

techniques such as pyRDF2Vec. Finally, Degraeve et al. [6] qualitatively compare embeddings produced by pyRDF2Vec with embeddings produced by their proposed RR-GCN through a t-SNE plot.

5   Discussion

In the previous sections, we showed how and why we designed pyRDF2Vec. The number of downloads or the number of stars shows the interest in the created package, but it does not directly show its research impact. Many researchers already depend upon this resource as shown in the previous section. They use embeddings in a wide research field, far beyond the scopes of the semantic web community. This is also reflected in the questions asked as GitHub issues, where the authors of this paper frequently have to explain some key concepts within our community (such as Literals, SPARQL, remote endpoints, etc.).

Besides its popularity, the pyRDF2Vec package is created to be extended and used in many application domains. The original RDF2Vec package had some limitations regarding extendability. To make sure new research ideas could be implemented based on the original RDF2Vec idea, a redesign of the Graph-Transformer-Walker-Embedder was, to our knowledge, needed. Separating all these key components in a new architecture benefits both the maintenance of this package and it resulted in the optimizations to deal with larger and more complex KGs.

6   Conclusion and Future Work

This paper presented the pyRDF2Vec software package. It reimplements the well-known RDF2Vec algorithm in Python, as this language is several significantly more popular in the data science community than Java, in which RDF2Vec was originally implemented. This reimplementation allows data scientists to integrate RDF2Vec immediately into their pipeline. Many optimisations regarding the walking algorithm were added to ensure this package can extract embeddings fast while handling large knowledge graphs. In addition to the original algorithm, pyRDF2Vec implements many extensions that have already been published, provides additional information and can handle literals. The fact that these extensions are bundled in a single place could facilitate future research. The pyRDF2Vec architecture is set up in such a way, in combination with automatic styling, testing, and documentation to foster future external contributions. Several research projects and use cases have already used pyRDF2Vec in their experimentation or as a basis for their code, which we discuss in this paper.

Resource Availability Statement: pyRDF2Vec is available under a MIT license on Github[10].

---

[10] https://github.com/IBCNServices/pyRDF2Vec.

A   Appendix: Example Usage

We now provide a simple code snippet in Listing 1 that demonstrates how a user can generate embeddings for nodes of interest in his/her KG with just a few lines of code.

Listing 1: Example usage of pyRDF2Vec

```
 1 # entities is a list of URIs which we want to embed.
 2 entities = [ ... ]
 3
 4 # Loads a KG object from hard disk, removes triples with
 5 # "dl#isMutagenic" as predicate, and specifies the paths
 6 # where literals can be found.
 7 dl = "http://dl-learner.org/carcinogenesis"
 8 kg = KG(
 9     "mutag.owl",
10     skip_predicates={dl + "#isMutagenic"},
11     literals=[
12         [
13             dl + "#hasBond",
14             dl + "#inBond",
15         ],
16         [
17             dl + "#hasAtom",
18             dl + "#charge",
19         ],
20     ]
21 )
22
23 # Create a Word2Vec embedder that trains for ten epochs.
24 embedder = Word2Vec(workers=1, epochs=10)
25
26 # Create a Sampler that uses PageRank (damping 0.85).
27 sampler = PageRankSampler(alpha=0.85)
28
29 # Use HALK strategy to extract all walks of depth 2.
30 walker1 = HALKWalker(2, None, n_jobs=4, sampler=None)
31
32 # Create walker that samples 100 walks per entity.
33 walker2 = RandomWalker(2, 100, n_jobs=4, sampler=sampler)
34
35 # Create our transformer object.
36 transformer = RDF2VecTransformer(
37     embedder,
38     walkers=[walker1, walker2]
39 )
40
41 # Extract the embeddings and literals.
42 embeddings, literals = transformer.fit_transform(kg, entities)
```

References

1. Bordes, A., Usunier, N., Garcia-Duran, A., Weston, J., Yakhnenko, O.: Translating embeddings for modeling multi-relational data. In: Advances in Neural Information Processing Systems, vol. 26 (2013)
2. Chen, J., Hu, P., Jimenez-Ruiz, E., Holter, O.M., Antonyrajah, D., Horrocks, I.: OWL2Vec*: embedding of owl ontologies. Mach. Learn. **110**(7), 1813–1845 (2021)
3. Choudhary, S., Luthra, T., Mittal, A., Singh, R.: A survey of knowledge graph embedding and their applications. arXiv preprint arXiv:2107.07842 (2021)
4. Cochez, M., Ristoski, P., Ponzetto, S.P., Paulheim, H.: Biased graph walks for RDF graph embeddings. In: Proceedings of the 7th International Conference on Web Intelligence, Mining and Semantics, pp. 1–12 (2017)
5. De Vries, G.K.D., De Rooij, S.: Substructure counting graph kernels for machine learning from RDF data. J. Web Semant. **35**, 71–84 (2015)
6. Degraeve, V., Vandewiele, G., Ongenae, F., Van Hoecke, S.: R-GCN: the R could stand for random. arXiv preprint arXiv:2203.02424 (2022)
7. Engleitner, N., Kreiner, W., Schwarz, N., Kopetzky, T., Ehrlinger, L.: Knowledge graph embeddings for news article tag recommendation. In: Joint Proceedings of the Semantics Co-located Events: Poster\&Demo Track and Workshop on Ontology-Driven Conceptual Modelling of Digital Twins co-located with Semantics 2021, Amsterdam and Online, 6–9 September 2021. CEUR-WS. org (2021)
8. Gkotse, B., Jouvelot, P., Ravotti, F.: Ontology embeddings with ontowalk2vec: an application to UI personalisation. Ph.D. thesis, MINES ParisTech-PSL Research University; CERN-Suisse (2022)
9. Grave, E., Bojanowski, P., Gupta, P., Joulin, A., Mikolov, T.: Learning word vectors for 157 languages. In: Proceedings of the International Conference on Language Resources and Evaluation (LREC 2018) (2018)
10. Gurbuz, O., et al.: Knowledge graphs for indication expansion: an explainable target-disease prediction method. Front. Genet. **13**, 814093 (2022)
11. Iana, A., Paulheim, H.: More is not always better: the negative impact of A-box materialization on RDF2Vec knowledge graph embeddings. arXiv preprint arXiv:2009.00318 (2020)
12. Jain, N., Kalo, J.-C., Balke, W.-T., Krestel, R.: Do embeddings actually capture knowledge graph semantics? In: Verborgh, R., et al. (eds.) ESWC 2021. LNCS, vol. 12731, pp. 143–159. Springer, Cham (2021). https://doi.org/10.1007/978-3-030-77385-4_9
13. Mikolov, T., Chen, K., Corrado, G., Dean, J.: Efficient estimation of word representations in vector space (2013)
14. Mukherjee, S., Oates, T., Wright, R.: Graph node embeddings using domain-aware biased random walks. arXiv preprint arXiv:1908.02947 (2019)
15. Nickel, M., Murphy, K., Tresp, V., Gabrilovich, E.: A review of relational machine learning for knowledge graphs. Proc. IEEE **104**(1), 11–33 (2015)
16. Portisch, J., Heist, N., Paulheim, H.: Knowledge graph embedding for data mining vs. knowledge graph embedding for link prediction-two sides of the same coin? Semant. Web **13**(3), 399–422 (2022)
17. Portisch, J., Paulheim, H.: Putting RDF2Vec in order. arXiv preprint arXiv:2108.05280 (2021)
18. Ristoski, P., Rosati, J., Di Noia, T., De Leone, R., Paulheim, H.: RDF2Vec: RDF graph embeddings and their applications. Semant. Web **10**(4), 721–752 (2019)

19. Schlichtkrull, M., Kipf, T.N., Bloem, P., van den Berg, R., Titov, I., Welling, M.: Modeling relational data with graph convolutional networks. In: Gangemi, A., et al. (eds.) ESWC 2018. LNCS, vol. 10843, pp. 593–607. Springer, Cham (2018). https://doi.org/10.1007/978-3-319-93417-4_38

20. Shi, Y., Cheng, G., Tran, T.K., Kharlamov, E., Shen, Y.: Efficient computation of semantically cohesive subgraphs for keyword-based knowledge graph exploration. In: Proceedings of the Web Conference 2021, pp. 1410–1421 (2021)

21. Shi, Y., Cheng, G., Tran, T.K., Tang, J., Kharlamov, E.: Keyword-based knowledge graph exploration based on quadratic group Steiner trees. In: IJCAI, vol. 2021, pp. 1555–1562 (2021)

22. Sousa, R.T., Silva, S., Pesquita, C.: Supervised semantic similarity. bioRxiv (2021)

23. Steenwinckel, B., et al.: Walk extraction strategies for node embeddings with RDF2Vec in knowledge graphs. In: Kotsis, G., et al. (eds.) DEXA 2021. CCIS, vol. 1479, pp. 70–80. Springer, Cham (2021). https://doi.org/10.1007/978-3-030-87101-7_8

24. Steenwinckel, B., Vandewiele, G., Weyns, M., Agozzino, T., Turck, F.D., Ongenae, F.: INK: knowledge graph embeddings for node classification. Data Min. Knowl. Discov. **36**, 620–667 (2022)

25. Taweel, A.A., Paulheim, H.: Towards exploiting implicit human feedback for improving RDF2Vec embeddings. arXiv preprint arXiv:2004.04423 (2020)

26. Wang, Q., Mao, Z., Wang, B., Guo, L.: Knowledge graph embedding: a survey of approaches and applications. IEEE Trans. Knowl. Data Eng. **29**(12), 2724–2743 (2017)

27. Zhang, S., Lin, X., Zhang, X.: Discovering DTI and DDI by knowledge graph with MHRW and improved neural network. In: 2021 IEEE International Conference on Bioinformatics and Biomedicine (BIBM), pp. 588–593. IEEE (2021)

Boosting Knowledge Graph Generation from Tabular Data with RML Views

Julián Arenas-Guerrero(✉)(iD), Ahmad Alobaid(iD), María Navas-Loro(iD),
María S. Pérez(iD), and Oscar Corcho(iD)

Ontology Engineering Group, Universidad Politécnica de Madrid, Madrid, Spain
{julian.arenas.guerrero,ahmad.alobaid,m.navas,
maria.s.perez,oscar.corcho}@upm.es

Abstract. A large amount of data is available in tabular form. RML
is commonly used to declare how such data can be transformed into
RDF. However, RML presents limitations that lead, in many cases, to
the need for additional preprocessing using scripting. Although some
proposed extensions (e.g., FnO or RML fields) address some of these
limitations, they are verbose, unfamiliar to most data engineers, and
implemented in systems that do not scale up when large volumes of data
need to be processed. In this work, we expand RML views to tabular
sources so as to address the limitations of this mapping language. In this
way, transformation functions, complex joins, or mixed syntax can be
defined directly in SQL queries. We present our extension of Morph-KGC
to efficiently support RML views for tabular sources. We validate our
implementation adapting R2RML test cases with views and compare
it against state-of-the-art RML+FnO systems showing that our system
is significantly more scalable. Moreover, we present specific examples
of a real use case in the public procurement domain where basic RML
mappings could not be used without additional preprocessing.
Resource type: Software framework
License: Apache 2.0
DOI: 10.5281/zenodo.7385488
URL: https://github.com/morph-kgc/morph-kgc

Keywords: Knowledge Graph · RML · CSV · Data Integration

1 Introduction

An extensive amount of data is stored as CSV, Microsoft Excel spreadsheets,
and other tabular formats such as Apache Parquet [3] or Apache ORC [2].
Many organizations are also transforming these data sources into RDF knowledge graphs [30] (KGs), given their potential to integrate, represent, and publish
heterogeneous data according to the model given by one or several ontologies.

Data transformations from tabular sources into RDF are typically defined in
a systematic manner using mapping languages [43]. These languages increase the
maintainability of the data integration pipelines and prevent the use of external scripting [13]. In addition, mappings leverage specialized data integration

© The Author(s), under exclusive license to Springer Nature Switzerland AG 2023
C. Pesquita et al. (Eds.): ESWC 2023, LNCS 13870, pp. 484–501, 2023.
https://doi.org/10.1007/978-3-031-33455-9_29

systems that come with rich functionality and are optimized for large-scale use cases.

The RDF Mapping Language [23] (RML) is a popular language [10] that extends the W3C Recommendation RDB to RDF Mapping Language [17] (R2RML) to data formats beyond relational databases (RDBs). In real-world data integration scenarios, some computations, such as transformation functions, complex joins, or extraction of embedded values, need to be applied to the input data. R2RML enables these computations by wrangling the data using SQL queries in the mappings that are executed over RDBs. However, RML does not allow this for tabular sources, which limits the capabilities of the mapping language for these common scenarios.

Although RML has already been extended with additional constructs to enable complex operations (e.g., FnO [19] and FunUL [16] for transformation functions, or RML fields [21] and mixed-syntax paths [36] for nested data), relying on SQL may ease the development of mappings by data engineers who know this query language well and are generally unfamiliar with semantic web technologies. Moreover, current implementations of these RML extensions, such as RMLMapper [38], RocketRML [39] and RMLStreamer [40], do not scale to large volumes of data [10]. This may impact the adoption of RML and its associated systems in particular, and maintainability and scalability of data integration pipelines in the broader scope.

In this work, we (i) analyze the limitations of RML and its implementations for handling tabular data, (ii) address them with RML views, (iii) extend a state-of-the-art system, Morph-KGC [8], to use SQL to define computations over the tabular sources, (iv) validate it with test cases and two benchmarks in the literature, and (v) apply our implementation to a real-world use case in the public procurement domain.

The manuscript is structured as follows. Section 2 presents an overview of RML, analyzes its limitations for tabular data, and expands RML views to tabular sources. Section 3 introduces our implementation as an extension of Morph-KGC. Section 4 validates the implementation using test cases and compares it with current alternatives. Section 5 applies our extension to a real use case in the public procurement domain. Finally, Sect. 6 presents the related work, and Sect. 7 wraps up with some conclusions and future work lines.

2 RML Tabular Views

In this section, we introduce the main limitations of RML for handling tabular data, as well as extensions that address part of them. After analyzing these limitations, we present our approach and show how it solves them relying on SQL.

2.1 RML Overview

RML is an extension of R2RML, a mapping language recommended by the W3C to generate RDF from RDBs. It generalizes R2RML to any data source.

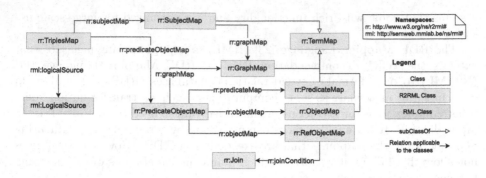

Fig. 1. RML overview (in Chowlk visual notation [24]).

Figure 1 depicts the structure of the RML mapping language, which includes `rml:LogicalSource` as an extension of R2RML's logical table.

An *RML mapping document* is an RDF document consisting of one or more *triples maps*. A triples map has one *logical source* which can be (according to the latest version of the RML specification [22]):

- A base source (any input source or a base table).
- A view (in the case of databases) given by a query.

For RDBs and tabular data sources, logical tables are iterated on a row basis to generate triples. However, for other data models such as XML or JSON, it is necessary to specify how this iteration occurs. This can be defined in RML via the property `rml:iterator`, which can be optionally accompanied by a `rml:referenceFormulation` specifying how the data is referred to, e.g., with XPath or JSONPath.

RDF terms in RML are generated through functions known as *term maps*, which describe how to generate them (using constants, references, or templates). Term maps can be subject, predicate, object, or graph maps determined by the position that the generated RDF terms take in the output RDF triples (or quads). Two triples maps can be joined with a *referencing object map*, which uses the subject map of the *parent triples map* to generate the object RDF terms.

2.2   Limitations of RML for Tabular Data Sources

As noted in the R2RML Recommendation, sometimes specific computations need to be performed over the input data, such as transformations or filtering. This can be achieved with R2RML views and the SQL query language by pushing down the computations to relational database management systems (RDBMSs). However, views in RML do not cover tabular data sources, which are restricted to RML's base source [22]. This reduces the capabilities of the mapping language and led to a number of proposals extending RML using additional constructs. In the following, we analyze the limitations of RML for tabular data along with some extensions in the literature that address them.

Transformation Functions [19]. Transformations of the data need to be defined in the mapping to handle data cleaning and computations such as reshaping, aggregating, or filtering. RML's base source uses the data source as is, without additional modifications. Projections of the source may still be computed using the references in the term maps [31] to avoid processing unnecessary data. To allow declarative transformation functions in mappings, RML has been extended with additional constructs, such as FnO [18,19] or FunUL [16].

Joins. RML is restricted regarding join operations over tabular sources. Referencing object maps join two triples maps (with their associated tabular base sources) for which join conditions can be defined using rr:Join. Some of the limitations of referencing object maps are:

- *Multiple joins.* A referencing object map involves two triples maps, consequently, RML does not support joining three or more tabular sources. To the best of our knowledge, no specific solution addressed this. A workaround to enable multiple joins is to create a relational schema for the tabular sources, load the data to an RDBMS and use an RML mapping with views to encode the joins in SQL queries. This implies increased complexity, due to the cost of defining the SQL schema, the addition of an RDBMS to the data integration pipeline, and the overhead of loading the data to it.
- *Theta joins* [32]. The class of join conditions in RML (i.e., rr:Join) only allows for equality conditions. This is shown in the R2RML Recommendation, where the *joint SQL query*[1] resulting from a referencing object map is an equijoin. However, some data integration scenarios require theta joins (or inequality joins). We are not aware of specific proposals tackling this limitation, for which the workaround described for multiple joins could be used.
- *Literal generation with joins* [20]. Referencing object maps use the subject map of parent triples maps to generate the object RDF terms of the output triples. Given that the term type of a subject map cannot be a literal (enforced by the RDF data model), it is not possible in RML to generate literals with RML's base source. Recently, Debruyne [20] has proposed an extension of RML enabling the generation of literals with joins.

Mixed Content [36]. Tabular sources in real data integration use cases usually present composite data values: values such as JSON or lists are embedded in cells. This has been referred to as *mixed content* [36]. RML does not allow for mixed content, although solutions such as *fields* [21] or *mixed-syntax paths* [36] addressed this limitation.

2.3 RML Views over Tabular Data

The approach of R2RML to solve the limitations above is R2RML views, which uses the SQL query language to push down computations to RDBMSs. It must be noted that R2RML views are different from *materialized views* [26]; the former

---

[1] https://www.w3.org/TR/r2rml/#dfn-joint-sql-query.

is an SQL query that is executed once and whose results are not persisted in the RDBMS, the latter is a table in the database resulting from the execution of a query for which refreshing policies apply (incremental, at regular time intervals, or on demand).

The RML specification [22] currently limits the scope of RML views to databases (the `rr:R2RMLView` class is not extended). The seminal work of RML [23] already devised that logical sources could be extended to support views over other data sources to allow data cleaning and transformation. However, views have not yet been considered for tabular sources.

We extend RML views to tabular data, which address the limitations of RML's base source. An RML view over tabular sources is a logical table populated with data resulting from the execution of an SQL query against the input tabular sources. It is represented by a resource with:

- One `rml:query` property (which extends R2RML's `rr:sqlQuery`), whose value is a literal with a lexical form that is a valid SELECT SQL query. The query result set cannot have duplicate column names, and projected columns resulting from an expression (e.g., aggregates) must be aliased to allow for referenciation from term maps.
- Zero or one `rml:referenceFormulation` property. Because of backwards compatibility with R2RML the property `rr:sqlVersion` can also be used. RML predefines `ql:CSV` to refer to CSV files using columns. In the case of RML views, the default is `rr:SQL2008` but others could be used[2]. This reference formulation applies to CSV and other tabular data formats such as Apache Parquet.
- Zero or one `rml:iterator` property. This is optional, since the default per-row iteration is assumed.

R2RML processors require an SQL connection[3] to access the input database. RML views over tabular sources do not need this connection, being the input sources directly referenced in the SQL query (using absolute or relative paths to the tabular files in the system or a URL for a remote file), which can be conveniently aliased. Since tabular sources are referenced as they are (in an RDBMS two tables with the same name can coexist in different databases), a default catalogue and schema are used.

3   Morph-KGC: An Extension for RML Tabular Views

Our implementation of RML views over tabular data is based on Morph-KGC [8]. This data integration system is optimized to process large volumes of data and supports the R2RML, RML, and RML-star [9] mapping languages. Due to the latter, our extension also generates graphs in the emerging RDF-star [27] data model. The system is implemented in Python and is built on top of the Pandas library [35].

---

[2] https://www.w3.org/2001/sw/wiki/RDB2RDF/SQL_Version_IRIs.
[3] https://www.w3.org/TR/r2rml/#dfn-sql-connection.

The mapping parser component was expanded to RML views. A logical source is now defined internally by two variables: a type and a value. The type can be a view, a source, or a table name, and the values are an SQL query, a path to a data file, or a table in an RDB, respectively. Additionally, the source format for a view (RDB or tabular, needed by the data loader component) is determined by the presence or lack of presence of a database connection. If the RML view is accompanied by a database connection, it is associated to the RDB format, otherwise it is associated to the tabular format.

Tabular data is ingested into Morph-KGC using Pandas for RML's base source and DuckDB [37] for RML views, for which a new connector to this state-of-the-art embedded analytical database has been implemented. The connector currently supports CSV (with any delimiter, inferred on the fly) and Apache Parquet, which are accessed locally or remotely (hosted by cloud providers). After evaluating a view, the query result set is transformed into a Pandas DataFrame, which is the internal structure used by Morph-KGC for processing data. If the logical source is related to a referencing object map or a star map, it will be further joined internally. Given the modular design of the system and the use of a source-independent internal data structure, the materialization procedure is not affected.

This extension of Morph-KGC allows pushing down some operations in the mappings, such as duplicate removal (using the DISTINCT clause), NULL elimination (IS NOT NULL statement) or joins (replacing referencing object maps) that can improve its performance. To the authors' knowledge, Morph-KGC is the first system that implements RML views over tabular data, solving the issues of RML's base source presented in Sect. 2.2, and avoiding the use of additional constructs such as RML+FnO or RML fields. The flexibility of views also enables the creation of identifiers when they are missing from tabular sources[4], and can potentially solve more limitations of base RML that may arise. The supported SQL syntax in the mapping is that of DuckDB (it can be consulted in its documentation[5]), which is derived from PostgreSQL. The main limitation of the system is the lack of user-defined functions; however, built-in SQL functions cover most data integration use cases [13] and we are already working to support them[6].

Regarding scalability, the core optimization of Morph-KGC is based on *mapping partitioning* [8]. This technique consists in creating groups of mapping rules that produce disjoint (i.e., non-overlapping) sets of triples. Each group of mappings can then be independently processed, generating a KG which is free of duplicate triples. If a parallel execution of the mapping groups is used, then the materialization time is minimized, and when they are sequentially processed, memory consumption is reduced. RML+FnO prevents good mapping partitioning (i.e., obtaining a mapping partition with a high number of groups), while our extension does not affect the partitioning. This is because to obtain a mapping

[4] https://github.com/morph-kgc/morph-kgc/discussions/102.
[5] https://duckdb.org/docs/sql/introduction.
[6] https://github.com/morph-kgc/morph-kgc/issues/117.

partition, the constant part of term maps (in `rr:constant` and `rr:template`) is used; however, for function maps it is not possible to make assumptions of constant parts of the generated RDF terms. By encoding transformation functions in RML views, we avoid the need of function maps in Morph-KGC, thus obtaining better mapping partitions and consequently, ensuring scalability.

Availability. The source code of Morph-KGC is actively maintained in a public GitHub repository[7]. The releases are archived in Zenodo [5] with their corresponding DOIs and distributed through the Python Package Index[8] (PyPi). The system is available under the Apache License 2.0 and its documentation is licensed under CC BY-SA 4.0.

Reusability. Morph-KGC is accompanied by detailed documentation hosted in Read the Docs[9]. A tutorial of the system is available on the Google Collaboration[10] platform using Python Notebooks with guide descriptions for users, and it has also been presented in tutorials. Morph-KGC is also used in semantic web courses in Universidad Politécnica de Madrid at the undergraduate and postgraduate levels and could be reused for similar courses by other universities. Furthermore, Morph-KGC is currently being used in several projects where the Ontology Engineering Group is involved, including domains such as public procurement (presented in Sect. 5) or labour (the EU project AI4LABOUR[11], where occupations and skills are linked to training courses for employees). In addition, we are also supporting large private organizations (in the insurance and manufacturing sectors[12]) in their data integration pipelines with tabular sources, and the issues in the GitHub repository show that Morph-KGC is being used by external organizations.

Design and Technical Quality. We carried out extensive evaluations validating that our RML views extension of Morph-KGC performs similar to the original system. As it will be explained in Sect. 4.1, we developed test cases for RML views and added them to the continuous integration pipeline of the system.

4   Evaluation

In this section, we present the evaluation of RML views in Morph-KGC. First, we extend the R2RML test cases using R2RML views to tabular sources and RML. Next, we compare the performance of our system with respect to state-of-the-art RML+FnO engines using GTFS-Madrid-Bench [14]. Finally, we use the LUBM4OBDA benchmark to validate that our system performs similarly to using an RDBMS populated with the tabular data. All experiments are run

---

[7] https://github.com/morph-kgc/morph-kgc.
[8] https://pypi.org/project/morph-kgc/.
[9] https://morph-kgc.readthedocs.io.
[10] https://github.com/morph-kgc/morph-kgc/tree/main/examples/tutorial.
[11] https://doi.org/10.3030/101007961.
[12] Names are not disclosed for confidentiality reasons.

using Morph-KGC v2.3.1. The evaluation was performed on an Intel® Core™ i7-1165G7 (2.80 GHz) and a memory of 40 GB RAM DDR4 (3200 MHz). All the times reported are the average time of 5 executions, and we set the timeout to 24 h.

4.1   Validation with Test Cases

The R2RML test cases [44] are a companion of the R2RML Recommendation to validate the compliance of systems with respect to the mapping language. Later, they were extended to RML [28]. However, given the lack of RML views for tabular data sources at that time, test cases with R2RML views were only considered for RDBs and excluded for the CSV data format. In order to validate the compliance of Morph-KGC, we extended these R2RML test cases to RML views. Table 1 lists them along with a description and an alternative solution using RML's base source with additional constructs. It must be noted that the test cases RMLTVTC0015a, RMLTVTC0015b and RMLTVTC0019a were included in the RML test cases for CSV [28], but the tabular files were preprocessed to enable RML's base source. Here, we maintain the original structure of the data in the R2RML test cases. We also created four additional test cases (RMLTVTC0026a, RMLTVTC0027a, RMLTVTC0028a, RMLTVTC0029a) to further validate some of the limitations described in Sect. 2.2.

Morph-KGC successfully passes all test cases, hence validating the compliance of the system with respect to RML views. Test cases are publicly available in the GitHub repository[13] and Zenodo [6]. They are used for automated and continuous testing of Morph-KGC with GitHub Actions.

4.2   Transformation Functions with GTFS-Madrid-Bench

In this experiment, we compare RML views to RML+FnO, and also evaluate the performance of the RML view extension of Morph-KGC to state-of-the-art RML+FnO systems. Materials are publicly available in Zenodo [4].

We use GTFS-Madrid-Bench, a benchmark in the transport domain which is widely used to evaluate ontology-based data integration systems. The benchmark consists of 10 CSV files and the materialized KG for scaling factor 100 contains more than 35 millions of triples. The target data model includes 9 data properties with xsd:boolean datatypes. Given that the benchmark produces 1s and 0s as boolean values, the CSV data needs to be transformed to "true" and "false" respectively to prevent the generation of *ill-typed literals*[14]. However, the mappings provided by the benchmark do not take this into account, so we extended them to address this issue using RML views and RML+FnO. Listing 1.1 shows an example mapping rule (in the human-readable YARRRML [29] syntax) for RML views, which employs two replace functions (other alternatives, such as casting to boolean, are possible). Listing 1.2 shows the same example

---

[13] https://github.com/morph-kgc/morph-kgc/tree/main/test/rmltv.
[14] https://www.w3.org/TR/r2rml/#dfn-ill-typed.

Table 1. Test cases that are not supported by RML's base source.

Test Case	Description	RML Support
RMLTVTC0002d	Concatenation of a column and a string	RML+FnO
RMLTVTC0002g	Tests the presence of an invalid SQL query	N/A
RMLTVTC0002h	Tests the presence of duplicate column names in the SELECT list of the SQL query	N/A
RMLTVTC0002i	Two columns mapping, SQL version identifier	N/A
RMLTVTC0002j	Two columns mapping, qualified column names	N/A
RMLTVTC0003b	Concatenation of two columns and a string	RML+FnO
RMLTVTC0009c	Concatenation of two columns and a string	RML+FnO
RMLTVTC0009d	Aggregation of a column	RML+FnO
RMLTVTC0011a	M to M relation, by using an SQL query	Yes (by using an additional Triples Map)
RMLTVTC0014d	Replacement of data values	RML+FnO
RMLTVTC0015a	Filtering	RML+FnO
RMLTVTC0015b	Filtering	RML+FnO
RMLTVTC0019a	Filtering	RML+FnO
RMLTVTC0026a	Embedded list in a column	RML+FnO
RMLTVTC0027a	Embedded JSON in a column	RML+Fields
RMLTVTC0028a	Generation of literals with joins	RML+ [20]
RMLTVTC0029a	Join of multiple sources	No

mapping with RML+FnO using a composite function: a condition for filtering the 1s/0s and a replace function to transform the values to true/false. As can be observed, RML+FnO results in a more verbose mapping that may impact their maintainability.

For the performance evaluation of both approaches, we compare Morph-KGC v2.3.1 to RMLMapper v6.0.0 [38] and RocketRML 2.1.0 [39]. For RMLMapper we employed predefined functions (as shown in Listing 1.2), and for RocketRML we implemented a user-defined function (since the provided function set of the system is more limited). Figure 2(a) depicts the materialization times of the systems for data scaling factors 1, 10 and 100 of GTFS-Madrid-Bench. Morph-KGC is one order of magnitude faster than RocketRML, and the difference increases even more with respect to RMLMapper. In fact, the former yields an out-of-memory error and the latter produces timeouts when materializing the KG for scaling factor 100.

Listing 1.1. RML views mapping example for GTFS-Madrid-Bench and Morph-KGC.

```
mappings:
  calendar_date_rules:
    sources:
      - query: |
          SELECT service_id, date, REPLACE(REPLACE(
              exception_type, '1', 'true'), '0', 'false') AS
              exception_type
          FROM 'data/CALENDAR_DATES.csv'
      s: \url{http://transport.linkeddata.es/madrid/metro/
        calendar_date_rule/{service_id}-{date}}
      po:
        - [gtfs:dateAddition, $(exception_type), xsd:boolean]
```

Listing 1.2. RML+FnO mapping example for GTFS-Madrid-Bench and RMLMapper.

```
mappings:
  calendar_date_rules:
    sources:
      - [data/CALENDAR_DATES.csv~csv]
      s: \url{http://transport.linkeddata.es/madrid/metro/
        calendar_date_rule/$(service_id)-$(date)}
      po:
        - predicates: gtfs:dateAddition
          objects:
            datatype: xsd:boolean
            function: grel:string_replace
            parameters:
              - [grel:valueParameter, $(exception_type)]
              - [grel:p_string_find, "1"]
              - [grel:p_string_replace, "true"]
          condition:
            function: idlab-fn:stringContainsOtherString
            parameters:
              - [idlab-fn:str, $(exception_type)]
              - [idlab-fn:otherStr, "1"]
              - [idlab-fn:delimiter, ""]
        - predicates: gtfs:dateAddition
          objects:
            datatype: xsd:boolean
            function: grel:string_replace
            parameters:
              - [grel:valueParameter, $(exception_type)]
              - [grel:p_string_find, "0"]
              - [grel:p_string_replace, "false"]
          condition:
            function: idlab-fn:stringContainsOtherString
            parameters:
              - [idlab-fn:str, $(exception_type)]
              - [idlab-fn:otherStr, "0"]
              - [idlab-fn:delimiter, ""]
```

4.3   Multiple Joins with the LUBM4OBDA Benchmark

Real data integration use cases over tabular data usually involve performing complex joins. In these cases, RML views is the only solution that does not require preprocessing, since RML's base source cannot deal with them even with extensions. The aim of this experiment is to show how our extension of Morph-KGC can handle complex joins efficiently even in the presence of large volumes of data.

To evaluate Morph-KGC in data integration scenarios with multiple joins over tabular data, we used the LUBM4OBDA benchmark[15]. LUBM4OBDA is an ontology-based data access benchmark (in the university domain) over RDBs that involves R2RML views with up to four joins in the SQL queries. Since the benchmark provides the data as SQL dumps, we exported the tables as tabular data in CSV and Apache Parquet (in a similar manner as done by GTFS-Madrid-Bench) formats. The benchmark consists of 14 tabular files, that result in an output KG of more than 150 million triples for scaling factor 1000. This data and the mappings are openly available in Zenodo [7]. We exclude RMLMapper and RocketRML from this experiment since they do not allow multiple joins. As an alternative, we considered a setup in which a relational representation of the tabular sources is created, the tabular data is loaded into an RDBMS, and mappings using standard R2RML views are used (as explained in Sect. 2.2). We just take into account the materialization times, ignoring the additional cost of creating the relational representation, and the overhead of loading the data into an RDBMS. We use PostgreSQL 15.0, MySQL 8.0.31 and data scaling factors 1, 10, 100 and 1000 of LUBM4OBDA.

Figure 2(b) shows the materialization times obtained. It is observed that Morph-KGC is faster when materializing directly from tabular sources compared to relying on RDBMSs. Differences are appreciated between RDBMSs, in particular, while PostgreSQL is not far from the materialization times obtained for tabular data, times significantly increase for MySQL when the scaling factor is large. This proves that our implementation supports multiple joins and that it is even more efficient than relying on RDBMSs.

5   A Real World Use Case in Public Procurement

Public procurement represents a relevant budget expense of many states worldwide. For example, the European Union spends around 14% of its annual gross domestic product on the purchase of services, utilities, and supplies[16]. Free access to this data facilitates accountability and transparency. Therefore, many public administrations (at the local, regional, and international levels) provide these data on their own open data portals [41].

---

[15] https://github.com/oeg-upm/lubm4obda.
[16] https://ec.europa.eu/growth/single-market/public-procurement_en.

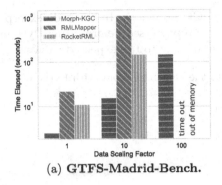
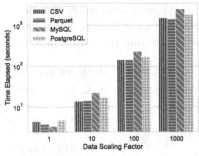

(a) **GTFS-Madrid-Bench.**   (b) **LUBM4OBDA benchmark.**

Fig. 2. Execution times for GTFS-Madrid-Bench in CSV format (Morph-KGC with RML views and RMLMapper and RocketRML with RML+FnO), and the LUBM4ODDA benchmark (Morph-KGC over different tabular formats and RDBMSs). Times are reported using a logarithmic scale.

In NextProcurement[17] we are developing an open, harmonized, and enriched public procurement data platform for Europe. In this case, the extension of Morph-KGC with RML views has been successfully used to transform Spanish public procurement data available in Apache Parquet format (mainly obtained from the national portal PLACE/PLASCP[18], together with some regional contracting platforms) into RDF according to the Open Contracting Data Standard (OCDS) ontology [41]. Prior to the use of RML views, the RDF was being generated by applying programmatic preprocessing in Python, and then using base sources in the mappings. The final public procurement service will be deployed on an external server, and the fact of directly using Morph-KGC without additional preprocessing simplifies the deployment and its maintainability.

In the following we introduce two specific situations where RML's base source is not enough to generate the output RDF, and how RML views have been used to overcome this.

5.1 Translating Spanish Codes to the Range Represented in the OCDS Ontology

Spanish public procurement procedures are usually categorized following a numeric typology[19], whose codes are defined upon the European Directive 2004/18/CE[20] and by the IDABC (Interoperable Delivery of Pan-European eGovernment Services to Public Administrations, Business and Citizens) Functional Requirements. However, these codes do not always have a direct mapping

---

[17] http://nextprocurement-project.com/.
[18] https://contrataciondelestado.es.
[19] https://contrataciondelestado.es/codice/cl/2.04/SyndicationTenderingProcessCode-2.04.gc.
[20] https://eur-lex.europa.eu/legal-content/EN/ALL/?uri=CELEX%3A32004L0018.

to the types of procedures detailed in the OCDS ontology. In the code excerpt below (Listing 1.3) it is shown how this was preprocessed before, using Python scripting to map the values in a Pandas DataFrame to the expected values.

Listing 1.3. Translating spanish codes to the OCDS ontology with Python.

```
tipos_contrato = { 1:   "goods",
                   2:   "services",
                   3:   "works",
                   21:  "services",
                   31:  "works" }
df["Tipo␣de␣Contrato"] = df["Tipo␣de␣Contrato"].map(
   tipos_contrato).fillna("other")
```

When we shifted to RML views, this mapping could be solved with the CASE statement in the SQL query (Listing 1.4). A similar solution[21] is exemplified in the R2RML Recommendation, which until now was only possible for RDBs.

Listing 1.4. Translating spanish codes to the OCDS ontology with SQL.

```
SELECT NextProcurement.*,
       CASE "Tipo␣de␣Contrato"
           WHEN 1  THEN 'goods'
           WHEN 2  THEN 'services'
           WHEN 3  THEN 'works'
           WHEN 21 THEN 'services'
           WHEN 31 THEN 'works'
           ELSE 'other'
       END AS TipoContrato
FROM 'NextProcurement.parquet' AS NextProcurement
```

5.2   Handling Embedded Lists of Lots in Procedures

Public procurement procedures may involve several tasks of different types (e.g., when a school starts operating, both the new materials and vacancies for the employees must be tendered). To facilitate organizations to apply only for the parts of the service that they are interested in, public procurement procedures are usually divided into lots. In our case, the input data associated with lots are in the form of lists embedded in the cells of an Apache Parquet file. RML views and Morph-KGC enable the processing of these lists by using unnesting, casting and splitting operations, as shown in the code excerpt below (Listing 1.5).

Listing 1.5. Processing embedded lists of lots in procedures with SQL.

```
SELECT "Número␣de␣Expediente",
   UNNEST("Lote"::DOUBLE[]) AS Lotes,
   UNNEST(
       (string_split
```

---

[21] https://www.w3.org/TR/r2rml/#example-translationtable.

```
        (replace("Número_de_Licitadores_Participantes", '
            NULL', '0')[2:-1], ',')
          ::DOUBLE[])
      ::INT[]) AS NumTenders
FROM 'NextProcurement.parquet'
```

6 Related Work

The SPARQL query language has been extended in several works, such as SPARQL-Anything [11], SPARQL-Generate [33] or Tarql [1], to generate RDF KGs from tabular data. Similarly to SQL in RML views, SPARQL functions allow for data transformation using the GENERATE clause in SPARQL-Generate and the CONSTRUCT query form in SPARQL-Anything (by overloading the SERVICE clause) and Tarql (via the FROM clause). Complex joins are enabled through nested GENERATE and CONSTRUCT clauses, but mixed content is not supported. The main difference with respect to our work is that SPARQL-based approaches use a query language over the target ontology, while RML views use a query language over the tabular sources (these approaches are known as local and global as view [34], respectively). Semantic web practitioners may prefer these alternatives, since they are familiar with SPARQL, while data engineers who are used to SQL may lean towards RML views.

García-González et al. [25] proposed using Shape Expressions [12] to map heterogeneous data to RDF. The Shape Expressions Mapping Language (ShExML) relies on a data validation language instead of a query language. ShExML is more limited regarding transformation functions, for which only matchers and string operations are supported, and filtering or mixed content is not possible. Also, limited join functionality can be achieved with shape linking and the JOIN clause.

Szekely et al. [42] proposed the T2WML language to allow layouts beyond the canonical tabular representation (one column for each variable). T2WML maps on a cell-centric basis rather than the row-centric model of RML's base source. Although T2WML allows transformation functions, it does not support joins between different tabular sources or mixed content. YAML is used to write T2WML rules, similar to YARRRML [29], a popular human-readable serialization of RML.

As already discussed during the paper, several mechanism extending RML have been proposed to increase the flexibility of the mapping language. RML has been aligned to FnO [19] and FunUL [16], which define functions in a generic and reusable way. While these approaches define functions within term maps, RML views define them directly in the logical source. RML fields introduces a nested iteration model to handle mixed-content, and the work presented in [36] proposes the concatenation of path expressions using the *mixed-syntax paths* constructs. RML+FnO and RML fields are now under the hood of the W3C Knowledge

Graph Construction Community Group[22]. Chaves-Fraga et al. [15] studied how to efficiently load tabular sources to an RDBMS, and perform SPARQL-to-SQL query translation to enable virtualization over tabular sources. This also allows complex joins similarly to RML views by delegating on the RDBMS. However it tackles virtualization, while we focus on the generation of the KG.

7   Conclusions and Future Work

This paper presents an open-source extension of Morph-KGC for KG generation from tabular data with RML views. Our implementation enables transformation functions, complex joins, and mixed content using SQL queries within RML mappings. In this way, Morph-KGC can potentially boost the adoption of RML, especially by data engineers, since they are usually more familiar with SQL than with RML extensions used so far for these purposes.

To validate the capabilities of our implementation, we extended some R2RML test cases for tabular data. We showed that our system significantly outperforms state-of-the-art RML+FnO for transformation functions and that it is the only one that allows complex joins over tabular sources. Furthermore, we demonstrated how Morph-KGC and RML views are being applied in a real use case in public procurement, replacing programmatic preprocessing.

We made publicly available (via Zenodo and GitHub) all the resources: the RML tabular views test cases, the RML+FnO mappings for GTFS-Madrid-Bench and the tabular data dumps and mappings for the LUBM4OBDA benchmark. The system is under active development and outlining its road map, we have already started working to support user-defined functions with RML+FnO and we plan to enhance its usability allowing the YARRRML human-friendly serialization of RML.

Acknowledgments. This work was funded partially by the project Knowledge Spaces: Técnicas y herramientas para la gestión de grafos de conocimientos para dar soporte a espacios de datos (Grant PID2020-118274RB-I00, funded by MCIN/AEI/ 10.13039/501100011033).

References

1. Tarql: SPARQL for Tables (2019). https://tarql.github.io/
2. Apache Software Foundation: Apache ORC. https://orc.apache.org/
3. Apache Software Foundation: Apache Parquet. https://parquet.apache.org/
4. Arenas-Guerrero, J.: Evaluation of RML tabular views with GTFS-Madrid-Bench (2022). https://doi.org/10.5281/zenodo.7389828
5. Arenas-Guerrero, J.: oeg-upm/morph-kgc (2022). https://doi.org/10.5281/zenodo.5543552
6. Arenas-Guerrero, J.: RML tabular views test cases (2022). https://doi.org/10.5281/zenodo.7389760

---

[22] https://www.w3.org/community/kg-construct/.

7. Arenas-Guerrero, J.: The LUBM4OBDA benchmark for tabular sources (2022). https://doi.org/10.5281/zenodo.7389705

8. Arenas-Guerrero, J., Chaves-Fraga, D., Toledo, J., Pérez, M.S., Corcho, O.: Morph-KGC: scalable knowledge graph materialization with mapping partitions. Semant. Web (2022). https://doi.org/10.3233/SW-223135

9. Arenas-Guerrero, J., Iglesias-Molina, A., Chaves-Fraga, D., Garijo, D., Corcho, O., Dimou, A.: Morph-KGCstar: declarative generation of RDF-star graphs from heterogeneous data. Submitted to Semantic Web (2023). https://www.semantic-web-journal.net/system/files/swj3238.pdf

10. Arenas-Guerrero, J., et al.: Knowledge Graph Construction with R2RML and RML: an ETL System-based Overview. In: Proceedings of the 2nd International Workshop on Knowledge Graph Construction, vol. 2873. CEUR Workshop Proceedings (2021). http://ceur-ws.org/Vol-2873/paper11.pdf

11. Asprino, L., Daga, E., Gangemi, A., Mulholland, P.: Knowledge graph construction with a façade: a unified method to access heterogeneous data sources on the web. ACM Trans. Internet Technol. (2022). https://doi.org/10.1145/3555312

12. Boneva, I., Labra Gayo, J.E., Prud'hommeaux, E.G.: Semantics and validation of shapes schemas for RDF. In: d'Amato, C., et al. (eds.) ISWC 2017. LNCS, vol. 10587, pp. 104–120. Springer, Cham (2017). https://doi.org/10.1007/978-3-319-68288-4_7

13. Chaves-Fraga, D., Corcho, O., Yedro, F., Moreno, R., Olías, J., De La Azuela, A.: Systematic construction of knowledge graphs for research-performing organizations. Information 13(12), 562 (2022). https://doi.org/10.3390/info13120562

14. Chaves-Fraga, D., Priyatna, F., Cimmino, A., Toledo, J., Ruckhaus, E., Corcho, O.: GTFS-Madrid-Bench: a benchmark for virtual knowledge graph access in the transport domain. J. Web Semant. 65, 100596 (2020). https://doi.org/10.1016/j.websem.2020.100596

15. Chaves-Fraga, D., Ruckhaus, E., Priyatna, F., Vidal, M.E., Corcho, O.: Enhancing virtual ontology based access over tabular data with Morph-CSV. Semant. Web 12(6), 869–902 (2021). https://doi.org/10.3233/SW-210432

16. Crotti Junior, A., Debruyne, C., Brennan, R., O'Sullivan, D.: An evaluation of uplift mapping languages. Int. J. Web Inf. Syst. 13(4), 405–424 (2017). https://doi.org/10.1108/IJWIS-04-2017-0036

17. Das, S., Sundara, S., Cyganiak, R.: R2RML: RDB to RDF mapping language. W3C Recommendation, World Wide Web Consortium (W3C) (2012). http://www.w3.org/TR/r2rml/

18. De Meester, B., Maroy, W., Dimou, A., Verborgh, R., Mannens, E.: Declarative data transformations for linked data generation: the case of DBpedia. In: Blomqvist, E., Maynard, D., Gangemi, A., Hoekstra, R., Hitzler, P., Hartig, O. (eds.) ESWC 2017. LNCS, vol. 10250, pp. 33–48. Springer, Cham (2017). https://doi.org/10.1007/978-3-319-58451-5_3

19. De Meester, B., Seymoens, T., Dimou, A., Verborgh, R.: Implementation-independent function reuse. Futur. Gener. Comput. Syst. 110, 946–959 (2020). https://doi.org/10.1016/j.future.2019.10.006

20. Debruyne, C.: Supporting relational database joins for generating literals in R2RML. In: Proceedings of the 3rd International Workshop on Knowledge Graph Construction, vol. 3141. CEUR Workshop Proceedings (2022). http://ceur-ws.org/Vol-3141/paper7.pdf

21. Delva, T., Van Assche, D., Heyvaert, P., De Meester, B., Dimou, A.: Integrating nested data into knowledge graphs with RML Fields. In: Proceedings of the

2nd International Workshop on Knowledge Graph Construction, vol. 2873. CEUR Workshop Proceedings (2021). http://ceur-ws.org/Vol-2873/paper9.pdf

22. Dimou, A., Vander Sande, M.: RDF mapping language (RML). Technical report, World Wide Web Consortium (W3C) (2022). https://rml.io/specs/rml/

23. Dimou, A., Vander Sande, M., Colpaert, P., Verborgh, R., Mannens, E., Van de Walle, R.: RML: a generic language for integrated RDF mappings of heterogeneous data. In: Proceedings of the 7th Workshop on Linked Data on the Web, vol. 1184. CEUR Workshop Proceedings (2014). http://ceur-ws.org/Vol-1184/ldow2014_paper_01.pdf

24. Feria, S.C., García-Castro, R., Poveda-Villalón, M.: Chowlk: from UML-based ontology conceptualizations to OWL. In: Groth, P., et al. (eds.) ESWC 2022. LNCS, vol. 13261, pp. 338–352. Springer, Cham (2022). https://doi.org/10.1007/978-3-031-06981-9_20

25. García-González, H., Boneva, I., Staworko, S., Labra-Gayo, J.E., Lovelle, J.M.C.: ShExML: improving the usability of heterogeneous data mapping languages for first-time users. PeerJ Comput. Sci. **6**, e318 (2020). https://doi.org/10.7717/peerj-cs.318

26. Goldstein, J., Larson, P.R.: Optimizing queries using materialized views: a practical, scalable solution. SIGMOD Rec. **30**(2), 331–342 (2001). https://doi.org/10.1145/376284.375706

27. Hartig, O.: Foundations of RDF* and SPARQL* (an alternative approach to statement-level metadata in RDF). In: Proceedings of the 11th Alberto Mendelzon International Workshop on Foundations of Data Management and the Web, vol. 1912. CEUR Workshop Proceedings (2017). http://ceur-ws.org/Vol-1912/paper12.pdf

28. Heyvaert, P., et al.: Conformance test cases for the RDF mapping language (RML). In: Villazón-Terrazas, B., Hidalgo-Delgado, Y. (eds.) KGSWC 2019. CCIS, vol. 1029, pp. 162–173. Springer, Cham (2019). https://doi.org/10.1007/978-3-030-21395-4_12

29. Heyvaert, P., De Meester, B., Dimou, A., Verborgh, R.: Declarative rules for linked data generation at your fingertips! In: Gangemi, A., et al. (eds.) ESWC 2018. LNCS, vol. 11155, pp. 213–217. Springer, Cham (2018). https://doi.org/10.1007/978-3-319-98192-5_40

30. Hogan, A., et al.: Knowledge graphs. ACM Comput. Surv. **54**(4) (2021). https://doi.org/10.1145/3447772

31. Jozashoori, S., Vidal, M.-E.: MapSDI: a scaled-up semantic data integration framework for knowledge graph creation. In: Panetto, H., Debruyne, C., Hepp, M., Lewis, D., Ardagna, C.A., Meersman, R. (eds.) OTM 2019. LNCS, vol. 11877, pp. 58–75. Springer, Cham (2019). https://doi.org/10.1007/978-3-030-33246-4_4

32. Khayyat, Z., Lucia, W., Singh, M., Ouzzani, M., Papotti, P., Quiané-Ruiz, J.-A., Tang, N., Kalnis, P.: Fast and scalable inequality joins. VLDB J. **26**(1), 125–150 (2016). https://doi.org/10.1007/s00778-016-0441-6

33. Lefrançois, M., Zimmermann, A., Bakerally, N.: A SPARQL extension for generating RDF from heterogeneous formats. In: Blomqvist, E., Maynard, D., Gangemi, A., Hoekstra, R., Hitzler, P., Hartig, O. (eds.) ESWC 2017. LNCS, vol. 10249, pp. 35–50. Springer, Cham (2017). https://doi.org/10.1007/978-3-319-58068-5_3

34. Lenzerini, M.: Data integration: a theoretical perspective. In: Proceedings of the 21st ACM SIGMOD-SIGACT-SIGART Symposium on Principles of Database Systems, PODS, pp. 233–246. Association for Computing Machinery (2002). https://doi.org/10.1145/543613.543644

35. McKinney, W.: Data structures for statistical computing in Python. In: Proceedings of the 9th Python in Science Conference, pp. 56–61 (2010). https://doi.org/10.25080/Majora-92bf1922-00a
36. Michel, F., Djimenou, L., Zucker, C.F., Montagnat, J.: Translation of relational and non-relational databases into RDF with xR2RML. In: Proceedings of the 11th International Conference on Web Information Systems and Technologies, vol. 1, pp. 443–454. SciTePress (2015). https://doi.org/10.5220/0005448304430454
37. Raasveldt, M., Mühleisen, H.: DuckDB: an embeddable analytical database. In: Proceedings of the 2019 International Conference on Management of Data, pp. 1981–1984. Association for Computing Machinery (2019). https://doi.org/10.1145/3299869.3320212
38. RMLio: RMLMapper (2022). https://github.com/RMLio/rmlmapper-java
39. Şimşek, U., Kärle, E., Fensel, D.: RocketRML - a NodeJS implementation of a use-case specific RML mapper. In: Proceedings of the 1st International Workshop on Knowledge Graph Building, vol. 2489, pp. 46–53. CEUR Workshop Proceedings (2019). http://ceur-ws.org/Vol-2489/paper5.pdf
40. Sitt Min, O., Gerald, H., Ben, D.M., Anastasia, D.: RMLStreamer-SISO: an RDF stream generator from streaming heterogeneous data. In: Sattler, U., et al. (eds.) ISWC 2022. LNCS, vol. 13489, pp. 697–713. Springer, Cham (2022). https://doi.org/10.1007/978-3-031-19433-7_40
41. Soylu, A., et al.: TheyBuyForYou platform and knowledge graph: expanding horizons in public procurement with open linked data. Semant. Web 13(2), 265–291 (2022). https://doi.org/10.3233/SW-210442
42. Szekely, P., Garijo, D., Bhatia, D., Wu, J., Yao, Y., Pujara, J.: T2WML: table to wikidata mapping language. In: Proceedings of the 10th International Conference on Knowledge Capture, pp. 267–270. Association for Computing Machinery, New York (2019). https://doi.org/10.1145/3360901.3364448
43. Van Assche, D., Delva, T., Haesendonck, G., Heyvaert, P., De Meester, B., Dimou, A.: Declarative RDF graph generation from heterogeneous (semi-)structured data: a systematic literature review. J. Web Semant. 75, 100753 (2023). https://doi.org/10.1016/j.websem.2022.100753
44. Villazón-Terrazas, B., Hausenblas, M.: R2RML and direct mapping test cases. W3C Note, World Wide Web Consortium (W3C) (2012). http://www.w3.org/TR/rdb2rdf-test-cases/

A Knowledge Graph of Contentious Terminology for Inclusive Representation of Cultural Heritage

Andrei Nesterov[1]([✉]) [iD], Laura Hollink[1] [iD], Marieke van Erp[2] [iD],
and Jacco van Ossenbruggen[3] [iD]

[1] Centrum Wiskunde & Informatica, Amsterdam, The Netherlands
{nesterov,hollink}@cwi.nl
[2] KNAW Humanities Cluster, Amsterdam, The Netherlands
marieke.van.erp@dh.huc.knaw.nl
[3] VU University Amsterdam, Amsterdam, The Netherlands
jacco.van.ossenbruggen@vu.nl

Abstract. Cultural heritage collections available as linked open data (LOD) may contain harmful stereotypes about people and cultures, for example, in outdated textual descriptions of objects. Galleries, libraries, archives, and museums (GLAM) have suggested various approaches to tackle potentially problematic content in digital collections. However, the domain expertise and discussions about words and phrases used in LOD-collections are scattered across different resources and detached from the collections themselves. In this paper, we capture domain expertise about English and Dutch contentious heritage terminology in a knowledge graph. Contentious terms in the resulting graph are then linked to entities from other LOD-resources used in the cultural domain and beyond, including Wikidata and WordNet. We make our design decisions explicit and report on the linking process. The developed knowledge graph makes expert knowledge interoperable, so it can be reused by the cultural heritage community and other LOD-developers to contribute to a more inclusive representation of cultural heritage on the Web.

Keywords: Knowledge Graph · Linked Open Data · Contentious Terms · Cultural Heritage

Resource type: Knowledge graph
License: CC BY-SA 4.0
DOI: 10.5281/zenodo.7456064
URL: https://w3id.org/culco#

Disclaimer. This paper contains derogatory words and phrases. They are provided solely as illustrations of the research results and do not reflect the opinions of the authors or their organisations. The derogatory and potentially offensive content is presented in *"quotes, boldfaced and italicised"*.

1   Introduction

Large collections of cultural objects are made available online as linked open data (LOD) on the websites of galleries, libraries, archives, and museums (or GLAM) [16,29]. Textual descriptions of objects in these collections may be originally written long time ago before digitisation. As a consequence, outdated language in digital cultural heritage may communicate historical stereotypes about people and cultures. In modern context, such stereotypes take forms of racism, ableism, homophobia, and other kinds of discrimination negatively affecting users [7,17]. Moreover, the stereotypes in LOD-collections might permeate applications built on top of such data [11,24].

The risks of problematic language are recognised by the cultural sector. GLAM have been developing approaches for more inclusive representation of objects in their collections [30]. For example, institutions provide explanations about inappropriate terminology in content warnings accompanying online collections[1] or publish general statements on their websites.[2] There is expert knowledge about problematic terminology that GLAM and other actors have produced, however, this knowledge is often detached from digital collections [18]. While object descriptions in collections are structured and often interconnected in knowledge organisation systems (KOS) used by heritage institutions, the domain expertise and discussions about problematic words in these collections exist in separate publications in different formats. To illustrate, the association Archives for Black Lives in Philadelphia published the document "Anti-racist description resources" [1], which recommends how to describe objects related to slavery, suggesting to use the terms "enslaved" or "captive" instead of *"slave"* when referring to people. At the same time, users do not see such discussions around the term's usage when they find the word *"slave"* in LOD-collections.[3]

Curators of digital cultural heritage collections and other LOD-contributors can benefit from machine-readable resources that connect expert knowledge to potentially harmful content in their data. This paper aims to incorporate GLAM professionals' domain knowledge about problematic terms into a knowledge graph to make the expert knowledge reusable and interoperable.

As a source of expert knowledge, we adopted the English and Dutch glossaries of problematic words and phrases found in museum databases. These glossaries are contained in the publication "Words Matter: An Unfinished Guide to Word Choices in the Cultural Sector" [22]. We refer to the problematic words and phrases from "Words Matter" as "contentious". The "Words Matter" glossaries give explanations on why a certain term is considered contentious and suggests how to use terms appropriately including synonyms. The consistency of the

---

[1] A content warning in the Europeana gallery "Black people in European art": https://www.europeana.eu/en/galleries/black-people-in-european-art. Accessed on 10.12.2022.

[2] The Getty Research Institute "Anti-Racist Statement": https://www.getty.edu/research/institute/antiracist_statement.html. Accessed on 10.12.2022.

[3] For example, the image entitled "slave from "[Across Africa, etc. [With a map and plates.]]"" in the Europeana collection: https://edu.nl/nttgk. Accessed on 30.11.2022.

glossaries' structure was the main motivation for selecting "Words Matter" as a knowledge source, because it enabled identifying conceptual elements of the glossaries and modelling the relationships between them as a knowledge graph.

We formulated two research questions:

- **RQ1.** How can we model expert knowledge about the usage of English and Dutch contentious terms in the cultural heritage domain?
- **RQ2.** How can contentious terms from the developed knowledge graph be linked to other LOD-resources?

For RQ1, we elicited knowledge from the "Words Matter" glossaries. First, we examined the structure and content of the glossaries in two languages to define their conceptual elements. Second, we verified our conceptualisation conducting structured and unstructured interviews with the experts involved in the glossaries production. Third, we populated the knowledge graph with the original content of the glossaries based on the conceptualisation and interviews.

To answer RQ2, we selected two groups of resources to link them to the developed knowledge graph. The first group includes controlled vocabularies used in the cultural domain: Thesaurus Wereldculturen (NMVW) of the Dutch National Museum of World Cultures[4] that produced "Words Matter" and the Getty Art & Architecture Thesaurus,[5] which is used by many institutions. The second group consists of commonly used LOD-resources: Wikidata[6] and Princeton WordNet 3.1.[7]. In each of the selected resources, we manually found entities that are the most relevant to the contentious terms in our knowledge graph, which we call "related matches". We linked both English and Dutch contentious terms to Wikidata and Getty AAT, only English terms to Princeton WordNet and only Dutch terms to the NMVW-thesaurus.

The main contribution of this paper is a knowledge graph representing domain expertise about English and Dutch contentious terminology used in cultural heritage. The contentious terms are linked to related entities from four LOD-resources frequently used in the cultural heritage sector and beyond. We report on our modelling choices and explain the process of identifying related matches of contentious terms in other LOD-resources. Having expert knowledge in machine readable format would facilitate the development of (semi-)automatic approaches to tackle potentially problematic terminology in LOD-collections making them more inclusive for users.

---

[4] Thesaurus Wereldculturen: https://collectie.wereldculturen.nl/thesaurus. Accessed on 10.12.2022.

[5] Getty Vocabularies: https://www.getty.edu/research/tools/vocabularies. Accessed on 10.12.2022.

[6] Wikidata: https://www.wikidata.org/wiki/Wikidata:Main_Page. Accessed on 10.12.2022.

[7] Princeton University "About WordNet": https://wordnet.princeton.edu/ Princeton University. 2010. Accessed on 09.12.2022.

2   Related Work

Approaches to Contentious Terminology in the Cultural Sector.
GLAM practitioners and researchers have formulated various approaches to
tackle problematic terminology in heritage collections to make them more inclusive for users. Two groups of such approaches are especially relevant to our work.
First, there are approaches directed at exposing controversies. They include
marking offensive terms in objects metadata with special symbols (brackets and
quotes), displaying content warnings, and providing appropriate synonyms next
to offensive terms [6,7,32]. The second group is related to contextualisation:
enriching offensive terms with additional information about why they are used to
describe objects, who used them and during which historical periods [10,14,17].

The knowledge graph we developed aims at connecting contentious terms
to their alternatives and explanations from experts. It relates to both making
contentious terms visible in LOD and their contextualisation.

Modelling Problematic Language in LOD. Datasets of problematic language are used in various areas of computer science, one of them being hate-
speech detection in social media in the field of natural language processing.
Hurtlex is a multilingual lexicon with several categories of offensive terms, including "negative stereotypes" [2], the category closely related to contentious terms in
our knowledge graph. Although Hurtlex is not available as linked open data, the
terms are given identifiers and mapped to their equivalents in other languages.
Apart from lexicons, there are ontologies developed to formalise offensive language for its detection. These ontologies are based on categorisations of offensive
terms drawn from corpus analysis [20] and conceptualisation of definitions and
theories of hate speech [3].

Another direction to systematise offensive terms for their auto-detection is
developing extensions to existing LOD-resources. The Open Multilingual Wordnet (OMW)[8] is enriched with Japanese offensive terms taken from several lexicons [4]. The researchers, who proposed this enrichment, analysed how offensive
terms can be categorised looking at Princeton WordNet. They also manually
mapped offensive terms to synsets in OMW. In another research project, Princeton WordNet synsets are linked to the terms scraped from social media, including the "vulgar" terms, based on manual annotations [21]. This is similar to our
approach of matching contentious terms to synsets in Princeton WordNet.

One LOD-resource that contains such categories of terms as "slurs" and "historical" is "Homosaurus", a controlled vocabulary of LGBTQ+ terms.[9] Besides
this categorisation, the vocabulary contains textual explanations of offensiveness
(literal values of the property *"rdfs:comment"*). A use-case with "Homosaurus"

---

[8] Global WordNet Association on GitHub: https://github.com/globalwordnet/OMW.
Accessed on 18.12.2022.

[9] Homosaurus.   An   international   LGBTQ+   linked   data   vocabulary: https://
homosaurus.org. Accessed on 18.12.2022.

illustrated how additional information about terms' usage can contextualise discriminatory terms in Library of Congress Subject Headings (LCSH)[10] and move to the terminology accepted by the community [15].

There are three key differences between the knowledge graph we developed and existing lists and LOD-vocabularies of offensive terms. First, our knowledge graph is based on cultural heritage domain expertise containing suggestions and alternatives for contentious terms in English and Dutch. In our modelling process, we do not categorise offensive terms ourselves, but preserve the experts' judgments. Second, our modelling allows to mark terms as contentious depending on context. Third, contentious terms are linked to four LOD-resources used both in the cultural sector and on the Semantic Web in general. These links are helpful in gathering more background information about the terms.

The development of a knowledge graph in this paper extends our previous work, in which we constructed a crowdsource-annotated corpus of contentious terms in contexts taken from historical newspapers [5]. The corpus was used for machine-learning based detection of contentiousness. The combination of this corpus and the knowledge graph can be used to improve the detection of contentious terms in heritage collections.

3 Eliciting Knowledge About Contentious Terms

A selection of common contentious terms in the cultural heritage domain is described in the publication "Words Matter: an unfinished guide to word choices in the cultural section". It is freely available online as a PDF-file on the website of the Dutch National Museum of World Cultures.[11] The publication's goal is to provide guidance on word use to cultural heritage professionals, so that their choices of describing heritage objects "are more conscious and informed" [22]. "Words Matter" provides glossaries of contentious terms in English and Dutch, which we took as a source of expert knowledge.

We elicited knowledge about contentious terms in two steps applying direct and indirect knowledge elicitation techniques described in [8,31]. First, we analysed the structure of the "Words Matter" glossaries and identified their conceptual elements. These conceptual elements served as building blocks of the knowledge graph schema. Second, we conducted structured and unstructured interviews with experts, who took part in producing the publication.

3.1 Identifying Conceptual Elements in "Words Matter"

Contentious and Suggested Terms. The "Words Matter" glossaries include terms "that are sensitive to particular groups, that can cause offense, that elide important context, and that are understood as derogatory" [22]. We refer to such

---

[10] Library of Congress. Controlled Vocabularies: https://www.loc.gov/librarians/controlled-vocabularies/. Accessed on 10.12.2022.
[11] "Words Matter - Publication": https://www.tropenmuseum.nl/en/about-tropenmuseum/words-matter-publication. Accessed on 02.12.2022.

terms as "contentious". "Suggested terms" are the words and phrases mentioned in "Words Matter" that serve as alternatives to contentious terms.

The nature of the contentious terms in "Words Matter" is heterogeneous, although most of them refer to (historically) marginalised people and cultures of the Dutch colonial period. Some of the terms are archaisms (*"Bombay"* as the former name of the city Mumbai in India), others have sensitive connotations only in specific contexts (for example, the term *"primitive"* when referring to peoples, cultures, styles and art). Many terms in the list may be defined as "one-sided terms" from the framing bias perspective [26] (for example, referring to the Dutch-Indonesian war as *"police actions"*). All terms from the glossaries can be seen as "sensitive lexical items" from the lexicographic perspective [19]. Many terms in the glossaries appear as contentious only in particular senses and contexts, because one term can have several meanings (polysemy) or share the same spelling with a term that have a different meaning (homonymy).

The Structure of the Glossaries' Entries. A single entry of the glossary has three main parts: a title which is a contentious word or a phrase, a textual part below it entitled "History, use, and possible sensitivities" (which we call a description), and the section "Suggestions". We present conceptual elements of the "Words Matter" glossaries on Fig. 1.

Apart from the title, contentious terms also appear in descriptions. For example, the entry *"Aboriginal"* mentions other terms that are marked as "controversial": *"Indian"*, *"Inuit"*, and *"Métis"*. In some of these cases, entries reference other entries with the text "see also". The section "Suggestions" has individual suggestions in a bulleted list, which include various content:

- A general suggestion that can be applicable to several entries (for example, "The term is appropriate when used respectfully");
- A word or a phrase that can be used instead of a contentious term ("Asian" for the term *"Oriental"*);
- A synonym that can be used only in some contexts and does not fully replace a contentious term (for example, the term "Moroccan-Dutch" is one of the possible alternatives for the term *"Allochtoon"*);
- An example of how a contentious term or its synonym can be used appropriately in speech; usually, it is a phrase providing additional context in which it is appropriate to use the mentioned terms, for example, the phrase "There was an artistic movement called 'primitivism'" for the term *"Primitive"*; this kind of usage examples are italicised in the publication.

Differences Between the English and Dutch Glossaries. Most of the entries in the "Words Matter" glossaries were originally written in Dutch and then translated into English. The Dutch and English versions contain 56 and 55 entries, respectively. In the English glossary, five entries have Dutch titles: *"Blank"* (meaning "white"), *"Inboorling"* ("native"), *"Indisch"* (refers to the former Dutch East Indies), *"Jappenkampen"* ("Japanese concentration

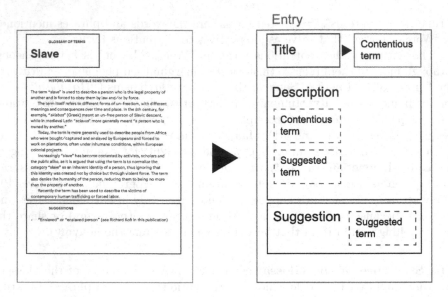

Fig. 1. The conceptualisation of the "Words Matter" glossary entries. A page from the glossary is on the left, and its conceptual elements are on the right. The dashed line shows that contentious and suggested terms are optional in the description text and suggestions.

camps"), and *"Politionele actie"* ("police action"), however, their descriptions and suggestions are in English. As the experts explained to us, these terms are kept in Dutch, because they would lose their meaning and context after translation. For the same reason, the entries *"Inlander"* ("native") and *"Islamiet"* ("Muslim") are not translated into English and are unique to the Dutch glossary. In the English version, the entry *"Native"* is not a translation of *"Inlander"*, it has unique description text and suggestions. These differences were important in our decision to separate the English and Dutch entries while populating the knowledge graph (Sect. 4.3).

3.2   Interviews with Domain Experts

We verified our work with two experts from the Dutch National Museum of World Cultures, who were involved in the creation of "Words Matter". We held a meeting with the experts conducting both structured and unstructured interviews. During the unstructured interview, we presented our preliminary work to the experts and discussed the identified conceptual elements as well as the modeling choices we made while creating the knowledge graph (see Sect. 4.2 for modeling choices). The structured interview consisted of detailed questions about difficult cases, which arose when populating the knowledge graph with the glossary entries (Sect. 4.3). After the consultation, we refined the schema and content of the knowledge graph. The meeting notes and the experts' responses are documented and published in the resource repository.[12]

3.3 Motivation to Select "Words Matter"

Other cultural heritage institutions and communities also bring awareness to problematic language used in heritage collections. Results of such initiatives are published in different forms such as blog posts,[13] policy documents, as the aforementioned "Anti-racist description resources". The website "The Cataloging Lab" lists 57 organisations that published statements about offensive language in various forms.[14] On this website, users can suggest potentially problematic terminology from Library of Congress Subject Headings (LCSH).[15] A similar possibility to users is offered by Triangle Research Libraries Network (TRLN).[16] This organisation has also made available a list of the subject headings remappings: 216 pairs of problematic and suggested words and phrases.[17]

An example from the Dutch context is a report of the Cultural Heritage Agency of the Netherlands about "traces of slavery" in art collections [25], which contain list of terms used to search records about slavery. It is stated in the report that some of the search terms are derogatory and offensive, although it is not specified which terms were considered as such and by whom.

Compared to other resources, "Words Matter" provides more comprehensive information about contentious terms. It includes English and Dutch glossaries of contentious terms often found in museum databases not limiting the scope to a specific topic (such as "slavery"). There is background information about contentious terms and suggestions on their usage in a modern context. These glossaries have a consistent structure with relationships between contentious terms and suggestions. This motivated our selection of "Words Matter" as a source of expert knowledge to develop the first version of a knowledge graph of contentious terminology, but in future work, others can be added.

---

[12] Interviews with domain experts. Meeting notes: https://github.com/cultural-ai/wordsmatter/raw/main/Meeting_Notes_12Oct2021.pdf.

[13] "California State University Libraries to change the display of the subject heading 'Illegal Aliens' in joint public catalog": https://libraries.calstate.edu/csu-libraries-change-subject-heading-illegal-aliens/. Accessed on 02.12.2022.

[14] "List of Statements on Bias in Library and Archives Description": http://cataloginglab.org/list-of-statements-on-bias-in-library-and-archives-description/. Accessed on 02.12.2022.

[15] "Problem LCSH": https://cataloginglab.org/problem-lcsh/. Accessed on 02.12.2022.

[16] "TRLN Discovery Subject Remapping": https://trln.org/resources/subject-remapping/. Accessed on 02.12.2022.

[17] The GitHub repository "marc-to-argot" of Triangle Research Libraries Network: https://edu.nl/kbaxv. Accessed on 02.12.2022.

4   Developing a Knowledge Graph of Contentious Terms

The conceptual elements identified in the "Words Matter" glossaries were transformed into classes and properties following the principles we formulated. This section explains the modelling decisions and population of the knowledge graph.

4.1   Modelling Principles

Before converting the glossaries into a knowledge graph, we set three principles to guide the modelling process: (1) preserving the integrity of the original publication, (2) reusing existing LOD vocabularies when possible, and (3) allowing extension and reuse of the developed knowledge graph and its schema in other cases not limited to "Words Matter".

The first principle stems from the fact that the "Words Matter" publication represents domain expert knowledge generated by a team of cultural heritage professionals and researchers, and any modification of the publication structure and content might influence the integrity of this knowledge. We held interviews with the experts to ensure that the first principle is respected. The second and third principles represent best practices of ontology development in the Semantic Web community [23]. The third principle enables reusing the knowledge graph in future work.

4.2   Modelling Choices: Classes and Properties

We present the knowledge graph schema in Fig 2. Following our second modelling principle, we searched for existing properties and classes in the W3C Data recommendations[18] and the "Linked Open Vocabularies" register.[19]

It is important to differentiate between a (SKOS) concept or (Wiki) entity (for example, a Wikidata item Q12773225 with the label *"slave"*[20]) versus a discussion *about* the term (e.g. a discussion about *"Slave"* being a contentious issue). To avoid confusion, we introduced a new class *ContentiousIssue* for the latter, instead of reusing, for example, *skos:Concept*. In "Words Matter", a term can be contentious while serving as a suggestion for another contentious term. To model this and other discussions about terms, we assigned each term an URI using the "SKOS eXtension for Labels" schema (SKOS-XL).[21] We modelled contentious and suggested terms as instances of the *skosxl:Label* class with its *skosxl:literalForm* taken from "Words Matter" text as is.

---

[18] W3C "All standards and Drafts": https://www.w3.org/TR/?tag=data& status=REC. Accessed on 05.12.2022.

[19] Linked Open Vocabularies (LOV): https://lov.linkeddata.es/dataset/lov/. Accessed on 05.12.2022.

[20] Wikidata entity "slave" (Q12773225): https://www.wikidata.org/wiki/Q12773225. Accessed on 06.12.2022.

[21] SKOS Simple Knowledge Organization System eXtension for Labels (SKOS-XL) Namespace Document - HTML Variant: https://www.w3.org/TR/skos-reference/ skos-xl.html. Accessed on 06.12.2022.

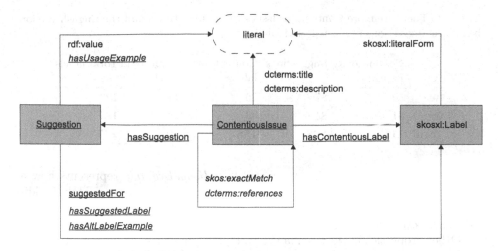

Fig. 2. The knowledge graph schema with custom classes and properties underlined. The italicized properties are optional.

To differentiate between contentious terms as a concept (*skosxl:Label*) and as a name of the glossary entry, we used the *dcterms:title* property from the DCMI Metadata Terms.[22] So, each glossary entry has a title as a literal value and the contentious term it describes as an URI.

The instances of the *Suggestion* class represent individual suggestions that are given as separate bullet points of the section "Suggestions". There is at least one suggestion item in every entry of the glossary. In several entries, suggestions have similar meanings but are phrased differently. For example, the suggestion "Use terms that people find respectful and acceptable for others to call them" (for the term *"Colored"*) is similar to "Adopt the terminology used and accepted as respectful by the people themselves" (for the term *"Aboriginal"*). We decided to count these suggestions as equivalents, giving them the same textual value. It allows inferring which contentious terms share similar suggestions. We preserved the original suggestions in a separate file.[23]

We modelled the relationships between the classes *ContentiousIssue* and *Suggestion* with the property *hasSuggestion*. *ContentiousIssue* is connected to *skosxl:Label* with another custom property *hasContentiousLabel*. For example, *ContentiousIssue* entitled *"Slave"* has contentious label with the literal form *"Slave@en"*, and there is one suggestion for this contentious issue with two suggested labels (*hasSuggestedLabel*) "Enslaved@en" and "enslaved person@en".

Individual suggestions may have different content, modelled by different properties. If an instance of *Suggestion* has a concrete term or a phrase to be used instead, it has the property *hasSuggestedLabel*. Another property *hasAlt-LabelExample* indicates that a suggestion gives a suggested contextual synonym

---

[22] DCMI Metadata Terms: https://www.dublincore.org/specifications/dublin-core/dcmi-terms/. Accessed on 06.12.2022.
[23] https://edu.nl/t7n7v.

Table 1. There are more Contentious Issues with Dutch titles, and the English version has more Suggestions and Suggested labels.

	Contentious Issues	Suggestions	Contentious labels	Suggested labels	Total labels
@en	50	87	75	48	123
@nl	61	81	83	41	124
Total	**111**	**168**	**158**	**89**	**247**

for a contentious term, while the value of *hasUsageExample* represents how a contentious or suggested term might be used in speech appropriately. Additionally, we explicitly stated for every *Suggestion* for which contentious label (*skosxl:Label*) it is a suggestion by using *suggestedFor*.

Other properties in the schema were adopted from existing vocabularies. The value of the *dcterms:description* property from DCMI Metadata Terms is the text from the "History, use, and possible sensitivities" section, which describes the glossary entry. Although this section gives extensive information about the usage of contentious terms, their cultural contexts, and etymology, we kept it as a literal value. Breaking down this textual information into semantically related parts requires more complex modelling. We model implicit "see also" references in the description text as explicit *dcterms:references* between Contentious Issues. The textual content of each *Suggestion* is a literal value of the property *rdf:value*. In total, we have introduced three custom classes and six custom properties.

4.3   Populating the Knowledge Graph

The knowledge graph schema was manually populated with the original content from the "Words Matter" glossaries in English and Dutch. Terms (*skosxl:Label*), the entries they appear in (*ContentiousIssue*), and suggestions (*Suggestion*) were given URIs. We decided to use meaningless URIs to avoid offensive URIs containing more meaningful terms. Textual content has been tagged "@en" or "@nl" where appropriate.

Because of the differences between the English and Dutch glossaries (see Sect. 3.1), we gave the entries of the two versions separate identifiers. In cases when the entities in both languages were equivalent (if translated), we connected them with the property *skos:exactMatch*.[24] For example, the contentious issue *"Slaaf"* is a *skos:exactMatch* of its English equivalent *"Slave"* with a different URI. The number of instances of the populated knowledge graph in two languages is given in Table 1.

Competency Questions. We formulated competency questions to ensure that the knowledge graph follows the structure of the original glossaries. The competency questions check the relationships between the English and Dutch versions

---

[24] SKOS Simple Knowledge Organization System Reference: https://www.w3.org/TR/skos-reference/#L4858 Accessed on 06.12.2022.

of the glossaries and their parts, such as entries, suggestions, and terms. For example, we checked with a SPARQL-query which contentious terms had suggested terms. There are 10 competency questions, answers to which serve as evaluation of the developed knowledge graph. The questions and the SPARQL-queries we used to answer them are available in the resource documentation.[25]

Availability and Reuse. The knowledge graph schema is available at https:// w3id.org/culco#. We documented it following the FAIR practices [12,13]. The glossary itself can be downloaded in Turtle format at https://w3id.org/culco/ wordsmatter/. The developed resource is published on GitHub[26] and registered on Zenodo.[27]

5 Linking Contentious Terms to LOD-Resources

The resulting knowledge graph has URIs of contentious labels, which we link to four LOD-resources. This section explains the linking process based on the guidelines we set and gives an overview of the obtained links.

5.1 Selecting LOD-Resources

We link contentious terms from the knowledge graph to other LOD-resources for two reasons: 1) it enriches contentious terms with related concepts, in literal values of which they are used, and 2) it connects the found occurrences of contentious terms in external LOD-resources to their suggested labels and explanations from experts in the knowledge graph. We selected four LOD-resources to be linked to contentious labels in the knowledge graph: controlled vocabularies used by cultural heritage institutions (Wereldculturen Thesaurus (NMVW) and Getty AAT) and commonly used LOD-resources (Wikidata and Princeton WordNet 3.1). In every resource, we searched for a related match (the term derives from the property in the SKOS-vocabulary *skos:relatedMatch*) of every contentious label. A related match is a concept that uses a contentious term in its labels, and the meaning of the term is the closest to the meaning in "Words Matter". In the case of Princeton WordNet, it is a synset with a contentious term as a lemma. Table 2 lists the LOD-resources selected for linking, their properties used for labelling, and the number of the found related matches.

Wikidata is one of the largest knowledge graphs on the Web with a variety of application areas, including cultural heritage [16,27]. Princeton WordNet can provide lexical information about contentious terms, including their synonyms, definitions, and examples. Getty AAT serves as a reference resource to many cultural heritage institutions [9]. Having related matches of contentious labels in Getty AAT can be helpful in finding links to more cultural heritage datasets.

Table 2. SKOS is used in Wikidata and NMVW for labeling entities. In Wikidata, there are two other equivalent properties for a preferred label. Getty AAT adopts SKOS-XL. Princeton WordNet uses OntoLex vocabulary for written representation of lemmas.

Resource	Properties for labelling	Language	# related matches
Wikidata	skos:prefLabel (rdfs:label, schema:name); skos:altLabel	EN	61
		NL	70
Princeton WordNet 3.1	ontolex:writtenRep	EN	56
Getty AAT	xl:prefLabel/xl:literalForm; xl:altLabel/xl:literalForm	EN	42
		NL	27
NMVW	skos:prefLabel; skos:altLabel	NL	19

The NMVW-thesaurus is used by the Dutch National Museum of World Cultures that published "Words Matter". We link contentious terms in our graph based on knowledge of experts from this museum to the actual thesaurus that is used to represent its collection.

5.2 Identifying Related Matches

Querying LOD-Resources. We linked contentious terms to external entities in the selected LOD-resources at the level of the *Label* class. For linking, we took only labels that are in the object position of a triple $<ContentiousIssue\ hasContentiousLabel\ Label>$. It means that these labels are marked as contentious in the glossary entry. In total, there are 75 English and 83 Dutch contentious labels.

The literal values of the contentious labels are mostly in a singular form. To find contentious labels in other resources that occur in plural or comparative (for adjectives) forms and other variations (spelling differences), we collected word forms for every contentious label using external datasets. Word forms for English terms were obtained from DBnary using their API [28]. For Dutch terms, we used a HTTP-request service provided by INT, the Dutch Language Institute.[28] After the manual inspection of the extracted word forms in both languages, we observed that word forms for some labels were still missing. We added more word forms for 18 labels. As a results of this step, every contentious label was given a list of word forms, which resulted in 154 English and 242 Dutch query tokens. This is expected as Dutch is a morphologically richer language than English.

To find entities that have contentious terms in their literal values, we searched every token in the selected LOD-resources. In Wikidata and Getty AAT, we searched both English and Dutch tokens. Princeton WordNet 3.1 (PWN) were

---

[28] Dutch Language Institute. GiGaNT: https://ivdnt.org/corpora-lexica/gigant/. Accessed on 18.12.2022.

searched for English tokens. NMVW is only available in Dutch, so we searched for Dutch tokens in this thesaurus.

Guidelines to Select Related Matches. For most of the query tokens, there was a large number of query results in the resources. For example, the term "black" has more than 134,000 hits in Wikidata. As our goal was to select only related matches, we performed this selection manually. To be consistent during selection, we formulated the following guidelines:

1. A query token of a contentious term is used in literal values of the corresponding properties of the resources (see the column "Properties for labelling" in Table 2);
2. The found token should be used in a similar meaning to the meaning it has in the associated "Words Matter" glossary entry;
3. If multiple entities are found, we pick one entity which is the closest in meaning and scope to what is intended in the "Words Matter" entry. An exception is made for PWN.

In some cases in PWN, it was not possible to differentiate the meanings of the found related synsets, so we allowed more than one related match. This resulted in 24 English contentious labels having more than one related synset in PWN.

The literal values of the resources, in which a query token was found, were taken into account to judge the meaning of a token (guideline 2). For example, apart from preferred and alternative labels (aliases) in Wikidata, we also looked at "Description".

To ensure high-quality of the related matches selection, two authors of the paper, of whom one is a native Dutch speaker, performed this step independently. The disagreements and mismatches were resolved during a discussion between the authors.

Linking Results. We obtained 275 related matches from four LOD-resources, 159 of which are for English labels, 116 are for Dutch labels. Almost half (131) of these related matches come from Wikidata (Table 2 provides the number of matches per resource). 142 out of all 158 contentious labels in English and Dutch were linked to at least one of the selected LOD-resources. 29 out of 75 English and 10 out of 83 Dutch contentious labels have related matches in all the corresponding resources. In the knowledge graph, contentious labels are linked to the URIs of their related matches with the property *skos:relatedMatch*.

Looking at the occurrences of contentious labels in the literal values of the related matches, we found that 46 English and 50 Dutch contentious labels from our knowledge graph are used as preferred labels of the related Wikidata items. 23 English and 25 Dutch (out of 27 found) contentious labels are used as preferred labels of the related concepts in Getty AAT. Dutch contentious labels in NMVW were used as preferred labels in 7 out of 19 found concepts.

To illustrate the found related matches, we give an example of the label with the literal value *"Slave@en"*. It has three related matches from Getty

AAT,[29] Wikidata,[30] and PWN (one synset).[31] In the related concept of Getty AAT, the term is used 4 times in alternative labels. The preferred label of this concept is "enslaved people", which is similar to the suggestion for this term in our knowledge graph ("enslaved person"). On the contrary, in Wikidata, the related item uses the contentious term as preferred label, which aliases are "enslaved person" and "enslaved". PWN does not give any synonyms of the term in the related synset. None of the resources contain any information about the term's contentiousness and its potentially inappropriate usage.

6   Conclusions and Future Work

We constructed a knowledge graph representing English and Dutch contentious terminology often used in museum object descriptions. The resource is based on domain expert knowledge elicited from the publication "Words Matter" [22]. The publication's consistent structure enabled identifying its conceptual elements that constituted the knowledge graph schema. Two domain experts verified our modelling choices and decisions regarding the knowledge graph population.

In total, there are 75 English and 83 Dutch terms in the knowledge graph that are potentially contentious depending on context. These terms are linked to explanations of their usage, suggestions, and alternatives given by experts. Additionally, we linked contentious terms to other LOD-resources used in the cultural sector and beyond: Wikidata, Princeton WordNet, Getty AAT, and the NMVW thesaurus. The resulting resource has been made openly available with a CC BY-SA 4.0 license following FAIR practices. In future work, the knowledge graph can be used to develop applications that highlight and contextualise offensive and outdated terms in cultural heritage objects' descriptions, making their representation more inclusive for users.

The publication, on which the knowledge graph is based, originates from one organisation presenting a viewpoint of the European cultural context. Since 2017, when the publication was produced, new discussions about contentious terms have emerged. When using the knowledge graph, its limitations, such as time and scope, should be acknowledged and included, along with other sources, in future updates of the knowledge graph.

We observed that contentious terms in the literal values of the LOD-resources studied in this paper often appear without information about their potential sensitivities. In future work, our knowledge graph can be used for further research into how contentious and suggested terms are used in other LOD resources. A large-scale inspection of such cases could identify problematic aspects of using culturally-sensitive language on the Semantic Web.

Acknowledgements. This work is a part of the "Culturally Aware AI" project funded by NWO (Dutch Research Council). We thank the Dutch National Museum of World

---

[29] http://vocab.getty.edu/aat/300230899. Accessed on 18.12.2022.
[30] https://www.wikidata.org/wiki/Q12773225. Accessed on 18.12.2022.
[31] http://wordnet-rdf.princeton.edu/id/10628841-n. Accessed on 18.12.2022.

Cultures for collaboration and personally Cindy Zalm, Marijke Kunst, Marjolijn van Beelen, and Richard van Alphen. Thanks to Antoine Isaac (Europeana Foundation) for giving recommendations at the first stages of the knowledge graph modelling.

References

1. Antracoli A.A., et al.: Archives for black lives in Philadelphia: anti-racist description resources (2020). https://github.com/a4blip/A4BLiP
2. Bassignana, E., Basile, V., Patti, V.: Hurtlex: a multilingual lexicon of words to hurt. In: Cabrio, E., Mazzei, A., Tamburini, F. (eds.) Proceedings of the Fifth Italian Conference on Computational Linguistics (CLiC-it 2018). CEUR Workshop Proceedings, vol. 2253. CEUR (2018). https://ceur-ws.org/Vol-2253/#paper49
3. Battistelli, D., Bruneau, C., Dragos, V.: Building a formal model for hate detection in French corpora. Procedia Comput. Sci. **176**, 2358–2365 (2020). https://doi.org/10.1016/j.procs.2020.09.299. Knowledge-Based and Intelligent Information & Engineering Systems: Proceedings of the 24th International Conference KES2020
4. Bond, F., Choo, M.Y.H.: Taboo wordnet. In: Proceedings of the 11th Global Wordnet Conference, pp. 36–43. Global Wordnet Association, University of South Africa (UNISA) (2021). https://aclanthology.org/2021.gwc-1.5
5. Brate, R., Nesterov, A., Vogelmann, V., van Ossenbruggen, J., Hollink, L., van Erp, M.: Capturing contentiousness: constructing the contentious terms in context corpus. In: Proceedings of the 11th on Knowledge Capture Conference, K-CAP 2021, pp. 17–24. Association for Computing Machinery, New York (2021). https://doi.org/10.1145/3460210.3493553
6. Brown, L., Gutierrez, C., Okmin, J., McCullough, S.: Desegregating conversations about race and identity in culturally specific museums. J. Museum Educ. **42**(2), 120–131 (2017). https://doi.org/10.1080/10598650.2017.1303602
7. Chilcott, A.: Towards protocols for describing racially offensive language in UK public archives. Arch. Sci. **19**(4), 359–376 (2019). https://doi.org/10.1007/s10502-019-09314-y
8. Cooke, N.J.: Varieties of knowledge elicitation techniques. Int. J. Hum.-Comput. Stud. Int. J. Man-Mach. Stud. (1994). https://doi.org/10.1006/ijhc.1994.1083
9. Díaz-Corona, D., Lacasta, J., Latre, M.Á., Zarazaga-Soria, F.J., Nogueras-Iso, J.: Profiling of knowledge organisation systems for the annotation of linked data cultural resources. Inf. Syst. **84**, 17–28 (2019). https://doi.org/10.1016/j.is.2019.04.008
10. Dodd, J., Sandell, R., Delin, A., Gay, J.: Arts and humanities research board: buried in the footnotes: the representation of disabled people in museum and gallery collections. Technical report, Leicester, RCMG (2004). https://leicester.figshare.com/articles/report/Buried_in_the_footnotes_the_representation_of_disabled_people_in_museum_and_gallery_collections/10077098
11. van Erp, M., de Boer, V.: A polyvocal and contextualised semantic web. In: Verborgh, R., et al. (eds.) ESWC 2021. LNCS, vol. 12731, pp. 506–512. Springer, Cham (2021). https://doi.org/10.1007/978-3-030-77385-4_30
12. Garijo, D.: WIDOCO: a wizard for documenting ontologies. In: d'Amato, C., et al. (eds.) ISWC 2017. LNCS, vol. 10588, pp. 94–102. Springer, Cham (2017). https://doi.org/10.1007/978-3-319-68204-4_9
13. Garijo, D., Poveda-Villalón, M.: Best Practices for Implementing FAIR Vocabularies and Ontologies on the Web, vol. 49, pp. 39–54. IOS Press (2020). https://doi.org/10.3233/SSW200034

14. Guiliano, J., Heitman, C.: Difficult heritage and the complexities of indigenous data. J. Cult. Anal. **4**(1) (2019). https://doi.org/10.22148/16.044
15. Hardesty, J., Nolan, A.: Mitigating bias in metadata. Inf. Technol. Libr. **40**(3) (2021). https://doi.org/10.6017/ital.v40i3.13053
16. Hawkins, A.: Archives, linked data and the digital humanities: increasing access to digitised and born-digital archives via the semantic web. Arch. Sci. **22**(3), 319–344 (2022). https://doi.org/10.1007/s10502-021-09381-0
17. Holterhoff, K.: From disclaimer to critique: race and the digital image archivist. Digit. Humanit. Q. **011**(3) (2017). http://www.digitalhumanities.org/dhq/vol/11/3/000324/000324.html
18. Kahn, R., Simon, R.: Feast and famine: the problem of sources for linked data creation. In: Andrews, T., Diehr, F., Efer, T., Kuczera, A., Zundert, J.V. (eds.) Graph Technologies in the Humanities - Proceedings 2020. CEUR Workshop Proceedings, vol. 3110, p. 86. CEUR (2020). http://ceur-ws.org/Vol-3110/#paper5
19. Lazić, D., Mihaljević, A.: Stereotypes and taboo words in dictionaries from a diachronic and a synchronic perspective - the case study of Croatian and Croatian Church Slavonic. In: Proceedings of XIX EURALEX Congress: Lexicography for Inclusion, vol. II, no. 2, pp. 643–653 (2021). https://www.euralex.org/elx_proceedings/Euralex2020-2021/EURALEX2020-2021_Vol2-p643-653.pdf
20. Lewandowska-Tomaszczyk, B., Žitnik, S., Bączkowska, A., Liebeskind, C., Mitrović, J., Oleskeviciene, G.V.: LOD-connected offensive language ontology and tagset enrichment. In: Carvalho, S., et al. (eds.) Proceedings of the Workshops and Tutorials held at LDK 2021. CEUR Workshop Proceedings, vol. 3064, pp. 135–150. CEUR (2021). https://ceur-ws.org/Vol-3064/#salld-03
21. McCrae, J.P., Wood, I., Hicks, A.: The colloquial wordnet: extending princeton wordnet with neologisms. In: Gracia, J., Bond, F., McCrae, J.P., Buitelaar, P., Chiarcos, C., Hellmann, S. (eds.) LDK 2017. LNCS (LNAI), vol. 10318, pp. 194–202. Springer, Cham (2017). https://doi.org/10.1007/978-3-319-59888-8_17
22. Modest, W., Lelijveld, R.: Words matter: an unfinished guide to word choices in the cultural sector (2018). https://www.tropenmuseum.nl/en/about-tropenmuseum/words-matter-publication
23. Noy, N., Mcguinness, D.: Ontology development 101: a guide to creating your first ontology. Knowl. Syst. Lab. **32** (2001). https://protege.stanford.edu/publications/ontology_development/ontology101.pdf
24. Ortolja-Baird, A., Nyhan, J.: Encoding the haunting of an object catalogue: on the potential of digital technologies to perpetuate or subvert the silence and bias of the early-modern archive. Digit. Scholarsh. Humanit. **37**(3), 844–867 (2021). https://doi.org/10.1093/llc/fqab065
25. Ras, G., Gootjes, E., Pennock, H., Vermaat, S.: Handreiking 'Onderzoek naar sporen van slavernij en het koloniale verleden in de collectieregistratie' (2021). https://www.cultureelerfgoed.nl/publicaties/publicaties/2021/01/01/handreiking-onderzoek-naar-sporen-van-slavernij-en-het-koloniale-verleden-in-de-collectieregistratie
26. Recasens, M., Danescu-Niculescu-Mizil, C., Jurafsky, D.: Linguistic models for analyzing and detecting biased language. In: Proceedings of the 51st Annual Meeting of the Association for Computational Linguistics (Volume 1: Long Papers), pp. 1650–1659. Association for Computational Linguistics, Sofia (2013). https://aclanthology.org/P13-1162
27. Rossenova, L., Duchesne, P., Blümel, I.: Wikidata and Wikibase as complementary research data management services for cultural heritage data. In: Kaffee, L.A.,

Razniewski, S., Amaral, G., Alghamdi, K.S. (eds.) Proceedings of the 3rd Wikidata Workshop 2022. CEUR Workshop Proceedings, vol. 3262. CEUR (2022). https://ceur-ws.org/Vol-3262/#paper15

28. Sérasset, G.: DBnary: wiktionary as a Lemon-based multilingual lexical resource in RDF. Semant. Web **6**(4), 355–361 (2015). https://doi.org/10.3233/SW-140147

29. Simou, N., Chortaras, A., Stamou, G., Kollias, S.: Enriching and publishing cultural heritage as linked open data. In: Ioannides, M., Magnenat-Thalmann, N., Papagiannakis, G. (eds.) Mixed Reality and Gamification for Cultural Heritage, pp. 201–223. Springer, Cham (2017). https://doi.org/10.1007/978-3-319-49607-8_7

30. Sinn, D.H.: Archival description and records from historically marginalized cultures: a view from a postmodern window. J. Korean Soc. Libr. Inf. Sci. **44**(4), 115–130 (2010). https://doi.org/10.4275/KSLIS.2010.44.4.115

31. Vásquez-Bravo, D.-M., Sánchez-Segura, M.-I., Medina-Domínguez, F., Amescua, A.: Guideline to select knowledge elicitation techniques. In: Lytras, M.D., Ruan, D., Tennyson, R.D., Ordonez De Pablos, P., García Peñalvo, F.J., Rusu, L. (eds.) WSKS 2011. CCIS, vol. 278, pp. 374–384. Springer, Heidelberg (2013). https://doi.org/10.1007/978-3-642-35879-1_45

32. Wright, K.: Archival interventions and the language we use. Arch. Sci. **19**(4), 331–348 (2019). https://doi.org/10.1007/s10502-019-09306-y

LegalHTML: A Representation Language for Legal Acts

Armando Stellato(✉) ⓘ and Manuel Fiorelli ⓘ

Department of Enterprise Engineering, University of Rome Tor Vergata, Via del Politecnico 1, 00133 Rome, Italy
{stellato,manuel.fiorelli}@uniroma2.it

Abstract. The Publications Office (OP) of European Union (EU) expressed the need to simplify the Official Journal production workflow, which required different formats and, consequently, document instances at different stages of the process. We met this need by developing LegalHTML, which unifies the formal, structural and semantic representation of legal acts, as well allowing for diverse typographic requirements for publication. This streamlines the production workflow and publication/fruition of content as well, since a single document instance is first drafted and then incrementally enriched. LegalHTML consists of an extension of HTML for the structural representation of legal acts (e.g., articles, paragraphs, items, and references), while a supplementary ontology enables the annotation (using RDFa) of domain references (e.g., signatories, people and their role in organizations, the scope of the document). LegalHTML also supports the consolidation of an act and its subsequent changes into a single document using a tree-based representation. Finally, we implemented a CSS stylesheet for the default rendering of the model and a JavaScript file imbuing documents with an API that supports TOC generation, footnote cross-references and point-in-time visualization of legal acts.

Keywords: legal document · consolidation · metadata · HTML · Semantic Web

Resource type: HTML extension for the legal domain and support ontology
License: European Union Public License 1.2 (EUPL-1.2)
  Linked Open Vocabularies (LOV): https://w3id.org/legalhtml/
DOI: https://doi.org/10.5281/zenodo.7454918
URL: https://w3id.org/legalhtml/

1 Introduction

With the large improvements in all aspects of information representation, management and content storage, a new generation of repositories for legal content, with documents rich in metadata, annotations, and cross-references, emerged.

Concrete actions such as the European Directive on open data and the re-use of public sector information [1], also known as the Open Data Directive, and initiatives such as Open Gov [2], have encouraged and possibly pushed institutions, governments, and any sort of actor in the public administration on publishing and sharing their data according to open standards and best practices.

With such scenario occurring and evolving at a fast pace, it is important to share and adopt solutions supporting the representation of legal content and of its jurisdictional existence and lifecycle (e.g., when a regulation is published, enters into force, etc..), facilitating all aspects of content production, publication and fruition.

In 2021, we conducted a study, funded by the Publications Office (OP) of the European Union (EU), exploring the possibility of an efficient solution for the publication of legal acts, streamlining an overly complex publication workflow that included several steps, including drafting, proof-reading, finalization and production of several manifestations scoped to different objectives, such as official journal publication, semantic indexing, dissemination, etc.

With the intent of covering the aforementioned objectives through a single solution, we have realized an HTML-based language for representing legal content, dubbed LegalHTML, featuring all structural aspects of an act, such as articles, paragraphs, items, references, supporting a semantically-rich representation of all such elements and references to entities of the legal domain. Furthermore, LegalHTML addresses consolidation of an act and its subsequent modifications into a single document using an efficient tree-based model. Finally, we imbued the document model with API supporting rendering and point-in-time visualization of legal acts. Metadata, consolidation information and other relevant information are represented by a dedicated ontology. In fact, other ontologies and controlled vocabularies can be combined to ground LegalHTML in different legal traditions (i.e., different ways to represent laws in different countries), without violating the integrity and generality of the language. The outcome of the study has been recently accepted and scheduled for adoption by the Publications Office.

2 Related Work

We can identify two classes of works that are relevant to our contribution, either bound by the domain (the legal domain) or the similarity of the approach (extending HTML).

For what concerns the first class, several initiatives for legal document publishing eventually developed XML formats for the representation of legal acts; these initiatives originated from individual countries or from international efforts seeking at accommodating different jurisdictions and legal traditions [3].

CEN MetaLex [4] has been designed in the context of *CEN Workshop on an Open XML Interchange Format for Legal and Legislative Resources (MetaLex)*, while the name comes from a substantially different model developed in a previous effort focused on Dutch legislation [5]. CEN MetaLex facilitates legal information exchange among software applications, by establishing a least common denominator between different jurisdiction-specific standards and vendor-specific formats. Interestingly, this standard foresees the translation of documents to RDF using a dedicated ontology, and the possibility of external RDF assertions on parts of the document each identified by a URI.

Substantial efforts toward a legal representation standard were pursued on both sides of the Atlantic Ocean, through the foundation of Legal XML [6] in 1998 and LEXML [7] in 2000, in the USA and Europe, respectively. While Legal XML pursued the agreement on a single schema per document type, the diversity of jurisdictions in Europe drove LEXML toward a bottom-up approach with different communities developing their own schemas, in the hope that eventually there would be a limited set of schemas to make the establishment of mappings feasible. With this regard, a Legal RDF Dictionary, being developed in a concerted effort between the two initiatives, would be key to integration of different schemas [8]. This effort was inspired by John McClure's ideas on Legal-RDF [9], utilizing an ontology to represent the structure and meaning of legal documents through inline annotations of XHTML documents.

Akoma Ntoso (Architecture for Knowledge Oriented Management of African Normative Texts using Open Standards and Ontologies) [10, 11], often shortened as AKN, is an international standard for the technological representation of judicial, legislative, and parliamentary documents. AKN was created by the initiative of the "Africa i-Parliament Action Plan", which is a program of the UNDESA (United Nations Department of Economic and Social Affairs). The project aims to achieve transparency, open access, exchange, and ultimately the maximum democratization of legal information produced by parliaments, courts, and government institutions. Past its original conception AKN has further development by the aforementioned Legal XML as an OASIS [12] standard, called OASIS LegalDocumentML, meant to offer specifications for a standard of legal documents of parliamentary, legislative and judicial origin. Akoma Ntoso addresses interoperability concerns including document identification, structure, and semantics. Akoma Ntoso was designed as an XML application, discarding alternatives such as HTML which – specifically – was considered weak on structural constraints, and geared much more towards presentation than structure and semantics. Having partnered with the Library of Congress in a data challenge aiming at the conversion of national legislation schemas to Akoma Ntoso, the United Kingdom National Archives not only adopted that standard but also developed an HTML serialization of Akoma Ntoso [13]. Nonetheless, these are just derivate formats, which are generated from their own XML format, the Crown Legislation Markup Language (CLML).

FORMEX (Formalized Exchange of Electronic Publications) [14] is the standard used by the Publications Office of the EU to exchange data with service providers. Introduced in 1985 as an SGML application defined by a DTD, the fourth revision of the standard became an XML application defined by an XML Schema. FORMEX captures the structure of documents published in the Official Journal of the EU.

A complement to legal document formats is represented by metadata vocabularies for legal acts: the European Legislation Identifier (ELI) is a European effort at harmonizing the way legislation is published. ELI's ontology is based on three pillars [15]:

1. every piece of legislation is identified by an HTTP URI;
2. the same metadata elements are used across the different jurisdictions;
3. metadata is shared in a machine-readable form, reusing the ELI Ontology.

The implementation level of ELI varies (only a core part of ELI is shared among various jurisdictions and indeed each EU country coined its own specialization of the ELI ontology for metadata representation of documents).

A more recent effort combining document formats and ontologies is represented by Lynx [16, 17]. In Lynx, a knowledge graph for the legal domain (Legal Knowledge

Graph, LKG) has been generated and made available for semantic processing, analysis, and enrichment of documents from the legal domain. As the objectives of Lynx did not require the complexity provided by document models such as Akoma Ntoso, they realized a simpler document model based on annotations taken after an ad-hoc ontology, the Legal Knowledge Graph Ontology.

A further, orthogonal, exploration on the semantics dimension of legal acts is given by LegalRuleML [18], an OASIS standard for writing legal rules in a machine-readable format. It extends RuleML with features specific to legal norms, such as defeasibility, deontic operators, negation and temporality. Developed by (part of) the same authors of Akoma Ntoso and thought to complement its representational aspects with reasoning and deontics, LegalRuleML can in fact be adopted in other legal document models.

Moving to other solutions sharing with LegalHTML the approach (extending HTML) rather than the domain, dokieli [19] is a browser-based platform that uses several web standards to enable decentralized authoring, publication, and annotation of documents. The "default UI" of a document in dokieli is a single-page application within the document itself: the necessary JavaScript files are to be linked from the document itself or injected (in any web document) by a dedicated browser extension. Not tied to a specific kind of documents, dokieli suggests combining HTML and RDFa to fully capture the (more specific) document semantics. The dokieli UI allows users to dynamically switch between different stylesheets (e.g., to support different presentation options). Dokieli supports the whole life cycle of a document, as it also covers discussing an already published document. This aspect is of relevance to scientific publication, enabling a more transparent and continuous scrutiny of publications by the scientific community than it is possible with current reviewing approaches. Dokieli is built on a separation between the application logic and the underlying storage, embracing the SOLID [20] platform to "true data ownership" with *personal data storages*.

RASH [21] is a framework for scholarly publishing using a subset of HTML consisting only of 32 elements. RASH leverages semantic elements introduced in HTML5 such as *figure*, *caption*, *section* to represent the components of scholarly publications. A publication can also embed RDF annotations. The framework also includes a schema for the defined subset of HTML using the RELAX NG [22] language.

Originally thought for authoring W3 specifications, ReSpec [23] simplifies writing technical documentation in HTML. Similarly to what has been already discussed about dokieli, a ReSpec document must include the JavaScript file implementing the browser-based support logic and follow certain convention about its content. Unlike dokieli, ReSpec does not implement actual editing of documents, observing that any HTML editor is sufficient. Indeed, the support logic is mostly concerned with generating a live-preview of the document, identifying errors and – most importantly – implementing cross references within the document and across specifications. Actually, ReSpec is not meant to be included in the final published documents, as it offers a few options to export the specification being authored to (X)HTML, EPUB 3 or PDF. ReSpec borrows from software development the idea to store documents on source code hosting sites, such as GitHub [24], Bitbucket [25] and GitLab [26], which support version control, issue management and distributed authoring through pull requests. Indeed, a ReSpec document should include references to these three services, thus fostering feedback and contributions from the wider audience.

3 Motivation

Most attempts at achieving machine-readable and shareable legal texts have resulted in the definition of XML schemas. These attempts also took advantage of the possibility – offered by XML – to combine different schemas for different needs, such as reuse and extensibility. Reused XML applications included (X)HTML for tables and complex formatting, MathML for math, ChemML for chemistry and ATOM for metadata.

However, as a (meta)markup language, XML is in fact representing data for the purpose of information exchange rather than viewable documents that can be consumed by end users. Although XML documents could be associated with CSS stylesheets and XSL transformations for visualization, these technologies are not generally adopted, and initiatives related to legal XML schemas usually assume to generate parallel, distinct versions of the documents for visualization (resorting to common standards, such as HTML). Akoma Ntoso, just to name a notable example, differentiates on purpose semantics and structure from presentation, providing support for structural and semantic markup with the aim to "move digital documents from the presentation to the semantic era" [27]. Along this line of thought, a blog post [28] on the popular akomantoso.io site provides rationale for the choice of XML in Akoma Ntoso as the driving channel for representing legal documents. In particular, HTML was regarded as a simple format designed to primarily support presentation, lacking in support for print publication and semantic service access. In the perspective of the author, HTML has limited support for representing structure (which is also defective in not being imposed strictly), and total lack of support for semantics related to legislation.

We argue that these claims related to HTML are no longer valid because of a general shift of this standard to semantic markup, focusing on the purpose and role of the marked-up content rather than its appearance, this latter depending on a combination of the associated stylesheets and of the user agent visualization preferences [29]. Indeed, simply selecting a different stylesheet can completely alter the presentation (i.e., rendering) of the same document (as discussed about dokieli in Sect. 2). Concerning the lack of support for print publication, it is clear that HTML has all the necessary tools (i.e. CSS) for describing how a document should be represented when printed. About the lack of semantics, the current HTML Living standard features several mechanisms for representing semantics and for extending the language [30], so that a specific language for the legal domain could indeed be developed. HTML as-is is not thought for legal documents, as much as XML as-is is not, it is indeed not even a language, it's a syntax. Finally, concerning the few structural rules and the non-strict application of the existing ones, we observe similar phenomena in both Akoma Ntoso and, on a lesser extent, in FORMEX as well. Akoma Ntoso has different admitted structures because of the respect for "different traditions" which does not make its validation mechanism a strict one. Conversely, HTML has its own validation mechanism that is based on general requirements for documents, not for legal documents. For certain aspects, it is even too strict. The main complication in choosing HTML for the representation of a(ny) specific kind of document is indeed that it might be difficult to embed certain structures given the already existing restrictions of HTML. The opposite phenomenon (too loose validation) described in the blog is indeed not a problem: in the economy of defining a new standard by extending HTML, the creation of an ad-hoc validator is not an issue, it is indeed part of the outcome.

Furthermore, there are two serializations of HTML: traditional HTML and XHTML. The latter is based on XML, enabling the use of validating schemas and the combination of several schemas that address different concerns. While the web usually relies on transport-level security concerning the transmission of HTML documents, an XHTML document could be digitally signed using XAdES [31].

Given the above considerations, we argue that a document format like (X)HTML is not only adequate, but it should indeed be used – being it the standard for representation of documents on the web – unless strong incompatibility is found. Accordingly, we have extended HTML, producing an explicit domain language, featuring all structural aspects of an act, as in Akoma Ntoso or FORMEX, with a neat structure and rich semantics. Our goal is indeed to improve the quality of representation in terms of efficiency and standard compliancy, streamlining the publication workflow by unifying different aspects and phases, such as drafting, semantics and dissemination, into a single format binding them all. Finally, we provided API for the specification oriented at rendering the documents and offering point-in-time visualization of legal acts.

4 Approach

LegalHTML is an extension of HTML that enables a simple and semantically explicit representation of legal acts. Given the current stance of HTML towards the semantics of content rather than its presentation, our aim first required us to focus on the semantics of a legal act. As such, we defined three semantic layers that address different concerns:

- document semantics, which is all about the document (i.e., the legal act) itself, further divided into:

  - global information: document metadata
  - structure: document organization

- external domain knowledge (i.e., non-document classes in Akoma Ntoso).

Table 1 lists the extension mechanisms of HTML against the semantic layers just mentioned. All the Ys represent the mechanisms that could definitely fit the description of a given semantic layer, of which bold ones represent those that we concretely selected for our specification. "N"-valued cells represent solutions not matching the considered layer whereas "P"-valued ones represent mechanisms that may possibly be used but are not convenient – for a matter of clarity or conciseness – for the scope (e.g., refer to the later discussion on RDFa to represent the structure of a legal act).

LegalHTML primarily uses script-embedded RDF (specifically, in Turtle syntax) to represent stand-off metadata describing the document and its editorial/jurisdictional lifecycle. RDFa is used, instead, when metadata is naturally reflected in the act content, as in case of the signatures, which must appear at the end of the act. LegalHTML also uses RDFa to represent external knowledge, again exemplified by signatures, where there is a need to annotate the *people* that sign on behalf of some *organization* playing a given *role*. For these purposes, we introduced a supplementary LegalHTML ontology, which – in most cases – has to be used in conjunction with other ontologies and controlled vocabularies. These are needed to express semantic concepts that are specific to a particular legal tradition and therefore cannot be included in the general LegalHTML model. Describing the use of the model for the European legislation, the examples in this paper often make use of the ELI ontology and authority tables managed by the Publications Office of the European Union.

Table 1. Matching extension mechanisms found in HTML to our semantic layers. Bold faced Y indicates that the corresponding row has been adopted to support the corresponding column

	Structure	Metadata	External knowledge
custom elements	**Y**	Y	N
data- attribute	**Y**	Y	Y
class attribute	Y	Y	Y
reuse of semantic elements	**Y**	Y	Y
embedded web annotations	N	P	N
microformats	Y	Y	Y
HTML **rel** attribute	**Y**	Y	Y
RDFa	P	**Y**	Y
microdata	P	Y	Y
script-embedded RDF	N	**Y**	Y
<meta> element	N	**Y**	N

For representing the structure of a legal act, LegalHTML commits on mixing existing HTML elements, when applicable, to new custom elements. As there are two types of custom elements, we defined the following policy for their adoption in legal HTML:

- *customized built-in elements* (`<div is="lh-citation">...</div>`) are used to represent the structural elements of a legal act, by inheriting the semantics of an existing HTML element;
- *autonomous custom elements* (`<lh-version id="art_2">...</lh-version>`), not inheriting from existing HTML elements, are used for control code (e.g., for consolidation), which is in any case beyond the semantics defined by HTML.

The problem with customized built-in elements is that defining a new element, say *lh-citation*, we must choose the one and only one HTML element it inherits from. Compound with the strict constraints associated with some HTML elements, this led to the adoption of somewhat generic elements such as `div` and `span`, as more specific elements might not fit all usages of the customized elements. Customized built-in elements must be used with *data-* attributes, as they cannot introduce new attributes.

LegalHTML borrows from previous standards, including Akoma Ntoso, the idea to avoid generated text, i.e., any visible content should be traceable back to source text. LegalHTML cannot thus rely on automatic numbering of articles, items, and so on.

We discarded RDFa and Microdata to describe the structure of a legal document, as both are not really about the document but about mentions of external entities, and their adoption might require the introduction of additional div and span elements, which is not tolerable to describe the structure of a document. The *class* attribute should be used to hold *semantic classes*, which in turn are used as anchors by styling rules. However, in practice it is used for all sorts of *classes*, including ones that are solely geared towards presentation concerns. Given the pollution of the value space of this attribute, we discarded it in LegalHTML in favor of custom elements. In fact, CSS classes can be used within a LegalHTML, when it is necessary to fine tune the semantics and the presentation of a legal document. The semantics of LegalHTML includes the "behavior" of the representation elements. Benefiting from the ability of HTML user agents (e.g., the browsers) to execute JavaScript code, we complemented LegalHTML with a programming API, making compliant documents "active" (as detailed in Sect. 8).

Overall, the combination of HTML, its extensions, RDFa, and script+embedded-RDF offers separated "channels" for structure, semantics and presentation, and yet provides a single locus for them all, streamlining production and publication workflows.

5 Evolution and Maturity

LegalHTML evolved across two efforts. A first study proved feasibility of the realization of a language based on HTML for representing the structure and semantics of legal acts. The study also produced a first draft specification and a few sample documents transformed from other existing formats adopted within the Publications Office (OP). Besides the draft specifications, the study did not produce a formal public deliverable, rather a series of presentations reporting on challenges, issues, solutions, etc.. The study was followed by a second stage, aimed at finalizing the specifications and ensuring coverage and soundness of the solution. The latter objective was achieved through the development of a systematic mapping for CoV (Common Vocabulary) [32], an internal standard at the Publications Office reflecting "interinstitutional agreement on business level regarding the semantic concepts that represent the text of exchanged documents". As a further contribution, we validated LegalHTML by converting all the 47 documents that are used as examples in the CoV specifications.

Both study and finalization were supported by legal experts on our side, interviews with staff (several groups with different competencies and duties) from the OP concerning all aspects and steps of the production and publication workflow, and finally various steps of feedback provided by legal document experts from the OP. At the time of writing, these documents are on imminent publication. Additionally, these docs offered a plethora of different use cases and document types (https://w3id.org/legalhtml/specs/#eu-legal-document-types) considered to be sufficient by the OP. These efforts culminated in a final decision to adopt the model for the representation of legal acts on the EUR-Lex portal, equaling a TRL (Technology Readiness Level) of 8.

6 The LegalHTML Document Model

We report the main aspects of the LegalHTML document model, referring to the online specifications for a complete description, which would not fit into this article.

6.1 Overall Document Structure

The overall structure of a document is determined by customized `section` elements, such as `lh-preamble`, `lh-title`, `lh-enacting-terms`, etc. Conversely, we reused the `article` element for the basic unit of the normative content.

6.2 Paragraphs and Items

An *article* is articulated into one or more *paragraphs*, possibly associated with an explicit numeration. The obvious equation of such paragraphs to `p` elements in not possible, as HTML constraints these elements to only contain phrasing content (i.e. text and inline markup), whereas legal paragraphs can be in fact the root of a complex structure, including lists, nested paragraphs, etc.

Consequently, we had introduced a customized `div` element called `lh-paragraph` to surround an entire paragraph. Consecutive unnumbered paragraphs are represented as more elements of this kind in a row. Conversely, for numbered paragraphs we defined a customized `ol` element as in the following example.

```
<ol is="lh-paragraphs">
  <li>
    <span is="lh-number" data-value="1">1.</span>
    <div is="lh-paragraph">
      <p>The specific control and inspection [...]</p>
      <ol is="lh-points">
        <li>
          <span is="lh-number" data-value="a">(a)</span>
          <div is="lh-point">fishing [...]</div>
        </li>
        [...]
      </ol>
    </div>
  </li>
  [...]
</ol>
```

Adhering to the approach (also found in Akoma Ntoso) to avoid generated content, the paragraph number is made explicit as an `lh-number` paired to an `lh-paragraph` by putting both inside a `li` element. The paragraph in the example contains in a turn a list of items indexed by lowercase Latin letters, which have been modeled in an analogous manner. The first `p` element inside the paragraph corresponds to the introductory phrase of the subsequent list.

6.3 Semantic Annotation

While custom elements are great for representing the structure of a legal act, domain references and, to a certain extent, metadata are best captured as semantic annotations using RDFa. The key insight is the introduction of an ontology providing a core vocabulary to represent such annotations (see (Fig. 2), the values of which are taken from external resources, decoupling LegalHTML from the terminology and procedure of any jurisdiction, including that of the European Union, which guided its development.

In the following example, we annotate the *acting entity* that adopted an act (in this cases, two entities: the European Parliament and the Council of the European Union), thanks to the *corporate body* [33] authority table from the Publications Office.

```
<span rel="lh:actingEntity" resource="corpbody:EP">THE EUROPEAN
PARLIAMENT</span> AND <span rel="lh:actingEntity" re-
source="corpbody:EURCOU">THE COUNCIL OF THE EUROPEAN
UNION</span>
</div>
```

In the following example, we annotate the direct applicability of an EU regulation to all member states, denoted by `corpbody:EUMS` by the *corporate body* authority.

```
<section is="lh-direct-applicability">
  <p rel="lh:applicability" resource="corpbody:EUMS">This Regu-
lation shall be binding in its entirety and directly applicable
in all Member States.</p>
</section>
```

A legal act contains an explicit section for the *concluding formulas*, which hosts the place and date it was approved and who signed it. However, details like the actual date and place, and the identity of who signed for a certain organization with a given role are instead annotated using RDFa accommodating different approaches to write this information. In the example, we used the place [34] authority table (e.g., for Brussels), the role [35] authority table (e.g., for president) and again the corporate body.

```
<section is="lh-concluding-formulas">
  <div is="lh-placedate">
    Done at <span rel="lh:signaturePlace" re-
source="place:BEL_BRU">Brussels</span>, <time property="lh:sig-
natureDate" datatype="xsd:date" content="2014-12-18"
datetime="2014-12-18">18 December 2014</time>.
  </div>
  <div is="lh-signature" rel="lh:signature" re-
source="#borgsign">
    <div>For the <span rel="lh:signatoryOrganization" re-
source="corpbody:EP">European Parliament</span></div>
    <div rel="lh:signatoryRole" resource="role:PRESID">The Pres-
ident</div>
    <div rel="lh:signatory" resource="dbr:Martin_Schulz">M.
SCHULZ</div>
  </div>
  [... ]
</section>
```

7 Consolidation

Legal acts evolve over time through subsequent amendments and corrigenda. There is thus a need to consolidate the base act and all documents making changes to it into a single *consolidated resource*, which in turn should allow to build a view of the act in any given point of time according to some criterion. The view of an act as applicable in each date, for example, contains the terms that are binding at that date. However, this view might include corrigenda that have been published on a later date, as they are usually retroactive. In this case, someone defending his good faith in a trial might argue the ignorance of errors corrected by retroactive corrigenda, by referring to the view only containing documents that have published at given and thus excluding corrigenda that were not published at that date.

LegalHTML adopts a tree-based multiversion model for consolidation (see Fig. 1 on the left) allowing to represent a *superposition* of the different versions of a legal act within a single document. Starting from the document root, when a portion of the act has been changed, LegalHTML introduces control lh-cons element containing a few lh-version elements associated with different "versions" of that part of the document each identified by a distinguished (technical) identifier (see Fig. 1 on the right).

Within an lh-version there can be another lh-cons, when portions thereof have been changed in turn (before the outer version has been deleted or replaced by a different version). The recursive application of consolidation-related elements produces the tree data structure depicted in Fig. 1 on the left. Indeed, the HTML elements described so far must be complemented by metadata (embedded inside a script element) that describes the different sets of changes in time.

We thus equipped the LegalHTML Ontology with a vocabulary related to consolidated resources (Fig. 2), allowing for a description roughly matching the analysis, lifecycle, temporal data and workflow sections of Akoma Ntoso (see Fig. 3).

- A new class: `lh:ConsolidatedResource`, extends `eli:LegalResource`.
- A property `lh:changeSet` links the consolidated resource to different sets of changes in time. A `lh:ChangeSet` describes a set of changes brought by a single amending doc.
- For each change set:

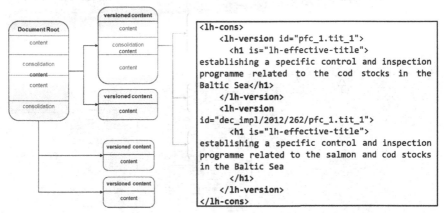

Fig. 1. Tree-based multiversion consolidation model (left) and control code to consolidate the effective title (right)

- the properties `lh:changingAct`, `lh:published`, `lh:entryIntoForce` and `lh:startOfApplicability` link the act providing the amendments described by the change set, and determine when these changes have been published, enter into force and start to be applicable;
- other properties, such as `lh:forceChange` and `lh:textualChange`, link to the different kinds of change that might occur in the change set described by specific claseses, such as: `lh:EntryIntoForce` or `lh:Substitution`;

- Each type of change is detailed by its dedicated properties, such as – in the case of `lh:Substitution` – `dct:type`, `lh:amendingText`, `lh:amendedText`, `lh:replaced`, `lh:replacement`. The latter two properties hold relative URLs with fragment identifiers referencing the `lh-version` elements by (technical) id.

Given a date of interest d, it is possible to construct a view of the act v_d as it is applicable on d using the following algorithm.

Let *act* be the base act of a consolidated resource and CS_{act} be the change sets affecting *act*. Let us write the members of CS_{act} as the sequence cs_1, cs_2, $..cs_n$, such that $\forall i \in [1, n-1].startOfApplicability(cs_i) < startOfApplicability(cs_{i+1})$ where the function *startOfApplicability* returns when a change set starts to be applicable.

For $i \in [1, n]$:

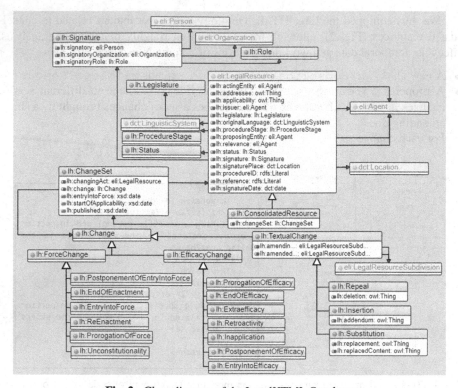

Fig. 2. Class diagram of the LegalHTML Ontology

- if *startOfApplicability*(cs_i) < d, then apply the changeset.

  For each change $c \in cs_i$, depending on the type of c:

  - lh:Insertion: ensure that the version pointed by lh:addendum is displayed;
  - lh:Repeal: ensure that the version pointed by lh:deletion is hidden;
  - lh:Substitution: ensure that the version pointed by lh:replacedContent is hidden while the version pointed by lh:replacement is displayed;

- otherwise, the changeset is not applicable and we must ensure that content introduced by any change in this set is hidden. For each change $c \in cs_i$, depending on the type of c:

  - lh:Insertion: ensure that the version pointed by lh:addendum is hidden;
  - lh:Substitution: ensure that the version pointed by lh:replacement is hidden.

```
<http://data.europa.eu/eli/dec/2008/589/2012-08-10>
    a         lh:ConsolidatedResource ;
    eli:type_document     <http://publications.europa.eu/resource/authority/resource-
type/CONS_TEXT> ;
    eli:consolidates
            <http://data.europa.eu/eli/dec/2008/589>,   # original doc
            <http://data.europa.eu/eli/dec/2011/114(1)>, # 1st amending doc
            <http://data.europa.eu/eli/dec_impl/2012/262>, # 2nd amending doc
            <http://data.europa.eu/eli/dec_impl/2012/468> ; #3rd amending doc, indirectly
amending this by amending
            <http://data.europa.eu/eli/dec_impl/2012/262>
    lh:changeSet
            <http://data.europa.eu/eli/dec/2008/589/2008-06-12/changeset_0>   ,
            <http://data.europa.eu/eli/dec/2008/589/2011-02-19/changeset_1>   ,
            <http://data.europa.eu/eli/dec/2008/589/2012-05-18/changeset_2>   ,
            <http://data.europa.eu/eli/dec/2008/589/2012-08-10/changeset_3>   .

[...]

<http://data.europa.eu/eli/dec/2008/589/2012-05-18/changeset_2>
    a                         lh:ChangeSet ;
    lh:changingAct            <http://data.europa.eu/eli/dec_impl/2012/262> ;
    lh:published              "2012-05-16"^^xsd:date ;
    lh:entryIntoForce         "2012-05-18"^^xsd:date ;
    lh:startOfApplicability   "2012-05-18"^^xsd:date ;
    lh:textualChange
            <http://data.europa.eu/eli/dec/2008/589/2012-05-18/change_1>   ,
            <http://data.europa.eu/eli/dec/2008/589/2012-05-18/change_2>,
            <http://data.europa.eu/eli/dec/2008/589/2012-05-18/change_3>   .

<http://data.europa.eu/eli/dec/2008/589/2012-05-18/change_1>
    a               lh:Substitution ;
    lh:amendingText  <http://data.europa.eu/eli/dec_impl/2012/262/art_1/unp_1/pnt_1/oj>;
    lh:amendedText   <http://data.europa.eu/eli/dec/2008/589/pfc_1/tit_1> ;
    dct:type         <http://publications.europa.eu/resource/authority/modification-
type/REPLACEMENT> ;
    lh:replacedContent  <#pfc_1.tit_1> ;
    lh:replacement    <#dec_impl/2012/262/pfc_1.tit_1>   .
[...]
```

Fig. 3. Excerpt of consolidation-related metadata

8   Implementation

We developed an implementation of LegalHTML consisting of a JavaScript file and CSS stylesheet, which implement, respectively, the semantics (behavior) and default presentation of a LegalHTML document. Figure 4 shows how the LegalHTML encoding of the Commission Decision 2008/589/EC looks like in a web browser. This example is also available online [36]. Although we did not aim at a pixel-perfect match, the default presentation of LegalHTML is heavily inspired by EUR-Lex, to reinforce the point that a semantically explicit representation can be used to target any presentation template, as long as presentation rules are consistently applied to semantic elements.

The implementation also includes the behavior for LegalHTML documents and an API for them, which support:

- the automatic generation of an interactive table of contents (see the box on the top-left corner of Fig. 4);

Fig. 4. Proof-of-concept of a Commission Decision in LegalHTML

- switching between different views of the document as it is applicable in different points-of-time (see the box on the bottom-left corner of Fig. 4), starting from the current date;
- management of backlinks from footnotes to in-text references.

The resolution includes different scenarios not limited to the time-variable. While the links provided by the standard view refer to points in time in which a certain modification of the act starts its applicability, the API support other more elaborated cases, e.g. restricting the view of the document to all changes that, at a certain data, have been not only entered into force and made applicable, but have been also published, so to analyze the case of the "good intentions" of a person who, in that date, was not aware of a retroactive modification of a law because it was not yet published.

9 Conclusion

The recent diffusion of linked open data standards and best practices for the publication of legal information produced by institutions, governments and, more in general, the public sector, require effective and efficient solutions for its representation, production, publication and fruition.

In the attempt to realize a single specification covering all the above aspects and thus replacing the different models being currently adopted by several institutions for their implementation, we have developed LegalHTML, an extension of the HTML language thought for representing legal acts. LegalHTML has proven to be a convenient solution for realizing electronic versions of legal acts, since their first drafting and through all other steps of the document preparation and publication, with a dedicated domain markup for structuring the act, a reference ontology for the legal domain, embedded document metadata for describing the editorial and jurisdictional history of the act and a dedicated model for representing the full history of modifications to the act brought by other acts into a single document. The LegalHTML API complete the picture by providing different ways to reconcile this change-tracked document according to different parameters such as a specific point in time and a combination of the jurisdictional characteristics of the modifications (publication, entry into force, efficacy). LegalHTML is scheduled for entering into application at the Publications Office by the end of 2023.

Acknowledgements. The authors want to thank by first Willem van Gemert and Maria Westermann for believing in the concept behind LegalHTML and for starting the discussion within the OP. A special acknowledgement to the work of Edyta Posel-Czescik, Camilo Soares and Dominika Uhrikova, for making it real through the end. Last, but surely not the least, we mention the devoted effort of Véronique Parisse who carefully reviewed our work and of all other staff who supported our preliminary investigation (Zilvinas Bubnys, Maria Kardami, Christian Marien and Tamas Schlemmer, among the many).

References

1. Directive (EU) 2019/1024 of the European Parliament and of the Council of 20 June 2019 on open data and the re-use of public sector information (recast). http://data.europa.eu/eli/dir/2019/1024/oj
2. Open Government Initiative. https://obamawhitehouse.archives.gov/open
3. Lupo, C., et al.: Deliverable 3.1: General XML format(s) for legal Sources. ESTRELLA Project (2007)
4. CEN MetaLex: Open XML Interchange Format for Legal and Legislative Resources. http://www.metalex.eu/
5. Boer, A., Hoekstra, R., Winkels, R.: METALex: legislation in XML. In: Bench-Capon, T.J.M., Daskalopulu, A., Winkels, R. (eds.) Legal Knowledge and Information Systems: Jurix 2002. IOS Press (2002)
6. Legal XML. http://www.legalxml.org/
7. LEXML. http://www.lexml.de/mission_english.htm
8. Muller, M.: Legal RDF dictionary. In: XML Europe 2002, Barcelona, May 2002 (2002)
9. McClure, J.: Legal-RDF vocabularies, requirements & design rationale. In: Proceedings of the V Legislative XML Workshop (2006)

10. Palmirani, M., Vitali, F.: Akoma-Ntoso for legal documents. In: Sartor, G., Palmirani, M., Francesconi, E., Biasiotti, M. (eds.) Legislative XML for the Semantic Web. LGTS, vol. 4, pp. 75–100. Springer, Dordrecht (2011)

11. Akoma Ntoso. http://www.akomantoso.org/

12. OASIS Open. http://www.oasis-open.org/

13. Mangiafico, J.: Legislative Data Challenges, One Year Later. https://blogs.loc.gov/law/2015/01/legislative-data-challenges-one-year-later/. Accessed 20 Jan 2015

14. Formex: Formalized Exchange of Electronic Publications. In: EU Vocabularies. https://op.europa.eu/en/web/eu-vocabularies/formex

15. About ELI. https://eur-lex.europa.eu/eli-register/about.html

16. Schneider, J.M., et al.: Lynx: a knowledge-based AI service platform for content processing, enrichment and analysis for the legal domain. Inf. Syst. **106**, 101966 (2022)

17. Rodriguez-Doncel, V., Montiel-Ponsoda, E.: Lynx: towards a legal knowledge graph for multilingual Europe. Law in Context **37**(1), 175–178 (2020)

18. Athan, T., Boley, H., Governatori, G., Palmirani, M., Paschke, A., Wyner, A.: OASIS Legal-RuleML. In: Fourteenth International Conference on Artificial Intelligence and Law, New York, pp.3–12 (2013)

19. Capadisli, S., Guy, A., Verborgh, R., Lange, C., Auer, S., Berners-Lee, T.: Decentralised authoring, annotations and notifications for a read-write web with dokieli. In: Cabot, J., De Virgilio, R., Torlone, R. (eds.) ICWE 2017. LNCS, vol. 10360, pp. 469–481. Springer, Cham (2017). https://doi.org/10.1007/978-3-319-60131-1_33

20. Solid. https://solid.mit.edu/

21. Peroni, S., et al.: Research articles in simplified HTML: a web-first format for HTML-based scholarly articles. PeerJ Comput. Sci. **3**, e132 (2017)

22. RELAX NG. https://relaxng.org/

23. ReSpec. https://respec.org/

24. GitHub: Where the world builds software. In: GitHub: Where the world builds software. https://github.com/

25. Bitbucket. https://bitbucket.org/

26. The One DevOps Platform | GitLab. https://gitlab.com/

27. Cervone, L., Palmirani, M., Vitali, F.: What it is | Akoma Ntoso. http://www.akomantoso.org/?page_id=25

28. Hariharan, A.: Why is Akoma Ntoso in XML and not HTML or JSON or PDF? In: AkomaNtoso.io - A Resource on Learning and using the Akoma Ntoso Schema. https://akomantoso.io/faq/why-is-akoma-ntoso-in-xml-and-not-html-or-json-or-pdf/. Accessed 25 Oct 2019

29. MDN contributors: Semantics - MDN Web Docs Glossary: Definitions of Web-related terms. In: MDN Web Docs. https://developer.mozilla.org/en-US/docs/Glossary/Semantics. Accessed 21 Sept 2022

30. WHATWG: Extensibility. In: HTML - Living Standard. https://html.spec.whatwg.org/multipage/introduction.html#extensibility. Accessed 8 Dec 2022

31. Cruellas, J.C., Karlinger, G., Pinkas, D., Ross, J.: XML advanced electronic signatures (XAdES). In: World Wide Web Consortium - Web Standards. http://www.w3.org/TR/XAdES/. Accessed 20 Feb 2003

32. Publications Office of the European Union: IMFC Common Vocabulary. In: EU Vocabularies. https://op.europa.eu/en/web/eu-vocabularies/cov. Accessed 2021

33. Publications Office of the European Union: Corporate body Named Authority List. http://data.europa.eu/88u/dataset/corporate-body. Accessed 2011

34. Publications Office of the European Union: Place Named Authority List. http://data.europa.eu/88u/dataset/place. Accessed 2009

35. Publications Office of the European Union: Role Named Authority List. http://data.europa.eu/88u/dataset/role. Accessed 2009
36. Stellato, A., Fiorelli, M.: Example representation in LegalHTML of the Commission Decision 2008/589/EC. In: LegalHTML. https://w3id.org/legalhtml/examples/OJ/L_2008190EN.01001101/L_2008190EN.01001101.xhtml. Accessed 18 Dec 2022

Whyis 2: An Open Source Framework for Knowledge Graph Development and Research

Jamie McCusker$^{(\boxtimes)}$⑩ and Deborah L. McGuinness⑩

Rensselaer Polytechnic Institute, Troy, NY 12180, USA
{mccusj2,dlm}@rpi.edu

Abstract. Whyis is the first open source framework for creating custom provenance-driven knowledge graph applications, or *KGApps*, supporting three principal tasks: knowledge curation, inference, and interaction. It has been used in knowledge graph projects in materials science, health informatics, and radio spectrum policy. All knowledge in Whyis graphs are encapsulated in nanopublications, which simplifies and standardizes the production of qualified knowledge in knowledge graphs. The architecture of Whyis enables what we consider to be essential requirements for knowledge graph construction, maintenance, and use. These requirements include support for automated and manual curation of knowledge from diverse sources, provenance traces of all knowledge, domain-specific user interaction, and generalized distributed knowledge inference. We coin the term "Nano-scale knowledge graph" to refer to nanopublication-driven knowledge graphs. Knowledge graph developers can use Whyis to configure custom sets of knowledge curation pipelines using custom data importers and semantic extract, transform, and load scripts. The flexible, nanopublication-based architecture of Whyis lets knowledge graph developers integrate, extend, and publish knowledge from heterogeneous sources on the web. Whyis KGApps and are easily developed locally, managed using source control, and deployable via continuous integration, server deployment scripts, and as docker containers.

Keywords: knowledge graphs · software framework · research framework

Resource type: Software framework
Python Package Index: whyis
License: Apache 2.0 License

This work was funded by the National Institute of Environmental Health Sciences (NIEHS) Award 0255-0236-4609/1U2CES026555-01, National Science Foundation (NSF) Award DMR-1310292, IBM Research AI through the AI Horizons Network, the National Spectrum Consortium (NSC) project number NSC-17-7030, and by the Gates Foundation through Healthy Birth, Growth, and Development knowledge integration (HBGDki). Any opinions, findings and conclusions or recommendations expressed in this material are those the authors and do not necessarily reflect the views of AFRL, IBM, or the Gates Foundation.

Documentation URL: https://whyis.readthedocs.io
Docker pull command: docker pull tetherlessworld/whyis
Source Code URL: https://github.com/tetherless-world/whyis
Example Project URL: https://github.com/whyiskg/les-mis-demo

1   Introduction

Knowledge graphs have become an important component of commercial and research applications on the Web. Google was one of the first to promote a semantic metadata organizational model described as a "knowledge graph," [33] and many other organizations have since used the term in the literature and in less formal communication. We believe that that successful knowledge graph construction requires more than simply storing and serving graph-oriented data, or even data in the Resource Description Format [6] or Linked Data [4]. Knowledge graphs need to be easily maintainable and usable in sometimes complex application settings. For instance, keeping a knowledge graph up to date can require developing a knowledge curation pipeline that either replaces the graph wholesale whenever updates are made, or requires detailed tracking of knowledge provenance across multiple data sources. Additionally, applying reasoning systems to graphs from diverse, potentially conflicting sources becomes very difficult, which has resulted in investigations of new kinds of reasoning paradigms [19].

Beyond this, it is becoming clear that other sorts of knowledge inference have become important to knowledge graph construction. NLP methods and other machine learning methods are commonly demonstrated as potential sources of knowledge graph construction. User interfaces are also key to the success of a knowledge graph, especially when supporting computational users. It is insufficient simply to provide a SPARQL endpoint or to list out the statements relevant to a single entity for most tasks. Google's knowledge graph, for instance, takes the semantic type of the entity into account when rendering information about that entity. Domain-specific APIs also help smooth the integration of knowledge graphs into existing systems. Finally, these challenges are dependent on high-quality knowledge provenance that is inherent in the design of any knowledge graph system, and not merely an afterthought.

The above challenges are not currently met by a reusable knowledge graph framework or architecture. We have therefore developed Whyis as a framework for developing knowledge graphs to support the above challenges. As shown in Fig. 1, Whyis provides a semantic analysis ecosystem: an environment that supports research and development of semantic analytics that we have previously had to build custom applications for [21,23]. Users interact through a suite of views into the knowledge graph, driven by the type of node and view requested in the URL. Knowledge is curated into the graph through knowledge curation methods, including Semantic ETL, external linked data mapping, and Natural Language Processing (NLP). Autonomous inference agents expand the available knowledge using traditional deductive reasoning as well as inductive methods that can include predictive models, statistical reasoners, and machine learning. We review case studies of projects that have used Whyis for knowledge graph development in materials science, health informatics, and radio spectrum policy.

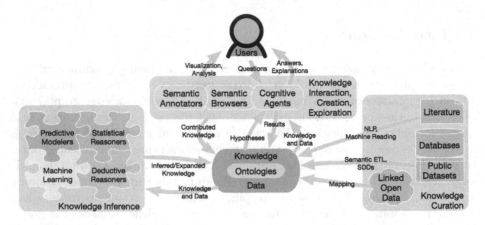

Fig. 1. The semantic ecosystem enabled by the Whyis framework for knowledge creation, interaction, and inference.

2   Approach

Whyis is a framework for developing nano-scale knowledge graph applications. It is a code-focused approach that enables software developers to create knowledge graph applications (KGApps) using minimal modifications, allowing for the use of code-oriented deployment and management tools like GitHub, Docker, and other DevOps tools. While it is possible and useful to use Whyis 2 to create KGApps without changing any code, much of the customization capabilities will only be useful if it is customized to some degree. We expect that most knowledge graph creators will use Javascript and Python to customize their KGApp for better user interaction, knowledge curation, and inference. In the software industry, this is called a low code/no code approach, allowing creators of knowledge graphs to do so without coding, but if they need to add code, it would be minimal.

Nano-scale knowledge graphs use *nanpublications* to encapsulate every piece of knowledge introduced into knowledge graphs it manages. Introduced in [24] and expanded on in [10], a nanopublication is composed of three named RDF graphs: an *Assertion* graph, knowledge encoded in RDF (which can be however many RDF statements as appropriate); a *Provenance* graph, which explains what the justification for the assertion is, and a *Publication Info* graph, which provides publication details, including attribution, of the nanopublication itself. We see knowledge graphs that include the level of granularity supported by nanopublications (thus nano-scale) as essential to fine-grained management of knowledge in knowledge graphs that are curated and inferred from diverse sources and can change on an ongoing basis. Other systems, like DBpedia [1] and Uniprot [28], have very rough grained management of knowledge using very large named graphs, which limit the ability to version, explain, infer from, and annotate the knowledge.

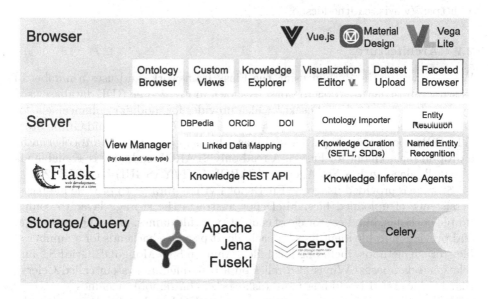

Fig. 2. The Whyis technology stack. Nanopublications are stored in the RDF database. Files can be uploaded and stored in a special File Depot instance as well. Celery is used to invoke and manage a set of autonomic inference agents, which listen for graph changes and respond with additional nanopublications. Users interact with the graph through a set of views that are configured by node type and are based on the Flask templating system Jinja2.

2.1 Whyis 2 Changes and Improvements

While Whyis 1 was only available as a Flask application, Whyis 2 is available as a python package through the Python Package Index as "whyis", and can be installed using Python 3.7 or later. Whyis 2 provides a number of additional capabilities and modes of operation above Whyis 1. It is now possible to run Whyis in "embedded" mode, which does not require users to install system services for Celery, Redis, and Fuseki. It also provides a number of auto-generated deployment scripts to create production servers from initial KGApps with minimal customization. We also included the ability to back up and restore KGApp RDF databases and file repositories to improve deployment and maintenance of production knowledge graphs. In order to improve long-term support, we also migrated Whyis from Blazegraph, which hadn't been recently maintained, to

Fuseki, which is still being actively improved. We also found Fuseki to be the only RDF database that could sustain ongoing edits while still providing performant read access to the database. Since it uses Apache Jena Fuseki, it also requires Java JDK 11 or later. Whyis 2 is also available as a Docker hub image using the tag "tetherlessworld/whyis", and has detailed documentation available at https://whyis.readthedocs.io.

2.2   Architecture

Whyis is written in Python using the Flask framework, and uses a number of existing infrastructure tools to work, as shown in Fig. 2. The RDF database used by default is Apache Jena Fuseki,[1] which provides for modular enhancement for additional capabilities. Whyis uses the SPARQL 1.1 Query [11], and Graph Store HTTP Protocols [25]. Any RDF database that supports those protocols can be a drop-in replacement for Fuseki. A read-only SPARQL endpoint is available via '/sparql', along with a Yet Another SPARQL GUI (YASGUI)-based UI [29].

Storage is provided using the FileDepot Python library[2] to provide file-based persistence of uploaded files. FileDepot abstracts the storage layer to configurable backends, handles storage of content type, file names, and other metadata, and provides durable identifiers for each file. It provides backends for a number of file storage methods, including local files, Amazon S3,[3] MongoDB GridFS,[4] and relational databases. Whyis also relies on a task queuing system called Celery[5] that can be scaled by adding more task workers on remote machines.

Knowledge graph developers create a new KGApp by simply running the "whyis" command in an empty directory. The system will generate a python module that contains the configuration, templates, and starter code files that allow developers to customize Whyis to their purposes. Views, templates, and code all live within this revision control-friendly Python project to better enable the management and staging of a production system.

To illustrate the capabilities and structure of Whyis, we created a demonstration knowledge graph of characters and their interactions from the novel *Les Miserables*, as originally created by Donald Knuth and maintained by Media and Design Studio[6] The demonstration graph is available at the Example Project URL. We have loaded the graph with an initial description of the network as a *dcat:Dataset*,[7], as shown in Fig. 3.

---

[1] https://jena.apache.org/documentation/fuseki2/.
[2] http://depot.readthedocs.io.
[3] https://aws.amazon.com/s3.
[4] https://docs.mongodb.com/manual/core/gridfs.
[5] http://www.celeryproject.org.
[6] Available at https://github.com/MADStudioNU/lesmiserables-character-network.
[7] https://github.com/whyiskg/les-mis-demo/blob/main/data/les-miserables.ttl.

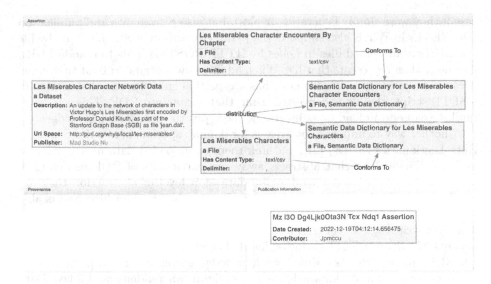

Fig. 3. A rendering of the *dcat:Dataset* "Les Miserables Character Network Data" with its nanopublication. Metadata is uploaded to the system to allow for future discovery, download, and/or processing. The "Publication Info" graph traces that the assertion was created by the user 'jpmccu' on 2022-12-19, which was captured automatically. There is no other provenance of the graph.

2.3   Enabling Knowledge Curation

Whyis supports knowledge curation through several pipelines: direct user interaction, direct loading of RDF, semantic ETL (sETL) scripts, semantic data dictionaries, and on-demand loading of linked data from the linked data web. These approaches can be mixed and matched as needed by knowledge graph developers.

Users can interact with the default Whyis user interface to annotate graph entities with links between entities (using defined Object Properties), add attributes to entities (using Datatype Properties), and add types to entities (using OWL or RDFS Classes). Users can also upload pre-generated RDF using the web interface or KGApp developers can use the *whyis load* command available from the command line.

A commonly used approach to integrate knowledge into a KGApp is using the Semantic Extract, Transform, and Load-r (SETLr) [20] to support conversion of tabular data, tabular and non-tabular JSON, XML, HTML, and other custom formats (through embedded python) into RDF suitable for the knowledge graph, as well as transforming existing RDF into a better desired representation. By loading SETL scripts (written in RDF) into the knowledge graph, the SETLr inference agent is triggered, which runs the script and imports the generated RDF. SETLr itself is powerful enough to support the creation of named graphs, which lets users control not just nanopublication assertions (as would be the case if they were simply generating triples), but also provenance and publication info. SETLr in Whyis also supports the parameterization of SETL scripts by file type. Users can upload files to nodes by HTTP POSTing a file to a node's URI. The node then represents that file. When adding new metadata about that node, it can include *rdf:type*. If a file node has a type that matches one that is used in a SETL script, the file is converted using that script into RDF. This lets users (and developers) upload domain-specific file types to contribute knowledge.

Another way to import knowledge is for domain specialists to write Semantic Data Dictionaries (SDDs) [27], and link them to uploaded data files. A SDD is an Excel spreadsheet that abstracts away the particulars of RDF modeling to allow for domain scientists to describe data at a level of abstraction they are familiar with. The SDDAgent looks for SDDs attached to data files, and is able to compile a SETL script for the SETLr agent to process. The end result is that users can write high-level descriptions of their data, while gaining the scalability benefits of writing a SETL script by hand. The structure[8] needed to process the two SDDs used in the *Les Miserables* knowledge graph are shown in Fig. 3.

The last to import knowledge is to configure an on-demand Linked Data importer. Whyis provides a flexible Linked Data importer that can load RDF from remote Linked Data sources by URL prefix. We have successfully tested use of this importer with DOI [26], OBO Foundries [34], Uniprot [28], DBPedia [1], and other project-specific resources. It supports the insertion of API keys, content negotiation, and HTTP authentication using a netrc file. It tracks the last modified time of remote RDF to only update when remote data has changed and provides provenance indicating that the imported RDF *prov:wasQuotedFrom* the original URL. Examples are available in the default configuration file in the *NAMESPACES* entry.[9] Whyis also provides a file importer that, rather than parsing the remote file as RDF, loads the file into the file depot. This can be invoked on-demand, so that metadata can be loaded from one SETL script about a collection of files, then other SETL scripts can process those files based on the types added, and the files would be dynamically downloaded to Whyis for processing.

2.4   Enabling Knowledge Interaction

To support the Knowledge Interaction user stories, developers of Whyis knowledge graphs can create custom views for nodes by both the *rdf:type* of the node and the *view* URL parameter. These views are looked up as templates and rendered using the Jinja2 templating engine.[10] This is configured in a turtle file in the KGApp directory (vocab.ttl), where viewed classes and view properties are defined. For more details, please see the view documentation.[11]

Through the use of nanopublications, developers can provide explanation for all assertions made in the graph by accessing the linked provenance graph

---

[8] https://github.com/whyiskg/les-mis-demo/blob/main/data/les-miserables.ttl.
[9] https://github.com/tetherless-world/whyis/blob/main/whyis/config/default.py.
[10] http://jinja.pocoo.org/docs/2.10.
[11] https://whyis.readthedocs.io/en/latest/views.html.

when a user asks for more details. Search is also supported through an entity resolution-based autocomplete and a full text search page.

Whyis provides a number of built-in views that can be customized as needed. In Fig. 4, we see standard entity views (Figs. 4a and 4b). Whyis also provides the ability to create custom visualizations using a SPARQL query and Vega Lite [31], as explained in Deagen *et al.* Fig. 5 demonstrates how it can be used to generate custom, dynamic visualizations of data using many different approaches.

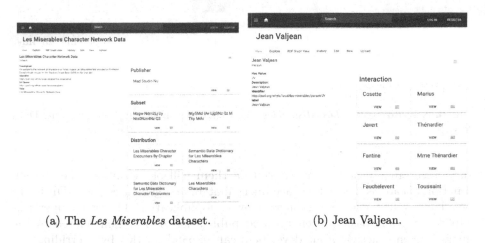

(a) The *Les Miserables* dataset.   (b) Jean Valjean.

Fig. 4. Views for entities in knowledge graphs are fairly flexible, but also extensible.

2.5   Enabling Knowledge Inference

Knowledge Inference in Whyis is performed by a suite of inference agents, each performing the analogue to a single rule in traditional deductive inferencing. Inference agents support a much broader means of creating inference "rules" than simple if-then entailments. Inference agents identify entities of interest using a SPARQL query (effectively the antecedent) and a python function that generates new RDF as the consequent. Agent developers create these queries and functions as a way to expand the capabilities of their knowledge graphs, and use integration at the knowledge modeling level to provide knowledge processing workflows. The agent framework provides custom inference capability, and is composed of a SPARQL query that serves as the "rule" "body" and a python function that serves has the "head", which generates additional RDF. The agent is invoked when new nanopublications are added to the knowledge graph that match the SPARQL query defined by the agent. Developers can choose to run this query either on just the single nanopublication that has been added, or on the entire graph. Whole-graph queries will need to exclude query matches that would cause the agent to be invoked over and over. This can take some consideration for complex cases, but excluding similar knowledge to the expected output or nodes

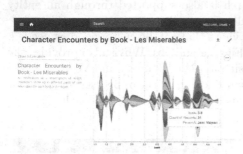
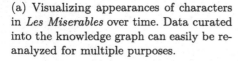
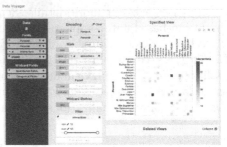

(a) Visualizing appearances of characters in *Les Miserables* over time. Data curated into the knowledge graph can easily be re-analyzed for multiple purposes.

(b) Creating a visualization using Data Voyager in Whyis. By supplying an initial query, users can then compose many Vega Lite visualizations using an embedded Data Voyager [36] instance.

Fig. 5. Visualizing the *Les Miserables* knowledge graph using Vega Lite and Data Voyager.

that have already had the agent run on them will often suffice. The Python function "head" is invoked on each query match, and generates new RDF for to be added to the knowledge graph as a new nanopublication. The agent superclass will assign some basic provenance and publication information related to the given inference activity, but developers can expand on this by overriding the *explain()* function.

These inference agents are run using the Celery distributed task queueing system. As knowledge is added to the graph on a per-nanopublication basis, an update function in the task queue is called to invoke the agent body query, and any matches are added to the queue. As each agent processes the relevant instances, they create new nanopublications, which are also published. The update function is in turn called on these, and the process continues until there are no more matches.

Prebuilt inference agent types include some NLP support, including entity detection using noun phrase extraction, basic entity resolution against other knowledge graph nodes, and Inverse Document Frequency computation for resolved nodes. It also includes agents for knowledge curation (processing SETL scripts and SDD files), an email notifier, a nanopublication versioning archive, and an ontology import closure loader. Because of the forward-chaining nature of the inference agent system, Whyis also provides support for custom deductive rules using the autonomic.Deductor class. Developers can write rules by providing a *construct* clause as the head and a *where* clause as the body. Further, Whyis also provides customized Deductor instances that are collected up into OWL and RDFS partial profiles for RDFS, OWL 2 EL, RL, and QL. OWL 2 property chain support is still in-progress.

An example inference agent is provided in the documentation.[12] The example shows a very simple example of how an external Python library, BeautifulSoup, can be used to extract the text from a node that has HTML associated with it. The agent mostly consists of a SPARQL query that looks for entities that have have *sioc:content*. The Python function then extracts that content as HTML from an RDFlib Resource in the "i" variable, parses it using BeautifulSoup, and adds a new schema:text statement to the entity as a Resource in a new graph (as "o"). While very simple, this agent is key to other downstream agents that can extract named entites from the text. Similar agents can be written to extract text from PDFs, Word Documents, or other custom data. If they use the same *schema:text* predicate, existing downstream agents will see those statements the same way as the HTML2Text agent, streamlining knowledge processing pipelines. Many other examples are available in the Whyis source code.[13]

3   Related Work

We see the following frameworks as providing some, but not all, aspects of knowledge graphs as we define them:

Stardog According to their current marketing literature, Stardog[14] includes OWL reasoning, mapping of data silos into RDF, and custom rules.

Ontowiki provides a user interface on top of a RDF database that tracks history, allows users to browse and edit knowledge, and supports user interface extensions [2].

Callimachus calls itself a "Semantic Content Manager" and lets developers provide custom templates by object type using RDFa, and supports versioning of the knowledge graph [3].

Virtuoso Openlink Data Spaces is a linked data publishing tool for Openlink Virtuoso. It provides a set of pre-defined data import tools and a fixed set of views on the linked data it creates.[15]

Vitro is part of the Vivo project [5]. It is "a general-purpose web-based ontology and instance editor with customizable public browsing."[16] It supports the creation of new ontology classes and instances that are driven by the ontology, to view, browse, and search those instances, but does not allow users to create custom interfaces.

iTelos (in preprint [9]) is a knowledge graph development methodology for which no software framework has been provided. It provides a method for separating schema development of knowledge graphs (Entity Type Graphs, or ETGs) from entity development (Entity Graphs, or EGs). Some tools are have been developed for creation of ETGs, and nothing seems to be offered for EGs.

---

[12] https://whyis.readthedocs.io/en/latest/inference.html.
[13] https://github.com/tetherless-world/whyis/tree/main/whyis/autonomic.
[14] A case study: https://www.stardog.com/blog/nasas-knowledge-graph/.
[15] Documentation: https://ods.openlinksw.com/wiki/ODS.
[16] Available: https://github.com/vivo-project/Vitro.

Semantic MediaWiki [14] is an extension to MediaWiki that allows editors to annotate wiki articles with RDF triples relative to the entity represented by the current article. Semantic MediaWiki was one of the first attempts at providing semantics to the Wikipedia project. It is limited to what could be expressed in the wiki page format extension, does not provide custom user interfaces, although it does offer the ability to push annotations to a SPARQL database, some of which offer reasoning.

Wikibase [37] is the technology platform for Wikidata. It provides a user interface for editing a knowledge graph as well as APIs for large scale knowledge import. Wikibase supports the introduction of provenance through reification using RDF* [12], but it does not allow for extensible inference nor does it allow for type-oriented custom user interfaces.

None of these tools support general-purpose inference beyond Datalog-like rules (Stardog), and only Stardog provides a general purpose method for importing data. Stardog does provide truth maintenance within the scope of its reasoning methods, and Ontowiki and Callimachus provide version histories, but do not provide reasoning. None of these tools allow for arbitrary knowledge inference extensions, NLP or otherwise, and only Callimachus and Ontowiki provide extensible user interfaces.

4   Case Studies and Evaluation

We present three case studies from our projects with Whyis for the use of it as a knowledge graph development framework. While these are all published examples, Whyis has been used many times for knowledge graph development on a smaller scale for prototyping, knowledge explorations, or for proofs of concept. We also note that because the underlying database is Fuseki, the performance of Fuseki through Whyis is comparable to using Fuseki directly when using the SPARQL endpoint.

4.1   MaterialsMine: A Materials Science Knowledge Graph

The MaterialsMine knowledge graph was initially introduced as NanoMine, a knowledge graph for curating experimental results from nanocomposite materials [22]. MaterialsMine is a collaboration between RPI, Duke University, California Institute of Technology, Northwestern University, and University of Vermont. Whyis is being used by materials scientists at all of these institutions to publish curated experimental and simulation data as an integrated materials science knowledge graph. Part of the Materials Genome Initiative (MGI) [35], MaterialsMine has expanded into providing data uploads for any materials science data using the Dataset Catalog (DCAT) [18], visualization of materials science knowledge [7], and curation of metamaterial computational experiment results into the knowledge graph.

MaterialsMine uses SETLr [20] to convert the detailed XML files originally supported by Nanomine into RDF nanopublications. Tabular data, mostly generated by the metamaterials community, is described using SDDs [27], which are annotated to DCAT dataset files using *dcterms:conformsTo*. The SDDAgent is then keyed to notice these links and process those files into the knowledge graph. Currently, MaterialsMine supports the processing of static properties of metamaterials through SDDs.

Users of MaterialsMine can explore the merged results using a gallery of visualizations (see Fig. 6), which are produced using a combination of SPARQL queries against the knowledge graph and a Vega Lite grammar of graphics specification [31]. This approach was discussed in Deagen *et al.* [7], and produced over 150 visualizations of the knowledge graph.

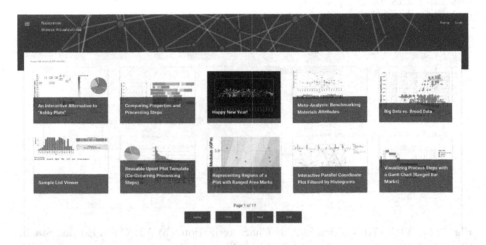

Fig. 6. A current view of the MaterialsMine visualization gallery, available at https:// materialsmine.org/wi/gallery.

4.2   Dynamic Spectrum Access Policy Framework

Normally, radio spectrum allocation is performed manually by humans over the course of months. Dynamic Spectrum Access (DSA) promises to accellerate that allocation to allow for allocation of spectrum use on-demand within hours or minutes of request. The DSA Policy Framework project [30] encoded a number of radio spectrum policies as OWL Ontology fragments for fast, automated validation of radio frequency allocation requests. The Whyis knowledge graph was used to manage the domain ontology that described types of equipment used, geographic regions managed, and the backing ontologies, as well as the actual policies expressed as OWL constraints. The DSA Policy Framework was deployed as a docker application with Whyis embedded in the deliverable to manage policies and supporting terminology.

4.3   Semantic Breast Cancer Restaging

The American Joint Committee on Cancer (AJCC) periodically updates its criteria for severity of different cancers into stages. In 2018, the AJCC release its first breast cancer staging guidelines, the 8th edition [13], based on biological and molecular markers (biomarkers), which dramatically improved the accuracy of breast cancer staging, but also complicated its assessment. Seneviratne *et al.* [32] were able to use OWL ontology-based rules for cancer staging of the 7th and 8th editions and were able to automatically recompute cancer stages for a number of example breast cancer cases. The project used the Whyis reasoning framework to classify cases into relevant cancer stages in both guidelines, and was also able to explain through recorded provenance traces how it had performed that classification. The Whyis view system was also used to produce user interfaces for the project, as shown in Fig. 7 (previously published in [32]), including the ability to show inference agent explanations to users.

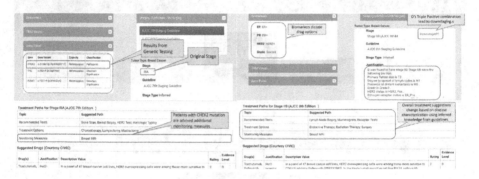

Fig. 7. (a) AJCC 7th Edition Staging Characterization. (b) AJCC 8th Edition Staging Characterization (previously published in [32]).

5   Discussion

Managing knowledge graphs at nano-scale within the Whyis semantic ecosystem has made it simple to realize core knowledge graph requirements for knowledge curation, integration and exploration. Knowledge curation from diverse sources can occur with detailed provenance of where everything comes from and what knowledge is contingent on other knowledge, using existing provenance standards. User interfaces can query knowledge provenance to provide deep explanations of what they show. Inference agents become more scalable when much of the analysis can be performed on knowledge fragments, rather than the entire knowledge graph. Whyis, through SETLr, supports the transformation of databases into rigorously modeled knowledge, regardless of the source format.

The inherent use of provenance standards opens up the ability to capture contingent knowledge that may or may not be consistent. Questions of "Who or what made this claim?", "What other knowledge have they added?", "Do we trust them?" can be asked by knowledge graph developers so that users can decide what knowledge they want to trust. We also have the option to provide services that look for evidence for a statement as well as evidence for the negation of a statement. For knowledge inference, the use of update-based general inference provides an inherent forward-chaining paradigm – when an agent adds new knowledge, the other agents are checked to see if they can provide new conclusions from that output. Further, the use of a distributed task queuing system (Celery) for implementation means that, while the inference engine may not be as fast as an in-database reasoner, it is potentially more scalable, because additional compute nodes can be added to serve as Celery workers. The central database is only responsible for recording changes and answering queries, which means that it can serve whatever knowledge has been computed so far, rather than waiting for a complete answer to be returned.

We see Whyis as a potential unifying testbed and integration point for algorithms and methods used in working with knowledge graphs. For example, NLP algorithms that purport to generate knowledge graphs and deductive or inference algorithms that expand knowledge graphs, graph learning algorithms that can infer new links between entities. This work has the potential to encourage algorithm developers to work on common knowledge representations, which will make comparisons easier across algorithms. A unified approach could make it easier to put new algorithms into practice by providing a context in which those algorithms can operate, including a common representation for existing entities in the knowledge graph and pre-loaded knowledge, and for algorithms to build off of each others' output. The challenge here is to provide a guide for NLP and other algorithm developers to map their output into a useful knowledge graph representation.

5.1   Limitations

There are a number of limitations to consider when evaluating Whyis for implementation. The inference engine is not as fast as in-database reasoners because it needs to query the database remotely, parse, and then serialize new knowledge back into the database. Currently, inference agents must be written in Python or have a Python wrapper around an external script or service. Also, the process of revising knowledge in largest imports can be slowed if there are many pre-existing revisions to retire. The commitment to using nanopublications as a transactional atom has also complicated our adoption of standards like the Linked Data Platform (LDP) [16]. LDP itself makes assumptions about the best way to manage knowledge graph fragments that are incompatible with arbitrarily-scoped nanopublications. Whyis does support LDP POST, DELETE, and PUT for nanopublication edits, but not for entities.

5.2   Future Work

Work and research on Whyis is active and ongoing; we have a number of improvements and research projects planned. While the immediate future of Whyis is secured by a number of research grants, we will be looking to plan out the long term sustainability of Whyis. Additionally, with the release of Whyis 2.0, we plan to expand usage by others, we will be providing tutorials at academic conferences and online video tutorials on using Whyis to create knowledge graphs. While most KGApp development has been driven by projects the authors were driving, we feel that Whyis is ready for use by a broader audience of knowledge graph developers.

We plan to perform a benchmark of the inference agent framework to compare both the capabilities and performance against other inference systems. We also plan to include support for the RDF Mapping Language (RML), a more familiar method of knowledge curation for the Semantic Web community than SETLr and SDDs. We are also going to research new methods for display in the knowledge explorer user interface, including custom renderings and layout using the Cytoscape.js [8], and to support the original use case developed in [21]. We are working on a suite of integrated inference agents. Inductive agents will utilize statistics and machine learning algorithms to automatically infer new knowledge and relationships in the knowledge graph. For example, we plan to investigate graph learning algorithms like [17] that can learn from the structure of published knowledge graphs to find new relations. Finally, with the increased uptake of ActivityPub-based standards in the "Fediverse" [15], we hope to explore the role of knowledge graphs and conversational agents in social networks by augmenting our commentary system to conform to the ActivityPub standard. This will allow Whyis knowledge graphs to serve as Fediverse nodes, and for Whyis computational agents to interact with humans through a medium they are already familiar with.

6   Conclusions

We introduce Whyis as the first provenance-aware open source framework for knowledge graph development that fulfills key user stories in knowledge graph curation, interaction, and inference within a unified ecosystem. We discussed the importance of nanopublications in the architecture of Whyis, and why it is valuable to develop nano-scale knowledge graphs that are built on nanopublications. The architecture of Whyis was designed to support use cases in three key areas of knowledge graph development: curation, inference, and interaction. As a result we were able to show how Whyis has been used in materials science, radio spectrum policy, and breast cancer restaging to produce valuable knowledge resources to those communities. Finally, we discussed the potential for Whyis to be a testbed of algorithms for curation of, interaction with, and inference from knowledge graphs, including algorithms that automatically build knowledge graphs using NLP, probabilistic network analysis, and machine learning methods for graph learning and statistical inference.

References

1. Auer, S., Bizer, C., Kobilarov, G., Lehmann, J., Cyganiak, R., Ives, Z.: DBpedia: a nucleus for a web of open data. In: Aberer, K., et al. (eds.) ASWC/ISWC -2007. LNCS, vol. 4825, pp. 722–735. Springer, Heidelberg (2007). https://doi.org/10.1007/978-3-540-76298-0_52
2. Auer, S., Dietzold, S., Riechert, T.: OntoWiki – a tool for social, semantic collaboration. In: Cruz, I., et al. (eds.) ISWC 2006. LNCS, vol. 4273, pp. 736–749. Springer, Heidelberg (2006). https://doi.org/10.1007/11926078_53
3. Battle, S., Wood, D., Leigh, J., Ruth, L.: The Callimachus project: RDFA as a web template language. In: Proceedings of the Third International Conference on Consuming Linked Data, vol. 905, pp. 1–14. CEUR-WS.org (2012)
4. Bizer, C., et al.: DBpedia - a crystallization point for the Web of Data. Web Semant.: Sci. Serv. Agents World Wide Web **7**(3), 154–165 (2009). https://doi.org/10.1016/j.websem.2009.07.002
5. Corson-Rikert, J., Cramer, E.J.: Vivo: enabling national networking of scientists. In: International Association for Social Science Information Services and Technology (2010)
6. Cyganiak, R., Wood, D., Lanthaler, M.: RDF 1.1 concepts and abstract syntax. W3C Recommendation (2014)
7. Deagen, M.E., et al.: Fair and interactive data graphics from a scientific knowledge graph. Sci. Data **9** (2022)
8. Franz, M., Lopes, C.T., Huck, G., Dong, Y., Sumer, O., Bader, G.D.: Cytoscape.js: a graph theory library for visualisation and analysis. Bioinformatics **32**(2), 309–311 (2016)
9. Giunchiglia, F., Bocca, S., Fumagalli, M., Bagchi, M., Zamboni, A.: iTelos- building reusable knowledge graphs. CoRR abs/2105.09418 (2021). https://arxiv.org/abs/2105.09418
10. Groth, P., Gibson, A., Velterop, J.: The anatomy of a nanopublication. Inf. Serv. Use **30**(1), 51–56 (2010). https://doi.org/10.3233/ISU-2010-0613
11. Harris, S., Seaborne, A.: SPARQL 1.1 query language. W3C recommendation, W3C (2013). http://www.w3.org/TR/2013/REC-sparql11-query-20130321/
12. Hartig, O.: Foundations of RDF* and SPARQL*: (an alternative approach to statement-level metadata in RDF). In: AMW 2017 11th Alberto Mendelzon International Workshop on Foundations of Data Management and the Web, Montevideo, Uruguay, 7–9 June 2017, vol. 1912. Juan Reutter, Divesh Srivastava (2017)
13. Kalli, S., Semine, A., Cohen, S., Naber, S.P., Makim, S.S., Bahl, M.: American joint committee on cancer's staging system for breast cancer, eighth edition: what the radiologist needs to know. RadioGraphics **38**(7), 1921–1933 (2018). https://doi.org/10.1148/rg.2018180056, pMID: 30265613
14. Krötzsch, M., Vrandečić, D., Völkel, M.: Semantic MediaWiki. In: Cruz, I., et al. (eds.) ISWC 2006. LNCS, vol. 4273, pp. 935–942. Springer, Heidelberg (2006). https://doi.org/10.1007/11926078_68
15. La Cava, L., Greco, S., Tagarelli, A.: Understanding the growth of the Fediverse through the lens of Mastodon. Appl. Netw. Sci. **6**(1), 1–35 (2021)
16. Le Hors, A.J., Speicher, S.: The linked data platform (LDP). In: Proceedings of the 22nd International Conference on World Wide Web, pp. 1–2 (2013)
17. Lin, Y., Liu, Z., Sun, M., Liu, Y., Zhu, X.: Learning entity and relation embeddings for knowledge graph completion. In: AAAI, vol. 15, pp. 2181–2187 (2015)
18. Maali, F., Erickson, J., Archer, P.: Data catalog vocabulary (DCAT). W3C recommendation. World Wide Web Consortium, pp. 29–126 (2014)

19. Margara, A., Urbani, J., Van Harmelen, F., Bal, H.: Streaming the web: reasoning over dynamic data. Web Semant.: Sci. Serv. Agents World Wide Web **25**, 24–44 (2014)
20. McCusker, J.P., Chastain, K., Rashid, S., Norris, S., McGuinness, D.L.: SETLr: the semantic extract, transform, and load-r. PeerJ Preprints **6**, e26476v1 (2018)
21. McCusker, J.P., Dumontier, M., Yan, R., He, S., Dordick, J.S., McGuinness, D.L.: Finding melanoma drugs through a probabilistic knowledge graph. PeerJ Comput. Sci. **3**, e106 (2017). https://doi.org/10.7717/peerj-cs.106
22. McCusker, J.P., Keshan, N., Rashid, S., Deagen, M., Brinson, C., McGuinness, D.L.: NanoMine: a knowledge graph for nanocomposite materials science. In: Pan, J.Z., et al. (eds.) ISWC 2020. LNCS, vol. 12507, pp. 144–159. Springer, Cham (2020). https://doi.org/10.1007/978-3-030-62466-8_10
23. McGuinness, D.L., Bennett, K.: Integrating semantics and numerics: case study on enhancing genomic and disease data using linked data technologies. In: Proceedings of SmartData, pp. 18–20 (2015)
24. Mons, B., Velterop, J.: Nano-publication in the e-science era. In: Workshop on Semantic Web Applications in Scientific Discourse (SWASD 2009), pp. 14–15 (2009)
25. Ogbuji, C.: SPARQL 1.1 graph store HTTP protocol. W3C recommendation, W3C (2013). http://www.w3.org/TR/2013/REC-sparql11-http-rdf-update-20130321/
26. Paskin, N.: Digital object identifier (doi®) system. Encyclopedia Libr. Inf. Sci. **3**, 1586–1592 (2010)
27. Rashid, S.M., et al.: The semantic data dictionary - an approach for describing and annotating data. Data Intell. **2**, 443–486 (2020)
28. Redaschi, N.: UniProt in RDF: tackling data integration and distributed annotation with the semantic web. Nat. Precedings 1 (2009)
29. Rietveld, L., Hoekstra, R.: The YASGUI family of SPARQL clients 1. Semant. Web **8**(3), 373–383 (2017)
30. Santos, H., et al.: A semantic framework for enabling radio spectrum policy management and evaluation. In: Pan, J.Z., et al. (eds.) ISWC 2020. LNCS, vol. 12507, pp. 482–498. Springer, Cham (2020). https://doi.org/10.1007/978-3-030-62466-8_30
31. Satyanarayan, A., Moritz, D., Wongsuphasawat, K., Heer, J.: Vega-lite: a grammar of interactive graphics. IEEE Trans. Vis. Comput. Graph. **23**(1), 341–350 (2016)
32. Seneviratne, O., et al.: Knowledge integration for disease characterization: a breast cancer example. In: Vrandečić, D., et al. (eds.) ISWC 2018. LNCS, vol. 11137, pp. 223–238. Springer, Cham (2018). https://doi.org/10.1007/978-3-030-00668-6_14
33. Singhal, A.: Introducing the knowledge graph: things, not strings. Official Google Blog (2012). https://googleblog.blogspot.com/2012/05/introducing-knowledge-graph-things-not.html. Accessed 11 Apr 2016
34. Smith, B., et al.: The OBO foundry: coordinated evolution of ontologies to support biomedical data integration. Nat. Biotechnol. **25**(11), 1251 (2007)
35. Ward, C.H.: Materials genome initiative for global competitiveness (2012). https://www.mgi.gov/sites/default/files/documents/materials_genome_initiative-final.pdf
36. Wongsuphasawat, K., Moritz, D., Anand, A., Mackinlay, J., Howe, B., Heer, J.: Voyager: Exploratory analysis via faceted browsing of visualization recommendations. IEEE Trans. Vis. Comput. Graph. **22**(1), 649–658 (2015)
37. Zhou, L., et al.: The enslaved dataset: a real-world complex ontology alignment benchmark using wikibase. In: Proceedings of the 29th ACM International Conference on Information & Knowledge Management, pp. 3197–3204 (2020)

In-Use

Prototyping an End-User User Interface for the Solid Application Interoperability Specification Under GDPR

Hadrien Bailly[1](✉), Anoop Papanna[1], and Rob Brennan[2]

[1] Dublin City University, Glasnevin Campus, Dublin 9, Ireland
{hadrien.bailly2,anoop.papanna2}@mail.dcu.ie
[2] ADAPT, University College Dublin, Belfield, Dublin 4, Ireland
rob.brennan@adaptcentre.ie

Abstract. This paper describes prototyping of the draft Solid application interoperability specification (INTEROP). We developed and evaluated a dynamic user interface (UI) for the new Solid application access request and authorization extended with the Data Privacy Vocabulary. Solid places responsibility on users to control their data. INTEROP adds new declarative access controls. Solid applications to date have provided few policy interfaces with high usability. GDPR controls on usage are rarely addressed. Implementation identified specification and Semantic Web tool issues and also in the understandability of declarative policies, a key concern under GDPR or data ethics best practices. The prototype was evaluated in a usability and task accuracy experiment, where the UI enabled users to create access and usage control policies with an accuracy of between 72 and 37%. Overall, the UI had a poor usability rating, with a median SUS (system usability scale) score of 37.67. Experimental participants were classified according to the Westin privacy scale to investigate the impact of user attitudes to privacy on the results. The paper discusses the findings of the study and their consequences for future data sovereignty access request and authorization UI designs.

Keywords: Solid · Access Control · User Interface · GDPR · Consent

1 Introduction

The Solid Platform was designed to address the loss of control over personal data [30]: enabling users from all backgrounds to regain control over their personal data and freely choose with whom to or not to share it. However, to date little attention has been given to how users - and particularly non-power users - would actually exert their control of access to their Solid Personal Online Datastore (*POD*). Another deficit has been Solid's use of Access Control List (ACL) policies to specify who can access which data [7], a process that is tedious and prone to errors [1], and does not allow users to specify what usage of their data is allowed – in spite of the fact that they are frequently unhappy with what happens

C. Pesquita et al. (Eds.): ESWC 2023, LNCS 13870, pp. 557–573, 2023.
https://doi.org/10.1007/978-3-031-33455-9_33

to their data after it was shared [24]. In 2022, the *Solid Data Interoperability Panel* (INTEROP) proposed a new, more intuitive specification to represent application access requests and user grants [2] with a more flexible policy model. In parallel, the Data Privacy Vocabulary (DPV) [22] has emerged for describing data processing purposes based on the European General Data Protection Regulation (GDPR). This legal exactness also comes with a potential cost in usability for non-experts. The INTEROP specification and DPV ontology are more expressive than Solid's original ACL approach and create innovation possibilities, but it is still not obvious how end users will be able to understand and manipulate their complex expressions.

This paper explores the following research question: *"To what extent can an access request and authorization UI effectively enable Solid users to specify INTEROP access policies and DPV usage control policies?"* It describes the design and evaluation of a new application access request and authorization UI for end users, based on first independent prototyping of the *Solid Data Interoperability Panel* (INTEROP) specification [2] combined with the *Data Privacy Vocabulary* (DPV) [22].

The contributions of the paper are as follows:

1. A new UI design for presenting Solid users with the access needs and intended processing actions of an application requesting access to their POD using the INTEROP specification;
2. A validation of the INTEROP specification through prototyping, resulting in a set of identified design issues and improvement suggestions;
3. A new open source prototype UI implementation of the INTEROP specification extended with the DPV, that generates fine-grained access and usage control authorizations according to the INTEROP data shape format;
4. A user evaluation of the new UI usability and user satisfaction, based on task completion accuracy, the System Usability Scale (SUS), Net Promoter Score (NPS) and a profile of users using the Westin Privacy scale.

The paper is structured as follows: Sect. 2 provides a motivating use case and lists the UI requirements; Sect. 3 overviews related work in Solid access and usage control and policy UI usability; Sect. 4 describes the UI design and its implementation; Sect. 5 details the user experiment; Finally, Sect. 6 describes conclusions.

2   Use Case and Requirements

This section illustrates the use of an application access request and authorization UI with an example use case drawn from the INTEROP specification [2].

Alice is a Solid User: she owns a POD, in which she stores both professional and personal data. Alice has several projects and tasks stored in her POD, and has found the Projectron app to manage them. Alice has never authorized Projectron before, so when she starts the app, she is presented with the application access request and authorization UI. First, Alice reviews Projectron's access needs, as defined by Projectron developers. These needs outline which (types of) data Projectron needs to access, what operations it will perform, and for what purpose, so Alice can understand what access she is asked to grant. Alice inspects each need, and decides that she will allow Projectron access her POD as described in the access request. She configures the scope of access for each need, then approves the request: the UI automatically generates a set of authorizations for Projectron. Projectron is now authorized. Later, when Projectron attempts to perform an operation on data in Alice's POD, the set of authorizations is used by an authorization agent to check if Projectron 1) was authorized by Alice; 2) is allowed to access that particular data in Alice's POD, and perform the requested operations on it; 3) has a purpose for performing the operation agreed to by Alice in the authorizations. If the attempt passes all checks, it can proceed, otherwise it is rejected.

This leads to these user and technical requirements for the application access request and authorization UI:

R1 When an arbitrary collection of access requirements in INTEROP format is present in a Solid request from an application, the UI shall graphically present it to the user. It must precisely identify what data the application requires and what operations it intends to conduct.

R2 The UI shall directly consume and produce Solid and RDF resources.

R3 The UI shall produce authorizations that can be used to allow/deny specified operations by a given application on any existing or future resource located in the user' POD.

R4 The UI shall enable users to "consent to the processing of their personal data for one or more specific purposes" (*EU General Data Protection Regulation (GDPR)*, art. 6.) [21].

R5 The UI shall support users "deciding whether it makes sense for them to share their personal data" [16], but avoid information overload.

R6 The UI shall be user-oriented [29], task-based [28], and enable users to create accurate authorizations.

3   Related Work

This section briefly describes Solid, Solid access and usage control schemes, Solid access control user interfaces, and usability evaluation techniques.

Solid and Usage and Access Control. Solid aims to return data sovereignty to web users [18]. It has two declared ambitions: 1) allow users to store data in a decentralized POD, and reuse it for multiple purposes (applications), 2) allow users to share data from their POD securely with multiple service providers. Solid relies on the *Resource Description Framework* (RDF), which enables third parties to locate and interact with a user's resources. Sharing resources requires that their owners can protect it from unwanted or unauthorized access. The ability of a data owner to authorize access and use of a resource has two dimensions:

access and usage control [27], where **access** denotes the authorization to read and edit some resources, and **usage** the conditions and obligations associated with this authorization. Traditionally, access control models encompass *Mandatory Access Control* (MAC), *Discretionary Access Control* (DAC), *Role-Based Access Control* (RBAC), and *View-Based Access Control* (VBAC) models. Additional models have been proposed, the most notable being the *Attribute-Based Access Control* (ABAC), and *Context-Based Access Control* (CBAC) models [15].

Simple access control models using access control lists (ACL) can take a document-centric view of RDF that applies to groups of triples in a document. More fine-grained controls use declarative constraint languages to describe what a resource contains (or should contain). To that end, RDF systems can make use of two constraint languages: SHACL[1] and ShEx (*Shape Expression*)[2], which define the *shape* with which the graph of a given resource is expected to comply. To describe complex sets of resources, multiple shapes can be assembled together to form *Shape Trees*[3]. Shapes and shape trees can be used to scope access or usage controls in the INTEROP specification.

Table 1. Access & Usage Control Protocols in Solid

Protocol		Personal Data Sovereignty				User experience	
		Model	Access	Usage	GDPR	UI	Task-based
Web Access Control (WAC)	[6]	DAC	✓	✗	✗	✓ [12]	✗
Access Control Policy (ACP)	[3]	CBAC	✓	✓	✗	✗	✗
Data Interoperability Panel Specification (INTEROP)	[2]	DAC	✓	✗	✗	?	✓
eXtensible Access Control Markup Language (XACML)	[26]	ABAC	✓	✗	✗	✗	✗
Open Data Rights Language (ODRL)	[11]	CBAC	✓	✓	✗	✗	✗
Open Regulatory Compliance Profile (ORCP)	[14]	CBAC	✓	✓	✓	✗	✗
ODRL Profile for Access Control (OAC)	[9]	CBAC	✓	✓	✓	✓SOPE [8]	✗

Currently, Solid resources are mainly secured using the DAC model and ACLs. Table 1 summarises the main protocols that have been proposed for Solid. *Web Access Control* (WAC) [6] is the current Solid standard. It uses ACL permission files to define the operations that an application can execute on a given resource. WAC offers only unrestricted read, write, append or control access to a resource, or no access at all – context or usage restrictions can only be supplied by the application. *Access Control Policy* (ACP) [3] was presented as an alternative, using context and conditions to limit operations on resources beyond binary access authorization. In the new INTEROP specification [2] rather than controlling individual resources or resource containers, users dynamically create policies for the needs of applications as a whole. When connecting with a new application, users are presented with an access request outlining a set of access needs for the application. Users can define either explicit authorizations to given

---

[1] https://www.w3.org/TR/shacl/.

[2] https://shex.io/shex-semantics/index.html.

[3] https://shapetrees.org/TR/specification/.

resources, or implicit ones to (existing or future) resources of a given data shape and location. An authorization agent is then responsible for inferring effective permissions for each resource in the POD. The access policies created under the INTEROP specification do not include usage control. The Open Data Rights Language (ODRL) Profile for Access Control (OAC) [9] aligns access and usage permissions with the GDPR for Solid. It ensures usage control policies can be written in compliance with the GDPR's requirements using the Data Privacy Vocabulary (DPV) [22].

Solid Access Control User Interfaces. Solid users can only currently create and manage WAC and OAC policies, using off-the-shelf file editors [12], and summarized in Table 1. The INTEROP specification has not to date been implemented in a user interface – although a wireframe design[4] was presented. Off the shelf editors are inappropriate to manage security: the policy editing workload is often too heavy, even for simple tasks [5] and most users, even experts, fail to recognize the implications of changes [1]. The design of Access Control UIs must balance between the need for accurate information and the reluctance or inability of users to process lengthy policies [19]. These UIs should be simple and task-oriented, and not require previous knowledge of the underlying technical model [28]. The level of understanding of ACL permissions, and security policies in general, is dependent on two factors: the technical knowledge of the user and the design of the UI [10]. Solid aims to address all categories of users, including members of the public. The access control UI design must reflect this.

Usability and Satisfaction Evaluation for Privacy Systems. The System Usability Scale (SUS) [4] is one of the most frequently used techniques to evaluate usability. SUS is a 10-item questionnaire that generates a 0–100 score from each participant. A system is considered above average usability if it scores above 68 for more than 50% of the participants. SUS does not identify causes of usability problems. To detect these, software engineers can instead use the Nielsen's 10 Design Heuristics and think-aloud [20]. This allows a limited number of evaluators to consistently identify most of the issues in a UI.

User satisfaction is also important in the success of a system. The *Net Promoter Score* (NPS) [25] is a tool frequently used to quickly evaluate the user satisfaction. It consists of a single rating question, ranging from 1 to 10 and asking whether a user is likely to recommend a product to family, colleague or friend. If the respondents rate the UI under 7, then they are said to be *detractors*. NPS can be followed by an open question to allow the respondents to elaborate. The pertinence of the NPS alone as an accurate measure for user satisfaction is debated [31], and it is advised to cross-check with other metrics and feedback.

Finally, it has been shown that the *profile* of users also plays a significant role in their perceived user experience [17]. When it comes to sharing private

---

[4] https://github.com/solid/data-interoperability-panel/blob/main/proposals/primer/images/authorization-screen.svg.

data, the popular Westin Scale defines three classes of users [16], which can be uncovered with a short 5-item questionnaire: 1) 34% of users are *fundamentalists*. They are concerned about their privacy, and proactively refuse to provide data; 2) 8% of users are *unconcerned*, least protective of their data and considering that the benefits of sharing outweigh the risks of breach; 3) The remaining users (58%) are *pragmatic* in their approach to privacy. They evaluate the pros and cons, and share data if it makes sense to them.

In summary, Solid relies heavily on the personal control of data sharing, yet the current access control protocols are coarse-grained and based on DAC models that do not support application needs well (**R2, R3**). The INTEROP specification aims to fix this with more expressive shape-based policies based on application needs (**R1, R5**), but users are not currently supported by appropriate access control UIs (**R1, R5, R6**) and INTEROP will place even more demands on them. In addition, GDPR-compliant usage control (**R4**) is not directly addressed.

4   A Proposed Application Access Request and Authorization User Interface for INTEROP

This section describes the architecture, features and implementation of a new dynamic access control UI for INTEROP (Fig. 1). The UI prototyping discussed identified gaps and two design issues in the draft INTEROP specification.

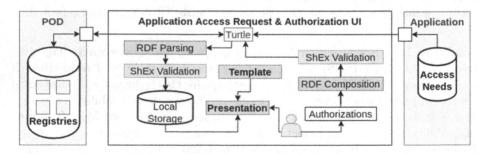

Fig. 1. Application Access Request and Authorization User Interface Architecture

4.1   Design

This UI was designed to meet the requirements in Sect. 2. It enables users to review arbitrary access requests from applications (**R1**) to use RDF resources (needs) (**R2**), and create INTEROP authorizations corresponding to the access needs (**R3**). When presenting a request, the UI provides explicit information about which resources are needed and for what GDPR-style purpose (**R4**), and gives users the opportunity to grant or refuse access (**R5**).

To display the access request and create the authorization, the UI requires input from two sources: 1) information about the content (registries) from the user's POD, and 2) the collection of access needs requested by an application. As per INTEROP, the input is received in RDF, parsed, and validated against ShEx shapes. When data has been received, an application access request UI is dynamically generated from a template and presented to the user for review (as show in Fig. 1). The user can inspect the request, select/deselect optional access needs, specify the extent (scope of) access, and decide whether to accept the request (**R1, R5**). If accepted, then the corresponding access and data authorizations are generated according to the user specification, composed into RDF triples and validated against ShEx, before being returned to the POD for enforcement by the INTEROP authorization agent (**R3**).

The design combines the INTEROP specification and the DPV to provide users with structured information about the application access request (**R1, R4**). It uses the INTEROP definition of access needs to present the access requirements of the application – in terms of type of resources accessed (shapes) and technical ACL permissions. Then this is supplemented with DPV terminology: first to describe the sensitivity of the data access and the purpose of use, and second to record the purpose to which the users consent to (e.g. *dpv:Service Provision* vs *dpv:Analytics*).

To discover what are the access needs of an application, and generate the access request UI, it draws a directed tree containing all the access needs and descriptions, starting from the application profile resource (`interop:Application`). However, this is currently impeded by two INTEROP design choices: (1) the use of collections and (2) several predicates incompatible with a directed tree structure (*backlinks*). For instance, a description is linked to an access need using the predicate `AccessNeedDescription.hasAccessNeed`, while no other node in the graph possesses an IRI pointing to this description. As a result, to obtain the description of an access need, one needs to 1) return to the parent access need group, 2) retrieve the corresponding access description set and unnamed collection of descriptions, and 3) iterate over all access need descriptions resources until one is found with a backlink `hasAccessNeed` to the need.

To overcome these issues, new predicates were introduced into the shape expressions:

- `accessNeed.hasAccessNeed` to obtain the list of dependent access needs, and
- `accessNeedGroup.hasAccessNeedGroupDescription` and `accessNeed.hasAccessNeedDescription` to obtain the corresponding descriptions by language.

It was also detected that the INTEROP specification is inconsistent in its use of the predicates `skos:prefLabel` and `skos:definition` to provide labels and descriptions. Several shapes miss either a label, a description, or both – such as `SocialAgent` or `DataInstance` (cf. Table 2). Other shapes use them inconsistently, e.g. between `AccessNeedDescription` using `prefLabel` as label and `AccessNeedGroupDescription` as definition. This does not prevent the creation of directed trees or presentation of authorization requests, but it precludes the use of human-readable labels over IRI in a dynamic user interface and violates ontology design best practices P20 [23]. New (`skos`) predicates were again introduced into the shape expressions of a number of resources to enforce the presence of these predicates for access request UI generation (cf. Table 4).

Table 2. INTEROP Concepts Missing Labels and Descriptions

Resource	Has Label	Has Description
Social Agent	✖	✖
Access Need Group*	✔	✔
Access Need*	✖	✔
Data Registry	✖	✖
Data Instance	✖	✖

resources using linked description

Finally, we propose the following changes in the INTEROP specification: (1) to alter the signification of the scope of access `Inherited` and (2) to include a new scope `Dependent`. This new scope of access enables users to reuse – instead of duplicate – the scope of access that has been selected in a similar access need. See Table 3 and Listing 1 for a comprehensive description of the new scope `Dependent` and revision of the existing scope `Inherited`, and Fig. 2 for an example.

Table 3. Revised Scopes of Access

Scope of Access	Dependency	Inheritance
Keyword	**Dependent**	**Inherited**
Predicate	**hasAccessNeed**	**inheritsFromNeed**
Relationship	Links to access needs whose registered shape tree is referenced by the shape tree associated with the current access need	Links to another access need whose registered shape tree is the same as the current access need
Example	*Assignees depend on a project*	*Assignees inherit from contacts*

Listing 1. Proposed DataAuthorizationDependentShape

```
<DataAuthorizationDependentShape> {
  a [ interop : DataAuthorization ] ,
    interop : grantee                    IRI  ,
    interop : registeredShapeTree        IRI  ,
    interop : satisfiesAccessNeed        IRI? ,
    interop : accessMode                 @<#AccessModes>+ ,
    interop : creatorAccessMode          @<#AccessModes>* ,
  interop : scopeOfAuthorization         [ interop : Dependent ] ,
  interop : dependsFromAuthorization     IRI
}
```

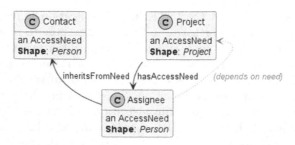

Fig. 2. Revised Scope of Access - Example

Table 4. INTEROP Shapes Suggested Predicates Changes Summary

Shape	Predicates Changes
AccessNeedShape	+ interop:hasAccessNeed
	+ interop:hasAccessNeedDescription
	+ interop:hasPurpose
AccessNeedGroupShape	+ interop:hasAccessNeedGroupDescription
	− interop:hasAccessDescriptionSet
AccessNeedDescriptionShape	+ skos:definition
DataRegistrationShape	+ ldp:contains
DataAuthorization-SelectedFromRegistryShape	− interop:hasDataRegistration
SocialAgentShape	+ foaf:name
	+ foaf:givenName
	+ foaf:familyName

4.2   Implementation

The open source prototype implementation is a Vue.js web application with a Java/PostgreSQL back-end[5] available under a GNU GPL v3.0 license.

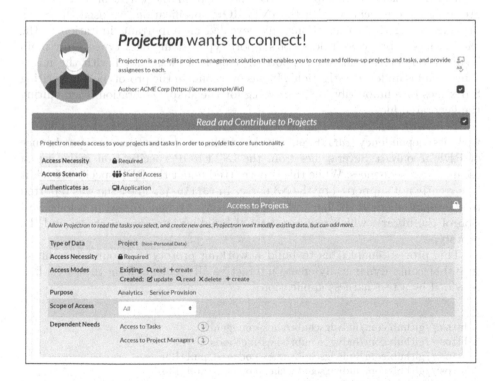

Fig. 3. Solid INTEROP Application Access Request User Interface

---

[5] **Source Code**: https://github.com/HBailly/solid-auth-ui/.

It has two goals: 1) implement the application access requests and authorization from the INTEROP specification, and 2) prototype our UI architecture for experiments enabling users to view and interact with application requests, and create corresponding authorizations. The scope does not include realizing an INTEROP authorization agent, nor enforcing the authorizations (although they are validated, see experiment).

The prototype dynamically loads access requests from a set of files stored on the server, validates the contents, and populates a Vue.js template. Users are presented with the populated template (Fig. 3), and can review the application access needs, then customize the authorizations they want to grant. On submission, the server stores the authorizations in a PostgreSQL database. All data exchanges are handled natively in RDF. The front-end depends on the `shex-codegen`[6] and `shex-methods`[7] Node.js libraries to parse and interact with the turtle files: All inputs/outputs are converted from and to RDF triples, and verified against ShEx models. The implementation uses the referenced RDF ontologies to fetch term descriptions and generate UI elements and tooltips.

`shex-codegen` is used during development to generate JavaScript objects (*sha-pes*) from a list of ShExes. These shapes can then be used at runtime with `shex-methods` to manipulate RDF nodes from the turtle files. To generate all shapes associated with the INTEROP specification, we used the ShEx provided along the specification. This revealed an important limitation in the `shex-codegen` library, as it does not support typed string data types. Only plain RDF literals are adequately supported. This issue was raised with the maintainer, and is under investigation[8]. It was overcome in the prototype by rewriting ShEx files to temporarily use `xsd:string` for the shape generation, then editing the generated files.

This work also revealed an issue with the `shex-methods` library, specifically with its dependency `rdflib.js`, which handles the creation and persistence of RDF resources. Several files from the INTEROP specification make use of escaped text sequences. While this is permitted under the RDF specification[9], it is currently not supported by the N3 parser in `rdflib.js`. The issue was reported to the maintainers of the library[10]. A temporary fix was applied in a local version of the library, which requires manual building into `shex-methods`, and the prototype[11].

This process enabled us to build a working prototype of our UI architecture that could dynamically create interactive UI elements from the turtle files provided by a test harness application.

[6] https://github.com/ludwigschubi/shex-codegen.
[7] https://github.com/ludwigschubi/shex-methods.
[8] https://github.com/ludwigschubi/shex-codegen/pull/139
    https://github.com/ludwigschubi/shex-codegen/pull/140.
[9] https://www.w3.org/TR/turtle/.
[10] https://github.com/linkeddata/rdflib.js/pull/523
    https://github.com/linkeddata/rdflib.js/pull/557.
[11] https://github.com/HBailly/solid-auth-ui/blob/main/pom.xml#942.

5   Evaluation

This section presents two evaluations of the prototype, verifying whether the design met the requirements **R5** and **R6**. The first evaluation was based on the Nielsen Heuristics and took place during the design and implementation phase of the prototype, while the second evaluation focused on the SUS, NPS and user feedback about the definitive version in a structured online experiment.

5.1   Demos and Usability Heuristics

The prototype was first demoed to participants of the *COST EU Workshop on Privacy Issues in Distributed Social Knowledge Graphs* (PIDSKG)[12]. Approximately 20 attendees were introduced to the research, shown the user interface, and were able to ask questions or raise concerns. The most frequently expressed concerns were about the ease of use, and the lack of an option to quickly select/deselect all optional access needs.

Next, the prototype was submitted to three preliminary evaluators from the ADAPT Research Centre, who were familiar with Linked Data and programming. They were tasked with evaluating the prototype using Nielsen's design heuristics. The evaluations took place remotely, in short sessions of 30 min, where the evaluators were also introduced to the research topic. They were then invited to use the UI and find violations of the heuristics (see Table 5). They raised issues regarding the vocabulary used in the interface, which was often complex and technical. They also pointed out several visibility issues with the appearance of buttons and relations between sections of the UI.

Table 5. Heuristics Breaches Identified Count

Heuristic	Description	Severity				
		Minor	Moderate	Serious	Severe	Critical
1 Visibility	*Visibility of system status*	0	0	0	0	0
2 Information	*Match between system and real world*	2	2	1	0	0
3 Consistency	*Consistency and standards*	0	0	0	0	0
4 Recognition	*Recognition rather than recall*	2	1	0	0	0
5 Flexibility	*Flexibility and efficiency of use*	0	0	0	0	0
6 Minimalism	*Aesthetic and minimalist design*	0	0	0	0	0

Post-Evaluation UI Refinement. The UI was reworked partially to include cascading selection of access needs and other shortcuts. The INTEROP ontology was also locally edited, and the terms identified as too technical by the evaluators were updated.

5.2   SUS, NPS, Access Authorization Validity and User Feedback

The second evaluation was a formal experiment to validate the prototype usability and user-friendliness, that it met the requirements from Sect. 2, and

---

[12] https://cost-dkg.eu/.

empowered users to correctly create access authorizations. It was an asynchronous, opt-in experiment.

Participants were selected from two categories in two areas of expertise: experts in the Solid ecosystem and/or in GDPR legal requirements, and students in computing or in privacy law. The participants were invited from: the COST ACTION DKG Conference on SOLID 2022 attendees, the Solid community Forum, the Solid Data Interoperability Panel Gitter, LinkedIn, the DCU Master in Computing 2022, and personal communications. The experiment was freely available online: any person with the link could connect, complete the tasks and the questionnaires. A major power failure in the host site reduced participant numbers during the collection period.

The experiment itself was designed as follows: 1) Participants first completed a questionnaire on demographic data, relevant expertise and the Westin privacy classification questions. 2) Participants were then introduced to the research topic and provided with brief background, as well as links to further internet resources, short videos[13] introducing the user interface, and a glossary of terms. 3) Participants received guidelines on three directed tasks. During each task, they were requested to grant access authorizations corresponding to a gold standard, using the prototype. They were also presented with the situation they were asked to imagine themselves in (next paragraph). Participants conducted the three tasks sequentially in the same order. The task output and execution time were recorded. 4) Participants were invited to score the user interface using SUS and NPS questionnaires, and to provide feedback about their experience[14].

The three directed tasks placed the participant into the position of *Alice* as per our Use Case (Sect. 2) derived from the INTEROP specification. Alice is presented with the application's access request and must decide what access to authorize (*permissions*). Each task is a variation of the access request, and requires the user to select the same permissions each time. The variations are of increasing complexity: i) a simple access request with five access needs (*flat hierarchy*); ii) introduces dependency between the access needs, and similar needs within different dependencies (*nested hierarchy*); and iii) includes inheritance on top of the dependency (*nested hierarchy with inheritance*).

5.3 Results and Discussion

In total, there were **15** participants to the experiment: Most were male, aged less than 36, and all had at least a bachelor's degree. Using Jensen 2005's Westin classification questionnaire [13], we observed a slightly more privacy-concerned distribution of the participants (ordinarily 26-64-10% [16], 33.3-60-6.7% in the experiment). Many had previous experience with programming, and there were experts in Solid, INTEROP and/or GDPR privacy law.

Tasks: On average, it took between 2.5 and 4.5 min to complete a task. The observed the number of errors follows the increasing complexity of the tasks.

---

[13] https://github.com/HBailly/solid-auth-ui/tree/main/tutorials/.

[14] https://github.com/HBailly/solid-auth-ui/tree/main/docs/questionnaires.

The sharing of contacts proved to be the most challenging part of the directed tasks (78.5% average error rate). Moreover, none of the participants de-selected an optional access need during any of the directed tasks, even if they had a high desire for privacy (perhaps due to the low stakes or personal involvement in the tasks). Table 6 summarizes the authorizations crafted by the participants, and compares them with the gold standard requested by the tasks.

Table 6. User-granted Authorization Deviations from Gold Standard

Access Need	Gold Standard	OK	Authorization granted when deviating from gold standard[a]							Total
			All	All From Registry	Selected From Registry	All From Agent	Dependent	Inherited	None	
Version 1										
need-project	*All from Registry*	9 60.0%	2 13.3%	0 0%	3 20/0%	1 6.7%	0 0%	0 0%	0 0%	15
need-task	*All from Registry*	11 73.3%	2 13.3%	1 6.7%	1 6.7%	0 0%	0 0%	0 0%	0 0%	15
need-contact	*Selected From Registry*	10 66.7%	0 0%	2 13.3%	0 0%	0 0%	3 3.%	0 0%	0 0%	15
need-account-details	*All*	13 86.7%	0 0%	1 6.7%	0 0%	1 6.7%	0 0%	0 0%	0 0%	15
need-credit-details	*Selected From Registry*	11 73.3%	1 6.7%	3 20.0%	0 0%	0 0%	0 0%	0 0%	0 0%	15
Version 2										
need-project	*All from Registry*	10 66.7%	1 6.7%	0 0%	3 20%	1 6.7%	0 0%	0 0%	0 0%	15
need-task	*All from Agent*	10 66.7%	1 6.7%	2 13.3%	2 13.3%	0 0%	0 0%	0 0%	0 0%	15
need-contact-project	*None*	0 0%	3 10.3%	0 0%	7 0%	1 6.7%	4 26.7%	0 0%	0 0%	15
need-contact-task	*Selected From Registry*	5 33.3%	1 6.7%	1 6.7%	2 13.3%	2 13.3%	4 26.7%	0 0%	0 0%	15
need-account-details	*All*	11 73.3%	0 0%	4 26.7%	0 0%	0 0%	0 0%	0 0%	0 0%	15
need-credit-details	*Selected From Registry*	13 86.7%	0 0%	2 13.3%	0 0%	0 0%	0 0%	0 0%	0 0%	15
Version 3[b]										
need-project	*All from Registry*	7 50%	5 35.7%	0 0%	1 7.1%	1 7.1%	0 0%	0 0%	0 0%	14
need-task	*All from Agent*	7 50%	3 21.4%	2 14.3%	2 14.3%	0 0%	0 0%	0 0%	0 0%	14
need-contact	*None*	0 0%	4 28.6%	0 0%	9 64.3%	1 7.1%	0 0%	0 0%	0 0%	14
need-contact-project	*None*	3 21.4%	0 0%	0 0%	1 7.1%	1 7.1%	0 0%	9 64.3%	0 0%	14
need-contact-task	*Selected From Registry*	1 7.1%	1 7.1%	0 0%	1 7.1%	1 7.1%	0 0%	10 71.4%	0 0%	14
need-account-details	*All*	10 71.4%	0 0%	4 28.6%	0 0%	0 0%	0 0%	0 0%	0 0%	14
need-credit-details	*Selected From Registry*	11 78.6%	1 7.1%	2 14.3%	0 0%	0 0%	0 0%	0 0%	0 0%	14

[a] A deviation value of 1 with the same scope as the gold standard (e.g. *All from Registry*) indicates that a participant selected the right type of scope (*All from Registry*), but a wrong value (an incorrect registry).
[b] One of the participants skipped the version 3 task, and is thus excluded from the analysis of this version.

Usability: Overall, the prototype only scored over 37.67 for more than 50% of the participants of the survey using the System Usability Scale (the details of which are presented in Table 7), which indicates *poor* usability. This score was independent of the nationality, level of education, expertise, or Westin privacy classes. Participants were primarily concerned by the technicality, complexity and cumbersomeness of the UI, which directly exposed the complex application resource requests. Most participants also found that the process was too long, but more than half thought that it was worthwhile. The participants with the most negative attitude towards the UI were also those finding the duration excessive.

Table 7. SUS Questionnaire

Question	Strongly disagree	Disagree	Neutral	Agree	Strongly agree
I think that I would like to use this system frequently	4 26.7%	2 13.3%	4 26.7%	5 33.3%	0 0%
I found the system unnecessarily complex	1 6.7%	4 26.7%	3 20%	3 20%	4 26.7%
I thought the system was easy to use	4 26.7%	3 20%	4 26.7%	4 26.7%	0 0%
I think that I would need the support of a technical person to be able to use this system	1 6.7%	4 26.7%	1 6.7%	9 60%	0 0%
I found the various functions in this system were well integrated	0 0%	2 13.3%	5 33.3%	7 46.7%	1 6.7%
I thought there was too much inconsistency in this system	2 13.3%	7 46.7%	5 33.3%	0 0%	1 6.7%
I would imagine that most people would learn to use this system very quickly	6 40%	4 26.7%	1 6.7%	4 26.7%	0 0%
I found the system very cumbersome to use	0 0%	3 20%	3 20%	7 46.7%	2 13.3%
I felt very confident using the system	7 46.7%	2 13.3%	4 26.7%	1 6.7%	1 6.7%
I needed to learn a lot of things before I could get going with this system	0 0%	6 40%	2 13.3%	5 33.3%	2 13.3%

Participants were divided when declaring their satisfaction with the prototype, as highlighted by the Net Promoter Score (5.4 on average - *detractor* stance), and the propensity to use it again (*Positive*: 5; *Neutral*: 4; *Negative*: 6). Noticeably, participants belonging to the fundamentalists were more positive about the prototype (*average*: 8; *count*: 5), whereas participants belonging to the pragmatic class were more likely to be detractors (*average*: 3.67; *count*: 9)[15]. Participants with a strong Solid or interop background also had a higher Net Promoter Score than the others.

When asked what version of the task they found the most appropriate/informative, participants either chose the first (*flat hierarchy*) (in majority) or the third version (*nested hierarchy with inheritance*). We found that the dividing line was also the Westin classification of participants: pragmatic users largely preferred the flat version (80%), while fundamentalists preferred the nested version (40%) or none (40%) (See Footnote 15). The most frequent reasons given by the pragmatic users were that it was simpler and offered less choice, hence less

---

[15] There was not enough data to evaluate the unconcerned.

confusion, and that the dependency and inheritance mechanisms were not given away by the prototype. On the contrary, 60% of the fundamentalists praised the hierarchy, as it allowed them to better assess the consequences of granting access (the other 40% did not notice the difference). More generally, participants were united in pointing out how there was too much information displayed, with many technical terms, whereas they would have preferred a more incremental process, perhaps with a wizard, or a multilayered UI.

Finally, participants rated positively the visual and textual aids of the prototype. No participant questioned the actual contents of the shapes requested, even the fundamentalists, and found them moderately to very informative. Participants did not agree on the utility of the GDPR purpose added in this design: participants without little knowledge of privacy law and fundamentalists found them informative, whereas pragmatics and people with declared expertise did not notice them. Interestingly, 67% of participants rated the access modes informative. When investigating whether they knew the difference between the modes for existing instances, and instances created by the application after it was authorized, only the participants with Solid expertise could tell correctly.

6   Conclusion

This paper prototyped the Solid INTEROP specification with an original UI to enable users to review application access requirements and define access and usage authorizations. We identified areas for improvement in the INTEROP draft specification, both in terms of Semantic Web best practice and to better support dynamic access control UI generation (Sect. 4). We showed that Solid is not using best practices in policy interfaces (Sect. 3) by relying on text editors, and that usage control remains an open issue under INTEROP. Our dynamic UI prototype based on Semantic Web tools identified limitations with current Semantic Web tools and libraries. Usability evidence collected also suggested that the fine-grained and expressive controls of INTEROP will require careful UI design to avoid overwhelming users (Sect. 5). The main reasons were the length and complexity of the requests and the terminology used. Participants felt in control of their data, but repeatedly failed in tasks to correctly generate authorizations and could not explain what access modes they granted. This is a limited study (n = 15), mainly conducted with experts, and a broader study should be conducted next.

Acknowledgement. This research had the financial support of Science Foundation Ireland under the ADAPT Centre for AI-driven Digital Content Technology, SFI Research Centres Programme (Grant 13/RC/2106_P2). For the purpose of Open Access, the authors have applied a CC-BY public copyright license to any author accepted manuscript version arising from this submission.

References

1. Beznosov, K., et al.: Usability meets access control, vol. 2807, p. 73. ACM Press (2009). https://doi.org/10.1145/1542207.1542220
2. Bingham, J., Prud'Hommeaux, E., Pavlik, E.: Solid Application Interoperability. W3C Editor's Draft (2022). https://solid.github.io/data-interoperability-panel/specification/
3. Bosquet, M.: Access Control Policy (ACP). Solid Editor's Draft (2022). https://solid.github.io/authorization-panel/acp-specification/
4. Brooke, J.: SUS: a quick and dirty usability scale. In: Usability Evaluation In Industry. CRC Press (1996). Chap. Off-the-Shelf Evaluation Methods. https://doi.org/10.1201/9781498710411-35
5. Cao, X., Iverson, L.: Intentional access management: making access control usable for end-users. In: Proceedings of the Second Symposium on Usable Privacy and Security, SOUPS 2006, Pittsburgh, Pennsylvania, USA, pp. 20–31. Association for Computing Machinery (2006). https://doi.org/10.1145/1143120.1143124
6. Capadisli, S., Berners-Lee, T.: Web Access Control. Version 1.0.0. Editor's Draft (2022). https://solid.github.io/web-access-control-spec/
7. Capadisli, S., et al.: Solid Protocol. Version 0.9.0 (2021). https://solidproject.org/TR/protocol
8. Esteves, B.: Solid ODRL access control Policies Editor. GitHub (2022). https://github.com/besteves4/solid-sope
9. Esteves, B., et al.: Using the ODRL profile for access control for solid pod resource governance. In: Extended Semantic Web Conference (ESWC) (2022). https://doi.org/10.5281/zenodo.6614777
10. Hamid, E., Jaafar, A., Choo, A.M.: A review of 'human-computer interaction' influence to home network. Jurnal Teknologi 75, 21–27 (2015). https://doi.org/10.11113/jt.v75.5038
11. Iannella, R., Villata, S.: ODRL Information Model. Version 2.2. W3C Recommendation (2018). https://www.w3.org/TR/odrl-model
12. Inrupt Inc., Access Policies: Universal API (2022). https://docs.inrupt.com/developer-tools/javascript/client-libraries/tutorial/manage-access-policies/
13. Jensen, C., Potts, C., Jensen, C.: Privacy practices of Internet users: self-reports versus observed behavior. Int. J. Hum.-Comput. Stud. 63(1–2), 203–227 (2005). https://doi.org/10.1016/j.ijhcs.2005.04.019
14. Kirrane, S., De Vos, M., Padget, J.: ODRL Regulatory Compliance Profile. Version 0.2. W3C Unofficial Draft (2020). https://ai.wu.ac.at/policies/orcp/regulatory-model.html
15. Kirrane, S., Mileo, A., Decker, S.: Access control and the resource description framework: a survey. In: Grau, B.C. (ed.) Semantic Web 8, pp. 311–352 (2016). https://doi.org/10.3233/SW-160236
16. Kumaraguru, P., Cranor, L.: Privacy indexes: a survey of Westin's studies. Technical report, Carnegie Mellon University, Pittsburgh, PA (2005). https://www.cs.cmu.edu/ponguru/CMU-ISRI-05-138.pdf
17. Liu, Y., Osvalder, A.-L., Karlsso, M.A.: Considering the importance of user profiles in interface design. In: User Interfaces, p. 270 (2010). https://doi.org/10.5772/8903
18. Mansour, E., et al.: A demonstration of the solid platform for social web applications. In: Proceedings of the 25th International Conference Companion on World Wide Web, WWW 2016, Companion, pp. 223–226. ACM Press, New York (2016). https://doi.org/10.1145/2872518.2890529

19. Meier, Y., Schäwel, J., Krämer, N.C.: The shorter the better? Effects of privacy policy length on online privacy decision- making. Media Commun. **8**, 291–301 (2020). https://doi.org/10.17645/mac.v8i2.2846
20. Nielsen, J.: Thinking Aloud: The #1 Usability Tool. Nielsen Norman Group (2012). https://www.nngroup.com/articles/thinking-aloud-the-1-usability-tool/
21. Official Journal of the European Union. General Data Protection Regulation (2016/679). Brussels (2016). http://eur-lex.europa.eu/legal-content/EN/TXT/PDF/?uri=CELEX:32016R0679
22. Pandit, H.J., et al.: Creating a vocabulary for data privacy. In: Panetto, H., Debruyne, C., Hepp, M., Lewis, D., Ardagna, C.A., Meersman, R. (eds.) OTM 2019. LNCS, vol. 11877, pp. 714–730. Springer, Cham (2019). https://doi.org/10.1007/978-3-030-33246-4_44
23. Poveda-Villalón, M., Gómez-Pérez, A., Suárez-Figueroa, M.C.: OOPS! (OntOlogy Pitfall Scanner!): an on-line tool for ontology evaluation. Int. J. Semant. Web Inf. Syst. (IJSWIS) **10**(2), 7–34 (2014)
24. Rainie, L., Duggan, M.: Americans' Opinions on Privacy and Information Sharing. Pew Research Center (2016). https://www.pewresearch.org/internet/2016/01/14/privacy-and-informationsharing/
25. Reichheld, F.F.: The One Number You Need to Grow. Growth Strategy (2003). https://hbr.org/2003/12/the-one-number-youneed-to-grow
26. Rissanen, E.: eXtensible Access Control Markup Language (XACML). Committee Draft 03. Version 3.0. Oasis (2010). http://docs.oasis-open.org/xacml/3.0/xacml-3.0-core-spec-cd-03-en.pdf
27. Sandhu, R., Park, J.: Usage control: a vision for next generation access control. In: Gorodetsky, V., Popyack, L., Skormin, V. (eds.) MMM-ACNS 2003. LNCS, vol. 2776, pp. 17–31. Springer, Heidelberg (2003). https://doi.org/10.1007/978-3-540-45215-7_2
28. Thomas, R.K., Sandhu, R.S.: Conceptual foundations for a model of task-based authorizations. In: Proceedings of the Computer Security Foundations Workshop, pp. 66–79 (1995). https://doi.org/10.1109/CSFW.1994.315946
29. Vaniea, K., et al.: Access control policy analysis and visualization tools for security professionals. In: SOUPS Workshop on Usable IT Security Management (USM) 2008, Pittsburgh, PA, USA, pp. 7–15 (2008). https://cups.cs.cmu.edu/soups/2008/USM/vaniea.pdf
30. Verborgh, R.: Re-decentralizing the Web, for good this time. In: Seneviratne, O., Hendler, J. (eds.) Linking the World's Information: A Collection of Essays on the Work of Sir Tim Berners-Lee. ACM (2022). https://ruben.verborgh.org/articles/redecentralizing-the-web/
31. Zaki, M., et al.: The Fallacy of the Net Promoter Score: Customer Loyalty Predictive Model. University of Cambridge (2016). https://cambridgeservicealliance.eng.cam.ac.uk/system/files/documents/2016OctoberPaper_FallacyoftheNetPromoterScore.pdf

SemReasoner - A High-Performance Knowledge Graph Store and Rule-Based Reasoner

Kevin Angele[1,3]($\boxtimes$), Jürgen Angele[2], Umutcan Simsek[1], and Dieter Fensel[1]

[1] Semantic Technology Institute Innsbruck, University of Innsbruck, Technikerstrasse 21a, 6020 Innsbruck, Austria
{`kevin.angele,umutcan.simsek,dieter.fensel`}`@sti2.at`
[2] adesso, Competence Center Artificial Intelligence, Pariser Bogen 5, 44269 Dortmund, Germany
`juergen.angele@adesso.de`
[3] Onlim GmbH, Weintraubengasse 22, 1020 Vienna, Austria
`kevin.angele@onlim.com`

Abstract. Knowledge graphs have become essential for integrating data from heterogeneous sources powering intelligent applications. Integrating data from various sources often results in incomplete knowledge that needs to be enriched based on custom inference rules. Handling a large number of facts requires a scalable storage layer that must be seamlessly integrated into the reasoning algorithms to guarantee efficient evaluation of rules and query answering over the knowledge graph. To this end, we present SemReasoner, a comprehensive, scalable, high-performance knowledge graph store and rule-based reasoner. SemReasoner includes a deductive reasoning engine and fully supports document store functionality for JSON documents. SemReasoner's modular architecture is easy to extend and integrate into existing IT landscapes and applications. We evaluate SemReasoner against the state-of-the-art rule-based reasoning engines using test cases from OpenRuleBench. The results show that SemReasoner outperforms existing engines in most test cases.

Keywords: SemReasoner · OO-Logic · Rules · Knowledge Graph Store · Triple Store · Reasoner

1 Introduction

In recent years knowledge graphs have become essential for powering intelligent applications like Siri or Alexa. A knowledge graph is a vast semantic net representing entities and their relationships [11], integrating data from heterogeneous sources that are often incomplete. Therefore, in many applications (e.g., data integration or information extraction), it is essential to infer implicit knowledge based on the given statements using rules (so-called inference rules). Rules allow the decoupling of the domain logic from the underlying application code.

C. Pesquita et al. (Eds.): ESWC 2023, LNCS 13870, pp. 574–590, 2023.
https://doi.org/10.1007/978-3-031-33455-9_34

The logic not hardcoded within an application but represented by rules is easily exchangeable when needed allowing applications to be much more generic. Besides, the behavior of applications can be defined in a low-/no-code way using rules. Additionally, integrating the logic into the model makes the queries much shorter and more straightforward.

The importance of rules for knowledge graphs is also visible when following the developments in recent years. Many new rule engines [6,9,19] have been developed. For a rule engine to be broadly adopted, it is essential to provide simple and well-known APIs to access and manage the data stored within it. Developers unfamiliar with the W3C recommendations should be able to integrate a rule engine into their system architecture. But, a semantic web expert should also have full expressivity when using the rule engine. Building a bridge between developers' technologies, formats, query languages, and the W3C recommendations is essential.

This paper presents SemReasoner, a high-performance knowledge graph store and rule-based reasoner. SemReasoner is used successfully in several industrial projects powering intelligent applications.

SemReasoner provides a comprehensive, scalable, and high-performance deductive database. It stores the data in the form of triples and provides Horn logic with negation as well as OO-logic [1] (a successor of F-logic [15]) for defining rules. Additionally, SemReasoner fully supports document store functionality and allows returning JSON documents in their initial structure without recreating them. Based on SemReasoner, ontology-based applications can be developed which offer the following advantages:

- The shared meaning (semantics) of information in a knowledge model
- The capturing of complex relationships with the help of rules

Rules allow for modeling the know-how and the business logic separately from the execution logic. Hence, users can flexibly adapt and extend the application logic without modifying code. SemReasoner is mainly accessed using OO-logic queries, but GraphQL, a query language simplifying developers' access, is also supported. Furthermore, we are currently working on supporting SPARQL queries.

The remainder of the paper is structured as follows. Section 2 will lay the foundations to follow the presentation in this paper. Afterward, Sect. 3 highlights SemReasoner's key characteristics and gives insights into use cases relying on it. SemReasoner's modular architecture is presented in Sect. 4. Then, we present the evaluation against the state-of-the-art rule engines (Sect. 5). The related work section offers a comparison with those engines (Sect. 6). Finally, we conclude the paper and give an outlook on the future work in Sect. 7.

2 Background

SemReasoner provides two languages for querying, namely OO-logic and GraphQL, and for verifying the data, JSON Schema is supported.

OO-logic [1] is a successor of F-Logic [2,15]. It combines the advantages of conceptual modeling from object-oriented frame-based languages with the declarative style, compact and simple syntax, and the well-defined semantics of a logic-based language (based on first order logic). OO-logic supports typing, meta-reasoning, complex objects, methods, classes, inheritance, rules, queries, modularization, and scoped inference. It can be translated to Horn logic with non-monotonic negation, a subset of predicate logic with highly efficient reasoning algorithms. It is "Turing complete" (computationally universal), which means that everything that can be expressed by a computer can also be expressed in OO-logic. This is very important for industrial applications. For example, use cases requiring recursive functions cannot be directly expressed in a language like OWL. Further, OO-logic is more lightweight than F-Logic. For schema definition, no special constructs are available. Instead, schema definition is done precisely the same way as the definition of instances. For classes, properties are defined and used in their instances, and properties of classes are defined in the same way. This clears the syntax given for F-Logic without losing functionality and makes it much easier to describe ontologies and rules. Our commercial experience shows that OO-logic is an excellent language for industrial applications. For better support of knowledge graph use cases, OO-logic has been extended by powerful path expressions, for instance, to recursively follow edges in the graph and thus retrieve whole paths.

GraphQL. JSON objects may be queried using GraphQL[1]. GraphQL is a query language to retrieve data from a data store. Usually, GraphQL is used as an alternative to an ordinary REST call. It allows retrieving the relevant information only instead of a sometimes extensive JSON object. As its syntax is closely related to JSON, it fits very well with JSON. GraphQL allows simple queries but is less powerful than OO-logic queries. SemReasoner supports the GraphQL constructs like *aliases, unions, fragments, nested fragments, inline fragments, arguments, variables, default variables,* and *directives (@include, @skip)*. Furthermore, introspection and mutation are supported, and arguments can contain OO-logic paths. A GraphQL response is returned as a JSON document with the same structure as the query structure. Furthermore, only properties specified in the query are returned.

JSON Schema is used for verifying JSON objects. The relation between a JSON schema[2] and a JSON object is given by the class (`@type`) of the JSON object. The name of the class is the property value of the `@id` property of the schema. An extension to JSON Schema is the support for inheriting properties from super-schemas [3]. The relation of a sub-schema to its super-schema is expressed using the property `@subClassOf`. Additionally, constraints can be expressed using OO-logic by using the `@constraints` property. In SemReasoner schema objects are stored as JSON objects. Whenever a schema is available for a given type, every added instance of that type is verified against this schema.

---

[1] https://graphql.org.

[2] https://json-schema.org/.

3 Key Characteristics and Use Cases

We present the key characteristics (Sect. 3.1) together with industry-related use cases (Sect. 3.2) in the following.

3.1 Key Characteristics

Document Store. SemReasoner's JSON API stores added JSON documents with their initial structure. This allows retrieving the documents quickly without reconstructing them from triples. Even more important, the original structure is kept, which can not be guaranteed when recreating them from triples.

Persistent Storage. The persistent storage layer stores the triples in B+ trees. A shadow implementation of those B+ trees allows safe transactions. This implies facts added or deleted during a transaction only modify shadows of the B+ tree nodes. Further, SemReasoner partitions the extensional database vertically using the property names, i.e., each property has its relation. For instance, *abc[hasDollarPrice:5]* is stored in a B+ tree containing ternary tuples only. The member relation (member of a class) is partitioned using the class names, i.e., each class has its member relation. For instance, *abc:Product* is stored in a B+ tree containing binary tuples only. An additional horizontal partitioning splits the database into subgraphs. In that case, the B+ trees have tuples with an additional argument: the subgraph identifier.

Reasoning. Join operations are used instead of resolution for evaluating rules. Both *Merge*[3] joins and *Nested Loop*[4] joins are implemented and a heuristic chooses one of them for each join operation. The intermediate rule results are kept in the main memory, and the indices are created dynamically. For B+ relations, those are B+ trees as well. For main memory relations, those are realized either by specialized hash tables or AVL-trees, decided based on a heuristics. Cross products are managed differently, they are not executed. Relations are not joined and the cross product is forwarded to the next operator. The same holds for join operations concerning two triple sets, which are known to have a one-to-one relation. Constants in rule literals are used as additional filters for join operations (lazy filtering). Lazy projection means that projections are not applied immediately but during the next join operation. Rules with a single head literal and a single body literal do not create intermediate results. All those optimizations allow fast evaluation of rules with huge sets of facts in the extensional database.

Transactions. SemReasoner is transactional, i.e., it provides snapshot and long transactions. Snapshot transactions allow clients to add or remove facts and pose queries without influencing parallel accessing clients. The changes become

---

[3] https://sqlserverfast.com/epr/merge-join/.
[4] https://sqlserverfast.com/epr/nested-loops/.

visible to other clients only after committing the transaction. Such transactions can also be rolled back, leaving the original state in the extensional database as before the transaction. A rollback means that the changes in the shadow nodes are ignored, and the shadow nodes are freed up. A commit switches to the shadow nodes, and the original nodes are freed up. Long transactions are open for a long time, e.g., days, and they still allow parallel accessing clients to pose queries. Those queries are independent of the changes in the long transaction. The shadow implementation again accomplishes this. Long transactions create shadow nodes only, thus not affecting the use of the original nodes.

3.2 Use Cases

SemReasoner has been successfully used in industrial projects and applications. adesso SE[5], a listed consulting and IT service company with more than 8000 employees, employs SemReasoner in various projects and products. Some of those we describe in the following.

- **adesso insurance solutions**, a subsidiary of adesso, uses SemReasoner at the core of an *in/sure workflow* & *in/sure workplace* product. The business architecture is completely described with an ontology, and rules represent decisions. This is an excellent example of a no-code/low-code system, where ontologies describe all the concrete domain-specific issues.
- **Banking** is one line of business inside adesso using SemReasoner to analyze embargo restrictions. Large banks process millions of SWIFT payment messages daily with real-time response requirements. OO-logic rules describe conditions when a payment message violates an embargo, and SemReasoner evaluates those conditions in real-time. This use case shows the high performance of SemReasoner

Further, SemReasoner is used in Onlim[6], a leading conversational AI platform provider in the DACH-Region, to host knowledge graphs and power intelligent applications like chatbots and voice assistants.

4   SemReasoner's Architecture

SemReasoner combines a graph store with a deductive reasoning engine and comes with a search index for efficiently searching ontologies and documents. The architecture is optimized to use SemReasoner as a runtime system in semantic applications or at the core of ontology-based services. Therefore, SemReasoner comes with well-documented APIs, extension possibilities, and interfaces[7]. Figure 1 presents an overview of SemReasoner's architecture components.

---

[5] https://www.adesso.de/en/.
[6] https://onlim.com/.
[7] see https://kev-ang.github.io/SemReasoner/.

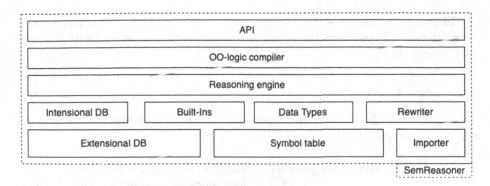

Fig. 1. SemReasoner's architecture

4.1   Storage Layer

The storage layer consists of three parts, the *Extensional Database* (EDB), *Symbol Table*, and *Importer*. While the first two are used for storing the data, the third imports the data from various formats into the EDB and Symbol Table.

Facts are separated from the rules and stored in the EDB. This EDB may either be configured to reside in the main memory (*memory mode*) or in its graph store (*persistent mode*)[8]. Additionally, a *mixed mode* keeps as much data as possible in the main memory and swaps (remove data from memory and load data from disk) whenever needed. Different data structures are used for the two modes. The graph store (persistent mode) is based on B+ trees [10]. Indices are generated and stored on disk for supporting joins and negations in reasoning. This persistent layer ensures rapid loading, rollback, parallel snapshot transactions, and backups. It has been tested for up to 34 billion triples while loading a billion facts in roughly 3.5 h on an ordinary PC. The loading time grows linearly with the number of triples. Binary trees (AVL trees) are used as the central data structure for the in-memory mode.

The storage of symbols is separated from the storage of triples. Symbols are encoded and stored within the *Symbol Table*. Therefore, the triples contain the codes of the symbols only. This allows fast comparisons of triples because only codes have to be compared. The encoding of symbols is done during the loading of the facts. The symbols are stored as B+ trees in the persistent mode, whereas hash tables are used for the in-memory mode.

Several importers are provided to load the data into memory or the graph store. SemReasoner currently supports the formats *JSON, OO-logic facts, Raw (files containing triples, with every element of a triple in a different line)* and all formats supported by the Jena[9] and Rio (RDF4J)[10]. In addition, SemReasoner provides an interface for implementing custom importers to add support for other formats.

---

[8] For performance reasons, the first configuration is preferable.

[9] https://jena.apache.org/documentation/io/.

[10] https://rdf4j.org/.

The storage layer is seamlessly integrated into the reasoning algorithms. It thus dramatically increases the performance compared to reasoners with a decoupled storage layer.

4.2 Logic Layer

Intensional DB, Built-Ins, Data Types, and *Rewriters* form the logic layer, containing the domain logic.

Intensional DB. Rules and queries are located in the *Intensional database*. They are arranged in a graph describing the dependency relation of the rules. A rule A is dependent on another rule B if the head atom of B unifies with one of the body literals of A. Cycles and double-connected components can be computed with the appropriate graph algorithms. Thus stratification of rules can be determined for non-monotonic negation. In addition, this allows deciding quickly which rule can contribute to the answer and which rules can be omitted.

Built-Ins. Some aspects cannot be easily described using logic. For example, complex mathematical algorithms should be described procedurally instead. SemReasoner can easily be extended with such procedural algorithms. Within OO-logic, these procedural attachments are called built-ins. They may be used inside rules or queries using predicate logic literals. For example, all mathematical built-ins are internally given in the same way. If we want to multiply numbers, we could use the multiply built-in (_mult) that can take two numbers as input and returns the output into a variable: _mult(2,3,?Y), which results in ?Y=6. Built-ins are identified by a leading underscore ("_"). The extension of such a built-in is not a given set of facts. Instead, the extension is computed by an algorithm. Built-ins are written in Java, are compiled against the SemReasoner code, and are registered as new built-ins. Then, they are subsequently available within queries and rules. Additionally, SemReasoner supports action built-ins. Action built-ins occur in the head of a rule and perform actions like writing a file or sending an e-mail. So far, SemReasoner comes with more than 200 built-ins, including the math and string functions from Java.

Data Types are assigned to facts and define how to interpret the data[11]. For example, adding two facts heavily depends on the assigned data type. Adding two integers results in the sum, whereas adding two strings is interpreted as concatenation. SemReasoner comes with a predefined set of data types consisting of *Boolean, Calendar, Double, Duration, Float, Integer, Long*, and *String*. As for the built-ins and the importers, extending the given set of data types is possible by implementing a given interface.

---

[11] https://foldoc.org/type.

Rewriter. Rewriters are used for optimizing the set of rules during the reasoning process. Optimizing the rules before evaluating them is essential for an efficient reasoning process. Without those optimizations, no real-time responses would be possible in many cases. The optimization is done by modifying the rules while ensuring that the revised rules evaluate the same answer as the original rules. An example is the magic set rewriter (see Sect. 4.3). SemReasoner comes with predefined rewriters, e.g., eliminating duplicate literals in rules or rewriting rules into SQL statements when integrating SQL databases.

4.3 Reasoning Engine

The reasoning engine operates on the existing facts stored in the Extensional DB. It uses the logic layer for inferring new knowledge or answering given queries. In the following, we will elaborate on the inference algorithms used. Afterward, the reasoning process is described, and finally, we briefly present SemReasoner's materialization abilities.

Inference Algorithms. In the kernel of SemReasoner, there are two reasoning methods available: a bottom-up reasoner (also called semi-naive evaluation, or forward chaining reasoner) [23], and a top-down reasoner based on the magic-set technology [7] (simulated backward-chaining reasoner).

A bottom-up reasoner (forward-chaining reasoner) takes the given facts, applies the rules, and creates derived facts. Afterward, the rules are applied again to derive more facts, including the derived facts of the first rule evaluation. This process continues until no new facts can be derived. Bottom-up reasoning is a simple method with the disadvantage that many (intermediate) facts are generated, which are generally unnecessary for answering the query. On the other hand, top-down reasoning sometimes provides so much overhead that this simple reasoning strategy performs best of all.

Magic set reasoning modifies the rules and processes them using a bottom-up reasoner. The rule transformation process creates a magic fact and a new rule from the given rule. This transformation directly brings a restricting ground term to the rule to be evaluated. The introduced ground term restricts the intermediate results at the bottom of the rule graph. Transforming the rules and processing the resulting rule set in a bottom-up way reduces the number of intermediate results that do not contribute to the answer. By creating these rules, we observe a trade-off between this reduction effect and the additional performance loss for magic set reasoning. We have seen queries better evaluated in a purely bottom-up fashion and others better evaluated by magic sets.

The Reasoning Process. A query is processed in several successive steps (see Fig. 2). First, the query is parsed and compiled (*OO-logic compiling*) into an internal data structure. Afterward, all rules that may contribute to the query are selected (*Selecting rules*) from all the rules stored in the Intensional DB. The resulting rules are then optimized by so-called rewriters (*Rule rewriting*).

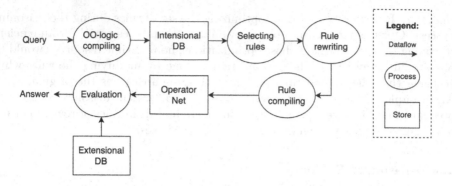

Fig. 2. Query processing in SemReasoner

Then a rule compiler creates a so-called operator net (*Rule compiling*). An operator net is a low-level representation of the operations needed for processing the set of rules. Such an operator net contains operations like *join, match, access to the EDB, projection, operations for built-ins*, and *operations for connectors*. Move operations move tuples to another node, collectors store intermediate results, and distributors distribute tuples to several other nodes.

Such an operator net is purely data flow-oriented, with every operator performing its operation and sending the results to the successor nodes.

The whole query processing is multi-user-capable. This means multiple users can send queries simultaneously, which are processed in parallel.

Materialization. The same reasoning methods (bottom-up and top-down) can be used to materialize inferences. This means that rules are evaluated directly after loading. The results are stored in the internal triple store, which means that, during query evaluation, these facts have to be accessed and retrieved only so that no evaluation takes place during query time. This drastically improves response times but may also increase the amount of stored data. SemReasoner provides functions for incrementally materializing models. Suppose a new triple is added/deleted to/from the model. Then, the materialization process must only be repeated for a small subset of the model rather than for the entire model. Materialization for the SemReasoner can be enabled when needed. Typically, it is used without materialization.

4.4 OO-logic Compiler

The OO-logic compiler parses incoming rules and queries by using ANTLR[12] (ANother Tool for Language Recognition). This parser builds and walks parse trees. Based on the resulting parse tree, the internal Java representation of the given rules and queries is compiled. Compiling rules into the internal Java representation includes transformations for exceptional cases. Rules may contain

---

[12] https://www.antlr.org/.

several heads and an OR operation in the body. For such cases, the OO-logic compiler performs a lightweight version of Lloyd-Topor transformation [18]. This transformation compiles such a complex rule into several Horn rules. Another exceptional case is aggregations, usable in rules and queries, which are transformed into several intermediate rules.

4.5   API

SemReasoner provides three ways to integrate it into an application. Those Java APIs allow adding/removing facts and sending OO-logic queries to be evaluated. Furthermore, the APIs allow adding built-ins, data types, importers, and rules. In the following, we will briefly introduce the three APIs *Deductive Database*, *JSON Deductive Database*, and *Streaming Database*.

Deductive Database. The Deductive Database is all about OO-logic. OO-logic facts and OO-logic rules are managed, and OO-logic queries can be posted. OO-logic facts are compiled into internal triples or quads (if a context is provided). OO-logic rules and queries are stored in their internal Java representation. This API is transactional, i.e., it provides snapshot and long transactions (see Sect. 3.1 for details). The deductive database is a client to the data, i.e., several deductive databases can be used in parallel for the same core.

JSON Deductive Database. SemReasoner provides a particular API for storing and retrieving JSON objects. JSON objects can be used together with logic rules and queried as a whole or specific parts using OO-logic queries. A significant advantage of the JSON API is its document store ability. JSON objects added to SemReasoner are stored as a whole with their original structure. Therefore, the JSON object is encoded and stored in the Symbol Table, and the code is then stored in a separate JSON table. Further, the JSON Deductive Database converts the JSON objects into triples. It adds the symbols to the Symbol Table and the triples consisting of the symbol codes into the Extensional DB. For verifying JSON objects, SemReasoner supports JSON schemas.

Streaming Database. The standard way to use SemReasoner is to fill it with ontologies, ontology instances, and rules and pose queries answered by the system. This is similar to the way a database is used. For complex event processing (stream-based reasoning) the system is filled with ontologies, instances, rules, and queries. External events are streamed into SemReasoner, creating new instances which are added to the set of instances, and these events cause the stored queries to come up with new answers. SemReasoner does this incrementally. Adding a new instance does not mean that the full original query must be evaluated. Instead, the query evaluation considers the previously evaluated partial results. Only an incremental effort is necessary to derive the additional answers.

5   Evaluation

This section evaluates SemReasoner against state-of-the-art rule engines using the RUBEN [4] framework. RUBEN is a Rule Engine Benchmarking Framework with a predefined set of test cases from the OpenRuleBench [17]. Due to the limited space, we show only a selected test case for each category Open-RuleBench provides. This section first presents the experimental setup, then the methodology, and finally, the evaluation results.

Experimental Setup. RUBEN was hosted on a server with an *Intel® Core^{TM} i9-9900K Octa-Core, 8 Cores/16 Threads, 3.60 GHz Base Frequency, 5.00 GHz Max Turbo Frequency* processor, 64 GB RAM, and Debian GNU/Linux 10. The memory was limited to 60GB to evaluate the various rule engines.

We selected rule-engines that purely evaluate rules during query evaluation time and rule-engines materializing the rules upfront[13].

- **No materialization** - Apache Jena (4.4), SemReasoner, and Stardog (8.2.2)
- **Materialization** - RDFox (6.1), SemReasoner (5.6.7), and VLog (0.8.0)

Apache Jena and Stardog are rule engines evaluating the rules during query time. Further, for those two rule engines, there is no possibility of materializing the rules upfront. Rule engines entirely relying on materialization are RDFox and VLog. In contrast to the selected engines supporting either materialization or no materialization, SemReasoner can be configured to operate in one or the other mode. Therefore, SemReasoner is placed in both categories and evaluated against both types of engines.

Methodology. RUBEN is a Java framework providing an interface to be implemented for evaluating rule engines. The data and rules need to be manually converted into the format of the particular rule engine. Each test case contains a file for the facts, a rule file, and a file with queries. Then, the materialization (if used) and afterward, the query is evaluated three times with a timeout of 15 min for each evaluation. The evaluation results are then used to calculate the average time for materialization and query response and the standard deviation.

For the scope of this paper, we have chosen the following three test cases from the OpenRuleBench[14]:

- **Large join tests - Join1** - non-recursive tree of binary joins relying on 250000 facts.
- **Datalog recursion - same-generation** - find all siblings in the same generation using cyclic and acyclic data with a data size of 24000.
- **Stratified negation - same-generation** - modified same-generation problem using cyclic data with a data size of 24000.

---

[13] see Sect. 6 for a detailed description of the rule-engines.
[14] For a full list and detailed description of those test cases consider [17].

Those test cases were selected based on the ability of the given rule engines. All rule engines can execute the selected test cases for the *large join tests* and *datalog recursion*. For example, some rule engines do not support n-ary predicates, which prevents them from evaluating the *Join2* test case from the OpenRuleBench. Jena and Stardog do not support negation. Therefore, no results are shown for the negation test case for both rule engines.

Results. For the presentation of the evaluation results, Table 1 shows the results of the engines without materialization. Further, in Table 2 a comparison of engines doing materialization is shown. The test cases for all engines were executed three times. After each run, the engines were restarted, and the data reloaded. Then, we calculated the average materialization time or query response time. For the non-materialized engines, we consider the query response time. In contrast, for engines running materialization, we only consider the materialization time as the query response time is the time for accessing the precomputed data, which does not give any essential insights. Besides the average of the materialization or query response time, we calculated the standard deviation. All times in the tables are given in milliseconds. The first time is the average materialization or query response time, and the standard deviation is given in brackets.

Table 1. Evaluation results not materialized (average query response time in ms, the standard deviation in ms in brackets, and the fastest times are marked bold)

Engine	**Join1**			Datalog Recursion	
	a	b1	b2	Cyc	No Cyc
Jena	timeout	timeout	51,134	timeout	timeout
Sem-Reasoner (Memory)	**46,547.00** (1,420.65)	**18,638.67** (299.95)	**2,774.67** (104.51)	**2,330.67** (85.99)	**2,270.00** (89.37)
Sem-Reasoner (Persistent)	96,903.67 (1,896.41)	37,542.33 (500.44)	8,103.67 (148.29)	3,325.67 (48.22)	3,257.00 (54.74)
Stardog	Exception	419,156.67 (25,884.61)	3,366.00 (253.15)	Error	Error

Jena and Stardog do not support negation in rules. Therefore, for the nonmaterialized engines, we left out the negation test. Due to the limited space, we only show the results of the queries without binding[15]. Only the bottom-up reasoning algorithm for SemReasoner was used, as the top-down approach only makes sense for queries with bindings. Comparing the results of the *Join1* test,

---

[15] for more results and the benchmarking data check https://github.com/kev-ang/SemReasoner and the ESWC branch in https://github.com/kev-ang/RUBEN.

SemReasoner is the fastest for the three given queries. A too large result causes the exception thrown by Stardog for the query a. For the *Datalog Recursion*, Stardog did not deliver a correct result, and the logs showed that the rule is not supported[16]. Out of the three rule engines, the open-source implementation of Jena either times out or is always the slowest. Jena delivers only a result for the b2 query in one run. Therefore, no standard deviation can be calculated.

Table 2. Evaluation results materialized (average materialization time in ms, the standard deviation in ms in brackets, and the fastest times are marked bold)

Engine	Join1	Datalog Recursion		Negation
		Cyc	No Cyc	
RDFox	–	–	–	–
SemReasoner (Memory)	**18,157.33** (991.95)	**1,733.00** (99.06)	**1,611.00** (91.02)	45,353.67 (2,796.67)
VLog	518,676.22 (369.55)	24,245.67 (78.68)	21,467.00 (54.11)	**9,135.00** (7.94)

Besides evaluating rules during the query evaluation, SemReasoner supports materialization. SemReasoner was run in the `MEMORY` mode for this part of the evaluation using the bottom-up reasoning algorithm. This configuration was chosen as it is comparable to how the other engines run the reasoning. Table 2 presents the performance comparison between engines supporting materialization. SemReasoner supports parallel materialization and is, therefore, faster than VLog. SemReasoner's speed-up compared to VLog reaches a factor between 13 and 28 for the *Join1*, *Cyc* and *No Cyc* test of *Datalog Recursion*. However, VLog is nearly five times faster for the negation. This seems to be a terrible use case for our implementation of negation and must be investigated in detail. SemReasoner is the slowest of the evaluated engines for the negation test case. Unfortunately, for RDFox, we did not get approval for the benchmarking results before the submission deadline. Therefore, we replaced the numbers by dashes in Table 2.

6   Related Work

OO-logic is a successor of F-logic and comes with the same expressivity. In [14], the author elaborates on the relationship of F-logic and Description Logics (DLs). F-logic is computationally complete, not so DLs. While F-logic's expressivity allows simple specifications of many problems beyond the expressivity of DLs, F-logic knowledge bases can not provide computational guarantees. But, those problems can be neglected because the exponential complexity of problems in DLs provides little comfort in practice.

---

[16] https://docs.stardog.com/inference-engine/#known-issues.

Further, many computational problems in F-logic are decidable within polynomial time. Those are especially all queries without function symbols and a large subclass of queries beyond DLs' expressive power. Further, there are knowledge bases with decidable query answering, including function symbols. DLs are more flexible regarding representing existential information or admitting disjunctive information to the knowledge base [15].

The following briefly introduces and discusses the rule engines from the evaluation section and includes GraphDB and the Fact++ reasoner.

GraphDB uses rules in the format and semantics analogous to R-entailment[17]. R-entailment is less expressive than DLs but improves the complexity and adds meta-modeling expressivity [13]. The reasoning engine inside GraphDB is called TRREE, performing forward-chaining reasoning relying on total materialization. All data is stored in files in the storage directory.

FaCT++ is a DL reasoner based on the tableaux decision procedure [22]. It comes with a persistent and incremental reasoning mode [21]. The persistent mode stores the internal state, and precomputed inferences and reloads them when needed. Further, the incremental reasoning mode avoids reloading and reclassifying the ontology for a few changed axioms but approximates the affected subsumptions. However, it does not have an integrated persistency layer but does the reasoning in memory.

Jena is an open-source framework for Semantic Web applications[18]. Jena comes with a triple store and inference support by various reasoning engines. For this paper, only the general-purpose rule engine[19] is of interest. The reasoning engine provides forward chaining, backward chaining, and a hybrid mode. Further, the rule engine provides built-in functions like string and mathematical functions that can be extended by the user [20]. The rule engine comes with its own rules called *Jena rule*, which is comparable to Notation3. Explicitly stating the expressivity of N3Logic is difficult [8]. It is more expressive than Datalog but less expressive than FOL, and, unlike DL, it is not decidable [8].

RDFox is a main-memory RDF store supporting parallel Datalog reasoning relying on materialization [19]. It comes with a highly efficient parallel reasoning algorithm and efficient handling of owl:sameAs statements. Further, RDFox supports datalog rules, a subset of horn logic rules.

Stardog is an Enterprise Knowledge Graph Platform[20]. Stardog does not materialize inferences but evaluates rules at query time, allowing maximum flexibility. Further, it comes with its rule language based on SPARQL and supports

---

[17] https://graphdb.ontotext.com/documentation/10.0/reasoning.html#rule-format-and-semantics.
[18] https://jena.apache.org/.
[19] https://jena.apache.org/documentation/inference/#rules.
[20] https://www.stardog.com/.

SWRL rules [12]. The expressivity of SPARQL is equivalent to recursive safe Datalog with negation [5]. SWRL is a combination of OWL-DL and OWL-Lite, sublanguages of OWL and Unary/Binary Datalog RuleML [12], allowing positive, function-free horn clauses [16]. Additionally, built-in functions like string or mathematical functions are supported.

Focusing on the supported rules and especially the procedural extension of those, SemReasoner's rule language is more expressive than the rule languages of the presented rule engines. The presented rule engines rely on DL or Datalog, which are Horn Logic formulas without functions and are less expressive than SemReasoner's rule language. Besides SemReasoner, only GraphDB provides an integrated persistency layer. The other engines rely on a decoupled storage layer or operate only in memory. RDFox, for example, needs to have all data available in memory. SemReasoner provides forward- and (simulated) backward-chaining. From the other engines, only Jena also provides both. The others either rely on forward- or backward-chaining. Besides, SemReasoner supports materialization as well as reasoning during query-time. In contrast, GraphDB, RDFox, and VLog fully rely on materialization and Jena and Stardog on reasoning during query-time. Further, SemReasoner has an integrated document store, while others need to rely on external system integrations. Many use cases require retrieving the initial JSON document from the underlying knowledge graph. Here, storing the JSON document in its initial structure brings performance benefits and allows to return the document as it was entered. This is not possible when recreating the JSON from triples. Also, SemReasoner comes with an extensive number of built-ins.

7   Conclusion and Future Work

This paper presented SemReasoner, a comprehensive, scalable, high-performance knowledge graph store, and rule-based reasoner. SemReasoner has an integrated storage layer and a rule language based on Horn logic extended by non-monotonic negation. Further, rules can be extended by built-ins that are procedural attachments to the declarative rules.

We introduced SemReasoner's modular architecture and various APIs, allowing easy and quick integration into existing applications. SemReasoner's integrated document store functionality for JSON documents is a benefit. With SemReasoner's ability to handle a vast amount of data[21] and its reasoning performance, it outperforms other reasoning engines in most of the selected test cases.

We are currently working on integrating SPARQL as a query language to access the stored data. Besides, sameAs reasoning based on equivalence classes is currently being implemented. Additionally, a clustered version allows for efficiently storing and operating on larger datasets using a cluster network in the future. Further, we plan a more extended evaluation and discussion of the configuration options supported by SemReasoner.

---

[21] SemReasoner has been tested with up to 32B triples.

References

1. Angele, J., Angele, K.: OO-logic: a successor of F-logic. In: RuleML+ RR (Supplement) (2019)
2. Angele, J., Kifer, M., Lausen, G.: Ontologies in F-logic. In: Staab, S., Studer, R. (eds.) Handbook on Ontologies. IHIS, pp. 45–70. Springer, Heidelberg (2009). https://doi.org/10.1007/978-3-540-92673-3_2
3. Angele, K., Angele, J.: JSON towards a simple ontology and rule (2021)
4. Angele, K., Angele, J., Şimşek, U., Fensel, D.: RUBEN: a rule engine benchmarking framework (2022)
5. Angles, R., Gutierrez, C.: The expressive power of SPARQL. In: Sheth, A., et al. (eds.) ISWC 2008. LNCS, vol. 5318, pp. 114–129. Springer, Heidelberg (2008). https://doi.org/10.1007/978-3-540-88564-1_8
6. Baget, J.-F., Leclère, M., Mugnier, M.-L., Rocher, S., Sipieter, C.: Graal: a toolkit for query answering with existential rules. In: Bassiliades, N., Gottlob, G., Sadri, F., Paschke, A., Roman, D. (eds.) RuleML 2015. LNCS, vol. 9202, pp. 328–344. Springer, Cham (2015). https://doi.org/10.1007/978-3-319-21542-6_21
7. Bancilhon, F., Maier, D., Sagiv, Y., Ullman, J.D.: Magic sets and other strange ways to implement logic programs. In: Proceedings of the Fifth ACM SIGACT-SIGMOD Symposium on Principles of Database Systems, pp. 1–15 (1985)
8. Berners-Lee, T., Connolly, D., Kagal, L., Scharf, Y., Hendler, J.: N3Logic: a logical framework for the World Wide Web. Theory Pract. Logic Program. 8(3), 249–269 (2008). https://doi.org/10.1017/S1471068407003213
9. Carral, D., Dragoste, I., González, L., Jacobs, C., Krötzsch, M., Urbani, J.: VLog: a rule engine for knowledge graphs. In: Ghidini, C., et al. (eds.) ISWC 2019. LNCS, vol. 11779, pp. 19–35. Springer, Cham (2019). https://doi.org/10.1007/978-3-030-30796-7_2
10. Cormen, T.H., Leiserson, C.E., Rivest, R.L., Stein, C.: Introduction to Algorithms (2022)
11. Fensel, D., et al.: Knowledge Graphs. Springer, Heidelberg (2020). https://doi.org/10.1007/978-3-030-37439-6
12. Horrocks, I., et al.: SWRL: a semantic web rule language combining OWL and RuleML. W3C Member Submission 21(79), 1–31 (2004)
13. Horst, H.J.: Combining RDF and part of OWL with rules: semantics, decidability, complexity. In: Gil, Y., Motta, E., Benjamins, V.R., Musen, M.A. (eds.) ISWC 2005. LNCS, vol. 3729, pp. 668–684. Springer, Heidelberg (2005). https://doi.org/10.1007/11574620_48
14. Kifer, M.: Rules and ontologies in F-logic. In: Eisinger, N., Małuszyński, J. (eds.) Reasoning Web. LNCS, vol. 3564, pp. 22–34. Springer, Heidelberg (2005). https://doi.org/10.1007/11526988_2
15. Kifer, M., Lausen, G., Wu, J.: Logical foundations of object-oriented and frame-based languages. J. ACM (JACM) 42(4), 741–843 (1995). https://doi.org/10.1145/210332.210335
16. Lawan, A., Rakib, A.: The semantic web rule language expressiveness extensions - a survey (2019). https://doi.org/10.48550/arXiv.1903.11723
17. Liang, S., Fodor, P., Wan, H., Kifer, M.: OpenRuleBench: an analysis of the performance of rule engines. In: Proceedings of the 18th International Conference on World Wide Web, pp. 601–610 (2009). https://doi.org/10.1145/1526709.1526790
18. Lloyd, J.W.: Foundations of Logic Programming. Springer, Heidelberg (2012)

19. Nenov, Y., Piro, R., Motik, B., Horrocks, I., Wu, Z., Banerjee, J.: RDFox: a highly-scalable RDF store. In: Arenas, M., et al. (eds.) ISWC 2015. LNCS, vol. 9367, pp. 3–20. Springer, Cham (2015). https://doi.org/10.1007/978-3-319-25010-6_1

20. Rattanasawad, T., Saikaew, K.R., Buranarach, M., Supnithi, T.: A review and comparison of rule languages and rule-based inference engines for the semantic web. In: 2013 International Computer Science and Engineering Conference (ICSEC), pp. 1–6. IEEE (2013). https://doi.org/10.1109/ICSEC.2013.6694743

21. Tsarkov, D.: Incremental and persistent reasoning in FaCT++. In: International Workshop on OWL Reasoner Evaluation, pp. 16–22 (2014)

22. Tsarkov, D., Horrocks, I.: FaCT++ description logic reasoner: system description. In: Furbach, U., Shankar, N. (eds.) IJCAR 2006. LNCS (LNAI), vol. 4130, pp. 292–297. Springer, Heidelberg (2006). https://doi.org/10.1007/11814771_26

23. Ullman, J.D.: Principles of database and knowledge-base systems, vol. I. Principles of computer science series, vol. 14. Computer Science Press (1988). https://www.worldcat.org/oclc/310956623. ISBN 0-7167-8069-0

LIS: A Knowledge Graph-Based Line Information System

Irlan Grangel-González[1]([✉]), Marc Rickart[2], Oliver Rudolph[2], and Fasal Shah[3]

[1] Robert Bosch GmbH, Corporate Research, Renningen, Germany
Irlan.GrangelGonzalez@de.bosch.com
[2] Robert Bosch GmbH, Automotive Electronics, Reutlingen, Germany
[3] Robert Bosch Engineering and Business Solutions Private Limited, Karnataka, India

Abstract. In a manufacturing enterprise, like Bosch, answering business questions regarding production lines, involves different stakeholders. Production planning, product and production process development, quality management, and purchase have different views on the same entity "production line". These different views are reflected in data residing in silos as Manufacturing Execution Systems (MES), Enterprise Resource Planning (ERP) systems as well as Master Data (MD) systems. To answer these questions, all data have to be integrated and semantically harmonized conciliating the different views in a uniform understanding of the domain. To fulfill these requirements in this specific domain, we present the Line Information System (LIS). LIS is a Knowledge Graph (KG)-based ecosystem capable of semantically integrating data from MES, ERP, and MD. LIS enables a 360° view of manufacturing data for all stakeholders involved while resolving Semantic Interoperability Conflicts (SICs) in a scalable manner. Furthermore, as a part of the LIS ecosystem, we developed the LIS ontology, mappings, and a procedure to ensure the quality of the data in the KG. The LIS application comprises many functionalities to answer business questions that were not possible without LIS. LIS is currently in use in 12 Bosch plants semantically integrating data of more than 1.100 production lines, 16.000 physical machines, as well as more than 400 manufacturing processes. After the rollout of LIS, we performed a study with 21 colleagues. In general, the study showed that LIS in particular, and KG-based solutions in general, paves the way of exploiting the knowledge in manufacturing settings in a reusable and scalable way.

Keywords: Knowledge Graph · Industry 4.0 · Smart Manufacturing · Semantic Data Integration · Ontology

1 Introduction

In numerous corporate-level manufacturing organizations, the *digital transformation*, which has seen its onset a few years back and is still ongoing, is considered a key-enabler in order to remain competitive as a company. In essence, digital transformation involves not only establishing connectivity, but also driving

C. Pesquita et al. (Eds.): ESWC 2023, LNCS 13870, pp. 591–608, 2023.
https://doi.org/10.1007/978-3-031-33455-9_35

accessibility and especially an understanding of the increasingly present digital assets. An essential part of the digital transformation thus is faster provisioning of easily digestible data to answer business-crucial questions used in decision-making processes. Data required for production planning purposes, traceability of products, production process optimization, and production operation is currently distributed in different IT-systems as there are ERP, MES, and MD. Also non-IT-available data of production process experts is of high interest, but is not directly accessible. These data typically rely in the head of experts as well as in unstructured formats, e.g., intranets, word, and pdf documents. The collection of all data required for decision-making causes high efforts in terms of time and cost to draw the right conclusions. Typically, data reside in above described silos which are not interconnected but contain semantically related terms with redundant but inconsistent information. Unlocking the potential of these data in a combined set-up by creating knowledge out of it is one of the biggest challenges of competing enterprises. Of particular importance in this setting is to achieve semantic interoperability among all data assets. Achieving semantic interoperability is challenging due to the fact that SICs demand to be resolved accordingly. This, in turn, requires domain knowledge and organizational consensus [12]. To that end, and particularly in the context of the Industry 4.0 movement, KGs have demonstrated to be a solution for that problem [1,6,9,14,16]. At this point, it is worth to give a word on SICs. In general, interoperability can be defined as a measure of the degree to which diverse systems, organizations, and/or individuals are able to work together to achieve a common goal. A more detailed overview on SICs in this context is available in [5,11].

To tackle this problem, we propose a KG-based solution for efficient integration and quick access of manufacturing data. The above described solution has been implemented at Bosch in a KG-based approach called *Line Information System* (LIS). We show the implementation of this approach on integration of heterogeneous data sources by a specially developed user interface according to user experience requirements. The proposed approach enables semantic harmonization of the data on production lines as this was found already in precedent works [3,8]. Key to the success of the presented approach is the encoded domain knowledge in the ontology combined with the semantically enriched KG mappings. The mappings bridge the mismatch between the data layer and the ontology layer as semantically heterogeneous data from different sources using distinct representations are integrated by these mappings to resolve SICs at the level of the KG. This allows querying available data in an integrated way by exploiting the semantics of the provided information. In the following, we present the contributions of the LIS approach. *(i)* We developed the LIS ontology describing the concepts and properties of a production line together with domain knowledge from various experts. This ontology is the basis of the KG-based approach for semantic data integration in manufacturing. *(ii)* We built a mapping layer that semantically connects the LIS ontology to the ERP, MES, and MD data sources. *(iii)* We integrated data from 12 Bosch plants around the world while providing a structured way of dealing with SICs. *(iv)* We devel-

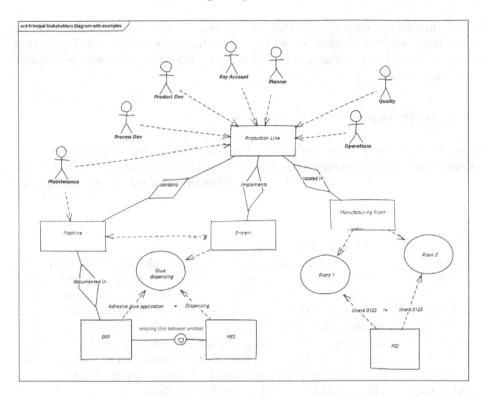

Fig. 1. Motivating example. The *Production Line* exposes multiple entities, e.g., *Machines* and *Processes*, to different stakeholders such as process and product developers, key accountants, planners, maintenance crew, quality engineers, and shopfloor operations. These stakeholders hold differing responsibilities and interest in these entities, hence leading to fundamentally different views. Different views on top of the data silos generate SICs. The example depicted is on the *Process* entity, which lives in both data assets *ERP* and *MES* under differing names yet referring to the exact same process in reality. One further example of such conflicts is the use of an identical production line identifier *lineId* used separately for completely different lines on two geo-locations.

oped the LIS ecosystem comprising a dedicated Web application that access the semantically harmonized data; a validation process to ensure that the data have the demanded quality so that it can be used by the domain experts, as well as a data sharing service on top of the LIS KG. In addition, LIS acts as a master data management system and a procedure to share as well as reporting on top of the semantically harmonized data. (v) We provided an automatic procedure to check that the data in the KG is correct with a set of dashboards to make the data quality transparent.

The paper is organized as follows: Sect. 2 provides background and motivation for this work. Section 3 describes the available components for the KG-based approach and the challenges for integrating data from these systems with the correct semantic description. In Sect. 4 we performed and study to get the feedback from the main stakeholders. In Sect. 5 we discuss the lessons learned. Section 6 presents the related endeavours and Sect. 7 concludes the paper with an outlook and future work.

2   Motivation

One of the larger pain points observed is that information is spread heterogeneously within the organization, be it in terms of the technology applied or the terminology in use within the data sets. This drives a culture of "expertism" and siloed applications. Instead of company-wide shared access to knowledge, a funneling approach that requires mostly human resources to retrieve and provide information by case can lead to bottlenecks and delays in the provisioning of those business-relevant details. Data collection to answer consumer-specific questions hence becomes time consuming and tedious, already starting with the search for the right expert or domain owner. In case the question asked renders certain levels of complexity, multiple entities and domain experts may become necessary, adding further to the resource constraints. If the right expert cannot be identified, typically data exploration and search with the risk of misinterpretations based on incorrect assumptions or outdated records can be the result, possibly posing risk to the business. The entities present in a manufacturing organization with varying functions and responsibilities, may have very differing and domain-specific questions regarding production lines.

A production line consists of a defined number and sequence of production processes with specified capabilities to manufacture or assemble a product until ready for shipment to the customer. These processes are realized by physical assets or machines. Along the processes, value is added to the product by materials and resource consumption, e.g., operations personnel, machine wear, maintenance and so forth. In this context, a plethora of questions can arise. While some plants make use of the MES in a similar way, lack of standardization across all plants causes differences in the usage and consequently population of certain fields. Next, we present some concrete examples (cf. Fig. 1).

1. Manufacturing planning generates a forecast about production requirements from one up to eight years. This requires a complete overview about available production lines in the plants in an international production network (IPN). Furthermore, these data need to be correlated with the customers demand of products to take investments decisions. The identification of the production lines is usually a number which is unique only in one plant but not across the IPN. As concrete example we found the case that in two plants, *different lines were having the same identifier but actually were referring to distinct lines in the reality*. Thus, a SIC of type *homonym* is present here (cf. [11]).
2. Data about machines and production processes with their names are distributed in different ERP and MES systems. A process is implemented by a machine as a physical asset. The description of a machine refers in most

cases to the process and can be found like this in the ERP system. In MES the description of a process is defined by its name. There is no possibility to link *physical assets with logical processes* in the current setting. Thus, a SIC of type *missing items* is detected here.

3. Due to missing standardization rules, processes have different names in one or even many MESs but referring to the identical process in the reality. To optimize the adhesive dispensing process[1] across multiple manufacturing plants in the IPN, process development requires the count, location, and manufacturer of assets implementing this process along with a means to identify the sources for process data. This data is usually connected to the name of the production process. Unfortunately the name of the process is not standardized and many names for our example adhesive dispensing are found in the systems as e.g., *dispense sealant* and *dispensing sealing compound*. Here a SIC of type *synonym* is required to be resolved.

To achieve a semantically correct answer, SICs have to be resolved. In addition, a scalable approach has to provide a common semantic understanding of the domain that can be exploited and further enhanced. The challenges which we address here are the time consumption and iterations found in human-based communication to retrieve information from knowledge domains in a manufacturing enterprise, i.e., Bosch. Additionally, the risk of interpretative errors causing misinformation, and the SICs present in data queries employing multiple tables or sources. To tackle these challenges, we propose LIS: a KG-based approach to enable a semantically harmonized access to knowledge for stakeholders within an organizational unit of Bosch.

3   LIS: A Knowledge Graph-Based Line Information System

In this section, we present a KG-based approach for semantically integrating data and its specific application at Bosch. Based on the architectural view in Fig. 2, we describe the key elements required to establish the LIS ecosystem from bottom to top.

3.1   Data Sources

In this section, we describe the key data sources to provide the information from various domains, i.e., from MES, tools, i.e., ERP, and reference, i.e., MD.

MES. Manufacturing execution systems act as control instance to assert proper sequence, completion, and performance of the work in progress during manufacturing. As such, MES is a primary source of information in each value-adding

---

[1] A production process used to mix, meter, and dispense adhesives, i.e., glues and thermal interface materials on one or more components of a product to bond those components with each other to withstand defined stress-levels.

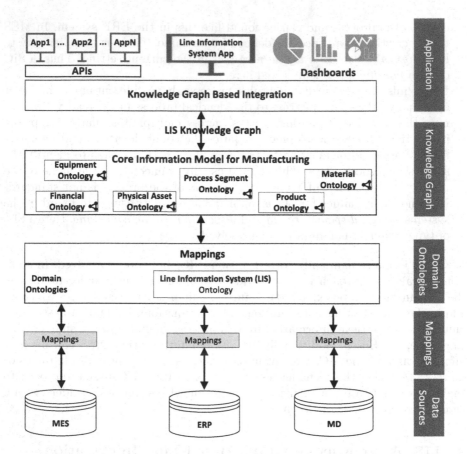

Fig. 2. The architecture in use for the proposed KG-based *Line Information System (LIS)* The LIS architecture comprises five layers, i.e., Data Sources, Mappings, Domain Ontologies, Knowledge Graph, and Application. *Data Sources* provide the information combined with the *Domain Ontologies* to shape the LIS KG. *Mappings* ensure the correct connection between the tables and fields within the underlying structured sources. The LIS Ontology is maintained in a central repository, and serves as the merging layer of interoperability between the sources. The KG provides semantically connected data, which can be retrieved from the *Application* via *SPARQL* queries, visualized using dashboards, as well as served to other applications via an API service.

step, as it typically involves part, machine, and process information, and possibly even results. In case of LIS, MES data serves as the logical view on the production line, as it abstracts the actual physical implementation by an asset or machine from the viewpoint of the mere process. In other words, MES describes what needs to happen in which sequence to a product, but does not interfere with the actual doing which is taken over by the equipment. As MES is close to real-time critical for manufacturing, in an effort to decouple loads the data sources are split into OLTP and OLAP stores. This aims at satisfying both, the immediate execution request from the connected equipment and the retroactive analysis of records taken. OLAP sources thus provide the point of connection.

ERP. Tools for enterprise resource-planning are mainly centered around the financial and controlling aspects of the company. In case of a manufacturing line, information such as asset tags, procurement or maintenance cost, depreciation cost, total cost of ownership, spare part stocks, and similar is present. In contrast to MES, ERP is more involved in the aspects of planning activities and customer-delivery fulfillment rather than day to day operations on the shop floor.

MD. Master data are crucial for clustering, categorizing, and querying correctly. Along other aspects, MD is considered to be a single source of truth with the intent to serve the organization in the endeavor of like treatment of data assets. In our example, the naming of plants, lines, and processes is to be considered unique and present. As with any organization undergoing the digital transformation, however, we have found this not to be the case in every situation. Thus, missing or redundant records have to be addressed. Since improvement data quality is a process and cannot be achieved within a short duration, intermediate solutions based on mere comma-separated value files have been installed as mitigating action. With increasing maturity of the organization, these sources can be replaced by their improved versions at a later time, requiring updates to the mappings but concealing these changes to the layers above. Hence, the application and users will not notice those changes. As a result of organically grown organizational diversity, while integrating our various sources, we have observed SICs frequently.

3.2   Mappings

A *mapping* is a set of assertions specifying how the classes and properties of the ontology are populated with data from our sources described in Sect. 3.1.

```
INSERT DATA {
GRAPH <http://bosch.com/kg/lis#> {
  ?line_instance a lis:LISLine ; lis:lineId ?line_id .
} }
WHERE {
    ?uri    a    tmpschema:MESClass ;
                 tmpschema:plant_id     ?plant_id ;
                 tmpschema:system_id    ?system_id ;
                 tmpschema:line_number  ?line_number .
    # generate unique key
BIND (CONCAT("Plant", ?plant_id, "_System", ?system_id, "_line", ?
    line_number) AS ?line_id)
    # instantiate classes based on their unique keys
BIND (IRI(CONCAT("http://bosch.com/ontologies/lis#LISLine_", ?line_id))) AS
    ?line_instance) }
```

Listing 1. Example of a mapping for URI creation. For every production line across all plants a unique key is generated based on several attributes to be consequently used in the instantiations of the `lis:LISLine` class.

Accordingly, they link the records from the sources to the concepts described in the ontology. Typically, mappings are used to resolve SICs. One of the central features for LIS is the creation of correct URI for every instance of the classes. As described in the motivation, lines are not uniquely identify across different plants causing a SIC of type homonym. We resolve this SIC by generating an unique identifier of the lines combining the plant and the system to where they belong in addition to its number (cf. Listing 1).

```
INSERT DATA {
GRAPH <http://bosch.com/kg/lis#> {
  ?process_instance a proc:Process ;
                    proc:processNumber  ?process_number;
                    proc:processName    ?process_name .
} }
WHERE{
     ?uri   a         tmpschema:MESClass ;
                      tmpschema:process_number    ?process_number .
                      tmpschema:process_name      ?process_name .

BIND (IRI (CONCAT("https://open-manufacturing.org/ontologies/I4.0/
    ProcessSegment#Process_", ?process_number))) AS ?process_instance)
}
```

Listing 2. Example of a mapping for creating an instance of process. Processes instances are created based on process number since the process name can vary or not exist. This resolves the synonym SIC.

Next, to resolve the synonym SIC we first employed the Listing 2. In this particular case, despite the process names may be distinct in different plants, the process number remains the same. Thus, we created the process instance based on the process number. We do not intent here to provide an exhaustive list of all the SICs that occur in the manufacturing context. On the contrary, the goal is to set the basis to resolve some of the most important ones and show that the LIS approach can scale in this context.

3.3   LIS Ontology

The LIS ontology serves as an abstraction over the manufacturing-related sources and is used by the domain experts to formulate queries over the data. The LIS ontology reuses most of the concepts and relations described in the set of ontologies that are part of the Core Information Model for Manufacturing (**CIMM**) [3]. This set of ontologies are published in the context of the Industrial Digital Twin association[2]. With the aim to create the LIS ontology, several iterations were performed with different groups of experts. It is important to note that the aim was to cover, as much as possible, the manufacturing domain in LIS by directly reusing the concepts included in CIMM. For instance, a Bosch plant which is described in CIMM as a class belonging to the equipment ontology, i.e., eq:Plant (cf. Fig. 3). Then, specific concepts and relationships were introduced to capture the particularities of the LIS approach. These concepts are not included in the CIMM but are demanded to be incorporated in the LIS ontology to capture the requirements of the manufacturing domain and the proposed approach.

---

[2] https://github.com/eclipse-esmf/esmf-manufacturing-information-model.

3.4 LIS Knowledge Graph

After executing the mappings, the data that rely on the three data sources under use is transformed into an RDF KG. It is important to realize that every data transformation process may lead to data leakage. We took this fact into account and developed a procedure to ensure that no data leakage is occurring. For instance, part of the procedure is focused on determining whether the number of instances of the classes that are built, e.g., lis:LISLine, eq:Plant, proc:Process, match with what exist in the data sources. LIS is intended to be used by manufacturing experts and for them, the quality of the presented data is of key relevance. The LIS KG comprises data from 12 Bosch plants around the globe, distributed in different regions and time zones. Additionally, it contains semantically integrated data of more than 1.100 production lines, more than 16.000 physical machines, as well as more than 100 manufacturing processes.

Writing Links into the LIS KG. In what follows, we outline two of the main requirements where we need to not only use the typical ETL process but also to enrich the LIS KG by including the input from the domain experts.

Linking Physical Machines and Logical Work Units. Despite the huge effort employed in data harmonization, an automatic link between physical machines presented in ERP and logical stations in MES was not possible to realize. Thus, we provide a user interface to enable domain experts for the manual creation of these links. Of core relevance here is to note that this approach is not only transforming the data that relies in existing sources but also creating links that do not exist. In this case, the experts in the plants are linking a physical machine with a logical work unit. The link is described in the ontology with the property c:isImplementedBy which has the eq:WorkUnit as domain and phys:Machine as range. This link is then written and maintained in the LIS KG.

Master Data Management. Combining data from different plants across countries and time zones is a challenging task, particularly, when it comes to semantic data integration. For instance, the line names were maintained manually in CSV files in the plants. We used the CSV files as starting point. The files were ingested into the LIS KG. Then, LIS also provides the possibility to maintain these and other data relevant to many different stakeholders in a centralized and harmonized manner. In this case, the line names are not maintained in the local CSV files anymore rather using LIS as a centralized solution.

3.5 Application

LIS is focused to create an ecosystem that integrates and harmonizes different heterogeneous data sources in the manufacturing domain. The integration has the goal to enable users to answer business-relevant questions (cf. Sect. 2). To that end, we designed the Application layer at the top of the LIS architecture. This layer comprises: 1) the web-based LIS application, with different

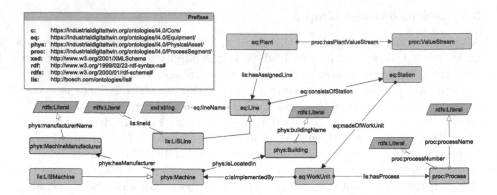

Fig. 3. Main classes and relations of the LIS Ontology. The LIS Ontology reuses classes from the **CIMM**, e.g., `phys:Machine` and `eq:Line` and further specifies subclasses, e.g., `lis:LISMachine` and `lis:LISLine` to reflect a more fine grained representation of the concepts in the manufacturing scenario in the Bosch Plants.

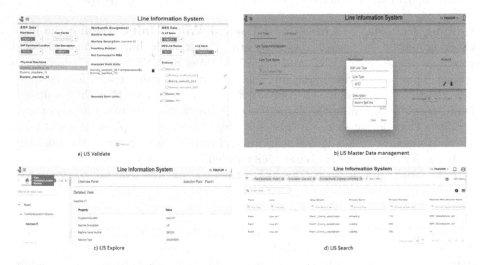

Fig. 4. Core functionalities of the LIS application. The Figure depicts four of the core functionalities of the **LIS** application. a) The Validate, which enables users to manually create links between ERP and MES; b) The Master Data management, which allows users to add new Lines or Statuses; c) The Explore, that aims to browse the integrated data of the plants; and d) The Search, which permit to access the data in any order on various entities, e.g., lines, processes, machines.

functionalities to browse and edit the LIS KG; 2) APIs service to enable data sharing by accessing the LIS KG from other applications; and 3) a set of dynamic dashboards to directly interact with LIS KG covering a huge range of possible combinations of data requirements to answer business questions.

```
SELECT DISTINCT ?plant_id ?work_unit_label ?process_name ?process_number ?
    building_name ?manufacturer_name
WHERE {
  ?plant eq:plantId ?plant_id ;
         lis:hasAssignedLine ?line .
  ?line eq:consistsOfStation   ?station ;
        eq:madeOfWorkUnit ?work_unit .
    ?work_unit   c:isImplementedBy   ?machine ;
                 rdfs:label          ?work_unit_label ;
                 lis:hasProcess      ?process .
    ?machine     phys:isLocatedIn  ?building ;
                 phys:hasManufacturer ?manufacturer .
    ?building    phys:buildingName ?building_name .
    ?manufacturer phys:manufacturerName ?manufacturer_name .
    ?process proc:processNumber   ?process_number ;
  OPTIONAL{
    ?work_unit c:isImplementedBy   ?machine .
    ?process proc:processName   ?process_name .
  }
}
```

Listing 3. **SPARQL** query linking data from the physical assets and the
logical processes

LIS Web Application. The LIS Web application is developed with KG at
its crux. The application comprises different functionalities like explore, search,
master data management, and linking information across data silos. Figure 4
depicts four of the core functionalities of the LIS web application. As discussed
in Sect. 3.4 LIS provides a user interface for domain experts to perform the link
creation between ERP and MES systems. This function is named "Validate"
since for the domain experts they are performing a validation on top of the data.
Currently, the application supports two types of validation. Firstly, it allows
domain experts to select their respective plant, once selected it proceeds to
query the KG and fetch the list of physical machines from the ERP system.
These machines are manually mapped to the respective work units under MES
data by the experts. Links are stored in the form of triples and are colored green
once assigned (cf. Fig. 4a). The second form of the validation is done when a
physical machine cannot be mapped to the MES system and is marked as "Not
Connected to MES", displayed in red color. This leads to the creation of new
relations within the KG which were not present earlier and hence semantically
connecting the two data silos.

Another important feature of LIS is the data management system. It replaces
the traditional way of maintaining CSV files with a centralized and semantically
harmonized system. For instance, lines can be maintained locally but linked to
the central line entity. The newly created data is appended into LIS KG as RDF
triples (cf. Fig. 4b). Even more, the LIS application provides functionality to
browse/explore and search across the KG (cf. Figs. 4c and 4d). Search allows
domain experts to access the data in a non-sequential manner based on values
selected, e.g., plants, lines, etc. Listing 3 showcases the query used in the search
feature to fetch data like work unit, process name, and number from the MES
system along with building and manufacturer name from the ERP system. This
is possible since LIS enables the possibility to create links between the two
systems. Thus resolving the missing items SIC. Particularly, the resolution of

this SIC has made LIS very attractive for other applications since these links are typically non existing in the manufacturing domain.

LIS API Service. In the manufacturing context, there exist other applications that require the data managed by LIS. Typically, these applications create their own data silos on top of what already existed. LIS enables the reuse of data between these applications by providing an easy way of sharing the data. With that we ensure that the applications access to the same harmonized data which is also maintained and semantically curated in LIS. To meet this requirement, we implemented an API service based on the needs of every application. The requirements of the consumer applications are transformed into SPARQL queries. They are then executed against the LIS KG and then served as a JSON-LD payload.

Dashboards on Top of the LIS KG. The LIS application is designed to cover main business questions regarding manufacturing. However, once the data from the plants is integrated many more questions can be answered. The complete set of possible questions is not covered by the LIS application. Thus, as a part of the LIS ecosystem, we provided the possibility to create dashboards on top of the LIS KG. The goal of the dashboards is twofold. First, to be able to provide to a different set of stakeholders the freedom of interacting with the semantically harmonized data to get answers to many different business questions. Second, the dashboards are also used by the developers in order to continuously validate the data quality. For instance, to ensure that the same amount of instances of processes, lines, machines is on the LIS KG as in the original sources.

4 Feedback of Main Stakeholders

In this section we report on the results of a study performed to collect feedback from the main stakeholders. A questionnaire is designed with eight questions to specific topics of interest. Seven questions are measured following the five-point Likert scale with values ranging between Strongly agree and Strongly disagree. We employ the mode to measure them since the data have ordinal nature. The first five questions, i.e., from **Q1** to **Q5**, are specifically evaluating LIS as a solution. **Q6** collects the current vision regarding the use of KGs for manufacturing and engineering domain. Further, the importance and availability of training courses in this regard in the manufacturing industry is included in **Q7**. Finally, **Q8** is a free-text question to collect feedback w.r.t. the possible obstacles that the stakeholders perceive to apply solutions like LIS. Table 1 outlines the questions and the mode value of the answers, depicting what is the general consensus of the stakeholders. A total of 21 stakeholders participated in the study. They are divided in three different groups of seven participants. The characteristics of the groups are as follows: **Managers**: They are business responsible and as such have a high interest in trust-worthy data. In digital transformation, they have the role of project sponsors, dedicate resources to projects, and need to trust in the technology. As the provided data offers completely new insights they are challenged to think out of the box for further business improvements. **Users**:

Table 1. Questions of the questionnaire and answers of the stakeholders

Question (with Mode values M we provide general consensus of our survey)	M
Q1. Did the developed **LIS** semantic model (ontology) meet your expectations?	Agree
Q2. How do you evaluate the perceived benefit of **LIS**?	Agree
Q3. How do you evaluate the benefit of data curation and integration in the **LIS** and its impact on data quality?	Strongly Agree
Q4. Do you think investing in knowledge graph-based technologies as **LIS** is based on can result in a good Return of Invest (ROI) in future?	Strongly Agree
Q5. Do you consider a high value of reuse data from **LIS** as a semantically curated central Master Data System in your organization?	Strongly Agree
Q6. Do you consider knowledge graph-based technologies fit for usage in the manufacturing and engineering domain?	Strongly Agree
Q7. Do you think a broader community should achieve the knowledge about and get trained in knowledge engineering?	Strongly Agree

Free-text questions:

Q8. What would be the biggest obstacles for the successful use of knowledge graph-based technologies at Bosch?

Mostly domain experts use the application and interact with the data. Partially they are also use case providers who specified their requirements for consideration for implementation. Their feedback is strongly required to improve the solution. They are mainly responsible for data curation and validation to raise the quality of the data in the systems and avoid SICs. **Developers**: This group has the deepest insight in the technology, i.e., understanding of the functionality, vision of the potential, but also the risks of this new technology. The developers have a strong identification with the product as they know the value of a solution like this for the organization. Figure 5 depicts the results of the questionnaire for the first seven questions. Regarding **Q8** we received some useful feedback w.r.t. possible obstacles for the adoption of **LIS** but also regarding KG-related technologies at Bosch. For instance, "degree of novelty of the technologies employed very high", and "tools for developing and maintaining ontologies and KGs need to get easier to use for non-experts" thus the need to have KG experts to ensure the success is crucial; "huge effort to bring humans to a shared understanding", and "management is lacking the deeper understanding of the importance of semantics for data sharing, reusability, and its economic impact" requires better communication for management level to achieve the right awareness for the topic.

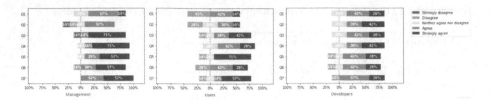

Fig. 5. Results of the questionnaire. The Figure shows the results of the questionnaire divided in three groups, i.e., Management, Users, and Developers. In general, the feedback from stakeholders is highly positive regarding LIS as well as for KG-based solutions.

5   Discussion and Lessons Learned

In this section, we analyze the outcome of the performed study. Initially, we discuss the results of the study. Further, we describe main lessons learned. The overall result is a very positive reception of the approach as the majority of the answers of all groups agreed or even strongly agreed with the LIS approach and the technology behind it. Though the group of users shows more a critical view on the application as this might be related to their role of use case providers and like this a high expectation is present. Moreover this group has the task of data cleansing which causes extra effort not seen before as this limits the advantage of usage of the application in their view. The question related to the perceived benefit of LIS was in the group of managers connected with some disagreement due to wrong expectation for a fast ROI than a strategic development. Furthermore the application revealed a data quality in the investigated systems which raises directly efforts to be taken in order to clean the data properly for the responsible system owners. From management side this is noted as a risk as possibly high personnel effort is required to ensure the data quality. Nevertheless the overall introduction of KG-based technology is seen as positive in all three groups and a strong belief in a success of KG-based technologies is present in the community. Further use cases were discussed with managers and users group to see a benefit of reusing the data of the LIS as this application as once the data set is curated, it can be used as a Master Data System for other applications. The developers group has a different view on this topic as technological requirements of a Master Data System is in principal possible but might require some adaptions. The usage of KG-based technologies in the domains engineering and manufacturing is perceived as appropriate to introduce as it offers more opportunities specifically for data re-use. All groups give a clear feedback that the introduction of a new technology requires setup of training possibilities to face future tasks with sufficient skills and competency. The result of the good acceptance of the application might be surprising, because compared to the developer group the managers and users have not the detailed insight of the technology used. Both groups see only a graphical user interface which hides any underlying technology.

In general, the LIS approach was well acknowledged in the organization. In the following we describe the main lessons learned for a production enterprise.

Main difficulty in the beginning was to understand how to use available data in different systems and to connect them to one and the same semantic model. The data base received from the different plants was required to be cleaned, sorted, and newly adjusted. These data bases are to be consumed in a way that users from other domains as manufacturing, e.g., product development or process engineering were able to understand the provided data. Corresponding table structures would have to be defined with their data models. The effort would have been to fit into these models. However, the reality is much more heterogeneous due to historical circumstances. In this respect, the use of a KG is of core importance here, as the ontology and thus also a semantically harmonization of the data can be handled and integrated much more flexibly. The possibility of easily adding further information by mapping of new data sources was found to be most efficient in terms of time and cost. The lesson learned of this approach was the power and flexibility of the KG-based technology. Even without data cleansing the information at once glance saves already many engineering hours to search for the right information in the organization. LIS is far more than a proof on concept and it is currently in use in one Bosch division. LIS will be stabilized as a product for re-use in other Bosch divisions. Though it has some limitations due to actuality of data[3], it serves already as a single source of truth for many other applications depending on data from manufacturing domain. Next, we list the essential points of our lessons learned.

Integrated View of Data Provided by LIS Ontology: For the first time, data from ERP, MES, and MD was integrated. This enabled the possibility that domain experts formulate their information needs as queries, as they were working on the level of incompatible raw data sources before. The integration of MD was required to harmonize the data available in the plant specific master data systems.

Impact on Data Quality: For the first time it was possible to make the data quality of the integrated systems transparent. The findings were used to fix undetected failures which were not present to the data stewards responsible for these systems. For example, the location identifier in the MES was in some cases too short and will probably lead into a failure. A correction of the location identifier was initiated.

Involvement of Domain Experts: Involving domain experts in the process of building, and maintaining the LIS approach is of paramount importance for its success. Training in KG-based technologies are provided to help experts to better understand the problems which LIS is tackling. Despite initial resistance to the KG-related technologies, the impact of the semantically integrated data has convinced most of the domain experts.

---

[3] The LIS KG is generated periodically once a day. The plant ERP and MES systems are mirrored accurately with a one-day uncertainty which is due to the definition of the use-cases acceptable.

LIS as Data Provider for Different Applications: Associated to the previous lesson, we observed an increasing need for other applications requesting data to LIS. This re-use of data enables the whole organization to refer with its questions to one single source of truth. The availability of a reliable master data system with all information about production lines is of high interest for implementation in other applications. The need for information typically arises in non-manufacturing domains such as product engineering or controlling and planning. By connecting to the LIS via an API these data can be retrieved now easily with the additional benefit that it is actual.

6   Related Work

In this section, we survey the current state of the art presenting similar approaches as LIS. Yan *et al.* [17] outlines an approach for building KGs in the context of manufacturing equipment. In this work, several data sources are integrated with particular focus on lathes, conveyors, and robots. Cheng *et al.* [2] designed an ontological approach for dealing with production lines in the context of Industry 4.0. Five ontologies for representing knowledge regarding production lines are developed, i.e., Base, Product, Device, Parameter, Process. Petersen *et al.* [13] utilize an RDF-based information model to semantically integrate different data sources in a manufacturing company. Kasrin *et al.* [7] present an RDF-based framework for system architecture and domain modelling to create semantic data management solutions for manufacturing. The framework comprises heterogeneous data utilising data lake and enhances knowledge with semantic metadata. Kalayci *et al.* [6] outlined a virtual KG approach for semantically integrating data for Surface Mount Technologies. Mehdi *et al.* [10] tackle a similar problem for performing semantic data integration on top of manufacturing related data. In the previously mentioned works, no extended and concrete implementation and rollout of such a KG-based solution was performed. Furthermore, no scalable way of describing and semantically harmonizing and resolving SICs in manufacturing context is provided.

7   Conclusions and Outlook

In this paper, we presented the LIS, a Knowledge Graph-based ecosystem capable of semantically harmonizing and integrating manufacturing data at Bosch. LIS enables a 360° view of manufacturing data while resolving Semantic Interoperability Conflicts in a scalable manner. Furthermore, we developed the LIS ontology, mappings, and a procedure to ensure the quality of the data in the LIS KG. The LIS application comprises many functionalities to answer business questions that were not possible without LIS. LIS is currently in use in 12 Bosch plants integrating data of more than 1.100 production lines, 16.000 physical machines, as well as more than 400 manufacturing processes. The feedback collected showed that LIS in particular, and KG-based solutions in general, paves the way of exploiting the knowledge in manufacturing settings in a reusable and scalable way. Despite the efforts employed in the data integration to create the LIS KG, still some room for improvement exists regarding its completeness and the semantic disambiguation of some of the core entities, e.g., processes. In future work, we envision to develop entity disambiguation algorithms on top of the LIS KG. Moreover, we plan to applying Machine Learning techniques to further improve the completeness of a manufacturing KG like the one presented here, e.g., in terms of Link Prediction [4,15].

References

1. Buchgeher, G., Gabauer, D., Gil, J.M., Ehrlinger, L.: Knowledge graphs in manufacturing and production: a systematic literature review. IEEE Access **9**, 55537–55554 (2021)
2. Cheng, H., Zeng, P., Xue, L., Shi, Z., Wang, P., Yu, H.: Manufacturing ontology development based on Industry 4.0 demonstration production line. In: 2016 Third International Conference on Trustworthy Systems and their Applications (TSA), pp. 42–47 IEEE (2016)
3. Grangel-González, I., Lösch, F., ul Mehdi, A.: Knowledge graphs for efficient integration and access of manufacturing data. In: 25th IEEE International Conference on Emerging Technologies and Factory Automation, ETFA, Vienna, Austria, 8–11 September, pp. 93–100. IEEE (2020)
4. Grangel-González, I., Shah, F.: Link prediction with supervised learning on an industry 4.0 related knowledge graph. In: 26th IEEE International Conference on Emerging Technologies and Factory Automation, ETFA, Vasteras, Sweden, 7–10 September, pp. 1–8. IEEE (2021)
5. Jirkovský, V., Obitko, M., Marík, V.: Understanding data heterogeneity in the context of cyber-physical systems integration. IEEE Trans. Ind. Inform. **13**(2), 660–667 (2017)
6. Kalaycı, E.G., et al.: Semantic integration of Bosch manufacturing data using virtual knowledge graphs. In: Pan, J.Z., et al. (eds.) ISWC 2020. LNCS, vol. 12507, pp. 464–481. Springer, Cham (2020). https://doi.org/10.1007/978-3-030-62466-8_29
7. Kasrin, N., Qureshi, M., Steuer, S., Nicklas, D.: Semantic data management for experimental manufacturing technologies. Datenbank-Spektrum **18**(1), 27–37 (2018)
8. Kharlamov, E., et al.: Semantic access to streaming and static data at siemens. J. Web Semant. **44**, 54–74 (2017)
9. Li, X., Lyu, M., Wang, Z., Chen, C.H., Zheng, P.: Exploiting knowledge graphs in industrial products and services: a survey of key aspects, challenges, and future perspectives. Comput. Ind. **129**, 103449 (2021)
10. Mehdi, A., Kharlamov, E., Stepanova, D., Loesch, F., Grangel-Gonzalez, I.: Towards semantic integration of Bosch manufacturing data. In: Proceedings of ISWC, pp. 303–304 (2019)
11. Melluso, N., Grangel-González, I., Fantoni, G.: Enhancing industry 4.0 standards interoperability via knowledge graphs with natural language processing. Comput. Ind. **140**, 103676 (2022)
12. Nilsson, J., Sandin, F.: Semantic interoperability in industry 4.0: survey of recent developments and outlook. In: 2018 IEEE 16th International Conference on Industrial Informatics (INDIN), pp. 127–132. IEEE (2018)

13. Petersen, N., Halilaj, L., Grangel-González, I., Lohmann, S., Lange, C., Auer, S.: Realizing an RDF-based information model for a manufacturing company - A case study. In: ISWC-17, pp. 350–366 (2017)
14. Sjarov, M., Franke, J.: Towards knowledge graphs for industrial end-to-end data integration: technologies, architectures and potentials. In: Behrens, B.-A., Brosius, A., Drossel, W.-G., Hintze, W., Ihlenfeldt, S., Nyhuis, P. (eds.) WGP 2021. LNPE, pp. 545–553. Springer, Cham (2022). https://doi.org/10.1007/978-3-030-78424-9_60
15. Xia, L., et al.: A knowledge graph-based link prediction for interpretable maintenance planning in complex equipment. In: 2022 13th International Conference on Reliability, Maintainability, and Safety (ICRMS), pp. 301–305. IEEE (2022)
16. Yahya, M., Breslin, J.G., Ali, Intizar, M.: Semantic web and knowledge graphs for industry 4.0. Appl. Sci. 11(11), 5110 (2021)
17. Yan, H., Yang, J., Wan, J.: KnowIME: a system to construct a knowledge graph for intelligent manufacturing equipment. IEEE Access 8, 41805–41813 (2020)

Combining Semantic Web and Machine Learning for Auditable Legal Key Element Extraction

Anna Breit[1], Laura Waltersdorfer[2], Fajar J. Ekaputra[2,3(✉)],
Sotirios Karampatakis[1], Tomasz Miksa[2], and Gregor Käfer[2]

[1] Semantic Web Company, Vienna, Austria
{anna.breit,sotirios.karampatakis}@semantic-web.com
[2] TU Wien, Vienna, Austria
{laura.waltersdorfer,fajar.ekaputra,tomasz.miksa,
gregor.kafer}@tuwien.ac.at
[3] Vienna University of Economics and Business, Vienna, Austria
fajar.ekaputra@wu.ac.at

Abstract. Based on a real world use case, we developed and evaluated a hybrid AI system that aims to extract key elements from legal permits by combining methods from the Semantic Web and Machine Learning. Specifically, we modelled the available background knowledge in a custom Knowledge Graph, which we exploited together with the usage of different language- and text-embedding-models in order to extract different information from official Austrian permits, including the Issuing Authority, the Operator of the facility in question, the Reference Number, and the Issuing Date. Additionally, we implemented mechanisms to capture automatically auditable traces of the system to ensure the transparency of the processes. Our quantitative evaluation showed overall promising results, while the in-depth qualitative analysis revealed concrete error types, providing guidance on how to improve the current prototype.

Keywords: legal permits · information extraction · semantic web · machine learning · auditability

1 Introduction

Given its manifold and distributed nature combined with a large number of associated exceptions and exemptions, the legal domain can be considered one of the most complex areas. In addition, most of the knowledge is stored (e.g., in laws) and distributed (e.g., in permits) in unstructured, textual form, that makes use of highly convoluted and composite language. In order to facilitate the searchability and processability of such legal documents, specific *key elements* – representing the most important actors and aspects of the document – are added as metadata. If not added at creation time of the document, these key elements need to be extracted manually in a later point in time. Due to the high cost of jurists, this extraction is often performed by laypersons for whom this task can be demanding and resource-intense.

C. Pesquita et al. (Eds.): ESWC 2023, LNCS 13870, pp. 609–624, 2023.
https://doi.org/10.1007/978-3-031-33455-9_36

In this work, we introduce a system that aims at assisting laypersons in their task of extracting key elements from official permits. For doing so, we collect requirements from and perform an evaluation along a real-world use case situated in Austria. Specifically, we build a hybrid AI system, which combines methods from Machine Learning and Semantic Web technologies to provide suggestions for specific key elements, while providing auditable traces of the extraction procedure, which increase the transparency of the system.

The rest of the paper is structured as follows. Section 2 describes the use case and the associated requirements in more detail, while Sect. 3 introduces the developed system. Section 4 explains methods and evaluation setup, results of our quantitative and qualitative analysis are shown in Sect. 5. Finally, we report our conclusions and future work in Sect. 6.

2   The Use Case

The use case concerns the operation of an electronic permit management system (EPMS) which facilitates the organisational and bureaucratic processes around official permits in Austria, including application, decision, and amendments, as it provides a common platform for all involved stakeholders. Alongside the digitized version of the permit document, the EPMS also provides a summary of *key elements* characterizing the most important aspects of the permit.

The task of filling these structured summaries is currently conducted by data management staff. However, as they are usually not specifically trained for this highly complex exercise, the task completion requires a lot of efforts and can end in poor data quality. Therefore, our goal is to provide a system that supports the administrators for extracting information by providing suggestions for the key elements that need to be extracted.

Specifically, for this use case, we are focusing on the following key elements (cf. Fig. 1): (1) the *Operator* of the installation a permit is targeting, (this could either be a legal or natural person), (2) the *Issuing Authority* in charge of the content of the permit, (3) the *Reference Number* of the permit, being its unique identifier, and (4) the *Issuing Date*. Along these key elements, which are mentioned in the permit content, we are further interested in extracting additional meta-information concerning the *Permit Types* including (5) the *Object Type* describing whom the permit is for (e.g., for an Installation Site), (6) the *Processing Type* describing the type of request and outcome of the permit (e.g., application, amendment, withdrawal), and (7) the *Procedure Type* describing the legal procedure under which the permit was issued (e.g., simplified procedure).

Requirements: Different requirements arise from the presented use case. First, the extracted key elements should be matched to pre-defined entities to ensure data quality. Second, the system must be able incorporate symbolic expert knowledge. Specifically, expert-created mappings of legal regulations to the different Permit Types should be exploitable by the system. Finally, to ensure the transparency of the provided suggestions and thus the acceptance of the users,

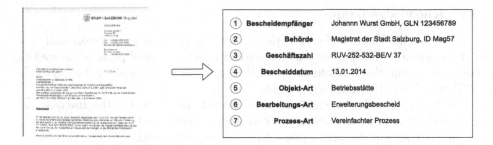

Fig. 1. Example of a structured summary of permit key elements.

auditability capabilities to conduct regular internal audits for error detection of past system executions should be included in the system. To this end the following audit requirements should be fulfilled: (A1) availability of audit traces logging complete system executions, (A2) automation of audit trace collection, transformation and management and (A3) the capability and ease of use to ask and answer to audit questions based on stakeholder input.

3 The System

The implemented solution consists of three main components, being (1) a knowledge graph (KG) containing the background knowledge and corresponding entities, (2) the Key Element Extraction Module, comprising of a main pipeline that orchestrates a set of extraction services, and (3) the AuditBox, responsible for collecting and providing audit traces of the system. To facilitate the accessibility of the developed system, a simple web interface was added through which user interaction can take place. An overview over the system is shown in Fig. 2.

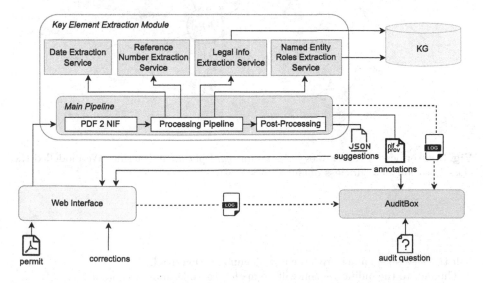

Fig. 2. Overview over the developed Auditable Key Element Extraction System

3.1 Knowledge Graph

We developed a knowledge graph (KG) as a central component to store and provide information both about the involved entities (e.g., legal persons) as well as background knowledge about these entities (e.g., associations of legal regulations to Permit Types) within legal permits.

To build such a KG, we first identified relevant datasets. For this use case, we collected (i) a *geo-location dataset* structured according to Geonames ontology[1], (ii) a *legal person dataset*, representing our operator entities, (iii) *authorities dataset*, (iv) *regulations dataset* structuring relevant Austrian law, and (v) the *Permit Types dataset* mapping the regulations to the different types. Afterwards, we develop an ontology which described the data model of the data from these datasets and the links between these data (e.g., the location of a legal person from legal person databases should be in the location registered in the geo-location dataset). The ontology is summarized in Fig. 3 and online available[2]. With the ontology in place, we transformed the source data into its KG representation, by integrating the transformed data from individual data sources in a triplestore. Finally, we enriched the generated KG with additional information, e.g., SKOS hierarchies based on the inputs from domain experts.

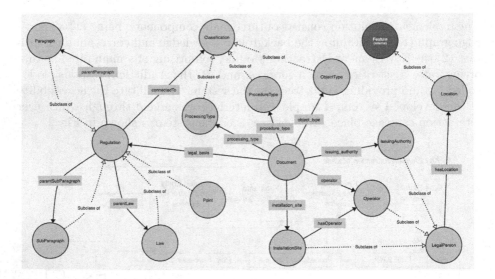

Fig. 3. Overview of the ontology classes for legal permit extraction. We modelled the class Location as a subclass of GeoNames Feature.

---

[1] http://www.geonames.org/ontology/documentation.html.
[2] The link to the online version will be made available upon acceptance.

3.2   Key Element Extraction Module

The Key Element Extraction Module of the developed system follows the paradigm of a microservice architecture, where the module is structured as a collection of decoupled services. Each microservice can be developed and deployed independently, providing flexibility on using different programming languages for their implementation. Microservices are by design minimal and autonomous, in contrast to monolithic integrated systems, thus can be developed more efficiently [12]. Furthermore, deployment can be automated to a large extent, making the solution easy to scale based on demand.

Main Pipeline. The use of a microservice architecture mandates the use of a management tool in order to orchestrate the execution of the different services and steps needed to accomplish more complex tasks. To this end, we used UnifiedViews ETL[3] [6] – an Extract-Transform-Load (ETL) framework and platform that allows users to define, execute, monitor, debug, schedule, and share data processing tasks as a pipeline – as it has the advantage of natively supporting the processing of RDF data. There, we defined a main pipeline which orchestrates the processing step needed to perform 1) the parsing and pre-processing of the legal document, 2) the execution of the extraction services, and 3) a number of post-processing steps needed to produce the final outcome of the main pipeline. Additionally, for each extraction service, we define a secondary annotation pipeline, in order to decouple configuration needs of each service from the main pipeline and enable parallel execution of the services. Fault tolerance is achieved through this design, as in case an error occurs on any of the extraction services, the main pipeline will continue to process.

By design, all extraction services use the NIF ontology as I/O format (see below). We developed a Data Processing Unit (DPU), a pluggable processing component for UnifiedViews, with the task to parse a document in PDF format and convert it into NIF. The DPU uses the DKPro-core Library [2] to achieve the conversion. Then, the NIF document is sent to next DPU in the pipeline, which triggers the secondary pipeline for each of the extraction services. Upon completion of all secondary pipelines, a set of post-processing steps is executed. First, the results are merged, then we filter the annotation units produced by the annotation services based on a confidence threshold. Finally, we serialize the results in JSON, by utilizing JSON-LD framing [9]. Thus the final results can be presented on the user interface of the system.

The NLP Interchange Format. The NLP Interchange Format (NIF) [5] is an RDF/OWL-based format that aims to achieve interoperability between Natural Language Processing (NLP) tools, language resources and annotations. The NIF 2.0 Core Ontology[4] provides classes and properties to describe the relations

---

[3] https://www.poolparty.biz/agile-data-integration/.
[4] http://persistence.uni-leipzig.org/nlp2rdf/ontologies/nif-core#.

between substrings, text, documents by assigning URIs to strings. These URIs can then be used as subjects in RDF triples and therefore enable easy annotation.

In the course of the presented use case, NIF 2.1[5] is used as the base data model for all annotation services. Each service should be able to parse NIF data as input for process. Additionally, output of each annotation service is expected as NIF. Thus, interoperability between all annotation services of the developed system is achieved through the NIF data model. Through the extensive usage of nif:AnnotationUnit, results from each service can be merged effortless to produce the final results of the annotation pipelines. Moreover, the use of provenance metadata on each of nif:AnnotationUnit ensures the auditability of the results produced by the annotation pipelines. An example of the output of an annotation service is shown in Listing 1.1.

```
@prefix nif: <http://persistence.uni-leipzig.org/nlp2rdf/ontologies/nif-core#> .
@prefix alkees-nif: <https://alkees.org/ontology/nif-alkees#> .
@prefix its-rdf: <http://www.w3.org/2005/11/its/rdf#> .
@prefix alkees-permit: <https://w3id.org/alkees/ns/permit#> .
@prefix alkees-authority: <http://w3id.org/alkees/id/authority/> .
@prefix alkees-service: <http://alkees.org/ns/service/> .

<file:///data/CONTENT17_71708645.pdf#offset_0_9672>
    a nif:Context, nif:OffsetBasedString, nif:String ;
    nif:beginIndex 0;
    nif:endIndex 9672;
    nif:isString "Lots of text...";
    alkees-nif:annotations  <file:///data/CONTENT17_71708645.pdf#offset_177_223> .

<file:///data/CONTENT17_71708645.pdf#offset_177_223>
    a alkees-nif:MatchedResourceOccurrence, nif:Annotation, nif:OffsetBasedString;
    nif:beginIndex 177;
    nif:endIndex 223;
    nif:referenceContext <file:///data/CONTENT17_71708645.pdf#offset_0_9672> ;
    nif:anchorOf "Bezirkshauptmannschaft Baden";
    nif:annotationUnit [ a nif:AnnotationUnit;
                    its-rdf:taAnnotatorRef
                           alkees-service:pp-concept-extraction-annotator-v1;
                    its-rdf:taClassRef alkees-permit:ConceptAnnotation;
                    its-rdf:taConfidence 1.0E0;
                    its-rdf:taIdentRef alkees-authority:308 .
                ] .
```

Listing 1.1. Example NIF output of an annotation service.

Extraction Services. In total, we developed four microservices to extract the five types of key elements, which we describe below in more detail. The communication of the services is based on well defined REST interfaces, simplifying the communication and allowing decoupling the client from the server.

Date Extraction: There is a variety of tools and libraries available that target the recognition and parsing of dates from textual data. After analyzing a selection of

---

[5] Please note, that version 2.1 has not yet officially been released yet, but is the latest develop branch of the ontology.

these libraries, (including *dateutil*[6], *dateparser*[7], and *datefinder*[8]) we decided for heideltime[9] as it provided the best range of functions and performance for the intended use case. This Java tool developed by Heidelberg University supports a wide variety of languages and date formats, captures the type of annotation (full date, relative date, ...), and directly annotates these mentions within the text. This gives the advantage of being able to easily filter out irrelevant dates, e.g., for our use case, where the goal is to extract the issuing date of the legal permit, we would only take into consideration full dates.

Reference Number Extraction. For extracting the reference numbers, we chose a two step-approach, being (1) candidate identification and (2) classification.

First, candidates are identified based on a set of RegEx patterns. Specifically, for the presented use case, we used a recall-optimized pattern to collect candidates, which we further refined by automatically filtering out groups of false positives such as all-caps words, or gendered terms (containing a "Binnen-I") with corresponding patterns to improve the quality.

In the second step, the reference number candidates are ingested into a string classifier. We decided for a 1-dimensional-CNN-based architecture to generate character embeddings for the candidates, which are then further fed into a binary classification layer.

Legal Info Extraction. For mapping the legal documents to the Permit Types, we chose a two-step approach: (1) we extracted and normalized the mentions of laws from the text, and then (2) mapped these mentions to the specific types.

Unfortunately, existing legal annotation tools (e.g., [14]) did not show sufficient quality in preliminary experiments. Therefore, we decided to develop our own reference parsing tool based on a context-free grammar. The basis for the grammar is different legislature elements such as article, paragraph, subparagraph, point, and sentence. These elements were organized in a transitive hierarchical way, so that different levels can be skipped to still form a valid overall mention. We also included known separators including commas, but also phrases such as "as well as", or "in combination with".

To automatically map the annotated and normalized legislature mentions to the different Permit Types, we queried the corresponding information provided in the KG.

Named Entity Role Extraction. We chose a two-step approach to extract the Operator and Issuing Authority from a legal permit: (1) we annotated all known entities in the text as candidates, and then (2) classified the candidates whether or not they appear in the role of interest.

---

[6] https://github.com/dateutil/dateutil.
[7] https://github.com/scrapinghub/dateparser.
[8] https://github.com/akoumjian/datefinder.
[9] https://github.com/HeidelTime/heideltime.

In order to annotate the entity candidates, we used PoolParty Extractor[10] to identify all mentions of concepts from the relevant sub-branch of the taxonomy from our KG. For being able to also identify surface forms that are unknown to the KG, we further deployed a BERT-based Named Entity Recognition (NER) model (`bert-base-german-cased` model with token classification head) which we fine-tuned on a German Legal NER dataset [7]. The candidates are then matched to their corresponding entity in the KG, using a fuzzy-string matching algorithm based on n-gram tf-idf-scores, with a empirically determined negative dot product cutoff of -0.8.

The extracted candidates are then used as fine-tuning examples for a disambiguation classifier, which decides whether the concept is used in the target role or not. The classifier consists of a `bert-base-german-cased` model with a binary classification layer. Specifically, the task of role disambiguation is re-formulated in as Target Sense Verification task [1], so that –given a context containing the target entity, as well as a label and definition of the target role– the task is to decide whether the entity in the context is used in the target role or not. This task formulation leads to flexibility regarding the target roles, but also allows to show ambiguities, e.g., when an entity embodies multiple roles in one sentence.

Finally, to overcome the problem of deprecated names used in the permits due to e.g., re-branding of companies, we automatically extracted the installation sites from the permits using RegEx queries parsing the real-estate numbers and used them to retrieve corresponding operators by querying the KG.

3.3 AuditBox

AuditBox offers a flexible and adaptable implementation to collect and transform audit traces from heterogeneous sources into a unified representation. This representation is built upon a workflow model in RDF-format which defines main activities with relevant in- and outputs (e.g. file uploads, suggestions for key elements etc.) and their data sources (e.g. extraction services, user interface). For our use case, traces are collected for each system execution ranging from permit upload to users, permit transformation, information extraction and users being able to correct extracted key elements.

Core components of the AuditBox include:

Audit Collection supports the automatic generation of endpoints (APIs) where traces from different sources and applications can be sent to. AuditBox collectors are REST APIs allowing a flexible and standardised coupling of services. A custom service ontology aides their automatic generation.

Audit Transformation: is responsible for the integration of the heterogeneous audit traces. A set of RML mappings is used to transform data from different sources into RDF format aligned to the workflow model. The transformed data is stored in a graph-based repository, for which we use GraphDB.

Audit Management supports the querying of transformed data from the repository and provides pre-defined queries for users without SPARQL expertise.

---

[10] https://www.poolparty.biz/poolparty-extractor.

Non-functional (security) capabilities include: User authentication and authorization to ensure that only authorized entities can send audit traces and query the stored data.

4   Methods

4.1   Evaluation Setup of Extraction Performance

The basis for this use case were 4612 historic permits that had been entered and annotated in the EPMS system. For evaluation purposes, we reserved 777 permits which were not used in the training of the models. For each of these permits, we performed the extraction of the relevant key elements, using the meta-data from EPMS as silver labels to compare against. As all services – with exception to the Legal Info Extraction – provide a confidence-sorted list of the extracted entities, we chose hits@k as an appropriate evaluation metric, i.e., the proportion of times the correct instance was within the top k ranked predictions. We chose k to be in $\{1, 3, all\}$.

For the extracted Reference Number, we decided to perform a two evaluation settings. a While the *strict* setting required an exact string match, the *lenient* setting allowed sub-string matches. Finally, for errors that occur in services with a two-step approach, we analyse whether the correct annotation was in the candidates or not, indicating if the error occurred in the candidate annotation step, or in the classification step.

4.2   Training of ML Models

While the Date and Legal Info Extraction services only require configuration, the models behind Reference Number and Named Entity Roles Extraction need to go through a training phase before they can be applied to the presented use case. As the legal permits provided for training only consisted of the documents themselves and their associated labels, but no annotations, we created the training data in an distant supervised fashion, where we used the corresponding candidate creation modules of the services to create the instances, and annotated all instances that target the correct entity as true, while others as false. Finally, we balanced the created instance sets to contain an equal number of positive and negative examples, and split into training and validation. It shall be noted that the outcomes of this procedure can contain noisy instances, as a context containing the target might be using this entity in a completely different role, but still serve as a positive example. However, we assumed that these noisy instances are mitigated during the training process.

For the CNN-based classifier, we were able to generate over 30.000 training instances. After 10 epochs of training, the model was able to reach an accuracy of 98%, and F_1 score of 92% (precision of 94%, recall of 90%) on the validation set. For the BERT-based classifier, due to hardware restrictions (Intel Xeon CPU E5-2640, 6x, 2.5 GHz) and the size of the model, we only used a training-set of

2000 instances and a validation set of 500 instances to optimize the model. After 10 epochs, the model achieved an accuracy and F_1 of 94%, (precision of 91%, recall of 97%) on the validation data.

4.3   Evaluation Setup of Auditability

Several methods were proposed to scope the context information to be collected for a given system and environment: A generic provenance-focused methodology e.g., [10], more specialised approaches for AI-supported systems, such as from an accountability perspective e.g. [13], or artefact-focused e.g., [15]. However, they do not focus on automatic collection and management of such context information. To this end, we adapted and refined the method presented in [4]. The three main phases are (cf. Fig. 4):

During the *Scoping Phase*, goal and aims of the audit are defined to identify main activities and entities to be included in the workflow. In the *Preparation Phase*, the workflow model and mappings to transform collected traces are created, to support the automatic management of audit traces. These two outputs are also needed to orchestrate the AuditBox. The *Execution Phase* is concerned with the execution of audits: audit traces are automatically collected and sent to the generated endpoints by the AuditBox. The traces are then transformed according to the mappings and stored in a graph-based format. Audit questions can be answered in the form of SPARQL queries prepared in the AuditBox or also by writing custom ones.

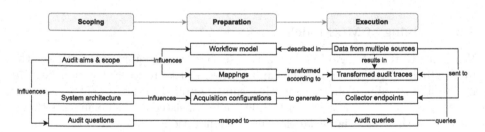

Fig. 4. Auditability method

Such audit questions (and the requirements from Sect. 2) form the main basis for our evaluation. Similar to the scenario-based and question-driven approaches to achieve explainable AI [3,8], we collected a set of audit questions (similar to competency questions) from relevant stakeholders involved in the operation of the EPMS to guide the audit scope. The structure of such a question:

As a <stakeholder>, I want <some goal> so that <some reason>.

One concrete example:

As a technical support staff, I want to know which suggestions of metadata has been corrected by a user so that either the system can ideally learn from errors or areas for enhancement can be detected.

5   Results

5.1   Quantitative Analysis

The results from the quantitative analysis are summarized in Table 1. The extraction of the Issuing Date is the most successful across all key elements and yielded in 79% of the cases the correct result on the first rank of the suggestions, while the consideration of later ranks would not bring too much benefit to the overall performance. In contrast, for other ranked key elements, a longer list of suggestions would result in an increased recall of the correct entity.

The Reference Number Extraction Service, despite the good performance on the training examples, was only able to achieve hits@all of 0.76 for the lenient and 0.55 for the strict setting. The performance difference in the two evaluation settings is quite large, with a total of 165 cases where the extracted reference number was only correct under the lenient scenario, indicating that the boundary detection capabilities of the Reference Number Extraction Service can still be improved. Another interesting insight is that if only incorrect reference numbers are suggested, the probability that the correct one is annotated as a candidate is much higher than compared to cases where no suggestions were provided.

For the key elements originating from the NE-Roles service, i.e., Issuing Authority and Operator, we reach a performance of 0.62 and 0.77 hits@all rate, respectively. Interestingly, the ranking for the extracted Operator suggestions seems to be significantly worse than for the Issuing Authority, as the comparison between the corresponding hits@3 and hits@all rates show. This could be due to the fact that the number of operator candidates contained in a permit is considerably larger than the number of authorities, therefore, the possibility for false positives is increased. For both Issuing Authority and Operator, the vast majority of errors can be traced back to the failed annotation of the corresponding candidate entities in the permit.

When analysing the extraction performance of the installation site in isolation, we can see that the overall performance, while staying below 60%, is considerably high in precision, as only 2% of the suggestions only contained incorrect entities, and if the correct entity was with the suggestions, it was within the first three ranks. However, in 40% of the cases, no suggestion for the installation site was provided, indicating that the identification and parsing of the real-estate number alone is not sufficient to reliably extract this kind of information.

The coverage of Permit Types that we were able to achieve with the tested strategy of extracting and mapping law mentions was considerably low with 23%–39% for hits@all rate for the different types. In a large amount of cases, no suggestion for the different types could be extracted. The model has produced a maximum of 3 suggestions for Object Type and Processing Type, and a maximum of 6 suggestions for Procedure Type across all test permits. Interestingly, the error rate, i.e., when only incorrect types were suggested, varies a lot among the different types: 11% for Object Type to 30% for Processing Type. Concluding, it can be said that the hypothesis that the extraction of Permit Types could be achieved by solely the parsing of law mentions could not be verified.

Table 1. Extraction performance for the different key elements. For Reference Number, we report both the performance for strict (extract string match) as well as lenient (sub-string) evaluation. Incorrect denotes the percentage of cases, where only incorrect suggestions were provided, while Nothing denotes the cases where no suggestions were provided. For those key elements that are extracted in a two-step approach, we report the percentage of cases where the correct entity was not contained in the candidates in parenthesis.

Key Element	hits@1	hits@3	hits@all	Incorrect	Nothing
Issuing Date	0.79	0.82	0.82	0.18	0.00
Ref. Number (strict)	0.41	0.49	0.56	–	–
(lenient)	0.56	0.67	0.77	0.10 (0.09)	0.12 (0.07)
Issuing Authority	0.51	0.63	0.65	0.09 (0.08)	0.25 (0.24)
Operator	0.47	0.59	0.77	0.14 (0.13)	0.08 (0.04)
Installation Site	0.51	0.57	0.57	0.02	0.40
Object Type	–	–	0.25	0.11	0.64
Processing Type	–	–	0.23	0.30	0.47
Procedure Type	–	–	0.39	0.19	0.42

5.2   Qualitative Analysis

To better understand the details of when the different services failed, we performed a qualitative error analysis for the Reference Number, Issuing Authority, and Operator.

One interesting aspect of the Reference Number outcomes is the rather large performance difference of the strict and lenient evaluation setting. Analysing the 165 cases where the lenient setting brings a positive and the strict setting a negative hits@all result, we could find that in 65% of the cases, the matched Reference Number extracted from the permit seemed to be an addendum to the one entered into the EPMS system (e.g., RKU-2123987 vs RKU-2123987-v2). Adding this addendum Reference Number to the original entry would probably be of benefit regarding searchability. In 14% of the cases, the Reference Number entered into the EPMS could not be used directly to compare against, as they were followed by a describing string Finally, in 21% of the cases, the extractor indeed did not correctly identify the boundaries when extracting the Reference Number. More specifically, the Reference Number followed by the a date was extracted. This type of error could easily be mitigated by adjusting the candidate annotation algorithm. In addition to the errors produced during the extraction of the Reference Number, it is further noteworthy that the 9% and 7% of cases, where the correct entity was not among the candidates for only incorrect and no suggestions, respectively, way more than half of the times (i.e., 5% and 4%), this could be traced back to the fact that the string entered as Reference Number into the EPMS system was not present at all in the permit document.

For the key elements extracted by the NE-Roles Extraction service, we analysed why the correct entities were not among the candidates, since this scenario is extremely common in cases of errors. Together with domain experts, we categorised the different reasons into five different super classes: deficiencies in the metadata stored in the EPMS (A), deficiencies in the data contained in the KG

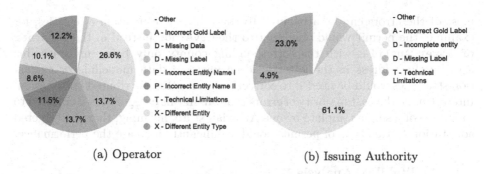

(a) Operator   (b) Issuing Authority

Fig. 5. Analysis of NE-Roles Extraction errors when the correct entity is not among the candidates.

(D), deficiencies contained in the permit itself (P), technical limitations of the developed system (T), and cases where it is not clear why the extraction failed (Other). Finally, we defined a sixth group (X) of errors, which we could identify, but not properly evaluate as crucial background information was missing, e.g., when the EPMS metadata contained a completely different entity type than mentioned in the permit (Fig. 5).

For the Operator, over 40% of the cases of missing correct candidates could be traced back to missing data in the KG. On the one hand, these were missing labels, especially when the Operator represented a natural person. On the other hand, the current version of the KG lacked some deeper insight, e.g., the renaming of companies.

Another fourth of the missed annotations could be attributed to the inaccurate usage of entity names in the permits. For companies, the usage of the exact wording is crucial to qualify their reference as correct, and therefore the permit as valid. In about 14% of the analysed cases, the permit authors would use slightly different wordings (e.g., `Umweltservice` vs `Umwelt Service`, `Umwelt Service` vs `Umwelt-Service`, or `&` vs `and`) to refer to the operating company. In these cases, despite the errors, it was rather obvious to the human which operator the permit was attributed to. However, in another 12% of the cases, the naming used in the permit diverged to a larger extent to the metadata annotated in the EPMS. For these instances, certain aspects (like first or last names, or business forms) are added, swapped, or removed from the registered company name. (e.g. `Johann Wurst GmbH` vs `Wurst Johann GmbH` vs `Wurst GmbH`, or `Wurst GmbH` vs `Wurst BaugmbH` vs `Wurst AG`). In these cases, it is hard to predict whether the true origin of these differences, i.e., from incorrect citation, or incorrectly annotated EPMS metadata. In a few cases, we could indeed verify that –despite the large similarity of the company names– the entity stored in the EPMS was a different from the one referred to in the permit.

In 8.6% of the cases, the missing annotation originated from technical limitations, e.g., when the entity was separated by a page break.

The reasons of missing candidate annotations for the Issuing Authority were quite different and less diverse then for the Operator. First, we could not identify any issues originating from deficiencies contained in the permit itself. Second, most of the errors can be attributed to the incomplete mention of entities, for example, the permit would only refer to the `Governor` instead of the `Governor of Lower Austria`, with the corresponding county only being unidentifiable e.g., by the address in the letter head. Additional data modelling or extraction strategies would be needed to correctly process this distributed information. Interestingly, the vast majority of errors that fall in this category are connected to the usage of a single template by one Austrian state, meaning, that the targeted adaptation to this type of permits could significantly increase the performance.

5.3   Auditability Analysis

We analyse our approach and report on lessons learned based on the audit requirements (A1–A3) (cf. Sect. 2):

Completeness of audit trace capturing: We analyse completeness on two levels: the use case level and the lifecycle level. For the concrete use case, the baseline for completeness is the set of audit questions (cf. Sect. 4.3). These audit questions were targeted with different SPARQL queries which can be divided into two different types: *overview queries* provide general logging information of past executions, including login, extraction, or error events. One example being Listing 1.2 showcasing all metadata elements suggestions that were changed by users. With this information specific executions can be inspected in further detail for the model id, occurring errors etc. The second type being *metric queries* calculating numeric summaries of past executions, e.g., the rate of successful extractions over a specific time period. With this set of queries, we were able to answer all audit questions of the stakeholders, resulting in the fulfilment of the completeness requirement for this use case.

Analysing the completeness of the developed system in a broader context, i.e., lifecycle view, we identified that the capturing of audit traces is focused on the operation phase, while auditability aspects of the development phase are partly neglected. Concretely, information about different ML model versions, associated high-level characteristics and hyperparameter are already captured, however, more detailed information (e.g. Model Cards [11] or data retrieved from MLOPs tools such as Weights & Biases[11] or MLflow[12]) are yet to be integrated.

Automatic Collection, Transformation and Management of Audit Traces: This requirement is completely fulfilled through the usage of AuditBox. After an initial set-up phase, all relevant information and traces are collected in a fully automatic way, validated according to the defined workflow model and stored in a graph format. *Ability to access results and Ease of Use:* In order to provide easy access to the audit results, we provided the SPARQL queries necessary to answer the audit questions as a set of over 20 templates. However, for complex queries and future work, a user interface to create custom audit dashboards leaves room for improvement to also enable users without SPARQL expertise to conduct regular audits with custom queries.

---

[11] https://wandb.ai/site.
[12] https://mlflow.org.

```
select ?uuid ?metadata_name ?metadata_extracted ?metadata_refined where {
    ?provenance rdf:type ep-plan:Bundle .
    ?provenance :uuid ?uuid .
    ?provenance ep-plan:hasTraceElement ?postProcessing .
    ?provenance ep-plan:hasTraceElement ?refineMetadata .
    ?postProcessing rdf:type :PostProcess .
    ?postProcessing prov:used ?metadata .
    ?metadata rdf:type ?metadata_name .
    ?metadata :value ?metadata_extracted .
    ?refineMetadata rdf:type :RefineMetadata .
    ?refinedMetadata rdf:type ?metadata_name .
    ?refinedMetadata prov:wasGeneratedBy ?refineMetadata .
    ?refinedMetadata :value ?metadata_refined .
    FILTER(?metadata_name != prov:Entity && ?metadata_name != ep-plan:Entity
&& ?metadata_name != prov:Metadata && ?metadata_name != prov:Metadata)
}
```

Listing 1.2. Overview query on corrected suggestions by user

6 Conclusion and Outlook

The extraction of key elements from legal documents is a complex task which is time-consuming and error-prone for non-trained experts. The heterogeneity of permits in information and format make it complex on multiple levels. The combination of symbolic and machine learning techniques for this use case allows to leverage strengths of both approaches: the ability to extract data through language and embedding models while incorporating background knowledge in the form of a knowledge graph can improve the overall detection of entities. Further improvements could be achieved by extending the ontology to e.g., cover historic changes in entity types or the complete set of labels. Another area for improvement could be expanding usable background knowledge in the form of explicit rules for issuing authorities or for specific responsibilities.

The auditability of the described system is a key feature to increase the user acceptance towards this AI-assisted solution approach. AuditBox, provides a generic tool for collecting and managing audit traces from multiple sources. Overall usability could be improved by providing a dashboard complementing the query-based approach. Further work in extending the audit traces to other system lifecycle phases (ML training) is planned.

Acknowledgements. This work has been supported by OBARIS (https://www.obaris.org/), a project funded by the Austrian Research Promotion Agency (FFG) under grant 877389.

References

1. Breit, A., Revenko, A., Rezaee, K., Pilehvar, M.T., Camacho-Collados, J.: WiC-TSV: an evaluation benchmark for target sense verification of words in context. In: Proceedings of the 16th Conference of the European Chapter of the Association for Computational Linguistics: Main Volume, pp. 1635–1645. Association for Computational Linguistics (2021). https://doi.org/10.18653/v1/2021.eacl-main.140, https://aclanthology.org/2021.eacl-main.140

2. Eckart de Castilho, R., Gurevych, I.: A broad-coverage collection of portable NLP components for building shareable analysis pipelines. In: Proceedings of the Workshop on Open Infrastructures and Analysis Frameworks for HLT, pp. 1–11. Association for Computational Linguistics and Dublin City University, Dublin (2014). https://doi.org/10.3115/v1/W14-5201, https://aclanthology.org/W14-5201

3. Eiband, M., Schneider, H., Bilandzic, M., Fazekas-Con, J., Haug, M., Hussmann, H.: Bringing transparency design into practice. In: 23rd International Conference on Intelligent User Interfaces, pp. 211–223 (2018)

4. Ekaputra, F.J., et al.: Semantic-enabled architecture for auditable privacy-preserving data analysis. Semant. Web (Preprint), 1–34 (2021)

5. Hellmann, S., Lehmann, J., Auer, S., Brümmer, M.: Integrating NLP using linked data. In: Alani, H., Kagal, L., Fokoue, A., Groth, P., Biemann, C., Parreira, J.X., Aroyo, L., Noy, N., Welty, C., Janowicz, K. (eds.) ISWC 2013. LNCS, vol. 8219, pp. 98–113. Springer, Heidelberg (2013). https://doi.org/10.1007/978-3-642-41338-4_7

6. Janowicz, K., et al.: UnifiedViews: an ETL tool for rdf data management. Semant. Web 9(5), 661–676 (2018). https://doi.org/10.3233/SW-180291

7. Leitner, E., Rehm, G., Moreno-Schneider, J.: Fine-grained named entity recognition in legal documents. In: Acosta, M., Cudré-Mauroux, P., Maleshkova, M., Pellegrini, T., Sack, H., Sure-Vetter, Y. (eds.) SEMANTiCS 2019. LNCS, vol. 11702, pp. 272–287. Springer, Cham (2019). https://doi.org/10.1007/978-3-030-33220-4_20

8. Liao, Q.V., Gruen, D., Miller, S.: Questioning the AI: informing design practices for explainable AI user experiences. In: Proceedings of the 2020 CHI Conference on Human Factors in Computing Systems, pp. 1–15 (2020)

9. Longley, D., Sporny, M., Kellogg, G., Lanthaler, M., Lindström, N.: JSON-LD 1.1 framing (2020). https://www.w3.org/TR/json-ld-framing/

10. Miles, S., Groth, P., Munroe, S., Moreau, L.: PrIMe: a methodology for developing provenance-aware applications. ACM Trans. Softw. Eng. Methodol. (TOSEM) 20(3), 1–42 (2011)

11. Mitchell, M., et al.: Model cards for model reporting. In: Proceedings of the Conference on Fairness, Accountability, and Transparency, pp. 220–229 (2019)

12. Moreno-Schneider, J., et al.: Orchestrating NLP services for the legal domain. In: Proceedings of the Twelfth Language Resources and Evaluation Conference, pp. 2332–2340. European Language Resources Association, Marseille (2020). https://aclanthology.org/2020.lrec-1.284

13. Naja, I., Markovic, M., Edwards, P., Cottrill, C.: A semantic framework to support AI system accountability and audit. In: Verborgh, R., et al. (eds.) ESWC 2021. LNCS, vol. 12731, pp. 160–176. Springer, Cham (2021). https://doi.org/10.1007/978-3-030-77385-4_10

14. Ostendorff, M., Blume, T., Ostendorff, S.: Towards an open platform for legal information. In: Proceedings of the ACM/IEEE Joint Conference on Digital Libraries in 2020, JCDL 2020, pp. 385–388. Association for Computing Machinery, New York (2020). https://doi.org/10.1145/3383583.3398616

15. Raji, I.D., et al.: Closing the AI accountability gap: Defining an end-to-end framework for internal algorithmic auditing. In: Proceedings of the 2020 Conference on Fairness, Accountability, and Transparency, pp. 33–44 (2020)

Understanding Customer Requirements

An Enterprise Knowledge Graph Approach

Basel Shbita[1,2], Anna Lisa Gentile[3(✉)], Pengyuan Li[3], Chad DeLuca[3],
and Guang-Jie Ren[3]

[1] University of Southern California, Los Angeles, CA, USA
shbita@usc.edu
[2] Information Sciences Institute, Marina del Rey, CA, USA
[3] IBM Research Almaden, San Jose, CA, USA
{annalisa.gentile,pengyuan}@ibm.com, {delucac,gren}@us.ibm.com

Abstract. Understanding customers demands and needs is one of the keys to success for large enterprises. Customers come to a large enterprise with a set of requirements and finding a mapping between the needs they are expressing and the scale of available products and services within the enterprise is a complex task. Formalizing the two sides of interaction - the requests and the offerings - is a way to achieve the matching. Enterprise Knowledge Graphs (EKG) are an effective method to represent enterprise information in ways that can be more easily interpreted by both humans and machines. In this work, we propose a solution to identify customer requirements from free text to represent them in terms of an EKG. We demonstrate the validity of the approach by matching customer requirements to their appropriate business units, using a dataset of historical requirement-offering records in IBM spanning over 10 years.

1 Introduction

Capturing domain knowledge is a critical task in many domains and applications - and especially so when dealing with capturing information about large organizations. In a large enterprise, the information landscape of assets, skills, intellectual properties, and customer requirements is very complicated, extremely dynamic, and often under-specified - and this is especially true for a company like IBM, that provides information technology solutions and consulting services spanning from AI, analytics, security, cloud, supply chain etc. to a vast spectrum of industries including banking, finance, education, energy, healthcare, government, travel and transportation to mention a few. In many cases, the Subject Matter Experts (SMEs) are the gatekeepers for matching customer needs with the multitude of the company's offerings - and they are perceived to hold the required knowledge to steer and develop business opportunities for the company.

B. Shbita—This work was conducted during Summer Internship at IBM Research Almaden.

A way to alleviate the issue is making sure that information is properly formalized, shared, and accessible within the organization. Knowledge Graphs (KG) are a popular way to represent information in a way that can be easily interpreted by both humans and machines. In fact, for more than a decade many organizations adopted KGs - oftentimes referred to as Enterprise KG (EKG) - to lay the foundation of next-generation enterprise data and metadata management, search, recommendation, analytics, intelligent agents, and more [33,60].

Nonetheless generating and maintaining a complete EKG that harmonizes all internal knowledge as well as data gathered from the vastness of open KGs on the Web can be expensive and difficult to achieve, for many reasons. Both internal organizational data and external customer requirements can be highly heterogeneous, cryptic, short, highly technically written, and only understood by a few. Those who actually have the expertise, experience, and procedural knowledge to understand such data often do not have the expertise to formalize it, nor the time to do so. External open knowledge available on the Web is vast, incomplete, imbalanced, highly distributed, and heterogeneous - and not easily accessible for SMEs without knowledge management skills. Without proper integration, the multitude of data repositories on the Web do not prove helpful in supporting decision-making systems.

In this work we address the problem of bootstrapping, populating, and maintaining an EKG - or a portion of it - relying on three main building blocks. Specifically we (i) extract information from internal unstructured data in the organization; (ii) use Open Knowledge gathered from the Web to augment the initial data either directly or by bootstrapping off-the-shelf weakly supervised data augmentation algorithms; and finally (iii) we rely on domain expertise to structure all acquired information into an EKG. Our proposal is a human-assisted pipeline that generates augmented representations of organizational concepts. Our humans-in-the-loop are SMEs internal to the organization who are familiar with the assets and can understand customer needs - and can help shape their semantic representation. The SMEs are involved in the selection of external knowledge to be included in the EKG, or to be used to bootstrap the training of the system. This approach lets us get high-quality, up-to-date insights from undersized, emerging corpora.

The main contribution of this work is a showcase of how the orchestration of NLP techniques, the usage of semantic resources, and human expertise can deliver industrial impact. We combine: (i) a method to tap into the vastness of open KG from the Web and retrieve, select, and distill instrumental knowledge to build and expand the EKG of interest; (ii) a method to extract structured information from unstructured technical text; and finally (iii) a user-driven mechanism to encapsulate the extracted knowledge within the existing EKG, and effectively expand it and populate it.

One of the most valuable uses of the constructed EKG is matching customer requirements to the available offerings in the organization. Specifically in this work we employ the extracted EKG to train automatic methods to help sales experts identify the correct business units and offerings to answer specific customer requirements. By using historical customer deal data within the organization, we show that our methodology can automatically retrieve the best business units and offerings that satisfy a customer requirement (compared against historical data). Specifically, we designed an in vitro classification task, using curated ground truth from 10 years of historical sales deals and show that by using the fully constructed EKG we improve the F_1 score of the business-units multi-classification task by as much as 4.1% when compared to a baseline method without the usage of the EKG, and by 1.3% when using the non-augmented version of the EKG.

2   Related Work

Capturing, representing, persisting, and sharing the vast amount of human knowledge in a way that is effectively accessible from both human and automated methods is a topic that attracted numerous research efforts and still presents many open challenges [55]. For many years Semantic Web technologies [34] have provided formal models to represent explicit semantics in a machine-interpretable form, and in the last decade Knowledge Graphs became the de facto standard to accumulate and convey knowledge of the real world, especially in industry settings [20]. As a representation of semantic relations between entities, KGs have proven to be particularly relevant for natural language processing (NLP) [42], both to inform the task of knowledge acquisition - i.e. using NLP to extract formal models from text [57] - or for the purpose of knowledge application - i.e. exploiting KGs to enhance NLP techniques and language models [6,28,54]. The recent survey paper by Schneider et al. [42] provides a detailed account of all recent works of KGs and NLP, classified under these two macro-classes. Our work falls under the knowledge acquisition category - where all techniques of information extraction and data integration are involved. At high level, the Information Extraction (IE) methods can be grouped in two categories: (i) Open IE - where the purpose is understanding the text - and (ii) targeted IE - where the goal is a focused extraction of domain specific information for the purpose of Knowledge Population [41].

Open IE can be considered a form of machine reading [2,13,36], where the target knowledge schema is not known and extractions are represented in the form of surface subject-relation-object triples. It is worth noting that there are many solutions for text understanding that do not extract human understandable facts, but rather use statistical information to model the language in text [10,25,37,61], and represent the information with numerical vectors that capture statistical patterns of words - with words embeddings [1] being a popular choice. While these data-driven models are impressive, they do not represent semantics explicitly - therefore data is unintelligible for a human - and they have no mechanism to logically reason about the captured knowledge. While we use some of these methodologies in our proposed pipeline, it is merely as a pre-processing step and we do not make specific contributions or claim novelties in this direction, therefore discussing them in detail is out of the scope of this work. On the other hand, some Open IE methods - more in line with our proposed approach - represent extracted information as a Knowledge Graph, including FRED [14], SHELDON [38], ClausIE [9], MinIE [15] and other similar methods [16,18]. The main difference with our proposed approach is that these methods do not assume domain specific target ontologies, therefore the extracted content can be way more than needed for the specific population task, thus requiring additional effort for the selection of relevant information.

Our work is similar to targeted IE methods, which collect the extracted information in formal models, i.e. ontology population from text [35,56]. Some of the earliest approaches for ontology population from text are based on pattern matching, string similarity functions, and external glossaries and knowledge bases [4,26,44,51,52]. Others exploit vector-feature similarity using terms and n-grams as features [5,17,47]. More recent works rely on: (i) machine learning, with standard NLP features extracted from text [24], or more sophisticated features such as type relational phrases [31], or type correlation based on co-occurring entities [39]; (ii) graph embedding models [40,59,62] and (iii) deep learning models [12,30,45,46,58].

There exist many established initiatives to foster research on targeted IE, such as the Knowledge Base Population task at TAC,[1] the TREC Knowledge Base Acceleration track,[2] and the Open Knowledge Extraction Challenge [32]. In these initiatives, systems are compared on the basis of recognizing individuals belonging to a few selected ontology classes, spanning from the common Person, Place and Organization [48], to more specific classes such as Facility, Weapon, Vehicle [11], Role [32] or Drug [43], among others. All these works tackle the KG completion in terms of "missing instances", i.e. finding entities belonging to pre-defined given classes. In the same direction, there is a plethora of tools for automatically detecting named entities in free text and aligning them to a predefined knowledge base, i.e., Spotlight [27], X-Lisa [63], Babelfy [29], Wikifier [3]. However, all these tools are able to identify only instances that already exist in a knowledge base, but do not cover the case of out-of-knowledge entities - which is a common case for very technical and niche domains.

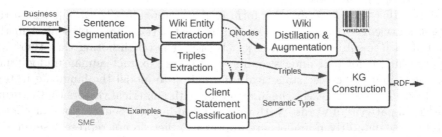

Fig. 1. EKG construction pipeline.

---

3   Building the EKG

The problem we address can be classified as a data and knowledge acquisition and integration task. Formally, we wish to populate and augment the Enterprise Knowledge Graph (EKG) by automatically integrating specialized and complementary knowledge coming from heterogeneous sources: proprietary messy unstructured data in the form of textual documents describing client requirements, open linked data on the Web (Open KGs), and non-formalized SME knowledge in the business domain.

Our proposed pipeline for the construction and enhancement of the EKG consists of several steps and components, as illustrated in Fig. 1. Each of the components is designed to address the data extraction and knowledge integration step in each of the data sources, then fuse them together to create an effective EKG. We firstly extract initial triples from the unstructured proprietary data (Sect. 3.2); then distill relevant knowledge from open KGs from the Web (Sect. 3.3); and finally structure all extracted information into an EKG with a user-driven method (Sect. 3.4).

3.1   Enterprise Knowledge Graph (EKG)

An Enterprise Knowledge Graph (EKG) is simply a KG of enterprise data with the goal of powering certain capabilities that are relevant to the business. The structure and content of the graph pertains to certain assets, clients, their requirements, and other relevant entities and offerings in the business domain.

In our problem setting, a manually-curated EKG is provided. The EKG contains triple statements about IBM business offerings/assets, organized in a hierarchical structure that reflects the organizational grouping of assets within business units and various topical verticals. The initial EKG used in this work contains 422 classes and 827 individuals.

In its initial form, the graph does not capture any knowledge about clients, their needs, or how these may relate to any of the pre-existing assets in the graph. Our task is: given client requirements in textual documents, we want to extract and represent client needs from text in a form that can be integrated and connected to the current EKG. This task requires materializing stakeholders, their needs, assets, and the relationships between all of the above within the text. While the EKG already contains information about assets, client needs are completely unknown to the EKG and they are expressed in text with a vocabulary that often has little or no intersection with the exiting EKG concepts. In order to tackle this problem, we enrich the extracted triples (both entities and relations) with additional knowledge existing on the open Web and benefit from prior knowledge provided by SMEs in the form of predefined examples of client statement types that are used to structure the final EKG. This allows us to capture corpus-specific information (both structural and semantic) and adapt to different scenarios effortlessly.

3.2 Extracting Triples from Proprietary Data: An NLP Approach

Business client requirement documents manifest as text snippets and include a diverse set of client-specific vocabularies, which vary by industry, client, or individual. These documents contain relevant and irrelevant information, which may be hard to distinguish even for an SME. Each document might contain multiple requirements, sometime expressed in the same short paragraph. Therefore, we must provide practical tools to achieve a complete analysis, considering particular and general needs and managing requirements in a comprehensive manner.

In this work we used a selection of "client cases", typically redacted by curation teams that summarise the profile of the client company, what kind of problem they are trying to address (the requirements), and which product(s) or service(s) they purchased from IBM that helped solved their problem. For the purposes of illustration, we will use the client case text shown in Listing 1.1 for all the examples.

```
<COMPANY NAME> uses a Microsoft Distributed File System to enable employees
to access data and files residing on different servers, usually to create
financial reports. Previously, <COMPANY NAME> was supporting its Microsoft
Distributed File System with older IBM Power 570 servers. Although the
incumbent technology had performed satisfactorily, the servers were nearing
the limits of their processing capacity and were starting to generate high
maintenance costs. In addition, <COMPANY NAME> recognized the opportunity
to increase storage capacity and streamline administration tasks within its
storage area network (SAN). Thus, <COMPANY NAME> sought a reliable IT provider
to help it refresh its server and storage technology and boost the performance
of its Microsoft Distributed File System.
```

Listing 1.1. An example of a short client case text.

We design a custom pipeline to perform triple extraction from technical text, based on linguistic parsing, statistical processing, and custom heuristics (Fig. 1). The first step is sentence segmentation, which is the process of identifying different sentences in a text paragraph. We perform the triple extraction step for each individual sentence, i.e. we identify the pairs of concepts (entities) and the relation between them, in the form of <concept> <relation> <concept> (example in Fig. 3).

The extraction is driven by (i) the part-of-speech (POS) annotation tags and (ii) the dependency tree of the sentence. POS tagging is the process of identifying the grammatical roles that explain how a particular word is used in a sentence (e.g., noun, adjective, verb). Dependency parsing is the process of extracting the dependency tree that represents the grammatical structure of the sentence (e.g. finding the subject and its relation to other words). An example of the extraction process is depicted in Fig. 2, where underneath each word in the sentence we denote its POS tag and over each edge we indicate the grammatical relation between the words. Both of these extraction steps are implemented using off-the-shelf tools. Specifically we rely on components from *SpaCy* [21], a comprehensive Natural Language Processing (NLP) library.

Once each sentence is annotated we use a rule-based algorithm to extract the relations in the form of individual triples. Specifically, we build on the hypothesis

Fig. 2. Dependency parse tree of an example sentence. POS tags are shown below each word. The grammatical relation between words is denoted over the edges.

that the main relation, i.e. the predicate of the triple, is the main verb in the sentence. We identify this verb first, and we concatenate any auxiliary, preposition, and negation words when present. This becomes the predicate of our triple. Starting from the detected predicate ("root" verb) we traverse backwards over the dependency tree to identify the candidate subject. Any compound, prefix, or modifier words preceding the candidate subject will be concatenated to it, with the exception of words with a POS tag that is neither a noun or an adjective. We run the same process forward (following compound elements) to determine the candidate object as well. This heuristic is not guaranteed to be optimal, yet it provides a sufficient solution for reaching a good, yet noisy, extractor that will steer additional components in our pipeline. As an example, consider the sentence shown in Fig. 2. In this case our technique will yield the verb "`were nearing`" as the predicate/relation. The subject/head is the company itself (employs the anonymized term "`<COMPANY NAME>`" to ensure confidentiality) and the object/-tail is "`high maintenance costs`".

The full document (including the sentence shown in Fig. 2) and the set of extracted triples are shown in Fig. 3 - note that we use the company who's request belongs to as the subject/head of all the predicate/objects, as we want to create a simplified customer-centric representation. Figure 3 also shows in red boxes entities that have been externally recognized as entities in Wikidata [53] - we extract those using the *Wikifier* [3] Named Entity Recognition (NER) service. This extraction is performed passing the full text snippet to Wikifier, completely in parallel to the triple extraction process. Full details on the Wikidata based augmentation are provided in Sect. 3.3.

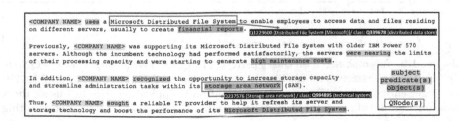

Fig. 3. Example document and its corresponding extracted triples (subjects are highlighted in yellow, predicates are highlighted in blue, and objects are highlighted in green), and linked QNodes (wrapped in a red, linked to the entity highlighted in black). (Color figure online)

3.3   Open KG from the Web: A Distillery Approach

The semantic Web and the Linked Open Data (LOD) cloud[3] are an invaluable source of knowledge, with a multitude of semantically connected datasets to exploit. For the scope of this work, we selected Wikidata [53] to perform our data augmentation process. Wikidata is a free, collaborative, fast-growing KG and importantly acts as a hub in the LOD cloud, in the sense that contains numerous incoming and outgoing links to external KGs and ontologies. These sources can also be exploited for further enrichment of the data and can be used for future approaches to this task. Moreover, there are plentiful state of the art tools to bootstrap the linkage from text to Wikidata - in fact we use the *Wikifier* [3] Named Entity Recognition (NER) service in our augmentation pipeline.

The sheer size of Wikidata makes it difficult for an SME to effectively tap into it. For this reason we design a KG distillation algorithm that: (i) constructs a salient subgraph of Wikidata entities - referred in Wikidata as QNodes - that are relevant to the extracted triples at hand (resulting from the process described in Sect. 3.2) and (ii) leverages the Wikidata taxonomy to integrate essential relations between the QNodes in the distilled subgraph.

Figure 3 depicts an example document, the result of the triple extraction, and the corresponding Wikidata entities. In the distillation process we were able to connect the phrase (and object) "`storage area network`" in the document to a corresponding entry in Wikidata. We found out that "`Storage area network`" corresponds to QNode Q237576 and is an instance of the concept "`technical system`" (Q994895), and we also retrieved all the corresponding successor concepts from Wikidata (as seen in Fig. 4).

To perform the distillation, we use the Wikidata SPARQL query service.[4] SPARQL is query language [7] and is one of the most powerful and most widely used services for accessing Linked Data. The core component of our KG distillation process is essentially a SPARQL query: the Subgraph Retrieval Query (SRQ). The SRQ query (depicted in Listing 1.2) starts with a target entity/-class that has been previously recognized by the Wikifier service; it retrieves all QNodes that are either direct instances of the target entity/class or of any of its sub-classes, recursively.

```
1   SELECT ?c ?cLabel WHERE {
2     wd:Q994895 wdt:P31?/wdt:P279* ?c .
3     SERVICE wikibase:label {
4       bd:serviceParam wikibase:language "en". } }
```

Listing 1.2. *Subgraph Retrieval Query (SRQ)*: The query has one target entity - QNode (Q994895) - and retrieves all entities that are *instance of* (P31) or *subclass of* (P279) the target entity (Q994895). The subclass relation is applied recursively - using the * notation. Line 3-4 of the query simply retrieve a human-readable label for each resulting QNodes.

---

[3] LOD cloud: https://lod-cloud.net/.

[4] Wikidata SPARQL query service: https://query.wikidata.org/.

Algorithm 1: Distilled Wikidata graph construction algorithm

Data: a set $\mathcal{Q}$ of QNodes
Result: a directed acyclic graph $\mathcal{G}$ of QNodes
1 **foreach** $q \in \mathcal{Q}$ **do**
2     $\lfloor$ $\mathcal{G}$.add(q); // add all QNodes to graph

3 **while** *True* **do**
4     $\mathcal{L}$ = list of nodes in $\mathcal{G}$ with no outgoing P31/P279 edges;
5     $\mathcal{Q}^*$ = getP31P279($\mathcal{L}$) $\setminus \mathcal{Q}$;
6   **foreach** $q^* \in \mathcal{Q}^*$ **do**
7       $\lfloor$ $\mathcal{G}$.add($\bigcup_{q_j^* \in P31P279(q)} q \mapsto q_j^*$); // add new nodes & edges

8   **if** $|\mathcal{Q}^*|$ == *0* **then**
9       $\lfloor$ break;
10   $\lfloor$ $\mathcal{Q} = \mathcal{Q}^* \cup \mathcal{Q}$

To handle the distillation task efficiently and avoid unnecessary calls to the SPARQL endpoint, we designed Algorithm 1. The algorithm performs the augmented subgraph construction. First, all recognized QNodes are inserted as nodes to the empty graph $\mathcal{G}$ (lines 1–2). Then, we retrieve *leaf nodes* - nodes without any outgoing edges of type P31/P279 - from the graph $\mathcal{G}$ to list $\mathcal{L}$ (line 4). The function getP31P279 (line 5) acts as a wrapper function which triggers the SRQ query for each input QNode in $\mathcal{L}$. The variable $\mathcal{Q}^*$ will hold the retrieved predecessor nodes (with respect to P31/P279) from Wikidata, not including QNodes that already exist in the graph (by subtracting $\mathcal{Q}$ in the same line). Next, we insert all the newly retrieved nodes and edges into the graph. The iterative addition over the set (line 7) is required since there may be one-to-many relations for each QNode, as expected in Wikidata, so we must execute over a set of nodes. We enforce a terminating case (line 8) that happens when there is no growth in the graph, meaning no new QNodes are retrieved, i.e. they already exist in our graph. The set $\mathcal{Q}$ is updated at each iteration (line 10) to reduce the lookup in the next repetition.

The relations between the nodes in the resulting graph $\mathcal{G}$ carry a semantic meaning between the different QNodes (a node is semantically similar to its predecessors and its successors) and will play a critical role in the RDF generation. Examples for such distilled subgraphs, are shown as green nodes in Fig. 4. As seen in the graph, the QNode Q994895, which was retrieved following the extraction of the object "storage area network", allowed the retrieval and addition of QNodes such as Q58778 system to the graph with the appropriate taxonomic relations from Wikidata.

3.4 Formalizing the Final EKG: A User-Assisted Semantic Typing Approach

Semantic typing is a group of fundamental natural language understanding problems aiming to classify tokens (or objects) of interest into semantic categories. In the context of our problem, this task aims to introduce meaningful semantic

634   B. Shbita et al.

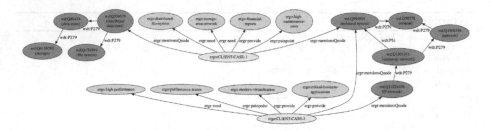

Fig. 4. A snippet of the EKG representing concepts extracted from client requirements with linkage to acquired QNodes. Client document nodes are shown in yellow. Extracted objects and concepts are shown in blue. QNodes are shown in green. (Color figure online)

labels and types to the extracted objects in each triple, and allow users to narrow the focus of the resulting EKG.

Conventionally, SMEs can find it challenging to articulate their domain knowledge with a formalism such as RDF. Considering the amount of data the EKG holds, modeling the entire EKG becomes intractable and tedious and is often susceptible to human error. While one obvious solution is to perform automated semantic labeling, it is a difficult task in a narrow and technical domain. A middle course to a fully automated solution is to design a data-driven procedure that can leverage SME knowledge to guide the data understanding and produce semi-automated labeling services.

Specifically for our problem, we are trying to model client needs and requirements in the EKG. While recognizing the triples can be mostly achieved automatically, typing them often requires the definition of new concept classes. To this end, we provide random samples of the extraction (triples, augmented entities) to the SME and ask them to group the samples where they see fit. The grouping is guided by the purpose of each particular statement (and the subsequent augmented triple) in the client requirement text; in fact, client requests contain snippets with different intents: some might describe their background, some might describe what they are struggling with, etc. As an example, consider the text: "[orgEntity] is one of the largest financial services ...". This type of sentence is typically present in client requirement text, where a background of the client itself is provided. Similarly, the snippet: "[orgEntity] relied on ... data warehouse environment to support ..." is a common type of sentence describing current struggles of the client. We rely on the SMEs to freely identify these different intents and create a desired label for them. In fact, we give the SME a collection of approximately 20 sentences at a time from different documents, sampled randomly - each of which contains at least a single triple. We ask them to identify sentences that express a similar type of intent and provide us with a label (name) of what that intent might be. The SME can, for example, return us the set of two sentences "[orgEntity] aims to be a personal bank in the digital age" and "[orgEntity] is one of the largest financial services companies in the United States" and declare that their intent is to "profile" an organization. Table 1 shows additional examples of different types of "Statement Types" that were defined with the help of SMEs. For the described four types, we engaged with one SME for a total annotation time of one hour. Technically speaking, we store this information (name of the intent, example sentences, etc.) in YAML files (Fig. 5), effectively translating the SME high-level reasoning into actionable training examples for the subsequent automated steps. A more technical SME can even introduce variance in the categorized sentences by introducing a "slot" that corresponds to entity types. In the example in Fig. 5, the orgEntity slot has a partial list of values (of type org) to provide structure and flexibility in the general classification method.

Table 1. Client statement semantic types, their descriptions, and examples.

Statement type	Description	Example
profileStatement	General attributes about the entity	*"is one of the largest financial services..."*
attemptStatement	Attempt or historical actions the entity has taken	*"relied on... data warehouse env. to support..."*
needStatement	Needs or desired outcomes the entity requires	*"wanted to build a system that..."*
painPointStatement	Pain points or obstacles the entity finds critical	*"struggled to process large volumes..."*

This process results in a categorical classification model that is later used to automatically translate the rest of the data into a formal EKG representation. Specifically the classification model id implemented using *Snips-NLU* [8], and trained with data generated by the SMEs. *Snips-NLU* uses a simple regular expression matching as a first stop to match against statements from training and logistic regression if there is no direct match. For logistic regression, TF-IDF and co-occurrence features are extracted from the text, and a classifier is trained with simple stochastic gradient descent. It is easy to add new training examples and custom statements by configuring YAML files similar to the discussed example (Fig. 5).

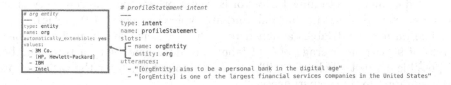

Fig. 5. Excerpts from a YAML file used to train the semantic typing engine.

The training process can be iterated several times: the SME initially only identifies a small set of examples, but is able to repeat the learning procedure until they consider the labeling performance satisfactory, thus incrementally improving the accuracy of "intent" representation. The modularity of the procedure allows SMEs to explore and experiment with different categorizations, slots, and filters as they see fit.

Finally, the extracted knowledge graph is materialized in an RDF format. In our implementation, the RDFLib[5] is used to construct the graph triples and convert the data to a semantic knowledge graph. Figure 4 shows an excerpt of the resulting knowledge graph. The yellow instances (i.e., CLIENT-CASE-X) represent two example client documents. Each one is the subject/head of the extracted triple, where their objects/tails are client statements (blue nodes) of some type - e.g. ClientPainpoint and ClientNeed, respectively matching the relation type leading to that object, i.e. ergr:painpoint and ergr:need. The rest of the instances are in green, representing the QNodes we acquired from Wikidata and the distillation process.

4   Evaluation and Discussion

The purpose of our experiment is to evaluate how our proposed method and pipeline impacts downstream tasks and the usefulness of the constructed EKG. Specifically we choose one of our downstream tasks - a multi-label classification [50] of customer requirement texts.

Dataset. The experimental dataset comprises 10 years of historical data of customer requirements and the corresponding sold assets and services. Specifically, the dataset contains 24,180 customer stories documents, each of them with an assigned set of business-unit labels - which indicate which business units within the company provided products/services to answer each specific customer requirement. A sample of some of the textual data can be explored on the "IBM Customer Stories: As told by our Customers" blog[6] where short articles classified by Topics and Industries describe successful collaborations between IBM and several customers. These stories are clearly redacted for broader audience, and can be richer and better elaborated that the raw data we use in our experiments, but they can give an idea of how use cases are described.[7]

The average length of each requirement document is 127 words, with the longest document containing 1,213 words, the shortest one 3 words (very short documents are discarded as invalid, and are typically a copy of the title).

The business-unit labels assigned to each document vary from 1 to a maximum of 9, with an average of 2.44 labels per document, with a total number of possible distinct labels of 13. These act as ground truth for the task and are used as target for our experiments.

Multi-label Classification Task. Our experimental task consists of classifying an unseen document (unstructured textual data) with one or several matching

---

[5] https://rdflib.readthedocs.io/.
[6] https://www.ibm.com/blogs/client-voices/.
[7] https://www.ibm.com/blog/sustainability-begins-with-design/.

business-units. After performing standard text pre-processing on the text (stemming, stop-words, removal etc.), we compare five different experimental settings, using: (i) text based features only; (ii) adding simple-KG features, (iii) adding SME-based augmented-KG features, (iv) adding Wikidata-based augmented-KG features, (v) adding all augmented-KG features (both SME and Wikidata).

Baseline. The first setting acts as baseline for our experiments. The constructed KG is not used at all in this case. Instead, we utilize a state-of-the-art document embedding model called *Doc2Vec* [23] to transform each document into a feature vector. *Doc2Vec* determines a low-dimensional representation (i.e., embedding) for a document: it learns a neural network using at each time one target word from the document and the words that surround it, as well as it uses a global contextual vector, associated with the document, as part of its predictive model. Although Transformer-based models have been outperforming other models in many NLP tasks [22], *Doc2Vec* is considered a simpler and faster model and can be a more useful choice for a medium-sized dataset [19].

In this setting, we use the embedding produced by the *Doc2Vec* model to train a One-vs-Rest (OvR) multi-label classification model that uses Support Vector Machines (SVM) with a linear kernel to classify input data into business units as a target. OvR constructs one classifier per class, which is trained to distinguish the samples in the single class from the samples in all remaining classes. This setting is denoted as "Doc2Vec" in Table 2.

KG Based Settings. To inject the KG in the classification model we employ *ComplEx* [49], a state-of-the-art KG embedding model. As described in Sect. 3, each client document becomes a graph (example in Fig. 4), which contains Wikidata-concepts nodes, "document" nodes (representing the whole document) and all other object nodes extracted by the triple extraction process. This whole graph is fed to *ComplEx*, which produces embedding vectors per each node and edge in the graph - we fix the size of each produced vector to 50.

The objective of *ComplEx* is to learn a fixed low-dimensional representation (i.e., embedding) of entities and relations in the KG while preserving their semantic meaning. By representing each node as a combination of vectors and computing their dot product, we are able to capture relationships between nodes. The dot product is passed through a complex-valued function that allows learning vector representation for each node in the knowledge graph, including those representing client documents. The choice of *ComplEx* vs other available KG embeddings techniques is that it uses complex valued vectors that better capture anti-symmetric relationships.

We experiment with four different versions of the KG (results in Table 2): (i) without applying the augmentation step ("Doc2Vec + KG"); (ii) only integrating the semantic types acquired with the help of SME ("Doc2Vec + Augmented KG (SME)"); (iii) only augmenting the with the Wikidata entities ("Doc2Vec + Augmented KG (Wiki)"); (iv) or using the fully augmented version of the KG, wuth both SME and Wiki based augmentations ("Doc2Vec + Augmented KG (Full)").

Similarly to the "Doc2Vec" baseline, we use the OvR multi-label SVM classifier with the business unit labels as a target, but we concatenate the *Doc2Vec* embedding with the appropriate KG embedding.

In each experimental setting, we utilized a 100-dimensional vector representation for training and testing the models. Having the same vector size of 100 for the embedding space across all settings was enforced to exclude that the benefit could be due to a bigger embedding space rather than the type of captured content. To ensure fairness in the information capacity between the different KG settings, we concatenated a 50-dimensional vector obtained from *Doc2Vec* with a 50-dimensional vector from the KG *ComplEx* embedding process. We evaluated the models based on precision, recall, and F_1 scores, using ten-fold cross-validation that split the data into mutually exclusive subsets. In this approach, one subset was used as the testing set, and the remaining subsets were used for training the model.

Table 2. Results summary for the business units multi-classification task.

Method	Precision	Recall	F_1
Doc2Vec	0.730	0.590	0.653
Doc2Vec + KG	0.741	0.605	0.666
Doc2Vec + Augmented KG (SME)	0.754	0.608	0.673
Doc2Vec + Augmented KG (Wiki)	**0.761**	0.621	0.684
Doc2Vec + Augmented KG (Full)	**0.761**	**0.638**	**0.694**

The evaluation results in Table 2 show the precision, recall and F_1 (harmonic mean of precision and recall) for the task of assigning the appropriate business unit(s) to an unstructured and unlabeled client request input, using the baseline method and the four KG augmentation variants. Compared to the baseline, the "Doc2Vec + KG" setting obtains slightly better results in all measures, while the fully augmented pipeline ("Doc2Vec + Augmented KG (Full)") achieves the best results in terms of precision, recall, and F_1, outperforming any other permutation. In this setting, we capture both semantic and contextual information, incorporate expert knowledge (SME), and leverage a vast and diverse source of structured data (Wikidata). The precision of 0.761, recall of 0.638, and F_1 score of 0.694 demonstrate that this model can achieve a balance between correctly identifying positive cases and minimizing false positives and false negatives, resulting in improved overall performance compared to a baseline model that relies only on text features.

Technical Specifications and Further Considerations. For the "Doc2Vec + KG" settings the total number of the generated triples was 150,022. The embeddings were computed in a matter of minutes using a workstation powered by NVIDIA GeForce RTX 2080 Ti GPU and Intel i7 CPU (GPU has 4352 cores and 11 GB DDR6 memory).

For the other augmentation settings, it is worth mentioning the importance of the size of graph $\mathcal{G}$ (Algorithm 1). Clearly, we could use the entire RDF dump of Wikidata to incorporate the linkage information, but this would result in a massive graph with a big number of QNodes, many of which not be useful for our task. This would generate an intractable number of computations when generating the KG embeddings - and many of those would be purposeless. This is where the distilled Wikidata graph comes into play. In this scenario, Algorithm 1 enriched our originally identified 3,729 QNodes to a total of 4,842 QNodes (connected within the directed graph $\mathcal{G}$), in 15 iterations (SPARQL calls - each with a response time averaging in 3–10 s) - again, in a matter of minutes. Following the semantic type assignments resulting from the SME inputs presented in Table 1, we retained statement of types: `attemptStatement, needStatement, painPointStatement` - and excluded statements of type `profileStatement` which simply describe the customer profile. It resulted in a total of 147,992 triples (including the materialized QNodes) - with 474 unique `needs`, 390 unique `painPoints`, and 123 unique `attempts` in the final EKG.

5   Conclusion and Future Work

In this work we introduce a method for constructing, modeling, and augmenting an Enterprise Knowledge Graph using (i) unstructured textual data from a collection of business requirement documents, (ii) open Knowledge Graphs from the Web - specifically Wikidata, and (iii) input from Subject Matter Experts. We evaluate our method using a dataset of historical records spanning over 10 years, capturing customer requests and products/services that have been provided to answer each specific customer requirement. We construct a graph from this data and quantify its the effect on informing a downstream task: classifying customer requests to one or more business units that can answer each specific customer need. The EKG improves the F_1 score of the classification task by as much as 4.1%. The aim of this work is for the augmented EKG to help the sales people navigating and browsing the multitude of company offerings along different business units, divisions and third party software offerings that we offer to our clients. Sometimes it can be difficult to understand what some of the assets accomplish (their descriptions can be highly technical). Having relations in the graph between a product and e.g. the pain-point extracted from client-stories (such as "`struggled to process large volumes of orders`") can be beneficial to understand their scope.

   We foresee multiple directions for our future work. We plan to test with a wider variety of fine grained targets for classification - e.g. item recommendation. We will also explore multi-lingual support: matching requests in other languages to our business offerings - for which we always have a representation in English. We envisage using the EKG for various additional tasks, including link prediction, assessing product similarities, understanding patterns etc. Finally, we plan to extend our approach by leveraging additional textual knowledge from open KBs to enrich each client document - this can provide additional context and insights for the embedding process.

References

1. Almeida, F., Xexéo, G.: Word embeddings: a survey. arXiv preprint arXiv:1901.09069 (2019)
2. Banko, M., Cafarella, M.J., Soderland, S., Broadhead, M., Etzioni, O.: Open information extraction from the web. In: Proceedings of the 20th International Joint Conference on Artificial Intelligence, IJCAI 2007, San Francisco, CA, USA, pp. 2670–2676. Morgan Kaufmann Publishers Inc. (2007). http://dl.acm.org/citation. cfm?id=1625275.1625705
3. Brank, J., Leban, G., Grobelnik, M.: Annotating documents with relevant Wikipedia concepts. In: Proceedings of SiKDD, p. 472 (2017)
4. Castano, S., et al.: Multimedia interpretation for dynamic ontology evolution. J. Log. Comput. **19**(5), 859–897 (2008)
5. Cimiano, P., Völker, J.: Towards large-scale, open-domain and ontology-based named entity classification. In: RANLP (2005)
6. Colon-Hernandez, P., Havasi, C., Alonso, J., Huggins, M., Breazeal, C.: Combining pre-trained language models and structured knowledge (2021). http://arxiv.org/ abs/2101.12294
7. World Wide Web Consortium, et al.: SPARQL 1.1 overview (2013)
8. Coucke, A., et al.: Snips voice platform: an embedded spoken language understanding system for private-by-design voice interfaces, pp. 12–16. arXiv preprint arXiv:1805.10190 (2018)
9. Del Corro, L., Gemulla, R.: ClausIE: clause-based open information extraction. In: WWW 2013 - Proceedings of the 22nd International Conference on World Wide Web (i), pp. 355–365 (2013)
10. Devlin, J., Chang, M.W., Lee, K., Toutanova, K.: BERT: pre-training of deep bidirectional transformers for language understanding. arXiv preprint arXiv:1810.04805 (2018)
11. Doddington, G.R., Mitchell, A., Przybocki, M.A., Ramshaw, L.A., Strassel, S., Weischedel, R.M.: The automatic content extraction (ACE) program-tasks, data, and evaluation. In: LREC (2004)
12. Dong, L., Wei, F., Sun, H., Zhou, M., Xu, K.: A hybrid neural model for type classification of entity mentions. In: IJCAI, pp. 1243–1249 (2015)
13. Etzioni, O., Fader, A., Christensen, J., Soderland, S., Mausam, M.: Open information extraction: the second generation. In: Proceedings of the Twenty-Second International Joint Conference on Artificial Intelligence, IJCAI 2011, vol. 1, pp. 3–10 (2011). https://doi.org/10.5591/978-1-57735-516-8/IJCAI11-012
14. Gangemi, A., Presutti, V., Reforgiato Recupero, D., Nuzzolese, A.G., Draicchio, F., Mongiovì, M.: Semantic web machine reading with FRED. Semant. Web **8**(6), 873–893 (2017)
15. Gashteovski, K., Gemulla, R., del Corro, L.: MinIE: minimizing facts in open information extraction. In: EMNLP 2017 - Conference on Empirical Methods in Natural Language Processing, Proceedings, pp. 2630–2640 (2017). https://doi.org/10. 18653/v1/d17-1278
16. Gerber, D., Hellmann, S., Bühmann, L., Soru, T., Usbeck, R., Ngonga Ngomo, A.-C.: Real-time RDF extraction from unstructured data streams. In: Alani, H., et al. (eds.) ISWC 2013. LNCS, vol. 8218, pp. 135–150. Springer, Heidelberg (2013). https://doi.org/10.1007/978-3-642-41335-3_9
17. Giuliano, C., Gliozzo, A.: Instance-based ontology population exploiting named-entity substitution. In: ACL 2008, pp. 265–272. ACL (2008)

18. Hamoudi, Y., Comebize, T.: Extracting RDF triples using the Stanford Parser (2016)
19. Hoberg, G., Knoblock, C.A., Phillips, G., Pujara, J., Raschid, L., Qiu, J.: Filling the private firm void: using representation learning to identify competitor relationships between businesses (2022)
20. Hogan, A., et al.: Knowledge graphs. ACM Comput. Surv. **54**(4), 1–37 (2021). https://doi.org/10.1145/3447772
21. Honnibal, M., Montani, I.: spaCy 2: natural language understanding with bloom embeddings, convolutional neural networks and incremental parsing (2017)
22. Kalyan, K.S., Rajasekharan, A., Sangeetha, S.: AMMUS: a survey of transformer-based pretrained models in natural language processing. arXiv preprint arXiv:2108.05542 (2021)
23. Le, Q., Mikolov, T.: Distributed representations of sentences and documents. In: International Conference on Machine Learning, pp. 1188–1196. PMLR (2014)
24. Ling, X., Weld, D.S.: Fine-grained entity recognition. In: AAAI 2012, pp. 94 100. AAAI Press (2012). http://dl.acm.org/citation.cfm?id=2900728.2900742
25. Liu, Y., et al.: RoBERTa: a robustly optimized BERT pretraining approach. arXiv preprint arXiv:1907.11692 (2019)
26. McDowell, L.K., Cafarella, M.: Ontology-driven, unsupervised instance population. Web Semant. Sci. Serv. Agents World Wide Web **6**(3), 218–236 (2008)
27. Mendes, P.N., Jakob, M., García-Silva, A., Bizer, C.: DBpedia Spotlight: shedding light on the web of documents. In: Proceedings of the 7th International Conference on Semantic Systems, pp. 1–8. ACM (2011)
28. Moiseev, F., Dong, Z., Alfonseca, E., Jaggi, M.: SKILL: structured knowledge infusion for large language models, pp. 1581–1588 (2022). https://doi.org/10.18653/v1/2022.naacl-main.113
29. Moro, A., Raganato, A., Navigli, R.: Entity linking meets word sense disambiguation: a unified approach. Trans. Assoc. Comput. Linguist. **2**, 231–244 (2014)
30. Murty, S., Verga, P., Vilnis, L., McCallum, A.: Finer grained entity typing with TypeNet. arXiv preprint arXiv:1711.05795 (2017)
31. Nakashole, N., Tylenda, T., Weikum, G.: Fine-grained semantic typing of emerging entities. In: ACL (1), pp. 1488–1497 (2013)
32. Nuzzolese, A.G., Gentile, A.L., Presutti, V., Gangemi, A., Garigliotti, D., Navigli, R.: Open knowledge extraction challenge. In: Gandon, F., Cabrio, E., Stankovic, M., Zimmermann, A. (eds.) SemWebEval 2015. CCIS, vol. 548, pp. 3–15. Springer, Cham (2015). https://doi.org/10.1007/978-3-319-25518-7_1
33. Pan, J.Z., Vetere, G., Gomez-Perez, J.M., Wu, H.: Exploiting Linked Data and Knowledge Graphs in Large Organisations. Springer, Cham (2017). https://doi.org/10.1007/978-3-319-45654-6
34. Patel, A., Jain, S.: Present and future of semantic web technologies: a research statement. Int. J. Comput. Appl. **43**(5), 413–422 (2021)
35. Paulheim, H.: Automatic knowledge graph refinement: a survey of approaches and evaluation methods. SWJ (2015). https://doi.org/10.3233/SW-160218
36. Presutti, V., Nuzzolese, A.G., Consoli, S., Gangemi, A., Reforgiato Recupero, D.: From hyperlinks to semantic web properties using open knowledge extraction. Semant. Web **7**(4), 351–378 (2016)
37. Radford, A., Wu, J., Child, R., Luan, D., Amodei, D., Sutskever, I.: Language models are unsupervised multitask learners. Technical report, OpenAI (2019)
38. Recupero, D.R., Nuzzolese, A.G., Consoli, S., Presutti, V., Peroni, S., Mongiovì, M.: Extracting knowledge from text using SHELDON, a semantic holistic framEwork for LinkeD ONtology data. In: WWW 2015 Companion - Proceedings of the

24th International Conference on World Wide Web, pp. 235–238 (2015). https://doi.org/10.1145/2740908.2742842

39. Ren, X., He, W., Qu, M., Huang, L., Ji, H., Han, J.: AFET: automatic fine-grained entity typing by hierarchical partial-label embedding. In: Proceedings of the Conference on Empirical Methods in Natural Language Processing (EMNLP) (2016)

40. Ristoski, P., Faralli, S., Ponzetto, S.P., Paulheim, H.: Large-scale taxonomy induction using entity and word embeddings. In: Proceedings - 2017 IEEE/WIC/ACM International Conference on Web Intelligence, WI 2017, pp. 81–87 (2017). https://doi.org/10.1145/3106426.3106465

41. Saggion, H., Funk, A., Maynard, D., Bontcheva, K.: Ontology-based information extraction for business intelligence. In: Aberer, K., et al. (eds.) ASWC/ISWC - 2007. LNCS, vol. 4825, pp. 843–856. Springer, Heidelberg (2007). https://doi.org/10.1007/978-3-540-76298-0_61

42. Schneider, P., Schopf, T., Vladika, J., Galkin, M., Simperl, E., Matthes, F.: A decade of knowledge graphs in natural language processing: a survey (2022). http://arxiv.org/abs/2210.00105

43. Segura-Bedmar, I., Martínez, P., Herrero Zazo, M.: SemEval-2013 Task 9: extraction of drug-drug interactions from biomedical texts (DDIExtraction 2013). In: SemEval 2013, pp. 341–350. ACL, June 2013

44. Shbita, B., Rajendran, A., Pujara, J., Knoblock, C.A.: Parsing, representing and transforming units of measure. In: Proceedings of the Conference on Modeling the World's Systems (2019)

45. Shimaoka, S., Stenetorp, P., Inui, K., Riedel, S.: An attentive neural architecture for fine-grained entity type classification. arXiv preprint arXiv:1604.05525 (2016)

46. Shimaoka, S., Stenetorp, P., Inui, K., Riedel, S.: Neural architectures for fine-grained entity type classification. arXiv preprint arXiv:1606.01341 (2016)

47. Tanev, H., Magnini, B.: Weakly supervised approaches for ontology population. Citeseer (2008)

48. Tjong Kim Sang, E.F., De Meulder, F.: Introduction to the CoNLL-2003 shared task: language-independent named entity recognition. In: Proceedings of the Seventh Conference on Natural Language Learning at HLT-NAACL 2003, CONLL 2003, Stroudsburg, PA, USA, vol. 4, pp. 142–147. Association for Computational Linguistics (2003)

49. Trouillon, T., Welbl, J., Riedel, S., Gaussier, É., Bouchard, G.: Complex embeddings for simple link prediction. In: International Conference on Machine Learning, pp. 2071–2080. PMLR (2016)

50. Tsoumakas, G., Katakis, I.: Multi-label classification: an overview. Int. J. Data Warehouse. Min. (IJDWM) 3(3), 1–13 (2007)

51. Velardi, P., Faralli, S., Navigli, R.: OntoLearn reloaded: a graph-based algorithm for taxonomy induction. Comput. Linguist. 39(3), 665–707 (2013)

52. Velardi, P., Navigli, R., Cuchiarelli, A., Neri, R.: Evaluation of OntoLearn, a methodology for automatic learning of domain ontologies. In: Ontology Learning from Text: Methods, Evaluation and Applications, vol. 123, no. 92 (2005)

53. Vrandecic, D., Krotzsch, M.: Wikidata: a free collaborative knowledgebase. Commun. ACM 57(10), 78–85 (2014)

54. Wang, S., Zhao, R., Chen, X., Zheng, Y., Liu, B.: Enquire one's parent and child before decision: fully exploit hierarchical structure for self-supervised taxonomy expansion. In: The Web Conference 2021 - Proceedings of the World Wide Web Conference, WWW 2021, pp. 3291–3304 (2021). https://doi.org/10.1145/3442381.3449948

55. Weikum, G., Dong, X.L., Razniewski, S., Suchanek, F.: Machine knowledge: creation and curation of comprehensive knowledge bases. Found. Trends Databases **10**(2–4), 108–490 (2021). https://doi.org/10.1561/1900000064
56. Weikum, G., Hoffart, J., Suchanek, F.: Ten years of knowledge harvesting: lessons and challenges. Data Eng. **5**, 41–50 (2016)
57. Wong, W., Liu, W., Bennamoun, M.: Ontology learning from text: a look back and into the future. ACM Comput. Surv. (CSUR) **44**(4), 1–36 (2012)
58. Yaghoobzadeh, Y., Adel, H., Schütze, H.: Noise mitigation for neural entity typing and relation extraction. arXiv preprint arXiv:1612.07495 (2016)
59. Yaghoobzadeh, Y., Schütze, H.: Corpus-level fine-grained entity typing using contextual information. arXiv preprint arXiv:1606.07901 (2016)
60. Yan, J., Wang, C., Cheng, W., Gao, M., Zhou, A.: A retrospective of knowledge graphs. Front. Comput. Sci. **12**(1), 55–74 (2018). https://doi.org/10.1007/s11704-016-5228-9
61. Yang, Z., Dai, Z., Yang, Y., Carbonell, J., Salakhutdinov, R.R., Le, Q.V.: XLNet: generalized autoregressive pretraining for language understanding. In: Advances in Neural Information Processing Systems, pp. 5753–5763 (2019)
62. Yogatama, D., Gillick, D., Lazic, N.: Embedding methods for fine grained entity type classification. In: ACL (2), pp. 291–296 (2015)
63. Zhang, L., Rettinger, A.: X-LiSA: cross-lingual semantic annotation. VLDB **7**(13), 1693–1696 (2014)

Investigating Ontology-Based Data Access with GitHub

Yahlieel Jafta[1,3]($\boxtimes$) (ID), Louise Leenen[1,3]($\boxtimes$) (ID), and Thomas Meyer[2,3] (ID)

[1] University of the Western Cape, Cape Town, South Africa
2858132@myuwc.ac.za, lleenen@uwc.ac.za
[2] University of Cape Town, Cape Town, South Africa
tmeyer@cair.org.za
[3] Centre for Artificial Intelligence Research (CAIR), Cape Town, South Africa

Abstract. Data analysis-based decision-making is performed daily by domain experts. As data grows, getting access to relevant data becomes a challenge. In an approach known as Ontology-based data access (OBDA), ontologies are advocated as a suitable formal tool to address complex data access. This technique combines a domain ontology with a data source by using a declarative mapping specification to enable data access using a domain vocabulary. We investigate this approach by studying the theoretical background; conducting a literature review on the implementation of OBDA in production systems; implementing OBDA on a relational dataset using an OBDA tool and; providing results and analysis of query answering. We selected Ontop (https://ontop-vkg.org) to illustrate how this technique enhances the data usage of the GitHub community. Ontop is an open-source OBDA tool applied in the domain of relational databases. The implementation consists of the GHTorrent dataset and an extended SemanGit ontology. We perform a set of queries to highlight a subset of the features of this data access approach. The results look positive and can assist various use cases related to GitHub data with a semantic approach. OBDA does provide benefits in practice, such as querying in domain vocabulary and making use of reasoning over the axioms in the ontology. However, the practical impediments we observe are in the "manual" development of a domain ontology and the creation of a mapping specification which requires deep knowledge of a domain and the data. Also, implementing OBDA within the practical context of an information system requires careful consideration for a suitable user interface to facilitate the query construction from ontology vocabulary. Finally, we conclude with a summary of the paper and direction for future research.

Keywords: Ontology-based data access · ontology · data access · relational databases · Git · GitHub

1 Introduction

Information retrieval is a critical process in organizations for extracting insights to achieve strategic organizational objectives. Large enterprises today use sev-

C. Pesquita et al. (Eds.): ESWC 2023, LNCS 13870, pp. 644–660, 2023.
https://doi.org/10.1007/978-3-031-33455-9_38

eral information systems each with its database to store input and functional data [14]. In various domains, clients require access to domain-specific services exported by systems [6]. However, gaining access to the required data in a heterogeneous environment is becoming a challenge due to data access generally being performed by technical experts who translate the requirements of domain experts into the necessary analytical output, creating a bottleneck at scale [17].

The two main ways to handle access to heterogeneous data are procedural and declarative [21]. A procedural methodology is a bottom-up approach where the problem is addressed at the data source level. However, this approach is expensive to maintain and requires updates for each change in the underlying data structure. The declarative approach, a top-down approach, defines a shared conceptualization that is valid for the domain of interest underlying the data sources. This conceptualization is constructed from the intentional level of the application domain terms, which is then linked to the actual data. These terms are then specified to access information [6]. The focus of this paper is based on the declarative approach. To realize such a solution an approach known as Ontology-based data access (OBDA) is advocated for, a technique that utilizes formalized domain knowledge (ontologies) as a suitable formal tool for data access [28]. In the literature, this formalism of domain knowledge is advocated for and applied in the space of problems around data integration and developing intelligent search systems [14]. The focus of this paper is on the latter, however, the literature considers this as a unified problem [14].

This paper applies Ontop, an open-source system that links relational databases with domain ontologies. Ontop transforms the relational database into a virtual Resource Description Framework (RDF) graph [4] that can be queried using SPARQL. This approach offers a powerful way to leverage existing databases for semantic web applications. Our implementation utilizes a GitHub relational dataset from the GHTorrent [11] project. Furthermore, there exists an RDF-linked dataset for GHTorrent called the Semantic Git (SemanGit) [19]. The SemanGit dataset was systematically built by transforming the GHTorrent dataset into linked data, and the SemanGit ontology was subsequently developed.

In this paper, the Ontop OBDA tool is used to illustrate how OBDA enhances the data usage of the GitHub community; Ontop is applied to the GHTorrent dataset and the SemanGit ontology. Section 2 provides the background on OBDA and Sect. 3 discusses related work. Section 4 discusses the Ontop system, the GHTorrent dataset, and the SemanGit ontology (including extensions to the ontology). Section 5 shows the implementation of Ontop on the selected dataset and ontology. Section 6 illustrates query answering with Ontop followed by a discussion in Sect. 7. Finally, we conclude in Sect. 8 with future work emanating from this research.

2 Ontology-Based Data Access

In the last decade, the database research community created the foundation for the utilization of columnar storage [1], allowing for efficient storage and processing of large data sets. As a result, relational database management systems (RDMS) have seen considerable growth, especially the wide adoption of database systems offered as cloud services [1]. Ontologies [13] express a shared conceptualization of the domain of interest at a high level of abstraction independent from the data sources. While ontologies are a good candidate for realizing this conceptualization, RDMS are natural candidates for the management of the data layer given the maturity of RDMS.

The Virtual Knowledge Graph (VKG) approach, also referred to in the literature as OBDA, is a well-known view for accessing and integrating data sources [34]. In this approach, the data sources are virtualized through mapping and an ontology, which is presented as a unified knowledge graph that can be queried by end-users using domain vocabulary [34]. When data is queried, the user query is translated over the ontology into SQL queries over the database. The mapping specification layer is responsible for binding the ontology and the data sources. This is achieved by linking the classes and properties in the ontology to SQL views over the data in the database. The ontology in combination with the mappings produces a VKG, which can be queried using SPARQL, the standard query language in the Semantic Web [4]. OBDA systems utilize the mapping specification and Description Logic [2] reasoning to automatically transform queries expressed in terms of the ontology into SQL queries that can be executed on the database.

The OBDA framework consists of an extensional instance, the data source, an intensional schema which is the ontology [32], and the link between the two consisting of a mapping specification.

Definition 1. *Formally, the extensional instance is represented as the* data source D *conforming to the data source schema* S. *The intensional schema is defined as the OBDA specification* $P = (O, M, S)$ *[32] where,*

- O *is an ontology*
- M *a mapping from* S *to* O
- S *the data source schema*

An OBDA specification P is instantiated by a database D compliant with the schema S. The pair (P, D) is referred to as an OBDA instance, or an instance of a VKG. The RDF graph, denoted $M(D)$, is the set of triples produced by combining M and D. Thus, the exposed virtual RDF graph, denoted $G_{P,D}$, provides the semantics of an OBDA instance (P, D) and comprises the triples derived from the triples in $M(D)$ by applying the axioms in O [33].

The most fundamental reasoning task in the OBDA approach is query answering over the KG [32]. Query answering is performed by utilizing SPARQL as a query language. A SPARQL query q over the OBDA instance (P, D) essentially returns the answer to q over the KG $G_{P,D}$, inline with the standard SPARQL semantics [33]. The primary method for query answering in this approach is query reformulation, which prevents physical materialization of the KG $G_{P,D}$. The SPARQL query q expressed over the KG is reformulated into a SQL query **Q** that can be directly executed on **D** [33]. During the query reformulation process, the SPARQL query **q** is processed through a set of transformations, which include rewriting the query **q** for the ontology **O** and unfolding it inline with the mapping **M**. The answers returned by the SQL query **Q**, after execution on **D**, are returned and transformed into RDF terms based on the mapping **M**. The mapping **M** connecting the ontology **O** to the database is responsible for specifying how the ontology assertions are populated by the data from the source **D**.

3 Related Work

Applications of knowledge graphs are gradually gaining momentum due to their agility and flexibility to apply to various data models [8]. This flexibility enables their application to the integration of heterogeneous sources and schema of data. There has been a lot of attention on converting legacy data to RDF knowledge graphs. Given the wide impact and implementations of relational databases, naturally, the focus shifted in this direction. The two main approaches for this integration were to materialize all data within a given data source as RDF triples or on-the-fly data access using a query language such as SPARQL and to delegate the actual retrieval of the data to the data source engine [26]. Once the data is exposed as VKGs, data can be processed using familiar vocabularies in the form of specific domain ontologies with automated reasoning capabilities.

Using Ontop, Massari et al. [26] apply OBDA to enable data integration of non-relational (NoSQL) data sources with the motivation to fill the gap between NoSQL and the Semantic web. They used Couchbase, a NoSQL document-oriented database with the following components defining the implementation; an OWL Ontology, an Access Interface, mappings, a NoSQL database, a SPARQL to NoSQL query adjustment, and a JSON export [26].

Siemens Energy used OBDA to address data access challenges on large-scale data [17]. The main motivation was the bottleneck for diagnostics in data gathering, which takes up to 80% of the overall time. Finding the right data for analytics is very hard due to the constraints of predefined queries, the complexity of data, the intricacy of query construction, and the limitation of explicitly stated information. Three ontologies, defining the turbine, sensor, and diagnostic data models, based on the Siemens database schemata were developed.

Geologists at the data-intensive petroleum company Statoil frequently use data stored in multiple data sources [16]. Due to the complexities of the data schemata, geologists often require IT personnel for data access support. For example, one of the data stores contains about 3000 tables with about 37000 columns. Given this large data model, query formulation by Statoil geologists is not feasible without the help of IT specialists [16]. OBDA was thus applied to address the data access challenge. Their approach includes an ontology that is connected to the data sources via mappings and query translation between user queries and underlying data sources. The Optique–platform [18] was used.

4   OBDA Tool, Dataset, and Ontology

4.1   Ontop System

In both academia and industry, more than a dozen VKG query answering systems have been developed [33]. To select a suitable query-answering system for our implementation we looked at systems that are open-source with the ability to perform ontological reasoning. Xiao et al. [33] reported on the most important query-answering systems that are compliant with industrial standards and in terms of query performance. The report includes systems that are both open-source and proprietary, irrespective of ontological reasoning capacity. The systems include D2RQ[1], Mastro [5], Morph [29], Ontop [4], Oracle Spatial and Graph[2], Stardog[3] and Ultrawrap [30]. From this list of query answering systems, D2RQ, Morph, and Ontop are open-source, however, both D2RQ and Morph projects do not support ontology inference and have not actively been maintained since January 2015 and June 2022 respectively. Given this, we opted for the Ontop system as the tool of choice.

Ontop has undergone four major releases since its inception in 2009, establishing it as the most mature and state-of-the-art OBDA open-source system [34]. Ontop support the World Wide Web Consortium (W3C) recommendations for SPARQL and the W3C RDB2RDF Mapping Language (R2RML) mappings. During query formulation, Ontop uses "a relational-algebra-type representation" [34] for queries in the intermediate query (IQ) language. Ontop has independent support for each RDMS vendor to produce the desired SQL results. The IQ is converted into the relevant SQL based on the applicable RDMS vendor SQL dialect. For further detail on Ontop, we direct the interested reader to the work of Xiao et al. [34].

4.2   The GHTorrent Dataset

The acquisition and curation of data from software repositories is a typical requirement to support empirical studies on software engineering [11], and GitHub is an attractive source for this as it provides access to its internal public data via a REST API [12]. However, access to the REST API is capped at a request limitation of 15,000 requests per hour per authentication token. Given this limitation, it is quite a cumbersome procedure to extract large amounts of data to support research depending on this data. As of February 2023, GitHub has over one hundred million developers across more than four million organizations contributing to more than three-hundred and thirty million repositories[4], making it a substantial source for software repository data. To address the need for making this data available, the GHTorrent project was established. GHTorrent is an offline mirror of GitHub's event streams and persistent data that is made available to the research community as a service.

---

[1] http://d2rq.org/.
[2] https://www.oracle.com/database/technologies/spatialandgraph.html.
[3] https://www.stardog.com/.
[4] https://github.com/about.

4.3   SemanGit Ontology

Utilizing an ontology that applies to the domain of the underlying data source is an essential step in OBDA. The GHTorrent dataset falls within the domain of the git version control system (VCS). A VCS keeps track of changes made to a file or set of files over time. Selected files can be restored to their previous state using this feature, promoting easy recovery of files and errors [9]. As part of the investigative procedure to identify the dataset, we had to keep in mind the ontology that will be used. For this, we had the option of developing or re-using an existing ontology for the domain of interest. While investigating a suitable dataset for the research, we found a novel RDF dataset based on the GHTorrent called SemanGit. Based on a git ontology, SemanGit is the first collection of linked data extracted from GitHub [19]. The SemanGit ontology[5] has been identified as a suitable ontology for this research as it was developed and used as the underlying ontology for the RDF-linked dataset created from the GHTorrent dataset [19]. In OBDA, the ontology is used directly over the data source via a mapping specification and keeps the data in its original state. In our work, the SemanGit ontology describes the concepts and relationships in the git domain, while the mapping specification provides a formal mapping between the ontology and the GHTorrent MySQL relational database schema. This enables queries to be expressed in terms of concepts from the ontology using SPARQL. At query time, a SPARQL query is first parsed and analyzed to identify the relevant concepts and relationships from the ontology. Next, the mapping specification is used to translate these ontology concepts and relationships into the corresponding SQL query (tables, columns, and joins) in the underlying relational database schema. Additionally, OBDA can integrate several data sources and should thus not be viewed as a specific data source.

The ontology differentiates between git conventions and provider-specific features. For example, based on git, the author of a commit is represented by a "Name [email]" pair whereas GitHub represents a "commit author" as a user containing additional attributes such as location, country code, creation date [19]. To accommodate this, the ontology was built in a hierarchical structure with the git protocol features forming the base classes, and provider-specific extensions being classes (denoted with the *"github_"* prefix) that inherit from the base classes.

We consider the ontology to be a base ontology with *Primitive* classes and no *Defined* classes. Classes with at least one set of necessary and sufficient requirements are known as defined classes; they have a definition, and every individual who meets the definition belongs to the class. Primitive classes are those that lack any sets of necessary and sufficient requirements [15].

In the SemanGit ontology, *github_pull_request* is a subclass of *pull_request* which says that if something is a *github_pull_request* it is necessarily a *pull_request*. According to GitHub's REST API, every pull request is an *issue*, but not all issues are considered pull requests. Given the ontology

---

[5] https://github.com/SemanGit/SemanGit.

description, if we consider an instance of a *pull_request*, the knowledge captured is not sufficient to determine that the pull request instance is a member of the class *github_pull_request* and that it is an *issue*. We must alter the conditions to make this possible, by extending the necessary conditions to necessary AND sufficient conditions. This means that the requirements for being a member of the class *github_pull_request* are not only necessary but also sufficient to establish that any given instance that satisfies the conditions must be a member of the class *github_pull_request*. Thus, the classes in the SemanGit ontology are considered to be primitive. The ontology also lacks inverse relations and object property characteristics which make it possible to enrich the meaning of properties [15]. We now outline the extensions made to the ontology. The approach used for extending the SemanGit ontology is based on the methodology defined by Noy et al. [27]. It is an iterative development process that repeats continuously to enhance the ontology. For our purpose, we renamed the classes and properties by removing the underscores and using UpperCamelCase for class names and lowerCamelCase for property names. We also focused on enriching existing class and property definitions. Since we are reusing an existing ontology, the domain *(git protocols)* and scope *(GitHub)* of the ontology is known with the key concepts being defined. Considering this, we are only focusing on the sub-processes related to the extension of class and property definitions. The instances are defined in the underlying database instance. The class extensions applied were minimal. We have converted the class descriptions of **GithubProject** and **GithubPullRequest** to *definitions*.

- If something is an instance of a **GithubProject** then it is necessary that it is a **Repository** and it is also necessary that it has exactly 1 owner that is a member of the class **User**.
    - $GithubProject \sqsubseteq Repository \sqcap \exists hasowner.User \sqcap$
      $(= 1 githubHasOwner.User)$
- If something is an instance of a **GithubPullRequest** then it is necessary that it is a **PullRequest** and it is also necessary that it has **exactly** 1 issue that is a member of the class **GithubIssue**.
    - $GithubPullRequest \sqsubseteq (PullRequest \sqcap GithubIssue) \sqcap$
      $\exists githubPullRequestIssue.GithubIssue \sqcap$
      $(= 1 githubPullRequestIssue.GithubIssue)$
- Furthermore, the **User** and **Repository** classes are disjoint from each other.
    - $User \sqsubseteq \neg Repository$

The following inverse properties were added.

- *githubOwnerOf* inverse of *githubHasOwner*
- *hasAuthoredComment* inverse of *commentAuthor*
- *hasAuthoredCommit* inverse of *commitAuthor*
- *hasCommittedCommit* inverse of *commitedBy*
- *repositoryHasCommit* inverse of *belongsToRepository*

In addition to this, each property was analyzed and updated with a characteristic where applicable. We show a visualization of the ontology in Fig. 1.

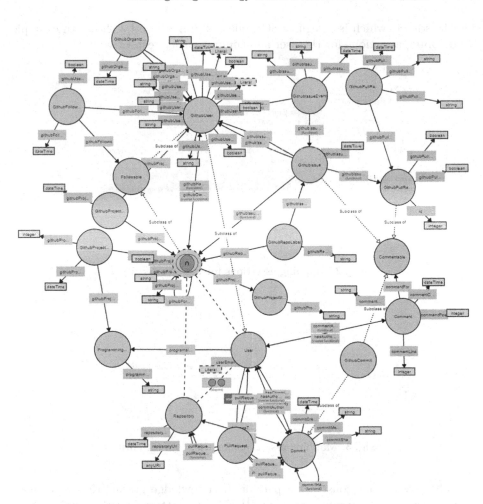

Fig. 1. Ontology visualisation using WebVOWL [24]

5   Mapping GHTorrent to the SemanGit Ontology

To create and manage the mapping assertions for the ontology and database
we use the open-source Protégé ontology editor[6] along with the Ontop plugin
to enable the management of mappings and querying from within the Protégé
editor. We used version 5.5.0 of Protégé and version 4.1.1 of the Ontop plugin.
A mapping assertion consists of three components; a unique mapping identifier,
a target, and a source. The target is a set of RDF triple patterns defined in the
Terse RDF Triple Language (Turtle)[7] syntax that captures the data returned

---

[6] https://protege.stanford.edu/.
[7] https://www.w3.org/TeamSubmission/turtle/.

by the source, which is a regular SQL query. Figures 2 and 3 shows an example of mapping assertions for the user and commit entity respectively.

Fig. 2. Mapping assertions for the User entity

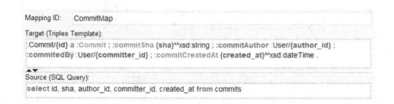

Fig. 3. Mapping assertions for the Commit entity

These assertions construct a part of the knowledge graph (KG) as defined in the target part, by populating the RDF triple pattern answer variables with the corresponding answer in the result set of the source SQL query. The answer variables are enclosed in braces "{" and "}". The "UserMap" mapping assertion populates the ontology User class with the relevant properties to the underlying database instance data. We note that the "UserMap" mapping assertion defines what an organization is considered to be, where an organization according to the dataset is a user database entry with the "type" column populated with the value "ORG". This mapping assertion allows the KG to assert whether a user is an organization based on the boolean value of the *githubUserIsOrg* property that is populated by the computed MySQL column "is_organization". The "CommitMap" mapping assertion populates the ontology Commit class.

6   Querying GHTorrent with SPARQL

To investigate the value of OBDA we performed query answering over the VKG using a select set of queries based on a user not being informed of specific data encoding schemes and schema structure of the data source. The query experiments were run on a computer with an AMD Ryzen 9 5900X 12-Core Processor running at 3.70 MHz using 32 GB of RAM, running Windows 10 Pro version 21H2. The MySQL database instance was installed on a Gigabyte GP-AG42TB AORUS 2TB M.2 2280 PCI-E 4.0 Solid State Drive with MySQL server version 8.0.

```
SELECT *
WHERE {
  ?organization a :User.
  ?organization :githubUserCountryCode true.
  ?organization :githubUserIsOrg "za".
}
```

Listing 1.1. Select GitHub organizations with country code "za"

```
SELECT v1.'id' AS 'id1m33'
FROM 'users' v1
WHERE ('ORG' = v1.'type' AND 'za' = v1.'country_code')
```

Listing 1.2. Generated SQL for listing 1.1

The query in Listing 1.1 selects the GitHub organizations from South Africa (country code "za"). GitHub identifies organizations and users as a **User** entity with a **type** column to distinguish whether an entity is an organization or a standard user. To model this in the ontology, a data property named *"githubUserIsOrg"* is defined with the domain *"githubUser"* and range the "boolean" datatype. In Fig. 2 we show how this property is mapped to the database. Listing 1.2 shows the SQL query translated from the SPARQL query. Here we observe the inclusion of the generated *'ORG' = v1.'type'* **WHERE** clause which is a result of the "UserMap" mapping specification in Fig. 2. With this query, we attempt to illustrate that a user does not need to know how the database encodes an "Organization". If the data encoding scheme changes in the database, it will require an update of the mapping assertion which will not affect the SPARQL query if there is no change in the ontology. Here we observe, selecting the organization subset by using the *"githubUserIsOrg"* property in the SPARQL clause (where *githubUserIsOrg* is *true*), unfolds in the *'ORG' = v1.'type'* SQL clause after query translation.

```
SELECT ?repo_name ?year (COUNT(?commit) AS ?commits)
WHERE
{
  ?commit :belongsToRepository ?project .
  ?project :githubProjectName ?repo_name .
  ?commit :commitCreatedAt ?date .
  FILTER (?project IN (repo:3905191, repo:12159636))
}
GROUP BY ?repo_name (year(?date) AS ?year)
```

Listing 1.3. Number of commits per year for Angular and React repositories

```
SELECT v7.'name1m32' AS 'name1m32', v7.'v2' AS 'v2',
COUNT(*) AS 'v4'
FROM (SELECT v5.'name1m32' AS 'name1m32',
EXTRACT(YEAR FROM v5.'created_at1m43') AS 'v2'
FROM (SELECT DISTINCT v1.'commit_id' AS 'commit_id1m4',
v3.'created_at' AS 'created_at1m43', v2.'name' AS 'name1m32',
v1.'project_id' AS 'project_id1m4'
FROM 'project_commits' v1, 'projects' v2, 'commits' v3
WHERE (
    (v1.'project_id' = 3905191 OR v1.'project_id' = 12159636)
    AND v1.'project_id' = v2.'id'
    AND v1.'commit_id' = v3.'id'
    )
) v5
) v7
GROUP BY v7.'v2', v7.'name1m32'
```

Listing 1.4. Generated SQL for listing 1.3

In Listing 1.3 we retrieve the number of commits per year for the repositories Angular and React. Angular and React are two popular GitHub repositories. Angular, developed at Google, is a web application development framework that uses Typescript/JavaScript and other languages to create mobile and desktop web applications. React, a JavaScript library for building user interfaces was developed at Meta (formerly known as Facebook). With this example, we illustrate query translation which includes an aggregate function with the commit table and a subset of the columns. We group the results by repository and year to see how the number of commits changed over time. The translated MySQL query can be seen in Listing 1.4.

```
SELECT ?author (COUNT(DISTINCT ?commit) as ?commits)
(COUNT(DISTINCT ?pr) AS ?prs)
WHERE {
  BIND (repo:12159636 AS ?repo)
  ?repo :repositoryHasCommit ?commit .
  ?author :hasAuthoredCommit ?commit .
  ?pr :pullRequestBaseProject ?repo .
  ?pr :pullRequestUser ?author .
}
GROUP BY ?author
```

Listing 1.5. Angular repository contributor commits and pull requests

```
SELECT v6.'author_id1m7' AS 'author_id1m7',
COUNT(DISTINCT(v6.'id1m28')) AS 'v3',
COUNT(DISTINCT(v6.'commit_id1m5')) AS 'v4'
FROM (SELECT DISTINCT v2.'author_id' AS 'author_id1m7',
v1.'commit_id' AS 'commit_id1m5', v3.'id' AS 'id1m28'
FROM 'project_commits' v1, 'commits' v2,
'pull_requests' v3, 'pull_request_history' v4
WHERE (
```

```
      v1.'commit_id' = v2.'id'
      AND v3.'id' = v4.'pull_request_id'
      AND v2.'author_id' = v4.'actor_id'
      AND 12159636 = v1.'project_id'
      AND 12159636 = v3.'base_repo_id'
      )
) v6
GROUP BY v6.'author_id1m7'
```

Listing 1.6. Generated SQL for listing 1.5

The query above, Listing 1.5 retrieves all the contributors with their total number of commits and pull requests. A **Pull Request** (PR) is a request to merge code changes made on a separate branch of the central repository into the base branch. The database table *"pull_request_history"* stores all the actions associated with a PR, including the user and type of action. We expect to receive results for this query by reasoning over the axioms in the ontology that declare inverse properties, even if we did not include any explicit mapping assertions for the object properties *repositoryHasCommit* and *hasAuthoredCommit*. We use the axioms that *repositoryHasCommit* is the inverse property of *belongsToRepository* and *hasAuthoredCommit* is the inverse property of *commitAuthor* in this scenario.

```
SELECT DISTINCT ?member
WHERE {
    VALUES ?project { repo:27601818 }
    ?member :githubUserFake false .
    ?pr :pullRequestBaseProject ?project .
    ?pr :githubPullRequestMerged true .
    ?pr :pullRequestUser ?member .
}
```

Listing 1.7. Core team members of Vue js project based on Pull Request contributions

```
SELECT DISTINCT v1.'id' AS 'id1m51' FROM 'users' v1,
'pull_requests' v2, 'pull_request_history' v3,
'pull_request_history' v4
WHERE (
    (v1.'fake' = 0) AND v2.'id' = v3.'pull_request_id'
    AND v2.'id' = v4.'pull_request_id'
    AND v1.'id' = v4.'actor_id'
    AND 27601818 = v2.'base_repo_id'
    AND 'merged' = v3.'action'
)
```

Listing 1.8. Generated SQL for listing 1.7

Listing 1.7 retrieves authentic users contributing to the popular GitHub repository Vue[8] based on merges of a **Pull Request** (PR). Authentic users can

---

[8] https://github.com/vuejs/vue.

own repositories and perform actions such as managing issues, pull requests, and commits. Unauthentic users only show up as commit authors or committers. The *fake* column is used to identify these types of users in the user table. We observe in the translated SQL query, Listing 1.8, the lookup into the *"pull_request_history"* table without explicitly defining it in the SPARQL query (Listing 1.7). This is a result of the mapping specification for the object property *githubPullRequestMerged*, which is populated based on the "merged" action related to a pull request that is stored in the *"pull_request_history"* table. We do note that the generated SQL query contains two self-joins on the *"pull_request_history"* table. The Ontop system uses unique constraints (primary key) for removing self-joins. In the mapping, we are referencing a non-unique constraint column (pull_request_id) for the pull_request_history table. As a test, we observed that when using the primary key in the mapping the self-join was removed.

We repeated each query ten times and took the mean average of the execution time. We compared the execution from within the Protégé SPARQL query editor against running the generated SQL directly in the MySQL Command-line client. We did not notice a major difference in the execution times. Each query was executed against the entire database by selecting "all results" in the Protégé SPARQL query editor. We show the SPARQL query execution time in Table 1.

Table 1. Query execution times

Query	Time (s)
Listing 1.1	9.515
Listing 1.3	0.6877
Listing 1.5	680.8
Listing 1.7	0.2202

7   Discussion

We performed a set of queries to highlight a subset of the features of the OBDA approach. During the execution of the experiments, the feature of querying in domain vocabulary without the need to understand the underlying database data encoding and schema as well as utilizing the ontology axioms during query executions does stand out. The results look positive and can assist various use cases related to GitHub data with a semantic approach. The ontology enables a more precise understanding of the relationships between different data elements, allowing for intelligent data querying. However, the practical impediments we observe are in the "manual" development of a domain ontology and the creation of a mapping specification which affects scalability.

The query volume, the size and complexity of the ontology, and the stability and performance of the underlying system all have an impact on scalability.

And while it is possible to scale OBDA systems in a production environment, in contrast to traditional database systems, it is a complex endeavor that requires deep knowledge to develop and maintain domain ontologies and mapping specifications that do not suffer semantic loss between the original data and associated ontologies. The mapping specification connecting the ontology to the database involves writing individual queries that must be consistent with the vocabulary of the ontology for each database table and column [4]. And while the development and maintenance of ontologies is a well-established topic with considerable research [31], the engineering of mapping specifications is still an emerging technology. Given this complexity, mapping engineering is a demanding procedure. Several mapping engineering methodologies and tools have been proposed to address this challenge. Xiao et al. [33] group the contributions into two categories: mapping bootstrappers and editors. A mapping bootstrapper attempts to automate a mapping specification for a relational data source. However, the generated ontology and mappings are data source specific, whereas a domain ontology aims at being used across multiple data sources within a domain. Mapping editors like the ontology editor Protégé provide an environment for mapping engineering but do not support features such as syntax highlighting and require deep-level knowledge about the underlying mapping language [33]. We also mention Ontopic Studio[9], a more recent no–code mapping editor to link databases and data lakes with knowledge graphs. For further detail, we direct the reader to https://ontopic.ai/en/ontopic-studio/.

Traditional relational database systems on the other hand have lower complexity, are scalable, and have defined best practices to achieve good performance in production given the level of maturity. In comparison to existing large systems and our experimental observation, OBDA currently falls short in terms of complexity, cost-effectiveness, and maturity. However, OBDA allows for a more detailed understanding of the connections that exist between data pieces. Thus the trade-off between scalability and the reasoning capacity of OBDA needs to be taken into consideration. Also, we note that actualizing OBDA within the context of an information system requires careful consideration for the implementation of a suitable user interface to facilitate the SPARQL query construction from ontology vocabulary, where users of such a system are querying from a client-facing user interface and not writing SPARQL queries. In this work, we assumed that a user performing queries is familiar with GitHub terminology and that the ontology is modeled as close as possible to this domain to enable query construction from the vocabulary terms. Another approach would be to look at the field of Natural Language Processing to assist in query formulation, such as integrating machine learning algorithms and knowledge representation to query knowledge graphs in natural language. This is however out of the scope of this research, we refer the interested reader to [10,22].

Given these impediments, the research in this field is very active. Such as semi-automating ontology development using an approach called Ontology Learning (OL), where machine learning techniques are applied to represent

---

[9] https://ontopic.ai/en/.

knowledge from heterogeneous data sources. Recent work in this area includes various proposals to apply OL in the scope of relational databases [3,20,23,25]. In the work by Calvanese et al. [7], the authors proposed an algorithm to automatically detect and map a relational schema to ontology mapping patterns.

The artifacts of this research can be found at this link, which includes the extended ontology and the full set of mapping specifications for each database table. We highlight that the GHTorrent dataset is not currently up to date, and the last data dump was released in March 2021. We also note that the website is not available anymore, however, the content is available on the GitHub repository. We are not aware of any future updates to the GHTorrent dataset.

8   Conclusion and Future Work

This paper describes the application of OBDA, specifically the use of the Ontop tool, on a well-defined open-source dataset called GHTorrent which is based on the GitHub platform. OBDA involves connecting an ontology to a data source using a mapping specification. The SemanGit ontology was used as the underlying ontology for this work, which we have extended. We documented the mapping procedure and demonstrated query answering using SPARQL. OBDA's querying in domain vocabulary, combined with reasoning over the ontology's axioms, shows promising results. There are opportunities for this work to be extended and applied for specific use cases applicable to GitHub and OBDA. This includes publishing the extended ontology and making this work publicly available to the GitHub community via an interface and API endpoint for further evaluation. Maintenance of the extended ontology will be ongoing and can take several directions depending on the scope of use cases. Furthermore, this research can facilitate the broader domain of artificial intelligence in the area of knowledge extraction from heterogeneous data. We thank the reviewers for their comments and suggestions. The authors used the Protégé editor, supported by grant GM10331601 from the National Institute of General Medical Sciences of the US National Institutes of Health.

References

1. Abadi, D., et al.: The Seattle report on database research. ACM SIGMOD Rec. **48**(4), 44–53 (2020). https://doi.org/10.1145/3385658.3385668
2. Baader, F., Horrocks, I., Lutz, C., Sattler, U.: Introduction to Description Logic. Cambridge University Press, Cambridge (2017). https://doi.org/10.1017/9781139025355
3. Ben Mahria, B., Chaker, I., Zahi, A.: A novel approach for learning ontology from relational database: from the construction to the evaluation. J. Big Data **8**(1), 1–22 (2021). https://doi.org/10.1186/s40537-021-00412-2
4. Calvanese, D., et al.: Ontop: answering SPARQL queries over relational databases. Semant. Web **8**(3), 471–487 (2017). https://doi.org/10.3233/SW-160217

5. Calvanese, D., et al.: The MASTRO system for ontology-based data access. Semant. Web **2**(1), 43–53 (2011). https://doi.org/10.3233/SW-2011-0029
6. Calvanese, D., De Giacomo, G., Lembo, D., Lenzerini, M., Poggi, A., Rosati, R.: Ontology-based database access. In: SEBD, pp. 324–331 (2007)
7. Calvanese, D., et al.: ADAMAP: automatic alignment of relational data sources using mapping patterns. In: La Rosa, M., Sadiq, S., Teniente, E. (eds.) CAiSE 2021. LNCS, vol. 12751, pp. 193–209. Springer, Cham (2021). https://doi.org/10.1007/978-3-030-79382-1_12
8. Calvanese, D., Lanti, D., De Farias, T.M., Mosca, A., Xiao, G.: Accessing scientific data through knowledge graphs with Ontop. Patterns **2**(10), 100346 (2021). https://doi.org/10.1016/j.patter.2021.100346
9. Chacon, S., Straub, B.: Pro Git. Springer, Heidelberg (2014)
10. Chen, Y.H., Lu, E.J.L., Ou, T.A.: Intelligent SPARQL query generation for natural language processing systems. IEEE Access **9**, 158638–158650 (2021). https://doi.org/10.1109/ACCESS.2021.3130667
11. Gousios, G.: The GHTorrent dataset and tool suite. In: Proceedings of the 10th Working Conference on Mining Software Repositories, MSR 2013, Piscataway, NJ, USA, pp. 233–236. IEEE Press (2013). https://doi.org/10.5555/2487085.2487132
12. Gousios, G., Spinellis, D.: GHTorrent: GitHub's data from a firehose. In: 2012 9th IEEE Working Conference on Mining Software Repositories (MSR), pp. 12–21. IEEE (2012). https://doi.org/10.1109/MSR.2012.6224294
13. Gruber, T.R.: A translation approach to portable ontology specifications. Knowl. Acquis. **5**(2), 199–220 (1993)
14. Gusenkov, A., Bukharaev, N., Birialtsev, E.: On ontology based data integration: problems and solutions. In: Journal of Physics: Conference Series, vol. 1203, p. 012059. IOP Publishing (2019). https://doi.org/10.1088/1742-6596/1203/1/012059
15. Horridge, M., Jupp, S., Moulton, G., Rector, A., Stevens, R., Wroe, C.: A practical guide to building "OWL" ontologies using protégé 4 and co-ode tools edition1. 2. The University of Manchester, vol. 107 (2009)
16. Kharlamov, E., et al.: Ontology based data access in Statoil. J. Web Semant. **44**, 3–36 (2017). https://doi.org/10.1016/j.websem.2017.05.005
17. Kharlamov, E., et al.: Semantic access to streaming and static data at Siemens. J. Web Semant. **44**, 54–74 (2017). https://doi.org/10.1016/j.websem.2017.02.001
18. Kharlamov, E., et al.: Optique: ontology-based data access platform (2015)
19. Kubitza, D.O., Böckmann, M., Graux, D.: SemanGit: a linked dataset from git. In: Ghidini, C., et al. (eds.) ISWC 2019. LNCS, vol. 11779, pp. 215–228. Springer, Cham (2019). https://doi.org/10.1007/978-3-030-30796-7_14
20. Lakzaei, B., Shamsfard, M.: Ontology learning from relational databases. Inf. Sci. **577**, 280–297 (2021). https://doi.org/10.1016/j.ins.2021.06.074
21. Lenzerini, M., Daraio, C.: Challenges, approaches and solutions in data integration for research and innovation. In: Glänzel, W., Moed, H.F., Schmoch, U., Thelwall, M. (eds.) Springer Handbook of Science and Technology Indicators. SH, pp. 397–420. Springer, Cham (2019). https://doi.org/10.1007/978-3-030-02511-3_15
22. Liang, S., Stockinger, K., de Farias, T.M., Anisimova, M., Gil, M.: Querying knowledge graphs in natural language. J. Big Data **8**(1), 1–23 (2021). https://doi.org/10.1186/s40537-020-00383-w
23. Liao, C., Wu, Y., King, G.: Research on learning OWL ontology from relational database. In: Journal of Physics: Conference Series, vol. 1176, p. 022031. IOP Publishing (2019). https://doi.org/10.1088/1742-6596/1176/2/022031

24. Lohmann, S., Link, V., Marbach, E., Negru, S.: WebVOWL: web-based visualization of ontologies. In: Lambrix, P., et al. (eds.) EKAW 2014. LNCS (LNAI), vol. 8982, pp. 154–158. Springer, Cham (2015). https://doi.org/10.1007/978-3-319-17966-7_21

25. Ma, C., Molnár, B.: Use of ontology learning in information system integration: a literature survey. In: Sitek, P., Pietranik, M., Krótkiewicz, M., Srinilta, C. (eds.) ACIIDS 2020. CCIS, vol. 1178, pp. 342–353. Springer, Singapore (2020). https://doi.org/10.1007/978-981-15-3380-8_30

26. El Massari, H., Mhammedi, S., Gherabi, N., Nasri, M.: Virtual OBDA mechanism Ontop for answering SPARQL queries over Couchbase. In: Saidi, R., El Bhiri, B., Maleh, Y., Mosallam, A., Essaaidi, M. (eds.) ICATH 2021. LNDECT, vol. 110, pp. 193–205. Springer, Cham (2022). https://doi.org/10.1007/978-3-030-94188-8_19

27. Noy, N.F., McGuinness, D.L., et al.: Ontology development 101: a guide to creating your first ontology (2001)

28. Poggi, A., Lembo, D., Calvanese, D., De Giacomo, G., Lenzerini, M., Rosati, R.: Linking data to ontologies. In: Spaccapietra, S. (ed.) Journal on Data Semantics X. LNCS, vol. 4900, pp. 133–173. Springer, Heidelberg (2008). https://doi.org/10.1007/978-3-540-77688-8_5

29. Priyatna, F., Corcho, O., Sequeda, J.: Formalisation and experiences of R2RML-based SPARQL to SQL query translation using Morph. In: Proceedings of the 23rd International Conference on World Wide Web, pp. 479–490 (2014). https://doi.org/10.1145/2566486.2567981

30. Sequeda, J.F., Miranker, D.P.: Ultrawrap: SPARQL execution on relational data. J. Web Semant. **22**, 19–39 (2013). https://doi.org/10.1016/j.websem.2013.08.002

31. Staab, S., Studer, R. (eds.): Handbook on Ontologies. IHIS, Springer, Heidelberg (2009). https://doi.org/10.1007/978-3-540-92673-3

32. Xiao, G., et al.: Ontology-based data access: a survey. In: International Joint Conferences on Artificial Intelligence (2018). https://doi.org/10.24963/ijcai.2018/777

33. Xiao, G., Ding, L., Cogrel, B., Calvanese, D.: Virtual knowledge graphs: an overview of systems and use cases. Data Intell. **1**(3), 201–223 (2019). https://doi.org/10.1162/dint_a_00011

34. Xiao, G., et al.: The virtual knowledge graph system Ontop. In: Pan, J.Z., et al. (eds.) ISWC 2020. LNCS, vol. 12507, pp. 259–277. Springer, Cham (2020). https://doi.org/10.1007/978-3-030-62466-8_17

Enabling Live SPARQL Queries over ConceptNet Using Triple Pattern Fragments

Marcelo Machado[1]([✉]), Guilherme Lima[1], Elton Soares[1], Rosario Uceda-Sosa[2], and Renato Cerqueira[1]

[1] IBM Research Brazil, Rio de Janeiro, Brazil
{mmachado,guilherme.lima,eltons}@ibm.com, rcerq@br.ibm.com
[2] IBM TJ Watson Research Center, Yorktown Heights, NY, USA
rosariou@us.ibm.com

Abstract. We describe how we used a Triple Pattern Fragments (TPF) interface and the Comunica knowledge graph querying framework to enable live SPARQL queries over ConceptNet, one of largest knowledge graphs for commonsense reasoning publicly available on the Web. Despite being a Linked Data resource, the official ConceptNet is not published in RDF and does not support SPARQL. Instead, it provides a REST-ful API for live queries, which are restricted to simple triple patterns. This limited API makes it hard for users to search for non-trivial patterns in the graph and hinders the possibility of federated queries offered by SPARQL. There have been attempts to convert ConceptNet to RDF but such proposals tend to quickly become obsolete. In this paper, we take a different route. We use TPF to expose a low-level RDF query interface to ConceptNet. This low-level interface is built on top of the ConceptNet API and can be used by TPF-compatible SPARQL engines such as Comunica. Using this approach, we were able evaluate non-trivial SPARQL queries, including federated queries, over ConceptNet on-the-fly. Our experiments showed that overhead incurred is small and can be further reduced by optimizing ConceptNet's internal edge representation. We argue that such overhead is justified by the gains in expressivity and flexibility. Moreover, the overall approach is general and can be extended to other non-RDF knowledge graphs.

Keywords: ConceptNet · RDF · Linked Data Fragments · Triple Pattern Fragments · Comunica · SPARQL

1 Introduction

ConceptNet [17] is a large public knowledge graph describing commonsense knowledge and its expression in various natural languages. It is a valuable resource for natural language processing applications in general, such as those based on word embeddings [18], and in particular for applications that seek

C. Pesquita et al. (Eds.): ESWC 2023, LNCS 13870, pp. 661–678, 2023.
https://doi.org/10.1007/978-3-031-33455-9_39

to emulate the kinds of commonsense reasoning performed by humans. These applications include question-answering [2,9], sentiment analysis [21], reading comprehension [1], image understanding [27], etc.

To access ConceptNet, users and applications can either use its live query interface or download one of its data dumps. The latter is the best approach if one is interested in processing the graph offline. However, for applications that want to query ConceptNet without ingesting the whole graph, the simplest approach is to use its live query interface (the ConceptNet API). This interface consists of a RESTful API [6] which accepts queries restricted to a single triple pattern, i.e., a combination of subject, predicate, and object. The triple pattern is matched against the components of edges in the graph and the results are returned in JSON-LD [19] format.

In this paper, we are concerned with overcoming what we think are the two main limitations of ConceptNet's live query interface: (i) its low expressivity and (ii) its lack of support for RDF [4] and SPARQL [26]. The first limitation makes it hard for users and applications to search for non-trivial patterns in the graph, while the second complicates the integration of ConceptNet into the Semantic Web ecosystem. The lack of support for SPARQL, in particular, hinders the possibility of more expressive queries and also of federated queries [15], which would allow users to match external references in ConceptNet against resources in DBpedia [8], Wikidata [25], WordNet [11], etc.

We remark that the absence of RDF support in ConceptNet is by design. It is a consequence of the choice of a relational database (PostgreSQL[1]) as its storage system. Although there have been proposals for converting ConceptNet to RDF [3,13], adopting one of these would require significant changes to its code base, including switching to a different storage system. That said, since ConceptNet 5.5.0, released in 2016, the lack of support for RDF is no longer a big issue. Version 5.5.0 changed the format of query responses to JSON-LD which can be easily converted to RDF on the client side [10]. The lack of support for SPARQL, however, is not so simple to overcome. Here is what the FAQ section of ConceptNet's documentation says about this:[2]

"*Can ConceptNet be queried using SPARQL?* No. SPARQL is computationally infeasible. Similar projects that use SPARQL have unacceptable latency and go down whenever anyone starts using them in earnest."

Indeed, SPARQL is known to be computationally intractable (query evaluation is PSPACE-complete [14]) but so is SQL (query evaluation in the relational calculus is also PSPACE-complete [22]). The problem is not with SPARQL per se but with exposing on the public Web what essentially is the query interface of the underlying database. Interestingly, the compromise reached by the designers of ConceptNet of exposing only a limited, triple pattern-based query interface is precisely the compromise advocated by the proponents of the Triple Pattern Fragments interface [24]:

---

[1] https://www.postgresql.org/.
[2] https://github.com/commonsense/conceptnet5/wiki/FAQ.

"Between the two extremes of data dumps and SPARQL endpoints lies a whole spectrum of possible (unexplored) Web interfaces. [...] Offering *triple-pattern*-based access to RDF knowledge graphs seems an interesting compromise because (i) triple patterns are the most basic building block of SPARQL queries, and (ii) servers can select triples that match a given pattern at low processing cost."

As suggested above, Triple Pattern Fragments (TPF) are a low-cost interface to RDF triples. They were introduced in the context of the Linked Data Fragments [23] framework with the goal of enabling the construction of reliable applications over public knowledge graphs. One crucial advantage of providing a TPF interface instead of a custom query interface, like ConceptNet API, is that the TPF results can be consumed by any TPF-compliant client, and this includes client-side SPARQL engines, like Comunica [20] and TPF client [24]. In this sense, TPF can be seen as a means of obtaining support for SPARQL.

This combination of TPF with a client-side SPARQL engine is exactly the approach we propose here for enabling live SPARQL queries over ConceptNet. To evaluate this proposal, we extended the TPF server Server.js[3] with a new datasource plugin[4] (released under the open-source MIT license) which allows it to communicate with the ConceptNet API. We then used the Comunica SPARQL engine [20] to create a SPARQL endpoint pointing to our modified TPF server. This setup is illustrated in Fig. 1.

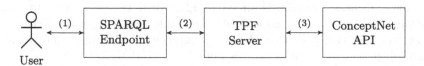

Fig. 1. The proposed approach for enabling SPARQL over ConceptNet.

We tested the viability of this setup through experiments that measured the overhead introduced at (1) and (2) in comparison to (3). The results indicate that the overhead is small and can be further reduced by simplifying the way edges are stored internally by ConceptNet. We argue that these overheads are justified by the gains in expressivity and flexibility obtained. Queries submitted at (1), for example, can contain any SPARQL feature supported by the query engine which, in the case of Comunica, includes property paths, filters, federation, etc. Also, the overall approach is general and can be extended to other non-RDF knowledge graphs.

The rest of the paper is organized as follows. Section 2 presents some background on the ConceptNet API, TPF, and Comunica. Section 3 presents our proposal and implementation. Section 4 presents the experimental evaluation and discusses its results. Section 5 discusses some related work. Finally, Sect. 6 presents our conclusions and future work.

---

[3] https://github.com/LinkedDataFragments/Server.js.
[4] https://github.com/IBM/tpf-conceptnet-datasource.

2   Background

2.1   ConceptNet API

ConceptNet [17] is a knowledge graph for commonsense reasoning that connects words and phrases in various languages using relations like "is a", "used for", "part of", etc. It originated from the MIT Media Lab's Open Mind Common Sense (OMCS) project [16] and has since been expanded with facts from many other resources, including Wiktionary[5], WordNet [11], DBpedia [8], etc.

The easiest way to query ConceptNet is through its public RESTful API. The latest version of the API (5.8.1) accepts simple requests like:

https://api.conceptnet.io/query?start=/c/en/cat&end=/c/en/milk

This particular request asks for all edges in the graph whose start node is "cat" (/c/en/cat) and end node is "milk" (/c/en/milk). Its response is a JSON-LD document which, among other things, contains this edge:

```
{ "@id":    "/a/[/r/Desires/,/c/en/cat/,/c/en/milk/]",
  "start": { "@id": "/c/en/cat",  ... },
  "rel":   { "@id": "/r/Desires", ... },
  "end":   { "@id": "/c/en/milk", ... }, ... }
```

This edge asserts that "cat" is related via "desires" to "milk". As illustrated here, every ConceptNet edge is directed and consists of a start node (start), a relation (rel), and an end node (end). The edge also has an id (derived from start, rel, and end) and can contain extra information like its weight (reliability measure), provenance (list of sources), etc.

The ConceptNet API supports essentially two kinds of queries:

1. *Start-rel-end queries.* These are queries in which any of the parameters start, rel, and end are given. The previous query is an example of such a query. It sets the parameter start to "cat" and end to "milk", which instructs the API to search for any edges leaving "cat" and reaching "milk".
2. *Node-other queries.* These are queries in which any of the parameters node or other are given. If only node or only other is given, the API searches for edges where the start or end of the edge matches the parameter. For example, the query ?node=/c/en/cat asks for edges where the start or end node is "cat". If both node and other are given, the API searches for edges where the start and end match the parameters regardless of their order. For example, the query ?node=/c/en/cat&other=/c/en/animal searches for any edges connecting "cat" and "animal" in either direction.

Start-rel-end queries can be seen as equivalent to SPARQL queries that contain a single triple-pattern, while node-other queries correspond to disjunctive SPARQL queries (i.e., queries that use the UNION operator to test for a match in either of the directions).

---

[5] https://en.wiktionary.org/.

By default, the ConceptNet API returns at most 50 edges per request. This number can be increased up to 1000 using the `limit` parameter. When the number of edges exceeds the limit, the extra results are put in separate pages which can be accessed either by setting the `offset` parameter in the request or by using the "next page" link returned at the end the JSON-LD response.

2.2   Triple Pattern Fragments

Triple Pattern Fragments (TPF) [24] are a lightweight interface to RDF graphs. They are part of the Linked Data Fragments (LDF) [23] initiative and were proposed as an intermediate alternative to RDF data dumps and SPARQL endpoints. LDF itself is a framework for the conceptual analysis of Linked Data interfaces. According to LDF, any such interface publishes only parts, or *(linked data) fragments*, of a given knowledge graph. These fragments are considered the "units of response" of the interface and are assumed to consist of three things:

1. *Data*: a subset of the triples of the graph;
2. *Metadata*: triples describing the data; and
3. *Controls*: links and forms that can be used to retrieve other fragments of the same or other knowledge graphs.

For example, a data dump of a knowledge graph can be described as single linked data fragment where the data is the whole content of the dump, the metadata consists of things like version, author, etc., and the controls are empty. Similarly, the response to a SPARQL CONSTRUCT query can be seen as a fragment where the data are the resulting triples, the metadata is empty, and the controls are any parameters used to paginate the result, such as limits and offsets.

A TPF interface provides access to an RDF graph based on a single triple-pattern. A *triple-pattern* is a pattern of the form (s, p, o) where s, p, and o are either fixed values (URIs or literals) or anonymous variables. When given a triple-pattern, the TPF interface responds with a fragment in which (i) the data are triples in the graph that match the pattern; (ii) the metadata are an estimate of the total number such triples; and (iii) the controls are a hypermedia form that allows clients to retrieve other fragments matching the same pattern.

Some popular knowledge graphs, like DBpedia [8] and Wikidata [25], already provide TPF interfaces. (Other public TPF interfaces can be found here[6].) Take the Wikidata TPF interface, for example. We can query it using a request like:

https://query.wikidata.org/bigdata/ldf?predicate=wdt:P31&object=wd:Q5

This request asks for every triple in Wikidata whose predicate component is `wdt:P31` (instance of) and object component is `wd:Q5` (human). That is, it selects the triples matching the pattern "$(s, \mathtt{wdt} : \mathtt{P31}, \mathtt{wd} : \mathtt{Q5})$" for any value of s. In other words, the triples such that subject s is an instance of human.

---

[6] https://linkeddatafragments.org/data/.

The response to this specific request is a single linked data fragment containing usually 100 triples matching the pattern. For instance, if you open the above URI in a Web browser, an HTML page with the matched triples will be shown. At the bottom of the page, you will see links (controls) to other pages (fragments) which contain the rest of the result. The actual format of the response depends on the value of the "Accept" header provided to the server in the HTTP request. This can be set to any of the popular RDF serialization formats, such as Turtle and JSON-LD.

Some TPF interfaces also support quad-patterns of the form (s, p, o, g) which take an additional parameter g specifying a named graph of an RDF dataset. If not set, g is assumed to be the default graph.

The advantage of TPF over other Linked Data interfaces is that it offers some query capability while being extremely lightweight. It is more convenient than a data dump and, it can be argued, it provides a more reasonable Web API than SPARQL in the sense that it exposes only a limited interface to the under-lying database. A further advantage has to do with caching. Because of their restricted syntax TPF requests are more cache-friendly than SPARQL requests. For instance, just by looking at the requested URI, it is straightforward for an HTTP proxy to determine whether two TPF requests are identical. The same cannot be said about SPARQL where there are many different ways to write essentially the same query.

2.3 Comunica

Comunica [20] is an advanced knowledge graph querying framework written in JavaScript and released under the open-source MIT license.[7] It is not tied to any particular storage system and can even run in the browser. Rather than functioning as a query engine itself, Comunica is a meta query engine that allows the creation of query engines by providing a set of modules that can be wired together in a flexible manner. The biggest differentiator of Comunica, however, is its support for federated queries over heterogeneous interfaces in which one can evaluate a federated SPARQL query over multiple interfaces, including TPF interfaces, SPARQL endpoints, and data dumps.

Comunica has full support for SPARQL 1.0 and implements a large subset of SPARQL 1.1[8]. It also has numerous other features, including support for other query languages (i.e., GraphQL), reasoning, etc. In this paper, however, we use Comunica mainly to evaluate simple (but non-trivial) SPARQL queries over our custom TPF interface which acts as a proxy to the ConceptNet API.

3 Proposal and Implementation

Our proposal to enable SPARQL queries over ConceptNet was summarized in Fig. 1 of Sect. 1. The idea is to build a TPF interface on top of the ConceptNet

---

[7] https://github.com/comunica/comunica.
[8] https://comunica.dev/docs/query/advanced/specifications/.

API. Then use a TPF-compatible SPARQL engine to create a SPARQL endpoint pointing to the TPF interface. A more detailed view of this proposal is given in Fig. 2.

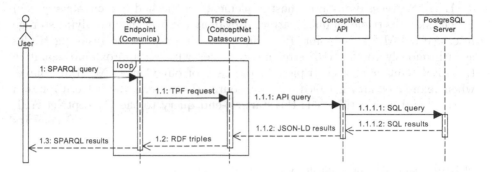

Fig. 2. The proposed approach for enabling SPARQL over ConceptNet. (Detailed)

To evaluate a SPARQL query over ConceptNet, the user sends a request to the SPARQL endpoint (1). This triggers one or more (triple-pattern) requests to our custom TPF server (1.1) each of which is translated into an equivalent (start-rel-end) query and sent to the ConceptNet API (1.1.1). As we mentioned previously, ConceptNet uses PostgreSQL as its storage system. So, each API query gives rise to one or more SQL queries (1.1.1.1) which are resolved by the PostgreSQL server. The other direction is similar: PostgreSQL's results are translated to JSON-LD (1.1.2), then to RDF triples (1.2), and finally to SPARQL results (1.3) which are delivered to the user.

The key element here is the TPF server. It needs to convert TPF queries, results, and controls into equivalent ConceptNet queries, results, and controls. In our case, we chose the TPF server Server.js.[9] We extended it with a new datasource that handles the input-output conversion and communication with the ConceptNet API. As the TPF-enabled SPARQL engine, we chose Comunica [20].

The rest of this section describes the challenges we had to overcome to implement the TPF protocol over the ConceptNet API. We describe two versions of this implementation. The first version, which we call *vanilla*, makes only minor changes to ConceptNet itself. The second version, which we call *simplified*, exposes the same API as the vanilla version but, in an attempt to speed up query evaluation, changes the way ConceptNet edges are represented in PostgreSQL.

3.1   The ConceptNet TPF Datasource

To create a TPF interface for ConceptNet, we extended the TPF server Server.js with a new datasource, called *ConceptNet Datasource* (MIT license).[10] In the

---

[9] https://github.com/LinkedDataFragments/Server.js.

[10] https://github.com/IBM/tpf-conceptnet-datasource.

Server.js architecture, the datasource is the component responsible for generating a stream of RDF triples from a given triple- or quad-pattern. The Server.js distribution comes with built-in datasources for generating triples from SPARQL endpoints and RDF files (including compressed HDT files [5]).

Every Server.js datasource must implement the method _executeQuery(p, s) which takes the triple- or quad-pattern p, evaluates it over the underlying storage interface (SPARQL endpoint, RDF file, etc.), and writes the resulting triples asynchronously to the RDF stream s together with an approximate count of the total number of such triples. In the case of our ConceptNet Datasource, when _executeQuery is called, the datasource (i) converts the pattern p into a start-rel-end query; (ii) sends the start-rel-end query to the ConceptNet API; (iii) awaits for the API's JSON-LD response and when it arrives (iv) converts the edges in the response into triples; and finally (v) writes the resulting triples into the stream s. The datasource also writes into s's metadata the total number of triples that will be eventually produced by the query.

We had to solve two issues to implement the behavior we have just described. The first one was the conversion of ConceptNet edges into RDF triples. Concept-Net uses a heavily reified representation for edges which, besides the endpoints (start and end) and label (rel), contain information like weight, license, list of sources (provenance), etc. This means that the standard conversion of a JSON-LD edge to RDF produces a complex result, usually consisting of many triples. Because this would complicate the format of the SPARQL queries, and because in this paper we are mainly interested in the edge data (instead of its metadata), we decided to extract just the ids of the start, rel, and end parts of the edge and, when necessary, make them into valid URIs by prefixing the namespace "http://conceptnet.io/". So, for example, the JSON-LD edge listed at the beginning of Sect. 2.1, which connects "cat" and "milk" via "desires", is translated into the RDF triple:

```
<http://conceptnet.io/c/en/cat>
<http://conceptnet.io/r/Desires>
<http://conceptnet.io/c/en/milk> .
```

The other issue we had to deal with while implementing the ConceptNet Datasource was obtaining the edge count of ConceptNet API queries. This count is returned by the TPF server as metadata and is used by TPF clients, such as Comunica, to optimize their query plan. Currently, the only way to obtain this information is by going through all the pages of the response adding up their edge counts. This of course is impractical. What we did then was to extend the ConceptNet API with a new *count* call which takes a query and returns the total number of matched edges (computed by PostgreSQL). For instance, a call to this count endpoint with the query start=/c/en/cat will trigger a SQL query in PostgreSQL that uses the COUNT function to count rows from the table of edges where the column start contains the string identifier /c/en/cat. The syntax of the count call is the same as that of the regular query call. The only difference is that its target URI ends in /query/count instead of /query.

The configuration we have just described is what we call *vanilla*. It consists of the ConceptNet TPF Datasource running on top of the original ConceptNet API extended with the /query/count API call. The other configuration or version we consider is the *simplified* version, which we describe next.

3.2   The Simplified Version

In the simplified version, the ConceptNet TPF Datasource runs on top of an optimized version of the ConceptNet API.[11] The syntax of this optimized version is the same as that of the vanilla API, i.e., it still consists of /query and /query/count calls, but the calls themselves are implemented differently. They use an alternative database table (actually, a materialized view) to obtain edge information. Before detailing the contents of this alternative table and the advantages of using it, we need to describe the layout of the tables involved in the process of query evaluation in the original, vanilla ConceptNet API.

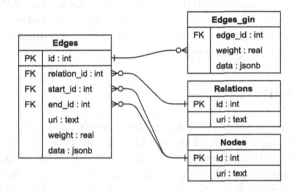

Fig. 3. Database tables involved in query evaluation in vanilla ConceptNet.

The entity-relationship diagram of the vanilla database tables is depicted in Fig. 3. The tables *Edges* and *Edges_gin* store edge data, *Relations* stores relation (predicate) data, and *Nodes* stores node data. The important thing to note is the "data" field present in *Edges* and *Edges_gin*. This field stores a JSON object similar to the one presented in Sect. 2.1 and is the field used for matching the query parameters in the vanilla version of /query and /query/count API calls. More specifically, in the vanilla version, queries are evaluated by first joining *Edges* and *Edges_gin* and then searching for the requested pattern within the JSON object stored in the data field. These JSON objects are indexed with GIN indices[12] which allows for efficient matching over composite objects using the containment operator "@>".

---

[11] https://github.com/IBM/tpf-conceptnet-datasource/tree/main/simplified-conceptnet5.

[12] https://www.postgresql.org/docs/current/datatype-json.html.

The reason for using this JSON-based matching approach, instead of simply matching the URIs in the *Nodes* and *Relations* tables, is that the vanilla API supports partial matches. For example, using the vanilla API, if we ask for edges matching `?start=/c/en/cat` the API returns not only edges whose start node is `/c/en/cat` but also any edge whose start node id is *prefixed* by `/c/en/cat` including, for example, `/c/en/cat/n/wn/animal`. The idea here is that `/c/en/cat/n/wn/animal`, i.e., the term "cat" interpreted as the noun (`/n`) used to name an animal (`/animal`) according to WordNet (`/wn`), is a more specific, disambiguated version of the term `/c/en/cat` ("cat").

In the simplified version, we wanted to avoid this partial matching feature for two reasons. First, because it is not compatible with the exact URI matches performed by SPARQL, and second because it complicates query evaluation. Thus, assuming that the support for partial matches was not desirable, we copied the contents of the data field to the columns of a new table, actually a materialized view, called *Simplified_edges*. This view is essentially the union of *Edges*, *Nodes* and *Relations* with indexes in the columns "start_uri", "rel_uri", and "end_uri". We then implemented simplified versions of the API calls `/query` and `/query/count` which use the *Simplified_edges* view instead of the original tables. A further advantage of this approach is that it eliminates the need for join operations during query evaluation.

4   Evaluation

In this section, we describe the experimental evaluation of our proposal. Our main goal was to measure the overhead in query evaluation time introduced by the TPF Server (extended with our ConceptNet TPF datasource) and by the SPARQL endpoint (Comunica) in comparison to the ConceptNet API.

We did two experiments, A and B, which dealt with the evaluation of start-rel-end and node-other queries, respectively. For each experiment, a pool of queries was generated by (i) selecting random triples in ConceptNet, (ii) masking some of their components, and (iii) counting the associated number of matches. We then picked enough queries from the pool to obtain a uniform distribution of queries with match-counts ranging from 1 to an upper limit of 12K matches in the vanilla ConceptNet.

The setup of both experiments was the same. We used an OpenShift cluster to run the following:

1. A private instance of ConceptNet[13] (API plus PostgreSQL server) with the modifications discussed in Sect. 3, deployed with 20 GiB of memory.
2. One instance of the TPF server Server.js[14] extended with our ConceptNet TPF datasource, deployed 24 GiB of memory. This TPF instance provided two endpoints: a vanilla TPF pointing to the vanilla ConceptNet API and a simplified TPF pointing to the simplified API.

---

[13] https://github.com/commonsense/ConceptNet5 (fda1b39, Sep. 7, 2021.).

[14] https://github.com/LinkedDataFragments/Server.js (b8cc6e3, Nov. 11, 2022.).

3. Two instances of Comunica[15], each deployed with 8 GiB of memory; one instance (vanilla Comunica) pointing to the vanilla TPF endpoint, and the other (simplified Comunica) pointing to the simplified TPF endpoint.
4. One instance of the script used to run the queries and collect the results.

To minimize the influence of network conditions, we ran the evaluation script in the same cluster as the servers, and we turned off the caches of the TPF server and Comunica. The numbers below constitute thus a worst-case scenario.

Both experiments used a fixed page size with 100 results per page. As remarked in [24], pages should be kept reasonably sized to not overload clients. We chose the value of 100 because it is default page size used by the TPF server Server.js. Note that the page size also determines the number of requests necessary to consume the full response of a query. For example, if a query produces 1000 results, with a page size of 100 it takes 10 HTTP requests (10 pages) to consume all of its results.

Next, we describe Experiments A and B in detail and discuss their results. At the end of the section, we present examples of more expressive SPARQL queries and discuss informally their evaluation using the same experimental setup.

4.1   Experiments A and B

For Experiment A, we used the method described above to generate 432 random start-rel-end queries with results ranging from 1 to about 10K matched edges in the vanilla ConceptNet. We then translated each of these queries into equivalent TPF and SPARQL queries and evaluated each version of a same query using both the vanilla configuration and the simplified configuration. The aggregated results of 5 runs of each query is shown in Fig. 4.

For Experiment B, we generated 382 random node-other queries with results ranging from 1 to about 10K matched edges in the vanilla ConceptNet. Node-other queries cannot be represented directly in TPF but can be emulated by disjunctive SPARQL queries, i.e., using the UNION operator to match the pattern in either direction of the edge. So, for Experiment B, we translated each query into an equivalent (disjunctive) SPARQL query and, as before, evaluated the versions of a same query using both the vanilla configuration and the simplified configuration. The aggregated results of 5 runs of the 382 random node-other queries are shown in Fig. 5.

Analysis. We start by analyzing the overhead of the TPF queries in Experiment A. As shown in Table 1, the average (median) difference between the evaluation time of vanilla TPF vs vanilla ConceptNet in Experiment A is 6.2s, and between simplified TPF vs vanilla ConceptNet is 5.6s. In other words, the simplification discussed in Sect. 3.2 contributed to an average reduction (delta) of 0.6s in the evaluation time of TPF queries.

---

[15] https://github.com/comunica/comunica (e4b91d5, Nov. 25, 2022.).

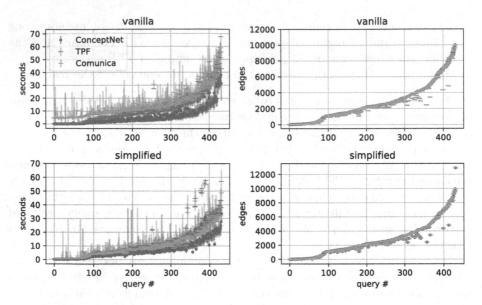

Fig. 4. *Experiment A*: Aggregated results of 5 runs of 432 random start-rel-end queries. The markers indicate the median of the 5 runs. The "query #" axis represents each one of the 432 queries sorted by the number of edges they return. Evaluation time (left) vs edge count (right). Vanilla ConceptNet API, TPF, Comunica (above) vs simplified ConceptNet API, TPF, Comunica (below).

Table 1. Average (median) overhead versus vanilla ConceptNet.

	TPF (A)	Comunica (A)	Comunica (B)
Vanilla	6.2s	9.5s	4.4s
Simplified	5.6s	3.6s	3.1s
delta	0.6s	5.9s	1.3s

Consider now the overhead of Comunica queries in Experiments A and B. The average difference between the evaluation time of vanilla Comunica vs vanilla ConceptNet is 9.5s in A and 4.4s in B, while the average difference between simplified Comunica vs vanilla ConceptNet is 3.6s in A and 3.1s in B. Hence, the proposed simplification seems to have contributed to an average reduction (delta) of 5.9s in the evaluation time of start-rel-end queries and of 1.3s for node-other queries using Comunica. This is a significant reduction considering that the average time of vanilla Comunica queries is 15.6s in A and 13.6s in B.

Surprisingly, the proposed simplification seems to affect more the first request performed by Comunica than the others. This first request is an empty request which Comunica uses to determine the type of the underlying endpoint. We noticed that this empty request, which is essentially a triple-pattern in which the three components are variables, takes about 3 times longer in the vanilla

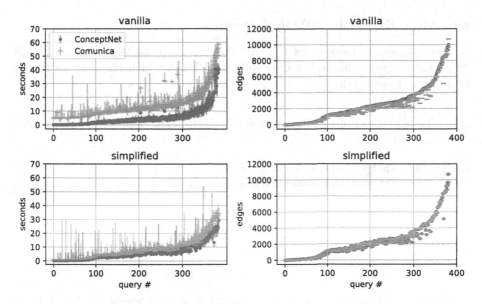

Fig. 5. *Experiment B*: Aggregated results of 5 runs of 382 random node-other queries. The markers indicate the median of the 5 runs. The "query #" axis represents each one of the 382 queries sorted by the number of edges they return. Evaluation time (left) vs edge count (right). Vanilla ConceptNet API, Comunica (above) vs simplified ConceptNet API, Comunica (below).

API than in the simplified API. To make matters worse, Comunica not even uses the results of this request, only its metadata. This suggests further paths for optimization. For example, we could extend the ConceptNet API to handle empty requests in an optimized manner; or we could modify Comunica to avoid such requests altogether by hard-coding in it the service metadata.

We conclude this analysis section by explaining two oddities in Figs. 4 and 5. The attentive reader might have noticed that Comunica sometimes seems to beat the ConceptNet API. This of course is impossible, as its requests should take at least the same time as those of the underlying API. The explanation is that Comunica uses parallel requests, while the results shown for ConceptNet and TPF assume serial requests. That said, even if the ConceptNet and TPF numbers could have been reduced via parallel requests, the overall improvement induced by our proposed simplification would still apply. Also, the support for parallel requests should count as a feature of the client and might not always be available (e.g., it is not supported by the TPF server).

The second oddity concerns the edge counts for the vanilla Comunica in Figs. 4 and 5, which seem to be smaller than those of ConceptNet for some queries. This is due to the partial match feature of vanilla ConceptNet which was explained in Sect. 3.2. Some vanilla queries return URIs which do not match the URIs in the pattern exactly. Different than the TPF server, Comunica always checks the returned URIs and discard those not matching the pattern exactly. This explains the difference in the number of results for some queries.

4.2   More Expressive SPARQL Queries

We now present some queries that illustrate non-trivial features of SPARQL which are not available in the ConceptNet API but which one gets for free by adopting our approach.

Q1. The first query illustrates the use of multiple triple patterns and regular-expression filters:

```
prefix cnc: <http://conceptnet.io/c/en/>
prefix cnr: <http://conceptnet.io/r/>
select ?x ?y where {
  cnc:cat cnr:Desires ?x.
  ?x cnr:Antonym ?y.
  filter(regex(str(?y), "ing$"))
} limit 10
```

It selects the terms x and y such that "cat" desires x which is an antonym of y and y ends in "ing". This query takes about 5s to execute in our experimental setup using the simplified Comunica endpoint and produces results like "(eat, drinking)", "(sleep, working)", etc.

Q2. The second query illustrates the use of property paths:

```
select ?x ?y where {
  cnc:chair (cnr:MadeOf/cnr:UsedFor) ?x.
  ?x cnr:IsA* ?y.
} limit 10
```

It selects the terms x and y such that "chair" is made of something which is used for x which itself is a type of y. This query takes about 20s to run using the simplified Comunica interface and includes among its results the tuple "(burning, chemical_reaction)".

Q3. The third and last query illustrates the use of federation:

```
prefix wd: <http://www.wikidata.org/entity/>
prefix wdt: <http://www.wikidata.org/prop/direct/>
select ?x where {
  cnc:police cnr:ExternalURL ?x.
  service <http://query.wikidata.org/sparql> {
    ?x wdt:P31 wd:Q5741069.
  }
} limit 10
```

This query selects the entities x in Wikidata such that x is listed as an external reference associated to the term "police" in ConceptNet and, according to Wikidata, is an instance of "rock group" (wd:Q5741069). The answer in this case is the Wikidata entity "The Police" (wd:Q178095). It takes about 10s to run this query using our simplified Comunica interface. Note that to evaluate it Comunica needs to query the public SPARQL endpoint of Wikidata.

5   Related Work

An early attempt to reconcile ConceptNet and the Semantic Web is [7]. In it the authors discuss the feasibility of an RDF encoding of ConceptNet (then version 3.0) and present a conceptual model of its core relations using OWL (the Web Ontology Language). No implementation or experimental evaluation is provided.

A more recent proposal for converting ConceptNet to RDF is [13]. It is an expansion of ConceptOnto [12], an upper ontology based on ConceptNet. In [13], the authors present an algorithm for extracting edges from ConceptNet 5 data dumps and for converting these edges to RDF. They also discuss use cases involving SPARQL queries, but these are assumed to run over the RDF files resulting from the offline conversion of the data dumps.

Yet another proposal for converting ConceptNet to RDF is [3]. In it the authors present a concise conversion model which attempts simplify the encoding proposed in [13]. They also discuss use cases and present illustrative SPARQL queries which, again, are assumed to be evaluated against the RDF files resulting from the offline conversion of ConceptNet's data dumps.

All of the above proposals have in common the fact that they operate over static data dumps of ConceptNet. The RDF files they produce quickly become obsolete and any attempt to use these files for live queries would require solving the same kind of problems which are already solved by the official ConceptNet API. To the best of our knowledge, our proposal is the first to expose a live RDF interface to ConceptNet which is built on top of the official interface and which supports SPARQL.

6   Conclusion

In this paper, we presented an approach for enabling live SPARQL queries over ConceptNet. Our approach is based on Linked Data Fragments and consists in building a TPF interface on top of the ConceptNet API. As we discussed, this requires only minimal changes to ConceptNet, and with such an interface in place one can then use TPF-compatible engines to evaluate SPARQL queries directly over the ConceptNet server. The experiments we did showed that the overhead incurred is small and can be further reduced by changing the way edges are represented internally by ConceptNet. Also, as discussed in Sect. 4, there are further opportunities for improvement if one takes into account the peculiarities of the SPARQL engine used.

In future work, we intend to investigate the possibility of making Comunica talk directly to the ConceptNet API, instead of having to go through a TPF interface. This could be done using a Comunica plugin developed for this purpose. Comunica adopts a plugin-based architecture and comes with built-in plugins for reading triples from standard sources like a TPF server. We could develop a custom input plugin that reads triples directly from a given ConceptNet endpoint (using the ConceptNet API) eliminating thus the need of the TPF layer.

References

1. Cai, H., Zhao, F., Jin, H.: Commonsense knowledge construction with concept and pretrained model. In: Zhao, X., Yang, S., Wang, X., Li, J. (eds.) WISA 2022. LNCS, vol. 13579, pp. 40–51. Springer, Cham (2022). https://doi.org/10.1007/978-3-031-20309-1_4

2. Chen, H., Trouve, A., Murakami, K.J., Fukuda, A.: An introduction to question answering with ConceptRDF. In: Proceedings of 2nd IEEE International Conference on Computational Intelligence and Applications (ICCIA), Beijing, China, 8–11 September 2017, pp. 537–541. IEEE (2017). https://doi.org/10.1109/CIAPP.2017.8167275

3. Chen, H., Trouve, A., Murakami, K.J., Fukuda, A.: A concise conversion model for improving the RDF expression of ConceptNet knowledge base. In: Lu, H., Xu, X. (eds.) Artificial Intelligence and Robotics. SCI, vol. 752, pp. 213–221. Springer, Cham (2018). https://doi.org/10.1007/978-3-319-69877-9_23

4. Cyganiak, R., Wood, D., Lanthaler, M.: RDF 1.1 concepts and abstract syntax. W3C recommendation, W3C (2014). http://www.w3.org/TR/2014/REC-rdf11-concepts-20140225/

5. Fernández, J.D., Martínez-Prieto, M.A., Gutiérrez, C., Polleres, A., Arias, M.: Binary RDF representation for publication and exchange (HDT). J. Web Semant. **19**, 22–41 (2013). https://doi.org/10.1016/j.websem.2013.01.002

6. Fielding, R.T.: Architectural styles and the design of network-based software architectures. Ph.D. thesis, University of California, Irvine (2000)

7. Grassi, M., Piazza, F.: Towards an RDF encoding of ConceptNet. In: Liu, D., Zhang, H., Polycarpou, M., Alippi, C., He, H. (eds.) ISNN 2011. LNCS, vol. 6677, pp. 558–565. Springer, Heidelberg (2011). https://doi.org/10.1007/978-3-642-21111-9_63

8. Lehmann, J., et al.: DBpedia - a large-scale, multilingual knowledge base extracted from Wikipedia. Semant. Web **6**, 167–195 (2015). https://doi.org/10.3233/SW-140134

9. Lin, B.Y., Wu, Z., Yang, Y., Lee, D.H., Ren, X.: RiddleSense: reasoning about riddle questions featuring linguistic creativity and commonsense knowledge. In: Findings of the Association for Computational Linguistics: ACL-IJCNLP 2021, pp. 1504–1515. ACL (2021). https://doi.org/10.18653/v1/2021.findings-acl.131

10. Longley, D., Kellogg, G., Lanthaler, M., Sporny, M., Lindström, N.: JSON-LD 1.1 processing algorithms and API. W3C recommendation, W3C (2020). https://www.w3.org/TR/json-ld11-api/
11. Miller, G.A.: WordNet: a lexical database for english. Commun. ACM **38**(11), 39–41 (1995). https://doi.org/10.1145/219717.219748
12. Najmi, E., Hashmi, K., Malik, Z., Rezgui, A., Khanz, H.U.: ConceptOnto: an upper ontology based on ConceptNet. In: Proceedings of the IEEE/ACS 11th International Conference on Computer Systems and Applications (AICCSA), pp. 366–372. IEEE (2014). https://doi.org/10.1109/AICCSA.2014.7073222
13. Najmi, E., Malik, Z., Hashmi, K., Rezgui, A.: ConceptRDF: an RDF presentation of ConceptNet knowledge base. In: Proceedings of 7th International Conference on Information and Communication Systems (ICICS), pp. 145–150. IEEE (2016)
14. Pérez, J., Arenas, M., Gutierrez, C.: Semantics and complexity of SPARQL. ACM Trans. Database Syst. **34**(3), 16:1–16:45 (2009). https://doi.org/10.1145/1567274.1567278
15. Prud'hommeaux, E., Buil-Aranda, C.: SPARQL 1.1 federated query. W3C recommendation, W3C (2013). https://www.w3.org/TR/2013/REC-sparql11-federated-query-20130321/
16. Singh, P.: The public acquisition of commonsense knowledge. In: Proceedings of the AAAI Spring Symposium: Acquiring (and Using) Linguistic (and World) Knowledge for Information Access. AAAI (2002)
17. Speer, R., Chin, J., Havasi, C.: ConceptNet 5.5: an open multilingual graph of general knowledge. In: Proceedings of the 31st AAAI Conference on Artificial Intelligence (AAAI-17), San Francisco, California, USA, 4–9 February 2017, pp. 4444–4451. AAAI (2017)
18. Speer, R., Lowry-Duda, J.: ConceptNet at SemEval-2017 task 2: extending word embeddings with multilingual relational knowledge. In: Proceedings of the 11th International Workshop on Semantic Evaluation (SemEval-2017), Vancouver, Canada, August 2017, pp. 85–89. ACL (2017). https://doi.org/10.18653/v1/S17-2008
19. Sporny, M., Longley, D., Kellogg, G., Lanthaler, M., Champin, P.A., Lindström, N.: JSON-LD 1.1: a JSON-based serialization for linked data. W3C recommendation, W3C (2020). https://www.w3.org/TR/json-ld/
20. Taelman, R., Van Herwegen, J., Vander Sande, M., Verborgh, R.: Comunica: a modular SPARQL query engine for the web. In: Vrandečić, D., et al. (eds.) ISWC 2018. LNCS, vol. 11137, pp. 239–255. Springer, Cham (2018). https://doi.org/10.1007/978-3-030-00668-6_15
21. Tamilselvam, S., Nagar, S., Mishra, A., Dey, K.: Graph based sentiment aggregation using ConceptNet ontology. In: Proceedings of the 8th International Joint Conference on Natural Language Processing, Taipei, Taiwan, November 2017 (Volume 1: Long Papers), pp. 525–535. Asian Federation of Natural Language Processing (2017)
22. Vardi, M.Y.: The complexity of relational query languages (extended abstract). In: Proceedings of the 14th Annual ACM Symposium on Theory of Computing (STOC 1982), San Francisco, California, USA, May 1982, pp. 137–146. ACM (1982). https://doi.org/10.1145/800070.802186
23. Verborgh, R., Sande, M.V., Colpaert, P., Coppens, S., Mannens, E., de Walle, R.V.: Web-scale querying through linked data fragments. In: Proceedings of the Workshop on Linked Data on the Web co-located with the 23rd International World Wide Web Conference (WWW 2014), Seoul, Korea, 8 April 2014. CEUR-WS.org (2014)

24. Verborgh, R., et al.: Triple pattern fragments: a low-cost knowledge graph interface for the web. J. Web Semantics **37–38**, 184–206 (2016). https://doi.org/10.1016/j.websem.2016.03.003
25. Vrandečić, D., Krötzsch, M.: WikiData: a free collaborative knowledgebase. Commun. ACM **57**(10), 78–85 (2014). https://doi.org/10.1145/2629489
26. W3C SPARQL working group: SPARQL 1.1 overview. W3C recommendation, W3C (2013). http://www.w3.org/TR/2013/REC-sparql11-overview-20130321/
27. Ye, S., Xie, Y., Chen, D., Xu, Y., Yuan, L., Zhu, C., Liao, J.: Improving commonsense in vision-language models via knowledge graph riddles (2022). https://doi.org/10.48550/ARXIV.2211.16504

Evaluation of a Representative Selection of SPARQL Query Engines Using Wikidata

An Ngoc Lam[✉][iD], Brian Elvesæter[iD], and Francisco Martin-Recuerda[iD]

SINTEF AS, Forskningsveien 1, 0373 Oslo, Norway
{an.lam,brian.elvesater,francisco.martin-recuerda}@sintef.no

Abstract. In this paper, we present an evaluation of the performance of five representative RDF triplestores, including GraphDB, Jena Fuseki, Neptune, RDFox, and Stardog, and one experimental SPARQL query engine, QLever. We compare importing time, loading time, and exporting time using a complete version of the knowledge graph Wikidata, and we also evaluate query performances using 328 queries defined by Wikidata users. To put this evaluation into context with respect to previous evaluations, we also analyze the query performances of these systems using a prominent synthetic benchmark: SP^2Bench. We observed that most of the systems we considered for the evaluation were able to complete the execution of almost all the queries defined by Wikidata users before the timeout we established. We noticed, however, that the time needed by most systems to import and export Wikidata might be longer than required in some industrial and academic projects, where information is represented, enriched, and stored using different representation means.

Keywords: RDF Triplestores · Knowledge Graphs · SPARQL Benchmarks · SP^2Bench · Wikidata

1 Introduction

Wikidata [34] is a collaboratively edited multilingual knowledge graph hosted by the Wikimedia Foundation. Wikidata is becoming a prominent software artifact in academia and industry, and offers a broad collection of terms and definitions that can improve data understandability, integration, and exchange. Wikidata is stored as an RDF [35] graph that can be queried with the SPARQL language [36]. With more than 16 billion triples and 100 million defined terms, as the size of the knowledge graph continuously increases, it might be challenging for state-of-the-art triplestores to import, export, and query Wikidata. This is also acknowledged by the Wikimedia Foundation, which is looking for alternatives to replace Blazegraph [11], an open-source triplestore no longer in development [39].

To investigate how efficiently RDF triplestores can handle Wikidata, in this paper, we present an evaluation of the performance of five representative RDF triplestores, including Ontotext GraphDB [20], Apache Jena Fuseki [6], Amazon

© The Author(s), under exclusive license to Springer Nature Switzerland AG 2023
C. Pesquita et al. (Eds.): ESWC 2023, LNCS 13870, pp. 679–696, 2023.
https://doi.org/10.1007/978-3-031-33455-9_40

Neptune [2], OST RDFox [24], and Stardog [31], and one experimental SPARQL query engine - QLever [9]. We compare importing, loading, and exporting time using a complete version of Wikidata, and we also evaluate query performances using 328 queries defined by Wikidata users.

Due to budget limitations, we limited our evaluation to only six representative tools. However, we tried to ensure a diverse selection. For instance, GraphDB, Neptune, RDFox, and Stardog are commercial applications, whereas QLever and Jena Fuseki are not. Neptune is based on Blazegraph, and it is available as a native cloud-based service. RDFox is an in-memory triplestore, while the others are persistent. QLever and Jena Fuseki are in the pool of tools considered by Wikimedia Foundation to replace Blazegraph. So we thought both could represent a good baseline for our study. After some deliberation, we also decided to conduct an evaluation of the six triplestores using the synthetic benchmark SP^2Bench [28], which has strong theoretical foundations and a main focus on query optimization, also very relevant in our analysis of query performances of SPARQL engines using Wikidata.

In our evaluation using a full version of Wikidata and large datasets generated by SP^2Bench, we study the query execution plan with query profiling information to understand better the difference in the performance of the triplestores on the same query. The ultimate goal is to obtain a thorough understanding of the impact of SPARQL features on the performance and confirm common best practices in the design of SPARQL queries. We also consider import and export time. As service-oriented and decentralized architecture has become a popular design for software infrastructure in recent years, importing and exporting performance may be critical to enable efficient data transformation and exchange, especially for big data applications (e.g., big data pipelines or Machine Learning pipelines). Therefore, it is important to optimize importing and exporting functionality to avoid bottlenecks in the execution of such applications.

Despite not considering the evaluation of the concurrent execution of SPARQL queries, we observed that most of the evaluated systems could complete the execution of almost all queries defined by Wikidata users before the timeout. However, most of them required a longer time to import and export a full Wikidata version than expected in many industrial and academic projects, where information is represented, enriched, and stored using a diverse selection of applications offering different representation means.

To help interested readers to dive into the details of this evaluation, all scripts, data, and results have been uploaded to an open repository [15]. The remainder of the paper is structured as follows. Section 2 discusses related work. Section 3 describes the evaluation setup. Section 4 provides a detailed discussion of the evaluation results using SP^2Bench and Wikidata. Finally, Sect. 5 concludes the paper and presents future work directions.

2   Related Work

To better relate our evaluation using Wikidata with previous evaluation papers, we reviewed existing benchmarks based on both synthetic and real-world datasets. Benchmarks that use synthetic datasets include *LUBM* (Lehigh University Benchmark) (2005) [16], *UOBM* (University Ontology Benchmark) (2006) [18], *BSBM* (Berlin SPARQL Benchmark) (2009) [10], SP^2Bench (SPARQL Performance Benchmark) (2009) [28], *Bowlognabench* (2011) [12], *WatDiv* (Waterloo SPARQL Diversity Test Suite) (2014) [1], *LDBC-SNB* (Linked Data Benchmark Council - Social Network Benchmark) (2015) [13], *TrainBench* (2018) [33] and *OWL2Bench* (2020) [29]. The sizes of the synthetic datasets used in the referenced papers ranged from 1M to 100M triples, and the numbers of SPARQL queries executed were between 12 and 29, with the exception of *WatDiv* that used a set of 12500 generated queries.

Amongst benchmarks that are based on real-world datasets or queries from real-world logs, we reviewed *DBPSB* (DBpedia SPARQL Benchmark) (2011) [19], *FishMark* (2012) [8], *BioBenchmark* (2014) [40], *FEASIBLE* (2015) [26], *WGPB* (Wikidata Graph Pattern Benchmark) (2019) [17] and *WDBench* (2022) [5]. The datasets for these benchmarks varied in size from 14M up to 8B triples, and the numbers of SPARQL queries defined were between 22 and 175, except for *WGPB* and *WDBench* that have 850 and more than 2000 queries respectively.

The study conducted by the Wikimedia Foundation to replace Blazegraph is the closest work we have been able to identify so far. This study provided a detailed analysis of relevant features of triplestores according to Wikimedia Foundation. This study, however, only considered open-source triplestores and did not include execution times for importing, loading, exporting, or querying Wikidata [37]. Another related study [14] discussed the possibility of hosting a full version of Wikidata, and it measured the import time of popular triplestores, including Jena Fuseki, QLever, and Stardog. This study, however, did not discuss export time or query performances. *WGPB* and *WDBench* rely on a substantially reduced version of full Wikidata, and they have very specific objectives. *WGPB* defines a large set of SPARQL basic graph patterns exhibiting a variety of increasingly complex join patterns for testing the benefits of worst-case optimal join algorithms. The design goal behind *WDBench* was to create an evaluation environment able to test not only graph databases supporting RDF data model and SPARQL query language. The authors of *WDBench* created a collection of more than 2000 SPARQL queries distributed in four different categories. These queries were selected from real Wikidata query logs. Due to budget constraints, we did not include the queries defined by *WDBench* in our study. Still, we would like to include them in an extended version of this evaluation and compare the results with the queries we selected.

3   Evaluation Setup

In this section we present the details of the evaluation by describing the operational setup.

Triplestores. To ensure that our limited selection of triple stores is representative and diverse, the following triplestores were evaluated: (1) Jena Fuseki 4.4.0 with Jena TDB2 RDF store, (2) Amazon Neptune Engine 1.0.5.1, (3) GraphDB Enterprise Edition 9.10.0, (4) RDFox 5.4, (5) QLever (commit version 742213facfcc80af11dade9a971fa6b09770f9ca), and (6) Stardog 7.8.0. In this selection: there are commercial and non-commercial (Jena Fuseki and QLever) applications; there is one triplestore distributed as native cloud-service (Neptune); and there is one in-memory triplestore (RDFox). All triplestores support SPARQL 1.1 syntax and provide querying services via SPARQL endpoints.

Datasets. We aim to evaluate the scalability and performance of the SPARQL query engines using large datasets. For SP^{2}Bench, we generated four different datasets with 125M, 250M, 500M, and 1B triples. For Wikidata, we used the full version `latest-all.nt.gz` (downloaded on 2021-11-19). Table 1 shows the general statistics of these datasets.

Table 1. Statistics of the datasets: number of distinct Triples, Sub[jects], Pred[idcates], Obj[ects], Class[es], Ind[ividuals], Obj[ect] Prop[erties] and Data Prop[erties].

Benchmark	Triples	Sub	Pred	Obj	Class	Ind	Obj Prop	Data Prop
SP^{2}Bench	125M	22.4M	78	59.5M	19	22.4M	64	21
	250M	45.9M	78	120.8M	19	46.2M	64	21
	500M	94M	78	244.9M	19	94.1M	64	21
	1B	190.3M	78	493M	19	190.5M	64	21
Wikidata	16.3B	1.78B	42.92K	2.93B	1.2K	1.77K	17.1K	27K

SPARQL Queries. SP^{2}Bench comes with a set of 14 SELECT and 3 ASK queries which were designed to cover several relevant SPARQL constructs and operators as well as to provide diverse execution characteristics in terms of difficulty and result size [28]. For Wikidata, the set of 356 SPARQL query examples defined by Wikidata users [38] was selected. Some of these queries use proprietary service extensions deployed for the Wikidata Query Service. We modified the queries to not use these service extensions and discarded some queries that are not compliant with SPARQL 1.1 specification or use proprietary built-in

Table 2. Coverage (%) of SPARQL features for each benchmark.

Benchmark	distinct	filter	optional	union	limit	order	bound	offset
SP^{2}Bench	35.29	58.82	17.65	17.65	5.88	11.76	11.76	5.88
Wikidata	33.14	30.84	31.12	5.19	14.7	48.7	2.59	0
	DateFnc	SetFnc	NumFnc	StringFnc	TermFnc	exists	notexists	in
SP^{2}Bench	0	0	0	0	0	0	0	0
Wikidata	8.65	27.67	2.59	9.8	16.14	0.58	3.75	1.44
	groupby	bind	values	minus	coalesce	if	having	PropPath
SP^{2}Bench	0	0	0	0	0	0	0	0
Wikidata	29.11	10.66	8.65	5.19	0.86	3.17	1.44	35.73

functions not supported by the evaluated triplestores. As a result, a set of 328 queries is used for the evaluation.

Table 2 presents an analysis of the queries from the two benchmarks regarding the SPARQL features and operators. These features may have a correlation with the execution time of the queries [25,27]. Hence, they need to be taken into consideration when designing a SPARQL query benchmark. It can be observed that Wikidata queries provide a broader coverage of SPARQL features and operators than SP^{2}Bench. Wikidata queries have more advanced features [36] such as Property Path, or built-in functions such as Dates and Times (DateFnc), Set (SetFnc), Strings (StringFnc), and RDF Terms (TermFnc) functions.

Amazon Web Services (AWS) Infrastructure. This evaluation was conducted on the AWS cloud. We used Amazon Elastic Compute Cloud (EC2) instances with Elastic Blob Store (EBS) volumes. Specifically, r5 instances with memory configurations of 128 GB, 256 GB, and 512 GB were selected. This corresponds to instances of type r5.4xlarge, r5.8xlarge, and r5.16xlarge [3]. This choice also matched the on-demand r5 instances available for the fully managed Neptune triplestore [4]. As RDFox is an in-memory triplestore, it needs additional memory to load a full version of Wikidata. None of the available r5 instances offers enough memory for RDFox. Therefore, x1 instances which offer up to 1,952 GB of memory were selected instead. In particular, x1.32xlarge [3] was employed to evaluate RDFox using Wikidata. Each EC2 instance was set up with a separate EBS gp3 volume for data storage with the performance of 3,000 IOPS and 125 MB/s throughput.

Configuration Details. We followed the recommended memory configuration for Stardog [30] and GraphDB [21], and applied it to all triplestores. We used the default settings for other configurations. In the case of RDFox, this implies that we use a persistence mode that stores incremental changes in a file [23]. RDFox can also be set up to run purely in-memory. According to the vendor, this would result in much lower import and export times than the ones presented in the paper. Similarly, RDFox offers the possibility to store datastores as binary files [22], which might significantly reduce loading times. These claims could not be verified before this study was submitted.

The evaluation was carried out simultaneously with one triplestore running on one instance. For SP^{2}Bench, r5.8xlarge was used to deploy all triplestores. For Wikidata, we ran the evaluation on r5.4xlarge, r5.8xlarge, and r5.16xlarge, except RDFox that was deployed only on x1.32xlarge. Due to some differences in the hardware configuration of r5 and x1, we performed a sensitivity analysis of their performance. The result of this analysis is discussed in Sect. 4.2.

To avoid the impact of network latency, the triplestores (i.e., SPARQL server) and the evaluation scripts (i.e., SPARQL client) were deployed on the same machine. Neptune is provided as database-as-a-service in the cloud. Thus, the SPARQL client needs to run on a separate machine. To estimate the effect of network latency, we set up a test with GraphDB where the SPARQL client was running on a separate machine. This analysis helped us to adjust and make the results for Neptune comparable with the others. Detail about this analysis is discussed in Sect. 4.2.

The evaluation is comprised of the following stages:

1. **Data Import.** All datasets were imported into the selected triplestores.
2. **System Restart and Warm-up.** The triplestores were restarted, and the evaluated dataset was loaded again (if needed). Then, one test query was executed to warm up the triplestores.
3. **Hot-run.** Each query was executed ten times. We set the query timeout to 30 min for the SP^{2}Bench and 5 min for the Wikidata.

The following metrics are recorded in this evaluation:

- **Import Time.** The time required to import the dataset for the first time. This step involves building indexes and persisting the datasets to storage.
- **(Re)Load Time.** The time required to (re)load the dataset after importing.
- **Export Time.** The time required to write imported data to an external file.
- **Query Execution Time**: The time needed to finish one query execution.
- **Success Indicators.** The numbers of success, error, and timeout queries.
- **Global Performance.** We follow the proposal in [28] to compute both well-known arithmetic mean and geometric mean (the nth root of the product over n number) of the execution times. Accordingly, the failed queries (e.g., timeout, error) were penalized with the double of timeout value. Arithmetic mean is used as an indicator of a high success and failure ratio (i.e., a smaller value indicates a higher ratio of success queries) while geometric mean is used to evaluate the overall performance over success queries (i.e., a smaller value as an indicator of shorter execution time for the success queries).

Although we ran our experiments on a cloud-based framework, it is worth mentioning that the executions of each run are remarkably consistent. Specifically, the standard deviation of the ten runs of 95% of the Wikidata queries is less than one millisecond.

4   Discussion of the Evaluation Results

In this section, we discuss the evaluation results using SP^{2}Bench and Wikidata. Additional supplementary information and all experimental results, including runtimes for individual queries on each engine tested, can be found online at [15].

4.1   Evaluation Results Using SP^{2}Bench

Import Time. Table 3 includes the import time of SP^{2}Bench datasets. For all triplestores, the import time increases proportionally to the size of the dataset.

Table 3. Global performance of the triplestores on SP^{2}Bench. To compute the mean, Timeout and Error queries were penalized with 3600 s seconds (1 h).

Triple stores	125M			250M			500M			1B		
	Imp Time	Arith Mean	Geo Mean	Imp Time	Arith Mean	Geo Mean	Imp Time	Arith Mean	Geo Mean	Imp Time	Arith Mean	Geo Mean
QLever	17m	1694.23	3.96	35m	1694.23	4.10	1h9m	1694.24	4.24	2h20m	1702.58	**5.74**
Fuseki	33m	1089.78	14.04	1h6m	1324.24	23.18	2h15m	1370.08	29.28	5h40m	1816.33	45.03
Neptune	18m	898.35	7.11	37m	974.22	9.89	1h16m	1323.48	13.83	2h22m	1781.18	26.40
RDFox	**3m**	1061.38	**1.75**	**5m**	1065.10	**2.42**	**9m**	1074.52	**2.91**	**18m**	1528.20	6.98
Stardog	18m	862.86	2.76	37m	878.88	3.62	1h17m	**917.33**	5.54	2h33m	1378.62	9.10
GraphDB	17m	**728.62**	3.97	36m	**766.16**	5.00	1h11m	995.00	7.55	2h23m	**1248.67**	11.75

Table 4. Success indicators (S[uc]C[ess], T[ime]O[ut], ERR[or]) on SP^{2}Bench.

Triplestore	125M			250M			500M			1B		
	SC	TO	ERR	SC	TO	ERR	SC	TO	ERR	SC	TO	ERR
QLever	9	0	8	9	0	8	9	0	8	9	0	8
Jena Fuseki	12	5	0	11	6	0	11	6	0	9	8	0
Amazon Neptune	13	4	0	13	4	0	11	6	0	9	8	0
RDFox	12	5	0	12	5	0	12	5	0	10	7	0
Stardog	13	4	0	13	4	0	13	4	0	11	6	0
GraphDB	15	2	0	15	2	0	14	3	0	13	4	0

Jena Fuseki showed poor import performance even though the `tdb2.xloader` [7] - a multi-threading bulk loader for very large datasets - was employed.

RDFox is the fastest when importing the datasets, even though it was configured using persistence mode. RDFox also exhibited similar loading times. As discussed in Sect. 3, RDFox importing and loading times might be reduced using a different configuration. The other triplestores show similar importing times and very fast loading times. For instance, they were able to restart and reload the synthetic dataset with 1B triples in less than a minute.

Query Execution Time. Tables 3 and 4 present success indicators and average execution time for the four SP^{2}Bench datasets. QLever is the only triplestore that had errors and no timeout. Seven queries could not be executed due to unsupported syntax or functions (e.g., ASK query, combined conditions in FILTER) and one "OutOfMemory" (OOM) error.

According to Table 4, the size of the dataset and results has a significant effect on the performance of all triplestores, in particular as the dataset grows from 125M to 1B triples. Neptune, as mentioned earlier, may suffer from network latency, especially for queries with large results because the server and client were deployed on different machines. For SP^{2}Bench, the timeout was set to 30 min which is relatively long enough for transferring big data between Amazon machines. In fact, in 8 timeout cases, Neptune failed to finish the execution of the queries and returned no result. Therefore, network latency is not the main issue for these timeout queries. Moreover, compared to the average execution time of the 17 SP^2Bench queries which is about 15 min, network latency may be considered as an insignificant factor. A thorough evaluation of network latency will be discussed in Sect. 4.2 using the Wikidata benchmark where there are a lot of queries executed in less than 100 milliseconds.

Regarding the global performance, the arithmetic means of GraphDB were superior to the others since it had a higher number of success queries. However, RDFox had better performance over successful queries, so its geometric means were the smallest; timeouts were limited to queries that introduce equi-joins using FILTER statements. In all cases, Stardog was always in the top two. It had more success queries than RDFox and executed difficult queries slightly faster than GraphDB. Jena Fuseki delivered the poorest performance while Neptune had mixed results on query execution. QLever was very fast on success queries, but it offered limited support for queries with complex SPARQL constructs. Moreover, QLever automatically puts a limit up to 100.000 results for all queries. Therefore, its reported execution times may not be comparable, especially for queries with large results.

Analysis of Query Execution Plan. A SPARQL query can be represented as a Basic Graph Pattern (BGP) which is a set of Triple Patterns (TPs) specified in the query [25]. Typically, the result of a BGP is obtained by joining the results of the TPs. Therefore, selective TPs that have smaller result sizes are usually executed first in order to minimize the number of intermediate results and therefore reduce the cost related to joining operations [17]. For the same purpose, filters are also moved closer to the part of the BGP where they apply. The execution order of the TPs in the BGP is the query execution plan. Typically, the query execution plan needs to be decided before the SPARQL engine executes the query. In order to do this, the triplestore requires precise estimation of the result size of each TP, which is done through building and updating different types of indexes [17]. In general, different triplestores may employ different data structures to implement their indexes and use different algorithms to optimize their query execution plan, therefore resulting in varying performance. In this study, except for QLever which does not provide the method to get the query plan, we investigated the execution plans of the other triplestores in order to gain a better understanding of their performances on the benchmarks.

In addition to the execution plan, RDFox, Neptune, and especially, Stardog also include very comprehensive profiling reports with the actual result sizes and the execution time of each TP. However, GraphDB provides only the estimation of the result sizes while Jena Fuseki produces only the complete results of each TP. Therefore, for these two triplestores, it was difficult to diagnose performance problems or identify expensive operations for the difficult queries.

Query 2 is one of the most difficult queries of the SP^2Bench where many triplestores timed out. It has a bushy BGP (i.e., single node linked to a multitude of other nodes) with 10 TPs, and the result size of this query grows with database size. Therefore, the execution time might be linear to the dataset size. According to the statistics provided by Stardog query profiler, the most expensive operation for this query is post-processing data (i.e., converting the results into the data structure that will be sent to the client). Similarly, Amazon Neptune also spent most of the execution time for this query on post-processing data. This observation illustrates the effect of large result sizes and large strings on the querying performance of SPARQL engines.

Query 3 (a, b, c) has just two TPs, one of which is of the form (?,?,?), and one FILTER with "equal to" operator. To avoid evaluating the TP (?,?,?) which may result in matching the whole dataset, all triplestores embedded the filter expression into this TP and transformed it into (?,p,?) form.

Query 4 is the most challenging query of the SP^{2}Bench benchmark. The result of the query is expected to be quadratic in the number of "journal" individuals in the dataset. To deal with this query, the author in [28] suggested that the query engines embed the FILTER expression into the computation of TPs (i.e., the same approach done in Query 3), which may help to reduce the intermediate results earlier. However, it is more challenging for all triplestores to embed the "greater than" operator in this query than the "equal to" operator. As a result, all of the triplestores failed to complete the query due to timeout.

Query 5a and 12a also test optimizations for embedding FILTER expression. The expression in these queries is the "equal to" comparison between two variables while Query 3 filters a variable with a constant value. GraphDB is the only triplestore handling Query 5a in 30 min. After rewriting this query by explicitly embedding the filtering expression, the triplestores can execute the query before timeout. However, as the dataset increased to 1B, timeout still occurred for the others. Query 12a replaces the SELECT construct of Query 5a with the ASK, which has a positive effect on query performances in all triplestores with the exception of Qlever and RDFox. This might indicate that collecting the results of Query 5a also has a significant impact on performances.

Query 6, 7, and 8 test another different optimization approach related to reusing TP results. These queries have several TPs repeated multiple times. Thus, intermediate results of those TPs can be reused to save cost for matching those triples. From the execution plan, it is unclear whether the triplestores implement this optimization approach or the same TPs were executed again.

Overall, when evaluating the execution plans, we observed that the triplestores did not pass several optimization tests designed by the authors of the benchmark. Despite being a synthetic benchmark with only 17 queries where some tests may not be practical (e.g., Query 4) or biased towards some specific constructs (e.g., FILTER), SP^{2}Bench proved to be very useful to test common query optimization techniques and to collect useful insights of the triplestores selected for this evaluation. Next, we will present the evaluation results using a completed version of Wikidata and 328 queries defined by its user community.

4.2   Evaluation Results Using Wikidata

Import and Export Time. The Wikidata dump used in this evaluation is available as a 112 GB gzip file (738 GB as unzip file). QLever is the only triple-

Table 5. Import and Export performance of the triplestores on Wikidata.

Triplestore	VM	Import Time	(Re)Load Time	Export Time	Persisted Storage
QLever	r5.4xlarge	1d 17h 2m	11m	n/a	871 GB
Jena Fuseki (TDB2)	r5.16xlarge	3d 15h 27m	<1m	Timeout	1.52 TB
Stardog	r5.4xlarge	2d 1h 9m	<1m	Error	862 GB
Amazon Neptune	r5.4xlarge	3d 1h 50m	7m	Error	3.98 TB
GraphDB	r5.4xlarge	1d 8h 13m	10m	Timeout	1.11 TB
RDFox	x1.32xlarge	0d 6h 25m	3h42m	5h28m	202 GB

store that has no support for gzip format. However, due to errors during importing, only Stardog, GraphDB, and RDFox managed to load the gzip file. Jena TDB2, in particular, was not able to import Wikidata due to 1319 URI syntax errors (e.g., special characters not allowed by Jena RIOT - the Jena syntax validator). After fixing these errors by replacing the special characters with their HTML numeric codes, we used this "clean" version to import into Jena Fuseki. Jena Fuseki also suffered from OOM error and succeeded in importing Wikidata only on r5.16xlarge machine (512 GB RAM).

Table 5 presents the performance for importing and exporting Wikidata. RDFox was much faster than the others. This result is consistent with the figures reported in SP^{2}Bench where all triplestores are evaluated using the same machine configuration. However, as the triplestores were restarted, RDFox required around 3.75 h (40% faster than its initial import time) to reload the data while the others took only a few minutes. As discussed in Sect. 3, RDFox importing and loading times might be reduced using a different configuration.

As QLever, Jena Fuseki, and Amazon Neptune used the unzip data and may not require any decompress operation during importing, their performance is expected to be slower on gzip Wikidata. Also, we observed that QLever reported a much larger number of loaded triples (21.5B triples). QLever may have a different way of building the statistics on the imported data.

To measure the export time, we set a timeout of 4 days for the triplestores. Except for QLever which has no support for data exporting, the other triplestores provide native functions to export the data. However, RDFox is the only triplestore that succeeded in exporting Wikidata within the timeout. Stardog did not show any progress or runtime output while Amazon Neptune encountered an error after exporting 503M statements in 1.5 h. GraphDB took 28 days and 8 h to export Wikidata. Due to cost constraints, we did not continue the exporting process for the others after 4 days. Based on this figure, it is obvious that exporting is not a prioritized feature of most triplestores.

Query Execution Time. Table 6 presents the success indicators and mean execution time of the triplestores on the Wikidata benchmark. QLever reported

Table 6. Global performance of the triplestores on Wikidata benchmark. To compute the mean, Timeout and Error queries were penalized with 600 s (10 min). The table also contains the estimated mean (in brackets) for RDFox on r5 machine and for Amazon Neptune r5.16x (r5.16xlarge VM) with network latency deducted.

Triplestore	VM	SC	TO	ERR	Arithmetic Mean	Geometric Mean
Qlever r5.4x	r5.4xlarge	106	0	222	404.87	12.33
Qlever r5.8x	r5.8xlarge	107	0	221	403.05	11.91
Qlever r5.16x	r5.16xlarge	108	0	220	401.23	11.73
Jena Fuseki r5.4x	r5.4xlarge	224	83	21	192.30	1.43
Jena Fuseki r5.8x	r5.8xlarge	231	76	21	180.21	1.29
Jena Fuseki r5.16x	r5.16xlarge	250	57	21	148.57	1.20
Amazon Neptune r5.4x	r5.4xlarge	309	18	1	39.29	0.34
Amazon Neptune r5.8x	r5.8xlarge	310	17	1	36.26	0.31
Amazon Neptune r5.16x	r5.16xlarge	312	15	1	31.65 (31.59)	0.28 (0.27)
Stardog r5.4x	r5.4xlarge	307	20	1	43.46	0.19
Stardog r5.8x	r5.8xlarge	308	19	1	42.01	0.16
Stardog r5.16x	r5.16xlarge	308	19	1	41.77	0.18
GraphDB r5.4x	r5.4xlarge	321	7	0	15.62	0.08
GraphDB r5.8x	r5.8xlarge	322	6	0	14.48	0.08
GraphDB r5.16x	r5.16xlarge	321	7	0	15.67	0.07
RDFox x1.32x	x1.32xlarge	324	4	0	12.11 (9.23)	0.04 (0.016)

the most errors (67% of all queries). Nearly all are syntax errors due to limited support for the SPARQL 1.1. Furthermore, there are 5 queries where QLever returns only the first 100.000 results. They were also classified as errors. QLever also has several OOM errors that were resolved on more powerful machines.

Jena Fuseki is the second triplestore with the most errors. It had 13 query syntax errors. Particularly, it does not allow using an existing variable name for the AS operator (e.g., (SAMPLE(?dob) AS ?dob)). Jena Fuseki also suffered from memory issues. This triplestore either crashed or froze and produced no output while executing the other 8 error queries. Amazon Neptune and Stardog accounted for one error which was reported as an internal failure exception.

If we look at the performance of each individual triplestore on the three different r5 configurations, GraphDB and Stardog were more robust with small variances among the machines. They had approximately the same query execution time and number of timeouts on the three machines. They may be optimized to work efficiently even on machines with less physical resources. In contrast, Jena Fuseki and Amazon Neptune performed better on more powerful machines as they had more success queries on those machines.

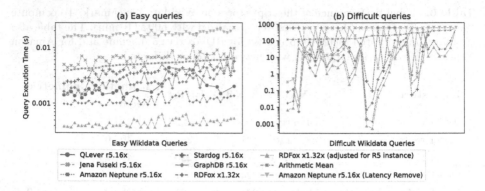

Fig. 1. Query execution time of the top 50 easy and difficult Wikidata queries on average (excluding error queries). The queries (x axis) are ordered by the arithmetic mean of the execution time of all triplestores.

When comparing the execution time of all triplestores, RDFox and GraphDB are the top two triplestores with the lowest arithmetic mean followed by Amazon Neptune. Jena Fuseki and QLever are the slowest triplestores due to a lot of errors and timeouts. Regarding geometric mean, RDFox is also the fastest with a value of 0.04 which is 50% smaller than the second best, GraphDB. Stardog is in the third place. Its geometric mean is around 0.18 which is 35% faster than Amazon Neptune. This insight can also be noticed from Fig. 1 that compares the best performance (i.e., on r5.16xlarge machines) of the triplestores for the top 50 easy and difficult queries (excluding error queries). Accordingly, for easy queries, it can be clearly identified the order of the triplestores where RDFox is the fastest and Amazon Neptune is the slowest. However, there is a mixed result for difficult queries.

Network Latency Analysis. In order to estimate network latency which can be incorporated into the execution time of Amazon Neptune, especially for those queries with large results, a separate experiment was conducted. Specifically, the same setting was deployed for GraphDB on two r5.4xlarge machines. On average, the latency amounted to 100 ms. In Fig. 1(a) and Table 6, we also have the execution time of Amazon Neptune adjusted by removing the latency for each individual query. As the latency is just a few milliseconds for easy queries, the adjusted figure is not different from the original value. Amazon Neptune is still the slowest on the top 50 easy queries.

Sensitivity Analysis of R5 and X1 Instances. To compare the performance of the triplestores on x1 and r5 instances, we performed a sensitivity analysis that: (1) evaluates the performance of GraphDB with Wikidata on x1e.4xlarge and r5.4xlarge machines, (2) evaluates the performance of RDFox with SP^{2}Bench on x1e.8xlarge and r5.8xlarge machines. On average,

GraphDB had approximately 50% performance degradation on `x1e.4xlarge` machine. Similarly, the performance of RDFox on SP^2Bench decreased about 59.75% on `x1e.8xlarge` machine. Thus, it is expected that RDFox may have better performance on `r5` instances for Wikidata queries if a suitable `r5` machine with sufficient RAM memory is available. To ensure the results of this analysis are reflected in the evaluation, in Table 6, we also provide the adjusted means for RDFox assuming the queries would be executed 59.75% on average faster.

Analysis of Query Execution Plan. To better understand the evaluation results discussed earlier, several queries are studied in more detail. In particular, the following selection criteria were applied:

1. Queries not executed by most of the triple stores due to timeout.
2. Queries with large variation in execution times (i.e., timeout for some triple-stores and executed in few seconds by the rest).
3. Queries where the numbers of results are not consistent (i.e., some triplestores returned different numbers of results for the same query).

Due to the page limitation, only a summary of the analysis is presented in this section. Firstly, for timeout queries, the most expensive operations are related to processing a large number of results, including both intermediate and final results. Therefore, to minimize overhead related to handling the results, highly selective triple patterns are usually prioritized to be executed earlier in order to reduce the scanning space for later triple patterns of the query. To do so, the query optimizer needs to have a good estimation of the outputs for each TP in the query. For queries with simple SPARQL constructs, most triplestores can manage to create an optimal execution plan. However, as the query employs complex constructs or features (e.g., nested SELECT query, built-in functions, property path, etc.), estimating a good execution plan becomes challenging. Based on the analysis of the query execution plans, the following observations can be considered when designing the queries for the evaluated triplestores:

- For queries with complicated patterns, most triplestores tend to keep the execution plan the same as the original order described in the query. In this case, it is recommended to rewrite the query using simple constructs. For example, the property path with arbitrary length can be rewritten explicitly with a sequence of TPs and UNION. For example, after we rewrite the property path of **Query 234** and **Query 235** with the sequence of three patterns explicitly, Stardog can produce a better plan and result in 2.6× and 4.2× faster respectively. If the query cannot be changed, the TPs need to be re-ordered manually to help the triplestores to optimize the execution plan. This can be done by repeating the execution with different orders [32].
- FILTER operations are usually moved earlier in the execution plan in order to reduce the number of intermediate results. However, filters with complex conditions (e.g., string and date-time functions) may slow down the execution, especially for a large number of results (e.g., **Query 192**, **Query 327**, **Query**

343 and **Query 350**). If possible, such condition should be rewritten in an equivalent form without using FILTER or applied later in the execution plan when there are fewer intermediate results.

- The TP of the form (?,?,?) should be considered carefully as it may result in a bottleneck in the execution of most triplestores (e.g., **Query 45**).

For queries with large variation in execution times, the following observations about the evaluated triplestores are recorded:

- Due to its in-memory solution, RDFox tends to perform better on scanning indexes and joining results, especially for large results or complicated operations such as string functions (e.g., **Query 13**, **Query 233**, **Query 237** and **Query 350**).
- Jena Fuseki had very poor performance on scanning and joining large results compared with the others. It also has very simple optimization algorithms. Mostly, it does not change the order of triple patterns, which results in inefficient execution plans and timeouts (e.g., **Query 45**, **Query 84** and **Query 286**). Therefore, the triple patterns need to be re-ordered manually in order to improve the performance of this triplestore.
- Stardog may have issues with queries having many OPTIONAL constructs. The triplestore tends to produce exponential intermediate results when matching such triple patterns (e.g.,   **Query 176** and **Query 326**) while the others produced much fewer results, and therefore resulting in timeout.
- For queries with sequence paths, Amazon Neptune tends to prioritize triple patterns with such property path syntax. This strategy may result in an exponential increase in the intermediate results if those patterns are not the most selective (e.g., **Query 84** and **Query 286**).
- For queries with UNION construct, RDFox tends to keep the triple patterns inside UNION unchanged while GraphDB tends to expand this construct by moving the JOIN operation inside each of the operands of UNION. Stardog and Amazon Neptune are more flexible in estimating the optimal plan for the UNION pattern. Therefore, if the optimal plan can be anticipated, it is recommended to rewrite the UNION patterns, especially for GraphDB and RDFox (e.g., **Query 184** and **Query 345**).

The third category of queries selected for further investigation is the one where the numbers of results are not consistent. Accordingly, we identified 10 queries where there is one triplestore that disagreed with the majority of other triplestores. As we only captured and compared the number of results, it is not sufficient to determine whether a triplestore is correct or not. However, if most of the triplestores report the same number of results, this might be a reasonable indication in terms of correctness. Based on the analysis of the execution plan, the following issues from the triplestores were identified:

- Amazon Neptune reported different results when executing a few queries with REGEX expressions. For instance, the triplestore returned no result after applying some filters with complex regex patterns (e.g., **Query 93**, **Query 133** and **Query 327**).

- Stardog reported different numbers of results for a few SELECT nested queries (e.g., **Query 82** and **Query 195**). Additionally, in **Query 284** which has a FILTER operator on date-time values, Stardog returned six more results than the others.
- GraphDB also had issues with a few nested SELECT queries. It returned no result for **Query 109** and **Query 319**. Additionally, in **Query 178** and **Query 233**, the triplestore returned much fewer results than the others.

5 Conclusions and Future Work

To the best of our knowledge, this study presents one of the most detailed analyses of the performances of a representative selection of the state-of-the-art triplestores using a complete version of the knowledge graph Wikidata. In this section, we conclude the paper with a summary of some of the most relevant observations produced by this evaluation.

With respect to the evaluation setup used in this study, all selected triplestores were tested on Amazon EC2 r5 or x1 instances. Despite some initial concerns about the reliability of the evaluation results, the execution times of each run were remarkably consistent. Amazon EC2 instances are also required to test Neptune, the only native cloud-based service in our evaluation. Some specific execution requirements posed by Neptune and RDFox difficult a fair comparative analysis. Sensitivity analyses were conducted to adjust the evaluation results for Neptune and RDFox and make them comparable with the others. While the impact of network latency in the Neptune client-server configuration seems to be small, the differences in performances between r5 and x1 instances seem to be significant (approximately 50% to 60% performance degrade).

SP^{2}Bench proved to be a great choice to test scalability and common query optimization techniques, which helps us to collect useful insights of the triplestores selected for this evaluation. RDFox was the fastest triplestore importing the synthetic datasets generated for this study and it has better performance over success queries. Regarding the global query performances, GraphDB was superior to the others, followed very close by Stardog. After analyzing query execution plans and query profiling information, we observed that the triplestores did not pass several optimization tests designed by the authors of SP^{2}Bench. It is worth mentioning that Stardog provides a comprehensive query profiling service, which establishes a reference for other triplestores.

SP^{2}Bench also has some limitations. It only provides 17 SPARQL queries offering limited coverage of some SPARQL constructs and features. Moreover, some of these queries and the synthetic datasets do not seem to be practical in real use case applications. Our evaluation employing a complete version of Wikidata with 328 queries defined by its users seems to overcome these limitations. This evaluation helps us to stress the triplestores and identify relevant insights. Importing Wikidata, and especially, exporting Wikidata was challenging for all triplestores, where RDFox was significantly more efficient. RDFox was also the only triplestore that managed to export Wikidata, and it completed this operation in a few hours. Loading Wikidata, however, was done much faster by the other triplestores, although a different configuration for RDFox might reduce loading time significantly.

Importing Wikidata was also difficult because of syntax errors reported by some rigorous parsers such as the ones implemented in RDFox and Jena Fuseki. It seems that the complete dumps published by Wikidata might not strictly follow W3C recommendations. For instance, it was possible to find values not formatted according to these recommendations. The same problem arises with some queries published by Wikidata users. Some of these queries use, for example, proprietary service extensions deployed by the Wikidata Query Service team.

In terms of query performances, RDFox reported the best overall performances followed by GraphDB. It is remarkable how consistent GraphDB and Stardog were, in terms of query performances independent of the memory configuration of the machine. This indicates a careful optimization of the design of both triplestores in terms of memory consumption. With the exception of QLever and Jena Fuseki, most triplestores reported none or just one error in the execution of the queries. Few discrepancies in the number of results were identified in the case of Stardog, GraphDB, and Neptune. The cause of these discrepancies could not be explained in this study and it will require further investigation.

As for future work, we plan to evaluate a larger collection of relevant triplestores or extend the queries used in the Wikidata evaluation with the queries defined by the benchmark WDBench.

Acknowledgment. The authors would like to thank the anonymous reviewers for their valuable feedback and the companies Ontotext and Oxford Semantic Technologies (OST) for their support during the evaluation. This work has been funded by The Research Council of Norway projects SkyTrack (No 309714), DataBench Norway (No 310134) and SIRIUS Centre (No 237898), and the European Commission projects DataBench (No 780966), VesselAI (No 957237), Iliad (No 101037643), enRichMyData (No 101070284) and Graph-Massivizer (No 101093202).

References

1. Aluç, G., Hartig, O., Özsu, M.T., Daudjee, K.: Diversified stress testing of RDF data management systems. In: Mika, P., et al. (eds.) ISWC 2014. LNCS, vol. 8796, pp. 197–212. Springer, Cham (2014). https://doi.org/10.1007/978-3-319-11964-9_13
2. Amazon AWS: Amazon Neptune Official Website. https://aws.amazon.com/neptune/
3. Amazon Web Services: Amazon EC2 Instance Types - Memory Optimized. https://aws.amazon.com/ec2/instance-types/#Memory_Optimized. Accessed 12 Dec 2022
4. Amazon Web Services: Amazon Neptune Pricing. https://aws.amazon.com/neptune/pricing/. Accessed 12 Dec 2022
5. Angles, R., Aranda, C.B., Hogan, A., Rojas, C., Vrgoč, D.: WDBench: A Wikidata Graph Query Benchmark. In: The Semantic Web–ISWC 2022. ISWC 2022. Lecture Notes in Computer Science, vol. pp. 714–731 13489. Springer, Cham. https://doi.org/10.1007/978-3-031-19433-7_41

6. Apache Jena: Apache Jena Fuseki Documentation. https://jena.apache.org/documentation/fuseki2/
7. Apache Jena: Apache Jena TDB xloader. https://jena.apache.org/documentation/tdb/tdb-xloader.html. Accessed 12 Dec 2022
8. Bail, S., et al.: FishMark: A Linked Data Application Benchmark. CEUR (2012)
9. Hannah, B., Björn, B.: QLever GitHub repository. https://github.com/ad-freiburg/qlever
10. Bizer, C., Schultz, A.: The berlin SPARQL benchmark. Int. J. Seman. Web Inf. Syst. (IJSWIS) **5**(2), 1–24 (2009)
11. Blazegraph: Blazegraph Official Website. https://blazegraph.com/
12. Demartini, G., Enchev, I., Wylot, M., Gapany, J., Cudré-Mauroux, P.: BowlognaBench—benchmarking RDF analytics. In: Aberer, K., Damiani, E., Dillon, T. (eds.) SIMPDA 2011. LNBIP, vol. 116, pp. 82–102. Springer, Heidelberg (2012). https://doi.org/10.1007/978-3-642-34044-4_5
13. Erling, O., et al.: The LDBC social network benchmark: interactive workload. In: Proceedings of the 2015 ACM SIGMOD International Conference on Management of Data, pp. 619–630 (2015)
14. Fahl, W., Holzheim, T., Westerinen, A., Lange, C., Decker, S.: Getting and hosting your own copy of Wikidata. In: Proceedings of the 3rd Wikidata Workshop 2022. CEUR-WS.org (2022). https://ceur-ws.org/Vol-3262/paper9.pdf
15. GitHub: Analysis and supplementary information for the paper, including queries, execution logs, query results and scripts. https://github.com/SINTEF-9012/rdf-triplestore-benchmark. Accessed 13 Mar 2023
16. Guo, Y., Pan, Z., Heflin, J.: LUBM: a benchmark for OWL knowledge base systems. J. Web Seman. **3**(2–3), 158–182 (2005)
17. Hogan, A., Riveros, C., Rojas, C., Soto, A.: A worst-case optimal join algorithm for SPARQL. In: Ghidini, C., et al. (eds.) ISWC 2019. LNCS, vol. 11778, pp. 258–275. Springer, Cham (2019). https://doi.org/10.1007/978-3-030-30793-6_15
18. Ma, L., Yang, Y., Qiu, Z., Xie, G., Pan, Y., Liu, S.: Towards a complete OWL ontology benchmark. In: Sure, Y., Domingue, J. (eds.) ESWC 2006. LNCS, vol. 4011, pp. 125–139. Springer, Heidelberg (2006). https://doi.org/10.1007/11762256_12
19. Morsey, M., Lehmann, J., Auer, S., Ngonga Ngomo, A.-C.: DBpedia SPARQL benchmark – performance assessment with real queries on real data. In: Aroyo, L., et al. (eds.) ISWC 2011. LNCS, vol. 7031, pp. 454–469. Springer, Heidelberg (2011). https://doi.org/10.1007/978-3-642-25073-6_29
20. Ontotext: GraphDB Official Website. https://graphdb.ontotext.com/
21. Ontotext: GraphDB Requirements. https://graphdb.ontotext.com/documentation/enterprise/requirements.html. Accessed 12 Dec 2022
22. OST: RDFox Documentation: Managing Data Stores. https://docs.oxfordsemantic.tech/5.4/data-stores.html#. Accessed 12 Dec 2022
23. OST: RDFox Documentation: Operations on Data Stores, persist-ds. https://docs.oxfordsemantic.tech/5.4/data-stores.html#persist-ds. Accessed 12 Dec 2022
24. Oxford Semantic Technologies: RDFox Official Website. https://www.oxfordsemantic.tech/product
25. Saleem, M., Ali, M.I., Hogan, A., Mehmood, Q., Ngomo, A.-C.N.: LSQ: the linked SPARQL queries dataset. In: Arenas, M., et al. (eds.) ISWC 2015. LNCS, vol. 9367, pp. 261–269. Springer, Cham (2015). https://doi.org/10.1007/978-3-319-25010-6_15
26. Saleem, M., Mehmood, Q., Ngonga Ngomo, A.-C.: FEASIBLE: a feature-based SPARQL benchmark generation framework. In: Arenas, M., et al. (eds.) ISWC

2015. LNCS, vol. 9366, pp. 52–69. Springer, Cham (2015). https://doi.org/10.1007/978-3-319-25007-6_4

27. Saleem, M., Szárnyas, G., Conrads, F., Bukhari, S.A.C., Mehmood, Q., Ngonga Ngomo, A.C.: How Representative Is a SPARQL Benchmark? An Analysis of RDF Triplestore Benchmarks. In: The World Wide Web Conference, pp. 1623–1633 (2019)

28. Schmidt, M., Hornung, T., Lausen, G., Pinkel, C.: SP^{2}Bench: A SPARQL performance benchmark. In: 2009 IEEE 25th International Conference on Data Engineering, pp. 222–233. IEEE (2009)

29. Singh, G., Bhatia, S., Mutharaju, R.: OWL2Bench: a benchmark for OWL 2 reasoners. In: Pan, J.Z., et al. (eds.) ISWC 2020. LNCS, vol. 12507, pp. 81–96. Springer, Cham (2020). https://doi.org/10.1007/978-3-030-62466-8_6

30. Stardog: Stardog Capacity Planning. https://docs.stardog.com/operating-stardog/server-administration/capacity-planning. Accessed 12 Dec 2022

31. Stardog: Stardog Official Website. https://www.stardog.com/

32. Stardog: 7 Steps to Fast SPARQL Queries. https://www.stardog.com/blog/7-steps-to-fast-sparql-queries/ (2017). Accessed 12 Dec 2022

33. Szárnyas, G., Izsó, B., Ráth, I., Varró, D.: The train benchmark: cross-technology performance evaluation of continuous model queries. Softw. Syst. Model. **17**(4), 1365–1393 (2018)

34. Vrandečić, D., Krötzsch, M.: Wikidata: a free collaborative knowledgebase. Commun. ACM **57**(10), 78–85 (2014)

35. W3C: RDF 1.1 Concepts and Abstract Syntax, W3C Recommendation (2014). https://www.w3.org/TR/rdf11-concepts/. Accessed 12 Dec 2022

36. W3C: SPARQL 1.1 Query Language, W3C Recommendation (2013). https://www.w3.org/TR/sparql11-query/. Accessed 12 Dec 2022

37. WDQS Search Team: WDQS Backend Alternatives: The process, details and result. Technical report, Wikimedia Foundation (2022). https://www.wikidata.org/wiki/File:WDQS_Backend_Alternatives_working_paper.pdf

38. Wikidata: SPARQL query service/queries/examples. https://www.wikidata.org/wiki/Wikidata:SPARQL_query_service/queries/examples. Accessed 12 Dec 2022

39. Wikidata: SPARQL query service/WDQS backend update. https://www.wikidata.org/wiki/Wikidata:SPARQL_query_service/WDQS_backend_update. Accessed 12 Dec 2022

40. Wu, H., Fujiwara, T., Yamamoto, Y., Bolleman, J., Yamaguchi, A.: BioBenchmark toyama 2012: an evaluation of the performance of triple stores on biological data. J. Biomed. Seman. **5**(1), 1–11 (2014)

MOSAIK: An Agent-Based Decentralized Control System with Stigmergy for a Transportation Scenario

Sebastian Schmid[1][(✉)] [iD], Daniel Schraudner[1] [iD], and Andreas Harth[1,2] [iD]

[1] Friedrich-Alexander-Universität Erlangen-Nürnberg, Chair of Technical Information Systems, Nuremberg, Germany
{sebastian.schmid,daniel.schraudner,andreas.harth}@fau.de
[2] Fraunhofer IIS, Fraunhofer Institute for Integrated Circuits IIS, Division Data Spaces and IoT Solutions, Nuremberg, Germany
andreas.harth@iis.fraunhofer.de

Abstract. We investigate possibilities for implementing the decentralized control of transporters with Semantic Web agents to fulfill a given transportation task. We present the MOSAIK framework as a system to build and simulate agents to control transporters using stigmergy for communication, and self-organize based on local decisions. Our framework uses Semantic Web technologies because the communication paradigm of stigmergy directly maps to the REST constraints of the application architecture of the web. The system achieves self-organization by implementing a combination of simple reflex web agents that coordinate using web resources as environment for stigmergy. Finally, we evaluate our system compared to an agent-based simulation and discuss requirements of decentralized systems on the Semantic Web using stigmergy.

Keywords: Self-organization · Transportation · Multi-agent system

1 Introduction

Research for industrial transportation and intralogistics focuses on decentralized control in transportation systems, promising scalability, adaptivity, and flexibility [6,27], in contrast to centralized control that is limited in data processing and scalability, and imposes the threat of a single point of failure [7].

The most promising approaches for decentralized control in transportation are multi-agent systems (MAS), where decision making to solve transportation orders happens in agents locally [27]. MAS are considered appropriate to solve transportation problems [35], are robust, scalable, and can cope with changing environments efficiently [6]. The question remains, how control of these transporter agents can be assured without losing the advantages of decentralized systems by introducing centralized control? Existing MAS approaches already

This work was funded by the German Federal Ministry of Education and Research through the MOSAIK project (grant no. 01IS18070A).

try to implement decentralized control, e.g. based on auctions [8], forecasting [22], negotiation [10], or hybrid approaches like local coordination and plan merging [1], but often centralized components remain as part of control.

We believe that an agent-based decentralized control system that fulfills the advantages of scalability, adaptivity, and flexibility needs to possess at least the following properties:

1. **Stateless, reactive agents**: Agents shall possess no internal states and only react to their perceived environment, as so-called simple reflex agents (SRA) [25]. SRAs scale well as SRAs do not get more computationally expensive with an increased problem size and still give a coherent outcome [34].
2. **Indirect communication**: The results of SRA's actions are not saved as agent state, but applied to the environment. Agents use their common environment as medium to communicate indirectly with each other, which is called stigmergy [20]. Indirect communication reduces coupling between agents, keeps the population flexible, and leads to resilience against breakdowns of individual agents by distribution of knowledge [3].
3. **Loose coupling between agents**: Agents shall not make assumptions about the agent population and only focus on their own task. For a single agent there shall be no difference if only itself or multiple agents are in the system. The system's adaptive behavior emerges from indirect interactions between agents [18].
4. **Use of local information**: Agents shall use only and thus adapt to locally available information to decide on their actions [17]. Together with stigmergy, the use of local information agents may achieve an overall goal by self-organization via explicit, directive stigmergy [33] that communicates opportunities and goal accomplishments between agents.

We put an emphasis on statelessness, indirect communication and loose coupling between agents, as we believe these form the major requirements for a decentralized control system.

To motivate the problem, we introduce the example of a driverless transportation systems (DTS) whose transporters shall be controlled by agents we realize with the MOSAIK framework [5]. We discern active components, agents, and reactive components, called artifacts that respond to agents' actions, and form together the agents' environment. The agents shall self-coordinate to explore the shop floor in a decentralized manner and use exclusively indirect communication. We assume that all data for agents to decide on is available in RDF (Resource Description Framework) in their environment. The environment shall be accessible for agents via a RESTful Read-Write Linked Data interface as well. We introduce our running example of a transportation scenario in Sect. 2.

We propose to use the advantages of stigmergy, that uses only indirect, decentralized communication for decentralized self-organization and control to keep the advantages of the overall decentralized system. Here, the Semantic Web offers a uniform interface for interaction between agents and artifacts as environment to share data with a common understanding by using established web technologies, as also the rising recent interest in the combination of autonomous agents and the Semantic Web shows [4]. Our presented combination of SRAs as stateless and independent agents, stigmergy for indirect communication, and the exclusive use of local information leads to a decentralized control system that consists of flexible software agents that can run in the cloud as well as on the edge, use local information without the need to crawl RDF graphs extensively, scale easily with problem sizes, and are resilient with graceful degradation, as agents' data survives in the environment.

We present our system, based on the MOSAIK model [5], consisting of transporters and workstations, which are reactive machines (called artifacts), and transporter agents, which control transporter artifacts via Linked Data technologies that is RDF as data model and HTTP for communication via RESTful interfaces. We built a decentralized transportation system according to the paradigms of stigmergy and Read-Write Linked Data, fulfilling the demands of Industry 4.0 for an agent-based system on state-of-the-art web technology level. Our contributions are:

- We implement the MOSAIK data model and interface for decentralized agents to control decentralized transporter artifacts via Linked Data.
- We present a formalization of the system's demanded behavior and implement the behavior in form of condition-action rules and derivation rules for agents, and state change rules and request processing rules for artifacts.
- We evaluate the performance of our system for a transportation task and compare the outcome to an agent-based simulation.

2 Running Example and Transportation Scenario

We introduce our example used throughout the paper of a transportation scenario, also depicted in Fig. 1.

Example 1. A shop floor, represented by a 3 × 6 grid, contains transporter1 at (2, 2), transporter5 at (3, 1), and two colored stations station1 at (0, 2) and station2 at (5, 2), all as artifacts. Station1 is a blue station and accepts blue products, station2 is a green station and accepts green products. Agents control the transporters, here ldfu5 controls transporter5.

Transporter5 holds a blue product, so ldfu5's reflexes try to find suitable adjacent floor tiles for transporter5 to move closer to station1 to deliver the product. Agents may only perceive information that is locally available to their controlled transporter, e.g. for ldfu5 transporter5's floor tile (3, 1), and the eight adjacent fields. Meanwhile, ldfu1, controlling transporter1, evaluated the surrounding floor tiles of transporter1 and perceived a so-called stigmergy mark (blue arrow) at (1, 2), which helps agents to find the nearest station by following the gradient in the direction of the respective station (see Sect. 3). ldfu1 creates a stigmergy mark at (2, 2) to extend the stigmergy gradient. ldfu5 orders transporter5 to follow these stigmergy marks successively to eventually arrive at station1. Therefore, ldfu5 perceives the now created blue stigmergy mark at (2, 2), concludes that transporter5 will get closer to station1 by moving to (2, 2), and thus orders transporter5 to move to (2, 2).

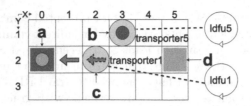

Fig. 1. Detail view of the used shop floor scenario: a) Blue `station1` with green product, b) `transporter5` with blue product, c) empty `transporter1`, d) empty green `station2`. All components are located on the shop floor's tiles (black and white grid). The blue arrows symbolize a gradient of blue stigmergy markers that point the way to the blue `station1` (the dashed stigmergy mark was just created). The respective transporters are controlled by agents (Color figure online).

Example 1 emphasizes our discussed properties from Sect. 1:

1. Stateless, reactive agent: `ldfu5` does not save information in internal states and only reacts to outside stimuli like the sigmergy mark at (2, 2)
2. Indirect communication: `ldfu1` saves stigmergy markers in the environment at (2, 2) to point the way to stations
3. Loose coupling between agents: `ldfu5` requires no knowledge about `ldfu1` and only perceives `ldfu1`'s action of putting a blue stigmergy mark to (2, 2)
4. Local information: `ldfu5` can only perceive the floor tiles that are next to `transporter5`'s location at (3, 1)

Example 1 and Fig. 1 are only a part of the bigger overall scenario, where transporters, as artifacts, have to fulfill transportation tasks [26]: A square shop floor with 7 × 7 floor tiles has four stations, each with one of four different colors green, red, blue and yellow. A station accepts only products of its own color. Stations randomly produce a product of a different color when their output port is empty. Three transporters have to bring colored products to the correct station of the same color. The agent controlling each transporter evaluates the transporter's own field and the eight adjacent fields.

Agents leave colored marks with values on floor tiles that gets higher the further away the tile is from a perceived station. An agent that follows the descending values will end up at a station [17]. Agents have no model of the shop floor, and do not communicate directly with other agents. The presented, simple scenario can be easily extended to a manufacturing shop floor that produce variants of a product along workstation, as for small batches of customer-specified products are manufactured, e.g. modular smartphones with different processor, memory size, and display as in [28].

3   Theoretical and Technical Background

3.1   Agent-Based Systems and Stigmergy

Russell and Norvig [25] describe the basic agent program for simple reflex agents (SRA), where an SRA is described as simplest possible agent form. SRAs base their actions only on their current perception during a so called perception-thought-action cycle, but have no memory. A set of condition-action rules gives the behavior, so called reflexes. A reflex triggers an action whenever the respective condition is fulfilled.

Stigmergy is the use of asynchronous interaction and information exchange between agents exclusively through changes in their environment, but not directly with each other [20]. Stigmergy is inspired by the indirect communication of insects like termites [11]. Stigmergy is the base for algorithms coming from ants [9] and has widespread usage [33,34]. The self-organization and coordination of agents is discussed in e.g. [12]. By changing and evaluating their environment, agents influence each others behavior indirectly [17,32]. Our SRAs manipulate their local environment based on their given rules [25]. Agents evaluate their surroundings for manipulations by other agents which then influences their own respective rules, which leads to indirect communication and achieving an overall goal by self-organization via explicit, directive stigmergy [33].

3.2   MOSAIK

We give the definitions of the MOSAIK model [5] for agents and artifacts, with focus on decentralization and stigmergy. Furthermore, we present the resources that were created and used during our research project to realize the model's vision for self-organized transportation in combination with the Semantic Web. We derive our formal definitions from Charpenay et al. [4].

Definition 1 (SRA). *We define simple reflex agents as proactive components (as opposed to artifacts) that make decisions on their own. Agents implement a perception-thought-action cycle to influence their environment, based on defined condition-action rules. We define an agent A as the tuple $A = \langle G, perc, appl, act \rangle$ where*

G, *set of all RDF graphs, representing the agent's possible knowledge*

$perc : D' \times G \rightarrow G$, *perception function, based on perceived environment states,*

$appl : G \rightarrow G$, *function for derivation rules,*

$act : G \rightarrow O$, *function for condition-action rules,*

with O, set of operations, as $\{GET, PUT, POST, DELETE\} \times U \times G$

and O_{GET} as $\langle GET, u, \emptyset \rangle$

where D' is the set of all finite datasets (the percepts) and D is the set of all RDF datasets (the environmental states) with $D' \subset D$ (cf. Definition 2).

Agent perception and actions are implemented via HTTP requests. Note that *act* realizes actions to influence the environment via unsafe requests (PUT, POST, DELETE) as well the agent's perception (GET), cf. Charpenay et al. [4].

Definition 2 (Artifact). *We define artifacts as reactive components (as opposed to agents) that form the agents' environment following [4]. Artifacts provide different ways for interaction via HTTP request, e.g. reading the artifact's* *state or manipulating the artifact's state via tasks. An internal logic defines the deterministic reaction to interaction, but artifacts do not act autonomously. We define the set of all artifacts as environment $E = \langle D, d_0, O, transfer, update, evolve \rangle$ where*

$$D, \text{set of all possible environment states as set of all RDF datasets}$$
$$d_0, \text{the environment's initial state}$$
$$transfer : O_{GET} \times D \to D', \text{function for agents to retrieve a finite percept } D' \subset D$$
$$update : (O \backslash O_{GET}) \times D \to D, \text{effectory function based on operations}$$
$$evolve : D \to D, \text{function for the environment's own developing state change.}$$

Artifact behavior is a black box for agents, but the behavior's result is observable via state changes and the *transfer* function. State changes can be triggered not only by agents, but also by the physical environment (e.g. machine error or mechanical overload), represented by *evolve*. In our setting, artifacts are transporter devices, workstations, and manipulable floor tiles.

Table 1 shows as a concluding comparison of agent and artifact rules, how the presented formal definitions of Sect. 1 and 2 map to each other, and how we implemented the rules (cf. Sect. 3.3 and 3.4).

Table 1. Comparison of defined rules for agents and artifacts

	Agents	Artifacts
Rule Definition Implementation	Derivation rules *appl* N3 Rules without HTTP Requests in Header	State change rules *evolve* SPARQL-Insert-Delete
Rule Definition Implementation	Condition-action rules *act* N3 Rules with HTTP Requests in Header	Request processing rule *update* Built-in BOLD rule

Interface. In order for the agents to be able to communicate with the artifacts via HTTP, we defined a common interface in MOSAIK which is based on Linked Data Platform [30] for Read-Write Linked Data. In line with the Interaction Affordances from Web of Things Thing Descriptions [21], agents interact with artifacts by either reading or writing their properties, by submitting tasks[1] to them, or by watching events:

– Agents read properties by sending a GET request to the URI of the artifact, write properties by sending a PUT request to the URI of the artifact.

---

[1] The difference between writing a property and submitting a task is that writing has to happen instantaneously while the task triggers an action that can take more time.

- A new task can be submitted to an artifact by sending a POST request to the task queue.
- Events can be watched by polling the event container via GET requests.

An extended description of our interface can be found in [29]. The rules to implement this interface on the artifact side can be found in Sect. 4.2. For our scenario we use tasks for transporter movement and properties for setting the stigmergy markers on the floor tiles; events are not used.

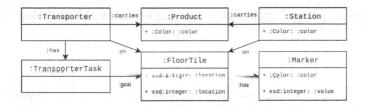

Fig. 2. Class diagram of the data model

Data Model. In our data model (Fig. 2) we have three types of artifacts that can be manipulated by agents: :Transporter, :Station, and :FloorTile, where each :FloorTile has a 2D location and each :Transporter and :Station has a reference to the floor tile they are standing on. Each :FloorTile furthermore has stigmergy :Markers for each color that save the stigmergy value for the color. :Transporters are moved by agents by submitting :TransporterTasks specifying the target :FloorTile to the task container of the :Transporter. :Transporters and :Stations may hold a :Product[2]. :Products and :Stations have :Colors (which must match for a :Station to accept a :Product). We created the ARENA vocabulary[3] to be able to use the data model from above in RDF. We use as its prefix **arena**.

3.3 Implementation of Agents

The data processing system Linked-Data Fu (ldfu)[4] [16] can retrieve, process and modify Linked Data based on logical rules and production rules in Notation3 (N3) [2]. We use N3 to implement the condition-action rules describing the behavior of the agent which controls the transporters, and interact with the artifacts via RESTful interfaces. ldfu has rules of the form $\{b_1...b_n\}$log:implies$\{h\}$., where we use **log:implies** (from the namespace **log**[5]) to express implication [15]. These rules realize the ldfu's *internalize* and

---

[2] :Products are not manipulated by the agents directly, but merely indirectly as consequence of manipulations of :Transporters or :Stations.

[3] https://solid.ti.rw.fau.de/public/ns/arena#.

[4] https://linked-data-fu.github.io/.

[5] http://www.w3.org/2000/10/swap/log#.

act functions to influence the agent's internal state or send HTTP requests as explained below. The antecedent of the rule, $b_1...b_n$, and the conclusion, h, are RDF triple patterns (s, p, o) as

$$(s, p, o) \in (U \cup B \cup V) \times (U \cup V) \times (U \cup B \cup L \cup V)$$

where a given U is the set of URIs, B a set of blank nodes, and L a set of literals. V is the set of variables that may replace constants to give patterns. The agent's rule set R is a finite set of rules. A conclusion h follows from a graph $g \in G$, if $h \in g$ or $\{b_1...b_n\} \subseteq g$.

ldfu has an internal graph (cf. $g \in G$ in Definition 1) that holds the agent's knowledge in volatile storage. During each cycle, ldfu starts by trying to instantiate its given N3 rules. ldfu may send an HTTP request to a URI given in h to interact with its environment, either to perceive (GET) or manipulate artifact states via unsafe requests (PUT, POST, DELETE). We use the namespaces http[6] and httpm[7] to express these requests. ldfu sends safe requests (cf. *act* O_{GET} in Definition 1) to all defined URIs in valid conclusions and merges the result to its knowledge (cf. *perc* in Definition 1) to apply the N3 rules again (cf. *appl* in Definition 1) - this is done as long as no fixpoint is reached, that is as long as there are still GET requests left to send and new triples are inserted in ldfu's graph. Only then, ldfu instantiates any unsafe requests e.g. to change its environment (cf. *act* with $O \backslash O_{GET}$ in Definition 1). Finally, the internal graph of ldfu is deleted and ldfu will start all over in the next cycle. Note that ldfu does not save triples or graphs between cycles internally (that is, ldfu has no persistent state), but has to apply results to the environment such that they are not lost.

Example 2. ldfu5 wants to steer `transporter5` to deliver the green product, so ldfu5 needs information about the current position. To get the information about the transporter's tile, ldfu5's N3 program (see below) has a rule that states whenever ldfu5 notices that a resource ?a has a `arena:tile` relation to another ressource ?b, ldfu5 will send an HTTP GET request to the URI of ressource ?b. As ldfu5 retrieves a triple `</transporters/5>` `arena:tile <shopfloor/3/1>` for transporter5, ldfu5 sends HTTP GET to `<shopfloor/3/1>`.

```
# Follow all foor:tile properties
{
  ?a arena:tile ?b .
} => {
  [] http:mthd httpm:GET ;
     http:requestURI ?b .       } .
```

---

[6] http://www.w3.org/2011/http#.
[7] http://www.w3.org/2011/http-methods#.

3.4 Implementation of Artifacts

BOLD[8] is a simulation environment that implements artifacts according to Definition 2. The artifacts' states are multiple RDF graphs, collected by BOLD in a single named graph representing the environment state D. Agents can read and manipulate artifacts via HTTP requests to HTTP resources under the URI of the named graph, as defined with *transfer* and *update*, cf. Definition 2. Each time step of the simulation, BOLD updates its graph by defined SPARQL INSERT / DELETE queries that take transferred states of agents into account (e.g. moving a transporter via a task), or by the environment's own development as defined in *evolve* (e.g. creating products). We give an example of a SPARQL query that BOLD applies for updates:

Example 3. `Transporter5` was busy as `ldfu5` has sent a task before. Thus, BOLD's graph contains that `transporter5` has still status busy via `</transporters/5> arena:status arena:busy`. But meanwhile `transporter5` executed the movement, so no tasks are left in `transporter5`'s task container. Hence, BOLD sets `transporter5`'s status to `arena:idle`.

```
# Set transporter to idle when no task available and busy
DELETE {  # delete triple with arena:busy as object
    GRAPH ?transporter {
        ?transporter arena:status arena:busy . }
} INSERT { # insert triple with arena:idle as object
    GRAPH ?transporter {
        ?transporter arena:status arena:idle . }
} WHERE {
    ?transporter a arena:Transporter ; #resource is a transporter
        arena:status arena:busy ; #resource has status busy
        arena:tasks ?taskContainer
    FILTER NOT EXISTS { #has no tasks in container
        ?taskContainer ldp:contains ?task .
    } };
```

We use BOLD as a centralized back end for our artifacts as we simulate the behavior and interactions among different artifacts. The (simulated) artifacts can influence each other (e.g. transporters blocking each other) and thus a decentralized simulation would continuously have to synchronize all artifact states. The interfaces offered by the artifacts, however, are independent of each other and thus can be easily distributed.

4 System Behavior

Below, we present an overview of the agent and artifact rules from Example 1, to show how `ldfu5` perceives stigmergy marks and gives a task for movement

---

[8] https://github.com/bold-benchmark/bold-server.

to `transporter5`, and how `transporter5` reacts to the task. All rules including code examples can be found in our online repository[9].

4.1   Agent Behavior

An ldfu program defines the agent behavior, whereas transporter, floor tiles, products, and stations are artifacts, simulated by BOLD. The ldfu agent reads the information provided by the artifacts and interacts with the artifacts, which in turn respond to the agent's tasks. Agents get a fixed entry URI of BOLD, the root resource /, to start their exploration, and obey their rule set in Notation3 to move the transporter and build a grid of stigmergy marks.

1. GET all links that are accessible as objects in triples at root
2. GET all tiles, their marks, and the stigmergy values
3. GET all links to transporter's neighboring tiles
4. If the transporter carries a product, GET the link to that product
5. If the transporter has a product, POST a task to move to the neighboring tile with the lowest stigmergy value of matching color to the transporter's task container, thus following the descending gradient of stigmergy values

4.2   Artifact Behavior

Transporters have internal reflexes as reaction to interactions from the outside, e.g. by the agent. These reflexes are given in SPARQL, as artifacts have a persistent state over the simulation time that we manipulate in a non-monotonic way (SRAs again have no internal state over the simulation time, so monotonic reasoning with N3 rules is sufficient), and handle move orders (given as `arena:TransporterTask`) and the pickup and delivery of products.

1. INSERT that the transporter is busy and DELETE that the transporter is idle, if the transporter is idle and has tasks in its task container
2. INSERT the goal tile given in a task as the transporter's new position and DELETE the old one, if the tile is free and adjacent
3. INSERT all neighboring tiles according to the transporter's current position
4. INSERT that the transporter is idle and DELETE that the transporter is busy, if the transporter is busy but has no tasks in its task container
5. DELETE all tasks that point to the transporter's current tile (e.g. after the transporter moved successfully to the goal tile)

The stations' reflexes, given in SPARQL, handle the creation and consumption of products:

1. If station's output port is empty, INSERT a new product of other color
2. If station's input port contains a link to a product of the station's color, DELETE the product

---

[9] https://github.com/wintechis/mosaik-runtime-documentation.

4.3 System Implementation

Our implementation as well as a demo video of our system in action are available in our online repository[10]. The overall system itself works as follows:

- ldfu executes the perception-thought-action cycle:
  - ldfu GETS the given entry point, a resource that links (indirectly) to all artifacts
  - ldfu GETS the current state of its transporter, follows the link to the transporter's current tile, and to all neighboring tiles and the markers.
  - ldfu derives that all perceived shop floor tiles without stigmergy markers get an internal value of 1000. Thus, tiles with a smaller stigmergy value are more attractive for ldfu to go to.
  - ldfu creates new unsafe HTTP requests (i. e. POST, PUT, or DELETE), according to derived statements in its knowledge graph.
- BOLD executes SPARQL queries periodically on its internal RDF graphs and updates the graphs of artifacts according to the stated behavior. BOLD checks also if the transporters have new tasks in their task containers and will initiate to execute the tasks.

Note that ldfu and BOLD are separate, concurrent systems. BOLD manages the shop floor as a grid with x- and y-coordinates, where all tiles are addressable by URIs. All fields are pre-initialized with value 1000 for color marks. Tiles outside the valid area are set to arena:nil and values to 1001, so ldfu discerns between invalid tiles outside the shop floor, tiles that were never visited and tiles that lead to a station, as these tiles have a smaller stigmergy mark value.

5   Evaluation

We evaluate our system compared to a simulation of agents that represents the expected behavior, implemented in GAMA, a modeling and simulation environment for building explicit agent-based simulations that provides an integrated environment for creating and testing distinct agents [31]. With the given algorithms of our agents and artifacts from ldfu and BOLD, GAMA can simulate multiple repetitions to show the system's correct behavior with statistical significance. As measurement for performance, we measure the cumulative amount of delivered products over time (TDI). The setup is the quadratic shop floor as presented in Sect. 2. Adjacency of transporters and stations is defined by the 3×3 floor tiles around them. We measure time in passed cycles during simulation, where one time step equals one cycle. We chose a cycle time of five seconds for ldfu. All repetitions were run with randomly chosen starting points for transporters on the shop floor. Figure 3 shows the TDI for 300 cycles with 1000 repetitions and the average development of the systems. On average, the GAMA simulation delivered 57.95 products after 300 cycles, where the first successful delivery was achieved after about 23 cycles. In comparison, MOSAIK

---

[10] https://github.com/wintechis/mosaik-runtime-documentation.

with ldfu and BOLD delivered 22.92 products after 300 cycles, with the first delivery after about 16 cycles. Note that the qualitative development of both systems resembles a "hockey stick", showing the state of the system without and with only few stigmergy marks (low performance), and with more marks to create direct paths (increasing performance). We focus on the implementation of MOSAIK in the application domain and include a general running example without comparison of different agent-based approaches or parameter optimization, as this is out of scope. For a discussion of different agent approaches in the DTS domain with a dynamic environment, see e.g. [26].

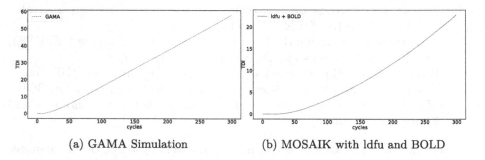

(a) GAMA Simulation   (b) MOSAIK with ldfu and BOLD

Fig. 3. Average behavior of our DTS compared to a simulation for the cumulative amount of delivered items, measured over 300 cycles with 1000 repetitions.

Example 4 explains the interaction between multiple, distinct agents in MOSAIK:

Example 4. Consider again Fig. 1 with agents ldfu1 and ldfu5, both controlling respectively transporter1 at (2, 2) and transporter5 at (3, 1). As transporter5 is carrying a blue product, ldfu5 prioritizes movement towards blue stigmergy markers such that the delivery can be fulfilled. At (3, 1), ldfu5 cannot perceive the blue station at (0, 2) or any marker towards the station, so the next move might be random. However, next to transporter1, at (1, 2), is a stigmergy marker pointing towards the blue station. ldfu1 cannot perceive the station, but perceives the adjacent marker. Agents GET all local information of their artifacts, e.g. ldfu1 also transporter1's floor tile or state, and meanwhile also adjacent floor tiles and respective stigmergy marks, see no. 1 Fig. 4. ldfu1's rules state to replicate adjacent stigmergy markers with increased value, so it PUTs a new blue marker with value 2 to transporter1's current tile, see no. 2 Fig. 4 (dashed arrow in Fig. 1). Finally, see no. 3 Fig. 4, ldfu5 GETs transporter5's floor tile (3, 1) and also the surrounding tiles including (2, 2). ldfu5 GETs (2, 2) and thus the stigmergy mark of blue with value 2, which is smaller than any other blue marker around. Hence, ldfu5 received the information, without direct communication, that a blue station can be reached, when following the stigmergy mark via the descending gradient and can decide to do so in a subsequent rule.

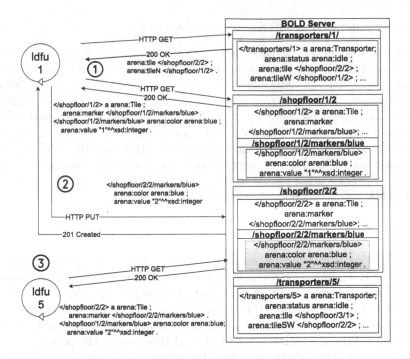

Fig. 4. Interaction between two agents to exchange information via stigmergy

6 Discussion

6.1 Simulation Results and System Performance

Considering the different performances of delivered items, we emphasize how GAMA works compared to BOLD and ldfu: GAMA simulates all agents and artifacts during one simulation cycle, e.g. all marks appear at the same time and can be evaluated in the successive cycle; BOLD+ldfu are unsynchronized, separate programs i.e. the environment's reaction (BOLD) might take longer to appear than the agents' action (ldfu). Thus, agents need additional cycles as they might miss other agents' actions as these are not applied to the environment in time. Still, MOSAIK and GAMA show the characteristic behavior of swarms that use the environment for positive feedback through stigmergy mark placement [14], similar to trails in Ant Colony Optimization [9]. Our agents decide autonomously, according to given rules, when to place marks to reflect the perceived truth. Artifacts act predominantly as producers of data - although their reflexes may also change the environment's state (e.g. picking up products) or its own (e.g. moving to a tile), these actions are only answers to an agent's stimulus.

6.2   Implementation of Distributed Control

MOSAIK discerns active agents (Sect. 4.1) that can perceive and interact with their environment, and reactive artifacts (Sect. 4.2) that represent external, reacting parts that are controlled by agents (the environment). As we focus on a decentralized control system, we demand agents to be stateless, use stigmergy, and have loose coupling (see Sect. 1). Semantic technologies offer sound inference algorithms for our agents, a uniform interface for interactions, and data sharing with a common understanding, implemented by RDF and RESTful interfaces. Our agents use MOSAIK and semantic technologies to self-coordinate and control, which enables other agents to take part pervasively.

Stateless agents amend each others knowledge by creating and changing perceived resources, but do not save any information internally. Thus, the knowledge of the agent population lies exclusively in the environment such that agents decide only on locally available information. RESTful interfaces and Linked Data technologies guarantee a common understanding and exchange of information.

Indirect communication has no dependence on explicit channels and protocols between agents, but agents need a shared medium to pass information, limited by agents' ability to perceive the world and the representation of useful states via stigmergy [20,24]. We use the artifacts to realize the agents' medium. Still, a distortion of the medium can lead to knowledge loss for the population [19].

With loose coupling between agents, the system is flexible and scalable as the population is independent such that single agents can be added to or removed from the population without impacting other agents. Without knowledge about other agents or their architectures, agents do not care if perceived information in the environment come from themselves or any other agent. Thus, new agents can adapt and work right away, as local knowledge is shared and perceivable. Removed agents only lead to graceful degradation of the system [3].

As we use RDF to represent the current state of a floor tile (and all other artifacts), an agent could crawl the environment's entire graph and thus have knowledge about all floor tiles and stations' locations. However, crawling the entire graph becomes infeasible when the environment's graph is very large and agents have a short perception cycle. Instead, we use stigmergy to make global information (possibly anywhere in the RDF graph, many links away) available locally [13]. Thus, agents get up-to-date information about the applied actions of others (or themselves before), and additionally agents can always be sure that the available information is at least a best guess with respect to the last available state of the environment, giving a minimum of resiliency. Unfortunately, the price of possibly suboptimal behavior comes when local information is heavily outdated or wrong, when the environment changed fundamentally, but can be repaired as part of robust self-organization [26].

We conclude that we successfully built a stateless, decentralized control system with MOSAIK building on indirect communication and loose coupling, using state-of-the-art Semantic Web technologies, with RDF as data model and RESTful communication. We designed our system according to the properties stated in the introduction and emphasize the merits of the Semantic Web for our application domain of decentralized transportation systems:

- Stateless agents can be stopped and started without the risk to loose internal information, as agents write their data to the environment. Agents can be thus be executed anywhere e.g. in an industrial cloud or on mobile transportation devices as edge.
- Loose coupling and indirect communication make it easy to create new agents, so the population can be scaled depending on outside requirements, e.g. if new transportation units have to be available in short time.
- Agents do not need to crawl whole RDF graphs for perception, when all required knowledge for decisions is locally available which reduces the overall network traffic and leads to faster decisions.

We see the following remaining challenges for the DTS domain:

- All artifacts need HTTP interfaces with a stable connection to their agents' network to be perceivable for agents.
- As agents regularly poll artifacts as part of the perception cycle, depending on the duration between polls, agents might not perceive artifact state changes in time. Also, artifacts have to respond to agents which uses electrical power. Thus, mobile transport units with limited battery cells might have an increased power consumption which influences the movement range.
- Precautions have to be taken that agents can find the required local information, otherwise the agent's perception of the local environment degenerates to a randomized perception search [13] of the RDF graph and gets inefficient.

7   Conclusion and Outlook

We realize a self-organizing, decentralized controlled transportation system using MOSAIK. We build on an agent-based system that uses Linked Data and stigmergy as technologies to implement stateless, reactive agents that rely on locally available information, retrieved from distributed artifacts. Agents and artifacts are described via declarative rules and communicate via HTTP. We show our system in the context of a defined transportation scenario that works in an abstract Industry 4.0 shop floor. Further usages include the control of stations, the optimization of path building and assigning transport orders. More research regarding the application of agent-based systems in the Semantic Web is needed, so we identified three problems during our research that will inevitably appear when scaling up our approach and thus must be tackled in the future:

- What is the optimal partitioning of artifacts that shall be controlled among agents? I.e. for how many artifacts should one agent be responsible? Or should agents only be responsible for certain aspects of the control, e.g. one agent for following stigmergy markers and one separate agent for random movement otherwise?

- When multiple agents act on the same artifacts, how to avoid conflicts between the actions agents submit to an artifact (e.g. one agent send the transporter to the left, one sends it to the right as both perceived that the transporter currently has no task)? As solution, HTTP would allow to use optimistic locking via the `If-Unmodified-Since` header, but this method is only efficient if conflicts are rare [23].
- Agent perception is limited to adjacent floor tiles – all other global information in the environment has to be made locally available via stigmergy. For other use cases, a different perception radius might be more efficient, i.e. agents could follow more link hops in the RDF graph to evaluate more distant floor tiles. How to find the optimal radius of the local perception is an open problem.

References

1. Alami, R., Fleury, S., Herrb, M., Ingrand, F., Robert, F.: Multi-robot cooperation in the MARTHA project. IEEE Robot. Autom. Mag. **5**(1), 36–47 (1998). https://doi.org/10.1109/100.667325
2. Berners-Lee, T.: Notation3 logic - an RDF language for the Semantic Web. https://www.w3.org/DesignIssues/Notation3.html
3. Bonabeau, E., Dorigo, M., Theraulaz, G.: Swarm Intelligence: From Natural to Artificial Systems. Oxford University Press, Santa Fe Institute Studies on the Sciences of Complexity (1999)
4. Charpenay, V., Käfer, T., Harth, A.: A unifying framework for agency in hypermedia environments. In: Alechina, N., Baldoni, M., Logan, B. (eds.) EMAS 2021. LNCS, pp. 42–61. Springer, Cham (2022). https://doi.org/10.1007/978-3-030-97457-2_3
5. Charpenay, V., et al.: MOSAIK: a formal model for self-organizing manufacturing systems. IEEE Pervasive Comput. **20**(1), 9–18 (2021). https://doi.org/10.1109/MPRV.2020.3035837
6. Chen, B., Cheng, H.: A review of the applications of agent technology in traffic and transportation systems. IEEE Trans. Intell. Transp. Syst. **11**(2), 485–497 (2010)
7. Chen, B., Wan, J., Shu, L., Li, P., Mukherjee, M., Yin, B.: Smart factory of industry 4.0: key technologies, application case, and challenges. IEEE Access **6**, 6505–6519 (2018). https://doi.org/10.1109/ACCESS.2017.2783682
8. Choi, H.L., Brunet, L., How, J.P.: Consensus-based decentralized auctions for robust task allocation. IEEE Trans. Rob. **25**(4), 912–926 (2009). https://doi.org/10.1109/TRO.2009.2022423
9. Dorigo, M., Birattari, M., Stutzle, T.: Ant colony optimization. IEEE Comput. Intell. Mag. **1**(4), 28–39 (2006). https://doi.org/10.1109/MCI.2006.329691
10. Giordani, S., Lujak, M., Martinelli, F.: A distributed multi-agent production planning and scheduling framework for mobile robots. Comput. Ind. Eng. **64**, 19–30 (2013). https://doi.org/10.1016/j.cie.2012.09.004
11. Grassé, P.: La reconstruction du nid et les coordinations interindividuelles chez Bellicositermes natalensis et Cubitermes sp. la théorie de la stigmergie: Essai d'interprétation du comportement des termites constructeurs. Insectes Sociaux **6**(1), 41–80 (1959). https://doi.org/10.1007/BF02223791

12. Hadeli, K., et al.: Self-organising in multi-agent coordination and control using stigmergy. In: Di Marzo Serugendo, G., Karageorgos, A., Rana, O.F., Zambonelli, F. (eds.) ESOA 2003. LNCS (LNAI), vol. 2977, pp. 105–123. Springer, Heidelberg (2004). https://doi.org/10.1007/978-3-540-24701-2_8

13. Hadeli, K., Valckenaers, P., Kollingbaum, M.J., Brussel, H.V.: Multi-agent coordination and control using stigmergy. Comput. Ind. **53**(1), 75–96 (2004)

14. Hamann, H.: Swarm Robotics: A Formal Approach, pp. 1–32. Springer, Cham (2018). https://doi.org/10.1007/978-3-319-74528-2_1

15. Harth, A.: Interoperation between information spaces on the web. In: Grust, T., et al. (eds.) EDBT 2006. LNCS, vol. 4254, pp. 44–53. Springer, Heidelberg (2006). https://doi.org/10.1007/11896548_5

16. Harth, A., Käfer, T.: Linked data techniques for the web of things: Tutorial. In: Proceedings of the 8th International Conference on the Internet of Things. IOT 2018, Association for Computing Machinery, New York (2018). https://doi.org/10.1145/3277593.3277641

17. Heylighen, F.. Stigmergy as a universal coordination mechanism i: Definition and components. Cogn. Syst. Res. **38**, 4–13 (2016). https://www.sciencedirect.com/science/article/pii/S1389041715000327

18. Heylighen, F.: The science of self-organization and adaptivity. Encycl. Life Support Syst. **5**, 253–280 (1970)

19. Heylighen, F.: Stigmergy as a universal coordination mechanism ii: varieties and evolution. Cogn. Syst. Res. **38**, 50–59 (2016)

20. Holland, O., Melhuish, C.: Stimergy, self-organization, and sorting in collective robotics. Artif. Life **5**, 173–202 (1999)

21. Kaebisch, S., Kamiya, T., McCool, M., Charpenay, V., Kovatsch, M.: Web of Things (WoT) Thing Description, W3C Recommendation. Accessed 18 Oct 2021 (2020)

22. Klein, N.: The impact of decentral dispatching strategies on the performance of intralogistics transport systems (2012). https://nbn-resolving.org/urn:nbn:de:bsz:14-qucosa-147739

23. Kung, H.T., Robinson, J.T.: On optimistic methods for concurrency control. ACM Trans. Database Syst. **6**(2), 213–226 (1981)

24. Parker, L.E.: Multiple Mobile Robot Systems, pp. 921–941. Springer, Heidelberg (2008). https://doi.org/10.1007/978-3-540-30301-5_41

25. Russell, S., Norvig, P.: Artificial Intelligence: A Modern Approach, 3rd edn. Prentice Hall Press, USA (2009)

26. Schmid, S., Schraudner, D., Harth, A.: Performance comparison of simple reflex agents using stigmergy with model-based agents in self-organizing transportation. In: 2021 IEEE International Conference on Autonomic Computing and Self-Organizing Systems Companion (ACSOS-C), pp. 93–98 (2021). https://doi.org/10.1109/ACSOS-C52956.2021.00071

27. Schmidt, T., Reith, K.B., Klein, N., Däumler, M.: Research on decentralized control strategies for automated vehicle-based in-house transport systems - a survey. Logistics Res. **13**, 10 (2020). https://doi.org/10.23773/2020_10

28. Schraudner, D.: Stigmergic multi-agent systems in the semantic web of things. In: Verborgh, R., et al. (eds.) ESWC 2021. LNCS, vol. 12739, pp. 218–229. Springer, Cham (2021). https://doi.org/10.1007/978-3-030-80418-3_34

29. Schraudner, D., Harth, A.: A RESTful interaction model for semantic digital twins. In: Proceedings of the Third International Workshop on Semantic Digital Twins co-located with the 19th Extended Semantic Web Conference (ESWC 2022) (2022)

30. Speicher, S., Arwe, J., Malhotra, A.: Linked data platform 1.0. W3C Recommendation (2015)
31. Taillandier, P., et al.: Building, composing and experimenting complex spatial models with the GAMA platform. GeoInformatica **23**(2), 299–322 (2019)
32. Theraulaz, G., Bonabeau, E.: A brief history of stigmergy. Artif. Life **5**, 97–116 (1999). https://doi.org/10.1162/106454699568700
33. Tummolini, L., Castelfranchi, C.: Trace signals: the meanings of stigmergy. In: Weyns, D., Parunak, H.V.D., Michel, F. (eds.) E4MAS 2006. LNCS, pp. 141–156. Springer, Heidelberg (2007). https://doi.org/10.1007/978-3-540-71103-2_8
34. Dyke Parunak, H.: A survey of environments and mechanisms for human-human stigmergy. In: Weyns, D., Van Dyke Parunak, H., Michel, F. (eds.) E4MAS 2005. LNCS (LNAI), vol. 3830, pp. 163–186. Springer, Heidelberg (2006). https://doi.org/10.1007/11678809_10
35. Zedadra, O., Jouandeau, N., Seridi, H., Fortino, G.: Multi-agent foraging: state-of-the-art and research challenges. Complex Adapt. Syst. Model. **5**(1), 3 (2017)

Correction to: IMKG: The Internet Meme Knowledge Graph

Riccardo Tommasini, Filip Ilievski, and Thilini Wijesiriwardene

Correction to:
Chapter "IMKG: The Internet Meme Knowledge Graph"
in: C. Pesquita et al. (Eds.): *The Semantic Web*, LNCS 13870,
https://doi.org/10.1007/978-3-031-33455-9_21

The chapter was inadvertently published with a typo in the family name of the second author so that it currently read "Illievski", i.e., an extra "l" was added whereas it should have read "Ilievski". This has been corrected.

The updated original version of this chapter can be found at
https://doi.org/10.1007/978-3-031-33455-9_21

Author Index

Printed in the United States
by Baker & Taylor Publisher Services